www.ingramcontent.com/pod-product-compliance
Lightning Source LLC
Chambersburg PA
CBHW051129120626
46547CB00012B/723

فرهنگ اشتقاق

واژه های فارسی

از ریشه های هند و اروپائی، سامی و غیره

دکتر علی نورائی

مقدمه

قبلاً در کتاب فرهنگ ریشه لغات فارسی با نمودار مشتقات (Persian Etymology Charts) ریشه های لغات فارسی و لغات همریشه آنها را در زبانهای هند و اروپایی، سامی و غیره در قالب شجره نامه هایی منتشر کرده بودم. شجره نامه میکند تا خواننده بتواند با یک نگاه اجمالی کلیه مشتقات یک ریشه را، در فارسی و زبانهای دیگر، یکجا مشاهده نماید ولی نمیتواند ریشه های مختلف یک لغت و ترکیب آنها را باهم نشان دهد. در کتاب مسیر اشتقاق لغات فارسی (The Origins of Persian Words) تلاش کردم که در نمودار های ساده تری ریشه های گوناگون هر لغت و مسیر اشتقاق و ترکیب آنها را باهم نشان دهم. فرهنگ حاضر بسط و گسترش این نمودار ها است که در آن منابع بیشتر و جدیدتری نیز بکارگرفته شده است.

هدف از تألیف این فرهنگ بیشتر توجه به مفاهیم اولیه یا ریشه ای لغات است که در مسیر اشتقاق ممکن است تغییراتی کرده یا فراموش شده باشند مانند معنی لغت پدر که "پاینده یا حافظ خانواده"، مادر که "ماده یا تغذیه کننده خانواده" و دخترکه "دوخنده یا شیر دوش خانواده" بوده اند. لذا، در این مختصر، توجه کمتری به تفکیک فرمهای دستوری لغات مانند اسم و فعل و مفرد و جمع شده که اثر چندانی روی مفاهیم لغات ندارند.

بیش از ۳۴۰۰ لغت فارسی در این فرهنگ ریشه یابی شده. مسیر اشتقاق آنها حدود ۴۰ زبان مختلف را دربر میگیرد که مهمترین آنها در نمودار زیر نشان داده شده است. در میان زبانهای غیر ایرانی، زبانهای عربی، یونانی و سانسکریت بیش از زبانهای دیگر روی لغات فارسی اثر گذار بوده اند. امیدوارم که این فرهنگ برای علاقمندان به زبان فارسی قابل استفاده باشد.

علی نورائی

بهمن ۱۴۰۲

زبانهای موثر در مهاجرت لغات به زبان فارسی

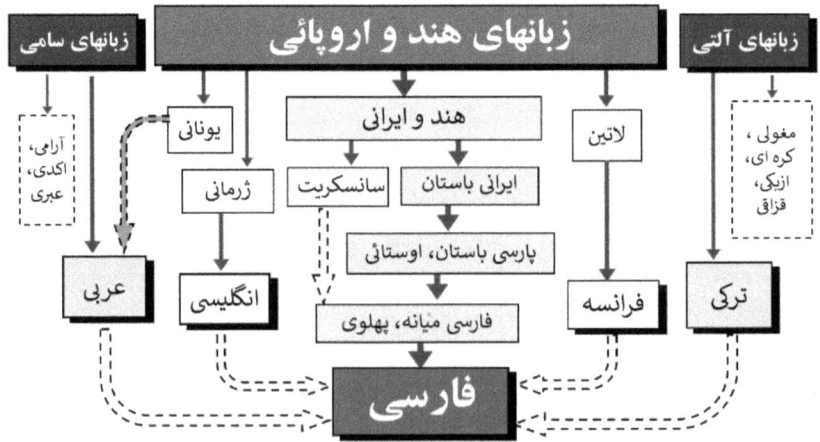

الف

راهنمای استفاده از این فرهنگ

لغات فارسی در این فرهنگ در سمت راست هر صفحه و اطلاعات مربوط به ریشه هایشان و اشتقاق و ترکیب هر یک از آنها در نمودار کوچکی زیر آن نشان داده شده است. اطلاعات مربوط به هر لغت داخل چهارچوبهای مستطیل شکل قرار دارد که در بالای آن نام زبان و در زیر آن دو حرف اختصاری منابع و مآخذ درج شده است مانند MO:389 که به صفحه ۳۸۹ فرهنگ معین رجوع میکند. همچنین علامت ستاره اشاره به استفاده از مراجع اینترنتی میباشد مانند DK* که اشاره به لغتنامه آنلاین دهخدا میباشد. علامت ستاره در مقابل بعضی از ریشه های هند و اروپایی نیز آمده که مأخوذ از منابعی است که بر بازسازی شده بودن آن ریشه ها تأکید دارند. گاهی اطلاعات بیشتری نظیر لغات همریشه یا معانی نا مأنوس برای بعضی از لغات نشان داده شده است. همچنین برای تلفظ لغات در زبانهای مختلف از حروف خاصی استفاده شده که در جدول زیر آمده است.

حروف مورد استفاده در تلفظ لغات

مثال انگلیسی	معادل فارسی	حروف تلفظ	مثال انگلیسی	معادل فارسی	حروف تلفظ
hot	ح ه	h	Far	آ	â
son	ث س ص	s	man	ا	a
zebra	ذ ز ض ظ	z	fun	ف	f
glottal stop	ء (ماخذ)	٫	boy	ب	b
strong guttural sound	ع	٬	pet	پ	p
boot	او (پول)	û (long)	cake	ک	k
old	اُ (استاد)	o (short)	goat	گ	g
toe	اُو (اوراق)	ô, ow (long)	lip	ل	l
machine	ای (ایمان)	î (long)	man	م	m
bee	ئی	ê (long)	noon	ن	n
gargling sound	غ	ğ [gh]	voice	و	v
emphatic k	ق	q [gh]	yard	ی	y
church	چ	č [ch]	joy	ج	j
Scottish loch	خ	x [kh]	day	د	d
vision	ژ	ž [jh, zh]	ray	ر	r
shop	ش	š [sh]	toy	ت ط	t

حروف داخل [ ] برای نوشتن لغات در متون انگلیسی میباشد.

صدای a در لغات سغدی با علامت (ٔ) نشان داده شده است.

ب

لیست منابع و مآخذ

AA   Asya Asbaghi, <u>Persische Lehnworter im Arabischen</u>, Otto Harrassowitz, Wiesbaden 1988

AD   W. Morris, <u>The American Heritage Dictionary</u>, New College Edition, 1975, Appendix on Indo-European Roots, pp 1505-1550.

AG1   M. Abolghâsemî, تاریخ مختصر زبان فارسی , Bonyâd Andîsheh Eslâmî Press, Tehran, 1373 (1994).

AG2   M. Abolghâsemî, ریشه شناسی - اتیمولوژی, Ghoghnoos Press, Tehran 1374 (1995).

AG3   M. Abolghâsemî, فعل های فارسی دری, Ghoghnoos Press, Tehran 1374 (1995).

AL   S. A. Starostin, A. V. Dybo, O. A. Mudrak, <u>An Etymological Dictionary of Altaic Languages</u>, ?

AP   M. Aryan Pour Kashani, فرهنگ ریشه های هند و اروپایی زبان فارسی, University of Esfahan, 1384 (2005).

AR   Andras Rajki, <u>Arabic Dictionary with Etymologies</u>, Version 2.2, 2005

AS   Addi Shir, Al-Alfâz Al-Fârsîyya Al-Mu`arraba, <u>A Dictionary of Persian Words in the Arabic Language</u>, Library of Lebanon, 1980.

AT   Asadî Tûsî, فرهنگ فرس, Khârazmî Press, Tehran 1365 (1986).

BK   C. D. Buck, <u>A Dictionary of the Selected Synonyms in the Principal Indo-European Languages</u>, University of Chicago press, 1949-1988.

BL1   H. W. Baily, <u>Indo-Scythian Studies</u> (Khotanese Texts - volume VI), Cambridge University Press, 1967.

BL2   H. W. Baily, <u>Hvatanica II</u>, (Glossary of some Khotanese words with reference to Avestan and Persian words), Bulletin of the School of Oriental and African Studies (BSOAS IX:1937-39) pp 69-78, University of London.

BQ   M. H. Tabrîzî (Borhân), برهان قاطع, Etymological footnotes by Dr. M. Mo`în, 4 vol, Amîr Kabîr Press, Tehran 1362 (1983).

BR   G. Badrehî, واژه های دخیل در قرآن مجید, translation of A. Jeffrey's <u>The Foreign Vocabulary of the Qur'ân</u>, Toos Publishers, Tehran 1372 (1993).

BT   C. Bartholomae, <u>Altiranisches Worterbuch Zusammen Mit Den Nacharbeiten Und Vorarbeiten</u>, Walter de Gruyter Press, 1979.

CH   J. Cheung, <u>Etymological Dictionary of the Iranian Verb, Vol. 2</u>, Leiden Indo-European Etymological Dictionary Series, Brill Press, Linden, Boston, 2007.

CL*   <u>Collins Dictionary</u> online, www.collinsdictionary.com

DG   A. Dâneshgar, فرهنگ اعلام فارسی, Hâfez Novîn Press, 1370 (1991).

DK* Ali Akbar Dehkhods, لغتنامه دهخدا , https://dehkhoda.ut.ac.ir/fa/dictionary

DS D. D. Y. Shapira, <u>Irano-Arabica: contamination and popular etymology</u>, in Christian East - New Series, vol. 5 (XI), Moscow, 2009

DV Michiel de Vaan, <u>Etymological Dictionary of Latin and other Italic Languages</u>, Lieden, Boston, 2008.

ED* <u>Online Etymology Dictionary</u>, www.etymonline.com

EE* <u>Visual Etymology Explorer</u>, Ver.2020, www.etymologyexplorer.com

ES S. M. A. Emâm Shûshtarî, فرهنگ واژه های فارسی در زبان عربی , Anjoman Âsâr Mellî, No 58, Bahman Press, Tehran, 1347 (1968).

FA Sallum Mohammed Daud, فرهنگ واژگان اكدی , translation: Nader Karimian Sardashti, Pajoheshkadeh zaban va gooyesh, Tehran 1384 (2006)

FJ F. Jonaydî, زندگی و مهاجرت آریائیان , Bonyâd Nayshâbûr, Tehran, 1374 (1995).

FV A. Farahvashî, ایرانویج , Tehran University Press, 1368 (1989).

GR B. Gharîb, فرهنگ سغدی. فارس. انگلیسی , Farhangân Press, Tehran, 1374 (1995).

GT S. K. Gupta, <u>A Comparative Etymologic Lexicon of Common Indo-European Words</u>, 6 Vol., Sverge Haus Publishers, Milton, Ma, 1997

GV I. Gershevitch, <u>The Avestan Hymn to Mithra</u>, Oriental Publications No.4, Cambridge University Press, 1959.

HM H. Hubschmann, <u>Persische Studien</u>, Verlag von Karl J. Trubner, Strassburg 1895.

HN1 W. Henning, <u>A List of Middle - Persian and Parthian Words</u>, Bulletin of the School of Oriental and African Studies (BSOAS IX:1937-39) pp 79-92, University of London.

HN2 W. B. Henning, <u>Sogdian Loan-words in New Persian</u>, Bulletin of the School of Oriental and African Studies (BSOAS X:1939-42) pp 93-106, University of London

IC Stuart E. Mann, <u>An Indo-European Comparative Dictionary</u>, Helmut Buske Verlag, Hamburg 1987

JD James Darmesteter, <u>Études Ieaniennes</u>, F. Vieweg , Libraire - Éditeur, 1888.

JS Jami Gilani Shakibi, <u>A Concise Etymologic Dictionary of the Persian Language</u>, three volumes, Babylon Books Publisher, 2007

KL D. Klein, <u>A comprehensive Etymological Dictionary of the English Language</u>, Two volumes, Elsevier Publishing Co., 1966.

KM Jalâl Khâleqî Motlaq, اساس اشتقاق فارسی ,Vol. I (خ . آ), Bonyâd Farhang Irân, 1977.

KT R. G. Kent, <u>Old Persian - Grammer, Text, Lexicon</u>, American Oriental Society, 1953.

LF   G. Laufer, <u>Sino-Iranica, Chinese Contributions to the History of Civilization in Ancient Iran</u>, Field museum of natural History, publication 201, Anthropological Series, Vol XV, No. 3, Chicago 1919.

MK   D. N. MacKenzie, <u>A Concise Pahlavi Dictionary</u>, Oxford University press, London 1971.

M. Moʿîn, فرهنگ فارسی معین, Six volumes, Amîr Kabîr press 1363 (1984).

NB   H. S. Nyberg, <u>A Manual of Pahlavi</u>, Wiesbaden 1974.

NS   A. H. Noushîn, فرهنگ شاهنامه فردوسی, Donyâ Press, Tehran 1363 (1984).

NV   S. M. Nahvî, فرهنگ وام واژه های عربی. دخیل, Tolûʿ Âzâdî Press 1368 (1989).

PA   Antonio Panaino, <u>Iran and the Caucasus 21</u> (2017) 150-195, "The Origins of Middle Persian Zamān and Related Words", *Università di Bologna, ,* Koninklijke Brill NV, Leiden, 2017

PH   Paul Horn, <u>Grundriss der NeuPersischen Etymology</u>, Verlag von Karl J. Trubner, Strassburg 1893-1974.

PK   J. Pokorny, <u>Indogermanisches Etymologisches Worterbuck</u>, Two volumes, Francke verlag, Bern 1959.

PT   B. Partridge, <u>Origins - A short Etymological Dictionary of Modern English</u>, MacMillan Co., NewYork 1958.

RB   Robert Beekes, <u>Etymological Dictionary of Greek, Vol 1</u>, Boston, 2010

RZ   M. H. Rokn Zâdeh - Âdammîyat, ارکان سخن, Sharq Press, Tehran 1347 (1968).

SH   J. T. Shipley, <u>The Origins of English Words</u>, The John Hopkins University Press, Baltimore 1984.

SK   W. W. Skeat, <u>A Concise Etymological Dictionary of the English Language</u>, Clarenden press, Oxford 1882-1967.

TU   T. Unaysî , <u>Tafsîr al-Alfâz al-Dakhîleh fe al-Loghat al-Arabîyeh</u>, Dâr al-Arab, Cairo, 1964.

TV   M. Tavoosî, واژه نامهٔ شایست نشایست, Shirâz University publications, 1986.

UT*   <u>Indo-European Lexicon</u>, Linguistics Research Center, University of Texas at Austin, https://lrc.la.utexas.edu/lex/master

WD   A. Walde, <u>Vergleichendes Worterbuch der Indogermanischen Sprachen</u>, two volumes, Walter de Gruyter & co., Leipzig 1930-1973.

YB   H. Yule & A. C. Burnel, <u>Hobson Jobson</u>, A Glossary of Colloqual Anglo-Indian Words, Oriental Publishers, Delhi 1903-1968.

ZM   H. Zimmern, <u>Akkadische Fremdworter Als Beweis</u>, Fur Babylonischen Kultureinfluss, Leipzig 1917.

ZV   Safia Zivingi, <u>Dictionary of Borrowed Foreign Vocabulary in Modern Arabic</u>, Democratic Arabic Center, Berlin, 2021

لغات

همراه با نمودار مسیر اشتقاق

از ریشه های هند و اروپایی،

سامی و غیره

این حرف گاهی به ی بدل شود.

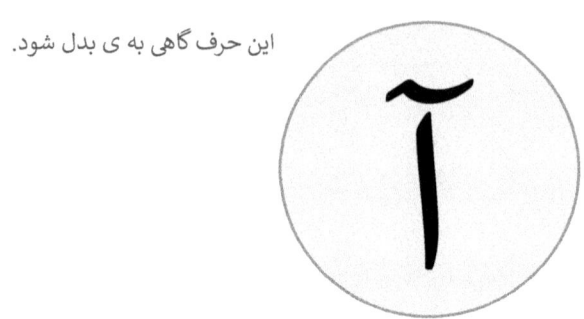

آ ـ ۱   پیشوند بعضی از افعال

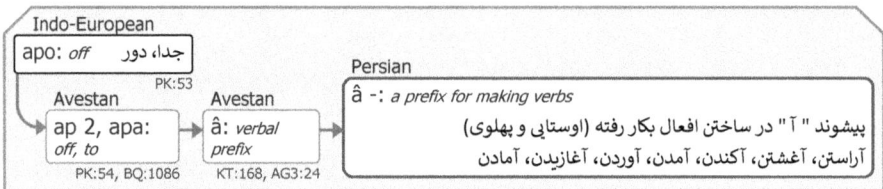

Indo-European
apo: *off*   جدا، دور
PK:53

Avestan
ap 2, apa: *off, to*
PK:54, BQ:1086

Avestan
â: *verbal prefix*
KT:168, AG3:24

Persian
â -: *a prefix for making verbs*
پیشوند " آ " در ساختن افعال بکار رفته (اوستایی و پهلوی)
آراستن، آغشتن، آکندن، آمدن، آوردن، آغازیدن، آمادن

1

آ ـ ۲   پیشوند نفی   مقایسه: آن ـ ۱

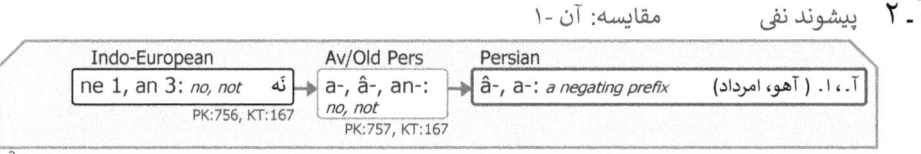

Indo-European
ne 1, an 3: *no, not*   نَه
PK:756, KT:167

Av/Old Pers
a-, â-, an-: *no, not*
PK:757, KT:167

Persian
â-, a-: *a negating prefix*   آ،۱. (آهو، امرداد)

2

آب۱: مایع

همریشه: Punjab

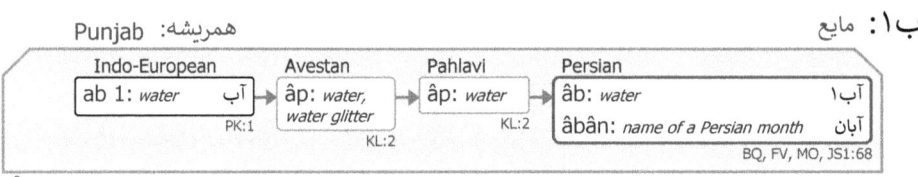

Indo-European
ab 1: *water*   آب
PK:1

Avestan
âp: *water, water glitter*
KL:2

Pahlavi
âp: *water*

Persian
âb: *water*   آب۱
âbân: *name of a Persian month*   آبان
BQ, FV, MO, JS1:68

3

آب۲: درخشش

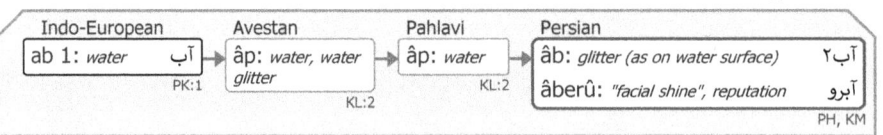

Indo-European
ab 1: *water*   آب
PK:1

Avestan
âp: *water, water glitter*
KL:2

Pahlavi
âp: *water*
KL:2

Persian
âb: *glitter (as on water surface)*   آب۲
âberû: *"facial shine", reputation*   آبرو
PH, KM

4

آباد

Indo-European
pa: *to protect, feed*
حفاظت کردن، غذا دادن
PK:787,842, BK:103

Av/Old Pers
pa: *to guard*
pâta: *protected*
PH:41,72, KL:114

Pahlavi
pây, â-pây: *to protect*
â-pât: *protected, thriving*
â-pât-ân: *name of a city (with protected waterways)*
FV:119, BQ:2, CH:288

Persian
Âbâd: *prosperous, cultivated*   آباد
Âbâdân: *a city in Iran*   آبادان
FV, BQ, CH

5

آبادان   . رجوع شود به   آباد

آبار: سرب سوخته

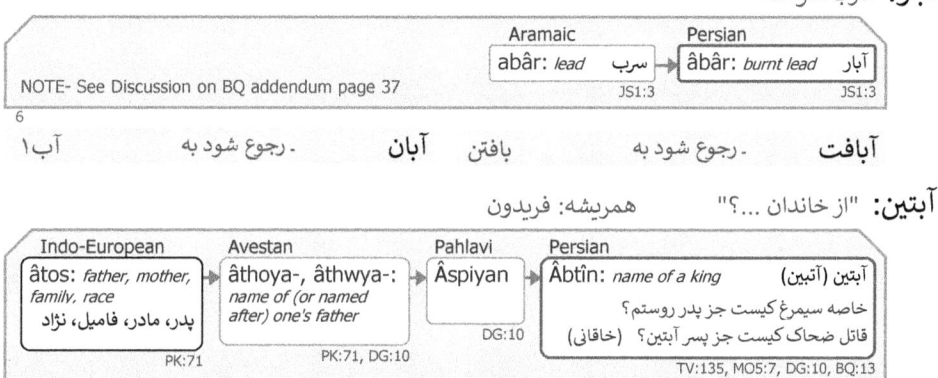

NOTE- See Discussion on BQ addendum page 37

6

آبافت ـ رجوع شود به **آبان**   بافتن ـ رجوع شود به   آب ۱

آبتین: "از خاندان ...؟"   همریشه: فریدون

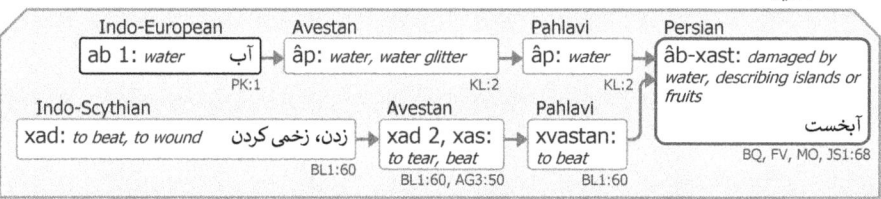

7

آبخست: جزیره

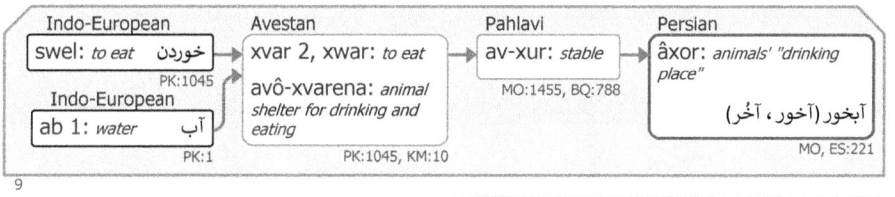

8

آبخور: محل آب خوردن جانور و آدمی

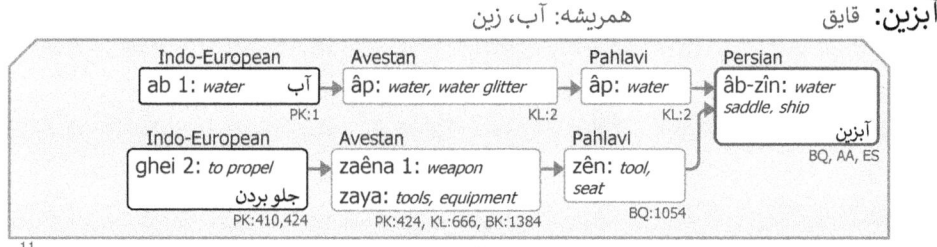

9

آبرو ـ رجوع شود به   آب ۲

آبریز

Indo-European: ab 1: *water* آب — PK:1
Avestan: âp: *water, water glitter* — KL:2
Pahlavi: âp-rex: *water container* — BR, BL1:3
Persian: âbrîz: *urn, pitcher*   آبریز — BL1:3

Indo-European: leigh 2, raič*: *leave* ترک کردن — PK:669, CH:307
Avestan: rêxt, rêz, hâek: *to pour out* — PK:669, AG3:72, GR:11
Pahlavi: rextan: *to pour*; âp-rex: *water pot, kettle* — BQ, PH:141,203, BR, TV:115

10

آبزین: قایق   همریشه: آب، زین

Indo-European: ab 1: *water* آب — PK:1
Avestan: âp: *water, water glitter* — KL:2
Pahlavi: âp: *water* — KL:2
Persian: âb-zîn: *water saddle, ship* آبزین — BQ, AA, ES

Indo-European: ghei 2: *to propel* جلو بردن — PK:410,424
Avestan: zaêna 1: *weapon*; zaya: *tools, equipment* — PK:424, KL:666, BK:1384
Pahlavi: zên: *tool, seat* — BQ:1054

11

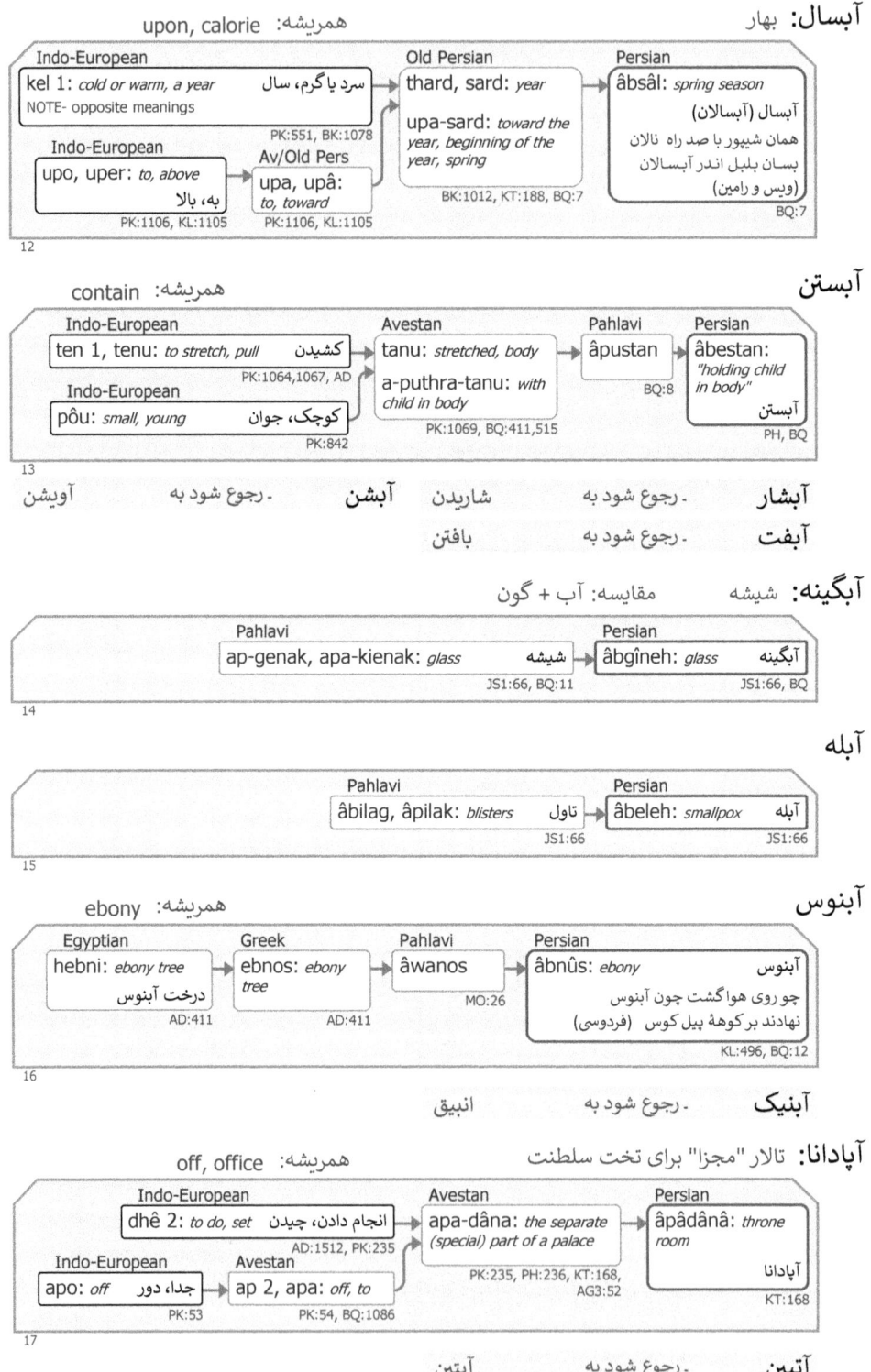

آبسال: بهار

همریشه: upon, calorie

Indo-European
kel 1: *cold or warm, a year*
NOTE- opposite meanings
سرد یا گرم، سال
PK:551, BK:1078

Indo-European
upo, uper: *to, above*
به، بالا
PK:1106, KL:1105

Av/Old Pers
upa, upâ:
to, toward
PK:1106, KL:1105

Old Persian
thard, sard: *year*

upa-sard: *toward the year, beginning of the year, spring*
BK:1012, KT:188, BQ:7

Persian
âbsâl: *spring season*
آبسال (آبسالان)
همان شیپور با صد راه نالان
بسان بلبل اندر آبسالان
(ویس و رامین)
BQ:7

12

آبستن

همریشه: contain

Indo-European
ten 1, tenu: *to stretch, pull*
کشیدن
PK:1064,1067, AD

Indo-European
pôu: *small, young*
کوچک، جوان
PK:842

Avestan
tanu: *stretched, body*

a-puthra-tanu: *with child in body*
PK:1069, BQ:411,515

Pahlavi
âpustan
BQ:8

Persian
âbestan:
"holding child in body"
آبستن
PH, BQ

13

| آبشار | ـ رجوع شود به | شاریدن | آبشن | ـ رجوع شود به | آویشن |
| آبفت | ـ رجوع شود به | بافتن | | | |

آبگینه: شیشه

مقایسه: آب + گون

Pahlavi
ap-genak, apa-kienak: *glass*
شیشه
JS1:66, BQ:11

Persian
âbgîneh: *glass*
آبگینه
JS1:66, BQ

14

آبله

Pahlavi
âbilag, âpilak: *blisters*
تاول
JS1:66

Persian
âbeleh: *smallpox*
آبله
JS1:66

15

آبنوس

همریشه: ebony

Egyptian
hebni: *ebony tree*
درخت آبنوس
AD:411

Greek
ebnos: *ebony tree*
AD:411

Pahlavi
âwanos
MO:26

Persian
âbnûs: *ebony*
آبنوس
چو روی هوا گشت چون آبنوس
نهادند بر کوههٔ پیل کوس (فردوسی)
KL:496, BQ:12

16

| آبنیک | ـ رجوع شود به | انبیق |

آپادانا: تالار "مجزا" برای تخت سلطنت

همریشه: off, office

Indo-European
dhê 2: *to do, set*
انجام دادن، چیدن
AD:1512, PK:235

Indo-European
apo: *off*
جدا، دور
PK:53

Avestan
ap 2, apa: *off, to*
PK:54, BQ:1086

Avestan
apa-dâna: *the separate (special) part of a palace*
PK:235, PH:236, KT:168, AG3:52

Persian
âpâdânâ: *throne room*
آپادانا
KT:168

17

| آتبین | ـ رجوع شود به | آبتین |

3

آتش

همریشه: atrium

Indo-European	Avestan	Pahlavi	Persian
ater: *fire* آتش	âtarš, âthra: *fire* âthur-pât-gan: *fire guard*	âtur: *fire*	âtaš: *fire* (آذر) آتش
PK:69	PK:69, KL:123	BQ:13	MO, AG2:59

18

آتمسفر: "کُره بخار"   همریشه: سپهر

همریشه: sphere

Indo-European	Greek	French	Persian
spher: *move* حرکت کردن	spairen: *to bounce like a ball* atmos-sphaira: *ball of vapor*		âtmosfer: *"sphere of vapor"* آتمسفر
PK:992	PK:992		MO:32

19

آجدن .رجوع شود به   آژدن

آجر

Akkadian / Aramaic	Old Persian	Pahlavi	Persian	Arabic	Persian
agurru: *baked clay, brick* گل پخته، آجر	aguru: *brick*	âgur	âgur: *brick* آگور	ajur: *brick*	âjor: *brick* آجر
ZM:31, KT:165	KT:165, AA:6	AA:6	AA:6, MO:78	AA:6, ZM:31, AS:7	MO:78

NOTE- This word could have entered Arabic directly from Akkadian / Aramaic

20

آجیدن: دوختن زینتهایی بر روی جامه با نخ یا رشتهٔ زر

Indo_European	Persian
čaih*: *to sew, stitch* دوختن، بخیه زدن	âjîdan: *to sew, stitch* (آزیدن، آژیدن) آجیدن کشیده پرستنده هر سورده همه جامه هاشان بزر آژده (فردوسی)
CH:29	MO:2599, CH:29, DK*

توجه . مقایسه شود با "آژدن" و سایر لغات متشابه

21

آخ

Indo-European	Avestan / Sanskrit	Pahlavi	Persian
agh(lo): *fear, disgust* ترس، چندش	ağô, ağâ: *bad, ugly* ağalâ: *a bad person*	âğ, âk: *trouble*	âx, ax: *a word of rejection and grief* آخ، اخ
PK:7,8	PK:8, JS1:77	TV:38	TV:38, BQ:90

22

آختن: بیرون کشیدن   همریشه: آهیختن

همریشه: tension, off

Indo-European	Avestan	Persian
ten 1, tenu: *to stretch, pull* کشیدن	thang, hanč, â-thax: *to pull*	âxtan: *to pull out* آختن axteh: *pulled out (testicles)* آخته
PK:1064,1067, AD	BQ:1481,2376, 2381, TV:7	JS1:107, BQ:92

Indo-European	Avestan	
apo: *off* جدا، دور	ap 2, apa: *off, to*	
PK:53	PK:54, BQ:1086	

23

آخُر ، آخور .رجوع شود به   آبخور   **آخوند** .رجوع شود به   خواندن

آداب .رجوع شود به   ادب

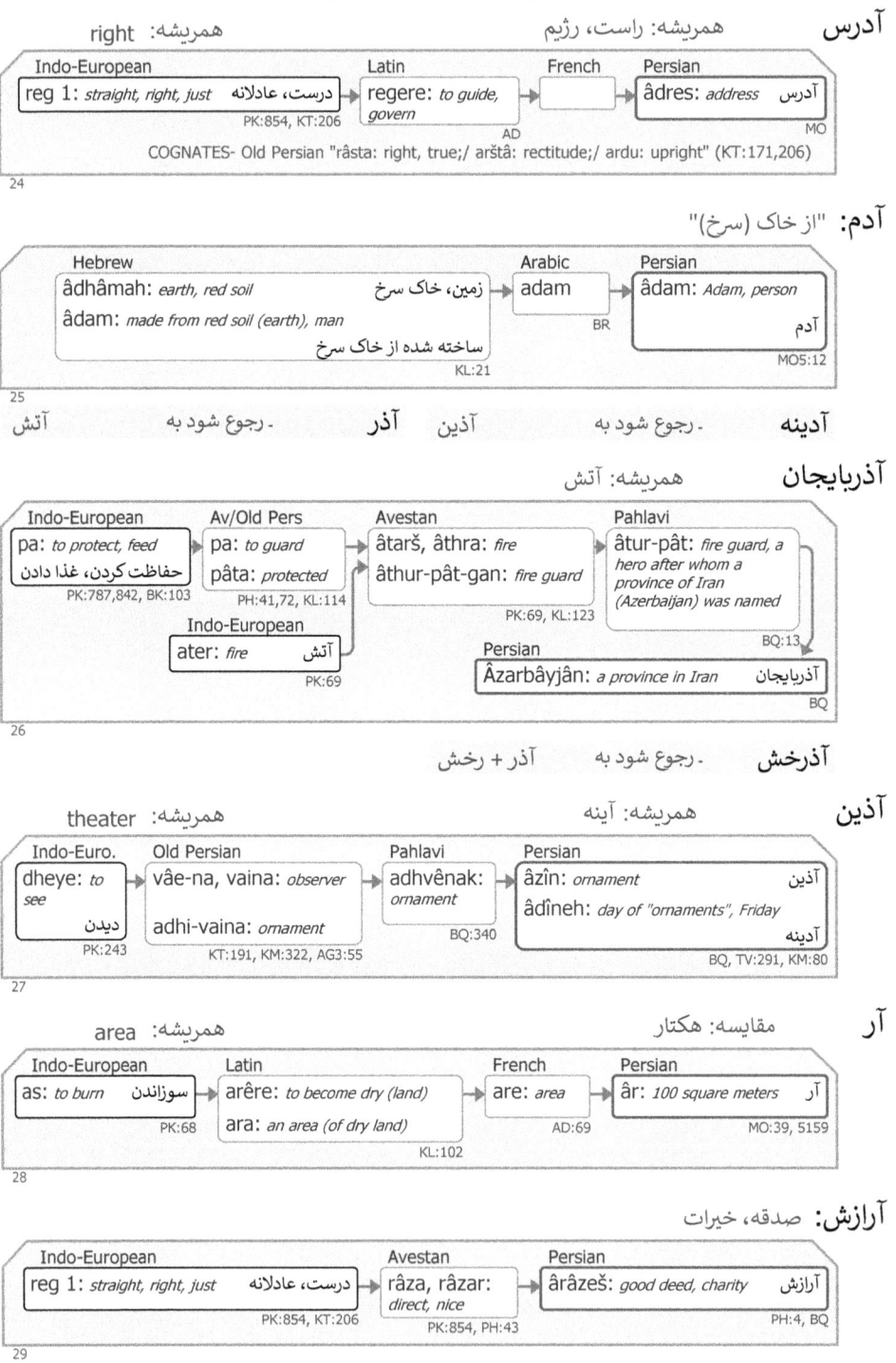

آدرس

همریشه: راست، رژیم

همریشه: right

Indo-European	Latin	French	Persian
reg 1: *straight, right, just* درست، عادلانه	regere: *to guide, govern*		âdres: *address* آدرس
PK:854, KT:206	AD		MO

COGNATES- Old Persian "râsta: right, true;/ arštâ: rectitude;/ ardu: upright" (KT:171,206)

24

آدم: "از خاک (سرخ)"

Hebrew	Arabic	Persian
âdhâmah: *earth, red soil* زمین، خاک سرخ	adam	âdam: *Adam, person* آدم
âdam: *made from red soil (earth), man* ساخته شده از خاک سرخ	BR	
KL:21		MO5:12

25

آدینه

_. رجوع شود به آذین آذر _. رجوع شود به آتش

آذربایجان

همریشه: آتش

Indo-European	Av/Old Pers	Avestan	Pahlavi
pa: *to protect, feed* حفاظت کردن، غذا دادن	pa: *to guard* pâta: *protected*	âtarš, âthra: *fire* âthur-pât-gan: *fire guard*	âtur-pât: *fire guard, a hero after whom a province of Iran (Azerbaijan) was named*
PK:787,842, BK:103	PH:41,72, KL:114	PK:69, KL:123	BQ:13

Indo-European			Persian
ater: *fire* آتش			Âzarbâyjân: *a province in Iran* آذربایجان
PK:69			BQ

26

آذرخش

_. رجوع شود به آذر + رخش

آذین

همریشه: آینه

همریشه: theater

Indo-Euro.	Old Persian	Pahlavi	Persian
dheye: *to see* دیدن	vâe-na, vaina: *observer* adhi-vaina: *ornament*	adhvênak: *ornament*	âzîn: *ornament* آذین âdîneh: *day of "ornaments", Friday* آدینه
PK:243	KT:191, KM:322, AG3:55	BQ:340	BQ, TV:291, KM:80

27

آر

مقایسه: هکتار

همریشه: area

Indo-European	Latin	French	Persian
as: *to burn* سوزاندن	arêre: *to become dry (land)* ara: *an area (of dry land)*	are: *area*	âr: *100 square meters* آر
PK:68	KL:102	AD:69	MO:39, 5159

28

آرازش: صدقه، خیرات

Indo-European	Avestan	Persian
reg 1: *straight, right, just* درست، عادلانه	râza, râzar: *direct, nice*	ârâzeš: *good deed, charity* آرازش
PK:854, KT:206	PK:854, PH:43	PH:4, BQ

29

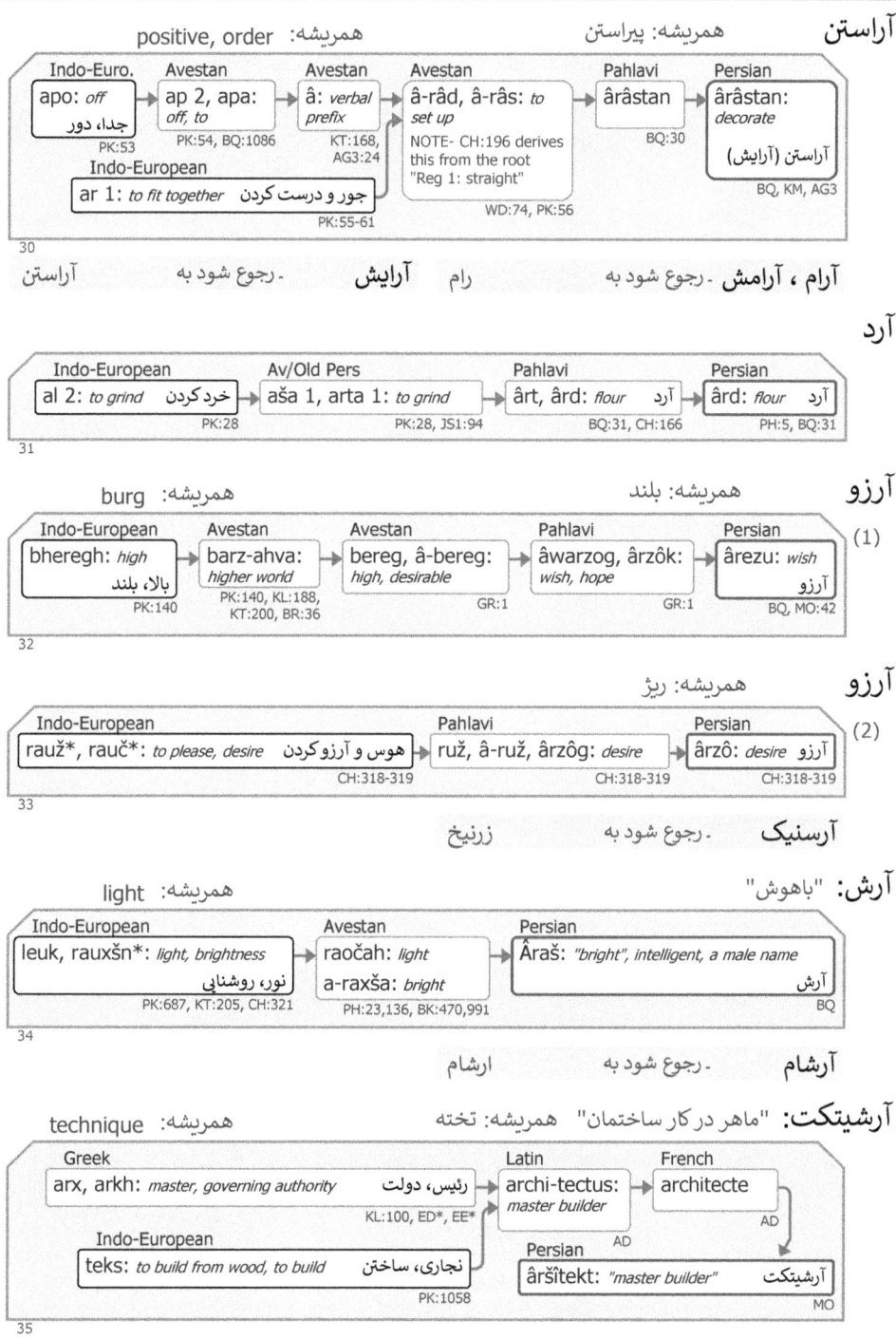

آرشیو: "پرونده های دولتی"

همریشه: archive, architect

Greek	Latin	French	Persian
arx, arkh: *master, governing authority* رئیس، دولت KL:100, ED*, EE*	archivum: *government records* AD	archive AD	âršîv: *archive* آرشیو MO

36

آرغنده   . رجوع شود به   ارغنده   **آرمئیتی**   . رجوع شود به   آرمَتی

آرمیدن   . رجوع شود به   رام

آرنج

همریشه: elbow

Indo-European	Avestan	Persian
el 1 : *to bend, elbow* خم کردن، آرنج PK:308, KL:509	arethna: *arm, elbow* PK:308	ârenj: *elbow* آرنج BQ:32, HN1:79

37

آرواره

Indo-European	Avestan	Pahlavi	Persian
aulos: *jaw* آرواره PK:88, AP:55	hanuharena: *jaw* AP:55	êrwârag AP:55	ârvâreh: *jaw* AP:55

38

آروغ

Indo-European	Persian
reug: *to vomit, belch, produce smoke or vapor* استفراغ ، آروغ زدن ، تولید دود یا بخار PK:871	roǧ: *belch* رُغ âroǧ: *belch* آروغ PK:871, MO

39

آری

همریشه: آور   همریشه: well

Indo-European	Old Persian	Pahlavi	Persian
en: *in, inside* داخل PK:311	adi-var: *in truth* PK:311	ê-var: *indeed* PH:6,20	ârî: *yes* آری PH
wel 1: *to wish, desire* آرزو کردن PK:1137			

40

آریا: "شریف"   همریشه: ایران   همریشه: Ireland

Indo-European	Indo-European	AV/Old Pers	Persian
al 1: *beyond, above* فراتر، بالاتر PK:24	Aryo, Ario: *Lord, ruler* PK:24,67	aria: *noble* PK, FV:7,28, BQ:179	Ârîyâ آریا MO5, FV, NS

41

آریغ   . رجوع شود به   ریغ

آز   همریشه: نیاز   همریشه: anger

Indo-European	Avestan	Pahlavi	Persian
angh: *compressed* فشرده az*: *to drive, lead* راندن (فشردن) PK:42, CH:171	âz, âzi: *need, desire, greed* NOTE- CH is not certain about this derivation. BQ:34, CH:172	âz: *greed* BQ:34, CH:172	âz: *need, desire, greed* آز BQ

42

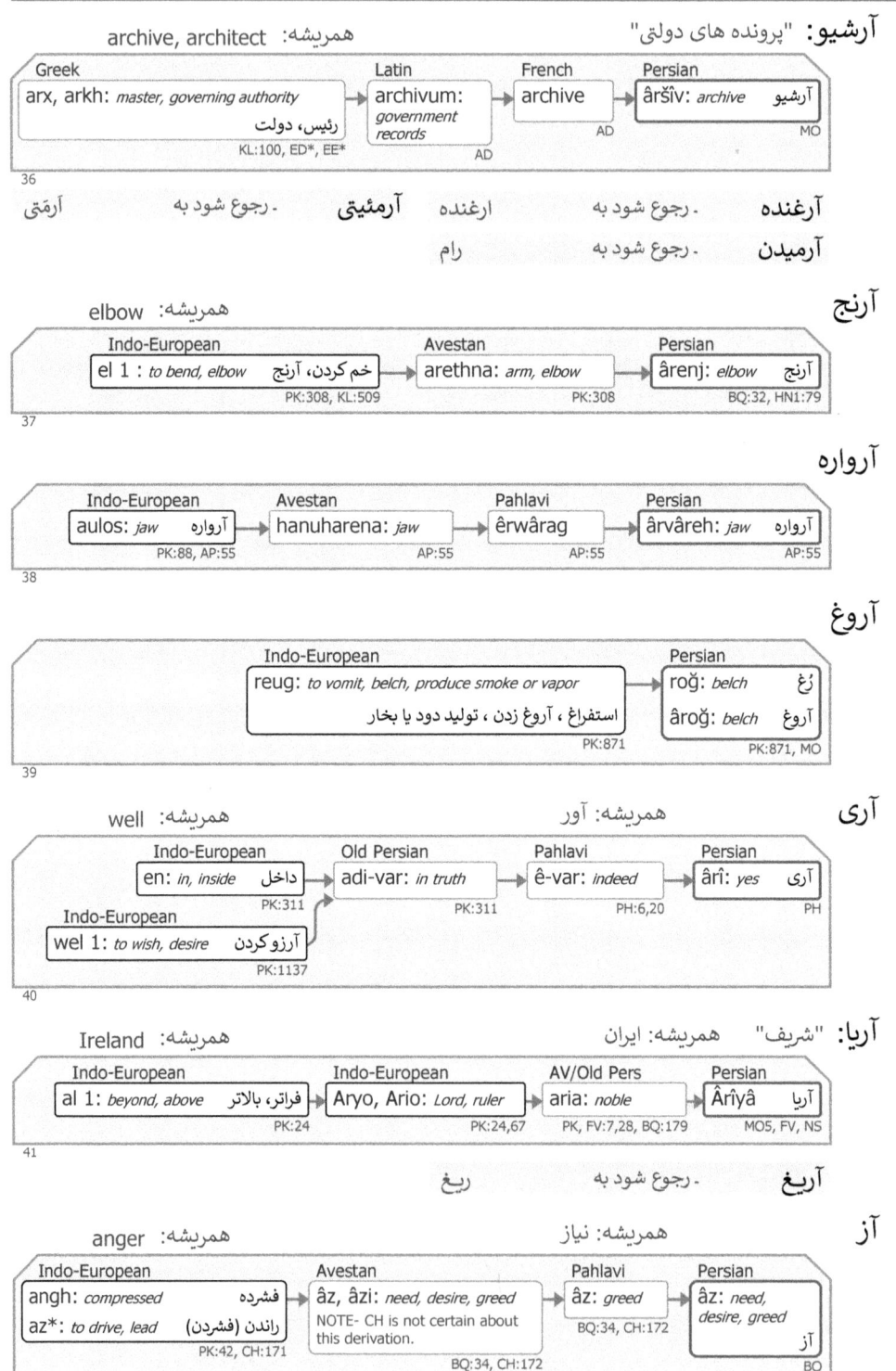

7

آزاد

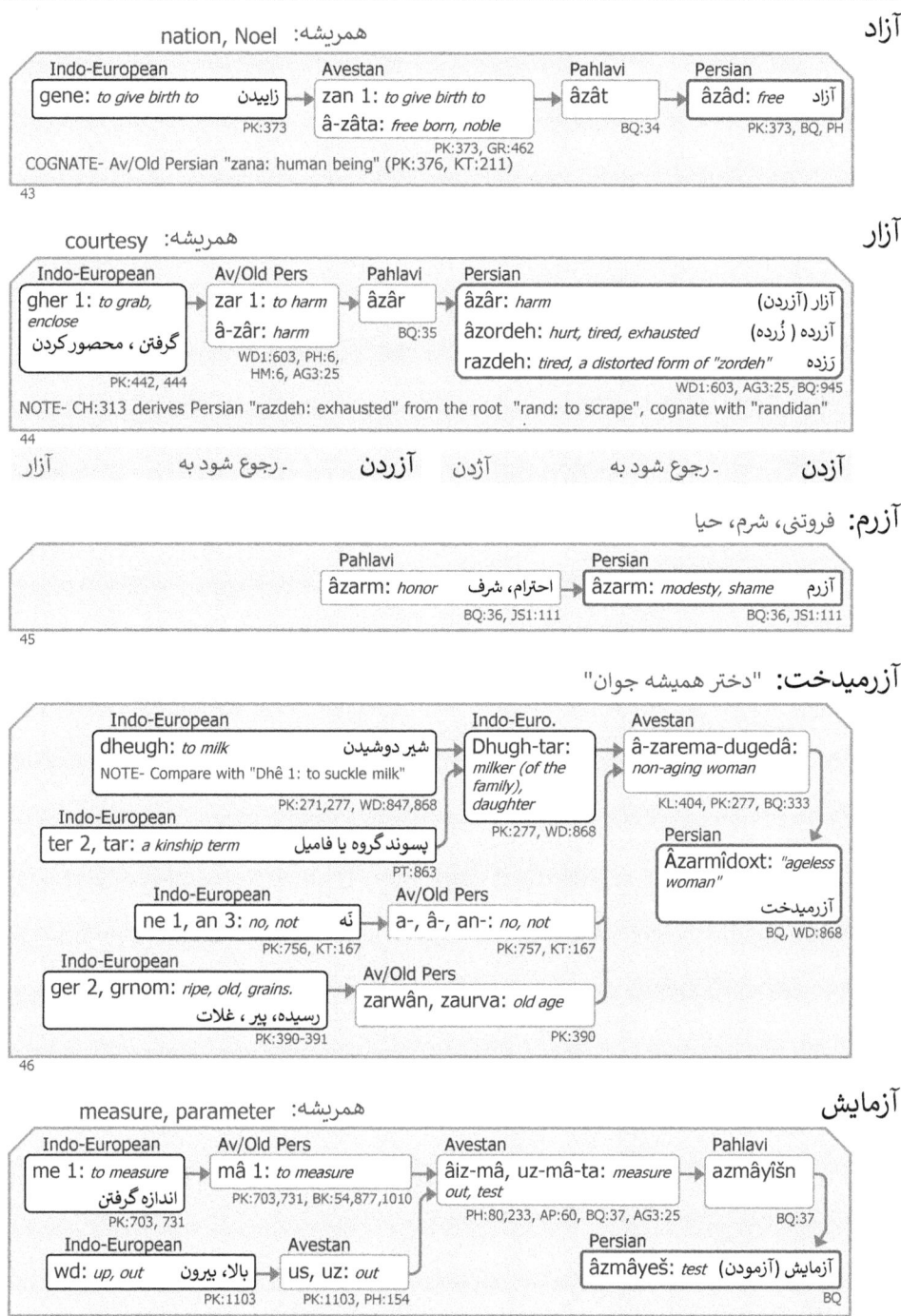

آزاد   همریشه: nation, Noel

Indo-European	Avestan	Pahlavi	Persian
gene: to give birth to زابیدن PK:373	zan 1: to give birth to â-zâta: free born, noble PK:373, GR:462	âzât BQ:34	âzâd: free آزاد PK:373, BQ, PH

COGNATE- Av/Old Persian "zana: human being" (PK:376, KT:211)
43

آزار   همریشه: courtesy

Indo-European	Av/Old Pers	Pahlavi	Persian
gher 1: to grab, enclose گرفتن ، محصور کردن PK:442, 444	zar 1: to harm â-zâr: harm WD1:603, PH:6, HM:6, AG3:25	âzâr BQ:35	âzâr: harm (آزار (آزردن âzordeh: hurt, tired, exhausted (آزرده (زُرده razdeh: tired, a distorted form of "zordeh" رزده WD1:603, AG3:25, BQ:945

NOTE- CH:313 derives Persian "razdeh: exhausted" from the root "rand: to scrape", cognate with "randidan"
44

آزار   آژدن رجوع شود به .   **آزردن**   آژدن رجوع شود به .   **آزدن**

آزرم: فروتنی، شرم، حیا

Pahlavi	Persian
âzarm: honor احترام، شرف BQ:36, JS1:111	âzarm: modesty, shame آزرم BQ:36, JS1:111

45

آزرمیدخت: "دختر همیشه جوان"

Indo-European	Indo-Euro.	Avestan
dheugh: to milk شیر دوشیدن NOTE- Compare with "Dhê 1: to suckle milk" PK:271,277, WD:847,868	Dhugh-tar: milker (of the family), daughter PK:277, WD:868	â-zarema-dugedâ: non-aging woman KL:404, PK:277, BQ:333

Indo-European		Persian
ter 2, tar: a kinship term پسوند گروه یا فامیل PT:863		Âzarmîdoxt: "ageless woman" آزرمیدخت BQ, WD:868

Indo-European	Av/Old Pers
ne 1, an 3: no, not نَه PK:756, KT:167	a-, â-, an-: no, not PK:757, KT:167

Indo-European	Av/Old Pers
ger 2, grnom: ripe, old, grains. رسیده، پیر ، غلات PK:390-391	zarwân, zaurva: old age PK:390

46

آزمایش   همریشه: measure, parameter

Indo-European	Av/Old Pers	Avestan	Pahlavi
me 1: to measure اندازه گرفتن PK:703, 731	mâ 1: to measure PK:703,731, BK:54,877,1010	âiz-mâ, uz-mâ-ta: measure out, test PH:80,233, AP:60, BQ:37, AG3:25	azmâyîšn BQ:37

Indo-European	Avestan	Persian
wd: up, out بالا، بیرون PK:1103	us, uz: out PK:1103, PH:154	âzmâyeš: test (آزمایش (آزمودن BQ

47

آجیدن   آزمایش رجوع شود به .   **آزدن**   آزمایش رجوع شود به .   **آزمودن**

8

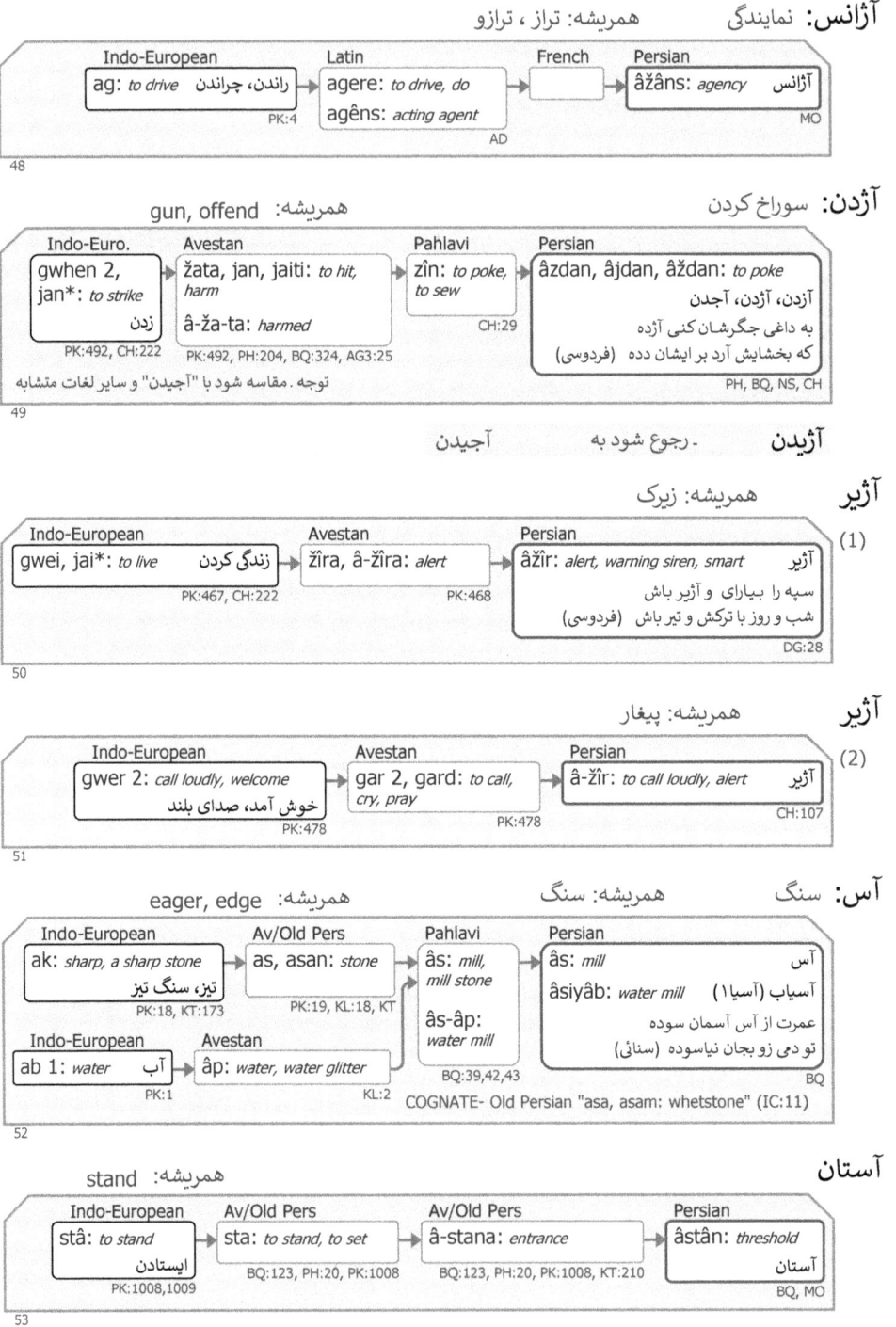

آژانس: نمایندگی   همریشه: تراز ، ترازو

Indo-European	Latin	French	Persian
ag: *to drive* راندن، چراندن	agere: *to drive, do* / agêns: *acting agent*		âžâns: *agency* آژانس
PK:4	AD		MO

48

آژدن: سوراخ کردن   همریشه: gun, offend

Indo-Euro.	Avestan	Pahlavi	Persian
gwhen 2, jan*: *to strike* زدن	žata, jan, jaiti: *to hit, harm* / â-ža-ta: *harmed*	zîn: *to poke, to sew*	âzdan, âjdan, âždan: *to poke* آزدن، آژدن، آجدن
PK:492, CH:222	PK:492, PH:204, BQ:324, AG3:25	CH:29	به داغی جگرشان کنی آژده / که بخشایش آرد بر ایشان دده (فردوسی)
			PH, BQ, NS, CH

توجه . مقایسه شود با "آجیدن" و سایر لغات متشابه

49

آژیدن   . رجوع شود به   آجیدن

آژیر   همریشه: زیرک   (1)

Indo-European	Avestan	Persian
gwei, jai*: *to live* زندگی کردن	žîra, â-žîra: *alert*	âžîr: *alert, warning siren, smart* آژیر
PK:467, CH:222	PK:468	سپه را بیارای و آژیر باش / شب و روز با ترکش و تیر باش (فردوسی)
		DG:28

50

آژیر   همریشه: پیغار   (2)

Indo-European	Avestan	Persian
gwer 2: *call loudly, welcome* خوش آمد، صدای بلند	gar 2, gard: *to call, cry, pray*	â-žîr: *to call loudly, alert* آژیر
PK:478	PK:478	CH:107

51

آس: سنگ   همریشه: eager, edge   همریشه: سنگ

Indo-European	Av/Old Pers	Pahlavi	Persian
ak: *sharp, a sharp stone* تیز، سنگ تیز	as, asan: *stone*	âs: *mill, mill stone*	âs: *mill* آس / âsiyâb: *water mill* آسیاب (آسیا۱)
PK:18, KT:173	PK:19, KL:18, KT	âs-âp: *water mill*	عمرت از آس آسمان سوده
Indo-European	Avestan		تو دی زو بجان نیاسوده (سنائی)
ab 1: *water* آب	âp: *water, water glitter*	BQ:39,42,43	BQ
PK:1	KL:2	COGNATE- Old Persian "asa, asam: whetstone" (IC:11)	

52

آستان   همریشه: stand

Indo-European	Av/Old Pers	Av/Old Pers	Persian
stâ: *to stand* ایستادن	sta: *to stand, to set*	â-stana: *entrance*	âstân: *threshold* آستان
PK:1008,1009	BQ:123, PH:20, PK:1008	BQ:123, PH:20, PK:1008, KT:210	BQ, MO

53

آستر

همریشه: wear, vest

Indo-European	Avestan	Pahlavi	Persian
wes 3: *to wear, put on* پوشیدن PK:1172	vah, vahna, vanhna, vasta: *cover, clothes* PK:1172, KT:219, AP:62	wastar: *lining* KL, AD, AP:62	âstar: *lining* آستر AP:62

54

آستین

همریشه: دست   همریشه: ambient

Indo-European	Avestan	Avestan	Persian
ambhi: *around* اطراف PK:34	abi: *up, around* PK:34	abi-dasta, a-dasta, a-dsta: *over hands, sleeve* GV:220	âstîn: *sleeve* آستین BQ:854, GV:220, MO
Indo-European	Avestan		
ghesto: *hand* دست PK:447	zasta, dasta: *hand* PK:447, KL:707, KT:190		

55

آسغده: آماده، ساخته شده

همریشه: ساختن

Indo-European	Avestan	Pahlavi	Persian
kak 1, sač: *to enable, prepare* فعال کردن، آماده PK:522, AP:352, CH:323	sak, sač, sâx: *to make, prepare* PK:522, PH:152, AG3:58	a-saxt-ak: *ready* pa-saxt-ak: *ready* JS1:135	âsaǧdeh: *prepared, ready* آسغده (بسغده) نشاید درون نابسغده شدن نباید که نئوائش بازآمدن (ابوشکور) CH:323-324, DK*

COGNATE- Avestan "čagad: *helped*" (PK:522)

56

آسفالت

. رجوع شود به   اسفالت

آسمان: "سنگ مانند"

همریشه: geometry, edge

Indo-European	Av/Old Pers	Pahlavi	Persian
ak: *sharp, a sharp stone* تیز، سنگ تیز PK:18, KT:173	as, asan: *stone* as-man: *like stone, sky* PK:19, KL:18, KT	âs-mân: *sky* BQ:39,42,43	âsmân: *sky* آسمان آسمان آسیای گردانست این چه خواهدت کردن آخر آس (عنصری) BQ
Indo-Euro. me 1: *to measure* اندازه گرفتن PK:703, 731	Indo-Euro. mân: *to resemble* شبیه بودن CH:272		

57

آسموغ

. رجوع شود به   آشموغ

آسه: محور

همریشه: axis

Indo-European	Avestan	Persian
asksâ, aksas: *axis* محور PK:6, AP:64	ašyâ: *axis* PK:6, AP:64	âseh: *axis* آسه AP:64, MO:57

58

آسیا۱

. رجوع شود به   آسیاب

آسیا۲: "محل طلوع آفتاب"

Akkadian	Greek	Latin	French	Persian
âsû : *to rise, come out (said of the sun)* بالا آمدن (خورشید) KL:113	asia: *land of sunrise, the East* KL:113			âsîyâ: *Asia* آسیا۲ MO5:37

59

آسیاب: ـ رجوع شود به   آس + آب

آسیدن: رسیدن

همریشه: enough

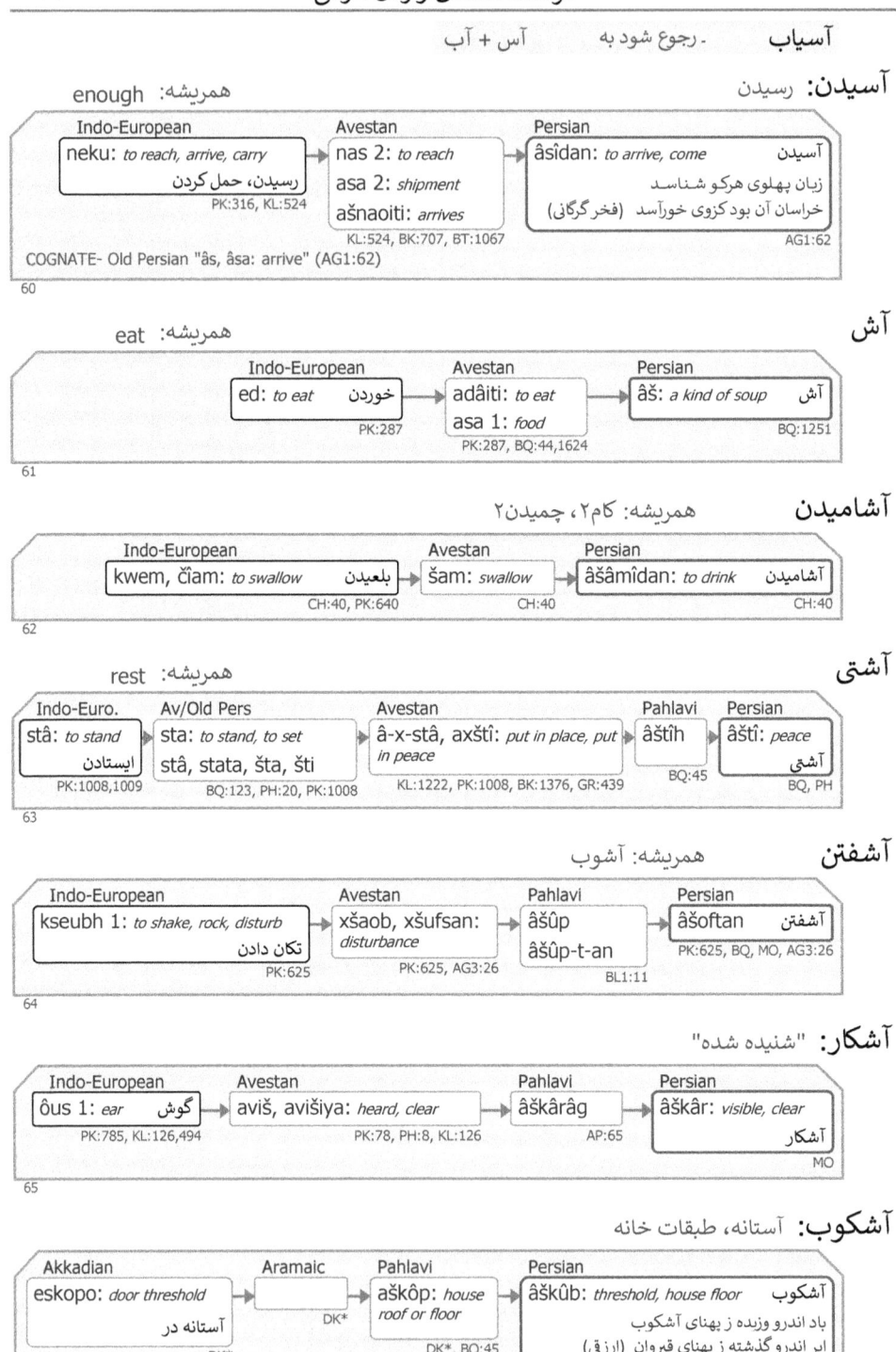

Indo-European	Avestan	Persian
neku: *to reach, arrive, carry* رسیدن، حمل کردن PK:316, KL:524	nas 2: *to reach* asa 2: *shipment* ašnaoiti: *arrives* KL:524, BK:707, BT:1067	âsîdan: *to arrive, come* آسیدن زبان پهلوی هرکو شناسـد خراسان آن بود کزوی خورآسد (فخر گرگانی) AG1:62

COGNATE- Old Persian "âs, âsa: arrive" (AG1:62)

60

آش

همریشه: eat

Indo-European	Avestan	Persian
ed: *to eat* خوردن PK:287	adâiti: *to eat* asa 1: *food* PK:287, BQ:44,1624	âš: *a kind of soup* آش BQ:1251

61

آشامیدن

همریشه: کام۲، چمیدن۲

Indo-European	Avestan	Persian
kwem, čǐam: *to swallow* بلعیدن CH:40, PK:640	šam: *swallow* CH:40	âšâmîdan: *to drink* آشامیدن CH:40

62

آشتی

همریشه: rest

Indo-Euro.	Av/Old Pers	Avestan	Pahlavi	Persian
stâ: *to stand* ایستادن PK:1008,1009	sta: *to stand, to set* stâ, stata, šta, šti BQ:123, PH:20, PK:1008	â-x-stâ, axštî: *put in place, put in peace* KL:1222, PK:1008, BK:1376, GR:439	âštîh BQ:45	âštî: *peace* آشتی BQ, PH

63

آشفتن

همریشه: آشوب

Indo-European	Avestan	Pahlavi	Persian
kseubh 1: *to shake, rock, disturb* تکان دادن PK:625	xšaob, xšufsan: *disturbance* PK:625, AG3:26	âšûp âšûp-t-an BL1:11	âšoftan آشفتن PK:625, BQ, MO, AG3:26

64

آشکار: "شنیده شده"

Indo-European	Avestan	Pahlavi	Persian
ôus 1: *ear* گوش PK:785, KL:126,494	aviš, avišiya: *heard, clear* PK:78, PH:8, KL:126	âškârâg AP:65	âškâr: *visible, clear* آشکار MO

65

آشکوب: آستانه، طبقات خانه

Akkadian	Aramaic	Pahlavi	Persian
eskopo: *door threshold* آستانه در DK*	DK*	aškôp: *house roof or floor* DK*, BQ:45	âškûb: *threshold, house floor* آشکوب باد اندرو وزده ز پهنای آشکوب ابر اندرو گذشته ز پهنای قیروان (ارزق) DK*, BQ:45

66

آشموغ: گمراه کننده و فریب دهنده

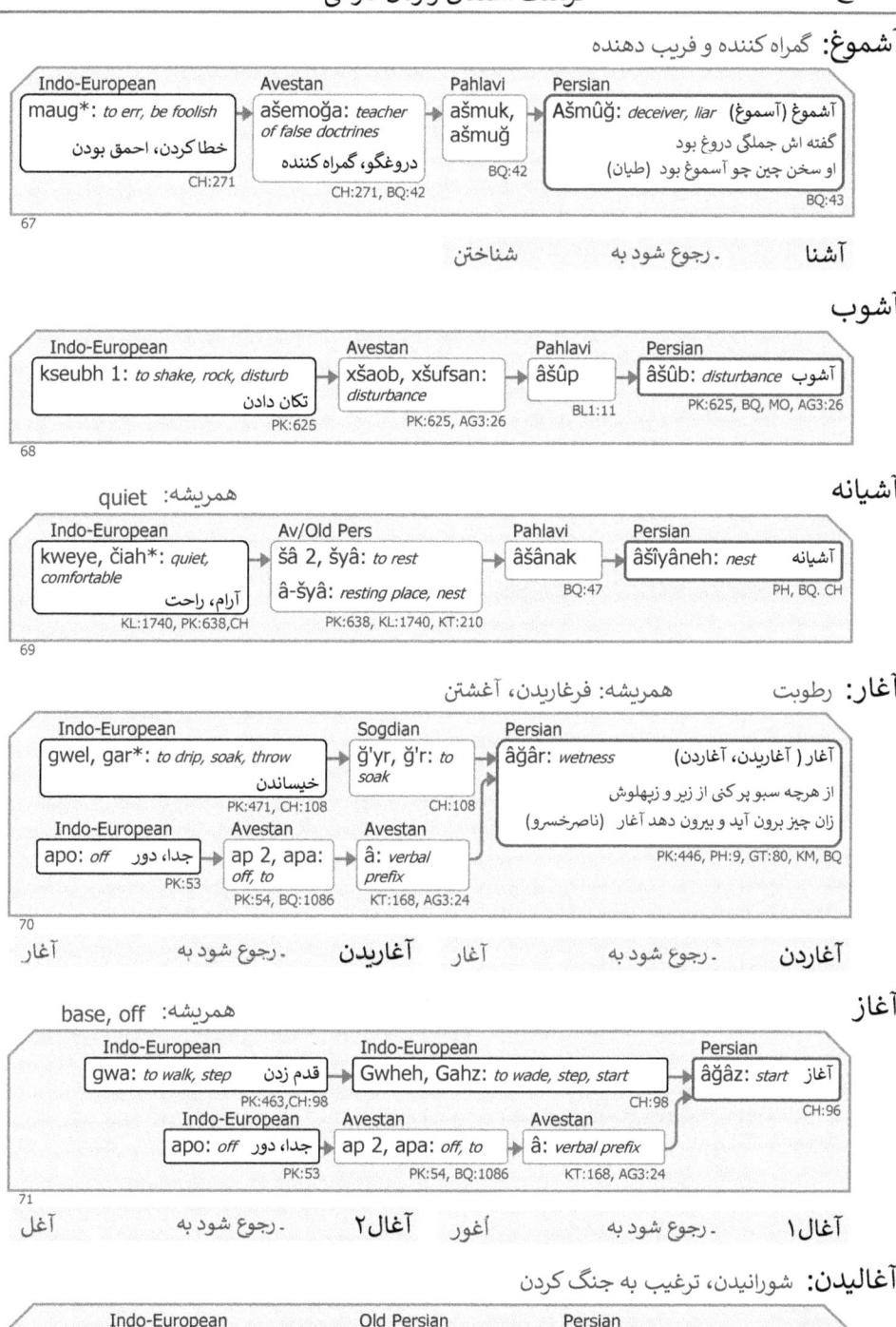

Indo-European	Avestan	Pahlavi	Persian
maug*: to err, be foolish — خطا کردن، احمق بودن — CH:271	ašemoğa: teacher of false doctrines — دروغگو، گمراه کننده — CH:271, BQ:42	ašmuk, ašmuğ — BQ:42	Ašmûğ: deceiver, liar — آشموغ (آسموغ) گفته اش جملگی دروغ بود او سخن چین چو آسموغ بود (طیان) — BQ:43

67

آشنا . رجوع شود به   شناختن

آشوب

Indo-European	Avestan	Pahlavi	Persian
kseubh 1: to shake, rock, disturb — تکان دادن — PK:625	xšaob, xšufsan: disturbance — PK:625, AG3:26	âšûp — BL1:11	âšûb: disturbance آشوب — PK:625, BQ, MO, AG3:26

68

آشیانه

همریشه: quiet

Indo-European	Av/Old Pers	Pahlavi	Persian
kweye, čiah*: quiet, comfortable — آرام، راحت — KL:1740, PK:638,CH	šâ 2, šyâ: to rest â-šyâ: resting place, nest — PK:638, KL:1740, KT:210	âšânak — BQ:47	âšîyâneh: nest آشیانه — PH, BQ. CH

69

آغار: رطوبت

همریشه: فرغاریدن، آغشتن

Indo-European	Sogdian	Persian
gwel, gar*: to drip, soak, throw — خیساندن — PK:471, CH:108	ğ'yr, ğ'r: to soak — CH:108	âğâr: wetness آغار (آغاریدن، آغاردن) از هرچه سبو پرکنی از زیر و زپهلوش زان چیز برون آید و بیرون دهد آغار (ناصرخسرو) — PK:446, PH:9, GT:80, KM, BQ

Indo-European	Avestan	Avestan
apo: off — جدا، دور — PK:53	ap 2, apa: off, to — PK:54, BQ:1086	â: verbal prefix — KT:168, AG3:24

70

آغاردن . رجوع شود به   آغار   آغاریدن   آغار . رجوع شود به   آغار

آغاز

همریشه: base, off

Indo-European	Indo-European	Persian
gwa: to walk, step — قدم زدن — PK:463,CH:98	Gwheh, Gahz: to wade, step, start — CH:98	âğâz: start آغاز — CH:96

Indo-European	Avestan	Avestan
apo: off — جدا، دور — PK:53	ap 2, apa: off, to — PK:54, BQ:1086	â: verbal prefix — KT:168, AG3:24

71

آغل   . رجوع شود به   اغور   آغال۲   . رجوع شود به   آغال۱

آغالیدن: شورانیدن، ترغیب به جنگ کردن

Indo-European	Old Persian	Persian
gheidh: wish for — آرزو کردن — PK:434	â-gard-ayatiy: he makes greedy, excites — JS1:90	âğâlîdan: to excite آغالیدن تو لشکر برآغال بر لشکرش بیکبار تا خیره گردد سرش (فردوسی) — JS1:90, DK*

COGNATE- Sanskrit "gridhyati: is greedy, violent" (PK:434, JS1:90)

72

آغر: ـ رجوع شود به   آغردن

آغردن: خیساندن   همریشه: فرغاریدن، آغار

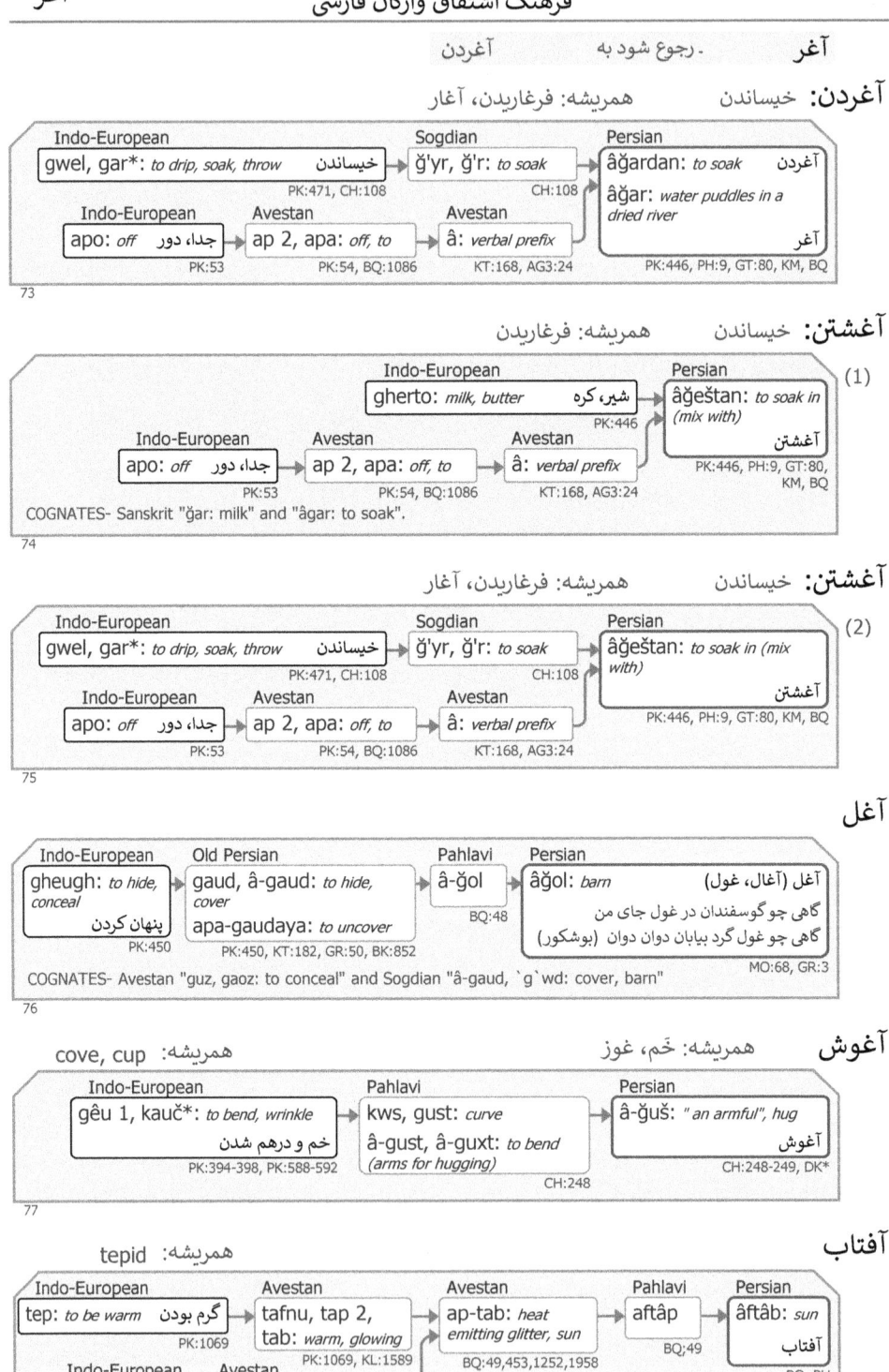

Indo-European
gwel, gar*: to drip, soak, throw   خیساندن
PK:471, CH:108

Sogdian
ǧ'yr, ǧ'r: to soak
CH:108

Persian
âǧardan: to soak   آغردن
âǧar: water puddles in a dried river
آغر
PK:446, PH:9, GT:80, KM, BQ

Indo-European
apo: off   جدا، دور
PK:53

Avestan
ap 2, apa: off, to
PK:54, BQ:1086

Avestan
â: verbal prefix
KT:168, AG3:24

73

آغشتن: خیساندن   همریشه: فرغاریدن   (1)

Indo-European
gherto: milk, butter   شیر، کره
PK:446

Persian
âǧeštan: to soak in (mix with)
آغشتن
PK:446, PH:9, GT:80, KM, BQ

Indo-European
apo: off   جدا، دور
PK:53

Avestan
ap 2, apa: off, to
PK:54, BQ:1086

Avestan
â: verbal prefix
KT:168, AG3:24

COGNATES- Sanskrit "ǧar: milk" and "âgar: to soak".

74

آغشتن: خیساندن   همریشه: فرغاریدن، آغار   (2)

Indo-European
gwel, gar*: to drip, soak, throw   خیساندن
PK:471, CH:108

Sogdian
ǧ'yr, ǧ'r: to soak
CH:108

Persian
âǧeštan: to soak in (mix with)
آغشتن
PK:446, PH:9, GT:80, KM, BQ

Indo-European
apo: off   جدا، دور
PK:53

Avestan
ap 2, apa: off, to
PK:54, BQ:1086

Avestan
â: verbal prefix
KT:168, AG3:24

75

آغل

Indo-European
gheugh: to hide, conceal   پنهان کردن
PK:450

Old Persian
gaud, â-gaud: to hide, cover
apa-gaudaya: to uncover
PK:450, KT:182, GR:50, BK:852

Pahlavi
â-ǧol
BQ:48

Persian
âǧol: barn
آغل (آغال، غول)
گاهی چو گوسفندان در غول جای من
گاهی چو غول گرد بیابان دوان دوان (بوشکور)
MO:68, GR:3

COGNATES- Avestan "guz, gaoz: to conceal" and Sogdian "â-gaud, `g`wd: cover, barn"

76

آغوش   همریشه: خَم، غوز   همریشه: cove, cup

Indo-European
gêu 1, kauč*: to bend, wrinkle
خم و درهم شدن
PK:394-398, PK:588-592

Pahlavi
kws, gust: curve
â-gust, â-guxt: to bend
(arms for hugging)
CH:248

Persian
â-ǧuš: "an armful", hug
آغوش
CH:248-249, DK*

77

آفتاب   همریشه: tepid

Indo-European
tep: to be warm   گرم بودن
PK:1069

Avestan
tafnu, tap 2, tab: warm, glowing
PK:1069, KL:1589

Avestan
ap-tab: heat emitting glitter, sun
BQ:49,453,1252,1958

Pahlavi
aftâp
BQ:49

Persian
âftâb: sun
آفتاب
BQ, PH

Indo-European
ab 1: water   آب
PK:1

Avestan
âp: water, water glitter
KL:2

78

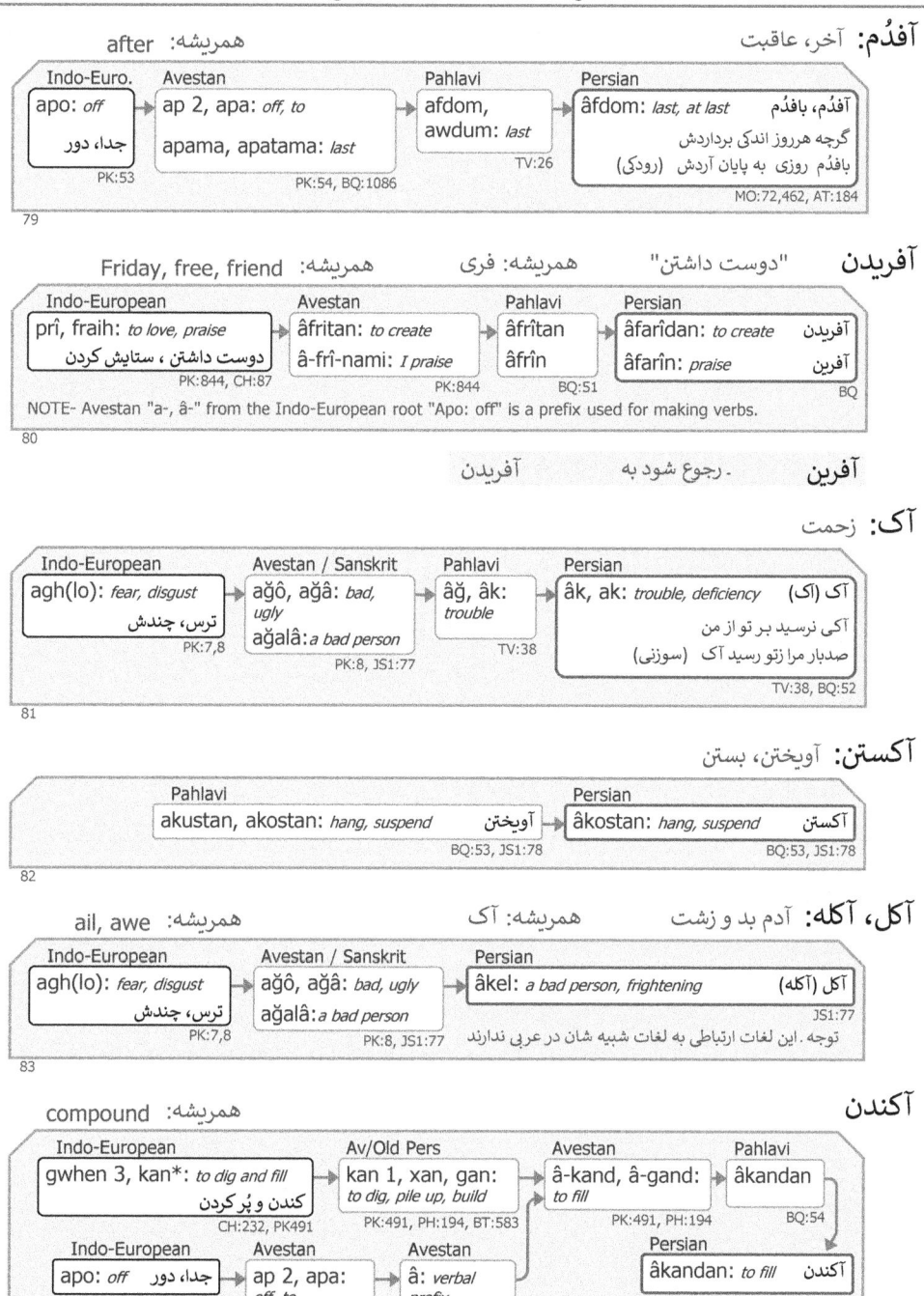

آفدُم: آخر، عاقبت

همریشه: after

Indo-Euro.	Avestan	Pahlavi	Persian
apo: off	ap 2, apa: off, to	afdom,	âfdom: last, at last آفدُم، بافدُم
جدا، دور	apama, apatama: last	awdum: last	گرچه هرروز اندکی برداردش
PK:53	PK:54, BQ:1086	TV:26	بافدُم روزی به پایان آردش (رودکی)
			MO:72,462, AT:184

79

آفریدن   "دوست داشتن"

همریشه: فری   همریشه: Friday, free, friend

Indo-European	Avestan	Pahlavi	Persian
prî, fraih: to love, praise	âfritan: to create	âfrîtan	âfarîdan: to create آفریدن
دوست داشتن ، ستایش کردن	â-frî-nami: I praise	âfrîn	âfarîn: praise آفرین
PK:844, CH:87	PK:844	BQ:51	BQ

NOTE- Avestan "a-, â-" from the Indo-European root "Apo: off" is a prefix used for making verbs.

80

آفرین   . رجوع شود به   آفریدن

آک: زحمت

Indo-European	Avestan / Sanskrit	Pahlavi	Persian
agh(lo): fear, disgust	ağô, ağâ: bad, ugly	âğ, âk: trouble	âk, ak: trouble, deficiency (آک) آک
ترس، چندش	ağalâ: a bad person		آکی نرسید بر تو از من
PK:7,8	PK:8, JS1:77	TV:38	صدبار مرا زتو رسید آک (سوزنی)
			TV:38, BQ:52

81

آکستن: آویختن، بستن

Pahlavi	Persian
akustan, akostan: hang, suspend آویختن	âkostan: hang, suspend آکستن
BQ:53, JS1:78	BQ:53, JS1:78

82

آکل، آکله: آدم بد و زشت   همریشه: آک

همریشه: ail, awe

Indo-European	Avestan / Sanskrit	Persian
agh(lo): fear, disgust	ağô, ağâ: bad, ugly	âkel: a bad person, frightening (آکله) آکل
ترس، چندش	ağalâ: a bad person	JS1:77
PK:7,8	PK:8, JS1:77	توجه. این لغات ارتباطی به لغات شبیه شان در عربی ندارند

83

آکندن

همریشه: compound

Indo-European	Av/Old Pers	Avestan	Pahlavi
gwhen 3, kan*: to dig and fill	kan 1, xan, gan: to dig, pile up, build	â-kand, â-gand: to fill	âkandan
کندن و پُرکردن			
CH:232, PK491	PK:491, PH:194, BT:583	PK:491, PH:194	BQ:54

Indo-European	Avestan	Avestan	Persian
apo: off جدا، دور	ap 2, apa: off, to	â: verbal prefix	âkandan: to fill آکندن
PK:53	PK:54, BQ:1086	KT:168, AG3:24	NOTE- compare with "Gwhen 1" BQ:54, TV:26

84

14

آگاه   همریشه: نگاه، ناگاه، گواه

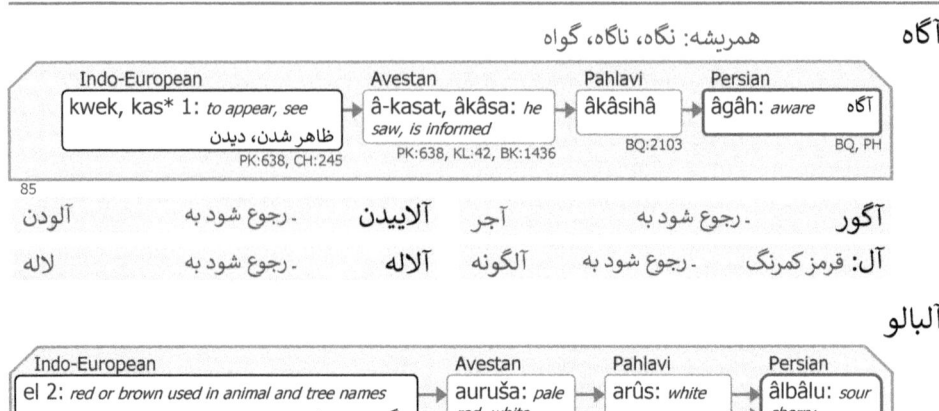

85

آلودن	. رجوع شود به	آلاییدن	آجر	. رجوع شود به	**آگور**
لاله	. رجوع شود به	آلاله	آلگونه	. رجوع شود به: قرمز کمرنگ	**آل**

آلبالو

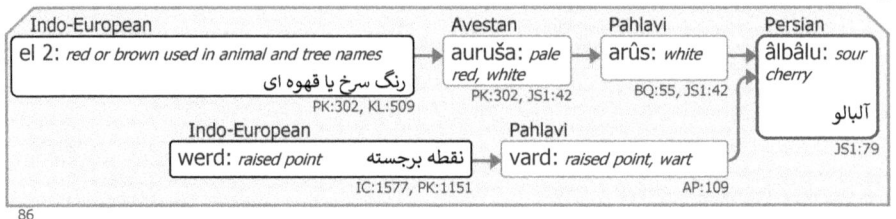

86

آلرژی: "عجیب، نا آشنا"

همریشه: alien, energy

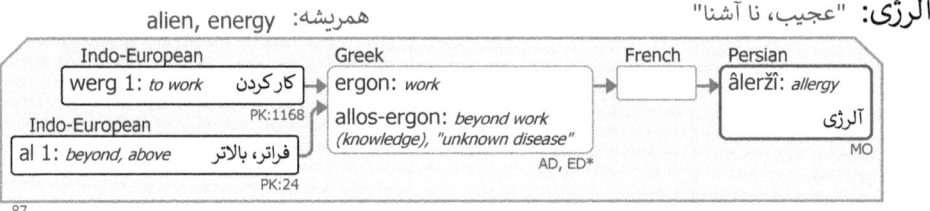

87

آلفاآلفا: "غذای اسب"

همریشه: hippo-, Philip

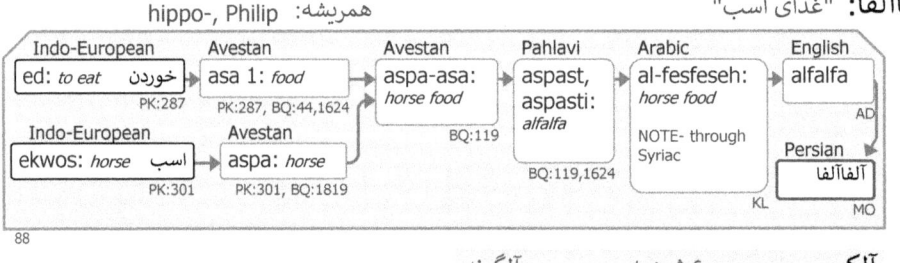

88

آلک   . رجوع شود به   آلگونه

آلگوریتم: روش محاسبه که بنام "خوارزمی" خوانده شد

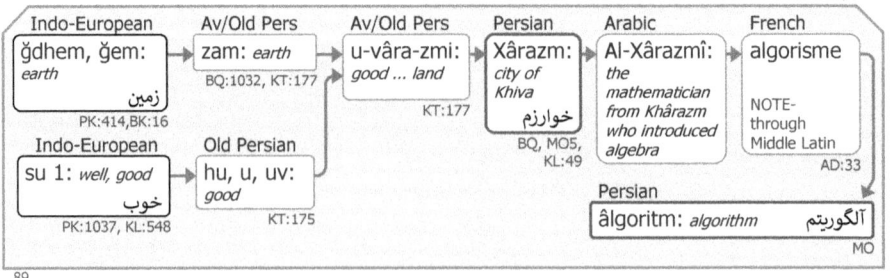

89

15

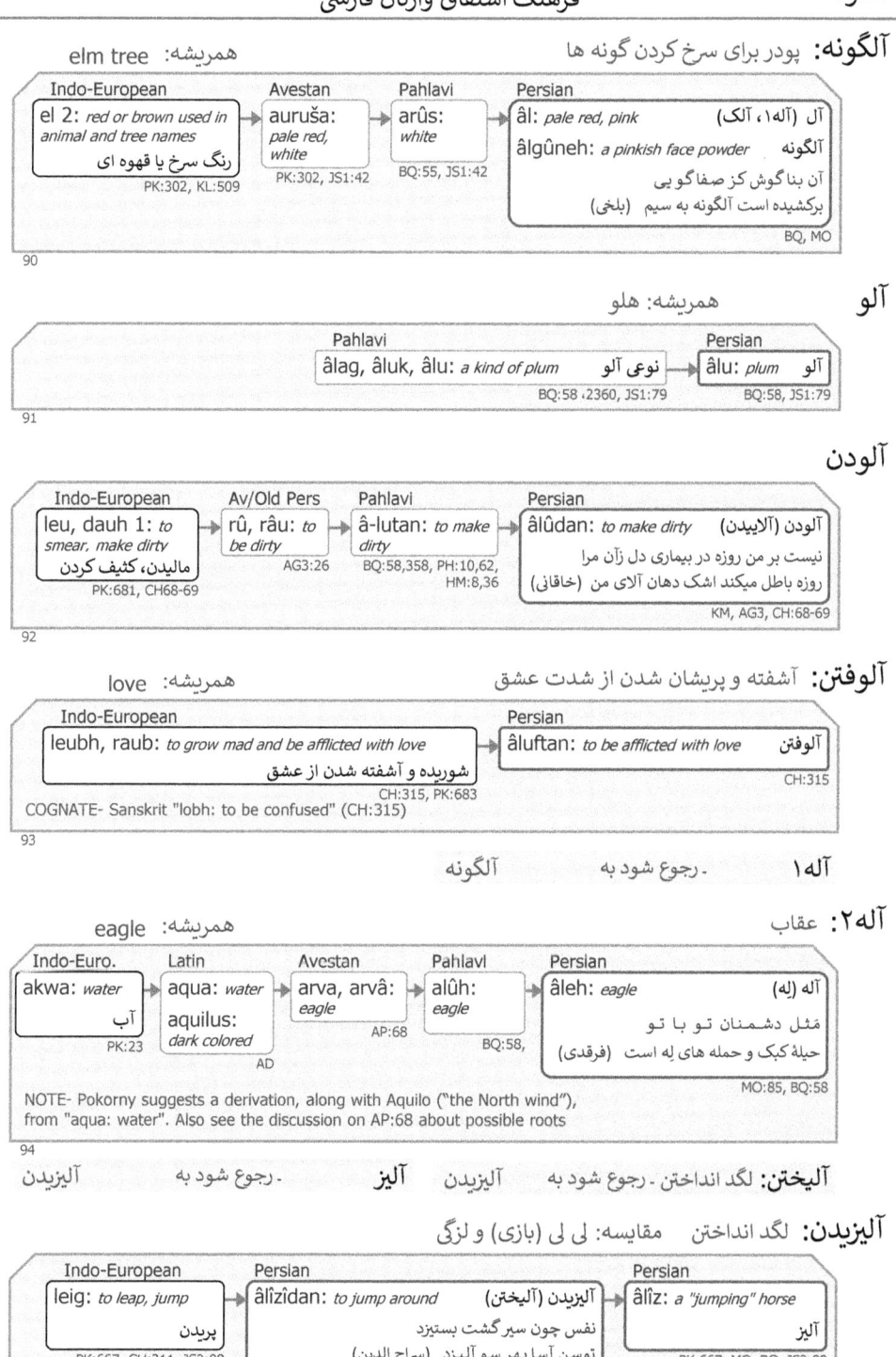

آلگونه: پودر برای سرخ کردن گونه ها   همریشه: elm tree

Indo-European	Avestan	Pahlavi	Persian
el 2: red or brown used in animal and tree names رنگ سرخ یا قهوه ای PK:302, KL:509	auruša: pale red, white PK:302, JS1:42	arûs: white BQ:55, JS1:42	آل (آله۱، آلک) âl: pale red, pink آلگونه âlgûneh: a pinkish face powder آن بناگوش کز صفا گویی برکشیده است آلگونه به سیم (بلخی) BQ, MO

90

آلو   همریشه: هلو

Pahlavi	Persian
âlag, âluk, âlu: a kind of plum نوعی آلو BQ:58, 2360، JS1:79	آلو âlu: plum BQ:58, JS1:79

91

آلودن

Indo-European	Av/Old Pers	Pahlavi	Persian
leu, dauh 1: to smear, make dirty مالیدن، کثیف کردن PK:681, CH68-69	rû, râu: to be dirty AG3:26	â-lutan: to make dirty BQ:58,358, PH:10,62, HM:8,36	âlûdan: to make dirty آلودن (آلاییدن) نیست بر من روزه در بیماری دل زآن مرا روزه باطل میکند اشک دهان آلای من (خاقانی) KM, AG3, CH:68-69

92

آلوفتن: آشفته و پریشان شدن از شدت عشق   همریشه: love

Indo-European	Persian
leubh, raub: to grow mad and be afflicted with love شوریده و آشفته شدن از عشق CH:315, PK:683	âluftan: to be afflicted with love آلوفتن CH:315
COGNATE- Sanskrit "lobh: to be confused" (CH:315)	

93

آله۱ . رجوع شود به   آلگونه

آله۲: عقاب   همریشه: eagle

Indo-Euro.	Latin	Avestan	Pahlavi	Persian
akwa: water آب PK:23	aqua: water aquilus: dark colored AD	arva, arvâ: eagle AP:68	alûh: eagle BQ:58	âleh: eagle آله (له) مثل دشمنان تو با تو حیله کبک و حمله های له است (فرقدی) MO:85, BQ:58
NOTE- Pokorny suggests a derivation, along with Aquilo ("the North wind"), from "aqua: water". Also see the discussion on AP:68 about possible roots				

94

آلیختن: لگد انداختن - رجوع شود به   آلیزیدن   **آلیز** . رجوع شود به   آلیزیدن

آلیزیدن: لگد انداختن   مقایسه: لی لی (بازی) و لزگی

Indo-European	Persian	Persian
leig: to leap, jump پریدن PK:667, CH:311, JS2:88	âlîzîdan: to jump around آلیزیدن (آلیختن) نفس چون سیرگشت بستیزد توسن آسا بهر سو آلیزد (سراج الدین) PK:667, MO, BQ, JS2:88	âlîz: a "jumping" horse آلیز PK:667, MO, BQ, JS2:88

95

16

آماج: گوآهن، تپه خاک هدف تیر اندازی

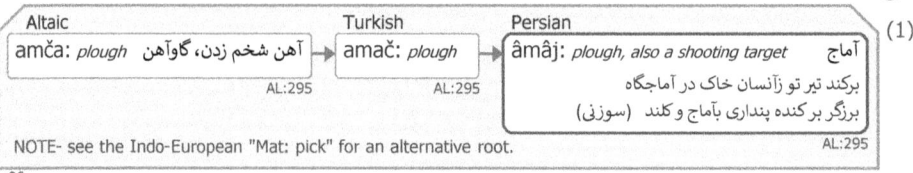

(1)

Altaic	Turkish	Persian
amča: *plough*	amač: *plough*	âmâj: *plough, also a shooting target* آماج

آهن شخم زدن،گوآهن

برکند تیر تو زآنسان خاک در آماجگاه

برزگر برکنده پنداری بآماج و کلند (سوزنی)

AL:295   AL:295   AL:295

NOTE- see the Indo-European "Mat: pick" for an alternative root.

96

آماج: گوآهن

همریشه: mattock

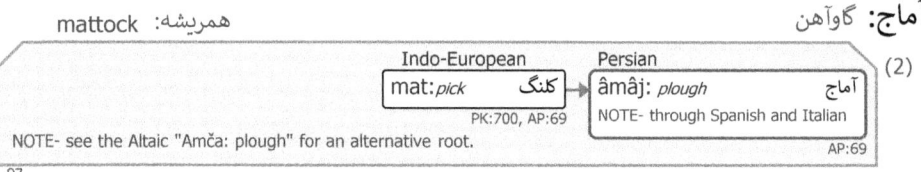

(2)

Indo-European	Persian
mat: *pick* کلنگ	âmâj: *plough* آماج
PK:700, AP:69	NOTE- through Spanish and Italian

NOTE- see the Altaic "Amča: plough" for an alternative root.

AP:69

97

آمادن، آماده

همریشه: measure, off

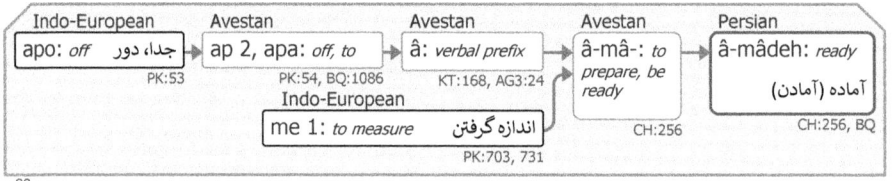

Indo-European	Avestan	Avestan	Avestan	Persian
apo: *off* جدا، دور	ap 2, apa: *off, to*	â: *verbal prefix*	â-mâ-: *to prepare, be ready*	â-mâdeh: *ready*
PK:53	PK:54, BQ:1086	KT:168, AG3:24		آماده (آمادن)

Indo-European

me 1: *to measure* اندازه گرفتن

PK:703, 731   CH:256   CH:256, BQ

98

آمار

همریشه: remember

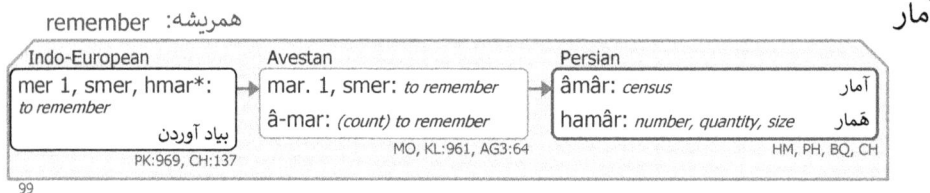

Indo-European	Avestan	Persian
mer 1, smer, hmar*: to remember	mar. 1, smer: *to remember*	âmâr: *census* آمار
بیاد آوردن	â-mar: *(count) to remember*	hamâr: *number, quantity, size* هَمار
PK:969, CH:137	MO, KL:961, AG3:64	HM, PH, BQ, CH

99

آماس: تورم   همریشه دَمیدن

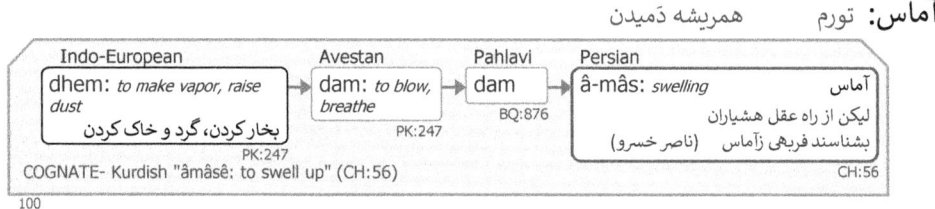

Indo-European	Avestan	Pahlavi	Persian
dhem: *to make vapor, raise dust*	dam: *to blow, breathe*	dam	â-mâs: *swelling* آماس
بخار کردن، گرد و خاک کردن		BQ:876	لیکن از راه عقل هشیاران
PK:247	PK:247		بشناسند فریهی زآماس (ناصر خسرو)
			CH:56

COGNATE- Kurdish "âmâsê: to swell up" (CH:56)

100

آمدن

همریشه: come, after

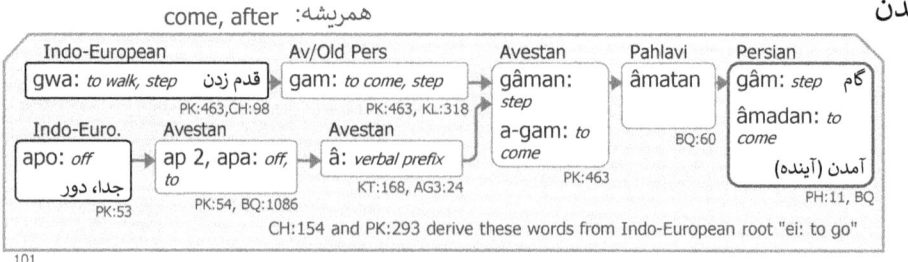

Indo-European	Av/Old Pers	Avestan	Pahlavi	Persian
gwa: *to walk, step* قدم زدن	gam: *to come, step*	gâman: *step*	âmatan	gâm: *step* گام
	PK:463, CH:98	PK:463, KL:318		âmadan: *to come*
Indo-Euro.	Avestan	Avestan	a-gam: *to come*	BQ:60	آمدن (آینده)
apo: *off* جدا، دور	ap 2, apa: *off, to*	â: *verbal prefix*	PK:463		PH:11, BQ
PK:53	PK:54, BQ:1086	KT:168, AG3:24		

CH:154 and PK:293 derive these words from Indo-European root "ei: to go"

101

17

آمرزیدن

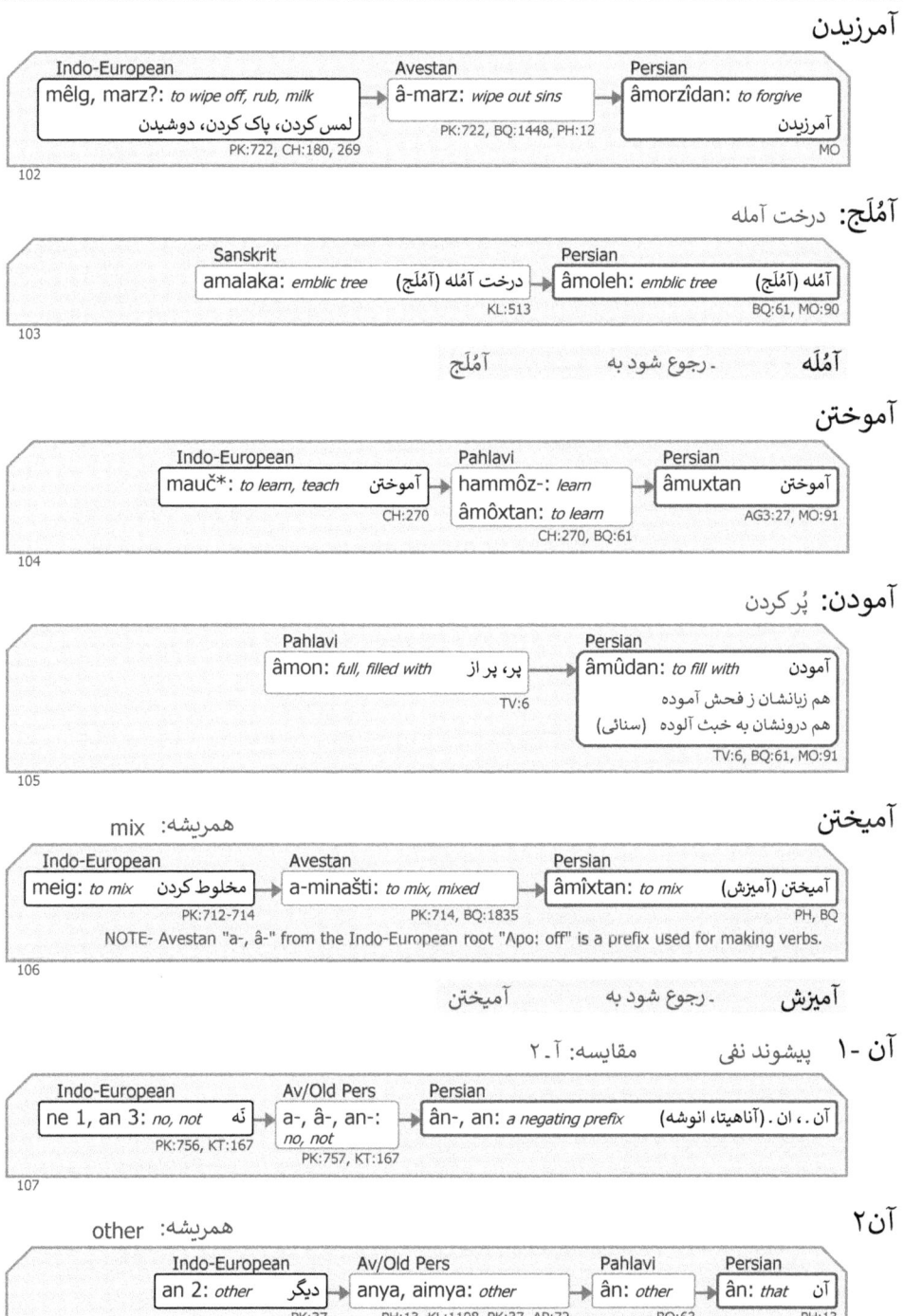

Indo-European	Avestan	Persian
mêlg, marz?: *to wipe off, rub, milk* لمس کردن، پاک کردن، دوشیدن PK:722, CH:180, 269	â-marz: *wipe out sins* PK:722, BQ:1448, PH:12	âmorzîdan: *to forgive* آمرزیدن MO

102

آمُلَج: درخت آمله

Sanskrit	Persian
amalaka: *emblic tree* درخت آمله (آمُلَج) KL:513	âmoleh: *emblic tree* آمله (آمُلَج) BQ:61, MO:90

103

آمُلَه   ـ رجوع شود به   آمُلَج

آموختن

Indo-European	Pahlavi	Persian
mauč*: *to learn, teach* آموختن CH:270	hammôz-: *learn* âmôxtan: *to learn* CH:270, BQ:61	âmuxtan آموختن AG3:27, MO:91

104

آمودن: پُر کردن

Pahlavi	Persian
âmon: *full, filled with* پر، پر از TV:6	âmûdan: *to fill with* آمودن هم زبانشان ز فحش آموده هم درونشان به خبث آلوده (سنائی) TV:6, BQ:61, MO:91

105

آمیختن

همریشه: mix

Indo-European	Avestan	Persian
meig: *to mix* مخلوط کردن PK:712-714	a-minašti: *to mix, mixed* PK:714, BQ:1835	âmîxtan: *to mix* آمیختن (آمیزش) PH, BQ
NOTE- Avestan "a-, â-" from the Indo-European root "Apo: off" is a prefix used for making verbs.		

106

آمیزش   ـ رجوع شود به   آمیختن

آن ۱-   پیشوند نفی   مقایسه: آ ـ ۲

Indo-European	Av/Old Pers	Persian
ne 1, an 3: *no, not* نَه PK:756, KT:167	a-, â-, an-: *no, not* PK:757, KT:167	ân-, an: *a negating prefix* آن ، ان . (آناهیتا، انوشه) KT:167

107

آن ۲

همریشه: other

Indo-European	Av/Old Pers	Pahlavi	Persian
an 2: *other* دیگر PK:37	anya, aimya: *other* PH:13, KL:1108, PK:37, AP:72	ân: *other* BQ:63	ân: *that* آن PH:13

108

آنا: پیرزن، مادربزرگ

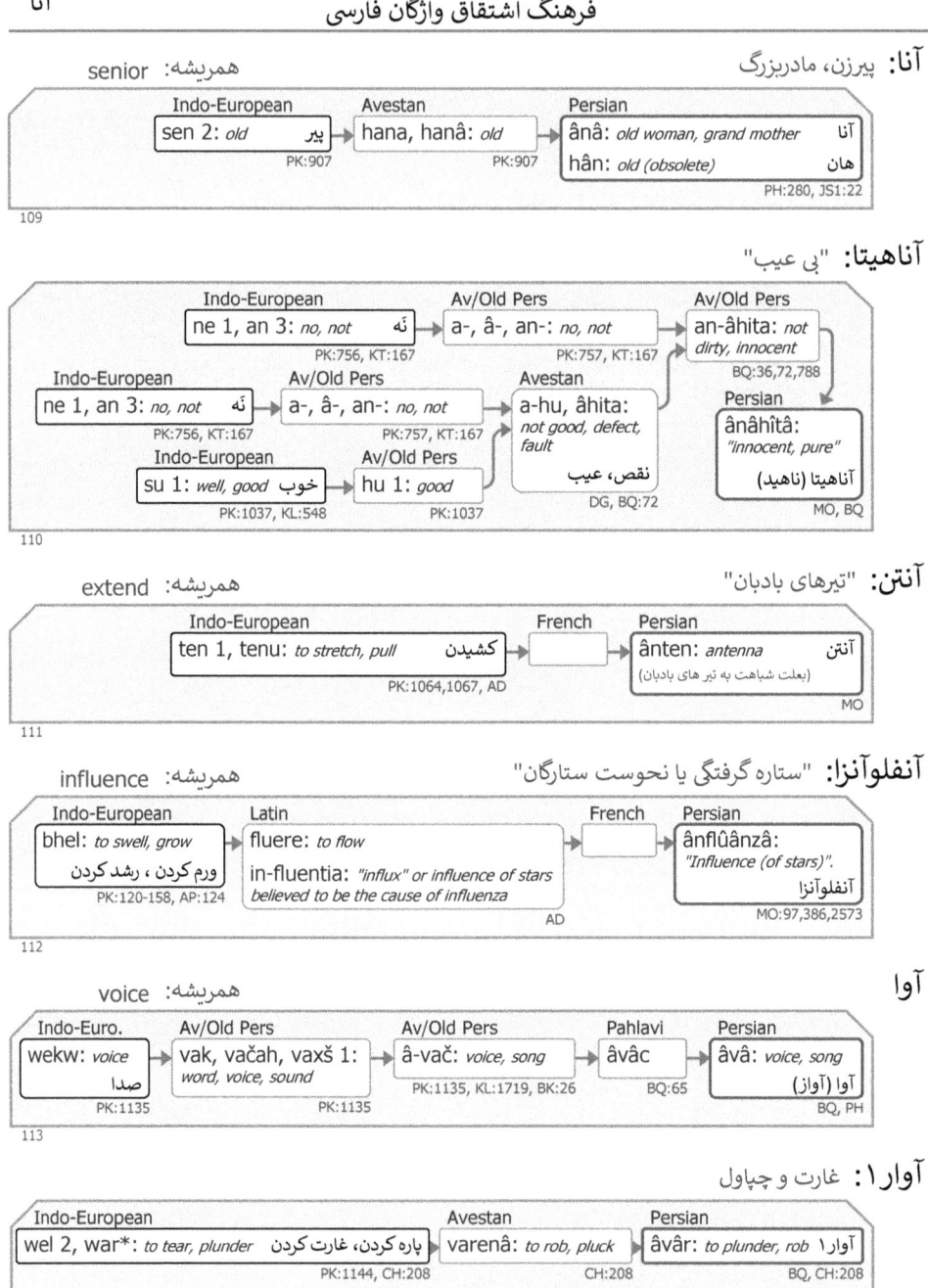

همریشه: senior

Indo-European	Avestan	Persian
sen 2: *old* پیر	hana, hanâ: *old*	ânâ: *old woman, grand mother* آنا
PK:907	PK:907	hân: *old (obsolete)* هان
		PH:280, JS1:22

109

آناهیتا: "بی عیب"

همریشه: influence (...)

Indo-European	Av/Old Pers	Av/Old Pers
ne 1, an 3: *no, not* نَه	a-, â-, an-: *no, not*	an-âhita: *not dirty, innocent*
PK:756, KT:167	PK:757, KT:167	BQ:36,72,788

Indo-European	Av/Old Pers	Avestan	Persian
ne 1, an 3: *no, not* نَه	a-, â-, an-: *no, not*	a-hu, âhita: *not good, defect, fault* نقص، عیب	ânâhîtâ: *"innocent, pure"* آناهیتا (ناهید)
PK:756, KT:167	PK:757, KT:167	DG, BQ:72	MO, BQ
Indo-European	Av/Old Pers		
su 1: *well, good* خوب	hu 1: *good*		
PK:1037, KL:548	PK:1037		

110

آنتن: "تیرهای بادبان"

همریشه: extend

Indo-European	French	Persian
ten 1, tenu: *to stretch, pull* کشیدن		ânten: *antenna* آنتن
PK:1064,1067, AD		(بعلت شباهت به تیر های بادبان)
		MO

111

آنفلوآنزا: "ستاره گرفتگی یا نحوست ستارگان"

همریشه: influence

Indo-European	Latin	French	Persian
bhel: *to swell, grow* ورم کردن ، رشد کردن	fluere: *to flow*		ânflûânzâ: *"Influence (of stars)".* آنفلوآنزا
PK:120-158, AP:124	in-fluentia: *"influx" or influence of stars believed to be the cause of influenza*		MO:97,386,2573
	AD		

112

آوا

همریشه: voice

Indo-Euro.	Av/Old Pers	Av/Old Pers	Pahlavi	Persian
wekw: *voice* صدا	vak, vačah, vaxš 1: *word, voice, sound*	â-vač: *voice, song*	âvâc	âvâ: *voice, song* آوا (آواز)
PK:1135	PK:1135	PK:1135, KL:1719, BK:26	BQ:65	BQ, PH

113

آوار ۱: غارت و چپاول

Indo-European	Avestan	Persian
wel 2, war*: *to tear, plunder* پاره کردن، غارت کردن	varenâ: *to rob, pluck*	âvâr: *to plunder, rob* آوار ۱
PK:1144, CH:208	CH:208	BQ, CH:208

114

آوار۲ . رجوع شود به   آواره

آواره

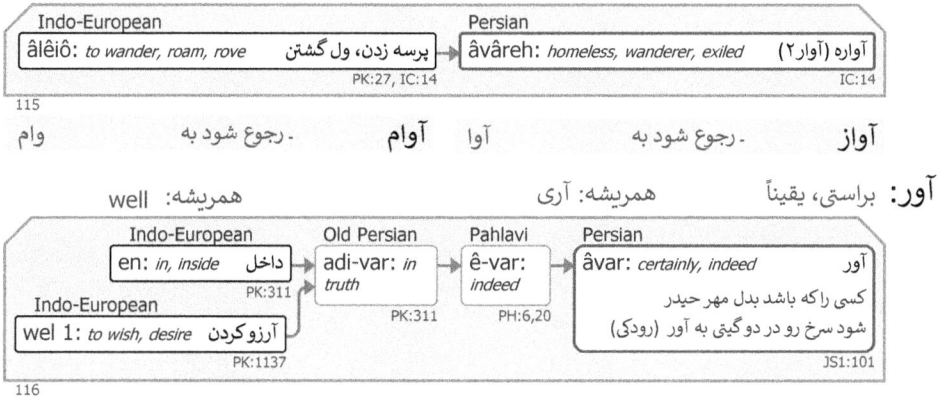

Indo-European		Persian
âlêiô: *to wander, roam, rove* پرسه زدن، ول گشتن PK:27, IC:14		âvâreh: *homeless, wanderer, exiled* آواره (آوار۲) IC:14

115

آواز .رجوع شود به **آوا** **آوام** .رجوع شود به **وام**

آور: براستی، یقیناً   همریشه: آری   همریشه: well

Indo-European	Old Persian	Pahlavi	Persian
en: *in, inside* داخل PK:311	adi-var: *in truth* PK:311	ê-var: *indeed* PH:6,20	âvar: *certainly, indeed* آور کسی راکه باشد بدل مهر حیدر شود سرخ رو در دو گیتی به آور (رودکی) JS1:101
Indo-European wel 1: *to wish, desire* آرزو کردن PK:1137			

116

آورد: جنگ و نبرد   همریشه: oppose, suppress

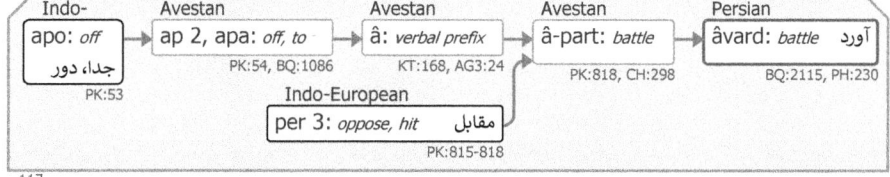

Indo- apo: *off* جدا، دور PK:53	Avestan ap 2, apa: *off, to* PK:54, BQ:1086	Avestan â: *verbal prefix* KT:168, AG3:24	Avestan â-part: *battle* PK:818, CH:298	Persian âvard: *battle* آورد BQ:2115, PH:230
		Indo-European per 3: *oppose, hit* مقابل PK:815-818		

117

آوردن

همریشه: bring, burden

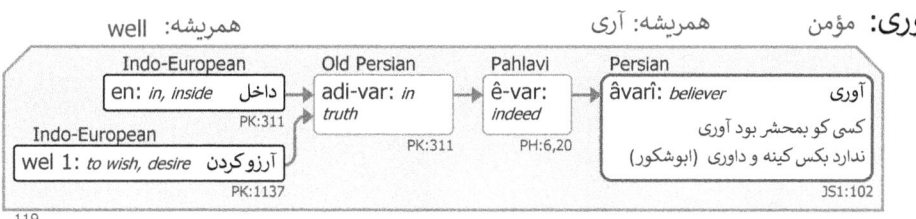

Indo-European	Av/Old Pers	Avestan	Pahlavi	Persian
bher 1: *to carry* حمل کردن PK:128,163, BK:107	bar: *to carry* PK:128	â-vare, â-bar-a: *bring* BQ:66, MO:1395, AG3:28, JD:292	âwutan BQ:66	âvardan: *to bring* آوردن BQ, NS:58

NOTE- Avestan "a-, â-" from the Indo-European root "Apo: off" is a prefix used for making verbs.

118

آوری: مؤمن   همریشه: آری   همریشه: well

Indo-European	Old Persian	Pahlavi	Persian
en: *in, inside* داخل PK:311	adi-var: *in truth* PK:311	ê-var: *indeed* PH:6,20	âvarî: *believer* آوری کسی کو بمحشر بود آوری ندارد بکس کینه و داوری (ابوشکور) JS1:102
Indo-European wel 1: *to wish, desire* آرزو کردن PK:1137			

119

آوند۱: پسوند مالکیت یا شامل بودن

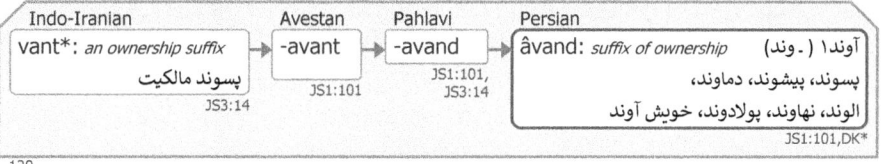

Indo-Iranian	Avestan	Pahlavi	Persian
vant*: *an ownership suffix* پسوند مالکیت JS3:14	-avant JS1:101	-avand JS1:101, JS3:14	âvand: *suffix of ownership* آوند۱ (ـ وند) پسوند، پیشوند، دماوند، الوند، نهاوند، پولادوند، خویش آوند JS1:101,DK*

120

آوند۲: ظرف آب، کوزه شراب

Indo-Iranian		Avestan	Pahlavi	Persian
vant*: *an ownership suffix* پسوند مالکیت		-avant	ap-avand: *containing water*	âvnd: *water container* آوند۲
JS3:14		JS1:101	JS1:101, JS3:14	JS1:101

Indo-European	Avestan
ab 1: *water* آب	âp: *water, water glitter*
PK:1	KL:2

121

آونگ

Indo-European	Av/Old Pers	Persian
weik 1: *to shake, swing* لرزاندن، تاب دادن	vyâxa, vyâxman: *assembly, collection*	âvang: *pendulum* آونگ
PK:1130	PK:1130	BQ, PH, MO

122

آویختن

مقایسه: بیختن

Indo-European	Av/Old Pers	Persian
weik 1: *to shake, swing* لرزاندن، تاب دادن	waix, waig: *to swing*	vîxtan: *to sling* ویختن âvîxtan: *to hang* آویختن (آویز)
PK:1130	PK:1130	BQ, PH, MO

123

آویز   ـ رجوع شود به   آویختن

آویشن

همریشه: آب

Indo-European	Avestan	Pahlavi	Persian
ab 1: *water* آب	âp: *water, water glitter*	âp: *water*	âvîšan: *thyme, spearmint*
PK:1	KL:2	KL:2	آویشن (آبشن)
Indo-European	Av/Old Pers	Pahlavi	JS1:103, BQ:68
gwhen 3, kan*: *to dig and fill* کندن و پُرکردن	šan, šyangh: *house, household*	šân: *house, shelter*	
CH:232, PK491	FJ:49-51	BQ:46, FJ:49-51	

124

آهختن   ـ رجوع شود به   آهیختن

آهسته

sitting :همریشه   همریشه: نشستن

Indo-European	Sanskrit	Persian
sed, had*: *to sit, step, go* نشستن، رفتن	satti: *sitting* a- satta: *slow*	âhesteh: *slow* آهسته
PK:884,887, KL:1075, CH:125	PK:884-887, JS1:75	JS1:75

125

آهن

Indo-European	Avestan	Pahlavi	Persian
aios: *metal* فلز	ayô, ayah, ayanh: *metal*	âsîn, âhên: *metal, iron*	Âhan: *iron, anything hard* آهن
PK:15, KL:1093	PK:15, KL:1093	BQ:70, PH:14	BQ:70, BK:612

NOTE- KL:1093 claims that this word may be from Ayashya, ancient name of Cyprus, meaning Cyprus metal.

126

آهنجیدن: کشیدن ـ رجوع شود به هنجیدن

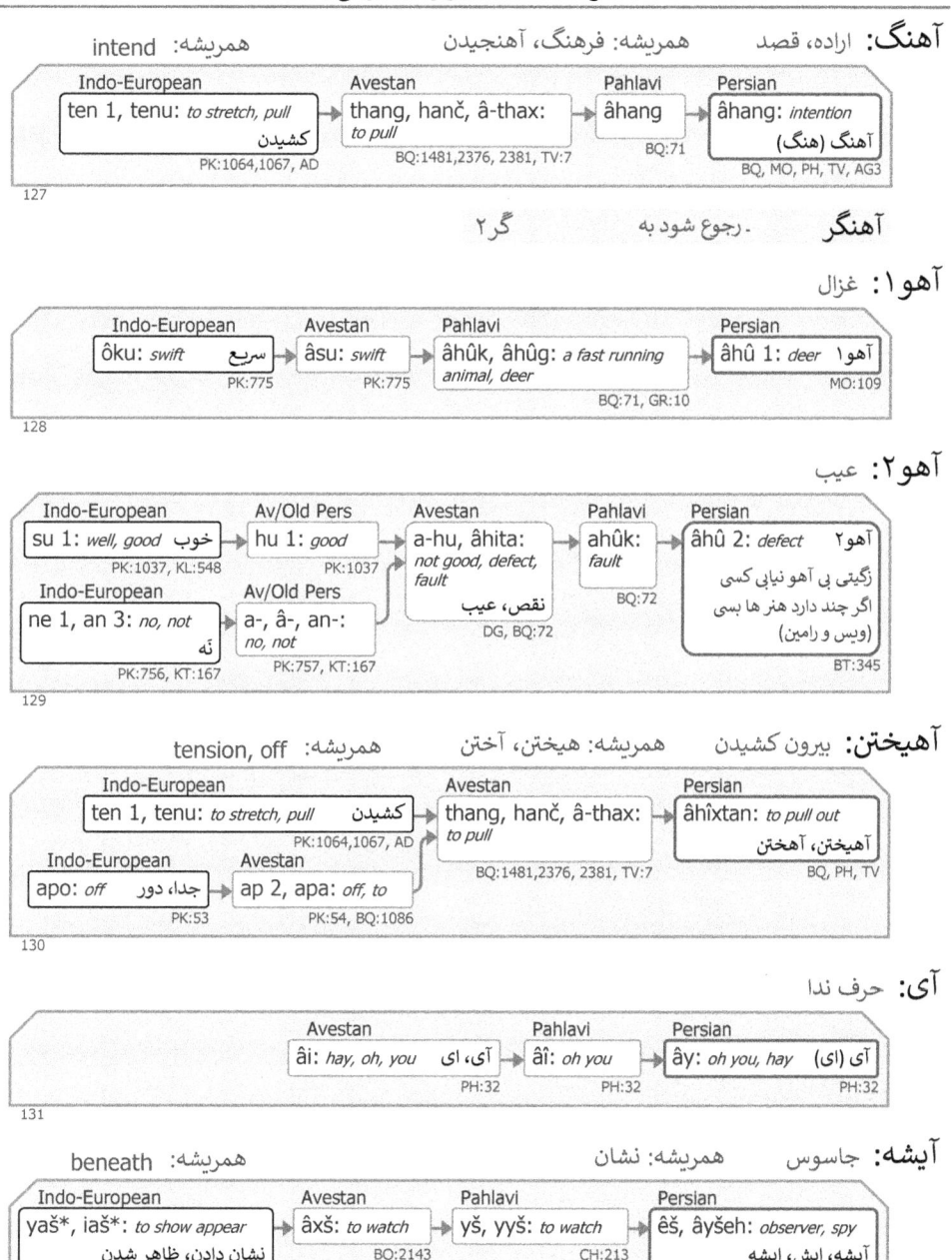

آهنگ: اراده، قصد — همریشه: فرهنگ، آهنجیدن — همریشه: intend

Indo-European	Avestan	Pahlavi	Persian
ten 1, tenu: *to stretch, pull* کشیدن	thang, hanč, â-thax: *to pull*	âhang	âhang: *intention* آهنگ (هنگ)
PK:1064,1067, AD	BQ:1481,2376, 2381, TV:7	BQ:71	BQ, MO, PH, TV, AG3

127

آهنگر رجوع شود به. گر ۲

آهو۱: غزال

Indo-European	Avestan	Pahlavi	Persian
ôku: *swift* سریع	âsu: *swift*	âhûk, âhûg: *a fast running animal, deer*	âhû 1: *deer* ۱ آهو
PK:775	PK:775	BQ:71, GR:10	MO:109

128

آهو۲: عیب

Indo-European	Av/Old Pers	Avestan	Pahlavi	Persian
su 1: *well, good* خوب	hu 1: *good*	a-hu, âhita: *not good, defect, fault*	ahûk: *fault*	âhû 2: *defect* ۲ آهو
PK:1037, KL:548	PK:1037		BQ:72	زگیتی بی آهو نیابی کسی
Indo-European	Av/Old Pers	نقص، عیب		اگر چند دارد هنر ها بسی
ne 1, an 3: *no, not* نه	a-, â-, an-: *no, not*			(ویس و رامین)
PK:756, KT:167	PK:757, KT:167	DG, BQ:72		BT:345

129

آهیختن: بیرون کشیدن — همریشه: هیختن، آختن — همریشه: tension, off

Indo-European	Avestan	Persian
ten 1, tenu: *to stretch, pull* کشیدن	thang, hanč, â-thax: *to pull*	âhîxtan: *to pull out* آهیختن، آختن
PK:1064,1067, AD	BQ:1481,2376, 2381, TV:7	BQ, PH, TV
Indo-European	Avestan	
apo: *off* جدا، دور	ap 2, apa: *off, to*	
PK:53	PK:54, BQ:1086	

130

آی: حرف ندا

Avestan	Pahlavi	Persian
âi: *hay, oh, you* آی، ای	âî: *oh you*	ây: *oh you, hay* آی (ای)
PH:32	PH:32	PH:32

131

آیشه: جاسوس — همریشه: نشان — همریشه: beneath

Indo-European	Avestan	Pahlavi	Persian
yaš*, iaš*: *to show appear* نشان دادن، ظاهر شدن	âxš: *to watch*	yš, yyš: *to watch*	êš, âyšeh: *observer, spy* آیشه، ایش، ایشه
CH:213	BQ:2143	CH:213	BQ:73, CH

132

آیفت نیاز، درخواست   همریشه: یافتن   همریشه: couple

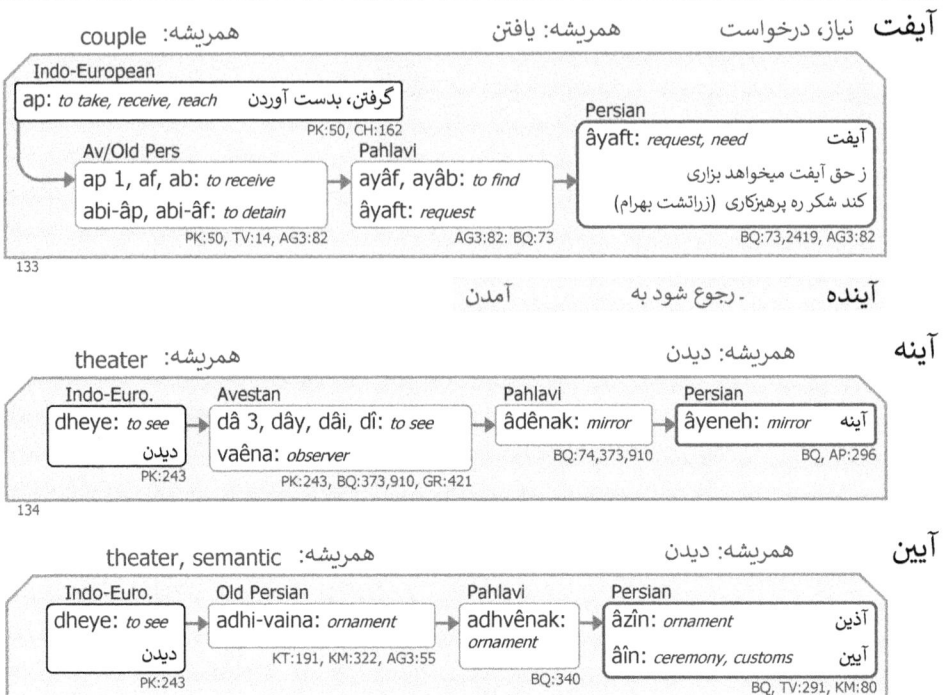

Indo-European

ap: *to take, receive, reach*   گرفتن، بدست آوردن

PK:50, CH:162

Av/Old Pers

ap 1, af, ab: *to receive*
abi-âp, abi-âf: *to detain*

PK:50, TV:14, AG3:82

Pahlavi

ayâf, ayâb: *to find*
âyaft: *request*

AG3:82, BQ:73

Persian

âyaft: *request, need*   آیفت

ز حق آیفت میخواهد بزاری
کند شکر ره پرهیزکاری (زراتشت بهرام)

BQ:73,2419, AG3:82

133

آینده ـ رجوع شود به   آمدن

آینه   همریشه: دیدن   همریشه: theater

Indo-Euro.

dheye: *to see*
دیدن

PK:243

Avestan

dâ 3, dây, dâi, dî: *to see*
vaêna: *observer*

PK:243, BQ:373,910, GR:421

Pahlavi

âdênak: *mirror*

BQ:74,373,910

Persian

âyeneh: *mirror*   آینه

BQ, AP:296

134

آیین   همریشه: دیدن   همریشه: theater, semantic

Indo-Euro.

dheye: *to see*
دیدن

PK:243

Old Persian

adhi-vaina: *ornament*

KT:191, KM:322, AG3:55

Pahlavi

adhvênak: *ornament*

BQ:340

Persian

âzîn: *ornament*   آذین
âîn: *ceremony, customs*   آیین

BQ, TV:291, KM:80

135

ا. ‐ رجوع شود به آ‐ ۲.

ابا: آش

همریشه: شوریا، نانوا، پختن همریشه: cook

Indo-European	Avestan	Pahlavi	Persian
pekw: *to cook* پختن PK:798	pax, pač, pačaiti: *to cook* -pâka: *a suffix referring to the cook.* PK:798, BQ:370, BK:336, AG3:40	pâk: *food, soup* BQ:76	abâ: *soup, food* ابا علم دیگ و آتش ار نبود ترا از شربتِ نیِ دیگ ماند نیِ ابا (مولوی) BQ:76

136

اباختر ‐ رجوع شود به باختر

أباردن: بلعیدن همریشه: پُر، انبار

Indo-European	Avestan	Pahlavi	Persian	(1)
baru: *to chew, swallow* جویدن، بلعیدن CH:12	badiriia: *chewable* CH:12	ôbâr: *to swallow* CH:12	aubardan: *to swallow* أباردن (أباشتن) CH:12	

137

أباردن: بلعیدن همریشه: پُر، انبار همریشه: full, plenty

Indo-European	Av/Old Pers	Avestan	Persian	(2)
au: *away, off, down* جدا، دور، پایین PK:72	ava 1, aorâ: *down* KL:132, PK:72	ava-par: *fill down* KM:175, BQ:180	obârdan: *to swallow* أباردن، اوباردن (أباشتن) پس بیوبارید ایشان را همه نیِ شبان را میش زنده، نیِ رمه (رودکی) BQ:180, KM:175, AG3:31	
Indo-European	Avestan			
pel 1: *to fill* پر کردن PK:799	par 1, perana: *full* PK:799			

138

أباشتن: بلعیدن ‐ رجوع شود به أباردن **ابر** ‐ رجوع شود به برٔ۲

ابر: "آب بار"

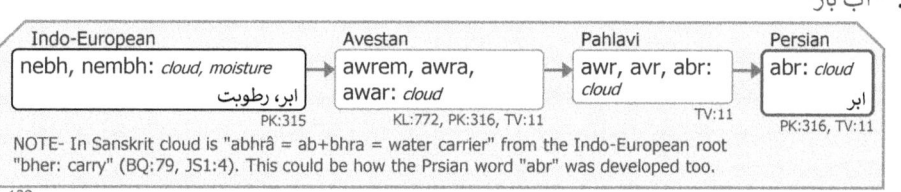

Indo-European	Avestan	Pahlavi	Persian
nebh, nembh: *cloud, moisture* ابر، رطوبت PK:315	awrem, awra, awar: *cloud* KL:772, PK:316, TV:11	awr, avr, abr: *cloud* TV:11	abr: *cloud* ابر PK:316, TV:11

NOTE- In Sanskrit cloud is "abhrâ = ab+bhra = water carrier" from the Indo-European root "bher: carry" (BQ:79, JS1:4). This could be how the Prsian word "abr" was developed too.

139

ابرآمون

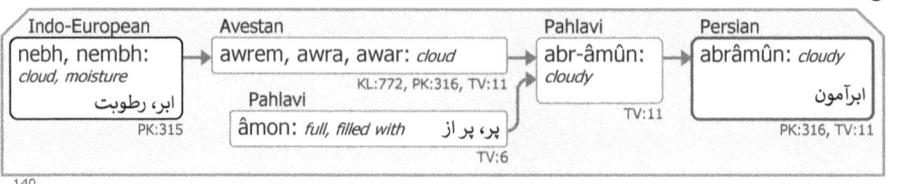

Indo-European	Avestan	Pahlavi	Persian
nebh, nembh: *cloud, moisture* ابر، رطوبت PK:315	awrem, awra, awar: *cloud* KL:772, PK:316, TV:11 Pahlavi âmon: *full, filled with* پر، پر از TV:6	abr-âmûn: *cloudy* TV:11	abrâmûn: *cloudy* ابرآمون PK:316, TV:11

140

ابراهیم: "پدر خاندان"

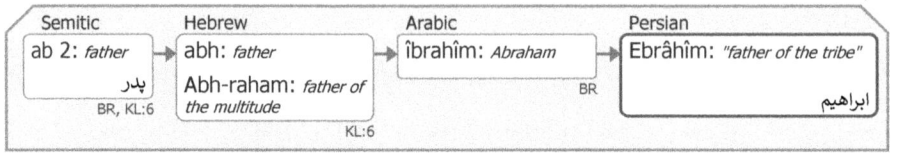

Semitic	Hebrew	Arabic	Persian
ab 2: *father* پدر BR, KL:6	abh: *father* Abh-raham: *father of the multitude* KL:6	îbrahîm: *Abraham* BR	Ebrâhîm: "*father of the tribe*" ابراهیم

141

ابرزین: انجمن بزرگان یا ابر اسلحه

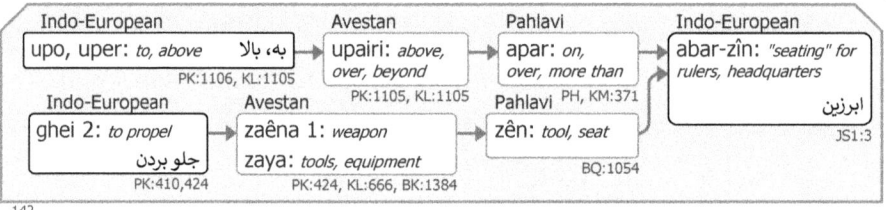

Indo-European	Avestan	Pahlavi	Indo-European
upo, uper: *to, above* به، بالا PK:1106, KL:1105	upairi: *above, over, beyond* PK:1105, KL:1105	apar: *on, over, more than* PH, KM:371	abar-zîn: "*seating*" for rulers, headquarters ابرزین JS1:3
ghei 2: *to propel* جلو بردن PK:410,424	zaêna 1: *weapon* zaya: *tools, equipment* PK:424, KL:666, BK:1384	zên: *tool, seat* BQ:1054	

142

ابرقوه، ابرکوه   . رجوع شود به   آبر + کوه

آبزَنجَن: حلقه سیم یا زر برای دست و پا   همریشه: اورنگ   همریشه: lacquer

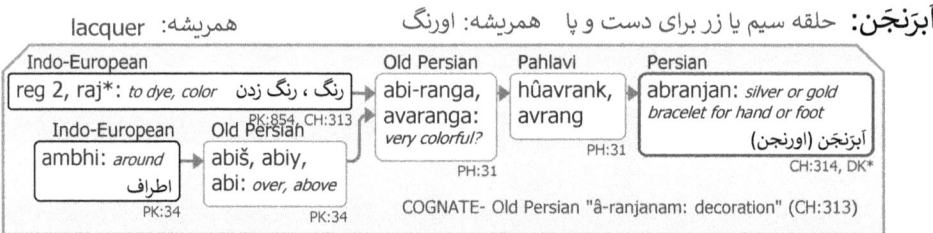

Indo-European	Old Persian	Pahlavi	Persian
reg 2, raj*: *to dye, color* رنگ ، رنگ زدن PK:854, CH:313	abi-ranga, avaranga: *very colorful?* PH:31	hûavrank, avrang PH:31	abranjan: *silver or gold bracelet for hand or foot* آبزنجَن (اورنجن) CH:314, DK*
ambhi: *around* اطراف PK:34	abiš, abiy, abi: *over, above* PK:34		

COGNATE- Old Persian "â-ranjanam: *decoration*" (CH:313)

143

ابرو

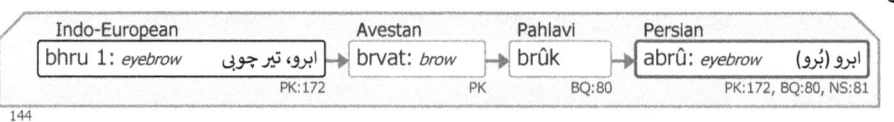

Indo-European	Avestan	Pahlavi	Persian
bhru 1: *eyebrow* ابرو، تیر چوبی PK:172	brvat: *brow* PK	brûk BQ:80	abrû: *eyebrow* ابرو (اَبرو) PK:172, BQ:80, NS:81

144

ابریشم   . رجوع شود به   ریشتن

اِبریق: آب ریز

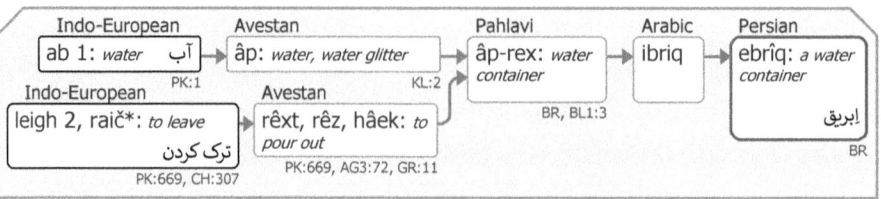

Indo-European	Avestan	Pahlavi	Arabic	Persian
ab 1: *water* آب PK:1	âp: *water, water glitter* KL:2	âp-rex: *water container* BR, BL1:3	ibriq	ebrîq: *a water container* اِبریق BR
leigh 2, raič*: *to leave* ترک کردن PK:669, CH:307	rêxt, rêz, hâek: *to pour out* PK:669, AG3:72, GR:11			

145

ابزار

(1)

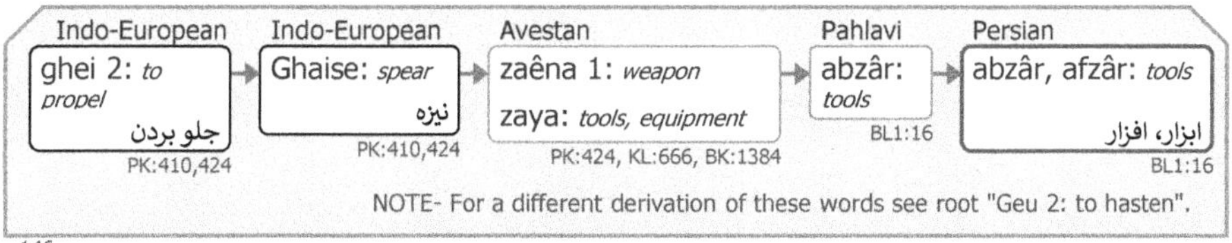

Indo-European	Indo-European	Avestan	Pahlavi	Persian
ghei 2: *to propel* جلو بردن PK:410,424	Ghaise: *spear* نیزه PK:410,424	zaêna 1: *weapon* zaya: *tools, equipment* PK:424, KL:666, BK:1384	abzâr: *tools* BL1:16	abzâr, afzâr: *tools* ابزار، افزار BL1:16

NOTE- For a different derivation of these words see root "Geu 2: to hasten".

146

ابزار

همریشه: choose

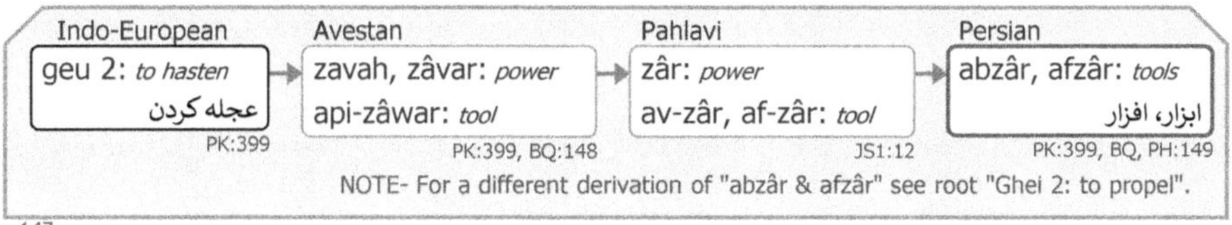

(2)

Indo-European	Avestan	Pahlavi	Persian
geu 2: *to hasten* عجله کردن PK:399	zavah, zâvar: *power* api-zâwar: *tool* PK:399, BQ:148	zâr: *power* av-zâr, af-zâr: *tool* JS1:12	abzâr, afzâr: *tools* ابزار، افزار PK:399, BQ, PH:149

NOTE- For a different derivation of "abzâr & afzâr" see root "Ghei 2: to propel".

147

آبفت: پارچه خشن   ـ رجوع شود به   بافتن

ابلق، ابلک: شراره آتش، دو رنگ

همریشه: bright

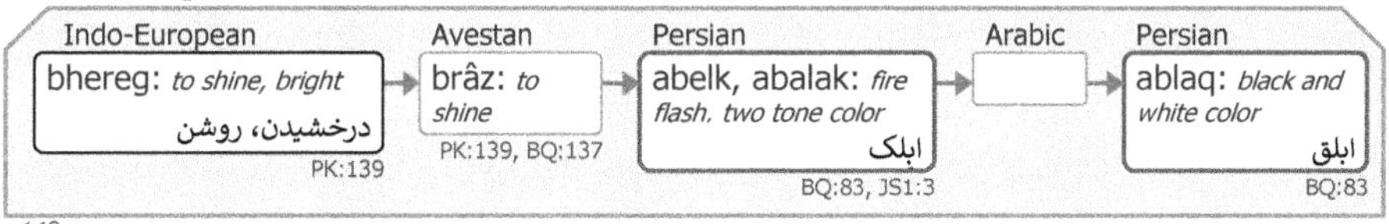

Indo-European	Avestan	Persian	Arabic	Persian
bhereg: *to shine, bright* درخشیدن، روشن PK:139	brâz: *to shine* PK:139, BQ:137	abelk, abalak: *fire flash, two tone color* ابلک BQ:83, JS1:3		ablaq: *black and white color* ابلق BQ:83

148

ابلیس: " تهمت زن "

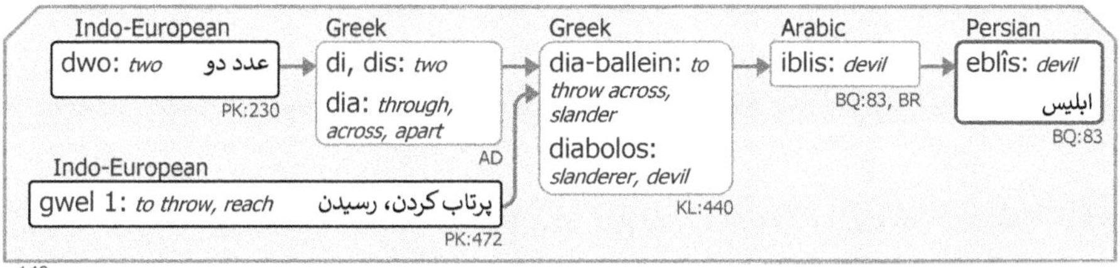

Indo-European	Greek	Greek	Arabic	Persian
dwo: *two* عدد دو PK:230	di, dis: *two* dia: *through, across, apart* AD	dia-ballein: *to throw across, slander* diabolos: *slanderer, devil* KL:440	iblis: *devil* BQ:83, BR	eblîs: *devil* ابلیس BQ:83
Indo-European				
gwel 1: *to throw, reach* پرتاب کردن، رسیدن PK:472				

149

اُبّهت

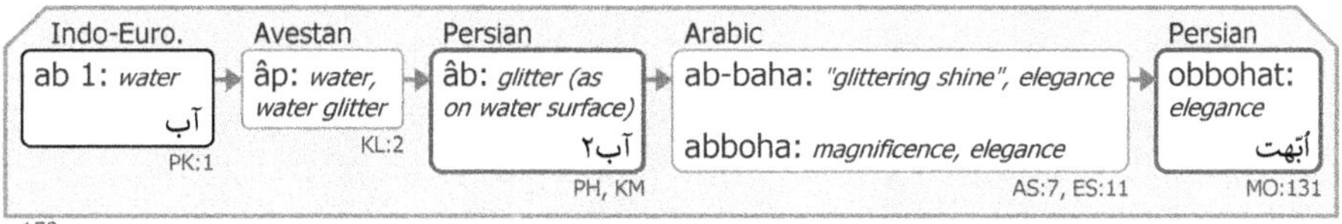

Indo-Euro.	Avestan	Persian	Arabic	Persian
ab 1: *water* آب PK:1	âp: *water, water glitter* KL:2	âb: *glitter (as on water surface)* آب۲ PH, KM	ab-baha: *"glittering shine", elegance* abboha: *magnificence, elegance* AS:7, ES:11	obbohat: *elegance* اُبّهت MO:131

150

ابی   ـ رجوع شود به   بی   **ابیورد**   ـ رجوع شود به   ـجرد

اتُم: "تقسیم نشدنی"

همریشه: negative, not

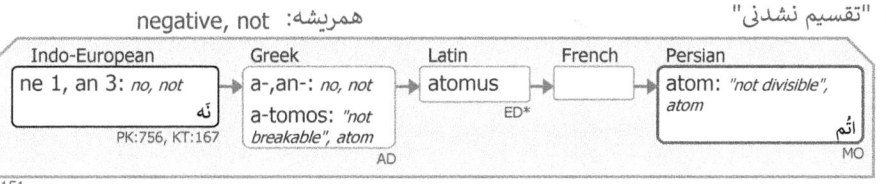

Indo-European	Greek	Latin	French	Persian
ne 1, an 3: *no, not* نَه PK:756, KT:167	a-,an-: *no, not* a-tomos: *"not breakable", atom* AD	atomus ED*		atom: *"not divisible", atom* اتُم MO

151

اپسان: ساییدن   ـ رجوع شود به   افسانیدن

اپیون

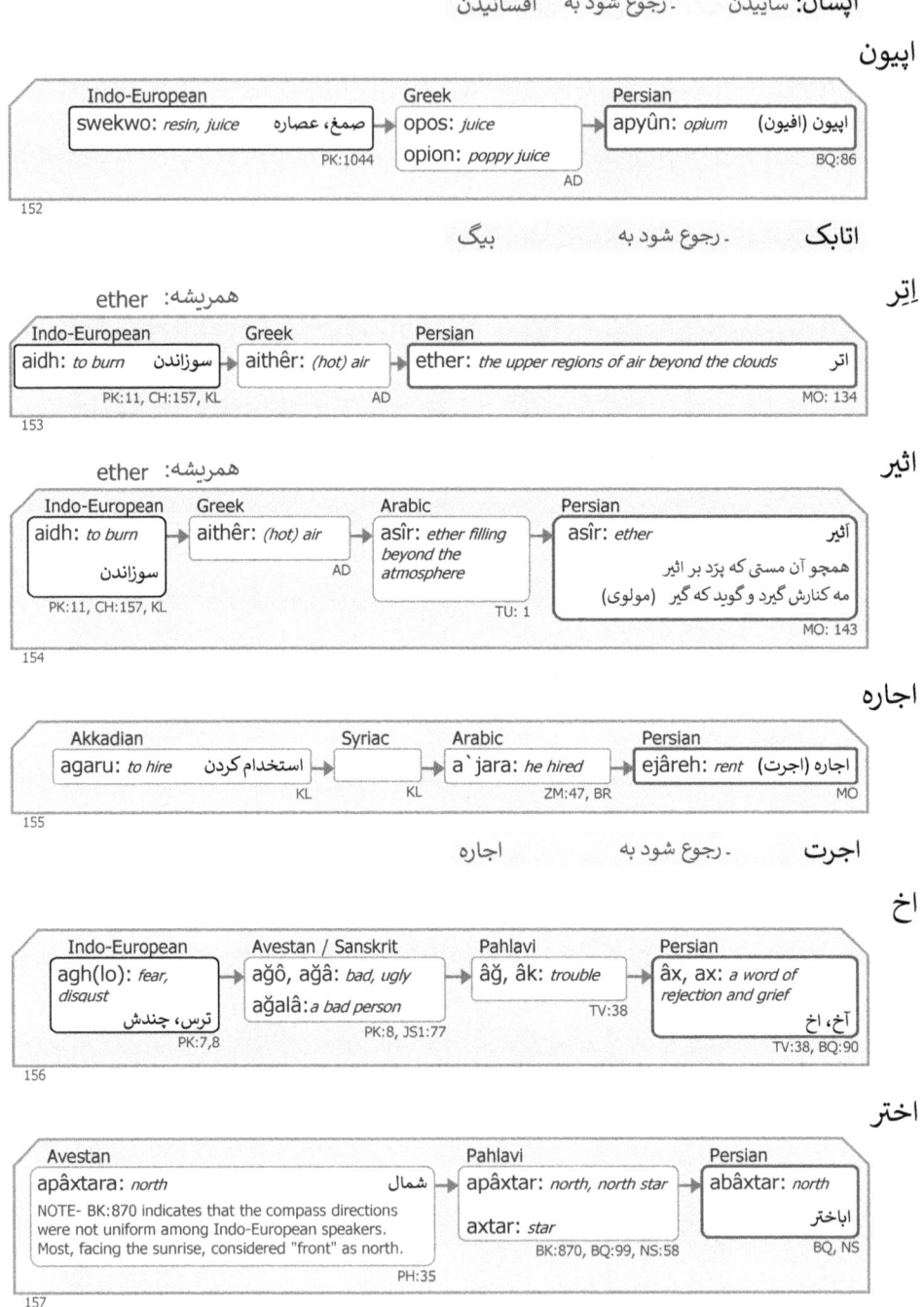

Indo-European	Greek	Persian
swekwo: *resin, juice* صمغ، عصاره	opos: *juice* opion: *poppy juice*	apyûn: *opium* اپیون (افیون)
PK:1044	AD	BQ:86

152

اتابک   ـ رجوع شود به   بیگ

اِتر

همریشه: ether

Indo-European	Greek	Persian
aidh: *to burn* سوزاندن	aithêr: *(hot) air*	ether: *the upper regions of air beyond the clouds* اتر
PK:11, CH:157, KL	AD	MO: 134

153

اثیر

همریشه: ether

Indo-European	Greek	Arabic	Persian
aidh: *to burn* سوزاندن	aithêr: *(hot) air*	asîr: *ether filling beyond the atmosphere*	asîr: *ether* اثیر همچو آن مستی که بِزَد بر اثیر مه کنارش گیرد و گوید که گیر (مولوی)
PK:11, CH:157, KL	AD	TU: 1	MO: 143

154

اجاره

Akkadian	Syriac	Arabic	Persian
agaru: *to hire* استخدام کردن		a`jara: *he hired*	ejâreh: *rent* اجاره (اجرت)
KL	KL	ZM:47, BR	MO

155

اجرت   ـ رجوع شود به   اجاره

اخ

Indo-European	Avestan / Sanskrit	Pahlavi	Persian
agh(lo): *fear, disgust* ترس، چندش	aĝô, aĝâ: *bad, ugly* aĝalâ: *a bad person*	âĝ, âk: *trouble*	âx, ax: *a word of rejection and grief* آخ، اخ
PK:7,8	PK:8, JS1:77	TV:38	TV:38, BQ:90

156

اختر

Avestan	Pahlavi	Persian
apâxtara: *north* شمال NOTE- BK:870 indicates that the compass directions were not uniform among Indo-European speakers. Most, facing the sunrise, considered "front" as north.	apâxtar: *north, north star* axtar: *star*	abâxtar: *north* اباختر
PH:35	BK:870, BQ:99, NS:58	BQ, NS

157

اخته: کشیده شده   ـ رجوع شود به   آختن

اخگر: زغال افروخته

همریشه: ignite

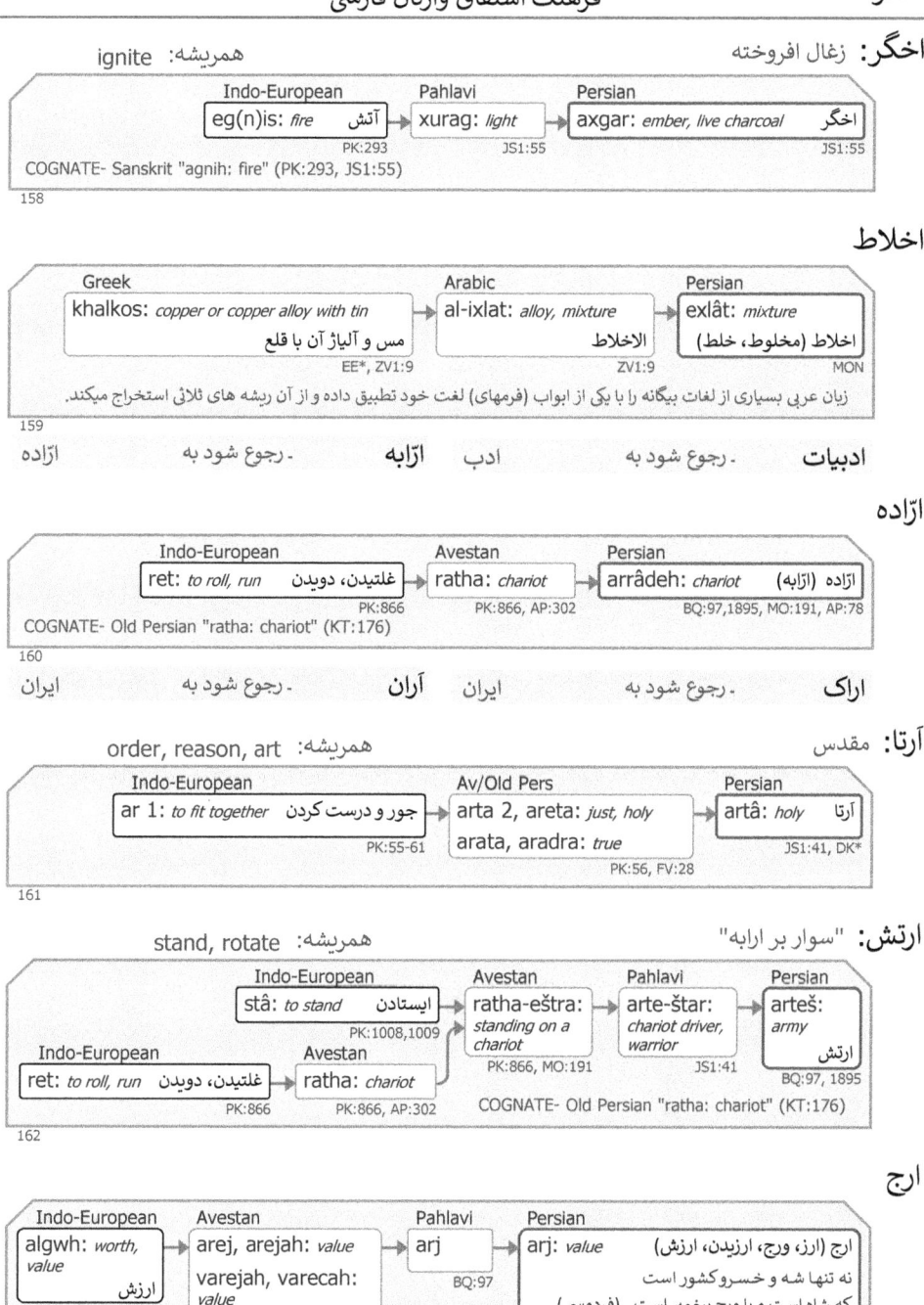

Indo-European	Pahlavi	Persian
eg(n)is: *fire* آتش	xurag: *light*	axgar: *ember, live charcoal* اخگر
PK:293	JS1:55	JS1:55

COGNATE- Sanskrit "agnih: fire" (PK:293, JS1:55)

158

اخلاط

Greek	Arabic	Persian
khalkos: *copper or copper alloy with tin* مس و آلیاژ آن با قلع	al-ixlat: *alloy, mixture* الاخلاط	exlât: *mixture* اخلاط (مخلوط، خلط)
EE*, ZV1:9	ZV1:9	MON

زبان عربی بسیاری از لغات بیگانه را با یکی از ابواب (فرمهای) لغت خود تطبیق داده و از آن ریشه های ثلاثی استخراج میکند.

159

ادبیات - رجوع شود به ادب   ارابه - رجوع شود به ازاده

ازاده

Indo-European	Avestan	Persian
ret: *to roll, run* غلتیدن، دویدن	ratha: *chariot*	arrâdeh: *chariot* ازاده (ارابه)
PK:866	PK:866, AP:302	BQ:97,1895, MO:191, AP:78

COGNATE- Old Persian "ratha: chariot" (KT:176)

160

اراک - رجوع شود به ایران   اران - رجوع شود به ایران

آرتا: مقدس

همریشه: order, reason, art

Indo-European	Av/Old Pers	Persian
ar 1: *to fit together* جور و درست کردن	arta 2, areta: *just, holy* arata, aradra: *true*	artâ: *holy* آرتا
PK:55-61	PK:56, FV:28	JS1:41, DK*

161

ارتش: "سوار بر ارابه"

همریشه: stand, rotate

Indo-European	Avestan	Pahlavi	Persian
stâ: *to stand* ایستادن	ratha-eštra: *standing on a chariot*	arte-štar: *chariot driver, warrior*	arteš: *army* ارتش
PK:1008,1009	PK:866, MO:191	JS1:41	BQ:97, 1895

Indo-European	Avestan		
ret: *to roll, run* غلتیدن، دویدن	ratha: *chariot*		
PK:866	PK:866, AP:302		

COGNATE- Old Persian "ratha: chariot" (KT:176)

162

ارج

Indo-European	Avestan	Pahlavi	Persian
algwh: *worth, value* ارزش	arej, arejah: *value* varejah, varecah: *value*	arj	arj: *value* ارج (ارز، ورج، ارزیدن، ارزش)
PK:32	PK:32, BK:826	BQ:97	BQ, PH:241, MO

نه تنها شـه و خسـروکشور است
که شاه است و با ورج پیغمبر است   (فردوسی)

163

28

ارجاسپ: "دارای اسبان ارزشمند"

همریشه: hippo-, equine

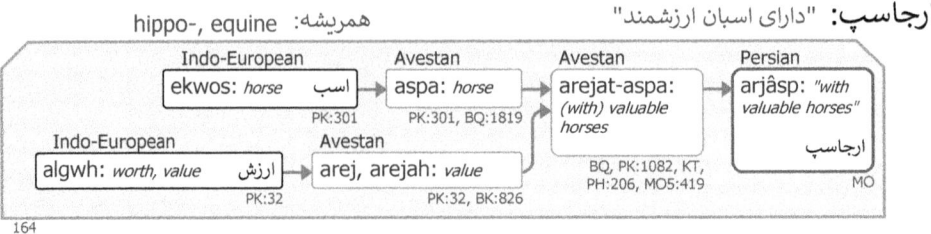

164

ارد: عدالت

همریشه: reason

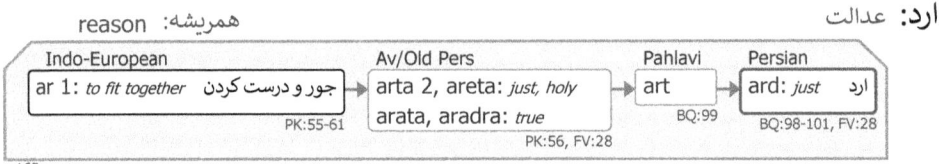

165

آردَب: پیمانه ای حدود یک پنجم متر مکعب

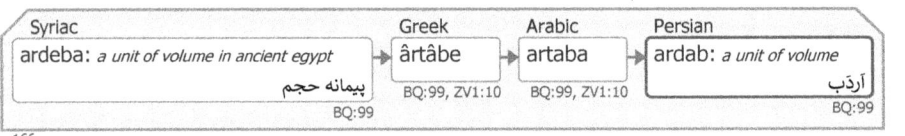

166

اردشیر: "شاه عادل"

همریشه: check, chess

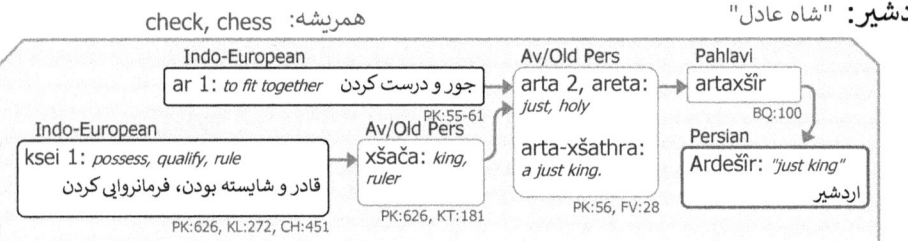

167

اردلان: "سرزمین شریف آرياييان"

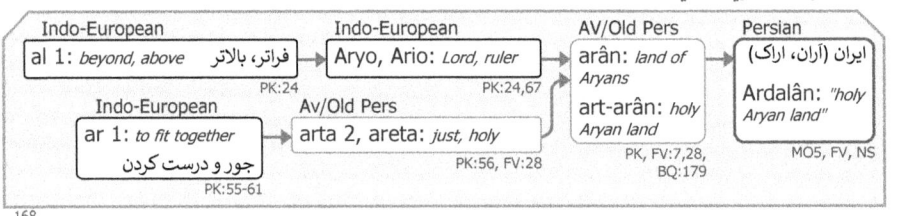

168

اردو

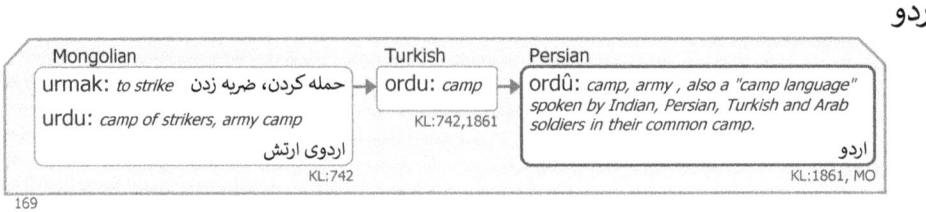

169

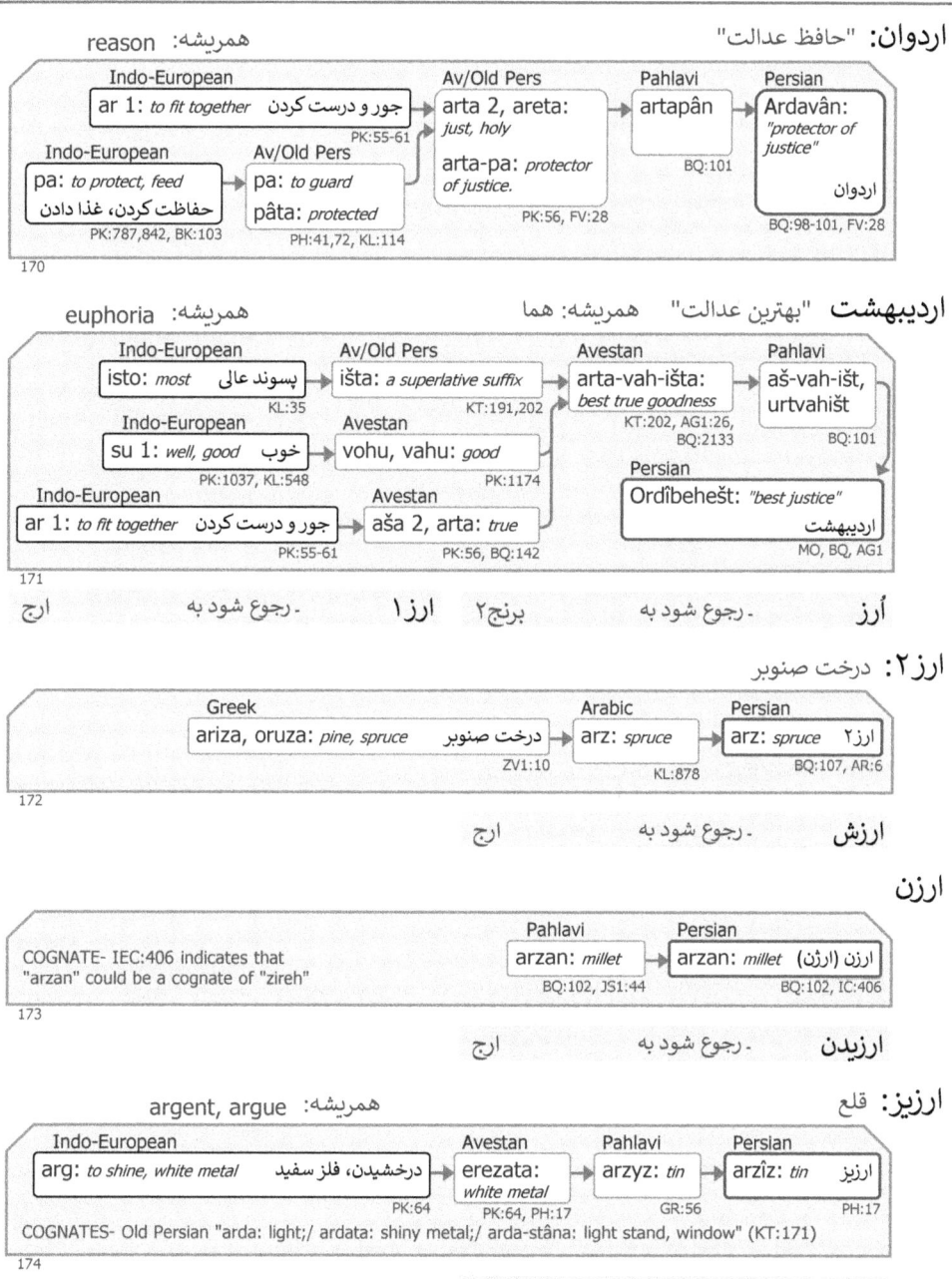

اردوان: "حافظ عدالت"   همریشه: reason

```
Indo-European
ar 1: to fit together   جور و درست کردن
                        PK:55-61
```
```
Indo-European          Av/Old Pers
pa: to protect, feed   pa: to guard
حفاظت کردن، غذا دادن    pâta: protected
PK:787,842, BK:103     PH:41,72, KL:114
```
```
Av/Old Pers
arta 2, areta: just, holy

arta-pa: protector of justice.
PK:56, FV:28
```
```
Pahlavi
artapân
BQ:101
```
```
Persian
Ardavân: "protector of justice"
اردوان
BQ:98-101, FV:28
```
170

اردیبهشت "بهترین عدالت"   همریشه: هما   همریشه: euphoria

```
Indo-European
isto: most   پسوند عالی
KL:35
```
```
Indo-European
su 1: well, good   خوب
PK:1037, KL:548
```
```
Indo-European
ar 1: to fit together   جور و درست کردن
PK:55-61
```
```
Av/Old Pers
išta: a superlative suffix
KT:191,202
```
```
Avestan
vohu, vahu: good
PK:1174
```
```
Avestan
aša 2, arta: true
PK:56, BQ:142
```
```
Avestan
arta-vah-išta: best true goodness
KT:202, AG1:26, BQ:2133
```
```
Pahlavi
aš-vah-išt, urtvahišt
BQ:101
```
```
Persian
Ordîbehešt: "best justice"
اردیبهشت
MO, BQ, AG1
```
171

أُرز   **ارز۱** برنج۲   ـ رجوع شود به   ارج

ارز۲: درخت صنوبر

```
Greek
ariza, oruza: pine, spruce   درخت صنوبر
ZV1:10
```
```
Arabic
arz: spruce
KL:878
```
```
Persian
arz: spruce   ارز۲
BQ:107, AR:6
```
172

ارزش   ـ رجوع شود به   ارج

ارزن

```
COGNATE- IEC:406 indicates that
"arzan" could be a cognate of "zireh"
```
```
Pahlavi
arzan: millet
BQ:102, JS1:44
```
```
Persian
arzan: millet (ارژن)   ارزن
BQ:102, IC:406
```
173

ارزیدن   ـ رجوع شود به   ارج

ارزیز: قلع   همریشه: argent, argue

```
Indo-European
arg: to shine, white metal   درخشیدن، فلز سفید
PK:64
```
```
Avestan
erezata: white metal
PK:64, PH:17
```
```
Pahlavi
arzyz: tin
GR:56
```
```
Persian
arzîz: tin   ارزیز
PH:17
```
COGNATES- Old Persian "arda: light;/ ardata: shiny metal;/ arda-stâna: light stand, window" (KT:171)

174

ارژن   ـ رجوع شود به   ارزن

ارژنگ: کتاب مانی با تصاویر زیبا

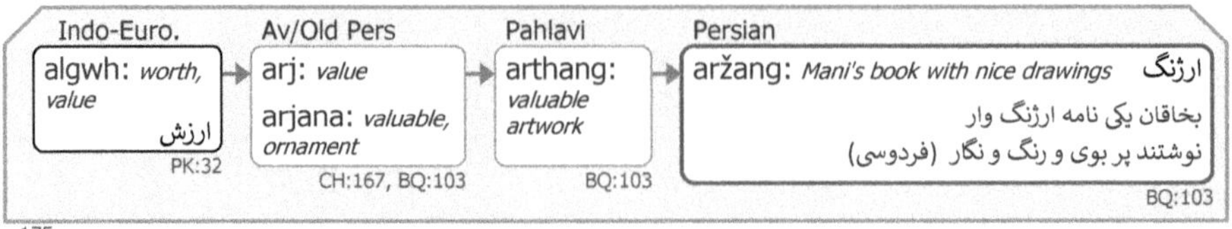

Indo-Euro.	Av/Old Pers	Pahlavi	Persian
algwh: *worth, value* ارزش PK:32	arj: *value* arjana: *valuable, ornament* CH:167, BQ:103	arthang: *valuable artwork* BQ:103	aržang: *Mani's book with nice drawings* ارژنگ بخاقان یکی نامه ارژنگ وار نوشتند پر بوی و رنگ و نگار (فردوسی) BQ:103

175

آرس ـ رجوع شود به   اشک

آرش۱: فاصله آرنج تا نوک انگشتان   همریشه: آرنج   همریشه: elbow

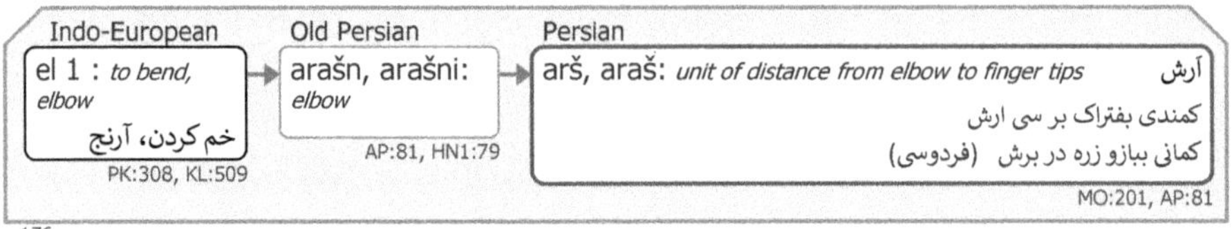

Indo-European	Old Persian	Persian
el 1 : *to bend, elbow* خم کردن، آرنج PK:308, KL:509	arašn, arašni: *elbow* AP:81, HN1:79	arš, araš: *unit of distance from elbow to finger tips* آرش کمندی بفتراک بر سی ارش کمانی ببازو زره در برش (فردوسی) MO:201, AP:81

176

آرش۲ ـ رجوع شود به   ارشیا

ارشاسپ: "دارای اسبان نر"   همریشه: ارشان و ارشک   همریشه: hippo-, equine

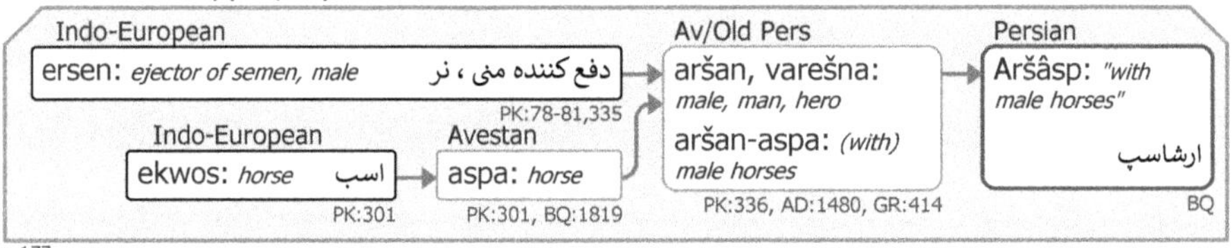

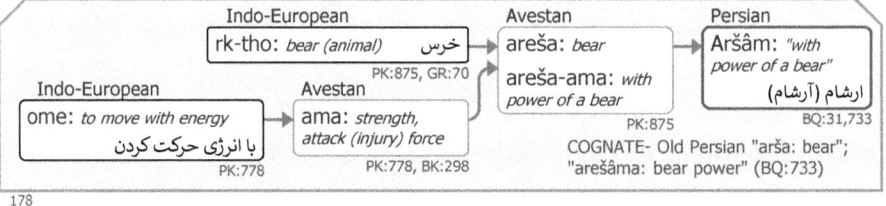

177

ارشام: "با نیروی خرس"

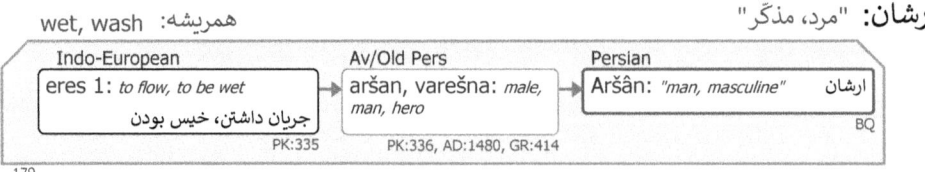

178

ارشان: "مرد، مذگر"   همریشه: wet, wash

Indo-European	Av/Old Pers	Persian
eres 1 : *to flow, to be wet* جریان داشتن، خیس بودن PK:335	aršan, varešna: *male, man, hero* PK:336, AD:1480, GR:414	Aršān: *"man, masculine"* ارشان BQ

179

ارشک۱: "مرد"، لقب بسیاری از پادشاهان اشکانی   همریشه: wet, wash

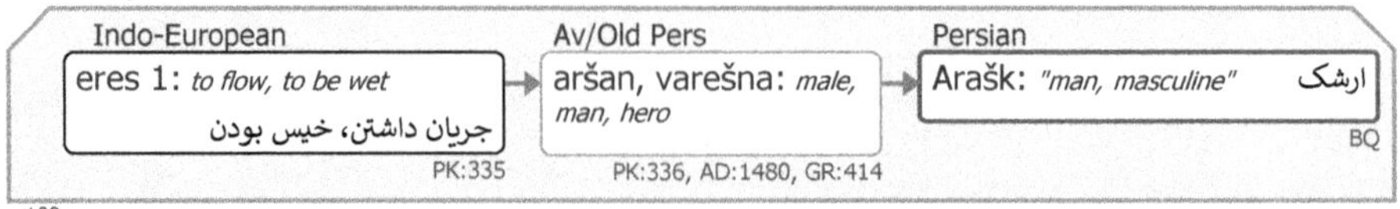

Indo-European	Av/Old Pers	Persian
eres 1 : *to flow, to be wet* جریان داشتن، خیس بودن PK:335	aršan, varešna: *male, man, hero* PK:336, AD:1480, GR:414	Arašk: *"man, masculine"* ارشک BQ

180

ارشک۲: رشک و حسادت

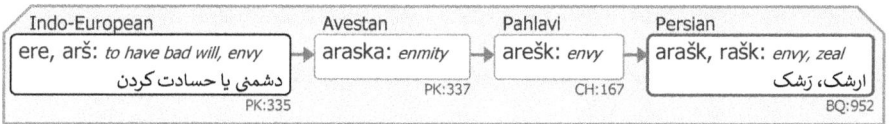

آرشیا: درست، راستین

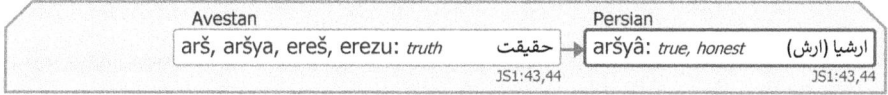

ارغنده: خشمگین

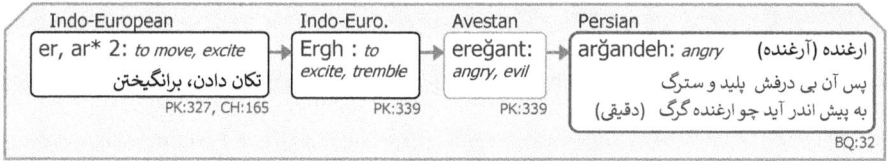

ارغنون

همریشه: organ, energy, work

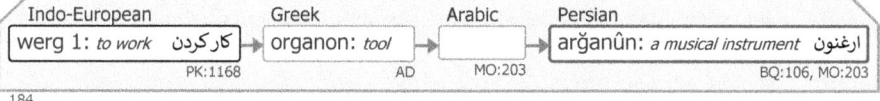

ارک: قلعه کوچک   همریشه: archer

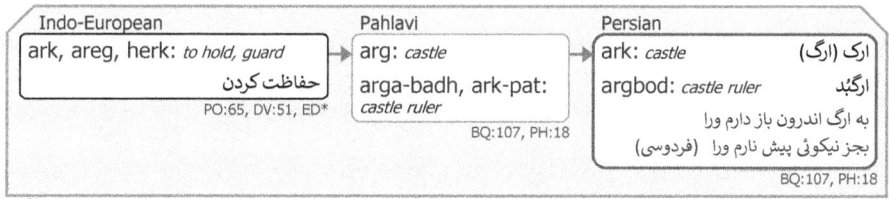

ارکیده

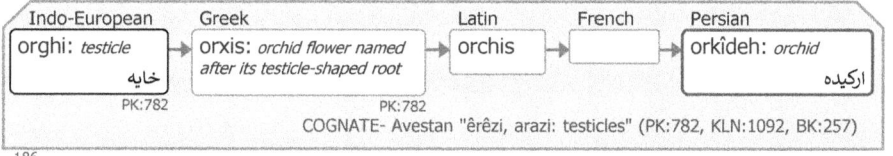

ارگ، ارگبُد ۔رجوع شود به   ارک

آرم: بازو   همریشه: اردلان, اردوان   همریشه: arm, army

آرمَتی: "صفات پسندیده"، فروتنی، بردباری، محبت

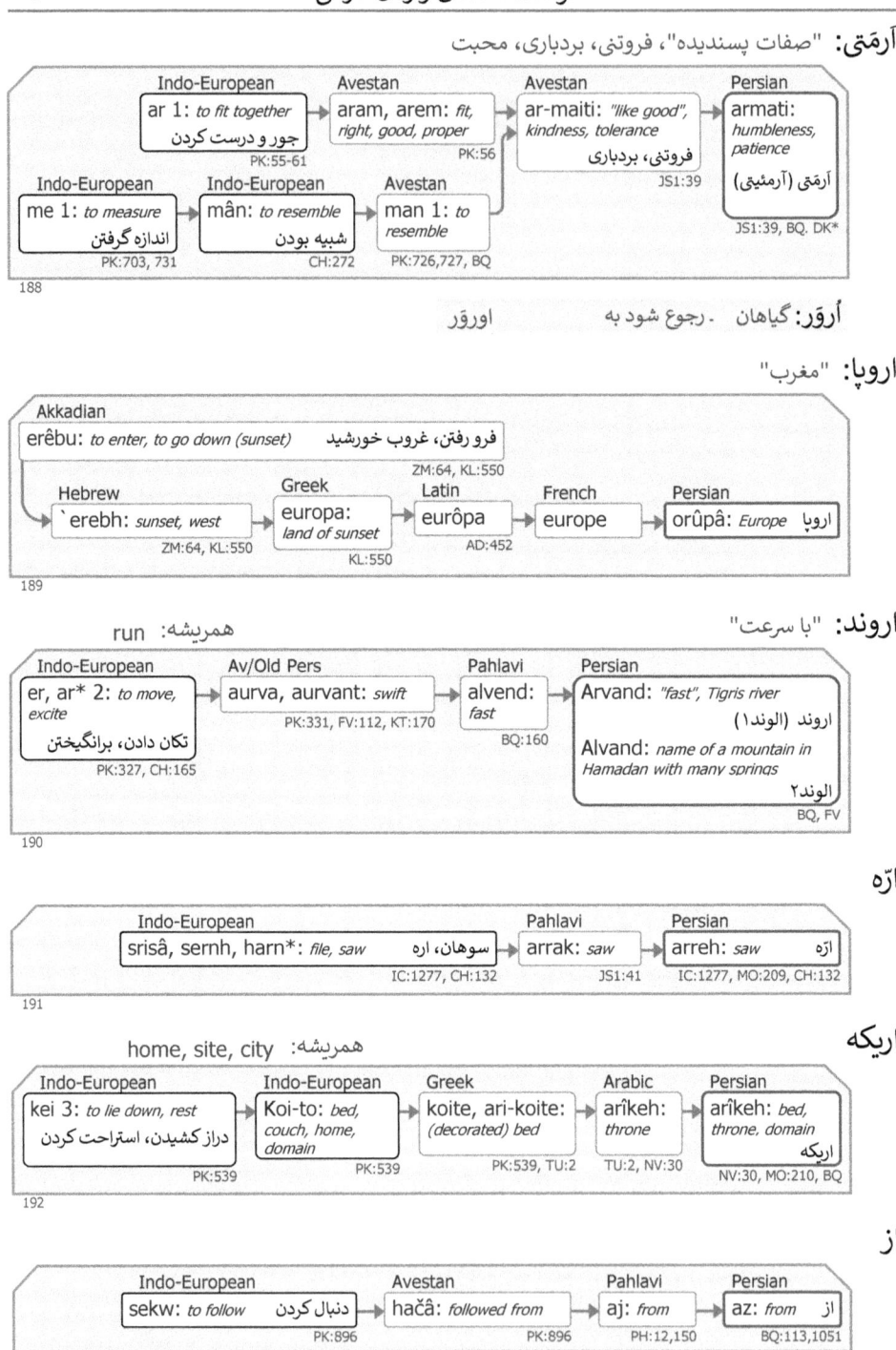

Box 188:

Indo-European — ar 1: *to fit together* — جور و درست کردن — PK:55-61

Avestan — aram, arem: *fit, right, good, proper* — PK:56

Avestan — ar-maiti: *"like good", kindness, tolerance* — فروتنی، بردباری — JS1:39

Persian — armati: *humbleness, patience* — آرمَتی (آرمئیی) — JS1:39, BQ. DK*

Indo-European — me 1: *to measure* — اندازه گرفتن — PK:703, 731

Indo-European — mân: *to resemble* — شبیه بودن — CH:272

Avestan — man 1: *to resemble* — PK:726,727, BQ

أُروَر: گیاهان   . رجوع شود به   اورور

اروپا: "مغرب"

Box 189:

Akkadian — erêbu: *to enter, to go down (sunset)* — فرو رفتن، غروب خورشید — ZM:64, KL:550

Hebrew — `erebh: *sunset, west* — ZM:64, KL:550

Greek — europa: *land of sunset* — KL:550

Latin — eurôpa — AD:452

French — europe

Persian — orûpâ: *Europe* اروپا

اروند: "با سرعت"

همریشه: run

Box 190:

Indo-European — er, ar* 2: *to move, excite* — تکان دادن، برانگیختن — PK:327, CH:165

Av/Old Pers — aurva, aurvant: *swift* — PK:331, FV:112, KT:170

Pahlavi — alvend: *fast* — BQ:160

Persian — Arvand: *"fast", Tigris river* اروند (الوند۱) — Alvand: *name of a mountain in Hamadan with many springs* الوند۲ — BQ, FV

اَرّه

Box 191:

Indo-European — srisâ, sernh, harn*: *file, saw* — سوهان، اره — IC:1277, CH:132

Pahlavi — arrak: *saw* — JS1:41

Persian — arreh: *saw* اَرّه — IC:1277, MO:209, CH:132

اریکه

همریشه: home, site, city

Box 192:

Indo-European — kei 3: *to lie down, rest* — دراز کشیدن، استراحت کردن — PK:539

Indo-European — Koi-to: *bed, couch, home, domain* — PK:539

Greek — koite, ari-koite: *(decorated) bed* — PK:539, TU:2

Arabic — arîkeh: *throne* — TU:2, NV:30

Persian — arîkeh: *bed, throne, domain* اریکه — NV:30, MO:210, BQ

از

Box 193:

Indo-European — sekw: *to follow* — دنبال کردن — PK:896

Avestan — hačâ: *followed from* — PK:896

Pahlavi — aj: *from* — PH:12,150

Persian — az: *from* از — BQ:113,1051

أَزدودن   . رجوع شود به   زدودن

33

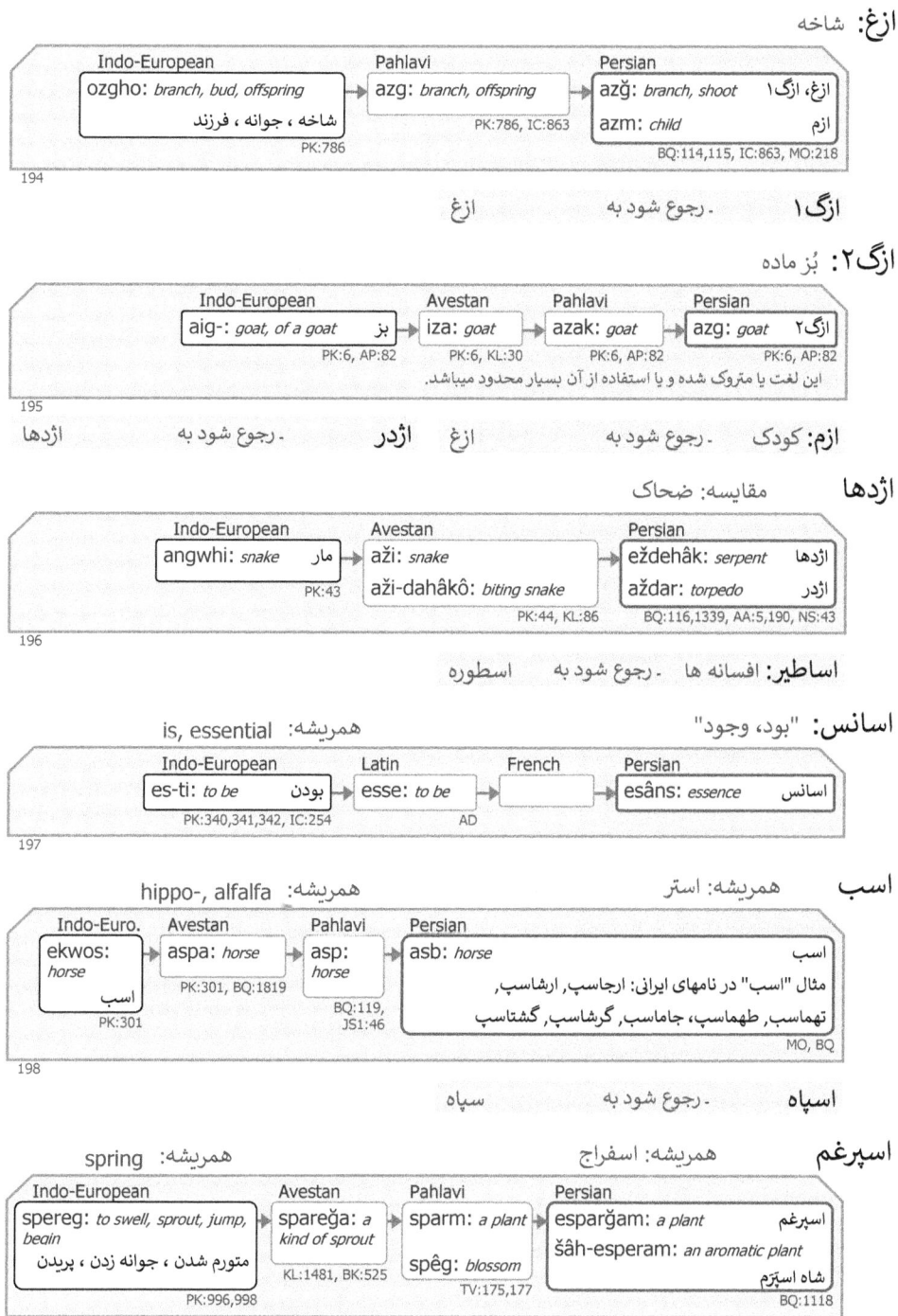

ازغ: شاخه

Indo-European	Pahlavi	Persian
ozgho: *branch, bud, offspring* شاخه ، جوانه ، فرزند PK:786	azg: *branch, offspring* PK:786, IC:863	azǧ: *branch, shoot* ۱ازغ، ازگ azm: *child* ازم BQ:114,115, IC:863, MO:218

194

ازگ۱   رجوع شود به.   **ازغ**

ازگ۲: بُز ماده

Indo-European	Avestan	Pahlavi	Persian
aig-: *goat, of a goat* بز PK:6	iza: *goat* PK:6, KL:30	azak: *goat* PK:6, AP:82	azg: *goat* ۲ازگ PK:6, AP:82

این لغت یا متروک شده و یا استفاده از آن بسیار محدود میباشد.

195

ازم: کودک   رجوع شود به.   **ازدر**   **ازغ**   اژدها

اژدها   مقایسه: ضحاک

Indo-European	Avestan	Persian
angwhi: *snake* مار PK:43	aži: *snake* aži-dahâkô: *biting snake* PK:44, KL:86	eždehâk: *serpent* اژدها aždar: *torpedo* اژدر BQ:116,1339, AA:5,190, NS:43

196

اساطیر: افسانه ها   رجوع شود به.   اسطوره

اسانس: "بود، وجود"   همریشه: is, essential

Indo-European	Latin	French	Persian
es-ti: *to be* بودن PK:340,341,342, IC:254	esse: *to be* AD		esâns: *essence* اسانس

197

اسب   همریشه: استر   همریشه: hippo-, alfalfa

Indo-Euro.	Avestan	Pahlavi	Persian
ekwos: *horse* اسب PK:301	aspa: *horse* PK:301, BQ:1819	asp: *horse* BQ:119, JS1:46	asb: *horse* اسب مثال "اسب" در نامهای ایرانی: ارجاسپ، ارشاسپ، تهماسپ، طهماسپ، گرشاسپ، گشتاسپ MO, BQ

198

اسپاه   رجوع شود به.   سپاه

اسپرغم   همریشه: اسفراج   همریشه: spring

Indo-European	Avestan	Pahlavi	Persian
spereg: *to swell, sprout, jump,* *begin* متورم شدن ، جوانه زدن ، پریدن PK:996,998	spareǧa: *a* *kind of sprout* KL:1481, BK:525	sparm: *a plant* spêg: *blossom* TV:175,177	esparǧam: *a plant* اسپرغم šâh-esperam: *an aromatic plant* شاه اسپَرم BQ:1118

199

34

اسپرود: گنجشک

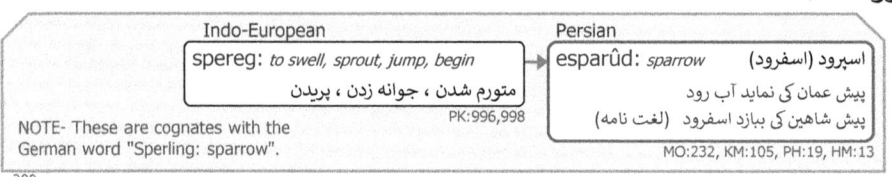

Indo-European	Persian
spereg: *to swell, sprout, jump, begin* متورم شدن ، جوانه زدن ، پریدن PK:996,998	esparûd: *sparrow* اسپرود (اسفرود) پیش عمان کی نماید آب رود پیش شاهین کی بباخت اسفرود (لغت نامه) MO:232, KM:105, PH:19, HM:13

NOTE- These are cognates with the German word "Sperling: sparrow".

200

اسپریس: میدان اسب دوانی یا جنگ

همریشه: equine, roll, round

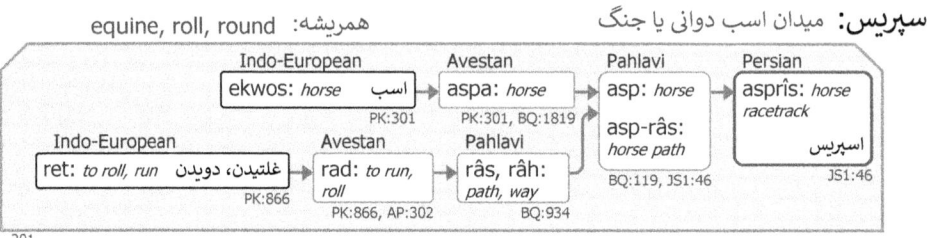

Indo-European	Avestan	Pahlavi	Persian
ekwos: *horse* اسب PK:301	aspa: *horse* PK:301, BQ:1819	asp: *horse* asp-râs: *horse path* BQ:119, JS1:46	asprîs: *horse racetrack* اسپریس JS1:46

Indo-European	Avestan	Pahlavi
ret: *to roll, run* غلتیدن، دویدن PK:866	rad: *to run, roll* PK:866, AP:302	râs, râh: *path, way* BQ:934

201

اسپست: "غذای اسب"

همریشه: alfalfa, hippo

Indo-European	Avestan	Avestan	Pahlavi
ekwos: *horse* اسب PK:301	aspa: *horse* PK:301, BQ:1819	aspa-asa: *horse food* BQ:1819	aspast: *horse food, alfalfa* BQ:119

Indo-European	Avestan
ed: *to eat* خوردن PK:287	asa 1: *food* PK:287, BQ:44,1624

Persian
 aspast: *alfalfa*   اسپست (سپست)
 سنبل و سوسن کجا آمد بدست از روضه ای
 کاندرو تخم سپست و سیر و سیسنبر برند (سنائی)
 MO

202

اسفند	.رجوع شود به	اسپنتا	اسفناج	.رجوع شود به	اسپناخ
			اسفند	.رجوع شود به	اسپند

اسپندارمذ: بردباری مقدس، آخرین ماه سال

همریشه: mind, reason, housel

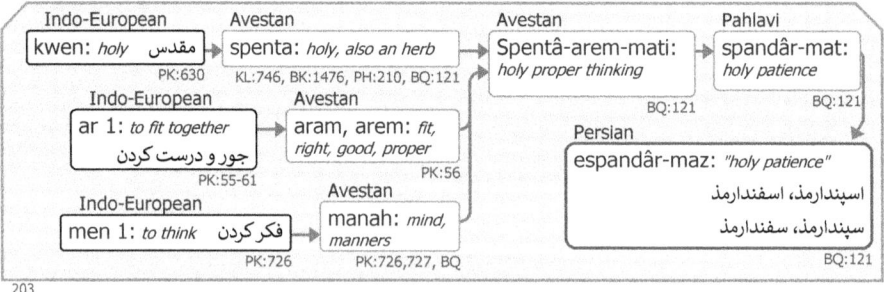

Indo-European	Avestan	Avestan	Pahlavi
kwen: *holy* مقدس PK:630	spenta: *holy, also an herb* KL:746, BK:1476, PH:210, BQ:121	Spentâ-arem-mati: *holy proper thinking* BQ:121	spandâr-mat: *holy patience* BQ:121

Indo-European	Avestan
ar 1: *to fit together* جور و درست کردن PK:55-61	aram, arem: *fit, right, good, proper* PK:56

Indo-European	Avestan
men 1: *to think* فکر کردن PK:726	manah: *mind, manners* PK:726,727, BQ

Persian
 espandâr-maz: *"holy patience"*
 اسپندارمذ، اسفندارمذ
 سپندارمذ، سفندارمذ
 BQ:121

203

سپهر	.رجوع شود به	اسپهر	اصفهان	.رجوع شود به	اسپهان
استخوان	.رجوع شود به	است۲	استن	هست-.رجوع شود به	است۱:
			ستاک	.رجوع شود به	اِستاخ: جسور

استاد: "آنکه اول یا جلو ایستاده"   همریشه: stand

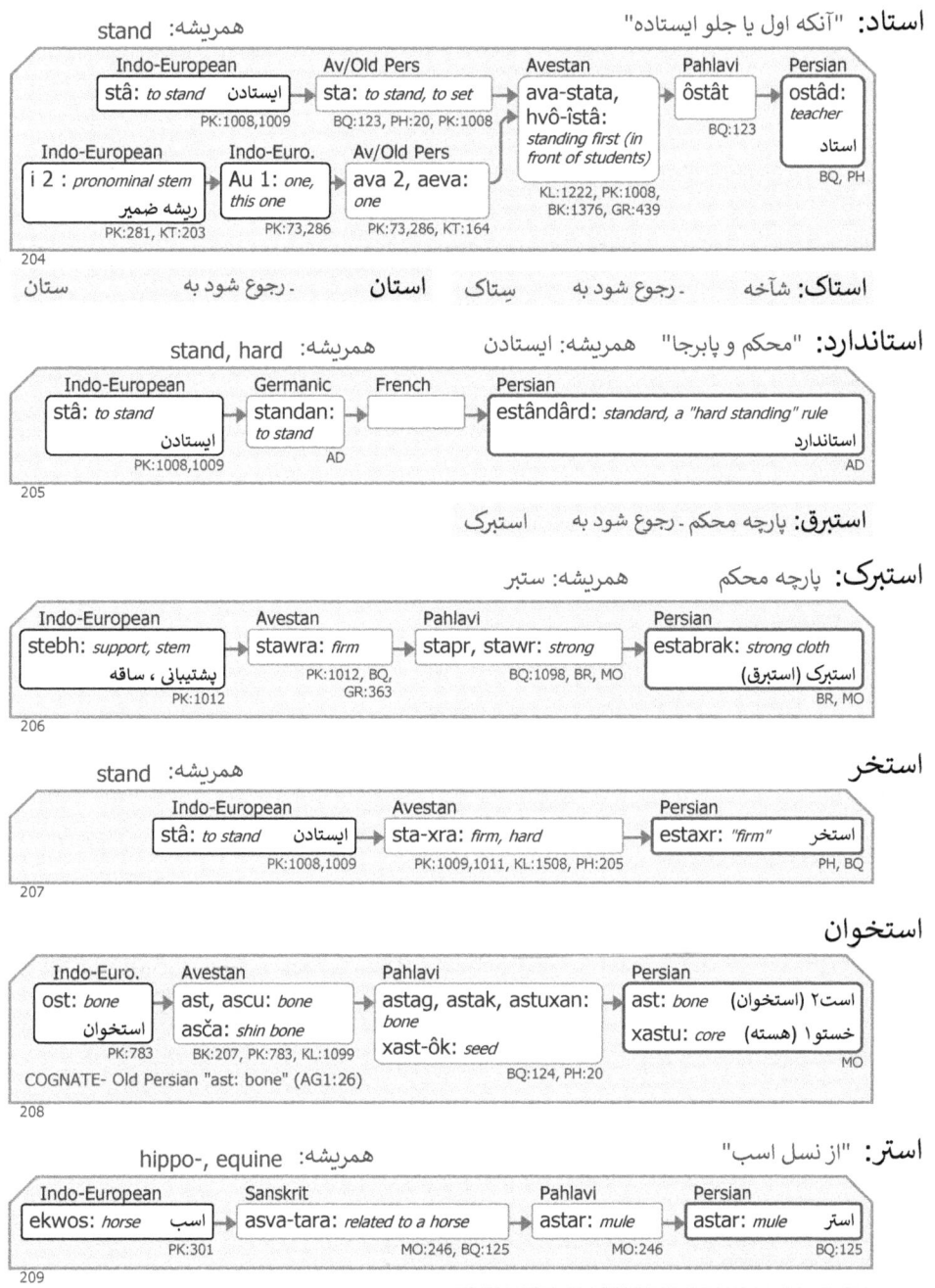

استاک: شآخه ۔ رجوع شود به   سِتاک   **استان**   ۔ رجوع شود به   ستان

استاندارد: "محکم و پابرجا"   همریشه: ایستادن   همریشه: stand, hard

استبرق: پارچه محکم ۔ رجوع شود به   استبرک

استبرک: پارچه محکم   همریشه: ستبر

استخر   همریشه: stand

استخوان

استر: "از نسل اسب"   همریشه: hippo-, equine

استردن   ۔ رجوع شود به   ستردن

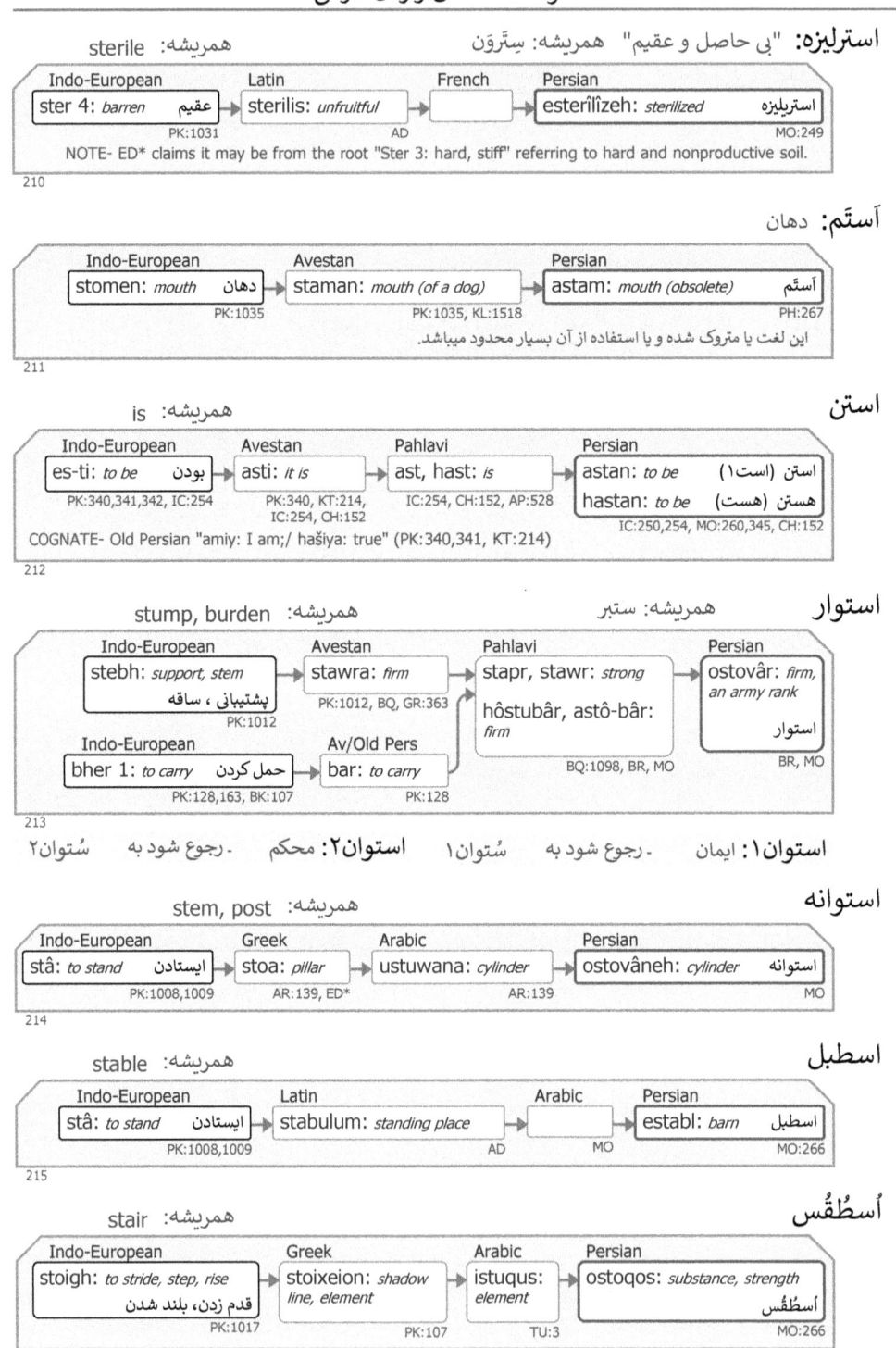

استرلیزه: "بی حاصل و عقیم"   همریشه: سِتَّروَن   همریشه: sterile

Indo-European	Latin	French	Persian
ster 4: *barren* عقیم	sterilis: *unfruitful*		esterîlîzeh: *sterilized* استرلیزه
PK:1031	AD		MO:249

NOTE- ED* claims it may be from the root "Ster 3: hard, stiff" referring to hard and nonproductive soil.

210

آستَم: دهان

Indo-European	Avestan	Persian
stomen: *mouth* دهان	staman: *mouth (of a dog)*	astam: *mouth (obsolete)* آستَم
PK:1035	PK:1035, KL:1518	PH:267

این لغت یا متروک شده و یا استفاده از آن بسیار محدود میباشد.

211

استن   همریشه: is

Indo-European	Avestan	Pahlavi	Persian
es-ti: *to be* بودن	asti: *it is*	ast, hast: *is*	astan: *to be* استن (است۱)
PK:340,341,342, IC:254	PK:340, KT:214, IC:254, CH:152	IC:254, CH:152, AP:528	hastan: *to be* هستن (هست)
			IC:250,254, MO:260,345, CH:152

COGNATE- Old Persian "amiy: I am;/ hašiya: true" (PK:340,341, KT:214)

212

استوار   همریشه: ستبر   همریشه: stump, burden

Indo-European	Avestan	Pahlavi	Persian
stebh: *support, stem* پشتیبانی ، ساقه	stawra: *firm*	stapr, stawr: *strong*	ostovâr: *firm, an army rank*
PK:1012	PK:1012, BQ, GR:363	hôstubâr, astô-bâr: *firm*	استوار
Indo-European	Av/Old Pers		BR, MO
bher 1: *to carry* حمل کردن	bar: *to carry*	BQ:1098, BR, MO	
PK:128,163, BK:107	PK:128		

213

استوان۱: ایمان   .رجوع شود به   سُتوان۱   **استوان۲:** محکم   .رجوع شود به   سُتوان۲

استوانه   همریشه: stem, post

Indo-European	Greek	Arabic	Persian
stâ: *to stand* ایستادن	stoa: *pillar*	ustuwana: *cylinder*	ostovâneh: *cylinder* استوانه
PK:1008,1009	AR:139, ED*	AR:139	MO

214

اسطبل   همریشه: stable

Indo-European	Latin	Arabic	Persian
stâ: *to stand* ایستادن	stabulum: *standing place*		establ: *barn* اسطبل
PK:1008,1009	AD	MO	MO:266

215

أسطُقُس   همریشه: stair

Indo-European	Greek	Arabic	Persian
stoigh: *to stride, step, rise* قدم زدن، بلند شدن	stoixeion: *shadow line, element*	istuqus: *element*	ostoqos: *substance, strength* أسطُقُس
PK:1017	PK:107	TU:3	MO:266

216

اسطوره: "داستان تاریخی"

همریشه: history

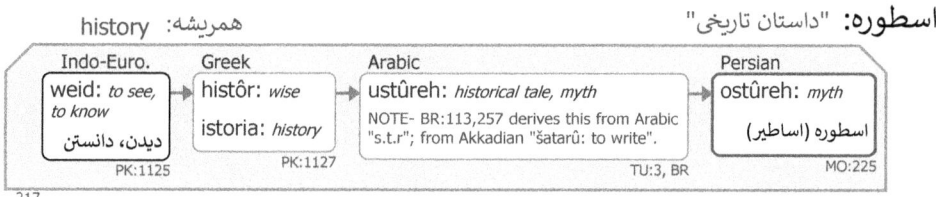

Indo-Euro.	Greek	Arabic	Persian
weid: to see, to know دیدن، دانستن PK:1125	histôr: wise istoria: history PK:1127	ustûreh: historical tale, myth NOTE- BR:113,257 derives this from Arabic "s.t.r"; from Akkadian "šatarû: to write". TU:3, BR	ostûreh: myth اسطوره (اساطیر) MO:225

217

اسفالت: "سطح غیر لغزنده"   همریشه: زفت

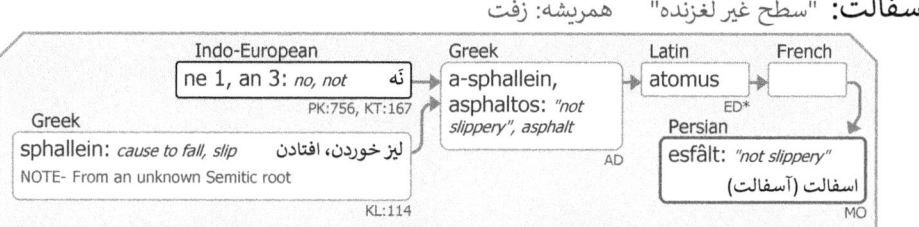

Indo-European	Greek	Latin	French
ne 1, an 3: no, not نَه PK:756, KT:167	a-sphallein, asphaltos: "not slippery", asphalt AD	atomus ED*	

Greek
sphallein: cause to fall, slip لیز خوردن، افتادن
NOTE- From an unknown Semitic root
KL:114

Persian
esfâlt: "not slippery"
اسفالت (آسفالت)
MO

218

اسفراج: مارچوبه

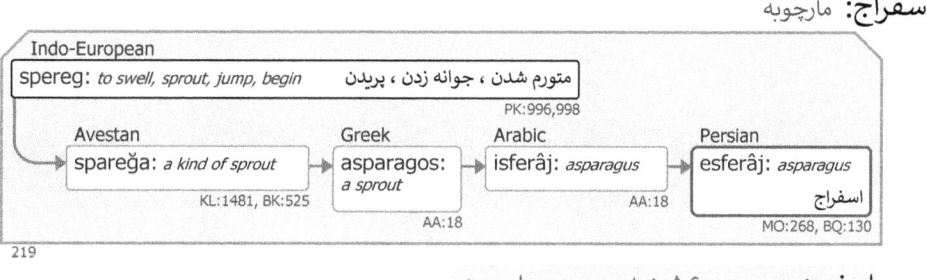

Indo-European
spereg: to swell, sprout, jump, begin متورم شدن ، جوانه زدن ، پریدن
PK:996,998

Avestan	Greek	Arabic	Persian
spareğa: a kind of sprout KL:1481, BK:525	asparagos: a sprout AA:18	isferâj: asparagus AA:18	esferâj: asparagus اسفراج MO:268, BQ:130

219

اسفرود

اسپرود   ـ رجوع شود به

اسفناج

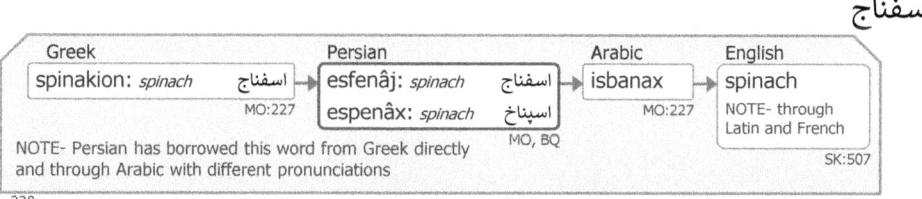

Greek	Persian	Arabic	English
spinakion: spinach اسفناج MO:227	esfenâj: spinach اسفناج espenâx: spinach اسپناخ MO, BQ	isbanax MO:227	spinach NOTE- through Latin and French SK:507

NOTE- Persian has borrowed this word from Greek directly and through Arabic with different pronunciations

220

اسفنج

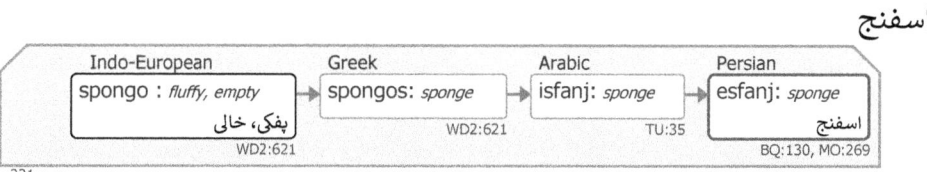

Indo-European	Greek	Arabic	Persian
spongo : fluffy, empty پفکی، خالی WD2:621	spongos: sponge WD2:621	isfanj: sponge TU:35	esfanj: sponge اسفنج BQ:130, MO:269

221

اسفند

همریشه: housel

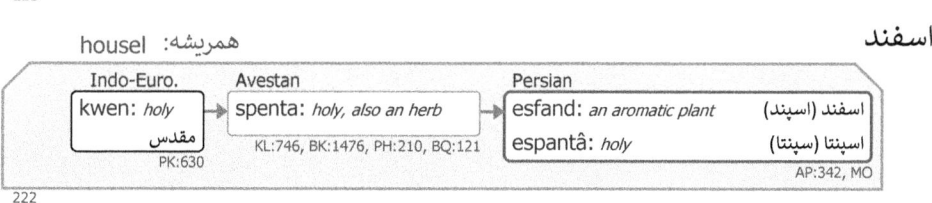

Indo-Euro.	Avestan	Persian
kwen: holy مقدس PK:630	spenta: holy, also an herb KL:746, BK:1476, PH:210, BQ:121	esfand: an aromatic plant اسفند (اسپند) espantâ: holy اسپنتا (سپنتا) AP:342, MO

222

اسفندارمذ ـ رجوع شود به اسپندارمذ

اسفندیار: "خلقت مقدس"

همریشه: housel

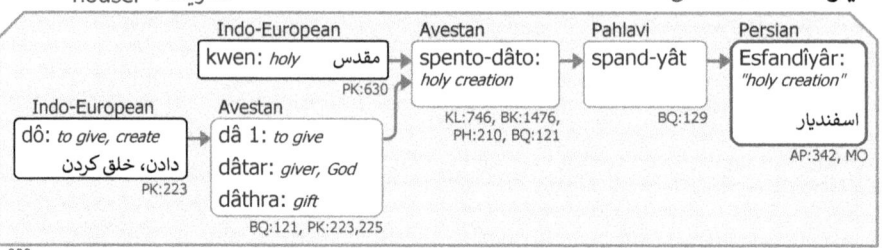

223

اسقف

همریشه: epidemic, scope

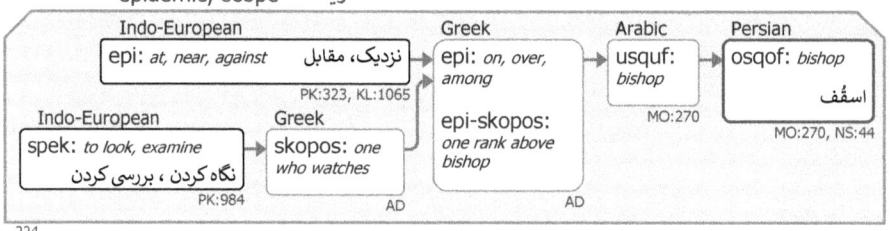

224

اسکاف: کفش دوز

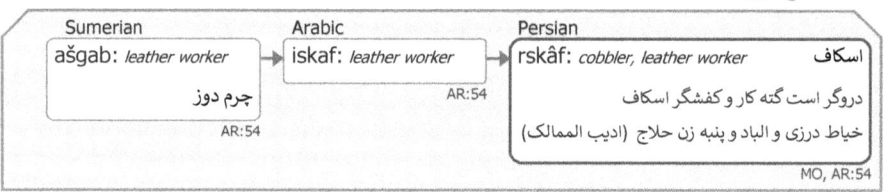

225

اسکله

226

اسکناس: "سفته"

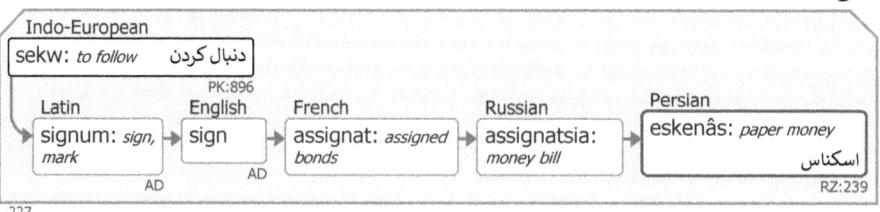

227

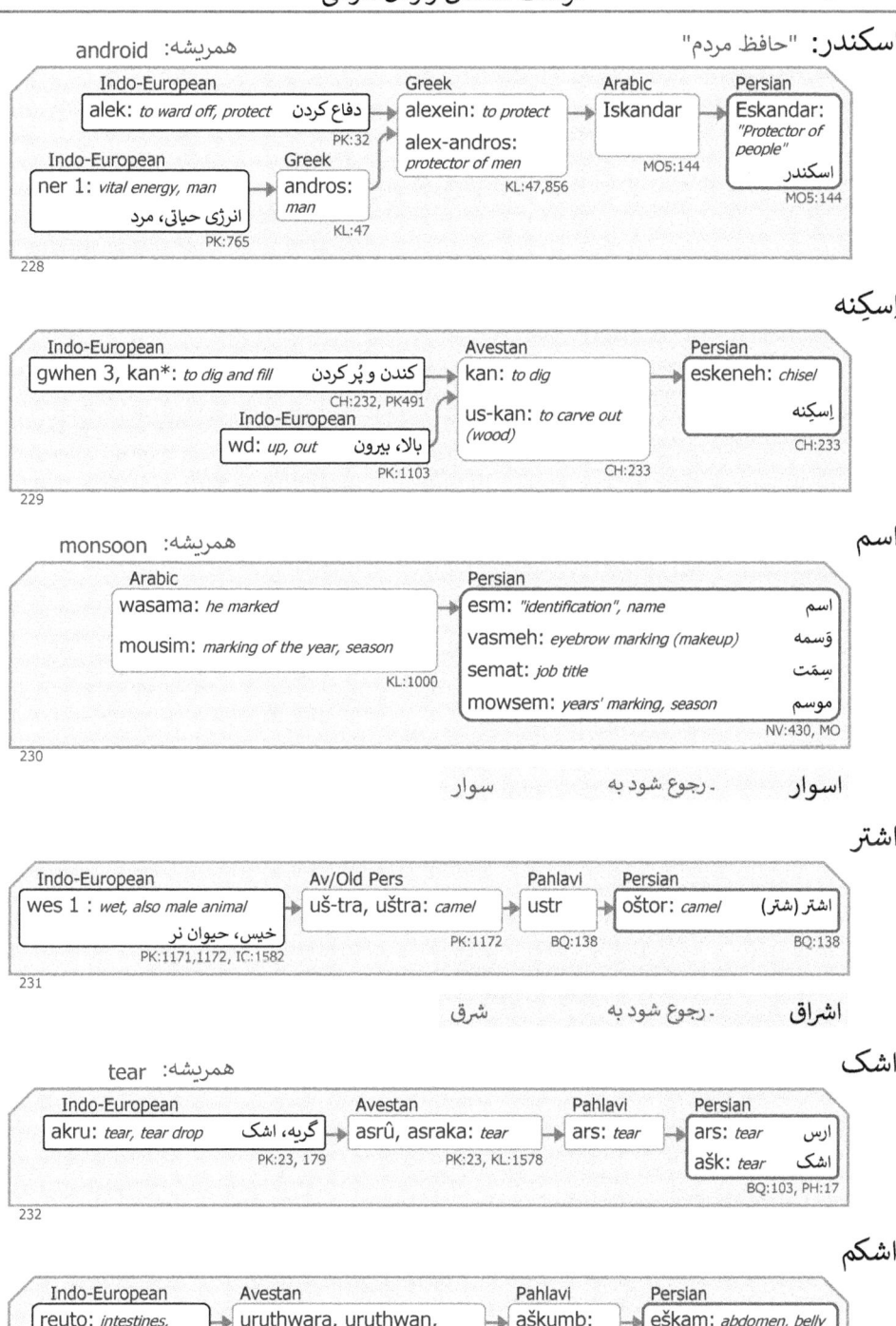

اسکندر: "حافظ مردم"

همریشه: android

Indo-European
alek: *to ward off, protect*   دفاع کردن
PK:32

Greek
alexein: *to protect*
alex-andros: *protector of men*
KL:47,856

Arabic
Iskandar
MO5:144

Persian
Eskandar: *"Protector of people"*
اسکندر
MO5:144

Indo-European
ner 1: *vital energy, man*   انرژی حیاتی، مرد
PK:765

Greek
andros: *man*
KL:47

228

إسکِنه

Indo-European
gwhen 3, kan*: *to dig and fill*   کندن و پُرکردن
CH:232, PK491

Indo-European
wd: *up, out*   بالا، بیرون
PK:1103

Avestan
kan: *to dig*
us-kan: *to carve out (wood)*
CH:233

Persian
eskeneh: *chisel*
إسکِنه
CH:233

229

اسم

همریشه: monsoon

Arabic
wasama: *he marked*
mousim: *marking of the year, season*
KL:1000

Persian
esm: *"identification", name*   اسم
vasmeh: *eyebrow marking (makeup)*   وَسمه
semat: *job title*   سِمَت
mowsem: *years' marking, season*   موسم
NV:430, MO

230

اسوار

ـ رجوع شود به   سوار

اشتر

Indo-European
wes 1 : *wet, also male animal*   خیس، حیوان نر
PK:1171,1172, IC:1582

Av/Old Pers
uš-tra, uštra: *camel*
PK:1172

Pahlavi
ustr
BQ:138

Persian
oštor: *camel*   اشتر (شتر)
BQ:138

231

اشراق

ـ رجوع شود به   شرق

اشک

همریشه: tear

Indo-European
akru: *tear, tear drop*   گریه، اشک
PK:23, 179

Avestan
asrû, asraka: *tear*
PK:23, KL:1578

Pahlavi
ars: *tear*

Persian
ars: *tear*   ارس
ašk: *tear*   اشک
BQ:103, PH:17

232

اشکم

Indo-European
reuto: *intestines, bowels*   دل و روده
PK:873

Avestan
uruthwara, uruthwan, uruthwasča: *abdomen, belly*
PK:874

Pahlavi
aškumb: *abdomen*
TV:36

Persian
eškam: *abdomen, belly*
اشکم (شکم)
TV:36

233

اُشنان: صابون

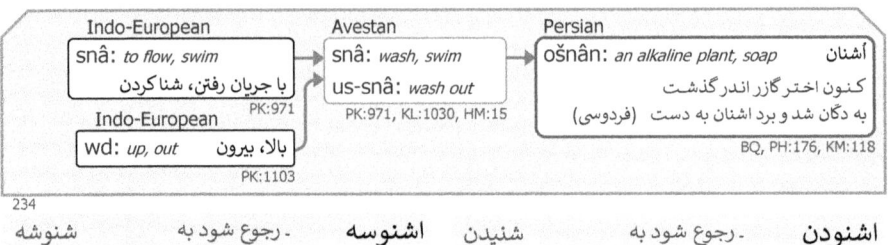

234

اشنودن - رجوع شود به **اشنوسه** شنیدن - رجوع شود به شنوشه

اُشنه: گلسنگ

همریشه: lichen

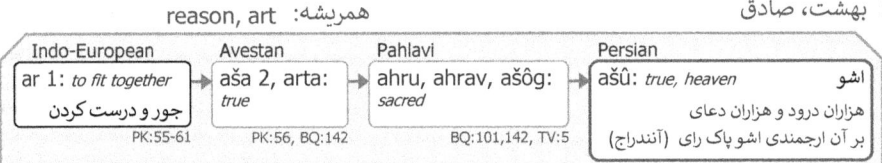

235

اشو: بهشت، صادق

همریشه: reason, art

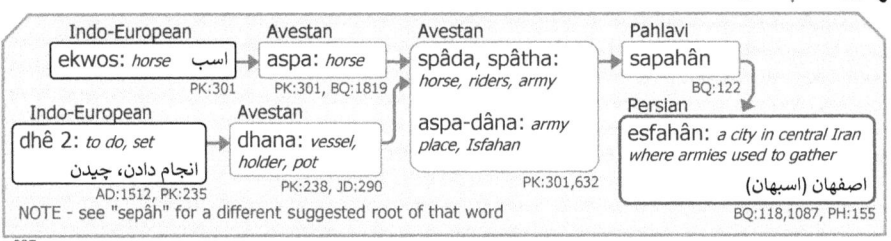

236

اصفهان: "سپاه دان"

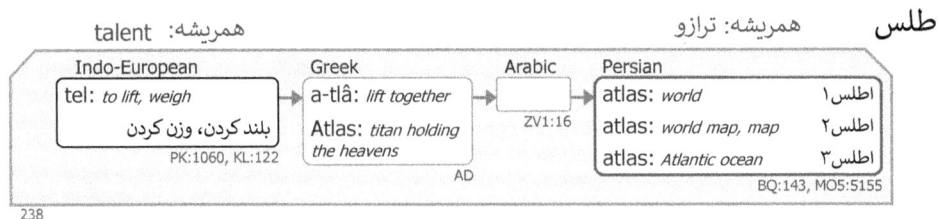

237

اطلس همریشه: ترازو   همریشه: talent

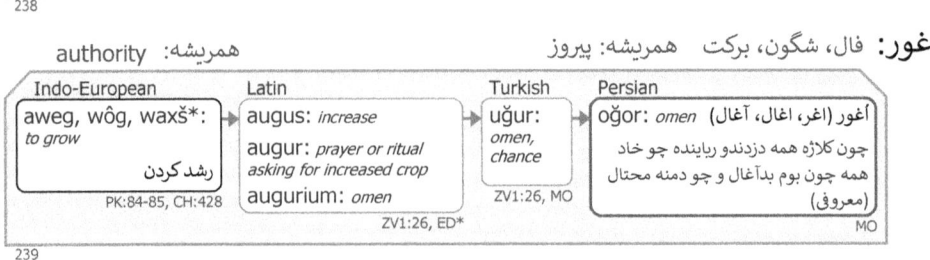

238

اُغور: فال، شگون، برکت   همریشه: پیروز   همریشه: authority

239

41

افتادن

همریشه: feather

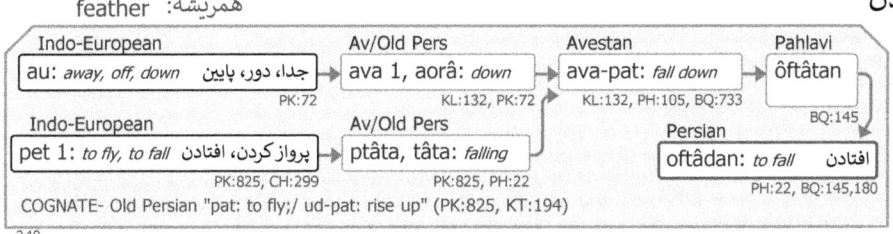

افتالیدن: پراکندن

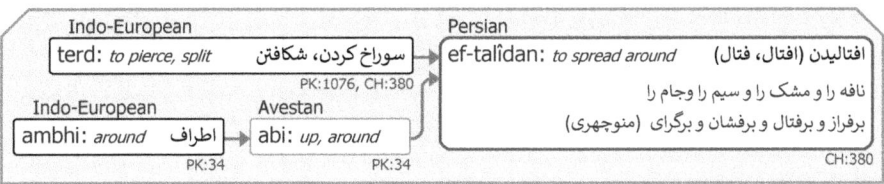

آفِد: تعجب کردن ۔رجوع شود به افدیدن

افدستا: ستایش بسیار یا شگفت

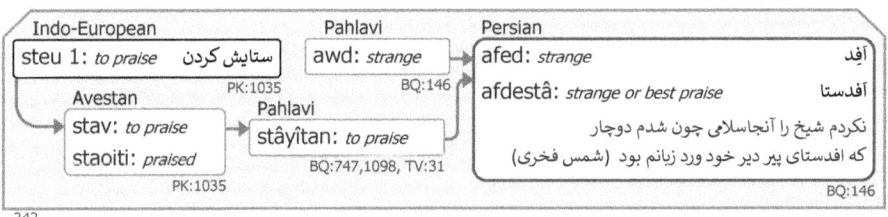

افدیدن: شگفتی کردن، تعجب کردن

همریشه: awe

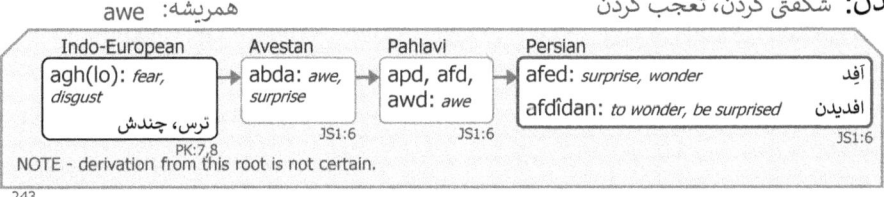

افراختن ۔رجوع شود به افراشتن افراز افراشتن ۔رجوع شود به افراشتن

افراسیاب: "ترسناک"

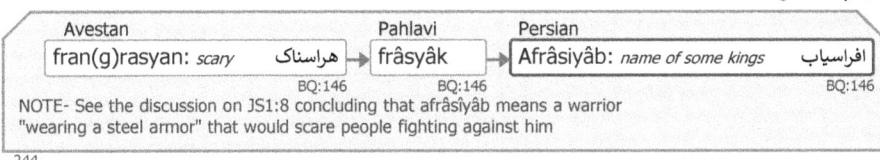

42

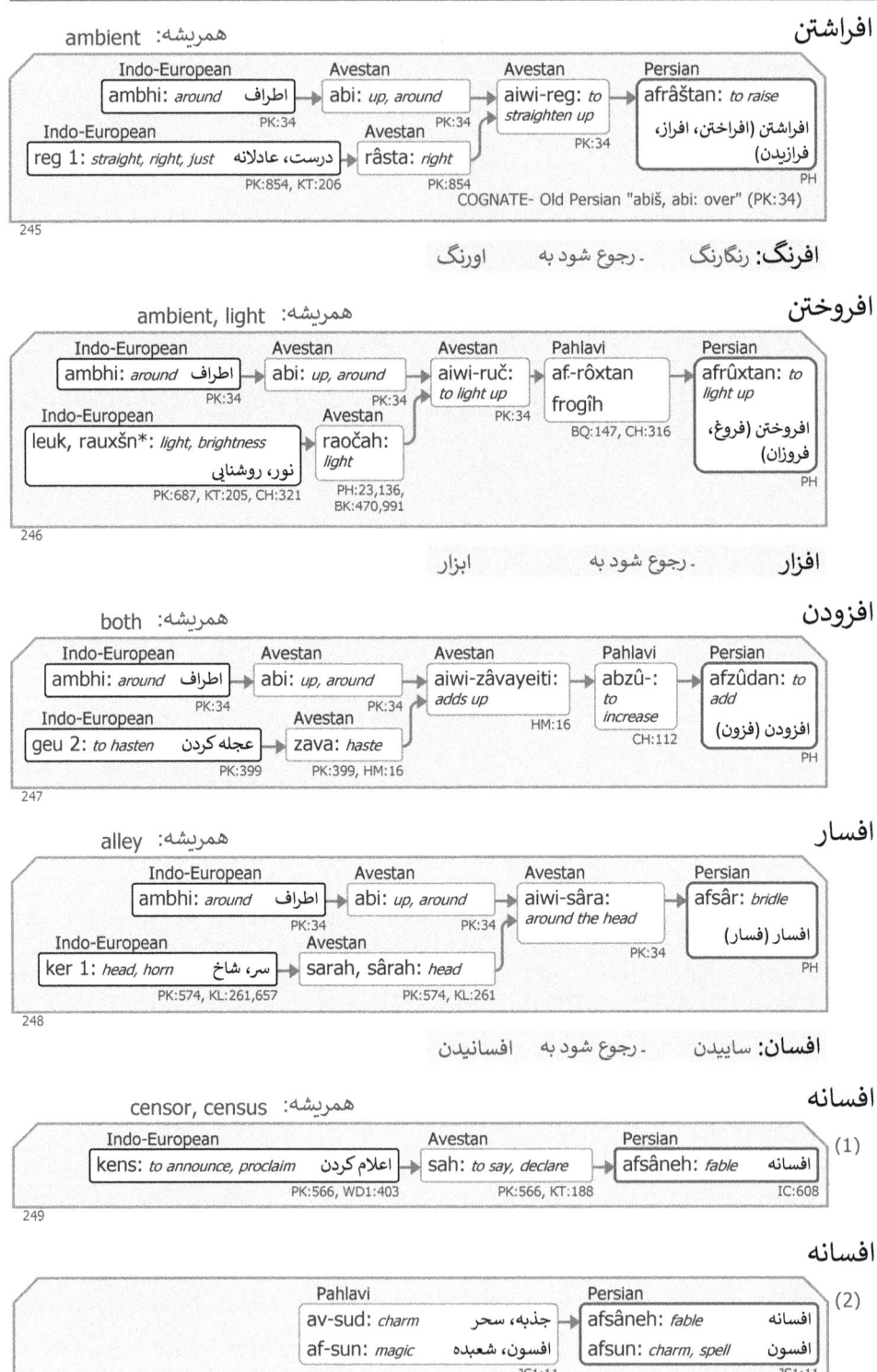

افراشتن

همریشه: ambient

Indo-European	Avestan	Avestan	Persian
ambhi: *around* اطراف PK:34	abi: *up, around* PK:34	aiwi-reg: *to straighten up* PK:34	afrâštan: *to raise* افراشتن (افراختن، افراز، فرازیدن) PH
Indo-European	Avestan		
reg 1: *straight, right, just* درست، عادلانه PK:854, KT:206	râsta: *right* PK:854		

COGNATE- Old Persian "abiš, abi: over" (PK:34)

245

افرنگ: رنگارنگ - رجوع شود به   اورنگ

افروختن

همریشه: ambient, light

Indo-European	Avestan	Avestan	Pahlavi	Persian
ambhi: *around* اطراف PK:34	abi: *up, around* PK:34	aiwi-ruč: *to light up* PK:34	af-rôxtan frogîh BQ:147, CH:316	afrûxtan: *to light up* افروختن (فروغ، فروزان) PH
Indo-European	Avestan			
leuk, rauxšn*: *light, brightness* نور، روشنایی PK:687, KT:205, CH:321	raočah: *light* PH:23,136, BK:470,991			

246

افزار - رجوع شود به   ابزار

افزودن

همریشه: both

Indo-European	Avestan	Avestan	Pahlavi	Persian
ambhi: *around* اطراف PK:34	abi: *up, around* PK:34	aiwi-zâvayeiti: *adds up* HM:16	abzû-: *to increase* CH:112	afzûdan: *to add* افزودن (فزون) PH
Indo-European	Avestan			
geu 2: *to hasten* عجله کردن PK:399	zava: *haste* PK:399, HM:16			

247

افسار

همریشه: alley

Indo-European	Avestan	Avestan	Persian
ambhi: *around* اطراف PK:34	abi: *up, around* PK:34	aiwi-sâra: *around the head* PK:34	afsâr: *bridle* افسار (فسار) PH
Indo-European	Avestan		
ker 1: *head, horn* سر، شاخ PK:574, KL:261,657	sarah, sârah: *head* PK:574, KL:261		

248

افسان: ساییدن - رجوع شود به   افسانیدن

افسانه

همریشه: censor, census

Indo-European	Avestan	Persian
kens: *to announce, proclaim* اعلام کردن PK:566, WD1:403	sah: *to say, declare* PK:566, KT:188	afsâneh: *fable* افسانه IC:608

(1)

249

افسانه

Pahlavi	Persian
av-sud: *charm* جذبه، سحر	afsâneh: *fable* افسانه
af-sun: *magic* افسون، شعبده JS1:11	afsun: *charm, spell* افسون JS1:11

(2)

250

43

افسانیدن

افسانیدن: ساییدن

همریشه فسانیدن، ساییدن

همریشه: edge, acute

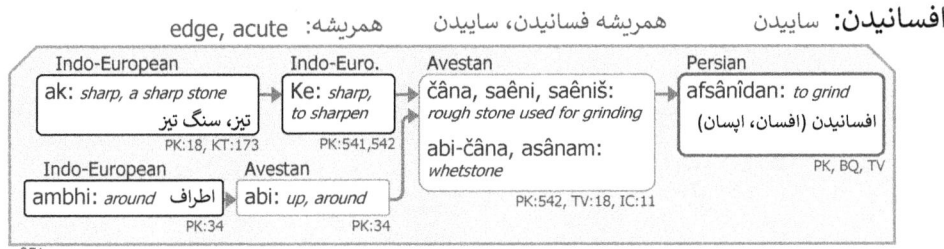

Indo-European	Indo-Euro.	Avestan	Persian
ak: sharp, a sharp stone / تیز، سنگ تیز	Ke: sharp, to sharpen	čâna, saêni, saêniš: rough stone used for grinding / abi-čâna, asânam: whetstone	afsânîdan: to grind / افسانیدن (افسان، اپسان)
PK:18, KT:173	PK:541,542	PK:542, TV:18, IC:11	PK, BQ, TV
Indo-European	Avestan		
ambhi: around اطراف	abi: up, around		
PK:34	PK:34		

251

افسر

همریشه: ambient

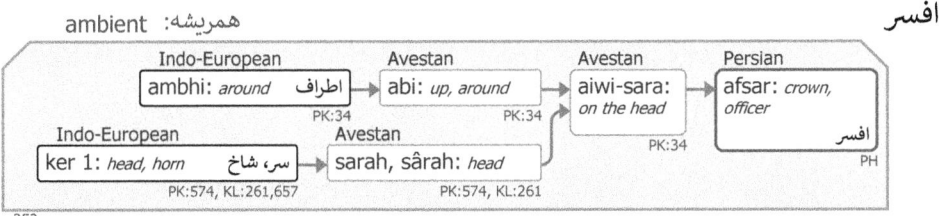

Indo-European	Avestan	Avestan	Persian
ambhi: around اطراف	abi: up, around	aiwi-sara: on the head	afsar: crown, officer / افسر
	PK:34	PK:34	PH
Indo-European	Avestan		
ker 1: head, horn سر، شاخ	sarah, sârah: head		
PK:574, KL:261,657	PK:574, KL:261		

252

افسردن

Indo-European	Avestan	Pahlavi	Persian
kel 1: cold or warm, a year / سرد یا گرم، سال / NOTE- opposite meanings	sarethâ: cold	awsartan: to become cold, to lose hope.	afsordan: to lose hope / افسردن
PK:551, BK:1078	PK:551, BK:1078	PH:23	PK:551, BK:1078, BQ

253

افسنتین

همریشه: اسفند

همریشه: housel

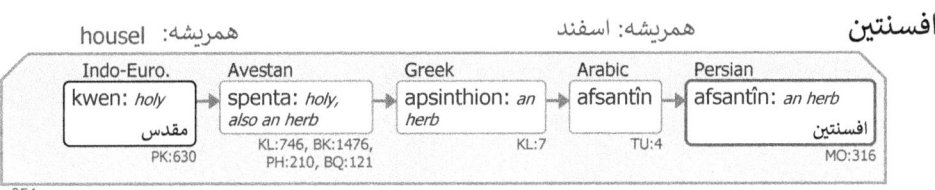

Indo-Euro.	Avestan	Greek	Arabic	Persian
kwen: holy / مقدس	spenta: holy, also an herb	apsinthion: an herb	afsantîn	afsantîn: an herb / افسنتین
PK:630	KL:746, BK:1476, PH:210, BQ:121	KL:7	TU:4	MO:316

254

افسوس

همریشه: سوختن

همریشه: ambulance

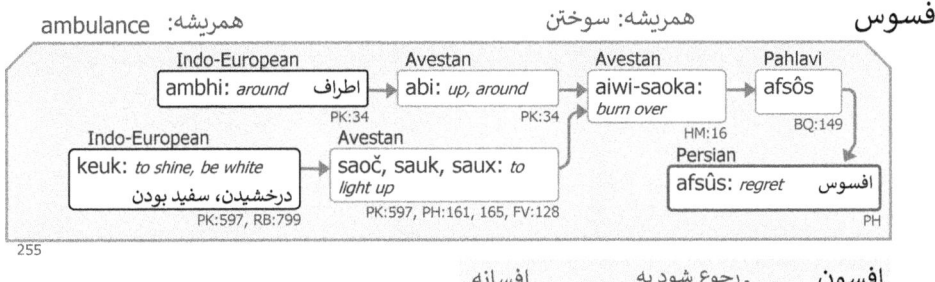

Indo-European	Avestan	Avestan	Pahlavi
ambhi: around اطراف	abi: up, around	aiwi-saoka: burn over	afsôs
	PK:34	PK:34	HM:16	BQ:149
Indo-European	Avestan		Persian
keuk: to shine, be white / درخشیدن، سفید بودن	saoč, sauk, saux: to light up		afsûs: regret افسوس
PK:597, RB:799	PK:597, PH:161, 165, FV:128		PH

255

افسون

ـ رجوع شود به   افسانه

افشاردن

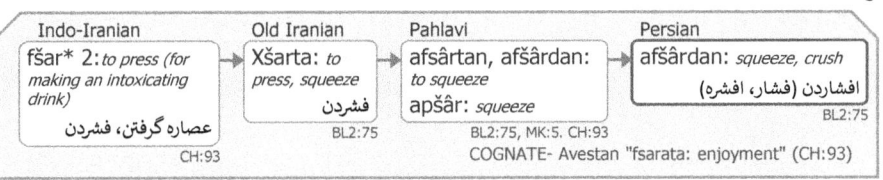

Indo-Iranian	Old Iranian	Pahlavi	Persian
fšar* 2: to press (for making an intoxicating drink) / عصاره گرفتن، فشردن	Xšarta: to press, squeeze / فشردن	afsârtan, afsârdan: to squeeze / apšâr: squeeze	afsârdan: squeeze, crush / افشاردن (فشار، افشره)
CH:93	BL2:75	BL2:75, MK:5. CH:93 / COGNATE- Avestan "fsarata: enjoyment" (CH:93)	BL2:75

256

افشاندن

همریشه: amphitheater

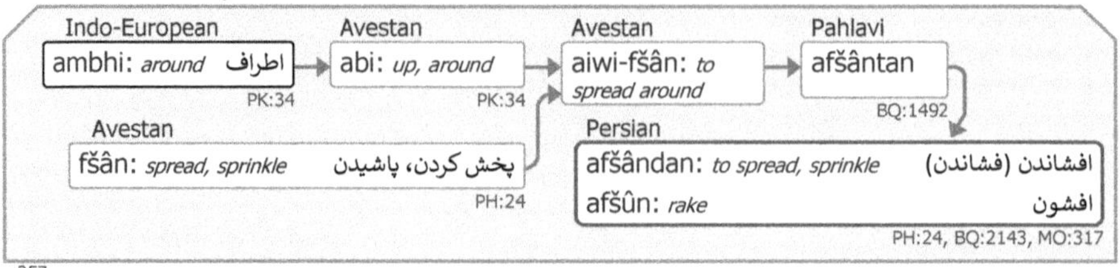

Indo-European	Avestan	Avestan	Pahlavi
ambhi: *around* اطراف PK:34	abi: *up, around* PK:34	aiwi-fšân: *to spread around*	afšântan BQ:1492

Avestan	Persian
fšân: *spread, sprinkle* پخش کردن، پاشیدن PH:24	afsândan: *to spread, sprinkle* افشاندن (فشاندن) afšûn: *rake* افشون PH:24, BQ:2143, MO:317

257

افشره   ـ رجوع شود به   افشاردن   **افشون**   ـ رجوع شود به   افشاندن

افشین

همریشه: check, chess

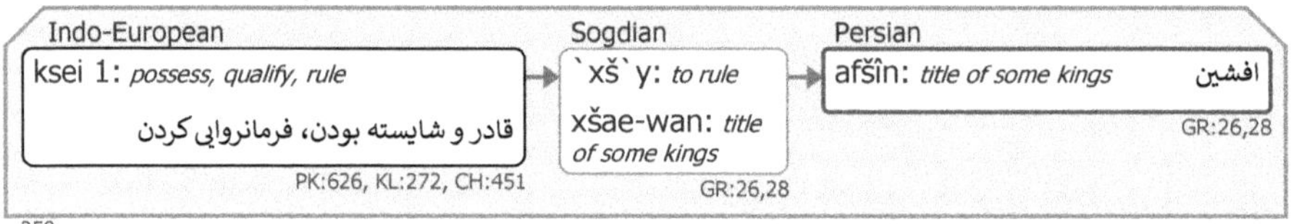

Indo-European	Sogdian	Persian
ksei 1: *possess, qualify, rule* قادر و شایسته بودن، فرمانروایی کردن PK:626, KL:272, CH:451	`xš`y: *to rule* xšae-wan: *title of some kings* GR:26,28	afšîn: *title of some kings* افشین GR:26,28

258

افغان

همریشه: خواندن

(1)

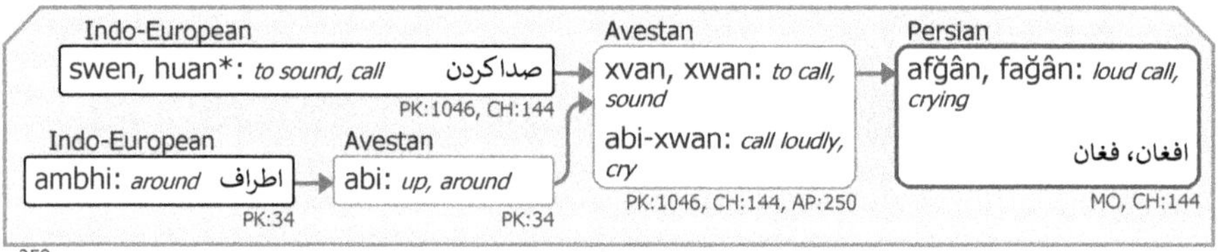

Indo-European	Avestan	Persian
swen, huan*: *to sound, call* صداکردن PK:1046, CH:144	xvan, xwan: *to call, sound* abi-xwan: *call loudly, cry* PK:1046, CH:144, AP:250	afğân, fağân: *loud call, crying* افغان، فغان MO, CH:144

Indo-European	Avestan
ambhi: *around* اطراف PK:34	abi: *up, around* PK:34

259

افغان

همریشه: گات, گاه۱۵ ,نیایش

(2)

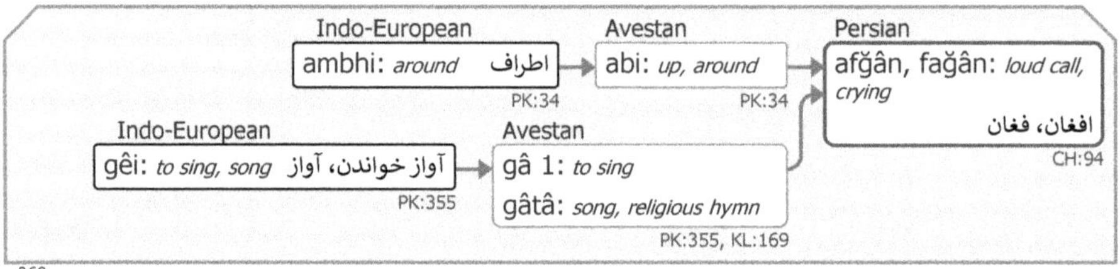

Indo-European	Avestan	Persian
ambhi: *around* اطراف PK:34	abi: *up, around* PK:34	afğân, fağân: *loud call, crying* افغان، فغان CH:94

Indo-European	Avestan
gêi: *to sing, song* آواز خواندن، آواز PK:355	gâ 1: *to sing* gâtâ: *song, religious hymn* PK:355, KL:169

260

افکندن

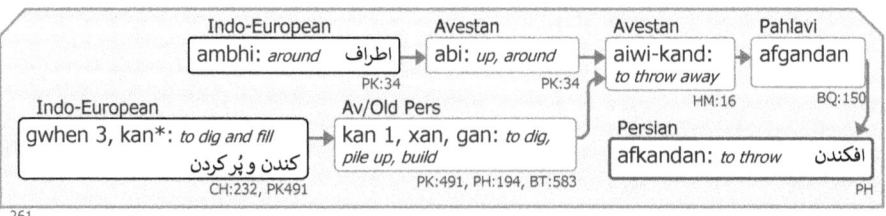

Indo-European	Avestan	Avestan	Pahlavi
ambhi: *around* اطراف PK:34	abi: *up, around* PK:34	aiwi-kand: *to throw away* HM:16	afgandan BQ:150

Indo-European	Av/Old Pers	Persian
gwhen 3, kan*: *to dig and fill* کندن و پُر کردن CH:232, PK491	kan 1, xan, gan: *to dig, pile up, build* PK:491, PH:194, BT:583	afkandan: *to throw* افکندن PH

261

45

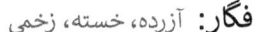

افگار: آزرده، خسته، زخمی

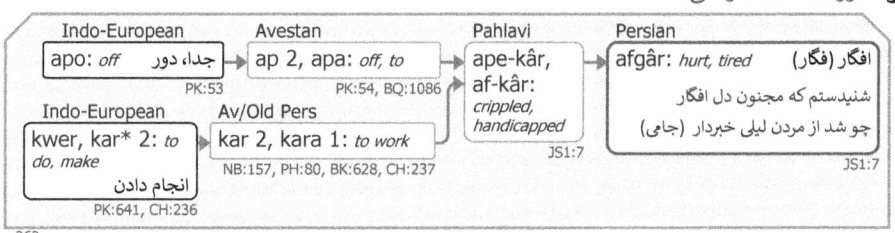

Indo-European	Avestan	Pahlavi	Persian
apo: *off* جدا، دور	ap 2, apa: *off, to*	ape-kâr, af-kâr: *crippled, handicapped*	afgâr: *hurt, tired* افگار (فگار)
PK:53	PK:54, BQ:1086	JS1:7	شنیدستم که مجنون دل افگار
Indo-European	Av/Old Pers		چو شد از مردم لیلی خبردار (جامی)
kwer, kar* 2: *to do, make* انجام دادن	kar 2, kara 1: *to work*		JS1:7
PK:641, CH:236	NB:157, PH:80, BK:628, CH:237		

262

افندی

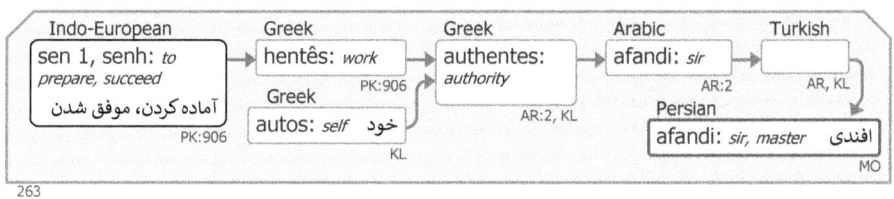

Indo-European	Greek	Greek	Arabic	Turkish
sen 1, senh: *to prepare, succeed* آماده کردن، موفق شدن	hentês: *work* PK:906	authentes: *authority*	afandi: *sir*	
	Greek		AR:2	AR, KL
	autos: *self* خود		Persian	
PK:906	KL	AR:2, KL	afandi: *sir, master* افندی	
			MO	

263

افیون ـ رجوع شود به اپیون

اقاقیا

همریشه: acacia

Indo-European	Greek	Persian
ak: *sharp, a sharp stone* تیز، سنگ تیز	akakiâ: *"thorny Egyptian tree", acacia*	aqâqîâ: *acacia* اقاقیا
PK:18, KT:173	ED*	BQ:151
		NOTE- etymology of the Greek word is not certain.

264

اقلیم

همریشه: lean, incline

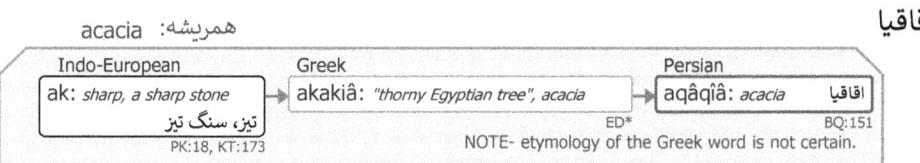

Indo-European	Greek	Arabic	Persian
klei: *to lean* مایل شدن، تکیه دادن	klîma: *sloping surface or land*	iqlîm: *a zone on earth, country*	eqlîm: *country, land* اقلیم
PK:600	PK:600	TU:57, ZV1:17	MO:326

COGNATE- Avestan "sray, srinu: to lean;/ srita: leaned" (PK:600)

265

اقیانوس

همریشه: ocean

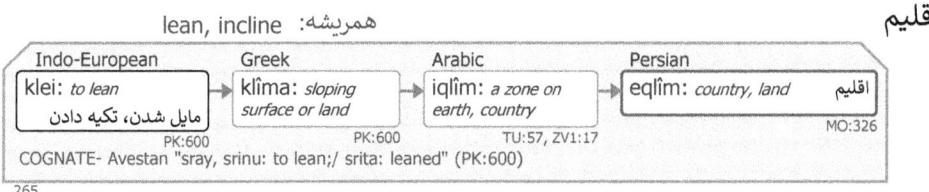

Greek	Greek	Arabic	Persian
keanos: *to lie down, sit* دراز کشیدن، نشستن	o-keanos: *lies around, water surrounding the earth*	uqyanûs: *ocean*	oqyânûs: *ocean* اقیانوس
KT:164	KT:164, AR:139	TU:5, AR:139	MO:327

266

آک ـ رجوع شود به آک

اکباتان: محل "گرد هم آیی" همریشه: هم و آمدن همریشه: base, same

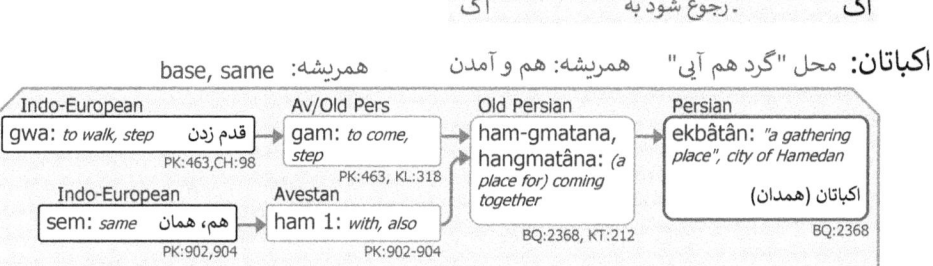

Indo-European	Av/Old Pers	Old Persian	Persian
gwa: *to walk, step* قدم زدن	gam: *to come, step*	ham-gmatana, hangmatâna: *(a place for) coming together*	ekbâtân: *"a gathering place", city of Hamedan*
PK:463,CH:98	PK:463, KL:318		اکباتان (همدان)
Indo-European	Avestan		
sem: *same* هم، همان	ham 1: *with, also*	BQ:2368, KT:212	BQ:2368
PK:902,904	PK:902-904		

267

اکسیر

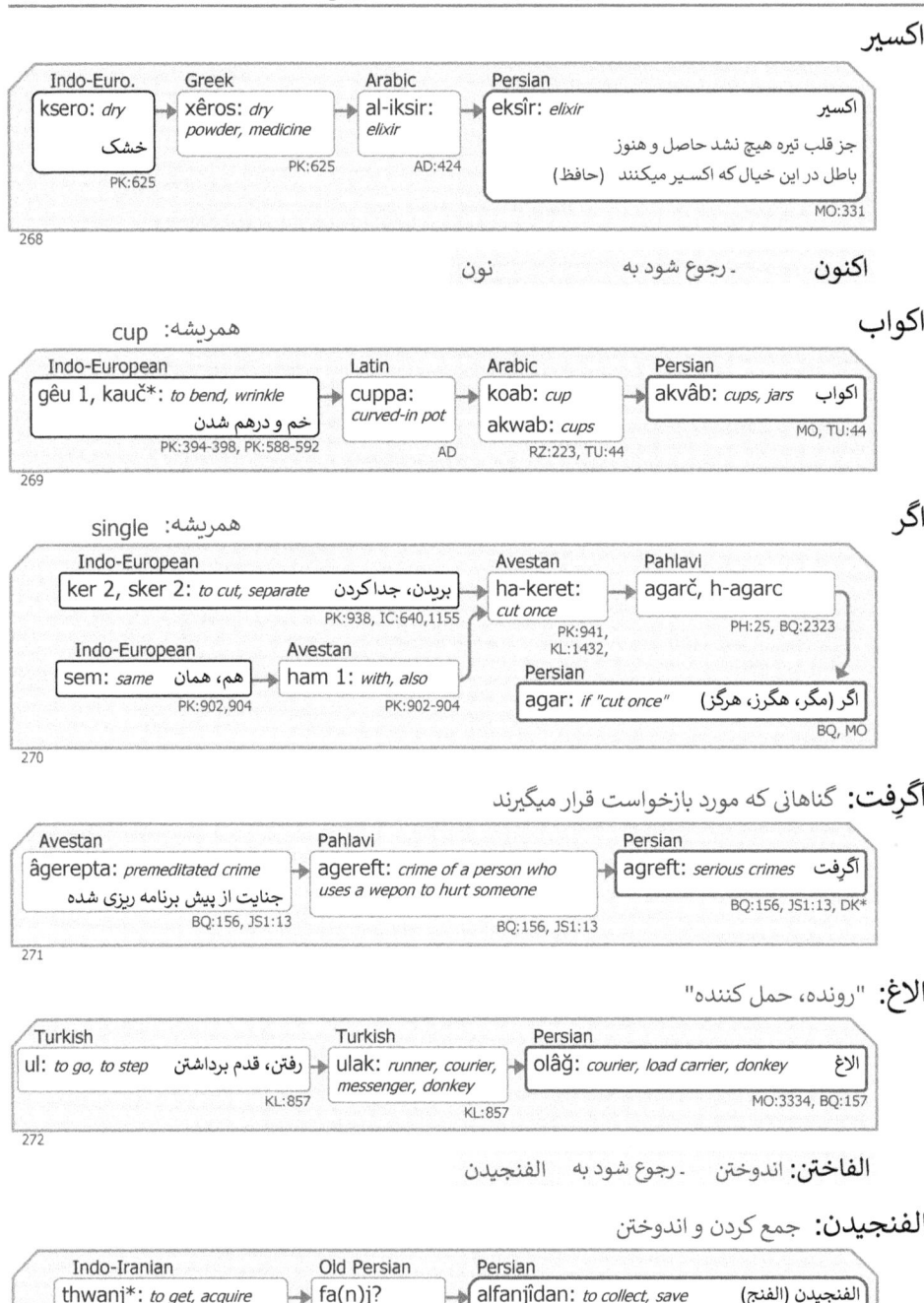

Indo-Euro.
ksero: *dry*
خشک
PK:625

Greek
xêros: *dry powder, medicine*
PK:625

Arabic
al-iksir: *elixir*
AD:424

Persian
eksîr: *elixir*
اکسیر
جز قلب تیره هیچ نشد حاصل و هنوز
باطل در این خیال که اکسیر میکنند (حافظ)
MO:331

268

اکنون - رجوع شود به "نون"   نون

اکواب

همریشه: cup

Indo-European
gêu 1, kauč*: *to bend, wrinkle*
خم و درهم شدن
PK:394-398, PK:588-592

Latin
cuppa: *curved-in pot*
AD

Arabic
koab: *cup*
akwab: *cups*
RZ:223, TU:44

Persian
akvâb: *cups, jars*
اکواب
MO, TU:44

269

اگر

همریشه: single

Indo-European
ker 2, sker 2: *to cut, separate*
بریدن، جدا کردن
PK:938, IC:640,1155

Avestan
ha-keret: *cut once*
PK:941, KL:1432,

Pahlavi
agarč, h-agarc
PH:25, BQ:2323

Indo-European
sem: *same*
هم، همان
PK:902,904

Avestan
ham 1: *with, also*
PK:902-904

Persian
agar: *if "cut once"*
اگر (مگر، هگرز، هرگز)
BQ, MO

270

اگرِفت: گناهانی که مورد بازخواست قرار میگیرند

Avestan
âgerepta: *premeditated crime*
جنایت از پیش برنامه ریزی شده
BQ:156, JS1:13

Pahlavi
agereft: *crime of a person who uses a wepon to hurt someone*
BQ:156, JS1:13

Persian
agreft: *serious crimes*
اگرِفت
BQ:156, JS1:13, DK*

271

الاغ: "رونده، حمل کننده"

Turkish
ul: *to go, to step*
رفتن، قدم برداشتن
KL:857

Turkish
ulak: *runner, courier, messenger, donkey*
KL:857

Persian
olâğ: *courier, load carrier, donkey*
الاغ
MO:3334, BQ:157

272

الفاختن: اندوختن - رجوع شود به الفنجیدن

الفنجیدن: جمع کردن و اندوختن

Indo-Iranian
thwanj*: *to get, acquire*
گرفتن، جمع کردن
CH:398

Old Persian
fa(n)j?
JS1:18

Persian
alfanjîdan: *to collect, save*
الفنجیدن (الفنج)
alfâxtan: *to collect, save*
الفاختن
ز الفنج دانش دلش گنج بود
جهاندیده و دانش الفنج بود (ابوشکور)
CH:398, JS1:18, DK*, BQ

NOTE- This word has reached Persian through the Bactrian (Balxi) language

273

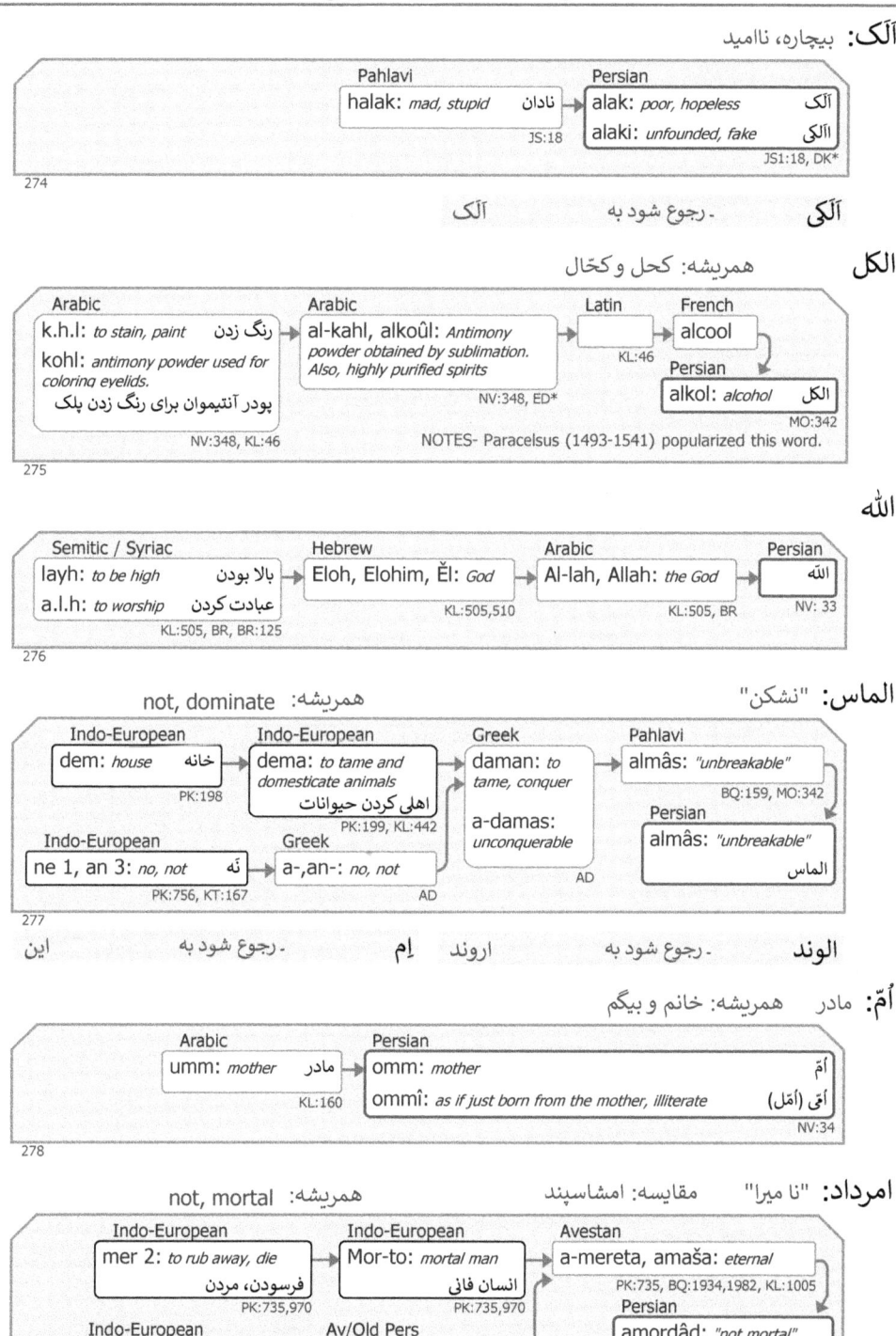

آلَک: بیچاره، ناامید

Pahlavi

halak: *mad, stupid*   نادان

JS:18

Persian

alak: *poor, hopeless*   آلَک

alaki: *unfounded, fake*   آلَکی

JS1:18, DK*

274

آلَکی   ـ رجوع شود به   آلَک

الکل   همریشه: کَحل و کَحّال

Arabic

k.h.l: *to stain, paint*   رنگ زدن

kohl: *antimony powder used for coloring eyelids.*

پودر آنتیموان برای رنگ زدن پلک

NV:348, KL:46

Arabic

al-kahl, alkoûl: *Antimony powder obtained by sublimation. Also, highly purified spirits*

NV:348, ED*

Latin

KL:46

French

alcool

Persian

alkol: *alcohol*   الکل

MO:342

NOTES- Paracelsus (1493-1541) popularized this word.

275

الله

Semitic / Syriac

layh: *to be high*   بالا بودن

a.l.h: *to worship*   عبادت کردن

KL:505, BR, BR:125

Hebrew

Eloh, Elohim, Ĕl: *God*

KL:505,510

Arabic

Al-lah, Allah: *the God*

KL:505, BR

Persian

الله

NV: 33

276

الماس: "نشکن"

همریشه: not, dominate

Indo-European

dem: *house*   خانه

PK:198

Indo-European

dema: *to tame and domesticate animals*

اهلی کردن حیوانات

PK:199, KL:442

Greek

daman: *to tame, conquer*

a-damas: *unconquerable*

AD

Pahlavi

almâs: *"unbreakable"*

BQ:159, MO:342

Persian

almâs: *"unbreakable"*

الماس

Indo-European

ne 1, an 3: *no, not*   نَه

PK:756, KT:167

Greek

a-,an-: *no, not*

AD

277

الوند   ـ رجوع شود به   اروند   اِم   ـ رجوع شود به   این

اُمّ:   مادر   همریشه: خانم و بیگم

Arabic

umm: *mother*   مادر

KL:160

Persian

omm: *mother*   اُمّ

ommî: *as if just born from the mother, illiterate*   اُمّی (اَمَل)

NV:34

278

امرداد: "نا میرا"   مقایسه: امشاسپند   همریشه: not, mortal

Indo-European

mer 2: *to rub away, die*

فرسودن، مردن

PK:735,970

Indo-European

Mor-to: *mortal man*

انسان فانی

PK:735,970

Avestan

a-mereta, amaša: *eternal*

PK:735, BQ:1934,1982, KL:1005

Persian

amordâd: *"not mortal"*

امرداد (مرداد)

BQ, PH, FJ

Indo-European

ne 1, an 3: *no, not*   نَه

PK:756, KT:167

Av/Old Pers

a-, â-, an-: *no, not*

PK:757, KT:167

279

امرود: گلابی

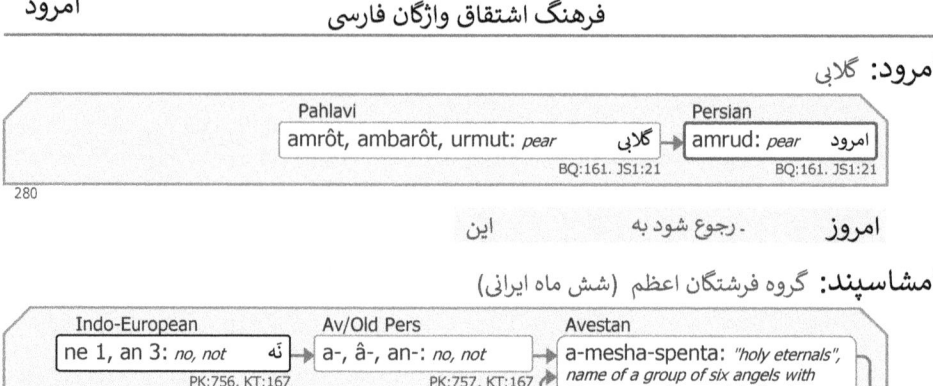

Pahlavi
amrôt, ambarôt, urmut: *pear*   گلابی
BQ:161. JS1:21

Persian
amrud: *pear*   امرود
BQ:161. JS1:21

280

امروز   ۔ رجوع شود به   این

امشاسپند: گروه فرشتگان اعظم (شش ماه ایرانی)

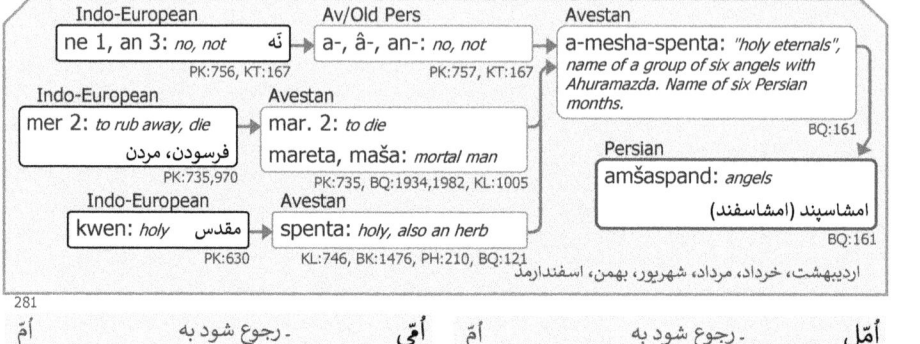

Indo-European
ne 1, an 3: *no, not*   نَه
PK:756, KT:167

Av/Old Pers
a-, â-, an-: *no, not*
PK:757, KT:167

Avestan
a-mesha-spenta: *"holy eternals"*, name of a group of six angels with Ahuramazda. Name of six Persian months.
BQ:161

Indo-European
mer 2: *to rub away, die*   فرسودن، مردن
PK:735,970

Avestan
mar. 2: *to die*
mareta, maša: *mortal man*
PK:735, BQ:1934,1982, KL:1005

Persian
amšaspand: *angels*
امشاسپند (امشاسفند)
BQ:161

Indo-European
kwen: *holy*   مقدس
PK:630

Avestan
spenta: *holy, also an herb*
KL:746, BK:1476, PH:210, BQ:121

اردیبهشت، خرداد، مرداد، شهریور، بهمن، اسفندارمذ

281

اُمّل   ۔ رجوع شود به   اَمّ   اُمّی   ۔ رجوع شود به   اُمّ

امید   همریشه: up, above

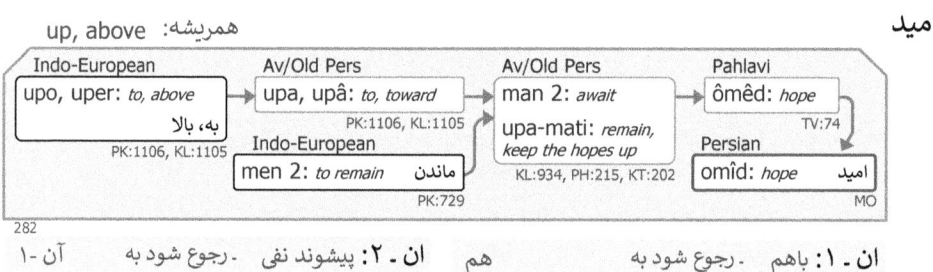

Indo-European
upo, uper: *to, above*   به، بالا
PK:1106, KL:1105

Av/Old Pers
upa, upâ: *to, toward*
PK:1106, KL:1105

Indo-European
men 2: *to remain*   ماندن
PK:729

Av/Old Pers
man 2: *await*
upa-mati: *remain, keep the hopes up*
KL:934, PH:215, KT:202

Pahlavi
ômêd: *hope*
TV:74

Persian
omîd: *hope*   امید
MO

282

ان ـ ۱: باهم   ۔ رجوع شود به   هم   ان ـ ۲: پیشوند نفی   ۔ رجوع شود به   آن ـ ۱

انار

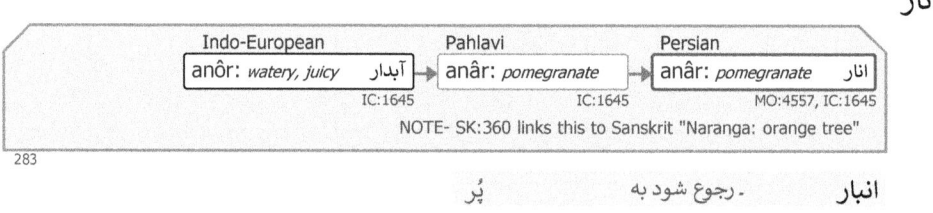

Indo-European
anôr: *watery, juicy*   آبدار
IC:1645

Pahlavi
anâr: *pomegranate*
IC:1645

Persian
anâr: *pomegranate*   انار
MO:4557, IC:1645

NOTE- SK:360 links this to Sanskrit "Naranga: orange tree"

283

انبار   ۔ رجوع شود به   پُر

انباز: همدم

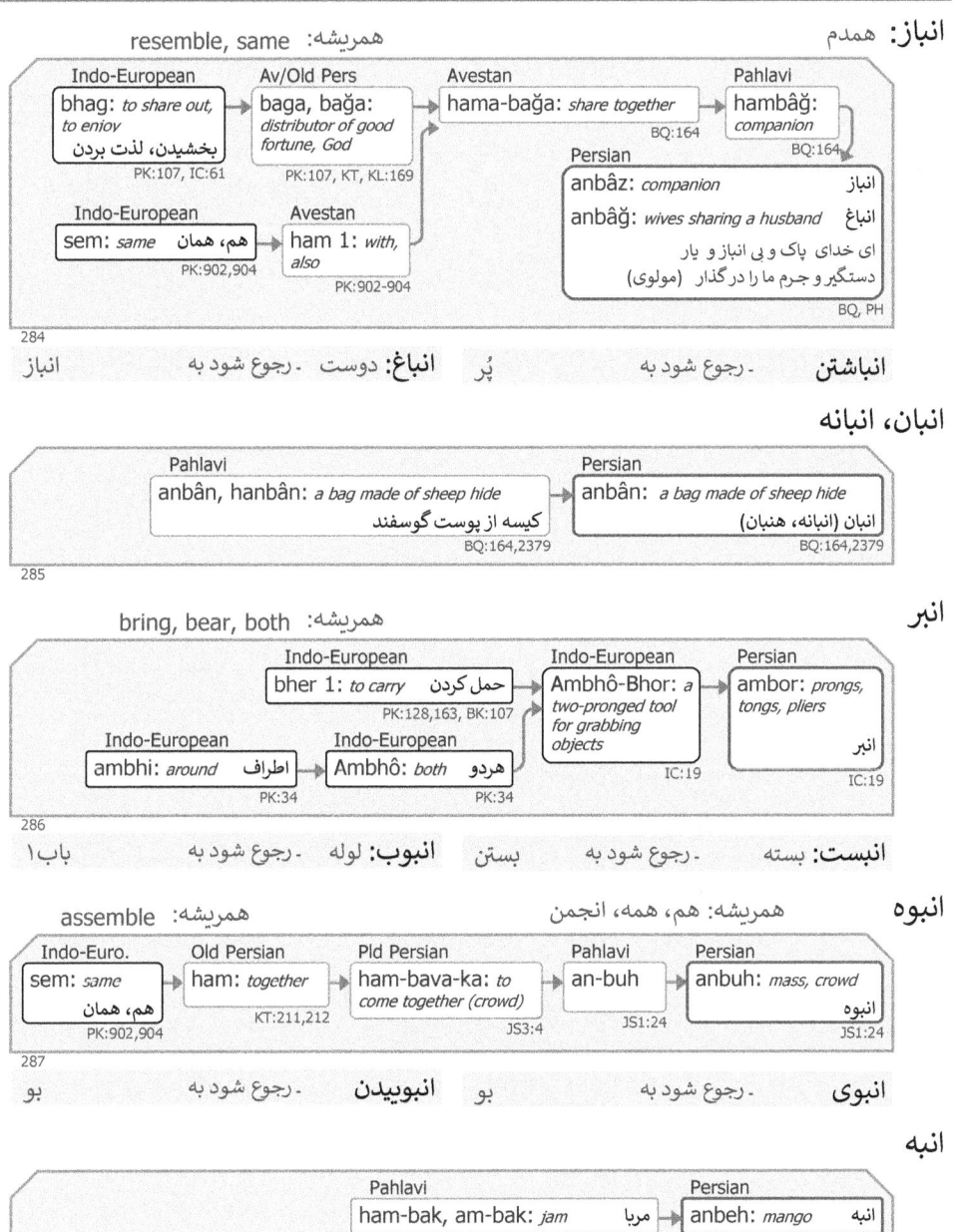

Indo-European	Av/Old Pers	Avestan	Pahlavi
bhag: to share out, to enjoy بخشیدن، لذت بردن PK:107, IC:61	baga, bağa: distributor of good fortune, God PK:107, KT, KL:169	hama-bağa: share together BQ:164	hambâğ: companion BQ:164

Persian
anbâz: companion انباز
anbâğ: wives sharing a husband انباغ
ای خدای پاک و بی انباز و یار
دستگیر و جرم ما را در گذار (مولوی)
BQ, PH

Indo-European	Avestan
sem: same هم، همان PK:902,904	ham 1: with, also PK:902-904

284

انباشتن ـ رجوع شود به پُر   **انباغ:** دوست   انباز

انبان، انبانه

Pahlavi	Persian
anbân, hanbân: a bag made of sheep hide کیسه از پوست گوسفند BQ:164,2379	anbân: a bag made of sheep hide انبان (انبانه، هنبان) BQ:164,2379

285

انبر

Indo-European	Indo-European	Persian
bher 1: to carry حمل کردن PK:128,163, BK:107	Ambhô-Bhor: a two-pronged tool for grabbing objects IC:19	ambor: prongs, tongs, pliers انبر IC:19

Indo-European	Indo-European
ambhi: around اطراف PK:34	Ambhô: both هردو PK:34

286

انبست: بسته ـ رجوع شود به بستن   **انبوب:** لوله ـ رجوع شود به باب۱

انبوه

Indo-Euro.	Old Persian	Pld Persian	Pahlavi	Persian
sem: same هم، همان PK:902,904	ham: together KT:211,212	ham-bava-ka: to come together (crowd) JS3:4	an-buh JS1:24	anbuh: mass, crowd انبوه JS1:24

287

انبوی ـ رجوع شود به بو   **انبوییدن** بو ـ رجوع شود به بو

انبه

Pahlavi	Persian
ham-bak, am-bak: jam مربا JS1:22	anbeh: mango انبه JS1:22

288

انبیق: وسیله تهیه "آب نیک"

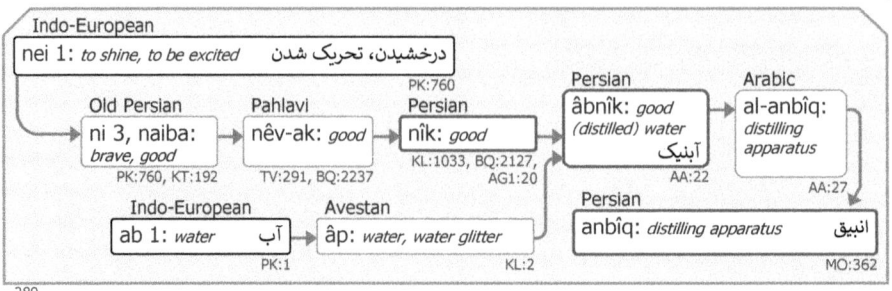

289

همریشه: simple, base   **انجام**

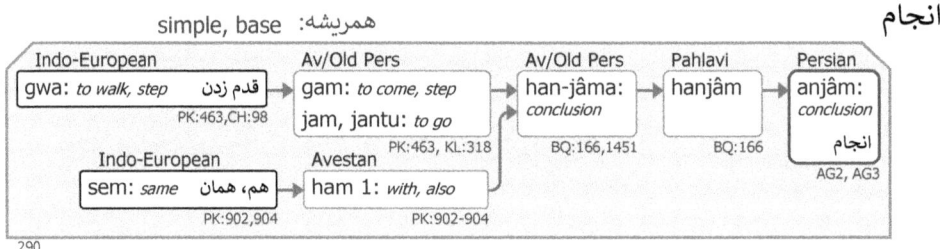

290

همریشه: come, assemble   **انجمن**

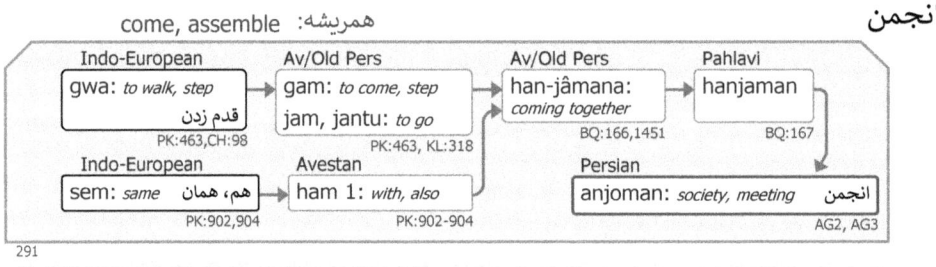

291

انجوخ: چین و چروک ـ رجوع شود به   انجوغ   **انجوختن:** چروکیدن ـ رجوع شود به   انجوغ

انجوغ: چین و چروک   همریشه: خم، غوز   همریشه: cove, cup

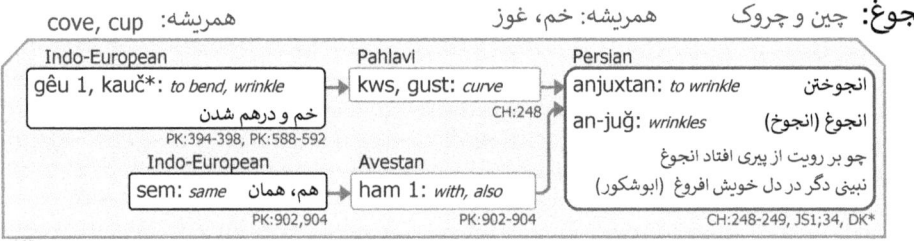

292

انجیدن: سوراخ کردن، تکه تکه کردن

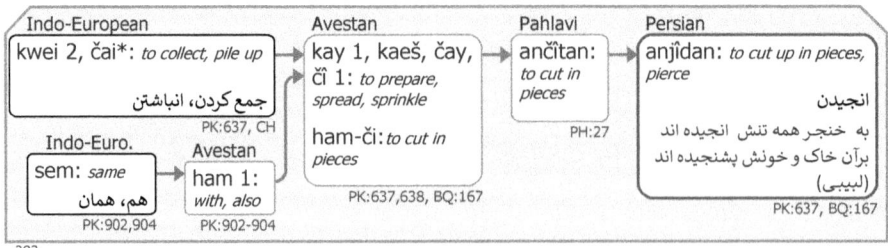

293

51

انجیر

Pahlavi
anjihr: *fig* انجیر → Persian
anjîr: *fig* انجیر
JS1:34 | JS1:34

COGNATE- Sanskrit "anjirah: fig" (JS1:34)

294

انجیل: "خبر خوش" همریشه:خوب، بهشت همریشه: angel

Akkadian
agaru: *to hire* استخدام کردن
KL

Indo-European
su 1: *well, good* خوب
PK:1037, KL:548

Greek
angelos: *hired messenger*
eu-angelos: *messenger of good news*
ev-angelion: *good news*
KL:74

Arabic
injîl: *good news, Bible*
TU:5

Persian
enjîl: *"Good News", the Bible*
انجیل
MO

295

آند: مقداری

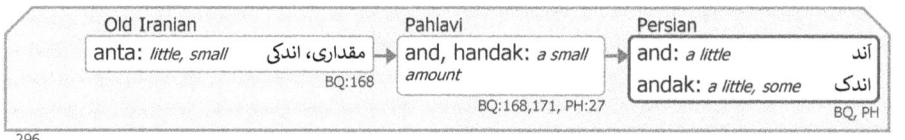

Old Iranian
anta: *little, small* مقداری، اندکی
BQ:168

Pahlavi
and, handak: *a small amount*
BQ:168,171, PH:27

Persian
and: *a little* آند
andak: *a little, some* اندک
BQ, PH

296

انداختن

همریشه: هندسه همریشه: assemble

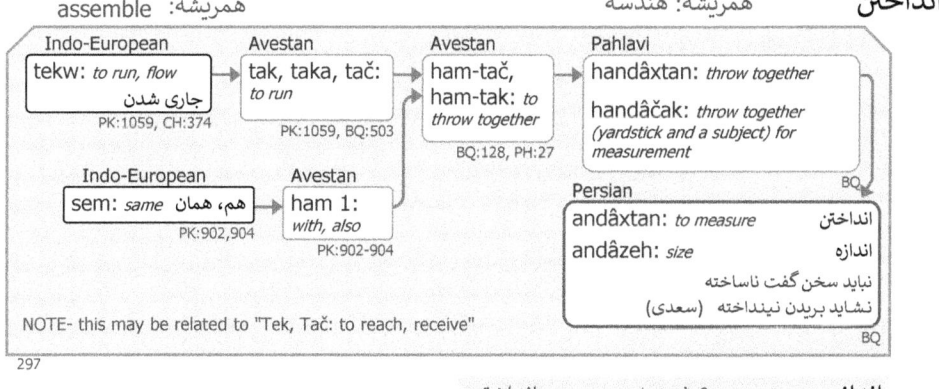

Indo-European
tekw: *to run, flow* جاری شدن
PK:1059, CH:374

Avestan
tak, taka, tač: *to run*
PK:1059, BQ:503

Avestan
ham-tač, ham-tak: *to throw together*
BQ:128, PH:27

Pahlavi
handâxtan: *throw together*
handâčak: *throw together (yardstick and a subject) for measurement*
BQ

Indo-European
sem: *same* هم، همان
PK:902,904

Avestan
ham 1: *with, also*
PK:902-904

Persian
andâxtan: *to measure* انداختن
andâzeh: *size* اندازه
نباید سخن گفت ناساخته
نشاید بریدن نینداخته (سعدی)
BQ

NOTE- this may be related to "Tek, Tač: to reach, receive"

297

اندازه .رجوع شود به انداختن

اندام

همریشه: assemble, deed

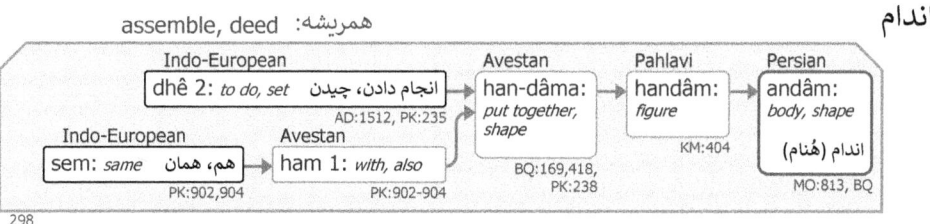

Indo-European
dhê 2: *to do, set* انجام دادن، چیدن
AD:1512, PK:235

Avestan
han-dâma: *put together, shape*
BQ:169,418, PK:238

Pahlavi
handâm: *figure*
KM:404

Persian
andâm: *body, shape*
اندام (هُنام)
MO:813, BQ

Indo-European
sem: *same* هم، همان
PK:902,904

Avestan
ham 1: *with, also*
PK:902-904

298

اندر۱

همریشه: in, intra, enter

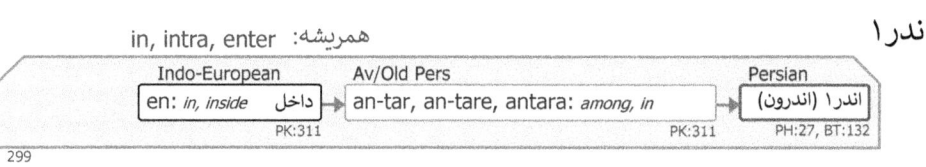

Indo-European
en: *in, inside* داخل
PK:311

Av/Old Pers
an-tar, an-tare, antara: *among, in*
PK:311

Persian
اندر۱ (اندرون)
PH:27, BT:132

299

اندر۲

همریشه: other

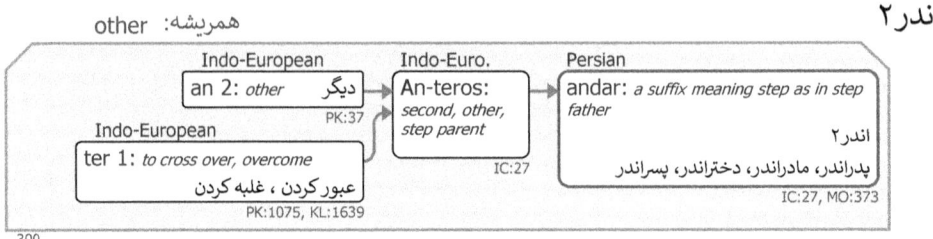

Indo-European
an 2: *other* دیگر
PK:37

Indo-European
ter 1: *to cross over, overcome*
عبور کردن ، غلبه کردن
PK:1075, KL:1639

Indo-Euro.
An-teros: *second, other, step parent*
IC:27

Persian
andar: *a suffix meaning step as in step father*
اندر۲
پدراندر، مادراندر، دختراندر، پسراندر
IC:27, MO:373

300

اندرز

همریشه: firm, simple

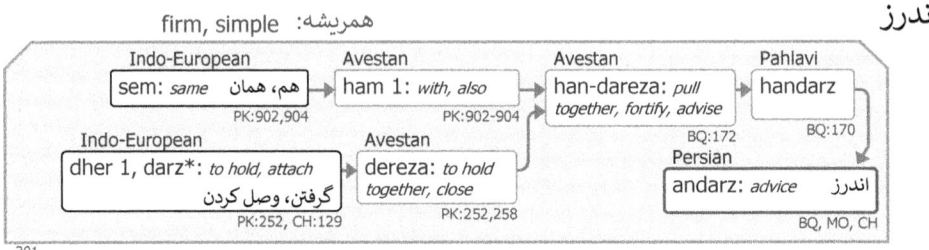

Indo-European
sem: *same* هم، همان
PK:902,904

Indo-European
dher 1, darz*: *to hold, attach*
گرفتن، وصل کردن
PK:252, CH:129

Avestan
ham 1: *with, also*
PK:902-904

Avestan
dereza: *to hold together, close*
PK:252,258

Avestan
han-dareza: *pull together, fortify, advise*
BQ:172

Pahlavi
handarz
BQ:170

Persian
andarz: *advice* اندرز
BQ, MO, CH

301

اندروا: "در هوا"

همریشه: in, wind

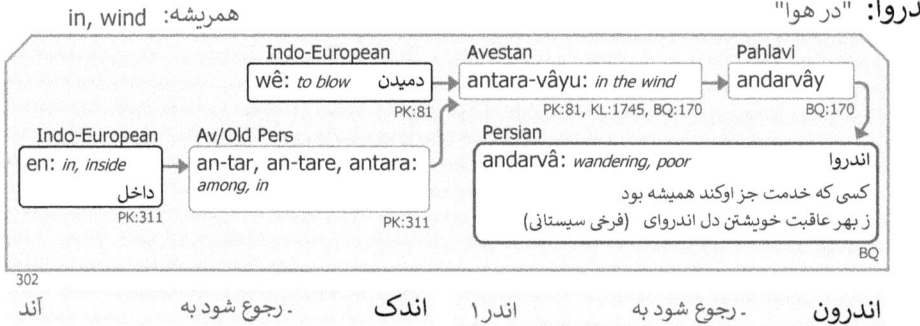

Indo-European
wê: *to blow* دمیدن
PK:81

Indo-European
en: *in, inside* داخل
PK:311

Av/Old Pers
an-tar, an-tare, antara: *among, in*
PK:311

Avestan
antara-vâyu: *in the wind*
PK:81, KL:1745, BQ:170

Pahlavi
andarvây
BQ:170

Persian
andarvâ: *wandering, poor* اندروا
کسی که خدمت جز اوکند همیشه بود
ز بهر عاقبت خویشتن دل اندروای (فرخی سیستانی)
BQ

302

اندرون - رجوع شود به اندر۱ اندک - رجوع شود به آند

اندوختن

همریشه: assemble

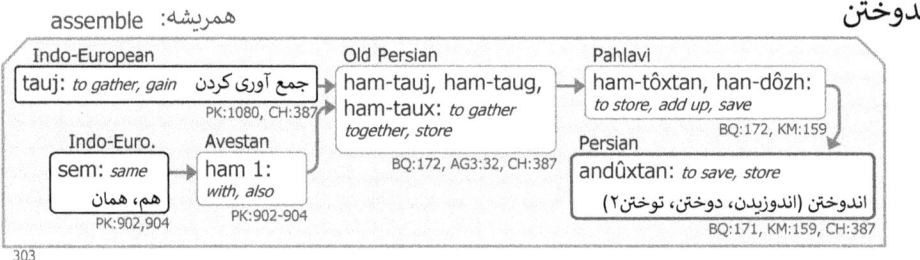

Indo-European
tauj: *to gather, gain* جمع آوری کردن
PK:1080, CH:387

Indo-Euro.
sem: *same* هم، همان
PK:902,904

Avestan
ham 1: *with, also*
PK:902-904

Old Persian
ham-tauj, ham-taug, ham-taux: *to gather together, store*
BQ:172, AG3:32, CH:387

Pahlavi
ham-tôxtan, han-dôzh: *to store, add up, save*
BQ:172, KM:159

Persian
andûxtan: *to save, store*
اندوختن (اندوزیدن، دوختن، توختن۲)
BQ:171, KM:159, CH:387

303

اندودن

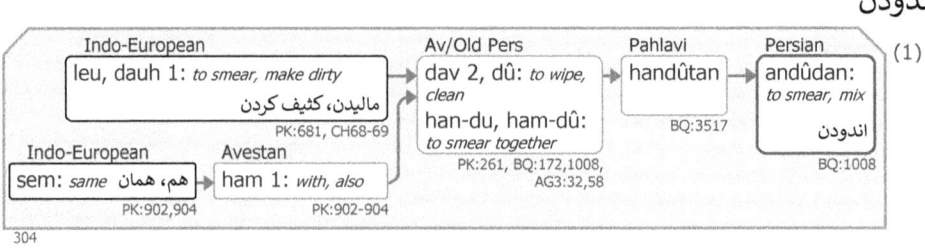

(1)

Indo-European
leu, dauh 1: *to smear, make dirty*
مالیدن، کثیف کردن
PK:681, CH68-69

Indo-European
sem: *same* هم، همان
PK:902,904

Avestan
ham 1: *with, also*
PK:902-904

Av/Old Pers
dav 2, dû: *to wipe, clean*
han-du, ham-dû: *to smear together*
PK:261, BQ:172,1008, AG3:32,58

Pahlavi
handûtan
BQ:3517

Persian
andûdan: *to smear, mix*
اندودن
BQ:1008

304

اندودن (2)

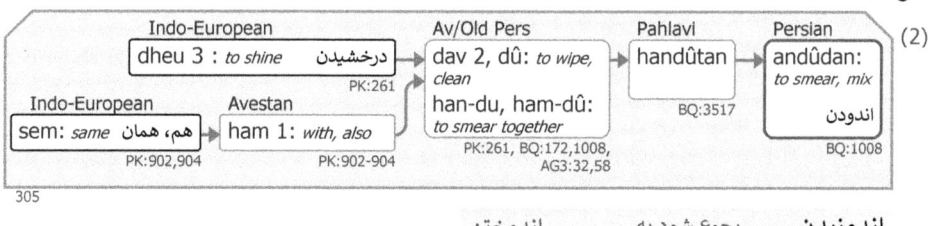

305

اندوزیدن ۔ رجوع شود به اندوختن

اندوه

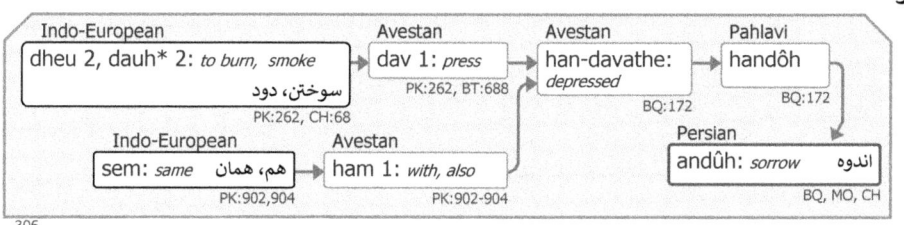

306

اندیشیدن همریشه: دیدن همریشه: assemble, semantic

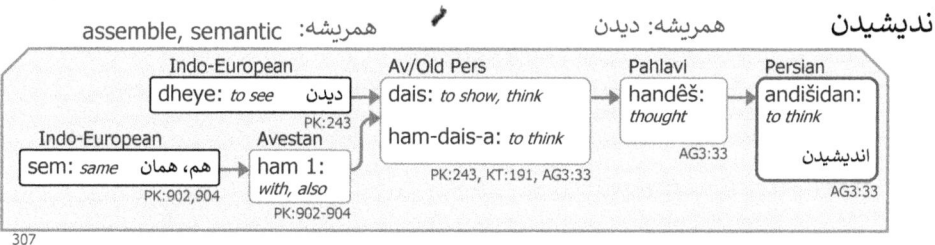

307

انرژی همریشه: آلرژی همریشه: allergy

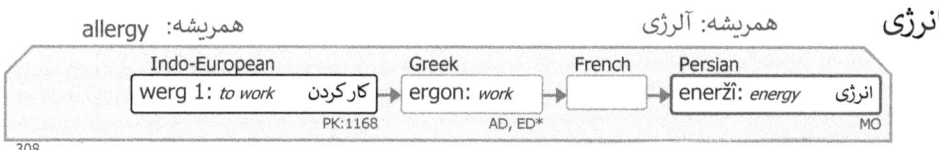

308

انغوزه: "صمغ شیرین"

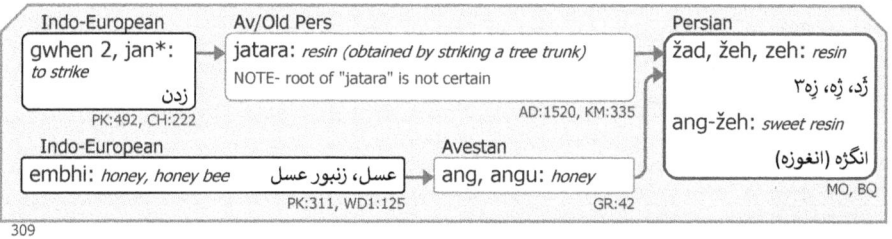

309

انفست: تار عنکبرت ۔ رجوع شود به بستن

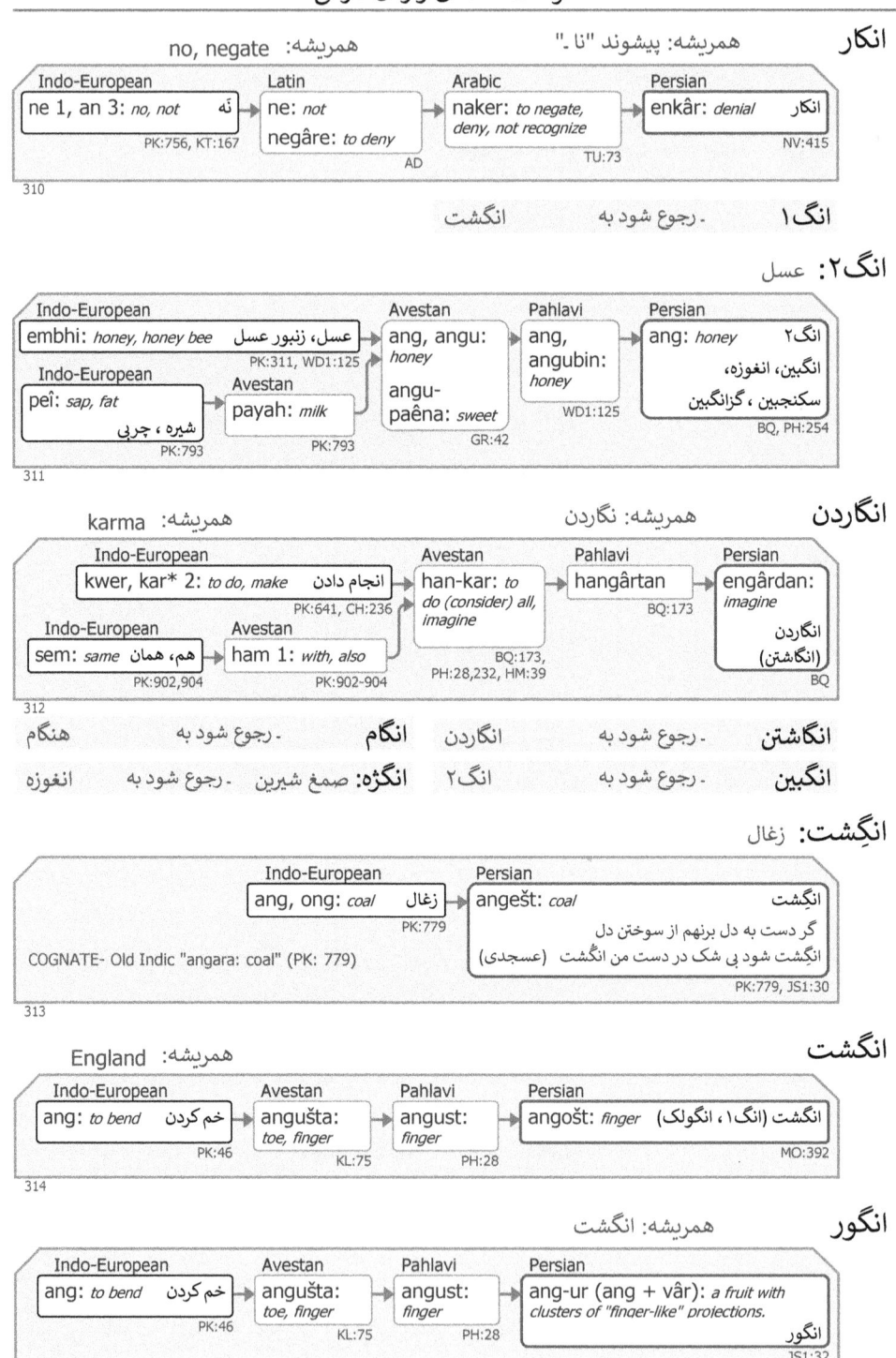

انکار

همریشه: پیشوند "نا ـ"   همریشه: no, negate

Indo-European	Latin	Arabic	Persian
ne 1, an 3: *no, not* نَه	ne: *not* negâre: *to deny*	naker: *to negate, deny, not recognize*	enkâr: *denial* انکار
PK:756, KT:167	AD	TU:73	NV:415

310

انگ۱   ـ رجوع شود به   انگشت

انگ۲: عسل

Indo-European	Avestan	Pahlavi	Persian
embhi: *honey, honey bee* عسل، زنبور عسل	ang, angu: *honey* angu-paêna: *sweet*	ang, angubin: *honey*	ang: *honey* انگ۲ انگبین، انغوزه، سکنجبین ، گزانگبین
PK:311, WD1:125		WD1:125	BQ, PH:254
Indo-European	Avestan		
peî: *sap, fat* شیره ، چربی	payah: *milk*		
PK:793	PK:793	GR:42	

311

انگاردن

همریشه: karma   همریشه: نگاردن

Indo-European	Avestan	Pahlavi	Persian
kwer, kar* 2: *to do, make* انجام دادن	han-kar: *to do (consider) all, imagine*	hangârtan	engârdan: *imagine* انگاردن (انگاشتن)
PK:641, CH:236		BQ:173	
Indo-European	Avestan	BQ:173,	
sem: *same* هم، همان	ham 1: *with, also*	PH:28,232, HM:39	
PK:902,904	PK:902-904		BQ

312

انگاشتن	ـ رجوع شود به	انگاردن	انگم	ـ رجوع شود به	هنگام
انگبین	ـ رجوع شود به	انگ۲	انگژه: صمغ شیرین	ـ رجوع شود به	انغوزه

انگِشت: زغال

Indo-European	Persian
ang, ong: *coal* زغال	angešt: *coal* انگشت گر دست به دل برنهم از سوختن دل انگِشت شود بی شک در دست من انگُشت (عسجدی)
PK:779	PK:779, JS1:30

COGNATE- Old Indic "angara: coal" (PK: 779)

313

انگشت

همریشه: England

Indo-European	Avestan	Pahlavi	Persian
ang: *to bend* خم کردن	angušta: *toe, finger*	angust: *finger*	angošt: *finger* انگشت (انگ۱، انگولک)
PK:46	KL:75	PH:28	MO:392

314

انگور

همریشه: انگشت

Indo-European	Avestan	Pahlavi	Persian
ang: *to bend* خم کردن	angušta: *toe, finger*	angust: *finger*	ang-ur (ang + vâr): *a fruit with clusters of "finger-like" projections.* انگور
PK:46	KL:75	PH:28	JS1:32

315

انگولک   ـ رجوع شود به   انگشت

انگیختن   همریشه: آویختن   همریشه: weak, single

```
┌─────────────────────────────────────────────────────────────────────────────────────┐
│  Indo-European              Av/Old Pers              Pahlavi            Persian    (1) │
│  ┌──────────────────────┐   ┌──────────────────┐    ┌─────────┐      ┌─────────────┐  │
│  │ weik 1: to shake, swing│─▶│ waix, waig: to swing│─▶│ han-   │──┐  │ angîxtan: to│  │
│  │ لرزاندن، تاب دادن      │   │           PK:1130 │    │ gêzitan: to│ ▶│ excite, motivate│ │
│  └──────────────────────┘   └──────────────────┘    │ motivate,│    │ انگیختن (انگیزه)│ │
│  Indo-European              Avestan                 │ excite  │    │             │  │
│  ┌──────────────────────┐   ┌──────────────────┐    │ KM:169, PH:30,│ BQ:178, KM:169│ │
│  │ sem: same  هم، همان   │──▶│ ham 1: with, also │    │ BQ:178,CH:97│  └─────────────┘  │
│  │           PK:902,904  │   │       PK:902-904  │    └─────────┘                     │
│  └──────────────────────┘   └──────────────────┘                                     │
└─────────────────────────────────────────────────────────────────────────────────────┘
316
```

انگیختن   همریشه: گیج

```
┌─────────────────────────────────────────────────────────────────────────────────────┐
│  Indo-Iranian                                    Pahlavi             Persian      (2) │
│  ┌──────────────────────────────────┐            ┌──────────────┐   ┌─────────────┐   │
│  │ gaiz*: to excite, stir           │───────────▶│ han-gêzitan: to│ ▶│ angîxtan: to│   │
│  │ برهم زدن، تحریک کردن              │            │ motivate, excite│  │ excite, motivate│ │
│  │                         CH:97     │            │ KM:169, PH:30, BQ:178,CH:97│ انگیختن (انگیزه)│ │
│  └──────────────────────────────────┘            └──────────────┘   │             │   │
│  Indo-European              Avestan                                  │  BQ:178, KM:169│ │
│  ┌──────────────────────┐   ┌──────────────────┐                    └─────────────┘   │
│  │ sem: same  هم، همان   │──▶│ ham 1: with, also │                                      │
│  │           PK:902,904  │   │       PK:902-904  │                                      │
│  └──────────────────────┘   └──────────────────┘                                      │
└─────────────────────────────────────────────────────────────────────────────────────┘
317
```

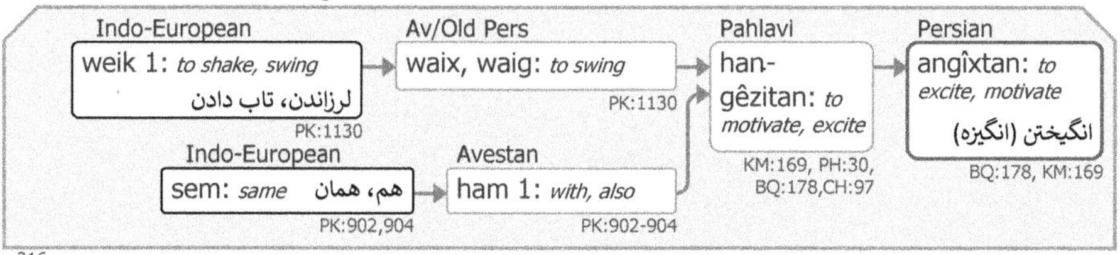

انگیزه   ـ رجوع شود به   انگیختن

انوشه: "بی مرگ"   همریشه: not, ear

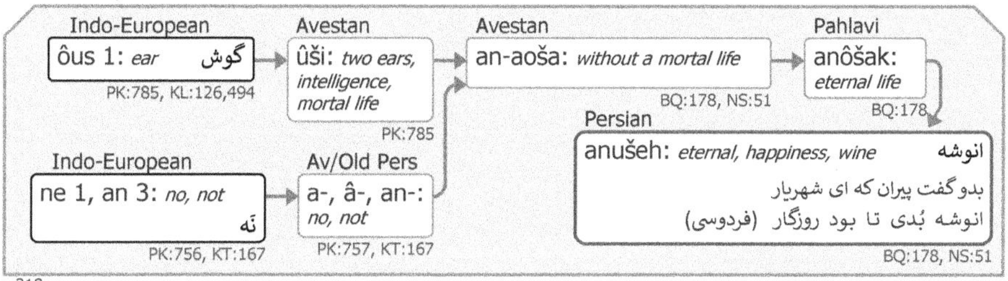

```
┌─────────────────────────────────────────────────────────────────────────────────────┐
│  Indo-European        Avestan           Avestan                       Pahlavi         │
│  ┌──────────────┐    ┌──────────────┐   ┌──────────────────────┐      ┌─────────────┐ │
│  │ ôus 1: ear گوش│──▶│ ûši: two ears,│─▶│ an-aoša: without a mortal life│▶│ anôšak:    │ │
│  │ PK:785, KL:126,494│ intelligence, │   │           BQ:178, NS:51 │    │ eternal life│ │
│  └──────────────┘    │ mortal life  │   └──────────────────────┘      │    BQ:178  │ │
│                      │      PK:785  │   Persian                        └─────────────┘ │
│  Indo-European        └──────────────┘   ┌──────────────────────────────────────────┐ │
│  ┌──────────────┐    Av/Old Pers         │ anušeh: eternal, happiness, wine  انوشه   │ │
│  │ ne 1, an 3: no, not│ ┌────────────┐    │ بدوگفت پیران که ای شهریار                 │ │
│  │           نَه  │   │ a-, â-, an-:│    │ انوشه بُدی تا بود روزگار  (فردوسی)          │ │
│  │ PK:756, KT:167│   │ no, not    │    │                          BQ:178, NS:51   │ │
│  └──────────────┘   │ PK:757, KT:167│    └──────────────────────────────────────────┘ │
│                     └────────────┘                                                    │
└─────────────────────────────────────────────────────────────────────────────────────┘
318
```

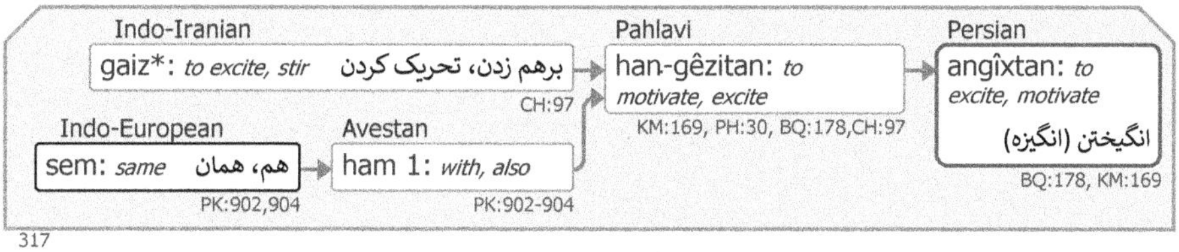

انوشیروان: "با روح جاوید"

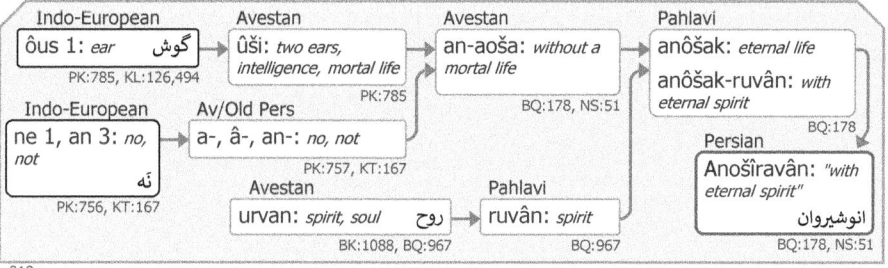

```
┌─────────────────────────────────────────────────────────────────────────────────────┐
│  Indo-European        Avestan               Avestan                Pahlavi            │
│  ┌──────────────┐    ┌──────────────────┐  ┌──────────────┐       ┌──────────────────┐│
│  │ ôus 1: ear گوش│──▶│ ûši: two ears,   │─▶│ an-aoša: without a│──▶│ anôšak: eternal life│ │
│  │ PK:785, KL:126,494│ intelligence, mortal life│ │ mortal life │     │ anôšak-ruvân: with│ │
│  └──────────────┘    │          PK:785  │  │ BQ:178, NS:51│       │ eternal spirit   ││
│  Indo-European        └──────────────────┘  └──────────────┘       │         BQ:178   ││
│  ┌──────────────┐    Av/Old Pers                                   └──────────────────┘│
│  │ ne 1, an 3: no,│  ┌────────────────┐                            Persian             │
│  │ not          │   │ a-, â-, an-: no, not│                        ┌──────────────────┐│
│  │          نَه  │   │    PK:757, KT:167│                          │ Anôšîravân: "with││
│  │ PK:756, KT:167│   └────────────────┘                           │ eternal spirit"  ││
│  └──────────────┘   Avestan            Pahlavi                     │ انوشیروان        ││
│                     ┌──────────────────┐ ┌──────────────┐          │   BQ:178, NS:51  ││
│                     │ urvan: spirit, soul روح│▶│ ruvân: spirit│       └──────────────────┘│
│                     │ BK:1088, BQ:967  │ │    BQ:967    │                              │
│                     └──────────────────┘ └──────────────┘                              │
└─────────────────────────────────────────────────────────────────────────────────────┘
319
```

انیر: بی شرافت، بد

همریشه: not, Aryan

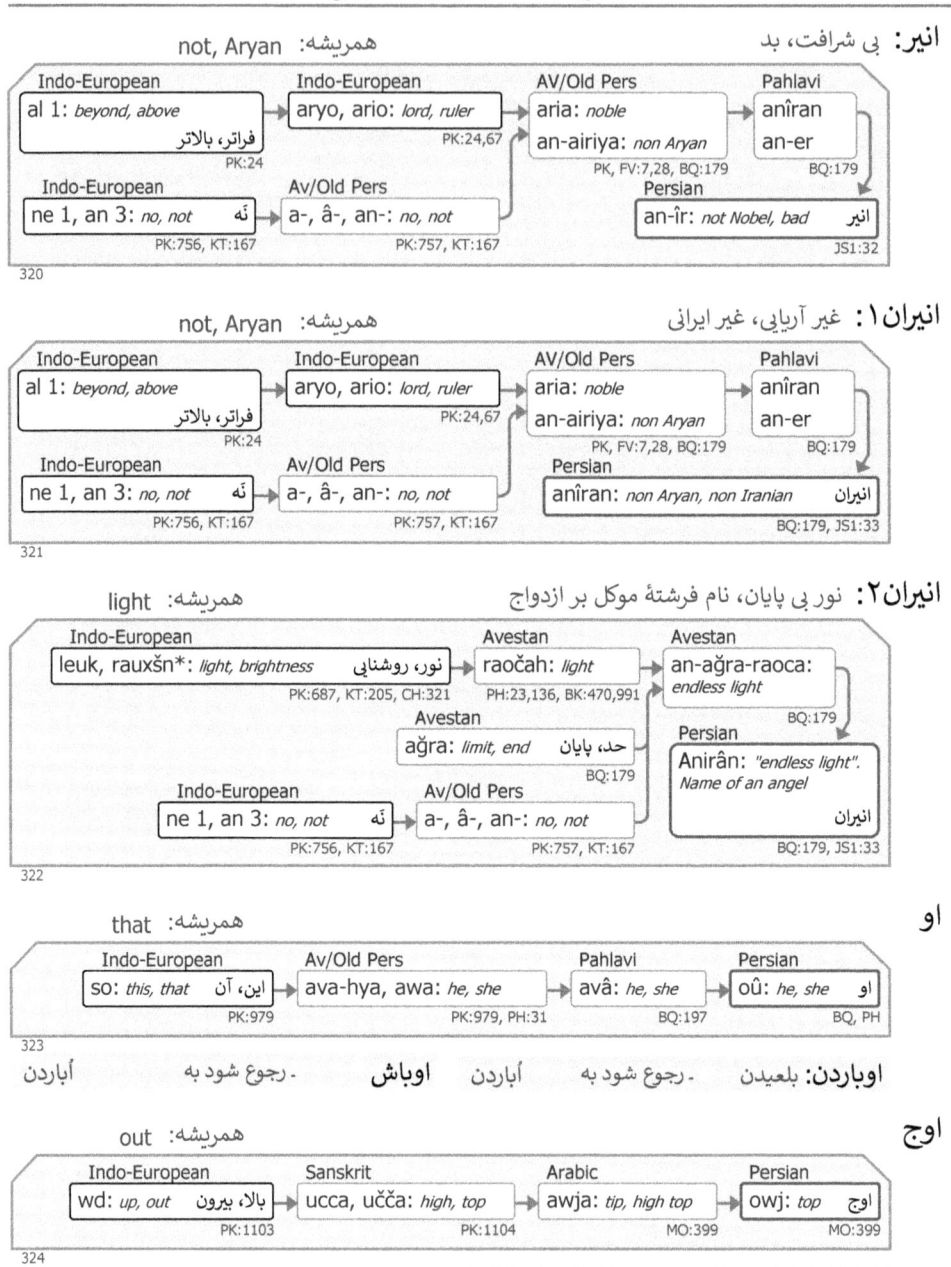

Indo-European	Indo-European	AV/Old Pers	Pahlavi
al 1: *beyond, above* فراتر، بالاتر PK:24	aryo, ario: *lord, ruler* PK:24,67	aria: *noble* an-airiya: *non Aryan* PK, FV:7,28, BQ:179	anîran an-er BQ:179

Indo-European	Av/Old Pers	Persian
ne 1, an 3: *no, not* نَه PK:756, KT:167	a-, â-, an-: *no, not* PK:757, KT:167	an-îr: *not Nobel, bad* انیر JS1:32

320

انیران۱: غیر آریایی، غیر ایرانی

همریشه: not, Aryan

Indo-European	Indo-European	AV/Old Pers	Pahlavi
al 1: *beyond, above* فراتر، بالاتر PK:24	aryo, ario: *lord, ruler* PK:24,67	aria: *noble* an-airiya: *non Aryan* PK, FV:7,28, BQ:179	anîran an-er BQ:179

Indo-European	Av/Old Pers	Persian
ne 1, an 3: *no, not* نَه PK:756, KT:167	a-, â-, an-: *no, not* PK:757, KT:167	anîran: *non Aryan, non Iranian* انیران BQ:179, JS1:33

321

انیران۲: نور بی پایان، نام فرشتهٔ موکل بر ازدواج

همریشه: light

Indo-European	Avestan	Avestan
leuk, rauxšn*: *light, brightness* نور، روشنایی PK:687, KT:205, CH:321	raočah: *light* PH:23,136, BK:470,991	an-ağra-raoca: *endless light* BQ:179

Avestan	Persian
ağra: *limit, end* حد، پایان BQ:179	Anirân: "*endless light*". *Name of an angel* انیران

Indo-European	Av/Old Pers
ne 1, an 3: *no, not* نَه PK:756, KT:167	a-, â-, an-: *no, not* PK:757, KT:167

BQ:179, JS1:33

322

او

همریشه: that

Indo-European	Av/Old Pers	Pahlavi	Persian
so: *this, that* این، آن PK:979	ava-hya, awa: *he, she* PK:979, PH:31	avâ: *he, she* BQ:197	oû: *he, she* او BQ, PH

323

اوباردن: بلعیدن   . رجوع شود به   أباردن   **اوباش**   أباردن   . رجوع شود به   أباردن

اوج

همریشه: out

Indo-European	Sanskrit	Arabic	Persian
wd: *up, out* بالا، بیرون PK:1103	ucca, učča: *high, top* PK:1104	awja: *tip, high top* MO:399	owj: *top* اوج MO:399

324

اورمزد   . رجوع شود به   اهورامزدا

اورنگ: "رنگارنگ"، تخت سلطنت   همریشه: اَبَرنجَن   همریشه: lacquer

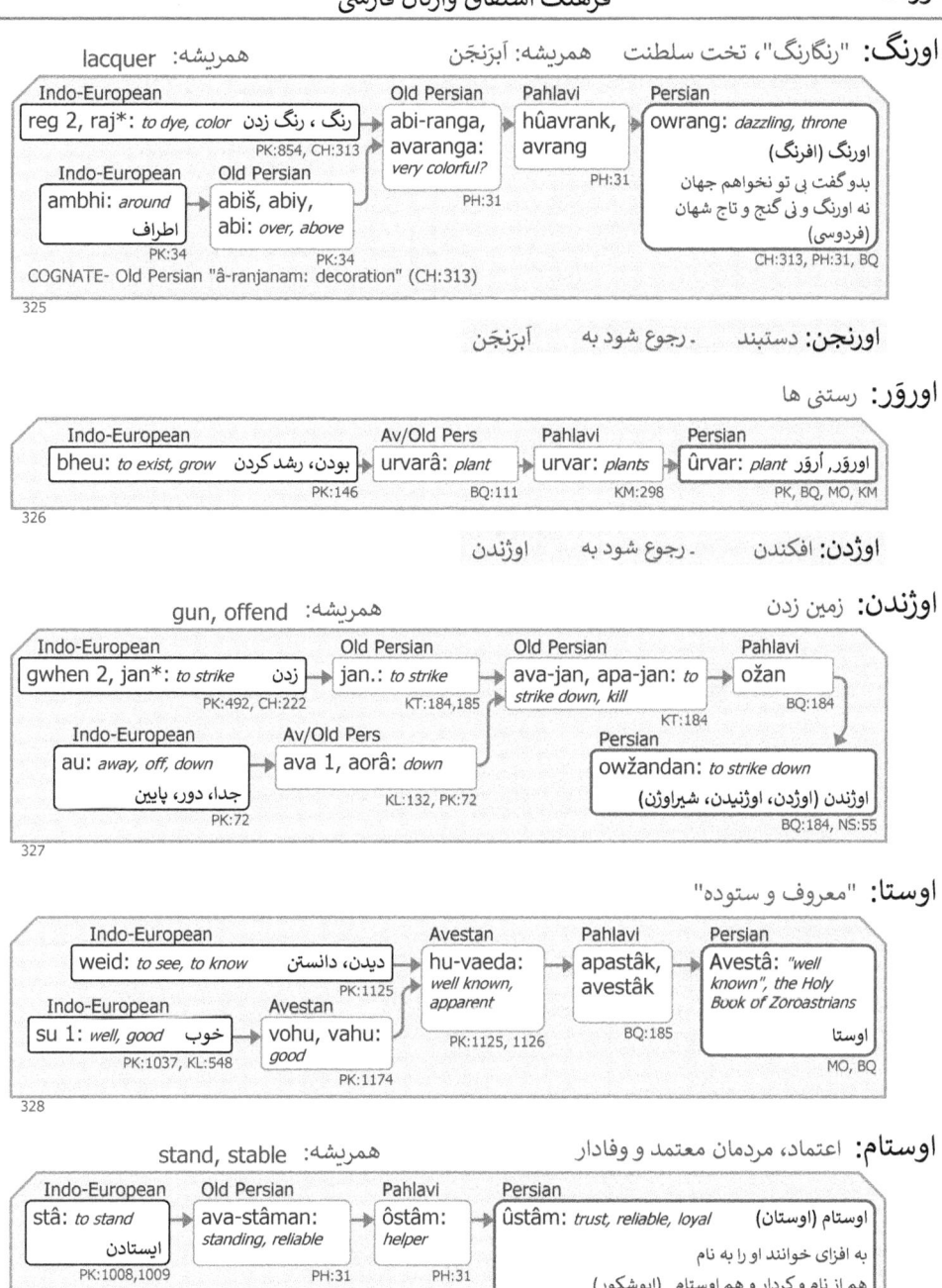

Indo-European	Old Persian	Pahlavi	Persian
reg 2, raj*: to dye, color رنگ ، رنگ زدن PK:854, CH:313	abi-ranga, avaranga: very colorful? PH:31	hûavrank, avrang PH:31	owrang: dazzling, throne اورنگ (افرنگ) بدو گفت بی تو نخواهم جهان نه اورنگ و نی گنج و تاج شهان (فردوسی) CH:313, PH:31, BQ

Indo-European	Old Persian
ambhi: around اطراف PK:34	abiš, abiy, abi: over, above PK:34

COGNATE- Old Persian "â-ranjanam: decoration" (CH:313)

325

اورنجن: دستبند   . رجوع شود به   اَبَرنجَن

اورَوَر: رستنی ها

Indo-European	Av/Old Pers	Pahlavi	Persian
bheu: to exist, grow بودن، رشد کردن PK:146	urvarâ: plant BQ:111	urvar: plants KM:298	ûrvar: plant اورَوَر، أرۆَر PK, BQ, MO, KM

326

اوژدن: افکندن   . رجوع شود به   اوژندن

اوژندن: زمین زدن   همریشه: gun, offend

Indo-European	Old Persian	Old Persian	Pahlavi
gwhen 2, jan*: to strike زدن PK:492, CH:222	jan.: to strike KT:184,185	ava-jan, apa-jan: to strike down, kill KT:184	ožan BQ:184

Indo-European	Av/Old Pers	Persian
au: away, off, down جدا، دور، پایین PK:72	ava 1, aorâ: down KL:132, PK:72	owžandan: to strike down اوژندن (اوژدن، اوژنیدن، شیراوژن) BQ:184, NS:55

327

اوستا: "معروف و ستوده"

Indo-European	Avestan	Pahlavi	Persian
weid: to see, to know دیدن، دانستن PK:1125	hu-vaeda: well known, apparent PK:1125, 1126	apastâk, avestâk BQ:185	Avestâ: "well known", the Holy Book of Zoroastrians اوستا MO, BQ

Indo-European	Avestan
su 1: well, good خوب PK:1037, KL:548	vohu, vahu: good PK:1174

328

اوستام: اعتماد، مردمان معتمد و وفادار   همریشه: stand, stable

Indo-European	Old Persian	Pahlavi	Persian
stâ: to stand ایستادن PK:1008,1009	ava-stâman: standing, reliable PH:31	ôstâm: helper PH:31	ûstâm: trust, reliable, loyal اوستام (اوستان) به افزای خواند او را به نام هم از نام و کردار و هم اوستام (ابوشکور) PH:31, BQ

329

اوستان: اعتماد   . رجوع شود به   اوستام   اویژه: پاک   ویژه

58

اهریمن: "با افکار خصمانه"

همریشه: mind

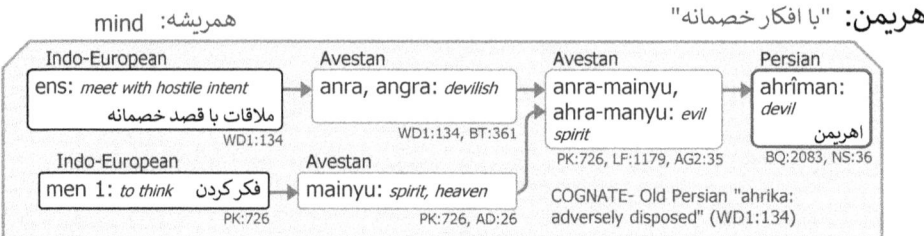

Indo-European	Avestan	Avestan	Persian
ens: *meet with hostile intent* ملاقات با قصد خصمانه WD1:134	anra, angra: *devilish* WD1:134, BT:361	anra-mainyu, ahra-manyu: *evil spirit* PK:726, LF:1179, AG2:35	ahrîman: *devil* اهریمن BQ:2083, NS:36

Indo-European	Avestan
men 1: *to think* فکر کردن PK:726	mainyu: *spirit, heaven* PK:726, AD:26

COGNATE- Old Persian "ahrika: *adversely disposed*" (WD1:134)

330

اهنوخوشی: صنف صنعتگران و پیشه وران دوره ساسانیان

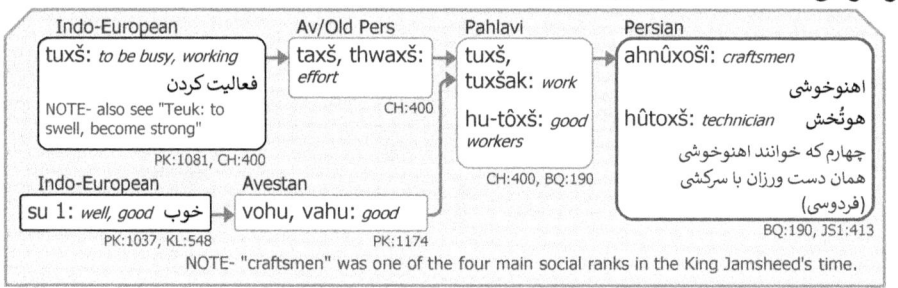

Indo-European	Av/Old Pers	Pahlavi	Persian
tuxš: *to be busy, working* فعالیت کردن NOTE- also see "Teuk: to swell, become strong" PK:1081, CH:400	taxš, thwaxš: *effort* CH:400	tuxš, tuxšak: *work* hu-tôxš: *good workers* CH:400, BQ:190	ahnûxošî: *craftsmen* اهنوخوشی hûtoxš: *technician* هوتُخش چهارم که خوانند اهنوخوشی همان دست ورزان با سرکشی (فردوسی) BQ:190, JS1:413

Indo-European	Avestan
su 1: *well, good* خوب PK:1037, KL:548	vohu, vahu: *good* PK:1174

NOTE- "craftsmen" was one of the four main social ranks in the King Jamsheed's time.

331

اهواز: جمع "هوز"

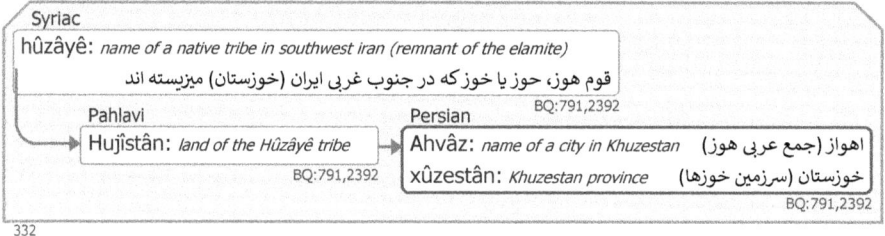

Syriac
hûzâyê: *name of a native tribe in southwest iran (remnant of the elamite)* قوم هوز، حوز یا خوز که در جنوب غربی ایران (خوزستان) میزیسته اند BQ:791,2392

Pahlavi	Persian
Hujîstân: *land of the Hûzâyê tribe* BQ:791,2392	Ahvâz: *name of a city in Khuzestan* اهواز (جمع عربی هوز) xûzestân: *Khuzestan province* خوزستان (سرزمین خوزها) BQ:791,2392

332

اهورا   . رجوع شود به   اهورامزدا

اهورامزدا: "روح عاقل"

همریشه: mind

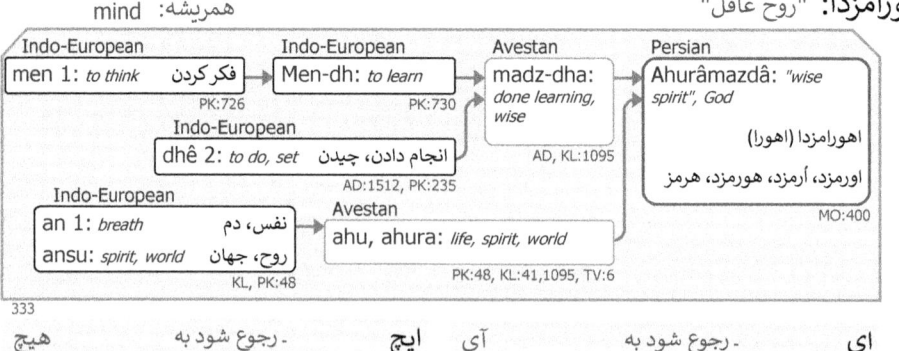

Indo-European	Indo-European	Avestan	Persian
men 1: *to think* فکر کردن PK:726	Men-dh: *to learn* PK:730	madz-dha: *done learning, wise* AD, KL:1095	Ahurâmazdâ: *"wise spirit", God* اهورامزدا (اهورا) اورمزد، أرمزد، هورمزد، هرمز MO:400

Indo-European
dhê 2: *to do, set* انجام دادن، چیدن AD:1512, PK:235

Indo-European	Avestan
an 1: *breath* نفس، دم ansu: *spirit, world* روح، جهان KL, PK:48	ahu, ahura: *life, spirit, world* PK:48, KL:41,1095, TV:6

333

هیچ   . رجوع شود به   ایچ   آی   ای   . رجوع شود به   ای

آیُخشُت: فلزات (آنچه قادر به ذوب کردن بودند)

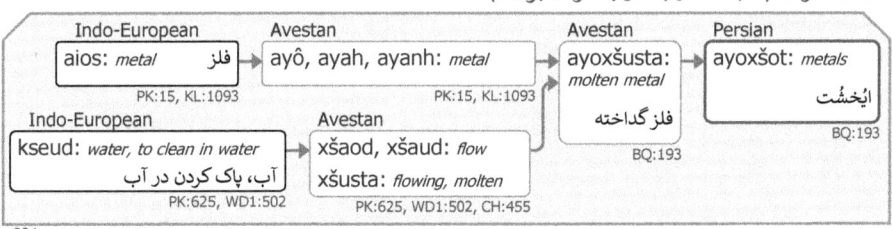

334

ایدر

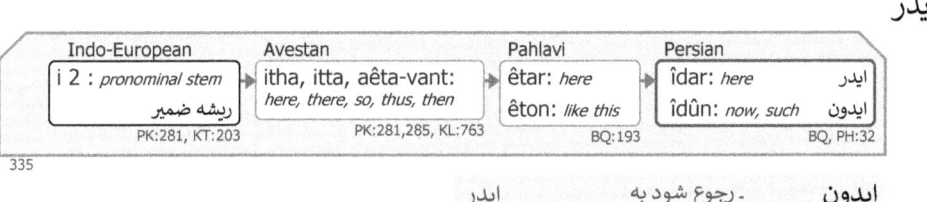

335

ایدون ـ رجوع شود به   ایدر

ایران   همریشه: آریا   همریشه: Ireland

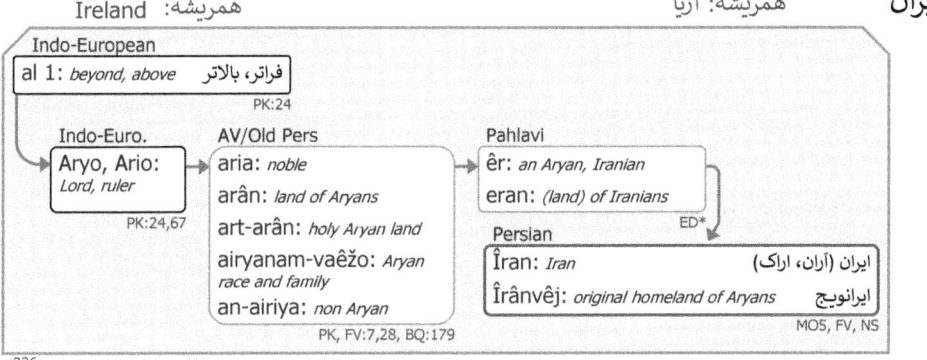

336

ایرانویج: "سرزمین آریاییان"

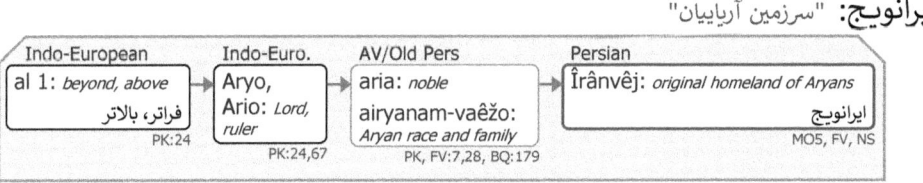

337

ایرج: "یار آریاییان"

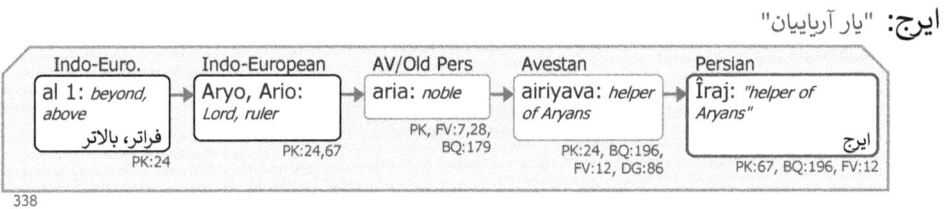

338

ایرمان: "میهمان محترم"

همریشه: mind, mentor

Indo-European	Indo-Euro.	AV/Old	Avestan	Pahlavi
al 1: *beyond, above* فراتر، بالاتر PK:24	Aryo, Ario: *Lord, ruler* PK:24,67	aria: *noble* PK, FV:7,28, BQ:179	airya-man: *noble mannered, friend, guest* PK:24, BQ:196, FV:12, DG:86	aêrmân BQ:196

Persian
îrmân: *guest*
ایرمان

Indo-European	Avestan
men 1: *to think* فکر کردن PK:726	manah: *mind, manners* man 1: *to resemble* PK:726,727, BQ

اگر کشته آید به دست تو گرگ
توباشی به روم ایرمانی بزرگ   (فردوسی)

PK:67, BQ:196, FV:12

339

ایزد

همریشه: hagios

Indo-European	Avestan	Pahlavi	Persian
yag: *to worship* ستایش کردن PK:501	yaz: *to worship* yazatanam: *God* PK:501, PH:95,252, KL:1759	yaztân: *plural of Yazd or Izad* BQ:2432	Îzad: *God* ایزد (یزدان، یزد) BQ, AG2

340

ایستادن

همریشه: in, standing

Indo-European	Av/Old Pers	Av/Old Pers	Pahlavi
stâ: *to stand* ایستادن PK:1008,1009	sta: *to stand, to set* BQ:123, PH:20, PK:1008	adi-sta: *in standing* BQ:123, PH:20, PK:1008, KT:210	êstâtan BQ:198

Persian
istâdan: *to stand*
ایستادن

Indo-European	Old Persian
en: *in, inside* داخل PK:311	adi, adyi: *in* PK:311

مثال فرم "ست": استاد، پرستار، تابستان، ستون
مثال فرم "شت یا ش": آشتی، فرشته، پشت، ارتش

BQ, MO

341

ایش: جاسوس . رجوع شود به   آیشه

ایشان

همریشه: this

Indo-European	Av/Old Pers	Pahlavi	Persian
SO: *this, that* این، آن PK:979	ava-hya, awa: *he, she* šim, šâm: *him, her* PK:979	avâ: *he, she* avâ-šam: *plural form used as a sign of respect* BQ:197	îŠân: *he/she, him/her* ایشان BQ, PH

342

ایشه: جاسوس . رجوع شود به   آیشه

ایمه: این، اکنون

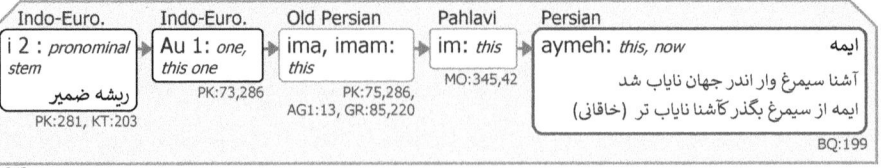

Indo-Euro.	Indo-Euro.	Old Persian	Pahlavi	Persian
i 2: *pronominal stem* ریشه ضمیر PK:281, KT:203	Au 1: *one, this one* PK:73,286	ima, imam: *this* PK:75,286, AG1:13, GR:85,220	im: *this* MO:345,42	aymeh: *this, now* ایمه

آشنا سیمرغ وار اندر جهان نایاب شد
ایمه از سیمرغ بگذر کآشنا نایاب تر   (خاقانی)

BQ:199

343

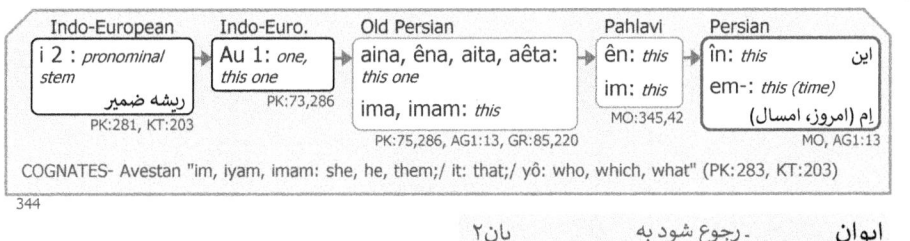

Indo-European	Indo-Euro.	Old Persian	Pahlavi	Persian
i 2 : *pronominal stem* ریشه ضمیر PK:281, KT:203	Au 1: *one, this one* PK:73,286	aina, êna, aita, aêta: *this one* ima, imam: *this* PK:75,286, AG1:13, GR:85,220	ên: *this* im: *this* MO:345,42	în: *this* این em-: *this (time)* اِم (امروز، امسال) MO, AG1:13

COGNATES- Avestan "im, iyam, imam: she, he, them;/ it: that;/ yô: who, which, what" (PK:283, KT:203)

344

ایوان ـ رجوع شود به بان۲

62

این حرف گاهی به م بدل شود.

بِ ـ : پیشوند برای تاکید افعال

Indo-European	Avestan	Persian
bhê: *indeed* واقعا	bâ, bê, beî: *indeed*	bî-, be-: *prefixes to emphasize verbs* (برو، بیا) بِ ، بی
PK:113, IC:59, WD2:136	PK:113, IC:59	IC:59, MO

345

با: شوریا ـ رجوع شود به پختن

باب۱ همریشه: Babel, Babylonia

Semitic	Akkadian	Persian
n.b.b: *to make hollow, dig a hole* حفره کندن، سوراخ کردن	bâbu: *door* bâb-ilu: *God's gate* imbûbu: *hollow tube*	bâb: *door* باب Bâbel: *"God's gate"* بابل anbûb: *pipe, flute* انبوب NOTES - through Aramaic and Arabic
	KL:138	KL:138, ZM:30	ZM:30, MO

346

باب۲ ـ رجوع شود به بابا

بابا همریشه: پدر همریشه: father

Indo-European	Pahlavi	Persian
pa: *to protect, feed* حفاظت کردن، غذا دادن	pâp, Pâpak: *father. Suffix -k indicates respect and love.* NOTE- possibly related to the Latin "papa".	bâbâ: *father* (باب، بابک) بابا NOTE- The words "bâb" and "bâbû" as a title of respect may be from a different root and mixed up with "bâbâ: father". See the word بَبه
PK:787,842, BK:103	BQ:202	
NOTE- This has probably started as a nursery word. Compare with the root "Baba".		BQ:202, PH:34, NB:150, MO:428, KM:197

347

بابک	ـ رجوع شود به مالیات	باج۱:			

بابک ـ رجوع شود به بابا بابل ـ رجوع شود به باب۱

باج۱: مالیات ـ رجوع شود به بخشیدن۱ باج۲: دعا ـ رجوع شود به واک

باختر

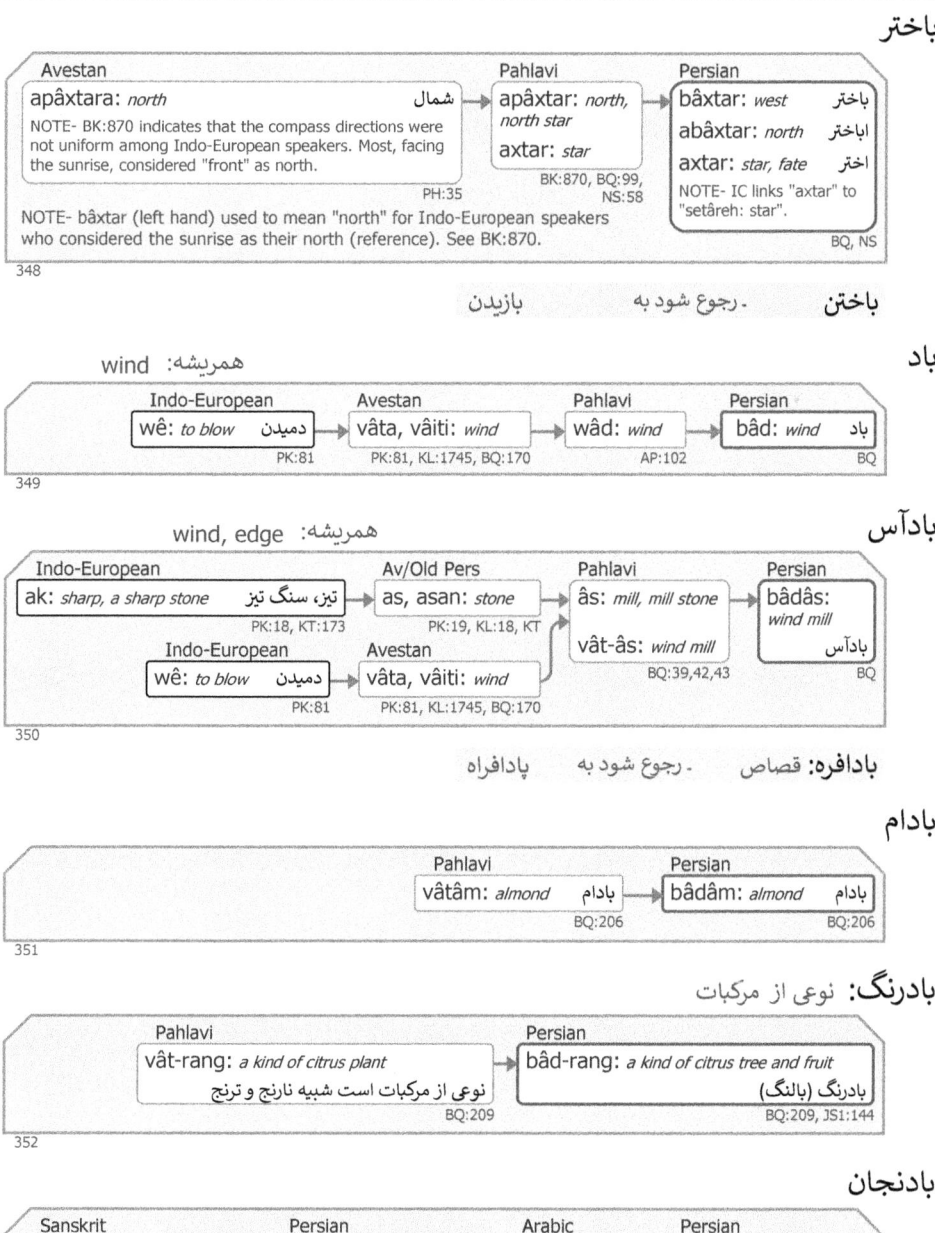

Avestan

apâxtara: *north*   شمال

NOTE- BK:870 indicates that the compass directions were not uniform among Indo-European speakers. Most, facing the sunrise, considered "front" as north.

PH:35

Pahlavi

apâxtar: *north, north star*

axtar: *star*

BK:870, BQ:99, NS:58

Persian

bâxtar: *west*   باختر

abâxtar: *north*   اباختر

axtar: *star, fate*   اختر

NOTE- IC links "axtar" to "setâreh: star".

BQ, NS

NOTE- bâxtar (left hand) used to mean "north" for Indo-European speakers who considered the sunrise as their north (reference). See BK:870.

348

باختن .رجوع شود به   بازیدن

باد

همریشه: wind

Indo-European

wê: *to blow*   دمیدن

PK:81

Avestan

vâta, vâiti: *wind*

PK:81, KL:1745, BQ:170

Pahlavi

wâd: *wind*

AP:102

Persian

bâd: *wind*   باد

BQ

349

بادآس

همریشه: wind, edge

Indo-European

ak: *sharp, a sharp stone*   تیز، سنگ تیز

PK:18, KT:173

Av/Old Pers

as, asan: *stone*

PK:19, KL:18, KT

Indo-European

wê: *to blow*   دمیدن

PK:81

Avestan

vâta, vâiti: *wind*

PK:81, KL:1745, BQ:170

Pahlavi

âs: *mill, mill stone*

vât-âs: *wind mill*

BQ:39,42,43

Persian

bâdâs: *wind mill*   بادآس

BQ

350

بادافره: قصاص .رجوع شود به   پادافراه

بادام

Pahlavi

vâtâm: *almond*   بادام

BQ:206

Persian

bâdâm: *almond*   بادام

BQ:206

351

بادرنگ: نوعی از مرکبات

Pahlavi

vât-rang: *a kind of citrus plant*

نوعی از مرکبات است شببه نارنج و ترنج

BQ:209

Persian

bâd-rang: *a kind of citrus tree and fruit*

بادرنگ (بالنگ)

BQ:209, JS1:144

352

بادنجان

Sanskrit

vatin-ganah: *eggplant*

بادنجان

KL:125

Persian

bâdengân: *eggplant*

بادنگان

KL:125, BQ:213, MO:444

Arabic

badinjan

KL:125,165

Persian

bâdenjân: *eggplant*

بادنجان (بادمجان)

BQ:213, MO:444

NOTE- Spanish "al-berginia" and French "au-bergine" are borrowed from Arabic "al-badinjan" (EE*)

353

64

باده

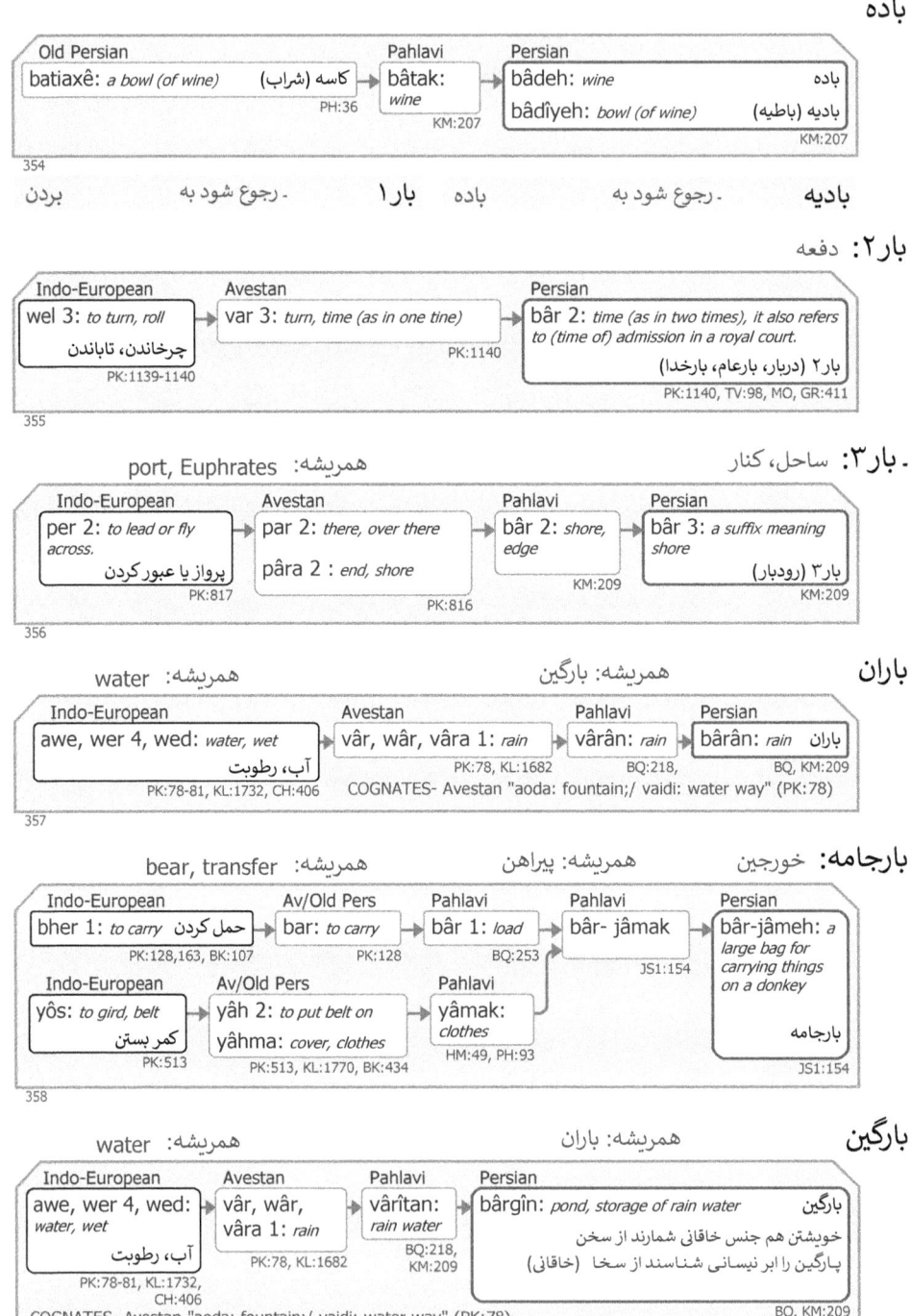

Old Persian — batiaxê: *a bowl (of wine)* کاسه (شراب) PH:36

Pahlavi — bâtak: *wine* KM:207

Persian — bâdeh: *wine* باده / bâdîyeh: *bowl (of wine)* باده (باطیه) KM:207

354

بادیه ـ رجوع شود به باده   بار۱ ـ رجوع شود به برده

بار۲: دفعه

Indo-European — wel 3: *to turn, roll* چرخاندن، تاباندن PK:1139-1140

Avestan — var 3: *turn, time (as in one tine)* PK:1140

Persian — bâr 2: *time (as in two times), it also refers to (time of) admission in a royal court.* بار۲ (دربار، بارعام، بارخدا) PK:1140, TV:98, MO, GR:411

355

ـ بار۳: ساحل، کنار   همریشه: port, Euphrates

Indo-European — per 2: *to lead or fly across.* پرواز یا عبور کردن PK:817

Avestan — par 2: *there, over there* / pâra 2 : *end, shore* PK:816

Pahlavi — bâr 2: *shore, edge* KM:209

Persian — bâr 3: *a suffix meaning shore* بار۳ (رودبار) KM:209

356

باران

همریشه: بارگین   همریشه: water

Indo-European — awe, wer 4, wed: *water, wet* آب، رطوبت PK:78-81, KL:1732, CH:406

Avestan — vâr, wâr, vâra 1: *rain* PK:78, KL:1682

Pahlavi — vârân: *rain* BQ:218,

Persian — bârân: *rain* باران BQ, KM:209

COGNATES- Avestan "aoda: fountain;/ vaidi: water way" (PK:78)

357

بارجامه: خورجین

همریشه: پیراهن   همریشه: bear, transfer

Indo-European — bher 1: *to carry* حمل کردن PK:128,163, BK:107

Av/Old Pers — bar: *to carry* PK:128

Pahlavi — bâr 1: *load* BQ:253

Pahlavi — bâr- jâmak JS1:154

Persian — bâr-jâmeh: *a large bag for carrying things on a donkey* بارجامه JS1:154

Indo-European — yôs: *to gird, belt* کمر بستن PK:513

Av/Old Pers — yâh 2: *to put belt on* / yâhma: *cover, clothes* PK:513, KL:1770, BK:434

Pahlavi — yâmak: *clothes* HM:49, PH:93

358

بارگین

همریشه: باران   همریشه: water

Indo-European — awe, wer 4, wed: *water, wet* آب، رطوبت PK:78-81, KL:1732, CH:406

Avestan — vâr, wâr, vâra 1: *rain* PK:78, KL:1682

Pahlavi — vârîtan: *rain water* BQ:218, KM:209

Persian — bârgin: *pond, storage of rain water* بارگین خویشتن هم جنس خاقانی شمارند از سخن پارگین را ابر نیسانی شـناسـند از سـخا (خاقانی) BQ, KM:209

COGNATES- Avestan "aoda: fountain;/ vaidi: water way" (PK:78)

359

باره۱: اسب

همریشه: burden, transfer

Indo-European	Av/Old Pers	Pahlavi	Persian
bher 1: *to carry* حمل کردن PK:128,163, BK:107	bar: *to carry* PK:128	bârag, bâr-ak: *horse mount* JS1:154	باره bâreh: *carrier, horse* یکی ترگ رومی به سر برنهاد یکی باره زیراندرش همچو باد (فردوسی) PK, BQ, KM

360

باره۲: دیوار قلعه

همریشه: cover

Indo-European	Av/Old Pers	Persian
wer 3, werg 2: *to cover, enclose* پوشاندن، محصور کردن PK:1168, IC:1599	var 1, vara, vâra 2: *cover, wall* PK:1168, KM:212, KT:207	بارو (باره) bâru: *castle wall* سر بارهٔ دژ بُد اندر هوا ندیدند جنگ هواکس روا (فردوسی) BQ

361

بارو: دیوار قلعه   .رجوع شود به   باره۲

باروت

همریشه: پودر

Indo-European	Latin	French	Turkish	Persian
pel 3: *dust, flour* خاک، آرد PK:802	pollen: *dust* AD	poudre: *dust, powder* AD:1024	pudra, barut BQ:216, TU:6	باروت bârût: *gun powder* BQ:216, TU:6

362

باریک

	Pahlavi	Persian
	bârig: *narrow* نازک JS1:154	باریک bârîk: *narrow* JS1:154

363

باز۱: واحد طول

Indo-European	Avestan	Persian
bhengh, banz*: *to be thick, dense* کلفت، غلیظ PK:127	bazah: *height, depth* PK:127, KL:1109	باز۱ bâz: *distance between stretched hands* بلندیش با چرخ همباز بود ستبریش بیش از چهل باز بود (اسدی طوسی) MO,CH

364

باز۲: شاهین

Indo-European	Avestan	Pahlavi	Persian
wegh: *to go, carry* رفتن، حمل کردن PK:1119	vaz: *fly* vaza 1: *a bird, hawk* PK:1119	bâza, bâž: *hawk* AP:105	باز۲ (باشه، واشه) bâz: *hawk, falcon* پس اندر دوان هفتصد باز۲ دار ابا واشه و چرخ و شاهین کار (فردوسی) BQ, MO

365

66

باز۳: گشاده

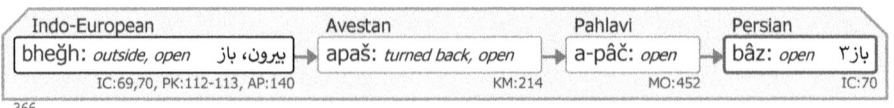

Indo-European	Avestan	Pahlavi	Persian
bheğh: outside, open بیرون، باز	apaš: turned back, open	a-pâč: open	bâz: open ۳باز
IC:69,70, PK:112-113, AP:140	KM:214	MO:452	IC:70

366

باز۴: دوباره

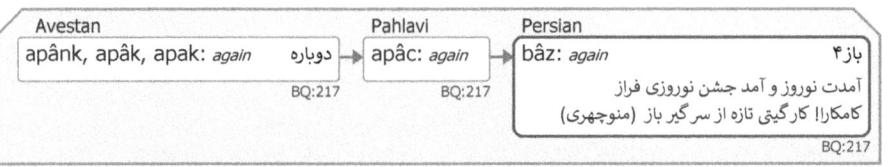

Avestan	Pahlavi	Persian
apânk, apâk, apak: again دوباره	apâc: again	bâz: again ۴باز
BQ:217	BQ:217	آمدت نوروز و آمد جشن نوروزی فراز
		کامکارا! کارگیتی تازه از سر گیر باز (منوچهری)
		BQ:217

367

بازار: "محل تجمع"   همریشه: wheel, cult

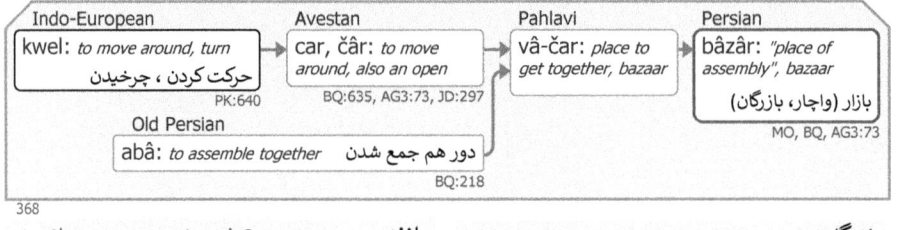

Indo-European	Avestan	Pahlavi	Persian
kwel: to move around, turn حرکت کردن ، چرخیدن	car, čar: to move around, also an open	vâ-čar: place to get together, bazaar	bâzâr: "place of assembly", bazaar
PK:640	BQ:635, AG3:73, JD:297		بازار (واچار، بازرگان)
Old Persian			MO, BQ, AG3:73
abâ: to assemble together دور هم جمع شدن			
BQ:218			

368

بازیدن   بازنده رجوع شود به .   بازار   رجوع شود به .   **بازنده**   **بازرگان**

بازو

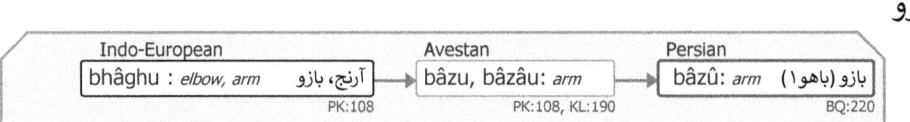

Indo-European	Avestan	Persian
bhâghu : elbow, arm آرنج، بازو	bâzu, bâzâu: arm	bâzû: arm بازو (باهو۱)
PK:108	PK:108, KL:190	BQ:220

369

بازیدن

Indo-European	Iranian	Pahlavi	Persian
weg 2: to be lively, strong سرزنده و قوی بودن	vâz, wâz: power, largeness or rising.	vâzîtan: to rise up, be active, play bâxtan: to rise up, play	bâzîdan: to play بازیدن (بازی، بازنده) bâxtan: to play, also to lose a game باختن
PK:1117	KM:201, IC:1499	HM:22, KM:201	KM:201, HM:22, IC:1499

370

باز۲ رجوع شود به .   **باشه:** شاهین   بخشیدن۱   رجوع شود به .   **باژ:** باج

باده رجوع شود به .   **باطیه:** کاسه شراب

باغ   همریشه: pagoda

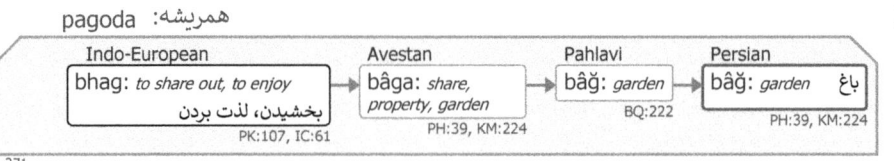

Indo-European	Avestan	Pahlavi	Persian
bhag: to share out, to enjoy بخشیدن، لذت بردن	bâga: share, property, garden	bâğ: garden	bâğ: garden باغ
PK:107, IC:61	PH:39, KM:224	BQ:222	PH:39, KM:224

371

بافتن

همریشه: weave

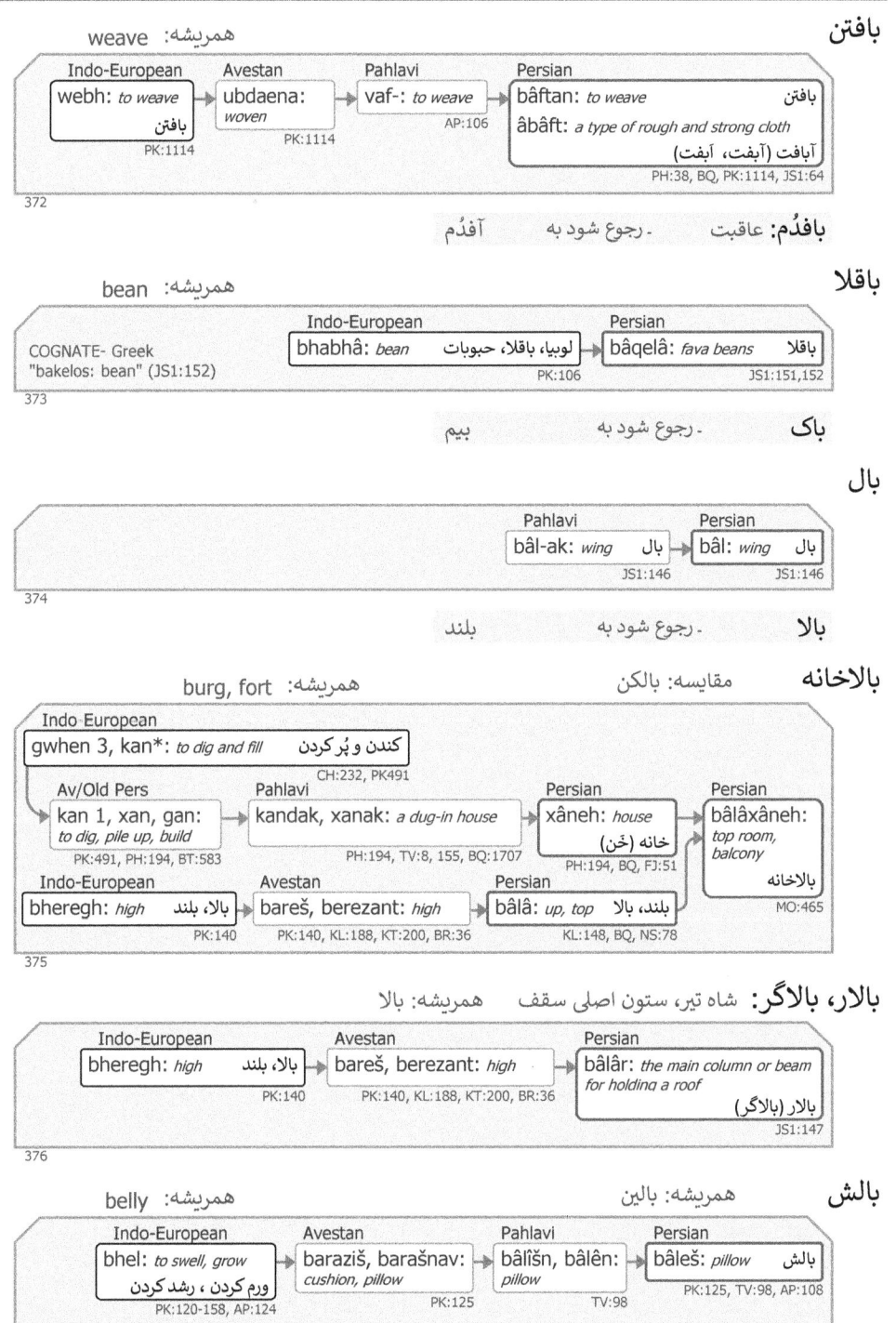

Indo-European	Avestan	Pahlavi	Persian
webh: *to weave* بافتن PK:1114	ubdaena: *woven* PK:1114	vaf-: *to weave* AP:106	bâftan: *to weave* بافتن âbâft: *a type of rough and strong cloth* آبافت (آبفت، آبفت) PH:38, BQ, PK:1114, JS1:64

372

بافدُم: عاقبت ـ رجوع شود به   آفدُم

باقلا

همریشه: bean

	Indo-European	Persian
COGNATE- Greek "bakelos: bean" (JS1:152)	bhabhâ: *bean* لوبیا، باقلا، حبوبات PK:106	bâqelâ: *fava beans* باقلا JS1:151,152

373

باک   ـ رجوع شود به   بیم

بال

Pahlavi	Persian
bâl-ak: *wing* بال JS1:146	bâl: *wing* بال JS1:146

374

بالا   ـ رجوع شود به   بلند

بالاخانه

مقایسه: بالکن   همریشه: burg, fort

Indo-European
gwhen 3, kan*: *to dig and fill* کندن و پُر کردن
CH:232, PK491

Av/Old Pers	Pahlavi	Persian	Persian
kan 1, xan, gan: *to dig, pile up, build* PK:491, PH:194, BT:583	kandak, xanak: *a dug-in house* PH:194, TV:8, 155, BQ:1707	xâneh: *house* خانه (خن) PH:194, BQ, FJ:51	bâlâxâneh: *top room, balcony* بالاخانه MO:465

Indo-European	Avestan	Persian	
bheregh: *high* بالا، بلند PK:140	bareš, berezant: *high* PK:140, KL:188, KT:200, BR:36	bâlâ: *up, top* بلند، بالا KL:148, BQ, NS:78	

375

بالار، بالاگر: شاه تیر، ستون اصلی سقف   همریشه: بالا

Indo-European	Avestan	Persian
bheregh: *high* بالا، بلند PK:140	bareš, berezant: *high* PK:140, KL:188, KT:200, BR:36	bâlâr: *the main column or beam for holding a roof* بالار (بالاگر) JS1:147

376

بالش

همریشه: بالین   همریشه: belly

Indo-European	Avestan	Pahlavi	Persian
bhel: *to swell, grow* ورم کردن ، رشد کردن PK:120-158, AP:124	baraziš, barašnav: *cushion, pillow* PK:125	bâlîšn, bâlên: *pillow* TV:98	bâleš: *pillow* بالش PK:125, TV:98, AP:108

377

68

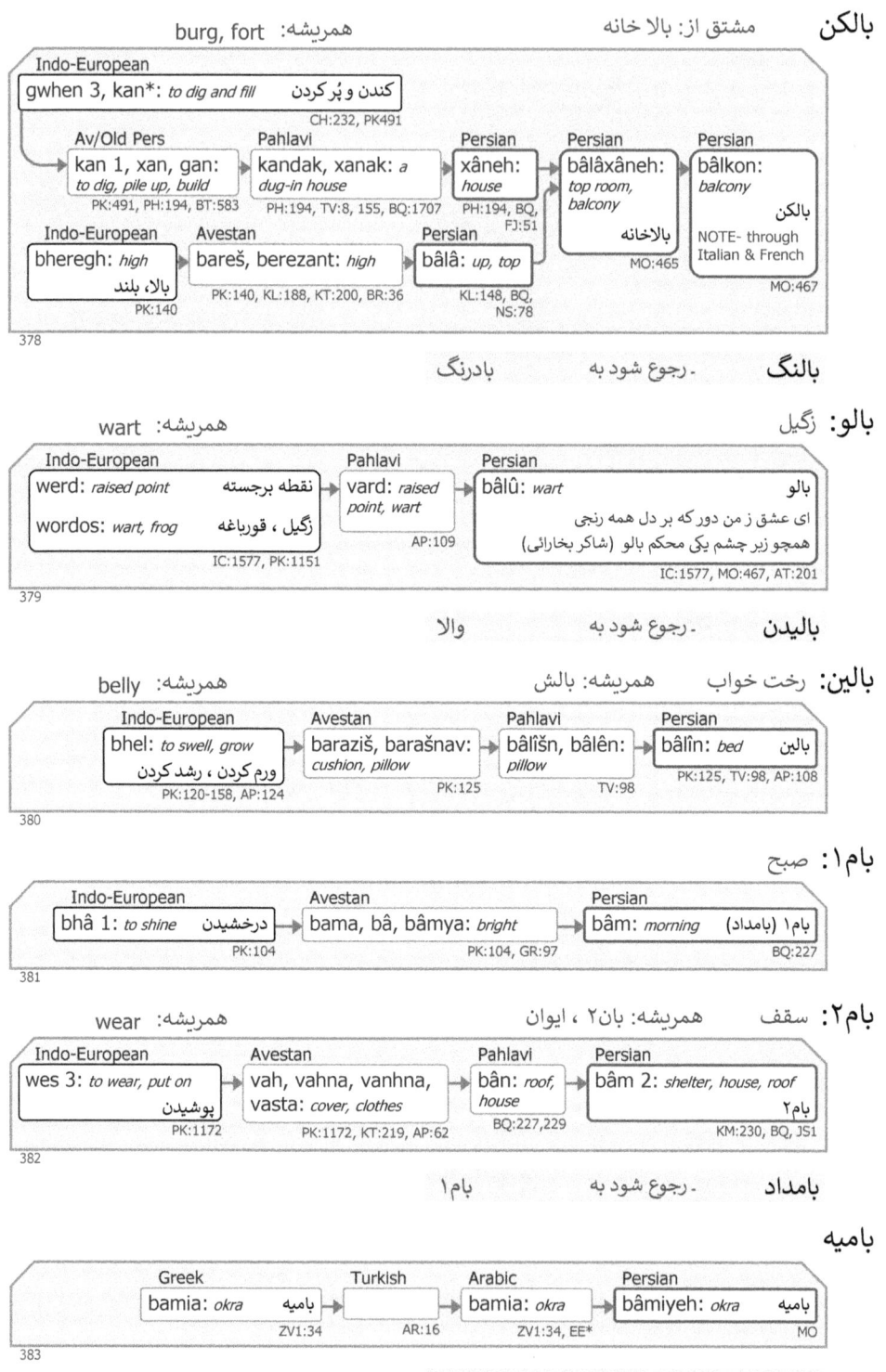

بالکن

مشتق از: بالا خانه   همریشه: burg, fort

Indo-European
gwhen 3, kan*: *to dig and fill*   کندن و پُر کردن
CH:232, PK491

Av/Old Pers
kan 1, xan, gan: *to dig, pile up, build*
PK:491, PH:194, BT:583

Pahlavi
kandak, xanak: *a dug-in house*
PH:194, TV:8, 155, BQ:1707

Persian
xâneh: *house*
PH:194, BQ

Persian
bâlâxâneh: *top room, balcony*
بالاخانه
MO:465
FJ:51

Persian
bâlkon: *balcony*
بالکن
NOTE- through Italian & French
MO:467

Indo-European
bheregh: *high*
بالا، بلند
PK:140

Avestan
bareš, berezant: *high*
PK:140, KL:188, KT:200, BR:36

Persian
bâlâ: *up, top*
KL:148, BQ, NS:78

378

بالنگ

ـ رجوع شود به   بادرنگ

بالو: زگیل

همریشه: wart

Indo-European
werd: *raised point*   نقطه برجسته
wordos: *wart, frog*   زگیل ، قورباغه
IC:1577, PK:1151

Pahlavi
vard: *raised point, wart*
AP:109

Persian
bâlû: *wart*
بالو
ای عشق ز من دور که بر دل همه رنجی
همچو زیر چشم یکی محکم بالو (شاکر بخارائی)
IC:1577, MO:467, AT:201

379

بالیدن

ـ رجوع شود به   والا

بالین: رخت خواب

همریشه: بالش   همریشه: belly

Indo-European
bhel: *to swell, grow*
ورم کردن، رشد کردن
PK:120-158, AP:124

Avestan
baraziš, barašnav: *cushion, pillow*
PK:125

Pahlavi
bâlîšn, bâlên: *pillow*
TV:98

Persian
bâlîn: *bed*
بالین
PK:125, TV:98, AP:108

380

بام۱: صبح

Indo-European
bhâ 1: *to shine*   درخشیدن
PK:104

Avestan
bama, bâ, bâmya: *bright*
PK:104, GR:97

Persian
bâm: *morning*   بام۱ (بامداد)
BQ:227

381

بام۲: سقف

همریشه: بان۲ ، ایوان   همریشه: wear

Indo-European
wes 3: *to wear, put on*
پوشیدن
PK:1172

Avestan
vah, vahna, vanhna, vasta: *cover, clothes*
PK:1172, KT:219, AP:62

Pahlavi
bân: *roof, house*
BQ:227,229

Persian
bâm 2: *shelter, house, roof*
بام۲
KM:230, BQ, JS1

382

بامداد

ـ رجوع شود به   بام۱

بامیه

Greek
bamia: *okra*   بامیه
ZV1:34

Turkish
AR:16

Arabic
bamia: *okra*
ZV1:34, EE*

Persian
bâmiyeh: *okra*   بامیه
MO

383

بان۱: نگاه دارنده

ـ رجوع شود به   پاییدن

بان۲: سقف   همریشه: بام۲   همریشه: wear

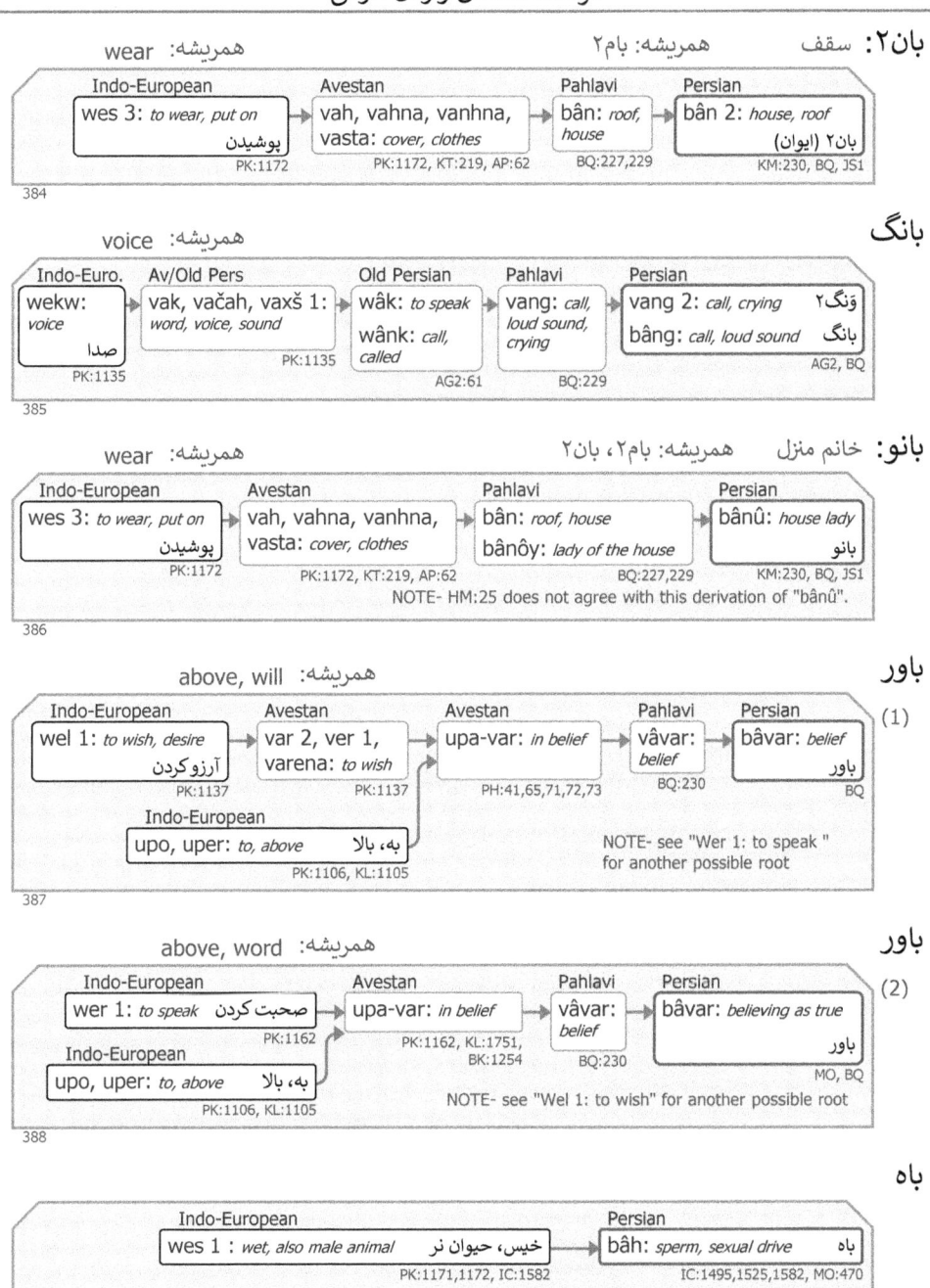

Indo-European	Avestan	Pahlavi	Persian
wes 3: *to wear, put on* پوشیدن PK:1172	vah, vahna, vanhna, vasta: *cover, clothes* PK:1172, KT:219, AP:62	bân: *roof, house* BQ:227,229	bân 2: *house, roof* بان۲ (ایوان) KM:230, BQ, JS1

384

بانگ

همریشه: voice

Indo-Euro.	Av/Old Pers	Old Persian	Pahlavi	Persian
wekw: *voice* صدا PK:1135	vak, vačah, vaxš 1: *word, voice, sound* PK:1135	wâk: *to speak* wânk: *call, called* AG2:61	vang: *call, loud sound, crying* BQ:229	vang 2: *call, crying* وَنگ۲ bâng: *call, loud sound* بانگ AG2, BQ

385

بانو: خانم منزل   همریشه: بام۲، بان۲   همریشه: wear

Indo-European	Avestan	Pahlavi	Persian
wes 3: *to wear, put on* پوشیدن PK:1172	vah, vahna, vanhna, vasta: *cover, clothes* PK:1172, KT:219, AP:62	bân: *roof, house* bânôy: *lady of the house* BQ:227,229	bânû: *house lady* بانو KM:230, BQ, JS1

NOTE- HM:25 does not agree with this derivation of "bânû".

386

باور (1)   همریشه: above, will

Indo-European	Avestan	Avestan	Pahlavi	Persian
wel 1: *to wish, desire* آرزو کردن PK:1137	var 2, ver 1, varena: *to wish* PK:1137	upa-var: *in belief* PH:41,65,71,72,73	vâvar: *belief* BQ:230	bâvar: *belief* باور BQ
Indo-European upo, uper: *to, above* به، بالا PK:1106, KL:1105				

NOTE- see "Wer 1: to speak " for another possible root

387

باور (2)   همریشه: above, word

Indo-European	Avestan	Pahlavi	Persian
wer 1: *to speak* صحبت کردن PK:1162	upa-var: *in belief* PK:1162, KL:1751, BK:1254	vâvar: *belief* BQ:230	bâvar: *believing as true* باور MO, BQ
Indo-European upo, uper: *to, above* به، بالا PK:1106, KL:1105			

NOTE- see "Wel 1: to wish" for another possible root

388

باه

Indo-European	Persian
wes 1 : *wet, also male animal* خیس، حیوان نر PK:1171,1172, IC:1582	bâh: *sperm, sexual drive* باه IC:1495,1525,1582, MO:470

389

باهو۱   رجوع شود به.   بازو

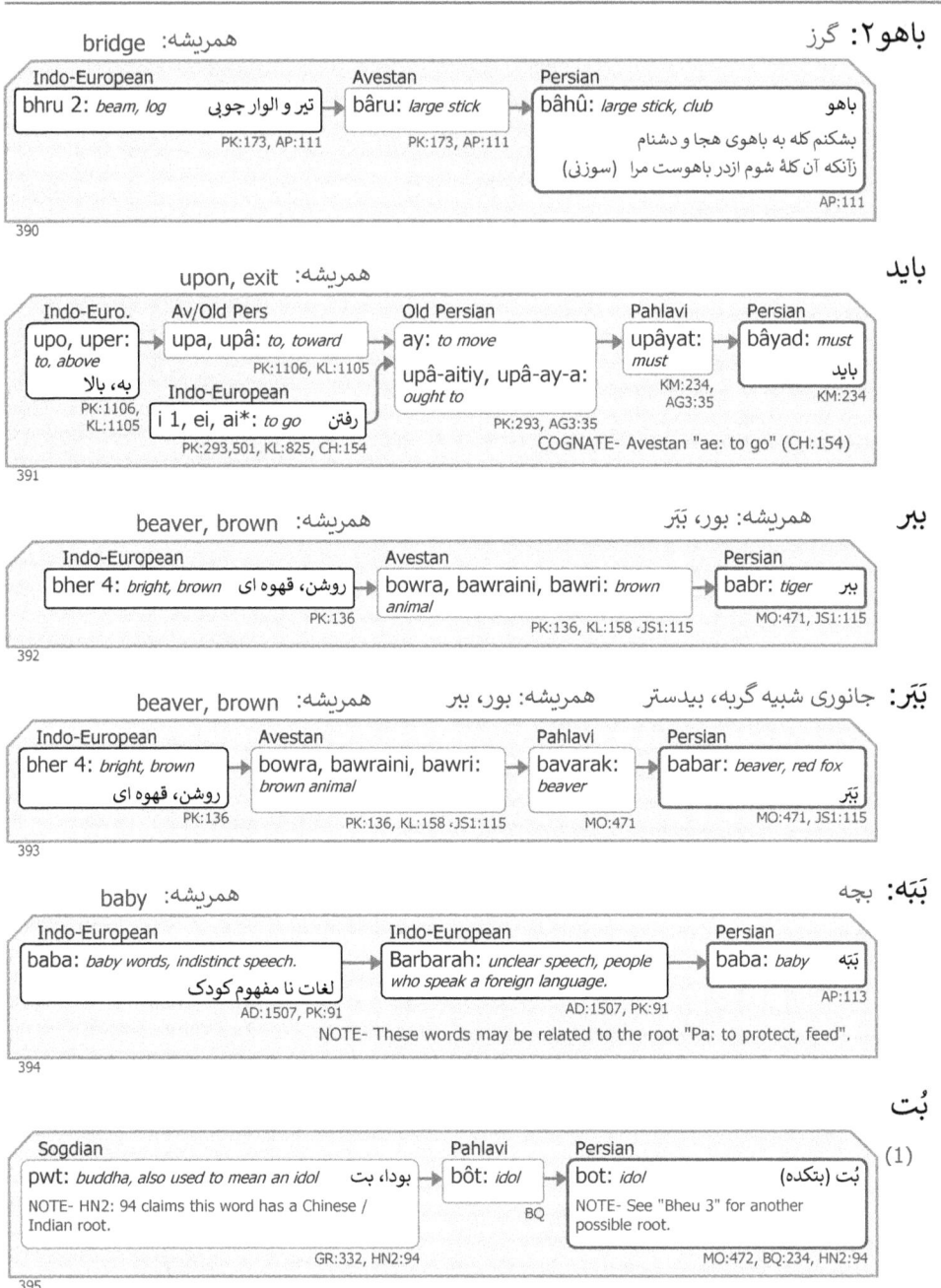

باهو۲: گرز

همریشه: bridge

Indo-European	Avestan	Persian
bhru 2: *beam, log* تیر و الوار چوبی	bâru: *large stick*	bâhû: *large stick, club* باهو
PK:173, AP:111	PK:173, AP:111	بشکنم کله به باهوی هجا و دشنام
		زآنکه آن کلهٔ شوم ازدر باهوست مرا (سوزنی)
		AP:111

390

باید

همریشه: upon, exit

Indo-Euro.	Av/Old Pers	Old Persian	Pahlavi	Persian
upo, uper: *to, above* به، بالا	upa, upâ: *to, toward*	ay: *to move*	upâyat: *must*	bâyad: *must* باید
PK:1106, KL:1105	PK:1106, KL:1105	upâ-aitiy, upâ-ay-a: *ought to*	KM:234, AG3:35	KM:234
	Indo-European			
	i 1, ei, ai*: *to go* رفتن	PK:293, AG3:35		
	PK:293,501, KL:825, CH:154	COGNATE- Avestan "ae: to go" (CH:154)		

391

بِبَر

همریشه: بور، بَبَر

همریشه: beaver, brown

Indo-European	Avestan	Persian
bher 4: *bright, brown* روشن، قهوه ای	bowra, bawraini, bawri: *brown animal*	babr: *tiger* ببر
PK:136	PK:136, KL:158، JS1:115	MO:471, JS1:115

392

بَبَر: جانوری شبیه گربه، بیدستر   همریشه: بور، ببر   همریشه: beaver, brown

Indo-European	Avestan	Pahlavi	Persian
bher 4: *bright, brown* روشن، قهوه ای	bowra, bawraini, bawri: *brown animal*	bavarak: *beaver*	babar: *beaver, red fox* بَبَر
PK:136	PK:136, KL:158، JS1:115	MO:471	MO:471, JS1:115

393

بَبَه: بچه

همریشه: baby

Indo-European	Indo-European	Persian
baba: *baby words, indistinct speech.* لغات نا مفهوم کودک	Barbarah: *unclear speech, people who speak a foreign language.*	baba: *baby* بَبَه
AD:1507, PK:91	AD:1507, PK:91	AP:113
	NOTE- These words may be related to the root "Pa: to protect, feed".	

394

بُت

(1)

Sogdian	Pahlavi	Persian
pwt: *buddha, also used to mean an idol* بودا، بت	bôt: *idol*	bot: *idol* بُت (بتکده)
NOTE- HN2: 94 claims this word has a Chinese / Indian root.	BQ	NOTE- See "Bheu 3" for another possible root.
GR:332, HN2:94		MO:472, BQ:234, HN2:94

395

بُت

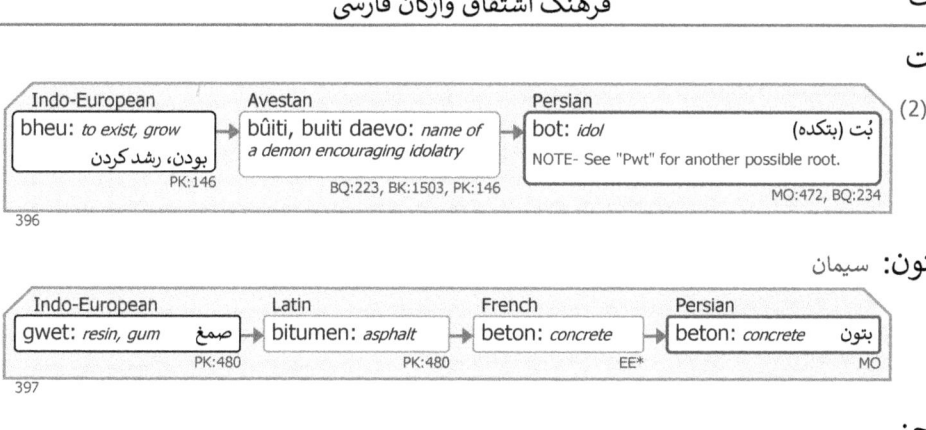

بُت (2)

Indo-European	Avestan	Persian
bheu: to exist, grow	bûiti, buiti daevo: name of a demon encouraging idolatry	bot: idol
بودن، رشد کردن		بُت (بتکده)
PK:146	BQ:223, BK:1503, PK:146	NOTE- See "Pwt" for another possible root. MO:472, BQ:234

396

بتون: سیمان

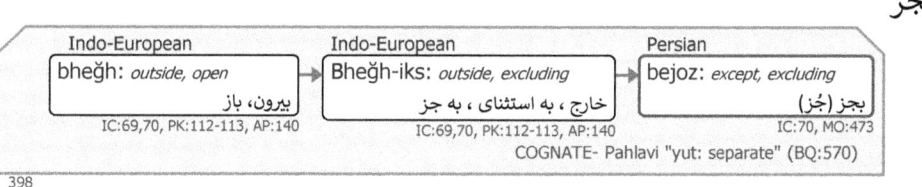

Indo-European	Latin	French	Persian
gwet: resin, gum صمغ	bitumen: asphalt	beton: concrete	beton: concrete بتون
PK:480	PK:480	EE*	MO

397

بجز

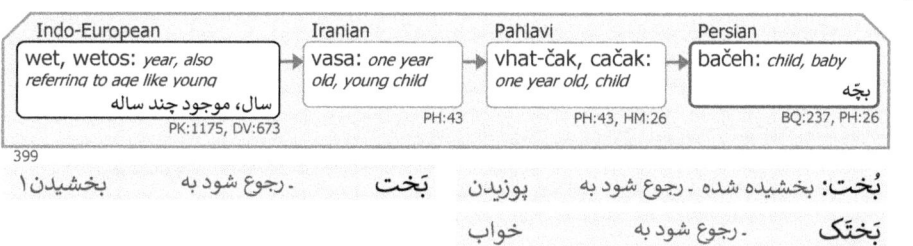

Indo-European	Indo-European	Persian
bheğh: outside, open	Bheğh-iks: outside, excluding	bejoz: except, excluding
بیرون، باز	خارج ، به استثنای ، به جز	بجز (جز)
IC:69,70, PK:112-113, AP:140	IC:69,70, PK:112-113, AP:140	IC:70, MO:473

COGNATE- Pahlavi "yut: separate" (BQ:570)

398

بچّه

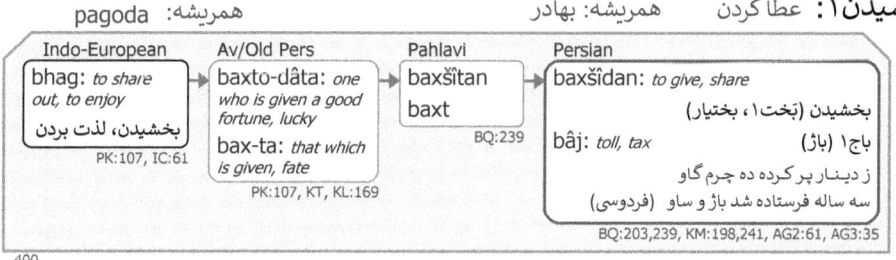

Indo-European	Iranian	Pahlavi	Persian
wet, wetos: year, also referring to age like young	vasa: one year old, young child	vhat-čak, cačak: one year old, child	bačeh: child, baby
سال، موجود چند ساله			بچّه
PK:1175, DV:673	PH:43	PH:43, HM:26	BQ:237, PH:26

399

بُخت: بخشیده شده ـ رجوع شود به   پوزیدن   تَخت   ـ رجوع شود به   بخشیدن۱

بَختَک   ـ رجوع شود به   خواب

بخشیدن۱: عطا کردن   همریشه: بهادر   همریشه: pagoda

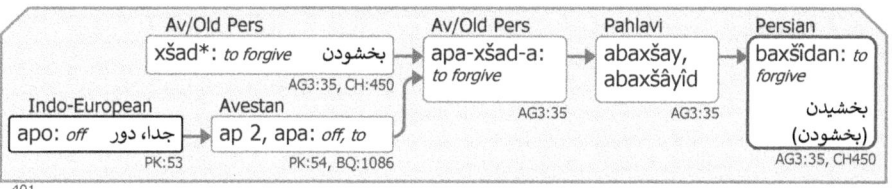

Indo-European	Av/Old Pers	Pahlavi	Persian
bhag: to share out, to enjoy	baxto-dâta: one who is given a good fortune, lucky	baxšîtan baxt	baxšîdan: to give, share
بخشیدن، لذت بردن			بخشیدن (تَخت۱، بختیار)
PK:107, IC:61	bax-ta: that which is given, fate	BQ:239	بٰاج۱ (باژ) bâj: toll, tax
	PK:107, KT, KL:169		ز دینار پر کرده ده چرم گاو سه ساله فرستاده شد باژ و ساو (فردوسی)
			BQ:203,239, KM:198,241, AG2:61, AG3:35

400

بخشیدن۲: گذشت کردن

	Av/Old Pers	Av/Old Pers	Pahlavi	Persian
	xšad*: to forgive بخشودن	apa-xšad-a: to forgive	abaxšay, abaxšâyîd	baxšîdan: to forgive
	AG3:35, CH:450	AG3:35	AG3:35	بخشیدن (بخشودن)
Indo-European	Avestan			AG3:35, CH450
apo: off جدا، دور	ap 2, apa: off, to			
PK:53	PK:54, BQ:1086			

401

بخشودن: عفو کردن ـ رجوع شود به   بخشیدن۲

بَد

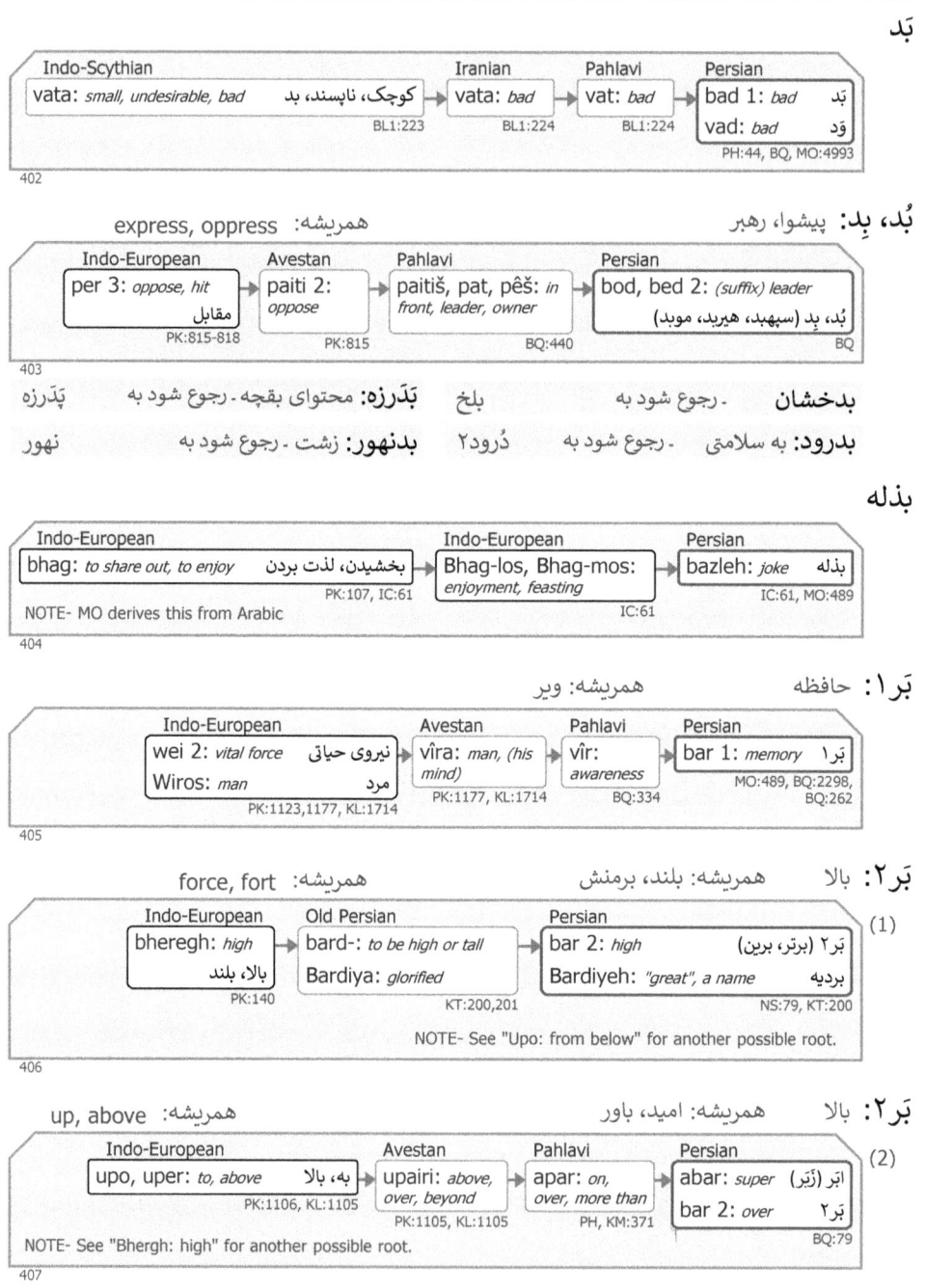

Indo-Scythian	Iranian	Pahlavi	Persian
vata: small, undesirable, bad کوچک، ناپسند، بد	vata: bad	vat: bad	bad 1: bad بَد / vad: bad وَد
BL1:223	BL1:224	BL1:224	PH:44, BQ, MO:4993

402

بُد، بِد: پیشوا، رهبر   همریشه: express, oppress

Indo-European	Avestan	Pahlavi	Persian
per 3: oppose, hit مقابل	paiti 2: oppose	paitiš, pat, pêš: in front, leader, owner	bod, bed 2: (suffix) leader بُد، بِد (سپهبد، هیربد، موبد)
PK:815-818	PK:815	BQ:440	BQ

403

بدخشان   ـ رجوع شود به   بلخ   بَدَرزه: محتوای بقچه ـ رجوع شود به   پَدَرزه

بدرود: به سلامتی   ـ رجوع شود به   دُرود۲   بدنهور: زشت ـ رجوع شود به   نهور

بذله

Indo-European	Indo-European	Persian
bhag: to share out, to enjoy بخشیدن، لذت بردن	Bhag-los, Bhag-mos: enjoyment, feasting	bazleh: joke بذله
PK:107, IC:61	IC:61	IC:61, MO:489
NOTE- MO derives this from Arabic		

404

بَر۱: حافظه   همریشه: ویر

Indo-European	Avestan	Pahlavi	Persian
wei 2: vital force نیروی حیاتی / Wiros: man مرد	vîra: man, (his mind)	vîr: awareness	bar 1: memory بَر۱
PK:1123,1177, KL:1714	PK:1177, KL:1714	BQ:334	MO:489, BQ:2298, BQ:262

405

بَر۲: بالا   همریشه: بلند، برمنش   force, fort :همریشه   (1)

Indo-European	Old Persian	Persian
bheregh: high بالا، بلند	bard-: to be high or tall / Bardiya: glorified	bar 2: high بَر۲ (برتر، برین) / Bardiyeh: "great", a name بردیه
PK:140	KT:200,201	NS:79, KT:200
		NOTE- See "Upo: from below" for another possible root.

406

بَر۲: بالا   همریشه: امید، باور   up, above :همریشه   (2)

Indo-European	Avestan	Pahlavi	Persian
upo, uper: to, above به، بالا	upairi: above, over, beyond	apar: on, over, more than	abar: super اتر (اَبَر) / bar 2: over بَر۲
PK:1106, KL:1105	PK:1105, KL:1105	PH, KM:371	BQ:79
NOTE- See "Bhergh: high" for another possible root.			

407

بَر۳: بار   ـ رجوع شود به   بردن

بَر ۴: سینه

همریشه: breast

Indo-European	Avestan	Pahlavi	Persian
bhreus: *swollen* متورم PK:170, AP:116	varang,varah: *swollen, breast* AP:116	war, bar: *breast* AP:116	bar: *breast, chest, appearance* بَر ۴ AP:116

408

برادر

همریشه: brother, bear

Indo-European	Indo-Euro.	Avestan	Pahlavi	Persian
bher 1: *to carry* حمل کردن PK:128,163, BK:107 Indo-European ter 2, tar: *a kinship term* پسوند گروه یا فامیل PT:863	Bhra-ter: *carrier of load or responsibility* PK, BK:103-107	brâ-tar: *carrier of family* KL, BK:103-107	barâtar BQ:246	barâdar: *"load or responsibility carrier of family", brother* برادر BQ

409

برازنده   ـ رجوع شود به   برازیدن

برازیدن: زیبا نمودن

همریشه: bright

Indo-European	Avestan	Persian
bhereg: *to shine, bright* درخشیدن، روشن PK:139	brâz: *to shine* PK:139, BQ:137	barâzîdan: *to look nice* برازیدن barâzandeh: *well suited, fit* برازنده BQ, MO, AP:118

410

بربط

Indo-European	Indo-European	Greek	Pahlavi	Persian
baba: *baby words, indistinct speech.* لغات نا مفهوم کودک AD:1507, PK:91	Barbarah: *unclear speech, people who speak a foreign* AD:1507, PK:91	barbitos: *foreign people or objects.* SH:22	barbut: *a stringed musical instrument* BQ:249, MO:497	barbat: *a musical instrument* بربط MO:497

411

برج

Greek	Arabic	Persian
purgos, pyrgos: *tower* برج RB:1262, AR:20, ED*	burj: *tower* NOTE- ZV1:36 claims this is from an Aramaic AR:20, BQ:250	borj: *tower* برج MO, AR:21

412

بَرخ: بهره، قسمت   همریشه: بهره

Indo-European	Avestan	Pahlavi	Persian
bhag: *to share out, to enjoy* بخشیدن، لذت بردن PK:107, IC:61	baxadra: *interest* BQ:251,324, TV:96	bahr, bahrak: *interest* KM:305	barx: *interest* بَرخ (برخی) تو ای دانشی چند نالی ز چرخ که ایزد بَدی دادت از چرخ برخ (اسدی طوسی) BQ, TV:96

413

بردن

همریشه: bear, transfer

Indo-European	Av/Old Pers	Pahlavi	Persian
bher 1: *to carry* حمل کردن PK:128,163, BK:107	bar: *to carry* PK:128	burtan: *to carry* bâr 1: *load* BQ:253	bordan: *to carry, take* بردن bâr 1: *load, fruit (tree load)* بار ۱ (بَر ۳) PK, BQ, KM

414

بَرده

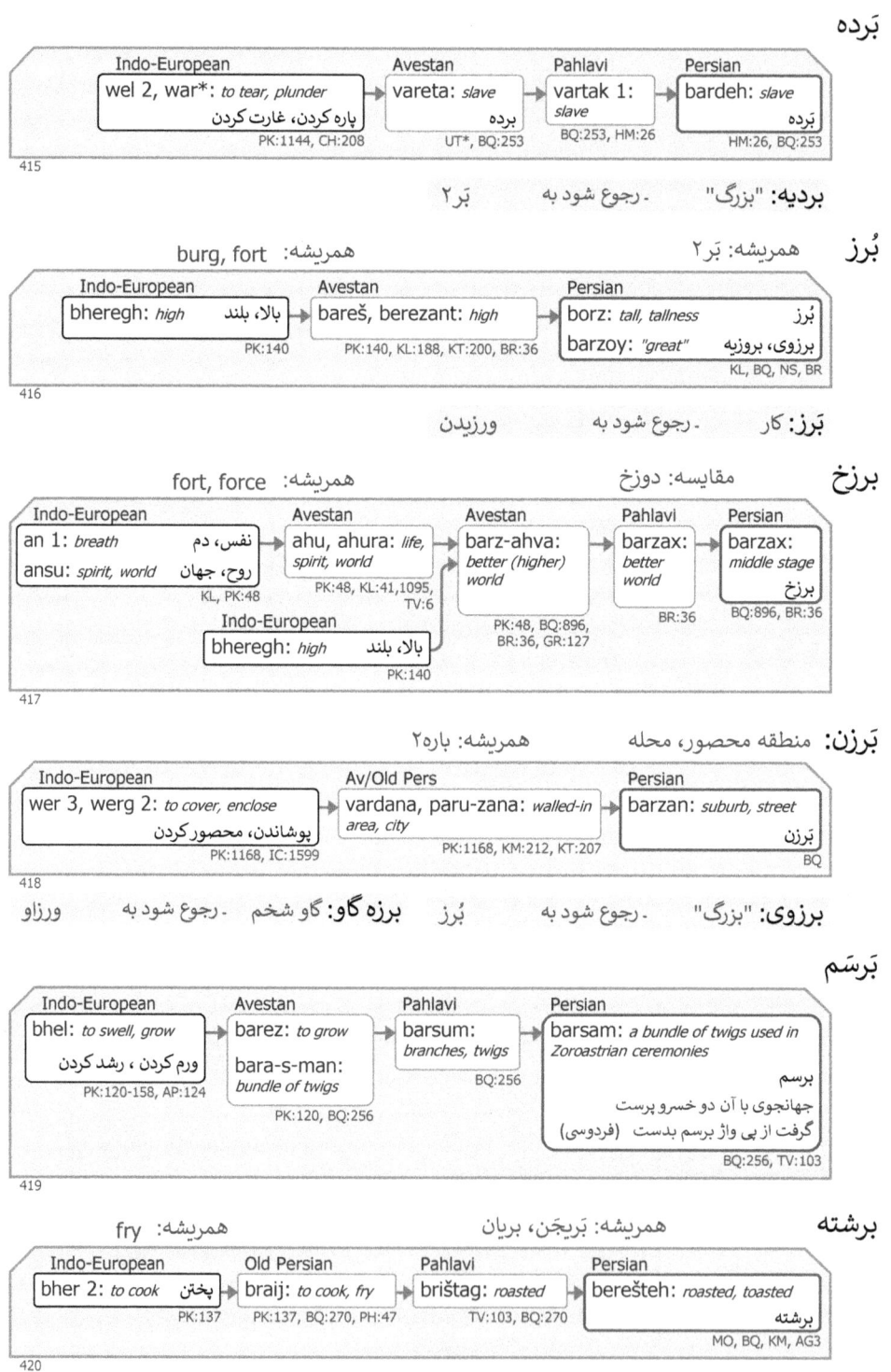

Indo-European	Avestan	Pahlavi	Persian
wel 2, war*: *to tear, plunder* پاره کردن، غارت کردن PK:1144, CH:208	vareta: *slave* برده UT*, BQ:253	vartak 1: *slave* BQ:253, HM:26	bardeh: *slave* بَرده HM:26, BQ:253

415

بَردیه: "بزرگ" ـ رجوع شود به   بَر ۲

بُرز

همریشه: بَر ۲   همریشه: burg, fort

Indo-European	Avestan	Persian
bheregh: *high* بالا، بلند PK:140	bareš, berezant: *high* PK:140, KL:188, KT:200, BR:36	بُرز borz: *tall, tallness* barzoy: *"great"* برزوی، بروزیه KL, BQ, NS, BR

416

بَرز: کار ـ رجوع شود به   ورزیدن

برزخ

مقایسه: دوزخ   همریشه: fort, force

Indo-European	Avestan	Avestan	Pahlavi	Persian
an 1: *breath* نفس، دم ansu: *spirit, world* روح، جهان KL, PK:48	ahu, ahura: *life, spirit, world* PK:48, KL:41,1095, TV:6	barz-ahva: *better (higher) world* PK:48, BQ:896, BR:36, GR:127	barzax: *better world* BR:36	barzax: *middle stage* برزخ BQ:896, BR:36
	Indo-European bheregh: *high* بالا، بلند PK:140			

417

بَرزن

همریشه: باره ۲   منطقه محصور، محله

Indo-European	Av/Old Pers	Persian
wer 3, werg 2: *to cover, enclose* پوشاندن، محصور کردن PK:1168, IC:1599	vardana, paru-zana: *walled-in area, city* PK:1168, KM:212, KT:207	barzan: *suburb, street* بَرزن BQ

418

برزوی: "بزرگ" ـ رجوع شود به   بُرز   **برزه گاو**: گاو شخم ـ رجوع شود به   ورزاو

بَرسَم

Indo-European	Avestan	Pahlavi	Persian
bhel: *to swell, grow* ورم کردن، رشد کردن PK:120-158, AP:124	barez: *to grow* bara-s-man: *bundle of twigs* PK:120, BQ:256	barsum: *branches, twigs* BQ:256	barsam: *a bundle of twigs used in Zoroastrian ceremonies* برسم جهانجوی با آن دو خسرو پرست گرفت از پی واژ برسم بدست (فردوسی) BQ:256, TV:103

419

برشته

همریشه: بَریجَن، بریان   همریشه: fry

Indo-European	Old Persian	Pahlavi	Persian
bher 2: *to cook* پختن PK:137	braij: *to cook, fry* PK:137, BQ:270, PH:47	brištag: *roasted* TV:103, BQ:270	berešteh: *roasted, toasted* برشته MO, BQ, KM, AG3

420

برغ، برغاب: بند آب ـ رجوع شود به   ورغ

برف

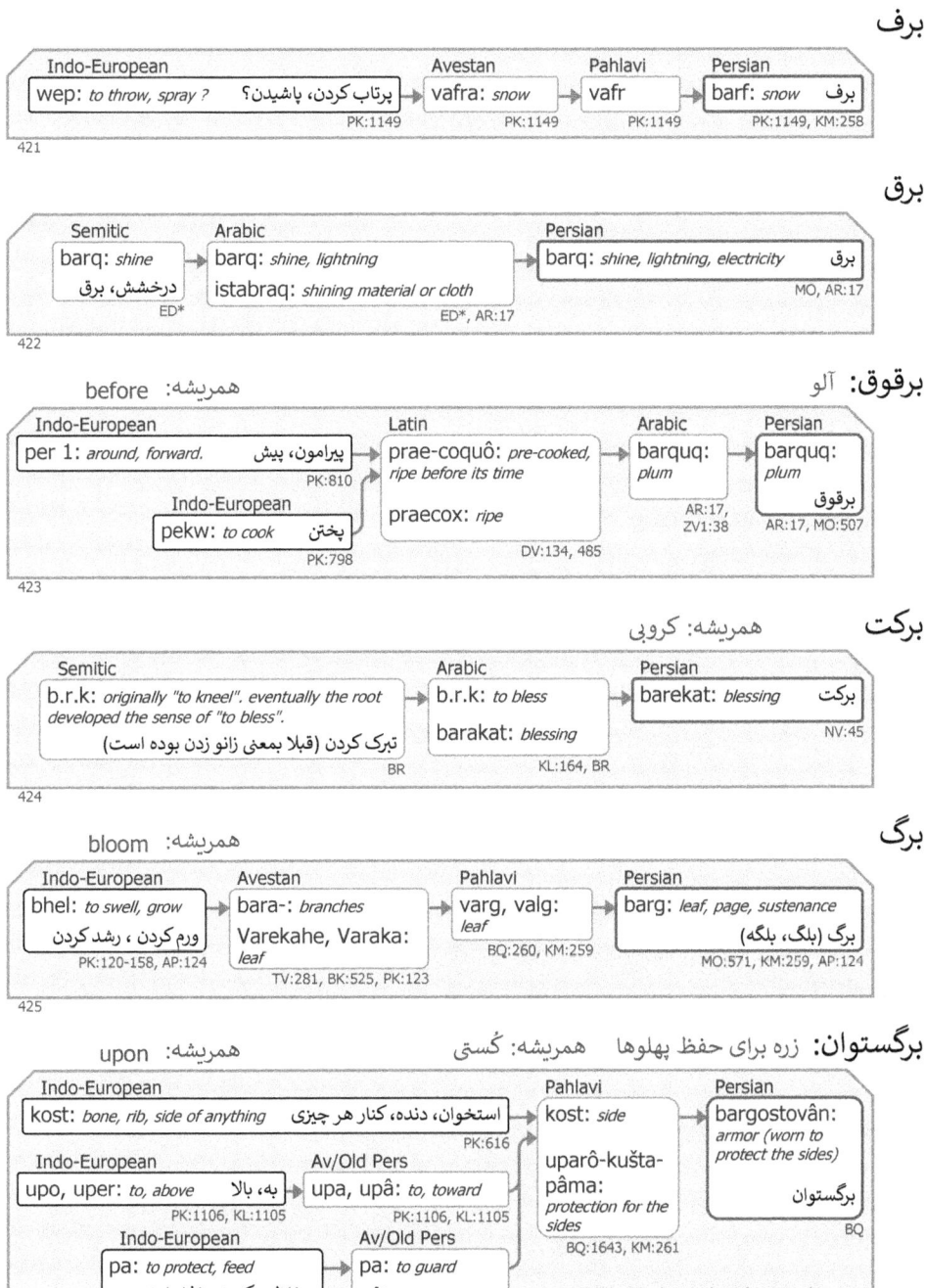

Indo-European	Avestan	Pahlavi	Persian
wep: to throw, spray ? پرتاب کردن، پاشیدن؟ PK:1149	vafra: snow PK:1149	vafr PK:1149	barf: snow برف PK:1149, KM:258

421

برق

Semitic	Arabic	Persian
barq: shine درخشش، برق ED*	barq: shine, lightning istabraq: shining material or cloth ED*, AR:17	barq: shine, lightning, electricity برق MO, AR:17

422

برقوق: آلو

همریشه: before

Indo-European	Latin	Arabic	Persian
per 1: around, forward. پیرامون، پیش PK:810 Indo-European pekw: to cook پختن PK:798	prae-coquô: pre-cooked, ripe before its time praecox: ripe DV:134, 485	barquq: plum AR:17, ZV1:38	barquq: plum برقوق AR:17, MO:507

423

برکت

همریشه: کروپی

Semitic	Arabic	Persian
b.r.k: originally "to kneel". eventually the root developed the sense of "to bless". تبرک کردن (قبلا بمعنی زانو زدن بوده است) BR	b.r.k: to bless barakat: blessing KL:164, BR	barekat: blessing برکت NV:45

424

برگ

همریشه: bloom

Indo-European	Avestan	Pahlavi	Persian
bhel: to swell, grow ورم کردن ، رشد کردن PK:120-158, AP:124	bara-: branches Varekahe, Varaka: leaf TV:281, BK:525, PK:123	varg, valg: leaf BQ:260, KM:259	barg: leaf, page, sustenance برگ (بلگ، بلگه) MO:571, KM:259, AP:124

425

برگستوان: زره برای حفظ پهلوها

همریشه: کُستی   همریشه: upon

Indo-European	Av/Old Pers	Pahlavi	Persian
kost: bone, rib, side of anything استخوان، دنده، کنار هر چیزی PK:616		kost: side uparô-kušta-pâma: protection for the sides BQ:1643, KM:261	bargostovân: armor (worn to protect the sides) برگستوان BQ
upo, uper: to, above به، بالا PK:1106, KL:1105	upa, upâ: to, toward PK:1106, KL:1105		
pa: to protect, feed حفاظت کردن، غذا دادن PK:787,842, BK:103	pa: to guard pâta: protected PH:41,72, KL:114	NOTE- AD claims that this may be related to the root "Ost: bone".	

426

برلیان

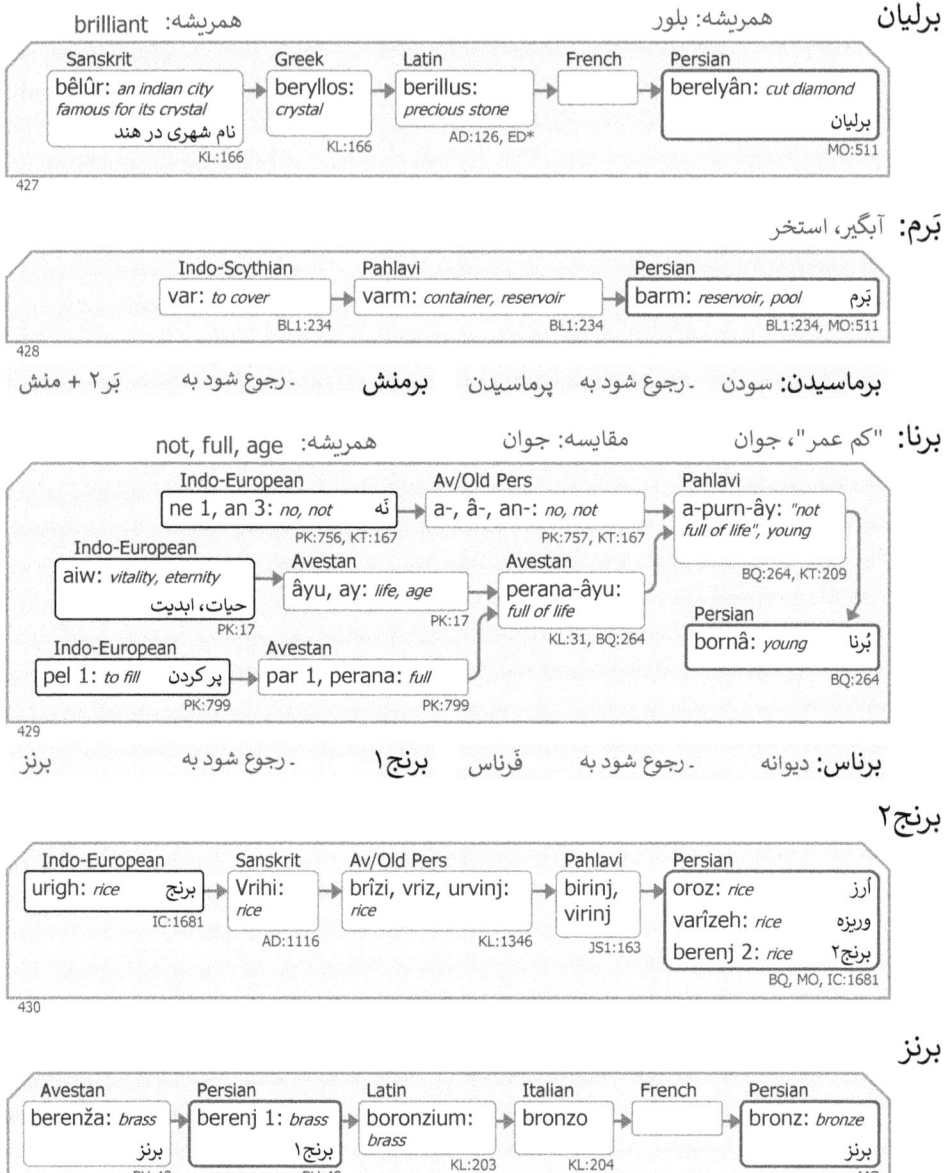

برلیان   همریشه: بلور   همریشه: brilliant

Sanskrit	Greek	Latin	French	Persian
bêlûr: an indian city famous for its crystal / نام شهری در هند	beryllos: crystal	berillus: precious stone		berelyân: cut diamond / برلیان
KL:166	KL:166	AD:126, ED*		MO:511

427

بَرم: آبگیر، استخر

Indo-Scythian	Pahlavi	Persian
var: to cover	varm: container, reservoir	barm: reservoir, pool بَرم
BL1:234	BL1:234	BL1:234, MO:511

428

برماسیدن: سودن ـ رجوع شود به پرماسیدن   **برمنش** ـ رجوع شود به بَر۲ + منش

برنا: "کم عمر"، جوان   مقایسه: جوان   همریشه: not, full, age

Indo-European	Av/Old Pers	Pahlavi
ne 1, an 3: no, not نَه	a-, â-, an-: no, not	a-purn-ây: "not full of life", young
PK:756, KT:167	PK:757, KT:167	BQ:264, KT:209

Indo-European	Avestan	Avestan	Persian
aiw: vitality, eternity / حیات، ابدیت	âyu, ay: life, age	perana-âyu: full of life	bornâ: young بُرنا
PK:17	PK:17	KL:31, BQ:264	BQ:264

Indo-European	Avestan
pel 1: to fill / پر کردن	par 1, perana: full
PK:799	PK:799

429

برناس: دیوانه   ـ رجوع شود به قَرناس   **برنج۱** ـ رجوع شود به برنز

برنج۲

Indo-European	Sanskrit	Av/Old Pers	Pahlavi	Persian
urigh: rice برنج	Vrihi: rice	brîzi, vriz, urvinj: rice	birinj, virinj	oroz: rice أرز varîzeh: rice وریزه berenj 2: rice برنج۲
IC:1681	AD:1116	KL:1346	JS1:163	BQ, MO, IC:1681

430

برنز

Avestan	Persian	Latin	Italian	French	Persian
berenža: brass برنز	berenj 1: brass برنج۱	boronzium: brass	bronzo		bronz: bronze برنز
PH:48	PH:48	KL:203	KL:204		MO

431

بُرو ـ رجوع شود به ابرو

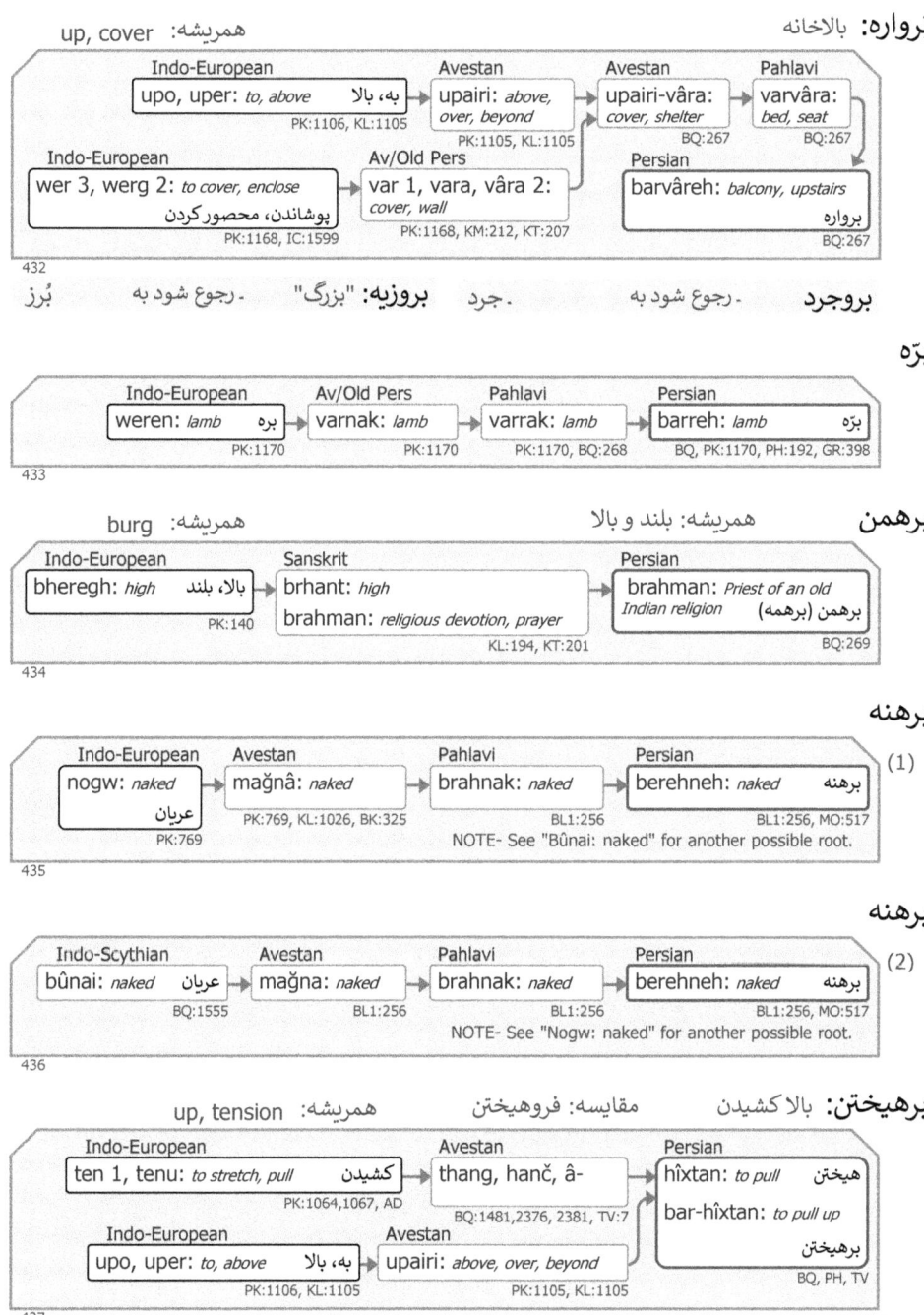

بَروارہ: بالاخانه

همریشه: up, cover

Indo-European
upo, uper: *to, above* به، بالا
PK:1106, KL:1105

Avestan
upairi: *above, over, beyond*
PK:1105, KL:1105

Avestan
upairi-vâra: *cover, shelter*
BQ:267

Pahlavi
varvâra: *bed, seat*
BQ:267

Indo-European
wer 3, werg 2: *to cover, enclose*
پوشاندن، محصورکردن
PK:1168, IC:1599

Av/Old Pers
var 1, vara, vâra 2: *cover, wall*
PK:1168, KM:212, KT:207

Persian
barvâreh: *balcony, upstairs*
برواره
BQ:267

432

بروجرد . رجوع شود به جرد **بروزیه:** "بزرگ" . رجوع شود به بُرز

بَرّہ

Indo-European
weren: *lamb* برہ
PK:1170

Av/Old Pers
varnak: *lamb*
PK:1170

Pahlavi
varrak: *lamb*
PK:1170, BQ:268

Persian
barreh: *lamb* بَرّہ
BQ, PK:1170, PH:192, GR:398

433

برهمن

همریشه: بلند و بالا

همریشه: burg

Indo-European
bheregh: *high* بالا، بلند
PK:140

Sanskrit
brhant: *high*
brahman: *religious devotion, prayer*
KL:194, KT:201

Persian
brahman: *Priest of an old Indian religion* برهمن (برهمه)
BQ:269

434

برهنه

Indo-European
nogw: *naked*
عریان
PK:769

Avestan
maǧnâ: *naked*
PK:769, KL:1026, BK:325

Pahlavi
brahnak: *naked*
BL1:256

Persian
berehneh: *naked* برهنه
BL1:256, MO:517

NOTE- See "Bûnai: naked" for another possible root.

(1)

435

برهنه

Indo-Scythian
bûnai: *naked* عریان
BQ:1555

Avestan
maǧna: *naked*
BL1:256

Pahlavi
brahnak: *naked*
BL1:256

Persian
berehneh: *naked* برهنه
BL1:256, MO:517

NOTE- See "Nogw: naked" for another possible root.

(2)

436

برهیختن: بالاکشیدن

مقایسه: فروهیختن

همریشه: up, tension

Indo-European
ten 1, tenu: *to stretch, pull* کشیدن
PK:1064,1067, AD

Avestan
thang, hanč, â-
BQ:1481,2376, 2381, TV:7

Persian
hîxtan: *to pull* هیختن
bar-hîxtan: *to pull up* برهیختن
BQ, PH, TV

Indo-European
upo, uper: *to, above* به، بالا
PK:1106, KL:1105

Avestan
upairi: *above, over, beyond*
PK:1105, KL:1105

437

78

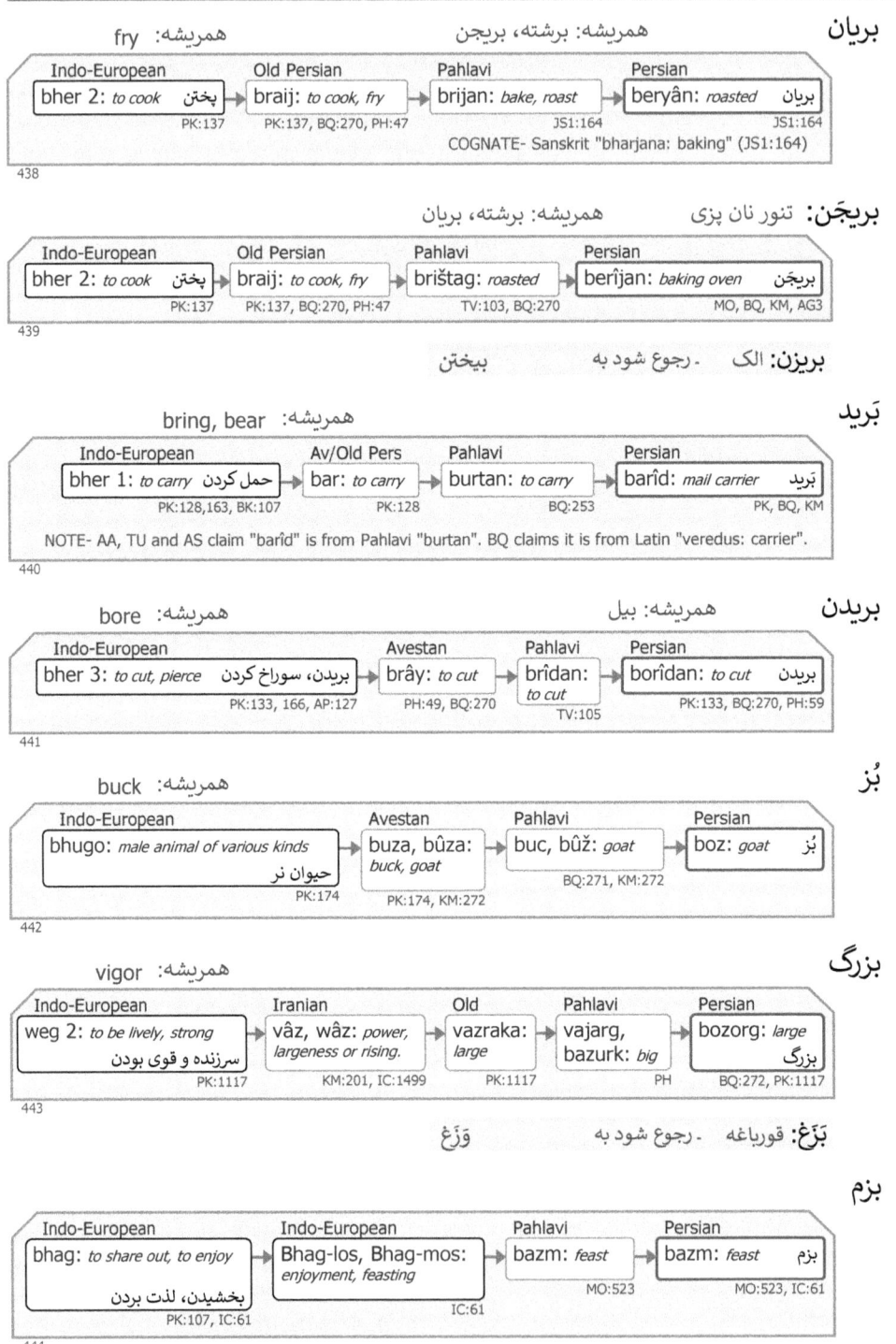

بریان

همریشه: fry   همریشه: برشته، بریجن

Indo-European	Old Persian	Pahlavi	Persian
bher 2: *to cook* پختن	braij: *to cook, fry*	brijan: *bake, roast*	beryân: *roasted* بریان
PK:137	PK:137, BQ:270, PH:47	JS1:164	JS1:164

COGNATE- Sanskrit "bharjana: baking" (JS1:164)

438

بریجَن: تنور نان پزی   همریشه: برشته، بریان

Indo-European	Old Persian	Pahlavi	Persian
bher 2: *to cook* پختن	braij: *to cook, fry*	brištag: *roasted*	berîjan: *baking oven* بریجَن
PK:137	PK:137, BQ:270, PH:47	TV:103, BQ:270	MO, BQ, KM, AG3

439

بریزن: الک ‐ رجوع شود به   بیختن

بَرید

همریشه: bring, bear

Indo-European	Av/Old Pers	Pahlavi	Persian
bher 1: *to carry* حمل کردن	bar: *to carry*	burtan: *to carry*	barîd: *mail carrier* بَرید
PK:128,163, BK:107	PK:128	BQ:253	PK, BQ, KM

NOTE- AA, TU and AS claim "barîd" is from Pahlavi "burtan". BQ claims it is from Latin "veredus: carrier".

440

بریدن

همریشه: bore   همریشه: بیل

Indo-European	Avestan	Pahlavi	Persian
bher 3: *to cut, pierce* بریدن، سوراخ کردن	brây: *to cut*	brîdan: *to cut*	borîdan: *to cut* بریدن
PK:133, 166, AP:127	PH:49, BQ:270	TV:105	PK:133, BQ:270, PH:59

441

بُز

همریشه: buck

Indo-European	Avestan	Pahlavi	Persian
bhugo: *male animal of various kinds* حیوان نر	buza, bûza: *buck, goat*	buc, bûž: *goat*	boz: *goat* بُز
PK:174	PK:174, KM:272	BQ:271, KM:272	

442

بزرگ

همریشه: vigor

Indo-European	Iranian	Old	Pahlavi	Persian
weg 2: *to be lively, strong* سرزنده و قوی بودن	vâz, wâz: *power, largeness or rising.*	vazraka: *large*	vajarg, bazurk: *big*	bozorg: *large* بزرگ
PK:1117	KM:201, IC:1499	PK:1117	PH	BQ:272, PK:1117

443

بَزَغ: قورباغه ‐ رجوع شود به   وَزَغ

بزم

Indo-European	Indo-European	Pahlavi	Persian
bhag: *to share out, to enjoy* بخشیدن، لذت بردن	Bhag-los, Bhag-mos: *enjoyment, feasting*	bazm: *feast*	bazm: *feast* بزم
PK:107, IC:61	IC:61	MO:523	MO:523, IC:61

444

بِزه: خطا، گناه

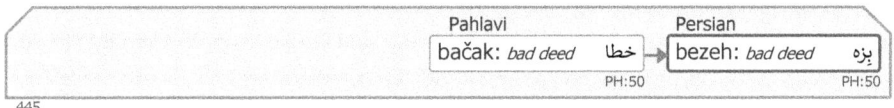

Pahlavi	Persian
bačak: *bad deed* خطا	bezeh: *bad deed* بِزه
PH:50	PH:50

445

بَس   همریشه: بسیار، هوس

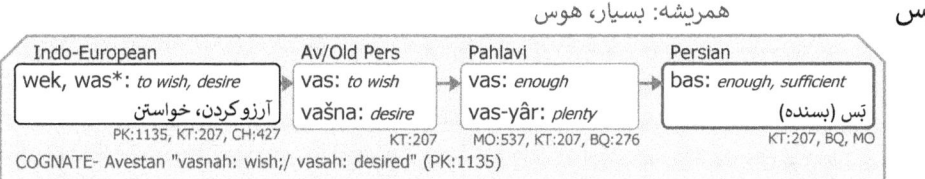

Indo-European	Av/Old Pers	Pahlavi	Persian
wek, was*: *to wish, desire* آرزو کردن، خواستن	vas: *to wish* vašna: *desire*	vas: *enough* vas-yâr: *plenty*	bas: *enough, sufficient* بَس (بسنده)
PK:1135, KT:207, CH:427	KT:207	MO:537, KT:207, BQ:276	KT:207, BQ, MO

COGNATE- Avestan "vasnah: wish;/ vasah: desired" (PK:1135)

446

تَساک: تاج گُل

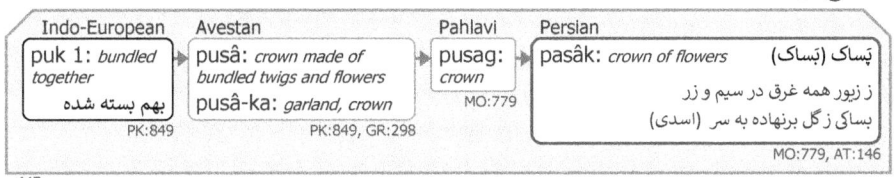

Indo-European	Avestan	Pahlavi	Persian
puk 1: *bundled together* بهم بسته شده	pusâ: *crown made of bundled twigs and flowers* pusâ-ka: *garland, crown*	pusag: *crown* MO:779	pasâk: *crown of flowers* (تَساک) تَساک ز زیور همه غرق در سیم و زر تَسای ز گل برنهاده به سر (اسدی)
PK:849	PK:849, GR:298		MO:779, AT:146

447

بستان   - رجوع شود به   بو

بستر   مقایسه: گستردن   همریشه: wide

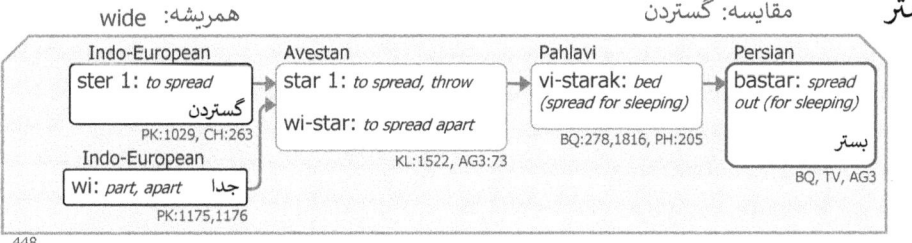

Indo-European	Avestan	Pahlavi	Persian
ster 1: *to spread* گستردن PK:1029, CH:263	star 1: *to spread, throw* wi-star: *to spread apart*	vi-starak: *bed* (spread for sleeping)	bastar: *spread out (for sleeping)* بستر
Indo-European wi: *part, apart* جدا PK:1175,1176	KL:1522, AG3:73	BQ:278,1816, PH:205	BQ, TV, AG3

448

بستن ۱   همریشه: bind

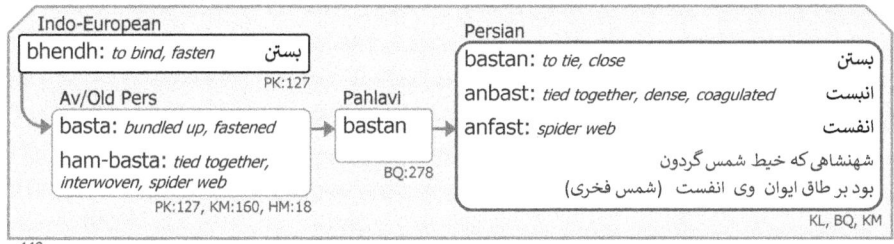

Indo-European		Pahlavi	Persian
bhendh: *to bind, fasten* بستن PK:127			bastan: *to tie, close* بستن
Av/Old Pers basta: *bundled up, fastened* ham-basta: *tied together, interwoven, spider web* PK:127, KM:160, HM:18		bastan BQ:278	anbast: *tied together, dense, coagulated* انبست anfast: *spider web* انفست شهنشاهی که خیط شمس گردون بود بر طاق ایوان وی انفست (شمس فخری) KL, BQ, KM

449

بستن ۲: سفت شدن نظیر ماست یا خون

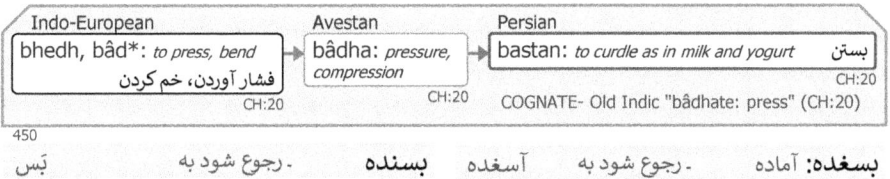

Indo-European	Avestan	Persian
bhedh, bâd*: *to press, bend* فشار آوردن، خم کردن CH:20	bâdha: *pressure, compression* CH:20	bastan: *to curdle as in milk and yogurt* بستن CH:20

COGNATE- Old Indic "bâdhate: press" (CH:20)

450

بسغده: آماده - رجوع شود به آسغده   بسنده - رجوع شود به بَس

بسیار همریشه: بَس، هوس

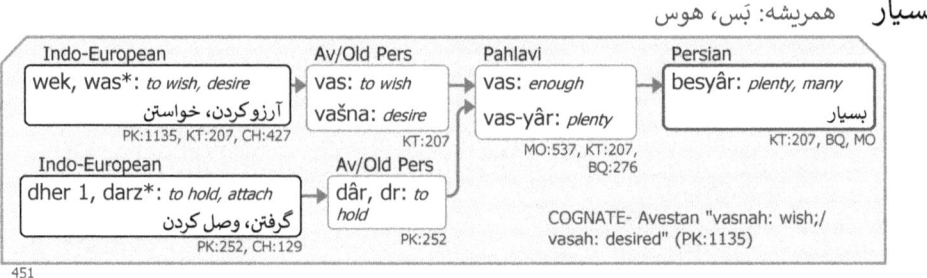

Indo-European	Av/Old Pers	Pahlavi	Persian
wek, was*: to wish, desire آرزو کردن، خواستن PK:1135, KT:207, CH:427	vas: to wish vašna: desire KT:207	vas: enough vas-yâr: plenty MO:537, KT:207, BQ:276	besyâr: plenty, many بسیار KT:207, BQ, MO
Indo-European	Av/Old Pers		
dher 1, darz*: to hold, attach گرفتن، وصل کردن PK:252, CH:129	dâr, dr: to hold PK:252		COGNATE- Avestan "vasnah: wish;/ vasah: desired" (PK:1135)

451

بسیج: کار سازی، آماده گردیدن   همریشه: ساختن

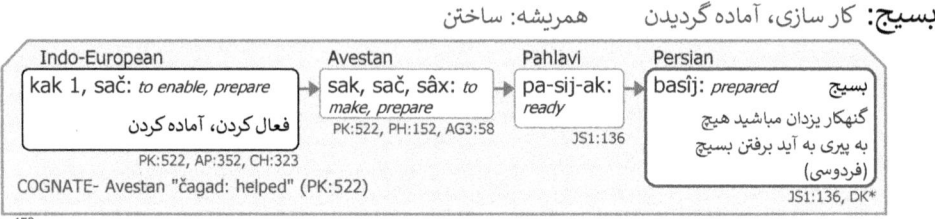

Indo-European	Avestan	Pahlavi	Persian
kak 1, sač: to enable, prepare فعال کردن، آماده کردن PK:522, AP:352, CH:323	sak, sač, sâx: to make, prepare PK:522, PH:152, AG3:58	pa-sij-ak: ready JS1:136	basîj: prepared بسیج گنهکار یزدان مباشید هیچ به پیری به آید برفتن بسیچ (فردوسی) JS1:136, DK*

COGNATE- Avestan "čagad: helped" (PK:522)

452

بُش: یال

همریشه: barrow

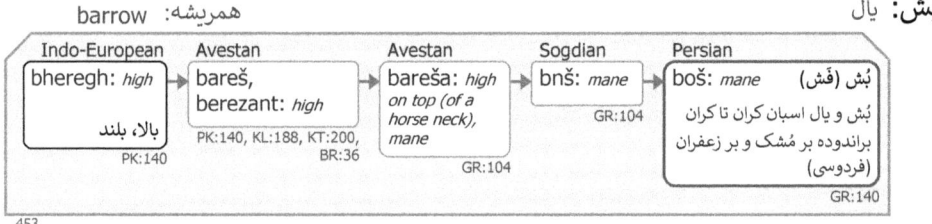

Indo-European	Avestan	Avestan	Sogdian	Persian
bheregh: high بالا، بلند PK:140	bareš, berezant: high PK:140, KL:188, KT:200, BR:36	bareša: high on top (of a horse neck), mane GR:104	bnš: mane GR:104	boš: mane (بُش (قَش بُش و یال اسبان کران تا کران براندوده بر مُشک و بر زعفران (فردوسی) GR:140

453

بَشن: قد و بالا

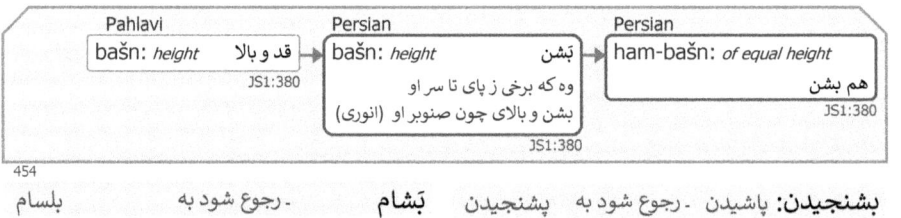

Pahlavi	Persian	Persian
bašn: height قد و بالا JS1:380	bašn: height بَشن وه که برخی ز پای تا سر او بشن و بالای چون صنوبر او (انوری) JS1:380	ham-bašn: of equal height هم بشن JS1:380

454

بشنجیدن: پاشیدن ۔ رجوع شود به   پشنجیدن   بَشام ۔ رجوع شود به   بلسام

بَط

NOTE- HM is not certain about this root

Indo-European	Persian
pad-: duck مرغابی AP:113	bat: duck بَط AP:113

455

بطریق

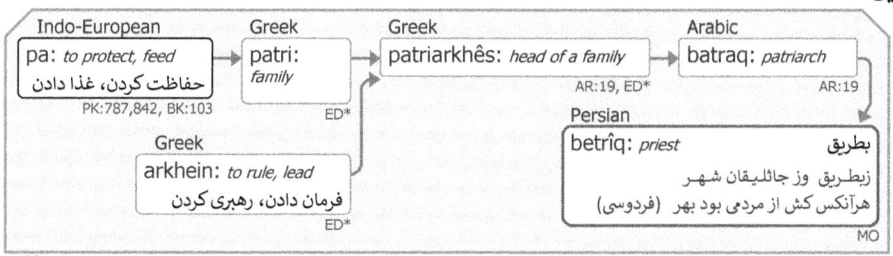

بغ: بخشنده

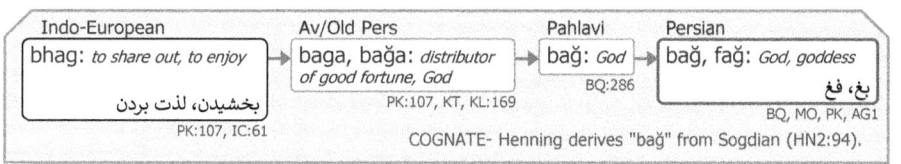

بغچه

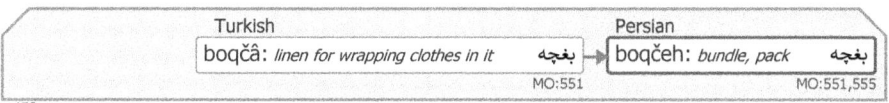

بغداد: "خدا داد" یا "باغ عدالت"

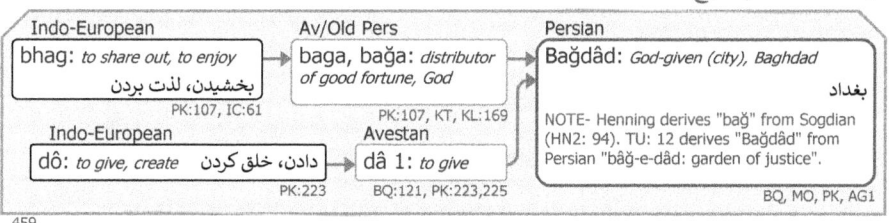

بغستان: "جایگاه خدا"

pagoda, stand :همریشه

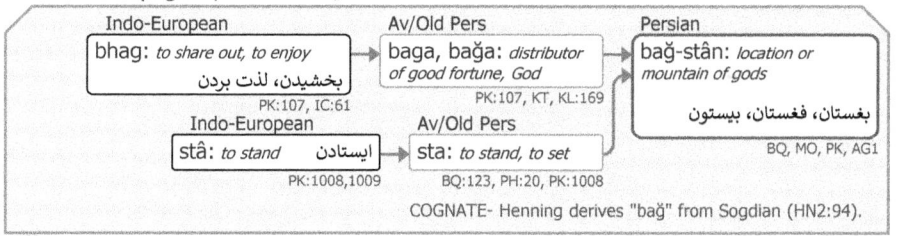

بَک: قورباغه، وزغ

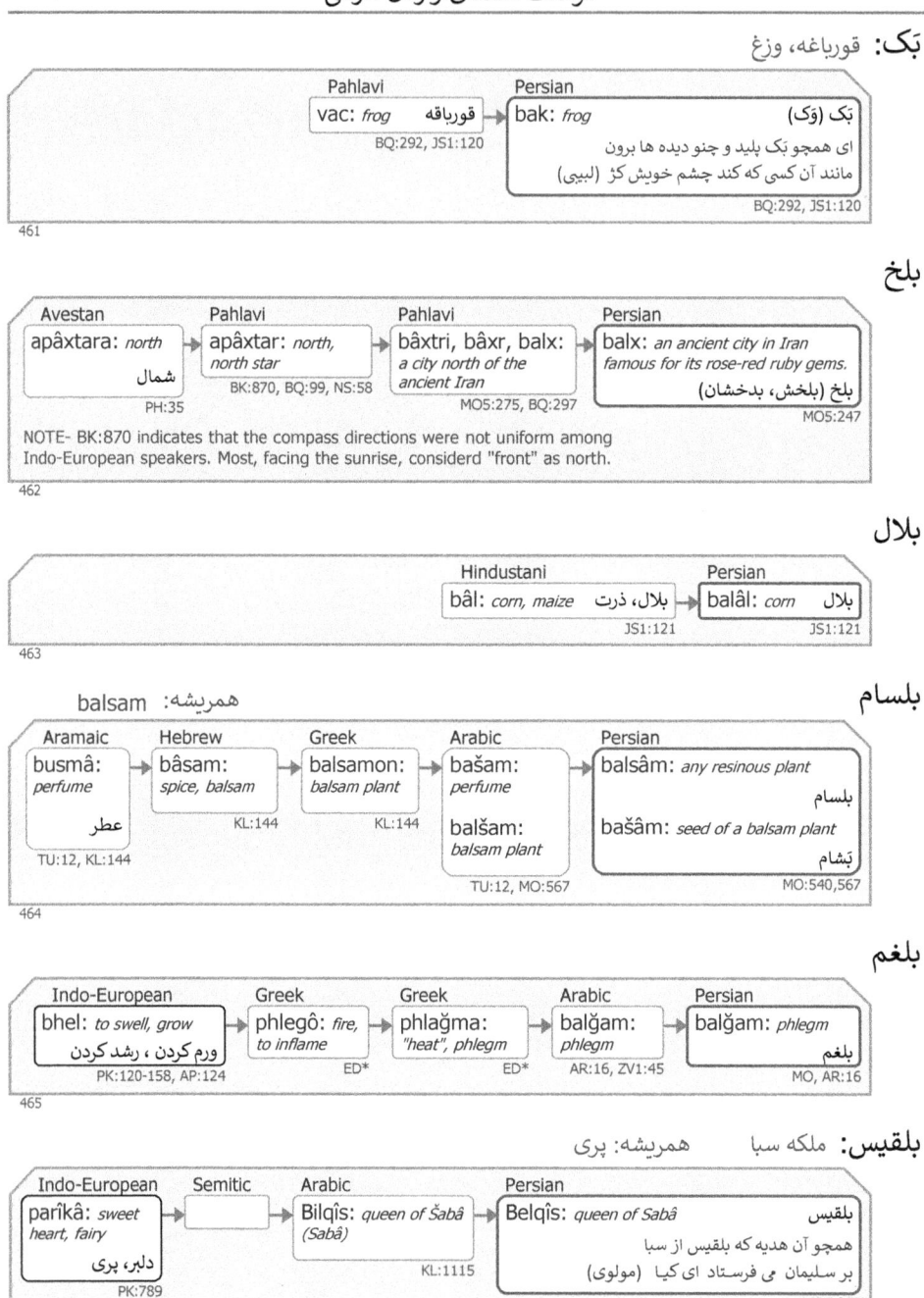

Pahlavi
vac: *frog* قورباقه
BQ:292, JS1:120

Persian
bak: *frog* بَک (وَک)
ای همچو بَک پلید و چنو دیده ها برون
مانند آن کسی که کند چشم خویش کژ (لبیبی)
BQ:292, JS1:120

461

بلخ

Avestan
apâxtara: *north*
شمال
PH:35

Pahlavi
apâxtar: *north, north star*
BK:870, BQ:99, NS:58

Pahlavi
bâxtri, bâxr, balx: *a city north of the ancient Iran*
MO5:275, BQ:297

Persian
balx: *an ancient city in Iran famous for its rose-red ruby gems*
بلخ (بلخش، بدخشان)
MO5:247

NOTE- BK:870 indicates that the compass directions were not uniform among Indo-European speakers. Most, facing the sunrise, considerd "front" as north.

462

بلال

Hindustani
bâl: *corn, maize* بلال، ذرت
JS1:121

Persian
balâl: *corn* بلال
JS1:121

463

بلسام

همریشه: balsam

Aramaic
busmâ: *perfume*
عطر
TU:12, KL:144

Hebrew
bâsam: *spice, balsam*
KL:144

Greek
balsamon: *balsam plant*
KL:144

Arabic
bašam: *perfume*
balšam: *balsam plant*
TU:12, MO:567

Persian
balsâm: *any resinous plant*
بلسام
bašâm: *seed of a balsam plant*
بَشام
MO:540,567

464

بلغم

Indo-European
bhel: *to swell, grow*
ورم کردن ، رشد کردن
PK:120-158, AP:124

Greek
phlegô: *fire, to inflame*
ED*

Greek
phlaǧma: *"heat", phlegm*
ED*

Arabic
balǧam: *phlegm*
AR:16, ZV1:45

Persian
balǧam: *phlegm*
بلغم
MO, AR:16

465

بلقیس: ملکه سبا   همریشه: پری

Indo-European
parîkâ: *sweet heart, fairy*
دلبر، پری
PK:789

Semitic

Arabic
Bilqîs: *queen of Šabâ (Sabâ)*
KL:1115

Persian
Belqîs: *queen of Sabâ*
بلقیس
همچو آن هدیه که بلقیس از سبا
بر سلیمان می فرستاد ای کیا (مولوی)
MO5:277

466

بلگه   ـ رجوع شود به   برگ

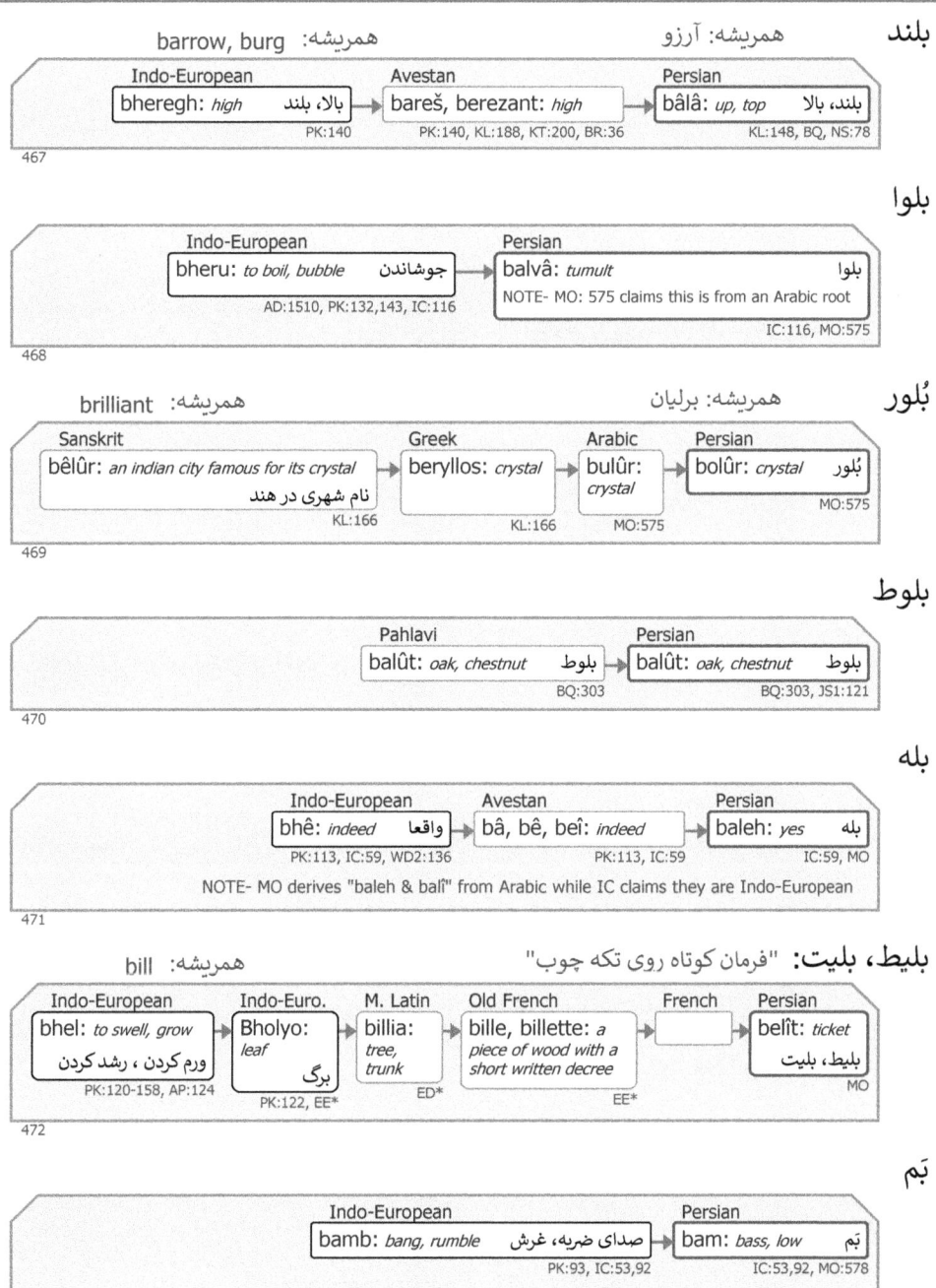

بلند

همریشه: آرزو   همریشه: barrow, burg

Indo-European	Avestan	Persian
bheregh: *high* بالا، بلند	bareš, berezant: *high*	bâlâ: *up, top* بلند، بالا
PK:140	PK:140, KL:188, KT:200, BR:36	KL:148, BQ, NS:78

467

بلوا

Indo-European	Persian
bheru: *to boil, bubble* جوشاندن	balvâ: *tumult* بلوا
AD:1510, PK:132,143, IC:116	NOTE- MO: 575 claims this is from an Arabic root
	IC:116, MO:575

468

بُلور

همریشه: برلیان   همریشه: brilliant

Sanskrit	Greek	Arabic	Persian
bêlûr: *an indian city famous for its crystal* نام شهری در هند	beryllos: *crystal*	bulûr: *crystal*	bolûr: *crystal* بُلور
KL:166	KL:166	MO:575	MO:575

469

بلوط

Pahlavi	Persian
balût: *oak, chestnut* بلوط	balût: *oak, chestnut* بلوط
BQ:303	BQ:303, JS1:121

470

بله

Indo-European	Avestan	Persian
bhê: *indeed* واقعا	bâ, bê, beî: *indeed*	baleh: *yes* بله
PK:113, IC:59, WD2:136	PK:113, IC:59	IC:59, MO

NOTE- MO derives "baleh & balî" from Arabic while IC claims they are Indo-European

471

بلیط، بلیت: "فرمان کوتاه روی تکه چوب"

همریشه: bill

Indo-European	Indo-Euro.	M. Latin	Old French	French	Persian
bhel: *to swell, grow* ورم کردن ، رشد کردن	Bholyo: *leaf* برگ	billia: *tree, trunk*	bille, billette: *a piece of wood with a short written decree*		belît: *ticket* بلیط، بلیت
PK:120-158, AP:124	PK:122, EE*	ED*	EE*		MO

472

بَم

Indo-European	Persian
bamb: *bang, rumble* صدای ضربه، غرش	bam: *bass, low* بَم
PK:93, IC:53,92	IC:53,92, MO:578

NOTE- MO derives this word from Arabic but IC claims it is Indo-European

473

بُن۱: پایه

همریشه: foundation

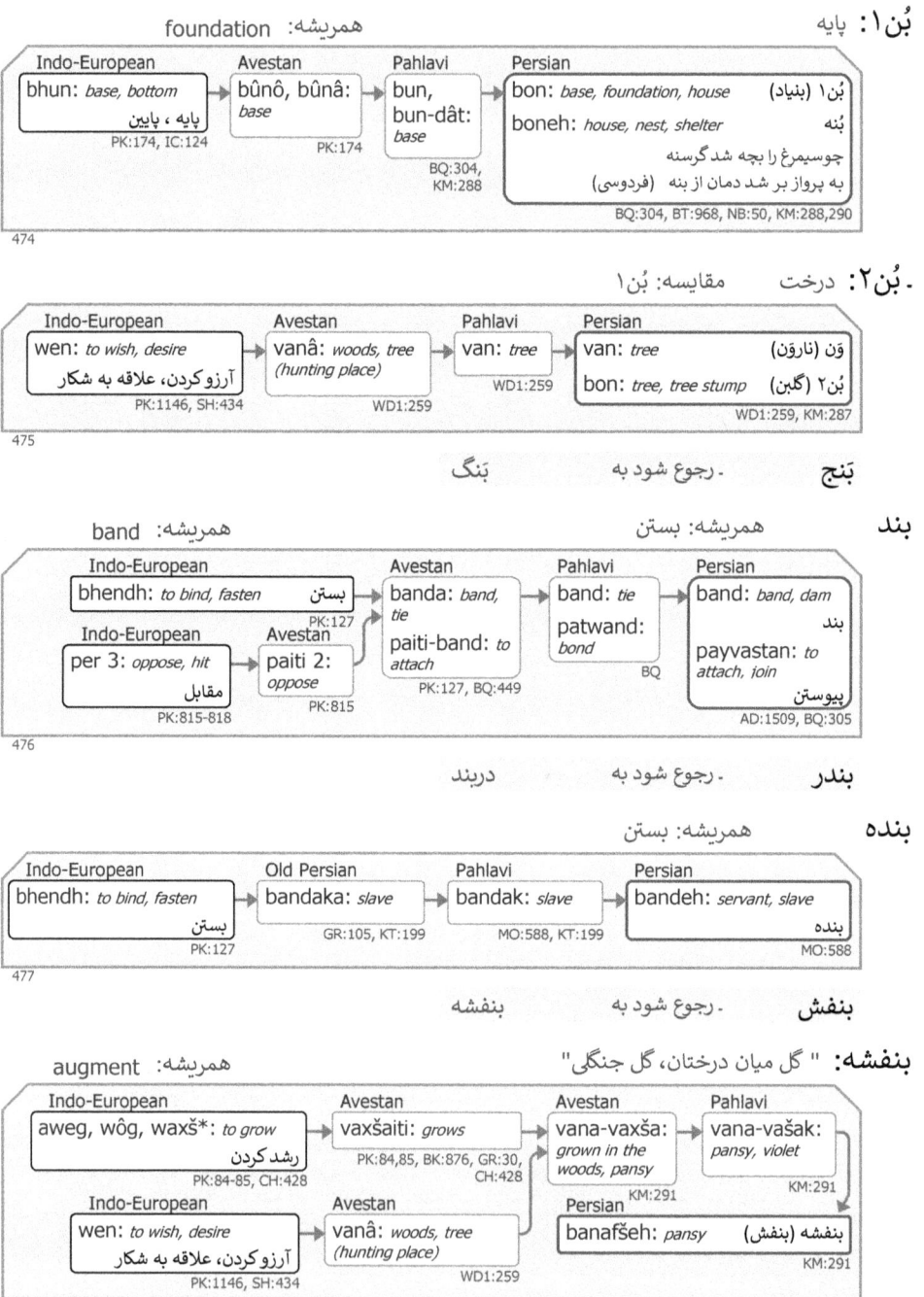

Indo-European	Avestan	Pahlavi	Persian
bhun: base, bottom / پایه ، پایین / PK:174, IC:124	bûnô, bûnâ: base / PK:174	bun, bun-dât: base / BQ:304, KM:288	بُن۱ (بنیاد) bon: base, foundation, house / بُنه boneh: house, nest, shelter / چوسیمرغ را بچه شد گرسنه / به پرواز بر شد دمان از بنه (فردوسی) / BQ:304, BT:968, NB:50, KM:288,290

474

ـ بُن۲: درخت   مقایسه: بُن۱

Indo-European	Avestan	Pahlavi	Persian
wen: to wish, desire / آرزو کردن، علاقه به شکار / PK:1146, SH:434	vanâ: woods, tree (hunting place) / WD1:259	van: tree / WD1:259	وَن (نارون) van: tree / بُن۲ (گبین) bon: tree, tree stump / WD1:259, KM:287

475

بَنج   ـ رجوع شود به   بَنگ

بند   همریشه: بستن   همریشه: band

Indo-European	Avestan	Pahlavi	Persian
bhendh: to bind, fasten / بستن / PK:127	banda: band, tie / paiti-band: to attach / PK:127, BQ:449	band: tie / patwand: bond / BQ	band: band, dam / بند / payvastan: to attach, join / پیوستن / AD:1509, BQ:305
Indo-European	Avestan		
per 3: oppose, hit / مقابل / PK:815-818	paiti 2: oppose / PK:815		

476

بندر   ـ رجوع شود به   دریند

بنده   همریشه: بستن

Indo-European	Old Persian	Pahlavi	Persian
bhendh: to bind, fasten / بستن / PK:127	bandaka: slave / GR:105, KT:199	bandak: slave / MO:588, KT:199	bandeh: servant, slave / بنده / MO:588

477

بنفش   ـ رجوع شود به   بنفشه

بنفشه: " گل میان درختان، گل جنگی"   همریشه: augment

Indo-European	Avestan	Avestan	Pahlavi
aweg, wôg, waxš*: to grow / رشد کردن / PK:84-85, CH:428	vaxšaiti: grows / PK:84,85, BK:876, GR:30, CH:428	vana-vaxša: grown in the woods, pansy / KM:291	vana-vašak: pansy, violet / KM:291
Indo-European	Avestan	Persian	
wen: to wish, desire / آرزو کردن، علاقه به شکار / PK:1146, SH:434	vanâ: woods, tree (hunting place) / WD1:259	banafšeh: pansy / بنفشه (بنفش) / KM:291	

478

بَنگ: نوعی از مواد مخدر

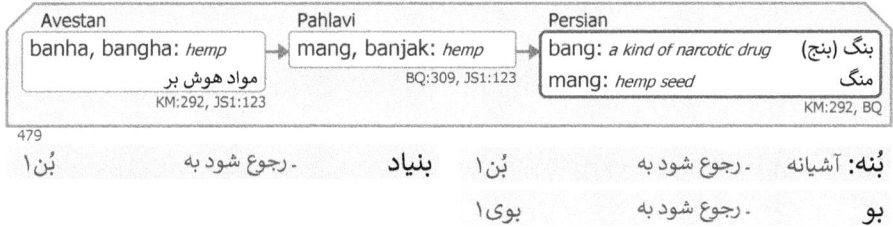

Avestan	Pahlavi	Persian
banha, bangha: *hemp*	mang, banjak: *hemp*	bang: *a kind of narcotic drug* (بنج) بَنگ
مواد هوش بر	BQ:309, JS1:123	mang: *hemp seed* مَنگ
KM:292, JS1:123		KM:292, BQ

479

بُنه: آشیانه ‧ رجوع شود به بُن۱   **بنیاد**   ‧ رجوع شود به بُن۱

بو ‧ رجوع شود به بوی۱

بوب

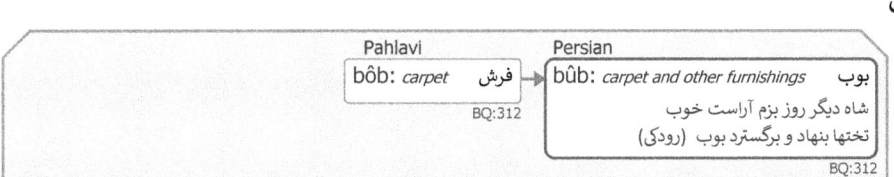

Pahlavi	Persian
bôb: *carpet* فرش	bûb: *carpet and other furnishings* بوب
BQ:312	شاه دیگر روز بزم آراست خوب
	تختها بنهاد و برگسترد بوب (رودکی)
	BQ:312

480

بوتیمار

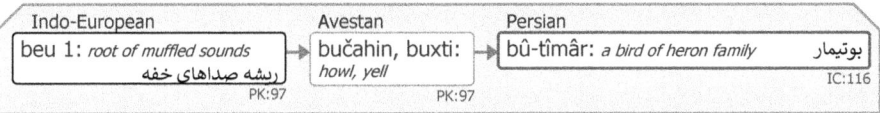

Indo-European	Avestan	Persian
beu 1: *root of muffled sounds*	bučahin, buxti: *howl, yell*	bû-tîmâr: *a bird of heron family* بوتیمار
ریشه صداهای خفه		IC:116
PK:97	PK:97	

481

بوختن: نجات دادن

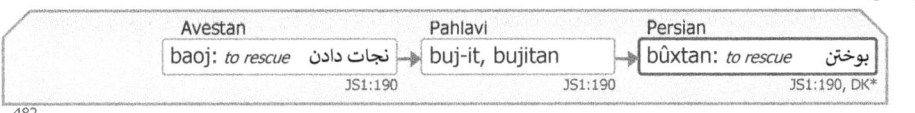

Avestan	Pahlavi	Persian
baoj: *to rescue* نجات دادن	buj-it, bujitan	bûxtan: *to rescue* بوختن
JS1:190	JS1:190	JS1:190, DK*

482

بودا

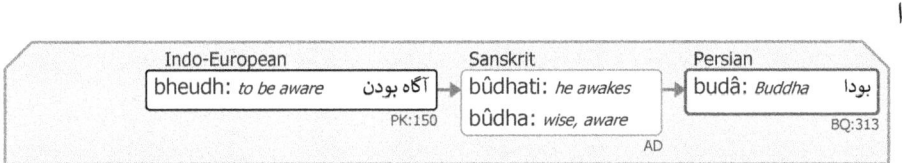

Indo-European	Sanskrit	Persian
bheudh: *to be aware* آگاه بودن	bûdhati: *he awakes*	budâ: *Buddha* بودا
PK:150	bûdha: *wise, aware*	BQ:313
	AD	

483

بودجه: "کیسه چرمی پول"

همریشه: budget

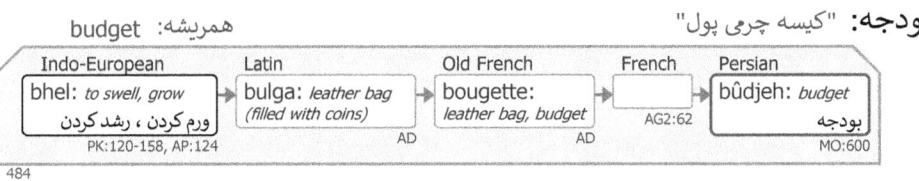

Indo-European	Latin	Old French	French	Persian
bhel: *to swell, grow*	bulga: *leather bag* (filled with coins)	bougette: *leather bag, budget*		bûdjeh: *budget* بودجه
ورم کردن ، رشد کردن	AD	AD	AG2:62	MO:600
PK:120-158, AP:124				

484

بودن

همریشه: be

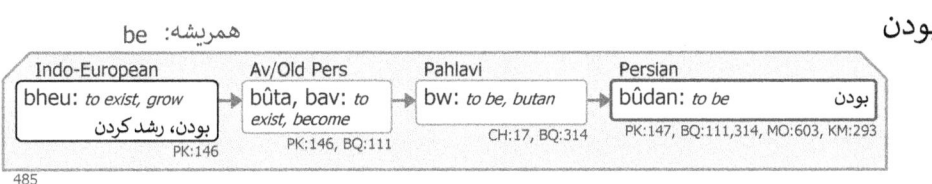

Indo-European	Av/Old Pers	Pahlavi	Persian
bheu: *to exist, grow*	bûta, bav: *to exist, become*	bw: *to be, butan*	bûdan: *to be* بودن
بودن ، رشد کردن	PK:146, BQ:111	CH:17, BQ:314	PK:147, BQ:111,314, MO:603, KM:293
PK:146			

485

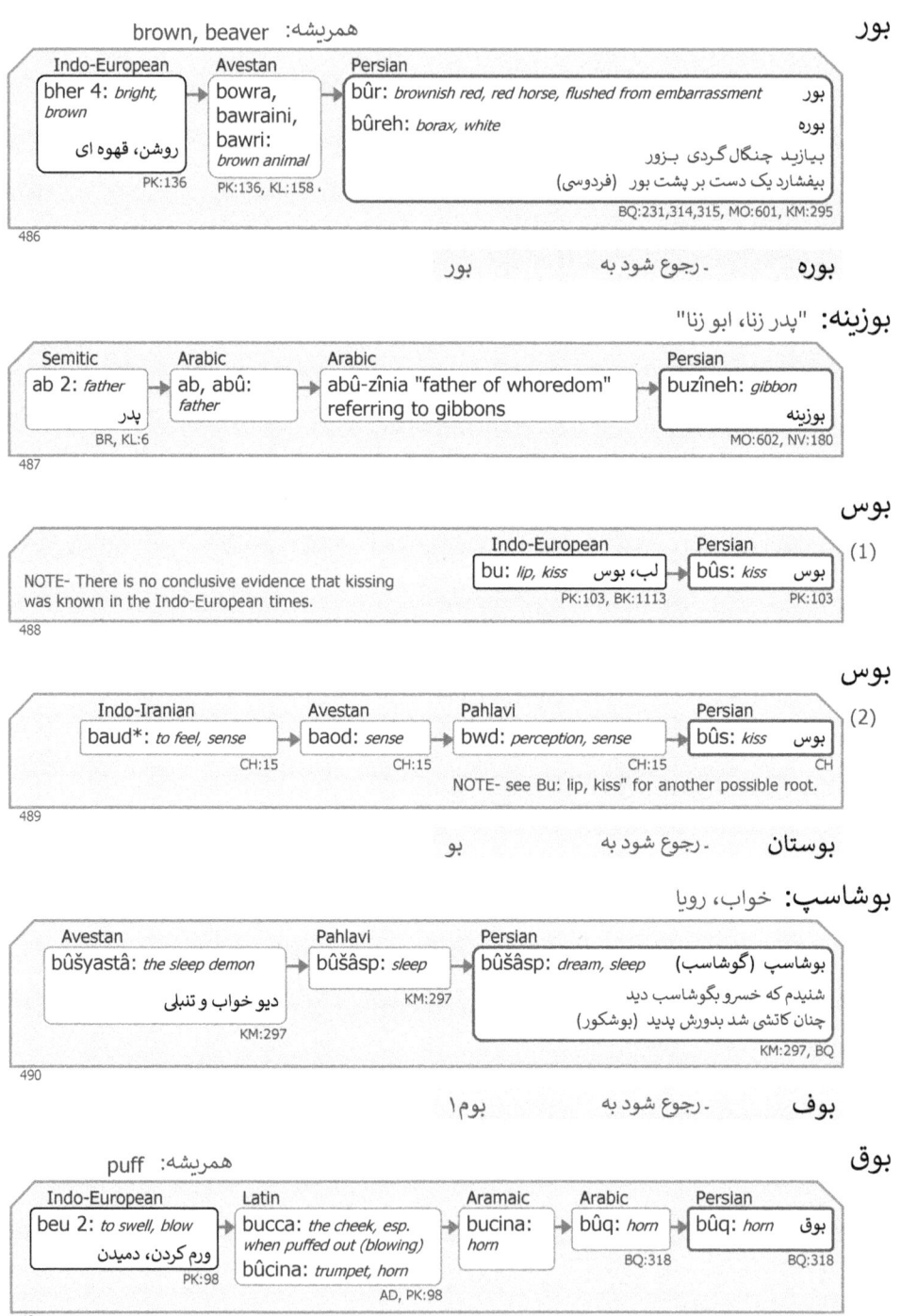

بور همریشه: brown, beaver

Indo-European	Avestan	Persian
bher 4: *bright, brown* روشن، قهوه ای	bowra, bawraini, bawri: *brown animal*	bûr: *brownish red, red horse, flushed from embarrassment* بور
		bûreh: *borax, white* بوره
PK:136	PK:136, KL:158،	بیازید چنگل گردی بـزور
		ببفشارد یک دست بر پشت بور (فردوسی)
486		BQ:231,314,315, MO:601, KM:295

بوره ـ رجوع شود به بور

بوزینه: "پدر زنا، ابو زنا"

Semitic	Arabic	Arabic	Persian
ab 2: *father* پدر	ab, abû: *father*	abû-zînia "father of whoredom" referring to gibbons	buzîneh: *gibbon* بوزینه
BR, KL:6			MO:602, NV:180
487			

بوس (1)

	Indo-European	Persian
NOTE- There is no conclusive evidence that kissing was known in the Indo-European times.	bu: *lip, kiss* لب، بوس	bûs: *kiss* بوس
	PK:103, BK:1113	PK:103
488		

بوس (2)

Indo-Iranian	Avestan	Pahlavi	Persian
baud*: *to feel, sense*	baod: *sense*	bwd: *perception, sense*	bûs: *kiss* بوس
CH:15	CH:15	CH:15	CH
		NOTE- see Bu: lip, kiss" for another possible root.	
489			

بوستان ـ رجوع شود به بو

بوشاسپ: خواب، رویا

Avestan	Pahlavi	Persian
bûšyastâ: *the sleep demon* دیو خواب و تنبلی	bûšâsp: *sleep*	bûšâsp: *dream, sleep* بوشاسپ (گوشاسب)
	KM:297	شنیدم که خسرو بگوشاسب دید
KM:297		چنان کاتشی شد بدورش پدید (بوشکور)
490		KM:297, BQ

بوف ـ رجوع شود به بوم۱

بوق همریشه: puff

Indo-European	Latin	Aramaic	Arabic	Persian
beu 2: *to swell, blow* ورم کردن، دمیدن	bucca: *the cheek, esp. when puffed out (blowing)*	bucina: *horn*	bûq: *horn*	bûq: *horn* بوق
PK:98	bûcina: *trumpet, horn*		BQ:318	BQ:318
	AD, PK:98			
491				

بوم۱: جغد

بوم۲: سرزمین

بوم‌مَهَن: زلزله

بوی۱: رایحه

بوی۲: آرزو

بویه   ـ رجوع شود به   بوی۲

بَه: خوب

به: بطرف

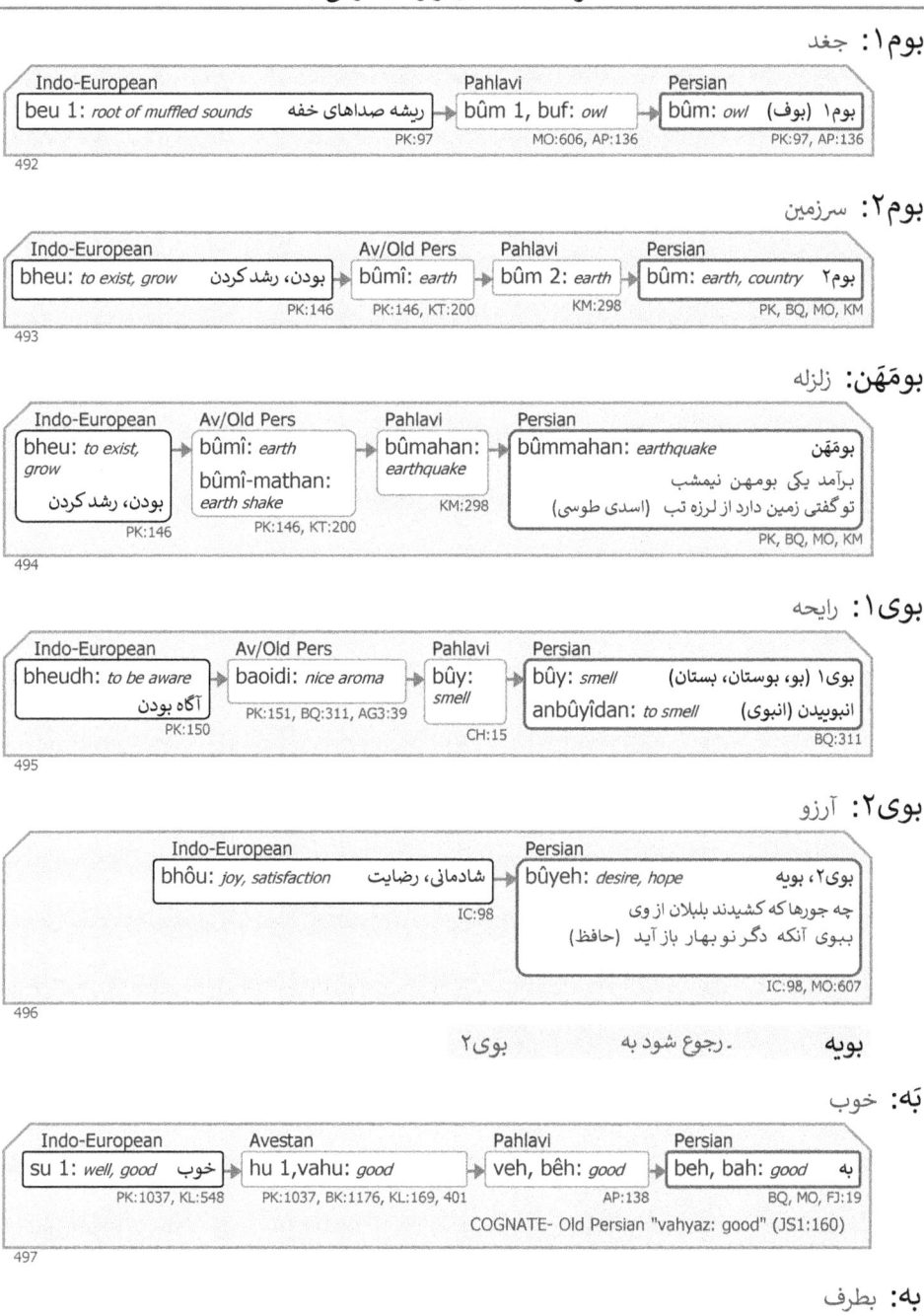

به: بطرف

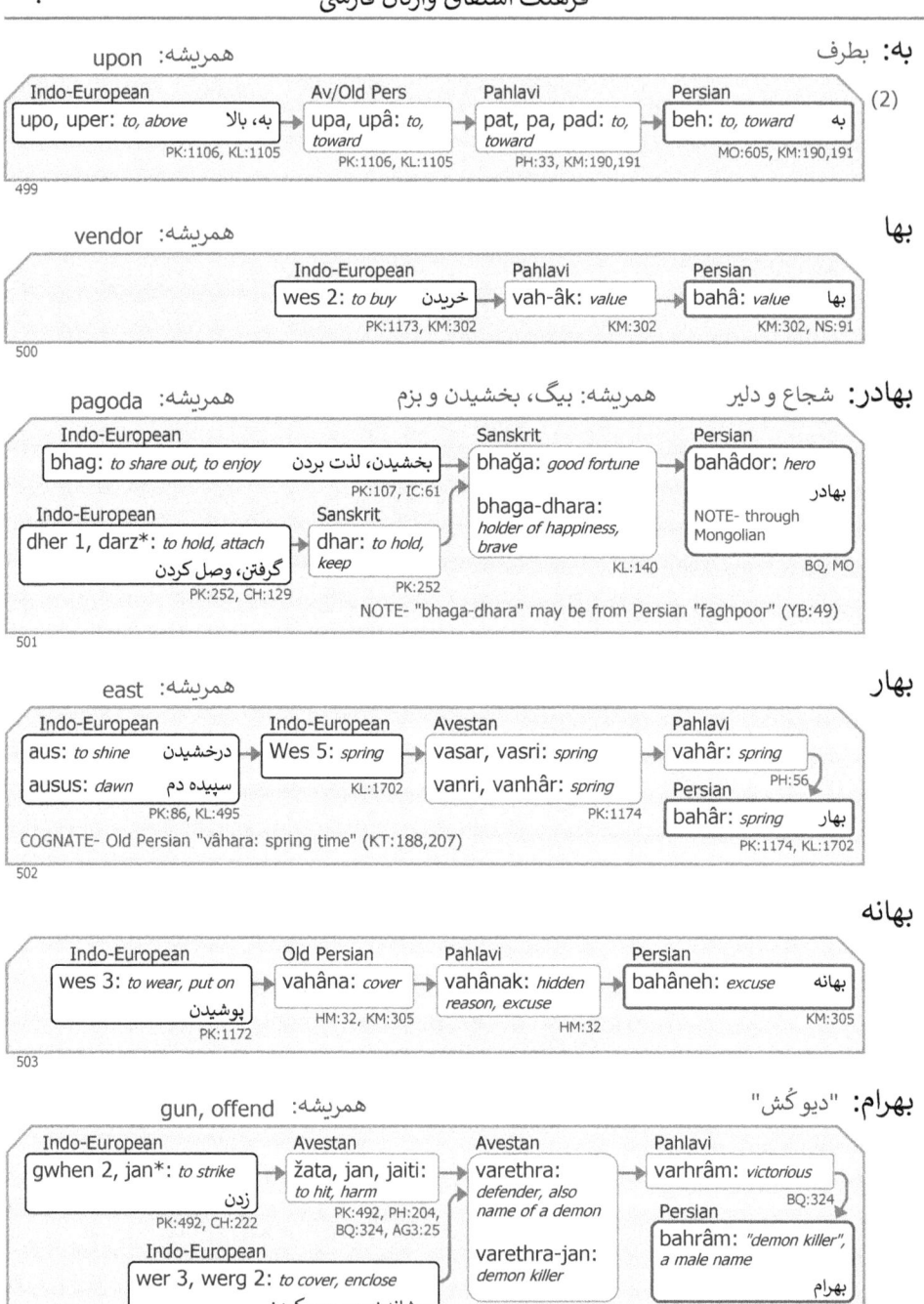

همریشه: upon

(2)

Indo-European	Av/Old Pers	Pahlavi	Persian
upo, uper: to, above به، بالا	upa, upâ: to, toward	pat, pa, pad: to, toward	beh: to, toward به
PK:1106, KL:1105	PK:1106, KL:1105	PH:33, KM:190,191	MO:605, KM:190,191

499

بها

همریشه: vendor

Indo-European	Pahlavi	Persian
wes 2: to buy خریدن	vah-âk: value	bahâ: value بها
PK:1173, KM:302	KM:302	KM:302, NS:91

500

بهادر: شجاع و دلیر

همریشه: بیگ، بخشیدن و بزم

همریشه: pagoda

Indo-European	Sanskrit	Persian
bhag: to share out, to enjoy بخشیدن، لذت بردن	bhağa: good fortune	bahâdor: hero بهادر
PK:107, IC:61		

Indo-European	Sanskrit	bhaga-dhara: holder of happiness, brave	NOTE- through Mongolian
dher 1, darz*: to hold, attach گرفتن، وصل کردن	dhar: to hold, keep		
PK:252, CH:129	PK:252	KL:140	BQ, MO

NOTE- "bhaga-dhara" may be from Persian "faghpoor" (YB:49)

501

بهار

همریشه: east

Indo-European	Indo-European	Avestan	Pahlavi
aus: to shine درخشیدن	Wes 5: spring	vasar, vasri: spring	vahâr: spring
ausus: dawn سپیده دم	KL:1702	vanri, vanhâr: spring	PH:56
PK:86, KL:495		PK:1174	Persian
			bahâr: spring بهار

COGNATE- Old Persian "vâhara: spring time" (KT:188,207)

PK:1174, KL:1702

502

بهانه

Indo-European	Old Persian	Pahlavi	Persian
wes 3: to wear, put on پوشیدن	vahâna: cover	vahânak: hidden reason, excuse	bahâneh: excuse بهانه
PK:1172	HM:32, KM:305	HM:32	KM:305

503

بهرام: "دیوکُش"

همریشه: gun, offend

Indo-European	Avestan	Avestan	Pahlavi
gwhen 2, jan*: to strike زدن	žata, jan, jaiti: to hit, harm	varethra: defender, also name of a demon	varhrâm: victorious
PK:492, CH:222	PK:492, PH:204, BQ:324, AG3:25		BQ:324
Indo-European			Persian
wer 3, werg 2: to cover, enclose پوشاندن، محصور کردن		varethra-jan: demon killer	bahrâm: "demon killer", a male name بهرام
PK:1168, IC:1599		PK:1116	BQ

504

بهره

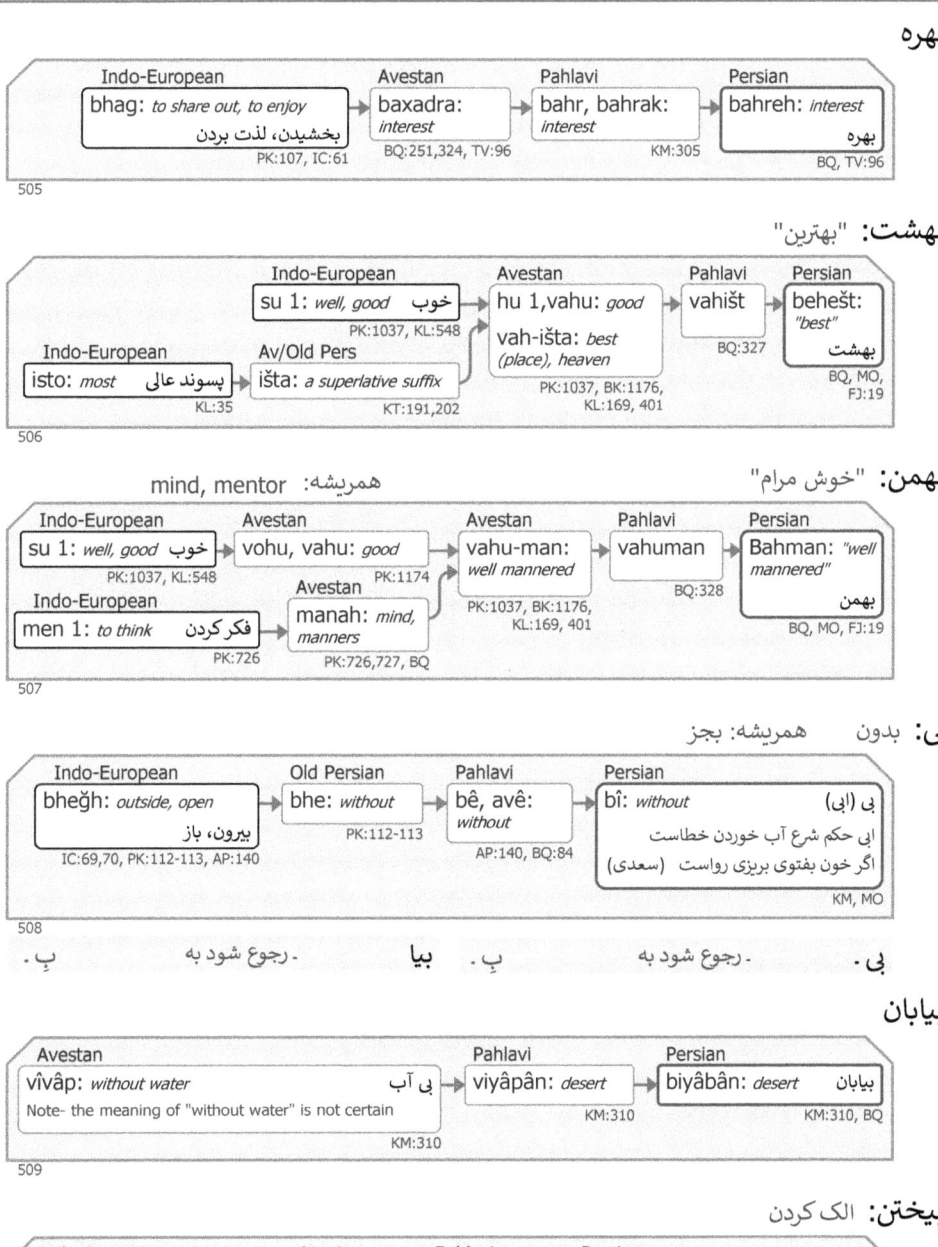

بهره

Indo-European	Avestan	Pahlavi	Persian
bhag: to share out, to enjoy بخشیدن، لذت بردن PK:107, IC:61	baxadra: interest BQ:251,324, TV:96	bahr, bahrak: interest KM:305	bahreh: interest بهره BQ, TV:96

505

بهشت: "بهترین"

Indo-European		Avestan	Pahlavi	Persian
su 1: well, good خوب PK:1037, KL:548		hu 1,vahu: good vah-išta: best (place), heaven PK:1037, BK:1176, KL:169, 401	vahišt BQ:327	behešt: "best" بهشت BQ, MO, FJ:19
Indo-European isto: most KL:35	Av/Old Pers išta: a superlative suffix KT:191,202			

506

بهمن: "خوش مرام"

همریشه: mind, mentor

Indo-European	Avestan	Avestan	Pahlavi	Persian
su 1: well, good خوب PK:1037, KL:548	vohu, vahu: good PK:1174	vahu-man: well mannered PK:1037, BK:1176, KL:169, 401	vahuman BQ:328	Bahman: "well mannered" بهمن BQ, MO, FJ:19
Indo-European men 1: to think فکر کردن PK:726	Avestan manah: mind, manners PK:726,727, BQ			

507

بی: بدون   همریشه: بجز

Indo-European	Old Persian	Pahlavi	Persian
bheĝh: outside, open بیرون، باز IC:69,70, PK:112-113, AP:140	bhe: without PK:112-113	bê, avê: without AP:140, BQ:84	bî: without (ابی) بی ابی بحکم شرع آب خوردن خطاست اگر خون بفتوی بریزی رواست (سعدی) KM, MO

508

بی .   - رجوع شود به   بِ .   بیا   . بِ .   - رجوع شود به   پِ .

بیابان

Avestan	Pahlavi	Persian
vîvâp: without water بی آب Note- the meaning of "without water" is not certain KM:310	viyâpân: desert KM:310	biyâbân: desert بیابان KM:310, BQ

509

بیختن: الک کردن

(1)

Indo-European	Avestan	Pahlavi	Persian
weidh: to select, separate انتخاب کردن، جدا کردن PK:1128, CH:407	vaêc: sift CH:407	wêz: sieve CH:407	bîxtan: to sieve بیختن (بیز، بیزش) parvîzan: sieve پرویزن (بریزن) CH:407
			NOTE- see "Weik: to shake, swing" for another possible root

510

بیختن: الک کردن

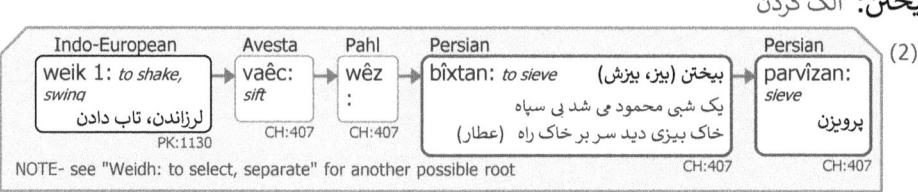

NOTE- see "Weidh: to select, separate" for another possible root

511

بید   همریشه: بیشه   همریشه: willow

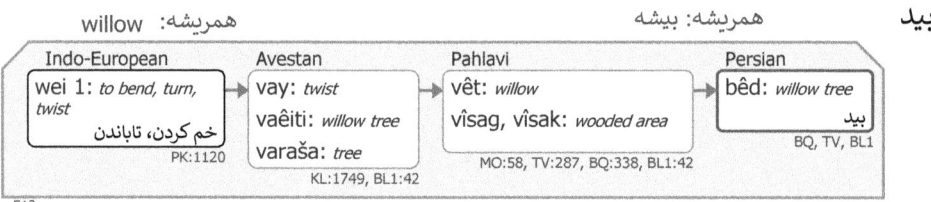

512

بیدار   همریشه: wide

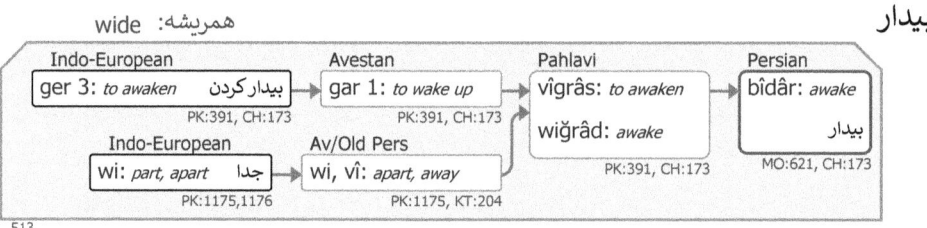

513

بیدخت: "دختر خدا"   مقایسه: فغفور

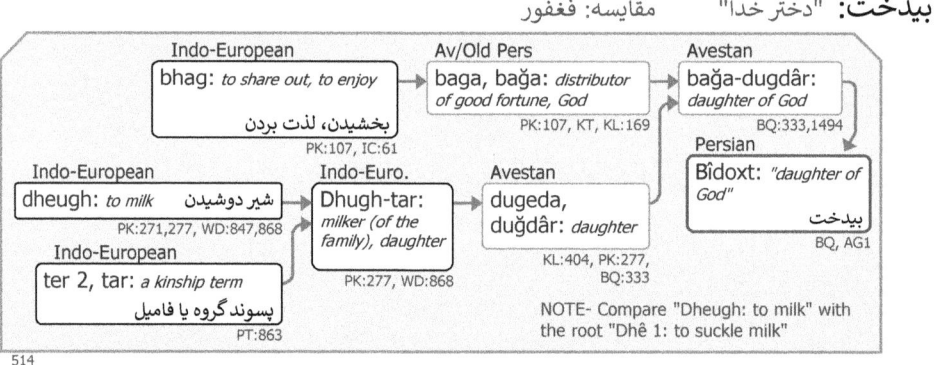

514

بیدستر: حیوانی که "بدون داس" درخت را قطع میکند

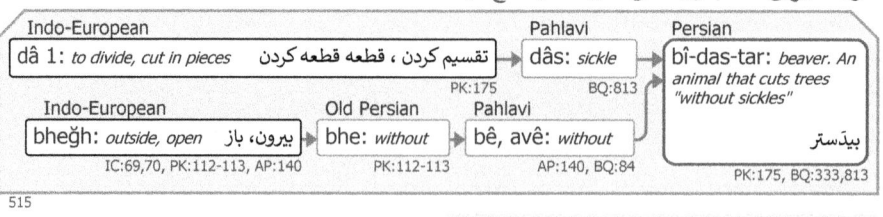

515

بیر: حافظه . رجوع شود به   ویر

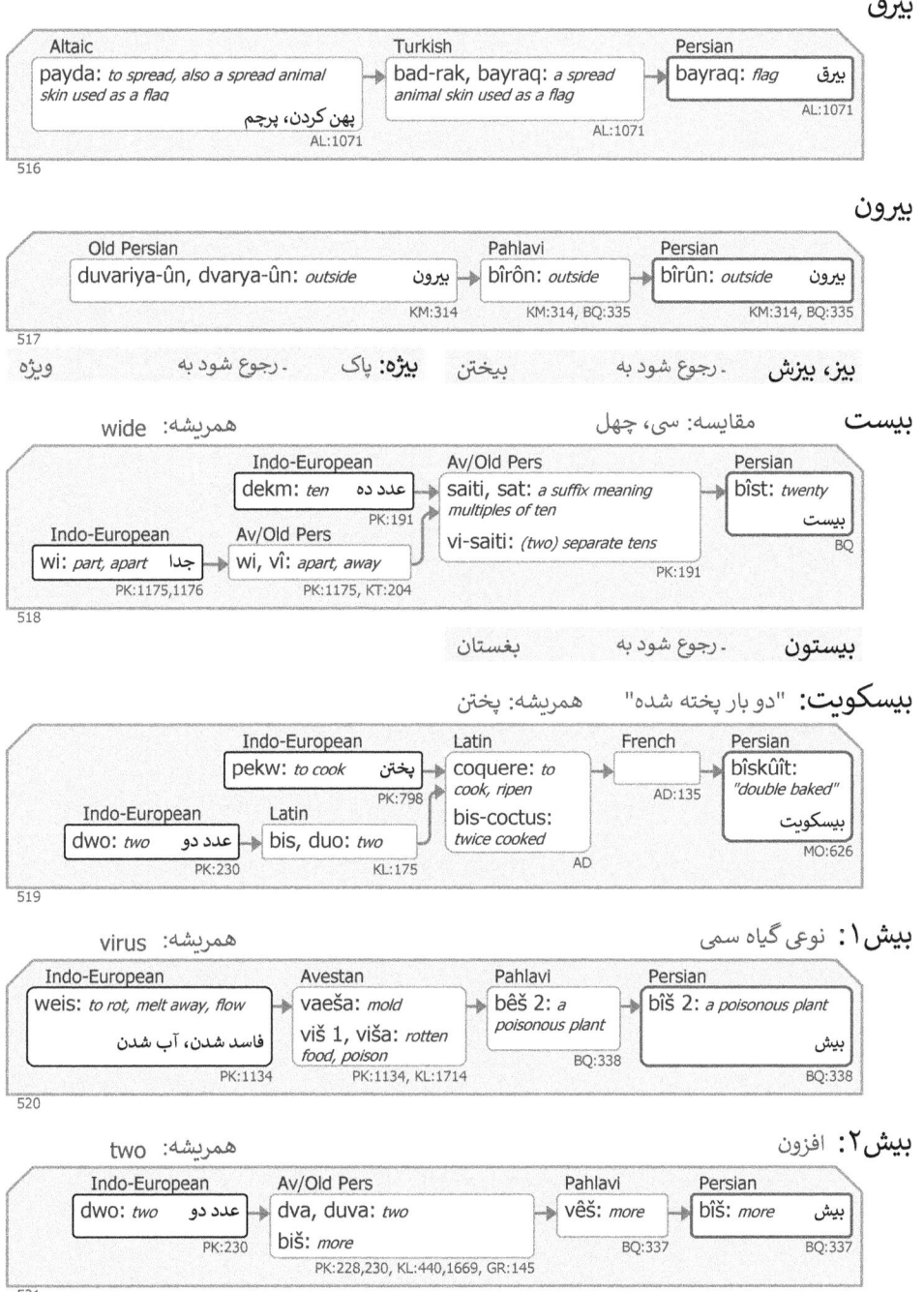

بیرق

Altaic
payda: *to spread, also a spread animal skin used as a flag*

پهن کردن، پرچم
AL:1071

Turkish
bad-rak, bayraq: *a spread animal skin used as a flag*
AL:1071

Persian
bayraq: *flag* بیرق
AL:1071

516

بیرون

Old Persian
duvariya-ûn, dvarya-ûn: *outside* بیرون
KM:314

Pahlavi
bîrôn: *outside*
KM:314, BQ:335

Persian
bîrûn: *outside* بیرون
KM:314, BQ:335

517

ویژه · رجوع شود به پاک :**بیژه** بیختن · رجوع شود به **بیز، بیزش**

بیست

مقایسه: سی، چهل
همریشه: wide

Indo-European
dekm: *ten* عدد ده
PK:191

Av/Old Pers
saiti, sat: *a suffix meaning multiples of ten*
vi-saiti: *(two) separate tens*
PK:191

Indo-European
wi: *part, apart* جدا
PK:1175,1176

Av/Old Pers
wi, vî: *apart, away*
PK:1175, KT:204

Persian
bîst: *twenty* بیست
BQ

518

بغستان · رجوع شود به **بیستون**

بیسکویت: "دو بار پخته شده"
همریشه: پختن

Indo-European
pekw: *to cook* پختن
PK:798

Latin
coquere: *to cook, ripen*
bis-coctus: *twice cooked*
AD

Indo-European
dwo: *two* عدد دو
PK:230

Latin
bis, duo: *two*
KL:175

French
AD:135

Persian
bîskûît: *"double baked"* بیسکویت
MO:626

519

بیش۱: نوعی گیاه سمی
همریشه: virus

Indo-European
weis: *to rot, melt away, flow* فاسد شدن، آب شدن
PK:1134

Avestan
vaeša: *mold*
viš 1, viša: *rotten food, poison*
PK:1134, KL:1714

Pahlavi
bêš 2: *a poisonous plant*
BQ:338

Persian
bîš 2: *a poisonous plant* بیش
BQ:338

520

بیش۲: افزون
همریشه: two

Indo-European
dwo: *two* عدد دو
PK:230

Av/Old Pers
dva, duva: *two*
biš: *more*
PK:228,230, KL:440,1669, GR:145

Pahlavi
vêš: *more*
BQ:337

Persian
bîš: *more* بیش
BQ:337

521

92

بیشه همریشه: بید همریشه: willow

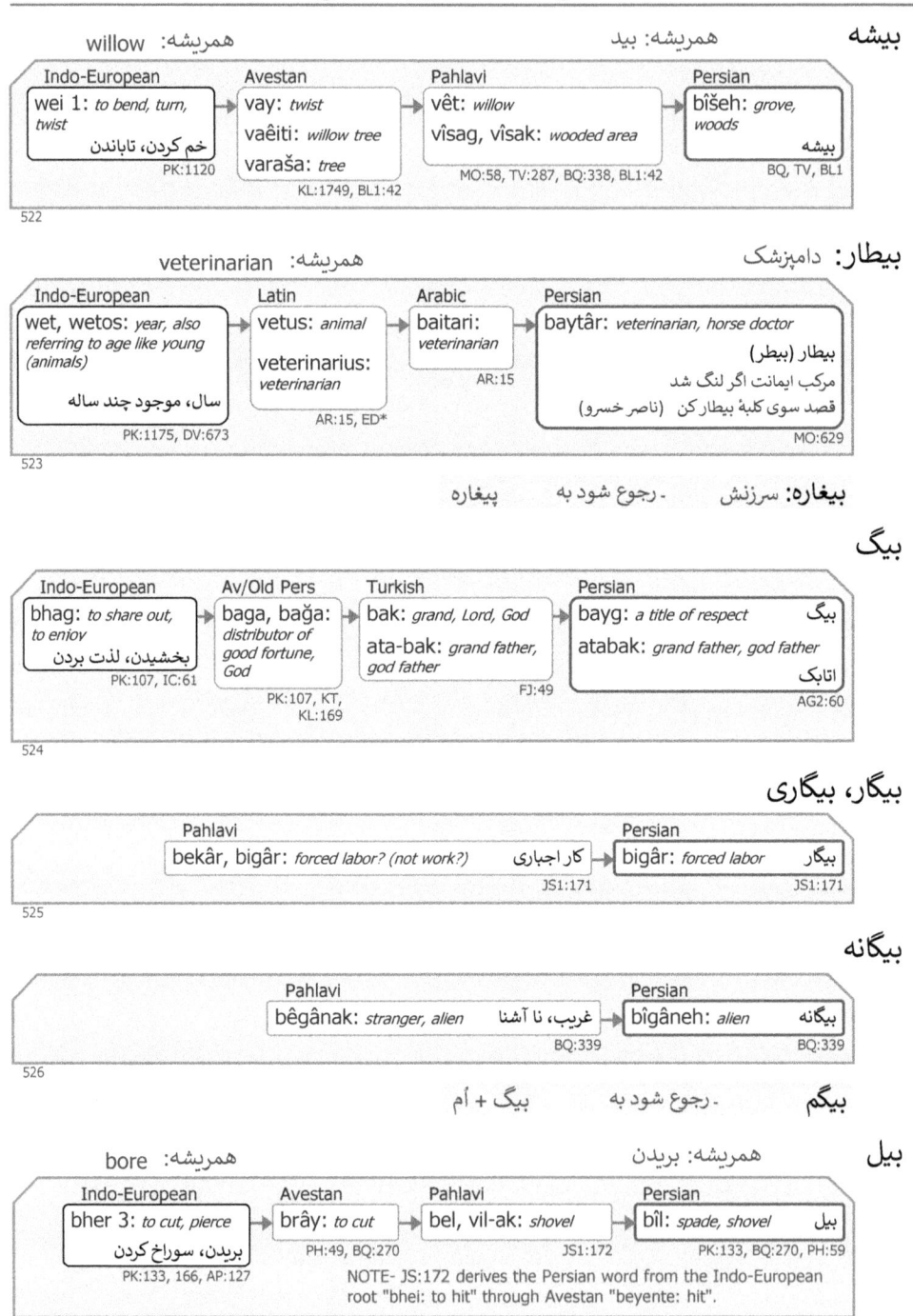

Indo-European	Avestan	Pahlavi	Persian
wei 1: *to bend, turn, twist* خم کردن، تاباندن PK:1120	vay: *twist* vaêiti: *willow tree* varaša: *tree* KL:1749, BL1:42	vêt: *willow* vîsag, vîsak: *wooded area* MO:58, TV:287, BQ:338, BL1:42	bîšeh: *grove, woods* بیشه BQ, TV, BL1

522

بیطار: دامپزشک همریشه: veterinarian

Indo-European	Latin	Arabic	Persian
wet, wetos: *year, also referring to age like young (animals)* سال، موجود چند ساله PK:1175, DV:673	vetus: *animal* veterinarius: *veterinarian* AR:15, ED*	baitari: *veterinarian* AR:15	baytâr: *veterinarian, horse doctor* بیطار (بیطر) مرکب ایمانت اگر لنگ شد قصد سوی کلبهٔ بیطار کن (ناصر خسرو) MO:629

523

بیغاره: سرزنش ـ رجوع شود به پیغاره

بیگ

Indo-European	Av/Old Pers	Turkish	Persian
bhag: *to share out, to enjoy* بخشیدن، لذت بردن PK:107, IC:61	baga, baǧa: *distributor of good fortune, God* PK:107, KT, KL:169	bak: *grand, Lord, God* ata-bak: *grand father, god father* FJ:49	bayg: *a title of respect* بیگ atabak: *grand father, god father* اتابک AG2:60

524

بیگار، بیگاری

Pahlavi	Persian
bekâr, bigâr: *forced labor? (not work?)* کار اجباری JS1:171	bigâr: *forced labor* بیگار JS1:171

525

بیگانه

Pahlavi	Persian
bêgânak: *stranger, alien* غریب، نا آشنا BQ:339	bîgâneh: *alien* بیگانه BQ:339

526

بیگم ـ رجوع شود به بیگ + اُم

بیل همریشه: بریدن همریشه: bore

Indo-European	Avestan	Pahlavi	Persian
bher 3: *to cut, pierce* بریدن، سوراخ کردن PK:133, 166, AP:127	brây: *to cut* PH:49, BQ:270	bel, vil-ak: *shovel* JS1:172	bîl: *spade, shovel* بیل PK:133, BQ:270, PH:59

NOTE- JS:172 derives the Persian word from the Indo-European root "bhei: to hit" through Avestan "beyente: hit".

527

بیم

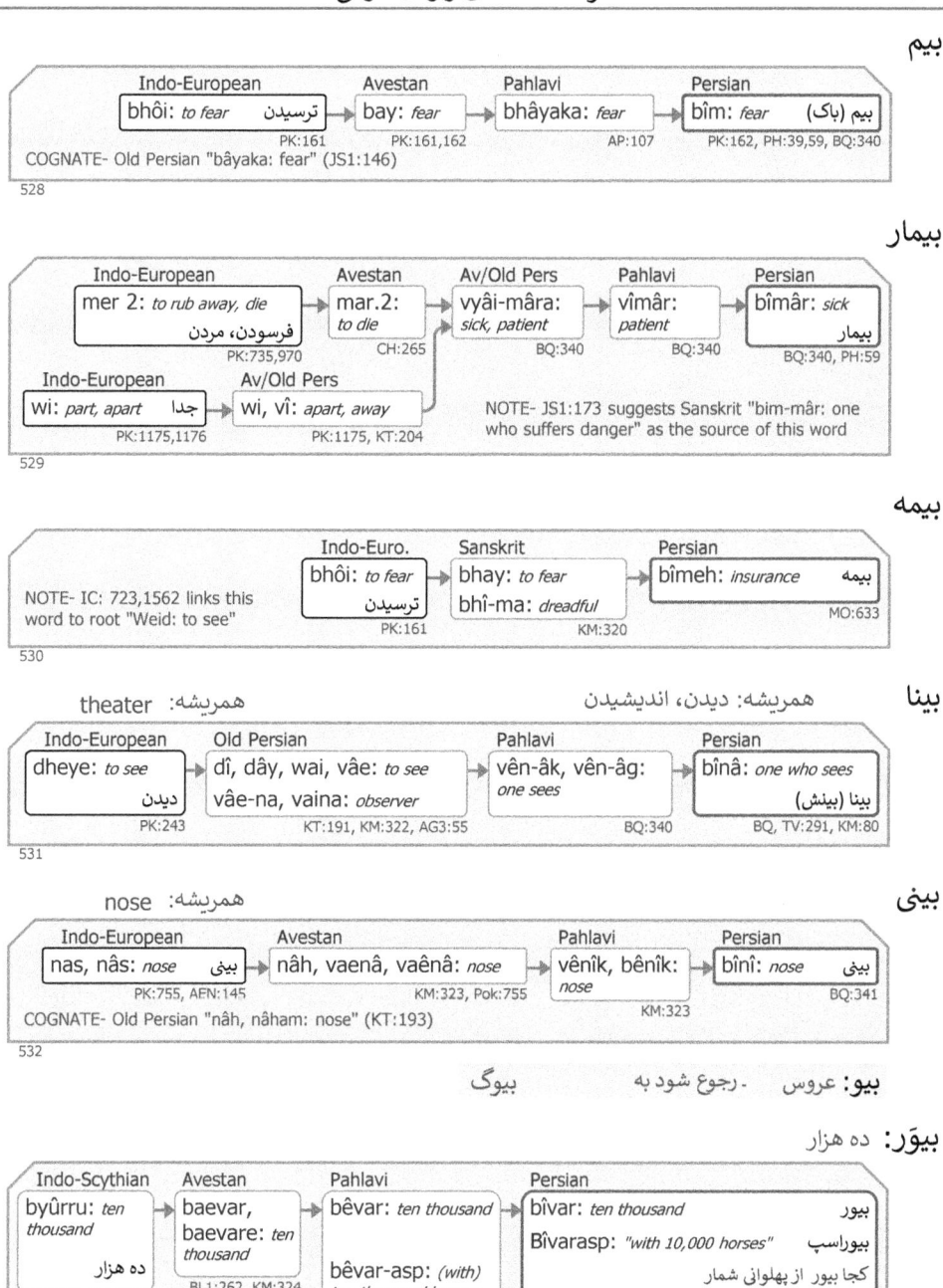

Page 528

Indo-European	Avestan	Pahlavi	Persian
bhôi: *to fear* ترسیدن	bay: *fear*	bhâyaka: *fear*	bîm: *fear* بیم (باک)
PK:161	PK:161,162	AP:107	PK:162, PH:39,59, BQ:340

COGNATE- Old Persian "bâyaka: fear" (JS1:146)

528

بیمار

Indo-European	Avestan	Av/Old Pers	Pahlavi	Persian
mer 2: *to rub away, die* فرسودن، مردن	mar.2: *to die*	vyâi-mâra: *sick, patient*	vîmâr: *patient*	bîmâr: *sick* بیمار
PK:735,970	CH:265	BQ:340	BQ:340	BQ:340, PH:59

Indo-European	Av/Old Pers
wi: *part, apart* جدا	wi, vî: *apart, away*
PK:1175,1176	PK:1175, KT:204

NOTE- JS1:173 suggests Sanskrit "bim-mâr: one who suffers danger" as the source of this word

529

بیمه

NOTE- IC: 723,1562 links this word to root "Weid: to see"

Indo-Euro.	Sanskrit	Persian
bhôi: *to fear* ترسیدن	bhay: *to fear* bhî-ma: *dreadful*	bîmeh: *insurance* بیمه
PK:161	KM:320	MO:633

530

بینا

همریشه: theater   همریشه: دیدن، اندیشیدن

Indo-European	Old Persian	Pahlavi	Persian
dheye: *to see* دیدن	dî, dây, wai, vâe: *to see* vâe-na, vaina: *observer*	vên-âk, vên-âg: *one sees*	bînâ: *one who sees* بینا (بینش)
PK:243	KT:191, KM:322, AG3:55	BQ:340	BQ, TV:291, KM:80

531

بینی

همریشه: nose

Indo-European	Avestan	Pahlavi	Persian
nas, nâs: *nose* بینی	nâh, vaenâ, vaênâ: *nose*	vênîk, bênîk: *nose*	bînî: *nose* بینی
PK:755, AEN:145	KM:323, Pok:755	KM:323	BQ:341

COGNATE- Old Persian "nâh, nâham: nose" (KT:193)

532

بیو: عروس .رجوع شود به   بیوگ

بیوَر: ده هزار

Indo-Scythian	Avestan	Pahlavi	Persian
byûrru: *ten thousand* ده هزار	baevar, baevare: *ten thousand*	bêvar: *ten thousand* bêvar-asp: *(with) ten thousand horses*	bîvar: *ten thousand* بیور Bîvarasp: *"with 10,000 horses"* بیوراسپ کجا بیور از پهلوانی شمار بود بر زبان دری ده هزار (فردوسی)
BL1:262	BL1:262, KM:324	KM:324	MO, NS:98

533

بیوراسپ   .رجوع شود به   بیور

بیوسیدن: انتظار داشتن

(1)

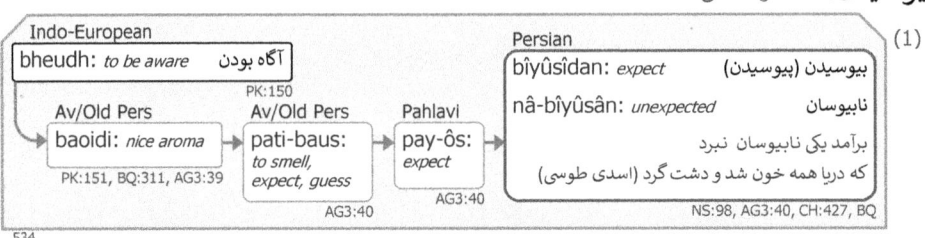

بیوسیدن: انتظار داشتن

(2)

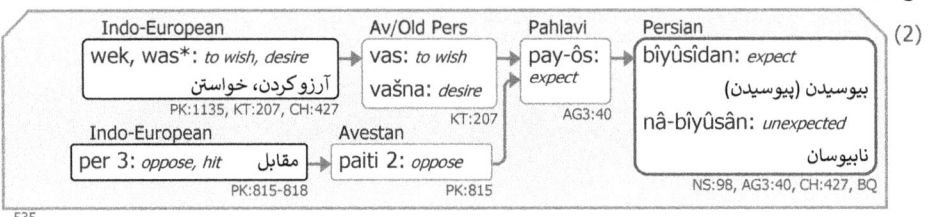

بیوگ: عروس

همریشه: upon, wedding

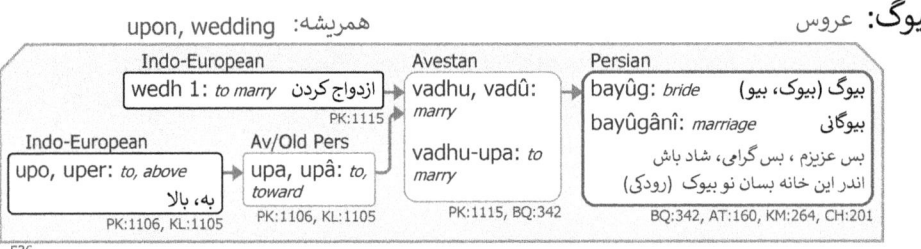

بیوه

همریشه: widow

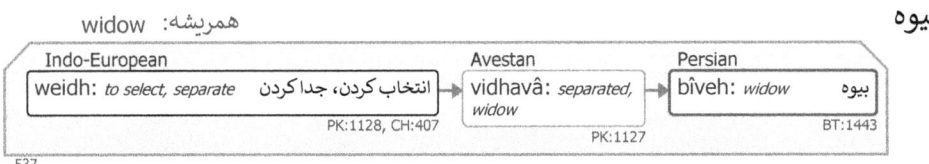

این حرف گاهی به ف بدل شود.

پ - : پیشوند به معنی ضد، مقابل یا پیش

همریشه: press, compress

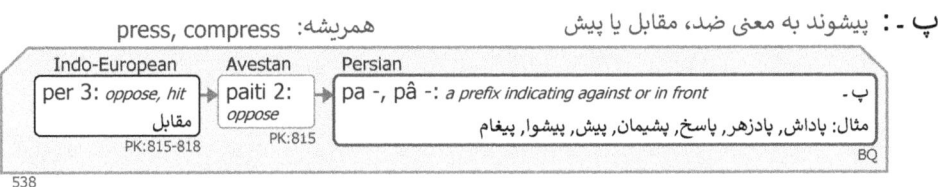

Indo-European	Avestan	Persian
per 3: *oppose, hit* مقابل	paiti 2: *oppose*	pa -, pâ -: *a prefix indicating against or in front* - پ
PK:815-818	PK:815	مثال: پاداش, پادزهر, پاسخ, پشیمان, پیش, پیشوا, پیغام
		BQ

538

پا

همریشه: foot, pedal

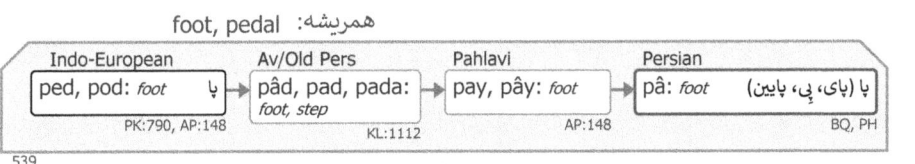

Indo-European	Av/Old Pers	Pahlavi	Persian
ped, pod: *foot* پا	pâd, pad, pada: *foot, step*	pay, pây: *foot*	pâ: *foot* (پای، پی، پایین) پا
PK:790, AP:148	KL:1112	AP:148	BQ, PH

539

پاپژ: دامنه کوه   همریشه: پژواک

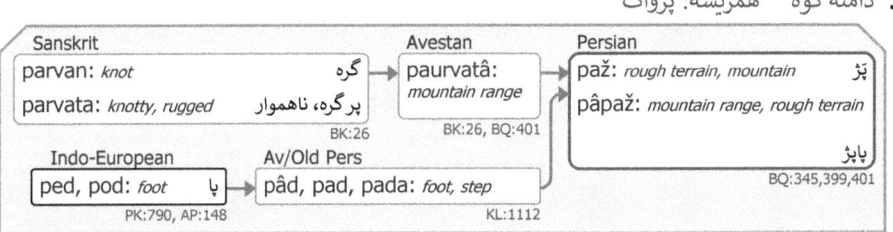

Sanskrit		Avestan	Persian
parvan: *knot* گره		paurvatâ: *mountain range*	paž: *rough terrain, mountain* پژ
parvata: *knotty, rugged* پرگره، ناهموار			pâpaž: *mountain range, rough terrain*
	BK:26	BK:26, BQ:401	پاپژ
Indo-European	Av/Old Pers		BQ:345,399,401
ped, pod: *foot* پا	pâd, pad, pada: *foot, step*		
PK:790, AP:148	KL:1112		

540

پاتیل

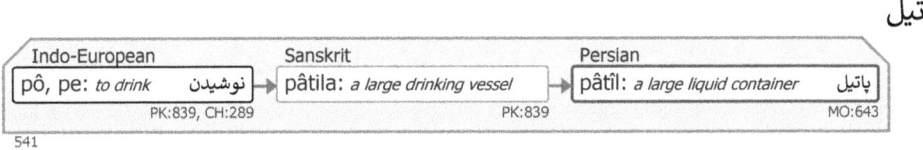

Indo-European	Sanskrit	Persian
pô, pe: *to drink* نوشیدن	pâtila: *a large drinking vessel*	pâtîl: *a large liquid container* پاتیل
PK:839, CH:289	PK:839	MO:643

541

پاجامه

همریشه: zone

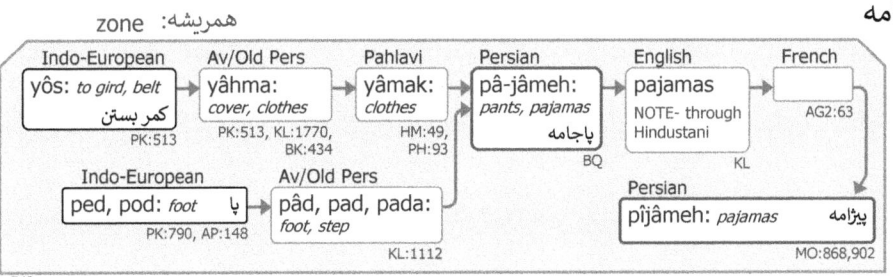

Indo-European	Av/Old Pers	Pahlavi	Persian	English	French
yôs: *to gird, belt* کمر بستن	yâhma: *cover, clothes*	yâmak: *clothes*	pâ-jâmeh: *pants, pajamas* پاجامه	pajamas NOTE- through Hindustani	
PK:513	PK:513, KL:1770, BK:434	HM:49, PH:93	BQ	KL	AG2:63
Indo-European	Av/Old Pers			Persian	
ped, pod: *foot* پا	pâd, pad, pada: *foot, step*			pîjâmeh: *pajamas* پیژامه	
PK:790, AP:148	KL:1112			MO:868,902	

542

پاداش

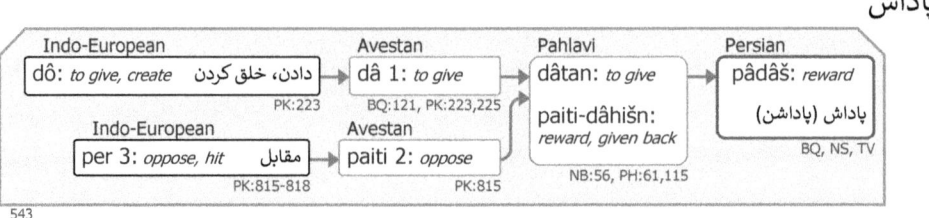

پادافراه: قصاص   مقایسه: پرسیدن

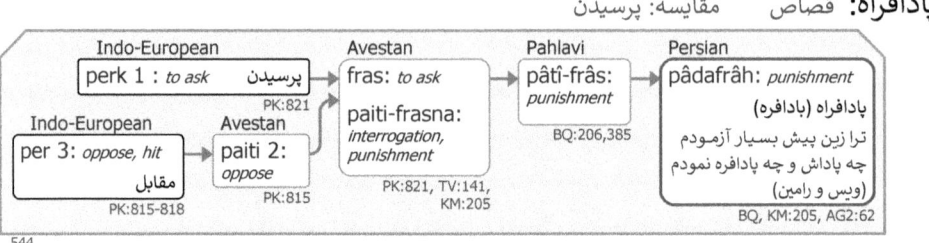

پادزهر

همریشه: suppress, offense

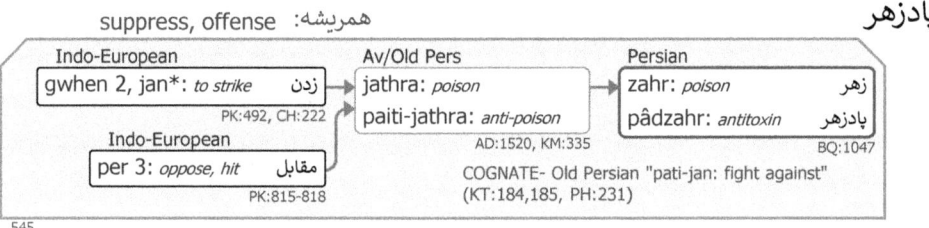

پادشاه

همریشه: check, chess

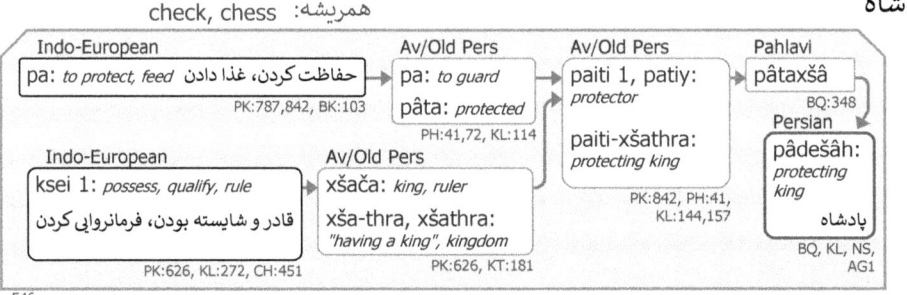

پاده: گله گاو و اسب   همریشه: پاییدن   پاسچر: pasture

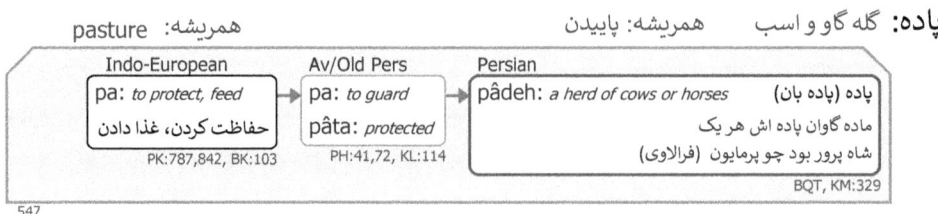

پار: "پیش"

همریشه: early

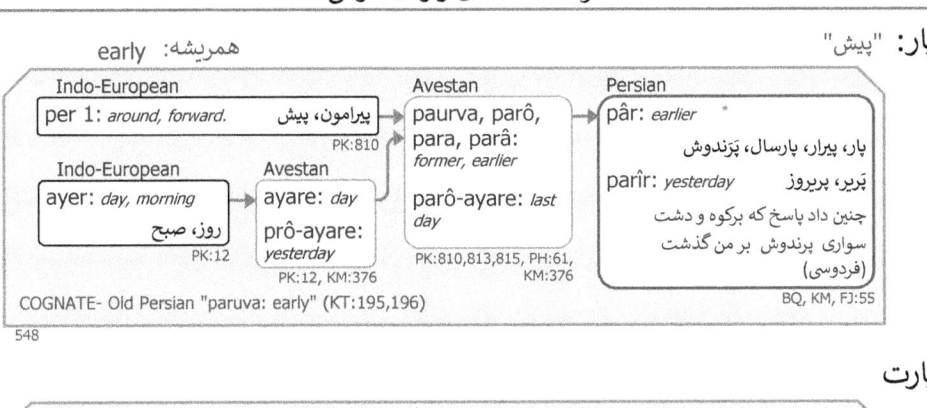

Indo-European	Avestan	Persian
per 1: *around, forward.* پیرامون، پیش PK:810	paurva, parô, para, parâ: *former, earlier*	pâr: *earlier* پار، پیرار، پارسال، پَرَندوش پریر، پریروز
Indo-European / Avestan	parô-ayare: *last day* PK:810,813,815, PH:61, KM:376	parîr: *yesterday* چنین داد پاسخ که برکوه و دشت سواری پرندوش بر من گذشت (فردوسی) BQ, KM, FJ:55
ayer: *day, morning* روز، صبح PK:12	ayare: *day* prô-ayare: *yesterday* PK:12, KM:376	

COGNATE- Old Persian "paruva: early" (KT:195,196)

548

پارت

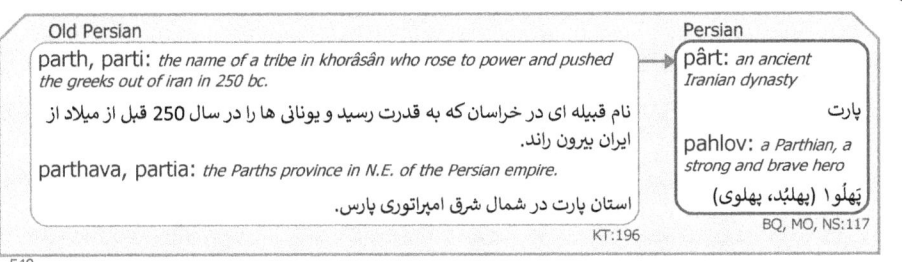

Old Persian	Persian
parth, parti: *the name of a tribe in khorâsân who rose to power and pushed the greeks out of iran in 250 bc.* نام قبیله ای در خراسان که به قدرت رسید و یونانی ها را در سال 250 قبل از میلاد از ایران بیرون راند. parthava, partia: *the Parths province in N.E. of the Persian empire.* استان پارت در شمال شرق امپراتوری پارس. KT:196	pârt: *an ancient Iranian dynasty* پارت pahlov: *a Parthian, a strong and brave hero* پهلو۱ (پهلبُد، پهلوی) BQ, MO, NS:117

549

پارد

همریشه: leopard

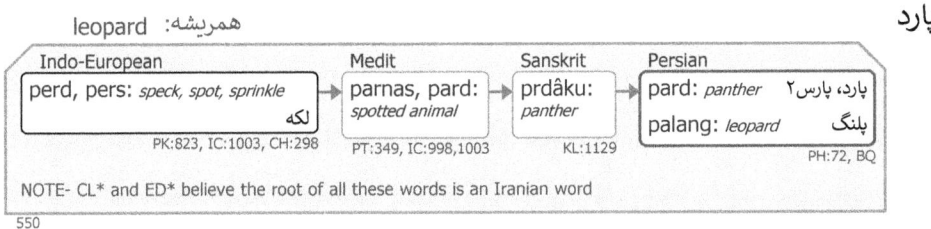

Indo-European	Medit	Sanskrit	Persian
perd, pers: *speck, spot, sprinkle* لکه PK:823, IC:1003, CH:298	parnas, pard: *spotted animal* PT:349, IC:998,1003	prdâku: *panther* KL:1129	pard: *panther* پارد، پارس۲ palang: *leopard* پلنگ PH:72, BQ

NOTE- CL* and ED* believe the root of all these words is an Iranian word

550

پارس۱

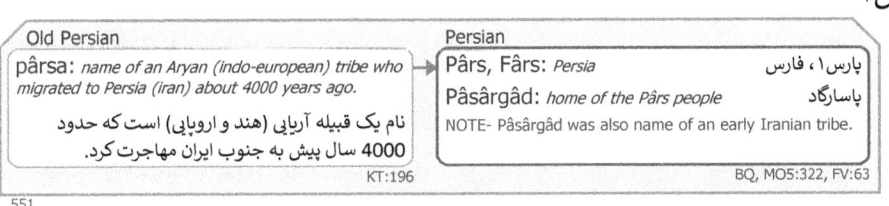

Old Persian	Persian
pârsa: *name of an Aryan (indo-european) tribe who migrated to Persia (iran) about 4000 years ago.* نام یک قبیله آریایی (هند و اروپایی) است که حدود 4000 سال پیش به جنوب ایران مهاجرت کرد. KT:196	Pârs, Fârs: *Persia* پارس۱، فارس Pâsârgâd: *home of the Pârs people* پاسارگاد NOTE- Pâsârgâd was also name of an early Iranian tribe. BQ, MO5:322, FV:63

551

پارس۲: پلنگ ـ رجوع شود به   پارد

پارسا

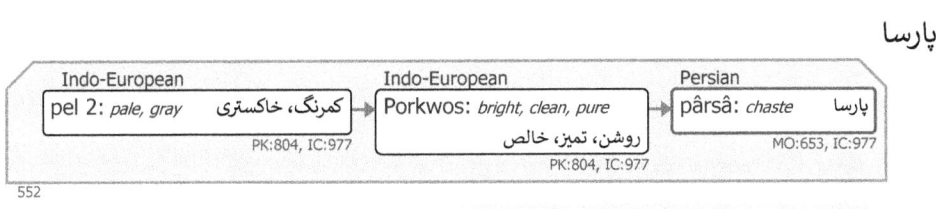

Indo-European	Indo-European	Persian
pel 2: *pale, gray* کمرنگ، خاکستری PK:804, IC:977	Porkwos: *bright, clean, pure* روشن، تمیز، خالص PK:804, IC:977	pârsâ: *chaste* پارسا MO:653, IC:977

552

پارسال ـ رجوع شود به   پار

پاره: تکه

همریشه: part

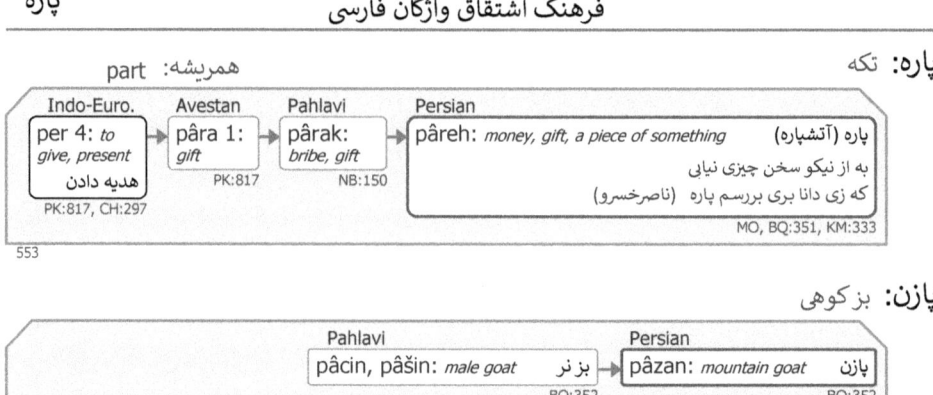

553

پازن: بزکوهی

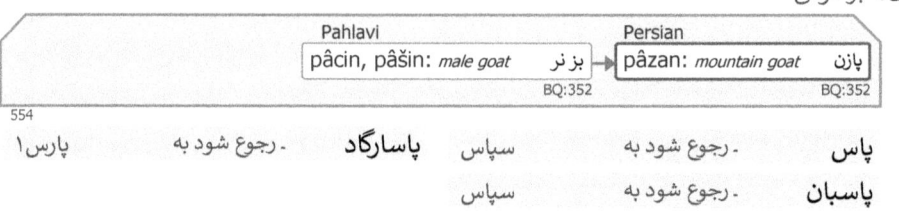

554

پاس . رجوع شود به سپاس   **پاسارگاد** سپاس . رجوع شود به   پارس۱

پاسبان . رجوع شود به سپاس

پاسخ

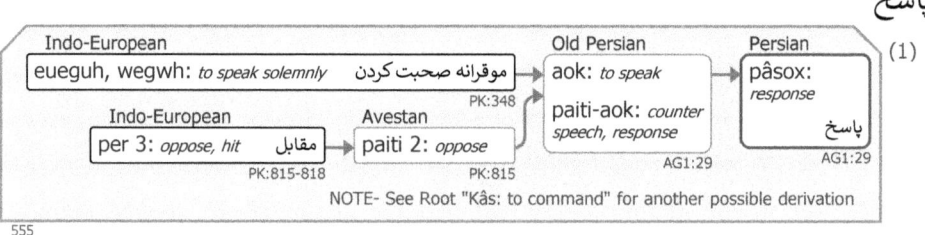

555

پاسخ

مقایسه: سخن

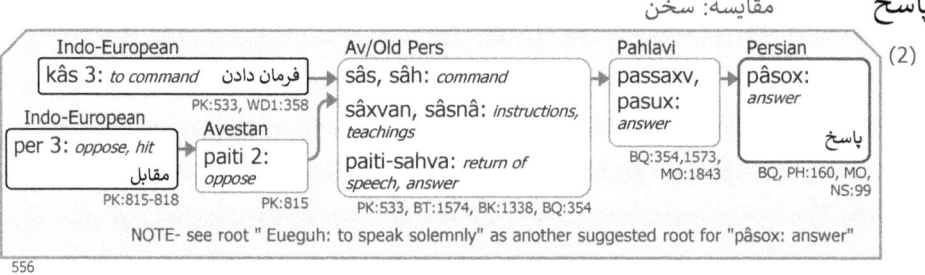

556

پاشنه

همریشه: pearl

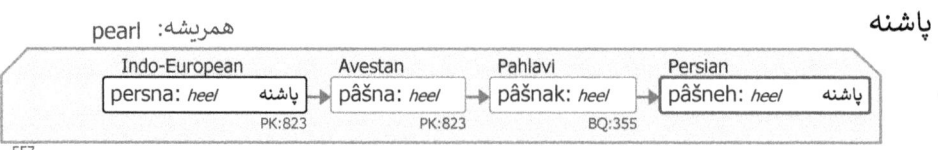

557

پاشیدن

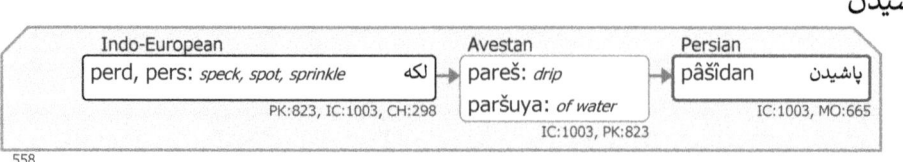

558

پاک

همریشه: pure

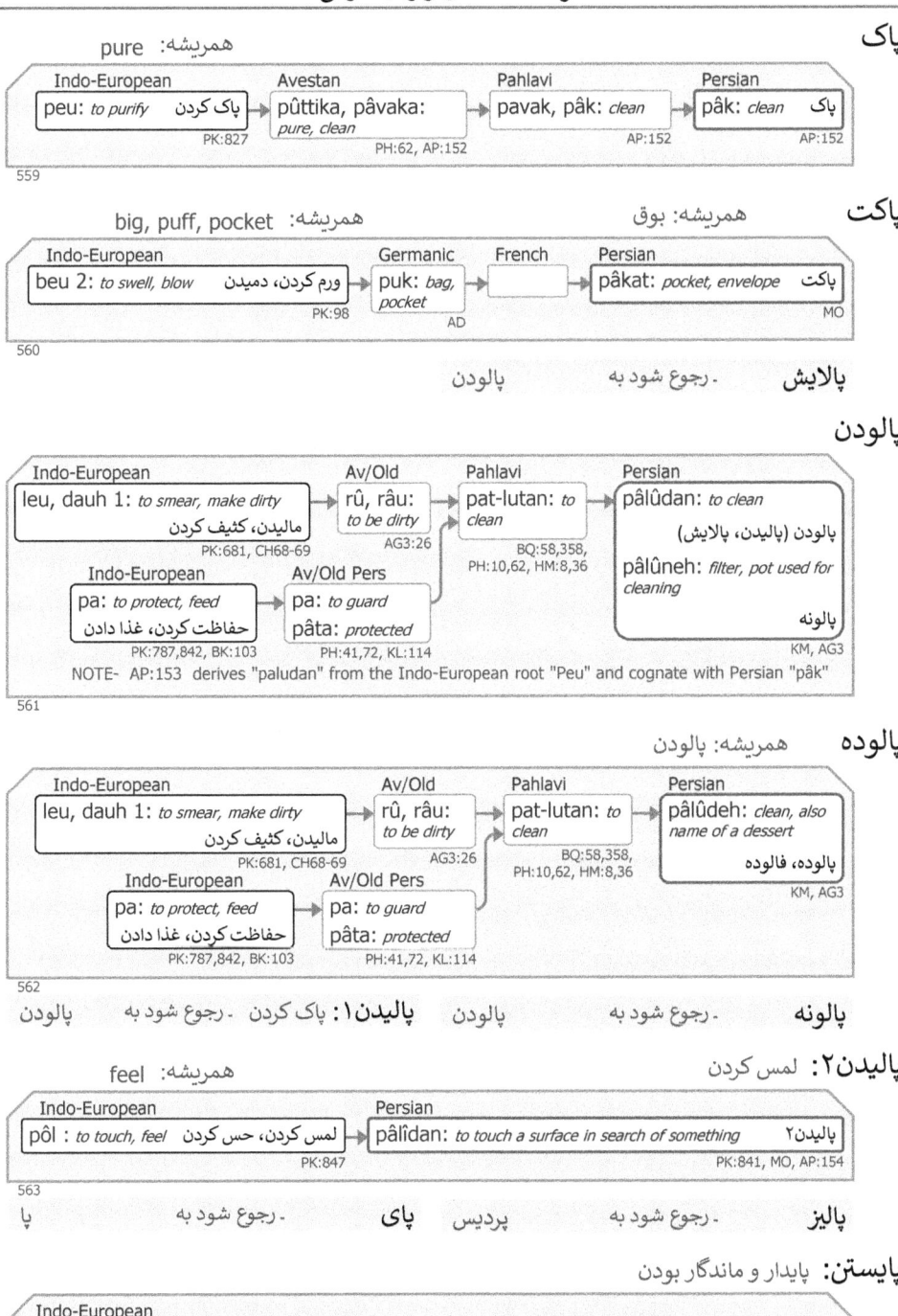

Indo-European	Avestan	Pahlavi	Persian
peu: *to purify* پاک کردن	pûttika, pâvaka: *pure, clean*	pavak, pâk: *clean*	pâk: *clean* پاک
PK:827	PH:62, AP:152	AP:152	AP:152

559

پاکت

همریشه: big, puff, pocket   همریشه: بوق

Indo-European	Germanic	French	Persian
beu 2: *to swell, blow* ورم کردن، دمیدن	puk: *bag, pocket*		pâkat: *pocket, envelope* پاکت
PK:98	AD		MO

560

پالایش   . رجوع شود به   پالودن

پالودن

Indo-European	Av/Old	Pahlavi	Persian
leu, dauh 1: *to smear, make dirty* مالیدن، کثیف کردن	rû, râu: *to be dirty*	pat-lutan: *to clean*	pâlûdan: *to clean* پالودن (پالیدن، پالایش) pâlûneh: *filter, pot used for cleaning* پالونه
PK:681, CH68-69	AG3:26	BQ:58,358, PH:10,62, HM:8,36	KM, AG3
Indo-European	Av/Old Pers		
pa: *to protect, feed* حفاظت کردن، غذا دادن	pa: *to guard* pâta: *protected*		
PK:787,842, BK:103	PH:41,72, KL:114		

NOTE- AP:153 derives "paludan" from the Indo-European root "Peu" and cognate with Persian "pâk"

561

پالوده   همریشه: پالودن

Indo-European	Av/Old	Pahlavi	Persian
leu, dauh 1: *to smear, make dirty* مالیدن، کثیف کردن	rû, râu: *to be dirty*	pat-lutan: *to clean*	pâlûdeh: *clean, also name of a dessert* پالوده، فالوده
PK:681, CH68-69	AG3:26	BQ:58,358, PH:10,62, HM:8,36	KM, AG3
Indo-European	Av/Old Pers		
pa: *to protect, feed* حفاظت کردن، غذا دادن	pa: *to guard* pâta: *protected*		
PK:787,842, BK:103	PH:41,72, KL:114		

562

پالونه   . رجوع شود به   پالودن   **پالیدن۱:** پاک کردن   . رجوع شود به   پالودن

پالیدن۲: لمس کردن

همریشه: feel

Indo-European	Persian
pôl : *to touch, feel* لمس کردن، حس کردن	pâlîdan: *to touch a surface in search of something* پالیدن۲
PK:847	PK:841, MO, AP:154

563

پالیز   . رجوع شود به   پردیس   **پای**   . رجوع شود به   پا

پایستن: پایدار و ماندگار بودن

Indo-European		Persian
pa: *to protect, feed* حفاظت کردن، غذا دادن		pâyastan: *to stay, remain* پایستن (پاینده)
PK:787,842, BK:103		جهانا چه در خورد و بایسته ای
Av/Old Pers	Av/Old Pers	اگر چند با کس نپایسته ای (ناصر خسرو)
pa: *to guard*	paiti 1, patiy: *protector*	BQ:364
PH:41,72, KL:114	PK:842, PH:41, KL:144,157	

564

پاینده: ـ رجوع شود به   پایستن

پاییدن   همریشه: feed

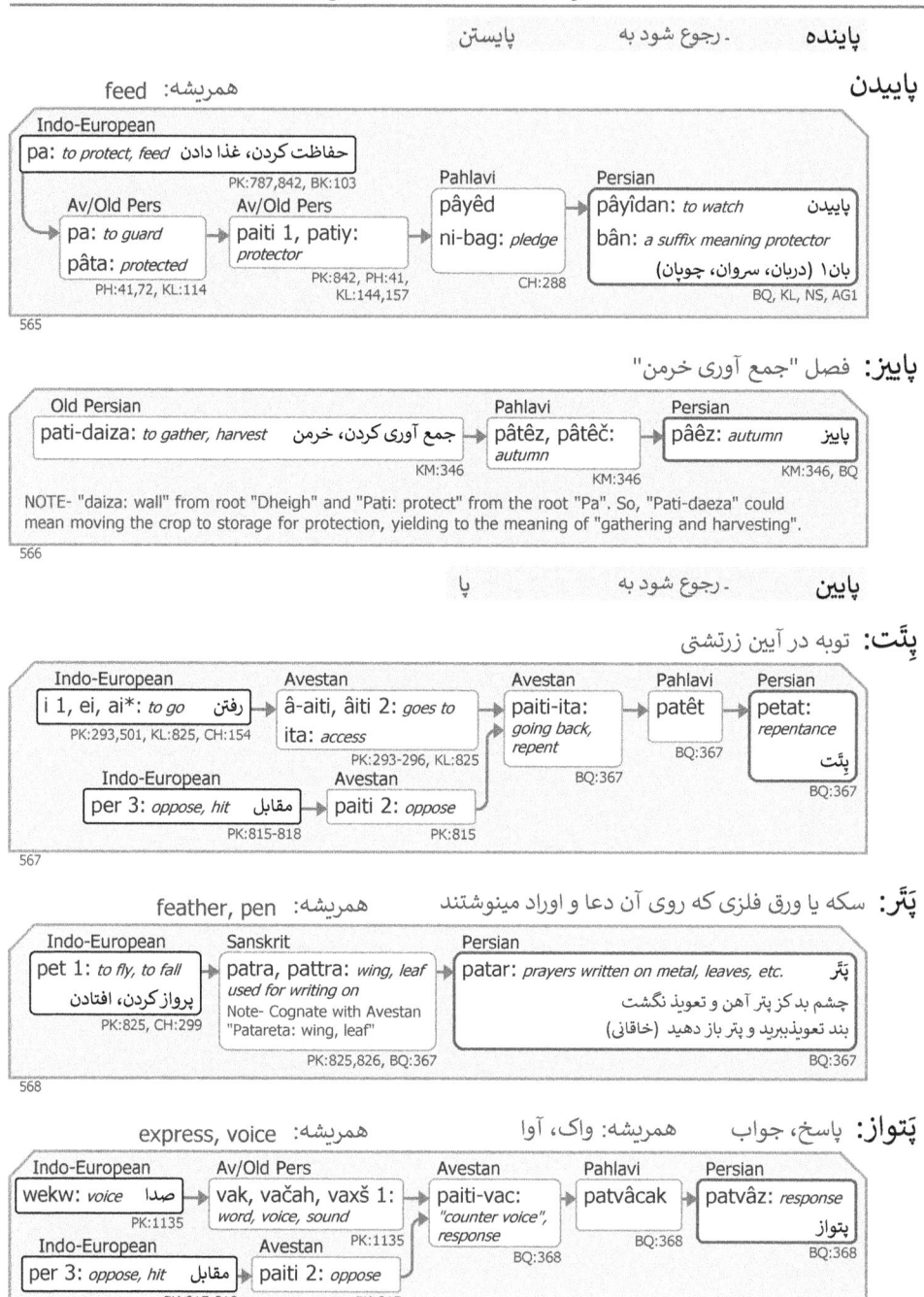

Indo-European

pa: *to protect, feed* حفاظت کردن، غذا دادن
PK:787,842, BK:103

Av/Old Pers
pa: *to guard*
pâta: *protected*
PH:41,72, KL:114

Av/Old Pers
paiti 1, patiy: *protector*
PK:842, PH:41, KL:144,157

Pahlavi
pâyêd
ni-bag: *pledge*
CH:288

Persian
pâyîdan: *to watch* پاییدن
bân: *a suffix meaning protector*
بان۱ (دریان، سروان، چوپان)
BQ, KL, NS, AG1

565

پاییز: فصل "جمع آوری خرمن"

Old Persian
pati-daiza: *to gather, harvest* جمع آوری کردن، خرمن
KM:346

Pahlavi
pâtêz, pâtêĉ: *autumn*
KM:346

Persian
pâêz: *autumn* پاییز
KM:346, BQ

NOTE- "daiza: wall" from root "Dheigh" and "Pati: protect" from the root "Pa". So, "Pati-daeza" could mean moving the crop to storage for protection, yielding to the meaning of "gathering and harvesting".

566

پایین: ـ رجوع شود به   پا

پِنَّت: توبه در آیین زرتشتی

Indo-European
i 1, ei, ai*: *to go* رفتن
PK:293,501, KL:825, CH:154

Avestan
â-aiti, âiti 2: *goes to*
ita: *access*
PK:293-296, KL:825

Avestan
paiti-ita: *going back, repent*
BQ:367

Pahlavi
patêt
BQ:367

Persian
petat: *repentance*
پِنَّت
BQ:367

Indo-European
per 3: *oppose, hit* مقابل
PK:815-818

Avestan
paiti 2: *oppose*
PK:815

567

پَتَّر: سکه یا ورق فلزی که روی آن دعا و اوراد مینوشتند   همریشه: feather, pen

Indo-European
pet 1: *to fly, to fall* پرواز کردن، افتادن
PK:825, CH:299

Sanskrit
patra, pattra: *wing, leaf used for writing on*
Note- Cognate with Avestan "Patareta: wing, leaf"
PK:825,826, BQ:367

Persian
patar: *prayers written on metal, leaves, etc.* پَتَّر
چشم بد کز پتر آهن و تعویذ نگشت
بند تعویذببرید و بتر باز دهید (خاقانی)
BQ:367

568

پَتواز: پاسخ، جواب   همریشه: واک، آوا   همریشه: express, voice

Indo-European
wekw: *voice* صدا
PK:1135

Av/Old Pers
vak, vačah, vaxš 1: *word, voice, sound*
PK:1135

Avestan
paiti-vac: *"counter voice", response*
BQ:368

Pahlavi
patvâcak
BQ:368

Persian
patvâz: *response* پَتواز
BQ:368

Indo-European
per 3: *oppose, hit* مقابل
PK:815-818

Avestan
paiti 2: *oppose*
PK:815

569

پتیاره: "مخالف پیشرفت"، ضدیت، مخالفت

همریشه: run

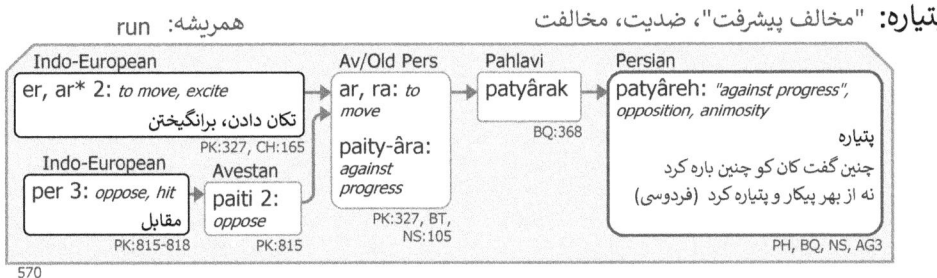

Indo-European
er, ar* 2: to move, excite
تکان دادن، برانگیختن
PK:327, CH:165

Indo-European
per 3: oppose, hit
مقابل
PK:815-818

Avestan
paiti 2: oppose
PK:815

Av/Old Pers
ar, ra: to move
paity-âra: against progress
PK:327, BT, NS:105

Pahlavi
patyârak
BQ:368

Persian
patyâreh: "against progress", opposition, animosity
پتیاره
چنین گفت کان کو چنین باره کرد
نه ز بهر پیکار و پتیاره کرد (فردوسی)
PH, BQ, NS, AG3

570

پِچگَم: خانه تابستانی

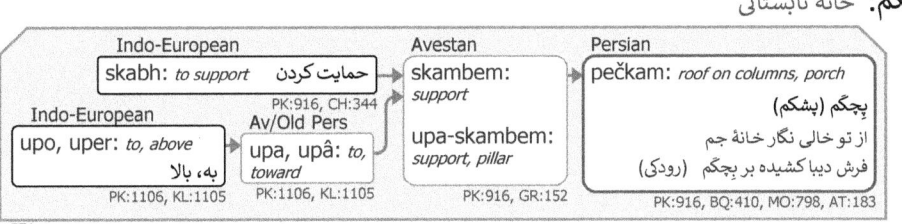

Indo-European
skabh: to support   حمایت کردن
PK:916, CH:344

Indo-European
upo, uper: to, above
به، بالا
PK:1106, KL:1105

Av/Old Pers
upa, upâ: to, toward
PK:1106, KL:1105

Avestan
skambem: support
upa-skambem: support, pillar
PK:916, GR:152

Persian
pečkam: roof on columns, porch
پچگم (پشکم)
از تو خالی نگار خانهٔ جم
فرش دیبا کشیده بر پچگم (رودکی)
PK:916, BQ:410, MO:798, AT:183

571

پختن

همریشه: cook

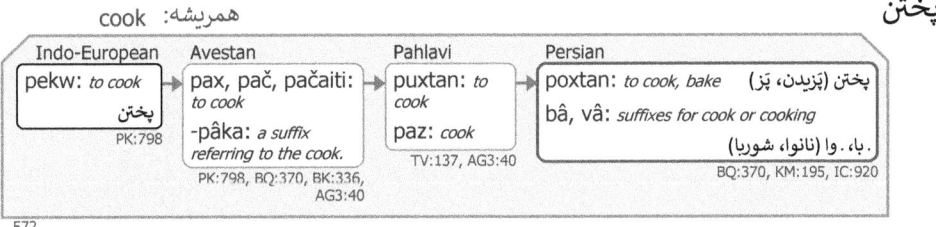

Indo-European
pekw: to cook
پختن
PK:798

Avestan
pax, pač, pačaiti: to cook
-pâka: a suffix referring to the cook.
PK:798, BQ:370, BK:336, AG3:40

Pahlavi
puxtan: to cook
paz: cook
TV:137, AG3:40

Persian
poxtan: to cook, bake   پختن (پزیدن، پز)
bâ, vâ: suffixes for cook or cooking
با، وا (نانوا، شوربا).
BQ:370, KM:195, IC:920

572

پدر: "حافظ خانواده"

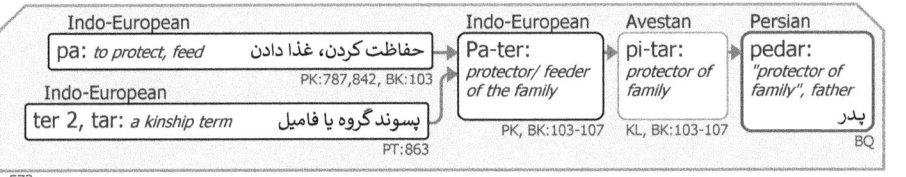

Indo-European
pa: to protect, feed   حفاظت کردن، غذا دادن
PK:787,842, BK:103

Indo-European
ter 2, tar: a kinship term   پسوند گروه یا فامیل
PT:863

Indo-European
Pa-ter: protector/ feeder of the family
PK, BK:103-107

Avestan
pi-tar: protector of family
KL, BK:103-107

Persian
pedar: "protector of family", father
پدر
BQ

573

پدرام: "آراسته، آرام"

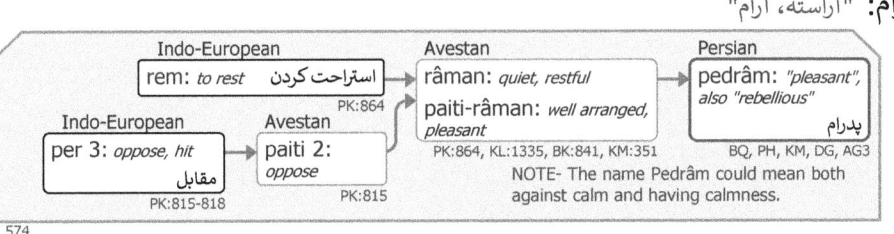

Indo-European
rem: to rest   استراحت کردن
PK:864

Indo-European
per 3: oppose, hit
مقابل
PK:815-818

Avestan
paiti 2: oppose
PK:815

Avestan
râman: quiet, restful
paiti-râman: well arranged, pleasant
PK:864, KL:1335, BK:841, KM:351

Persian
pedrâm: "pleasant", also "rebellious"
پدرام
BQ, PH, KM, DG, AG3

NOTE- The name Pedrâm could mean both against calm and having calmness.

574

پدراندر: پدرخوانده ـ رجوع شود به   اندر۲

پَدَرزه: چیزی که در جامه یا لنگی بسته باشند

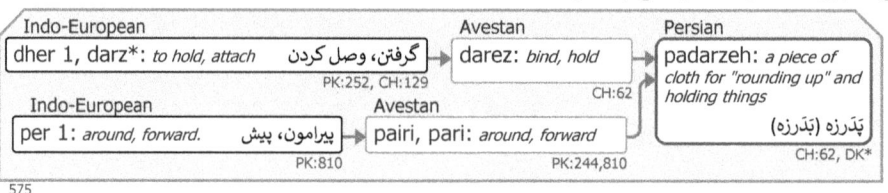

575

پدرود .رجوع شود به دُرود۲

همریشه: above, semantic   همریشه: دیدن   **پدید**

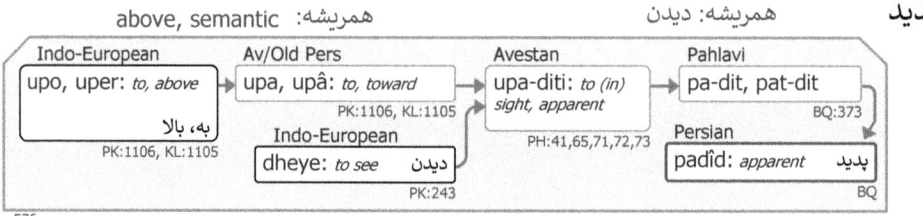

576

همریشه: grab   **پذیرفتن**

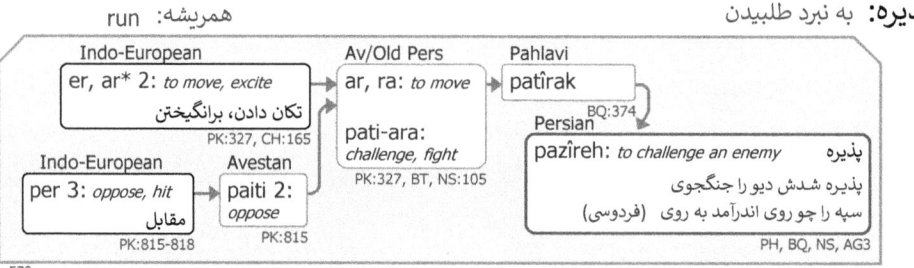

577

همریشه: run   **پذیره:** به نبرد طلبیدن

578

همریشه: full, assemble   **پُر**

579

پَر

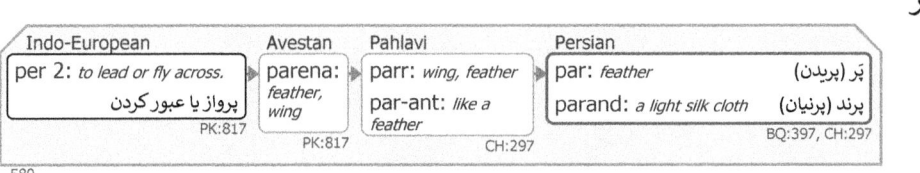

580

پراکندن

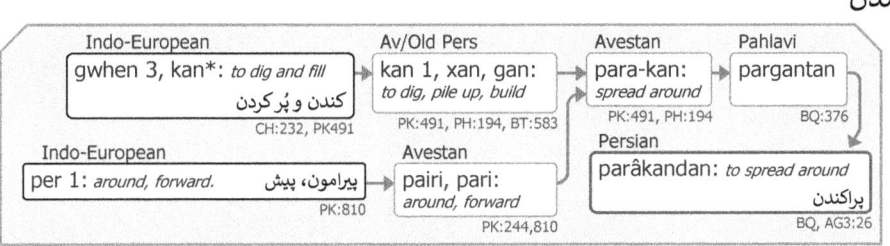

581

پرت، پرتاب

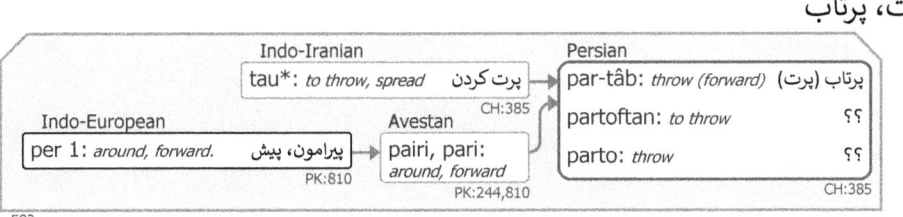

582

پرتو

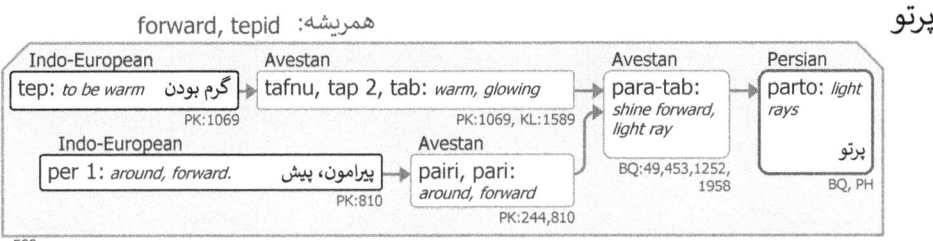

583

پرچین

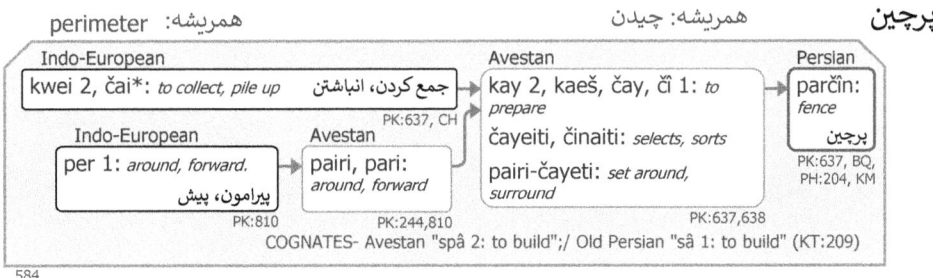

584

پرخاش: توهین، بد زبانی

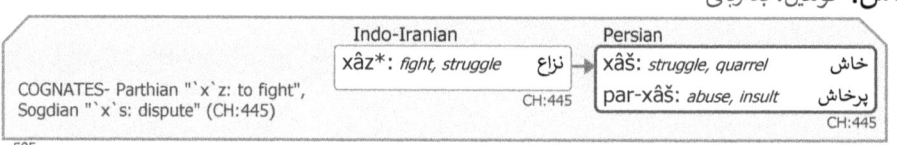

Indo-Iranian	Persian
xâz*: *fight, struggle* نزاع CH:445	xâš: *struggle, quarrel* خاش par-xâš: *abuse, insult* پرخاش CH:445

COGNATES- Parthian "`x`z: to fight",
Sogdian "`x`s: dispute" (CH:445)

585

پرداختن۱: انجام دادن   perform :همریشه

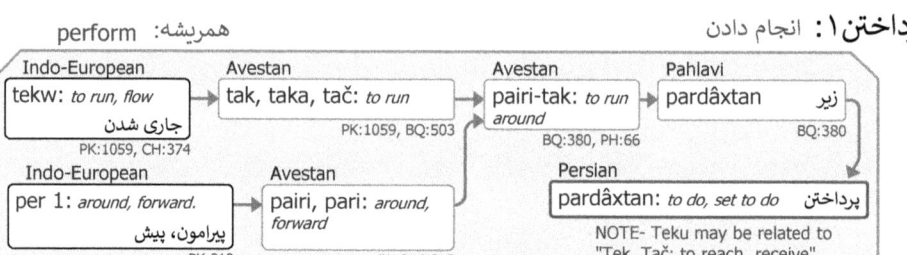

Indo-European	Avestan	Avestan	Pahlavi
tekw: *to run, flow* جاری شدن PK:1059, CH:374	tak, taka, tač: *to run* PK:1059, BQ:503	pairi-tak: *to run around* BQ:380, PH:66	pardâxtan زیر BQ:380
Indo-European	Avestan	Persian	
per 1: *around, forward.* پیرامون، پیش PK:810	pairi, pari: *around, forward* PK:244,810	pardâxtan: *to do, set to do* پرداختن	

NOTE- Teku may be related to
"Tek, Tač: to reach, receive"

586

پرداختن۲

Indo-European	Pahlavi	Persian
tek, tač*: *to stretch, reach, receive* دست دراز کردن، دریافت کردن PK:1057, CH:374	par-daz-: *to accomplish, pay* CH:374	pardâxtan: *to pay* پرداختن CH:374
Indo-European	Avestan	
per 1: *around, forward.* پیرامون، پیش PK:810	pairi, pari: *around, forward* PK:244,810	

NOTE- Teku may be related to
"Tek, Tač: to reach, receive"

587

پرده

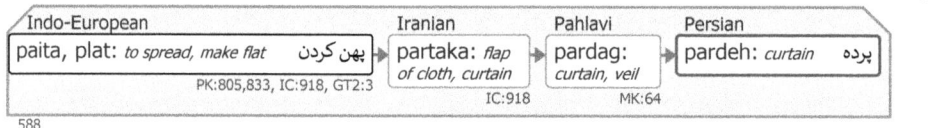

Indo-European	Iranian	Pahlavi	Persian
paita, plat: *to spread, make flat* پهن کردن PK:805,833, IC:918, GT2:3	partaka: *flap of cloth, curtain* IC:918	pardag: *curtain, veil* MK:64	pardeh: *curtain* پرده

588

پردیس: "محصور به دیوار"   همریشه: پیرامون و دیوار   همریشه: figure, lady

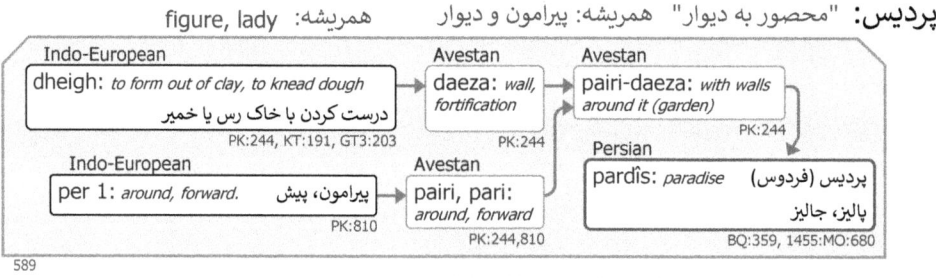

Indo-European	Avestan	Avestan
dheigh: *to form out of clay, to knead dough* درست کردن با خاک رس یا خمیر PK:244, KT:191, GT3:203	daeza: *wall, fortification* PK:244	pairi-daeza: *with walls around it (garden)* PK:244
Indo-European	Avestan	Persian
per 1: *around, forward.* پیرامون، پیش PK:810	pairi, pari: *around, forward* PK:244,810	pardîs: *paradise* پردیس (فردوس) پالیز، جالیز BQ:359, 1455:MO:680

589

پرستار   - رجوع شود به   پرستیدن

پرستو   همریشه: sparrow

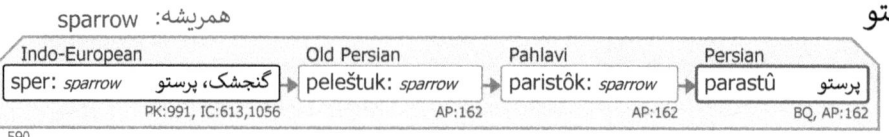

Indo-European	Old Persian	Pahlavi	Persian
sper: *sparrow* گنجشک، پرستو PK:991, IC:613,1056	peleštuk: *sparrow* AP:162	paristôk: *sparrow* AP:162	parastû پرستو BQ, AP:162

590

پرستیدن

همریشه: stand, before, perimeter

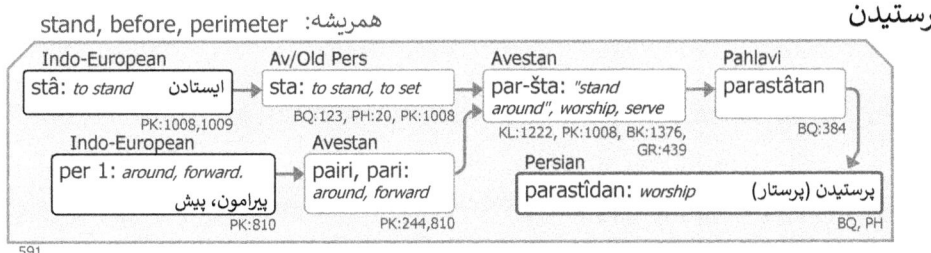

591

پَرسنگ

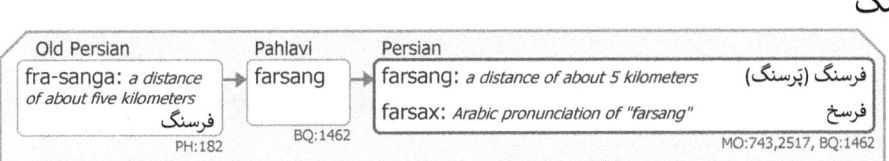

592

پرسیدن

مقایسه: پادافراه

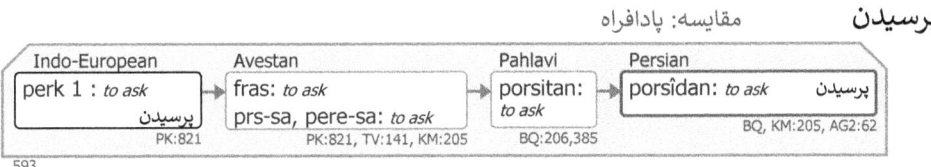

593

پرگار: "پیرامون نگار"

همریشه: perimeter

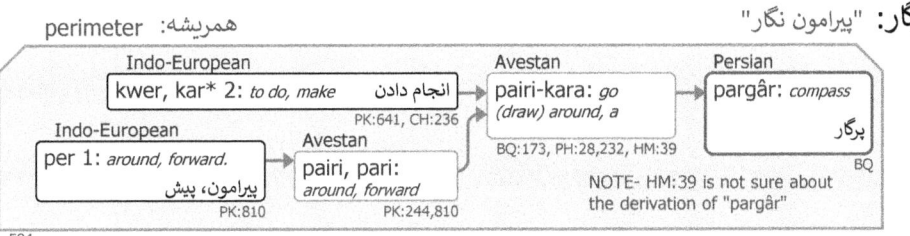

594

پَرگَنه: "زمینی که دور تا دورش خندق باشد"

همریشه: perimeter

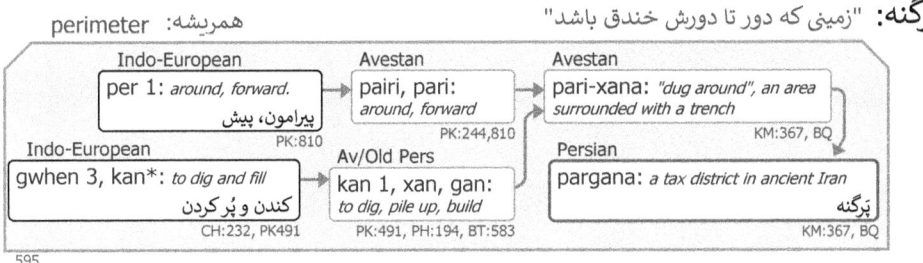

595

پَرماسیدن۱: لمس کردن، سودن

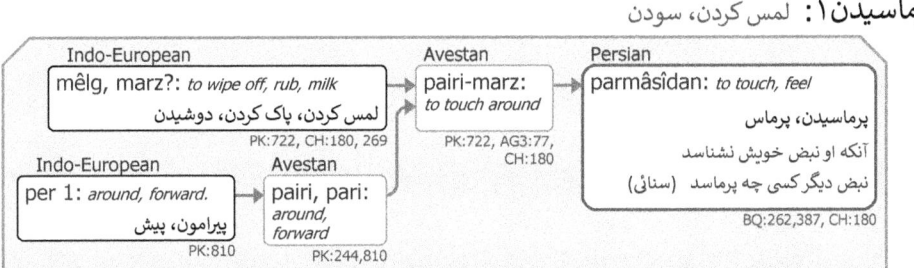

596

پَرماسیدن۲: دانستن

همریشه: per, measure

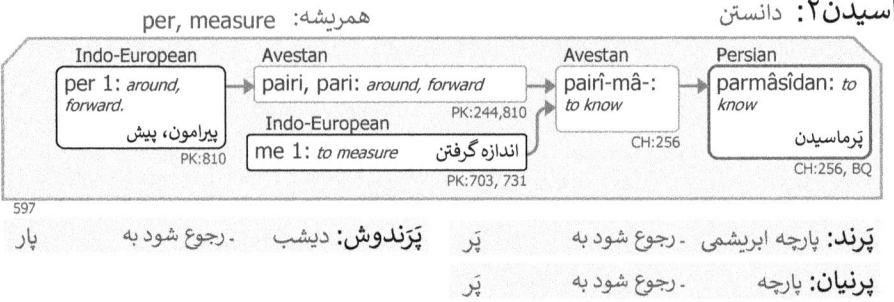

597

پَرند: پارچه ابریشمی - رجوع شود به   پَر   پَرَندوش: دیشب - رجوع شود به   پار

پرنیان: پارچه   - رجوع شود به   پَر

پروار: اسطبل، بزرگ شده در اسطبل (بدون فعالیت)

همریشه: cover, garage

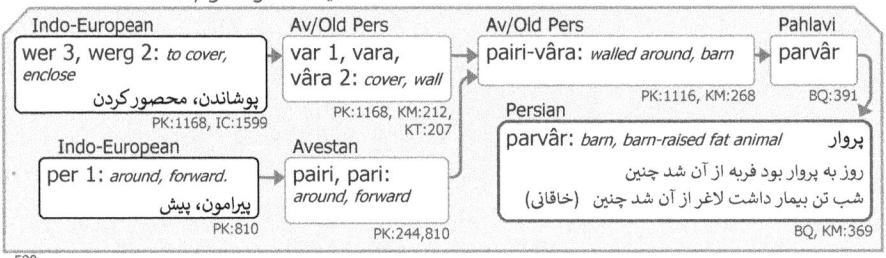

598

پرواز

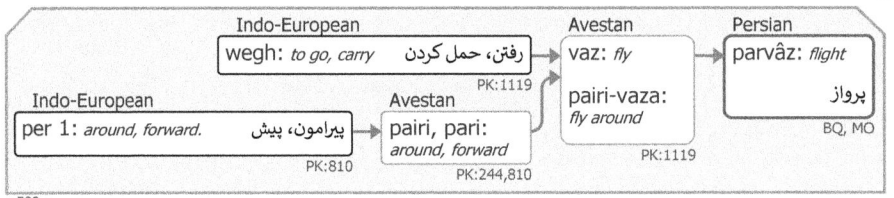

599

پروانه

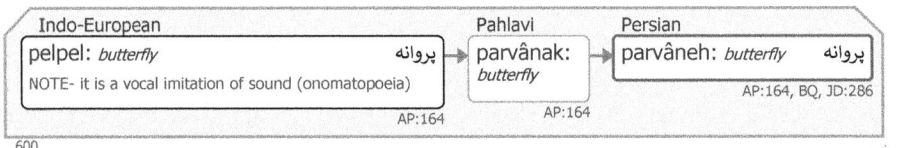

600

پروردن

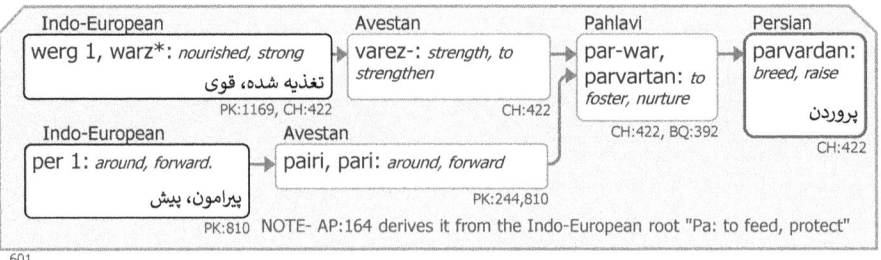

601

پرویز همریشه: ویژه   "پیروز، موفق"   همریشه: over, super

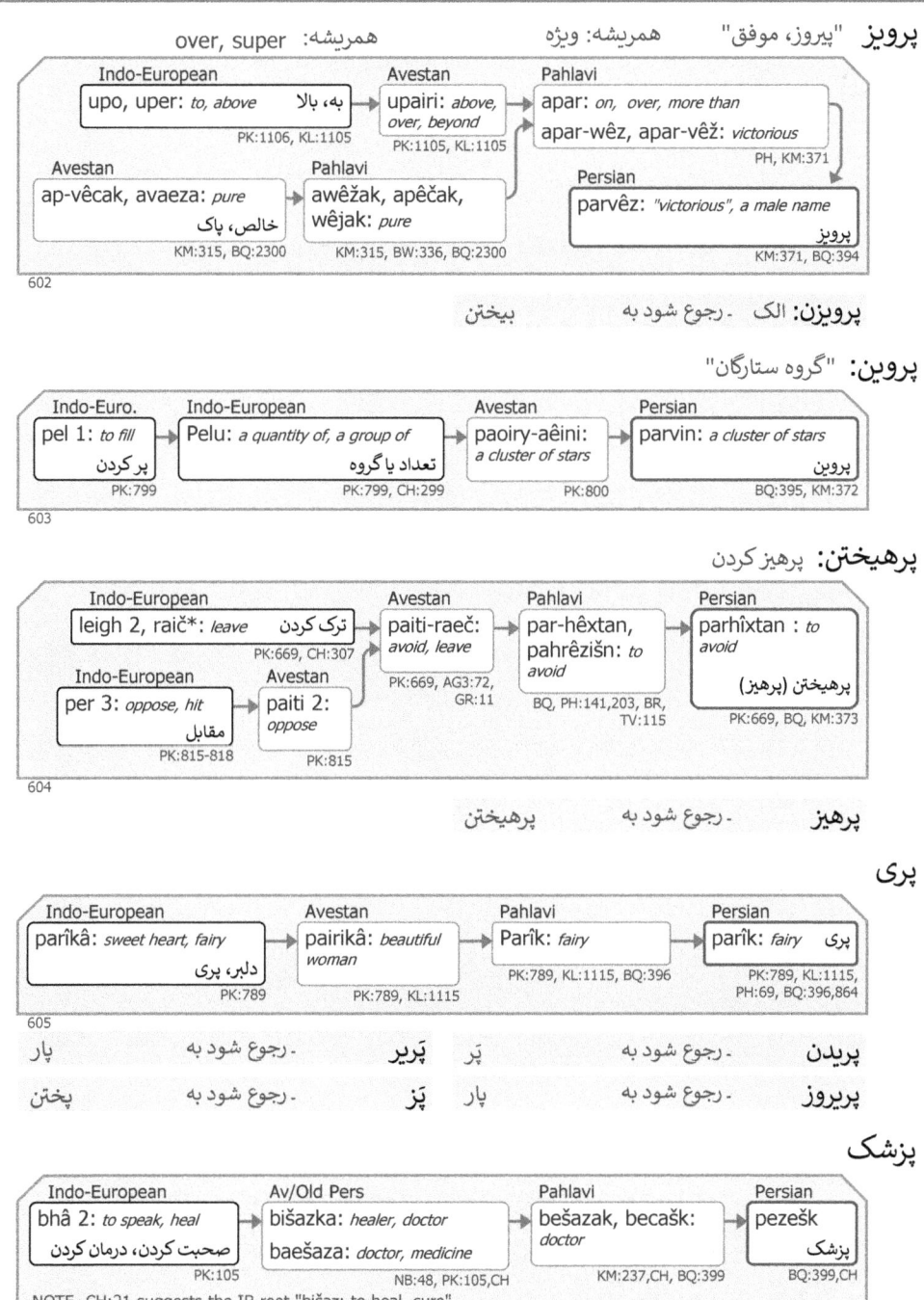

602

پرویزن: الک   ـ رجوع شود به   بیختن

پروین: "گروه ستارگان"

603

پرهیختن: پرهیز کردن

604

پرهیز   ـ رجوع شود به   پرهیختن

پری

605

| پریدن | ـ رجوع شود به | پَر | پَریر | ـ رجوع شود به | پار |
| پریروز | ـ رجوع شود به | پار | پَز | ـ رجوع شود به | پختن |

پزشک

606

پَزیدن   ـ رجوع شود به   پختن

108

پَژ: کوه   همریشه: پاپژ، پژواک

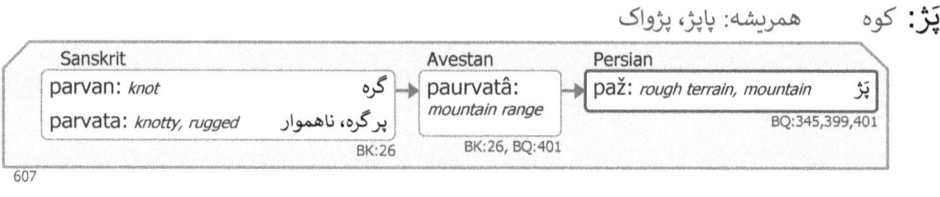

پژمان: پشیمان

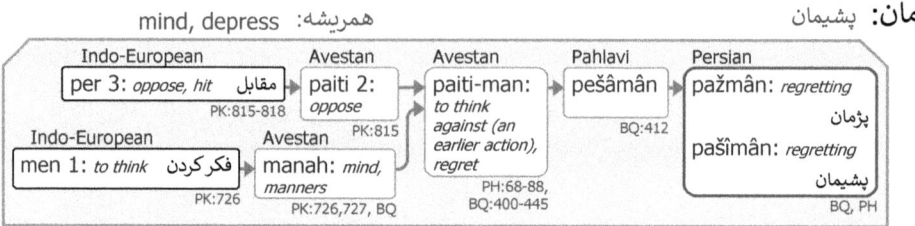

پژمردن

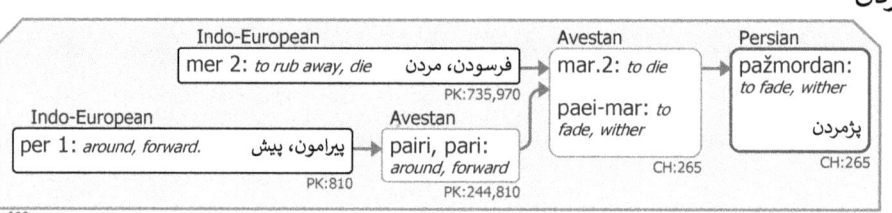

پژواک: "صدای کوه"   همریشه: پژ، پاپژ

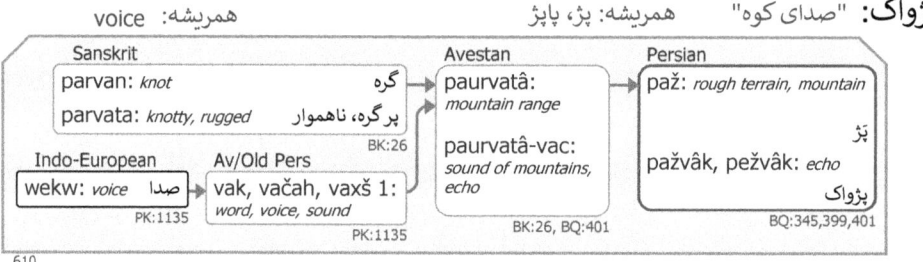

پژوهیدن

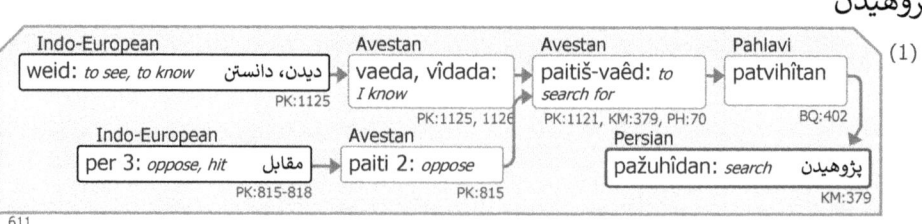

پژوهیدن

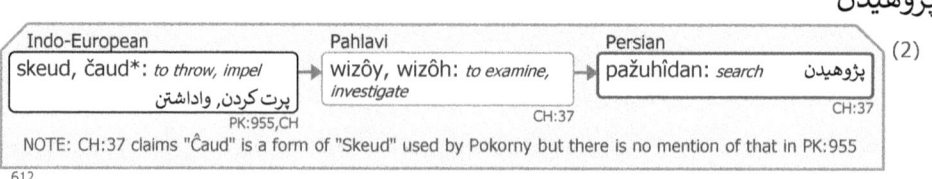

پس: پشت، پی، دنبال

همریشه: of, after

Indo-European	Indo-European	Av/Old Pers	Pahlavi	Persian
apo: *off* جدا، دور PK:53	Pos: *after, behind* PK:841	pasča, pasca, pasâ: *after, behind* PK:842	pas, pasin BQ:3673	pas: *later, after* پس PH:70, BQ:403, IC:29

613

پَساک: تاج گُل   ـ رجوع شود به   بَساک

پَست

همریشه: compete

Indo-European	Av/Old Pers	Avestan	Persian
pet 1: *to fly, to fall* پرواز کردن، افتادن PK:825, CH:299	ptâta, tâta: *falling* PK:825, PH:22	patta: *fallen, low, inferior* KM:382, HM:41	past: *low, inferior* پست۱ KM:382

614

پِست: آرد

Indo-European	Avestan	Pahlavi	Persian
pais, peis: *crush, grind* خرد کردن	pišant: *crushing, grinding* pîštra: *flour*	pest BQ:404	pest: *flour, crushed roasted wheat* پست۲ بیاورد جامی زیاقوت زرد پر از شکر و پست با آب سرد (فردوسی)
WD2:1, CH:292, PK:796	WD2:1, CH:292		HM:42, MO, CH:292

615

پستان

Indo-European	Avestan	Pahlavi	Persian
pestêno: *breast* پستان PK:990	fštâna: *breast* KL:1513, PK:990	pistân BQ:405	pestân: *breast* پستان PK:990, BQ:405

616

پسته

Pahlavi	Persian	Greek	Arabic	Persian
bistak: *pistachio* پسته	pesteh: *pistachio* پسته AA:210, AD:998	pistake, pistakion AA:210, KL:1190	fustug, fostoq: *pistachio* AA:210	fostoĝ: *pistachio* فُستُق MO:2545

NOTE- MO: 2545 claims this is from Aramaic, then passed to Greek.

617

پسر

همریشه: poor, pupil, puppet

Indo-European	Av/Old Pers	Pahlavi	Persian
pôu: *small, young* کوچک، جوان PK:842	pu 1, pu-thra, puthra: *child* PK:842	puhr, pus, pusar: *boy, child* BQ:425, AP:169	pesar: *son* پسر pûr: *son* پور (پوران) BQ, KM:384

COGNATE- Old Persian "puča: son" (AG1:13)

618

پِسراندر: پسرخوانده ـ رجوع شود به   اندر۲

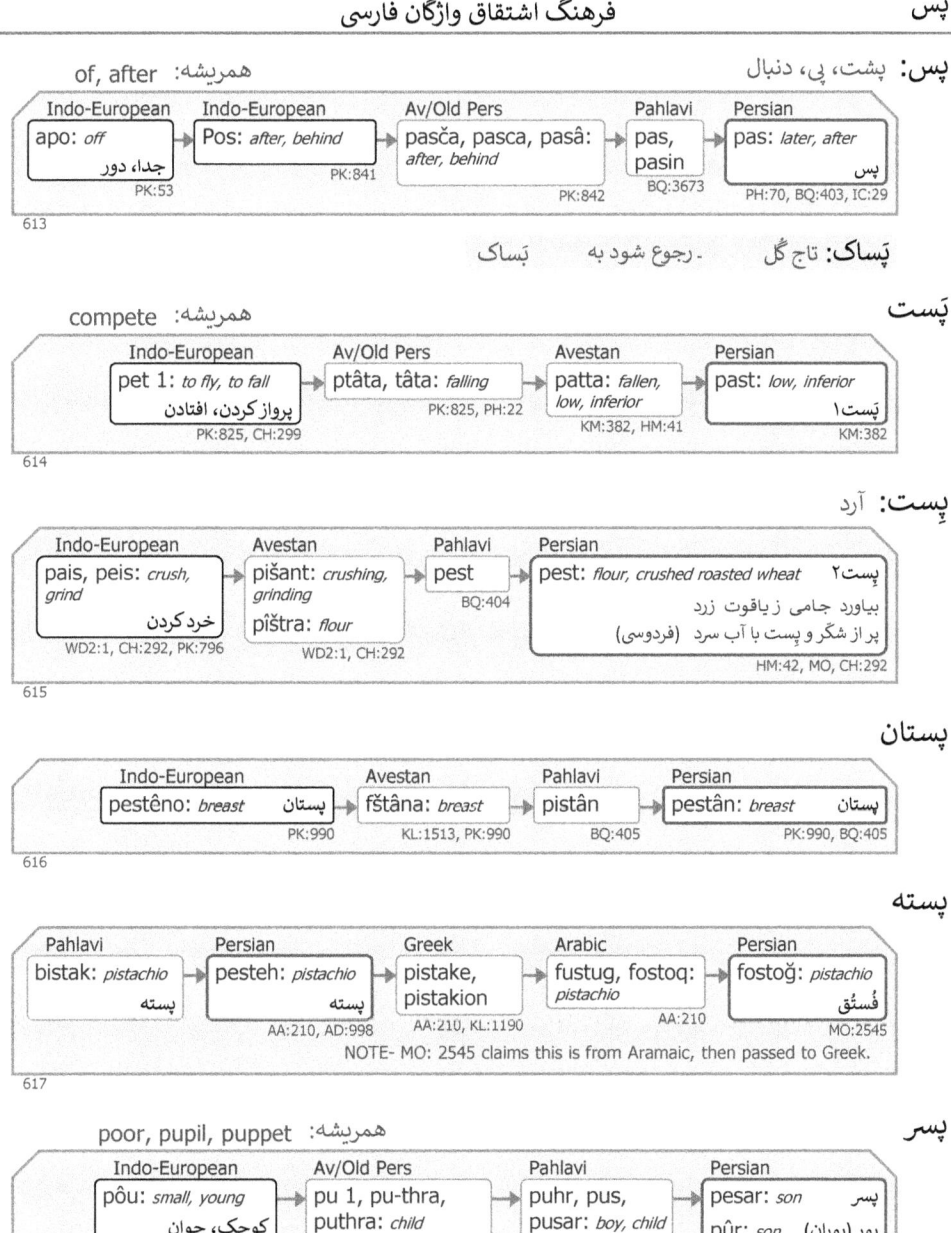

پسندیدن

همریشه: above, settle   همریشه: خرسند

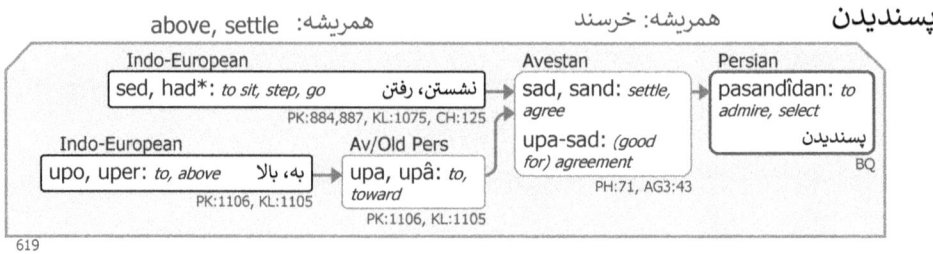

Indo-European — sed, had*: *to sit, step, go* نشستن، رفتن — PK:884,887, KL:1075, CH:125

Indo-European — upo, uper: *to, above* به، بالا — PK:1106, KL:1105

Av/Old Pers — upa, upâ: *to, toward* — PK:1106, KL:1105

Avestan — sad, sand: *settle, agree* — upa-sad: *(good for) agreement* — PH:71, AG3:43

Persian — pasandîdan: *to admire, select* پسندیدن — BQ

619

پشت

همریشه: stand, proper   همریشه: ستون

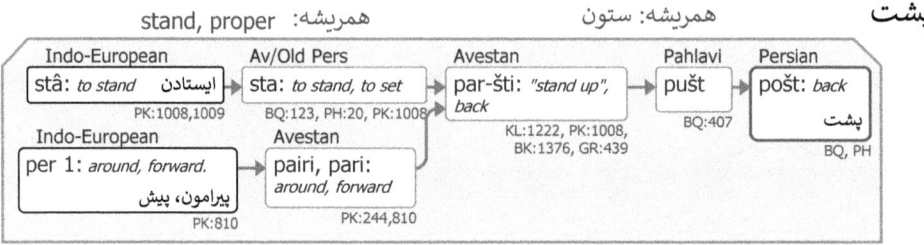

Indo-European — stâ: *to stand* ایستادن — PK:1008,1009

Indo-European — per 1: *around, forward.* پیرامون، پیش — PK:810

Av/Old Pers — sta: *to stand, to set* — BQ:123, PH:20, PK:1008

Avestan — pairi, pari: *around, forward* — PK:244,810

Avestan — par-šti: *"stand up", back* — KL:1222, PK:1008, BK:1376, GR:439

Pahlavi — pušt — BQ:407

Persian — pošt: *back* پشت — BQ, PH

620

پشگم: خانه تابستانی ـ رجوع شود به   پچگم

پشم

همریشه: fellow   همریشه: چوپان

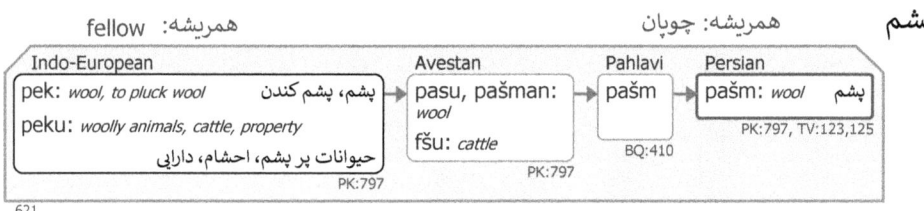

Indo-European — pek: *wool, to pluck wool* پشم، پشم کندن — peku: *woolly animals, cattle, property* حیوانات پر پشم، احشام، دارایی — PK:797

Avestan — pasu, pašman: *wool* — fšu: *cattle* — PK:797

Pahlavi — pašm — BQ:410

Persian — pašm: *wool* پشم — PK:797, TV:123,125

621

پشملبا: "بستنی سیب پارسی (هلو)"

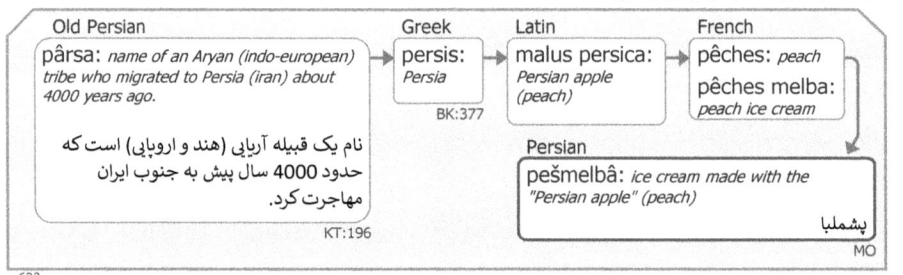

Old Persian — pârsa: *name of an Aryan (indo-european) tribe who migrated to Persia (iran) about 4000 years ago.* نام یک قبیله آریایی (هند و اروپایی) است که حدود 4000 سال پیش به جنوب ایران مهاجرت کرد. — KT:196

Greek — persis: *Persia* — BK:377

Latin — malus persica: *Persian apple (peach)*

French — pêches: *peach* — pêches melba: *peach ice cream*

Persian — pešmelbâ: *ice cream made with the "Persian apple" (peach)* پشملبا — MO

622

پشنجیدن: آب پاشیدن، نم زدن

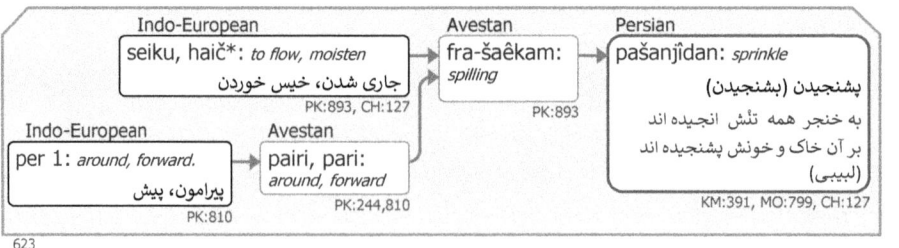

Indo-European — seiku, haič*: *to flow, moisten* جاری شدن، خیس خوردن — PK:893, CH:127

Indo-European — per 1: *around, forward.* پیرامون، پیش — PK:810

Avestan — fra-šaêkam: *spilling* — PK:893

Avestan — pairi, pari: *around, forward* — PK:244,810

Persian — pašanjîdan: *sprinkle* پشنجیدن (بشنجیدن) به خنجر همه تنش انجیده اند بر آن خاک و خونش پشنجیده اند (لبیبی) — KM:391, MO:799, CH:127

623

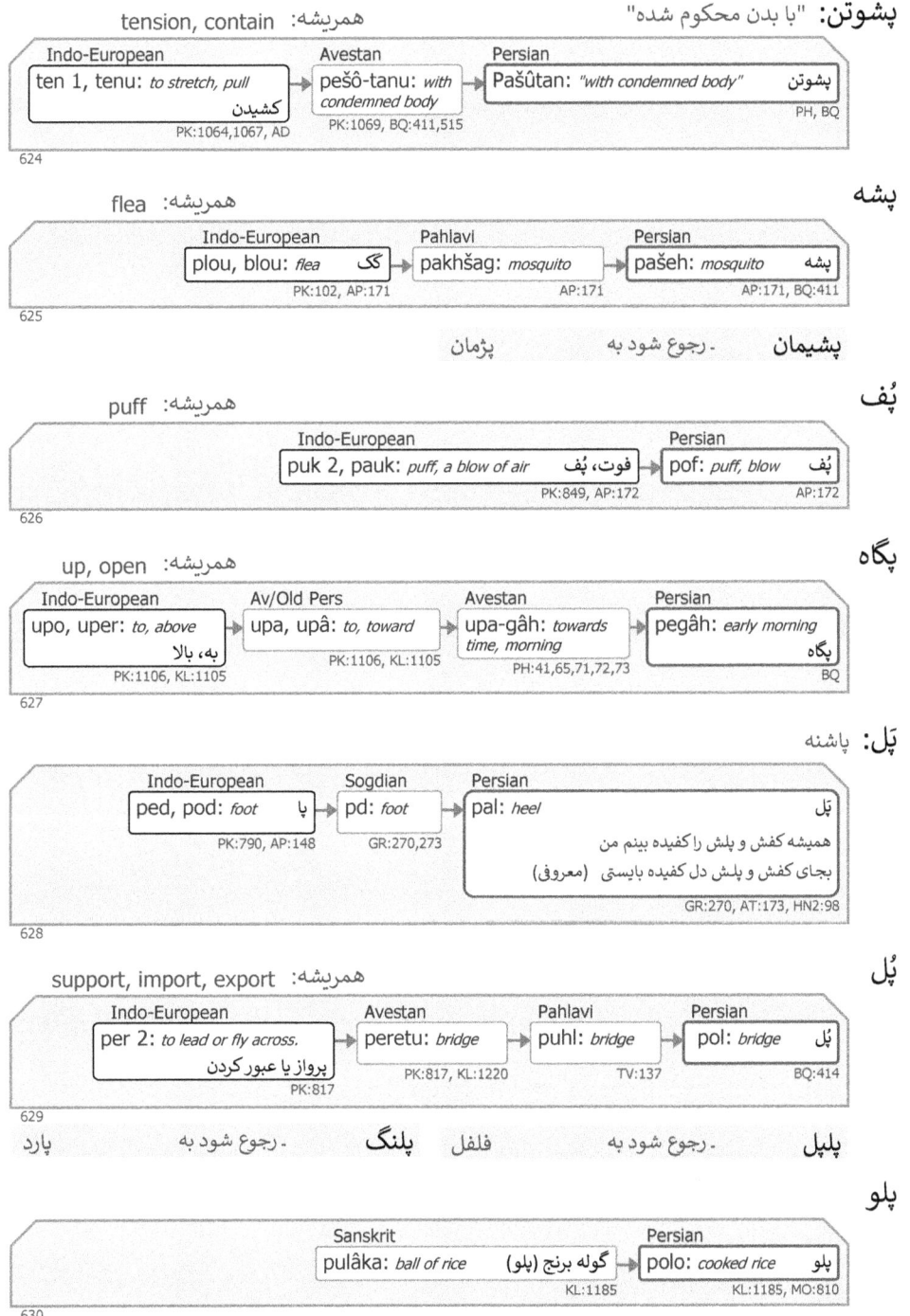

پشوتن: "با بدن محکوم شده"

همریشه: tension, contain

Indo-European — ten 1, tenu: *to stretch, pull* کشیدن — PK:1064,1067, AD

Avestan — pešô-tanu: *with condemned body* — PK:1069, BQ:411,515

Persian — Pašûtan: *"with condemned body"* پشوتن — PH, BQ

624

پشه

همریشه: flea

Indo-European — plou, blou: *flea* گگ — PK:102, AP:171

Pahlavi — pakhšag: *mosquito* — AP:171

Persian — pašeh: *mosquito* پشه — AP:171, BQ:411

625

پشیمان

. رجوع شود به   پژمان

پُف

همریشه: puff

Indo-European — puk 2, pauk: *puff, a blow of air* فوت، پُف — PK:849, AP:172

Persian — pof: *puff, blow* پُف — AP:172

626

پگاه

همریشه: up, open

Indo-European — upo, uper: *to, above* به، بالا — PK:1106, KL:1105

Av/Old Pers — upa, upâ: *to, toward* — PK:1106, KL:1105

Avestan — upa-gâh: *towards time, morning* — PH:41,65,71,72,73

Persian — pegâh: *early morning* پگاه — BQ

627

پِل: پاشنه

Indo-European — ped, pod: *foot* پا — PK:790, AP:148

Sogdian — pd: *foot* — GR:270,273

Persian — pal: *heel* پِل

همیشه کفش و پلش را کفیده بینم من
بجای کفش و پلش دل کفیده بایستی (معروق)

GR:270, AT:173, HN2:98

628

پُل

همریشه: support, import, export

Indo-European — per 2: *to lead or fly across.* پرواز یا عبور کردن — PK:817

Avestan — peretu: *bridge* — PK:817, KL:1220

Pahlavi — puhl: *bridge* — TV:137

Persian — pol: *bridge* پُل — BQ:414

629

پلپل

. رجوع شود به   فلفل   پلنگ   . رجوع شود به   پارد

پلو

Sanskrit — pulâka: *ball of rice* گوله برنج (پلو) — KL:1185

Persian — polo: *cooked rice* پلو — KL:1185, MO:810

630

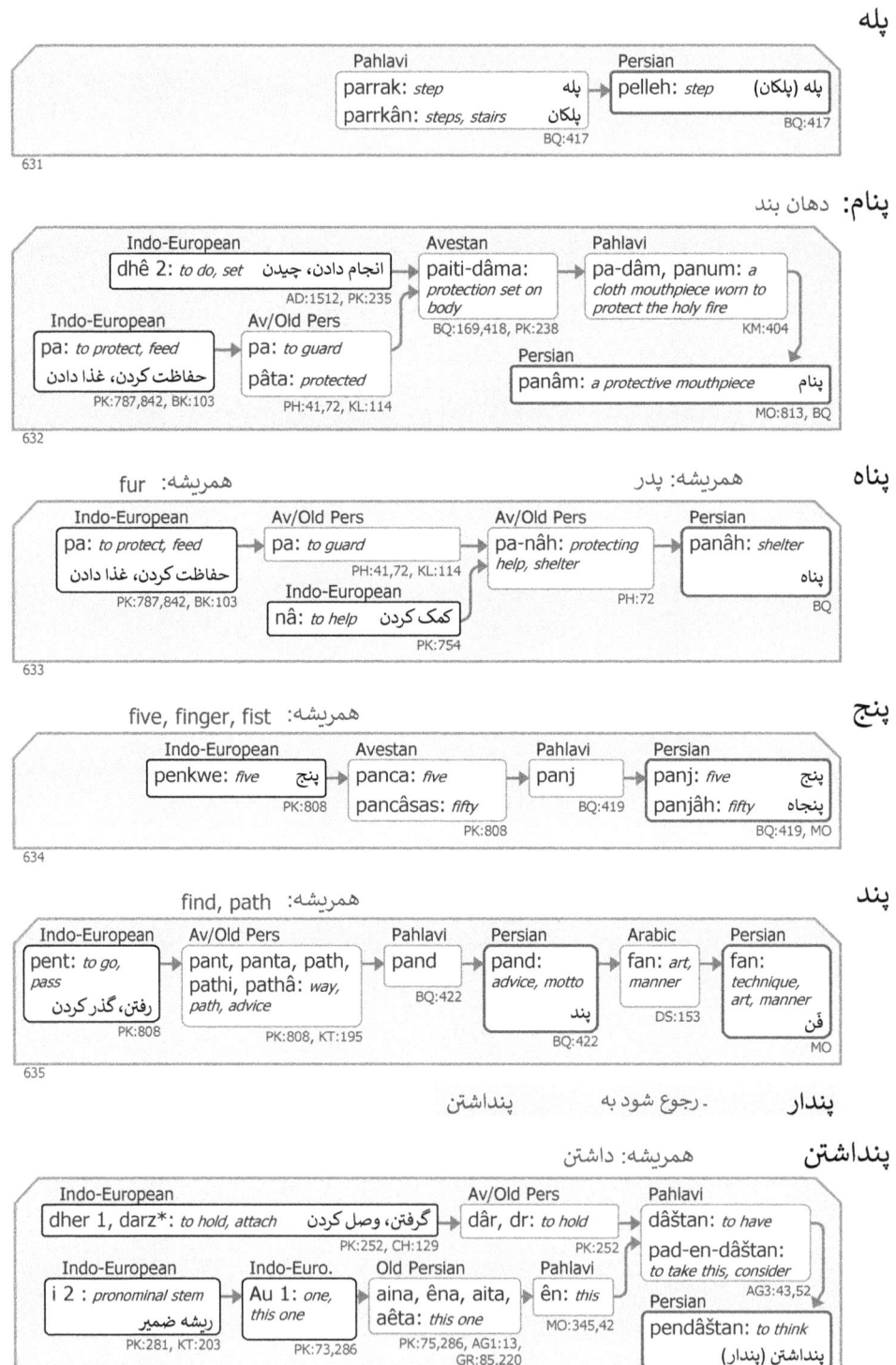

پله

Pahlavi
parrak: *step* پله
parrkân: *steps, stairs* پلکان
BQ:417

Persian
pelleh: *step* پله (پلکان)
BQ:417

631

پنام: دهان بند

Indo-European
dhê 2: *to do, set* انجام دادن، چیدن
AD:1512, PK:235

Indo-European
pa: *to protect, feed*
حفاظت کردن، غذا دادن
PK:787,842, BK:103

Av/Old Pers
pa: *to guard*
pâta: *protected*
PH:41,72, KL:114

Avestan
paiti-dâma: *protection set on body*
BQ:169,418, PK:238

Pahlavi
pa-dâm, panum: *a cloth mouthpiece worn to protect the holy fire*
KM:404

Persian
panâm: *a protective mouthpiece* پنام
MO:813, BQ

632

پناه

همریشه: fur   همریشه: پدر

Indo-European
pa: *to protect, feed*
حفاظت کردن، غذا دادن
PK:787,842, BK:103

Av/Old Pers
pa: *to guard*
PH:41,72, KL:114

Indo-European
nâ: *to help* کمک کردن
PK:754

Av/Old Pers
pa-nâh: *protecting help, shelter*
PH:72

Persian
panâh: *shelter*
پناه
BQ

633

پنج

همریشه: five, finger, fist

Indo-European
penkwe: *five* پنج
PK:808

Avestan
panca: *five*
pancâsas: *fifty*
PK:808

Pahlavi
panj
BQ:419

Persian
panj: *five* پنج
panjâh: *fifty* پنجاه
BQ:419, MO

634

پند

همریشه: find, path

Indo-European
pent: *to go, pass*
رفتن، گذر کردن
PK:808

Av/Old Pers
pant, panta, path, pathi, pathâ: *way, path, advice*
PK:808, KT:195

Pahlavi
pand
BQ:422

Persian
pand: *advice, motto*
پند
BQ:422

Arabic
fan: *art, manner*
DS:153

Persian
fan: *technique, art, manner*
فَن
MO

635

پندار

رجوع شود به .   پنداشتن

پنداشتن

همریشه: داشتن

Indo-European
dher 1, darz*: *to hold, attach* گرفتن، وصل کردن
PK:252, CH:129

Indo-European
i 2 : *pronominal stem*
ریشه ضمیر
PK:281, KT:203

Indo-Euro.
Au 1: *one, this one*
PK:73,286

Old Persian
aina, êna, aita, aêta: *this one*
PK:75,286, AG1:13, GR:85,220

Av/Old Pers
dâr, dr: *to hold*
PK:252

Pahlavi
ên: *this*
MO:345,42

Pahlavi
dâštan: *to have*
pad-en-dâštan: *to take this, consider*
AG3:43,52

Persian
pendâštan: *to think*
پنداشتن (پندار)
BQ:810, AG3:43

636

113

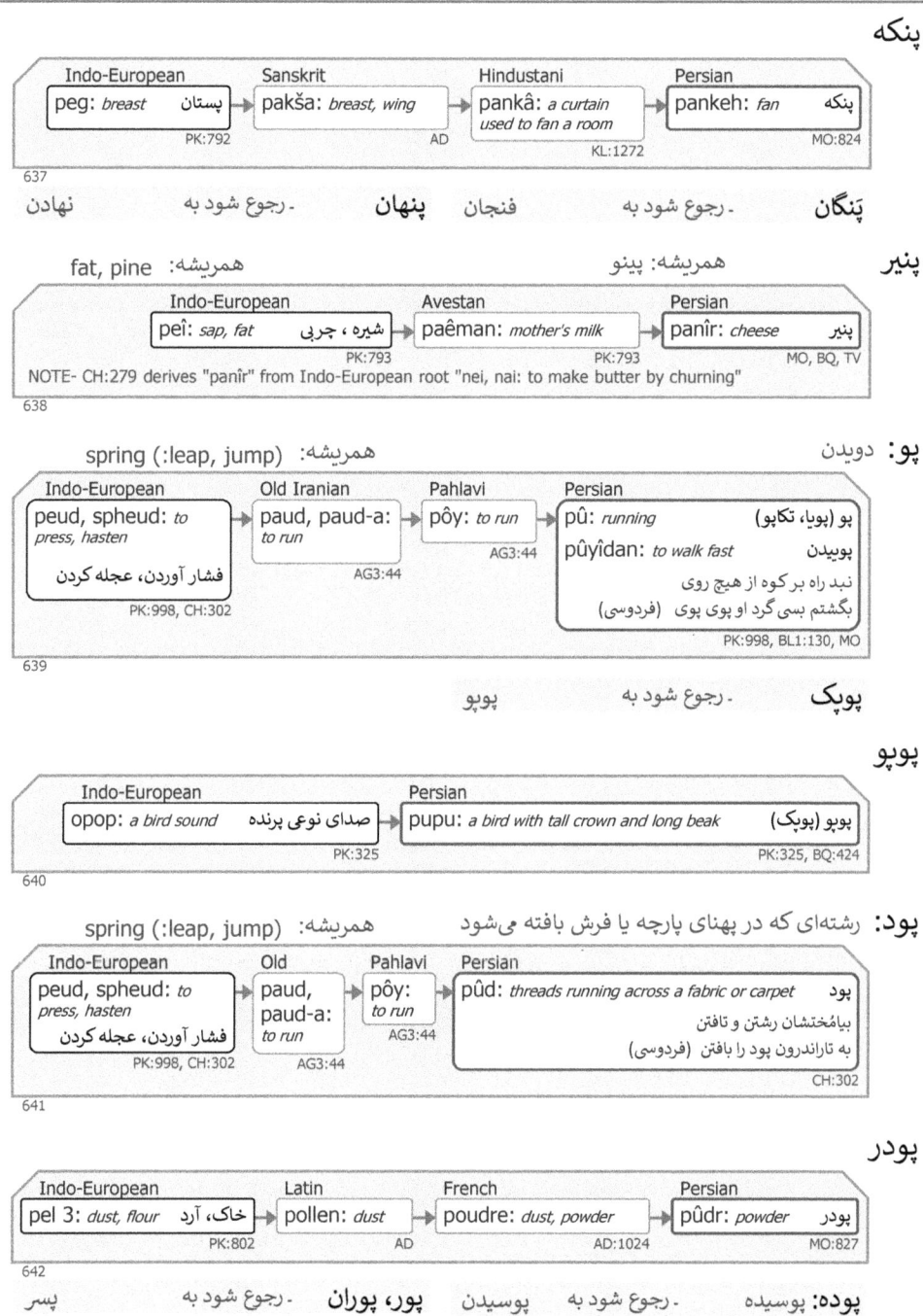

پنکه

Indo-European	Sanskrit	Hindustani	Persian
peg: *breast* پستان	pakša: *breast, wing*	panká: *a curtain used to fan a room*	pankeh: *fan* پنکه
PK:792	AD	KL:1272	MO:824

637

پَنگان ـ رجوع شود به **نهادن**

پنهان ـ رجوع شود به **فنجان**

پنیر همریشه: پینو

همریشه: fat, pine

Indo-European	Avestan	Persian
peî: *sap, fat* شیره ، چربی	paêman: *mother's milk*	panîr: *cheese* پنیر
PK:793	PK:793	MO, BQ, TV

NOTE- CH:279 derives "panîr" from Indo-European root "nei, nai: to make butter by churning"

638

پو: دویدن

همریشه: (spring (:leap, jump

Indo-European	Old Iranian	Pahlavi	Persian
peud, spheud: *to press, hasten* فشار آوردن، عجله کردن	paud, paud-a: *to run*	pôy: *to run*	pû: *running* پو (پویا، تکاپو)
			pûyîdan: *to walk fast* پوییدن
			نبد راه بر کوه از هیچ روی
			بگشتم بسی گرد او پوی پوی (فردوسی)
PK:998, CH:302	AG3:44	AG3:44	PK:998, BL1:130, MO

639

پوپک ـ رجوع شود به **پوپو**

پوپو

Indo-European	Persian
opop: *a bird sound* صدای نوعی پرنده	pupu: *a bird with tall crown and long beak* پوپو (پوپک)
PK:325	PK:325, BQ:424

640

پود: رشته‌ای که در پهنای پارچه یا فرش بافته می‌شود

همریشه: (spring (:leap, jump

Indo-European	Old	Pahlavi	Persian
peud, spheud: *to press, hasten* فشار آوردن، عجله کردن	paud, paud-a: *to run*	pôy: *to run*	pûd: *threads running across a fabric or carpet* پود
			بیامختشان رشتن و تافتن
			به تاراندرون پود را بافتن (فردوسی)
PK:998, CH:302	AG3:44	AG3:44	CH:302

641

پودر

Indo-European	Latin	French	Persian
pel 3: *dust, flour* خاک، آرد	pollen: *dust*	poudre: *dust, powder*	pûdr: *powder* پودر
PK:802	AD	AD:1024	MO:827

642

پوده: پوسیده ـ رجوع شود به **پوسیدن**

پور، پوران ـ رجوع شود به **پسر**

پوزش ـ رجوع شود به **پوزیدن**

پوزیدن

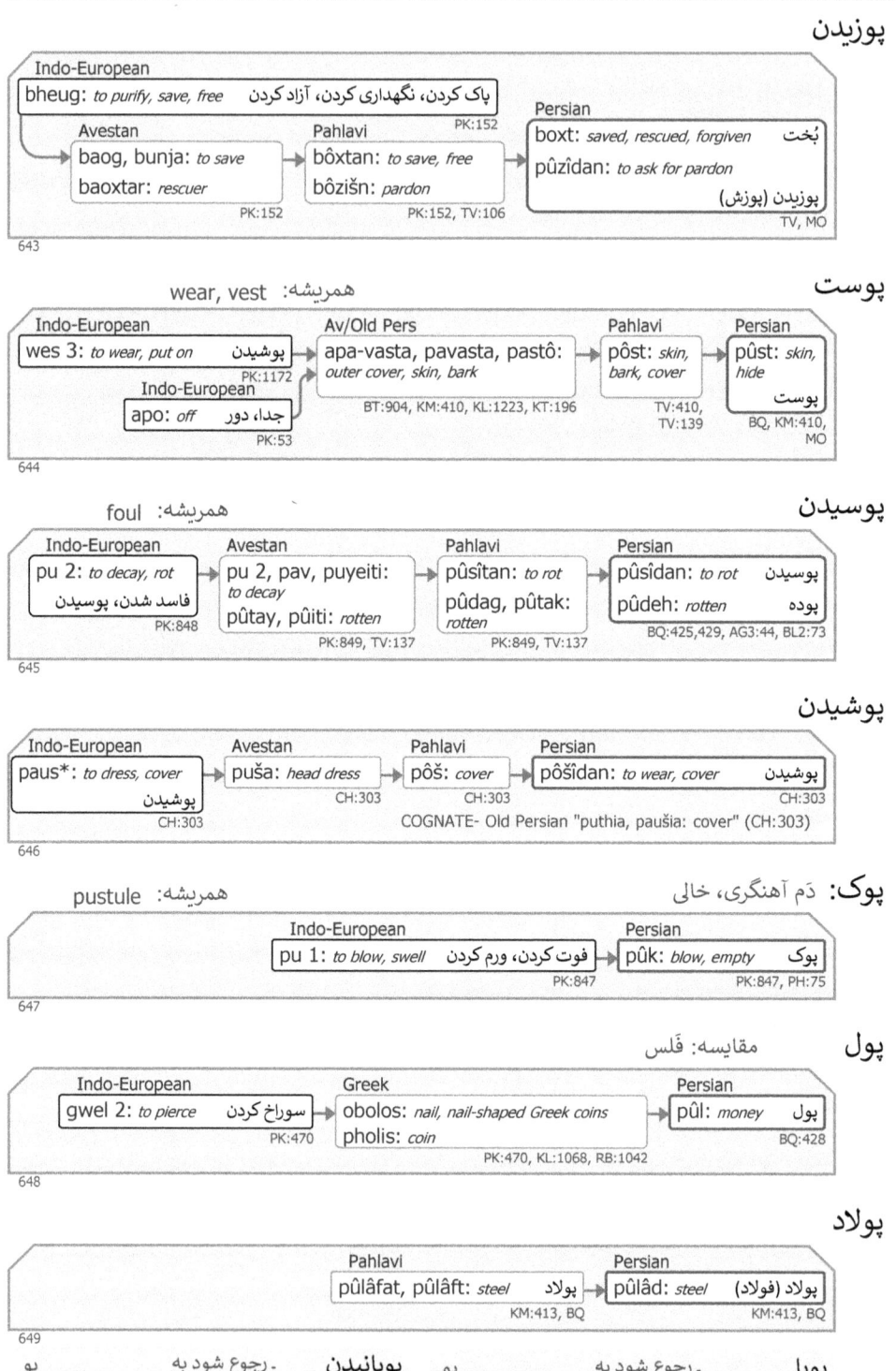

Indo-European
bheug: *to purify, save, free*   پاک کردن، نگهداری کردن، آزاد کردن
PK:152

Avestan
baog, bunja: *to save*
baoxtar: *rescuer*
PK:152

Pahlavi
bôxtan: *to save, free*
bôzišn: *pardon*
PK:152, TV:106

Persian
boxt: *saved, rescued, forgiven*   بُخت
pûzîdan: *to ask for pardon*
پوزیدن (پوزش)
TV, MO

643

پوست

همریشه: wear, vest

Indo-European
wes 3: *to wear, put on*   پوشیدن
PK:1172

Indo-European
apo: *off*   جدا، دور
PK:53

Av/Old Pers
apa-vasta, pavasta, pastô:
outer cover, skin, bark
BT:904, KM:410, KL:1223, KT:196

Pahlavi
pôst: *skin, bark, cover*
TV:410, TV:139

Persian
pûst: *skin, hide*
پوست
BQ, KM:410, MO

644

پوسیدن

همریشه: foul

Indo-European
pu 2: *to decay, rot*
فاسد شدن، پوسیدن
PK:848

Avestan
pu 2, pav, puyeiti: *to decay*
pûtay, pûiti: *rotten*
PK:849, TV:137

Pahlavi
pûsîtan: *to rot*
pûdag, pûtak: *rotten*
PK:849, TV:137

Persian
pûsîdan: *to rot*   پوسید
pûdeh: *rotten*   پوده
BQ:425,429, AG3:44, BL2:73

645

پوشیدن

Indo-European
paus*: *to dress, cover*
پوشیدن
CH:303

Avestan
puša: *head dress*
CH:303

Pahlavi
pôš: *cover*
CH:303

Persian
pôšîdan: *to wear, cover*   پوشید
CH:303

COGNATE- Old Persian "puthia, paušia: cover" (CH:303)

646

پوک: دَم آهنگری، خالی

همریشه: pustule

Indo-European
pu 1: *to blow, swell*   فوت کردن، ورم کردن
PK:847

Persian
pûk: *blow, empty*   پوک
PK:847, PH:75

647

پول

مقایسه: فَلس

Indo-European
gwel 2: *to pierce*   سوراخ کردن
PK:470

Greek
obolos: *nail, nail-shaped Greek coins*
pholis: *coin*
PK:470, KL:1068, RB:1042

Persian
pûl: *money*   پول
BQ:428

648

پولاد

Pahlavi
pûlâfat, pûlâft: *steel*   پولاد
KM:413, BQ

Persian
pûlâd: *steel*   (پولاد (فولاد
KM:413, BQ

649

پو   رجوع شود به -   **پویانیدن**   پو   رجوع شود به -   **پویا**

پوییدن   ـ رجوع شود به   **پو**   **پِه**   ـ رجوع شود به   پیه

پَهره: پاس و محافظت

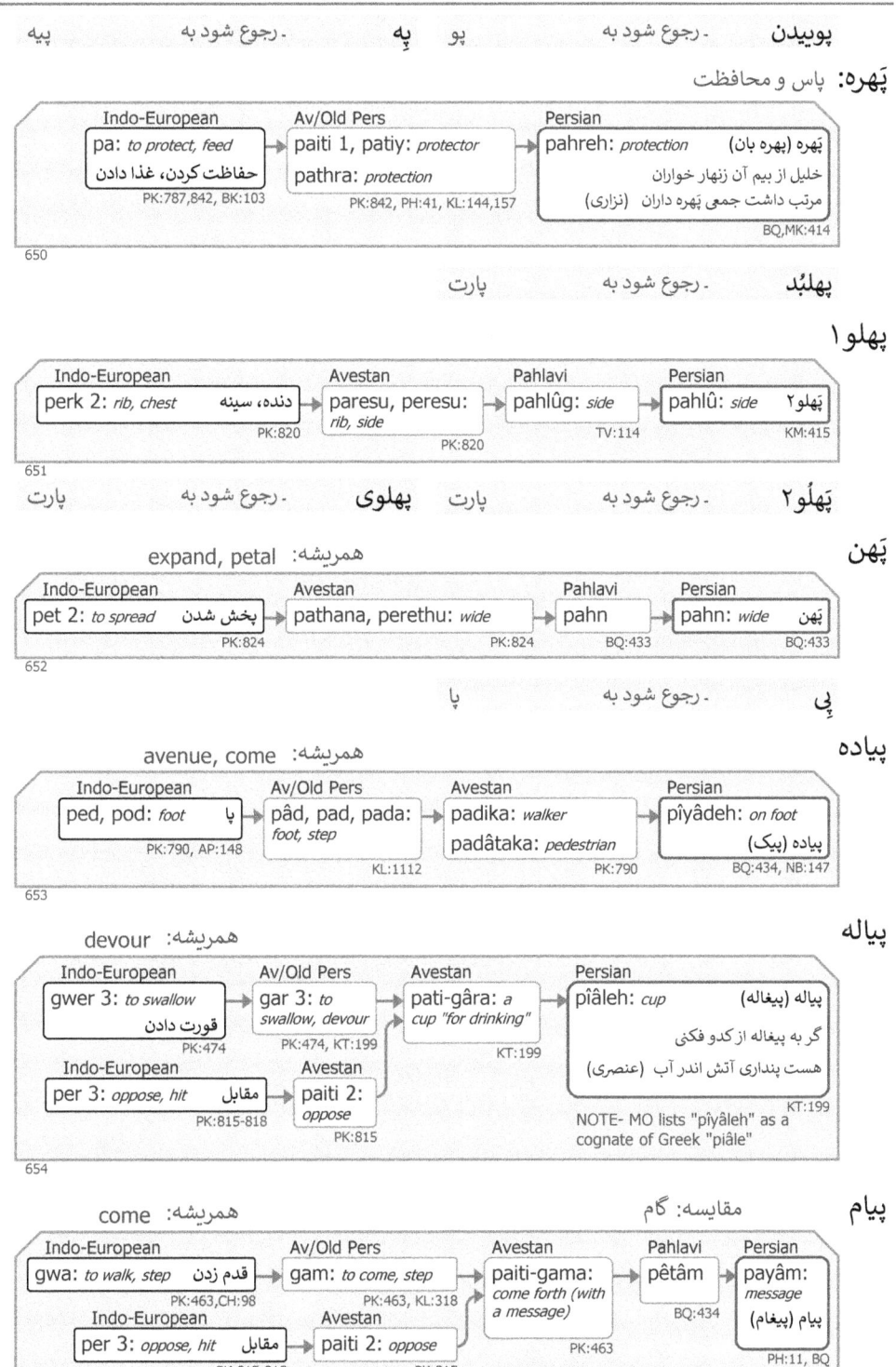

Indo-European
pa: to protect, feed
حفاظت کردن، غذا دادن
PK:787,842, BK:103

Av/Old Pers
paiti 1, patiy: protector
pathra: protection
PK:842, PH:41, KL:144,157

Persian
pahreh: protection   پَهره (پَهره بان)
خلیل از بیم آن زنهار خواران
مرتب داشت جمعی پَهره داران   (نزاری)
BQ,MK:414

650

پهلبُد   ـ رجوع شود به   پارت

پهلو ۱

Indo-European
perk 2: rib, chest   دنده، سینه
PK:820

Avestan
paresu, peresu: rib, side
PK:820

Pahlavi
pahlûg: side
TV:114

Persian
pahlû: side   پهلو ۲
KM:415

651

پَهلُو۲   پارت   ـ رجوع شود به   **پهلوی**   پارت   ـ رجوع شود به   پارت

پَهن   همریشه: expand, petal

Indo-European
pet 2: to spread   پخش شدن
PK:824

Avestan
pathana, perethu: wide
PK:824

Pahlavi
pahn
BQ:433

Persian
pahn: wide   پَهن
BQ:433

652

پِی   ـ رجوع شود به   پا

پیاده   همریشه: avenue, come

Indo-European
ped, pod: foot   پا
PK:790, AP:148

Av/Old Pers
pâd, pad, pada: foot, step
KL:1112

Avestan
padika: walker
padâtaka: pedestrian
PK:790

Persian
pîyâdeh: on foot
پیاده (پیک)
BQ:434, NB:147

653

پیاله   همریشه: devour

Indo-European
gwer 3: to swallow
قورت دادن
PK:474

Av/Old Pers
gar 3: to swallow, devour
PK:474, KT:199

Avestan
pati-gâra: a cup "for drinking"
KT:199

Persian
pîâleh: cup   پیاله (پیغاله)
گر به پیغاله از کدو فکنی
هست پنداری آتش اندر آب   (عنصری)
KT:199

Indo-European
per 3: oppose, hit   مقابل
PK:815-818

Avestan
paiti 2: oppose
PK:815

NOTE- MO lists "pîyâleh" as a cognate of Greek "piâle"

654

پیام   مقایسه: گام   همریشه: come

Indo-European
gwa: to walk, step   قدم زدن
PK:463,CH:98

Av/Old Pers
gam: to come, step
PK:463, KL:318

Avestan
paiti-gama: come forth (with a message)
PK:463

Pahlavi
pêtâm
BQ:434

Persian
payâm: message
پیام (پیغام)
PH:11, BQ

Indo-European
per 3: oppose, hit   مقابل
PK:815-818

Avestan
paiti 2: oppose
PK:815

655

پیچ .رجوع شود به   پیچیدن

پیچیدن

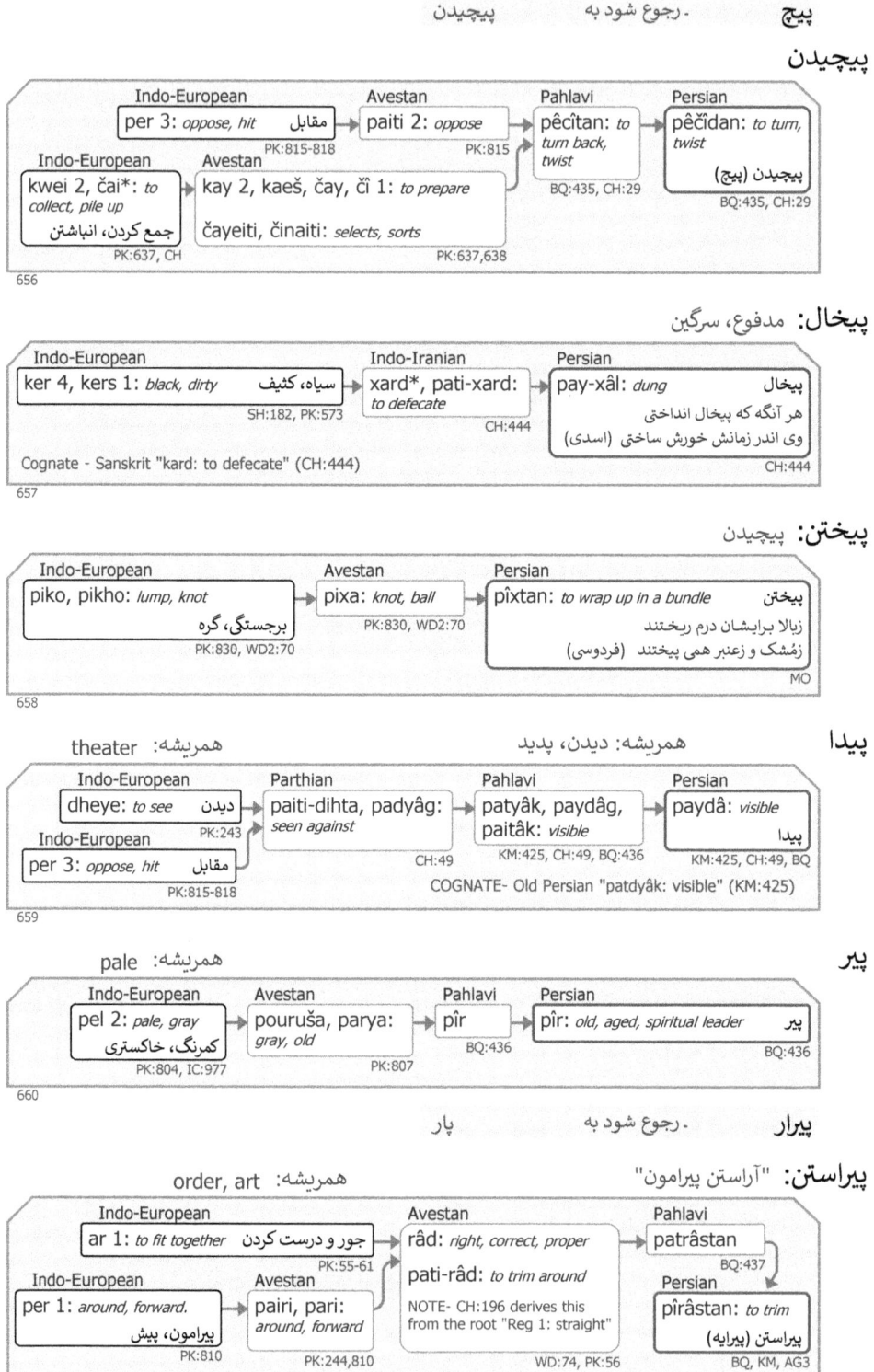

Indo-European	Avestan	Pahlavi	Persian
per 3: oppose, hit مقابل	paiti 2: oppose	pêcîtan: to turn back, twist	pêčîdan: to turn, twist
PK:815-818	PK:815		پیچیدن (پیچ)

Indo-European	Avestan
kwei 2, čai*: to collect, pile up جمع کردن، انباشتن	kay 2, kaeš, čay, čî 1: to prepare
	čayeiti, činaiti: selects, sorts
PK:637, CH	PK:637,638

BQ:435, CH:29

656

پیخال: مدفوع، سرگین

Indo-European	Indo-Iranian	Persian
ker 4, kers 1: black, dirty سیاه، کثیف	xard*, pati-xard: to defecate	pay-xâl: dung پیخال
SH:182, PK:573	CH:444	هر آنگه که پیخال انداخی وی اندر زمانش خورش ساخی (اسدی)

Cognate - Sanskrit "kard: to defecate" (CH:444)   CH:444

657

پیختن: پیچیدن

Indo-European	Avestan	Persian
piko, pikho: lump, knot برجستگی، گره	pixa: knot, ball	pîxtan: to wrap up in a bundle پیختن
PK:830, WD2:70	PK:830, WD2:70	زبالا برایشان درم ریختند زمشک و زعنبر همی پیختند (فردوسی)

MO

658

پیدا   همریشه: دیدن، پدید

theater :همریشه

Indo-European	Parthian	Pahlavi	Persian
dheye: to see دیدن	paiti-dihta, padyâg: seen against	patyâk, paydâg, paitâk: visible	paydâ: visible پیدا
PK:243		KM:425, CH:49, BQ:436	KM:425, CH:49, BQ

Indo-European
per 3: oppose, hit مقابل
PK:815-818

CH:49

COGNATE- Old Persian "patdyâk: visible" (KM:425)

659

پیر   pale :همریشه

Indo-European	Avestan	Pahlavi	Persian
pel 2: pale, gray کمرنگ، خاکستری	pouruša, parya: gray, old	pîr	pîr: old, aged, spiritual leader پیر
PK:804, IC:977	PK:807	BQ:436	BQ:436

660

پیرار .رجوع شود به   پار

پیراستن: "آراستن پیرامون"

order, art :همریشه

Indo-European	Avestan	Pahlavi	Persian
ar 1: to fit together جور و درست کردن	râd: right, correct, proper	patrâstan	pîrâstan: to trim
PK:55-61	pati-râd: to trim around	BQ:437	پیراستن (پیرایه)

Indo-European	Avestan
per 1: around, forward. پیرامون، پیش	pairi, pari: around, forward
PK:810	PK:244,810

NOTE- CH:196 derives this from the root "Reg 1: straight"

WD:74, PK:56   BQ, KM, AG3

661

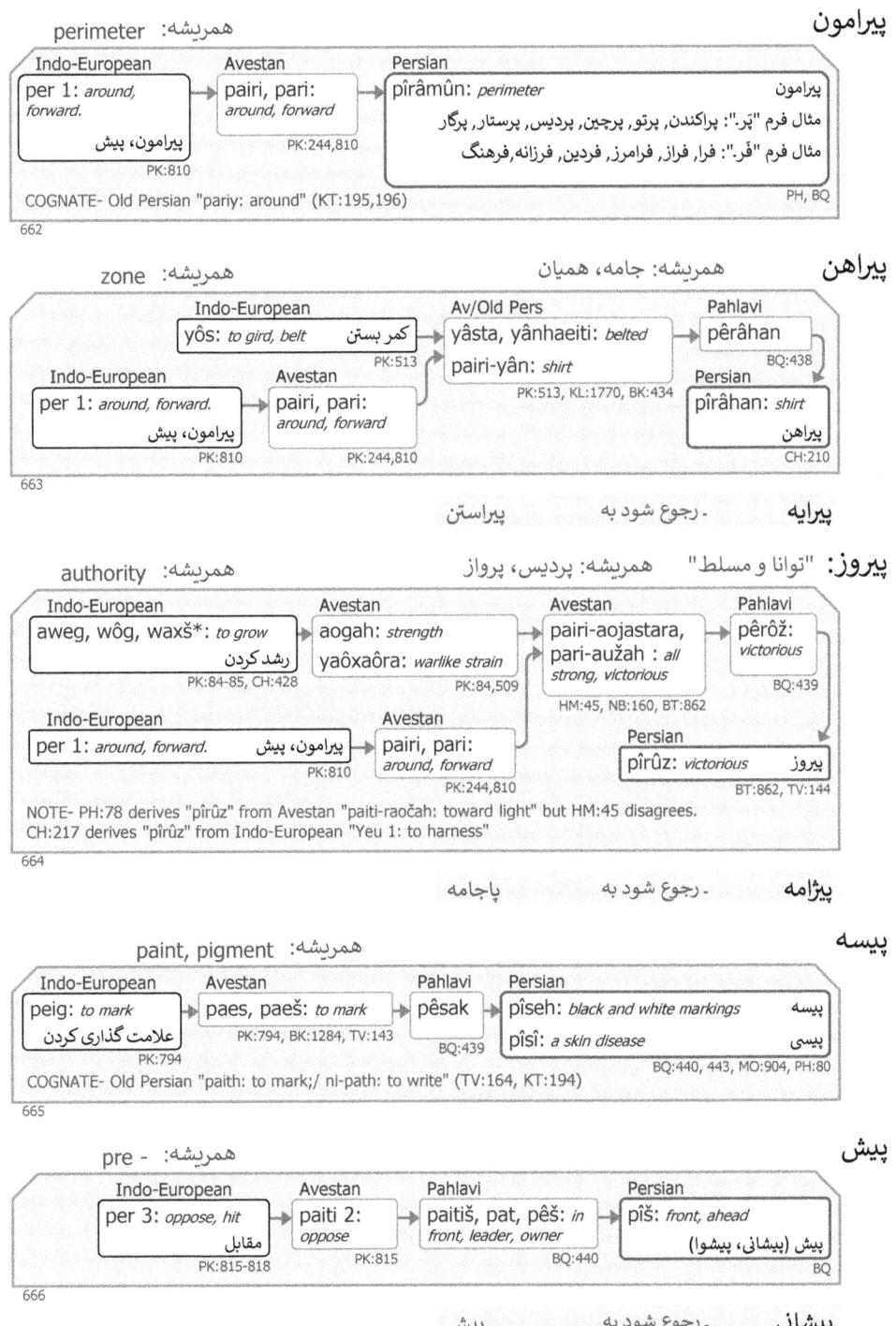

پیرامون

همریشه: perimeter

Indo-European
per 1: around, forward.
پیرامون، پیش
PK:810

Avestan
pairi, pari: around, forward
PK:244,810

Persian
pîrâmûn: perimeter

پیرامون

مثال فرم "پَر": پراکندن، پرتو، پرچین، پردیس، پرستار، پرگار

مثال فرم "فَر": فرا، فراز، فرامرز، فردین، فرزانه، فرهنگ

PH, BQ

COGNATE- Old Persian "pariy: around" (KT:195,196)

662

پیراهن

همریشه: جامه، همیان   همریشه: zone

Indo-European
yôs: to gird, belt
کمر بستن
PK:513

Av/Old Pers
yâsta, yânhaeiti: belted
pairi-yân: shirt
PK:513, KL:1770, BK:434

Pahlavi
pêrâhan
BQ:438

Indo-European
per 1: around, forward.
پیرامون، پیش
PK:810

Avestan
pairi, pari: around, forward
PK:244,810

Persian
pîrâhan: shirt
پیراهن
CH:210

663

پیرایه .رجوع شود به   پیراستن

پیروز: "توانا و مسلط"   همریشه: پردیس، پرواز   همریشه: authority

Indo-European
aweg, wôg, waxš*: to grow
رشد کردن
PK:84-85, CH:428

Avestan
aogah: strength
yaôxaôra: warlike strain
PK:84,509

Avestan
pairi-aojastara, pari-aužah : all strong, victorious
HM:45, NB:160, BT:862

Pahlavi
pêrôz: victorious
BQ:439

Indo-European
per 1: around, forward.
پیرامون، پیش
PK:810

Avestan
pairi, pari: around, forward
PK:244,810

Persian
pîrûz: victorious
پیروز
BT:862, TV:144

NOTE- PH:78 derives "pîrûz" from Avestan "paiti-raôčah: toward light" but HM:45 disagrees.
CH:217 derives "pîrûz" from Indo-European "Yeu 1: to harness"

664

پیژامه .رجوع شود به   پاجامه

پیسه

همریشه: paint, pigment

Indo-European
peig: to mark
علامت گذاری کردن
PK:794

Avestan
paes, paeš: to mark
PK:794, BK:1284, TV:143

Pahlavi
pêsak
BQ:439

Persian
pîseh: black and white markings پیسه
pîsî: a skin disease پیسی
BQ:440, 443, MO:904, PH:80

COGNATE- Old Persian "paith: to mark;/ ni-path: to write" (TV:164, KT:194)

665

پیش

همریشه: pre -

Indo-European
per 3: oppose, hit
مقابل
PK:815-818

Avestan
paiti 2: oppose
PK:815

Pahlavi
paitiš, pat, pêš: in front, leader, owner
BQ:440

Persian
pîš: front, ahead
پیش (پیشانی، پیشوا)
BQ

666

پیشانی .رجوع شود به   پیش

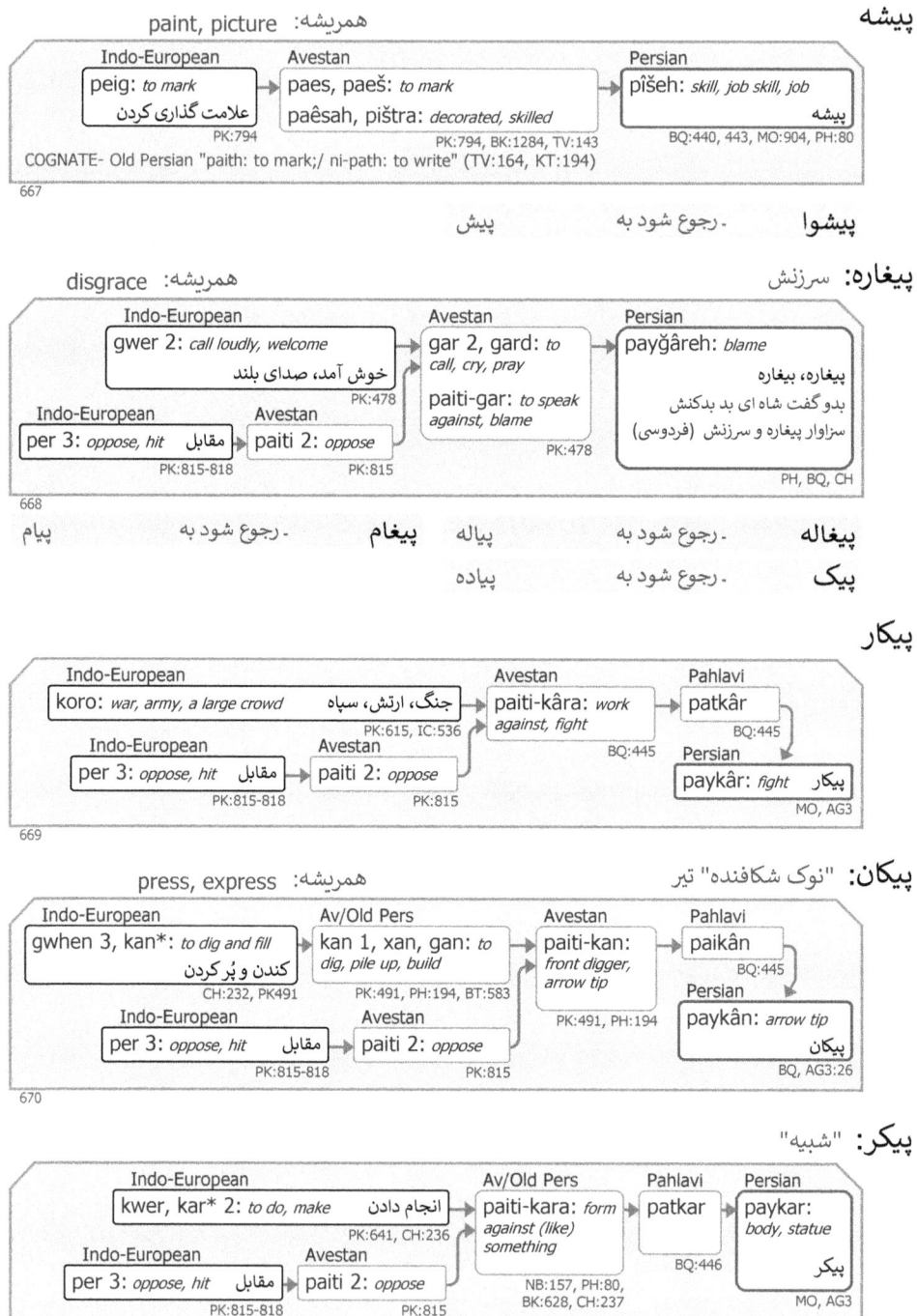

پیشه

همریشه: paint, picture

Indo-European
peig: *to mark*
علامت گذاری کردن
PK:794

Avestan
paes, paeš: *to mark*
paêsah, pištra: *decorated, skilled*
PK:794, BK:1284, TV:143

Persian
pîšeh: *skill, job skill, job*
پیشه
BQ:440, 443, MO:904, PH:80

COGNATE- Old Persian "paith: to mark;/ ni-path: to write" (TV:164, KT:194)

667

پیشوا   . رجوع شود به   پیش

پیغاره: سرزنش   همریشه: disgrace

Indo-European
gwer 2: *call loudly, welcome*
خوش آمد، صدای بلند
PK:478

Indo-European
per 3: *oppose, hit* مقابل
PK:815-818

Avestan
paiti 2: *oppose*
PK:815

Avestan
gar 2, gard: *to call, cry, pray*
paiti-gar: *to speak against, blame*
PK:478

Persian
payğâreh: *blame*
پیغاره، بیغاره
بدو گفت شاه ای بد بدکنش
سزاوار پیغاره و سرزنش (فردوسی)
PH, BQ, CH

668

پیغاله   . رجوع شود به   پیاله   پیغام   . رجوع شود به   پیام

پیک   . رجوع شود به   پیاده

پیکار

Indo-European
koro: *war, army, a large crowd* جنگ، ارتش، سپاه
PK:615, IC:536

Indo-European
per 3: *oppose, hit* مقابل
PK:815-818

Avestan
paiti 2: *oppose*
PK:815

Avestan
paiti-kâra: *work against, fight*
BQ:445

Pahlavi
patkâr
BQ:445

Persian
paykâr: *fight* پیکار
MO, AG3

669

پیکان: "نوک شکافنده" تیر   همریشه: press, express

Indo-European
gwhen 3, kan*: *to dig and fill*
کندن و پُر کردن
CH:232, PK491

Av/Old Pers
kan 1, xan, gan: *to dig, pile up, build*
PK:491, PH:194, BT:583

Indo-European
per 3: *oppose, hit* مقابل
PK:815-818

Avestan
paiti 2: *oppose*
PK:815

Avestan
paiti-kan: *front digger, arrow tip*
PK:491, PH:194

Pahlavi
paikân
BQ:445

Persian
paykân: *arrow tip*
پیکان
BQ, AG3:26

670

پیکر: "شبیه"

Indo-European
kwer, kar* 2: *to do, make* انجام دادن
PK:641, CH:236

Indo-European
per 3: *oppose, hit* مقابل
PK:815-818

Avestan
paiti 2: *oppose*
PK:815

Av/Old Pers
paiti-kara: *form against (like) something*
NB:157, PH:80, BK:628, CH:237

Pahlavi
patkar
BQ:446

Persian
paykar: *body, statue*
پیکر
MO, AG3

671

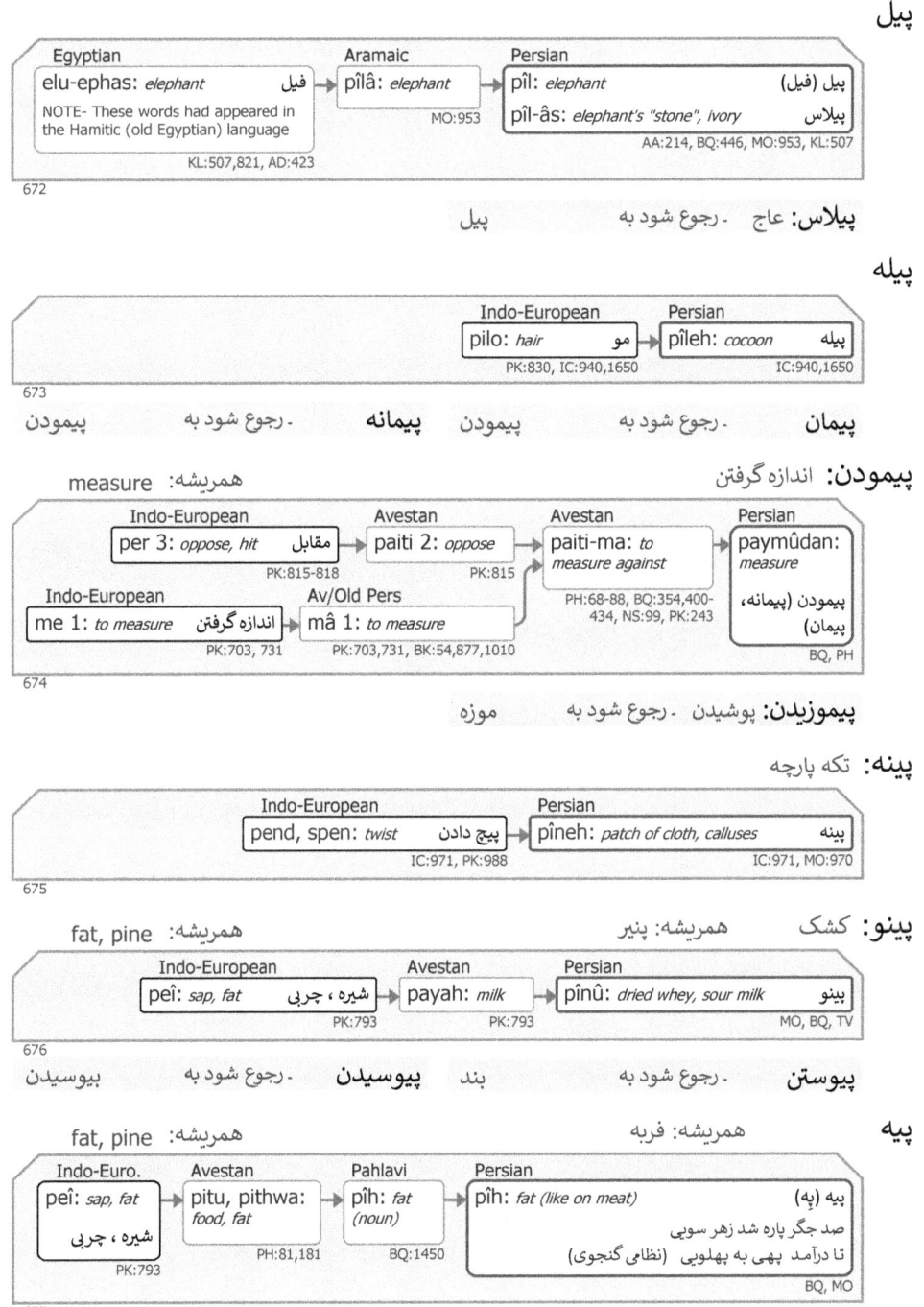

پیل

Egyptian
elu-ephas: *elephant*   فیل
NOTE- These words had appeared in the Hamitic (old Egyptian) language
KL:507,821, AD:423

Aramaic
pîlâ: *elephant*
MO:953

Persian
pîl: *elephant*   پیل (فیل)
pîl-âs: *elephant's "stone", ivory*   پیلاس
AA:214, BQ:446, MO:953, KL:507

672

پیلاس: عاج   ـ رجوع شود به   پیل

پیله

Indo-European
pilo: *hair*   مو
PK:830, IC:940,1650

Persian
pîleh: *cocoon*   پیله
IC:940,1650

673

پیمانه   **پیمانه**   پیمودن   ـ رجوع شود به   پیمودن   ـ رجوع شود به   **پیمان**

پیمودن: اندازه گرفتن

همریشه: measure

Indo-European
per 3: *oppose, hit*   مقابل
PK:815-818

Indo-European
me 1: *to measure*   اندازه گرفتن
PK:703, 731

Avestan
paiti 2: *oppose*
PK:815

Av/Old Pers
mâ 1: *to measure*
PK:703,731, BK:54,877,1010

Avestan
paiti-ma: *to measure against*
PH:68-88, BQ:354,400-434, NS:99, PK:243

Persian
paymûdan: *measure*
پیمودن (پیمانه، پیمان)
BQ, PH

674

پیموزیدن: پوشیدن   ـ رجوع شود به   موزه

پینه: تکه پارچه

Indo-European
pend, spen: *twist*   پیچ دادن
IC:971, PK:988

Persian
pîneh: *patch of cloth, calluses*   پینه
IC:971, MO:970

675

پینو: کشک   همریشه: پنیر   همریشه: fat, pine

Indo-European
peî: *sap, fat*   شیره ، چربی
PK:793

Avestan
payah: *milk*
PK:793

Persian
pînû: *dried whey, sour milk*   پینو
MO, BQ, TV

676

بیوسیدن   ـ رجوع شود به   **پیوسیدن**   بند   ـ رجوع شود به   **پیوستن**

پیه   همریشه: فربه   همریشه: fat, pine

Indo-Euro.
peî: *sap, fat* شیره ، چربی
PK:793

Avestan
pitu, pithwa: *food, fat*
PH:81,181

Pahlavi
pîh: *fat (noun)*
BQ:1450

Persian
pîh: *fat (like on meat)*   پیه (په)
صد جگر پاره شد زهر سویی
تا درآمد پهی به پهلویی (نظامی گنجوی)
BQ, MO

677

120

حرف ت.گاهی به د بدل شود.

تا: پسوند اعداد مثل دو تا. چین، لا

Old Persian	Pahlavi	Persian
tâvat, tâvant: *so much* چندان	tâk: *count, unit, one* عدد، دانه	tâ: *a number suffix, also a fold* تا (یکتا، دوتا) tak: *each, unique* تک
BQ:451	KM:467; BQ:451	KM:467; BQ:451

678

تاب ـ رجوع شود به تب   **تابان** تب ـ رجوع شود به   تب

تابستان   همریشه: تب   همریشه: tepid, stand

Indo-European	Av/Old Pers	Av/Old Pers
stâ: *to stand* ایستادن	sta: *to stand, to set*	tap-stana: *place (time) of heat*
PK:1008,1009	BQ:123, PH:20, PK:1008	BQ:123, PH:20, PK:1008, KT:210
Indo-European	Avestan	Persian
tep: *to be warm* گرم بودن	tafnu, tap 2, tab: *warm, glowing*	tâbestân: *summer* تابستان
PK:1069	PK:1069, KL:1589	BQ, MO

679

تابش ـ رجوع شود به تب

تابیدن۱   همریشه: tension

Indo-European	Avestan	Persian
ten 1, tenu: *to stretch, pull* کشیدن	tan, tapayati: *to pull, stretch, spin*	tâbîdan: *to spin, twist* تابیدن۱ (تافتن۱)
PK:1064,1067, AD	TV:147, AP:186	PK:1064, AP:186

680

تابیدن۲ ـ رجوع شود به تب   **تابه** تب   ـ رجوع شود به   تب

تاج   همریشه: تَجَر   همریشه: tile, protection

	Indo-European	Persian
COGNATE- cognate with Old Persian "tačara: cover" (KT:186)	steg: *to cover* پوشاندن	tâj: *crown* تاج (تاجور)
	PK:1013	KL:1510

681

تاجور ـ رجوع شود به تاج

تاختن

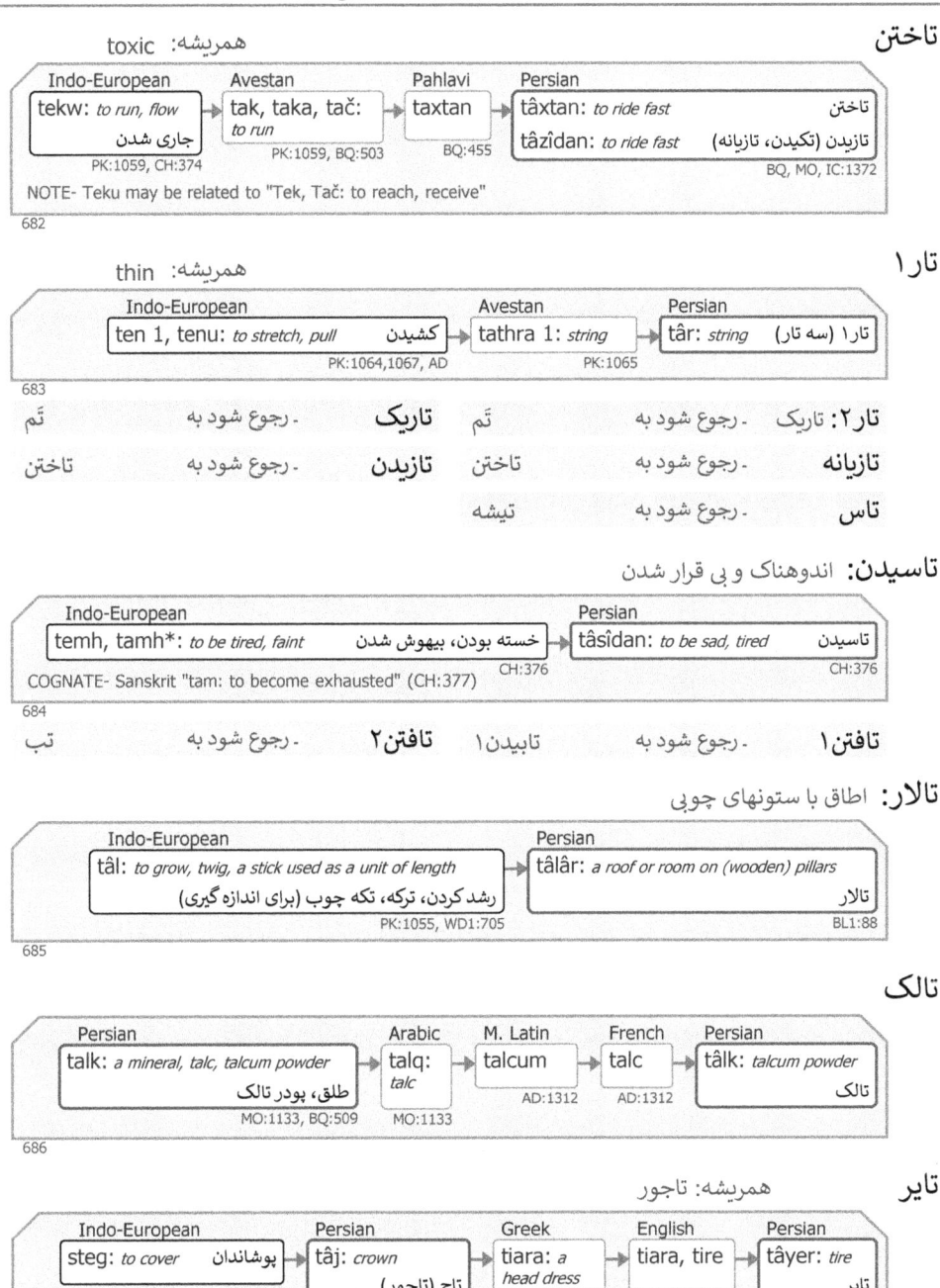

همریشه: toxic

Indo-European	Avestan	Pahlavi	Persian
tekw: *to run, flow* جاری شدن	tak, taka, tač: *to run*	taxtan	tâxtan: *to ride fast* تاختن tâzîdan: *to ride fast* تازیدن (تکیدن، تازیانه)
PK:1059, CH:374	PK:1059, BQ:503	BQ:455	BQ, MO, IC:1372

NOTE- Teku may be related to "Tek, Tač: to reach, receive"

682

تار۱

همریشه: thin

Indo-European	Avestan	Persian
ten 1, tenu: *to stretch, pull* کشیدن	tathra 1: *string*	târ: *string* تار۱ (سه تار)
PK:1064,1067, AD	PK:1065	

683

تَم	تاریک	تَم	تار۲: تاریک - رجوع شود به
تاختن	تازیدن	تاختن	تازیانه - رجوع شود به
		تیشه	تاس - رجوع شود به

تاسیدن: اندوهناک و بی قرار شدن

Indo-European	Persian
temh, tamh*: *to be tired, faint* خسته بودن، بیهوش شدن	tâsîdan: *to be sad, tired* تاسیدن
COGNATE- Sanskrit "tam: to become exhausted" (CH:377) CH:376	CH:376

684

تب	تابیدن۲	تافتن۲	تافتن۱ - رجوع شود به تابیدن۱ - رجوع شود به

تالار: اطاق با ستونهای چوبی

Indo-European	Persian
tâl: *to grow, twig, a stick used as a unit of length* رشد کردن، ترکه، تکه چوب (برای اندازه گیری)	tâlâr: *a roof or room on (wooden) pillars* تالار
PK:1055, WD1:705	BL1:88

685

تالک

Persian	Arabic	M. Latin	French	Persian
talk: *a mineral, talc, talcum powder* طلق، پودر تالک	talq: *talc*	talcum	talc	tâlk: *talcum powder* تالک
MO:1133, BQ:509	MO:1133	AD:1312	AD:1312	

686

تایر

همریشه: تاجور

Indo-European	Persian	Greek	English	Persian
steg: *to cover* پوشاندن	tâj: *crown* تاج (تاجور)	tiara: *a head dress*	tiara, tire	tâyer: *tire* تایر
PK:1013	KL:1510	PT:719	PT:358	MO:1014

687

تب

همریشه: tepid

Indo-European	Avestan	Pahlavi	Persian
tep: *to be warm* گرم بودن PK:1069	tafnu, tap 2, tab: *warm, glowing* PK:1069, KL:1589	tâb CH:378	tab: *fever, heat* tâbîdan: *shine* tafsîdan: *to become hot* تب (تاب، تابه، تفت) تابیدن۲ (تافتن۲، تابان، تابش) تفسیدن BQ, PH, CH:379

688

تباه

همریشه: pierce, stupid

Indo-European	Avestan	Pahlavi	Persian
steu 2: *to push, beat, hit, also throw* هل دادن، زدن، پرت کردن PK:1032	tap 1: *to hit, hurt, destroy* TV:147	tapâh BQ:465	tabâh: *ruined, destroyed, bad* تباه TV:147

NOTE- IC derives these words from Indo-European root "Tâbh: to rot"

689

تبر

Pahlavi	Persian
tabrak: *ax* تبر NOTE- not related to the Pahlavi "tabrak: break" KM:471	tabar: *ax* تبر KM:471

690

تبوراک   تنبور، طبل   ·رجوع شود به   تنبور، طبل   **تبیر**   ·رجوع شود به   تنبور، طبل

تپیدن

همریشه: تابیدن   همریشه: tepid

Indo-European	Avestan	Persian
tep: *to be warm* گرم بودن PK:1069	tafnu, tap 2, tab: *warm, glowing* PK:1069, KL:1589	tapîdan: *beat* (تپش) تپیدن BQ, PH

691

تَجَر: خانه زمستانی   همریشه: تاج   همریشه: tile, deck, protection

Indo-European	Old Persian	Persian
steg: *to cover* پوشاندن PK:1013	tačara: *cover, house, castle* KT:186	tajar: *winter house, castle* (تَژَر) تَجَر میان این تجر و گنبد فلک فرق است که هست این بثبات، آن نباشد آرامش (نزاری قهستانی) PH:84, BQ:472

692

تخته   ·رجوع شود به   تیشه

تخش   تیر و کمان

همریشه: toxic

Indo-European	Old Persian	Persian
tekw: *to run, flow* جاری شدن PK:1059, CH:374	taxša: *a type of bow & arrow* PK:1059	taxš: *bow and arrow* تخش همه بنده در پیش رخش مند جگر خستهٔ تیغ و تخش مند (فردوسی) BQ:476

NOTE- Teku may be related to "Tek, Tač: to reach, receive"

693

تخشا: کوشا   ·رجوع شود به   تخشیدن

تخشیدن   کوشیدن

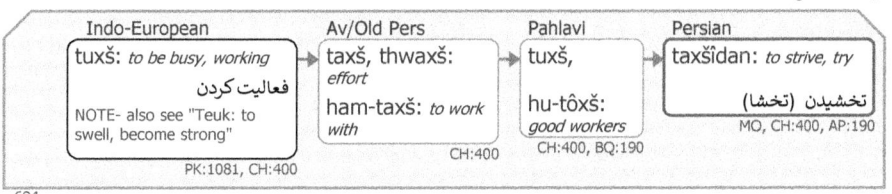

694

تخم

همریشه: tumor

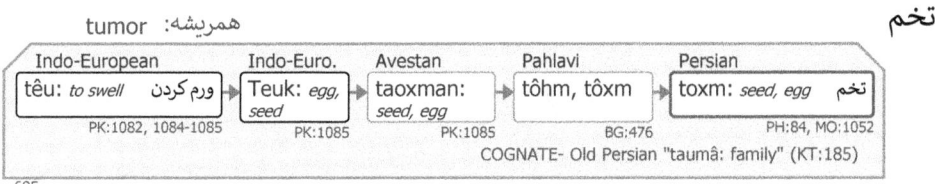

695

تذرو

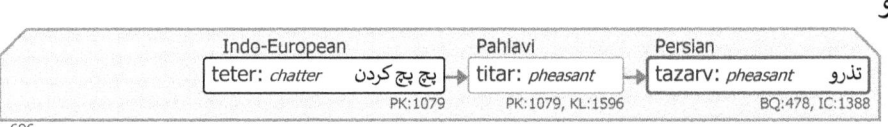

696

ـتَر۱: پسوند برای تفضیل (مثل بزرگ تر)

همریشه: determine

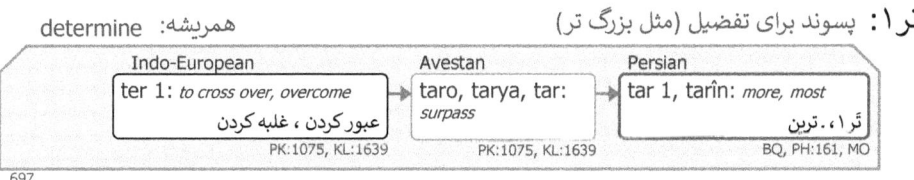

697

تَر۲: مرطوب، تازه، جوان، لطیف

همریشه: tender

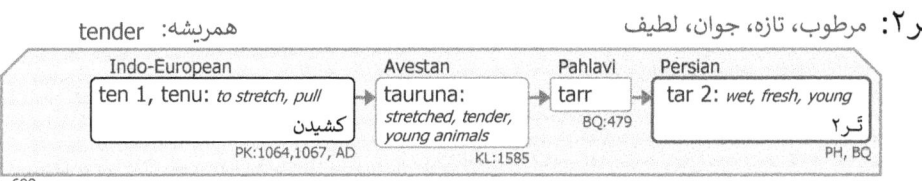

698

تَر۳: زودرنج، ماهر، نیرنگ باز

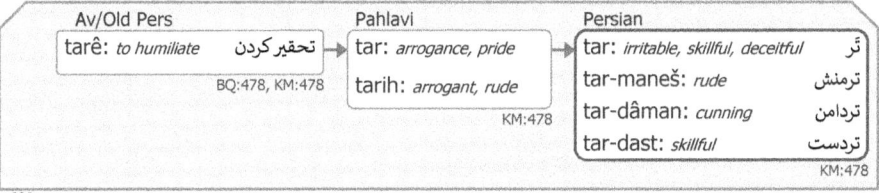

699

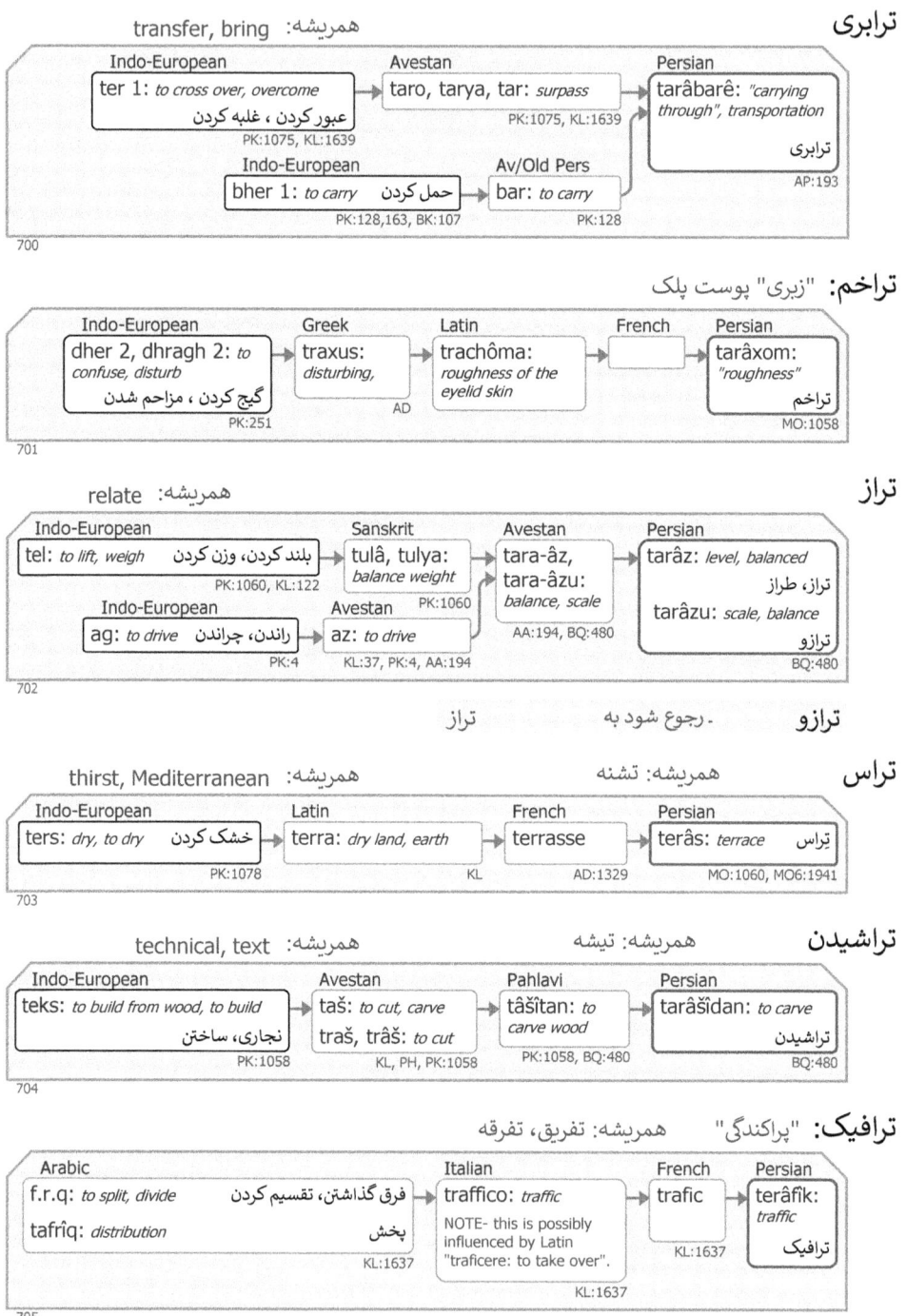

ترابری

همریشه: transfer, bring

Indo-European — ter 1: *to cross over, overcome* — عبور کردن ، غلبه کردن — PK:1075, KL:1639

Avestan — taro, tarya, tar: *surpass* — PK:1075, KL:1639

Persian — tarâbarê: *"carrying through", transportation* — ترابری — AP:193

Indo-European — bher 1: *to carry* — حمل کردن — PK:128,163, BK:107

Av/Old Pers — bar: *to carry* — PK:128

700

تراخم: "زبری" پوست پلک

Indo-European — dher 2, dhragh 2: *to confuse, disturb* — گیج کردن ، مزاحم شدن — PK:251

Greek — traxus: *disturbing,* — AD

Latin — trachôma: *roughness of the eyelid skin*

French

Persian — tarâxom: *"roughness"* — تراخم — MO:1058

701

تراز

همریشه: relate

Indo-European — tel: *to lift, weigh* — بلند کردن، وزن کردن — PK:1060, KL:122

Sanskrit — tulâ, tulya: *balance weight* — PK:1060

Avestan — tara-âz, tara-âzu: *balance, scale* — AA:194, BQ:480

Persian — tarâz: *level, balanced* — تراز، طراز — tarâzu: *scale, balance* — ترازو — BQ:480

Indo-European — ag: *to drive* — راندن، چراندن — PK:4

Avestan — az: *to drive* — KL:37, PK:4, AA:194

702

ترازو ۔ رجوع شود به تراز

تراس

همریشه: تشنه   همریشه: thirst, Mediterranean

Indo-European — ters: *dry, to dry* — خشک کردن — PK:1078

Latin — terra: *dry land, earth* — KL

French — terrasse — AD:1329

Persian — terâs: *terrace* — تراس — MO:1060, MO6:1941

703

تراشیدن

همریشه: تیشه   همریشه: technical, text

Indo-European — teks: *to build from wood, to build* — نجاری، ساختن — PK:1058

Avestan — taš: *to cut, carve* — traš, trâš: *to cut* — KL, PH, PK:1058

Pahlavi — tâšîtan: *to carve wood* — PK:1058, BQ:480

Persian — tarâšîdan: *to carve* — تراشیدن — BQ:480

704

ترافیک: "پراکندگی"   همریشه: تفریق، تفرقه

Arabic — f.r.q: *to split, divide* — فرق گذاشتن، تقسیم کردن — tafrîq: *distribution* — بخش — KL:1637

Italian — traffico: *traffic* — NOTE- this is possibly influenced by Latin "traficere: to take over". — KL:1637

French — trafic — KL:1637

Persian — terâfîk: *traffic* — ترافیک

705

ترانه: "لطیف"

همریشه: tender

Indo-European	Avestan	Persian
ten 1, tenu: *to stretch, pull* کشیدن	tauruna: *stretched, tender, young animals*	tarâneh: *"a tender" love song* ترانه
PK:1064,1067, AD	KL:1585	PH, BQ

706

تُرُب: "توده"

Indo-European		Persian
tulupos: *lump, ball, mass, crowd* توپ، توده، جمعیت		torob, torb: *radish* تُرُب
	IC:1455	IC:1455

707

تربیت ـ رجوع شود به رَبّ

ترجمه

Akkadian	Aramaic	Arabic	Persian
targumânu: *interpreter* مترجم	tûrgemânâ: *interpreter*	tarjama: *he translated*	tarjomeh: *translation* ترجمه tarjom: *speech, statement* تَرجُم (ترجمان)
KL:1573	AD:396, KL:1573	KL:1573	MO:1064

708

ترخون

Indo-European	Greek	Arabic	Persian
derk: *to see* دیدن	drakoon: *a dragon with devil eyes*	tarxûn: *an aromatic bushy plant*	tarxûn: *tarragon* ترخون
PK:218	KL:480,1574	KL:1554, TU:49	MO

709

ترخینه

همریشه: تنگ (خشک و سفت)   همریشه: tight

Indo-European	Av/Old Pers	Persian
tenk: *to become firm and thick* محکم و ضخیم شدن	tanj, taxma: *pulled together, tight, strong*	tarxêneh: *a food made with wheat and milk and dried to be eaten later* ترخینه (تلخینه)
PK:1068	PK:1068, KL:1617, MO5:405, BQ:511	AP:193

710

تُرد: شکننده

Indo-European	Old Persian	Persian
turd: *hard, strong* سخت، محکم	sparda, sfard: *stiff, hard*	tord: *brittle, stiff* تُرد
WD1:747, IC:1472	IC:1472	IC:1472, MO:1066

711

تردامن ـ رجوع شود به تَر ۳   **تردست** تَر ۳ ـ رجوع شود به تَر ۳

ترسا ـ رجوع شود به ترسیدن

ترسیدن

همریشه: سهمناک   همریشه: terror

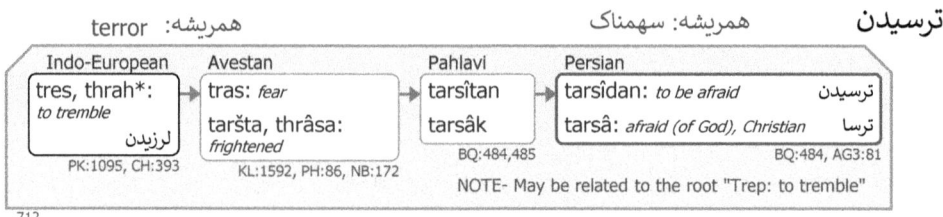

Indo-European	Avestan	Pahlavi	Persian
tres, thrah*: to tremble لرزیدن	tras: fear / taršta, thrâsa: frightened	tarsîtan / tarsâk	tarsîdan: to be afraid ترسیدن / tarsâ: afraid (of God), Christian ترسا
PK:1095, CH:393	KL:1592, PH:86, NB:172	BQ:484,485	BQ:484, AG3:81

NOTE- May be related to the root "Trep: to tremble"

712

تُرش

همریشه: starve

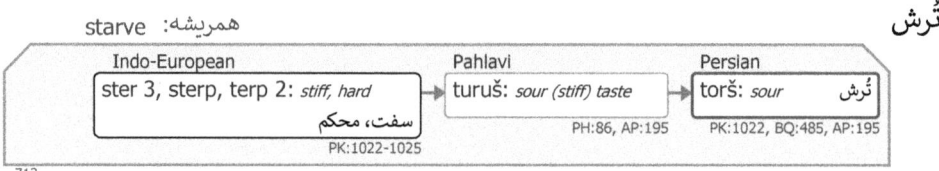

Indo-European	Pahlavi	Persian
ster 3, sterp, terp 2: stiff, hard سفت، محکم	turuš: sour (stiff) taste	torš: sour تُرش
PK:1022-1025	PH:86, AP:195	PK:1022, BQ:485, AP:195

713

تَرفند: مکر و حیله

Indo-European	Avestan	Pahlavi	Persian
tarp: to lie, steal دزدیدن، دروغ گفتن NOTE- derived from "Terp: enjoy" (PK:1077)	trap: to steal	turftag: stolen	tarfand: lie, fraud تَرفند، تروند
PK:1077, CH:383	PK:1077, CH:383	CH:383	CH:383

714

ترک: "مردمان قوی"

Chinese	Persian	Greek	Latin	French	English
tu-kûe: strong people مردمان قوی	tork: a Turk, a beautiful woman تُرک (ترکمن) NOTE- PHN: 363 derives these from Arabic "T.r.k: to leave", as Turks were originally nomads	tourxoi	turcus		turk, Turkey, turquoise
PT:743, SK:578	BQ:487	BQ:487			KL:1665

715

ترک	ـ رجوع شود به	**ترکمن**	کیش۲ ـ رجوع شود به **ترکش**
ترنجیدن	ـ رجوع شود به	**ترنج**	تَر۳ ـ رجوع شود به **ترمنش**

تَرنجیدن: چروکیدن

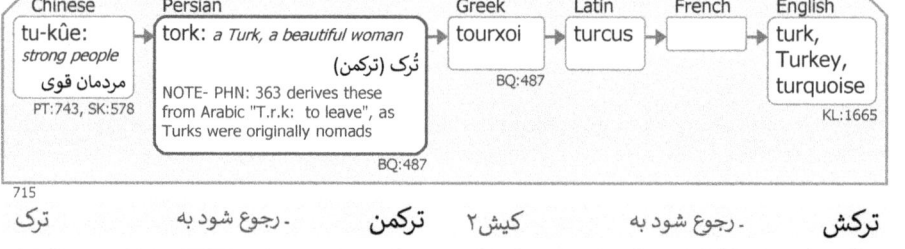

Indo-European	Avestan	Greek
trenk, thranč*: to compress فشردن	Thranc: to compress / traxtanam: pressed together	taranjîdan: to compress, to wrinkle تَرنجیدن / toranj: bergamot تُرنج
PK:1093, CH:395	PK:1092, KL:1612, CH:395	MO, CH:395

716

رَفتن	ـ رجوع شود به	**ترویج**	تَرفند ـ رجوع شود به **تروند**

تره

همریشه: thorn

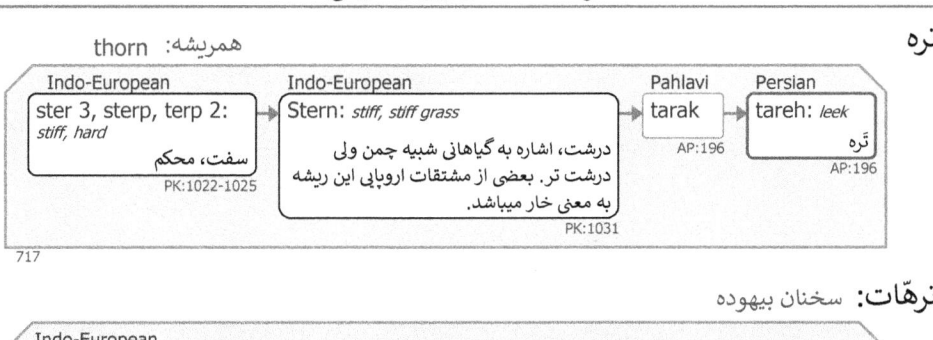

717

ترّهات: سخنان بیهوده

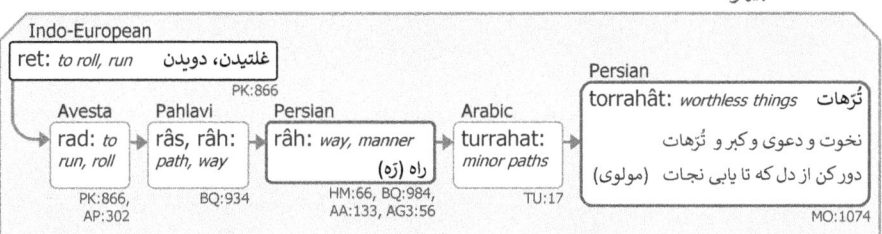

718

تریکو: پارچه کشباف حاصل "میل زدن"   همریشه: strike

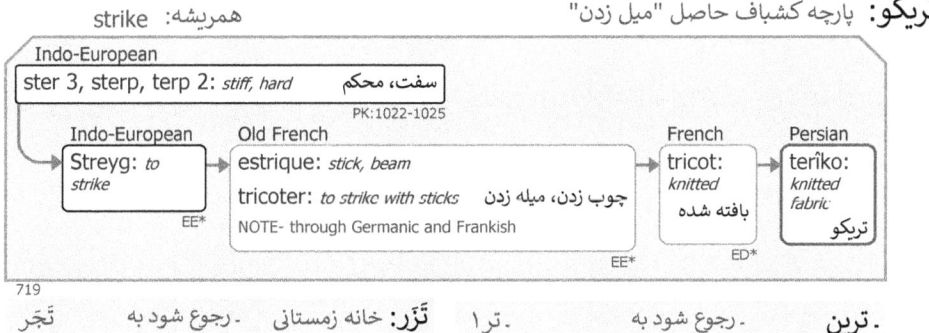

719

. ترین . رجوع شود به تَزَر: خانه زمستانی . رجوع شود به . تر ۱ تَجَر

تزویر   همریشه: زور۳

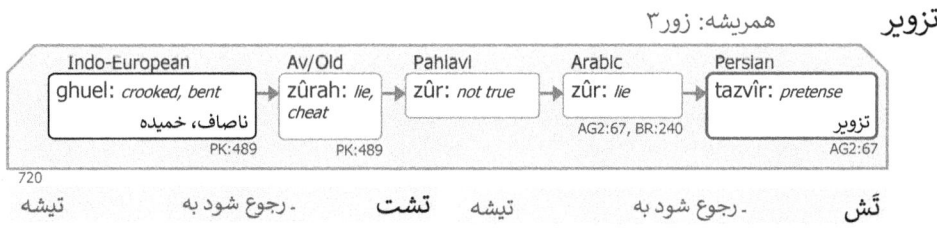

720

تَش . رجوع شود به تشت تیشه . رجوع شود به تیشه

تشنه   همریشه: thirsty

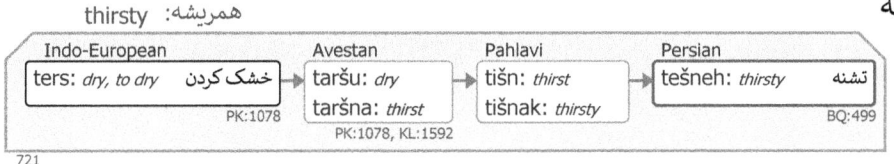

721

تُف

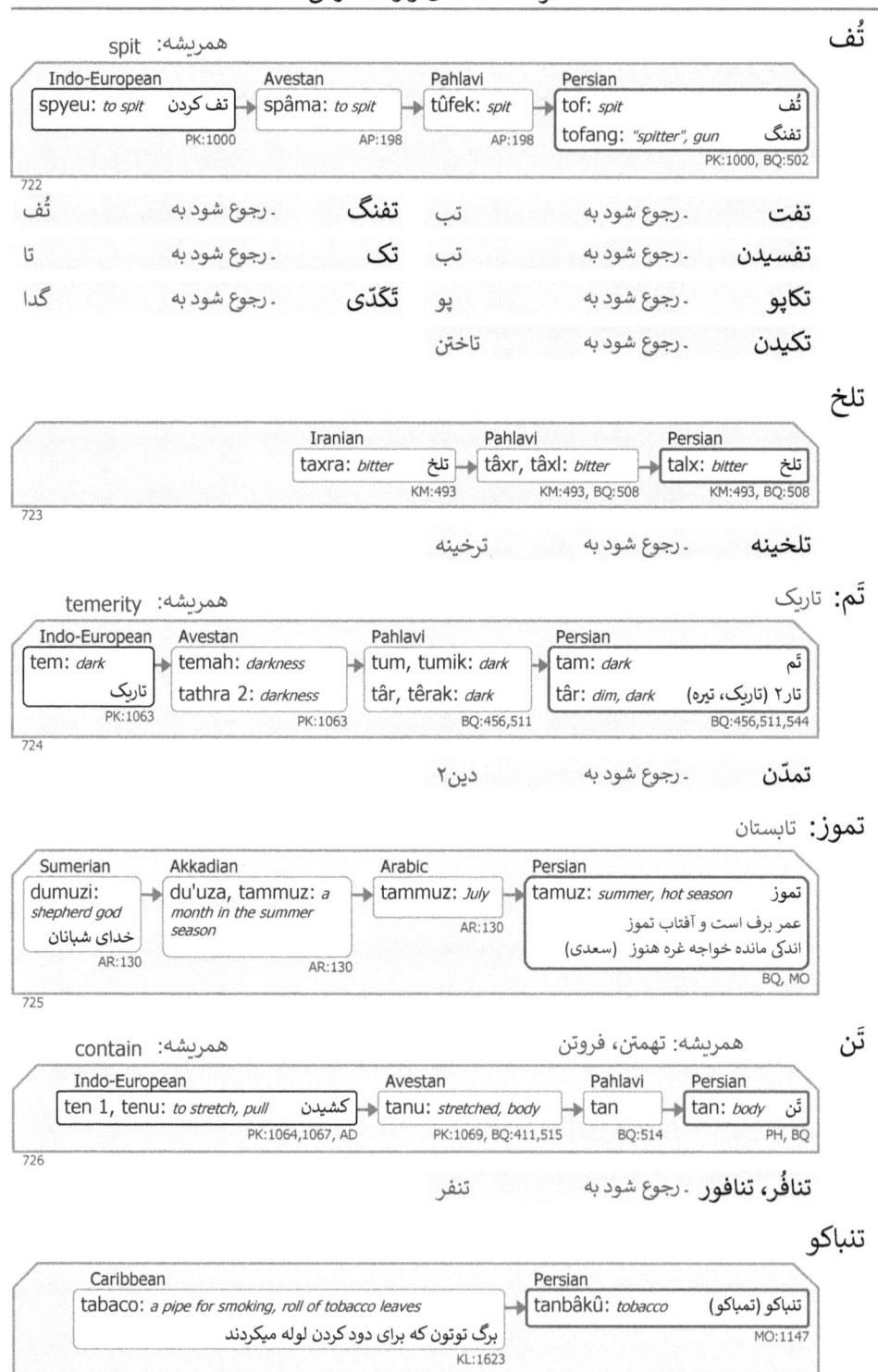

همریشه: spit

Indo-European	Avestan	Pahlavi	Persian
spyeu: *to spit* تف کردن	spâma: *to spit*	tûfek: *spit*	tof: *spit* تُف
PK:1000	AP:198	AP:198	tofang: *"spitter", gun* تفنگ
			PK:1000, BQ:502

722

تُف ← رجوع شود به **تفنگ** تب	رجوع شود به ← **تفت**
تا ← رجوع شود به **تک** تب	رجوع شود به ← **تفسیدن**
گدا ← رجوع شود به **تگّدی** پو	رجوع شود به ← **تکاپو**
	تاختن ← رجوع شود به **تکیدن**

تلخ

Iranian	Pahlavi	Persian
taxra: *bitter* تلخ	tâxr, tâxl: *bitter*	talx: *bitter* تلخ
KM:493	KM:493, BQ:508	KM:493, BQ:508

723

تلخینه ترخینه ← رجوع شود به

تَم: تاریک

همریشه: temerity

Indo-European	Avestan	Pahlavi	Persian
tem: *dark* تاریک	temah: *darkness*	tum, tumik: *dark*	tam: *dark* تَم
PK:1063	tathra 2: *darkness*	târ, têrak: *dark*	târ: *dim, dark* (تاریک، تیره) تار۲
	PK:1063	BQ:456,511	BQ:456,511,544

724

تمدّن دین۲ ← رجوع شود به

تموز: تابستان

Sumerian	Akkadian	Arabic	Persian
dumuzi: *shepherd god* خدای شبانان	du'uza, tammuz: *a month in the summer season*	tammuz: *July*	tamuz: *summer, hot season* تموز
AR:130	AR:130	AR:130	عمر برف است و آفتاب تموز
			اندکّ مانده خواجه غره هنوز (سعدی)
			BQ, MO

725

تَن

همریشه: تهمتن، فروتن

همریشه: contain

Indo-European	Avestan	Pahlavi	Persian
ten 1, tenu: *to stretch, pull* کشیدن	tanu: *stretched, body*	tan	tan: *body* تَن
PK:1064,1067, AD	PK:1069, BQ:411,515	BQ:514	PH, BQ

726

تنافُر، تنافور تنفر ← رجوع شود به

تنباکو

Caribbean	Persian
tabaco: *a pipe for smoking, roll of tobacco leaves*	tanbâkû: *tobacco* (تمباکو) تنباکو
برگ توتون که برای دود کردن لوله میکردند	MO:1147
KL:1623	

727

تنبک

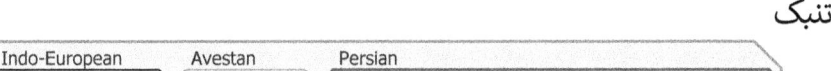

Indo-European	Avestan	Persian	
dumb: *tail* دُم	duma: *tail*	donbak, tonbak: *a long tailed drum*	دنبک، تنبک
PK:227	PK:227, PH:128		MO:1563

728

تنبل

همریشه: contain

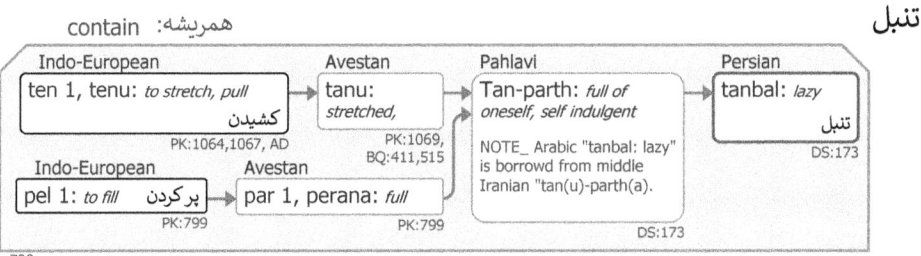

Indo-European	Avestan	Pahlavi	Persian
ten 1, tenu: *to stretch, pull* کشیدن	tanu: *stretched,*	Tan-parth: *full of oneself, self indulgent*	tanbal: *lazy* تنبل
PK:1064,1067	PK:1069, BQ:411,515	NOTE_ Arabic "tanbal: lazy" is borrowd from middle Iranian "tan(u)-parth(a)."	DS:173
Indo-European	Avestan		
pel 1: *to fill* پر کردن	par 1, perana: *full*		
PK:799	PK:799	DS:173	

729

تنبور

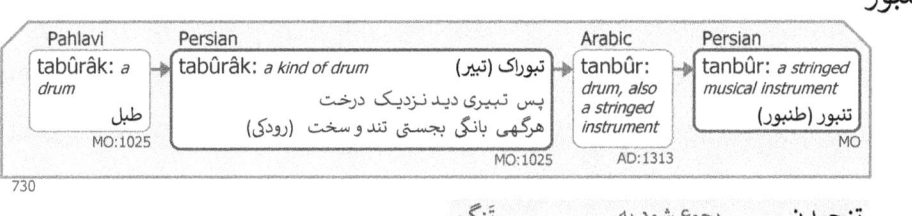

Pahlavi	Persian	Arabic	Persian
tabûrâk: *a drum* طبل	tabûrâk: *a kind of drum* تبوراک (تبیر) پس تبیری دید نزدیک درخت هرگهی بانگ بجستی تند و سخت (رودکی)	tanbûr: *drum, also a stringed instrument*	tanbûr: *a stringed musical instrument* تنبور (طنبور)
MO:1025	MO:1025	AD:1313	MO

730

تنجیدن ۔ رجوع شود به تَنگ

تُند۱: طعمی که دهان رابسوزاند، مانند طعم فلفل

همریشه: steep, pierce

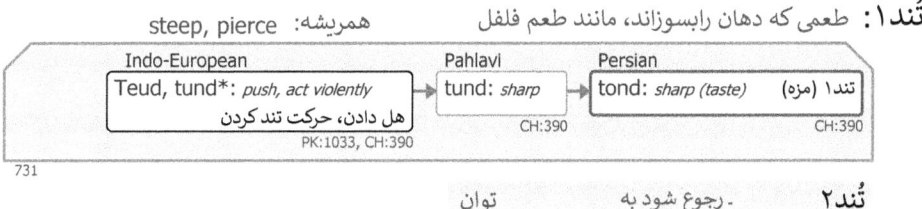

Indo-European	Pahlavi	Persian
Teud, tund*: *push, act violently* هل دادن، حرکت تند کردن	tund: *sharp*	tond: *sharp (taste)* تند۱ (مزه)
PK:1033, CH:390	CH:390	CH:390

731

تُند۲ ۔ رجوع شود به توان

تُندر

همریشه: thunder

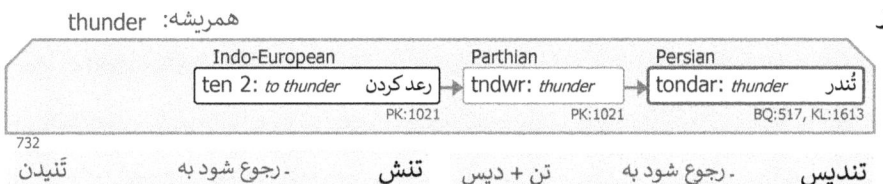

Indo-European	Parthian	Persian
ten 2: *to thunder* رعد کردن	tndwr: *thunder*	tondar: *thunder* تُندر
PK:1021	PK:1021	BQ:517, KL:1613

732

تندیس ۔ رجوع شود به تن + دیس **تنش** ۔ رجوع شود به تَنیدن

تنفر

همریشه: tension, pretend

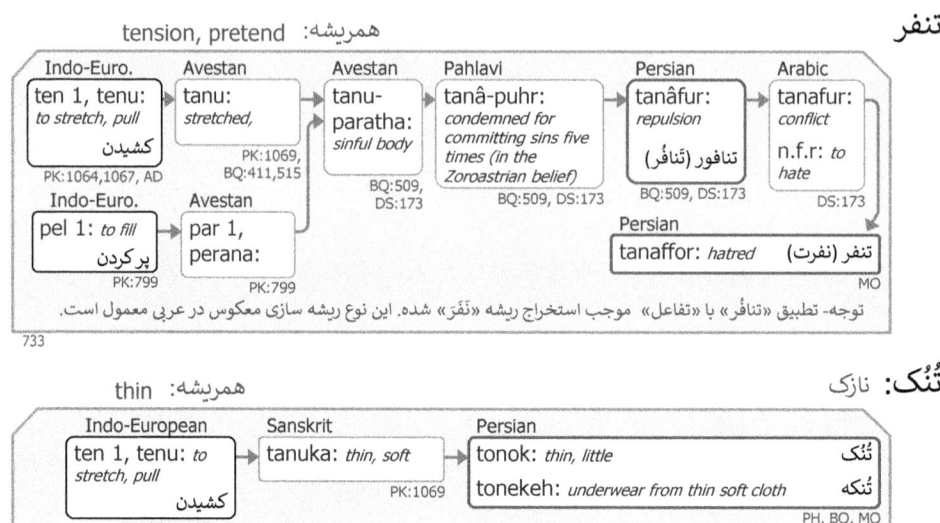

Indo-Euro.	Avestan	Avestan	Pahlavi	Persian	Arabic
ten 1, tenu: *to stretch, pull* کشیدن PK:1064,1067, AD	tanu: *stretched,* PK:1069,	tanu-paratha: *sinful body* BQ:411,515	tanâ-puhr: *condemned for committing sins five times (in the Zoroastrian belief)* BQ:509, DS:173	tanâfur: *repulsion* تنافر (تَنافُر) BQ:509, DS:173	tanafur: *conflict* n.f.r: *to hate* DS:173

Indo-Euro.	Avestan
pel 1: *to fill* پر کردن PK:799	par 1, perana: PK:799

Persian
tanaffor: *hatred*   تنفر (نفرت)
MO

توجه- تطبیق «تنافُر» با «تفاعل» موجب استخراج ریشه «نَفَر» شده. این نوع ریشه سازی معکوس در عربی معمول است.

733

تُنُک: نازک

همریشه: thin

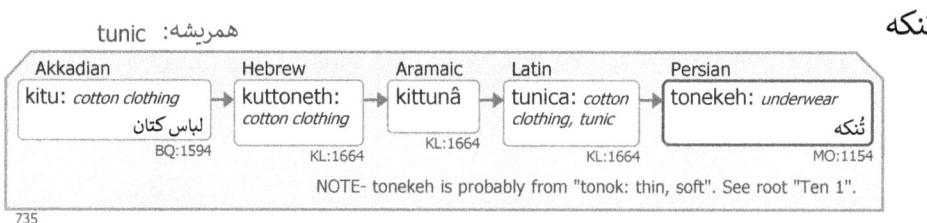

Indo-European	Sanskrit	Persian
ten 1, tenu: *to stretch, pull* کشیدن PK:1064,1067, AD	tanuka: *thin, soft* PK:1069	tonok: *thin, little* تُنُک tonekeh: *underwear from thin soft cloth* تُنُکه PH, BQ, MO

NOTE- See root "Kitu: cotton clothing" for another possible root of "tonekeh"

734

تُنُکه

همریشه: tunic

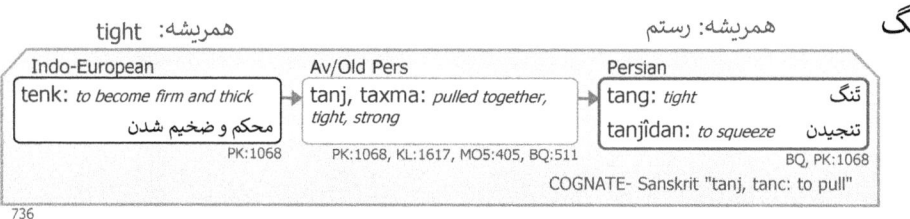

Akkadian	Hebrew	Aramaic	Latin	Persian
kitu: *cotton clothing* لباس کتان BQ:1594	kuttoneth: *cotton clothing* KL:1664	kittunâ KL:1664	tunica: *cotton clothing, tunic* KL:1664	tonekeh: *underwear* تُنُکه MO:1154

NOTE- tonekeh is probably from "tonok: thin, soft". See root "Ten 1".

735

تَنگ

همریشه: رستم   همریشه: tight

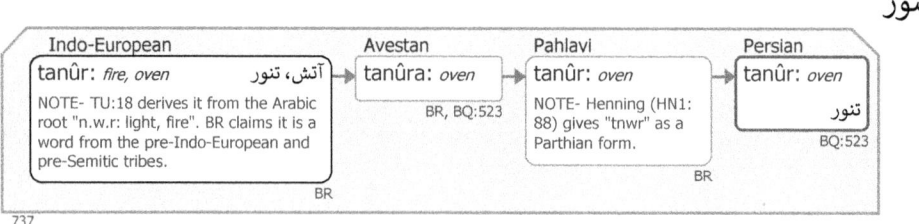

Indo-European	Av/Old Pers	Persian
tenk: *to become firm and thick* محکم و ضخیم شدن PK:1068	tanj, taxma: *pulled together, tight, strong* PK:1068, KL:1617, MO5:405, BQ:511	tang: *tight* تَنگ tanjîdan: *to squeeze* تنجیدن BQ, PK:1068

COGNATE- Sanskrit "tanj, tanc: to pull"

736

تنور

Indo-European	Avestan	Pahlavi	Persian
tanûr: *fire, oven* آتش، تنور NOTE- TU:18 derives it from the Arabic root "n.w.r: light, fire". BR claims it is a word from the pre-Indo-European and pre-Semitic tribes. BR	tanûra: *oven* BR, BQ:523	tanûr: *oven* NOTE- Henning (HN1: 88) gives as 'tnwr' a Parthian form. BR	tanûr: *oven* تنور BQ:523

737

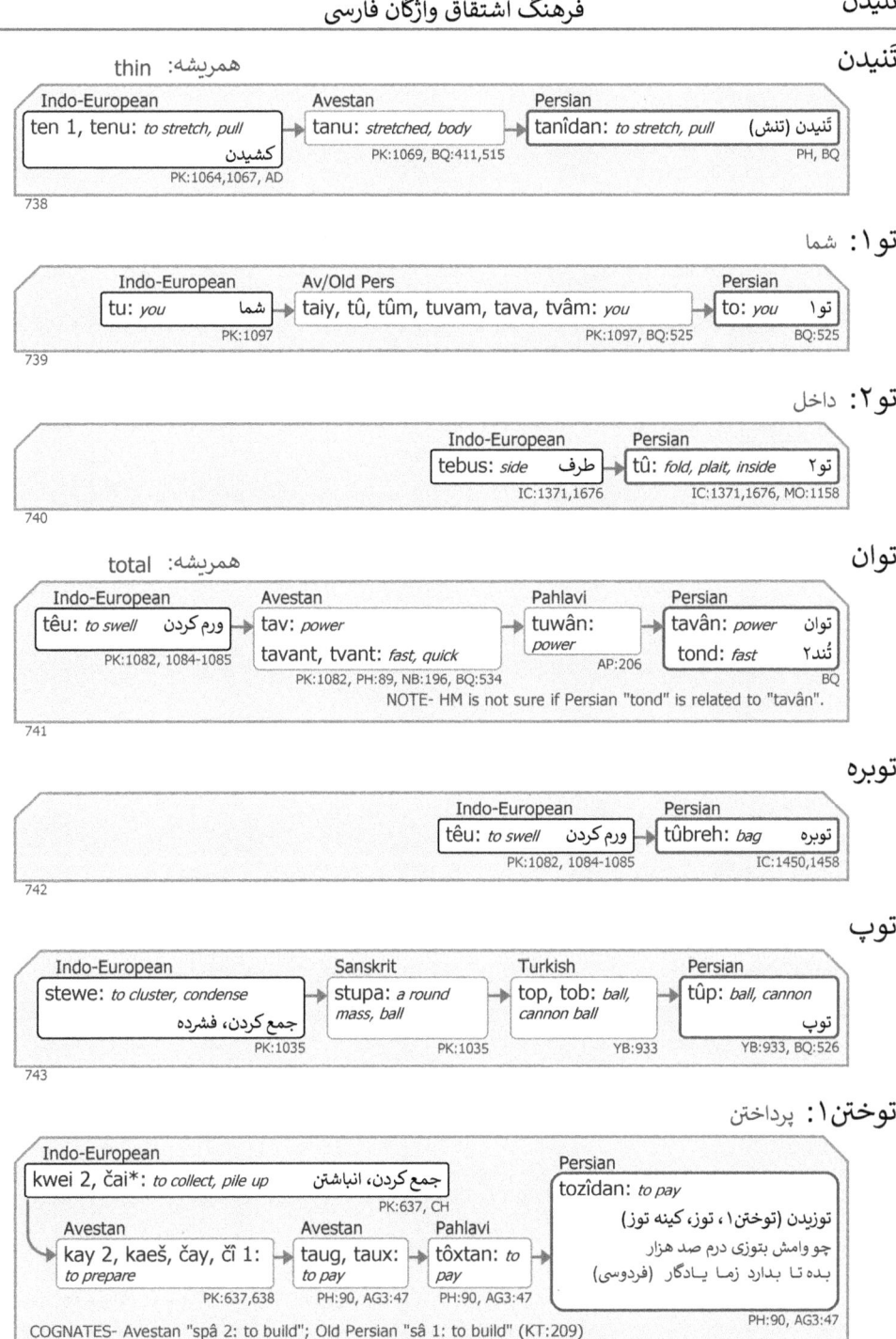

تَنیدن

همریشه: thin

Indo-European	Avestan	Persian
ten 1, tenu: *to stretch, pull* كشيدن	tanu: *stretched, body*	tanîdan: *to stretch, pull* تَنیدن (تنش)
PK:1064,1067, AD	PK:1069, BQ:411,515	PH, BQ

738

تو۱: شما

Indo-European	Av/Old Pers	Persian
tu: *you* شما	taiy, tû, tûm, tuvam, tava, tvâm: *you*	to: *you* تو۱
PK:1097	PK:1097, BQ:525	BQ:525

739

تو۲: داخل

Indo-European	Persian
tebus: *side* طرف	tû: *fold, plait, inside* تو۲
IC:1371,1676	IC:1371,1676, MO:1158

740

توان

همریشه: total

Indo-European	Avestan	Pahlavi	Persian
têu: *to swell* ورم كردن	tav: *power*	tuwân: *power*	tavân: *power* توان
PK:1082, 1084-1085	tavant, tvant: *fast, quick*	AP:206	tond: *fast* تُند۲
	PK:1082, PH:89, NB:196, BQ:534		BQ

NOTE- HM is not sure if Persian "tond" is related to "tavân".

741

توبره

Indo-European	Persian
têu: *to swell* ورم كردن	tûbreh: *bag* توبره
PK:1082, 1084-1085	IC:1450,1458

742

توپ

Indo-European	Sanskrit	Turkish	Persian
stewe: *to cluster, condense* جمع كردن، فشرده	stupa: *a round mass, ball*	top, tob: *ball, cannon ball*	tûp: *ball, cannon* توپ
PK:1035	PK:1035	YB:933	YB:933, BQ:526

743

توختن۱: پرداختن

Indo-European		Persian
kwei 2, čai*: *to collect, pile up* جمع كردن، انباشتن		tozîdan: *to pay*
PK:637, CH		توزیدن (توختن۱، توز، کینه توز)
Avestan	Avestan	Pahlavi	چو وامش بتوزی درم صد هزار
kay 2, kaeš, čay, čî 1: *to prepare*	taug, taux: *to pay*	tôxtan: *to pay*	بده تا بدارد زما یـادگار (فردوسی)
PK:637,638	PH:90, AG3:47	PH:90, AG3:47	PH:90, AG3:47

COGNATES- Avestan "spâ 2: to build"; Old Persian "sâ 1: to build" (KT:209)

744

توختن۲   . رجوع شود به   اندوختن

توده

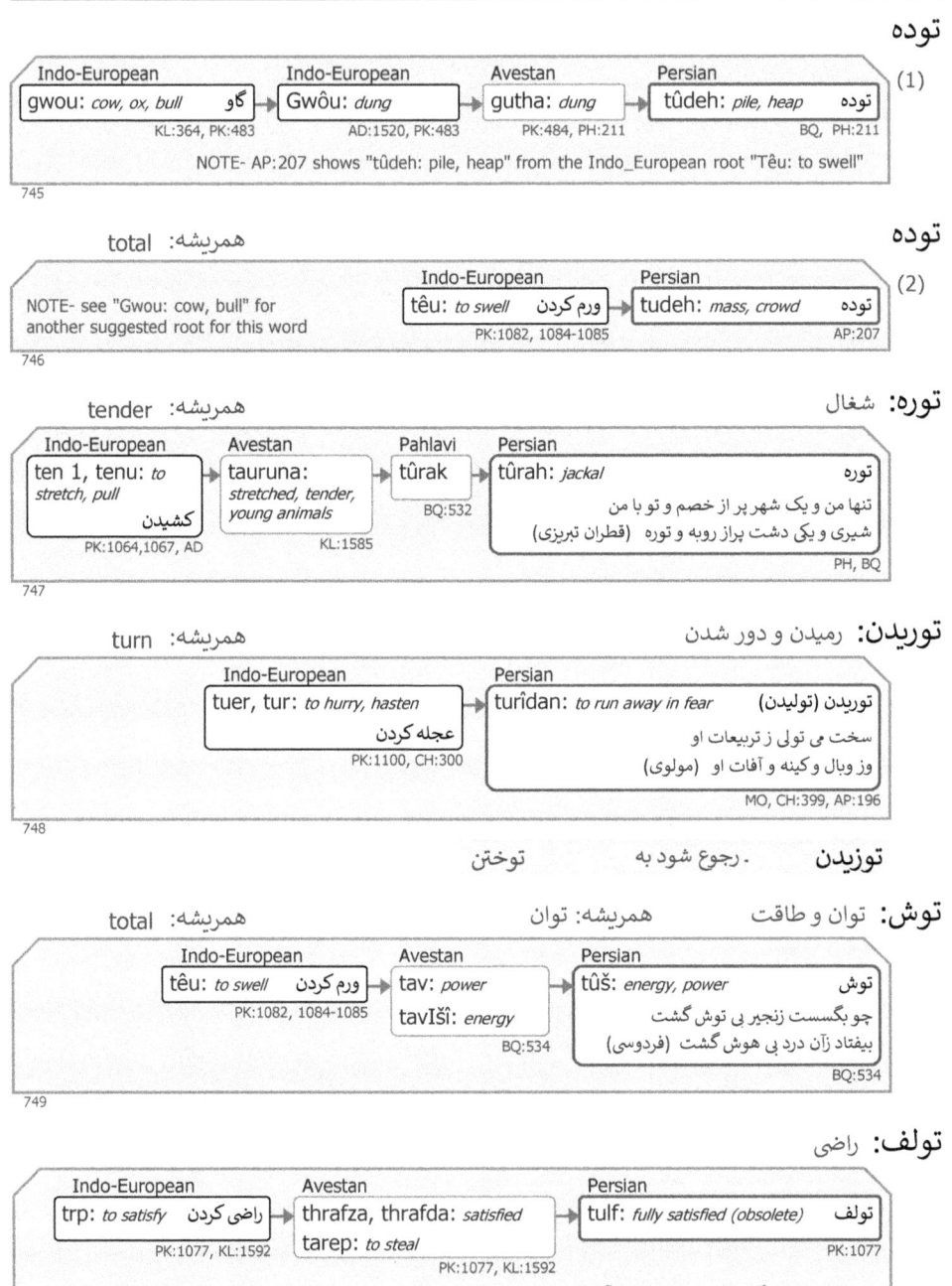

توده (1)

Indo-European	Indo-European	Avestan	Persian
gwou: *cow, ox, bull* گاو	Gwôu: *dung*	gutha: *dung*	tûdeh: *pile, heap* توده
KL:364, PK:483	AD:1520, PK:483	PK:484, PH:211	BQ, PH:211

NOTE- AP:207 shows "tûdeh: pile, heap" from the Indo_European root "Têu: to swell"

745

توده (2)

همریشه: total

	Indo-European	Persian
NOTE- see "Gwou: cow, bull" for another suggested root for this word	têu: *to swell* ورم کردن	tudeh: *mass, crowd* توده
	PK:1082, 1084-1085	AP:207

746

توره: شغال

همریشه: tender

Indo-European	Avestan	Pahlavi	Persian
ten 1, tenu: *to stretch, pull* کشیدن	tauruna: *stretched, tender, young animals*	tûrak BQ:532	tûrah: *jackal* توره
PK:1064,1067, AD	KL:1585		

تنها من و یک شهر پر از خصم و تو با من
شیری و یک دشت پراز روبه و توره (قطران تبریزی)

PH, BQ

747

توریدن: رمیدن و دور شدن

همریشه: turn

Indo-European	Persian
tuer, tur: *to hurry, hasten* عجله کردن	turîdan: *to run away in fear* توریدن (تولیدن)
PK:1100, CH:300	

سخت می تولی ز تربیعات او
وز وبال و کینه و آفات او (مولوی)

MO, CH:399, AP:196

748

توزیدن . رجوع شود به   توختن

توش: توان و طاقت   همریشه: توان   همریشه: total

Indo-European	Avestan	Persian
têu: *to swell* ورم کردن	tav: *power*	tûš: *energy, power* توش
PK:1082, 1084-1085	tavIšî: *energy*	
	BQ:534	

چو بگسست زنجیر بی توش گشت
بیفتاد زآن درد بی هوش گشت (فردوسی)

BQ:534

749

تولف: راضی

Indo-European	Avestan	Persian
trp: *to satisfy* راضی کردن	thrafza, thrafda: *satisfied*	tulf: *fully satisfied (obsolete)* تولف
PK:1077, KL:1592	tarep: *to steal*	PK:1077
	PK:1077, KL:1592	

این لغت یا متروک شده و یا استفاده از آن بسیار محدود میباشد.

750

توله

همریشه: tender

Indo-European	Avestan	Pahlavi	Persian
ten 1, tenu: *to stretch, pull* کشیدن	tauruna: *stretched, tender, young animals*	tôrag, tûrak: *baby animal*	tûleh: *"a tender" animal baby* توله
PK:1064,1067, AD	KL:1585	AP:207	PH, BQ

751

تولیدن: رمیدن   . رجوع شود به   توریدن

تَه

Indo-European	Av/Old Pers	Pahlavi	Persian
teus: *empty* خالی	taoš, tuš, tusen, tussya: *empty*	tihîk, tuhîk: *empty*	tah: *bottom* تَه / tahî, tohî: *empty* تهی
PK:1085	PK:1085, BK:933	BQ:539, TV:151	BQ:539,537, PH:90

752

تَهم: قوی محکم   همریشه: tight

Indo-European	Av/Old Pers	Persian
tenk: *to become firm and thick* محکم و ضخیم شدن	tanj, taxma: *pulled together, tight, strong*	تهم (تهمتن) tahm, taham: *strong*
PK:1068	PK:1068, KL:1617, MO5:405, BQ:511	تَهم رستم نیو با تیغ تیز / برآود از ایشان دم رستخیز (فردوسی)
		KM:514

753

تهماسب: "با اسبان قوی"   همریشه: تهمتن   همریشه: -total, hippo

Indo-European	Avestan	Persian
têu: *to swell* ورم کردن	tav: *power*	Tahmâsb: *"with strong horses"*
PK:1082, 1084-1085	tum-âspa: *(with) strong horses*	تهماسب (طهماسپ)
Indo-European ekwos: *horse* اسب	**Avestan** aspa: *horse*	BQ
PK:301	PK:1082, PH:89, NB:196, BQ:534	
	PK:301, BQ:1819	

754

تهمتن: بدن قوی   . رجوع شود به   تَهم + تن

تهمورث: "با سگهای قوی"   همریشه: tight

Indo-European	Indo-Euro.	Avestan	Av/Old Pers	Persian
ulk, ulkos: *wolf (with fiery eyes)* گرگ	Wlp: *wolf, dog*	urpa, urupis: *dog* / raopias: *fox*	taxma-urupa: *(with) strong dogs*	Tahmûras: *"with strong dogs"* تهمورث
PK:1144, 1179	PK:1179	PK:1179	PK:1068, KL:1617, MO5:405, BQ:511	BQ, PK:1068
Indo-European tenk: *to become firm and thick* محکم و ضخیم شدن				
		PK:1068	NOTE- The root "Ulk: wolf" may be from the root "Ulk: shine, fiery"	

755

تهی   . رجوع شود به   تَه

تیتو

Indo-European	Sanskrit	Persian
titi: *imitation of a bird song* تقلید صدای پرنده	tittibha: *a water bird*	tîtû: *a water bird* تیتو (طیطو)
PK:1086	PK:1086	BQ:1364

756

تیر

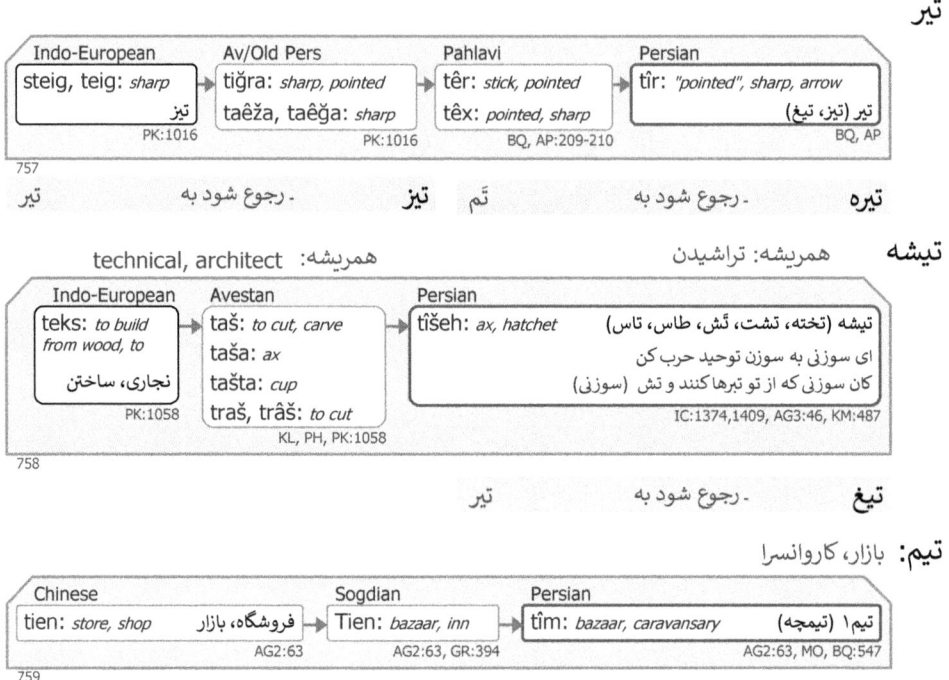

Indo-European	Av/Old Pers	Pahlavi	Persian
steig, teig: *sharp* تیز	tiğra: *sharp, pointed* taêža, taêğa: *sharp*	têr: *stick, pointed* têx: *pointed, sharp*	tîr: *"pointed", sharp, arrow* تیر (تیز، تیغ)
PK:1016	PK:1016	BQ, AP:209-210	BQ, AP

757

تیره ـ رجوع شود به ـ تَم   **تیز**   ـ رجوع شود به ـ تیر

تیشه   همریشه: تراشیدن   همریشه: technical, architect

Indo-European	Avestan	Persian
teks: *to build from wood, to* نجاری، ساختن	taš: *to cut, carve* taša: *ax* tašta: *cup* traš, trâš: *to cut*	tîšeh: *ax, hatchet* تیشه (تخته، تشت، تَش، طاس، تاس) ای سوزنی به سوزن توحید حرب کن کان سوزنی که از تو تبرها کنند و تش (سوزنی)
PK:1058	KL, PH, PK:1058	IC:1374,1409, AG3:46, KM:487

758

تیغ   ـ رجوع شود به ـ تیر

تیم: بازار، کاروانسرا

Chinese	Sogdian	Persian
tien: *store, shop* فروشگاه، بازار	Tien: *bazaar, inn*	tîm: *bazaar, caravansary* تیم۱ (تیمچه)
AG2:63	AG2:63, GR:394	AG2:63, MO, BQ:547

759

تیمچه: بازار   ـ رجوع شود به ـ تیم

ثور

همریشه: Taurus

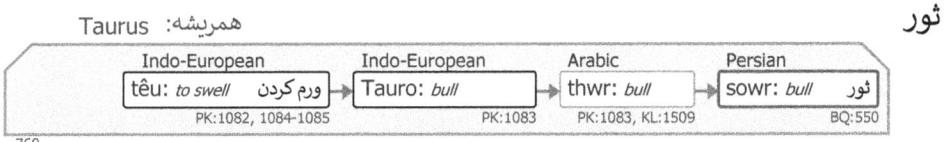

Indo-European	Indo-European	Arabic	Persian
têu: *to swell* ورم کردن	Tauro: *bull*	thwr: *bull*	sowr: *bull* ثور
PK:1082, 1084-1085	PK:1083	PK:1083, KL:1509	BQ:550

136

این حرف گاهی به ت، ز، گ، چ، ژ، ش یا ی بدل شود.

جا: مکان، رتبه، مقام

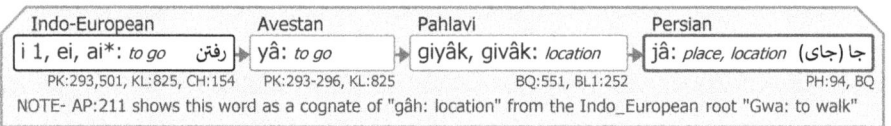

Indo-European	Avestan	Pahlavi	Persian
i 1, ei, ai*: *to go* رفتن	yâ: *to go*	giyâk, givâk: *location*	jâ: *place, location* (جای) جا
PK:293,501, KL:825, CH:154	PK:293-296, KL:825	BQ:551, BL1:252	PH:94, BQ

NOTE- AP:211 shows this word as a cognate of "gâh: location" from the Indo_European root "Gwa: to walk"

761

جاثلیق

همریشه: Catholic, solid, save

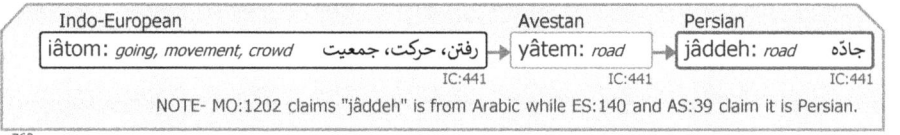

Indo-Euro.	Greek	Arabic	Persian
solo: *whole* تمام، کامل	holos: *whole* kata-holos, katholicos: *undivided church of Christ*	jaselîq: *a rank in the Catholic church.*	jâselîq: *a Catholic rank* جاثلیق زبطـریق وز جاثلیقان شـهـر هرآنکس کش از مردمی بود بهر (فردوسی)
	PK:979		
PK:979		TU:19	MO:1199, NS:141

762

جادّه

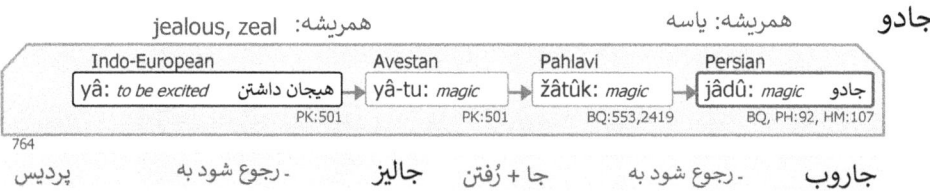

Indo-European	Avestan	Persian
iâtom: *going, movement, crowd* رفتن، حرکت، جمعیت	yâtem: *road*	jâddeh: *road* جادّه
IC:441	IC:441	IC:441

NOTE- MO:1202 claims "jâddeh" is from Arabic while ES:140 and AS:39 claim it is Persian.

763

جادو

همریشه: یاسه   همریشه: jealous, zeal

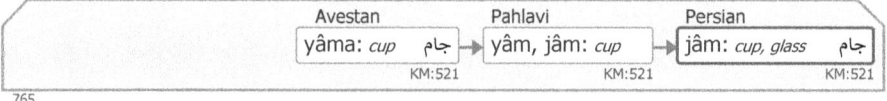

Indo-European	Avestan	Pahlavi	Persian
yâ: *to be excited* هیجان داشتن	yâ-tu: *magic*	žâtûk: *magic*	jâdû: *magic* جادو
PK:501	PK:501	BQ:553,2419	BQ, PH:92, HM:107

764

جاروب - رجوع شود به   جا + رُفتن   **جالیز** - رجوع شود به   پردیس

جام: پیاله، ساغر

Avestan	Pahlavi	Persian
yâma: *cup* جام	yâm, jâm: *cup*	jâm: *cup, glass* جام
KM:521	KM:521	KM:521

765

جاماسب: "اسب دار"

همریشه: -hippo

Indo-European	Avestan	Avestan	Persian
ekwos: *horse* اسب PK:301	aspa: *horse* PK:301, BQ:1819	jâm-âspa: *owning horses* BQ, PK:1082, KT, PH:206, MO5:419	Jamasb: *a name meaning "has horse(s)"* جاماسب MO

766

جامه   همریشه: پیراهن، همیان

همریشه: zone

Indo-European	Av/Old Pers	Pahlavi	Persian
yôs: *to gird, belt* کمر بستن PK:513	yâh 2: *to put belt on* yâhma: *cover, clothes* PK:513, KL:1770, BK:434	yâmak: *clothes* HM:49, PH:93	jâmeh: *clothes* جامه BQ

767

جان

همریشه: theater, semantic

Indo-European	Sanskrit	Pahlavi	Persian
dheye: *to see* دیدن PK:243	dhi: *to see, to think* dhyânah: *seeing mentally* PK:243	gyân, jân: *soul* BQ:558	jân: *life, soul* جان NOTE- PH: 93 derives this from AV "dhay: to see" HM:49, BQ:558

768

جاوید

همریشه: eternal

Indo-European	Avestan	Pahlavi	Persian
aiw: *vitality, eternity* حیات، ابدیت PK:17	âyu, ay: *life, age* yave: *forever* PK:17	yavê-tân: *ever lasting* BQ:564, PH:93	jâvîd: *eternal* جاوید

769

جاه

همریشه: base

Indo-Euro.	Av/Old Pers	Av/Old Pers	Persian	Arabic	Persian
gwa: *to walk, step* قدم زدن PK:463,CH:98	gam: *to come, step* PK:463, KL:318	gât, gâthu, gâv, gâtuš: *place, seat, throne* PK:463, KT:183	gâh 2: *place, position, rank* گاه2 BQ:1771,1773	jah: *rank* ES:144	jâh: *position, rank* جاه MO

COGNATE- Old Persian "yâtha: place, rank"

770

جبر

همریشه: algebra

Aramaic	Arabic	Persian
j.b.r: *to reunite, join together, force* بهم آوردن، وصل کردن، نیرو jabra: *powerful, man* نیرومند، مرد KL:633	J.b.r: *to reunite, force* Al-Jabr-w'al-Muqâbalah: *"Reunion and Comparison", the first book on Algebra by Al-Khârazmî* KL:633, NV:67	jabr: *force, algebra* جَبر NV:67

771

جبرئیل: "خدا قدرت من است"

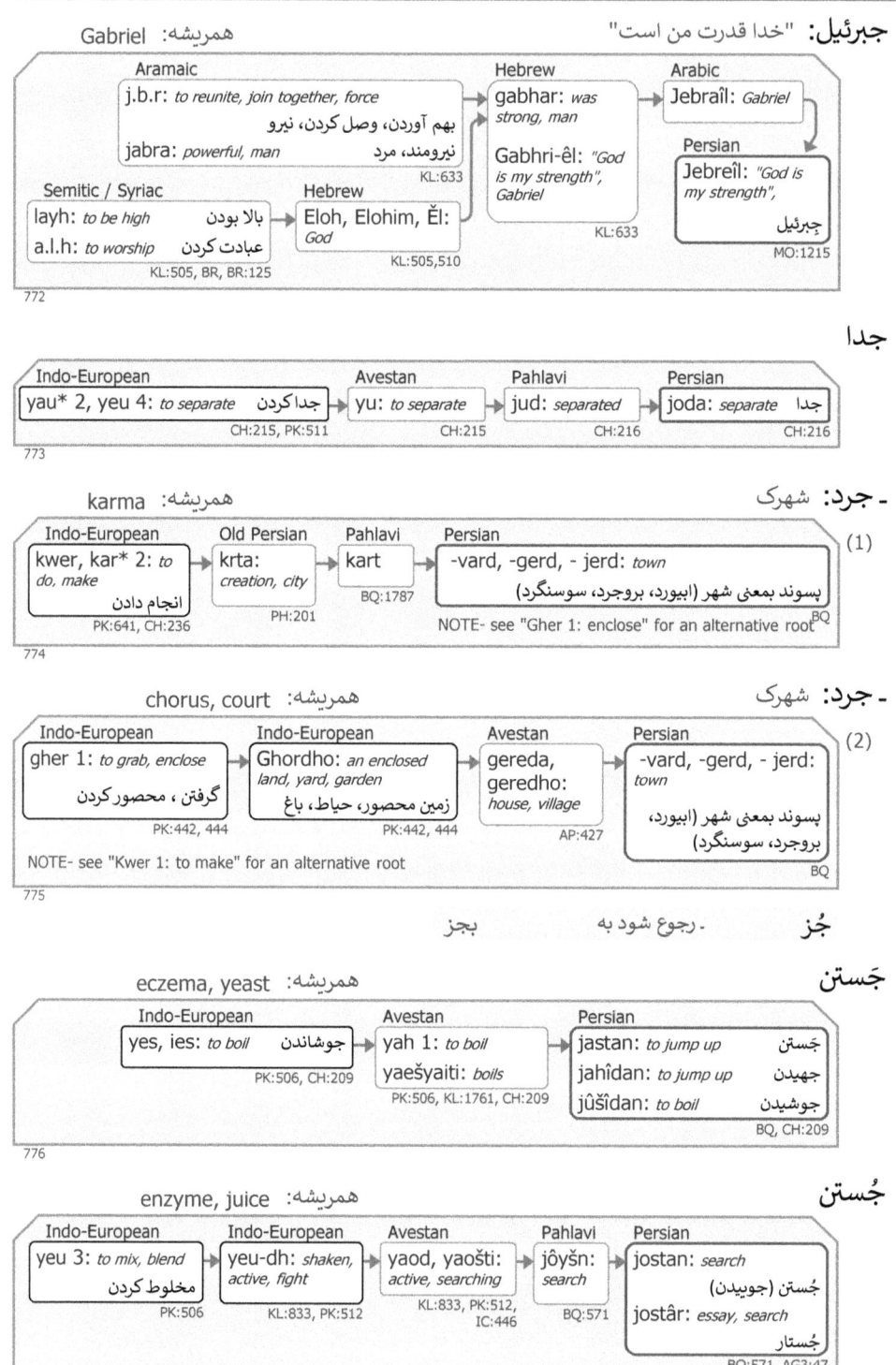

همریشه: Gabriel

Aramaic
j.b.r: to reunite, join together, force
بهم آوردن، وصل کردن، نیرو
jabra: powerful, man
نیرومند، مرد
KL:633

Hebrew
gabhar: was strong, man

Gabhri-êl: "God is my strength", Gabriel
KL:633

Arabic
Jebraîl: Gabriel

Persian
Jebreîl: "God is my strength",
جبرئیل
MO:1215

Semitic / Syriac
layh: to be high
بالا بودن
a.l.h: to worship
عبادت کردن
KL:505, BR, BR:125

Hebrew
Eloh, Elohim, Ěl: God
KL:505,510

772

جدا

Indo-European
yau* 2, yeu 4: to separate
جدا کردن
CH:215, PK:511

Avestan
yu: to separate
CH:215

Pahlavi
jud: separated
CH:216

Persian
joda: separate   جدا
CH:216

773

ـ جرد: شهرک

همریشه: karma

Indo-European
kwer, kar* 2: to do, make
انجام دادن
PK:641, CH:236

Old Persian
krta: creation, city

Pahlavi
kart
BQ:1787

Persian
-vard, -gerd, - jerd: town
پسوند بمعنی شهر (ابیورد، بروجرد، سوسنگرد)
NOTE- see "Gher 1: enclose" for an alternative root BQ

(1)

774

ـ جرد: شهرک

همریشه: chorus, court

Indo-European
gher 1: to grab, enclose
گرفتن ، محصور کردن
PK:442, 444

Indo-European
Ghordho: an enclosed land, yard, garden
زمین محصور، حیاط، باغ
PK:442, 444

Avestan
gereda, geredho: house, village
AP:427

Persian
-vard, -gerd, - jerd: town
پسوند بمعنی شهر (ابیورد، بروجرد، سوسنگرد)
BQ

(2)

NOTE- see "Kwer 1: to make" for an alternative root

775

جُز   . رجوع شود به   بجز

جَستن

همریشه: eczema, yeast

Indo-European
yes, ies: to boil
جوشاندن
PK:506, CH:209

Avestan
yah 1: to boil
yaešyaiti: boils
PK:506, KL:1761, CH:209

Persian
jastan: to jump up   جستن
jahîdan: to jump up   جهیدن
jûšîdan: to boil   جوشیدن
BQ, CH:209

776

جُستن

همریشه: enzyme, juice

Indo-European
yeu 3: to mix, blend
مخلوط کردن
PK:506

Indo-European
yeu-dh: shaken, active, fight
KL:833, PK:512

Avestan
yaod, yaošti: active, searching
KL:833, PK:512, IC:446

Pahlavi
jôyšn: search
BQ:571

Persian
jostan: search
جستن (جویدن)
jostâr: essay, search
جستار
BQ:571, AG3:47

777

جَسک: بلا و محنت

Avestan	Pahlavi	Persian
yaska: *sickness* بیماری	yask: *sickness*	jask: *misery, calamity* جَسک
KM:535, BQ:571	KM:535, BQ:571	گر بخواهم از کسی یک مشت نسک مرمرا گوید خمش کن مرگ و جسک (مولوی) KM:535, BQ:571

778

جشن   همریشه: ایزد، یزدان   همریشه: hagios

Indo-European	Avestan	Pahlavi	Persian
yag: *to worship* ستایش کردن	yesnya, yasna: *worship*	yašn	jašn: *celebration* جشن
PK:501	PK:501, PH:95,252, KL:1759	BQ:572	BQ, AG2
COGNATE- Old Persian "yad: worsjip"			

779

جُغ   ـ رجوع شود به   یوغ

جفت   همریشه: یوغ   همریشه: yoke

Indo-European	Avestan	Pahlavi	Persian
yeu 1, yauj*: *to join, harness* جفت کردن، مهار کردن	yuxta: *harnessed, joined*	juxt: *pair*	joft: *pair (union)* جفت
PK:509, CH:217	BQ:577,1228,2458, PK:509	BQ:577	BQ

780

جگر   همریشه: liver, hepatic

Indo-European	Avestan	Pahlavi	Persian
yekwer: *liver* جگر	yâkara: *liver*	jakar, jagar: *liver*	jegar: *liver* جگر
PK:504	PK:504	TV:317	BQ:579, PK:504

781

جلیقه   همریشه: ژیلت   همریشه: gilet

Turkish	Persian
ijlak, yelek: *sleeveless coat* کت بی آستین	jalîqeh: *waist coat without sleeves* جلیقه (جلیتقه)
KL:656	BQ:584

782

جم: "دوقلو"، لقب جمشید شاه که دوقلو بدنیا آمد   همریشه: Gemini, even

Indo-European	Avestan	Pahlavi	Persian
yem: *hold together (pair)* جفت، جفت کردن	yemô, yemâ, yîma: *twin (king)*	yam: *king*	jam: *king* جم
PK:505	KL:1763, BT:1301, FV:5	BQ:587	BQ:587, MO5:433, AG1:28
	NOTE- King Jamshîd's twin sister was also nicknamed "Yimâ: twin".		

783

جمشید   همریشه: Gemini, even

Indo-European	Avestan	Pahlavi	Persian
yem: *hold together (pair)* جفت، جفت کردن	yemô, yemâ, yîma: *twin (king)*	yam-šît: *brilliant twin,* *brilliant king*	Jamsîd: *"brilliant king"* جمشید
PK:505	yima-xšaetem: *brilliant king*	BQ:587	BQ:587, MO5:433, AG1:28
Indo-European	KL:1763, BT:1301, FV:5		
ksei 2: *bright* روشن		NOTE- King Jamshîd's twin sister was also nicknamed "Yimâ: twin".	
WD1:501, BT:541			

784

140

جَن: راه

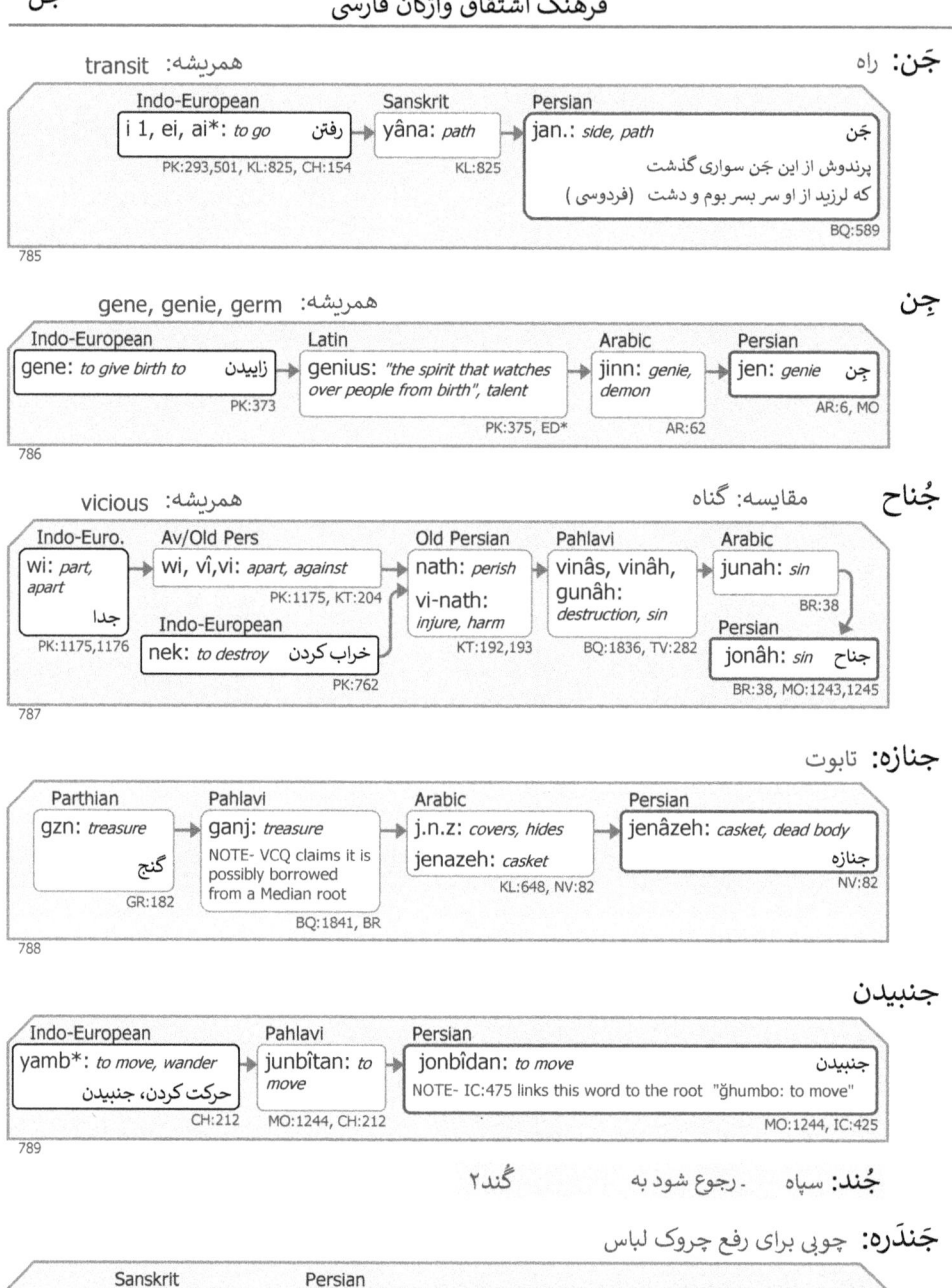

همریشه: transit

Indo-European — i 1, ei, ai*: *to go* رفتن — PK:293,501, KL:825, CH:154

Sanskrit — yâna: *path* — KL:825

Persian — jan.: *side, path* جَن

پرندوش از این جَن سواری گذشت

که لرزید از او سر بسر بوم و دشت (فردوسی)

BQ:589

785

چِن

همریشه: gene, genie, germ

Indo-European — gene: *to give birth to* زاییدن — PK:373

Latin — genius: *"the spirit that watches over people from birth", talent* — PK:375, ED*

Arabic — jinn: *genie, demon* — AR:62

Persian — jen: *genie* چِن — AR:6, MO

786

جُناح

مقایسه: گناه   همریشه: vicious

Indo-Euro. — wi: *part, apart* جدا — PK:1175,1176

Av/Old Pers — wi, vî,vi: *apart, against* — PK:1175, KT:204

Indo-European — nek: *to destroy* خراب کردن — PK:762

Old Persian — nath: *perish* / vi-nath: *injure, harm* — KT:192,193

Pahlavi — vinâs, vinâh, gunâh: *destruction, sin* — BQ:1836, TV:282

Arabic — junah: *sin* — BR:38

Persian — jonâh: *sin* جناح — BR:38, MO:1243,1245

787

جنازه: تابوت

Parthian — gzn: *treasure* گنج — GR:182

Pahlavi — ganj: *treasure* NOTE- VCQ claims it is possibly borrowed from a Median root — BQ:1841, BR

Arabic — j.n.z: *covers, hides* / jenazeh: *casket* — KL:648, NV:82

Persian — jenâzeh: *casket, dead body* جنازه — NV:82

788

جنبیدن

Indo-European — yamb*: *to move, wander* حرکت کردن، جنبیدن — CH:212

Pahlavi — junbîtan: *to move* — MO:1244, CH:212

Persian — jonbîdan: *to move* جنبیدن NOTE- IC:475 links this word to the root "ğhumbo: to move" — MO:1244, IC:425

789

جُند: سپاه   ـ رجوع شود به   گُند۲

جَندَره: چوبی برای رفع چروک لباس

Sanskrit — yantra: *tool* ابزار — BQ:591

Persian — jandareh: *a wood stick used to remove wrinkles from clothes* جَندَره — MON, BQ

790

141

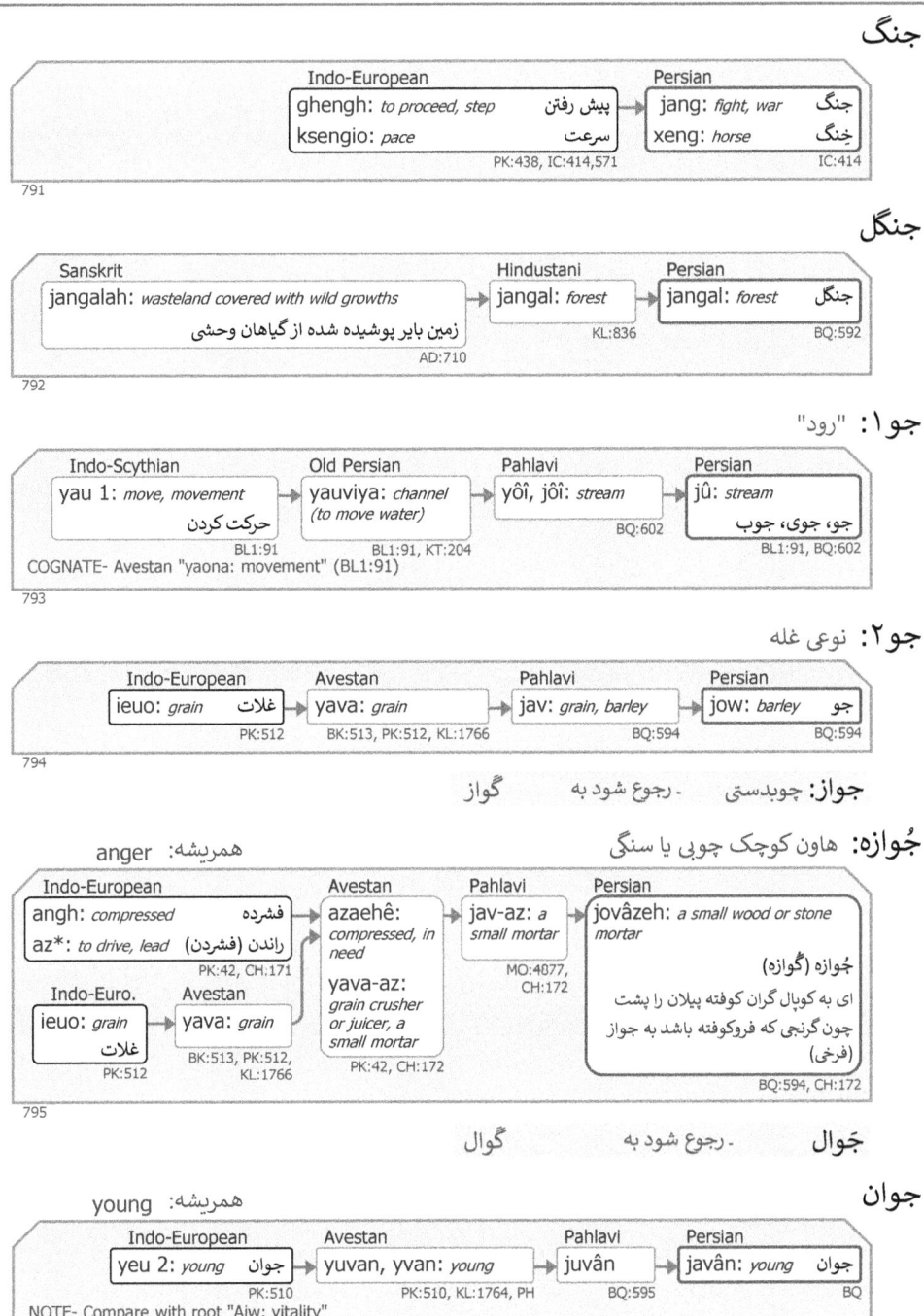

جنگ

Indo-European	Persian
ghengh: *to proceed, step* پیش رفتن	jang: *fight, war* جنگ
ksengio: *pace* سرعت	xeng: *horse* خنگ
PK:438, IC:414,571	IC:414

791

جنگل

Sanskrit	Hindustani	Persian
jangalah: *wasteland covered with wild growths* زمین بایر پوشیده شده از گیاهان وحشی	jangal: *forest*	jangal: *forest* جنگل
AD:710	KL:836	BQ:592

792

جو ۱: "رود"

Indo-Scythian	Old Persian	Pahlavi	Persian
yau 1: *move, movement* حرکت کردن	yauviya: *channel (to move water)*	yôî, jôî: *stream*	jû: *stream* جو، جوی، جوب
BL1:91	BL1:91, KT:204	BQ:602	BL1:91, BQ:602

COGNATE- Avestan "yaona: movement" (BL1:91)

793

جو ۲: نوعی غله

Indo-European	Avestan	Pahlavi	Persian
ieuo: *grain* غلات	yava: *grain*	jav: *grain, barley*	jow: *barley* جو
PK:512	BK:513, PK:512, KL:1766	BQ:594	BQ:594

794

جواز: چوبدستی ـ رجوع شود به گواز

جُوازه: هاون کوچک چوبی یا سنگی

همریشه: anger

Indo-European	Avestan	Pahlavi	Persian
angh: *compressed* فشرده	azaehê: *compressed, in need*	jav-az: *a small mortar*	jovâzeh: *a small wood or stone mortar*
az*: *to drive, lead* راندن (فشردن)			جُوازه (گُوازه)
PK:42, CH:171	yava-az: *grain crusher or juicer, a small mortar*		ای به کوپال گران کوفته پیلان را پشت چون گرنجی که فروکوفته باشد به جواز (فرخی)

Indo-Euro.	Avestan		
ieuo: *grain* غلات	yava: *grain*	MO:4877, CH:172	
PK:512	BK:513, PK:512, KL:1766	PK:42, CH:172	BQ:594, CH:172

795

جَوال ـ رجوع شود به گوال

جوان

همریشه: young

Indo-European	Avestan	Pahlavi	Persian
yeu 2: *young* جوان	yuvan, yvan: *young*	juvân	javân: *young* جوان
PK:510	PK:510, KL:1764, PH	BQ:595	BQ

NOTE- Compare with root "Aiw: vitality"

796

جوب ـ رجوع شود به جو ۱   جوجه ـ رجوع شود به ژوژه

جوراب

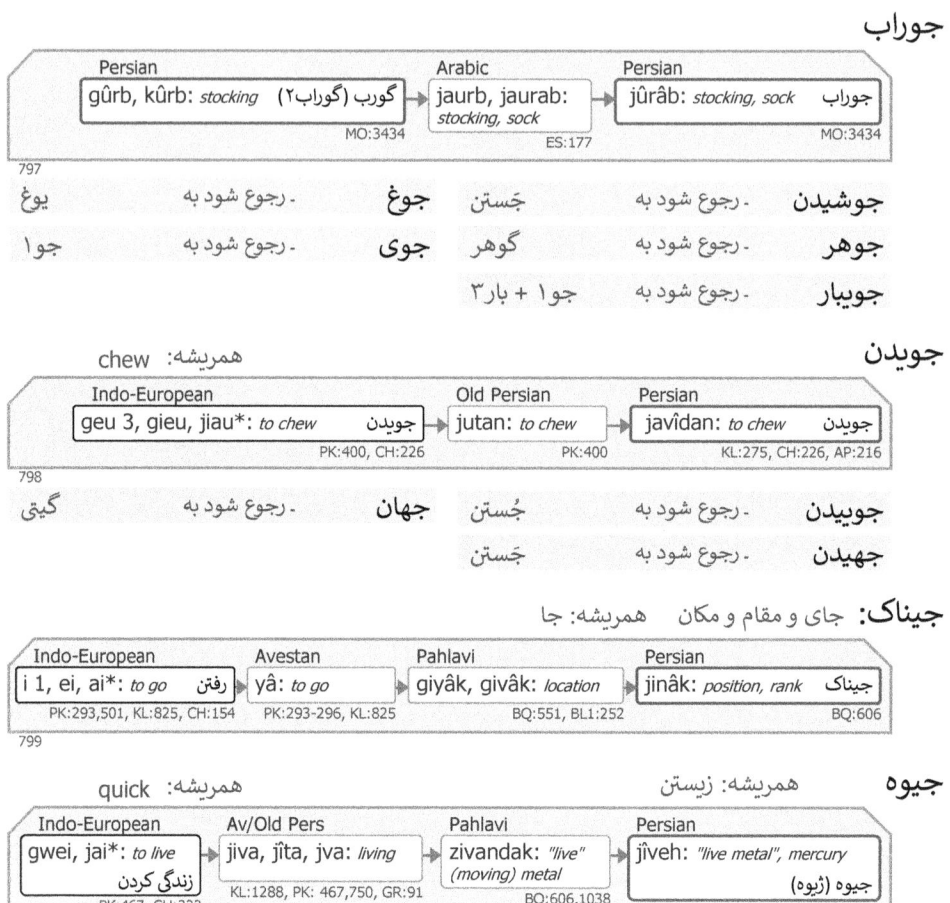

Persian	Arabic	Persian
گورب (گوراب۲) gûrb, kûrb: *stocking*	jaurb, jaurab: *stocking, sock*	جوراب jûrâb: *stocking, sock*
MO:3434	ES:177	MO:3434

797

جوغ	رجوع شود به	یوغ		جوشیدن	رجوع شود به	جُستن
جوی	رجوع شود به	جو۱		جوهر	رجوع شود به	گوهر
				جویبار	رجوع شود به	جو۱ + بار۳

جویدن

همریشه: chew

Indo-European	Old Persian	Persian
جویدن geu 3, gieu, jiau*: *to chew*	jutan: *to chew*	جویدن javîdan: *to chew*
PK:400, CH:226	PK:400	KL:275, CH:226, AP:216

798

جهان	رجوع شود به	گیتی		جویدن	رجوع شود به	جُستن
				جهیدن	رجوع شود به	جَستن

جیناک: جای و مقام و مکان   همریشه: جا

Indo-European	Avestan	Pahlavi	Persian
رفتن i 1, ei, ai*: *to go*	yâ: *to go*	giyâk, givâk: *location*	جیناک jinâk: *position, rank*
PK:293,501, KL:825, CH:154	PK:293-296, KL:825	BQ:551, BL1:252	BQ:606

799

جیوه

همریشه: quick   همریشه: زیستن

Indo-European	Av/Old Pers	Pahlavi	Persian
gwei, jai*: *to live* زندگی کردن	jiva, jîta, jva: *living*	zivandak: *"live" (moving) metal*	jîveh: *"live metal", mercury* جیوه (ژیوه)
PK:467, CH:222	KL:1288, PK: 467,750, GR:91	BQ:606,1038	MO, CH

800

این حرف گاهی به ش، ز، ژ، یا ص بدل شود.

چابک

همریشه: trepid   همریشه: سبُک

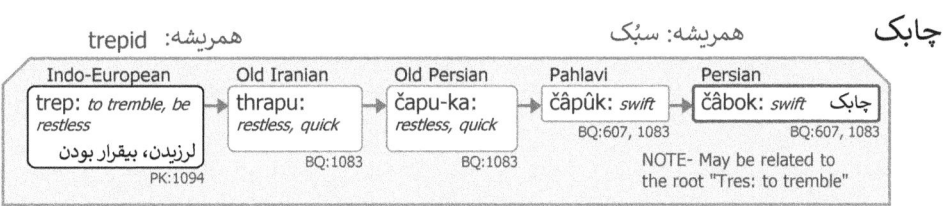

Indo-European	Old Iranian	Old Persian	Pahlavi	Persian
trep: *to tremble, be restless* لرزیدن، بیقرار بودن PK:1094	thrapu: *restless, quick* BQ:1083	čapu-ka: *restless, quick* BQ:1083	čâpûk: *swift* BQ:607, 1083	čâbok: *swift* چابک BQ:607, 1083 NOTE- May be related to the root "Tres: to tremble"

801

چاپ

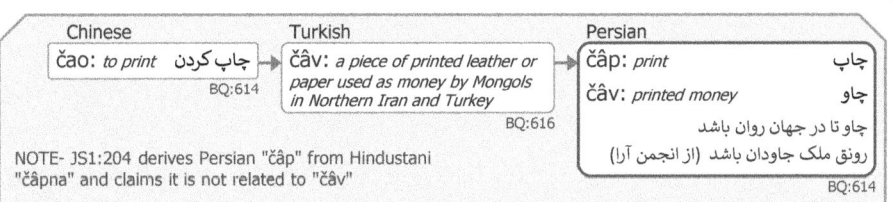

Chinese	Turkish	Persian
čao: *to print* چاپ کردن BQ:614	čâv: *a piece of printed leather or paper used as money by Mongols in Northern Iran and Turkey* BQ:616	čâp: *print* چاپ čâv: *printed money* چاو چاو تا در جهان روان باشد رونق ملک جاودان باشد (از انجمن آرا) BQ:614

NOTE- JS1:204 derives Persian "čâp" from Hindustani "čâpna" and claims it is not related to "čâv"

802

چاپیدن

همریشه: capture, have   همریشه: چسبیدن

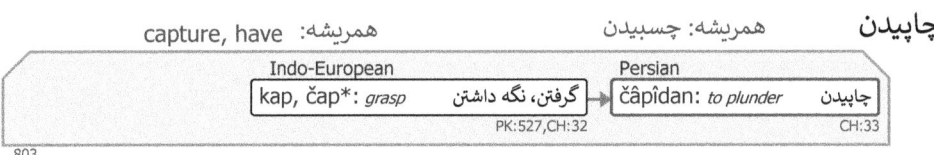

Indo-European	Persian
kap, čap*: *grasp* گرفتن، نگه داشتن PK:527,CH:32	čâpîdan: *to plunder* چاپیدن CH:33

803

چادر

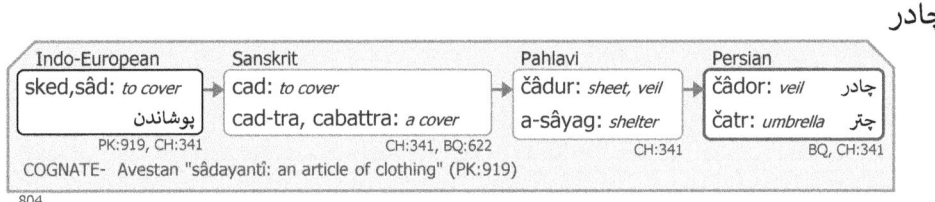

Indo-European	Sanskrit	Pahlavi	Persian
sked, sâd: *to cover* پوشاندن PK:919, CH:341	cad: *to cover* cad-tra, cabattra: *a cover* CH:341, BQ:622	čâdur: *sheet, veil* a-sâyag: *shelter* CH:341	čâdor: *veil* چادر čatr: *umbrella* چتر BQ, CH:341

COGNATE- Avestan "sâdayanti: an article of clothing" (PK:919)

804

چار، چاره

مقایسه: وچر   همریشه: گُزیدن   همریشه: Sanskrit "vi-cay"

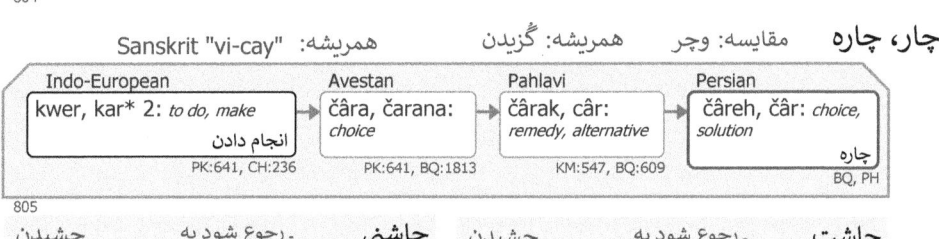

Indo-European	Avestan	Pahlavi	Persian
kwer, kar* 2: *to do, make* انجام دادن PK:641, CH:236	čâra, čarana: *choice* PK:641, BQ:1813	čârak, čâr: *remedy, alternative* KM:547, BQ:609	čâreh, čâr: *choice, solution* چاره BQ, PH

805

چاشت - رجوع شود به چشیدن   چاشنی - رجوع شود به چشیدن

چاقو

Indo-European
keku: *club*   گرز، چکش
WD1:381, PK:543, IC:1390

Avestan
kakuš, čakuš: *ax*
PK:543

Pahlavi
cakôč: *ax*
BQ:613

Persian
čakkoš: *hammer*   چکش
čâqû: *knife*   چاقو
PK:543, BK:597, BT:575, MO:1268, IC:1390

COGNATE- Old Persian "queke: club" (PK:543);/ IC:1390 links "čakkoš" to "čowgân" from "Čop: wood";/ Persian "čakoš" may be from Altaic "čekû: handle" (ST:422)

806

چاک

Indo-Iranian
čak*, čag*: *to strike, hit*   ضربه زدن، دریدن
CH:31

Persian
čâk: *rupture, crack*   چاک
CH:31

807

چاکر: فرمانبر، مطیع

Pahlavi
ča-kar: *obedient*   فرمانبردار، مطیع
JS1:202

Persian
čâker: *obedient*   چاکر
JS1:202

808

چال: رفتن ۔ رجوع شود به   چلیدن   **چالاک**   چلیدن ۔ رجوع شود به   چلیدن

چالش   چلیدن ۔ رجوع شود به   **چالیدن**   چلیدن ۔ رجوع شود به   چلیدن

چالیک: الک دولک   همریشه: چِلیک

Turkish (Ottoman)
člyk: *hit by a blow, a tapered piece of wood or steel*
ضربه خورده، چوب یا آهن شکل گرفته
EE*

Persian
čâlik: *tipcat, a game played with two pieces of tapered wood*   چالیک
گه تاج سلطانان شوم گه مکر شیطانان شوم
گه عقل چالاکی شوم گه طفل چالیکی شوم (مولوی)
DK*, EE*, BQ:615

809

چامیدن: ادرار کردن

Pahlavi
čamiš, čamišn, urine   ادرار
JS1:203

Persian
چامیدن (چامین)   čâmîdan: *to urinate*
شد طعمه طوطی شکر
وان زاغ را چامین خر (مولوی)
JS1:203, DK*

810

چامین: ادرار ۔ رجوع شود به   چامیدن

چانه   همریشه: زنخ   همریشه: chin

Indo-European
genu 2: *chin, jaw bone*   چانه، استخوان فک
PK:381

Avestan
zânu, zanva: *chin*
PK:381, BK:221

Persian
čâneh: *chin*   چانه
BK:221, BQ:1036, PH:148, AP:218

811

چاو: اسکناس چینی ۔ رجوع شود به   چاپ

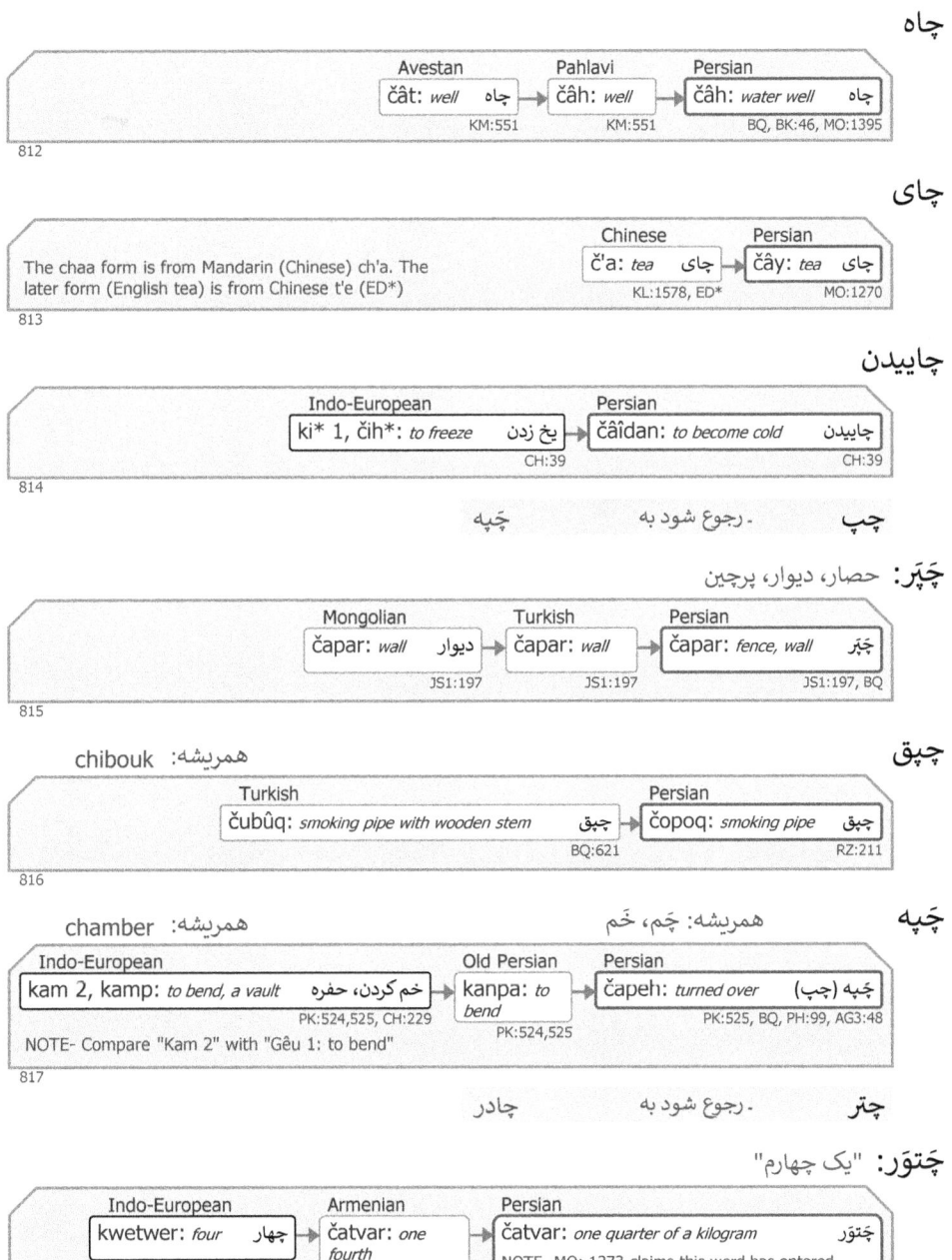

چاه

812

Avestan	Pahlavi	Persian
čât: *well* چاه	čâh: *well*	čâh: *water well* چاه
KM:551	KM:551	BQ, BK:46, MO:1395

چای

813

The chaa form is from Mandarin (Chinese) ch'a. The later form (English tea) is from Chinese t'e (ED*)

Chinese	Persian
č'a: *tea* چای	čây: *tea* چای
KL:1578, ED*	MO:1270

چاییدن

814

Indo-European	Persian
ki* 1, čih*: *to freeze* یخ زدن	čâîdan: *to become cold* چاییدن
CH:39	CH:39

چپ .رجوع شود به چَپه

چَپَر: حصار، دیوار، پرچین

815

Mongolian	Turkish	Persian
čapar: *wall* دیوار	čapar: *wall*	čapar: *fence, wall* چَپَر
JS1:197	JS1:197	JS1:197, BQ

چپق

همریشه: chibouk

816

Turkish	Persian
čubûq: *smoking pipe with wooden stem* چبق	čopoq: *smoking pipe* چبق
BQ:621	RZ:211

چَپه

همریشه: chamber   همریشه: چَم، خَم

817

Indo-European	Old Persian	Persian
kam 2, kamp: *to bend, a vault* خم کردن، حفره	kanpa: *to bend*	čapeh: *turned over* چَپه (چپ)
PK:524,525, CH:229	PK:524,525	PK:525, BQ, PH:99, AG3:48
NOTE- Compare "Kam 2" with "Gêu 1: to bend"		

چتر .رجوع شود به چادر

چَتوَر: "یک چهارم"

818

Indo-European	Armenian	Persian
kwetwer: *four* چهار	čatvar: *one fourth*	čatvar: *one quarter of a kilogram* چَتوَر
PK:642	TV:148	NOTE- MO: 1273 claims this word has entered Persian through Russian. TV:148

چِرا

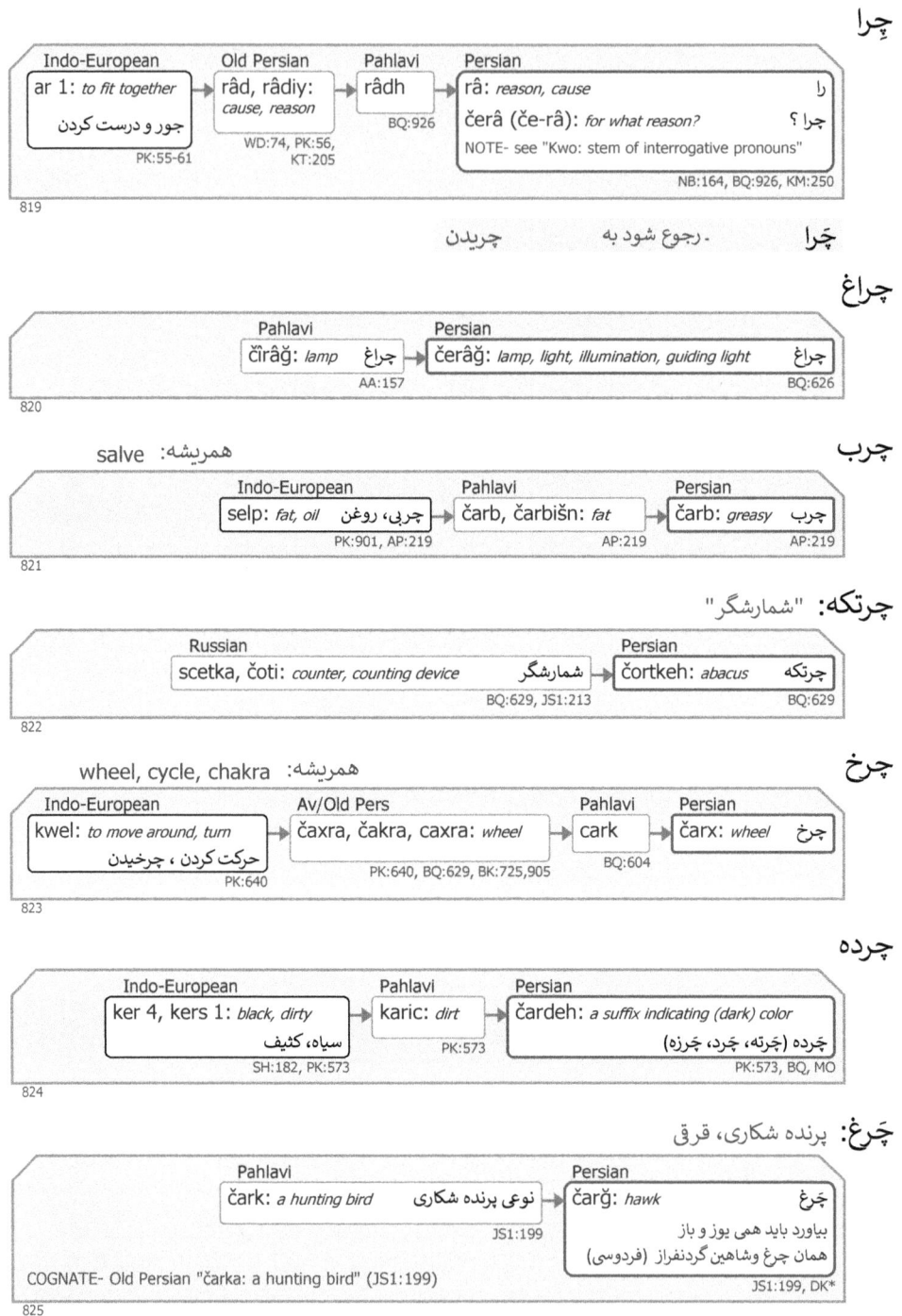

چِرا رجوع شود به.   **چریدن**

چراغ

چرب   همریشه: salve

چرتکه: "شمارشگر"

چرخ   همریشه: wheel, cycle, chakra

چرده

چَرغ: پرنده شکاری، قرق

چرک

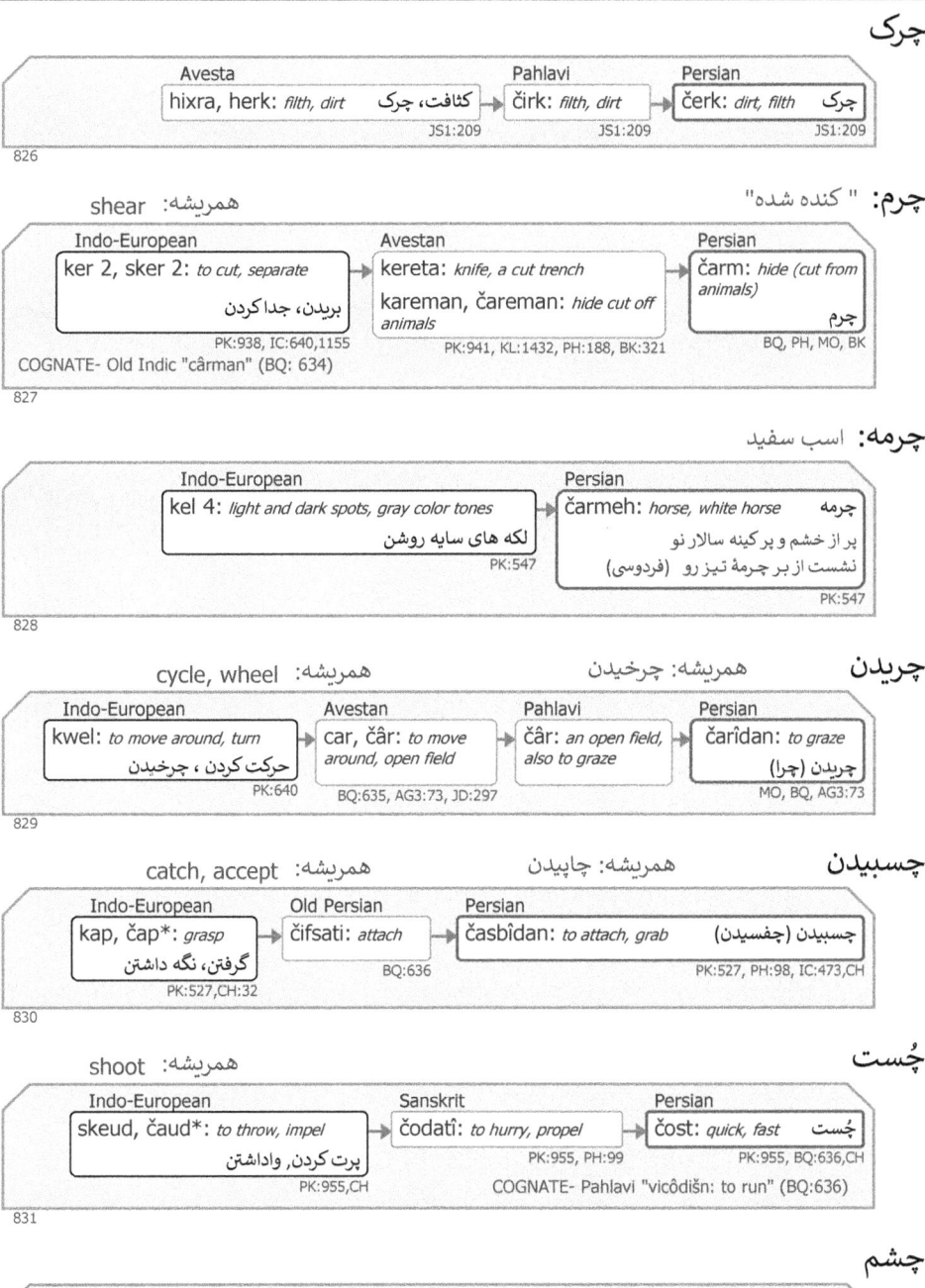

چرک

Avesta	Pahlavi	Persian
hixra, herk: *filth, dirt* کثافت، چرک	čirk: *filth, dirt*	čerk: *dirt, filth* چرک
JS1:209	JS1:209	JS1:209

826

چرم: " کنده شده"

همریشه: shear

Indo-European	Avestan	Persian
ker 2, sker 2: *to cut, separate* بریدن، جدا کردن	kereta: *knife, a cut trench* kareman, čareman: *hide cut off animals*	čarm: *hide (cut from animals)* چرم
PK:938, IC:640,1155	PK:941, KL:1432, PH:188, BK:321	BQ, PH, MO, BK

COGNATE- Old Indic "čârman" (BQ: 634)

827

چرمه: اسب سفید

Indo-European	Persian
kel 4: *light and dark spots, gray color tones* لکه های سایه روشن	čarmeh: *horse, white horse* چرمه پر از خشم و پر کینه سالار نو نشست از بر چرمهٔ تیز رو (فردوسی)
PK:547	PK:547

828

چریدن

همریشه: چرخیدن   همریشه: cycle, wheel

Indo-European	Avestan	Pahlavi	Persian
kwel: *to move around, turn* حرکت کردن ، چرخیدن	car, čâr: *to move around, open field*	čâr: *an open field, also to graze*	čarîdan: *to graze* چریدن (چرا)
PK:640	BQ:635, AG3:73, JD:297		MO, BQ, AG3:73

829

چسبیدن

همریشه: چاپیدن   همریشه: catch, accept

Indo-European	Old Persian	Persian
kap, čap*: *grasp* گرفتن، نگه داشتن	čifsati: *attach*	časbîdan: *to attach, grab* چسبید (چفسیدن)
PK:527,CH:32	BQ:636	PK:527, PH:98, IC:473,CH

830

چُست

همریشه: shoot

Indo-European	Sanskrit	Persian
skeud, čaud*: *to throw, impel* پرت کردن، واداشتن	čodatî: *to hurry, propel*	čost: *quick, fast* چُست
PK:955,CH	PK:955, PH:99	PK:955, BQ:636,CH

COGNATE- Pahlavi "vicôdišn: to run" (BQ:636)

831

چشم

Indo-European	Avestan	Pahlavi	Persian
kwek, kas* 1: *to appear, see* ظاهر شدن، دیدن	kas, čas, čaš: *to behold, see* čašman: *eyes*	čašm	čašm: *eye* چشم
PK:638, CH:245	PK:638, KL:42, BK:1436	BQ:638	BQ, PH

832

148

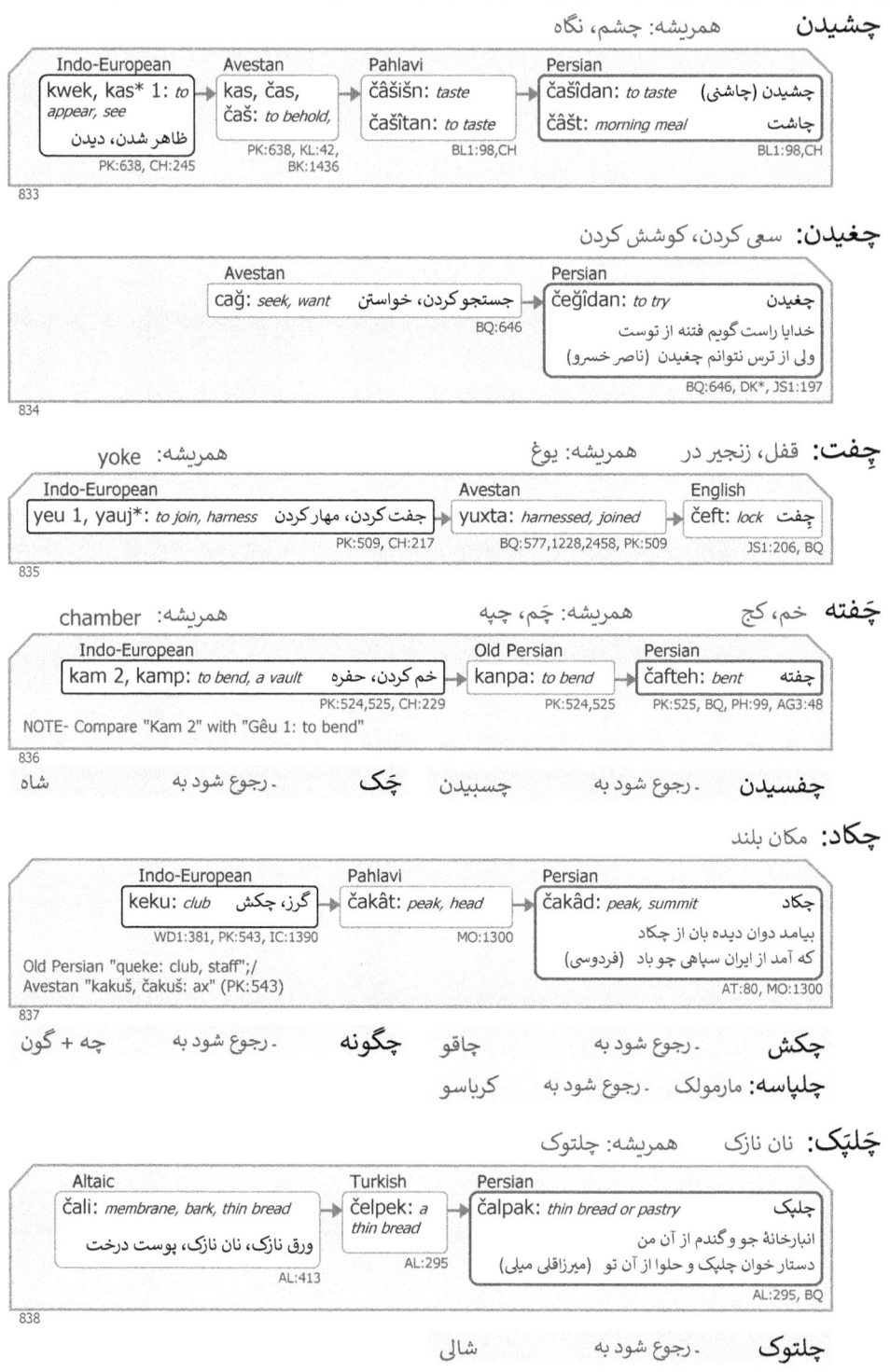

چشیدن   همریشه: چشم، نگاه

Indo-European	Avestan	Pahlavi	Persian
kwek, kas* 1: *to appear, see* ظاهر شدن، دیدن	kas, čas, čaš: *to behold,*	čâšišn: *taste* čašîtan: *to taste*	چشیدن (چاشی) čašîdan: *to taste* چاشت čâšt: *morning meal*
PK:638, CH:245	PK:638, KL:42, BK:1436	BL1:98,CH	BL1:98,CH

833

چغیدن: سعی کردن، کوشش کردن

Avestan	Persian
čağ: *seek, want* جستجو کردن، خواستن	čeğîdan: *to try* چغیدن خدایا راست گویم فتنه از توست ولی از ترس نتوانم چغیدن (ناصر خسرو)
BQ:646	BQ:646, DK*, JS1:197

834

چفت: قفل، زنجیر در   همریشه: یوغ   همریشه: yoke

Indo-European	Avestan	English
yeu 1, yauj*: *to join, harness* جفت کردن، مهار کردن	yuxta: *harnessed, joined*	čeft: *lock* چفت
PK:509, CH:217	BQ:577,1228,2458, PK:509	JS1:206, BQ

835

چفته خم، کج   همریشه: چم، چپه   chamber :همریشه

Indo-European	Old Persian	Persian
kam 2, kamp: *to bend, a vault* خم کردن، حفره	kanpa: *to bend*	čafteh: *bent* چفته
PK:524,525, CH:229	PK:524,525	PK:525, BQ, PH:99, AG3:48

NOTE- Compare "Kam 2" with "Gêu 1: to bend"

836

چفسیدن - رجوع شود به چسبیدن   **چَک** - رجوع شود به   شاه

چکاد: مکان بلند

Indo-European	Pahlavi	Persian
keku: *club* گرز، چکش	čakât: *peak, head*	čakâd: *peak, summit* چکاد بیامد دوان دیده بان از چکاد که آمد ز ایران سپاهی چو باد (فردوسی)
WD1:381, PK:543, IC:1390	MO:1300	AT:80, MO:1300

Old Persian "queke: club, staff";/
Avestan "kakuš, čakuš: ax" (PK:543)

837

چکش - رجوع شود به   چاقو   **چگونه** - رجوع شود به   چه + گون

چلپاسه: مارمولک   - رجوع شود به   کرباسو

چلپک: نان نازک   همریشه: چلتوک

Altaic	Turkish	Persian
čali: *membrane, bark, thin bread* ورق نازک، نان نازک، پوست درخت	čelpek: *a thin bread*	čalpak: *thin bread or pastry* چلپک انبارخانۀ جو و گندم از آن من دستار خوان چلپک و حلوا از آن تو (میرزاقلی میلی)
AL:413	AL:295	AL:295, BQ

838

چلتوک - رجوع شود به   شالی

چِلِم: سر قلیان

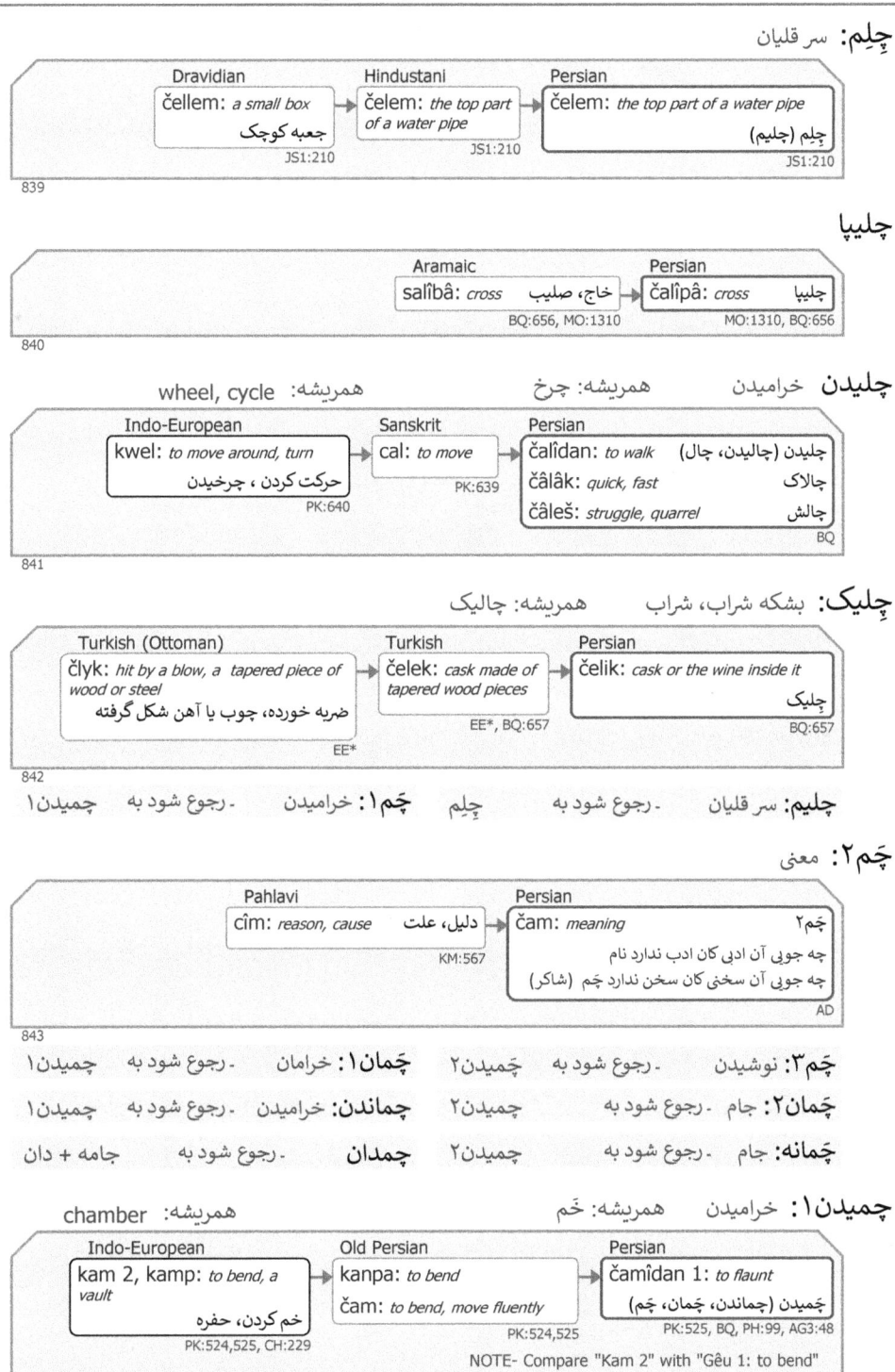

چِلِم: سر قلیان

Dravidian	Hindustani	Persian
čellem: *a small box*	čelem: *the top part of a water pipe*	čelem: *the top part of a water pipe*
جعبه کوچک		چِلِم (چلیم)
	JS1:210	JS1:210
	JS1:210	

839

چلیپا

	Aramaic	Persian
	salîbâ: *cross* خاج، صلیب	čalîpâ: *cross* چلیپا
	BQ:656, MO:1310	MO:1310, BQ:656

840

چلیدن خرامیدن — همریشه: چرخ — همریشه: چرخ، cycle

wheel, cycle :همریشه — چرخ :همریشه — چلیدن خرامیدن

Indo-European	Sanskrit	Persian
kwel: *to move around, turn*	cal: *to move*	čalîdan: *to walk* چلیدن (چالیدن، چال)
حرکت کردن ، چرخیدن	PK:639	čâlâk: *quick, fast* چالاک
PK:640		čâleš: *struggle, quarrel* چالش
		BQ

841

چِلیک: بشکه شراب، شراب — همریشه: چالیک

Turkish (Ottoman)	Turkish	Persian
člyk: *hit by a blow, a tapered piece of wood or steel*	čelek: *cask made of tapered wood pieces*	čelik: *cask or the wine inside it*
ضربه خورده، چوب یا آهن شکل گرفته	EE*, BQ:657	چِلیک
EE*		BQ:657

842

چِلیم: سر قلیان ـ رجوع شود به چِلِم   **چَم۱:** خرامیدن ـ رجوع شود به چمیدن۱

چَم۲: معنی

Pahlavi	Persian
cîm: *reason, cause* دلیل، علت	čam: *meaning* چَم۲
KM:567	چه جویی آن ادبی کان ادب ندارد نام
	چه جویی آن سخنی کان سخن ندارد چَم (شاکر)
	AD

843

چَم۳: نوشیدن ـ رجوع شود به چمیدن۲   **چَمان۱:** خرامان ـ رجوع شود به چمیدن۱

چَمان۲: جام ـ رجوع شود به چمیدن۲   **چَماندن:** خرامیدن ـ رجوع شود به چمیدن۱

چَمانه: جام ـ رجوع شود به چمیدن۲   **چمدان** ـ رجوع شود به جامه + دان

چمیدن۱: خرامیدن ـ همریشه: خَم — همریشه: chamber

chamber :همریشه — خَم :همریشه — خرامیدن

Indo-European	Old Persian	Persian
kam 2, kamp: *to bend, a vault*	kanpa: *to bend*	čamîdan 1: *to flaunt*
خم کردن، حفره	čam: *to bend, move fluently*	چمیدن (چماندن، چمان، چَم)
PK:524,525, CH:229	PK:524,525	PK:525, BQ, PH:99, AG3:48
	NOTE- Compare "Kam 2" with "Gêu 1: to bend"	

844

چمیدن۲: نوشیدن   همریشه: آشامیدن، کام۲

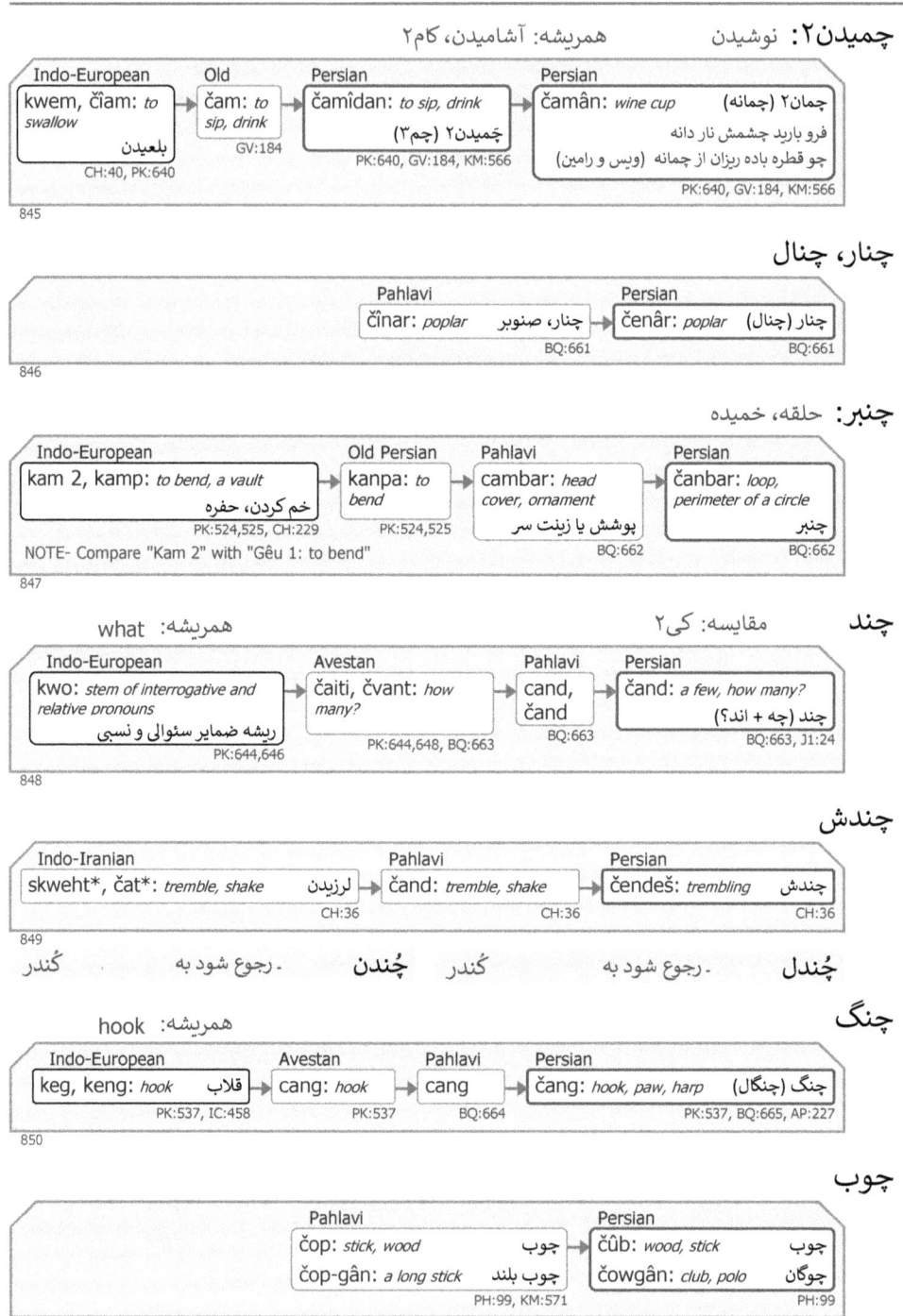

Indo-European	Old	Persian	Persian
kwem, čiam: *to swallow*	čam: *to sip, drink*	čamîdan: *to sip, drink*	čamân: *wine cup*
بلعیدن		چمیدن۲ (چم۳)	چمان۲ (چمانه)
CH:40, PK:640	GV:184	PK:640, GV:184, KM:566	فرو بارید چشمش نار دانه
			چو قطره باده ریزان از چمانه (ویس و رامین)
			PK:640, GV:184, KM:566

845

چنار، چنال

	Pahlavi	Persian
	čînar: *poplar*	čenâr: *poplar*
	چنار، صنوبر	چنار (چنال)
	BQ:661	BQ:661

846

چنبر: حلقه، خمیده

Indo-European	Old Persian	Pahlavi	Persian
kam 2, kamp: *to bend, a vault*	kanpa: *to bend*	cambar: *head cover, ornament*	čanbar: *loop, perimeter of a circle*
خم کردن، حفره		پوشش یا زینت سر	چنبر
PK:524,525, CH:229	PK:524,525	BQ:662	BQ:662
NOTE- Compare "Kam 2" with "Gêu 1: to bend"			

847

چند   مقایسه: کی۲   همریشه: what

Indo-European	Avestan	Pahlavi	Persian
kwo: *stem of interrogative and relative pronouns*	čaiti, čvant: *how many?*	cand, čand	čand: *a few, how many?*
ریشه ضمایر سئوالی و نسبی			چند (چه + اند؟)
PK:644,646	PK:644,648, BQ:663	BQ:663	BQ:663, J1:24

848

چندش

Indo-Iranian	Pahlavi	Persian
skweht*, čat*: *tremble, shake*	čand: *tremble, shake*	čendeš: *trembling*
لرزیدن		چندش
CH:36	CH:36	CH:36

849

چُندل   . رجوع شود به   کُندر   چُندن   . رجوع شود به   گُندر

چنگ   همریشه: hook

Indo-European	Avestan	Pahlavi	Persian
keg, keng: *hook* قلاب	cang: *hook*	cang	čang: *hook, paw, harp*
PK:537, IC:458	PK:537	BQ:664	چنگ (چنگال)
			PK:537, BQ:665, AP:227

850

چوب

	Pahlavi	Persian
	čop: *stick, wood* چوب	čûb: *wood, stick* چوب
	čop-gân: *a long stick* چوب بلند	čowgân: *club, polo* چوگان
	PH:99, KM:571	PH:99

851

چوپان   "گله بان"

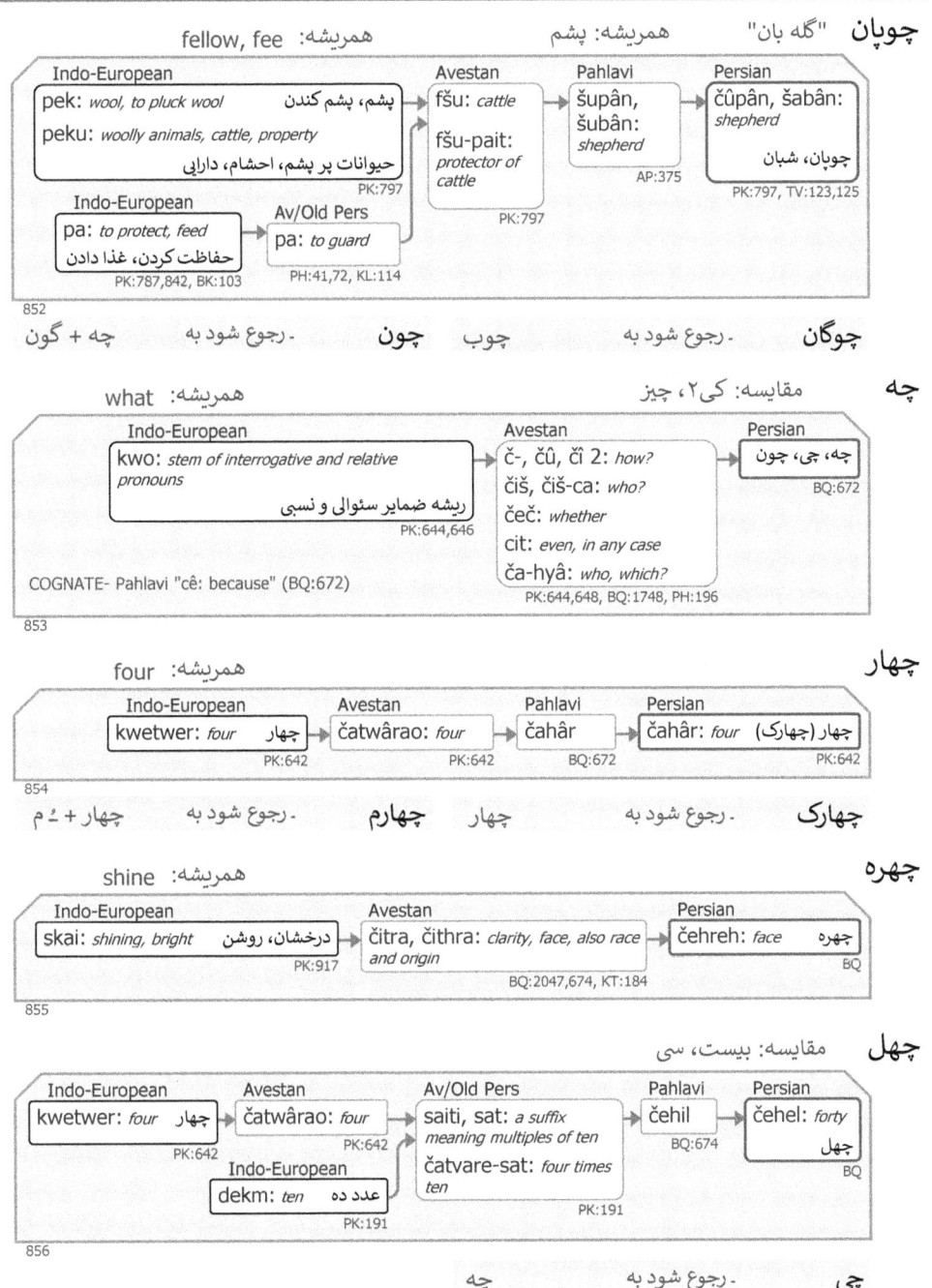

همریشه: fellow, fee   همریشه: پشم

Indo-European

pek: *wool, to pluck wool*   پشم، پشم کندن

peku: *woolly animals, cattle, property*

حیوانات پر پشم، احشام، دارایی

Indo-European

pa: *to protect, feed*

حفاظت کردن، غذا دادن

PK:787,842, BK:103

Av/Old Pers

pa: *to guard*

PH:41,72, KL:114

Avestan

fšu: *cattle*

fšu-pait: *protector of cattle*

PK:797

Pahlavi

šupân, šubân: *shepherd*

AP:375

Persian

čûpân, šabân: *shepherd*

چوپان، شبان

PK:797, TV:123,125

852

چوگان   چه + گون   .رجوع شود به   چون   چوب   .رجوع شود به

چه   مقایسه: کی۲، چیز

همریشه: what

Indo-European

kwo: *stem of interrogative and relative pronouns*

ریشه ضمایر سئوالی و نسبی

PK:644,646

COGNATE- Pahlavi "cê: *because*" (BQ:672)

Avestan

č-, čû, čî 2: *how?*

čiš, čiš-ca: *who?*

čeč: *whether*

cit: *even, in any case*

ča-hyâ: *who, which?*

PK:644,648, BQ:1748, PH:196

Persian

چه، چی، چون

BQ:672

853

چهار   همریشه: four

Indo-European

kwetwer: *four*   چهار

PK:642

Avestan

čatwârao: *four*

PK:642

Pahlavi

čahâr

BQ:672

Persian

چهار (چهارک) | čahâr: *four*

PK:642

854

چهارک   چهار + ـُ م   .رجوع شود به   چهارم   چهار   .رجوع شود به

چهره   همریشه: shine

Indo-European

skai: *shining, bright*   درخشان، روشن

PK:917

Avestan

čitra, čithra: *clarity, face, also race and origin*

BQ:2047,674, KT:184

Persian

čehreh: *face*   چهره

BQ

855

چهل   مقایسه: بیست، سی

Indo-European

kwetwer: *four*   چهار

PK:642

Indo-European

dekm: *ten*   عدد ده

PK:191

Avestan

čatwârao: *four*

PK:642

Av/Old Pers

saiti, sat: *a suffix meaning multiples of ten*

čatvare-sat: *four times ten*

PK:191

Pahlavi

čehil

BQ:674

Persian

čehel: *forty*

چهل

BQ

856

چی   چه   .رجوع شود به

152

چیچست: نام باستانی دریاچهٔ ارومیّه

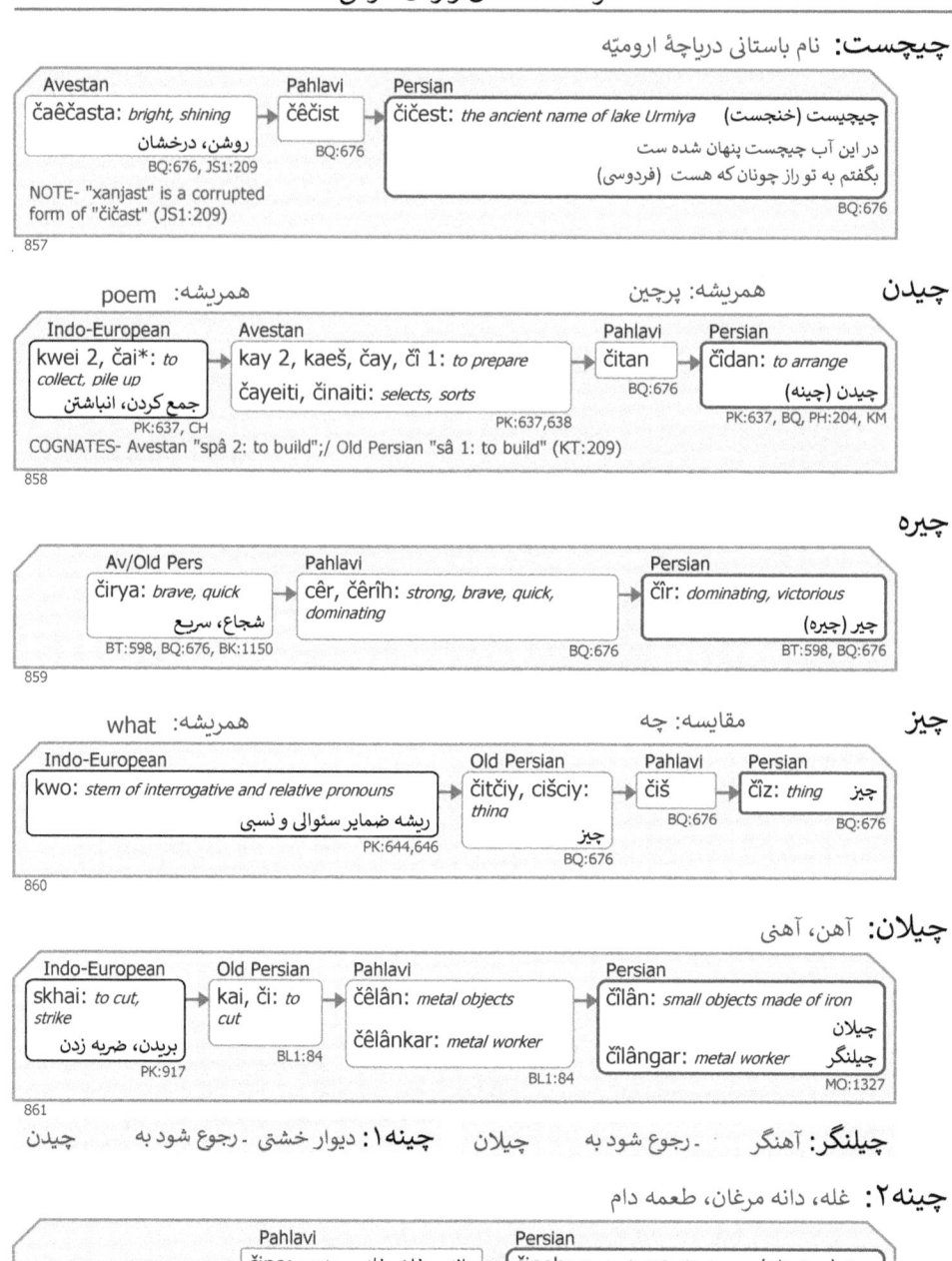

Avestan	Pahlavi	Persian

Avestan
čaêčasta: *bright, shining*
روشن، درخشان
BQ:676, JS1:209

NOTE- "xanjast" is a corrupted
form of "čičast" (JS1:209)

Pahlavi
čêčist
BQ:676

Persian
čičest: *the ancient name of lake Urmiya*
چیچیست (خنجست)
در این آب چیچست پنهان شده ست
بگفتم به تو راز چونان که هست   (فردوسی)
BQ:676

857

چیدن   همریشه: پرچین   همریشه: poem

Indo-European
kwei 2, čai*: *to collect, pile up*
جمع کردن، انباشتن
PK:637, CH

Avestan
kay 2, kaeš, čay, čī 1: *to prepare*
čayeiti, činaiti: *selects, sorts*
PK:637,638

Pahlavi
čitan
BQ:676

Persian
čīdan: *to arrange*
چیدن (چینه)
PK:637, BQ, PH:204, KM

COGNATES- Avestan "spâ 2: to build";/ Old Persian "sâ 1: to build" (KT:209)

858

چیره

Av/Old Pers
čirya: *brave, quick*
شجاع، سریع
BT:598, BQ:676, BK:1150

Pahlavi
cêr, čêrîh: *strong, brave, quick, dominating*
BQ:676

Persian
čīr: *dominating, victorious*
چیر (چیره)
BT:598, BQ:676

859

چیز   مقایسه: چه   همریشه: what

Indo-European
kwo: *stem of interrogative and relative pronouns*
ریشه ضمایر سئوالی و نسبی
PK:644,646

Old Persian
čitčiy, cisciy: *thing*
چیز
BQ:676

Pahlavi
čiš
BQ:676

Persian
čīz: *thing*   چیز
BQ:676

860

چیلان: آهن، آهنی

Indo-European
skhai: *to cut, strike*
بریدن، ضربه زدن
PK:917

Old Persian
kai, či: *to cut*
BL1:84

Pahlavi
čêlân: *metal objects*
čêlânkar: *metal worker*
BL1:84

Persian
čîlân: *small objects made of iron*
چیلان
čîlângar: *metal worker*   چیلنگر
MO:1327

861

چیلنگر: آهنگر   - رجوع شود به   چیلان   **چینه۱:** دیوار خشتی - رجوع شود به   چیدن

چینه۲: غله، دانه مرغان، طعمه دام

Pahlavi
čine: *grain*   دانه مرغان، غله
JS1:211

Persian
čineh: *grain, bait for birds*   چینه (چینه دان)
همه کارها را سرانجام بین
چو بدخواه چینه نهد دام بین   (اسدی)
JS1:211

COGNATE- Sanskrit "čima, kima: grain" (JS1:211)

862

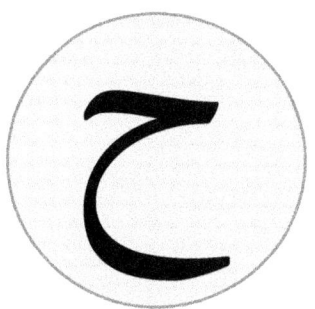

حبل

همریشه: کابل

همریشه: cable

Aramaic	Arabic	Persian
habl: *rope* طناب	habl: *rope, cable*	habl: *rope* حبل
BR:176	KL:216	NV:89

863

حِربا: آفتاپرست

همریشه: sun, helium

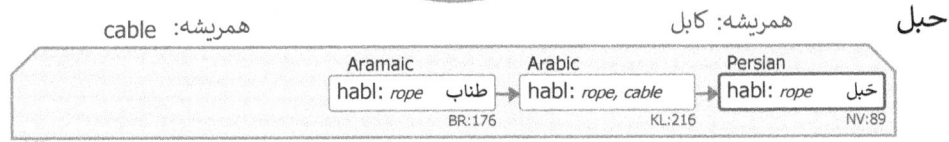

Indo-European	Avestan	Persian	Arabic
sâwel: *sun* آفتاب	hvare, xvar 1: *sun, light*	hûr 2: *sun, star* هور	herba'
PK:881	PK:881		ES:189, AS:50
Indo-European	Av/Old Pers	hûr-bân: "sun quard", chameleon. هوربان	Persian
pa: *to protect, feed* حفاظت کردن، غذا دادن	pa: *to guard* pâta: *protected*		herbâ: *chameleon* حربا
PK:787,842, BK:103	PH:41,72, KL:114	ES:189, AS:50, BQ	MO:1347

864

حشیش: "گیاه خشک شده"

همریشه: assassin

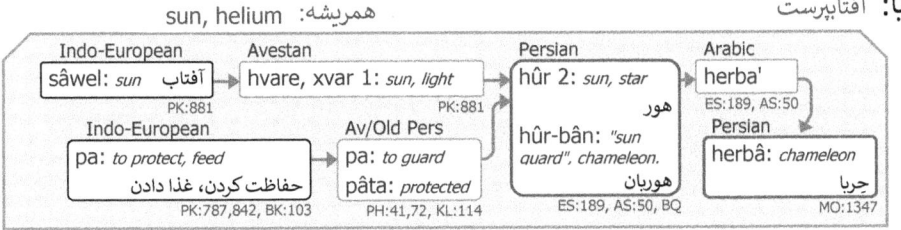

Arabic	Arabic	Persian
h.š.š: *to dry vegetable* خشک کردن گیاهان	hašîš: *hemp* haššašîn: *hemp users, followers of Hasan Sabbâh*	hašîš: *hemp* حشیش
NV:102, KL:706	NV:102, KL:706	NV:102

865

حوّا

۔ رجوع شود به   حیات

حور: "خوش اندام"

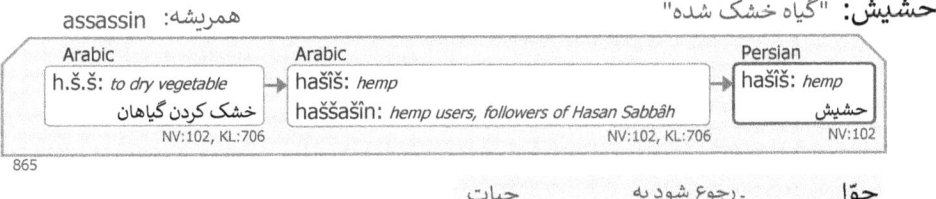

Indo-European	Av/Old Pers	Avestan	Pahlavi	Arabic
su 1: *well, good* خوب	hu 1: *good*	hava-rd: *well grown*	hu-rust: *well built*	hûr: *heavenly woman*
PK:1037, KL:548	PK:1037	BR:188-191	BR:188-191	
Indo-European	Avestan		Persian	
leudh, raud 2: *to grow* رشد کردن	raod 1, raodha: *growth, face*		hûr: *heavenly women* حور	
PK:684, KL:885, BK:874, BR:39	KL:885, BK:874		MO:1378	

NOTE- see BR:39,188-191for a discussion on the debated roots and meanings of the word "hûr".

866

حوز

۔ رجوع شود به   اهواز

حیات

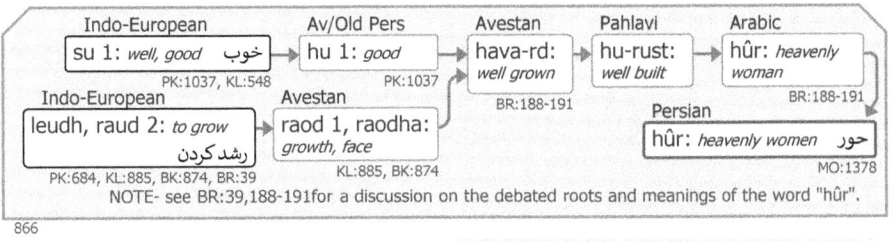

Semitic	Arabic	Persian
h.y.y: *to live* زیستن	hayat: *life* hawwa: *the living being, child bearing, Eve*	hayât: *life* حیات havvâ: *Eve* حوّا
KL:552, NV:118	KL:552, NV:118	NV:118

867

این حرف گاهی به ز، س، ش یا
غ بدل شود.

خاج

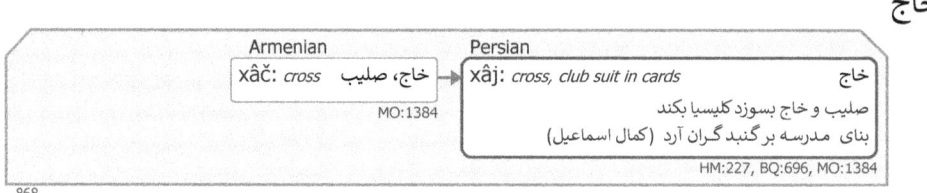

Armenian	Persian
xâč: cross خاج، صلیب	xâj: cross, club suit in cards خاج
MO:1384	صلیب و خاج بسوزد کلیسیا بکند
	بنای مدرسه برگنبد گران آرد (کمال اسماعیل)
	HM:227, BQ:696, MO:1384

868

خار

همریشه: hard

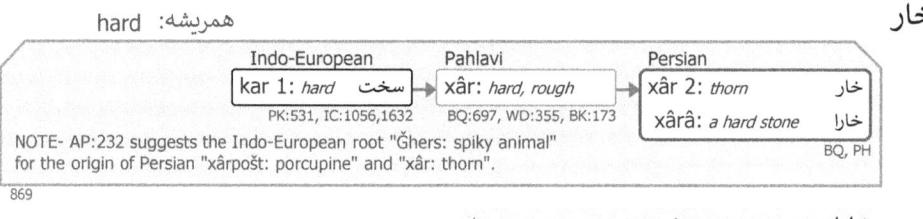

Indo-European	Pahlavi	Persian
kar 1: hard سخت	xâr: hard, rough	xâr 2: thorn خار
PK:531, IC:1056,1632	BQ:697, WD:355, BK:173	xârâ: a hard stone خارا
		BQ, PH

NOTE- AP:232 suggests the Indo-European root "Ğhers: spiky animal"
for the origin of Persian "xârpošt: porcupine" and "xâr: thorn".

869

خارا

خار   رجوع شود به .

خاراندن

همریشه: sore

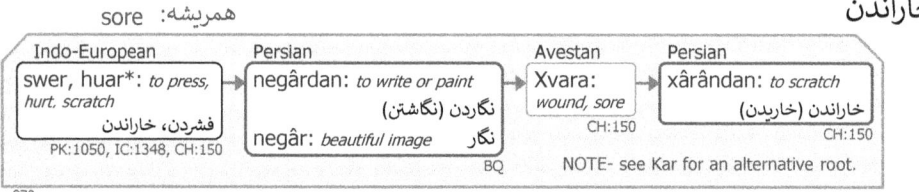

Indo-European	Persian	Avestan	Persian
swer, huar*: to press, hurt, scratch	negârdan: to write or paint	Xvara: wound, sore	xârândan: to scratch
فشردن، خاراندن	نگاردن (نگاشتن)	CH:150	خاراندن (خاریدن)
PK:1050, IC:1348, CH:150	negâr: beautiful image نگار		CH:150
	BQ	NOTE- see Kar for an alternative root.	

870

خاریدن

همریشه: خار

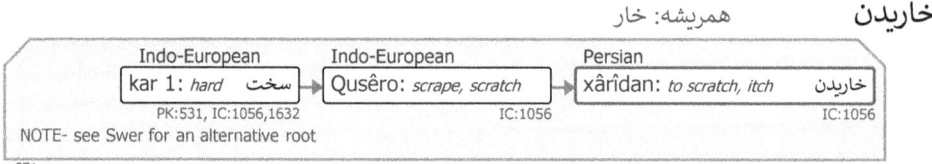

Indo-European	Indo-European	Persian
kar 1: hard سخت	Qusêro: scrape, scratch	xârîdan: to scratch, itch خاریدن
PK:531, IC:1056,1632	IC:1056	IC:1056

NOTE- see Swer for an alternative root

871

خاستن

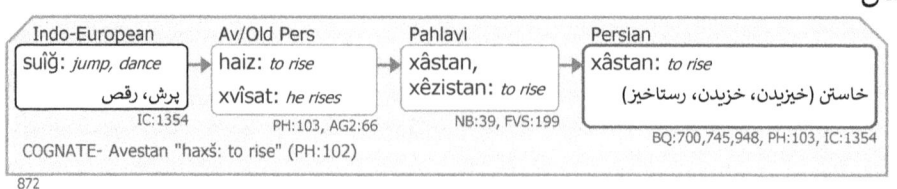

Indo-European	Av/Old Pers	Pahlavi	Persian
suîĝ: jump, dance	haiz: to rise	xâstan, xêzistan: to rise	xâstan: to rise
پرش، رقص	xvîsat: he rises		خاستن (خیزیدن، خزیدن، رستاخیز)
IC:1354	PH:103, AG2:66	NB:39, FVS:199	BQ:700,745,948, PH:103, IC:1354

COGNATE- Avestan "haxš: to rise" (PH:102)

872

خاش ـ رجوع شود به پرخاش

خاک

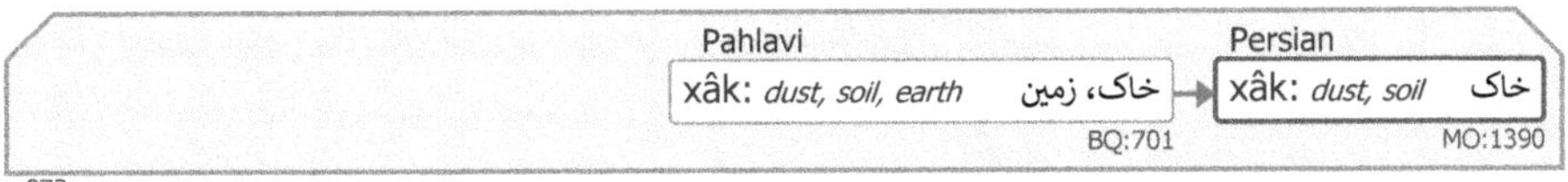

Pahlavi	Persian
xâk: *dust, soil, earth* خاک، زمین BQ:701	خاک xâk: *dust, soil* MO:1390

873

خاکستر

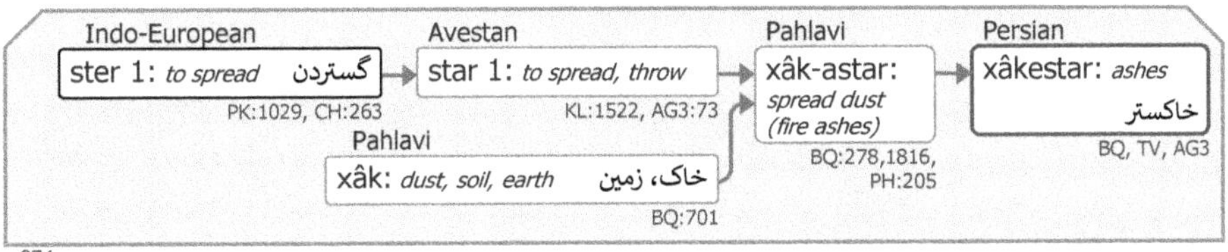

Indo-European	Avestan	Pahlavi	Persian
ster 1: *to spread* گستردن PK:1029, CH:263	star 1: *to spread, throw* KL:1522, AG3:73	xâk-astar: *spread dust* *(fire ashes)* BQ:278,1816, PH:205	xâkestar: *ashes* خاکستر BQ, TV, AG3
	Pahlavi xâk: *dust, soil, earth* خاک، زمین BQ:701		

874

خام

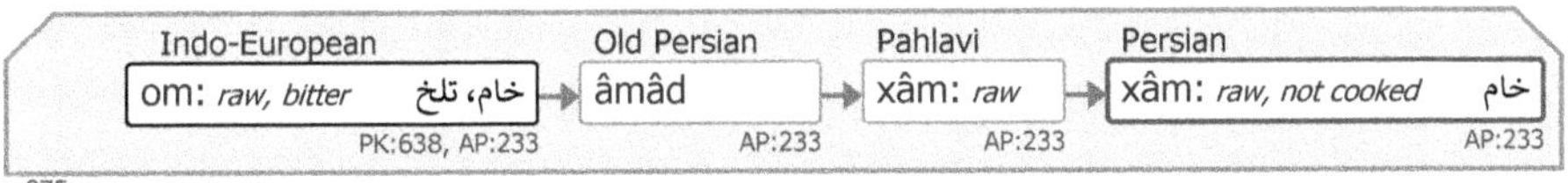

Indo-European	Old Persian	Pahlavi	Persian
om: *raw, bitter* خام، تلخ PK:638, AP:233	âmâd AP:233	xâm: *raw* AP:233	xâm: *raw, not cooked* خام AP:233

875

خاموش

مقایسه: مردن، فراموش از همین ریشه

Indo-European	Indo-European	Sanskrit	Persian
mer 2: *to rub away, die* فرسودن، مردن PK:735,970	Mers, Marš: *to forget* فراموش کردن PK:737, CH:268	â-marš: *to be* *patient (quiet)* BQ:708, 1448	xâmuš: *quiet, dark* خاموش BQ:706,1448

876

خان

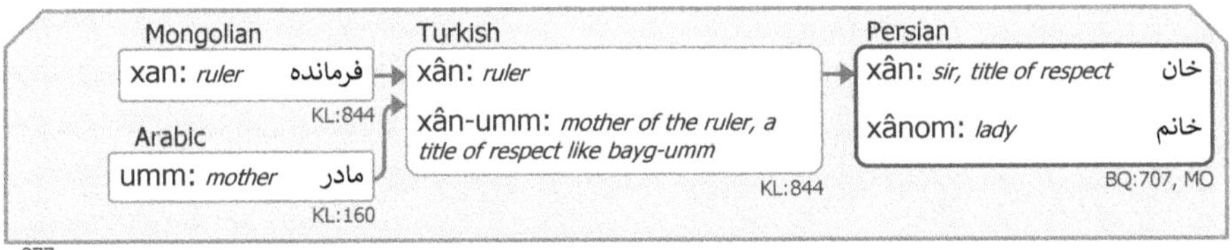

Mongolian	Turkish	Persian
xan: *ruler* فرمانده KL:844	xân: *ruler* xân-umm: *mother of the ruler, a* *title of respect like bayg-umm* KL:844	خان xân: *sir, title of respect* xânom: *lady* خانم BQ:707, MO
Arabic umm: *mother* مادر KL:160		

877

خانقاه ـ رجوع شود به خانه + ۲۵گا   خانم   خانه + ۲۵گا   خان

خانه

Indo-European	Av/Old Pers	Pahlavi	Persian
gwhen 3, kan*: *to dig and fill* کندن و پُر کردن CH:232, PK491	kan 1, xan, gan: *to dig, pile* PK:491, PH:194, BT:583	kantan, xandan: *to dig* kandak, xanak: *a dug-in house* PH:194, TV:8, 155, BQ:1707	xâneh: *house* خانه (خن) PH:194, BQ, FJ:51

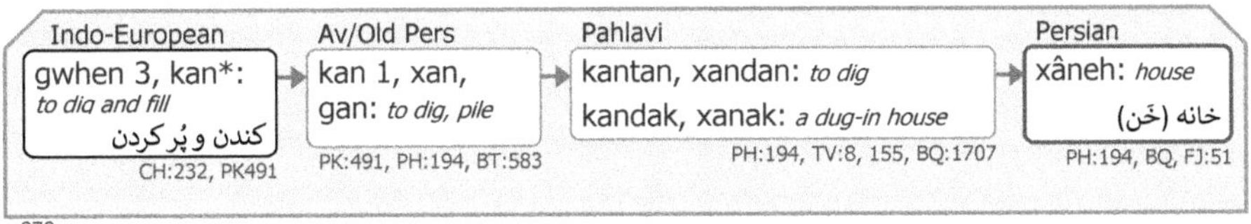

878

خانی: چشمه، حوض

همریشه: canal

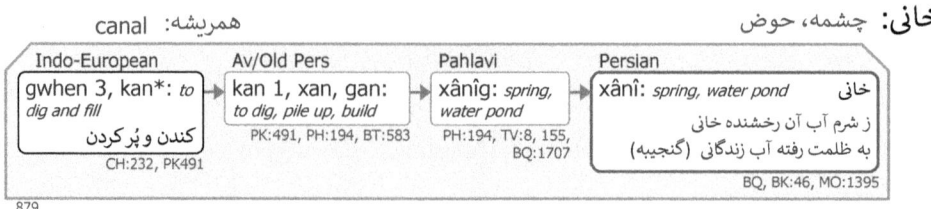

879

خاور

همریشه: bring, sun

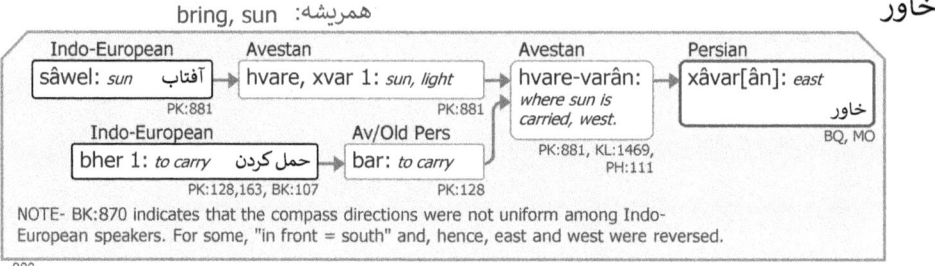

880

خاویار: ماهی "خایه بار"

همریشه: burden

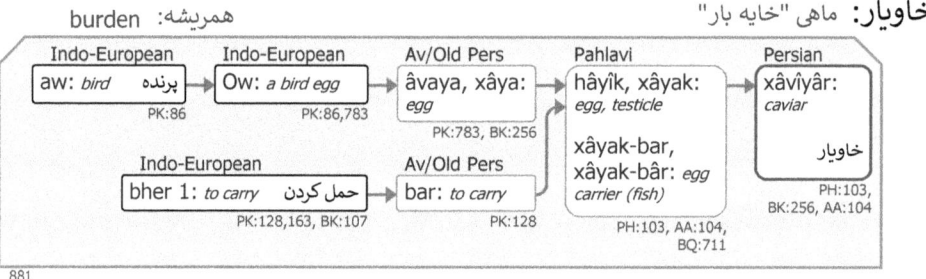

881

خایه

همریشه: egg

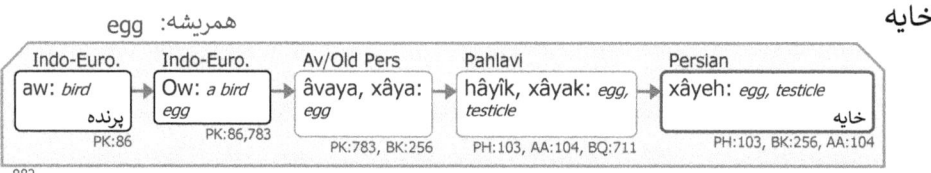

882

خاییدن: خوردن، جویدن

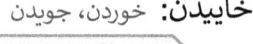

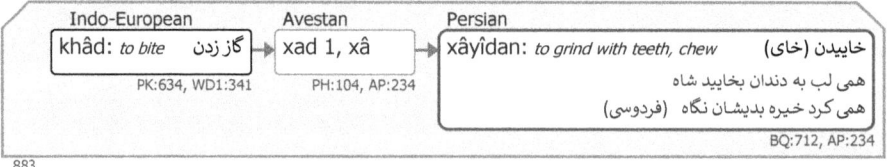

883

خَپَک، خَپه . رجوع شود به   خفه

ختن

همریشه: Cathay

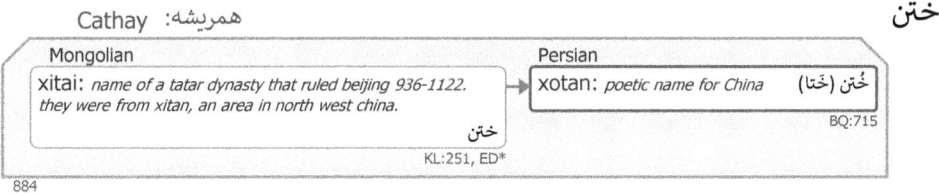

Mongolian	Persian
xitai: *name of a tatar dynasty that ruled beijing 936-1122. they were from xitan, an area in north west china.* ختن KL:251, ED*	xotan: *poetic name for China* (خُتا) خُتَن BQ:715

884

خجسته: مبارک

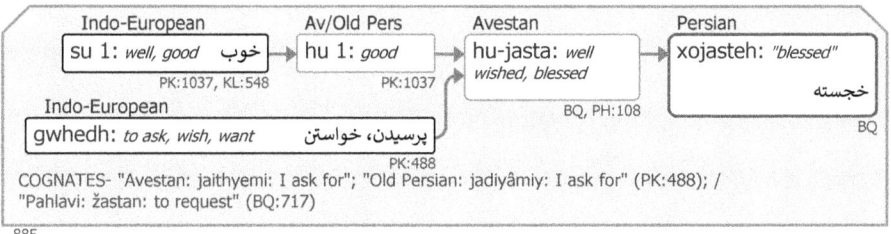

Indo-European	Av/Old Pers	Avestan	Persian
su 1: *well, good* خوب PK:1037, KL:548	hu 1: *good* PK:1037	hu-jasta: *well wished, blessed* BQ, PH:108	xojasteh: *"blessed"* خجسته BQ
Indo-European			
gwhedh: *to ask, wish, want* پرسیدن، خواستن PK:488			

COGNATES- "Avestan: jaithyemi: I ask for"; "Old Persian: jadiyâmiy: I ask for" (PK:488); / "Pahlavi: žastan: to request" (BQ:717)

885

خُجیر: نیک . رجوع شود به   هژیر

خدا: "کسی که از او کمک میطلبند"

(1)

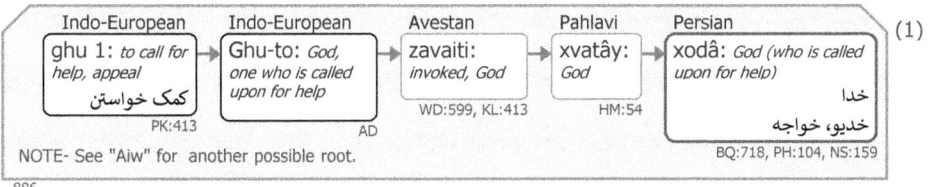

Indo-European	Indo-European	Avestan	Pahlavi	Persian
ghu 1: *to call for help, appeal* کمک خواستن PK:413	Ghu-to: *God, one who is called upon for help* AD	zavaiti: *invoked, God* WD:599, KL:413	xvatây: *God* HM:54	xodâ: *God (who is called upon for help)* خدا خدیو، خواجه BQ:718, PH:104, NS:159

NOTE- See "Aiw" for another possible root.

886

خدا: "زنده از خود"

(2)

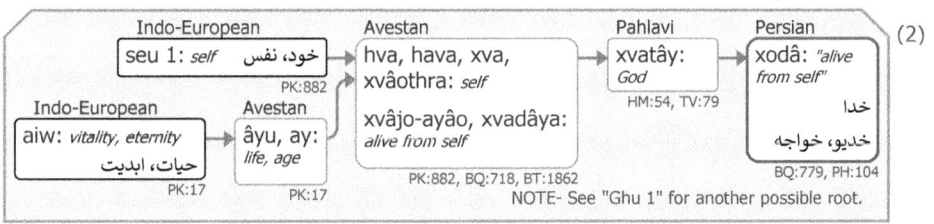

Indo-European	Avestan	Pahlavi	Persian
seu 1: *self* خود، نفس PK:882	hva, hava, xva, xvâothra: *self* xvâjo-ayâo, xvadâya: *alive from self* PK:882, BQ:718, BT:1862	xvatây: *God* HM:54, TV:79	xodâ: *"alive from self"* خدا خدیو، خواجه BQ:779, PH:104
Indo-European	Avestan		
aiw: *vitality, eternity* حیات، ابدیت PK:17	âyu, ay: *life, age* PK:17		

NOTE- See "Ghu 1" for another possible root.

887

خدنگ

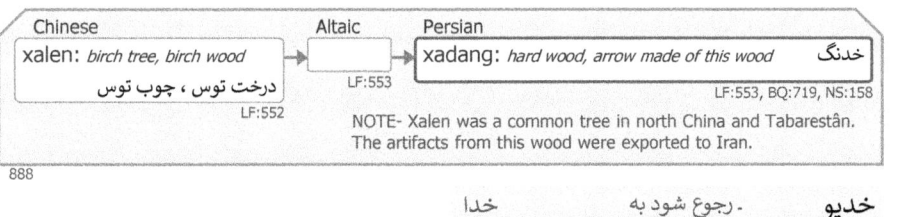

Chinese	Altaic	Persian
xalen: *birch tree, birch wood* درخت توس ، چوب توس LF:552	LF:553	xadang: *hard wood, arrow made of this wood* خدنگ LF:553, BQ:719, NS:158

NOTE- Xalen was a common tree in north China and Tabarestân. The artifacts from this wood were exported to Iran.

888

خدیو   . رجوع شود به   خدا

خر

همریشه: hard

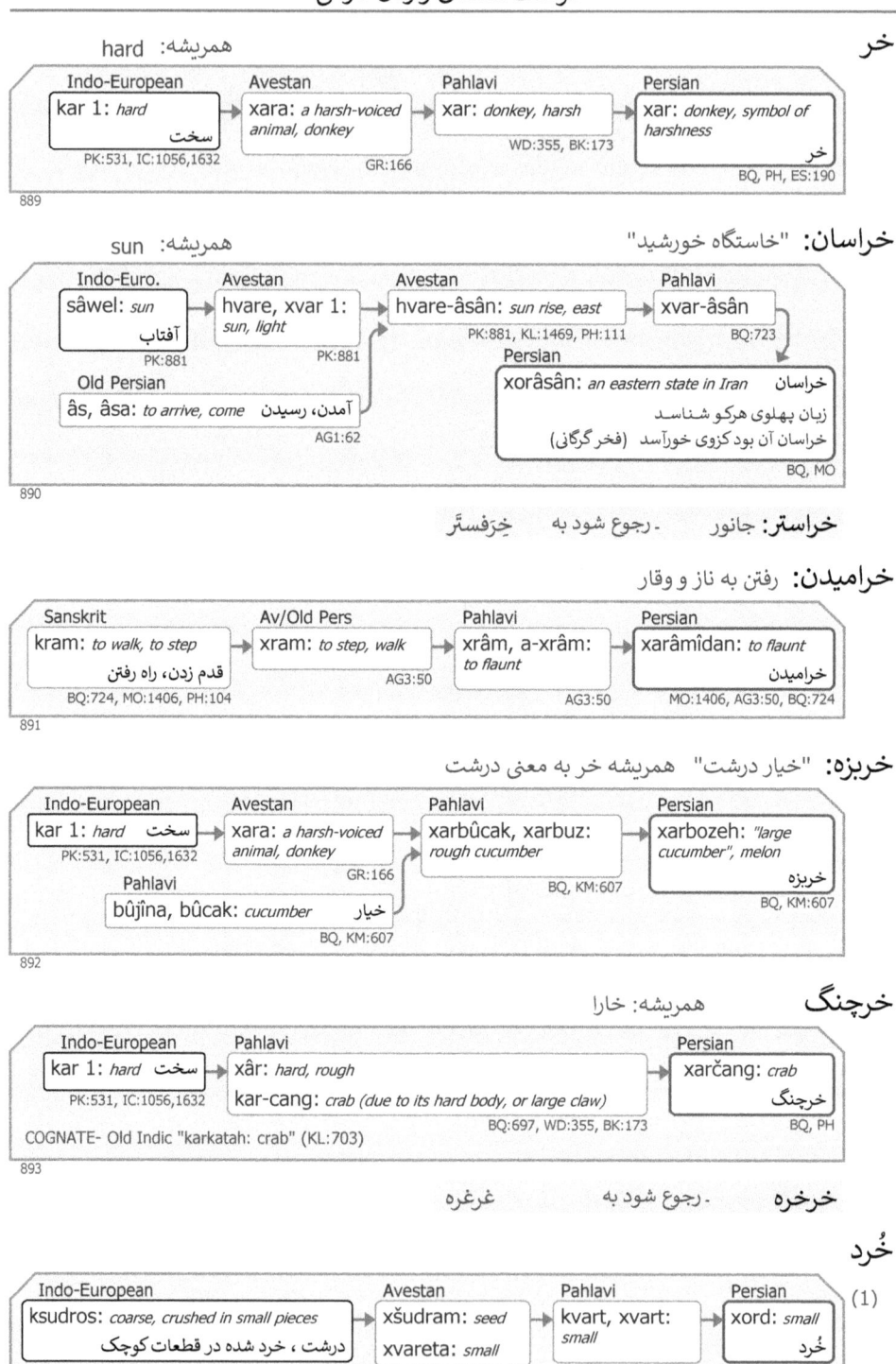

Indo-European	Avestan	Pahlavi	Persian
kar 1: *hard* سخت PK:531, IC:1056,1632	xara: *a harsh-voiced animal, donkey* GR:166	xar: *donkey, harsh* WD:355, BK:173	xar: *donkey, symbol of harshness* خر BQ, PH, ES:190

889

خراسان: "خاستگاه خورشید"

همریشه: sun

Indo-Euro.	Avestan	Avestan	Pahlavi
sâwel: *sun* آفتاب PK:881	hvare, xvar 1: *sun, light* PK:881	hvare-âsân: *sun rise, east* PK:881, KL:1469, PH:111	xvar-âsân BQ:723

Old Persian: âs, âsa: *to arrive, come* آمدن، رسیدن — AG1:62

Persian: xorâsân: *an eastern state in Iran* خراسان
زبان پهلوی هرکو شناسد
خراسان آن بود کزوی خورآسد (فخر گرگانی)
BQ, MO

890

خراستر: جانور. رجوع شود به   خِرَفسْتَر

خرامیدن: رفتن به ناز و وقار

Sanskrit	Av/Old Pers	Pahlavi	Persian
kram: *to walk, to step* قدم زدن، راه رفتن BQ:724, MO:1406, PH:104	xram: *to step, walk* AG3:50	xrâm, a-xrâm: *to flaunt* AG3:50	xarâmîdan: *to flaunt* خرامیدن MO:1406, AG3:50, BQ:724

891

خربزه: "خیار درشت"   همریشه خر به معنی درشت

Indo-European	Avestan	Pahlavi	Persian
kar 1: *hard* سخت PK:531, IC:1056,1632	xara: *a harsh-voiced animal, donkey* GR:166	xarbûcak, xarbuz: *rough cucumber* BQ, KM:607	xarbozeh: *"large cucumber", melon* خربزه BQ, KM:607

Pahlavi: bûjîna, bûcak: *cucumber* خیار — BQ, KM:607

892

خرچنگ

همریشه: خارا

Indo-European	Pahlavi	Persian
kar 1: *hard* سخت PK:531, IC:1056,1632	xâr: *hard, rough* kar-cang: *crab (due to its hard body, or large claw)* BQ:697, WD:355, BK:173	xarčang: *crab* خرچنگ BQ, PH

COGNATE- Old Indic "karkatah: crab" (KL:703)

893

خرخره: . رجوع شود به   غرغره

خُرد

(1)

Indo-European	Avestan	Pahlavi	Persian
ksudros: *coarse, crushed in small pieces* درشت، خرد شده در قطعات کوچک IC:576,1060	xšudram: *seed* xvareta: *small* BQ:729, IC:576,1060	kvart, xvart: *small* BQ:729	xord: *small* خُرد BQ:729, IC:576,1060

NOTE- see "Skordh: small" for another possible root of this word.

894

خُرد

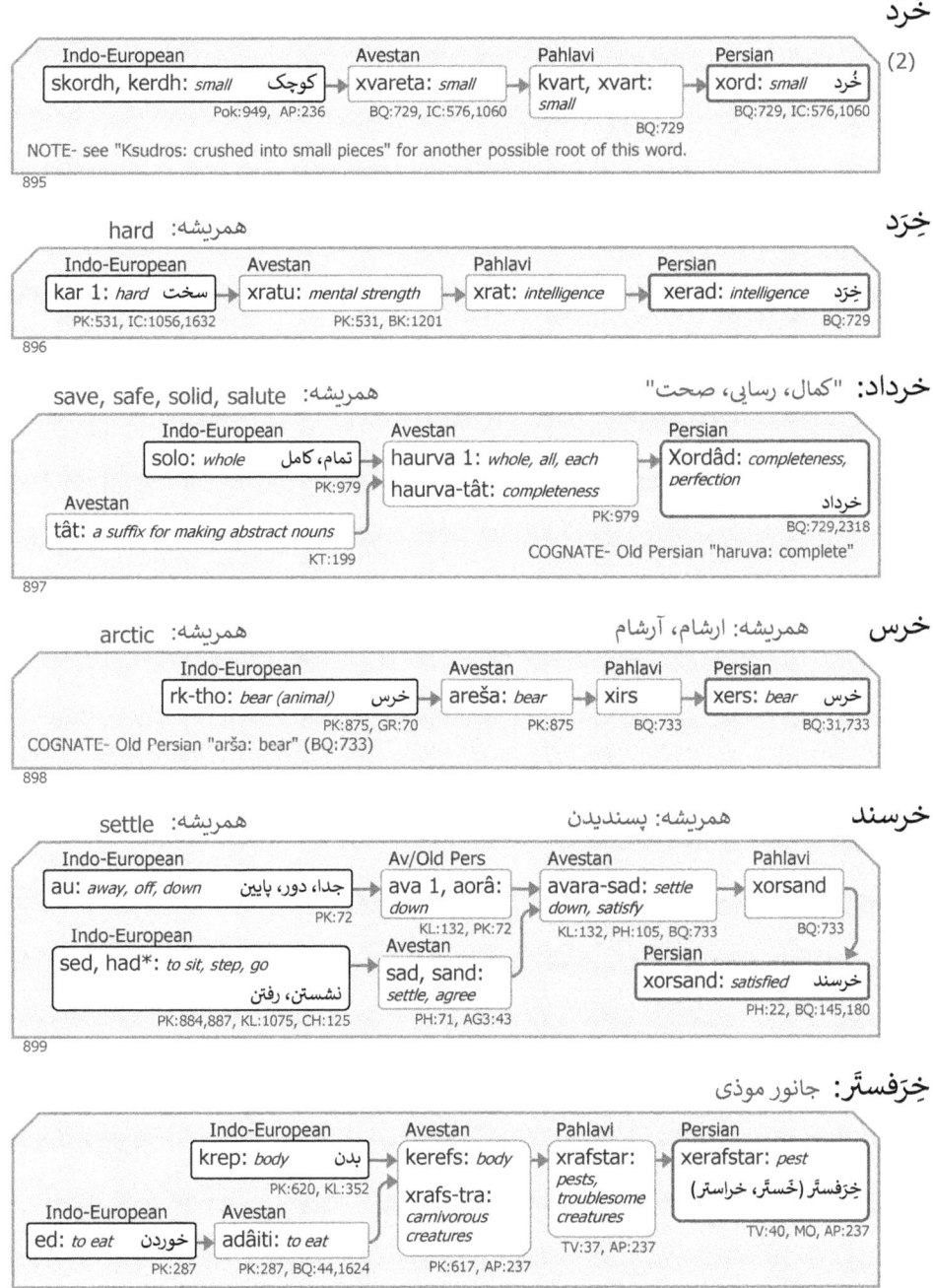

خُرد (2)

Indo-European
skordh, kerdh: *small* کوچک
Pok:949, AP:236

→ **Avestan**
xvareta: *small*
BQ:729, IC:576,1060

→ **Pahlavi**
kvart, xvart: *small*
BQ:729

→ **Persian**
xord: *small* خُرد
BQ:729, IC:576,1060

NOTE- see "Ksudros: crushed into small pieces" for another possible root of this word.
895

خِرَد

همریشه: hard

Indo-European
kar 1: *hard* سخت
PK:531, IC:1056,1632

→ **Avestan**
xratu: *mental strength*
PK:531, BK:1201

→ **Pahlavi**
xrat: *intelligence*

→ **Persian**
xerad: *intelligence* خِرَد
BQ:729

896

خِرداد: "کمال، رسایی، صحت"

همریشه: save, safe, solid, salute

Indo-European
solo: *whole* تمام، کامل
PK:979

Avestan
tât: *a suffix for making abstract nouns*
KT:199

→ **Avestan**
haurva 1: *whole, all, each*
haurva-tât: *completeness*
PK:979

→ **Persian**
Xordâd: *completeness, perfection*
خرداد
BQ:729,2318

COGNATE- Old Persian "haruva: complete"

897

خرس

همریشه: ارشام، آرشام

همریشه: arctic

Indo-European
rk-tho: *bear (animal)* خرس
PK:875, GR:70

→ **Avestan**
areša: *bear*
PK:875

→ **Pahlavi**
xirs
BQ:733

→ **Persian**
xers: *bear* خرس
BQ:31,733

COGNATE- Old Persian "arša: bear" (BQ:733)

898

خرسند

همریشه: پسندیدن

همریشه: settle

Indo-European
au: *away, off, down* جدا، دور، پایین
PK:72

Indo-European
sed, had*: *to sit, step, go* نشستن، رفتن
PK:884,887, KL:1075, CH:125

→ **Av/Old Pers**
ava 1, aorâ: *down*
KL:132, PK:72

Avestan
sad, sand: *settle, agree*
PH:71, AG3:43

→ **Avestan**
avara-sad: *settle down, satisfy*
KL:132, PH:105, BQ:733

→ **Pahlavi**
xorsand
BQ:733

→ **Persian**
xorsand: *satisfied* خرسند
PH:22, BQ:145,180

899

خِرَفسّتَر: جانور موذی

Indo-European
krep: *body* بدن
PK:620, KL:352

Indo-European
ed: *to eat* خوردن
PK:287

Avestan
adâiti: *to eat*
PK:287, BQ:44,1624

→ **Avestan**
kerefs: *body*

xrafs-tra: *carnivorous creatures*
PK:617, AP:237

→ **Pahlavi**
xrafstar: *pests, troublesome creatures*
TV:37, AP:237

→ **Persian**
xerafstar: *pest*
خِرَفسّر (خَسّر، خراسّر)
TV:40, MO, AP:237

900

خُرّم

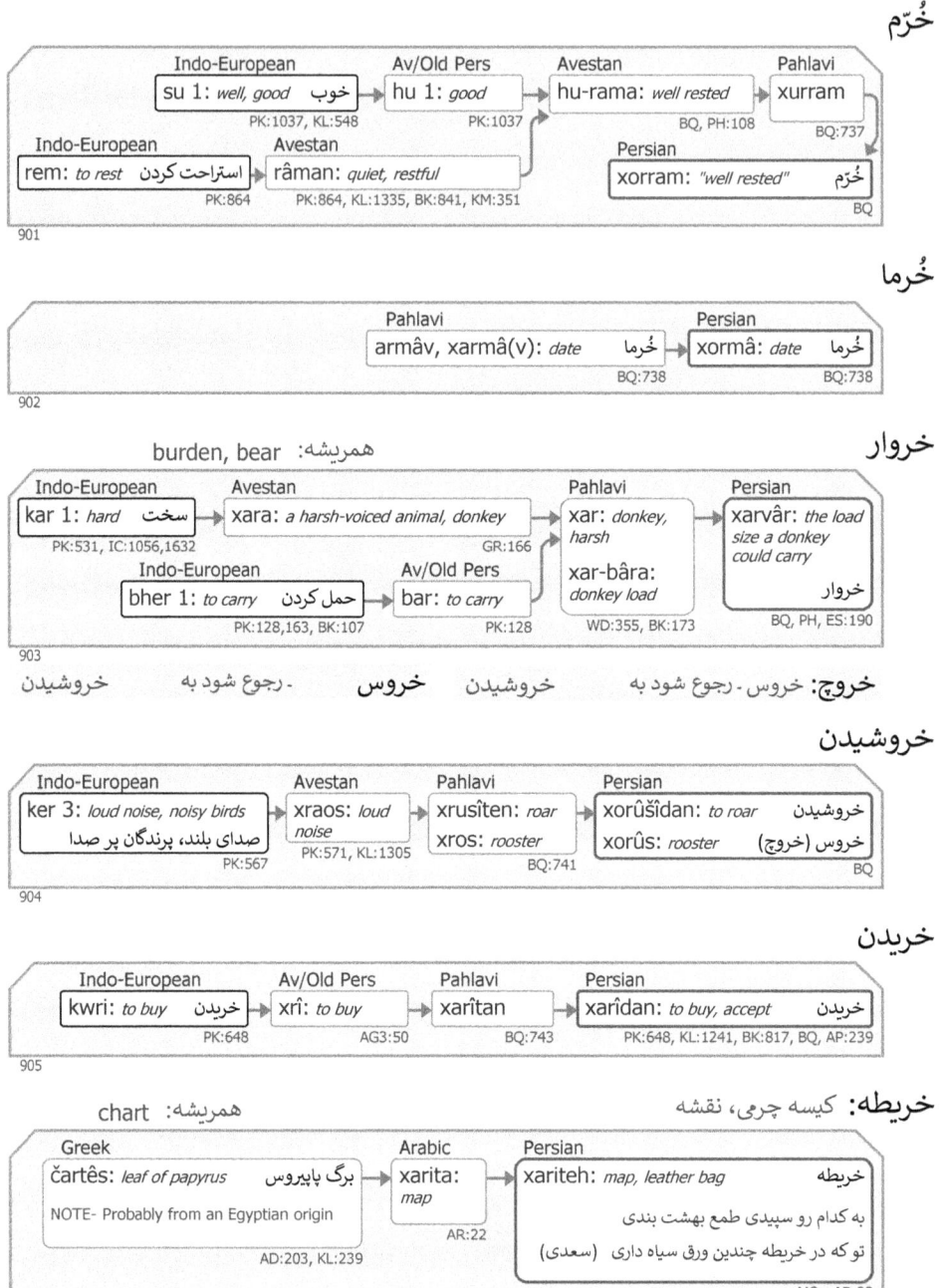

Indo-European	Av/Old Pers	Avestan	Pahlavi
su 1: *well, good* خوب PK:1037, KL:548	hu 1: *good* PK:1037	hu-rama: *well rested* BQ, PH:108	xurram BQ:737

Indo-European	Avestan	Persian
rem: *to rest* استراحت کردن PK:864	râman: *quiet, restful* PK:864, KL:1335, BK:841, KM:351	xorram: *"well rested"* خرّم BQ

901

خُرما

Pahlavi	Persian
armâv, xarmâ(v): *date* خرما BQ:738	xormâ: *date* خرما BQ:738

902

خروار

همریشه: burden, bear

Indo-European	Avestan	Pahlavi	Persian
kar 1: *hard* سخت PK:531, IC:1056,1632	xara: *a harsh-voiced animal, donkey* GR:166	xar: *donkey, harsh* xar-bâra: *donkey load* WD:355, BK:173	xarvâr: *the load size a donkey could carry* خروار BQ, PH, ES:190

Indo-European	Av/Old Pers		
bher 1: *to carry* حمل کردن PK:128,163, BK:107	bar: *to carry* PK:128		

903

خروج: خروس ـ رجوع شود به **خروس** ـ رجوع شود به خروشیدن خروشیدن

خروشیدن

Indo-European	Avestan	Pahlavi	Persian
ker 3: *loud noise, noisy birds* صدای بلند، پرندگان پر صدا PK:567	xraos: *loud noise* PK:571, KL:1305	xrusîten: *roar* xros: *rooster* BQ:741	xorûšîdan: *to roar* خروشیدن xorûs: *rooster* (خروج) خروس BQ

904

خریدن

Indo-European	Av/Old Pers	Pahlavi	Persian
kwri: *to buy* خریدن PK:648	xrî: *to buy* AG3:50	xarîtan BQ:743	xarîdan: *to buy, accept* خریدن PK:648, KL:1241, BK:817, BQ, AP:239

905

خریطه: کیسه چرمی، نقشه

همریشه: chart

Greek	Arabic	Persian
čartês: *leaf of papyrus* برگ پاپیروس NOTE- Probably from an Egyptian origin AD:203, KL:239	xarita: *map* AR:22	xariteh: *map, leather bag* خریطه به کدام رو سپیدی طمع بهشت بندی تو که در خریطه چندین ورق سیاه داری (سعدی) MO:, AR:22

906

خزانه

همریشه: magazine

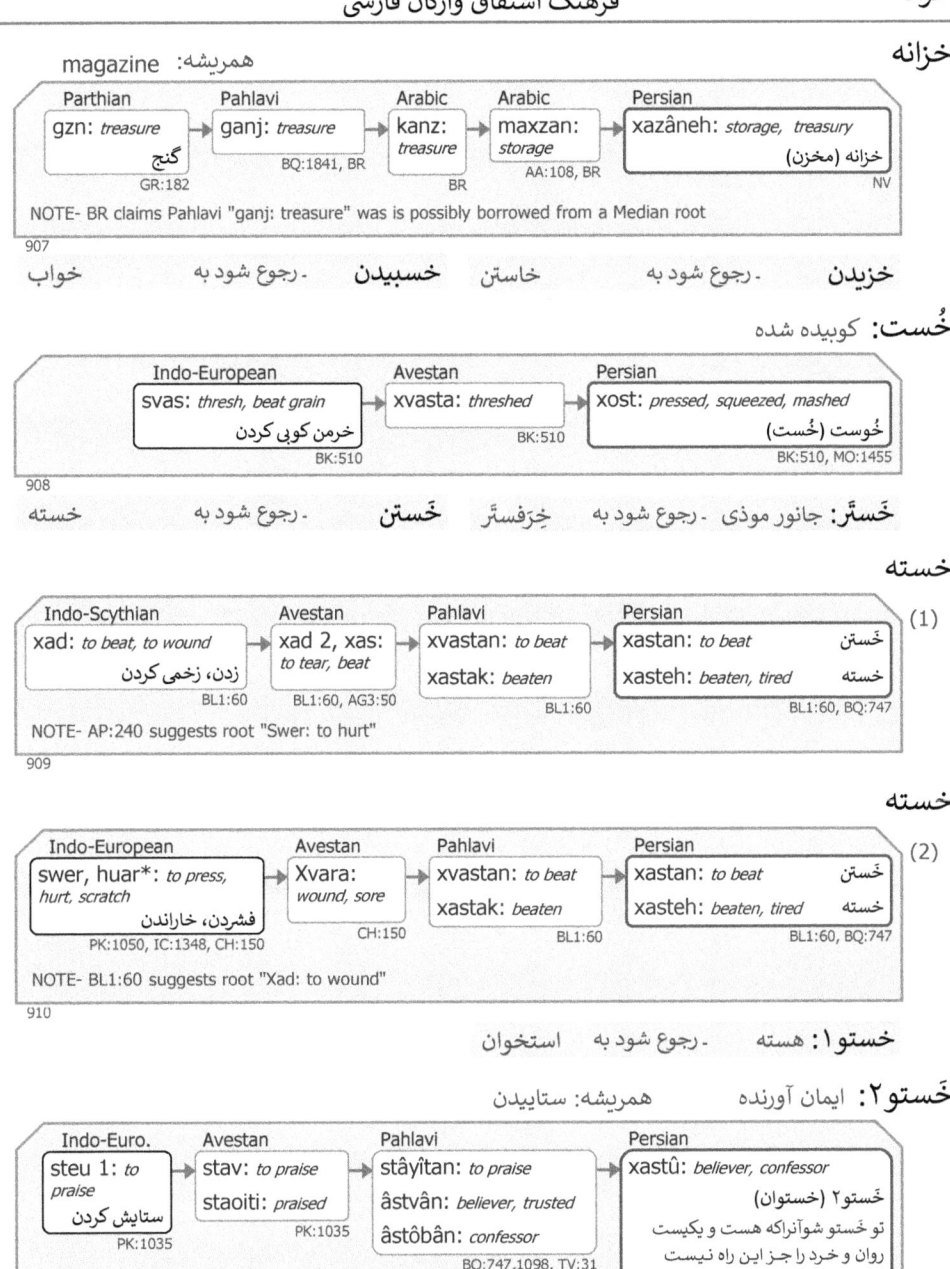

Parthian	Pahlavi	Arabic	Arabic	Persian
gzn: *treasure* گنج	ganj: *treasure*	kanz: *treasure*	maxzan: *storage*	xazâneh: *storage, treasury* خزانه (مخزن)
GR:182	BQ:1841, BR	BR	AA:108, BR	NV

NOTE- BR claims Pahlavi "ganj: treasure" was is possibly borrowed from a Median root

907

خزیدن . رجوع شود به خسبیدن خاستن . رجوع شود به خواب

خُست: کوبیده شده

Indo-European	Avestan	Persian
svas: *thresh, beat grain* خرمن کوبی کردن	xvasta: *threshed*	xost: *pressed, squeezed, mashed* خوست (خُست)
BK:510	BK:510	BK:510, MO:1455

908

خَستَّر: جانور موذی . رجوع شود به خِرَفسَّر خَستن . رجوع شود به خسته

خسته

Indo-Scythian	Avestan	Pahlavi	Persian	(1)
xad: *to beat, to wound* زدن، زخمی کردن	xad 2, xas: *to tear, beat*	xvastan: *to beat* xastak: *beaten*	xastan: *to beat* خَستن xasteh: *beaten, tired* خسته	
BL1:60	BL1:60, AG3:50	BL1:60	BL1:60, BQ:747	

NOTE- AP:240 suggests root "Swer: to hurt"

909

خسته

Indo-European	Avestan	Pahlavi	Persian	(2)
swer, huar*: *to press, hurt, scratch* فشردن، خاراندن	Xvara: *wound, sore*	xvastan: *to beat* xastak: *beaten*	xastan: *to beat* خَستن xasteh: *beaten, tired* خسته	
PK:1050, IC:1348, CH:150	CH:150	BL1:60	BL1:60, BQ:747	

NOTE- BL1:60 suggests root "Xad: to wound"

910

خستو۱: هسته . رجوع شود به استخوان

خَستو۲: ایمان آورنده همریشه: ستاییدن

Indo-Euro.	Avestan	Pahlavi	Persian
steu 1: *to praise* ستایش کردن	stav: *to praise* staoiti: *praised*	stâyitan: *to praise* âstvân: *believer, trusted* âstôbân: *confessor*	xastû: *believer, confessor* خَستو۲ (خستوان) تو خستو شوآنراکه هست و یکیست روان و خرد را جز این راه نیست (فردوسی)
	PK:1035		
PK:1035		BQ:747,1098, TV:31	BQ, PH:159, NB:180, TV:31

911

خُسُر: پدر همسر

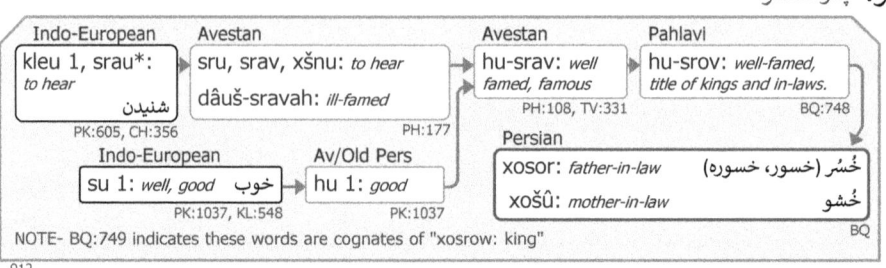

912

خسرو: "خوشنام"

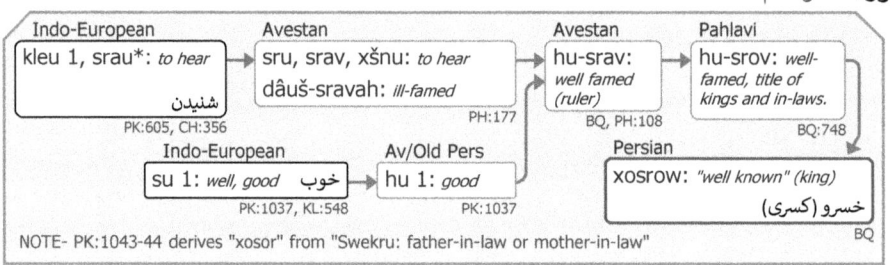

913

خُسور: پدر همسر ـ رجوع شود به خُسُر   خُسوره: پدر همسر ـ رجوع شود به خُسُر

خسوف ـ رجوع شود به کسوف

خَسیدن: جویدن

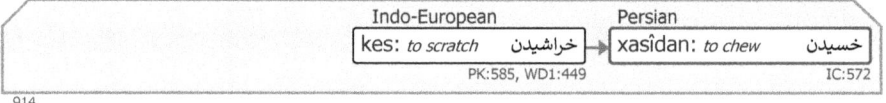

914

خشایار: "شاه مردان"   همریشه: check, chess

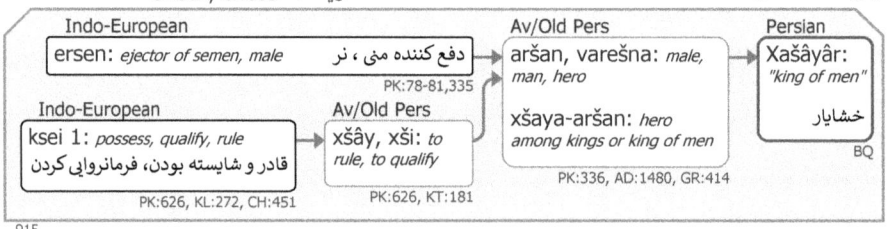

915

خشت۱: آجر خام   همریشه: هیزم

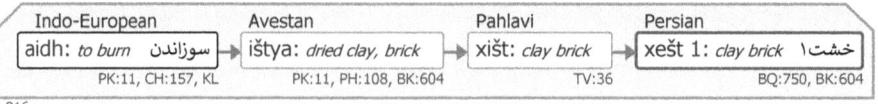

916

163

خِشت۲: نیزه کوتاه

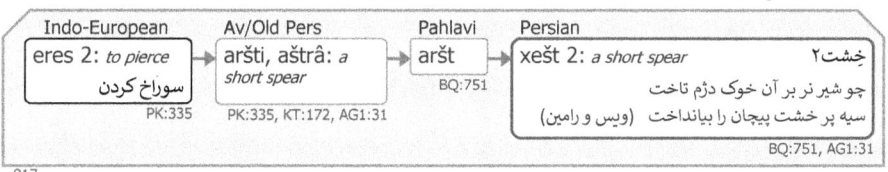

917

خشک

همریشه: austerity

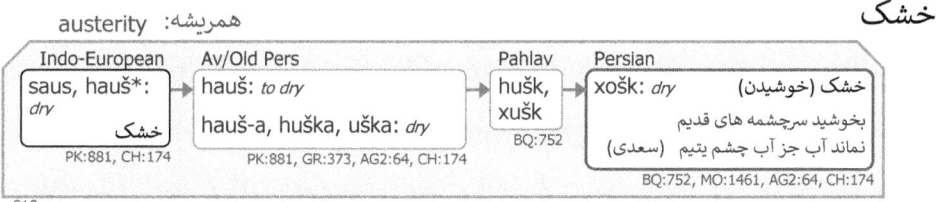

918

خشم، خِشمِن

همریشه: iron

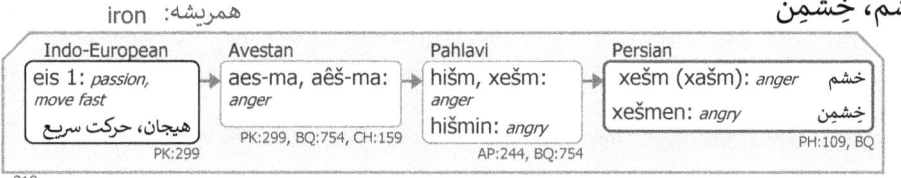

919

خَشَن: رنگ آبی تیره

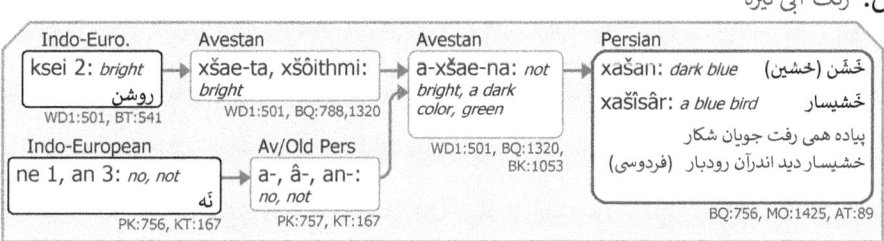

920

خشنود

همریشه: خوب

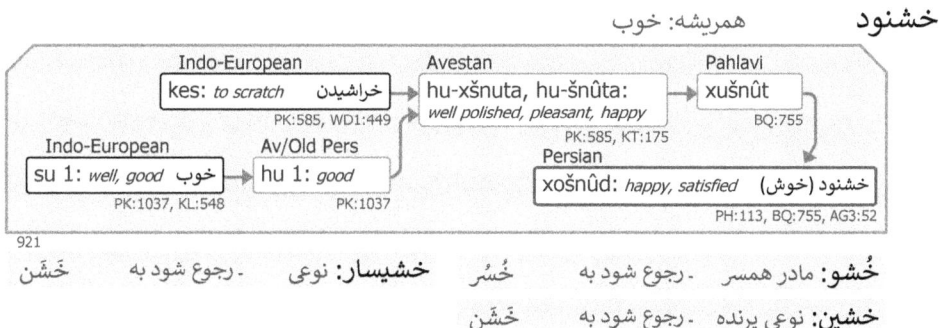

921

خُشو: مادر همسر ۔ رجوع شود به   خُسُر

خشین: نوعی پرنده ۔ رجوع شود به   خَشَن

خشیسار: نوعی ۔ رجوع شود به   خَشَن

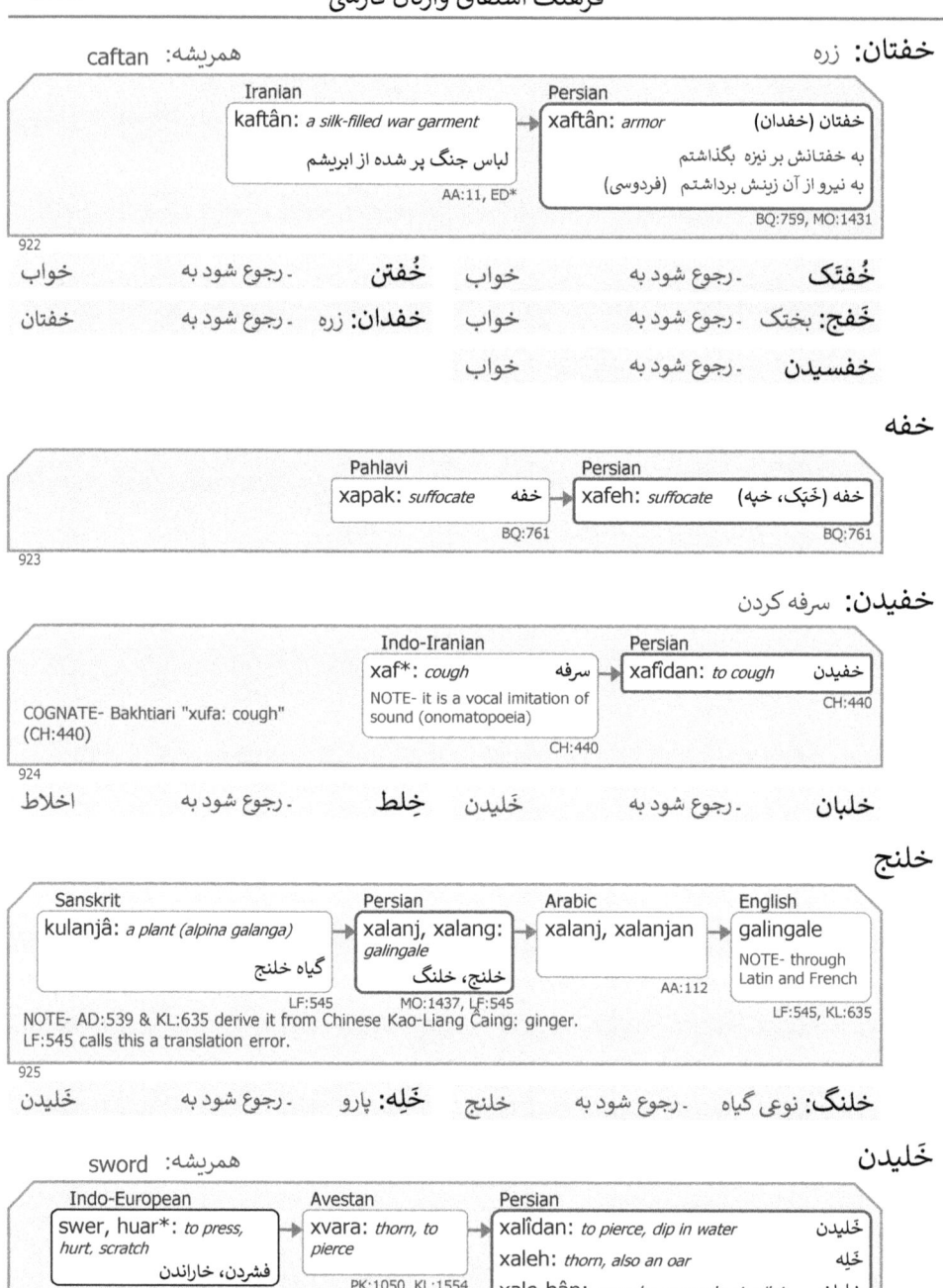

خفتان: زره   همریشه: caftan

Iranian	Persian
kaftân: *a silk-filled war garment*	xaftân: *armor* خفتان (خفدان)
لباس جنگ پر شده از ابریشم	به خفتانش بر نیزه بگذاشتم
AA:11, ED*	به نیرو از آن زینش برداشتم (فردوسی)
	BQ:759, MO:1431

922

خواب   . رجوع شود به   **خُفتَن**   خواب   . رجوع شود به   **خُفتک**

خفتان   . رجوع شود به   **خفدان: زره**   خواب   . رجوع شود به   **خَفج: بختک**

خواب   . رجوع شود به   **خفسیدن**

خفه

Pahlavi	Persian
xapak: *suffocate* خفه	xafeh: *suffocate* خفه (خَپَک، خپه)
BQ:761	BQ:761

923

خفیدن: سرفه کردن

Indo-Iranian	Persian
xaf*: *cough* سرفه	xafîdan: *to cough* خفیدن
NOTE- it is a vocal imitation of sound (onomatopoeia)	CH:440
CH:440	

COGNATE- Bakhtiari "xufa: cough" (CH:440)

924

اخلاط   . رجوع شود به   **خِلط**   خَلیدن   . رجوع شود به   **خلبان**

خلنج

Sanskrit	Persian	Arabic	English
kulanjâ: *a plant (alpina galanga)*	xalanj, xalang: *galingale*	xalanj, xalanjan	galingale
گیاه خلنج	خلنج، خلنگ	AA:112	NOTE- through Latin and French
	MO:1437, LF:545		LF:545, KL:635

NOTE- AD:539 & KL:635 derive it from Chinese Kao-Liang Caing: ginger. LF:545 calls this a translation error.

925

خَلیدن   . رجوع شود به   **خَلِه: پارو**   خلنج   . رجوع شود به   **خلنگ: نوعی گیاه**

خَلیدن   همریشه: sword

Indo-European	Avestan	Persian
swer, huar*: *to press, hurt, scratch*	xvara: *thorn, to pierce*	xalîdan: *to pierce, dip in water* خَلیدن
فشردن، خاراندن	PK:1050, KL:1554	xaleh: *thorn, also an oar* خَله
PK:1050, IC:1348, CH:150		xale-bân: *one who rows a boat, pilot* خلبان
		PH:109, BQ:766

926

165

خُم

همریشه: cup, cove

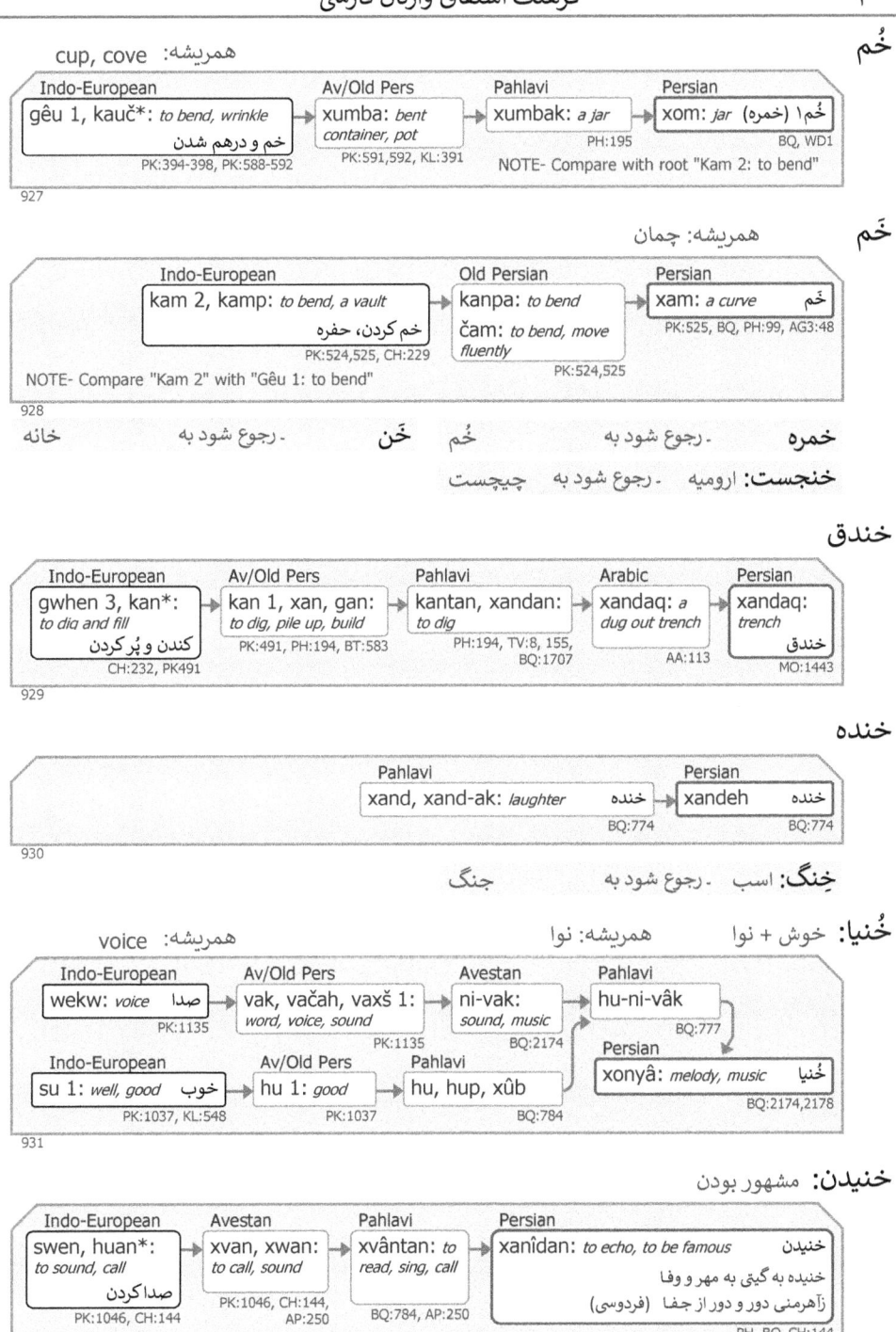

Indo-European
gêu 1, kauč*: *to bend, wrinkle*
خم و درهم شدن
PK:394-398, PK:588-592

Av/Old Pers
xumba: *bent container, pot*
PK:591,592, KL:391

Pahlavi
xumbak: *a jar*
PH:195

Persian
xom: *jar* (خمره) ۱خُم
BQ, WD1

NOTE- Compare with root "Kam 2: to bend"

927

خَم

همریشه: چمان

Indo-European
kam 2, kamp: *to bend, a vault*
خم کردن، حفره
PK:524,525, CH:229

Old Persian
kanpa: *to bend*
čam: *to bend, move fluently*
PK:524,525

Persian
xam: *a curve* خَم
PK:525, BQ, PH:99, AG3:48

NOTE- Compare "Kam 2" with "Gêu 1: to bend"

928

خمره ۔ رجوع شود به   خُم   خَن ۔ رجوع شود به   خانه

خنجست: ارومیه ۔ رجوع شود به   چیچست

خندق

Indo-European
gwhen 3, kan*: *to dig and fill*
کندن و پُر کردن
CH:232, PK491

Av/Old Pers
kan 1, xan, gan: *to dig, pile up, build*
PK:491, PH:194, BT:583

Pahlavi
kantan, xandan: *to dig*
PH:194, TV:8, 155, BQ:1707

Arabic
xandaq: *a dug out trench*
AA:113

Persian
xandaq: *trench*
خندق
MO:1443

929

خنده

Pahlavi
xand, xand-ak: *laughter* خنده
BQ:774

Persian
xandeh خنده
BQ:774

930

خِنگ: اسب ۔ رجوع شود به   جنگ

خُنیا: خوش + نوا   همریشه: نوا   همریشه: voice

Indo-European
wekw: *voice* صدا
PK:1135

Av/Old Pers
vak, vačah, vaxš 1: *word, voice, sound*
PK:1135

Avestan
ni-vak: *sound, music*
BQ:2174

Pahlavi
hu-ni-vâk
BQ:777

Indo-European
su 1: *well, good* خوب
PK:1037, KL:548

Av/Old Pers
hu 1: *good*
PK:1037

Pahlavi
hu, hup, xûb
BQ:784

Persian
xonyâ: *melody, music* خُنیا
BQ:2174,2178

931

خنیدن: مشهور بودن

Indo-European
swen, huan*: *to sound, call*
صداکردن
PK:1046, CH:144

Avestan
xvan, xwan: *to call, sound*
PK:1046, CH:144, AP:250

Pahlavi
xvântan: *to read, sing, call*
BQ:784, AP:250

Persian
xanîdan: *to echo, to be famous* خنیدن
خنیده به گیتی به مهر و وفا
زآهرمنی دور و دور از جفا   (فردوسی)
PH, BQ, CH:144

932

خو ۔ رجوع شود به   خود۱

خواب

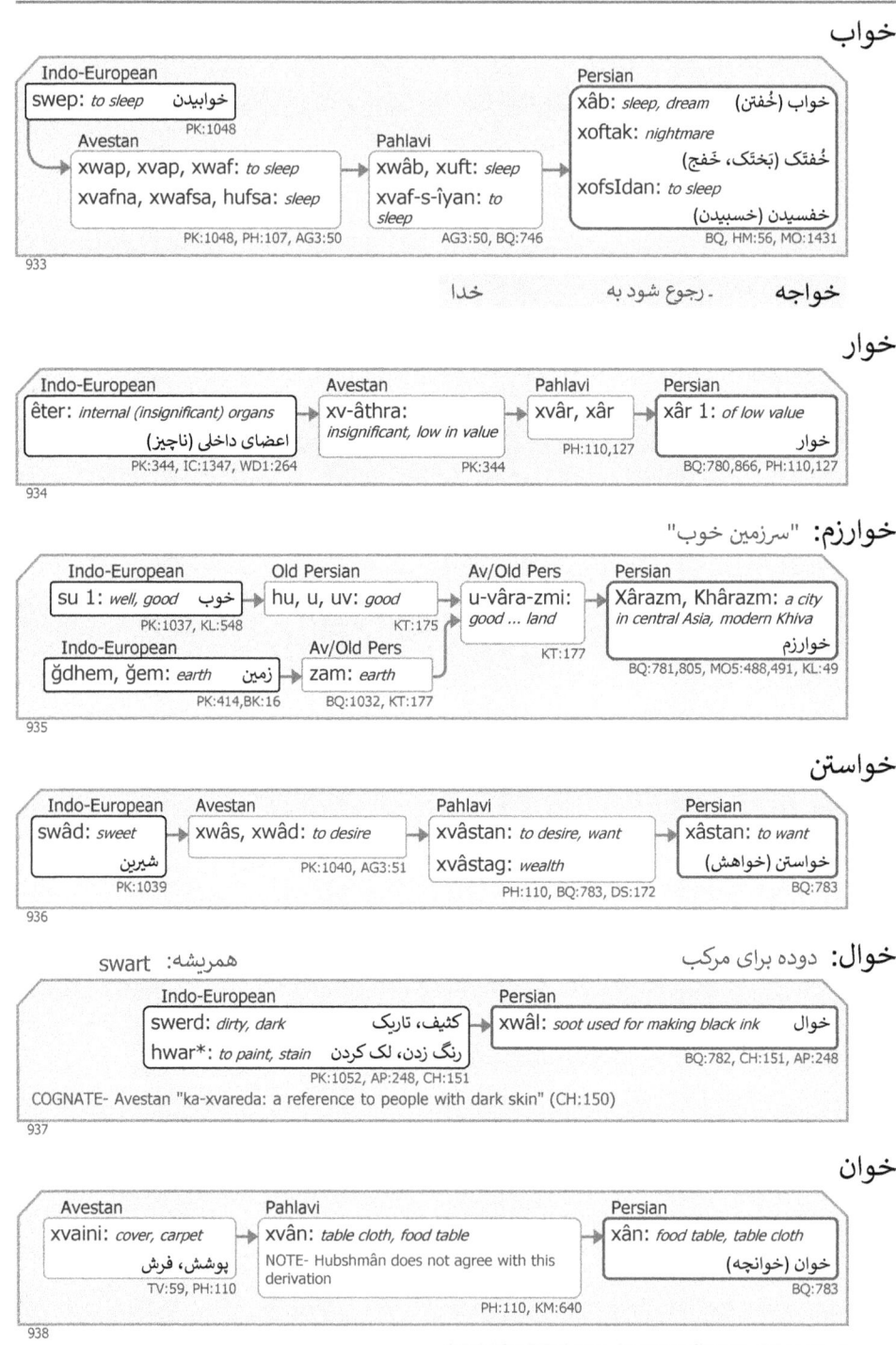

Indo-European
swep: to sleep　خوابیدن
PK:1048

Avestan
xwap, xvap, xwaf: to sleep
xvafna, xwafsa, hufsa: sleep
PK:1048, PH:107, AG3:50

Pahlavi
xwâb, xuft: sleep
xvaf-s-îyan: to sleep
AG3:50, BQ:746

Persian
xâb: sleep, dream　خواب (خُفتن)
xoftak: nightmare
خُفتَک (بَختَک، خفج)
xofsIdan: to sleep
خفسیدن (خسبیدن)
BQ, HM:56, MO:1431

933

خواجه　.رجوع شود به　خدا

خوار

Indo-European
êter: internal (insignificant) organs
اعضای داخلی (ناچیز)
PK:344, IC:1347, WD1:264

Avestan
xv-âthra:
insignificant, low in value
PK:344

Pahlavi
xvâr, xâr
PH:110,127

Persian
xâr 1: of low value
خوار
BQ:780,866, PH:110,127

934

خوارزم: "سرزمین خوب"

Indo-European
su 1: well, good　خوب
PK:1037, KL:548

Old Persian
hu, u, uv: good
KT:175

Av/Old Pers
u-vâra-zmi:
good ... land
KT:177

Persian
Xârazm, Khârazm: a city
in central Asia, modern Khiva
خوارزم
BQ:781,805, MO5:488,491, KL:49

Indo-European
ğdhem, ğem: earth　زمین
PK:414,BK:16

Av/Old Pers
zam: earth
BQ:1032, KT:177

935

خواستن

Indo-European
swâd: sweet
شیرین
PK:1039

Avestan
xwâs, xwâd: to desire
PK:1040, AG3:51

Pahlavi
xvâstan: to desire, want
xvâstag: wealth
PH:110, BQ:783, DS:172

Persian
xâstan: to want
خواستن (خواهش)
BQ:783

936

خوال: دوده برای مرکب

همریشه: swart

Indo-European
swerd: dirty, dark　کثیف، تاریک
hwar*: to paint, stain　رنگ زدن، لک کردن
PK:1052, AP:248, CH:151

Persian
xwâl: soot used for making black ink　خوال
BQ:782, CH:151, AP:248

COGNATE- Avestan "ka-xvareda: a reference to people with dark skin" (CH:150)

937

خوان

Avestan
xvaini: cover, carpet
پوشش، فرش
TV:59, PH:110

Pahlavi
xvân: table cloth, food table
NOTE- Hubshmân does not agree with this
derivation
PH:110, KM:640

Persian
xân: food table, table cloth
خوان (خوانچه)
BQ:783

938

خوانچه　.رجوع شود به　خوان

خواندن

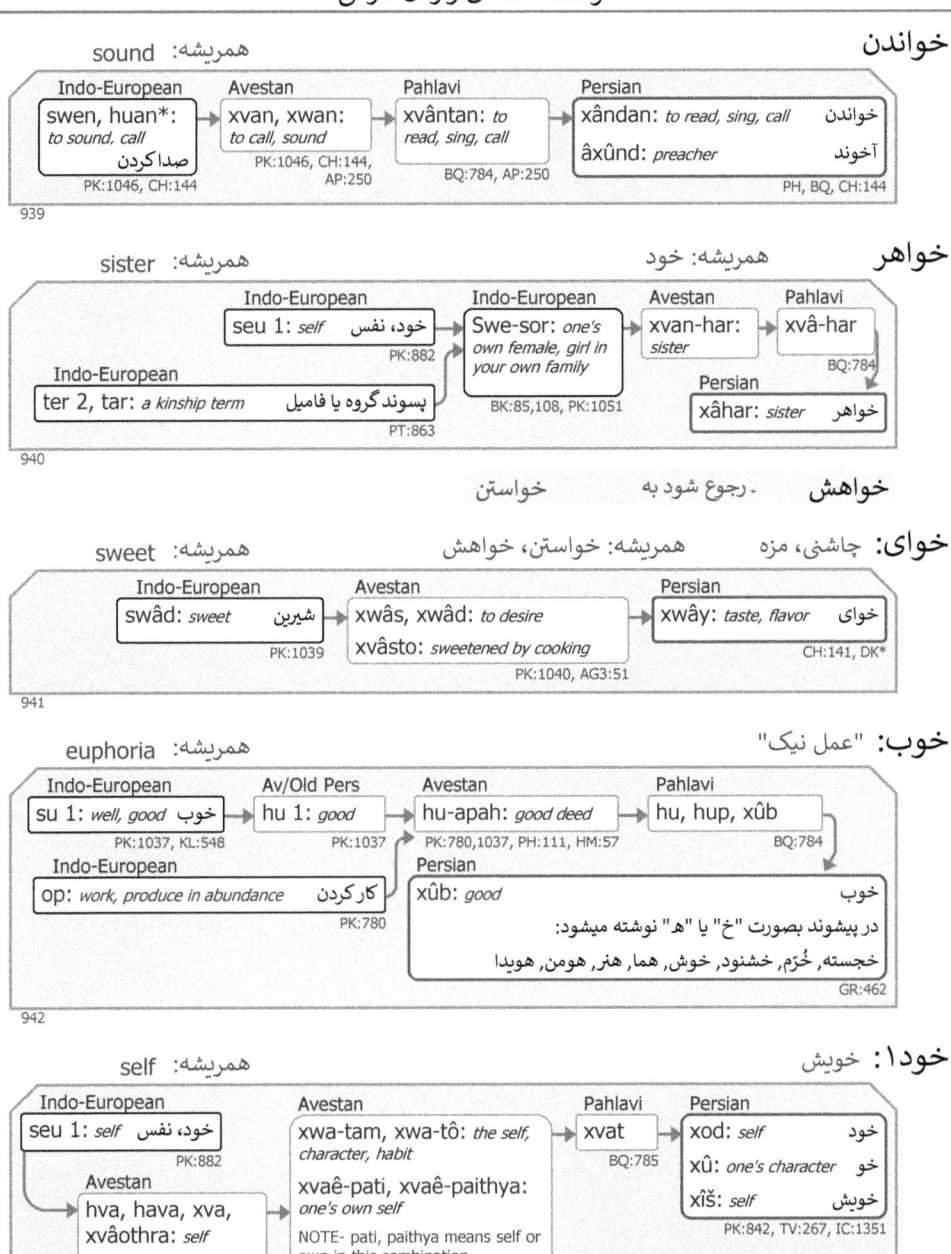

خواندن   همریشه: sound

Indo-European	Avestan	Pahlavi	Persian
swen, huan*: to sound, call صداکردن PK:1046, CH:144	xvan, xwan: to call, sound PK:1046, CH:144, AP:250	xvântan: to read, sing, call BQ:784, AP:250	xândan: to read, sing, call خواندن âxûnd: preacher PH, BQ, CH:144

939

خواهر   همریشه: خود   همریشه: sister

Indo-European	Indo-European	Avestan	Pahlavi
seu 1: self خود، نفس PK:882	Swe-sor: one's own female, girl in your own family BK:85,108, PK:1051	xvan-har: sister	xvâ-har BQ:784

Indo-European		Persian
ter 2, tar: a kinship term پسوند گروه یا فامیل PT:863		xâhar: sister خواهر

940

خواهش - رجوع شود به   خواستن

خوای: چاشنی، مزه   همریشه: خواستن، خواهش   همریشه: sweet

Indo-European	Avestan	Persian
swâd: sweet شیرین PK:1039	xwâs, xwâd: to desire xvâsto: sweetened by cooking PK:1040, AG3:51	xwây: taste, flavor خوای CH:141, DK*

941

خوب: "عمل نیک"

Indo-European	Av/Old Pers	Avestan	Pahlavi
su 1: well, good خوب PK:1037, KL:548	hu 1: good PK:1037	hu-apah: good deed PK:780,1037, PH:111, HM:57	hu, hup, xûb BQ:784

Indo-European		Persian
op: work, produce in abundance کارکردن PK:780		xûb: good خوب در پیشوند بصورت "خ" یا "ه" نوشته میشود: خجسته, خُرّم, خشنود, خوش, هما, هنر, هومن, هویدا GR:462

942

خود۱: خویش   همریشه: self

Indo-European	Avestan	Pahlavi	Persian
seu 1: self خود، نفس PK:882	xwa-tam, xwa-tô: the self, character, habit xvaê-pati, xvaê-paithya: one's own self NOTE- pati, paithya means self or own in this combination PK:842, TV:267, IC:1351	xvat BQ:785	xod: self خود xû: one's character خو xîš: self خویش PK:842, TV:267, IC:1351

	Avestan		
	hva, hava, xva, xvâothra: self PK:882, BQ:718, BT:1862		COGNATE- Old Persian "(h)uva: self" (BQ:785)

943

خود۲: کلاهخود

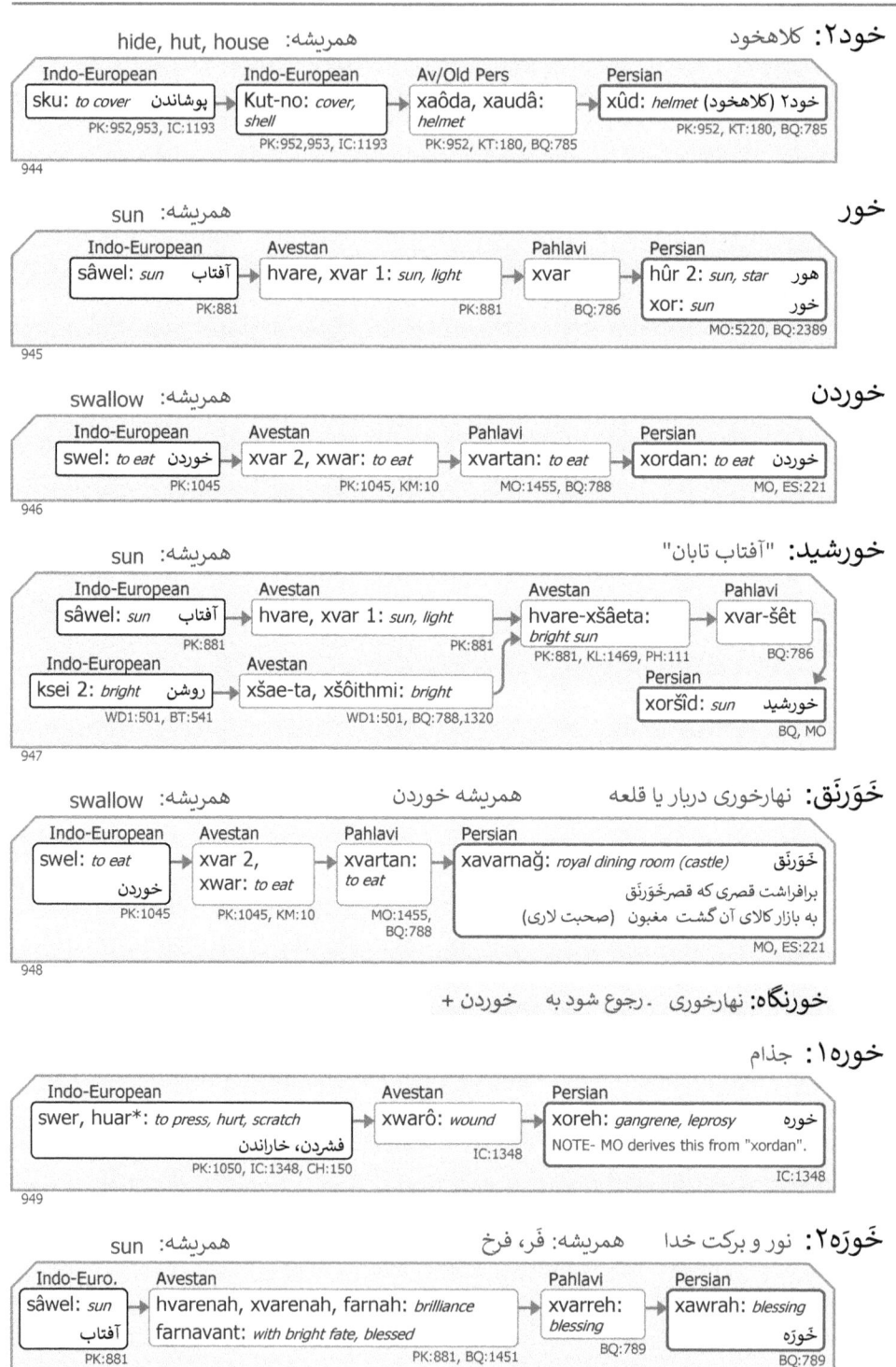

همریشه: hide, hut, house

Indo-European
sku: *to cover*   پوشاندن
PK:952,953, IC:1193

Indo-European
Kut-no: *cover, shell*
PK:952,953, IC:1193

Av/Old Pers
xaôda, xaudâ: *helmet*
PK:952, KT:180, BQ:785

Persian
xûd: *helmet* (خود۲ (کلاهخود
PK:952, KT:180, BQ:785

944

خور

همریشه: sun

Indo-European
sâwel: *sun*   آفتاب
PK:881

Avestan
hvare, xvar 1: *sun, light*
PK:881

Pahlavi
xvar
BQ:786

Persian
hûr 2: *sun, star*   هور
xor: *sun*   خور
MO:5220, BQ:2389

945

خوردن

همریشه: swallow

Indo-European
swel: *to eat*   خوردن
PK:1045

Avestan
xvar 2, xwar: *to eat*
PK:1045, KM:10

Pahlavi
xvartan: *to eat*
MO:1455, BQ:788

Persian
xordan: *to eat*   خوردن
MO, ES:221

946

خورشید: "آفتاب تابان"

همریشه: sun

Indo-European
sâwel: *sun*   آفتاب
PK:881

Avestan
hvare, xvar 1: *sun, light*
PK:881

Avestan
hvare-xšâeta: *bright sun*
PK:881, KL:1469, PH:111

Pahlavi
xvar-šêt
BQ:786

Indo-European
ksei 2: *bright*   روشن
WD1:501, BT:541

Avestan
xšae-ta, xšôithmi: *bright*
WD1:501, BQ:788,1320

Persian
xoršîd: *sun*   خورشید
BQ, MO

947

خَوَرنَق: نهارخوری دربار یا قلعه   همریشه خوردن

همریشه: swallow

Indo-European
swel: *to eat*   خوردن
PK:1045

Avestan
xvar 2, xwar: *to eat*
PK:1045, KM:10

Pahlavi
xvartan: *to eat*
MO:1455, BQ:788

Persian
xavarnağ: *royal dining room (castle)*   خَوَرنَق
برافراشت قصری که قصرخَوَرنَق
به بازار کالای آن گشت مغبون (صحبت لاری)
MO, ES:221

948

خورنگاه: نهارخوری . رجوع شود به خوردن +

خوره۱: جذام

Indo-European
swer, huar*: *to press, hurt, scratch*
فشردن، خاراندن
PK:1050, IC:1348, CH:150

Avestan
xwarô: *wound*
IC:1348

Persian
xoreh: *gangrene, leprosy*   خوره
NOTE- MO derives this from "xordan".
IC:1348

949

خَوَرَه۲: نور و برکت خدا   همریشه: فَر، فرخ

همریشه: sun

Indo-Euro.
sâwel: *sun*
آفتاب
PK:881

Avestan
hvarenah, xvarenah, farnah: *brilliance*
farnavant: *with bright fate, blessed*
PK:881, BQ:1451

Pahlavi
xvarreh: *blessing*
BQ:789

Persian
xawrah: *blessing*
خوزه
BQ:789

950

اهواز	ـ رجوع شود به	**خوزستان**	اهواز	ـ رجوع شود به	**خوز**
خشنود	ـ رجوع شود به	**خوش**	خُست	ـ رجوع شود به	**خُوست:** کوبیده
			خشک	ـ رجوع شود به	**خوشیدن**

خوک: " شبیه گراز"

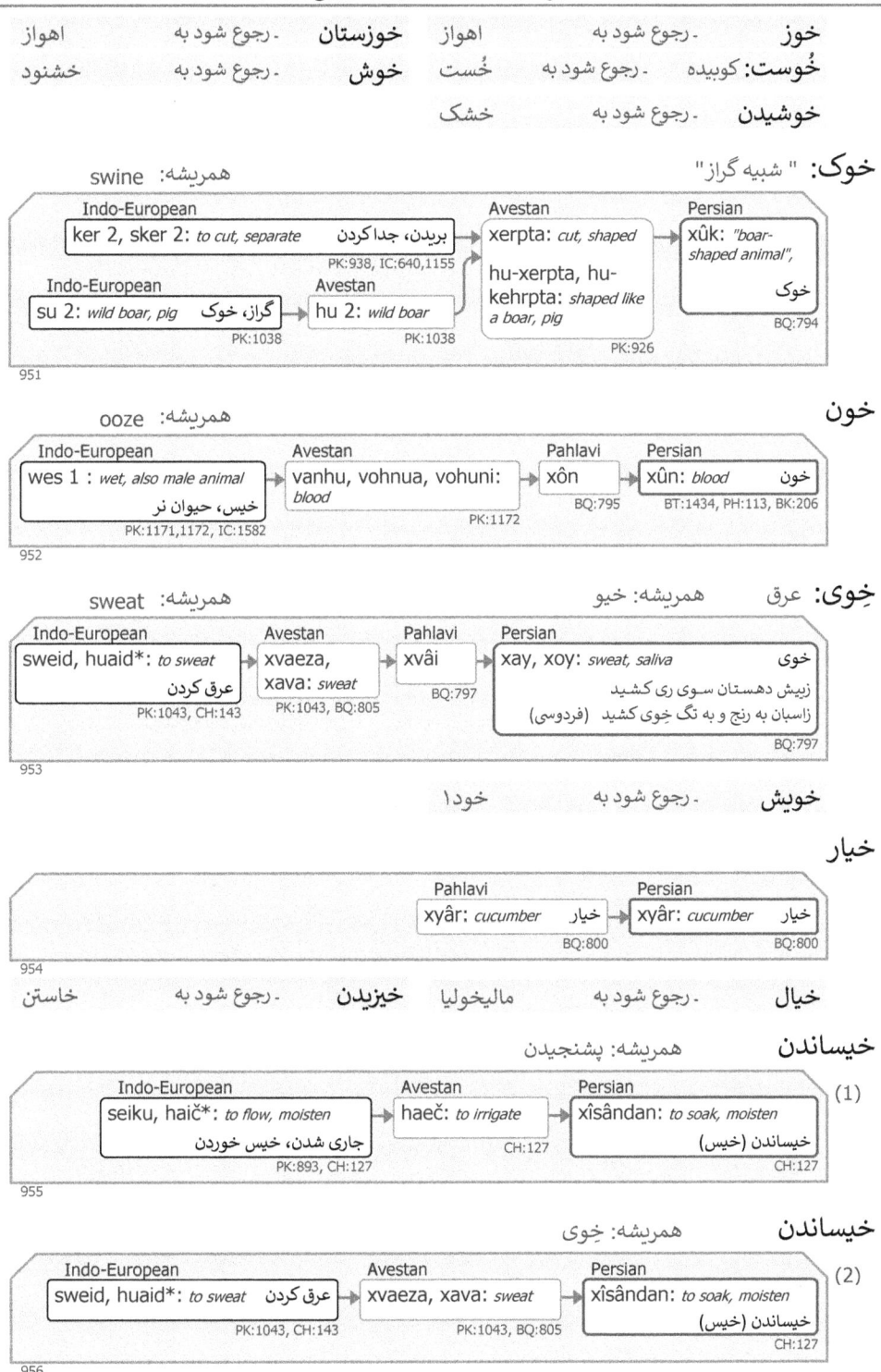

همریشه: swine

Indo-European
ker 2, sker 2: *to cut, separate*   بریدن، جدا کردن
PK:938, IC:640,1155

Indo-European
su 2: *wild boar, pig*   گراز، خوک
PK:1038

Avestan
hu 2: *wild boar*
PK:1038

Avestan
xerpta: *cut, shaped*
hu-xerpta, hu-kehrpta: *shaped like a boar, pig*
PK:926

Persian
xûk: *"boar-shaped animal"*,
خوک
BQ:794

951

خون

همریشه: ooze

Indo-European
wes 1 : *wet, also male animal*
خیس، حیوان نر
PK:1171,1172, IC:1582

Avestan
vanhu, vohnua, vohuni: *blood*
PK:1172

Pahlavi
xôn
BQ:795

Persian
xûn: *blood*   خون
BT:1434, PH:113, BK:206

952

خِوی: عرق   همریشه: خیو

همریشه: sweat

Indo-European
sweid, huaid*: *to sweat*
عرق کردن
PK:1043, CH:143

Avestan
xvaeza, xava: *sweat*
PK:1043, BQ:805

Pahlavi
xvâi
BQ:797

Persian
xay, xoy: *sweat, saliva*   خوی
زبش دهستان سـوی ری کشید
زاسبان به رنج و به تگ خِوی کشید   (فردوسی)
BQ:797

953

خویش   ـ رجوع شود به   خود۱

خیار

Pahlavi
xyâr: *cucumber*   خیار
BQ:800

Persian
xyâr: *cucumber*   خیار
BQ:800

954

| خاستن | ـ رجوع شود به | **خیزیدن** | مالیخولیا | ـ رجوع شود به | **خیال** |

خیساندن

همریشه: پشنجیدن

Indo-European
seiku, haič*: *to flow, moisten*
جاری شدن، خیس خوردن
PK:893, CH:127

Avestan
haeč: *to irrigate*
CH:127

Persian
xîsândan: *to soak, moisten*
خیساندن (خیس)
CH:127

(1)

955

خیساندن

همریشه: خِوی

Indo-European
sweid, huaid*: *to sweat*   عرق کردن
PK:1043, CH:143

Avestan
xvaeza, xava: *sweat*
PK:1043, BQ:805

Persian
xîsândan: *to soak, moisten*
خیساندن (خیس)
CH:127

(2)

956

170

خیش: گاوآهن

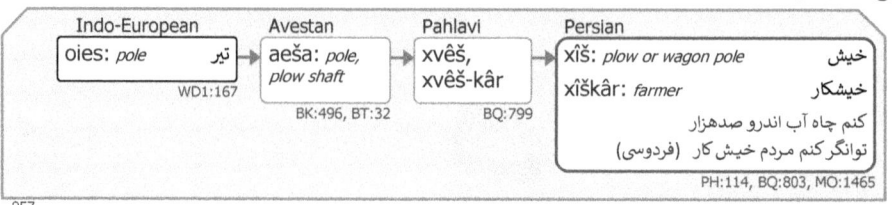

957

خیشکار: کشاورز ــ رجوع شود به خیش

خیم: خوی، طبیعت

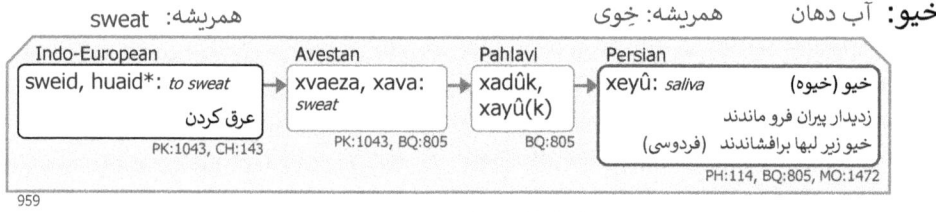

958

خیو: آب دهان ــ همریشه: خِوی ــ همریشه: sweat

Indo-European

sweid, huaid*: to sweat

عرق کردن

PK:1043, CH:143

Avestan

xvaeza, xava: sweat

PK:1043, BQ:805

Pahlavi

xadûk, xayû(k)

BQ:805

Persian

xeyû: saliva

خیو (خیوه)

زدیدار پیران فرو ماندند

خیو زیر لبها برافشاندند   (فردوسی)

PH:114, BQ:805, MO:1472

959

خیوه ــ رجوع شود به خیو

حرف د گاهی به ت بدل شود.

داد: عدالت

همریشه: certify, verify

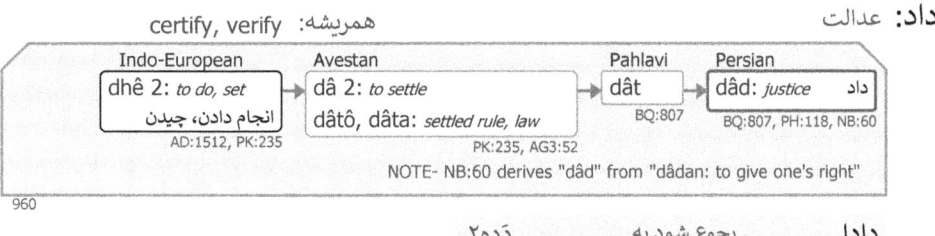

Indo-European	Avestan	Pahlavi	Persian
dhê 2: *to do, set* انجام دادن، چیدن AD:1512, PK:235	dâ 2: *to settle* dâtô, dâta: *settled rule, law* PK:235, AG3:52	dât BQ:807	dâd: *justice* داد BQ:807, PH:118, NB:60

NOTE- NB:60 derives "dâd" from "dâdan: to give one's right"

960

دادا . رجوع شود به   دَدِه٢

دادار

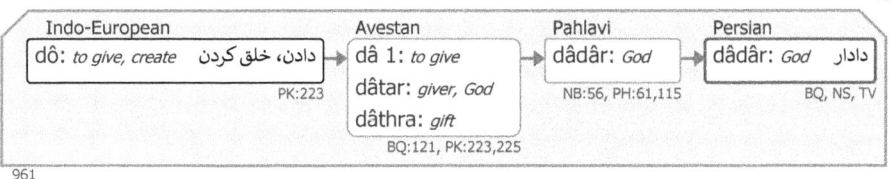

Indo-European	Avestan	Pahlavi	Persian
dô: *to give, create* دادن، خلق کردن PK:223	dâ 1: *to give* dâtar: *giver, God* dâthra: *gift* BQ:121, PK:223,225	dâdâr: *God* NB:56, PH:61,115	dâdâr: *God* دادار BQ, NS, TV

961

دادن

همریشه: donate, dose, rent

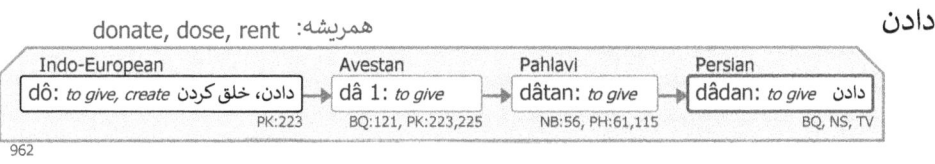

Indo-European	Avestan	Pahlavi	Persian
dô: *to give, create* دادن، خلق کردن PK:223	dâ 1: *to give* BQ:121, PK:223,225	dâtan: *to give* NB:56, PH:61,115	dâdan: *to give* دادن BQ, NS, TV

962

دار١: خانه، دنیا   همریشه: دایره

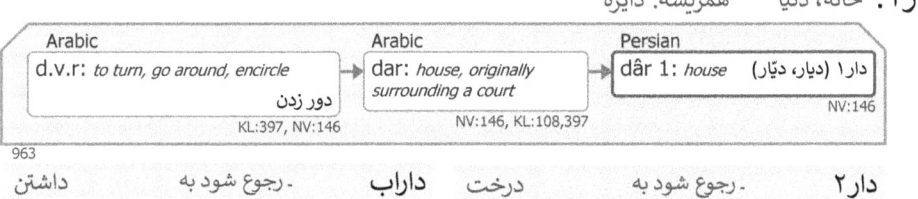

Arabic	Arabic	Persian
d.v.r: *to turn, go around, encircle* دور زدن KL:397, NV:146	dar: *house, originally surrounding a court* NV:146, KL:108,397	dâr 1: *house* دارا (دیار، دیّار) NV:146

963

دار٢ . رجوع شود به   درخت   **داراب** . رجوع شود به   داشتن

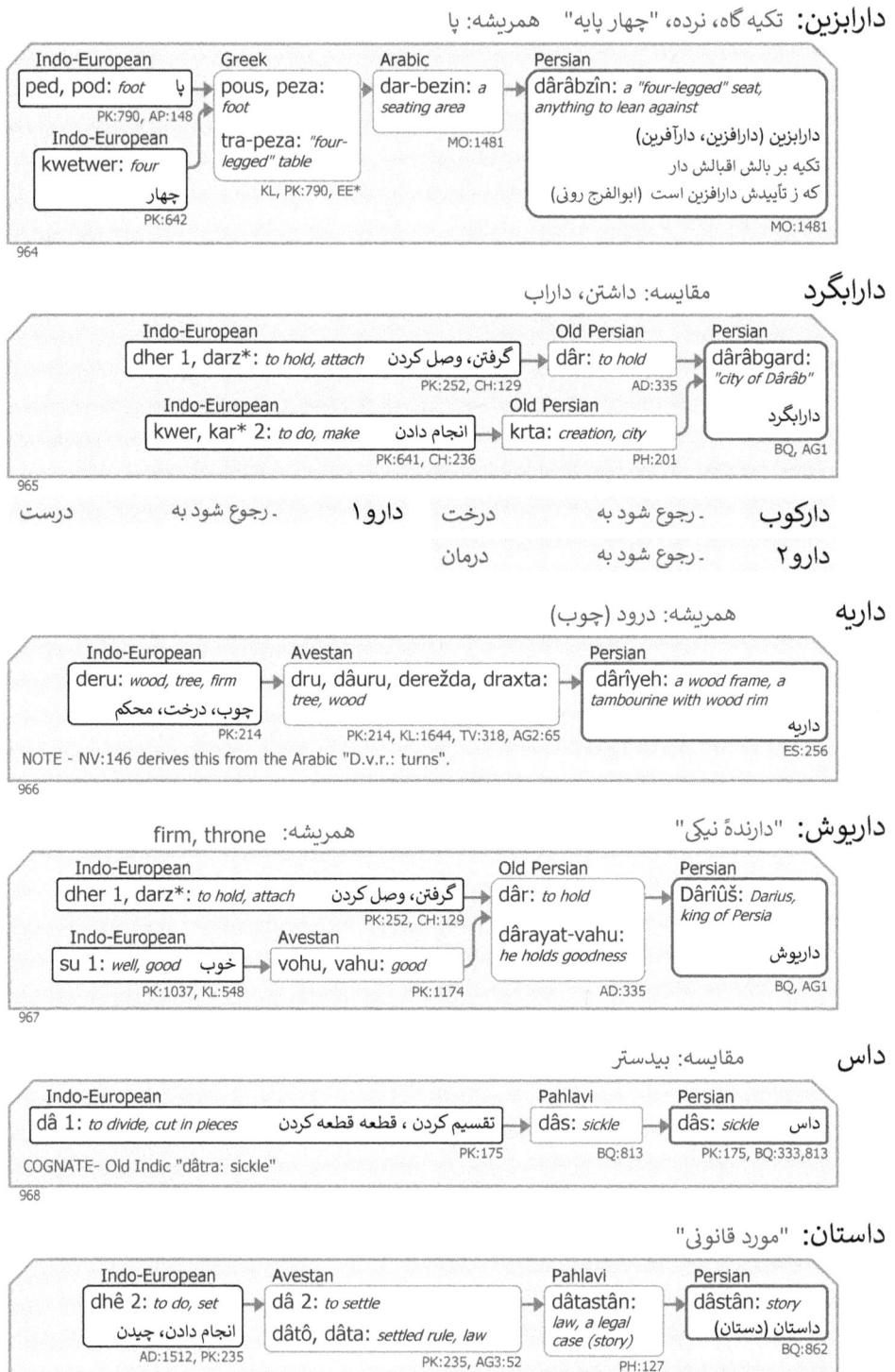

دارابزین: تکیه گاه، نرده، "چهار پایه" همریشه: پا

Indo-European	Greek	Arabic	Persian
ped, pod: *foot* پا PK:790, AP:148	pous, peza: *foot*	dar-bezin: *a seating area* MO:1481	dârâbzîn: *a "four-legged" seat, anything to lean against*
Indo-European	tra-peza: *"four-legged" table*		دارابزین (دارافزین، دارآفرین)
kwetwer: *four* چهار PK:642	KL, PK:790, EE*		تکیه بر بالش اقبالش دار که ز تأییدش دارافزین است (ابوالفرج رونی) MO:1481

964

دارابگرد مقایسه: داشتن، داراب

Indo-European	Old Persian	Persian
dher 1, darz*: *to hold, attach* گرفتن، وصل کردن PK:252, CH:129	dâr: *to hold* AD:335	dârâbgard: *"city of Dârâb"*
Indo-European	Old Persian	دارابگرد
kwer, kar* 2: *to do, make* انجام دادن PK:641, CH:236	krta: *creation, city* PH:201	BQ, AG1

965

درست	.رجوع شود به	**دارو ۱**	درخت	.رجوع شود به	**دارکوب**
		دارو ۲	درمان	.رجوع شود به	

داریه همریشه: درود (چوب)

Indo-European	Avestan	Persian
deru: *wood, tree, firm* چوب، درخت، محکم PK:214	dru, dâuru, derežda, draxta: *tree, wood* PK:214, KL:1644, TV:318, AG2:65	dârîyeh: *a wood frame, a tambourine with wood rim* داریه ES:256

NOTE - NV:146 derives this from the Arabic "D.v.r.: turns".

966

داریوش: "دارندهٔ نیکی" firm, throne :همریشه

Indo-European	Old Persian	Persian
dher 1, darz*: *to hold, attach* گرفتن، وصل کردن PK:252, CH:129	dâr: *to hold*	Dârîûš: *Darius, king of Persia*
Indo-European	Avestan	dârayat-vahu: *he holds goodness*	داریوش
su 1: *well, good* خوب PK:1037, KL:548	vohu, vahu: *good* PK:1174	AD:335	BQ, AG1

967

داس مقایسه: بیدستر

Indo-European	Pahlavi	Persian
dâ 1: *to divide, cut in pieces* تقسیم کردن، قطعه قطعه کردن	dâs: *sickle* PK:175	dâs: *sickle* داس PK:175, BQ:333,813
		BQ:813	

COGNATE- Old Indic "dâtra: sickle"

968

داستان: "مورد قانونی"

Indo-European	Avestan	Pahlavi	Persian
dhê 2: *to do, set* انجام دادن، چیدن AD:1512, PK:235	dâ 2: *to settle* dâtô, dâta: *settled rule, law* PK:235, AG3:52	dâtastân: *law, a legal case (story)* PH:127	dâstân: *story* داستان (دستان) BQ:862

969

داش: کوره آجر یا کوزه پزی   همریشه: داغ، دخش۲   همریشه: fever

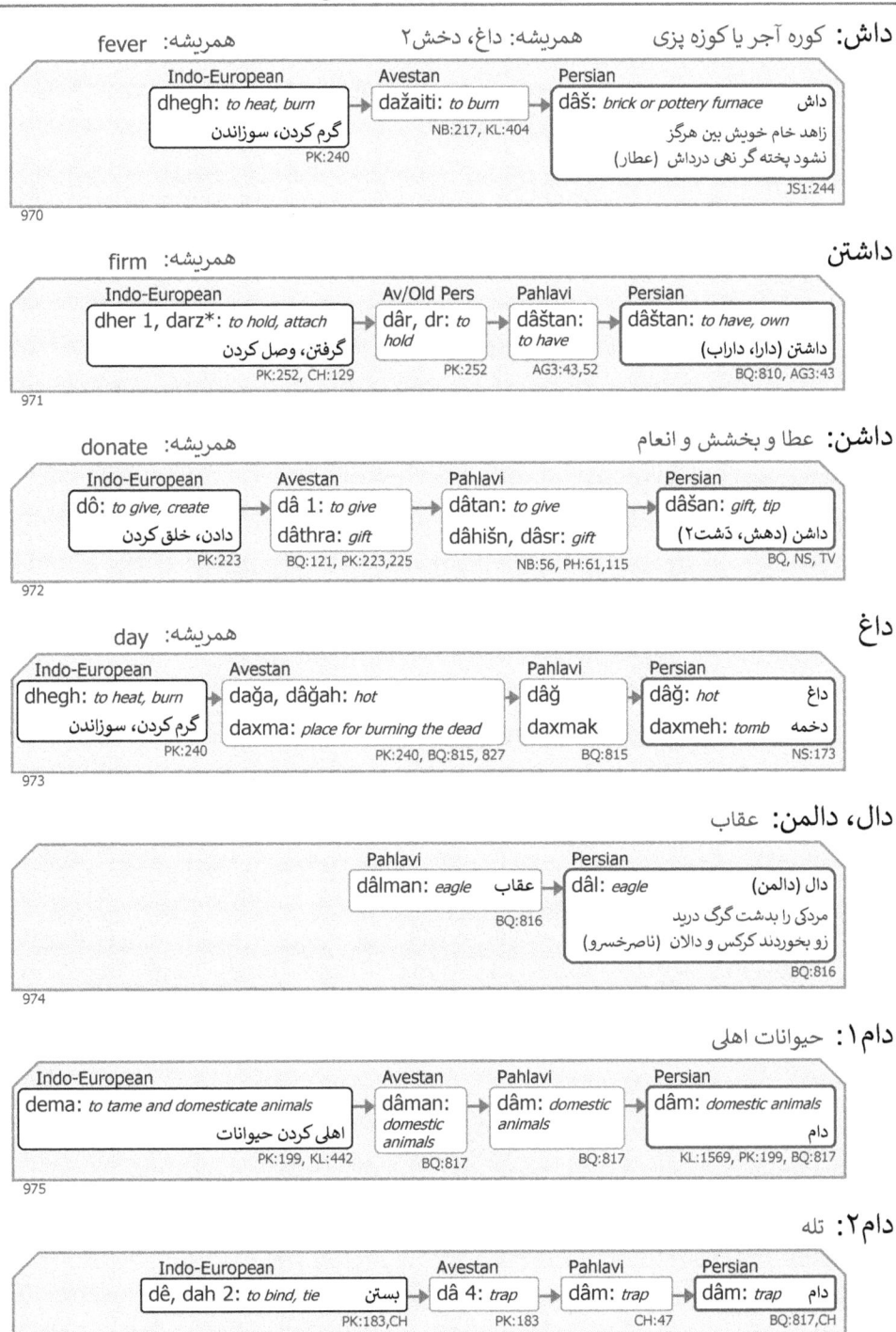

Indo-European	Avestan	Persian
dhegh: *to heat, burn* گرم کردن، سوزاندن PK:240	dažaiti: *to burn* NB:217, KL:404	dâš: *brick or pottery furnace* داش زاهد خام خویش بین هرگز نشود پخته گر نهی درداش (عطار) JS1:244

970

داشتن

همریشه: firm

Indo-European	Av/Old Pers	Pahlavi	Persian
dher 1, darz*: *to hold, attach* گرفتن، وصل کردن PK:252, CH:129	dâr, dr: *to hold* PK:252	dâštan: *to have* AG3:43,52	dâštan: *to have, own* داشتن (دارا، داراب) BQ:810, AG3:43

971

داشن: عطا و بخشش و انعام

همریشه: donate

Indo-European	Avestan	Pahlavi	Persian
dô: *to give, create* دادن، خلق کردن PK:223	dâ 1: *to give* dâthra: *gift* BQ:121, PK:223,225	dâtan: *to give* dâhišn, dâsr: *gift* NB:56, PH:61,115	dâšan: *gift, tip* داشن (دهش، دَشت۲) BQ, NS, TV

972

داغ

همریشه: day

Indo-European	Avestan	Pahlavi	Persian
dhegh: *to heat, burn* گرم کردن، سوزاندن PK:240	dağa, dâğah: *hot* daxma: *place for burning the dead* PK:240, BQ:815, 827	dâğ daxmak BQ:815	dâğ: *hot* داغ daxmeh: *tomb* دخمه NS:173

973

دال، دالمن: عقاب

Pahlavi	Persian
dâlman: *eagle* عقاب BQ:816	dâl: *eagle* دال (دالمن) مردکی را بدشت گرگ درید زو بخوردند کرکس و دالان (ناصرخسرو) BQ:816

974

دام۱: حیوانات اهلی

Indo-European	Avestan	Pahlavi	Persian
dema: *to tame and domesticate animals* اهلی کردن حیوانات PK:199, KL:442	dâman: *domestic animals* BQ:817	dâm: *domestic animals* BQ:817	dâm: *domestic animals* دام KL:1569, PK:199, BQ:817

975

دام۲: تله

Indo-European	Avestan	Pahlavi	Persian
dê, dah 2: *to bind, tie* بستن PK:183,CH	dâ 4: *trap* PK:183	dâm: *trap* CH:47	dâm: *trap* دام BQ:817,CH

976

174

داماد

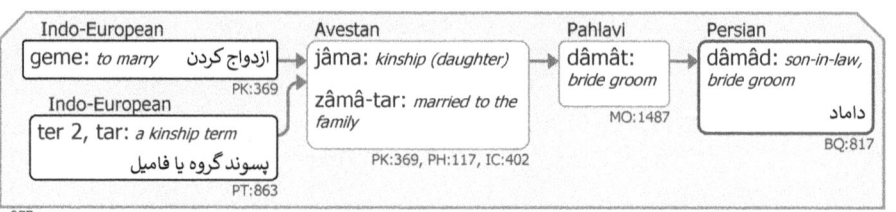

Indo-European	Avestan	Pahlavi	Persian
geme: *to marry* ازدواج کردن PK:369	jâma: *kinship (daughter)* zâmâ-tar: *married to the family* PK:369, PH:117, IC:402	dâmât: *bride groom* MO:1487	dâmâd: *son-in-law, bride groom* داماد BQ:817
Indo-European			
ter 2, tar: *a kinship term* پسوند گروه یا فامیل PT:863			

977

ـ دان

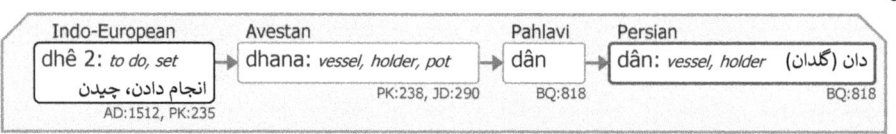

Indo-European	Avestan	Pahlavi	Persian
dhê 2: *to do, set* انجام دادن، چیدن AD:1512, PK:235	dhana: *vessel, holder, pot* PK:238, JD:290	dân BQ:818	dân: *vessel, holder* (دان (گدان BQ:818

978

دانستن

همریشه: know

Indo-European	Av/Old Pers	Pahlavi	Persian
gnô: *to know* دانستن PK:376	dan, dânâ: *to know* PK:376, BQ:1298	dânastan BQ:819	dânestan (دانستن (دانش BQ, AG3

979

دانش ـ رجوع شود به دانستن   **دانگ** ـ رجوع شود به دانه   دانه

دانه

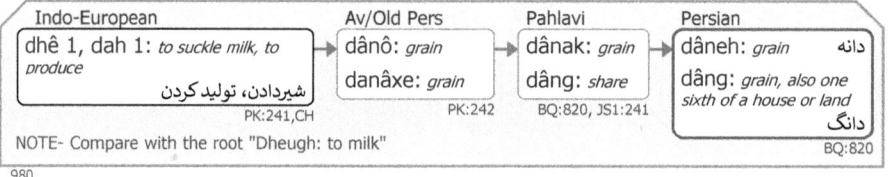

Indo-European	Av/Old Pers	Pahlavi	Persian
dhê 1, dah 1: *to suckle milk, to produce* شیردادن، تولید کردن PK:241,CH	dânô: *grain* danâxe: *grain* PK:242	dânak: *grain* dâng: *share* BQ:820, JS1:241	dâneh: *grain* دانه dâng: *grain, also one sixth of a house or land* دانگ BQ:820

NOTE- Compare with the root "Dheugh: to milk"

980

دانوب: "رودخانه"

Indo-European	Av/Old Pers	Greek	French	Persian
dâ 2: *to flow* جریان یافتن dânu: *river* رودخانه PK:175	dânu: *river, water* Dânavo: *Danube river* PK:175, FV:123	Dânao: *Danube* NOTE- This word apparently entered European languages through Scythians (7th century B.C.). PK:175, FV:123, MO5:772		Dânûb دانوب MO5:516

981

دانیدن: غلطانیدن

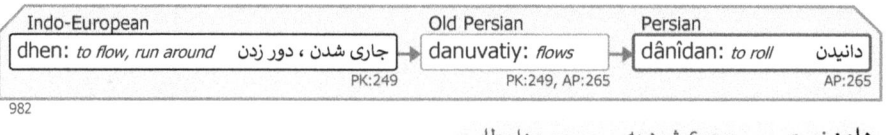

Indo-European	Old Persian	Persian
dhen: *to flow, run around* جاری شدن ، دور زدن PK:249	danuvatiy: *flows* PK:249, AP:265	dânîdan: *to roll* دانیدن AP:265

982

داو: نوبت ـ رجوع شود به   داوطلب

داور: "حامل قانون"

همریشه: reference

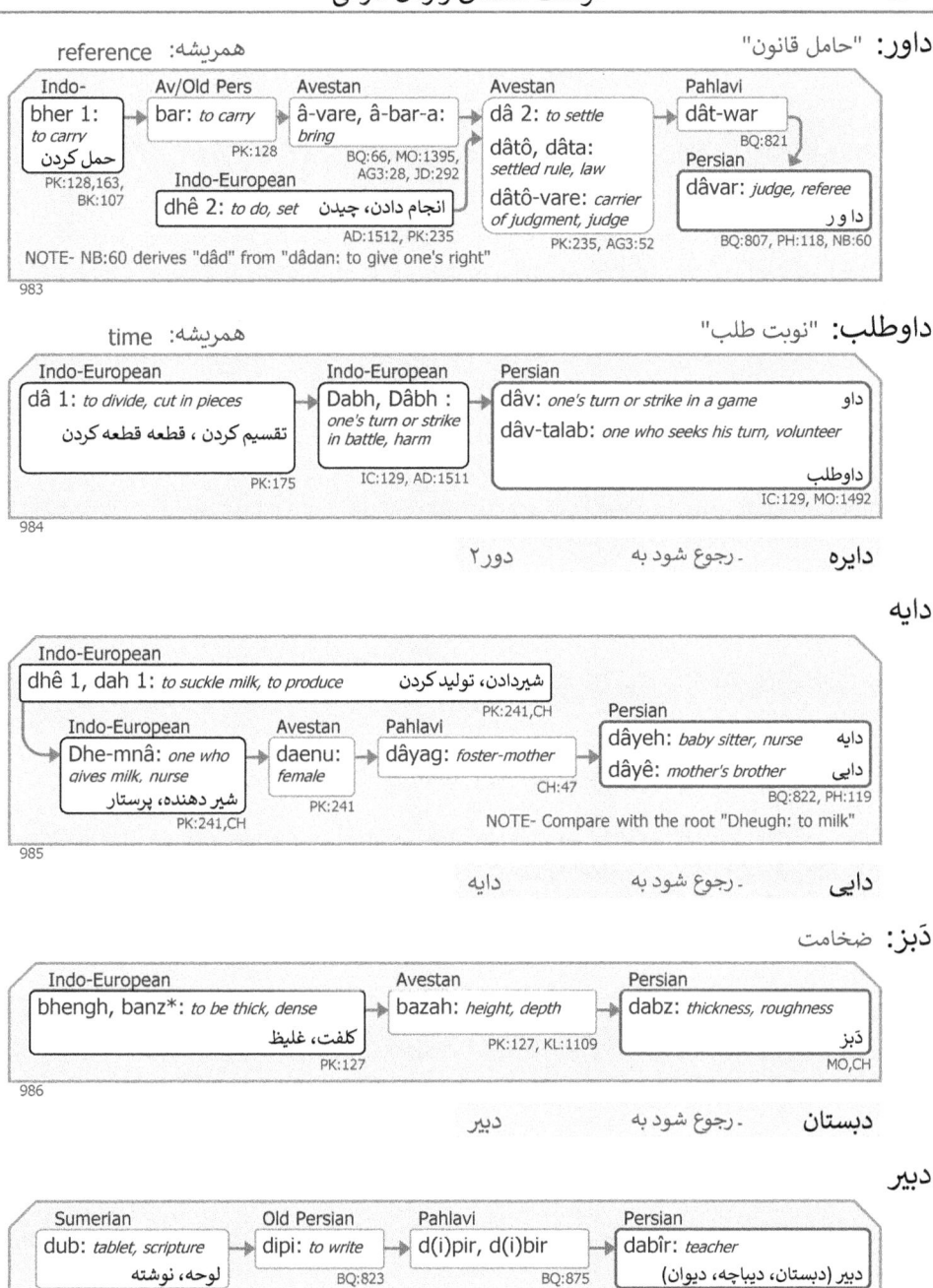

Indo-

bher 1: *to carry*

حمل کردن

PK:128,163,
BK:107

Av/Old Pers

bar: *to carry*

PK:128

Indo-European

dhê 2: *to do, set*

انجام دادن، چیدن

AD:1512, PK:235

Avestan

â-vare, â-bar-a: *bring*

BQ:66, MO:1395,
AG3:28, JD:292

Avestan

dâ 2: *to settle*

dâtô, dâta: *settled rule, law*

dâtô-vare: *carrier of judgment, judge*

PK:235, AG3:52

Pahlavi

dât-war

BQ:821

Persian

dâvar: *judge, referee*

داور

BQ:807, PH:118, NB:60

NOTE- NB:60 derives "dâd" from "dâdan: to give one's right"

983

داوطلب: "نوبت طلب"

همریشه: time

Indo-European

dâ 1: *to divide, cut in pieces*

تقسیم کردن ، قطعه قطعه کردن

PK:175

Indo-European

Dabh, Dâbh : *one's turn or strike in battle, harm*

IC:129, AD:1511

Persian

dâv: *one's turn or strike in a game*

dâv-talab: *one who seeks his turn, volunteer*

داو

داوطلب

IC:129, MO:1492

984

دایره ـ رجوع شود به ۲دور

دایه

Indo-European

dhê 1, dah 1: *to suckle milk, to produce* شیردادن، تولید کردن

PK:241,CH

Indo-European

Dhe-mnâ: *one who gives milk, nurse*

شیر دهنده، پرستار

PK:241,CH

Avestan

daenu: *female*

PK:241

Pahlavi

dâyag: *foster-mother*

CH:47

Persian

dâyeh: *baby sitter, nurse* دایه

dâyê: *mother's brother* دایی

BQ:822, PH:119

NOTE- Compare with the root "Dheugh: to milk"

985

دایی ـ رجوع شود به دایه

دَبز: ضخامت

Indo-European

bhengh, banz*: *to be thick, dense*

کلفت، غلیظ

PK:127

Avestan

bazah: *height, depth*

PK:127, KL:1109

Persian

dabz: *thickness, roughness*

دَبز

MO,CH

986

دبستان ـ رجوع شود به دبیر

دبیر

Sumerian

dub: *tablet, scripture*

لوحه، نوشته

ZM:19, BQ:823

Old Persian

dipi: *to write*

BQ:823

Pahlavi

d(i)pir, d(i)bir

BQ:875

Persian

dabîr: *teacher*

دبیر (دبستان، دیباچه، دیوان)

BQ:824, KL:467, ZM:19, AG2:36

987

دجله: "سریع"

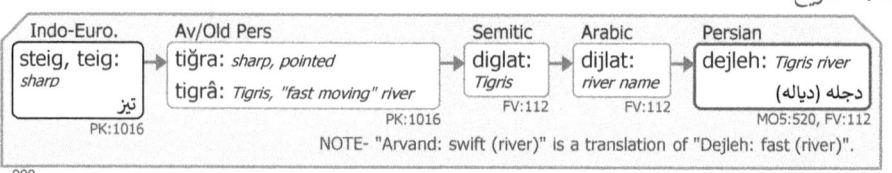

Indo-Euro.	Av/Old Pers	Semitic	Arabic	Persian
steig, teig: *sharp* تیز	tiğra: *sharp, pointed* tiğrâ: *Tigris, "fast moving" river*	diglat: *Tigris*	dijlat: *river name*	dejleh: *Tigris river* دجله (دیاله)
PK:1016	PK:1016	FV:112	FV:112	MO5:520, FV:112

NOTE- "Arvand: swift (river)" is a translation of "Dejleh: fast (river)".

988

دختر: "شیر دوش"

همریشه: daughter

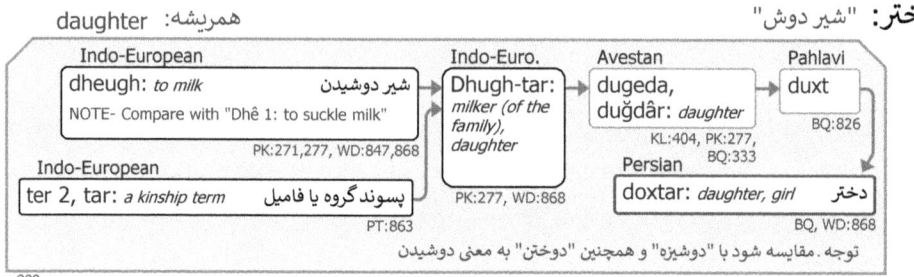

Indo-European	Indo-Euro.	Avestan	Pahlavi
dheugh: *to milk* شیر دوشیدن NOTE- Compare with "Dhê 1: to suckle milk" PK:271,277, WD:847,868	Dhugh-tar: *milker (of the family), daughter*	dugeda, duğdâr: *daughter* KL:404, PK:277, BQ:333	duxt BQ:826
Indo-European ter 2, tar: *a kinship term* پسوند گروه یا فامیل PT:863	PK:277, WD:868	Persian doxtar: *daughter, girl* دختر BQ, WD:868	

توجه . مقایسه شود با "دوشیزه" و همچنین "دوختن" به معنی دوشیدن

989

دختراندر ۰ رجوع شود به   اندر۲

دخش۱: حرفه

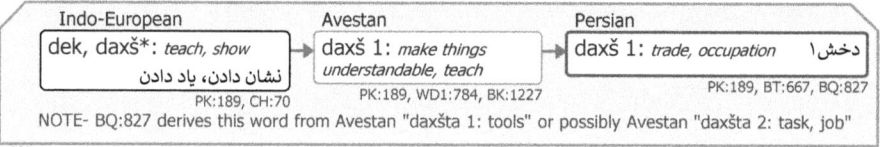

Indo-European	Avestan	Persian
dek, daxš*: *teach, show* نشان دادن، یاد دادن PK:189, CH:70	daxš 1: *make things understandable, teach* PK:189, WD1:784, BK:1227	daxš 1: *trade, occupation* دخش۱ PK:189, BT:667, BQ:827

NOTE- BQ:827 derives this word from Avestan "daxšta 1: tools" or possibly Avestan "daxšta 2: task, job"

990

دخش۲: تاریک

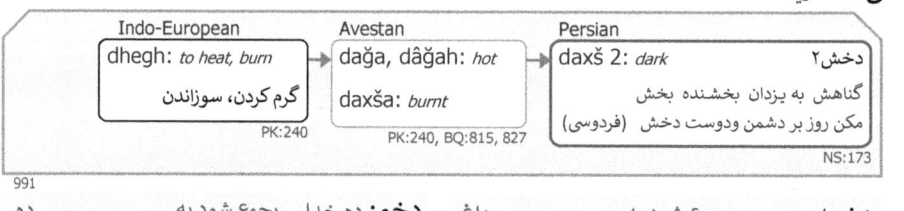

Indo-European	Avestan	Persian
dhegh: *to heat, burn* گرم کردن، سوزاندن PK:240	dağa, dâğah: *hot* daxša: *burnt* PK:240, BQ:815, 827	daxš 2: *dark* دخش۲ گناهش به یزدان بخشنده بخش مکن روز بر دشمن ودوست دخش (فردوسی) NS:173

991

دخمه ۰ رجوع شود به   دخو: ده خدا ۰رجوع شود به   داغ   دِه

دَد: حیوان وحشی   همریشه: دندان   همریشه: tooth

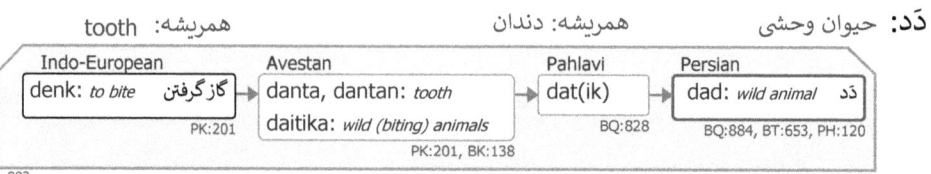

Indo-European	Avestan	Pahlavi	Persian
denk: *to bite* گاز گرفتن PK:201	danta, dantan: *tooth* daitika: *wild (biting) animals* PK:201, BK:138	dat(ik) BQ:828	dad: *wild animal* دَد BQ:884, BT:653, PH:120

992

ددَ۱۵: جد پدری یا مادری   همریشه: dad

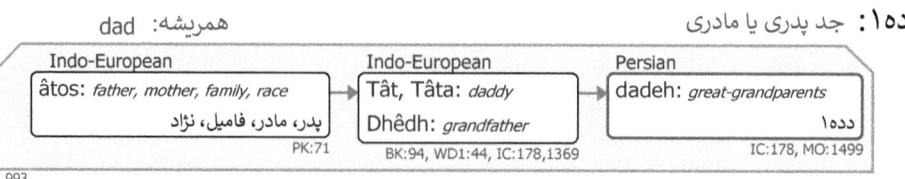

Indo-European	Indo-European	Persian
âtos: *father, mother, family, race* پدر، مادر، فامیل، نژاد PK:71	Tât, Tâta: *daddy* Dhêdh: *grandfather* BK:94, WD1:44, IC:178,1369	dadeh: *great-grandparents* ددِه۱۵ IC:178, MO:1499

993

دَدِه۲ه: پرستار بچه

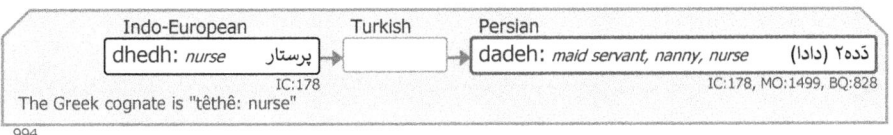

در

همریشه: door

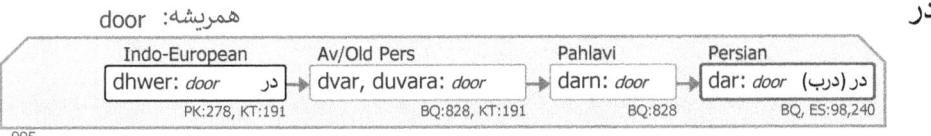

دراز

همریشه: درنگ، دیر   همریشه: long, length

درای: زنگ و جرس   همریشه: دراییدن

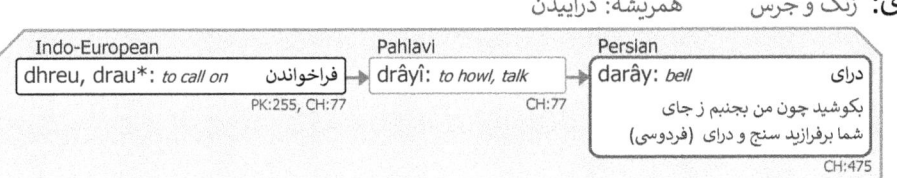

دراییدن: سخن گفتن   همریشه: درای

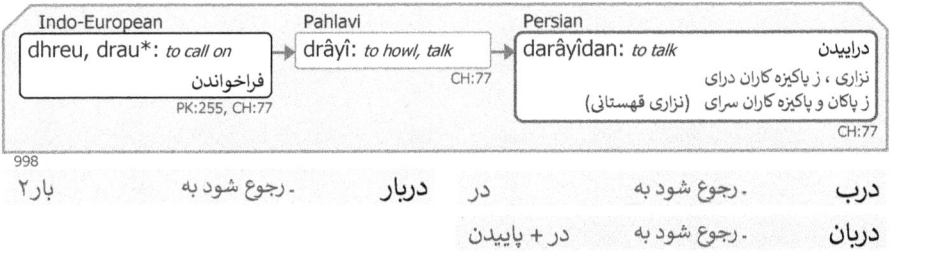

درب. رجوع شود به **در**   **دربار.** رجوع شود به **در**   بار۲

دربان. رجوع شود به در + پاییدن

دربند: "منطقه محصور"

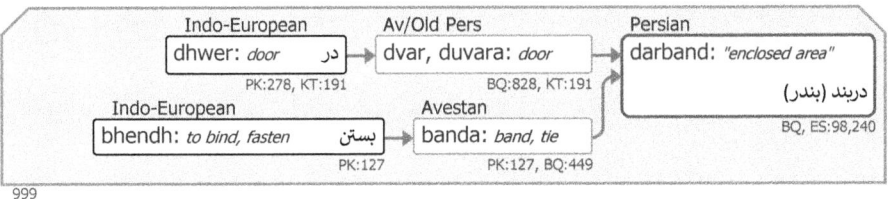

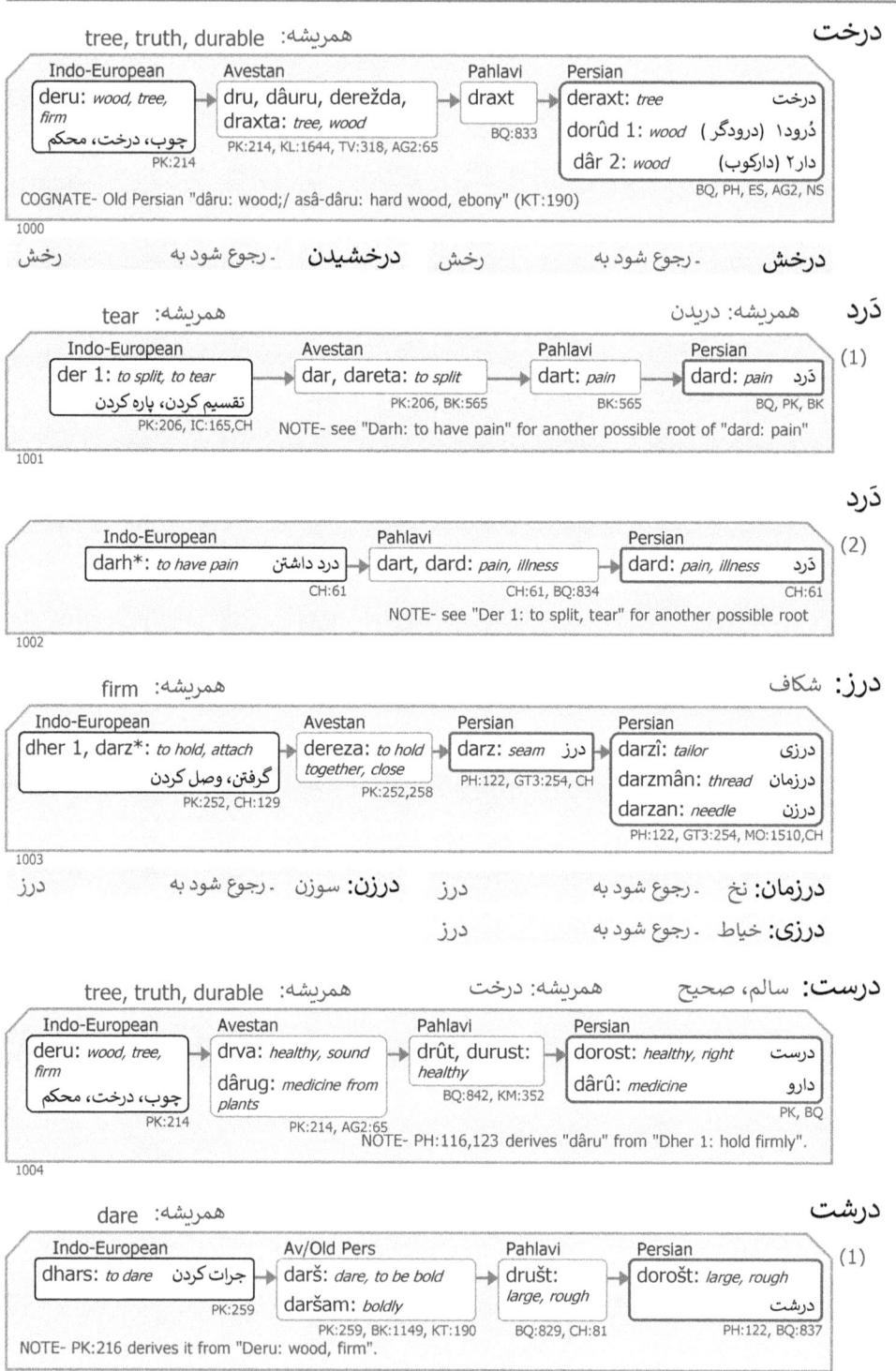

درخت

همریشه: tree, truth, durable

Indo-European	Avestan	Pahlavi	Persian
deru: *wood, tree, firm* چوب، درخت، محکم PK:214	dru, dâuru, derežda, draxta: *tree, wood* PK:214, KL:1644, TV:318, AG2:65	draxt BQ:833	deraxt: *tree* درخت dorûd 1: *wood* دُرودا (درودگر) dâr 2: *wood* ۲دار (دارکوب) BQ, PH, ES, AG2, NS

COGNATE- Old Persian "dâru: wood;/ asâ-dâru: hard wood, ebony" (KT:190)

1000

درخش . رجوع شود به   رخش   **درخشیدن** رخش . رجوع شود به   رخش

دَرد (1)   همریشه: دریدن   همریشه: tear

Indo-European	Avestan	Pahlavi	Persian
der 1: *to split, to tear* تقسیم کردن، پاره کردن PK:206, IC:165,CH	dar, dareta: *to split* PK:206, BK:565	dart: *pain* BK:565	dard: *pain* دَرد BQ, PK, BK

NOTE- see "Darh: to have pain" for another possible root of "dard: pain"

1001

دَرد (2)

Indo-European	Pahlavi	Persian
darh*: *to have pain* درد داشتن CH:61	dart, dard: *pain, illness* CH:61, BQ:834	dard: *pain, illness* دَرد CH:61

NOTE- see "Der 1: to split, tear" for another possible root

1002

درز: شکاف   همریشه: firm

Indo-European	Avestan	Persian	Persian
dher 1, darz*: *to hold, attach* گرفتن، وصل کردن PK:252, CH:129	dereza: *to hold together, close* PK:252,258	darz: *seam* درز PH:122, GT3:254, CH	darzî: *tailor* درزی darzmân: *thread* درزمان darzan: *needle* درزن PH:122, GT3:254, MO:1510,CH

1003

درزمان: نخ . رجوع شود به   درز   **درزن:** سوزن . رجوع شود به   درز

درزی: خیاط . رجوع شود به   درز

درست: سالم، صحیح   همریشه: درخت   همریشه: tree, truth, durable

Indo-European	Avestan	Pahlavi	Persian
deru: *wood, tree, firm* چوب، درخت، محکم PK:214	drva: *healthy, sound* dârug: *medicine from plants* PK:214, AG2:65	drût, durust: *healthy* BQ:842, KM:352	dorost: *healthy, right* درست dârû: *medicine* دارو PK, BQ

NOTE- PH:116,123 derives "dâru" from "Dher 1: hold firmly".

1004

درشت (1)   همریشه: dare

Indo-European	Av/Old Pers	Pahlavi	Persian
dhars: *to dare* جرات کردن PK:259	darš: *dare, to be bold* daršam: *boldly* PK:259, BK:1149, KT:190	društ: *large, rough* BQ:829, CH:81	dorošt: *large, rough* درشت PH:122, BQ:837

NOTE- PK:216 derives it from "Deru: wood, firm".

1005

179

درشت

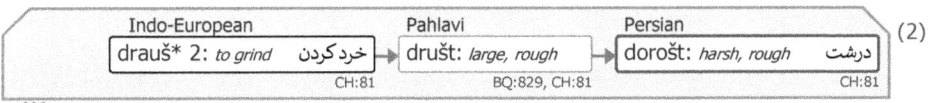

Indo-European	Pahlavi	Persian
drauš* 2: *to grind* خرد کردن	društ: *large, rough*	dorošt: *harsh, rough* درشت
CH:81	BQ:829, CH:81	CH:81

(2)

1006

درشکه

همریشه: drag

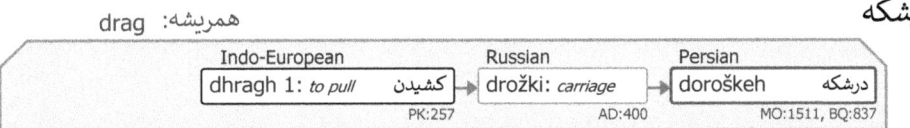

Indo-European	Russian	Persian
dhragh 1: *to pull* کشیدن	drožki: *carriage*	doroškeh درشکه
PK:257	AD:400	MO:1511, BQ:837

1007

درفش۱: پرچم

همریشه: light

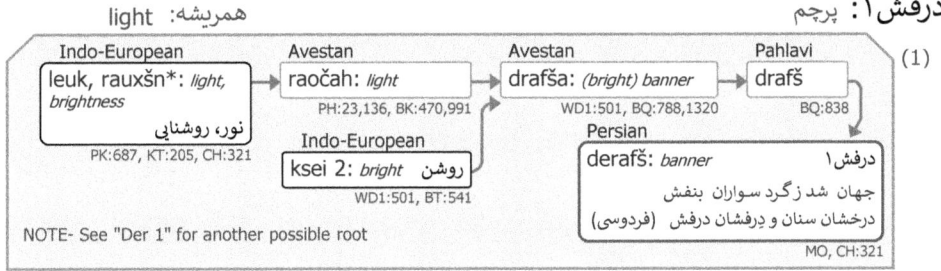

Indo-European	Avestan	Avestan	Pahlavi
leuk, rauxšn*: *light, brightness* نور، روشنایی	raočah: *light*	drafša: *(bright) banner*	drafš
PK:687, KT:205, CH:321	PH:23,136, BK:470,991	WD1:501, BQ:788,1320	BQ:838

Indo-European	Persian
ksei 2: *bright* روشن	derafš: *banner* درفش۱
WD1:501, BT:541	جهان شد زگرد سواران بنفش درخشان سنان و درفشان درفش (فردوسی)
	MO, CH:321

NOTE- See "Der 1" for another possible root

(1)

1008

درفش۱: پرچم

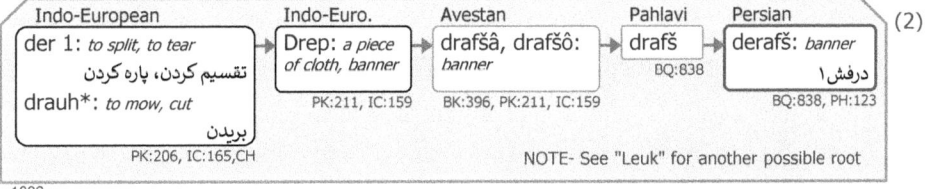

Indo-European	Indo-Euro.	Avestan	Pahlavi	Persian
der 1: *to split, to tear* تقسیم کردن، پاره کردن drauh*: *to mow, cut* بریدن	Drep: *a piece of cloth, banner*	drafšâ, drafšô: *banner*	drafš	derafš: *banner* درفش۱
PK:206, IC:165,CH	PK:211, IC:159	BK:396, PK:211, IC:159	BQ:838	BQ:838, PH:123

NOTE- See "Leuk" for another possible root

(2)

1009

درفش۲: وسیله سوراخ کردن

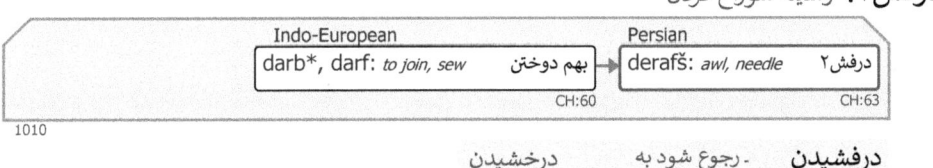

Indo-European	Persian
darb*, darf: *to join, sew* بهم دوختن	derafš: *awl, needle* درفش۲
CH:60	CH:63

1010

درفشیدن   - رجوع شود به   درخشیدن

دِرَم

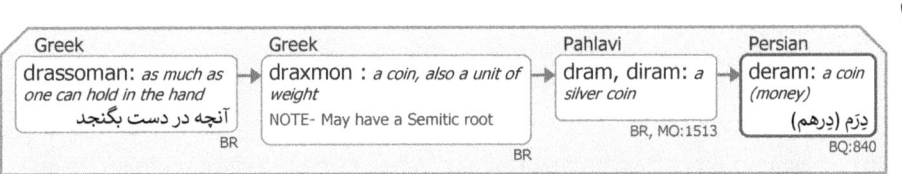

Greek	Greek	Pahlavi	Persian
drassoman: *as much as one can hold in the hand* آنچه در دست بگنجد	draxmon: *a coin, also a unit of weight* NOTE- May have a Semitic root	dram, diram: *a silver coin*	deram: *a coin (money)* دِرَم (درهم)
BR	BR	BR, MO:1513	BQ:840

1011

درمان

همریشه: firm, affirm

Indo-European	Av/Old Pers	Pahlavi	Persian
dher 1, darz*: *to hold, attach* گرفتن، وصل کردن PK:252, CH:129	dâr, dr: *to hold* PK:252	dârûk: *medication* durmân: *treatment* BQ:813,840	dâru: *medication* دارو darmân: *treatment* درمان BQ:840, PH:116,123

NOTE- AG2:65 derives these words from "Deru: wood (also firm and healthy)".

1012

درنگ

همریشه: long, linger   همریشه: دیر

Indo-Euro.	Avestan	Pahlavi	Persian
del: *long* دراز، طولانی PK:197, KT:190	daraga, darağa, drâjah: *long* drang: *hesitation* PK:197, BQ:829, TV:324	Dirang: *hesitation* BQ:841	derang: *length of time, hesitation* درنگ PK, BQ, TV

1013

دِرو

Indo-European	Avestan	Persian
der 1: *to split, to tear* تقسیم کردن، پاره کردن drauh*: *to mow, cut* بریدن PK:206, IC:165,CH	dereta: *cuts, harvests* deretô: *cut, mown* PK:208	dero: *harvest* دِرو dorûdan: *to harvest* دُرودن PK:208, PH:124

1014

درواخ: نقاهت

همریشه: tree, truth, durable   همریشه: سلامت

Indo-European	Avestan	Persian
deru: *wood, tree, firm* چوب، درخت، محکم PK:214	drva: *healthy, sound* dârug: *medicine from plants* PK:214, AG2:65	darvâx: *recovery from sickness* درواخ کرده خصمان بر او جهان فراخ تنگ تر از درون گه درواخ (سنایی) JS1:228

COGNATE- Old Persian "dorova: recovery" (JS1:228)

1015

دُرود۱ · رجوع شود به   درخت

دُرود۲: "سلامتی"

همریشه: tree, true, durable   همریشه: درخت

Indo-European	Avestan	Pahlavi	Persian
deru: *wood, tree, firm* چوب، درخت، محکم PK:214	drva: *healthy, sound* dârug: *medicine from plants* PK:214, AG2:65	drût, durust: *healthy* pa-drût: *to health* BQ:842, KM:352	dorûd 2: *greetings* دُرود۲ pedrûd: *greetings* پدرود (بدرود) PK, BQ
Indo-European	Avestan	Pahlavi	
per 3: *oppose, hit* مقابل PK:815-818	paiti 2: *oppose* PK:815	pad, pa: *to, toward* PH:33, KM:190	

1016

دُرودگر · رجوع شود به   درخت   دُرودن · رجوع شود به   دِرو

دِروش: داغ و مُهر

Indo-European	Avestan	Pahlavi	Persian
drauš* 1: *to make a mark, brand* مُهر و داغ کردن CH:80	drauša: *to mark, brand* CH:80	drôš: *to brand* CH:80	dirôš: *to mark, brand* دِروش به موسمی که ستوران دروش و داغ کنند ستوروار بر اعدا نهاده داغ و دروش (سوزنی) CH:80

1017

دروغ

همریشه: dream

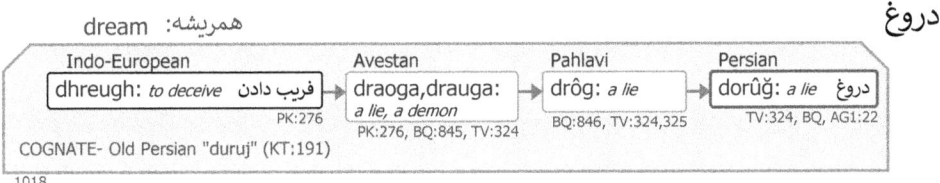

Indo-European	Avestan	Pahlavi	Persian
dhreugh: *to deceive* فریب دادن PK:276	draoga,drauga: *a lie, a demon* PK:276, BQ:845, TV:324	drôg: *a lie* BQ:846, TV:324,325	dorûĝ: *a lie* دروغ TV:324, BQ, AG1:22

COGNATE- Old Persian "duruj" (KT:191)

1018

درون: دعای زرتشتیان

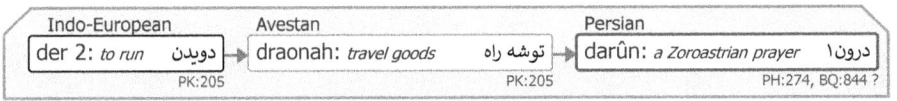

Indo-European	Avestan	Persian
der 2: *to run* دویدن PK:205	draonah: *travel goods* توشه راه PK:205	darûn: *a Zoroastrian prayer* درون۱ PH:274, BQ:844 ?

1019

دُرَوَند: خدا نشناس   همریشه: دروغ   همریشه: dream

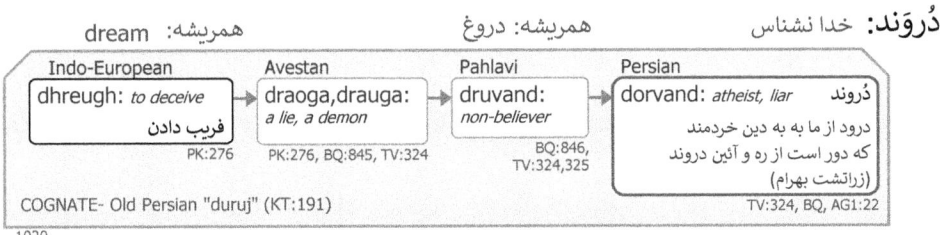

Indo-European	Avestan	Pahlavi	Persian
dhreugh: *to deceive* فریب دادن PK:276	draoga,drauga: *a lie, a demon* PK:276, BQ:845, TV:324	druvand: *non-believer* BQ:846, TV:324,325	dorvand: *atheist, liar* دُرَوَند درود از ما به به دین خردمند که دور است از ره و آئین دروند (زراتشت بهرام) TV:324, BQ, AG1:22

COGNATE- Old Persian "duruj" (KT:191)

1020

درونه: کمان

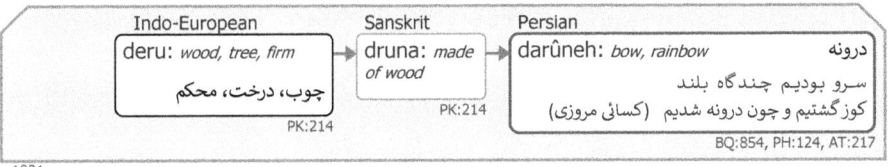

Indo-European	Sanskrit	Persian
deru: *wood, tree, firm* چوب، درخت، محکم PK:214	druna: *made of wood* PK:214	darûneh: *bow, rainbow* درونه سرو بودیم چندگاه بلند کوز گشتیم و چون درونه شدیم (کسائی مروزی) BQ:854, PH:124, AT:217

1021

درویش

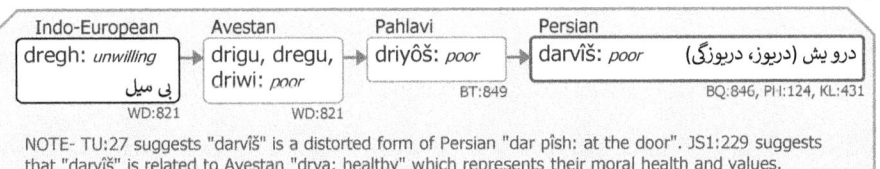

Indo-European	Avestan	Pahlavi	Persian
dregh: *unwilling* بی میل WD:821	drigu, dregu, driwi: *poor* WD:821	driyôš: *poor* BT:849	darvîš: *poor* درویش (دریوز، دریوزگی) BQ:846, PH:124, KL:431

NOTE- TU:27 suggests "darvîš" is a distorted form of Persian "dar pîsh: at the door". JS1:229 suggests that "darvîš" is related to Avestan "drva: healthy" which represents their moral health and values.

1022

دَرّه   همریشه: tear

Indo-European	Avestan	Persian
der 1: *to split, to tear* تقسیم کردن، پاره کردن drauh*: *to mow, cut* بریدن PK:206, IC:165,CH	darêna: *a cut in earth, ravine* PK:206	darreh: *valley* دَرّه BQ:845, HM:62, PH:124

1023

دِرهم   . رجوع شود به   دِرَم

دریا   همریشه: زراه

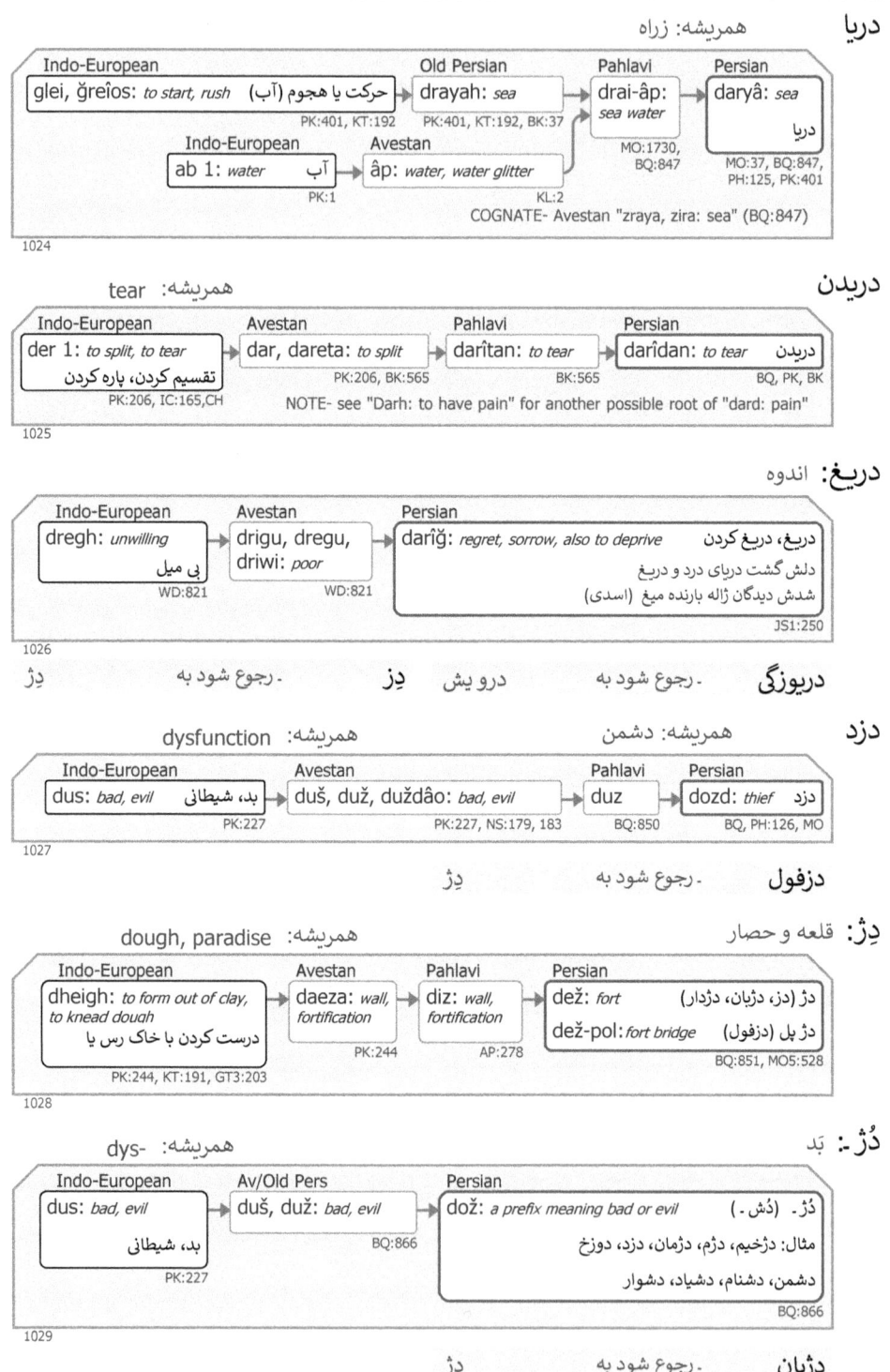

دریا

Indo-European
glei, ǧreîos: to start, rush   حرکت یا هجوم (آب)
PK:401, KT:192

Old Persian
drayah: sea
PK:401, KT:192, BK:37

Pahlavi
drai-âp:
sea water
MO:1730,
BQ:847

Persian
daryâ: sea
دریا
MO:37, BQ:847,
PH:125, PK:401

Indo-European
ab 1: water   آب
PK:1

Avestan
âp: water, water glitter
KL:2

COGNATE- Avestan "zraya, zira: sea" (BQ:847)

1024

دریدن   همریشه: tear

Indo-European
der 1: to split, to tear
تقسیم کردن، پاره کردن
PK:206, IC:165,CH

Avestan
dar, dareta: to split
PK:206, BK:565

Pahlavi
darîtan: to tear
BK:565

Persian
darîdan: to tear   دریدن
BQ, PK, BK

NOTE- see "Darh: to have pain" for another possible root of "dard: pain"

1025

دریغ: اندوه

Indo-European
dregh: unwilling
بی میل
WD:821

Avestan
drigu, dregu,
driwi: poor
WD:821

Persian
darîĝ: regret, sorrow, also to deprive   دریغ، دریغ کردن
دلش گشت دریای درد و دریغ
شدش دیدگان ژاله بارنده میغ   (اسدی)
JS1:250

1026

دریوزگی . رجوع شود به   دِز   درویش   دِژ

دزد   همریشه: دشمن   همریشه: dysfunction

Indo-European
dus: bad, evil   بد، شیطانی
PK:227

Avestan
duš, duž, duždâo: bad, evil
PK:227, NS:179, 183

Pahlavi
duz
BQ:850

Persian
dozd: thief   دزد
BQ, PH:126, MO

1027

دزفول . رجوع شود به   دِژ

دِژ: قلعه و حصار   همریشه: dough, paradise

Indo-European
dheigh: to form out of clay,
to knead dough
درست کردن با خاک رس یا
PK:244, KT:191, GT3:203

Avestan
daeza: wall,
fortification
PK:244

Pahlavi
diz: wall,
fortification
AP:278

Persian
dež: fort
dež-pol: fort bridge
دژ (دز، دژبان، دژدار)
دژ پل (دزفول)
BQ:851, MO5:528

1028

دُژ ـِ: بَد   همریشه: -dys

Indo-European
dus: bad, evil
بد، شیطانی
PK:227

Av/Old Pers
duš, duž: bad, evil
BQ:866

Persian
دُژ ـ (دُش ـ)   :dož: a prefix meaning bad or evil
مثال: دژخیم، دژم، دژمان، دزد، دوزخ
دشمن، دشنام، دشیاد، دشوار
BQ:866

1029

دژبان . رجوع شود به   دِژ

دُژپیه: غده ای بزرگ که زیر پوست برآید

همریشه: dys-, fat

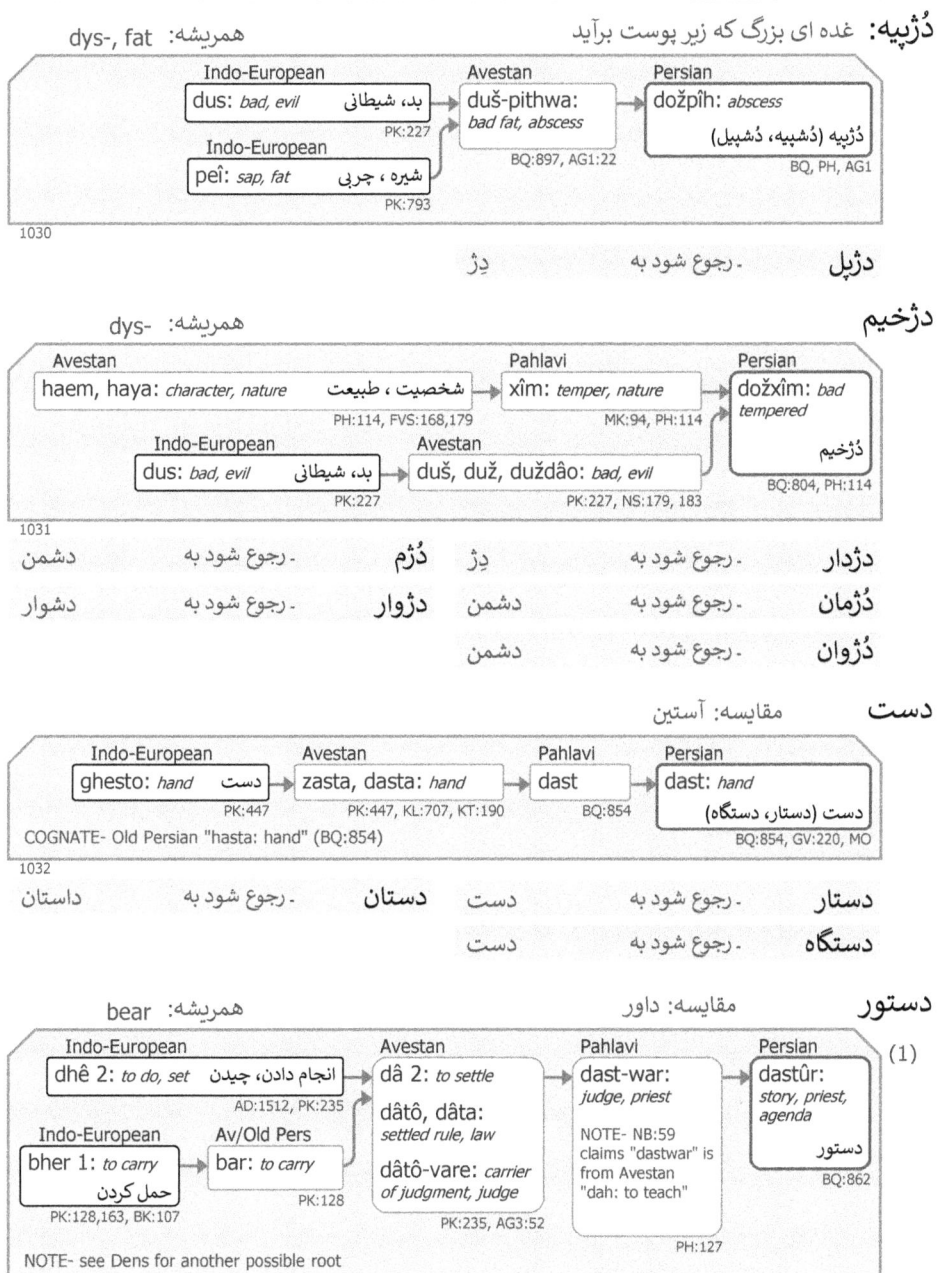

Indo-European
dus: *bad, evil* — بد، شیطانی
PK:227

Indo-European
peî: *sap, fat* — شیره ، چربی
PK:793

Avestan
duš-pithwa: *bad fat, abscess*
BQ:897, AG1:22

Persian
dožpîh: *abscess*
دُژپیه (دُشپیه، دُشپیل)
BQ, PH, AG1

1030

دژپل - رجوع شود به دِژ

دژخیم

همریشه: -dys

Avestan
haem, haya: *character, nature* — شخصیت ، طبیعت
PH:114, FVS:168,179

Pahlavi
xîm: *temper, nature* — xim
MK:94, PH:114

Persian
dožxîm: *bad tempered*
دُژخیم
BQ:804, PH:114

Indo-European
dus: *bad, evil* — بد، شیطانی
PK:227

Avestan
duš, duž, duždâo: *bad, evil*
PK:227, NS:179, 183

1031

دژدار	- رجوع شود به دِژ	دُژم	- رجوع شود به دشمن	دشمن
دُژمان	- رجوع شود به دشمن	دژوار	- رجوع شود به دشوار
دُژوان	- رجوع شود به دشمن		

دست

مقایسه: آستین

Indo-European
ghesto: *hand* — دست
PK:447

Avestan
zasta, dasta: *hand*
PK:447, KL:707, KT:190

Pahlavi
dast
BQ:854

Persian
dast: *hand*
دست (دستار، دستگاه)
BQ:854, GV:220, MO

COGNATE- Old Persian "hasta: hand" (BQ:854)

1032

| دستار | - رجوع شود به دست | دستان | - رجوع شود به دست | داستان |
| دستگاه | - رجوع شود به دست | | |

دستور (1)

مقایسه: داور   همریشه: bear

Indo-European
dhê 2: *to do, set* — انجام دادن، چیدن
AD:1512, PK:235

Indo-European
bher 1: *to carry* — حمل کردن
PK:128,163, BK:107

Av/Old Pers
bar: *to carry*
PK:128

Avestan
dâ 2: *to settle*
dâtô, dâta: *settled rule, law*
dâtô-vare: *carrier of judgment, judge*
PK:235, AG3:52

Pahlavi
dast-war: *judge, priest*
NOTE- NB:59 claims "dastwar" is from Avestan "dah: to teach"
PH:127

Persian
dastûr: *story, priest, agenda*
دستور
BQ:862

NOTE- see Dens for another possible root

1033

دستور

(2)

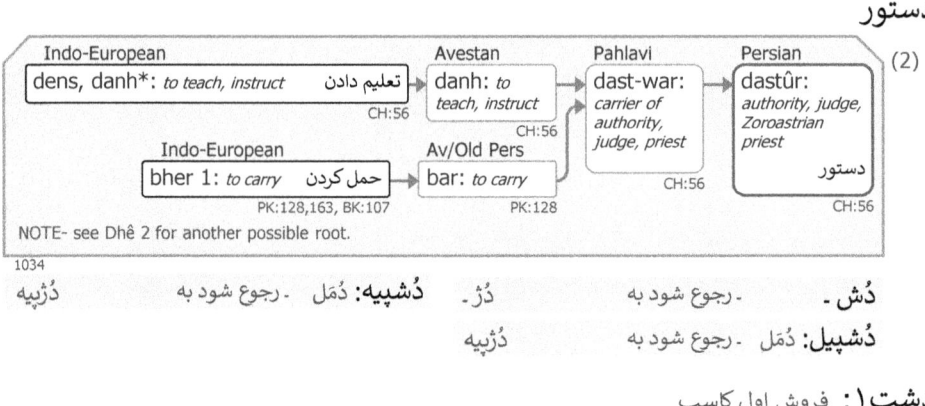

1034

دُش ـ ‌. رجوع شود به　ـ دُژ‌ ـ‌　دُشپیه: دُمَل　دُژپیه

دُشپیل: دُمَل ‌. رجوع شود به　دُژپیه

دشت۱: فروش اول کاسب

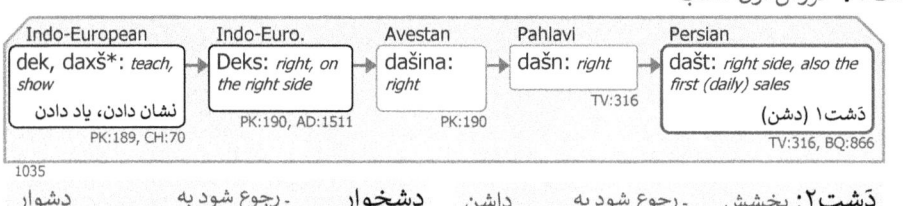

1035

دَشت۲: بخشش　ـ رجوع شود به　داشن　دشخوار　ـ رجوع شود به　دشوار

دشمن

همریشه: dys-, mind

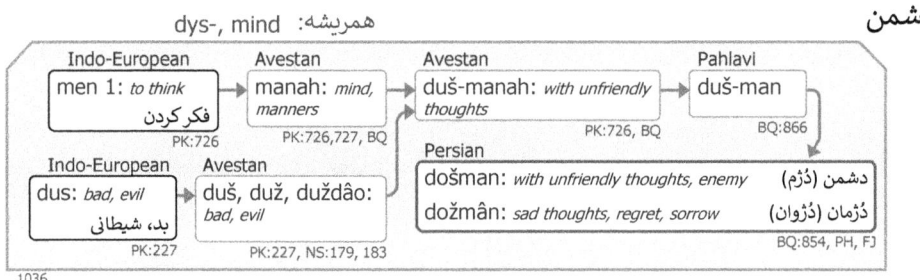

1036

دَشن: فروش اول　ـ رجوع شود به　دشت۱

دشنام

همریشه: dys-, name

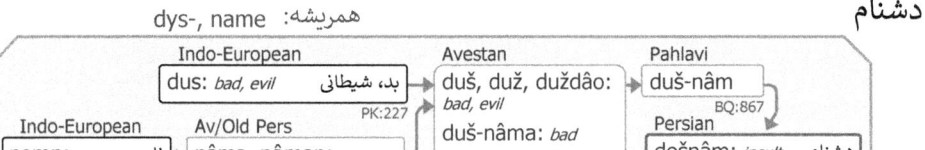

1037

دشوار: "بارِبَد" همریشه: دژم و بار　همریشه: dys-, bear

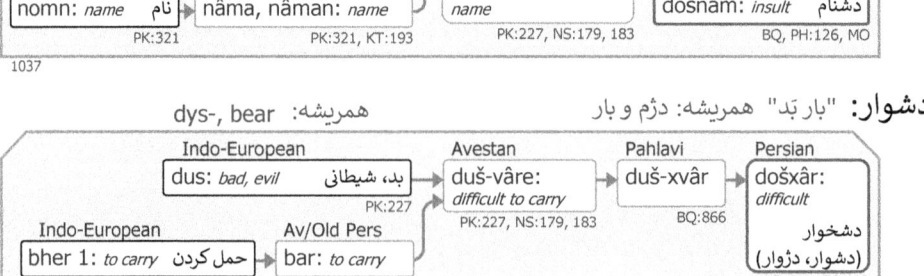

1038

185

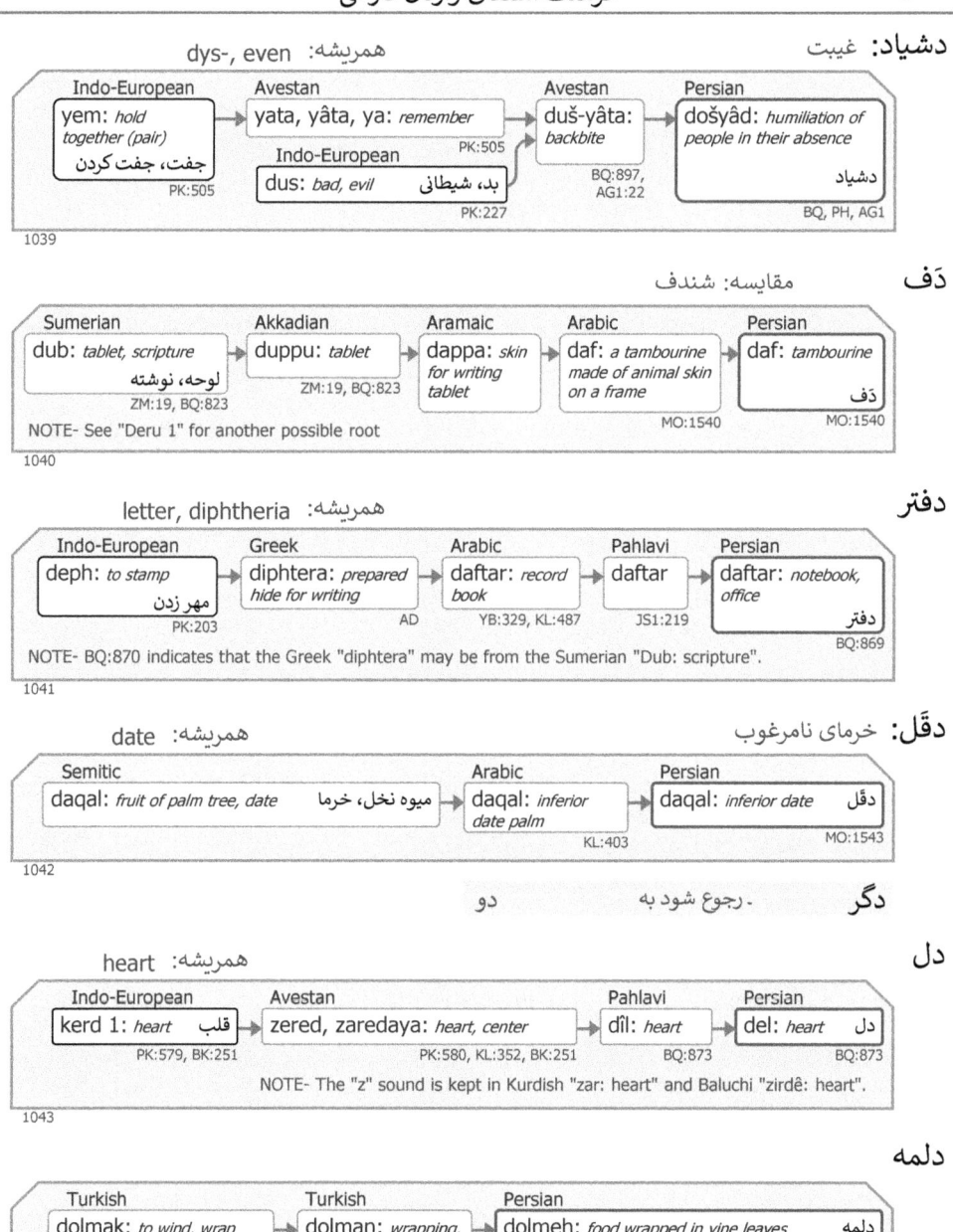

دشیاد: غیبت

همریشه: dys-, even

Indo-European	Avestan	Avestan	Persian
yem: *hold together (pair)* جفت، جفت کردن PK:505	yata, yâta, ya: *remember* PK:505	duš-yâta: *backbite* BQ:897, AG1:22	došyâd: *humiliation of people in their absence* دشیاد BQ, PH, AG1
	Indo-European dus: *bad, evil* بد، شیطانی PK:227		

1039

دَف

مقایسه: شندف

Sumerian	Akkadian	Aramaic	Arabic	Persian
dub: *tablet, scripture* لوحه، نوشته ZM:19, BQ:823	duppu: *tablet* ZM:19, BQ:823	dappa: *skin for writing tablet*	daf: *a tambourine made of animal skin on a frame* MO:1540	daf: *tambourine* دَف MO:1540

NOTE- See "Deru 1" for another possible root

1040

دفتر

همریشه: letter, diphtheria

Indo-European	Greek	Arabic	Pahlavi	Persian
deph: *to stamp* مهر زدن PK:203	diphtera: *prepared hide for writing* AD	daftar: *record book* YB:329, KL:487	daftar JS1:219	daftar: *notebook, office* دفتر BQ:869

NOTE- BQ:870 indicates that the Greek "diphtera" may be from the Sumerian "Dub: scripture".

1041

دقَل: خرمای نامرغوب

همریشه: date

Semitic	Arabic	Persian
daqal: *fruit of palm tree, date* میوه نخل، خرما	daqal: *inferior date palm* KL:403	daqal: *inferior date* دقَل MO:1543

1042

دگر   رجوع شود به . دو

دل

همریشه: heart

Indo-European	Avestan	Pahlavi	Persian
kerd 1: *heart* قلب PK:579, BK:251	zered, zaredaya: *heart, center* PK:580, KL:352, BK:251	dîl: *heart* BQ:873	del: *heart* دل BQ:873

NOTE- The "z" sound is kept in Kurdish "zar: heart" and Baluchi "zirdê: heart".

1043

دلمه

Turkish	Turkish	Persian
dolmak: *to wind, wrap* پیچیدن AD:389	dolman: *wrapping, cover, coating* AD:389	dolmeh: *food wrapped in vine leaves* دلمه MO:1554

1044

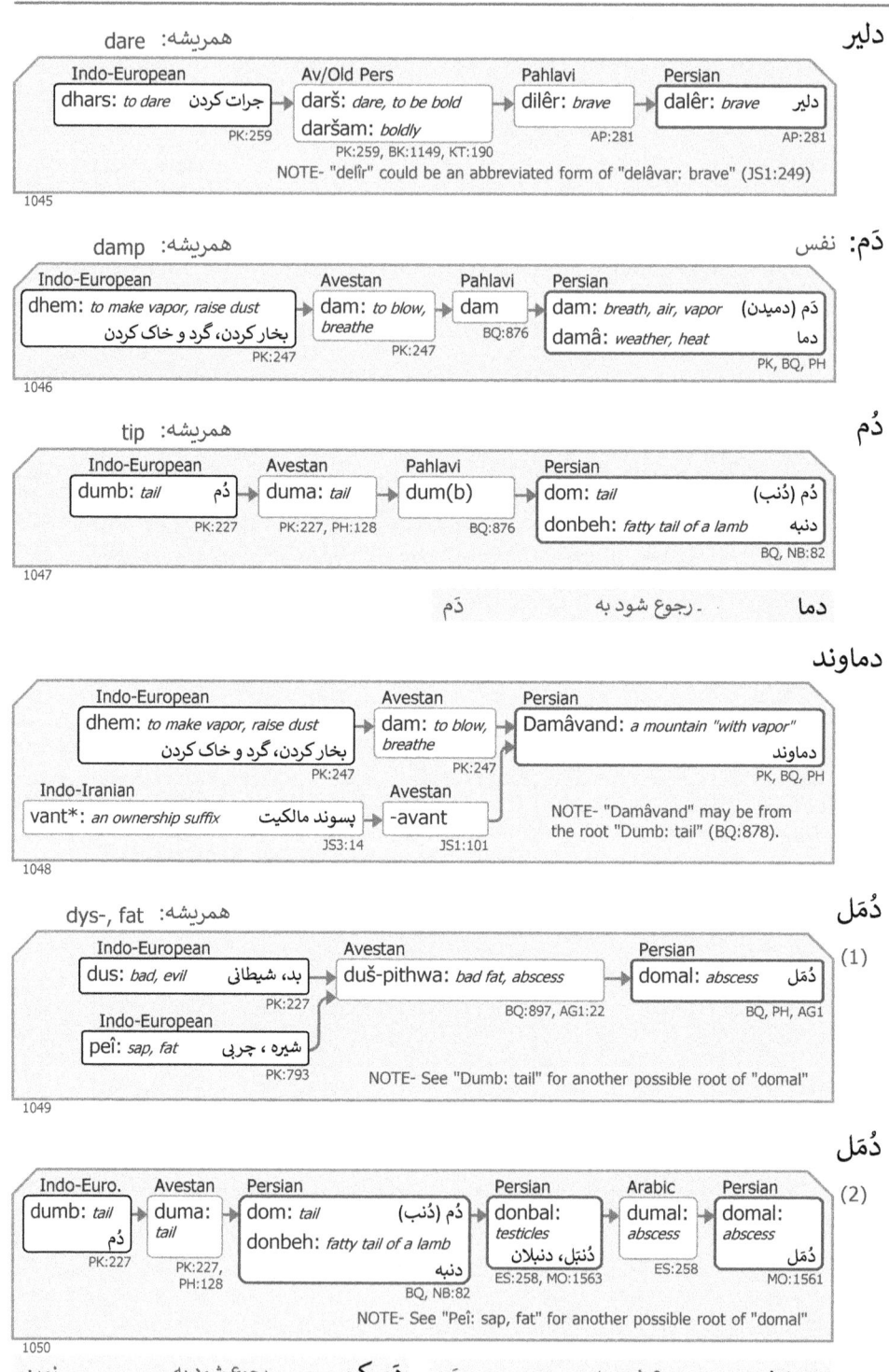

دلیر

همریشه: dare

Indo-European
dhars: to dare — جرات کردن
PK:259

Av/Old Pers
darš: dare, to be bold
daršam: boldly
PK:259, BK:1149, KT:190

Pahlavi
dilêr: brave
AP:281

Persian
dalêr: brave — دلیر
AP:281

NOTE- "delîr" could be an abbreviated form of "delâvar: brave" (JS1:249)

1045

دَم: نفس

همریشه: damp

Indo-European
dhem: to make vapor, raise dust
بخار کردن، گرد و خاک کردن
PK:247

Avestan
dam: to blow, breathe
PK:247

Pahlavi
dam
BQ:876

Persian
dam: breath, air, vapor — (دمیدن) دَم
damâ: weather, heat — دما
PK, BQ, PH

1046

دُم

همریشه: tip

Indo-European
dumb: tail — دُم
PK:227

Avestan
duma: tail
PK:227, PH:128

Pahlavi
dum(b)
BQ:876

Persian
dom: tail — (دُنب) دُم
donbeh: fatty tail of a lamb — دنبه
BQ, NB:82

1047

دما

. رجوع شود به دَم

دماوند

Indo-European
dhem: to make vapor, raise dust
بخار کردن، گرد و خاک کردن
PK:247

Avestan
dam: to blow, breathe
PK:247

Persian
Damâvand: a mountain "with vapor"
دماوند
PK, BQ, PH

Indo-Iranian
vant*: an ownership suffix — پسوند مالکیت
JS3:14

Avestan
-avant
JS1:101

NOTE- "Damâvand" may be from the root "Dumb: tail" (BQ:878).

1048

دُمَل (1)

همریشه: dys-, fat

Indo-European
dus: bad, evil — بد، شیطانی
PK:227

Indo-European
peî: sap, fat — شیره ، چربی
PK:793

Avestan
duš-pithwa: bad fat, abscess
BQ:897, AG1:22

Persian
domal: abscess — دُمَل
BQ, PH, AG1

NOTE- See "Dumb: tail" for another possible root of "domal"

1049

دُمَل (2)

Indo-Euro.
dumb: tail — دُم
PK:227

Avestan
duma: tail
PK:227, PH:128

Persian
dom: tail — (دُنب) دُم
donbeh: fatty tail of a lamb — دنبه
BQ, NB:82

Persian
donbal: testicles — دُنتِل، دنبلان
ES:258, MO:1563

Arabic
dumal: abscess
ES:258

Persian
domal: abscess — دُمَل
MO:1561

NOTE- See "Peî: sap, fat" for another possible root of "domal"

1050

دمیدن

. رجوع شود به دَم   دَمیک   . رجوع شود به زمین

دَن: فریاد شادی

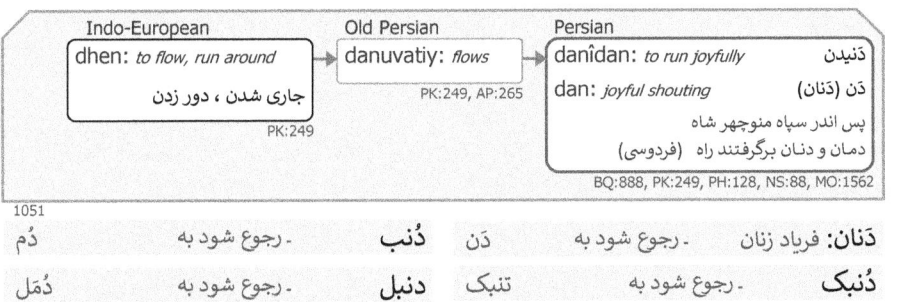

1051

دُم		دُنب	دَن		دَنان: فریاد زنان
ـ رجوع شود به			ـ رجوع شود به		
دُمَل	ـ رجوع شود به	دنبل	تنبک	ـ رجوع شود به	دُنبک

دنبلان

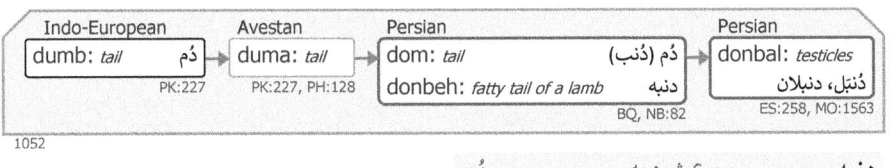

1052

دُم	ـ رجوع شود به		**دنبه**

دندان

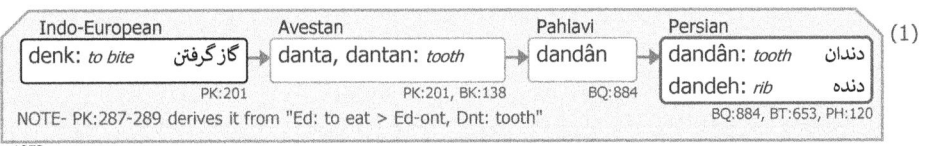

1053

دندان

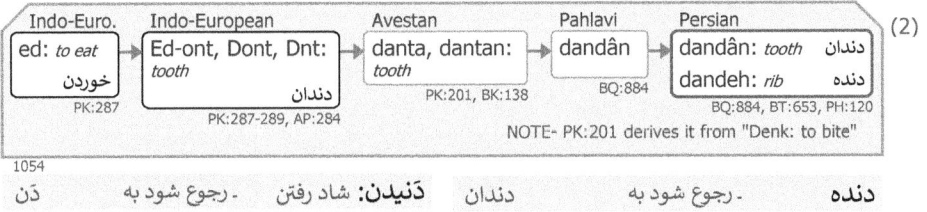

1054

دَن	ـ رجوع شود به شاد رفتن	**دَنیدن:**	دندان	ـ رجوع شود به	**دنده**

دو

همریشه: two

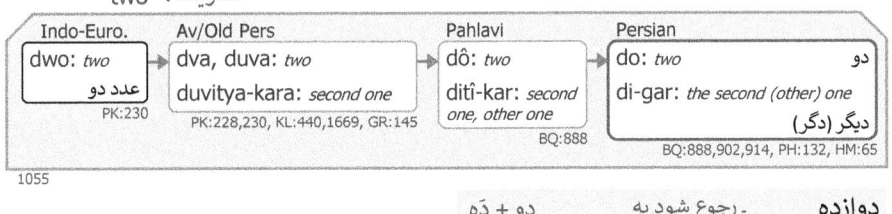

1055

دو و دَه	ـ رجوع شود به		**دوازده**

دوجین: "دو بالای ده"

همریشه: dozen

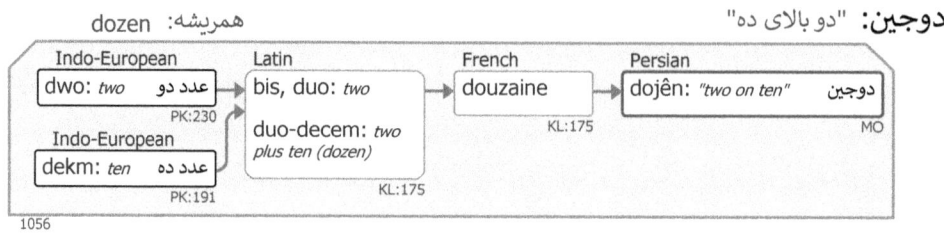

1056

دوختن۱

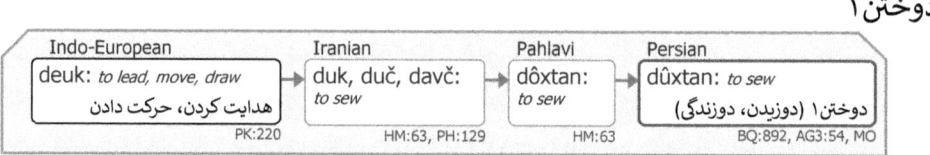

1057

دوختن۲: دوشیدن

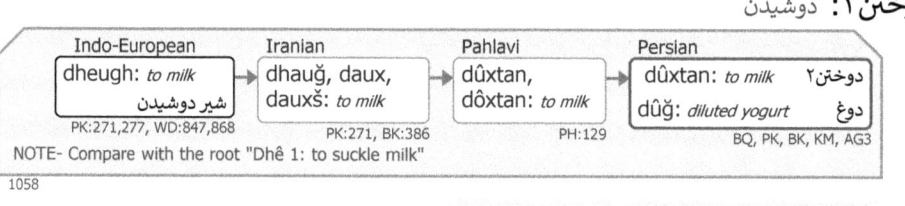

1058

دوختن۳ ـ رجوع شود به   اندوختن

دود

همریشه: fume

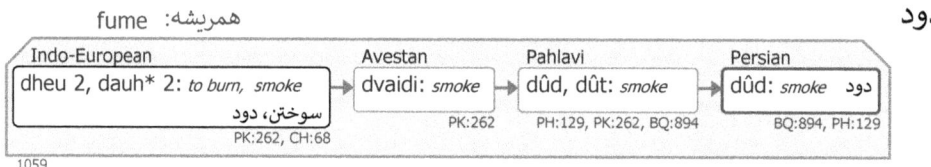

1059

دودمان: "جمع دور آتش در خانه"

همریشه: domestic, madam

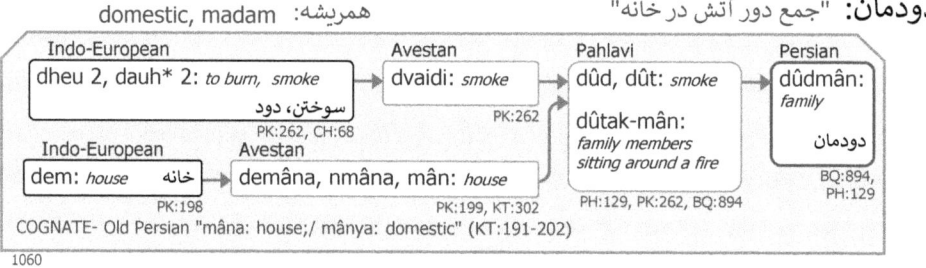

1060

دور۱: با فاصله

همریشه: endure, during

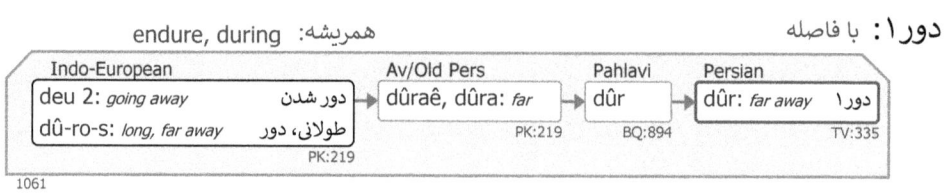

1061

189

دور۲: پیرامون   همریشه: دیار

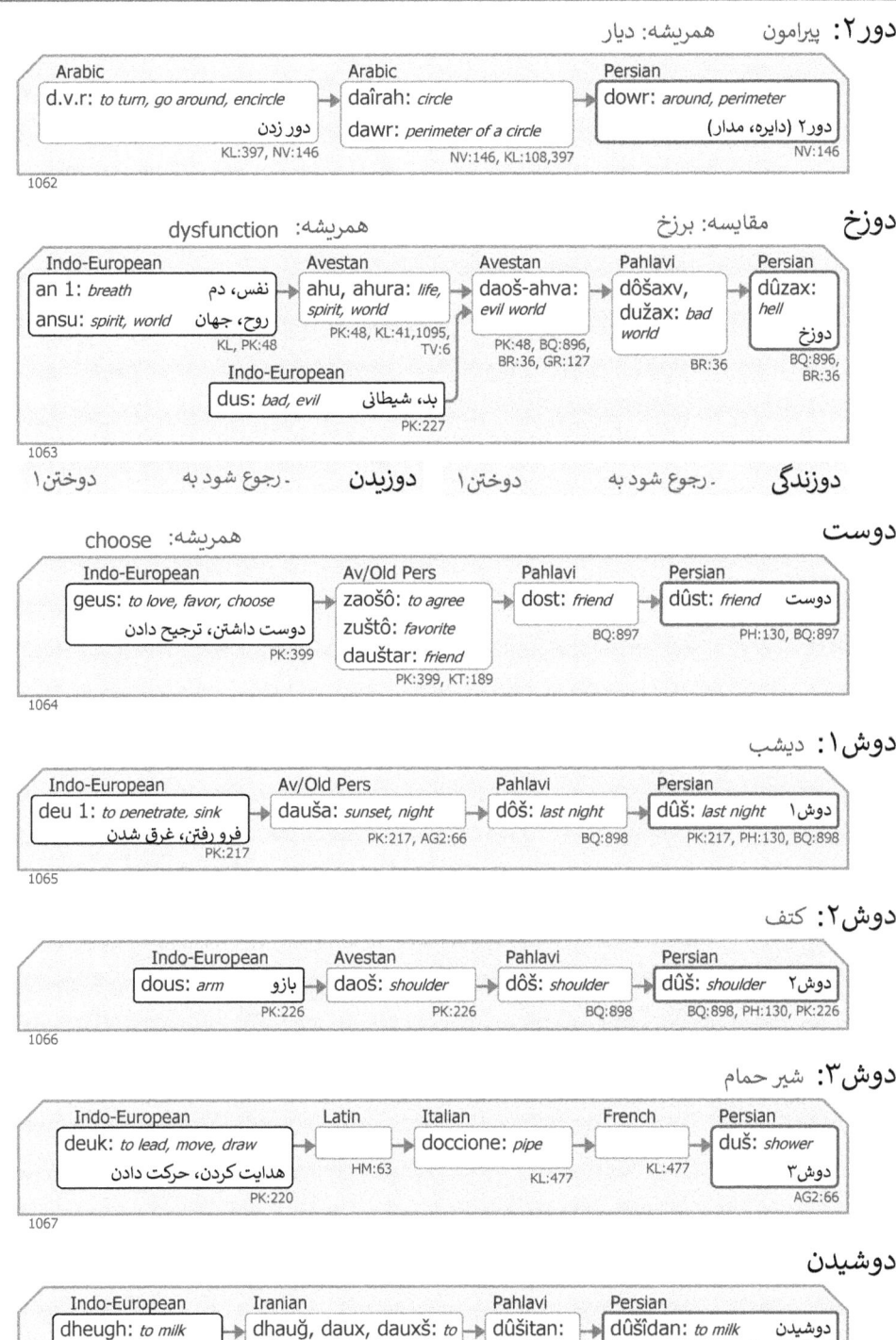

دوزخ   مقایسه: برزخ   همریشه: dysfunction

دوزندگی _. رجوع شود به دوختن۱_   **دوزیدن** دوختن۱ . رجوع شود به   دوختن۱

دوست   همریشه: choose

دوش۱: دیشب

دوش۲: کتف

دوش۳: شیر حمام

دوشیدن

190

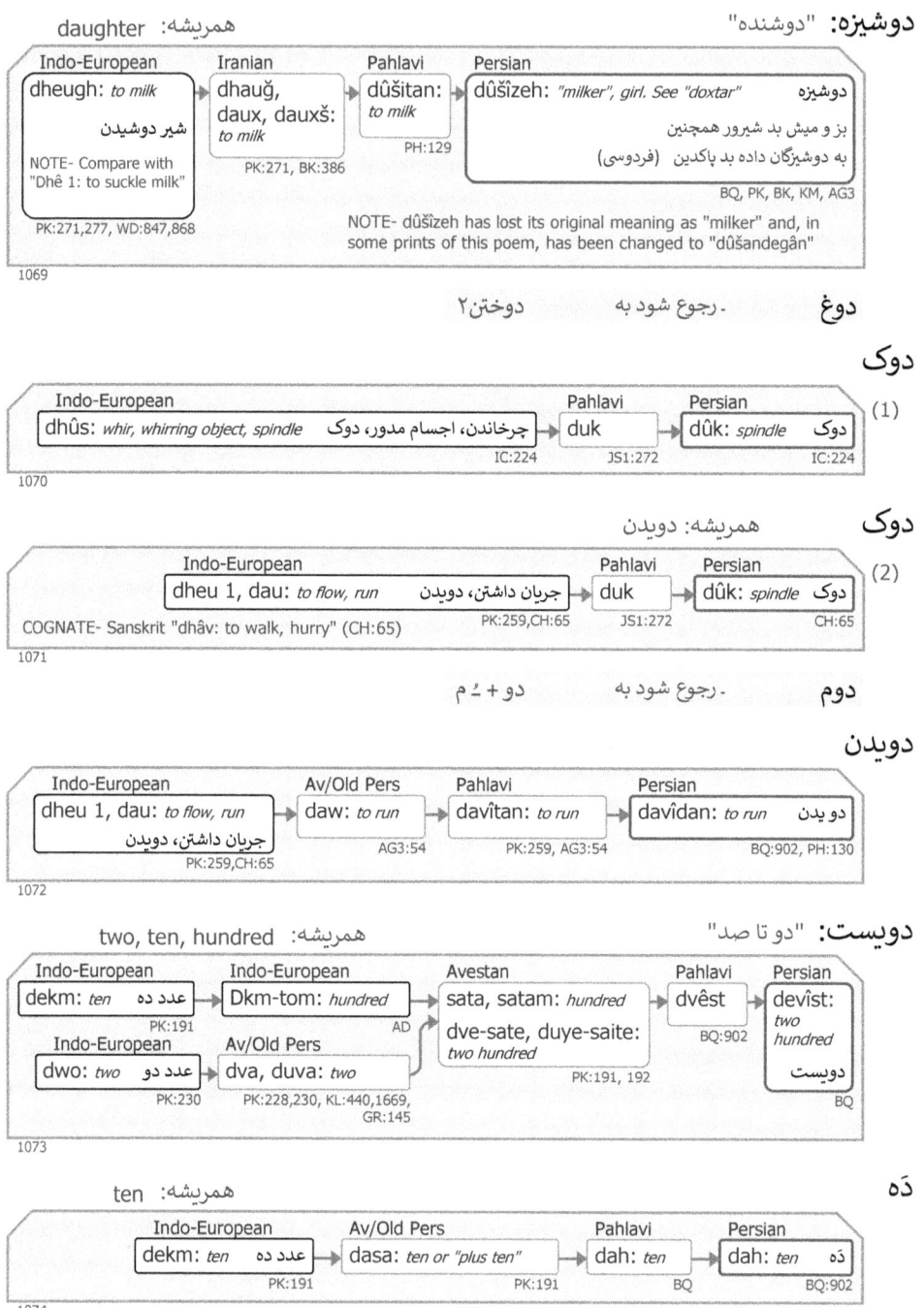

دوشیزه: "دوشنده"

همریشه: daughter

Indo-European
dheugh: *to milk*

شیر دوشیدن

NOTE- Compare with
"Dhê 1: to suckle milk"

PK:271,277, WD:847,868

Iranian
dhauǧ,
daux, dauxš:
to milk

PK:271, BK:386

Pahlavi
dûšitan:
to milk

PH:129

Persian
dûšîzeh: *"milker", girl. See "doxtar"*   دوشیزه

بز و میش بد شیرور همچنین
به دوشیزگان داده بد پاکدین (فردوسی)

BQ, PK, BK, KM, AG3

NOTE- dûšîzeh has lost its original meaning as "milker" and, in
some prints of this poem, has been changed to "dûšandegân"

1069

دوغ   . رجوع شود به   دوختن۲

دوک

(1)

Indo-European
dhûs: *whir, whirring object, spindle*   چرخاندن، اجسام مدور، دوک

IC:224

Pahlavi
duk

JS1:272

Persian
dûk: *spindle*   دوک

IC:224

1070

دوک

همریشه: دویدن

(2)

Indo-European
dheu 1, dau: *to flow, run*   جریان داشتن، دویدن

COGNATE- Sanskrit "dhâv: to walk, hurry" (CH:65)

PK:259,CH:65

Pahlavi
duk

JS1:272

Persian
dûk: *spindle*   دوک

CH:65

1071

دوم   . رجوع شود به   دو + ـُ م

دویدن

Indo-European
dheu 1, dau: *to flow, run*

جریان داشتن، دویدن

PK:259,CH:65

Av/Old Pers
daw: *to run*

AG3:54

Pahlavi
davîtan: *to run*

PK:259, AG3:54

Persian
davîdan: *to run*   دویدن

BQ:902, PH:130

1072

دویست: "دو تا صد"

همریشه: two, ten, hundred

Indo-European
dekm: *ten*   عدد ده

PK:191

Indo-European
Dkm-tom: *hundred*

AD

Indo-European
dwo: *two*   عدد دو

PK:230

Av/Old Pers
dva, duva: *two*

PK:228,230, KL:440,1669,
GR:145

Avestan
sata, satam: *hundred*

dve-sate, duye-saite:
two hundred

PK:191, 192

Pahlavi
dvêst

BQ:902

Persian
devîst:
*two
hundred*

دویست

BQ

1073

دَه   همریشه: ten

Indo-European
dekm: *ten*   عدد ده

PK:191

Av/Old Pers
dasa: *ten or "plus ten"*

PK:191

Pahlavi
dah: *ten*

BQ

Persian
dah: *ten*   دَه

BQ:902

1074

دِه

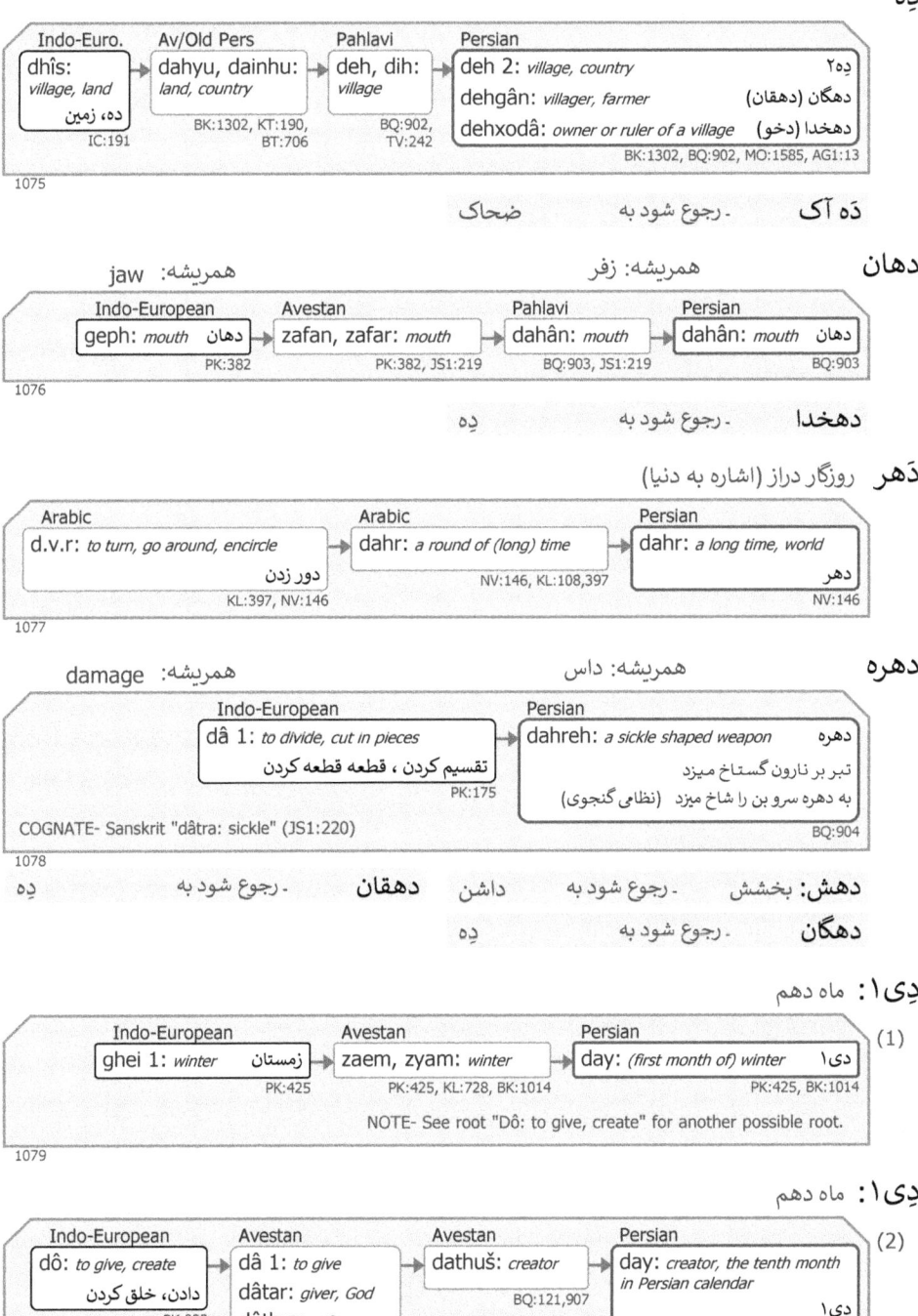

دِه

Indo-Euro.	Av/Old Pers	Pahlavi	Persian
dhîs: *village, land* ده، زمین IC:191	**dahyu, dainhu:** *land, country* BK:1302, KT:190, BT:706	**deh, dih:** *village* BQ:902, TV:242	**deh 2:** *village, country* دِه٢ دهگان (دهقان) **dehgân:** *villager, farmer* دهخدا (دخو) **dehxodâ:** *owner or ruler of a village* BK:1302, BQ:902, MO:1585, AG1:13

1075

دَه آک ۔ رجوع شود به ضحاک

دهان همریشه: زفر همریشه: jaw

Indo-European	Avestan	Pahlavi	Persian
geph: *mouth* دهان PK:382	**zafan, zafar:** *mouth* PK:382, JS1:219	**dahân:** *mouth* BQ:903, JS1:219	**dahân:** *mouth* دهان BQ:903

1076

دهخدا ۔ رجوع شود به دِه

دَهر روزگار دراز (اشاره به دنیا)

Arabic	Arabic	Persian
d.v.r: *to turn, go around, encircle* دور زدن KL:397, NV:146	**dahr:** *a round of (long) time* NV:146, KL:108,397	**dahr:** *a long time, world* دهر NV:146

1077

دهره همریشه: داس همریشه: damage

Indo-European	Persian
dâ 1: *to divide, cut in pieces* تقسیم کردن ، قطعه قطعه کردن PK:175	**dahreh:** *a sickle shaped weapon* دهره تبر بر نارون گستاخ میزد به دهره سرو بن را شاخ میزد (نظامی گنجوی) BQ:904

COGNATE- Sanskrit "dâtra: sickle" (JS1:220)

1078

دهش: بخشش ۔ رجوع شود به داشن **دهقان** ۔ رجوع شود به دِه

دهگان ۔ رجوع شود به دِه

دِی١: ماه دهم

Indo-European	Avestan	Persian	
ghei 1: *winter* زمستان PK:425	**zaem, zyam:** *winter* PK:425, KL:728, BK:1014	**day:** *(first month of) winter* دِی١ PK:425, BK:1014	(1)

NOTE- See root "Dô: to give, create" for another possible root.

1079

دِی١: ماه دهم

Indo-European	Avestan	Avestan	Persian	
dô: *to give, create* دادن، خلق کردن PK:223	**dâ 1:** *to give* **dâtar:** *giver, God* **dâthra:** *gift* BQ:121, PK:223,225	**dathuš:** *creator* BQ:121,907	**day:** *creator, the tenth month in Persian calendar* دِی١ MO:1588	(2)

NOTE- See root "Ghei 1: winter" for another possible root.

1080

192

دی۲: گذشته (دیروز، دیشب)

همریشه: yester

Indo-European	Avestan	Pahlavi	Persian
ghdies: yester دی (گذشته)	zyô: yester	dîk: yester	dî: yester دی۲ (دیروز)
PK:416	PK:416, KL:1762		MO:1588

1081

دیابت: "عبور". اشاره به تشنگی و ادرار زیاد در این بیماری

Indo-European	Greek		French	Persian
gwa: to walk, step قدم زدن	bainein: to go, walk, step dia-bainein: going across (referring to excessive thirst and urination due to diabetes)			dîâbet: diabetes دیابت
PK:463,CH:98	KL			MO

1082

دجله به رجوع شود به دیاله دار۱ رجوع شود به دیار، دیّار

دیبا

همریشه: divine

(1)

Indo-European	Sanskrit	Pahlavi	Persian
dei: to shine, heavenly spirits درخشیدن، ارواح آسمانی	dîp: to shine	dêpâk, dêbâg: a colorful type of cloth	dîbâ: a colorful cloth دیبا (دیباج، دیبه)
PK:183	PK:183	BQ:908, TV:313	BQ:908

NOTE- See root "Zi: to adorn" for another possible derivation.

1083

دیبا

(2)

Indo-Scythian	Pahlavi	Persian
zi: to adorn آراستن	dêpâk: a beautiful cloth, brocade	dîbâ: a colorful cloth دیبا (دیباج، دیبه)
BL1:16	BL1:16	BQ:908

NOTE- See root "Dei: to shine" for another possible derivation.

1084

دیبا به رجوع شود به دیبه دیبا رجوع شود به دیباج

دیدن

همریشه: آیین، آینه همریشه: theater

Indo-Euro.	Avestan	Pahlavi	Persian
dheye: to see دیدن	dâ 3, dây, dâi, dî: to see vaêna: observer	dîtan: to see	dîdan: to see دیدن
PK:243	PK:243, BQ:373,910, GR:421	BQ:74,373,910	BQ, AP:296

1085

دیر

همریشه: درنگ همریشه: long, linger

Indo-European	Avestan	Persian
del: long دراز، طولانی	daraga, darağa, drâjah: long drang: hesitation	dîr: late دیر
PK:197, KT:190	PK:197, BQ:829, TV:324	PK, BQ, TV

1086

دیرند: دیرپای   همریشه: دیر، دراز   همریشه: long, linger

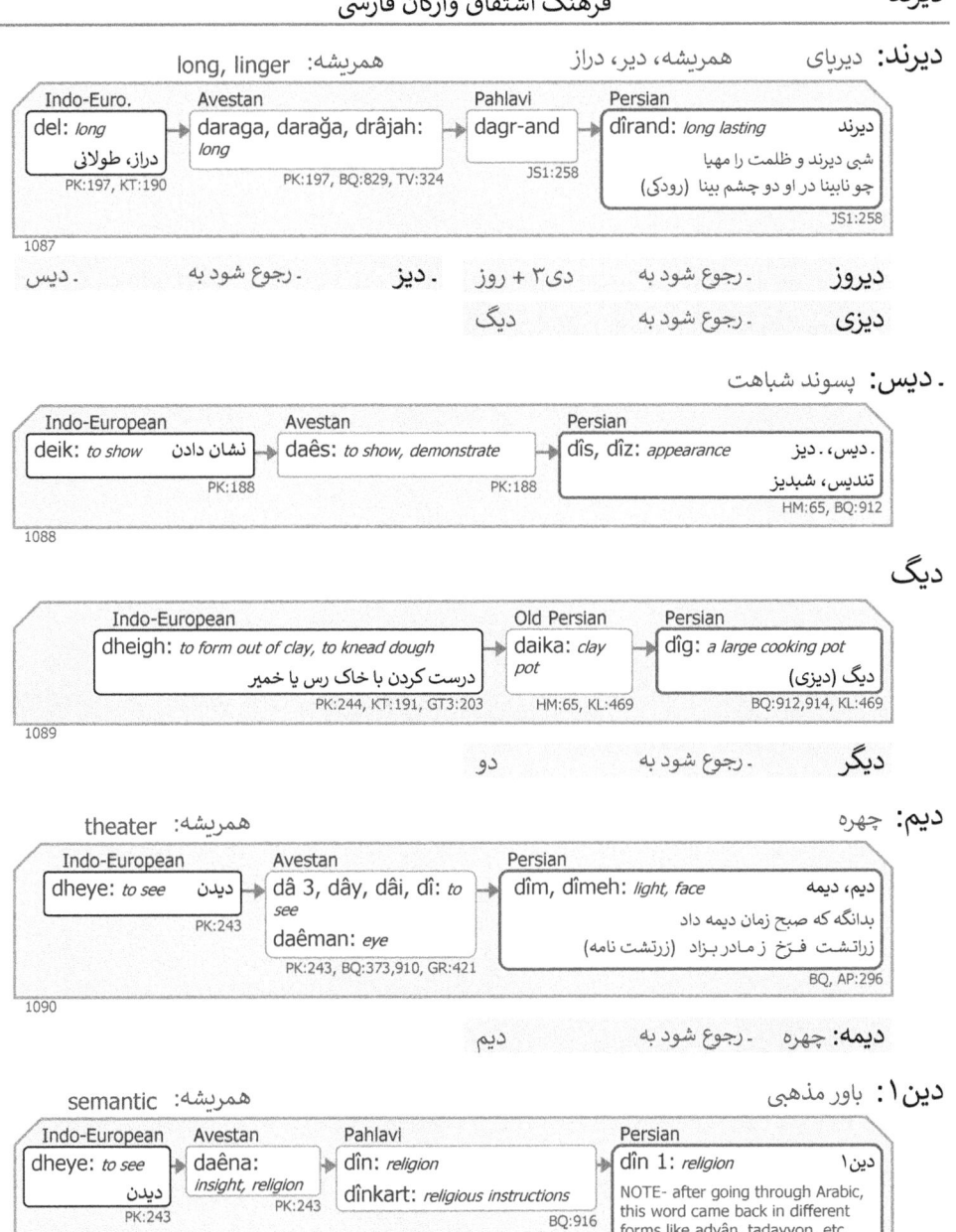

Indo-Euro.	Avestan	Pahlavi	Persian
del: *long* دراز، طولانی PK:197, KT:190	daraga, darağa, drâjah: *long* PK:197, BQ:829, TV:324	dagr-and JS1:258	dîrand: *long lasting* دیرند شی دیرند و ظلمت را مهیا چو نابینا در او دو چشم بینا (رودکی) JS1:258

1087

دیروز ۔رجوع شود به دی ۳ + روز   **دیز.** ۔رجوع شود به   دیس.

دیزی ۔رجوع شود به دیگ

دیس. پسوند شباهت

Indo-European	Avestan	Persian
deik: *to show* نشان دادن PK:188	daês: *to show, demonstrate* PK:188	dîs, dîz: *appearance* دیس، دیز. تندیس، شبدیز HM:65, BQ:912

1088

دیگ

Indo-European	Old Persian	Persian
dheigh: *to form out of clay, to knead dough* درست کردن با خاک رس یا خمیر PK:244, KT:191, GT3:203	daika: *clay pot* HM:65, KL:469	dîg: *a large cooking pot* دیگ (دیزی) BQ:912,914, KL:469

1089

دیگر ۔رجوع شود به   دو

دیم: چهره   همریشه: theater

Indo-European	Avestan	Persian
dheye: *to see* دیدن PK:243	dâ 3, dây, dâi, dî: *to see* daêman: *eye* PK:243, BQ:373,910, GR:421	dîm, dîmeh: *light, face* دیم، دیمه بدانگه که صبح زمان دیمه داد زراتشت فرّخ ز مادر بزاد (زرتشت نامه) BQ, AP:296

1090

دیمه: چهره   ۔رجوع شود به   دیم

دین۱: باور مذهبی   همریشه: semantic

Indo-European	Avestan	Pahlavi	Persian
dheye: *to see* دیدن PK:243	daêna: *insight, religion* PK:243	dîn: *religion* dînkart: *religious instructions* BQ:916	dîn 1: *religion* دین۱ NOTE- after going through Arabic, this word came back in different forms like adyân, tadayyon, etc. BQ:916, MO:1597, NS:191
NOTE- BR claims Arabic "dîn: religion" is borrowed from Iranian while "dîn: judgment" is borrowed from Aramaic and passed to Persian.			

1091

دین۲: قضاوت   همریشه: دانیال ("خدا قاضی است")

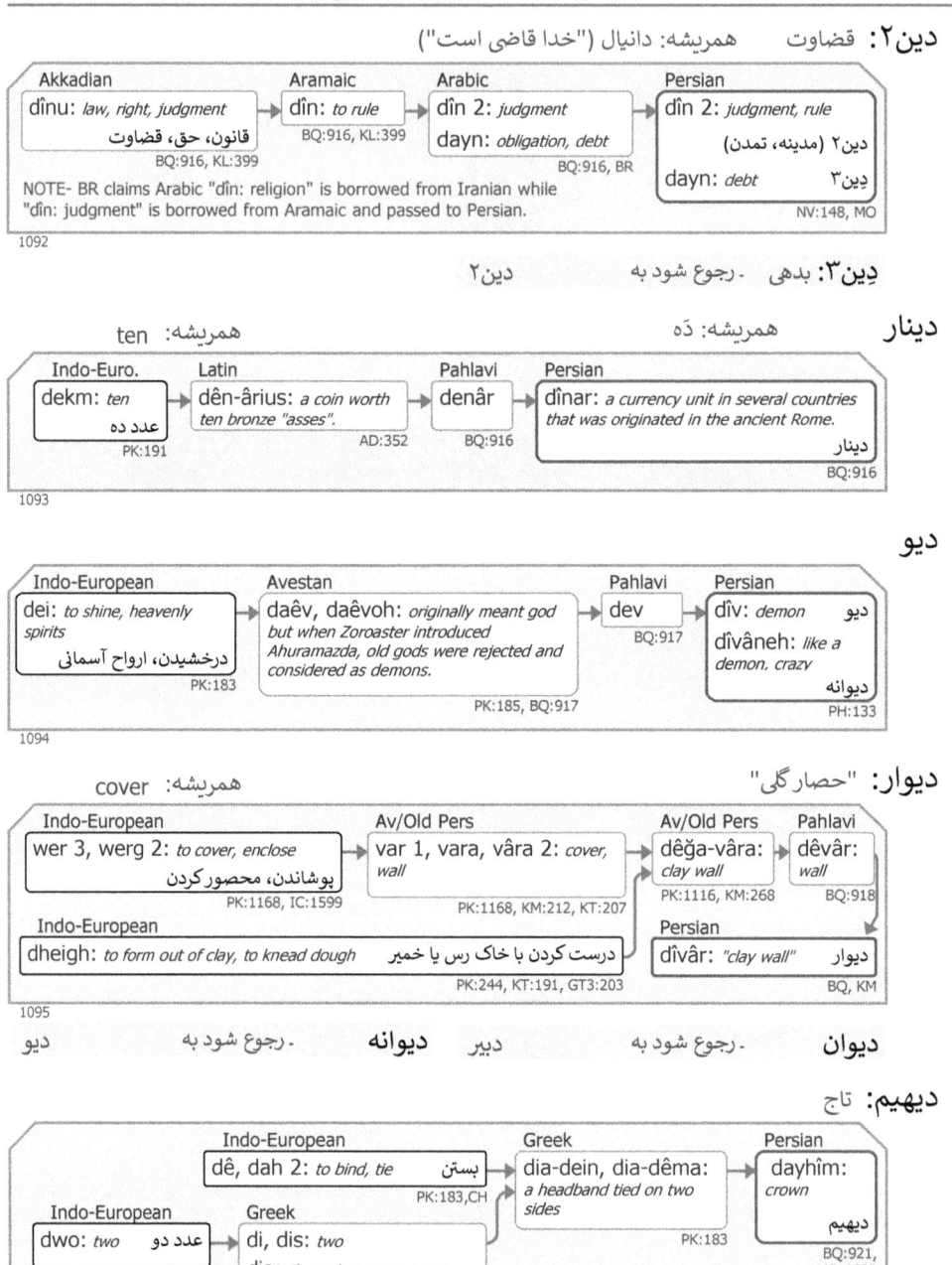

Akkadian
dînu: *law, right, judgment*
قانون، حق، قضاوت
BQ:916, KL:399

Aramaic
dîn: *to rule*
BQ:916, KL:399

Arabic
dîn 2: *judgment*
dayn: *obligation, debt*
BQ:916, BR

Persian
dîn 2: *judgment, rule*
دین۲ (مدینه، تمدن)
dayn: *debt*   دین۳
NV:148, MO

NOTE- BR claims Arabic "dîn: religion" is borrowed from Iranian while "dîn: judgment" is borrowed from Aramaic and passed to Persian.
1092

دِین۳: بدهی   .رجوع شود به   دین۲

دینار   همریشه: دَه   همریشه: ten

Indo-Euro.
dekm: *ten*
عدد ده
PK:191

Latin
dên-ârius: *a coin worth ten bronze "asses".*
AD:352

Pahlavi
denâr
BQ:916

Persian
dînar: *a currency unit in several countries that was originated in the ancient Rome.*
دینار
BQ:916
1093

دیو

Indo-European
dei: *to shine, heavenly spirits*
درخشیدن، ارواح آسمانی
PK:183

Avestan
daêv, daêvoh: *originally meant god but when Zoroaster introduced Ahuramazda, old gods were rejected and considered as demons.*
PK:185, BQ:917

Pahlavi
dev
BQ:917

Persian
dîv: *demon*   دیو
dîvâneh: *like a demon, crazy*
دیوانه
PH:133
1094

دیوار: "حصارگلی"   همریشه: cover

Indo-European
wer 3, werg 2: *to cover, enclose*
پوشاندن، محصور کردن
PK:1168, IC:1599

Av/Old Pers
var 1, vara, vâra 2: *cover, wall*
PK:1168, KM:212, KT:207

Av/Old Pers
dêğa-vâra: *clay wall*
PK:1116, KM:268

Pahlavi
dêvâr: *wall*
BQ:918

Indo-European
dheigh: *to form out of clay, to knead dough*
درست کردن با خاک رس یا خمیر
PK:244, KT:191, GT3:203

Persian
dîvâr: *"clay wall"*   دیوار
BQ, KM
1095

دیو   رجوع شود به.   دیوانه   دبیر   .رجوع شود به   دیوان

دیهیم: تاج

Indo-European
dê, dah 2: *to bind, tie*   بستن
PK:183,CH

Greek
dia-dein, dia-dêma: *a headband tied on two sides*
PK:183

Persian
dayhîm: *crown*
دیهیم
BQ:921, MO:1603

Indo-European
dwo: *two*   عدد دو
PK:230

Greek
di, dis: *two*
dia: *through, across, apart*
AD
1096

حرف ذ گاهی به د یا گ بدل
شود.

ذغال

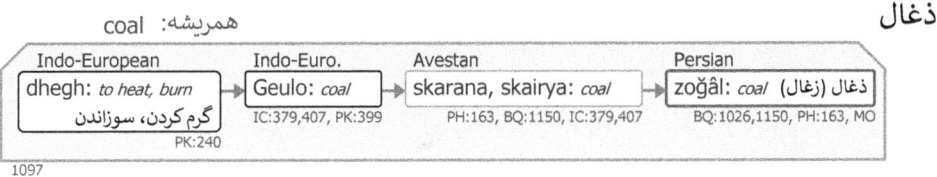

همریشه: coal

Indo-European	Indo-Euro.	Avestan	Persian
dhegh: *to heat, burn*	Geulo: *coal*	skarana, skairya: *coal*	ذغال (زغال) zoğâl: *coal*
گرم کردن، سوزاندن			
PK:240	IC:379,407, PK:399	PH:163, BQ:1150, IC:379,407	BQ:1026,1150, PH:163, MO

1097

196

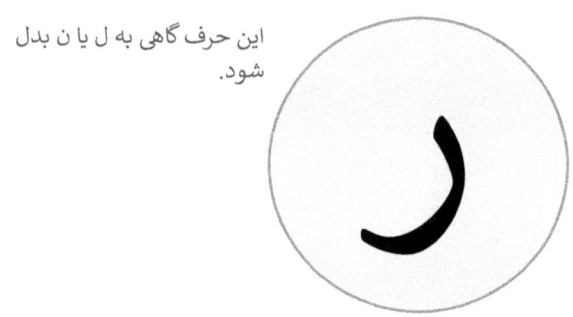

این حرف گاهی به ل یا ن بدل شود.

ـَر: پسوند "ر" پس از حرف مفتوح یعنی عضو خانواده   همریشه: er- as in mother

Indo-European	Avestan	Persian
ter 2, tar: *a kinship term* پسوند گروه یا فامیل PT:863	- tar, - dar, - har: *suffix used for family members* NOTE- see Avestan words in charts of the family members like mother, father, brother, etc. BQ	- ar: *suffix for family members* ـَر پدر، مادر، برادر، خواهر، دختر توجه . پسوند "ر" در لغات داماد و دخت حذف شده BQ

1098

را   - رجوع شود به   رای و چرا

راد۱: درست   همریشه: رَد   arm, art, order :همریشه

Indo-European	Avestan	Persian
ar 1: *to fit together* جور و درست کردن PK:55-61	râd: *right, correct, proper* NOTE- CH:196 derives this from the root "Reg 1: straight" WD:74, PK:56	râd: *proper, brave* راد۱ BQ, KM, AG3

1099

راد۲: بخشنده   همریشه: رای   real :همریشه

Indo-European	Avestan	Pahlavi	Persian
rei 1: *possession* مالکیت PK:860	râ: *to give* râiti, a-râiti: *generous* PK:860, BQ, AP:301	rât: *generous* BQ:926	râd: *generous* راد۲ BQ:926

1100

راز

Indo-European	Avestan	Pahlavi	Persian
redh, raz*: *to escape, leave* فرار کردن، رهیدن KT:205, CH:322	rah: *to escape, set free* razah: *isolation* KT:205, NB:167	râz: *secret* BQ:926	râz: *secret* راز BQ:926, PH:134, CH:322

1101

رازق   - رجوع شود به   رزق   **رازق، رازگی**   - رجوع شود به   ری

رازی   - رجوع شود به   ری

راست

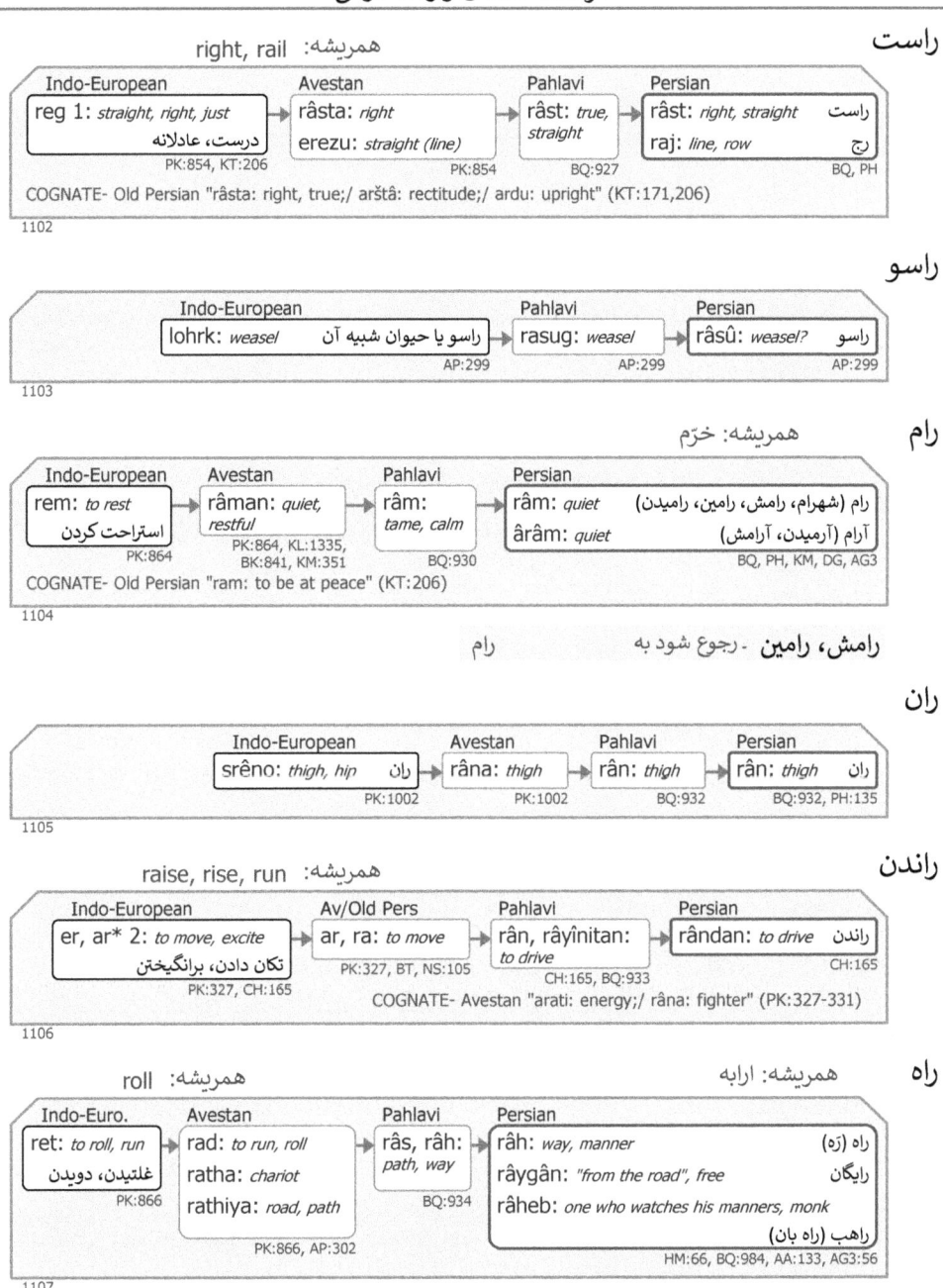

راست

همریشه: right, rail

Indo-European	Avestan	Pahlavi	Persian
reg 1: straight, right, just درست، عادلانه PK:854, KT:206	râsta: right erezu: straight (line) PK:854	râst: true, straight BQ:927	râst: right, straight راست raj: line, row رج BQ, PH

COGNATE- Old Persian "râsta: right, true;/ arštâ: rectitude;/ ardu: upright" (KT:171,206)

1102

راسو

Indo-European	Pahlavi	Persian
lohrk: weasel راسو یا حیوان شبیه آن AP:299	rasug: weasel AP:299	râsû: weasel? راسو AP:299

1103

رام

همریشه: خرّم

Indo-European	Avestan	Pahlavi	Persian
rem: to rest استراحت کردن PK:864	râman: quiet, restful PK:864, KL:1335, BK:841, KM:351	râm: tame, calm BQ:930	râm: quiet رام (شهرام، رامش، رامین، رامیدن) ârâm: quiet آرام (آرمیدن، آرامش) BQ, PH, KM, DG, AG3

COGNATE- Old Persian "ram: to be at peace" (KT:206)

1104

رامش، رامین - رجوع شود به رام

ران

Indo-European	Avestan	Pahlavi	Persian
srêno: thigh, hip ران PK:1002	râna: thigh PK:1002	rân: thigh BQ:932	rân: thigh ران BQ:932, PH:135

1105

راندن

همریشه: raise, rise, run

Indo-European	Av/Old Pers	Pahlavi	Persian
er, ar* 2: to move, excite تکان دادن، برانگیختن PK:327, CH:165	ar, ra: to move PK:327, BT, NS:105	rân, râyînitan: to drive CH:165, BQ:933	rândan: to drive راندن CH:165

COGNATE- Avestan "arati: energy;/ râna: fighter" (PK:327-331)

1106

راه

همریشه: ارابه   همریشه: roll

Indo-Euro.	Avestan	Pahlavi	Persian
ret: to roll, run غلتیدن، دویدن PK:866	rad: to run, roll ratha: chariot rathiya: road, path PK:866, AP:302	râs, râh: path, way BQ:934	râh: way, manner راه (رَه) râygân: "from the road", free رایگان râheb: one who watches his manners, monk راهب (راه بان) HM:66, BQ:984, AA:133, AG3:56

1107

راهب - رجوع شود به راه

رای: عقل   همریشه: راد۲   همریشه: real

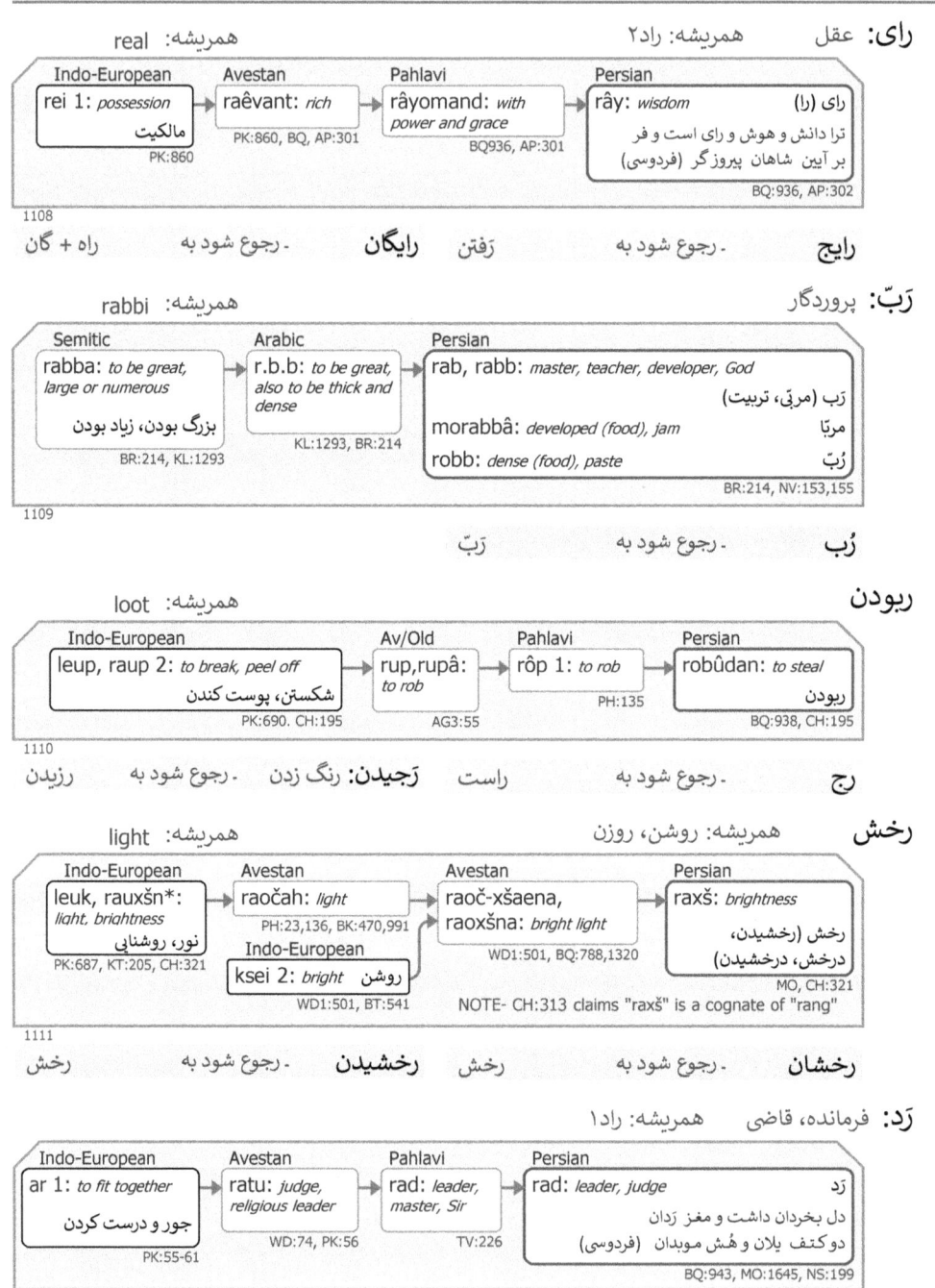

Indo-European
rei 1: *possession*
مالکیت
PK:860

Avestan
raêvant: *rich*
PK:860, BQ, AP:301

Pahlavi
râyomand: *with power and grace*
BQ936, AP:301

Persian
rây: *wisdom*
رای (را)
ترا دانش و هوش و رای است و فر
بر آیین شاهان پیروزگر (فردوسی)
BQ:936, AP:302

1108

رایج ـ رجوع شود به   **رایگان**   رفتن   ـ رجوع شود به   راه + گان

رَبّ: پروردگار   همریشه: rabbi

Semitic
rabba: *to be great, large or numerous*
بزرگ بودن، زیاد بودن
BR:214, KL:1293

Arabic
r.b.b: *to be great, also to be thick and dense*
KL:1293, BR:214

Persian
rab, rabb: *master, teacher, developer, God*
رَب (مربّی، تربیت)
morabbâ: *developed (food), jam*
مربّا
robb: *dense (food), paste*
رُبّ
BR:214, NV:153,155

1109

رُب   ـ رجوع شود به   رَبّ

ربودن   همریشه: loot

Indo-European
leup, raup 2: *to break, peel off*
شکستن، پوست کندن
PK:690. CH:195

Av/Old
rup,rupâ: *to rob*
AG3:55

Pahlavi
rôp 1: *to rob*
PH:135

Persian
robûdan: *to steal*
ربودن
BQ:938, CH:195

1110

رج ـ رجوع شود به   راست   **رَجیدن:** رنگ زدن ـ رجوع شود به   رزیدن

رخش   همریشه: روشن، روزن   همریشه: light

Indo-European
leuk, rauxšn*: *light, brightness*
نور، روشنایی
PK:687, KT:205, CH:321

Avestan
raočah: *light*
PH:23,136, BK:470,991
Indo-European
ksei 2: *bright*
روشن
WD1:501, BT:541

Avestan
raoč-xšaena, raoxšna: *bright light*
WD1:501, BQ:788,1320

Persian
raxš: *brightness*
رخش (رخشیدن، درخش، درخشیدن)
MO:321
NOTE- CH:313 claims "raxš" is a cognate of "rang"

1111

رخشان ـ رجوع شود به   رخش   **رخشیدن** ـ رجوع شود به   رخش

رَد: فرمانده، قاضی   همریشه: راد۱

Indo-European
ar 1: *to fit together*
جور و درست کردن
PK:55-61

Avestan
ratu: *judge, religious leader*
WD:74, PK:56

Pahlavi
rad: *leader, master, Sir*
TV:226

Persian
rad: *leader, judge*
رَد
دل بخردان داشت و مغز زدان
دو کتف یلان و هُش موبدان (فردوسی)
BQ:943, MO:1645, NS:199

1112

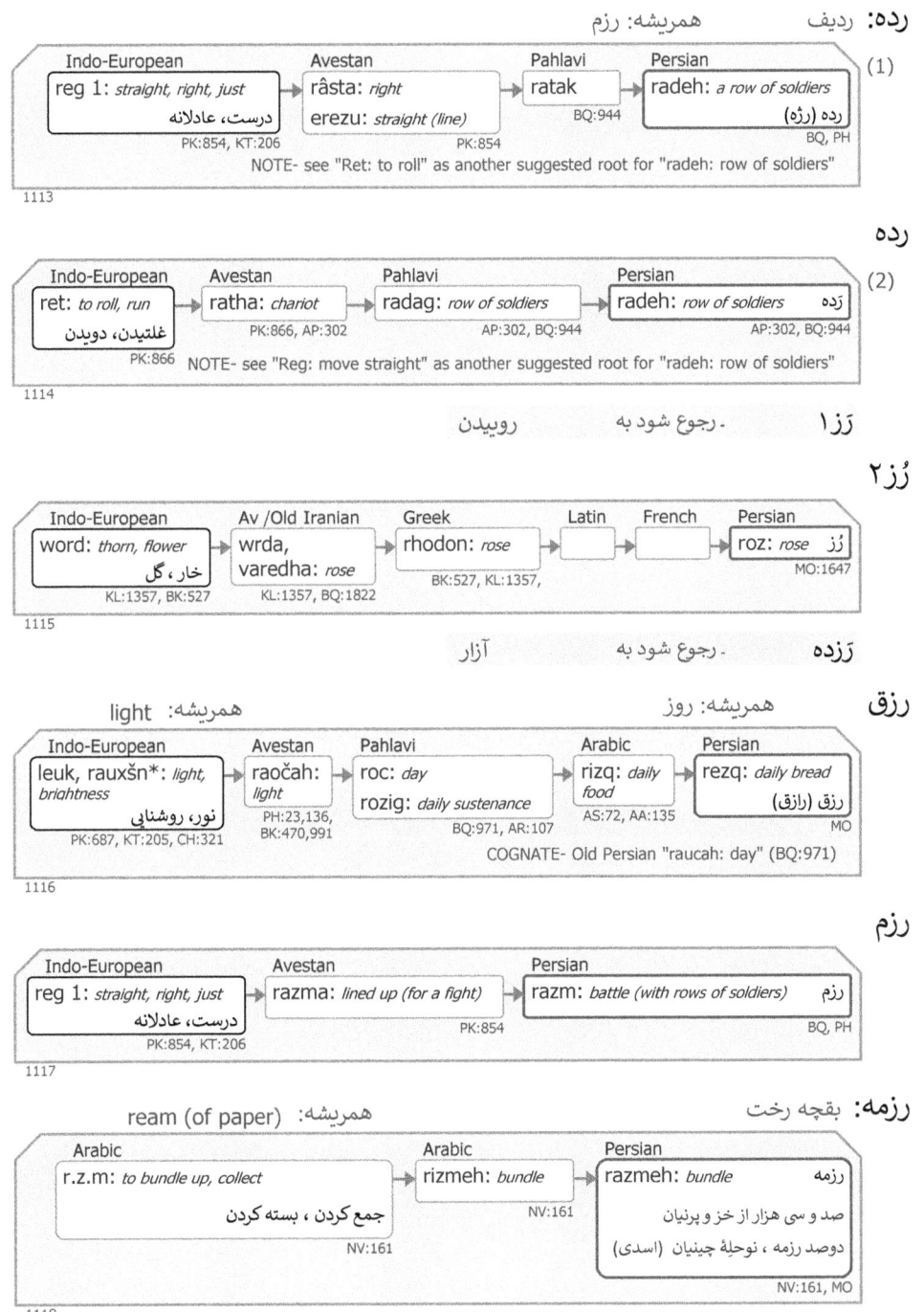

رده: ردیف   همریشه: رزم

(1)

Indo-European	Avestan	Pahlavi	Persian
reg 1: *straight, right, just* درست، عادلانه PK:854, KT:206	râsta: *right* erezu: *straight (line)* PK:854	ratak BQ:944	radeh: *a row of soldiers* رده (رژه) BQ, PH

NOTE- see "Ret: to roll" as another suggested root for "radeh: row of soldiers"

1113

رده

(2)

Indo-European	Avestan	Pahlavi	Persian
ret: *to roll, run* غلتیدن، دویدن PK:866	ratha: *chariot* PK:866, AP:302	radag: *row of soldiers* AP:302, BQ:944	radeh: *row of soldiers* رده AP:302, BQ:944

NOTE- see "Reg: move straight" as another suggested root for "radeh: row of soldiers"

1114

رزا۱ ـ رجوع شود به   روییدن

رُز۲

Indo-European	Av /Old Iranian	Greek	Latin	French	Persian
word: *thorn, flower* خار، گل KL:1357, BK:527	wrda, varedha: *rose* KL:1357, BQ:1822	rhodon: *rose* BK:527, KL:1357,			roz: *rose* رُز MO:1647

1115

رَزده ـ رجوع شود به   آزار

رزق   همریشه: روز   همریشه: light

Indo-European	Avestan	Pahlavi	Arabic	Persian
leuk, rauxšn*: *light, brightness* نور، روشنایی PK:687, KT:205, CH:321	raočah: *light* PH:23,136, BK:470,991	roc: *day* rozig: *daily sustenance* BQ:971, AR:107	rizq: *daily food* AS:72, AA:135	rezq: *daily bread* رزق (رازق) MO

COGNATE- Old Persian "raucah: day" (BQ:971)

1116

رزم

Indo-European	Avestan	Persian
reg 1: *straight, right, just* درست، عادلانه PK:854, KT:206	razma: *lined up (for a fight)* PK:854	razm: *battle (with rows of soldiers)* رزم BQ, PH

1117

رزمه: بقچه رخت   همریشه: ream (of paper)

Arabic	Arabic	Persian
r.z.m: *to bundle up, collect* جمع کردن، بسته کردن NV:161	rizmeh: *bundle* NV:161	razmeh: *bundle* رزمه صد و سی هزار از خز و پرنیان دوصد رزمه ، نوحلهٔ چینیان (اسدی) NV:161, MO

1118

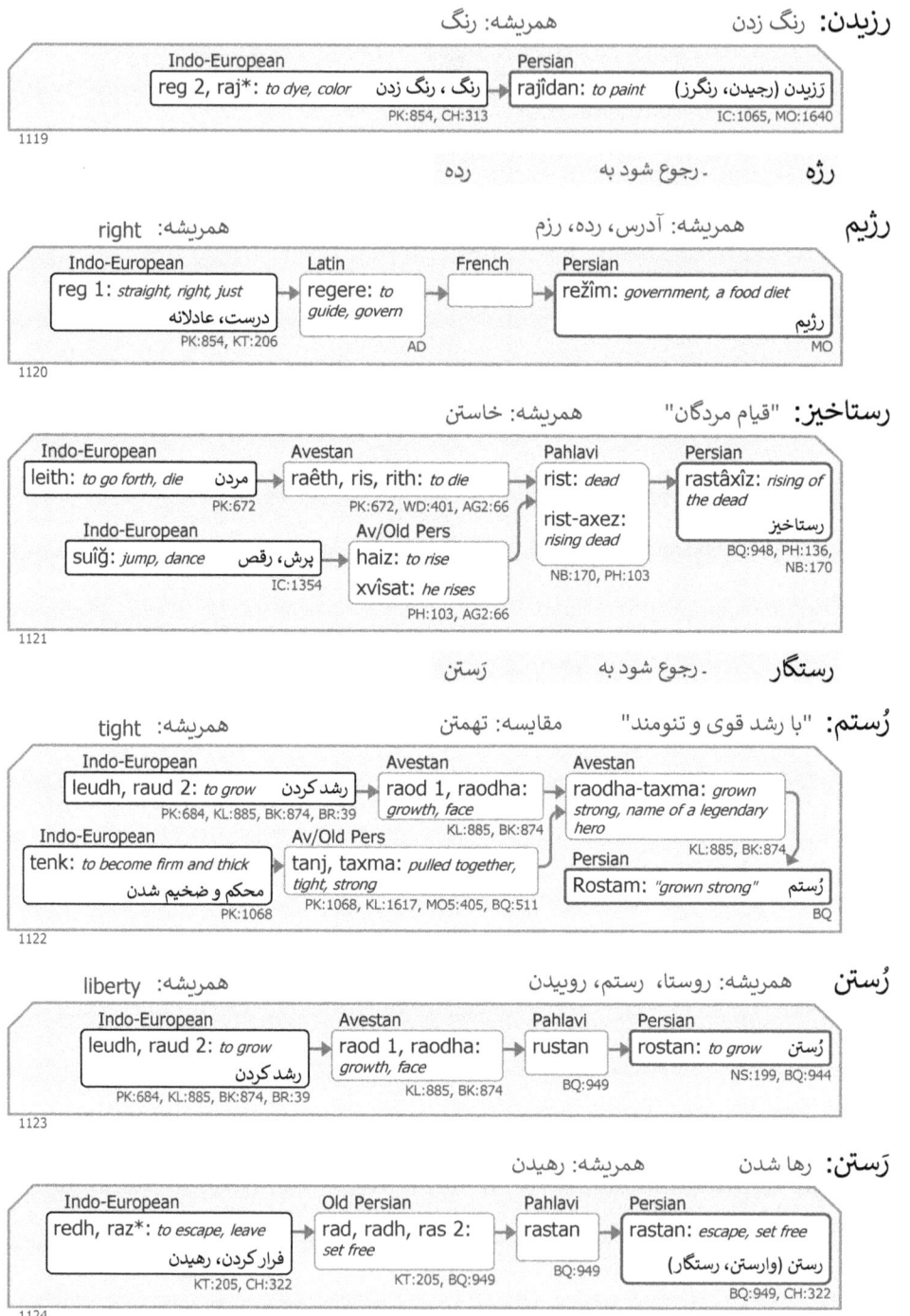

رزیدن: رنگ زدن   همریشه: رنگ

Indo-European
reg 2, raj*: *to dye, color*   رنگ ، رنگ زدن
PK:854, CH:313

Persian
rajîdan: *to paint*   رزیدن (رجیدن، رنگرز)
IC:1065, MO:1640

1119

رژه   ـ رجوع شود به   رده

رژیم   همریشه: آدرس، رده، رزم   همریشه: right

Indo-European
reg 1: *straight, right, just*   درست، عادلانه
PK:854, KT:206

Latin
regere: *to guide, govern*
AD

French

Persian
režîm: *government, a food diet*   رژیم
MO

1120

رستاخیز: "قیام مردگان"   همریشه: خاستن

Indo-European
leith: *to go forth, die*   مردن
PK:672

Avestan
raêth, ris, rith: *to die*
PK:672, WD:401, AG2:66

Pahlavi
rist: *dead*
rist-axez: *rising dead*
NB:170, PH:103

Persian
rastâxîz: *rising of the dead*   رستاخیز
BQ:948, PH:136, NB:170

Indo-European
suîǧ: *jump, dance*   پرش، رقص
IC:1354

Av/Old Pers
haiz: *to rise*
xvîsat: *he rises*
PH:103, AG2:66

1121

رستگار   ـ رجوع شود به   رَستن

رُستم: "با رشد قوی و تنومند"   مقایسه: تهمتن   همریشه: tight

Indo-European
leudh, raud 2: *to grow*   رشد کردن
PK:684, KL:885, BK:874, BR:39

Avestan
raod 1, raodha: *growth, face*
KL:885, BK:874

Avestan
raodha-taxma: *grown strong, name of a legendary hero*
KL:885, BK:874

Indo-European
tenk: *to become firm and thick*   محکم و ضخیم شدن
PK:1068

Av/Old Pers
tanj, taxma: *pulled together, tight, strong*
PK:1068, KL:1617, MO5:405, BQ:511

Persian
Rostam: *"grown strong"*   رُستم
BQ

1122

رُستن   همریشه: روستا، رستم، روییدن   همریشه: liberty

Indo-European
leudh, raud 2: *to grow*   رشد کردن
PK:684, KL:885, BK:874, BR:39

Avestan
raod 1, raodha: *growth, face*
KL:885, BK:874

Pahlavi
rustan
BQ:949

Persian
rostan: *to grow*   رُستن
NS:199, BQ:944

1123

رَستن: رها شدن   همریشه: رهیدن

Indo-European
redh, raz*: *to escape, leave*   فرار کردن، رهیدن
KT:205, CH:322

Old Persian
rad, radh, ras 2: *set free*
KT:205, BQ:949

Pahlavi
rastan
BQ:949

Persian
rastan: *escape, set free*   رستن (وارستن، رستگار)
BQ:949, CH:322

1124

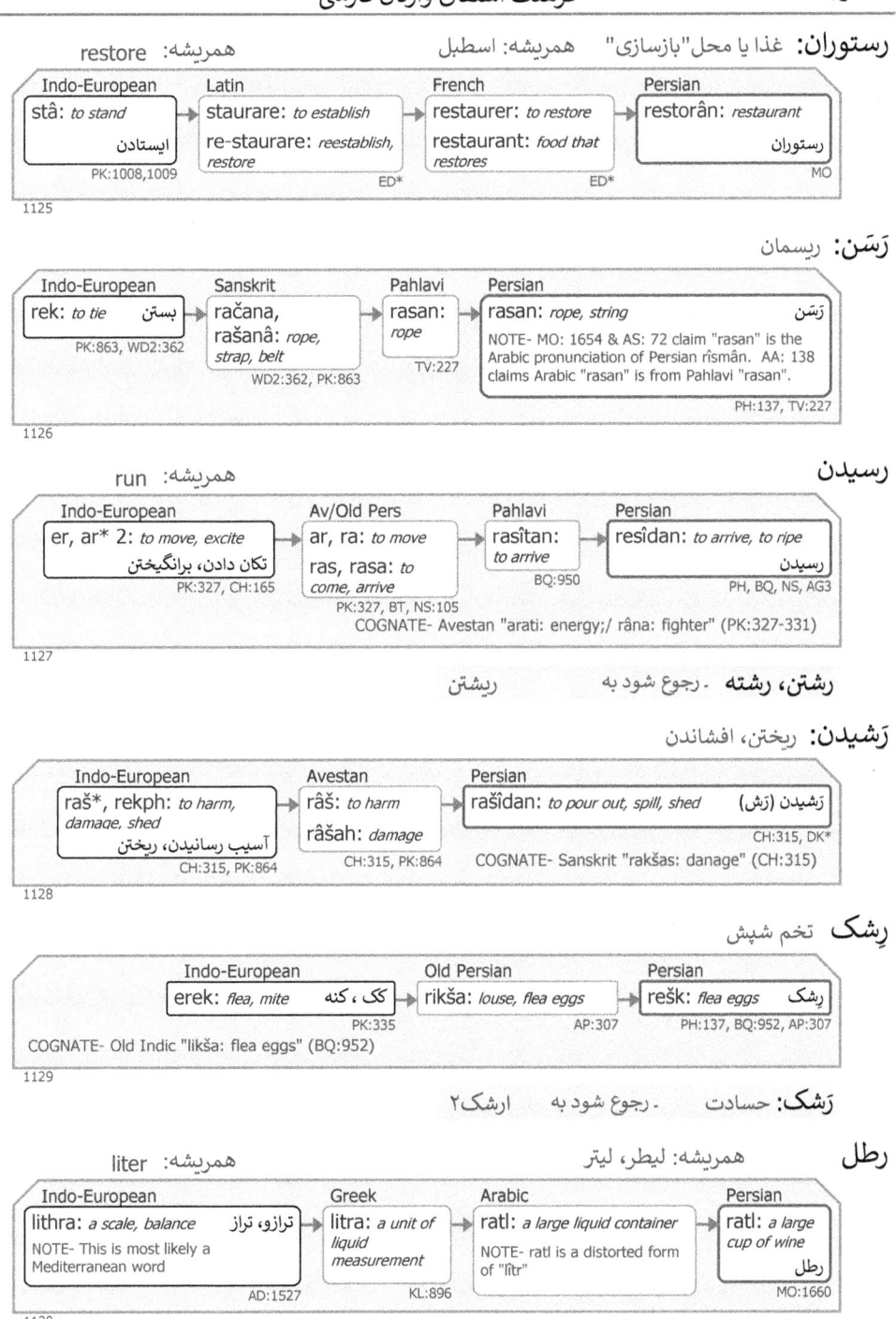

رستوران: غذا یا محل"بازسازی"   همریشه: اسطبل   همریشه: restore

Indo-European	Latin	French	Persian
stâ: *to stand* ایستادن	staurare: *to establish* re-staurare: *reestablish, restore*	restaurer: *to restore* restaurant: *food that restores*	restorân: *restaurant* رستوران
PK:1008,1009	ED*	ED*	MO

1125

رَسَن: ریسمان

Indo-European	Sanskrit	Pahlavi	Persian
rek: *to tie* بستن	račana, rašanâ: *rope, strap, belt*	rasan: *rope*	rasan: *rope, string* رَسَن NOTE- MO: 1654 & AS: 72 claim "rasan" is the Arabic pronunciation of Persian rîsmân. AA: 138 claims Arabic "rasan" is from Pahlavi "rasan".
PK:863, WD2:362	WD2:362, PK:863	TV:227	PH:137, TV:227

1126

رسیدن   همریشه: run

Indo-European	Av/Old Pers	Pahlavi	Persian
er, ar* 2: *to move, excite* تکان دادن، برانگیختن	ar, ra: *to move* ras, rasa: *to come, arrive*	rasîtan: *to arrive*	resîdan: *to arrive, to ripe* رسیدن
PK:327, CH:165	PK:327, BT, NS:105	BQ:950	PH, BQ, NS, AG3
	COGNATE- Avestan "arati: energy;/ râna: fighter" (PK:327-331)		

1127

رشتن، رشته ۔ رجوع شود به   ریشتن

رَشیدن: ریختن، افشاندن

Indo-European	Avestan	Persian
raš*, rekph: *to harm, damage, shed* آسیب رسانیدن، ریختن	râš: *to harm* râšah: *damage*	rašîdan: *to pour out, spill, shed* (رش) رشیدن
CH:315, PK:864	CH:315, PK:864	CH:315, DK* COGNATE- Sanskrit "rakšas: danage" (CH:315)

1128

رِشک تخم شپش

Indo-European	Old Persian	Persian
erek: *flea, mite* کک ، کنه	rikša: *louse, flea eggs*	rešk: *flea eggs* رِشک
PK:335	AP:307	PH:137, BQ:952, AP:307
COGNATE- Old Indic "likša: flea eggs" (BQ:952)		

1129

رَشک: حسادت   ۔ رجوع شود به   ارشک۲

رطل   همریشه: لیطر، لیتر   همریشه: liter

Indo-European	Greek	Arabic	Persian
lithra: *a scale, balance* ترازو، تراز NOTE- This is most likely a Mediterranean word	litra: *a unit of liquid measurement*	ratl: *a large liquid container* NOTE- ratl is a distorted form of "lîtr"	ratl: *a large cup of wine* رطل
AD:1527	KL:896		MO:1660

1130

رُغ ۔ رجوع شود به   آروغ

رَغزه: پوشش پشمی

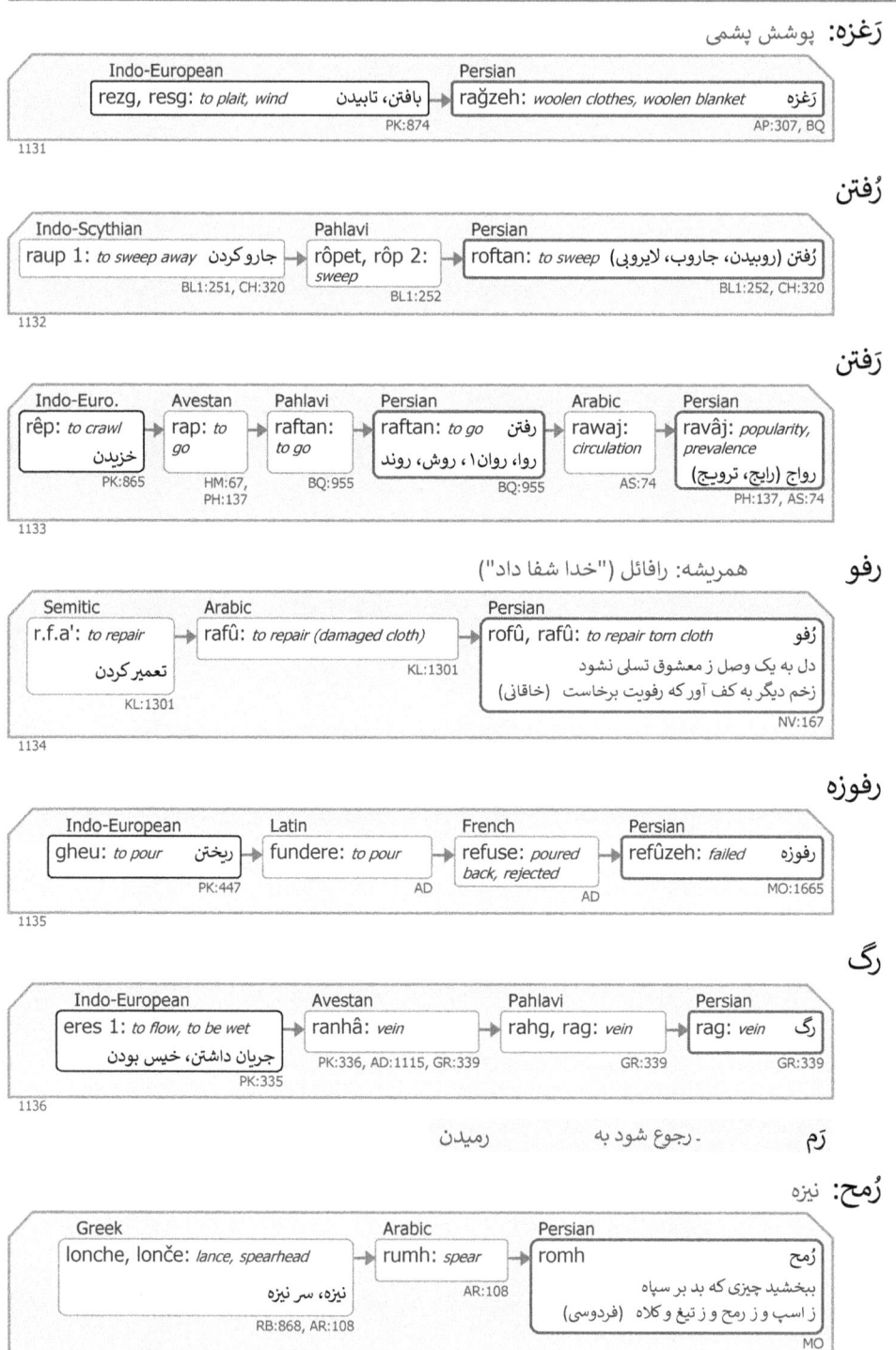

Indo-European	Persian
rezg, resg: *to plait, wind* بافتن، تابیدن	rağzeh: *woolen clothes, woolen blanket* زغزه
PK:874	AP:307, BQ

1131

رُفتن

Indo-Scythian	Pahlavi	Persian
raup 1: *to sweep away* جارو کردن	rôpet, rôp 2: *sweep*	رُفتن (روبیدن، جاروب، لایروبی) roftan: *to sweep*
BL1:251, CH:320	BL1:252	BL1:252, CH:320

1132

رَفتن

Indo-Euro.	Avestan	Pahlavi	Persian	Arabic	Persian
rêp: *to crawl* خزیدن	rap: *to go*	raftan: *to go*	raftan: *to go* رفتن روا، روان۱، روش، روند	rawaj: *circulation*	ravâj: *popularity, prevalence* رواج (رایج، ترویج)
PK:865	HM:67, PH:137	BQ:955	BQ:955	AS:74	PH:137, AS:74

1133

رفو

همریشه: رافائل ("خدا شفا داد")

Semitic	Arabic	Persian
r.f.a': *to repair* تعمیر کردن	rafû: *to repair (damaged cloth)*	rofû, rafû: *to repair torn cloth* زفو
KL:1301	KL:1301	دل ز یک وصل ز معشوق تسلی نشود
		زخم دیگر که به کف آورد که رفویت برخاست (خاقانی)
		NV:167

1134

رفوزه

Indo-European	Latin	French	Persian
gheu: *to pour* ریختن	fundere: *to pour*	refuse: *poured back, rejected*	refûzeh: *failed* رفوزه
PK:447	AD	AD	MO:1665

1135

رگ

Indo-European	Avestan	Pahlavi	Persian
eres 1: *to flow, to be wet* جریان داشتن، خیس بودن	ranhâ: *vein*	rahg, rag: *vein*	rag: *vein* رگ
PK:335	PK:336, AD:1115, GR:339	GR:339	GR:339

1136

رَم . رجوع شود به رمیدن

رُمح: نیزه

Greek	Arabic	Persian
lonche, lonče: *lance, spearhead* نیزه، سر نیزه	rumh: *spear*	romh رُمح
	AR:108	ببخشید چیزی که بد بر سپاه
RB:868, AR:108		ز اسپ و ز رمح و ز تیغ و کلاه (فردوسی)
		MO

1137

رمیدن

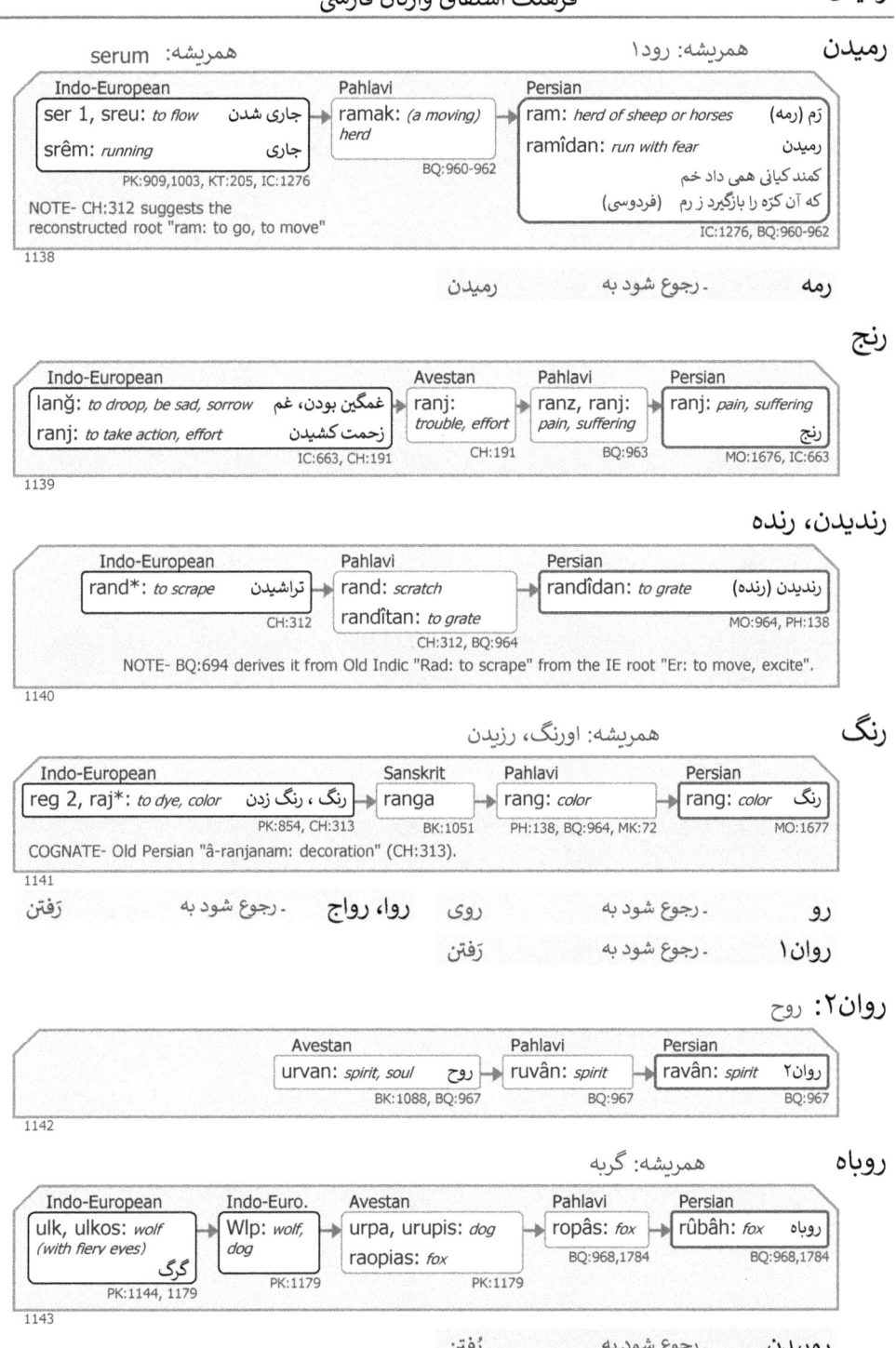

همریشه: رود۱

همریشه: serum

Indo-European	Pahlavi	Persian
ser 1, sreu: *to flow* جاری شدن	ramak: *(a moving) herd*	ram: *herd of sheep or horses* زَم (رمه)
srêm: *running* جاری		ramîdan: *run with fear* رمیدن
PK:909,1003, KT:205, IC:1276	BQ:960-962	کمند کیانی همی داد خم
NOTE- CH:312 suggests the reconstructed root "ram: to go, to move"		که آن کژه را بازگیرد ز رم (فردوسی)
		IC:1276, BQ:960-962

1138

رمه   - رجوع شود به   رمیدن

رنج

Indo-European	Avestan	Pahlavi	Persian
lanǧ: *to droop, be sad, sorrow* غمگین بودن، غم	ranj: *trouble, effort*	ranz, ranj: *pain, suffering*	ranj: *pain, suffering* رنج
ranj: *to take action, effort* زحمت کشیدن			
IC:663, CH:191	CH:191	BQ:963	MO:1676, IC:663

1139

رندیدن، رنده

Indo-European	Pahlavi	Persian
rand*: *to scrape* تراشیدن	rand: *scratch*	randîdan: *to grate* رندیدن (رنده)
CH:312	randîtan: *to grate*	MO:964, PH:138
	CH:312, BQ:964	
NOTE- BQ:694 derives it from Old Indic "Rad: to scrape" from the IE root "Er: to move, excite".		

1140

رنگ

همریشه: اورنگ، رزیدن

Indo-European	Sanskrit	Pahlavi	Persian
reg 2, raj*: *to dye, color* رنگ، رنگ زدن	ranga	rang: *color*	rang: *color* رنگ
PK:854, CH:313	BK:1051	PH:138, BQ:964, MK:72	MO:1677
COGNATE- Old Persian "â-ranjanam: decoration" (CH:313).			

1141

رو   - رجوع شود به   روی   روا، رواج   - رجوع شود به   رَفتن

روان۱   - رجوع شود به   رَفتن

روان۲: روح

	Avestan	Pahlavi	Persian
	urvan: *spirit, soul* روح	ruvân: *spirit*	ravân: *spirit* روان۲
	BK:1088, BQ:967	BQ:967	BQ:967

1142

روباه

همریشه: گربه

Indo-European	Indo-Euro.	Avestan	Pahlavi	Persian
ulk, ulkos: *wolf* (with fiery eyes) گرگ	Wlp: *wolf, dog*	urpa, urupis: *dog* raopias: *fox*	ropâs: *fox*	rûbâh: *fox* روباه
PK:1144, 1179	PK:1179	PK:1179	BQ:968,1784	BQ:968,1784

1143

روبیدن   - رجوع شود به   رُفتن

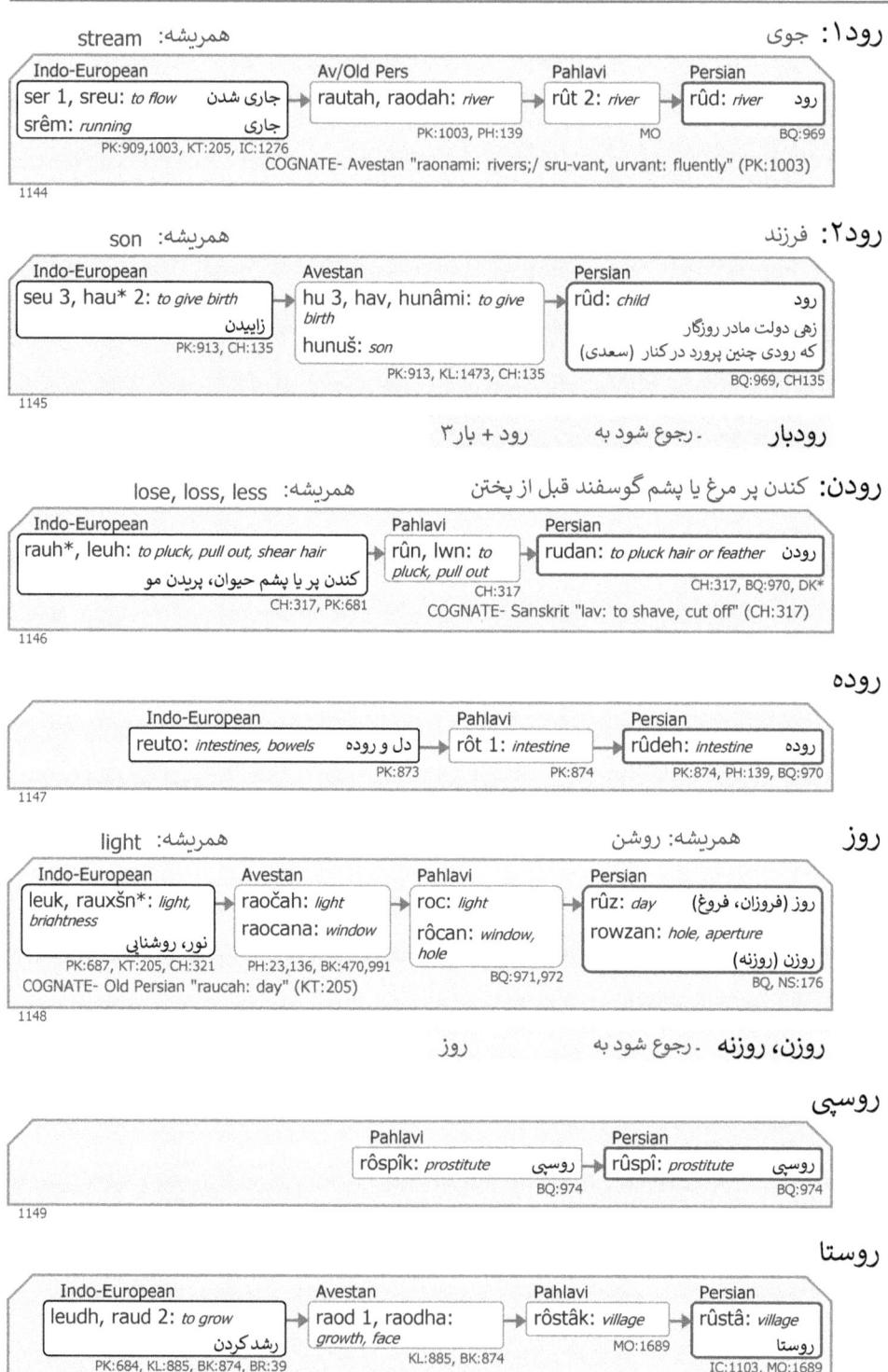

رود۱: جوی   همریشه: stream

Indo-European	Av/Old Pers	Pahlavi	Persian
ser 1, sreu: *to flow* جاری شدن srêm: *running* جاری PK:909,1003, KT:205, IC:1276	rautah, raodah: *river* PK:1003, PH:139	rût 2: *river* MO	rûd: *river* رود BQ:969

COGNATE- Avestan "raonami: rivers;/ sru-vant, urvant: fluently" (PK:1003)

1144

رود۲: فرزند   همریشه: son

Indo-European	Avestan	Persian
seu 3, hau* 2: *to give birth* زاییدن PK:913, CH:135	hu 3, hav, hunâmi: *to give birth* hunuš: *son* PK:913, KL:1473, CH:135	rûd: *child* رود زهی دولت مادر روزگار که رودی چنین پرورد در کنار (سعدی) BQ:969, CH135

1145

رودبار   - رجوع شود به   رود + بار۳

رودن: کندن پر مرغ یا پشم گوسفند قبل از پختن   همریشه: lose, loss, less

Indo-European	Pahlavi	Persian
rauh*, leuh: *to pluck, pull out, shear hair* کندن پر یا پشم حیوان، پریدن مو CH:317, PK:681	rûn, lwn: *to pluck, pull out* CH:317	rudan: *to pluck hair or feather* رودن CH:317, BQ:970, DK*

COGNATE- Sanskrit "lav: to shave, cut off" (CH:317)

1146

روده

Indo-European	Pahlavi	Persian
reuto: *intestines, bowels* دل و روده PK:873	rôt 1: *intestine* PK:874	rûdeh: *intestine* روده PK:874, PH:139, BQ:970

1147

روز   همریشه: روشن   همریشه: light

Indo-European	Avestan	Pahlavi	Persian
leuk, rauxšn*: *light, brightness* نور، روشنایی PK:687, KT:205, CH:321	raočah: *light* raocana: *window* PH:23,136, BK:470,991	roc: *light* rôcan: *window, hole* BQ:971,972	rûz: *day* روز (فروزان، فروغ) rowzan: *hole, aperture* روزن (روزنه) BQ, NS:176

COGNATE- Old Persian "raucah: day" (KT:205)

1148

روزن، روزنه   - رجوع شود به   روز

روسپی

Pahlavi	Persian
rôspîk: *prostitute* روسپی BQ:974	rûspî: *prostitute* روسپی BQ:974

1149

روستا

Indo-European	Avestan	Pahlavi	Persian
leudh, raud 2: *to grow* رشد کردن PK:684, KL:885, BK:874, BR:39	raod 1, raodha: *growth, face* KL:885, BK:874	rôstâk: *village* MO:1689	rûstâ: *village* روستا IC:1103, MO:1689

1150

روش ـ رجوع شود به رَفتن

روشن   همریشه: روز   همریشه: light

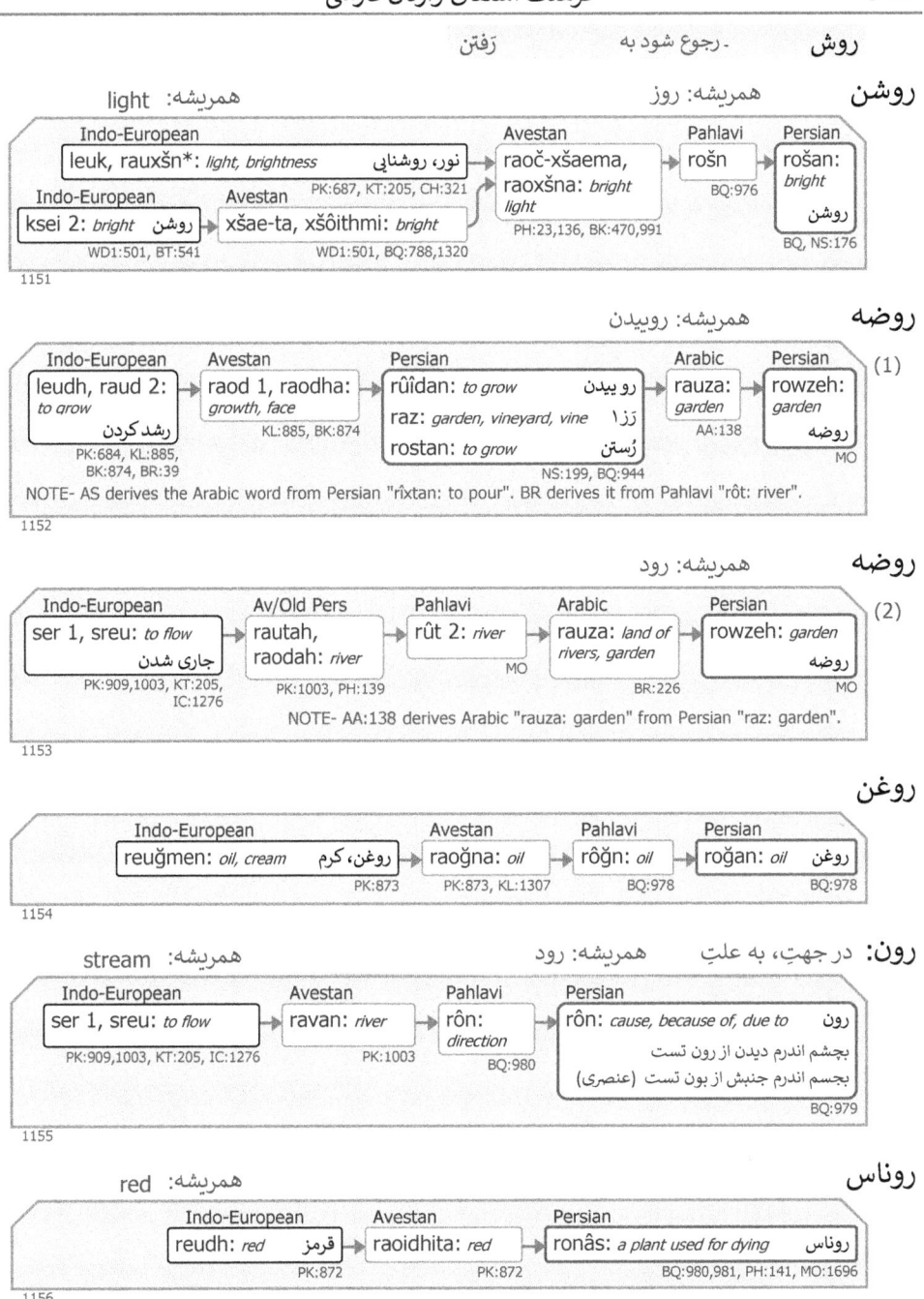

1151

روشن: Persian rošan: bright — Pahlavi rošn BQ:976 — Avestan raoč-xšaema, raoxšna: bright light PH:23,136, BK:470,991 — Indo-European leuk, rauxšn*: light, brightness نور، روشنایی PK:687, KT:205, CH:321 — Indo-European ksei 2: bright روشن WD1:501, BT:541 — Avestan xšae-ta, xšôithmi: bright WD1:501, BQ:788,1320 — BQ, NS:176

روضه (1)   همریشه: روییدن

Persian rowzeh: garden روضه MO — Arabic rauza: garden AA:138 — Persian rûîdan: to grow رو ییدن / raz: garden, vineyard, vine رَز / rostan: to grow رُستن NS:199, BQ:944 — Avestan raod 1, raodha: growth, face KL:885, BK:874 — Indo-European leudh, raud 2: to grow رشد کردن PK:684, KL:885, BK:874, BR:39

NOTE- AS derives the Arabic word from Persian "rîxtan: to pour". BR derives it from Pahlavi "rôt: river".

1152

روضه (2)   همریشه: رود

Persian rowzeh: garden روضه MO — Arabic rauza: land of rivers, garden BR:226 — Pahlavi rût 2: river MO — Av/Old Pers rautah, raodah: river PK:1003, PH:139 — Indo-European ser 1, sreu: to flow جاری شدن PK:909,1003, KT:205, IC:1276

NOTE- AA:138 derives Arabic "rauza: garden" from Persian "raz: garden".

1153

روغن

Persian rožan: oil روغن BQ:978 — Pahlavi rôğn: oil BQ:978 — Avestan raoğna: oil PK:873, KL:1307 — Indo-European reuğmen: oil, cream روغن، کرم PK:873

1154

رون: در جهتِ، به علتِ   همریشه: رود   همریشه: stream

Persian rôn: cause, because of, due to رون بچشم اندرم دیدن از رون تست بجسم اندرم جنبش از بون تست (عنصری) BQ:979 — Pahlavi rôn: direction BQ:980 — Avestan ravan: river PK:1003 — Indo-European ser 1, sreu: to flow PK:909,1003, KT:205, IC:1276

1155

روناس   همریشه: red

Persian ronâs: a plant used for dying روناس BQ:980,981, PH:141, MO:1696 — Avestan raoidhita: red PK:872 — Indo-European reudh: red قرمز PK:872

1156

روند ـ رجوع شود به رَفتن

رونق، رونیک

همریشه: روی، نیک، نیو، نیل،   همریشه: neat

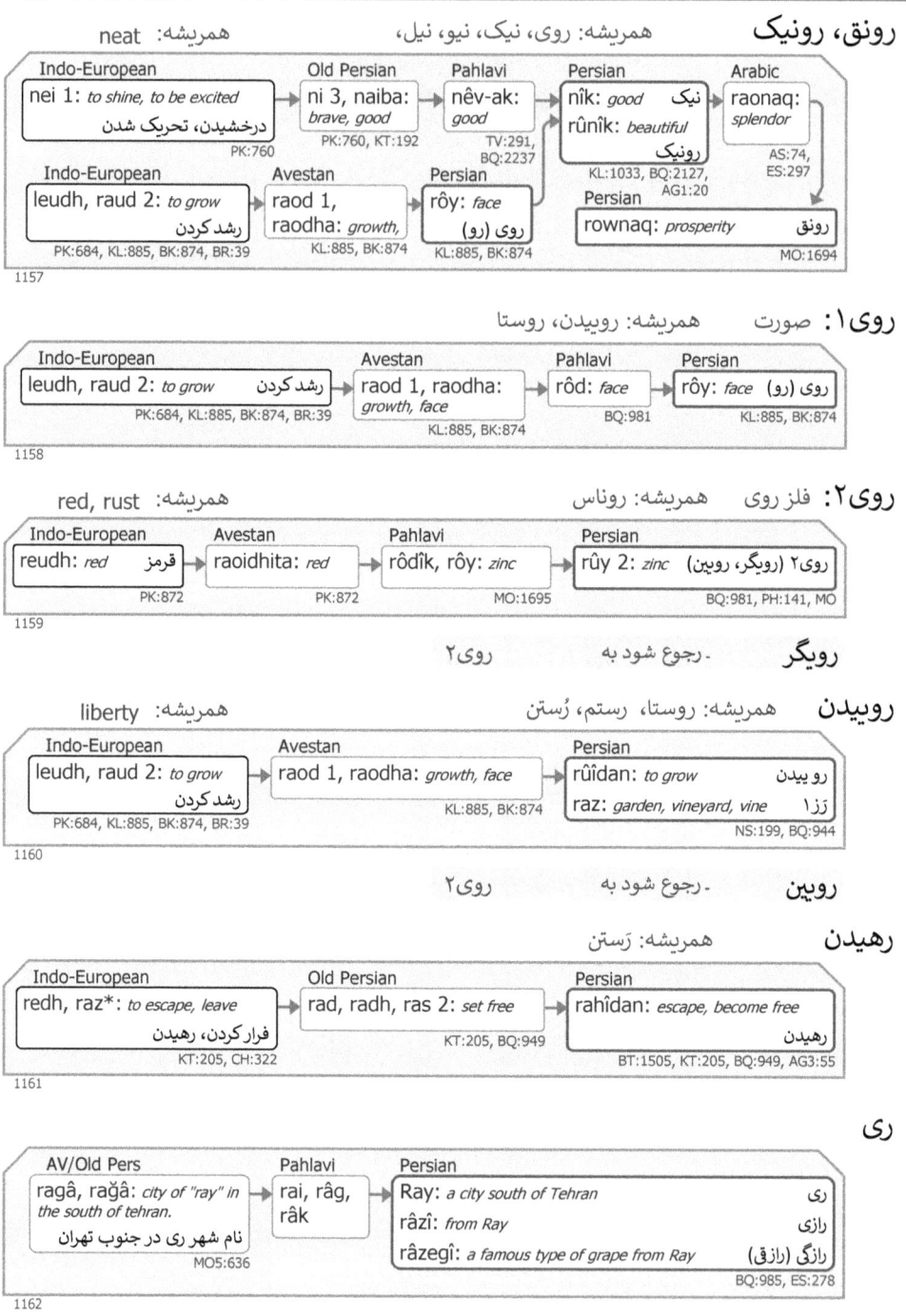

روی۱: صورت   همریشه: روییدن، روستا

روی۲: فلز روی   همریشه: روناس   همریشه: red, rust

رویگر - رجوع شود به   روی۲

روییدن   همریشه: روستا، رستم، رُستن   همریشه: liberty

روین - رجوع شود به   روی۲

رهیدن   همریشه: رَستن

ری

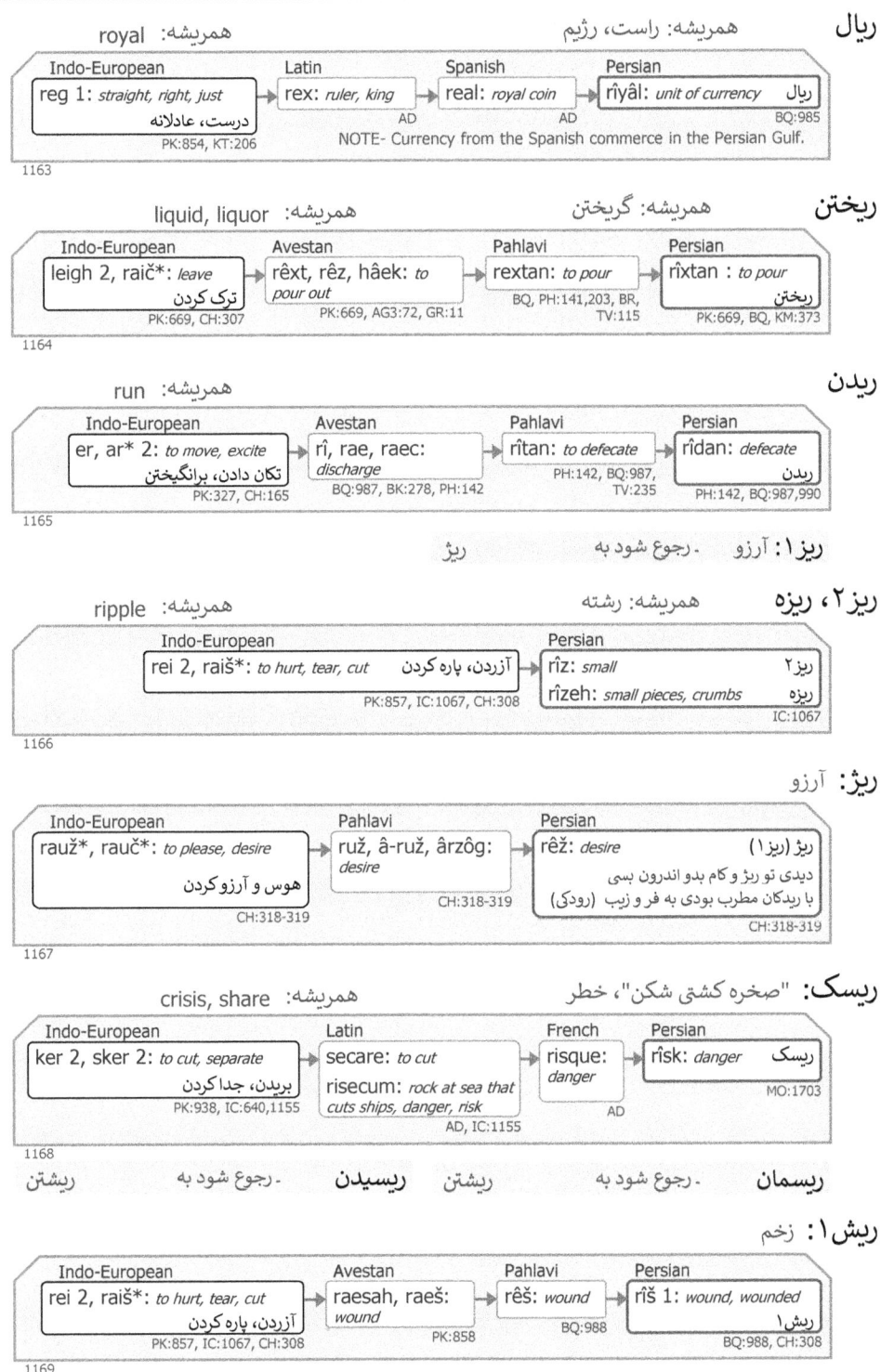

ریال   همریشه: راست، رژیم   همریشه: royal

Indo-European	Latin	Spanish	Persian
reg 1: *straight, right, just* درست، عادلانه PK:854, KT:206	rex: *ruler, king* AD	real: *royal coin* AD	rîyâl: *unit of currency* ریال BQ:985

NOTE- Currency from the Spanish commerce in the Persian Gulf.

1163

ریختن   همریشه: گریختن   همریشه: liquid, liquor

Indo-European	Avestan	Pahlavi	Persian
leigh 2, raič*: *leave* ترک کردن PK:669, CH:307	rêxt, rêz, hâek: *to pour out* PK:669, AG3:72, GR:11	rextan: *to pour* BQ, PH:141,203, BR, TV:115	rîxtan : *to pour* ریختن PK:669, BQ, KM:373

1164

ریدن   همریشه: run

Indo-European	Avestan	Pahlavi	Persian
er, ar* 2: *to move, excite discharge* تکان دادن، برانگیختن PK:327, CH:165	rî, rae, raec: *discharge* BQ:987, BK:278, PH:142	rîtan: *to defecate* PH:142, BQ:987, TV:235	rîdan: *defecate* ریدن PH:142, BQ:987,990

1165

ریز۱: آرزو   ۔رجوع شود به   ریژ

ریز۲، ریزه   همریشه: رشته   همریشه: ripple

Indo-European	Persian
rei 2, raiš*: *to hurt, tear, cut* آزردن، پاره کردن PK:857, IC:1067, CH:308	rîz: *small* ریز۲ rîzeh: *small pieces, crumbs* ریزه IC:1067

1166

ریژ: آرزو

Indo-European	Pahlavi	Persian
rauž*, rauč*: *to please, desire* هوس و آرزو کردن CH:318-319	ruž, â-ruž, ârzôg: *desire* CH:318-319	rêž: *desire* ریژ (ریز۱) دیدی تو ریژ و کام بدو اندرون بسی با ریدکان مطرب بودی به فر و زیب (رودکی) CH:318-319

1167

ریسک: "صخره کشتی شکن"، خطر   همریشه: crisis, share

Indo-European	Latin	French	Persian
ker 2, sker 2: *to cut, separate* بریدن، جدا کردن PK:938, IC:640,1155	secare: *to cut* risecum: *rock at sea that cuts ships, danger, risk* AD, IC:1155	risque: *danger* AD	rîsk: *danger* ریسک MO:1703

1168

ریسمان   ۔رجوع شود به   ریشتن   **ریسیدن**   ریشتن   ۔رجوع شود به   ریشتن

ریش۱: زخم

Indo-European	Avestan	Pahlavi	Persian
rei 2, raiš*: *to hurt, tear, cut* آزردن، پاره کردن PK:857, IC:1067, CH:308	raesah, raeš: *wound* PK:858	rêš: *wound* BQ:988	rîš 1: *wound, wounded* ریش۱ BQ:988, CH:308

1169

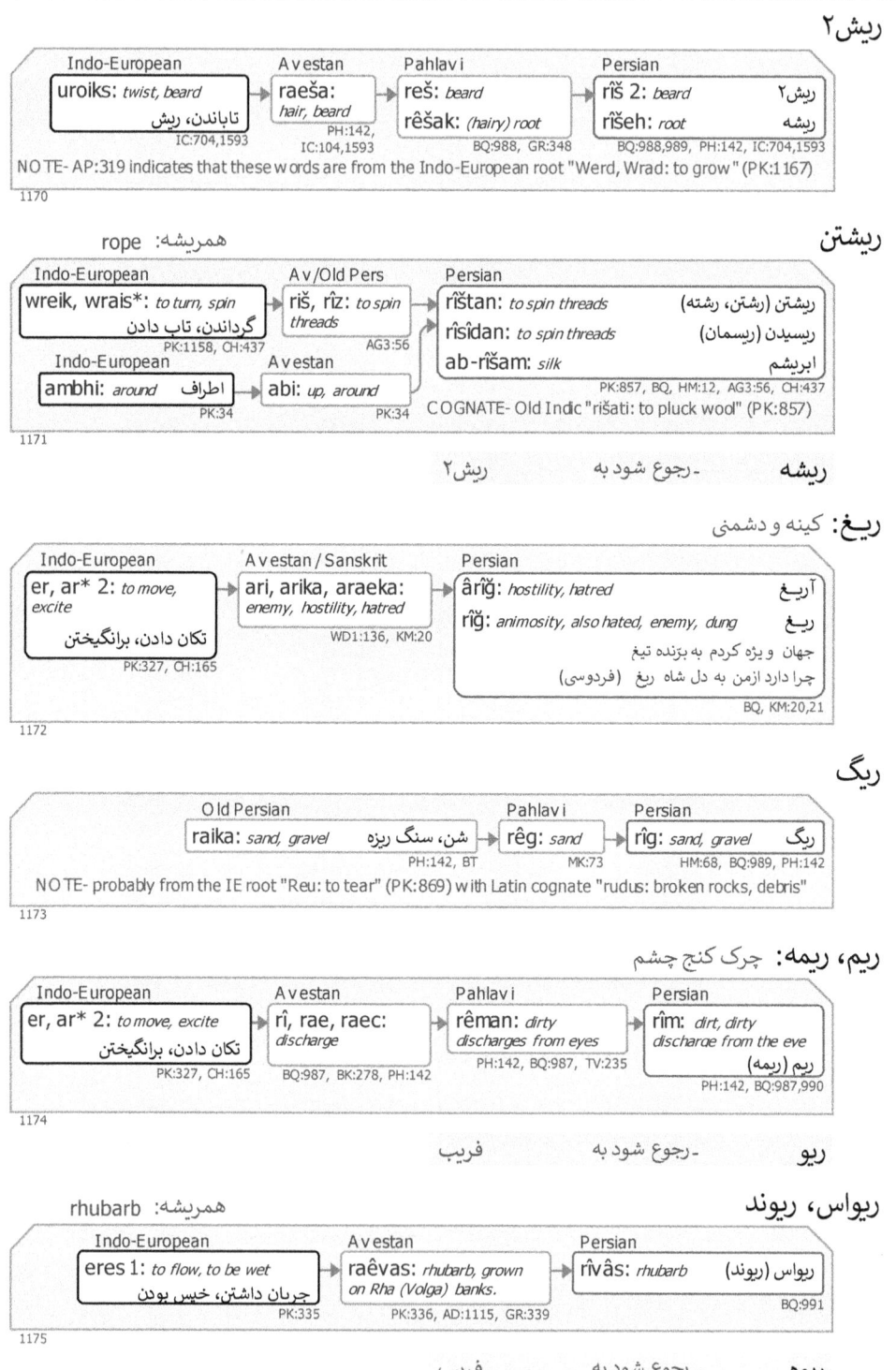

ریش۲

Indo-European	Avestan	Pahlavi	Persian	
uroiks: *twist, beard*	raeša: *hair, beard*	reš: *beard*	rîš 2: *beard*	ریش۲
تاباندن، ریش		rêšak: *(hairy) root*	rîšeh: *root*	ریشه
IC:704,1593	PH:142 IC:104,1593	BQ:988, GR:348	BQ:988,989, PH:142, IC:704,1593	

NOTE- AP:319 indicates that these words are from the Indo-European root "Werd, Wrad: to grow" (PK:1167)

1170

ریشتن

rope :همریشه

Indo-European	Av/Old Pers	Persian	
wreik, wrais*: *to turn, spin*	rîš, rîz: *to spin threads*	rîštan: *to spin threads*	(رشتن، رشته) ریشتن
گرداندن، تاب دادن		rîsîdan: *to spin threads*	(ریسمان) ریسیدن
PK:1158, CH:437	AG3:56	ab-rîšam: *silk*	ابریشم
Indo-European	Avestan		PK:857, BQ, HM:12, AG3:56, CH:437
ambhi: *around* اطراف	abi: *up, around*	COGNATE- Old Indic "rišati: to pluck wool" (PK:857)
PK:34	PK:34	

1171

ریشه   - رجوع شود به   ریش۲

ریغ: کینه و دشمنی

Indo-European	Avestan / Sanskrit	Persian	
er, ar* 2: *to move, excite*	ari, arika, araeka: *enemy, hostility, hatred*	ârîg: *hostility, hatred*	آریغ
تکان دادن، برانگیختن		rîg: *animosity, also hated, enemy, dung*	ریغ
PK:327, CH:165	WD1:136, KM:20	جهان وبژه کردم به بژنده تیغ	
		چرا دارد ازمن به دل شاه ریغ (فردوسی)	
		BQ, KM:20,21	

1172

ریگ

Old Persian	Pahlavi	Persian	
raika: *sand, gravel* شن، سنگ ریزه	rêg: *sand*	rîg: *sand, gravel* ریگ
PH:142, BT	MK:73	HM:68, BQ:989, PH:142

NOTE- probably from the IE root "Reu: to tear" (PK:869) with Latin cognate "rudus: broken rocks, debris"

1173

ریم، ریمه: چرک کنج چشم

Indo-European	Avestan	Pahlavi	Persian	
er, ar* 2: *to move, excite*	rî, rae, raec: *discharge*	rêman: *dirty discharges from eyes*	rîm: *dirt, dirty discharge from the eye*	
تکان دادن، برانگیختن			(ریمه) ریم	
PK:327, CH:165	BQ:987, BK:278, PH:142	PH:142, BQ:987, TV:235	PH:142, BQ:987,990	

1174

ریو   - رجوع شود به   فریب

ریواس، ریوند

rhubarb :همریشه

Indo-European	Avestan	Persian	
eres 1: *to flow, to be wet*	raêvas: *rhubarb, grown on Rha (Volga) banks.*	rîvâs: *rhubarb*	(ریوند) ریواس
جریان داشتن، خیس بودن		BQ:991	
PK:335	PK:336, AD:1115, GR:339	

1175

ریوه   - رجوع شود به   فریب

این حرف گاهی به ج، چ، غ یا س
بدل شود.

ز

زاب: چشمه ـ رجوع شود به   زهاب

زادن

همریشه: gene, generate, nation

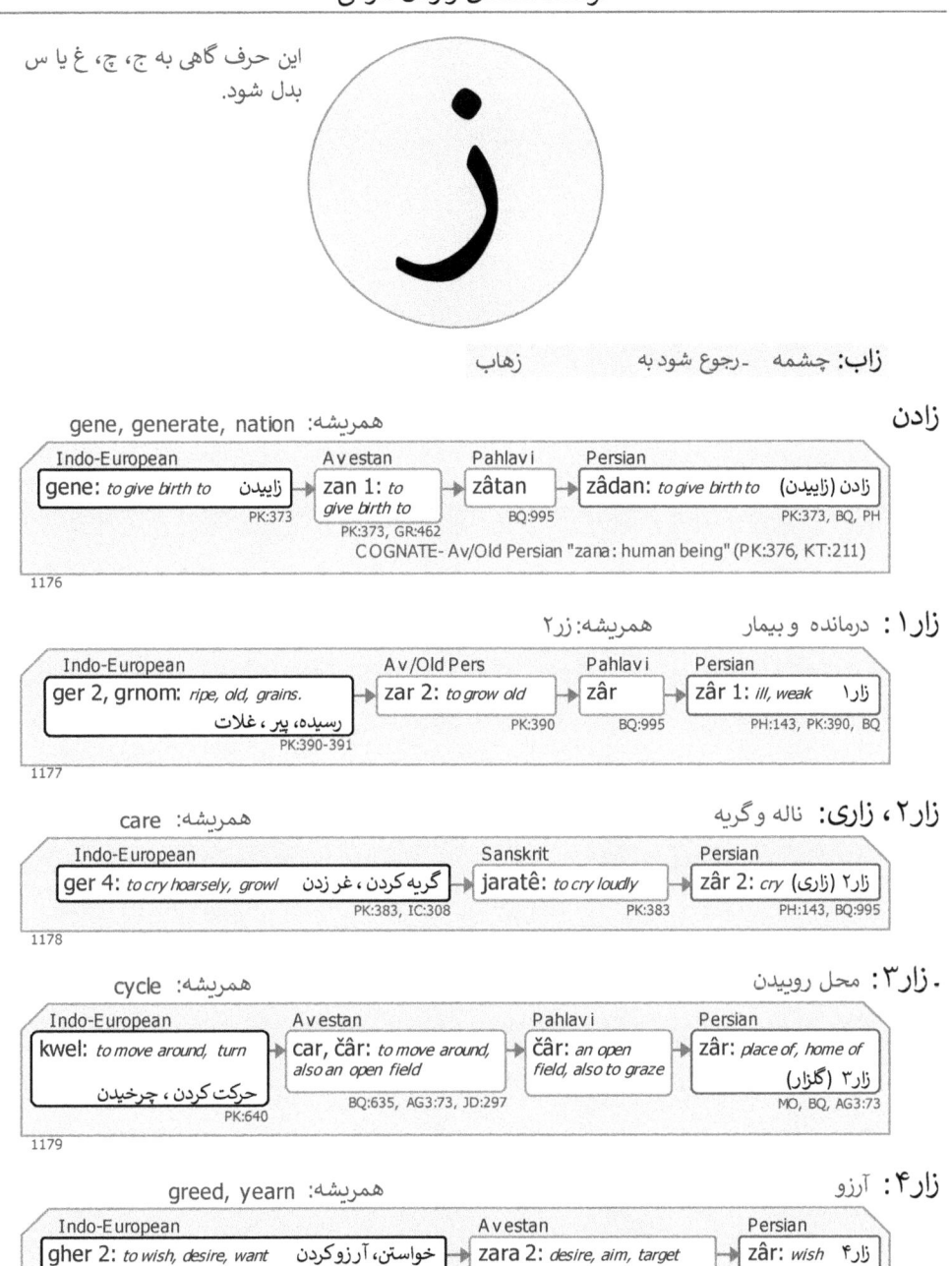

Indo-European	Avestan	Pahlavi	Persian
gene: to give birth to زاییدن	zan 1: to give birth to	zâtan	zâdan: to give birth to زادن (زاییدن)
PK:373	PK:373, GR:462	BQ:995	PK:373, BQ, PH

COGNATE- Av/Old Persian "zana: human being" (PK:376, KT:211)

1176

زار۱ : درمانده و بیمار   همریشه: زر۲

Indo-European	Av/Old Pers	Pahlavi	Persian
ger 2, grnom: ripe, old, grains. رسیده، پیر، غلات	zar 2: to grow old	zâr	zâr 1: ill, weak زار۱
PK:390-391	PK:390	BQ:995	PH:143, PK:390, BQ

1177

زار۲، زاری: ناله و گریه   همریشه: care

Indo-European	Sanskrit	Persian
ger 4: to cry hoarsely, growl گریه کردن، غر زدن	jaratê: to cry loudly	zâr 2: cry زار۲ (زاری)
PK:383, IC:308	PK:383	PH:143, BQ:995

1178

. زار۳: محل روییدن   همریشه: cycle

Indo-European	Avestan	Pahlavi	Persian
kwel: to move around, turn حرکت کردن ، چرخیدن	car, čâr: to move around, also an open field	čâr: an open field, also to graze	zâr: place of, home of زار۳ (گلزار)
PK:640	BQ:635, AG3:73, JD:297		MO, BQ, AG3:73

1179

زار۴: آرزو   همریشه: greed, yearn

Indo-European	Avestan	Persian
gher 2: to wish, desire, want خواستن، آرزو کردن	zara 2: desire, aim, target	zâr: wish زار۴
PK:440	PK:440	CH:104

این لغت یا متروک شده و یا استفاده از آن بسیار محدود میباشد.

1180

زاغ
(1)

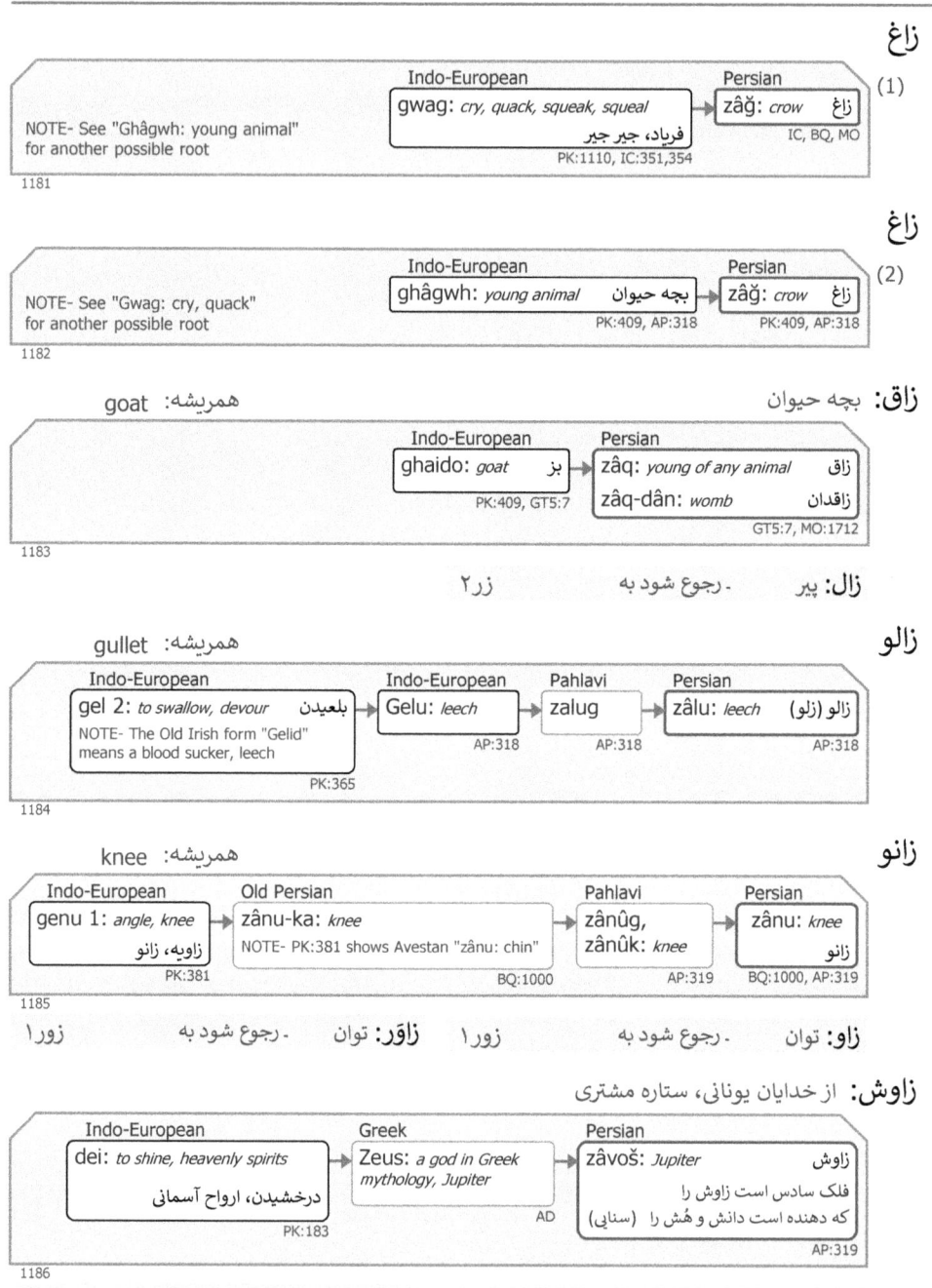

Indo-European
gwag: *cry, quack, squeak, squeal*
فریاد، جیر جیر
PK:1110, IC:351,354

Persian
zâğ: *crow* زاغ
IC, BQ, MO

NOTE- See "Ghâgwh: young animal"
for another possible root

1181

زاغ
(2)

Indo-European
ghâgwh: *young animal* بچه حیوان
PK:409, AP:318

Persian
zâğ: *crow* زاغ
PK:409, AP:318

NOTE- See "Gwag: cry, quack"
for another possible root

1182

زاق: بچه حیوان

همریشه: goat

Indo-European
ghaido: *goat* بز
PK:409, GT5:7

Persian
zâq: *young of any animal* زاق
zâq-dân: *womb* زاقدان
GT5:7, MO:1712

1183

زال: پیر ۰ رجوع شود به زر ۲

زالو

همریشه: gullet

Indo-European
gel 2: *to swallow, devour* بلعیدن
NOTE- The Old Irish form "Gelid"
means a blood sucker, leech
PK:365

Indo-European
Gelu: *leech*
AP:318

Pahlavi
zalug
AP:318

Persian
zâlu: *leech* (زلو) زالو
AP:318

1184

زانو

همریشه: knee

Indo-European
genu 1: *angle, knee*
زاویه، زانو
PK:381

Old Persian
zânu-ka: *knee*
NOTE- PK:381 shows Avestan "zânu: chin"
BQ:1000

Pahlavi
zânûg,
zânûk: *knee*
AP:319

Persian
zânu: *knee*
زانو
BQ:1000, AP:319

1185

زاو: توان ۰ رجوع شود به زور ۱ **زاوَر:** توان ۰ رجوع شود به زور ۱

زاوش: از خدایان یونانی، ستاره مشتری

Indo-European
dei: *to shine, heavenly spirits*
درخشیدن، ارواح آسمانی
PK:183

Greek
Zeus: *a god in Greek
mythology, Jupiter*
AD

Persian
zâvoš: *Jupiter* زاوش
فلک سادس است زاوش را
که دهنده است دانش و هُش را (سنایی)
AP:319

1186

زاهید: زادن ۰ رجوع شود به زه ۲ **زاییدن** ۰ رجوع شود به زادن

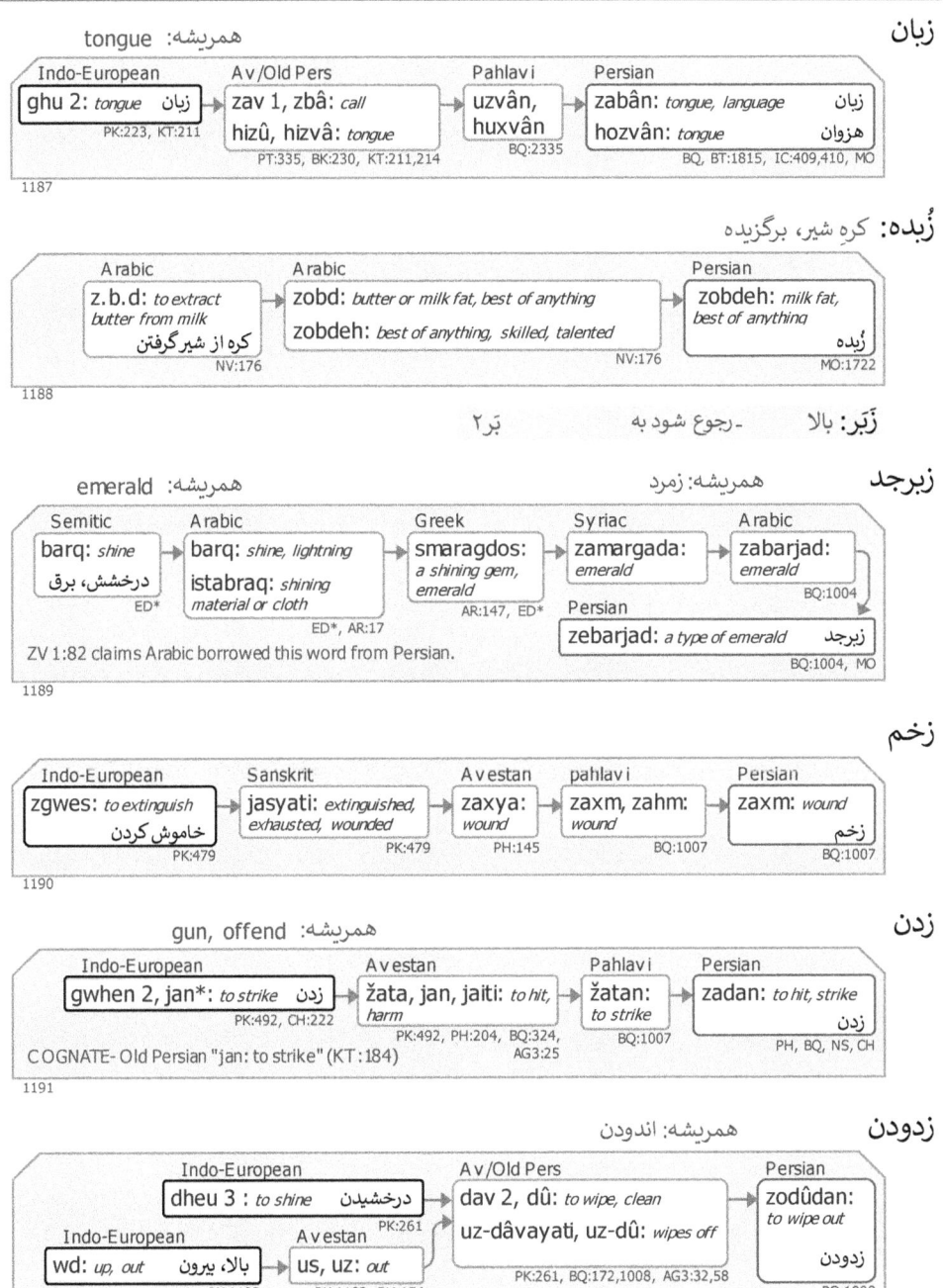

زبان

همریشه: tongue

Indo-European	Av/Old Pers	Pahlavi	Persian
ghu 2: *tongue* زبان PK:223, KT:211	zav 1, zbâ: *call* hizû, hizvâ: *tongue* PT:335, BK:230, KT:211,214	uzvân, huxvân BQ:2335	zabân: *tongue, language* زبان hozvân: *tongue* هزوان BQ, BT:1815, IC:409,410, MO

1187

زُبده: کرهِ شیر، برگزیده

Arabic	Arabic	Persian
z.b.d: *to extract butter from milk* کره از شیر گرفتن NV:176	zobd: *butter or milk fat, best of anything* zobdeh: *best of anything, skilled, talented* NV:176	zobdeh: *milk fat, best of anything* زُبده MO:1722

1188

زَبَر: بالا ـ رجوع شود به بَر۲

زبرجد

همریشه: زمرد ∙ همریشه: emerald

Semitic	Arabic	Greek	Syriac	Arabic
barq: *shine* درخشش، برق ED*	barq: *shine, lightning* istabraq: *shining material or cloth* ED*, AR:17	smaragdos: *a shining gem, emerald* AR:147, ED*	zamargada: *emerald*	zabarjad: *emerald* BQ:1004

Persian
zebarjad: *a type of emerald* زبرجد
BQ:1004, MO

ZV 1:82 claims Arabic borrowed this word from Persian.

1189

زخم

Indo-European	Sanskrit	Avestan	pahlavi	Persian
zgwes: *to extinguish* خاموش کردن PK:479	jasyati: *extinguished, exhausted, wounded* PK:479	zaxya: *wound* PH:145	zaxm, zahm: *wound* BQ:1007	zaxm: *wound* زخم BQ:1007

1190

زدن

همریشه: gun, offend

Indo-European	Avestan	Pahlavi	Persian
gwhen 2, jan*: *to strike* زدن PK:492, CH:222	žata, jan, jaiti: *to hit, harm* PK:492, PH:204, BQ:324, AG3:25	žatan: *to strike* BQ:1007	zadan: *to hit, strike* زدن PH, BQ, NS, CH

COGNATE- Old Persian "jan: to strike" (KT:184)

1191

زدودن

همریشه: اندودن

Indo-European	Av/Old Pers	Persian
dheu 3: *to shine* درخشیدن PK:261	dav 2, dû: *to wipe, clean* uz-dâvayati, uz-dû: *wipes off* PK:261, BQ:172,1008, AG3:32,58	zodûdan: *to wipe out* زدودن BQ:1008

Indo-European	Avestan	
wd: *up, out* بالا، بیرون PK:1103	us, uz: *out* PK:1103, PH:154	

1192

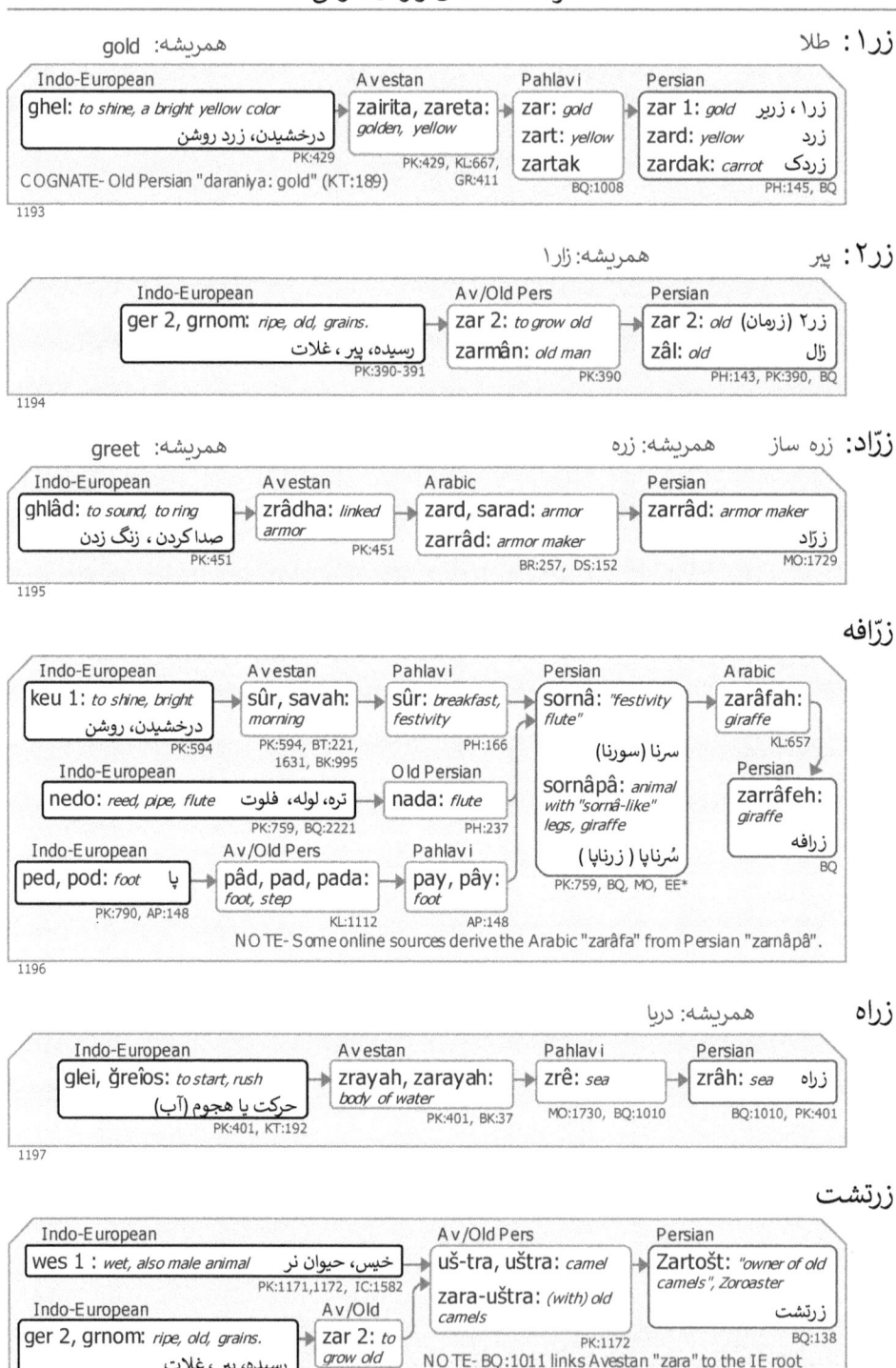

زر ۱: طلا

همریشه: gold

Indo-European	Avestan	Pahlavi	Persian
ghel: to shine, a bright yellow color درخشیدن، زرد روشن PK:429	zairita, zareta: golden, yellow PK:429, KL:667, GR:411	zar: gold zart: yellow zartak BQ:1008	zar 1: gold زریر، زر ۱ zard: yellow زرد zardak: carrot زردک PH:145, BQ

COGNATE- Old Persian "daraniya: gold" (KT:189)

1193

زر ۲: پیر

همریشه: زار ۱

Indo-European	Av/Old Pers	Persian
ger 2, grnom: ripe, old, grains. رسیده، پیر، غلات PK:390-391	zar 2: to grow old zarmân: old man PK:390	zar 2 (زمان) زر ۲: old zâl: old زال PH:143, PK:390, BQ

1194

زرّاد: زره ساز   همریشه: زره   همریشه: greet

Indo-European	Avestan	Arabic	Persian
ghlâd: to sound, to ring صدا کردن، زنگ زدن PK:451	zrâdha: linked armor PK:451	zard, sarad: armor zarrâd: armor maker BR:257, DS:152	zarrâd: armor maker زرّاد MO:1729

1195

زرّافه

Indo-European	Avestan	Pahlavi	Persian	Arabic
keu 1: to shine, bright درخشیدن، روشن PK:594	sûr, savah: morning PK:594, BT:221, 1631, BK:995	sûr: breakfast, festivity PH:166	sornâ: "festivity flute" سرنا (سورنا)	zarâfah: giraffe KL:657

Indo-European		Old Persian		Persian
nedo: reed, pipe, flute تره، لوله، فلوت PK:759, BQ:2221		nada: flute PH:237		zarrâfeh: giraffe زرّافه BQ

Indo-European	Av/Old Pers	Pahlavi	
ped, pod: foot پا PK:790, AP:148	pâd, pad, pada: foot, step KL:1112	pay, pây: foot AP:148	

sornâpâ: animal
with "sornâ-like"
legs, giraffe
(سُرناپا (زرناپا
PK:759, BQ, MO, EE*

NOTE- Some online sources derive the Arabic "zarâfa" from Persian "zarnâpâ".

1196

زراه

همریشه: دریا

Indo-European	Avestan	Pahlavi	Persian
glei, ğreîos: to start, rush (حرکت یا هجوم (آب PK:401, KT:192	zrayah, zarayah: body of water PK:401, BK:37	zrê: sea MO:1730, BQ:1010	zrâh: sea زراه BQ:1010, PK:401

1197

زرتشت

Indo-European	Av/Old Pers	Persian
wes 1: wet, also male animal خیس، حیوان نر PK:1171,1172, IC:1582	uš-tra, uštra: camel zara-uštra: (with) old camels PK:1172	Zartošt: "owner of old camels", Zoroaster زرتشت BQ:138

Indo-European	Av/Old	
ger 2, grnom: ripe, old, grains. رسیده، پیر، غلات PK:390-391	zar 2: to grow old PK:390	

NOTE- BQ:1011 links Avestan "zara" to the IE root
"Ghel: yellow", thus zara-uštra: (with) yellow camels.

1198

زرد، زردک   رجوع شود به-   زر ۱

زرگون

همریشه: ژَهره

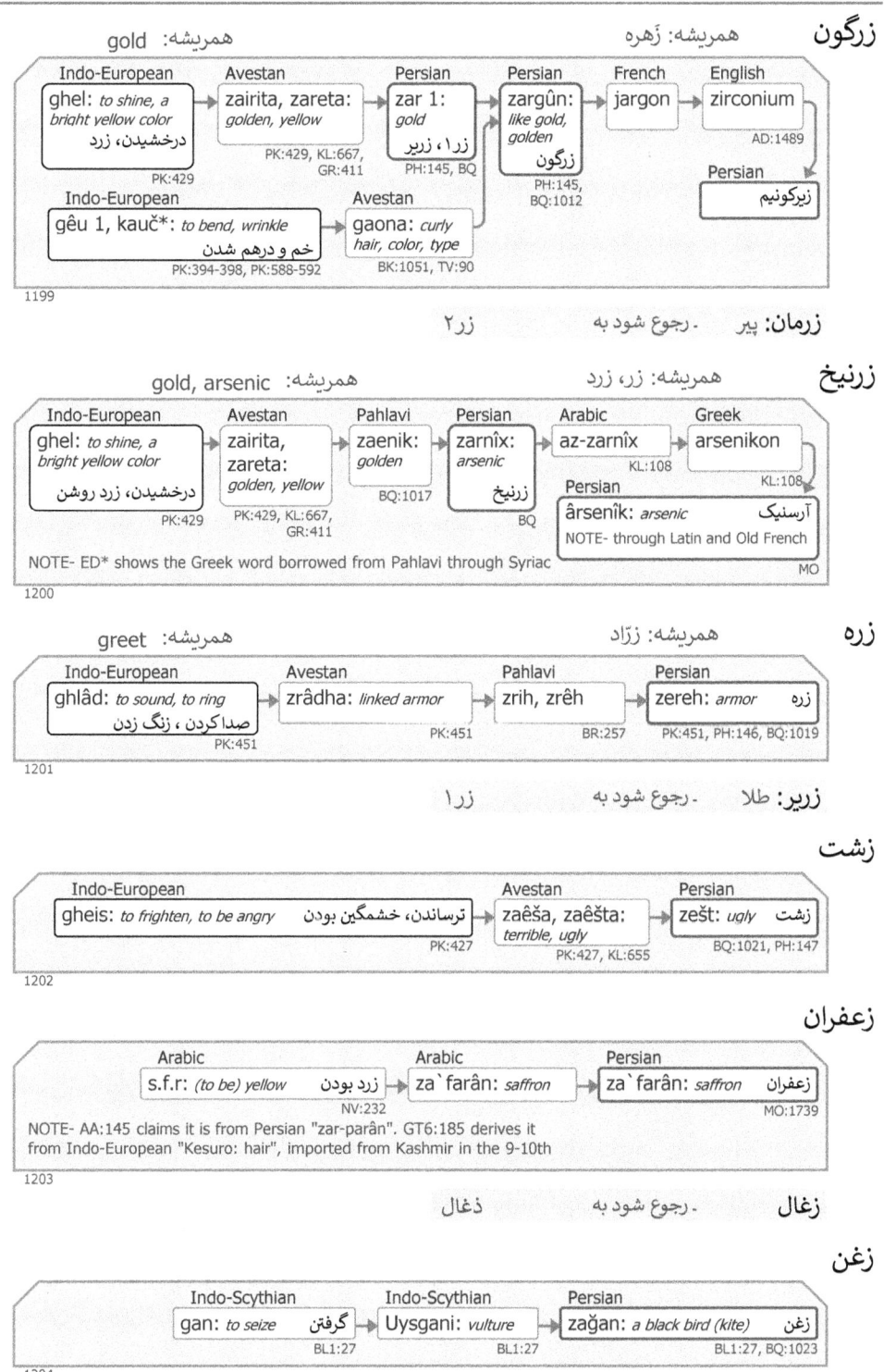

زرگون

همریشه: gold

Indo-European	Avestan	Persian	Persian	French	English
ghel: *to shine, a bright yellow color* درخشیدن، زرد PK:429	zairita, zareta: *golden, yellow* PK:429, KL:667, GR:411	zar 1: *gold* زر۱، زریر PH:145, BQ	zargûn: *like gold, golden* زرگون PH:145, BQ:1012	jargon	zirconium AD:1489

Persian: زیرکونیم

Indo-European	Avestan
gêu 1, kauč*: *to bend, wrinkle* خم و درهم شدن PK:394-398, PK:588-592	gaona: *curly hair, color, type* BK:1051, TV:90

1199

زرمان: پیر   . رجوع شود به   زر۲

زرنیخ

همریشه: زر، زرد

همریشه: gold, arsenic

Indo-European	Avestan	Pahlavi	Persian	Arabic	Greek
ghel: *to shine, a bright yellow color* درخشیدن، زرد روشن PK:429	zairita, zareta: *golden, yellow* PK:429, KL:667, GR:411	zaenik: *golden* BQ:1017	zarnîx: *arsenic* زرنیخ BQ	az-zarnîx KL:108	arsenikon KL:108

Persian: ârsenîk: *arsenic* آرسنیک
NOTE- through Latin and Old French   MO

NOTE- ED* shows the Greek word borrowed from Pahlavi through Syriac

1200

زره

همریشه: زرّاد

همریشه: greet

Indo-European	Avestan	Pahlavi	Persian
ghlâd: *to sound, to ring* صداکردن ، زنگ زدن PK:451	zrâdha: *linked armor* PK:451	zrih, zrêh BR:257	zereh: *armor* زره PK:451, PH:146, BQ:1019

1201

زریر: طلا   . رجوع شود به   زر۱

زشت

Indo-European	Avestan	Persian
gheis: *to frighten, to be angry* ترساندن، خشمگین بودن PK:427	zaêša, zaêšta: *terrible, ugly* PK:427, KL:655	zešt: *ugly* زشت BQ:1021, PH:147

1202

زعفران

Arabic	Arabic	Persian
s.f.r: *(to be) yellow* زرد بودن NV:232	za`farân: *saffron*	za`farân: *saffron* زعفران MO:1739

NOTE- AA:145 claims it is from Persian "zar-parân". GT6:185 derives it from Indo-European "Kesuro: hair", imported from Kashmir in the 9-10th

1203

زغال

زغال: . رجوع شود به   ذغال

زغن

Indo-Scythian	Indo-Scythian	Persian
gan: *to seize* گرفتن BL1:27	Uysgani: *vulture* BL1:27	zağan: *a black bird (kite)* زغن BL1:27, BQ:1023

1204

زفت

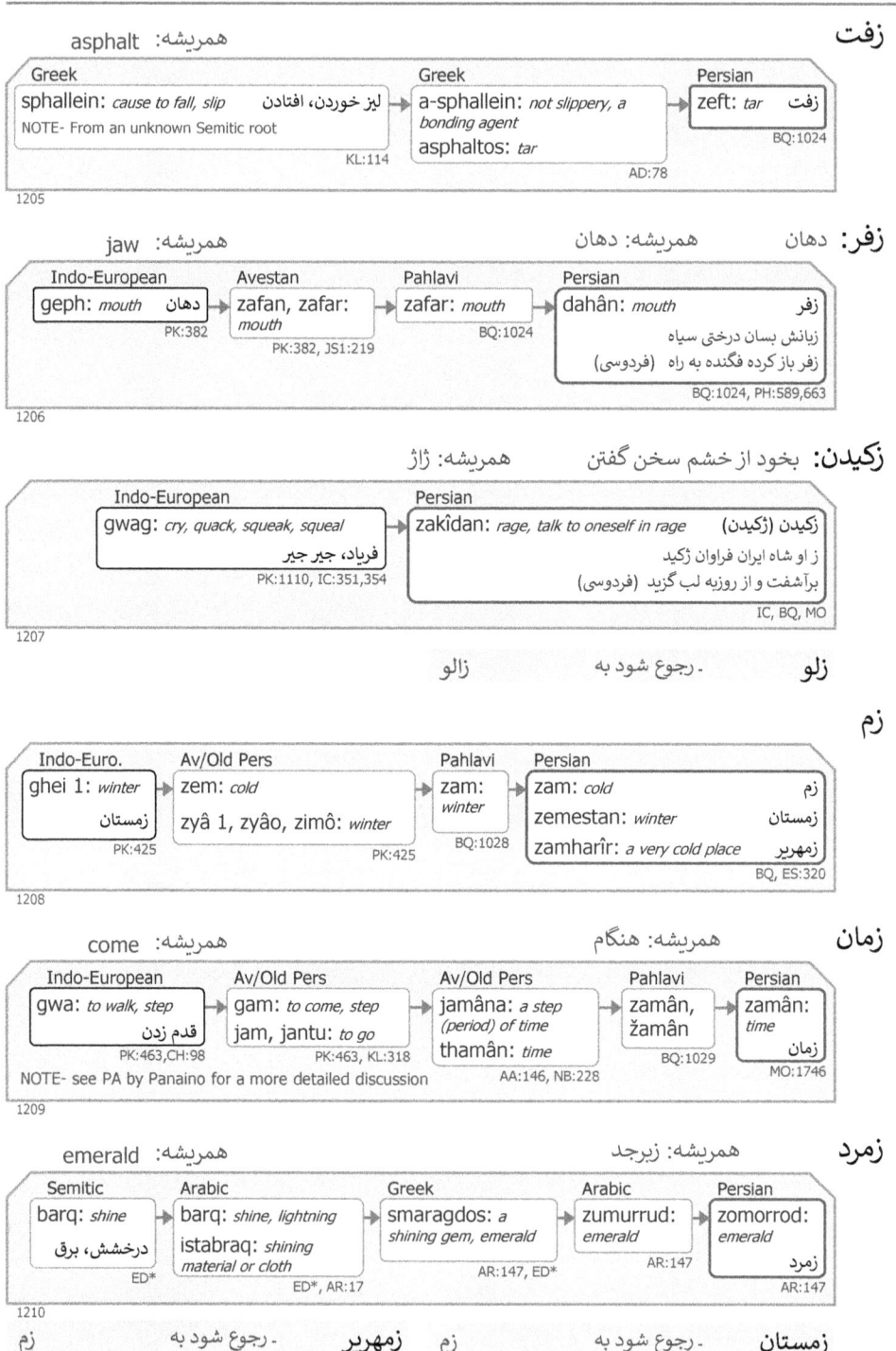

همریشه: asphalt

Greek
sphallein: *cause to fall, slip* لیز خوردن، افتادن
NOTE- From an unknown Semitic root
KL:114

Greek
a-sphallein: *not slippery, a bonding agent*
asphaltos: *tar*
AD:78

Persian
zeft: *tar* زفت
BQ:1024

1205

زفر: دهان

همریشه: jaw   همریشه: دهان

Indo-European
geph: *mouth* دهان
PK:382

Avestan
zafan, zafar: *mouth*
PK:382, JS1:219

Pahlavi
zafar: *mouth*
BQ:1024

Persian
dahân: *mouth* زفر
زبانش بسان درختی سیاه
زفر باز کرده فگنده به راه   (فردوسی)
BQ:1024, PH:589,663

1206

زکیدن: بخود از خشم سخن گفتن

همریشه: ژاژ

Indo-European
gwag: *cry, quack, squeak, squeal*
فریاد، جیر جیر
PK:1110, IC:351,354

Persian
zakîdan: *rage, talk to oneself in rage*   زکیدن (ژکیدن)
ز او و شاه ایران فراوان ژکید
برآشفت و از روزیه لب گزید   (فردوسی)
IC, BQ, MO

1207

زلو

رجوع شود به -   زالو

زم

Indo-Euro.
ghei 1: *winter*
زمستان
PK:425

Av/Old Pers
zem: *cold*
zyâ 1, zyâo, zimô: *winter*
PK:425

Pahlavi
zam: *winter*
BQ:1028

Persian
zam: *cold* زم
zemestan: *winter* زمستان
zamharîr: *a very cold place* زمهریر
BQ, ES:320

1208

زمان

همریشه: come   همریشه: هنگام

Indo-European
gwa: *to walk, step*
قدم زدن
PK:463,CH:98

Av/Old Pers
gam: *to come, step*
jam, jantu: *to go*
PK:463, KL:318

Av/Old Pers
jamâna: *a step (period) of time*
thamân: *time*
AA:146, NB:228

Pahlavi
zamân, žamân
BQ:1029

Persian
zamân: *time*
زمان
MO:1746

NOTE- see PA by Panaino for a more detailed discussion

1209

زمرد

همریشه: emerald   همریشه: زبرجد

Semitic
barq: *shine*
درخشش، برق
ED*

Arabic
barq: *shine, lightning*
istabraq: *shining material or cloth*
ED*, AR:17

Greek
smaragdos: *a shining gem, emerald*
AR:147, ED*

Arabic
zumurrud: *emerald*
AR:147

Persian
zomorrod: *emerald*
زمرد
AR:147

1210

زمستان   رجوع شود به -   زم   **زمهریر**   زم   رجوع شود به -   زم

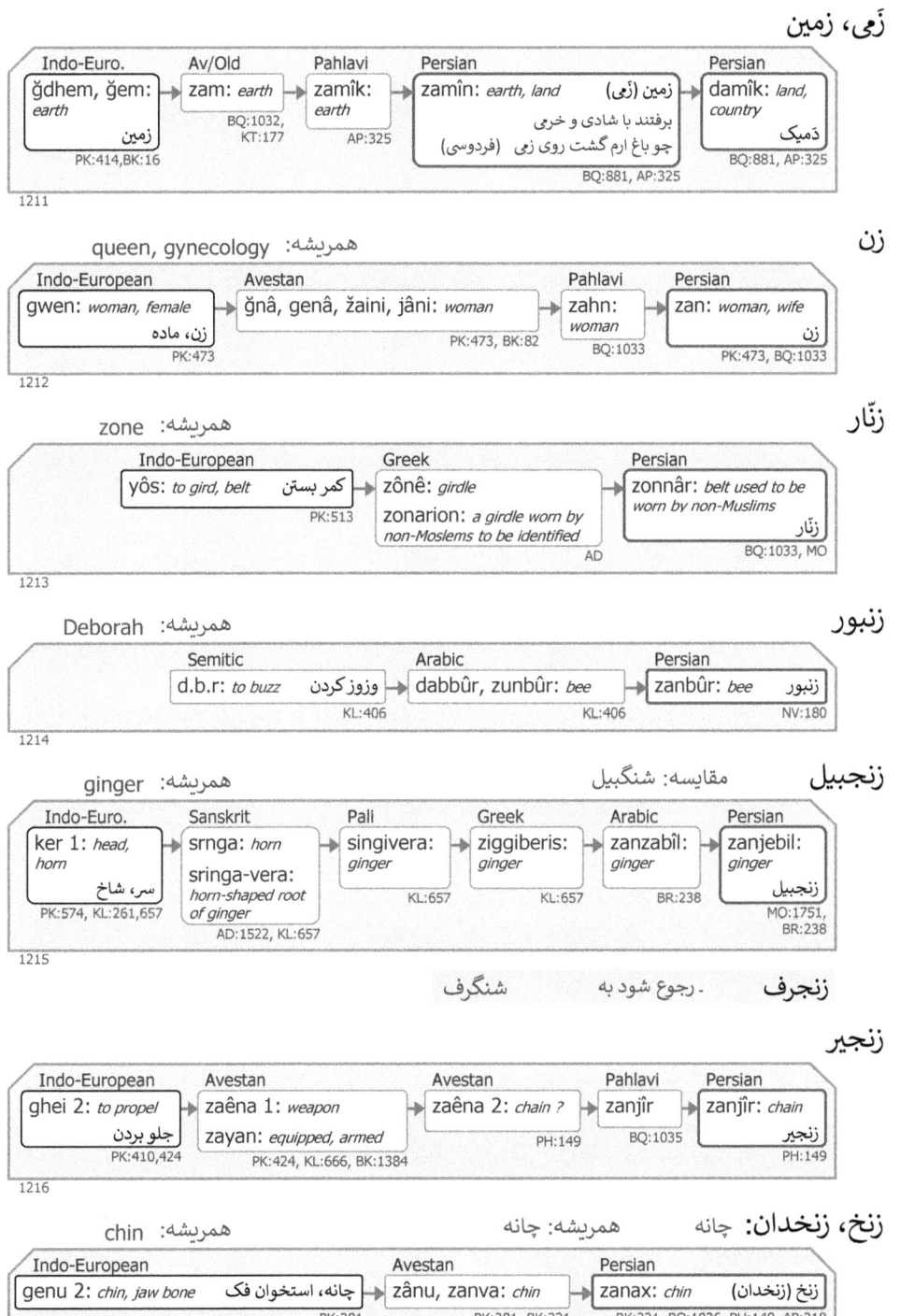

زَمی، زمین

1211

زن

همریشه: queen, gynecology

1212

زنّار

همریشه: zone

1213

زنبور

همریشه: Deborah

1214

زنجبیل

همریشه: ginger   مقایسه: شنگبیل

1215

زنجرف ‌ـ رجوع شود به   شنگرف

زنجیر

1216

زنخ، زنخدان: چانه   همریشه: چانه   همریشه: chin

1217

زند: تفسیر اوستا به پهلوی همریشه: دانش همریشه: knowledge

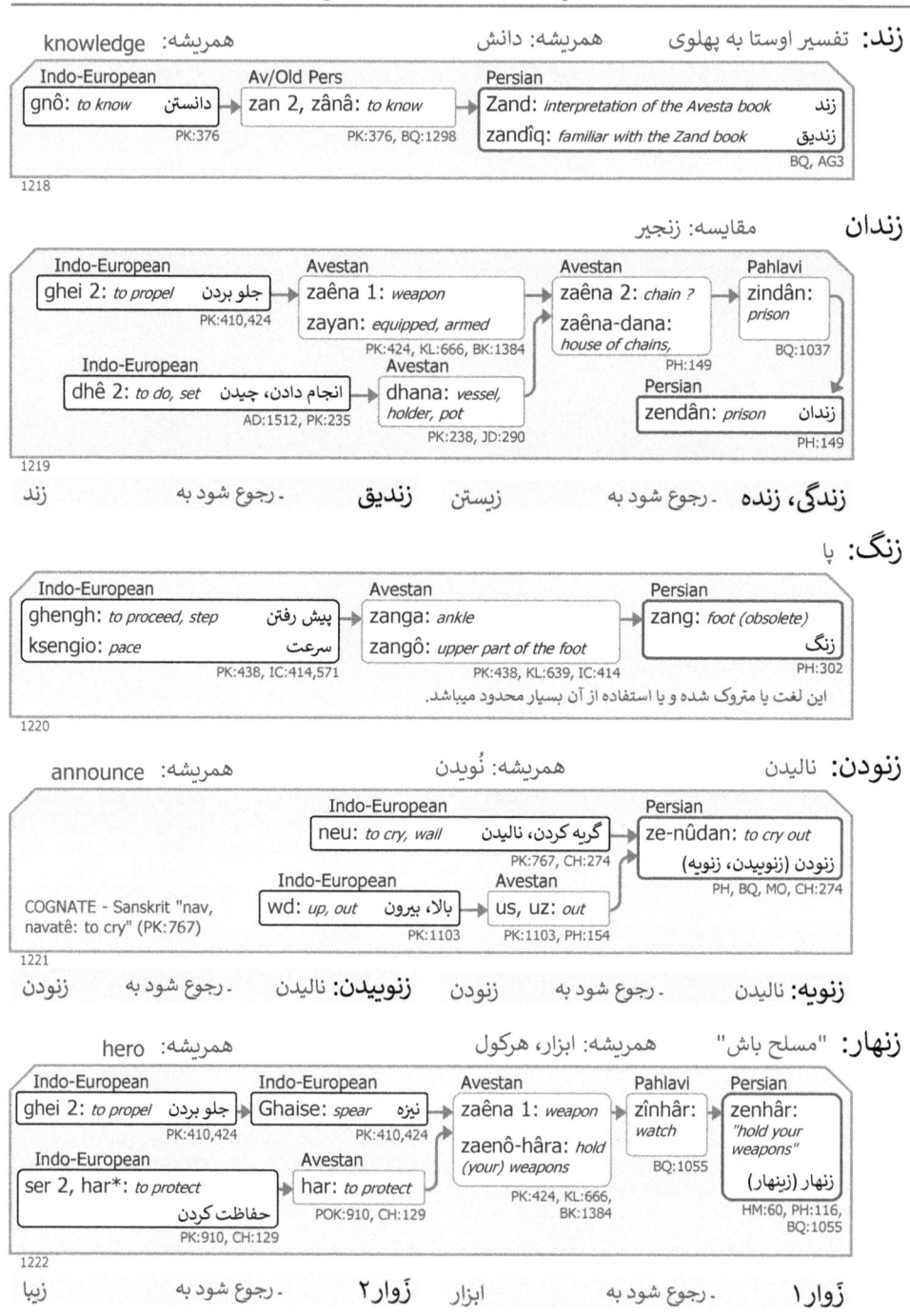

Indo-European	Av/Old Pers	Persian
gnô: *to know* دانستن	zan 2, zânâ: *to know*	Zand: *interpretation of the Avesta book* زند
PK:376	PK:376, BQ:1298	zandîq: *familiar with the Zand book* زندیق
		BQ, AG3

1218

زندان مقایسه: زنجیر

Indo-European	Avestan	Avestan	Pahlavi
ghei 2: *to propel* جلو بردن	zaêna 1: *weapon*	zaêna 2: *chain ?*	zindân: *prison*
PK:410,424	zayan: *equipped, armed*	zaêna-dana: *house of chains,*	BQ:1037
	PK:424, KL:666, BK:1384	PH:149	
Indo-European	Avestan		Persian
dhê 2: *to do, set* انجام دادن، چیدن	dhana: *vessel, holder, pot*		zendân: *prison* زندان
AD:1512, PK:235	PK:238, JD:290		PH:149

1219

زندگی، زنده ـ رجوع شود به **زیستن** **زندیق** ـ رجوع شود به زند

زنگ: پا

Indo-European	Avestan	Persian
ghengh: *to proceed, step* پیش رفتن	zanga: *ankle*	zang: *foot (obsolete)*
ksengio: *pace* سرعت	zangô: *upper part of the foot*	زنگ
PK:438, IC:414,571	PK:438, KL:639, IC:414	PH:302

این لغت یا متروک شده و یا استفاده از آن بسیار محدود میباشد.

1220

زنودن: نالیدن همریشه: نُوید همریشه: announce

	Indo-European	Persian
	neu: *to cry, wail* گریه کردن، نالیدن	ze-nûdan: *to cry out*
	PK:767, CH:274	زنودن (زنوییدن، زنویه)
	Indo-European	Avestan	PH, BQ, MO, CH:274
COGNATE - Sanskrit "nav, navatê: to cry" (PK:767)	wd: *up, out* بالا، بیرون	us, uz: *out*	
	PK:1103	PK:1103, PH:154	

1221

زنویه: نالیدن ـ رجوع شود به زنودن **زنوییدن:** نالیدن ـ رجوع شود به زنودن

زنهار: "مسلح باش" همریشه: ابزار، هرکول همریشه: hero

Indo-European	Indo-European	Avestan	Pahlavi	Persian
ghei 2: *to propel* جلو بردن	Ghaise: *spear* نیزه	zaêna 1: *weapon*	zînhâr: *watch*	zenhâr: "hold your weapons"
PK:410,424	PK:410,424	zaenô-hâra: *hold (your) weapons*	BQ:1055	زنهار (زینهار)
Indo-European	Avestan	PK:424, KL:666, BK:1384		HM:60, PH:116, BQ:1055
ser 2, har*: *to protect* حفاظت کردن	har: *to protect*			
PK:910, CH:129	POK:910, CH:129			

1222

ژوار ۱ ـ رجوع شود به زیبا **ژوار ۲** ابزار ـ رجوع شود به ژور ۲

زوت، زوتر: موبد ـ رجوع شود به ژور ۲

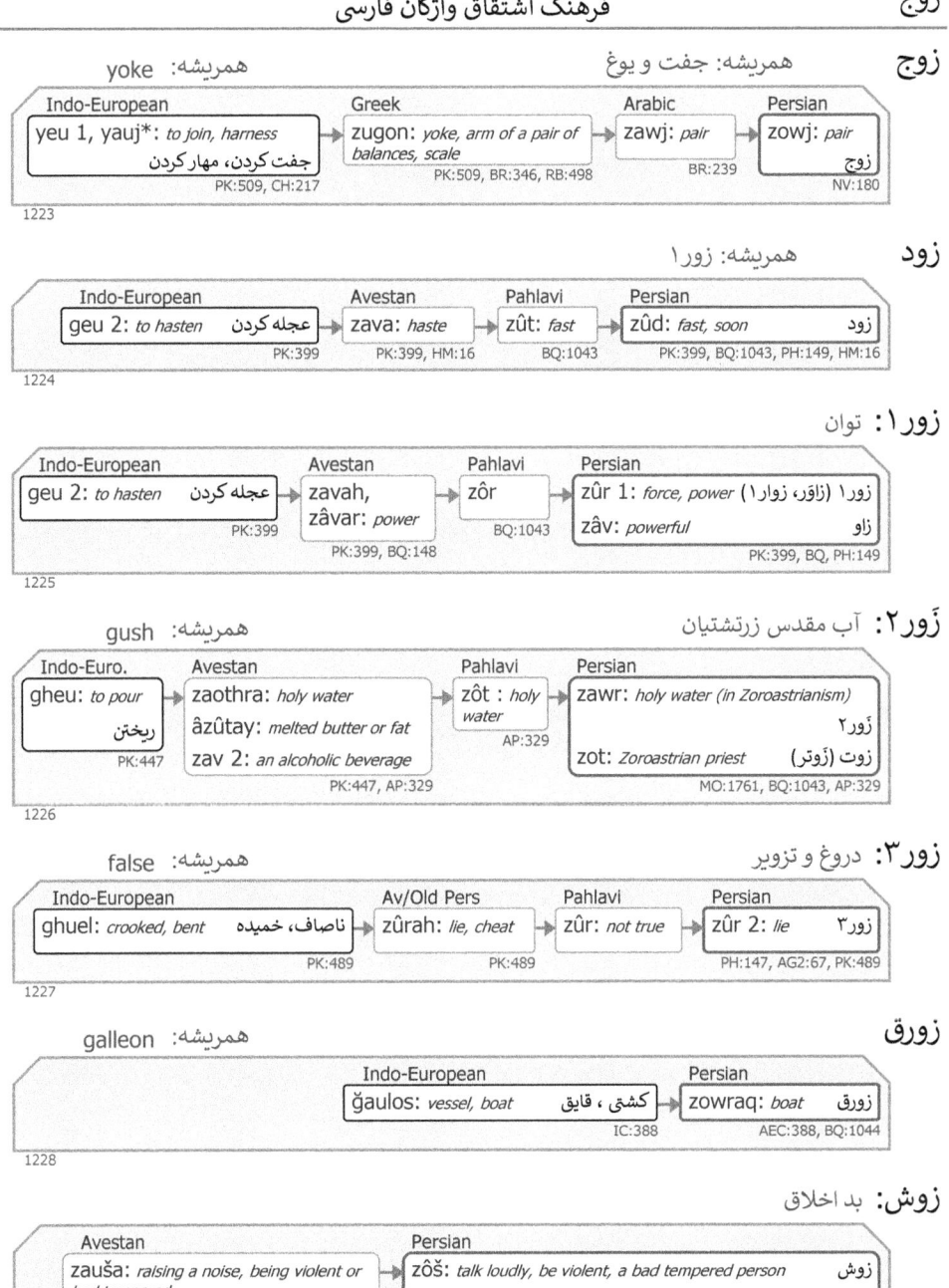

زوج   همریشه: جفت و یوغ

همریشه: yoke

Indo-European	Greek	Arabic	Persian
yeu 1, yauj*: to join, harness جفت کردن، مهار کردن	zugon: yoke, arm of a pair of balances, scale	zawj: pair	zowj: pair زوج
PK:509, CH:217	PK:509, BR:346, RB:498	BR:239	NV:180

1223

زود   همریشه: زور۱

Indo-European	Avestan	Pahlavi	Persian
geu 2: to hasten عجله کردن	zava: haste	zût: fast	zûd: fast, soon زود
PK:399	PK:399, HM:16	BQ:1043	PK:399, BQ:1043, PH:149, HM:16

1224

زور۱: توان

Indo-European	Avestan	Pahlavi	Persian
geu 2: to hasten عجله کردن	zavah, zâvar: power	zôr	زور۱ (زاوَر، زوار۱): force, power زاو zâv: powerful
PK:399	PK:399, BQ:148	BQ:1043	PK:399, BQ, PH:149

1225

زور۲: آب مقدس زرتشتیان

همریشه: gush

Indo-Euro.	Avestan	Pahlavi	Persian
gheu: to pour ریختن	zaothra: holy water âzûtay: melted butter or fat zav 2: an alcoholic beverage	zôt : holy water	zawr: holy water (in Zoroastrianism) زور۲ zot: Zoroastrian priest زوت (زَوتر)
PK:447	PK:447, AP:329	AP:329	MO:1761, BQ:1043, AP:329

1226

زور۳: دروغ و تزویر

همریشه: false

Indo-European	Av/Old Pers	Pahlavi	Persian
ghuel: crooked, bent ناصاف، خمیده	zûrah: lie, cheat	zûr: not true	zûr 2: lie زور۳
PK:489	PK:489		PH:147, AG2:67, PK:489

1227

زورق

همریشه: galleon

Indo-European	Persian
ğaulos: vessel, boat کشتی، قایق	zowraq: boat زورق
IC:388	AEC:388, BQ:1044

1228

زوش: بد اخلاق

Avestan	Persian
zauša: raising a noise, being violent or bad tempered داد زدن و بد اخلاقی کردن	zôš: talk loudly, be violent, a bad tempered person زوش بانگ کردمت ای بت سیمین زوش خواندم تراکه هستی زوش (رودکی)
GV:220	GV:220, BQ:1044, MO:1762

1229

فرهنگ اشتقاق واژگان فارسی

زه ۱۵: چلۀ کمان

همریشه: file, filet

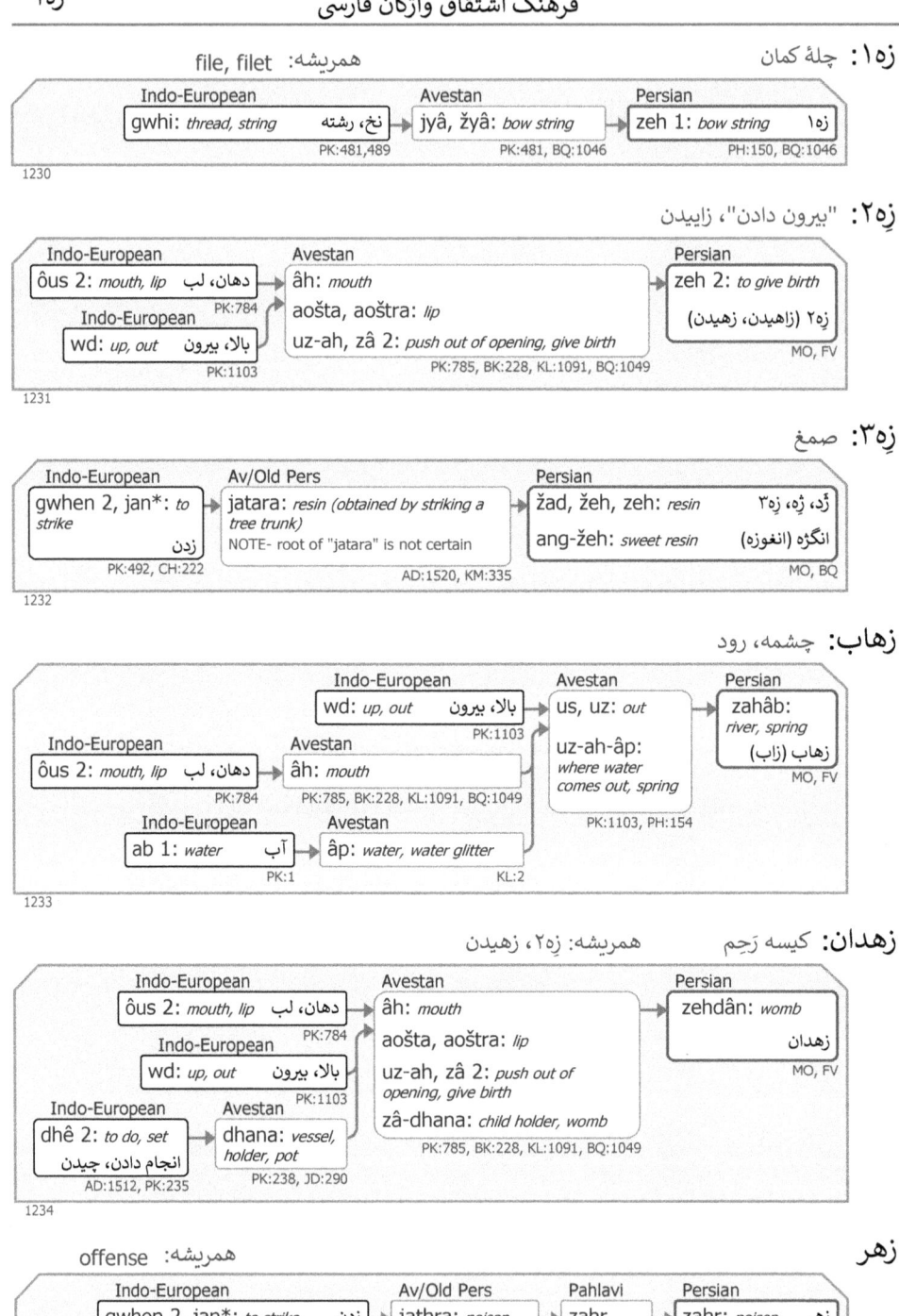

Indo-European	Avestan	Persian
gwhi: *thread, string* نخ، رشته	jyâ, žyâ: *bow string*	zeh 1: *bow string* زه ۱
PK:481,489	PK:481, BQ:1046	PH:150, BQ:1046

1230

زِه ۲: "بیرون دادن"، زاییدن

Indo-European	Avestan	Persian
ôus 2: *mouth, lip* دهان، لب	âh: *mouth*	zeh 2: *to give birth*
PK:784	aošta, aoštra: *lip*	زه ۲ (زاهیدن، زهیدن)
Indo-European	uz-ah, zâ 2: *push out of opening, give birth*	
wd: *up, out* بالا، بیرون		MO, FV
PK:1103	PK:785, BK:228, KL:1091, BQ:1049	

1231

زِه ۳: صمغ

Indo-European	Av/Old Pers	Persian
gwhen 2, jan*: *to strike*	jatara: *resin (obtained by striking a tree trunk)*	žad, žeh, zeh: *resin* ژَد، ژِه، زه ۳
زدن	NOTE- root of "jatara" is not certain	ang-žeh: *sweet resin* انگژه (انغوزه)
PK:492, CH:222	AD:1520, KM:335	MO, BQ

1232

زهاب: چشمه، رود

	Indo-European		Avestan	Persian
	wd: *up, out* بالا، بیرون		us, uz: *out*	zahâb: *river, spring* زهاب (زاب)
	PK:1103		uz-ah-âp: *where water comes out, spring*	
Indo-European	Avestan			MO, FV
ôus 2: *mouth, lip* دهان، لب	âh: *mouth*			
PK:784	PK:785, BK:228, KL:1091, BQ:1049		PK:1103, PH:154	
Indo-European	Avestan			
ab 1: *water* آب	âp: *water, water glitter*			
PK:1		KL:2		

1233

زهدان: کیسه رَحِم

همریشه: زِه ۲، زهیدن

Indo-European	Avestan	Persian
ôus 2: *mouth, lip* دهان، لب	âh: *mouth*	zehdân: *womb*
PK:784	aošta, aoštra: *lip*	زهدان
Indo-European	uz-ah, zâ 2: *push out of opening, give birth*	
wd: *up, out* بالا، بیرون		MO, FV
PK:1103	zâ-dhana: *child holder, womb*	
Indo-European	Avestan	
dhê 2: *to do, set* انجام دادن، چیدن	dhana: *vessel, holder, pot*	
AD:1512, PK:235	PK:238, JD:290	PK:785, BK:228, KL:1091, BQ:1049

1234

زهر

همریشه: offense

Indo-European	Av/Old Pers	Pahlavi	Persian
gwhen 2, jan*: *to strike* زدن	jathra: *poison*	zahr	zahr: *poison* زهر
PK:492, CH:222	AD:1520, KM:335	BQ:1047	BQ:1047

1235

219

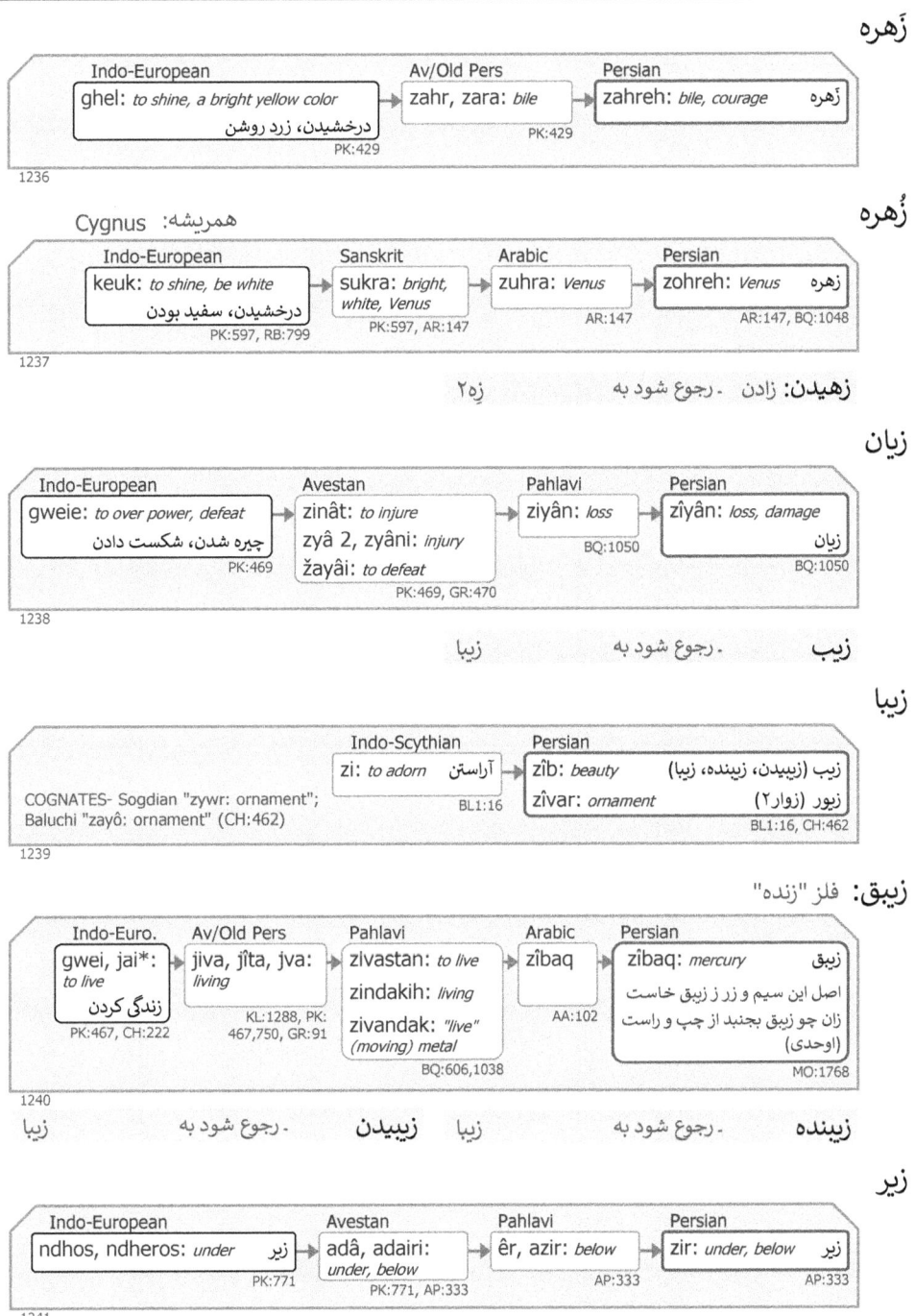

Indo-European ghel: to shine, a bright yellow color / درخشیدن، زرد روشن / PK:429 → **Av/Old Pers** zahr, zara: bile / PK:429 → **Persian** zahreh: bile, courage / زهره

1236

همریشه: Cygnus

Indo-European keuk: to shine, be white / درخشیدن، سفید بودن / PK:597, RB:799 → **Sanskrit** sukra: bright, white, Venus / PK:597, AR:147 → **Arabic** zuhra: Venus / AR:147 → **Persian** zohreh: Venus / زهره / AR:147, BQ:1048

1237

زهیدن: زادن ـ رجوع شود به زِه۲

زیان

Indo-European gweie: to over power, defeat / چیره شدن، شکست دادن / PK:469 → **Avestan** zinât: to injure / zyâ 2, zyâni: injury / žayâi: to defeat / PK:469, GR:470 → **Pahlavi** ziyân: loss / BQ:1050 → **Persian** zîyân: loss, damage / زیان / BQ:1050

1238

زیب ـ رجوع شود به زیبا

زیبا

COGNATES- Sogdian "zywr: ornament"; Baluchi "zayô: ornament" (CH:462) → **Indo-Scythian** zi: to adorn / آراستن / BL1:16 → **Persian** zîb: beauty (زیبیدن، زیبنده، زیبا) زیب / zîvar: ornament زیور (زوار۲) / BL1:16, CH:462

1239

زیبق: فلز "زنده"

Indo-Euro. gwei, jai*: to live / زندگی کردن / PK:467, CH:222 → **Av/Old Pers** jiva, jîta, jva: living / KL:1288, PK: 467,750, GR:91 → **Pahlavi** zîvastan: to live / zindakih: living / zivandak: "live" (moving) metal / BQ:606,1038 → **Arabic** zîbaq / AA:102 → **Persian** zîbaq: mercury زیبق / اصل این سیم و زر زِ زیبق خاست / زان چو زیبق بجنبد از چپ و راست (اوحدی) / MO:1768

1240

زیبنده ـ رجوع شود به زیبا **زیبیدن** زیبا ـ رجوع شود به زیبا

زیر

Indo-European ndhos, ndheros: under زیر / PK:771 → **Avestan** adâ, adairi: under, below / PK:771, AP:333 → **Pahlavi** êr, azir: below / AP:333 → **Persian** zir: under, below زیر / AP:333

1241

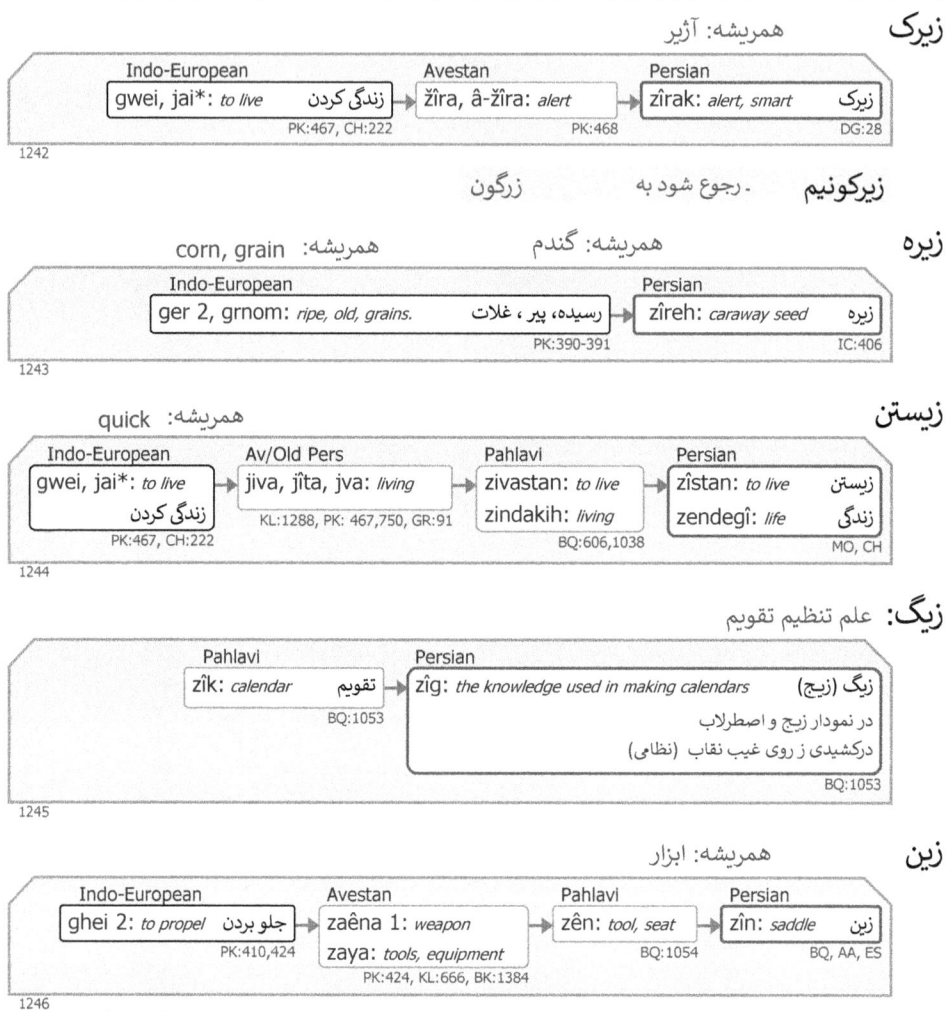

زیرک   همریشه: آژیر

Indo-European	Avestan	Persian
gwei, jai*: to live زندگی کردن	žîra, â-žîra: alert	zîrak: alert, smart زیرک
PK:467, CH:222	PK:468	DG:28

1242

زیرکونیم   ـ رجوع شود به   زرگون

زیره   همریشه: گندم   همریشه: corn, grain

Indo-European	Persian
ger 2, grnom: ripe, old, grains. رسیده، پیر ، غلات	zîreh: caraway seed زیره
PK:390-391	IC:406

1243

زیستن   همریشه: quick

Indo-European	Av/Old Pers	Pahlavi	Persian
gwei, jai*: to live زندگی کردن	jiva, jîta, jva: living	zivastan: to live zindakih: living	zîstan: to live زیستن zendegî: life زندگی
PK:467, CH:222	KL:1288, PK: 467,750, GR:91	BQ:606,1038	MO, CH

1244

زیگ: علم تنظیم تقویم

Pahlavi	Persian
zîk: calendar تقویم	zîg: the knowledge used in making calendars (زیج) زیگ در نمودار زیج و اصطرلاب درکشیدی ز روی غیب نقاب (نظامی)
BQ:1053	BQ:1053

1245

زین   همریشه: ابزار

Indo-European	Avestan	Pahlavi	Persian
ghei 2: to propel جلو بردن	zaêna 1: weapon zaya: tools, equipment	zên: tool, seat	zîn: saddle زین
PK:410,424	PK:424, KL:666, BK:1384	BQ:1054	BQ, AA, ES

1246

زینهار   ـ رجوع شود به   زنهار   زیور   ـ رجوع شود به   زیبا

221

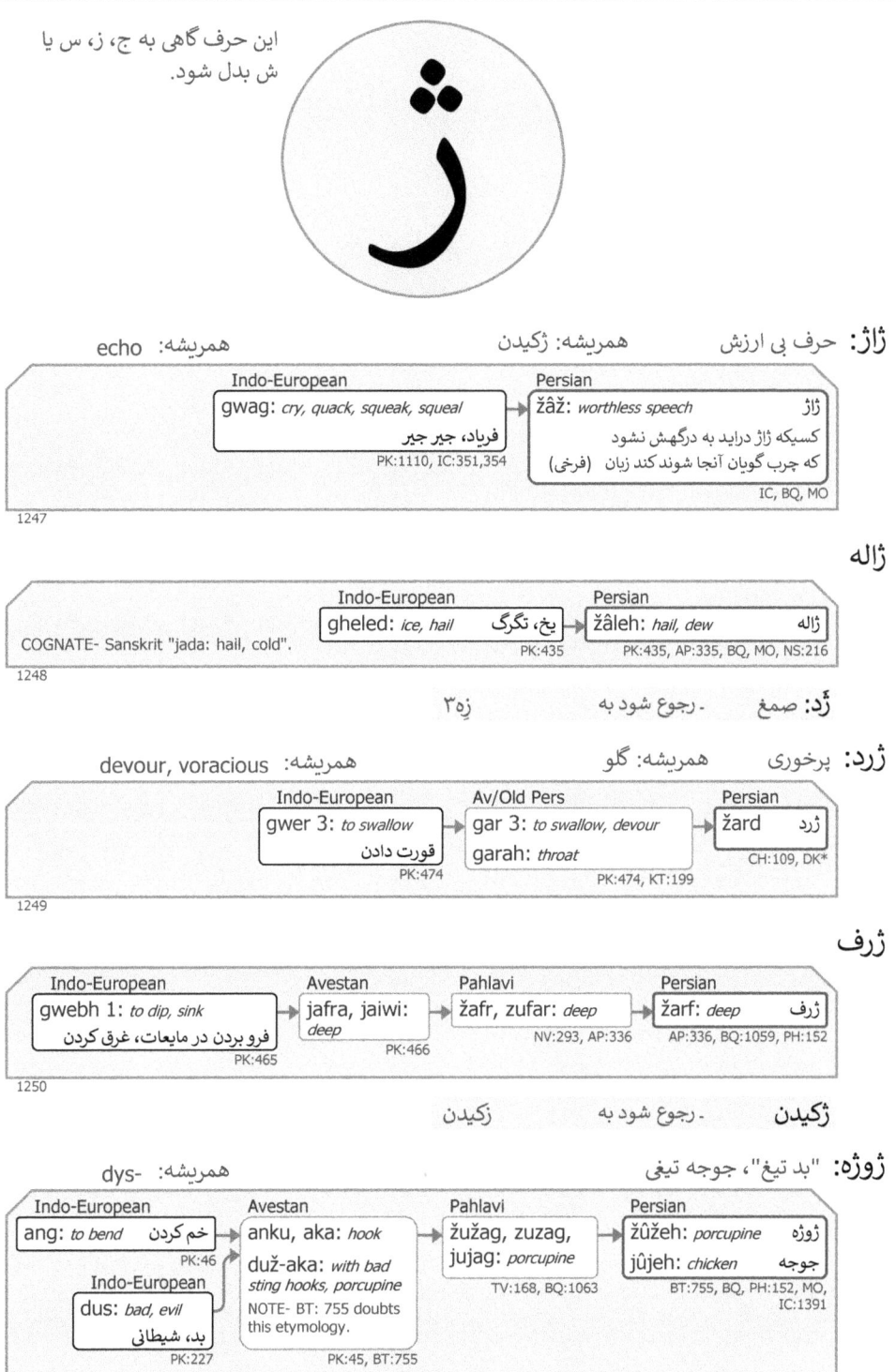

این حرف گاهی به ج، ز، س یا ش بدل شود.

ژاژ: حرف بی ارزش   همریشه: ژکیدن   همریشه: echo

Indo-European	Persian
gwag: *cry, quack, squeak, squeal* فریاد، جیر جیر PK:1110, IC:351,354	ژاژ žâž: *worthless speech* کسیکه ژاژ دراید به درگهش نشود که چرب گویان آنجا شوند کند زیان (فرخی) IC, BQ, MO

1247

ژاله

	Indo-European	Persian
COGNATE- Sanskrit "jada: hail, cold".	gheled: *ice, hail* یخ، تگرگ PK:435	žâleh: *hail, dew* ژاله PK:435, AP:335, BQ, MO, NS:216

1248

ژُد: صمغ   ـ رجوع شود به   زِه ۳

ژرد: پرخوری   همریشه: گلو   همریشه: devour, voracious

Indo-European	Av/Old Pers	Persian
gwer 3: *to swallow* قورت دادن PK:474	gar 3: *to swallow, devour* garah: *throat* PK:474, KT:199	žard ژرد CH:109, DK*

1249

ژرف

Indo-European	Avestan	Pahlavi	Persian
gwebh 1: *to dip, sink* فرو بردن در مایعات، غرق کردن PK:465	jafra, jaiwi: *deep* PK:466	žafr, zufar: *deep* NV:293, AP:336	žarf: *deep* ژرف AP:336, BQ:1059, PH:152

1250

ژکیدن   ـ رجوع شود به   زکیدن

ژوژه: "بد تیغ"، جوجه تیغی   همریشه: -dys

Indo-European	Avestan	Pahlavi	Persian
ang: *to bend* خم کردن PK:46	anku, aka: *hook* duž-aka: *with bad sting hooks, porcupine* NOTE- BT: 755 doubts this etymology.	žužag, zuzag, jujag: *porcupine* TV:168, BQ:1063	žûžeh: *porcupine* ژوژه jûjeh: *chicken* جوجه BT:755, BQ, PH:152, MO, IC:1391
Indo-European dus: *bad, evil* بد، شیطانی PK:227	PK:45, BT:755		

1251

ژه: صمغ   ـ رجوع شود به   زِه۳

ژیمناستیک: "تمرین ورزش بی لباس"   همریشه: برهنه   همریشه: nude

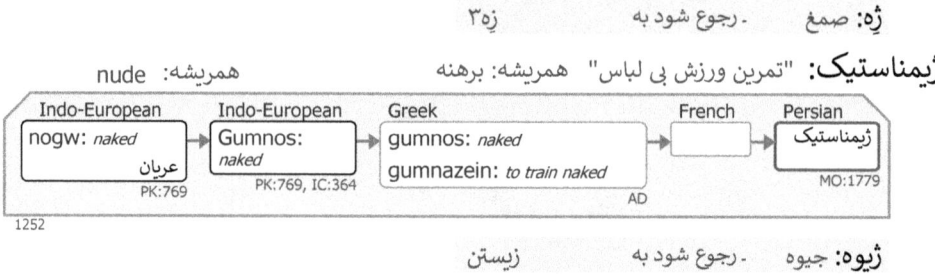

1252

ژیوه: جیوه   ـ رجوع شود به   زیستن

223

این حرف گاهی به ج، چ، ز، ه یا ی بدل شود.

ساج همریشه: teak

Sanskrit	Hindustani	Arabic	Persian
sakah: *teak wood* چوب درخت ساج	sâgun: *teak*	saj: *teak*	sâj: *teak tree* ساج
KL:1578	YB:910	YB:910, KL:1578	MO:1783

1253

ساخارین ـ رجوع شود به سوخاری

ساختن همریشه: آسغده

Indo-European	Avestan	Pahlavi	Persian
kak 1, sač: *to enable, prepare* فعال کردن، آماده کردن	sak, sač, sâx: *to make, prepare*	sâxtan: *make* saz: *to be fit*	sâxtan: *to build* ساختن (سازش)
PK:522, AP:352, CH:323	PK:522, PH:152, AG3:58	BQ:1055,CH:323	PH, BQ, PK:522

COGNATE- Avestan "čagad: *helped*" (PK:522)

1254

ـ سار۱ ـ رجوع شود به سرای

سار۲: غم و رنج همریشه: hate

Indo-European	Avestan	Persian
kâd: *sorrow, hatred* غم، تنفر	sâdra: *pain, grief*	sâr: *grief, pain* سار۲
PK:517	PK:517	بسا سار و نومید و بیمار و سست که مُردَش پزشک و ببود او درست (سعدی)
		BQ:1069, MO:1790

1255

سار۳: پرنده ای سیاه رنگ با خالهای سفید همریشه: sparling

	Indo-European	Pahlavi	Persian
(1)	storos: *a type of bird (sparrow?)* نوعی پرنده کوچک	sâr: *sparrow*	sâr: *sparrow* سار۳
	Pok:1036	AP:337	AP:337

NOTE- see "Sper" for a different suggested root

1256

سار۳: پرنده ای سیاه رنگ با خالهای سفید همریشه: sparrow

	Indo-European	Pahlavi	Persian
(2)	sper: *sparrow* گنجشک، پرستو	sâr: *sparrow*	sâr: *sparrow* سار۳
	PK:991, IC:613,1056	MO:1789	IC:613,1056, MO:1789

NOTE- see "Storos" for a different suggested root

1257

سار۴ ـ رجوع شود به سر   **سازش** ـ رجوع شود به ساختن

ساس۱: ـ رجوع شود به   سیستان

ساس۲: جانوری نظیر شپش

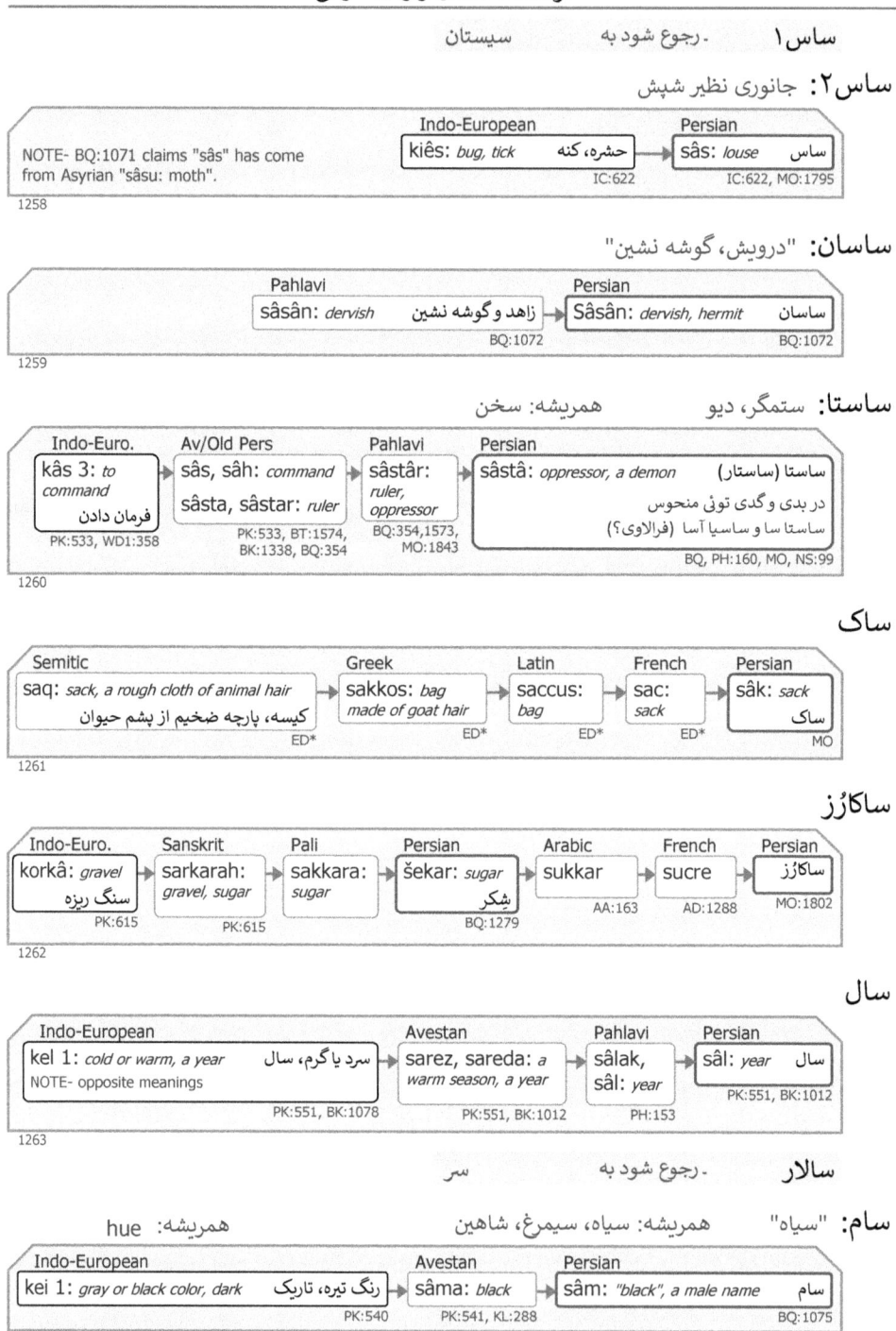

Indo-European — kiês: *bug, tick*   حشره، کنه   IC:622

Persian — sâs: *louse*   ساس   IC:622, MO:1795

NOTE- BQ:1071 claims "sâs" has come from Asyrian "sâsu: moth".

1258

ساسان: "درویش، گوشه نشین"

Pahlavi — sâsân: *dervish*   زاهد و گوشه نشین   BQ:1072

Persian — Sâsân: *dervish, hermit*   ساسان   BQ:1072

1259

ساستا: ستمگر، دیو   همریشه: سخن

Indo-Euro. — kâs 3: *to command*   فرمان دادن   PK:533, WD1:358

Av/Old Pers — sâs, sâh: *command* / sâsta, sâstar: *ruler*   PK:533, BT:1574, BK:1338, BQ:354

Pahlavi — sâstâr: *ruler, oppressor*   BQ:354,1573, MO:1843

Persian — sâstâ: *oppressor, a demon*   ساستا (ساستار)   در بدی و گدی توٚنٚ منحوس   ساستا سا و ساسیا آسا (فرالاوی؟)   BQ, PH:160, MO, NS:99

1260

ساک

Semitic — saq: *sack, a rough cloth of animal hair*   کیسه، پارچه ضخیم از پشم حیوان   ED*

Greek — sakkos: *bag made of goat hair*   ED*

Latin — saccus: *bag*   ED*

French — sac: *sack*   ED*

Persian — sâk: *sack*   ساک   MO

1261

ساکارٚز

Indo-Euro. — korkâ: *gravel*   سنگ ریزه   PK:615

Sanskrit — sarkarah: *gravel, sugar*   PK:615

Pali — sakkara: *sugar*

Persian — šekar: *sugar*   شِکَر   BQ:1279

Arabic — sukkar   AA:163

French — sucre   AD:1288

Persian — ساکارٚز   MO:1802

1262

سال

Indo-European — kel 1: *cold or warm, a year*   سرد یا گرم، سال   NOTE- opposite meanings   PK:551, BK:1078

Avestan — sarez, sareda: *a warm season, a year*   PK:551, BK:1012

Pahlavi — sâlak, sâl: *year*   PH:153

Persian — sâl: *year*   سال   PK:551, BK:1012

1263

سالار   ـ رجوع شود به   سر

سام: "سیاه"   همریشه: سیاه، سیمرغ، شاهین   همریشه: hue

Indo-European — kei 1: *gray or black color, dark*   رنگ تیره، تاریک   PK:540

Avestan — sâma: *black*   PK:541, KL:288

Persian — sâm: *"black", a male name*   سام   BQ:1075

1264

سامه: عهد و سوگند، امان

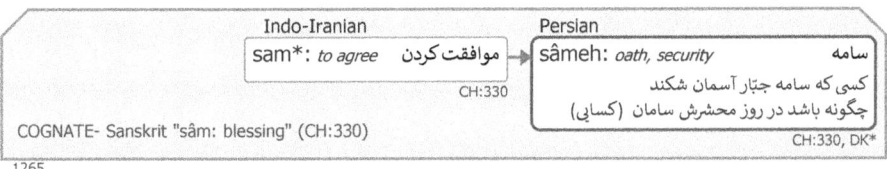

Indo-Iranian

sam*: *to agree*   موافقت کردن

CH:330

Persian

sâmeh: *oath, security*   سامه
کسی که سامه جبار آسمان شکند
چگونه باشد در روز محشرش سامان (کسایی)

CH:330, DK*

COGNATE- Sanskrit "sâm: blessing" (CH:330)

1265

سانتیگراد ـ رجوع شود به   کنگره۲

سایه: " بدون تابش"

همریشه: no, shine

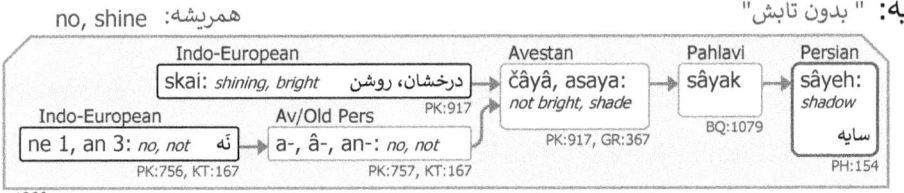

Indo-European

skai: *shining, bright*   درخشان، روشن

PK:917

Indo-European

ne 1, an 3: *no, not*   نَه

PK:756, KT:167

Av/Old Pers

a-, â-, an-: *no, not*

PK:757, KT:167

Avestan

čâyâ, asaya: *not bright, shade*

PK:917, GR:367

Pahlavi

sâyak

BQ:1079

Persian

sâyeh: *shadow*   سایه

PH:154

1266

ساییدن

همریشه: افسانیدن، فسانیدن

همریشه: edge, acute

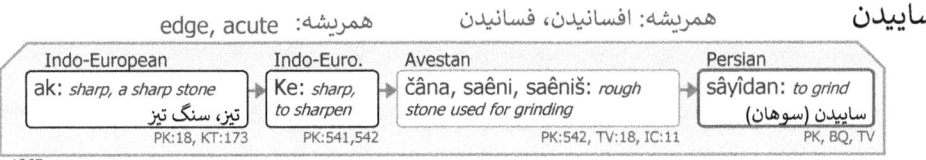

Indo-European

ak: *sharp, a sharp stone*   تیز، سنگ تیز

PK:18, KT:173

Indo-Euro.

Ke: *sharp, to sharpen*

PK:541,542

Avestan

čâna, saêni, saêniš: *rough stone used for grinding*

PK:542, TV:18, IC:11

Persian

sâyîdan: *to grind*   ساییدن (سوهان)

PK, BQ, TV

1267

سَبْت

همریشه: sabbatical

همریشه: شنبه

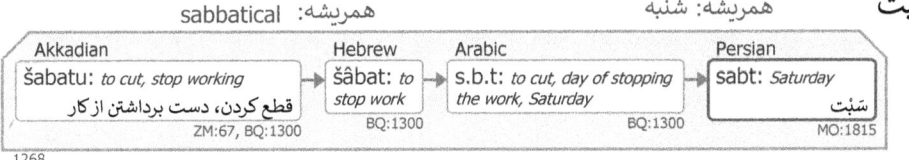

Akkadian

šabatu: *to cut, stop working*   قطع کردن، دست برداشتن از کار

ZM:67, BQ:1300

Hebrew

šâbat: *to stop work*

BQ:1300

Arabic

s.b.t: *to cut, day of stopping the work, Saturday*

BQ:1300

Persian

sabt: *Saturday*   سَبْت

MO:1815

1268

سبز

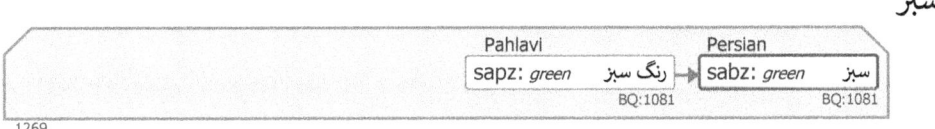

Pahlavi

sapz: *green*   رنگ سبز

BQ:1081

Persian

sabz: *green*   سبز

BQ:1081

1269

سُبک

همریشه: trepid

همریشه: چابک

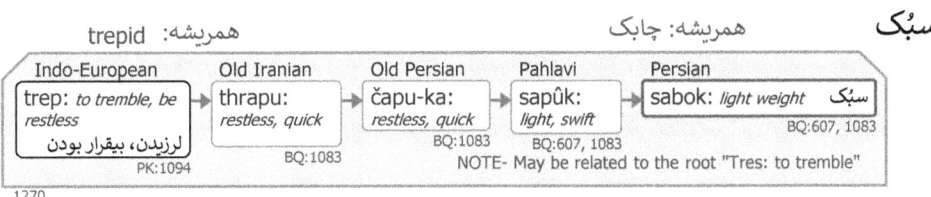

Indo-European

trep: *to tremble, be restless*   لرزیدن، بیقرار بودن

PK:1094

Old Iranian

thrapu: *restless, quick*

BQ:1083

Old Persian

čapu-ka: *restless, quick*

BQ:1083

Pahlavi

sapûk: *light, swift*

BQ:607, 1083

Persian

sabok: *light weight*   سُبک

BQ:607, 1083

NOTE- May be related to the root "Tres: to tremble"

1270

سپار: گاوآهن

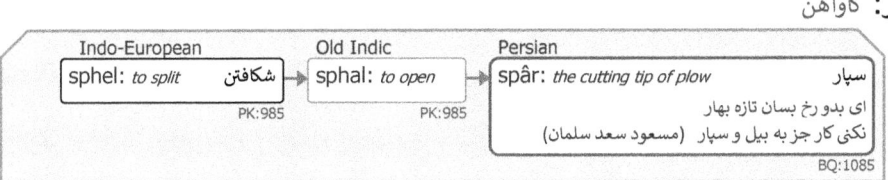

Indo-European

sphel: *to split*   شکافتن

PK:985

Old Indic

sphal: *to open*

PK:985

Persian

spâr: *the cutting tip of plow*   سپار
ای بدو رخ بسان تازه بهار
نکنی کار جز به بیل و سپار (مسعود سعد سلمان)

BQ:1085

1271

226

سپاردن

همریشه: deposit

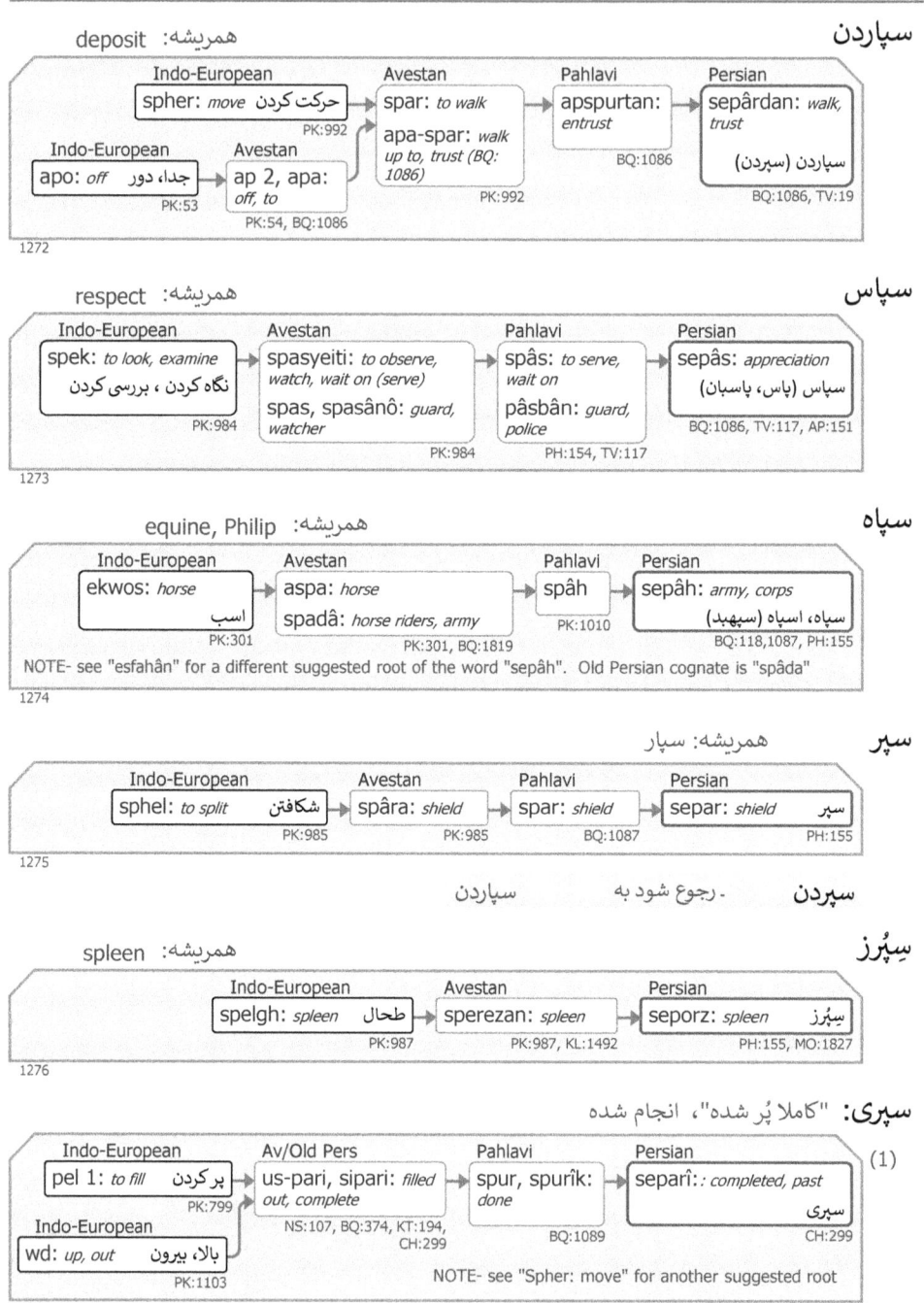

Indo-European
spher: *move* حرکت کردن
PK:992

Indo-European
apo: *off* جدا، دور
PK:53

Avestan
spar: *to walk*
apa-spar: *walk up to, trust (BQ: 1086)*
PK:992

Avestan
ap 2, apa: *off, to*
PK:54, BQ:1086

Pahlavi
apspurtan: *entrust*
BQ:1086

Persian
sepârdan: *walk, trust*
سپاردن (سپردن)
BQ:1086, TV:19

1272

سپاس

همریشه: respect

Indo-European
spek: *to look, examine*
نگاه کردن ، بررسی کردن
PK:984

Avestan
spasyeiti: *to observe, watch, wait on (serve)*
spas, spasânô: *guard, watcher*
PK:984

Pahlavi
spâs: *to serve, wait on*
pâsbân: *guard, police*
PH:154, TV:117

Persian
sepâs: *appreciation*
سپاس (پاس، پاسبان)
BQ:1086, TV:117, AP:151

1273

سپاه

همریشه: equine, Philip

Indo-European
ekwos: *horse*
اسب
PK:301

Avestan
aspa: *horse*
spadâ: *horse riders, army*
PK:301, BQ:1819

Pahlavi
spâh
PK:1010

Persian
sepâh: *army, corps*
سپاه، اسپاه (سپهبد)
BQ:118,1087, PH:155

NOTE- see "esfahân" for a different suggested root of the word "sepâh". Old Persian cognate is "spâda"

1274

سپر

همریشه: سپار

Indo-European
sphel: *to split* شکافتن
PK:985

Avestan
spâra: *shield*
PK:985

Pahlavi
spar: *shield*
BQ:1087

Persian
separ: *shield* سپر
PH:155

1275

سپردن

. رجوع شود به سپاردن

سِپُرز

همریشه: spleen

Indo-European
spelgh: *spleen* طحال
PK:987

Avestan
sperezan: *spleen*
PK:987, KL:1492

Persian
seporz: *spleen* سِپُرز
PH:155, MO:1827

1276

سپری: "کاملاً پُر شده"، انجام شده

(1)

Indo-European
pel 1: *to fill* پر کردن
PK:799

Indo-European
wd: *up, out* بالا، بیرون
PK:1103

Av/Old Pers
us-pari, sipari: *filled out, complete*
NS:107, BQ:374, KT:194, CH:299

Pahlavi
spur, spurîk: *done*
BQ:1089

Persian
separî: : *completed, past*
سپری
CH:299

NOTE- see "Spher: move" for another suggested root

1277

سپری: رفته، گذشته

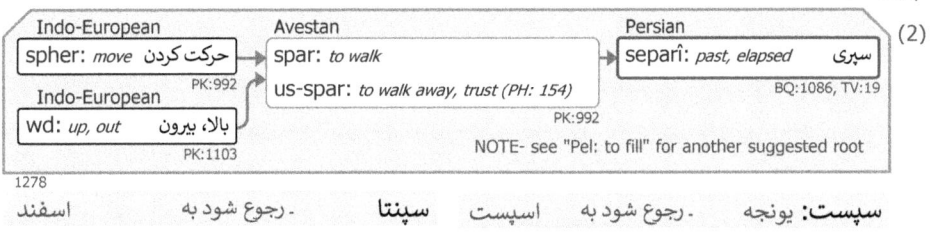

(2)

Indo-European	Avestan	Persian
spher: *move* حرکت کردن PK:992	spar: *to walk* us-spar: *to walk away, trust (PH: 154)* PK:992	separî: *past, elapsed* سپری BQ:1086, TV:19
Indo-European wd: *up, out* بالا، بیرون PK:1103		

NOTE- see "Pel: to fill" for another suggested root

1278

سپست: یونجه   ـ رجوع شود به   **اسپست**   **سپنتا**   ـ رجوع شود به   اسفند

سپنج: پوچ و بی ارزش

همریشه: sponge

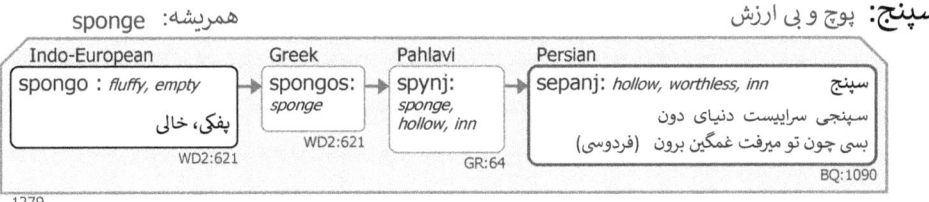

Indo-European	Greek	Pahlavi	Persian
spongo : *fluffy, empty* پفکی، خالی WD2:621	spongos: *sponge* WD2:621	spynj: *sponge, hollow, inn* GR:64	sepanj: *hollow, worthless, inn* سپنج سپنجی سرایست دنیای دون بسی چون تو میرفت غمگین برون (فردوسی) BQ:1090

1279

سپندارمذ: مقدس   ـ رجوع شود به   اسپندارمذ

سپوختن۱: انداختن، سوراخ کردن

همریشه: puncture

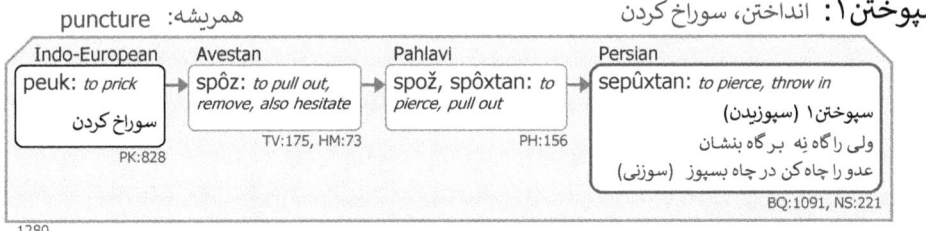

Indo-European	Avestan	Pahlavi	Persian
peuk: *to prick* سوراخ کردن PK:828	spôz: *to pull out, remove, also hesitate* TV:175, HM:73	spož, spôxtan: *to pierce, pull out* PH:156	sepûxtan: *to pierce, throw in* سپوختن۱ (سپوزیدن) ولی راگه نه بر گه بنشان عدو را چاه کن در چاه بسپوز (سوزنی) BQ:1091, NS:221

1280

سپوختن۲: به تاخیر انداختن

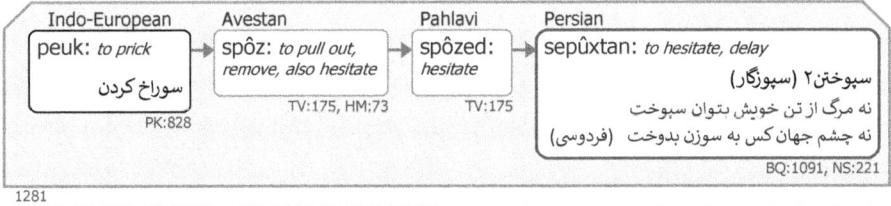

Indo-European	Avestan	Pahlavi	Persian
peuk: *to prick* سوراخ کردن PK:828	spôz: *to pull out, remove, also hesitate* TV:175, HM:73	spôzed: *hesitate* TV:175	sepûxtan: *to hesitate, delay* سپوختن۲ (سپوزگار) نه مرگ از تن خویش بتوان سپوخت نه چشم جهان کس به سوزن بدوخت (فردوسی) BQ:1091, NS:221

1281

سپوزگار: کاهل   ـ رجوع شود به   سپوختن۲   **سپوزیدن:** انداختن   ـ رجوع شود به   سپوختن۱

سپهبد   ـ رجوع شود به   سپاه + بُد

سپهر

همریشه: sphere

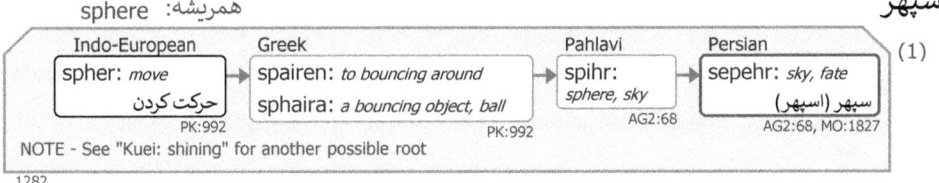

(1)

Indo-European	Greek	Pahlavi	Persian
spher: *move* حرکت کردن PK:992	spairen: *to bouncing around* sphaira: *a bouncing object, ball* PK:992	spihr: *sphere, sky* AG2:68	sepehr: *sky, fate* سپهر (اسپهر) AG2:68, MO:1827

NOTE - See "Kuei: shining" for another possible root

1282

سپهر (2)

همریشه: white

Indo-European		Old Persian	Pahlavi	Persian
kuei: *white, shining* سفید، درخشان	→	sipithra: *white, bright sky*	→ spihr: *sky*	→ sepehr: *sky, fate* سپهر
PK:629		BQ:1092, AP:343	BQ:1092, AP:343	BQ:1092, AP:343

NOTE- See "spher: move" for another possible root. It may have come from Sanskrit "čvitrâ" (BQ:1092)

1283

سپید

همریشه: white

Indo-European	Avestan	Pahlavi	Persian
kuei: *white, shining* سفید، درخشان	spaêta: *white* spiti-doithra: *bright*	→ spêt: *white*	→ sepîd: *white* سپید (سفید)
PK:629	PK:629	BQ:1093	PH:157

1284

ستادن

Indo-European	Old Persian	Pahlavi	Persian
stâi: *to steal* دزدیدن	→ stan, sta: *to steal*	→ stâtan: *to grab*	→ setâdan : *to grab, steal* ستادن
PK:1010	AG3:59	BQ:1095	PH:157, BQ, AG3:59

1285

ستاره

همریشه: star

Indo-European	Avestan	Pahlavi	Persian
ster 2: *star* ستاره	→ star 2	→ stârak, stârag, star: *star*	→ setâreh: *star* ستاره
PK:1027	PK:1027	AP:344	AD

NOTE- IC: 260 derives "setâreh" and "axtar" from the same root.

1286

سِتاک: شاخه

همریشه: stand, stem

Indo-Euro.	Av/Old Pers	Pahlavi	Persian
stâ: *to stand* ایستادن	→ sta: *to stand, to set*	→ stâk: *branch, stiff*	→ setâk: *branch* سِتاک (استاک) estâx: *brave, rude* إستاخ
PK:1008,1009	BQ:123, PH:20, PK:1008	PH:20	BQ, PH:20

NOTE- AP:345 indicates that this word may be from the Indo European root "Steug, Stugnos: stiff"

1287

ستان: محل تجمع

همریشه: ایستادن، ستون   همریشه: stand, state

Indo-European	Av/Old Pers	Pahlavi	Persian
stâ: *to stand* ایستادن	→ sta: *to stand, to set* stâna: *location of*	→ stân: *place of, location for*	→ - stân: *location of , center of* ستان (استان)
PK:1008,1009	BQ:123, PH:20, PK:1008	BQ:1097	BQ, PH:20

1288

ستایش

ـ رجوع شود به   ستاییدن

ستاییدن

Indo-European	Avestan	Pahlavi	Persian
steu 1: *to praise* ستایش کردن	→ stav: *to praise* staoiti: *praised*	→ stâyîtan: *to praise* âstvân: *believer, trusted*	→ setâyîdan: *to praise* ستاییدن (ستودن، ستایش)
PK:1035	PK:1035	BQ:747,1098, TV:31	BQ, PH:159, NB:180, TV:31, MO

1289

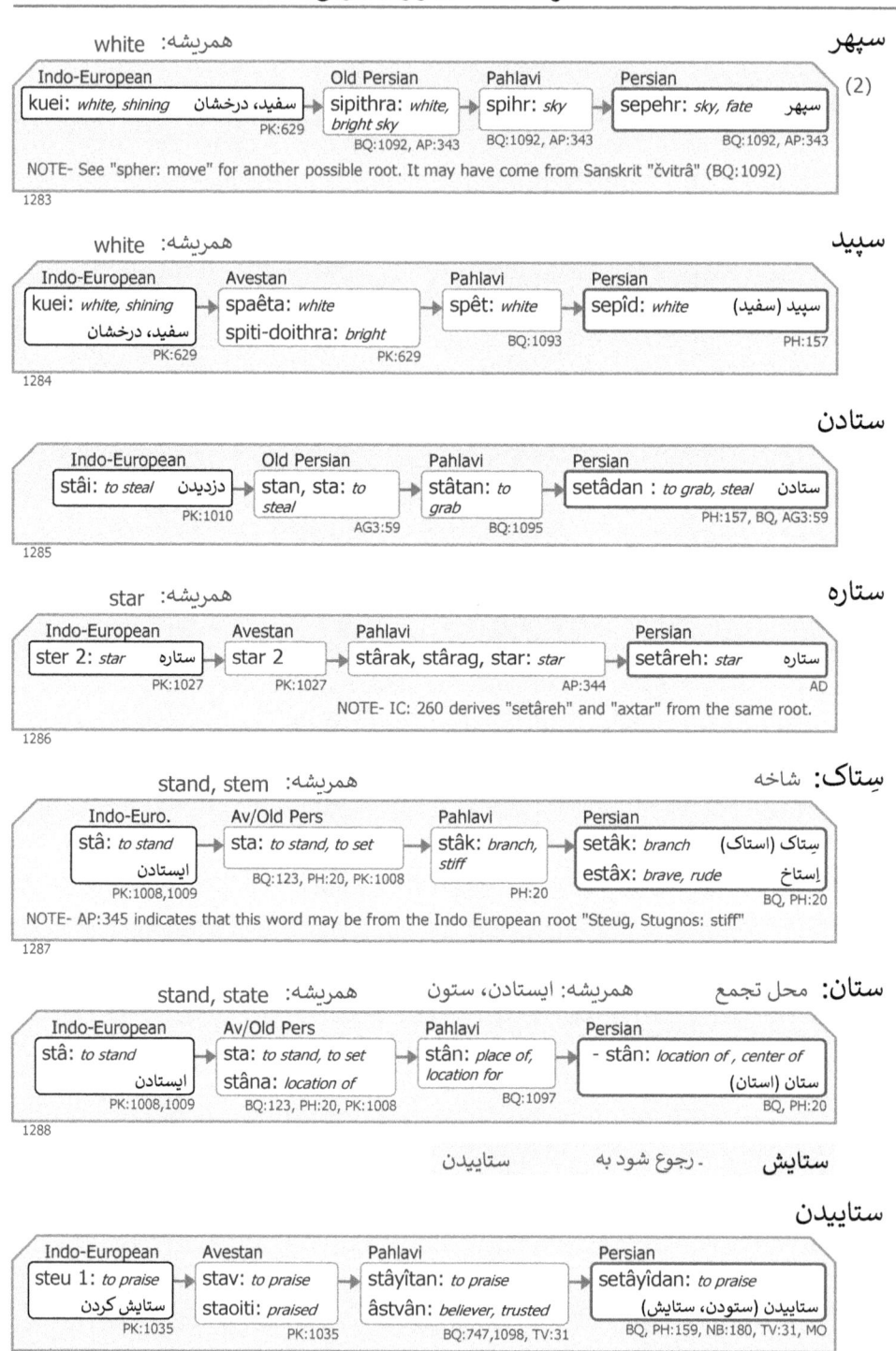

ستبر: محکم　　همریشه: استبرک، استوار　　همریشه: stamp

Indo-European	Avestan	Pahlavi	Persian
stebh: *support, stem* پشتیبانی ، ساقه PK:1012	stawra: *firm* PK:1012, BQ, GR:363	stapr, stawr: *strong* BQ:1098, BR, MO	setabr: *strong, thick* ستبر BR, MO

1290

ستردن: تراشیدن، محو کردن　　همریشه: contour

Indo-European		Persian
ter 3: *to rub, wipe, shave*　تراشیدن، پاک کردن PK:1071, CH:382		os-tordan: *to wipe out, shave* استردن (ستردن) PK:1071, CH:382
Indo-European	Avestan	
wd: *up, out*　بالا، بیرون PK:1103	us, uz: *out* PK:1103, PH:154	

1291

سُتُرگ: درشت و قوی　　همریشه: ستاک، ستون　　همریشه: stand

Indo-European	Avestan	Pahlavi	Persian
stâ: *to stand* ایستادن PK:1008,1009	stûra: *thick, large, husky* PK:1009,1011, KL:1508, PH:205	sturg: *big and strong* BQ:1099	sotorg: *"large and strong"* سُتُرگ PH, BQ

1292

سَتَروَن: عقیم　　همریشه: sterilized

	Indo-European	Persian
COGNATE- Old Indic "starî: infertile, barren"	ster 4: *barren*　عقیم PK:1031	satarvan: *sterile* سَتَروَن BQ:1100, MO:1833

1293

ستم

Indo-European	Avestan	Pahlavi	Persian
stâ: *to stand*　ایستادن PK:1008,1009	sta-xma, sta-mba: *hardship, cruelty* PK:1009,1011, KL:1508, PH:205	stahm BQ:1100	setam: *"hardship"*　ستم PH, BQ

1294

ستنبه: زشت و خشن

Indo-European	Old Persian	Persian
stebh: *support, stem* پشتیبانی ، ساقه PK:1012	stambaka: *strong* stamb: *stand firm, revolt* BQ:1100, KT:210	setonbeh: *strong, violent, ugly*　ستنبه گرفتش دایه و گفتش چه بودت ؟ ستنبه دیو بدخو چه نمودت ؟　(ویس و رامین) BQ, NS:223

1295

ستوان۱: مؤمن و معترف　　همریشه: ستاییدن

Indo-European	Avestan	Pahlavi	Persian
steu 1: *to praise* ستایش کردن PK:1035	stav: *to praise* staoiti: *praised* PK:1035	stâyîtan: *to praise* âstvân: *believer, trusted* âstôbân: *confessor* BQ:747,1098, TV:31	ostovân: *believer, confessor* أستوان۱ (ستوان۱) BQ, PH:159, NB:180, TV:31

1296

سُتوان۲: "محکم"

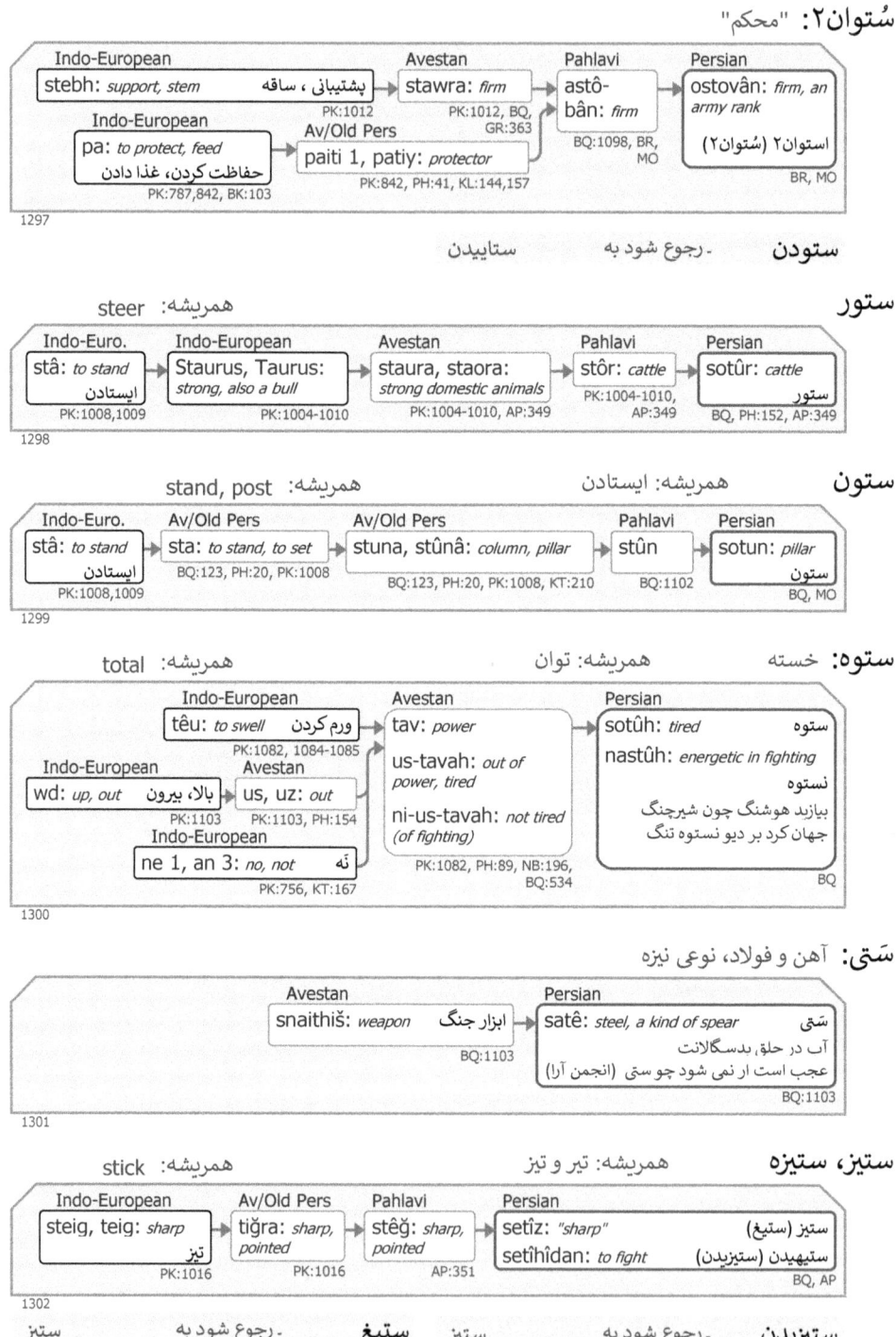

Indo-European	Avestan	Pahlavi	Persian
stebh: support, stem پشتیبانی ، ساقه PK:1012	stawra: firm PK:1012, BQ, GR:363	astô- bân: firm BQ:1098, BR, MO	ostovân: firm, an army rank استوان۲ (سُتوان۲) BR, MO

Indo-European	Av/Old Pers
pa: to protect, feed حفاظت کردن، غذا دادن PK:787,842, BK:103	paiti 1, patiy: protector PK:842, PH:41, KL:144,157

1297

ستودن   - رجوع شود به   ستاییدن   ستودن

ستور   همریشه: steer

Indo-Euro.	Indo-European	Avestan	Pahlavi	Persian
stâ: to stand ایستادن PK:1008,1009	Staurus, Taurus: strong, also a bull PK:1004-1010	staura, staora: strong domestic animals PK:1004-1010, AP:349	stôr: cattle PK:1004-1010, AP:349	sotûr: cattle ستور BQ, PH:152, AP:349

1298

ستون   همریشه: ایستادن   همریشه: stand, post

Indo-Euro.	Av/Old Pers	Av/Old Pers	Pahlavi	Persian
stâ: to stand ایستادن PK:1008,1009	sta: to stand, to set BQ:123, PH:20, PK:1008	stuna, stûnâ: column, pillar BQ:123, PH:20, PK:1008, KT:210	stûn BQ:1102	sotun: pillar ستون BQ, MO

1299

ستوه: خسته   همریشه: توان   همریشه: total

Indo-European	Avestan	Persian
têu: to swell ورم کردن PK:1082, 1084-1085	tav: power	sotûh: tired ستوه nastûh: energetic in fighting

Indo-European	Avestan
wd: up, out بالا، بیرون PK:1103, PH:154	us, uz: out PK:1103, PH:154

us-tavah: out of
power, tired

نستوه
بیازید هوشنگ چون شیرچنگ
جهان کرد بر دیو نستوه تنگ

Indo-European
ne 1, an 3: no, not   نَه PK:756, KT:167

ni-us-tavah: not tired
(of fighting)
PK:1082, PH:89, NB:196,
BQ:534

BQ

1300

سَتی: آهن و فولاد، نوعی نیزه

Avestan	Persian
snaithiš: weapon ابزار جنگ BQ:1103	satê: steel, a kind of spear سَتی آب در حلق، بدسگالانت عجب است ار نمی شود چو ستی (انجمن آرا) BQ:1103

1301

ستیز، ستیزه   همریشه: تیر و تیز   همریشه: stick

Indo-European	Av/Old Pers	Pahlavi	Persian
steig, teig: sharp تیز PK:1016	tiğra: sharp, pointed PK:1016	stêğ: sharp, pointed AP:351	setîz: "sharp" ستیز (ستیغ) setîhîdan: to fight ستیهیدن (ستیزیدن) BQ, AP

1302

ستیزیدن   - رجوع شود به   ستیز   ستیغ   - رجوع شود به   ستیز

ستیهیدن   - رجوع شود به   ستیز

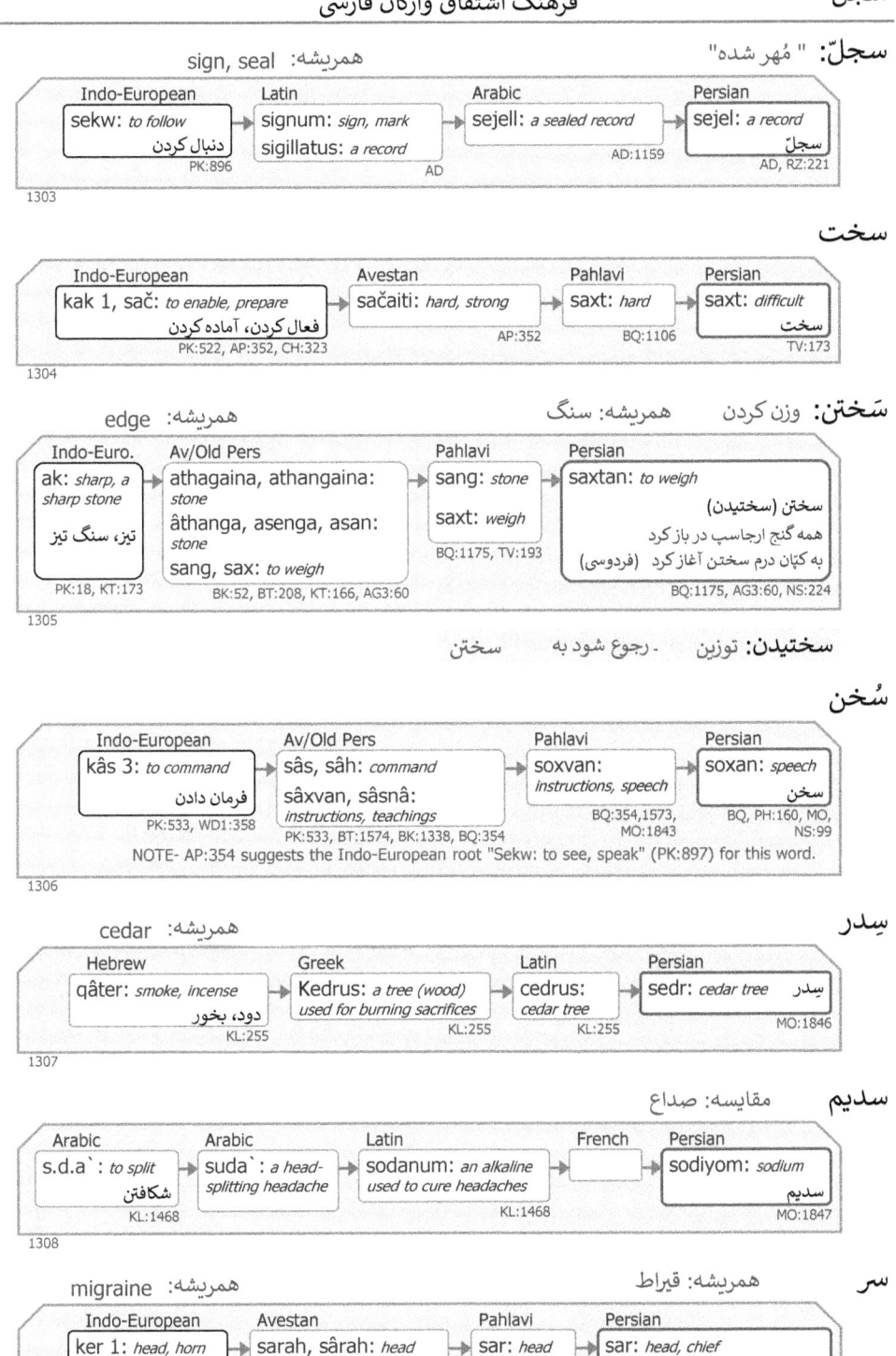

سجلّ: "مُهر شده"

همریشه: sign, seal

Indo-European	Latin	Arabic	Persian
sekw: to follow دنبال کردن PK:896	signum: sign, mark sigillatus: a record AD	sejell: a sealed record AD:1159	sejel: a record سجلّ AD, RZ:221

1303

سخت

Indo-European	Avestan	Pahlavi	Persian
kak 1, sač: to enable, prepare فعال کردن، آماده کردن PK:522, AP:352, CH:323	sačaiti: hard, strong AP:352	saxt: hard BQ:1106	saxt: difficult سخت TV:173

1304

سَختَن: وزن کردن   همریشه: سنگ   همریشه: edge

Indo-Euro.	Av/Old Pers	Pahlavi	Persian
ak: sharp, a sharp stone تیز، سنگ تیز PK:18, KT:173	athagaina, athangaina: stone âthanga, asenga, asan: stone sang, sax: to weigh BK:52, BT:208, KT:166, AG3:60	sang: stone saxt: weigh BQ:1175, TV:193	saxtan: to weigh سختن (سختیدن) همه گنج ارجاسپ در باز کرد به کپان درم سختن آغاز کرد (فردوسی) BQ:1175, AG3:60, NS:224

1305

سختیدن: توزین   ـ رجوع شود به   سختن

سُخن

Indo-European	Av/Old Pers	Pahlavi	Persian
kâs 3: to command فرمان دادن PK:533, WD1:358	sâs, sâh: command sâxvan, sâsnâ: instructions, teachings PK:533, BT:1574, BK:1338, BQ:354	soxvan: instructions, speech BQ:354,1573, MO:1843	soxan: speech سخن BQ, PH:160, MO, NS:99

NOTE- AP:354 suggests the Indo-European root "Sekw: to see, speak" (PK:897) for this word.

1306

سِدر   همریشه: cedar

Hebrew	Greek	Latin	Persian
qâter: smoke, incense دود، بخور KL:255	Kedrus: a tree (wood) used for burning sacrifices KL:255	cedrus: cedar tree KL:255	sedr: cedar tree سِدر MO:1846

1307

سدیم   مقایسه: صداع

Arabic	Arabic	Latin	French	Persian
s.d.a`: to split شکافتن KL:1468	suda`: a head-splitting headache	sodanum: an alkaline used to cure headaches KL:1468		sodiyom: sodium سدیم MO:1847

1308

سر   همریشه: قیراط   همریشه: migraine

Indo-European	Avestan	Pahlavi	Persian
ker 1: head, horn سر، شاخ PK:574, KL:261,657	sarah, sârah: head PK:574, KL:261	sar: head BQ:1111	sar: head, chief سر (سالار، سار، نگونسار) BQ

1309

سرا

سرا . رجوع شود به سرای

سراج

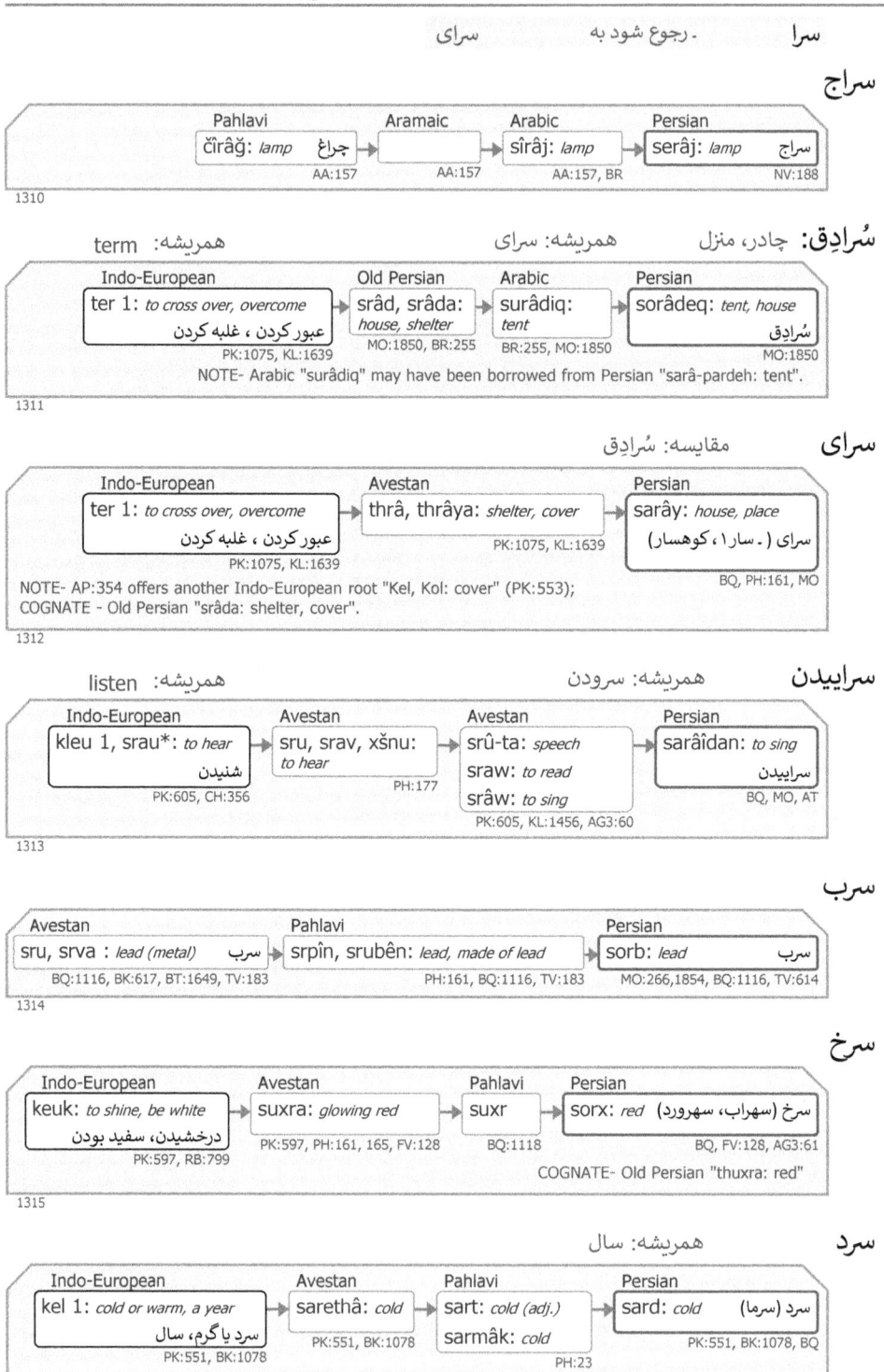

Pahlavi	Aramaic	Arabic	Persian
čîrâğ: *lamp* چراغ		sîrâj: *lamp*	serâj: *lamp* سراج
AA:157	AA:157	AA:157, BR	NV:188

1310

سُرادِق: چادر، منزل

همریشه: سرای   همریشه: term

Indo-European	Old Persian	Arabic	Persian
ter 1: *to cross over, overcome* عبور کردن ، غلبه کردن	srâd, srâda: *house, shelter*	surâdiq: *tent*	sorâdeq: *tent, house* سُرادِق
PK:1075, KL:1639	MO:1850, BR:255	BR:255, MO:1850	MO:1850

NOTE- Arabic "surâdiq" may have been borrowed from Persian "sarâ-pardeh: tent".

1311

سرای

مقایسه: سُرادِق

Indo-European	Avestan	Persian
ter 1: *to cross over, overcome* عبور کردن ، غلبه کردن	thrâ, thrâya: *shelter, cover*	sarây: *house, place* سرای (ـ سار۱، کوهسار)
PK:1075, KL:1639	PK:1075, KL:1639	BQ, PH:161, MO

NOTE- AP:354 offers another Indo-European root "Kel, Kol: cover" (PK:553);
COGNATE - Old Persian "srâda: shelter, cover".

1312

سراییدن

همریشه: سرودن   همریشه: listen

Indo-European	Avestan	Avestan	Persian
kleu 1, srau*: *to hear* شنیدن	sru, srav, xšnu: *to hear*	srû-ta: *speech* sraw: *to read* srâw: *to sing*	sarâîdan: *to sing* سراییدن
PK:605, CH:356	PH:177	PK:605, KL:1456, AG3:60	BQ, MO, AT

1313

سرب

Avestan	Pahlavi	Persian
sru, srva : *lead (metal)* سرب	srpîn, srubên: *lead, made of lead*	sorb: *lead* سرب
BQ:1116, BK:617, BT:1649, TV:183	PH:161, BQ:1116, TV:183	MO:266,1854, BQ:1116, TV:614

1314

سرخ

Indo-European	Avestan	Pahlavi	Persian
keuk: *to shine, be white* درخشیدن، سفید بودن	suxra: *glowing red*	suxr	sorx: *red* سرخ (سهراب، سهرورد)
PK:597, RB:799	PK:597, PH:161, 165, FV:128	BQ:1118	BQ, FV:128, AG3:61

COGNATE- Old Persian "thuxra: red"

1315

سرد

همریشه: سال

Indo-European	Avestan	Pahlavi	Persian
kel 1: *cold or warm, a year* سرد یا گرم، سال	sarethâ: *cold*	sart: *cold (adj.)* sarmâk: *cold*	sard: *cold* سرد (سرما)
PK:551, BK:1078	PK:551, BK:1078	PH:23	PK:551, BK:1078, BQ

1316

سرده: نژاد، نوع

همریشه: herd

Indo-European	Avestan	Pahlavi	Persian
kerd 2: *row, herd* گروه، گله PK:579	saredha: *way, kind, race, breed* PK:579	sartak: *breed*	sardeh: *race, breed, kind* سرده BQ:1122, TV:183

1317

سرشار - رجوع شود به شاریدن

سرشت: آمیزه، طبیعت   همریشه: سریش

Indo-European	Old Iranian	Avestan	Pahlavi	Persian
klis: *adhere* چسبیدن، پایبند بودن IC:1637	srîš, sraîš: *a plant resin used for making glue.* AG3:60	sraêš: *mixture, nature* PH:162, HM:75	sirištan BQ:1124	sereštan: *to mix* سرشتن serešt: *nature* سرشت BQ:1124, PH:162

1318

سرشک: قطره اشک

Indo-European	Avestan	Pahlavi	Persian
sresk: *to drip* چکیدن PK:1002	srask: *tear drop* PK:1002	srešk: *drop* BQ:1124, TV:183	serešk: *tear drop* سرشک PK:1002, BQ:1124

1319

سرفه

همریشه: scream

Indo-European	Persian
ker 3: *loud noise, noisy birds* صدای بلند، پرندگان پر صدا PK:567	sorfeh: *cough* سرفه PK:569

1320

سرکه

Altaic	Turkish	Persian
sure: *acid, bad smell* اسید، بوی بد AL:1319	sirke: *vinegar* AL:1319	serkeh: *vinegar* سرکه AL:1319

1321

سرگرد - رجوع شود به گُرد

سرگین: "دفع شده"، مدفوع   همریشه: excrement, shear

Indo-European	Avestan	Pahlavi
ker 2, sker 2: *to cut, separate* بریدن، جدا کردن PK:938, IC:640,1155	sairi-gaona: *like cut (dropped) from the body, dung* PK:578,920,947	sargîn BQ:1128

Indo-European	Avestan	Persian
gêu 1, kauč*: *to bend, wrinkle* خم و درهم شدن PK:394-398, PK:588-592	gaona: *curly hair, color, type* BK:1051, TV:90	sargin, sergin: *animal dung* سرگین PH, BQ, PK:578,947

1322

سِرُم   همریشه: رود   همریشه: stream

Indo-European	Latin	French	Persian
ser 1, sreu: *to flow* جاری شدن srêm: *running* جاری PK:909,1003, KT:205, IC:1276	serum: *liquid from animal tissue* AD		serom: *liquid from animal tissue* سِرُم MO

1323

سرما ـ رجوع شود به سرد

سرنا، سرنای: ساز هنگام سور و شادی مقایسه: کُرنا

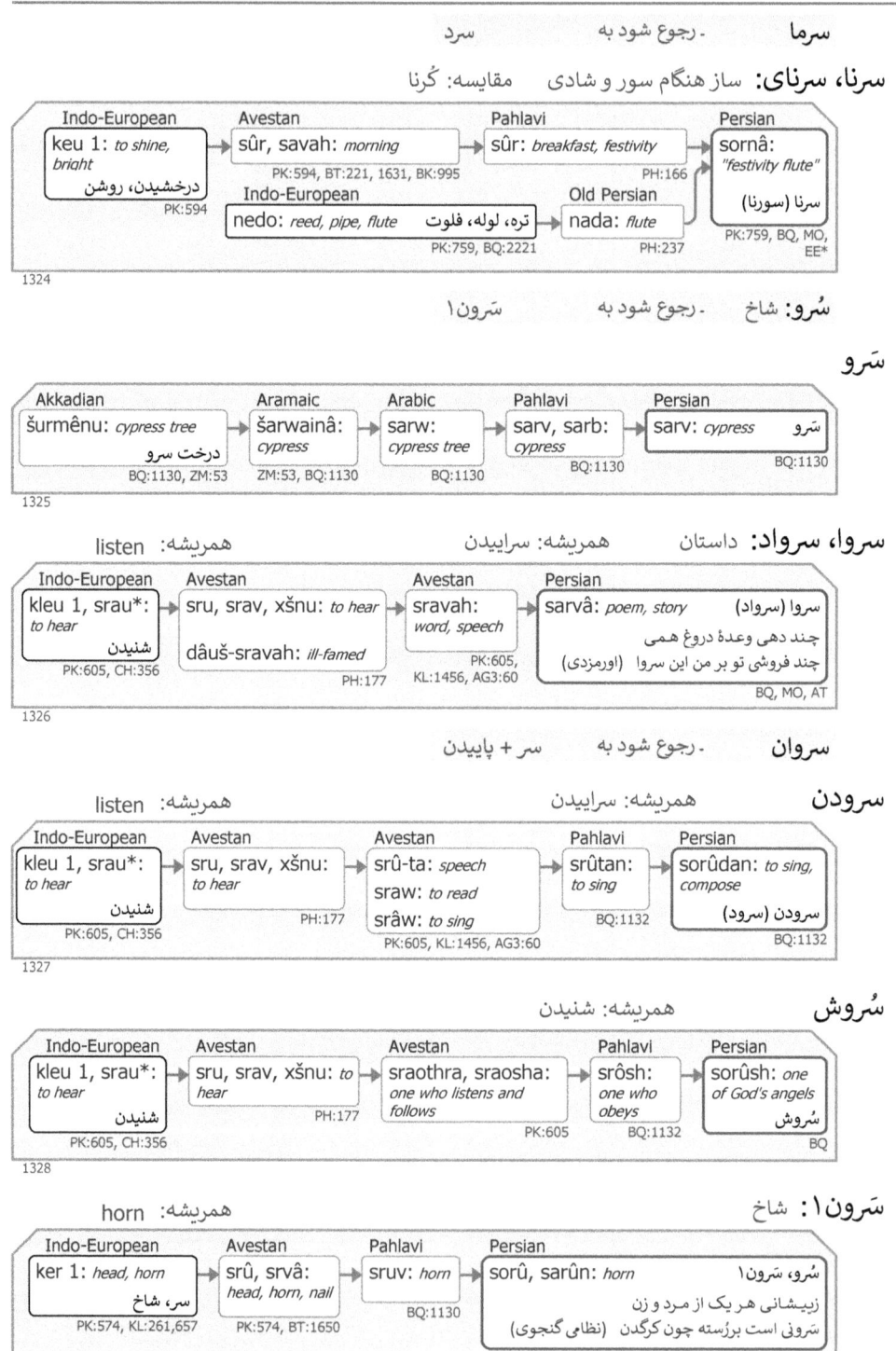

Indo-European	Avestan	Pahlavi	Persian
keu 1: to shine, bright درخشیدن، روشن PK:594	sûr, savah: morning PK:594, BT:221, 1631, BK:995	sûr: breakfast, festivity PH:166	sornâ: "festivity flute" سرنا (سورنا) PK:759, BQ, MO, EE*
	Indo-European nedo: reed, pipe, flute تره، لوله، فلوت PK:759, BQ:2221	Old Persian nada: flute PH:237	

1324

سُرو: شاخ ـ رجوع شود به سَرون۱

سَرو

Akkadian	Aramaic	Arabic	Pahlavi	Persian
šurmênu: cypress tree درخت سرو BQ:1130, ZM:53	šarwainâ: cypress ZM:53, BQ:1130	sarw: cypress tree BQ:1130	sarv, sarb: cypress BQ:1130	sarv: cypress سَرو BQ:1130

1325

سروا، سرواد: داستان همریشه: سراییدن همریشه: listen

Indo-European	Avestan	Avestan	Persian
kleu 1, srau*: to hear شنیدن PK:605, CH:356	sru, srav, xšnu: to hear dâuš-sravah: ill-famed PH:177	sravah: word, speech PK:605, KL:1456, AG3:60	sarvâ: poem, story سروا (سرواد) چند دهی وعدهٔ دروغ همی چند فروشی تو بر من این سروا (اورمزدی) BQ, MO, AT

1326

سروان ـ رجوع شود به سر + پاییدن

سرودن همریشه: سراییدن همریشه: listen

Indo-European	Avestan	Avestan	Pahlavi	Persian
kleu 1, srau*: to hear شنیدن PK:605, CH:356	sru, srav, xšnu: to hear PH:177	srû-ta: speech sraw: to read srâw: to sing PK:605, KL:1456, AG3:60	srûtan: to sing BQ:1132	sorûdan: to sing, compose سرودن (سرود) BQ:1132

1327

سُروش همریشه: شنیدن

Indo-European	Avestan	Avestan	Pahlavi	Persian
kleu 1, srau*: to hear شنیدن PK:605, CH:356	sru, srav, xšnu: to hear PH:177	sraothra, sraosha: one who listens and follows PK:605	srôsh: one who obeys BQ:1132	sorûsh: one of God's angels سُروش BQ

1328

سَرون۱: شاخ همریشه: horn

Indo-European	Avestan	Pahlavi	Persian
ker 1: head, horn سر، شاخ PK:574, KL:261,657	srû, srvâ: head, horn, nail PK:574, BT:1650	sruv: horn BQ:1130	sorû, sarûn: horn سُرو، سَرون۱ زیبشانی هر یک از مرد و زن سَرونی است برجسته چون کرگدن (نظامی گنجوی) BQ:1130, PH:162

1329

سُرون۲: کفل

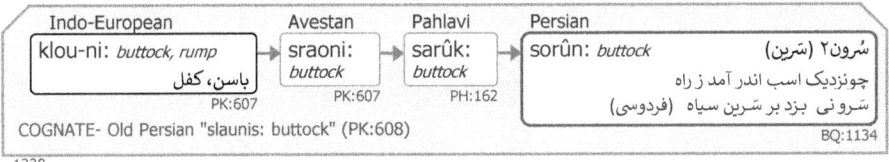

Indo-European
klou-ni: *buttock, rump*
باسن، کفل
PK:607

Avestan
sraoni: *buttock*
PK:607

Pahlavi
sarûk: *buttock*
PH:162

Persian
sorûn: *buttock*
سُرون۲ (سَرین)
چونزدیک اسب اندر آمد ز راه
سَرونی بزد بر سَرین سیاه   (فردوسی)
BQ:1134

COGNATE- Old Persian "slaunis: buttock" (PK:608)

1330

همریشه: هار   **سِری:** ردیف   همریشه: sort, series

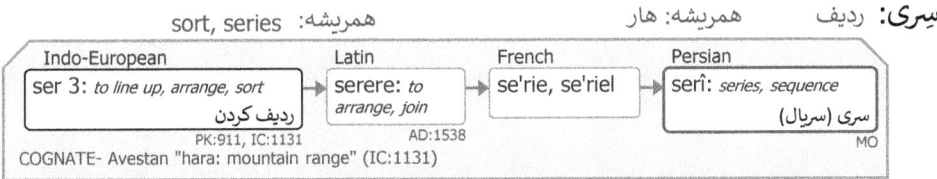

Indo-European
ser 3: *to line up, arrange, sort*
ردیف کردن
PK:911, IC:1131

Latin
serere: *to arrange, join*
AD:1538

French
se'rie, se'riel

Persian
serî: *series, sequence*
سری (سریال)
MO

COGNATE- Avestan "hara: mountain range" (IC:1131)

1331

همریشه: سرشت   **سِریش:** نوعی چسب

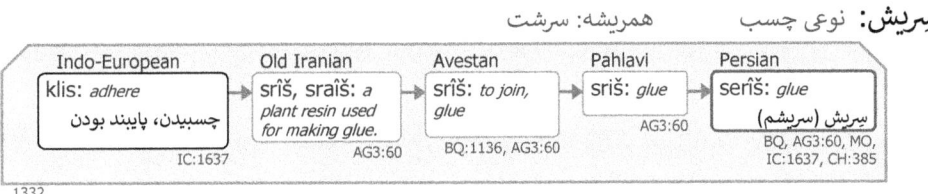

Indo-European
klis: *adhere*
چسبیدن، پایبند بودن
IC:1637

Old Iranian
srîš, sraîš: *a plant resin used for making glue.*
AG3:60

Avestan
srîš: *to join, glue*
BQ:1136, AG3:60

Pahlavi
sriš: *glue*
AG3:60

Persian
serîš: *glue*
سیریش (سریشم)
BQ, AG3:60, MO,
IC:1637, CH:385

1332

سُرون۲   **سَرین:** کفل   ـ رجوع شود به

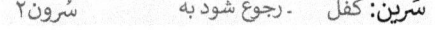

همریشه: ساختن، سازش   **سزا، سزیدن**

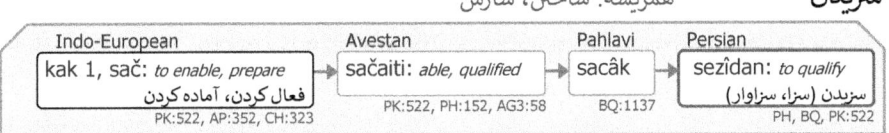

Indo-European
kak 1, sač: *to enable, prepare*
فعال کردن، آماده کردن
PK:522, AP:352, CH:323

Avestan
sačaiti: *able, qualified*
PK:522, PH:152, AG3:58

Pahlavi
sacâk
BQ:1137

Persian
sezîdan: *to qualify*
سزیدن (سزا، سزاوار)
PH, BQ, PK:522

1333

سُست

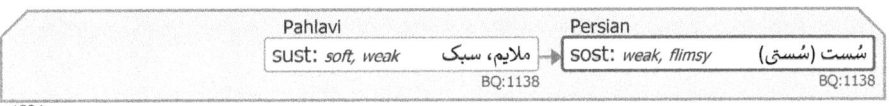

Pahlavi
sust: *soft, weak*
ملایم، سبک
BQ:1138

Persian
sost: *weak, flimsy*
سُست (سُستی)
BQ:1138

1334

سطل

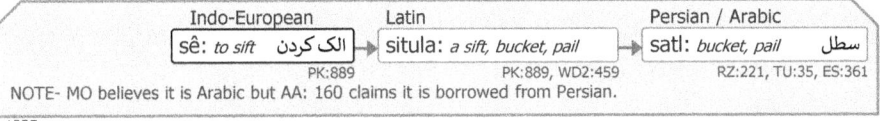

Indo-European
sê: *to sift*
الک کردن
PK:889

Latin
situla: *a sift, bucket, pail*
PK:889, WD2:459

Persian / Arabic
satl: *bucket, pail*   سطل
RZ:221, TU:35, ES:361

NOTE- MO believes it is Arabic but AA: 160 claims it is borrowed from Persian.

1335

سُغُر: جوجه تیغی، خارپشت

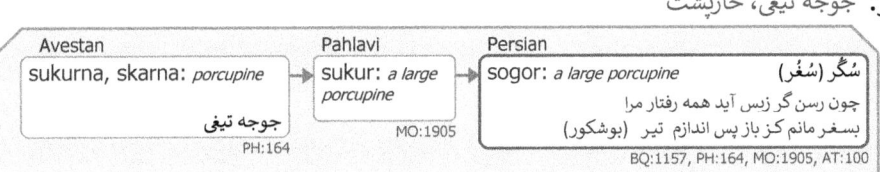

Avestan
sukurna, skarna: *porcupine*
جوجه تیغی

Pahlavi
sukur: *a large porcupine*
MO:1905

Persian
sogor: *a large porcupine*
سُگُر (سُغُر)
چون رسن گر زِس آید همه رفتار مرا
بسغر مانم کز باز پس اندازم تیر   (بوشکور)
BQ:1157, PH:164, MO:1905, AT:100

1336

سُفت: شانه

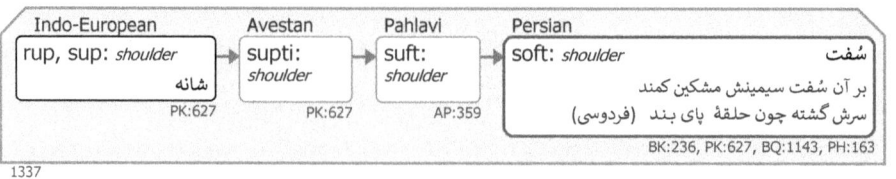

سُفتن: سوراخ کردن   همریشه: سوراخ   همریشه: cave

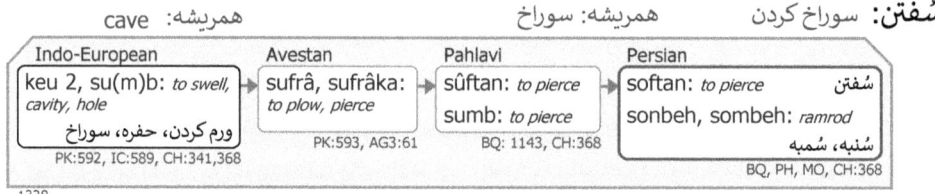

سفره

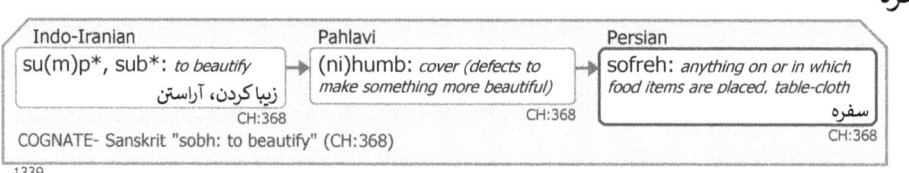

سفسطه: مغالطه

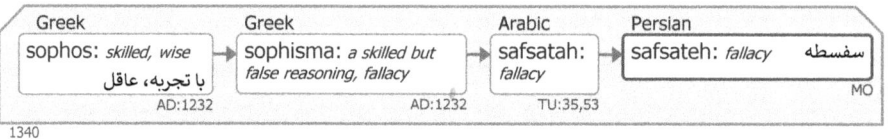

سَقَل: سُم   همریشه: سُم   همریشه: hoof

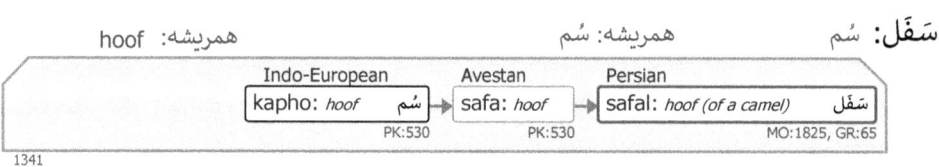

سفلیس   نام این بیماری از شعر "دوست خوکان" آمده   همریشه: swine

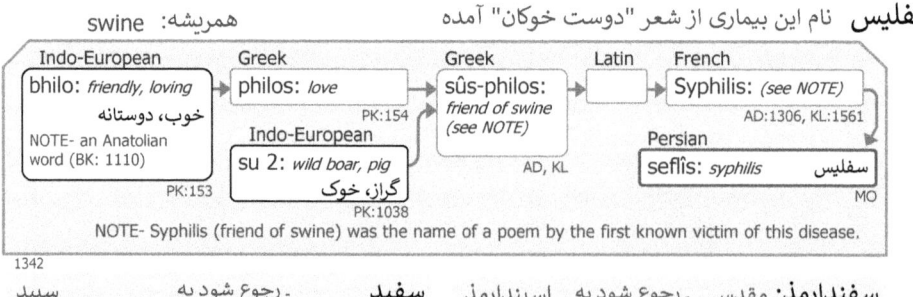

سفندارمذ: مقدس ـ رجوع شود به اسپندارمذ   سفید ـ رجوع شود به   سپید

سفینه

همریشه: goad

Indo-Euro.	Avestan	Persian	Arabic	Persian
ghei 2: *to propel* جلو بردن PK:410,424	zaêna 1: *weapon* zaya: *tools, equipment* PK:424, KL:666, BK:1384	zîn: *saddle* زین âb-zîn: *water saddle, ship* آبزین BQ, AA, ES	safîneh: *ship* AA:162, BR:260	safîneh: *ship* سفینه

1343

سقرلات: نوعی پارچه   همریشه: اسکناس, سجلّ   همریشه: scarlet

Indo-European	Latin	Arabic	Persian
sekw: *to follow* دنبال کردن PK:896	signum: *sign, mark* AD	siqillat: *with little images* AD:1159	saqarlât: *a rich red cloth* سقرلات AD, RZ:221

1344

سکا   . رجوع شود به   سیستان

سکار: ذغال   همریشه: coal

Indo-European	Indo-European	Avestan	Persian
dhegh: *to heat, burn* گرم کردن، سوزاندن PK:240	Geulo: *coal* IC:379,407, PK:399	skarana, skairya: *coal* PH:163, BQ:1150, IC:379,407	sekâr: *coal* سکار (سکارو) بدار دنیا چو برفروخت آتش ظلم سکار آن بجهنّم همی خورد چو ظلیم (سوزنی سمرقندی) BQ:1026,1150, PH:163, MO

1345

سکنجبین   . رجوع شود به   سرکه + انگ۲

سگّو

Altaic	Turkish	Persian
sik-ke: *detail of the house entrance* ساختار اطراف در ورودی منزل AL:1246	seku: *stone bench at the house entrance* AL:1246	sakku: *stone bench* سگّو AL:1246, BQ

1346

سکوبا: أسقُف   همریشه: spy

Indo-European	Greek	Old Persian	Persian
spek: *to look, examine* نگاه کردن ، بررسی کردن PK:984	skopos: *one who watches* AD	skuba: *bishop, priest* MO:1901, NS:228	sekubâ: *a Christian bishop* سکوبا نوشتند نامه به هر کشوری سکوبا و بطریق و هر مهتری (فردوسی) MO:1901, NS:228

1347

سکوره: کاسه سفالی   همریشه: کلاهخود   همریشه: sky, house

Indo-European	Persian
sku: *to cover* پوشاندن PK:952,953, IC:1193	skûreh: *earthen bowl* سکوره سکوره ای است ز پیروزه گر قیاس کنی بخوان همت او صحن گنبد خضرا (رضی الدین باباقزوینی) IC:594,1193, MO

1348

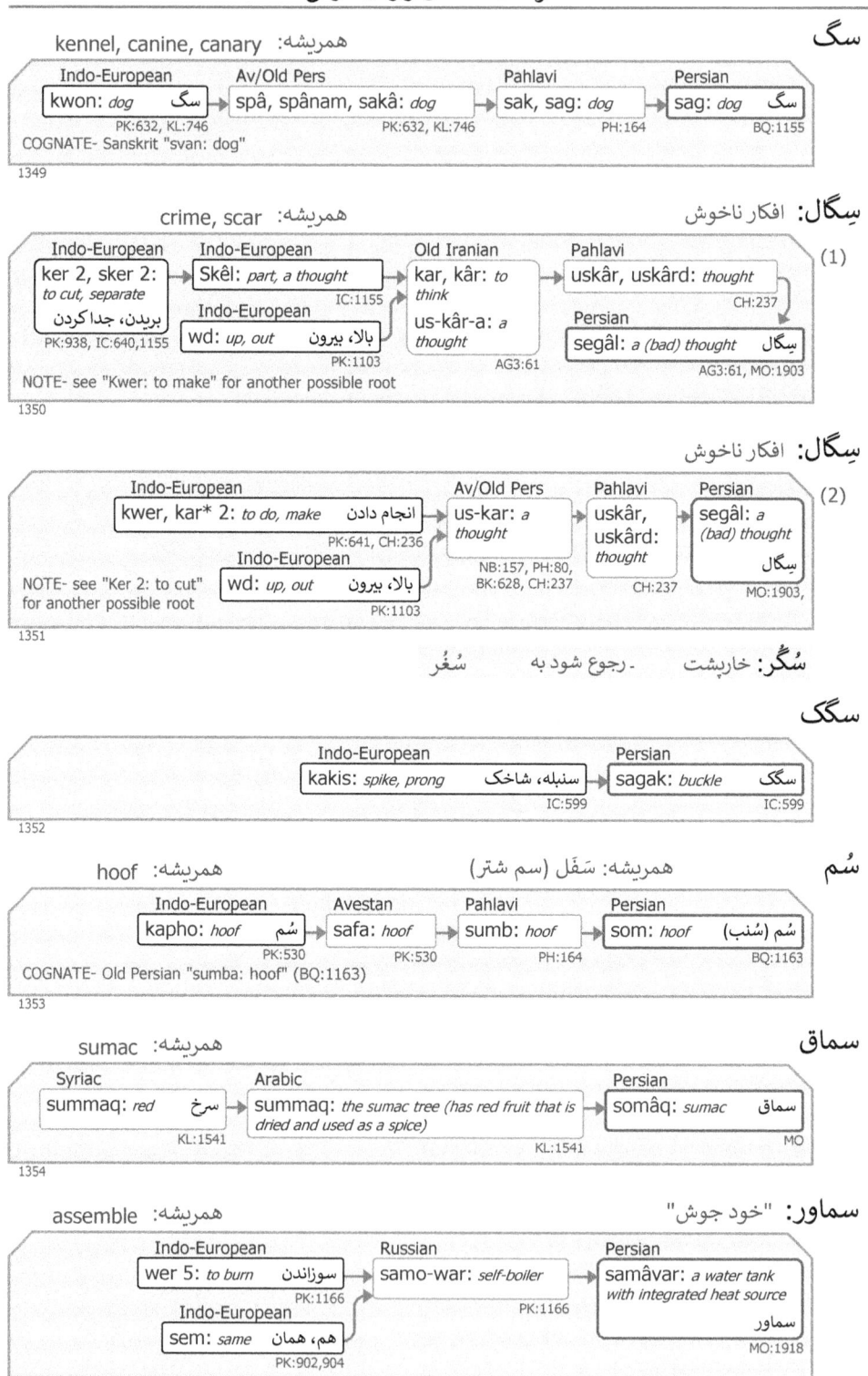

سگ

همریشه: kennel, canine, canary

Indo-European	Av/Old Pers	Pahlavi	Persian
kwon: *dog* سگ	spâ, spânam, sakâ: *dog*	sak, sag: *dog*	sag: *dog* سگ
PK:632, KL:746	PK:632, KL:746	PH:164	BQ:1155

COGNATE- Sanskrit "svan: dog"

1349

سِگال: افکار ناخوش (1)

همریشه: crime, scar

Indo-European	Indo-European	Old Iranian	Pahlavi
ker 2, sker 2: *to cut, separate* بریدن، جدا کردن	Skêl: *part, a thought* IC:1155	kar, kâr: *to think*	uskâr, uskârd: *thought* CH:237
PK:938, IC:640,1155	wd: *up, out* بالا، بیرون PK:1103	us-kâr-a: *a thought* AG3:61	Persian — segâl: *a (bad) thought* سگال AG3:61, MO:1903

NOTE- see "Kwer: to make" for another possible root

1350

سِگال: افکار ناخوش (2)

Indo-European	Av/Old Pers	Pahlavi	Persian
kwer, kar* 2: *to do, make* انجام دادن PK:641, CH:236	us-kar: *a thought* NB:157, PH:80, BK:628, CH:237	uskâr, uskârd: *thought* CH:237	segâl: *a (bad) thought* سگال MO:1903,
Indo-European — wd: *up, out* بالا، بیرون PK:1103			

NOTE- see "Ker 2: to cut" for another possible root

1351

سُگُر: خارپشت - رجوع شود به سُغُر

سگک

Indo-European	Persian
kakis: *spike, prong* سنبله، شاخک IC:599	sagak: *buckle* سگک IC:599

1352

سُم

همریشه: سَقَل (سم شتر) همریشه: hoof

Indo-European	Avestan	Pahlavi	Persian
kapho: *hoof* سُم PK:530	safa: *hoof* PK:530	sumb: *hoof* PH:164	som: *hoof* (سُنب) سُم BQ:1163

COGNATE- Old Persian "sumba: hoof" (BQ:1163)

1353

سماق

همریشه: sumac

Syriac	Arabic	Persian
summaq: *red* سرخ KL:1541	summaq: *the sumac tree (has red fruit that is dried and used as a spice)* KL:1541	somâq: *sumac* سماق MO

1354

سماور: "خود جوش"

همریشه: assemble

Indo-European	Russian	Persian
wer 5: *to burn* سوزاندن PK:1166	samo-war: *self-boiler* PK:1166	samâvar: *a water tank with integrated heat source* سماور MO:1918
Indo-European — sem: *same* هم، همان PK:902,904		

1355

سُمبه ۔ رجوع شود به سُفتن

سَمت

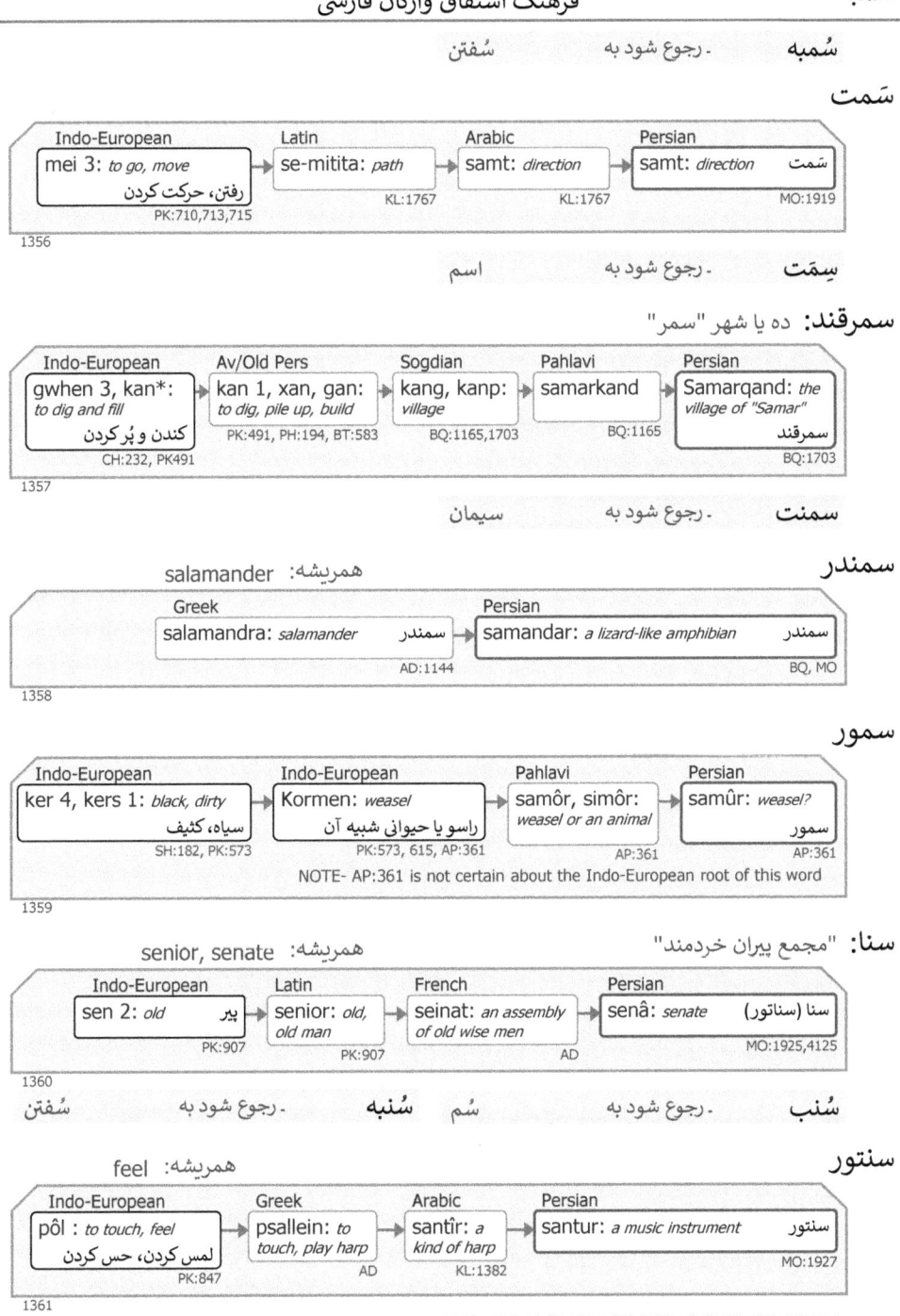

Indo-European	Latin	Arabic	Persian
mei 3: *to go, move* رفتن، حرکت کردن PK:710,713,715	se-mitita: *path* KL:1767	samt: *direction* KL:1767	samt: *direction* سَمت MO:1919

1356

سِمَت ۔ رجوع شود به اسم

سمرقند: ده یا شهر "سمر"

Indo-European	Av/Old Pers	Sogdian	Pahlavi	Persian
gwhen 3, kan*: *to dig and fill* کندن و پُر کردن CH:232, PK491	kan 1, xan, gan: *to dig, pile up, build* PK:491, PH:194, BT:583	kang, kanp: *village* BQ:1165,1703	samarkand BQ:1165	Samarqand: *the village of "Samar"* سمرقند BQ:1703

1357

سمنت ۔ رجوع شود به سیمان

سمندر

همریشه: salamander

Greek	Persian
salamandra: *salamander* سمندر AD:1144	samandar: *a lizard-like amphibian* سمندر BQ, MO

1358

سمور

Indo-European	Indo-European	Pahlavi	Persian
ker 4, kers 1: *black, dirty* سیاه، کثیف SH:182, PK:573	Kormen: *weasel* راسو یا حیوانی شبیه آن PK:573, 615, AP:361	samôr, simôr: *weasel or an animal* AP:361	samûr: *weasel?* سمور AP:361

NOTE- AP:361 is not certain about the Indo-European root of this word

1359

سنا: "مجمع پیران خردمند"

همریشه: senior, senate

Indo-European	Latin	French	Persian
sen 2: *old* پیر PK:907	senior: *old, old man* PK:907	seinat: *an assembly of old wise men* AD	senâ: *senate* سنا (سناتور) MO:1925,4125

1360

سُنب ۔ رجوع شود به سُم سُنبه ۔ رجوع شود به سُفتن

سنتور

همریشه: feel

Indo-European	Greek	Arabic	Persian
pôl: *to touch, feel* لمس کردن، حس کردن PK:847	psallein: *to touch, play harp* AD	santîr: *a kind of harp* KL:1382	santur: *a music instrument* سنتور MO:1927

1361

سنج ۔ رجوع شود به صنج

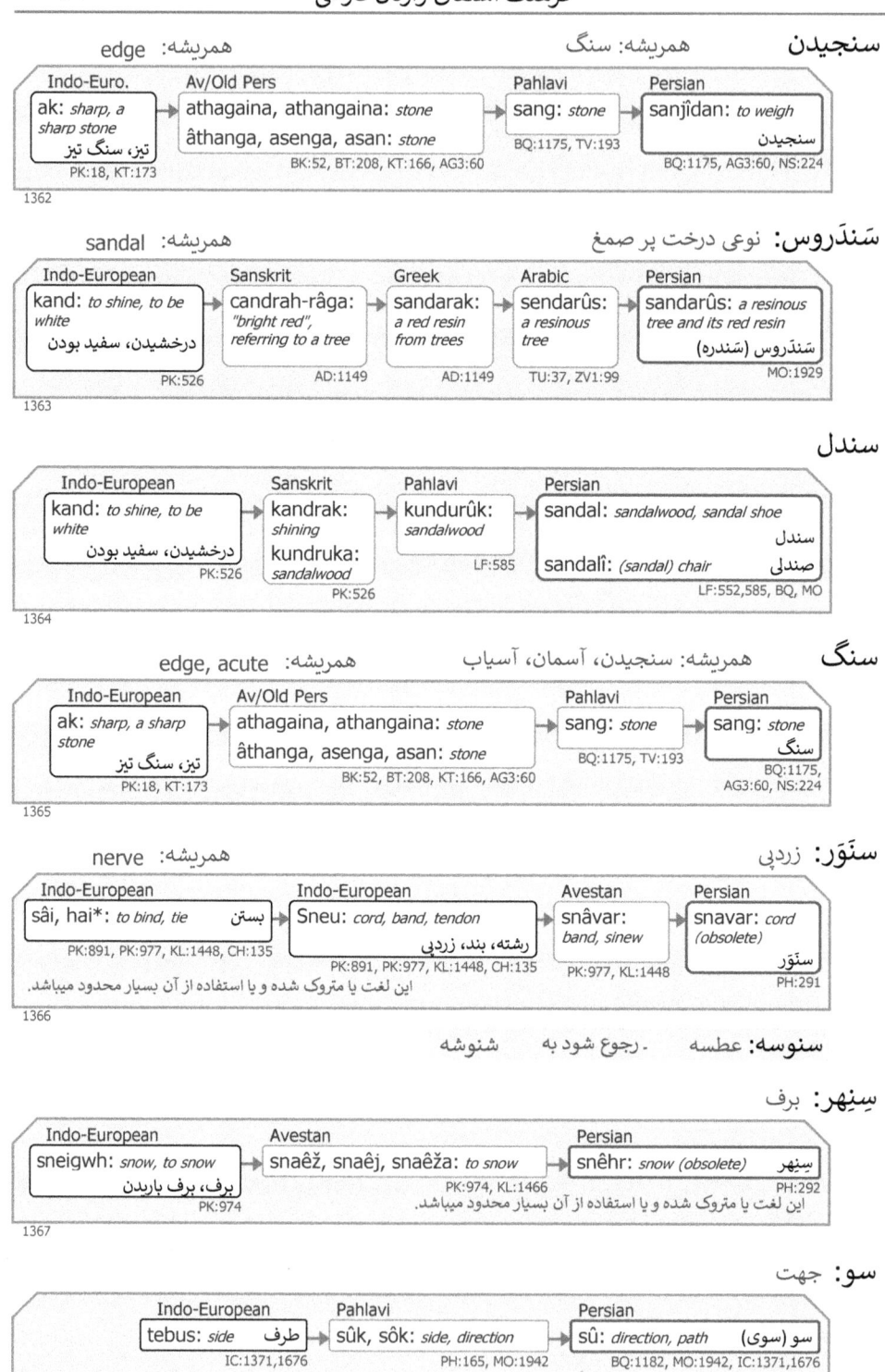

سنجیدن

همریشه: سنگ   همریشه: edge

Indo-Euro.	Av/Old Pers	Pahlavi	Persian
ak: *sharp, a sharp stone* / تیز، سنگ تیز / PK:18, KT:173	athagaina, athangaina: *stone* / âthanga, asenga, asan: *stone* / BK:52, BT:208, KT:166, AG3:60	sang: *stone* / BQ:1175, TV:193	sanjîdan: *to weigh* / سنجیدن / BQ:1175, AG3:60, NS:224

1362

سَندَروس: نوعی درخت پر صمغ

همریشه: sandal

Indo-European	Sanskrit	Greek	Arabic	Persian
kand: *to shine, to be white* / درخشیدن، سفید بودن / PK:526	candrah-râga: *"bright red", referring to a tree* / AD:1149	sandarak: *a red resin from trees* / AD:1149	sendarûs: *a resinous tree* / TU:37, ZV1:99	sandarûs: *a resinous tree and its red resin* / سَندَروس (سندره) / MO:1929

1363

سندل

Indo-European	Sanskrit	Pahlavi	Persian
kand: *to shine, to be white* / درخشیدن، سفید بودن / PK:526	kandrak: *shining* / kundruka: *sandalwood* / PK:526	kundurûk: *sandalwood* / LF:585	sandal: *sandalwood, sandal shoe* / سندل / sandalî: *(sandal) chair* / صندلی / LF:552,585, BQ, MO

1364

سنگ

همریشه: سنجیدن، آسمان، آسیاب   همریشه: edge, acute

Indo-European	Av/Old Pers	Pahlavi	Persian
ak: *sharp, a sharp stone* / تیز، سنگ تیز / PK:18, KT:173	athagaina, athangaina: *stone* / âthanga, asenga, asan: *stone* / BK:52, BT:208, KT:166, AG3:60	sang: *stone* / BQ:1175, TV:193	sang: *stone* / سنگ / BQ:1175, AG3:60, NS:224

1365

سنَوَر: زردپی

همریشه: nerve

Indo-European	Indo-European	Avestan	Persian
sâi, hai*: *to bind, tie* / بستن / PK:891, PK:977, KL:1448, CH:135	Sneu: *cord, band, tendon* / رشته، بند، زردپی / PK:891, PK:977, KL:1448, CH:135	snâvar: *band, sinew* / PK:977, KL:1448	snavar: *cord (obsolete)* / سنَوَر / PH:291

این لغت متروک شده و یا استفاده از آن بسیار محدود میباشد.

1366

سنوسه: عطسه   - رجوع شود به   شنوشه

سِنِهر: برف

Indo-European	Avestan	Persian
sneigwh: *snow, to snow* / برف، برف باریدن / PK:974	snaêž, snaêj, snaêža: *to snow* / PK:974, KL:1466	snêhr: *snow (obsolete)* / سِنِهر / PH:292

این لغت یا متروک شده و یا استفاده از آن بسیار محدود میباشد.

1367

سو: جهت

Indo-European	Pahlavi	Persian
tebus: *side* / طرف / IC:1371,1676	sûk, sôk: *side, direction* / PH:165, MO:1942	sû: *direction, path* / سو (سوی) / BQ:1182, MO:1942, IC:1371,1676

1368

سوار: "اسب بار"

همریشه: equine, burden

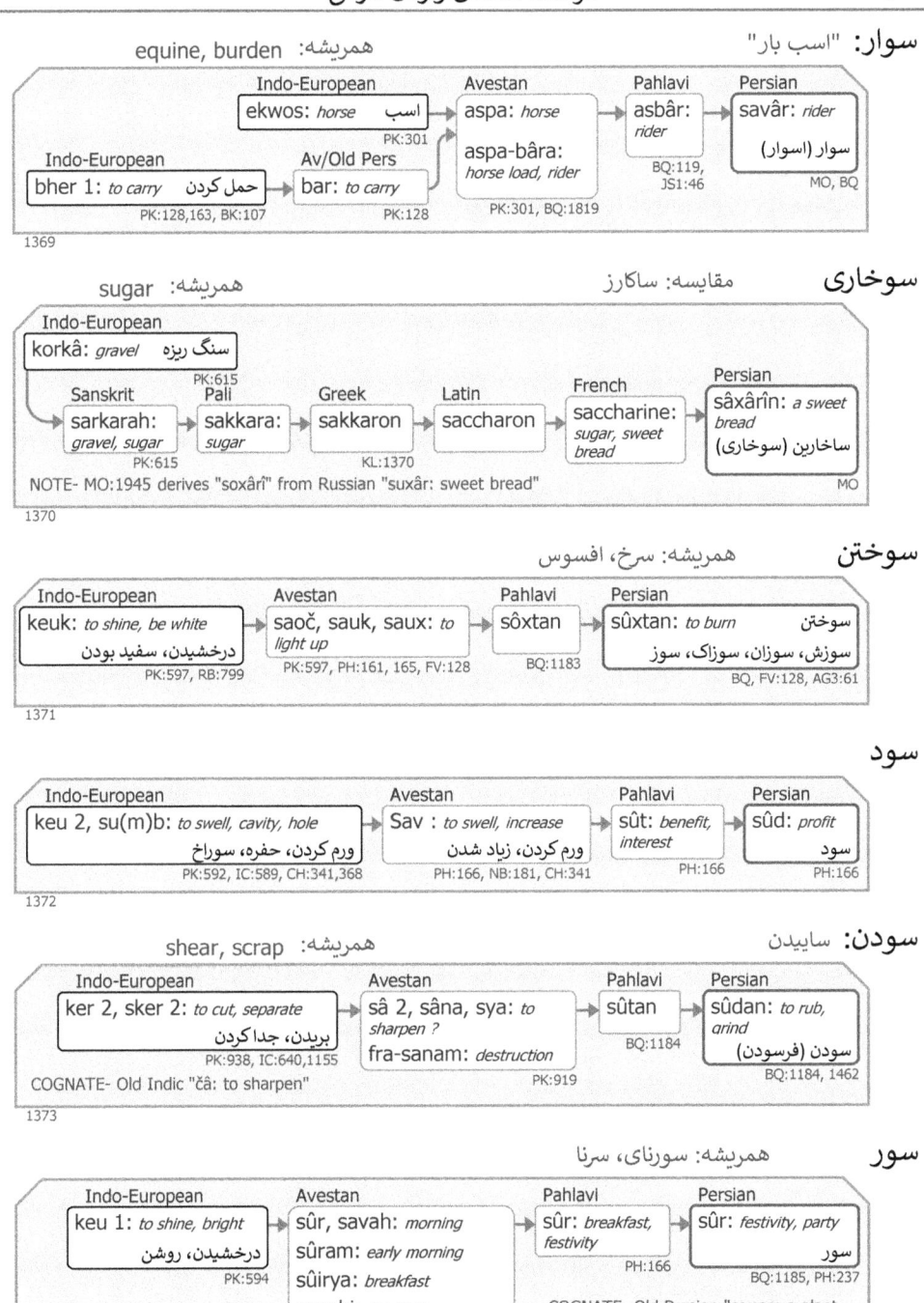

سوخاری   مقایسه: ساکارز   همریشه: sugar

NOTE- MO:1945 derives "soxârî" from Russian "suxâr: sweet bread"

سوختن

همریشه: سرخ، افسوس

سود

سودن: ساییدن

همریشه: shear, scrap

سور

همریشه: سورنای، سرنا

1369

1370

1371

1372

1373

1374

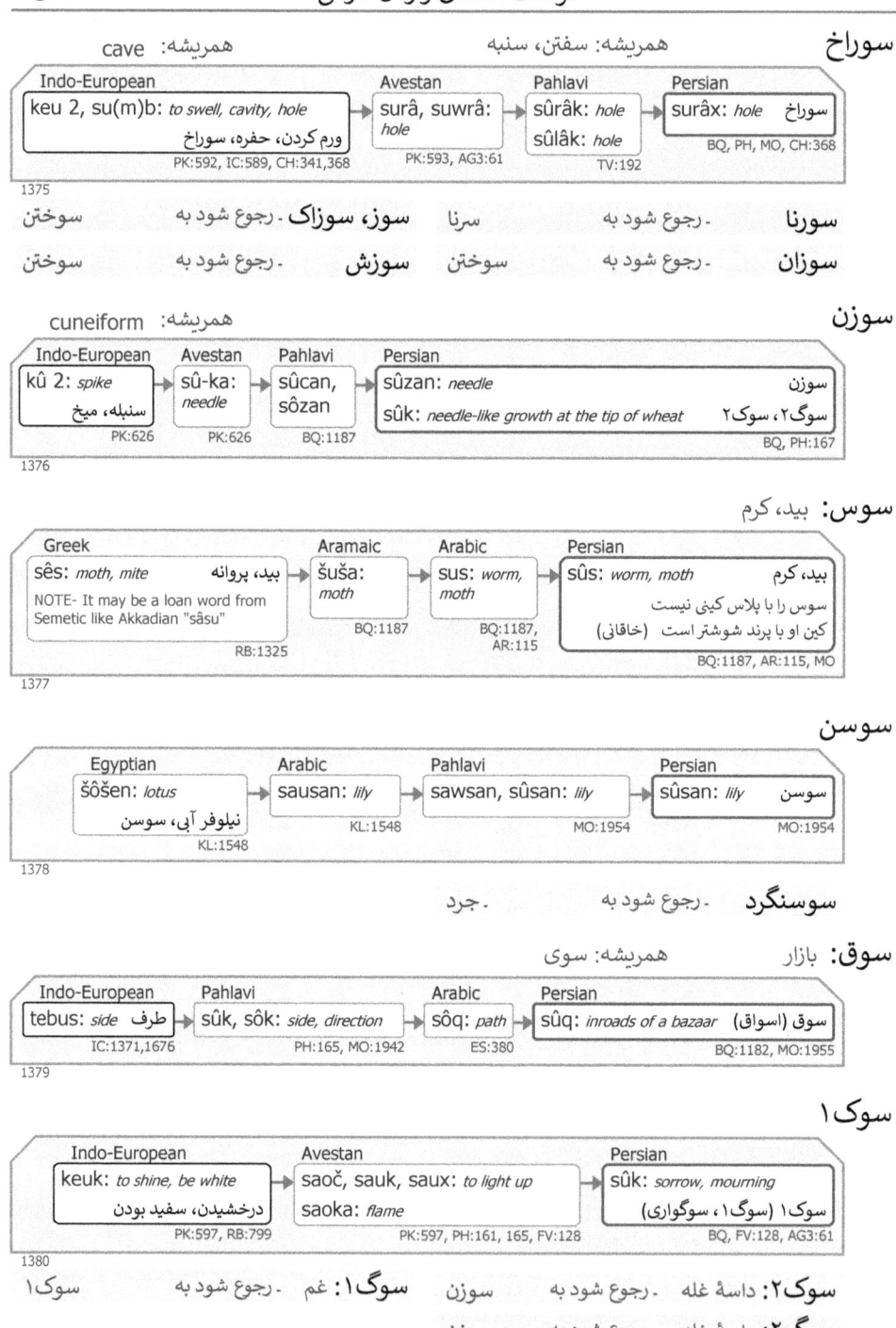

سوراخ

همریشه: سفتن، سنبه   همریشه: cave

Indo-European
keu 2, su(m)b: *to swell, cavity, hole*
ورم کردن، حفره، سوراخ
PK:592, IC:589, CH:341,368

Avestan
surâ, suwrâ: *hole*
PK:593, AG3:61

Pahlavi
sûrâk: *hole*
sûlâk: *hole*
TV:192

Persian
surâx: *hole* سوراخ
BQ, PH, MO, CH:368

1375

سورنا
رجوع شود به. سرنا   **سوز، سوزاک** ∙ رجوع شود به سوختن

سوزان
رجوع شود به. سوختن   **سوزش** ∙ رجوع شود به سوختن

سوزن

همریشه: cuneiform

Indo-European
kû 2: *spike*
سنبله، میخ
PK:626

Avestan
sû-ka: *needle*
PK:626

Pahlavi
sûcan, sôzan
BQ:1187

Persian
sûzan: *needle* سوزن
sûk: *needle-like growth at the tip of wheat* سوگ۲، سوک۲
BQ, PH:167

1376

سوس: بید، کرم

Greek
sês: *moth, mite* بید، پروانه
NOTE- It may be a loan word from
Semetic like Akkadian "sâsu"
RB:1325

Aramaic
šuša: *moth*
BQ:1187

Arabic
sus: *worm, moth*
BQ:1187, AR:115,

Persian
sûs: *worm, moth* بید، کرم
سوس را با پلاس کینی نیست
کین او با پرند شوشتر است (خاقانی)
BQ:1187, AR:115, MO

1377

سوسن

Egyptian
šôšen: *lotus*
نیلوفر آبی، سوسن
KL:1548

Arabic
sausan: *lily*
KL:1548

Pahlavi
sawsan, sûsan: *lily*
MO:1954

Persian
sûsan: *lily* سوسن
MO:1954

1378

سوسنگرد
رجوع شود به. جرد

سوق: بازار

همریشه: سوی

Indo-European
tebus: *side* طرف
IC:1371,1676

Pahlavi
sûk, sôk: *side, direction*
PH:165, MO:1942

Arabic
sôq: *path*
ES:380

Persian
sûq: *inroads of a bazaar* سوق (اسواق)
BQ:1182, MO:1955

1379

سوک۱

Indo-European
keuk: *to shine, be white*
درخشیدن، سفید بودن
PK:597, RB:799

Avestan
saoč, sauk, saux: *to light up*
saoka: *flame*
PK:597, PH:161, 165, FV:128

Persian
sûk: *sorrow, mourning*
سوک۱ (سوگ۱، سوگواری)
BQ, FV:128, AG3:61

1380

سوک۲: داسهٔ غله
رجوع شود به. سوزن   **سوگ۱:** غم ∙ رجوع شود به سوک۱

سوگ۲: داسهٔ غله
رجوع شود به. سوزن

سوگند: "آب گوگرد برای اثبات بیگناهی "

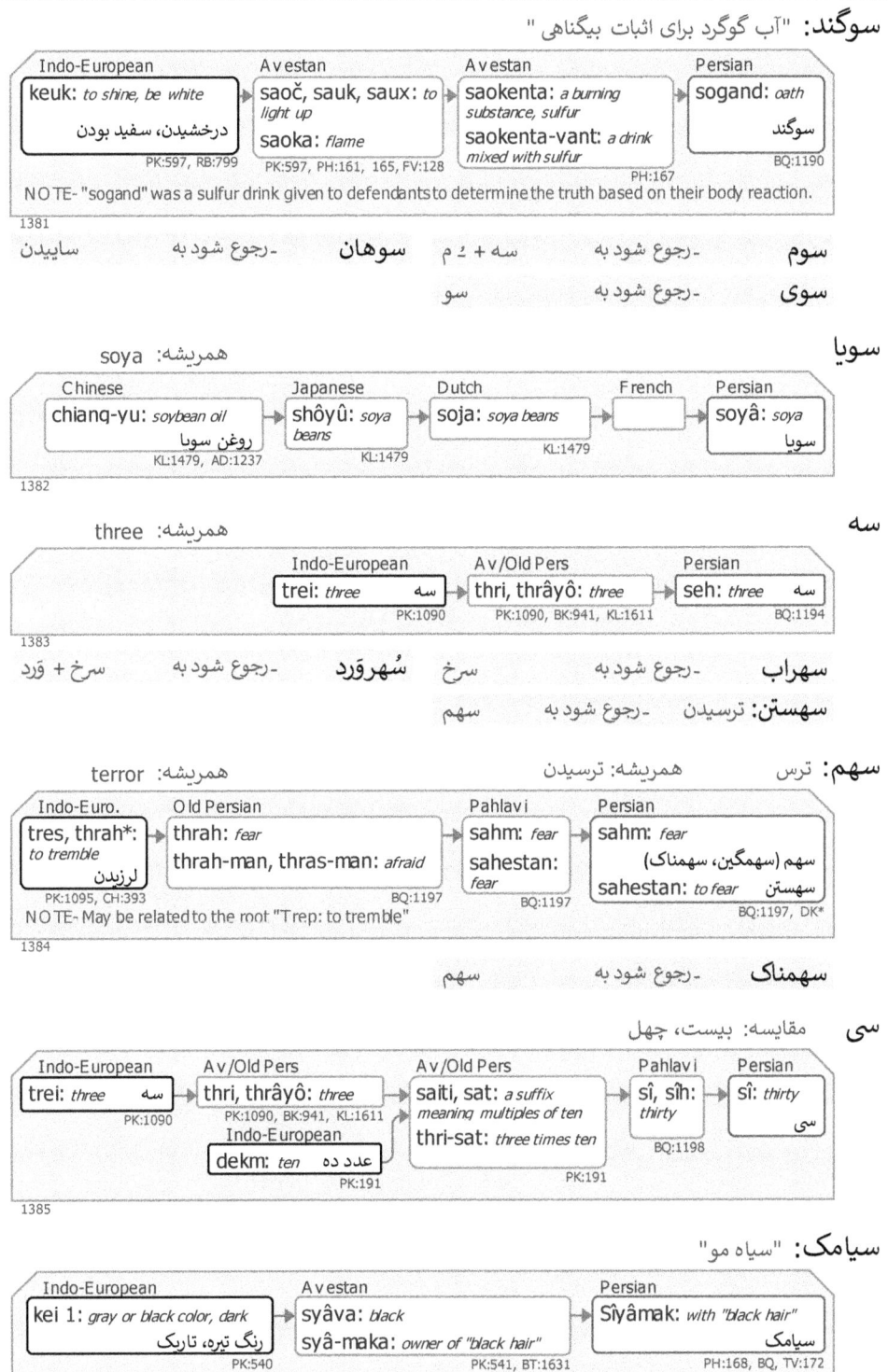

Indo-European	Avestan	Avestan	Persian
keuk: to shine, be white	saoč, sauk, saux: to light up	saokenta: a burning substance, sulfur	sogand: oath
درخشیدن، سفید بودن	saoka: flame	saokenta-vant: a drink mixed with sulfur	سوگند
PK:597, RB:799	PK:597, PH:161, 165, FV:128	PH:167	BQ:1190

NOTE- "sogand" was a sulfur drink given to defendants to determine the truth based on their body reaction.

1381

سوم	ـ رجوع شود به	سه + ‹ِ م	سوهان	ـ رجوع شود به	ساییدن
سوی	ـ رجوع شود به	سو			

سویا   همریشه: soya

Chinese	Japanese	Dutch	French	Persian
chiang-yu: soybean oil	shôyû: soya beans	soja: soya beans		soyâ: soya
روغن سویا				سویا
KL:1479, AD:1237	KL:1479	KL:1479		

1382

سه   همریشه: three

Indo-European	Av/Old Pers	Persian
trei: three سه	thri, thrâyô: three	seh: three سه
PK:1090	PK:1090, BK:941, KL:1611	BQ:1194

1383

سهراب	ـ رجوع شود به	سرخ	سُهرَورد	ـ رجوع شود به	سرخ + وَرد
سهستن: ترسیدن	ـ رجوع شود به	سهم			

سهم: ترس   همریشه: ترسیدن   همریشه: terror

Indo-Euro.	Old Persian	Pahlavi	Persian
tres, thrah*: to tremble	thrah: fear	sahm: fear	sahm: fear
لرزیدن	thrah-man, thras-man: afraid	sahestan: fear	سهم (سهمگین، سهمناک)
PK:1095, CH:393	BQ:1197	BQ:1197	sahestan: to fear سهستن
			BQ:1197, DK*

NOTE- May be related to the root "Trep: to tremble"

1384

سهمناک	ـ رجوع شود به	سهم

سی   مقایسه: بیست، چهل

Indo-European	Av/Old Pers	Av/Old Pers	Pahlavi	Persian
trei: three سه	thri, thrâyô: three	saiti, sat: a suffix meaning multiples of ten	sî, sîh: thirty	sî: thirty
PK:1090	PK:1090, BK:941, KL:1611	thri-sat: three times ten	BQ:1198	سی
	Indo-European			
	dekm: ten عدد ده			
	PK:191	PK:191		

1385

سیامک: "سیاه مو"

Indo-European	Avestan	Persian
kei 1: gray or black color, dark	syâva: black	Sîyâmak: with "black hair"
رنگ تیره، تاریک	syâ-maka: owner of "black hair"	سیامک
PK:540	PK:541, BT:1631	PH:168, BQ, TV:172

1386

سياوش: "با اسبان سياه"

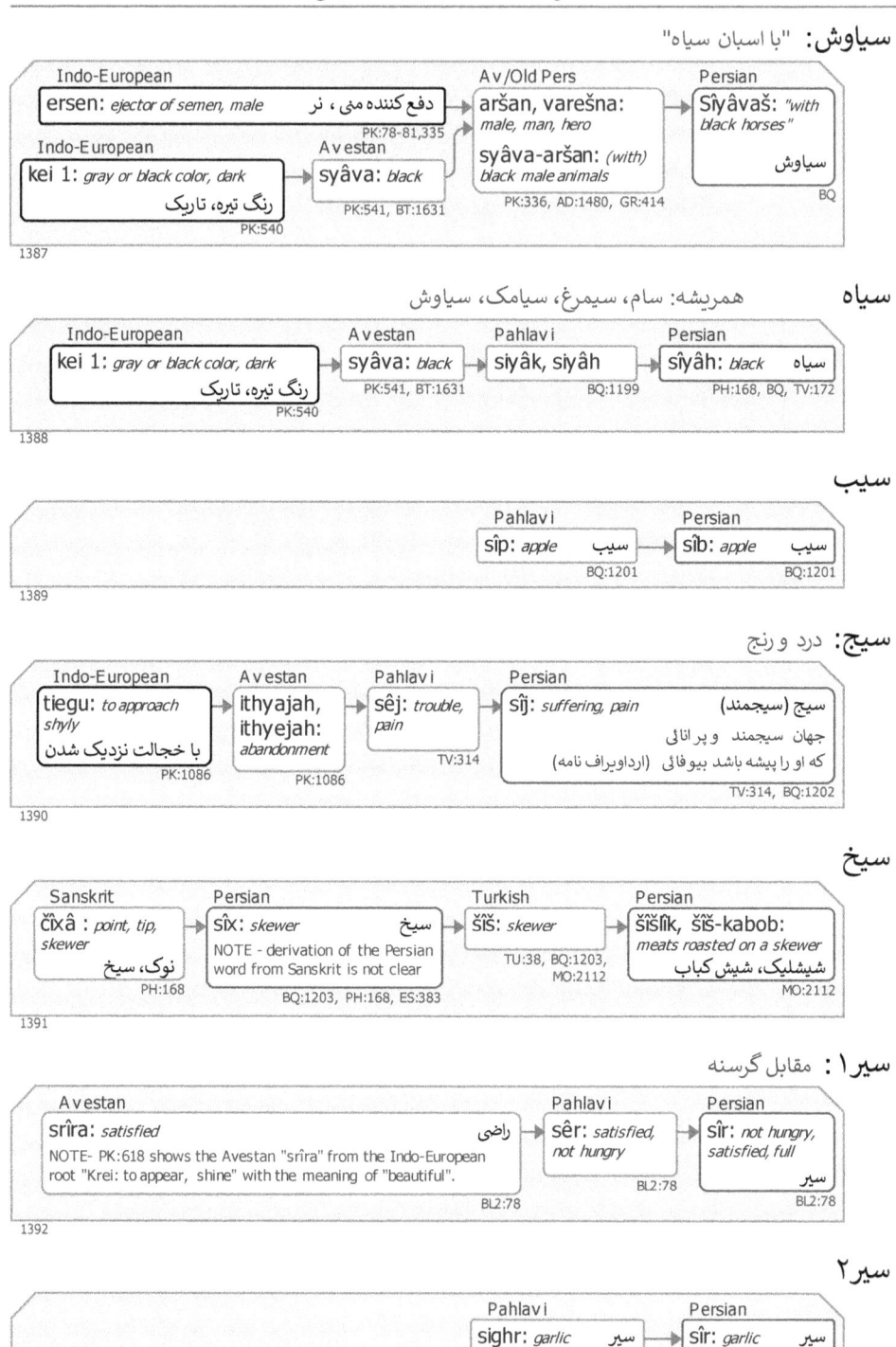

1387

همریشه: سام، سیمرغ، سیامک، سیاوش سياه

1388

سيب

1389

سيج: درد و رنج

1390

سيخ

1391

سير ۱: مقابل گرسنه

1392

سير ۲

1393

سیستان

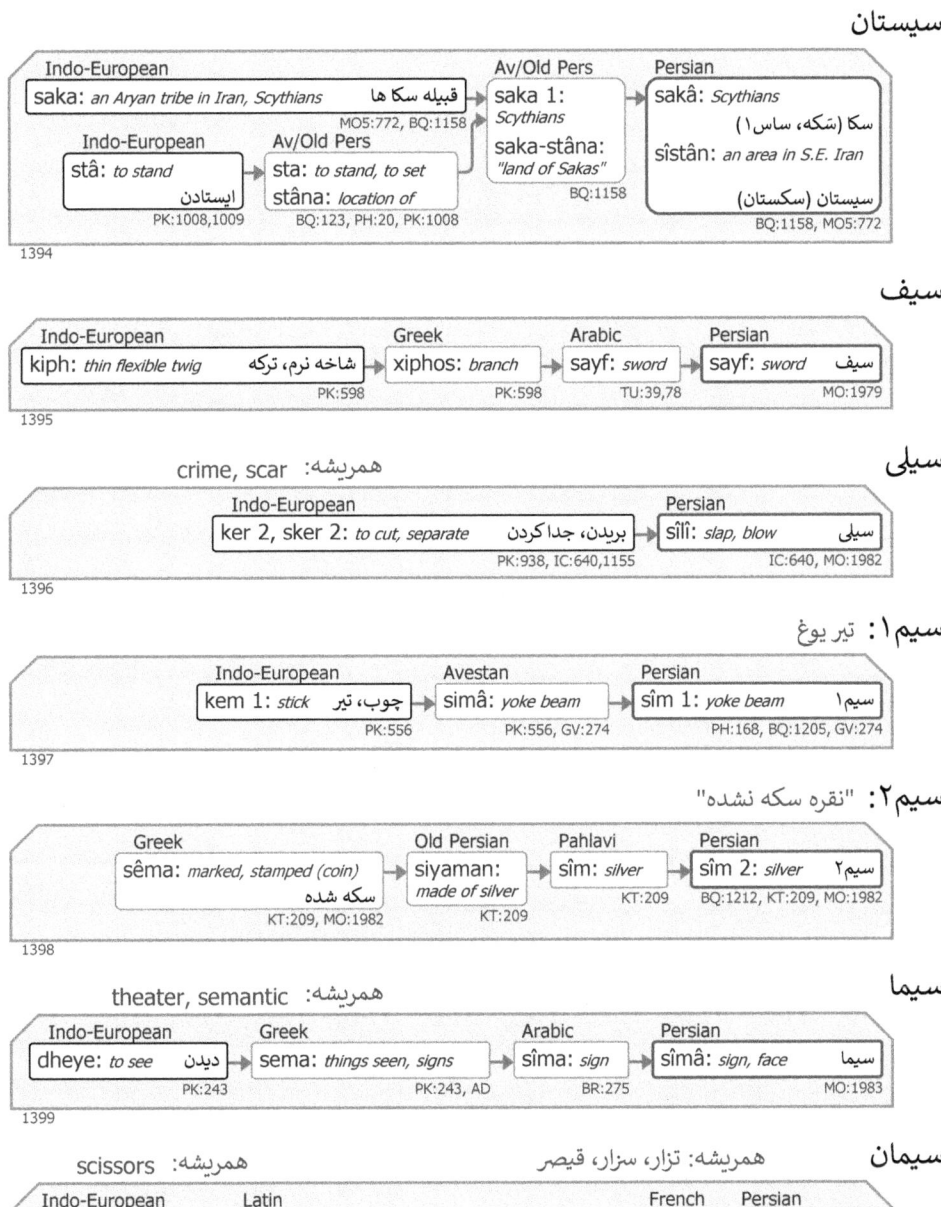

Indo-European		Av/Old Pers	Persian
saka: *an Aryan tribe in Iran, Scythians* قبیله سکا ها		saka 1: *Scythians*	sakâ: *Scythians*
			سکا (سَکه، ساس۱)
MO5:772, BQ:1158		saka-stâna: "land of Sakas"	sîstân: *an area in S.E. Iran*
Indo-European	Av/Old Pers		
stâ: *to stand*	sta: *to stand, to set*	BQ:1158	سیستان (سکستان)
ایستادن	stâna: *location of*		
PK:1008,1009	BQ:123, PH:20, PK:1008		BQ:1158, MO5:772

1394

سیف

Indo-European	Greek	Arabic	Persian
kiph: *thin flexible twig* شاخه نرم، ترکه	xiphos: *branch*	sayf: *sword*	sayf: *sword* سیف
PK:598	PK:598	TU:39,78	MO:1979

1395

سیلی

همریشه: crime, scar

Indo-European	Persian
ker 2, sker 2: *to cut, separate* بریدن، جداکردن	sîlî: *slap, blow* سیلی
PK:938, IC:640,1155	IC:640, MO:1982

1396

سیم۱: تیر یوغ

Indo-European	Avestan	Persian
kem 1: *stick* چوب، تیر	simâ: *yoke beam*	sîm 1: *yoke beam* سیم۱
PK:556	PK:556, GV:274	PH:168, BQ:1205, GV:274

1397

سیم۲: "نقره سکه نشده"

Greek	Old Persian	Pahlavi	Persian
sêma: *marked, stamped (coin)* سکه شده	siyaman: *made of silver*	sîm: *silver*	sîm 2: *silver* سیم۲
KT:209, MO:1982	KT:209	KT:209	BQ:1212, KT:209, MO:1982

1398

سیما

همریشه: theater, semantic

Indo-European	Greek	Arabic	Persian
dheye: *to see* دیدن	sema: *things seen, signs*	sîma: *sign*	sîmâ: *sign, face* سیما
PK:243	PK:243, AD	BR:275	MO:1983

1399

سیمان

همریشه: تزار، سزار، قیصر   همریشه: scissors

Indo-European	Latin	French	Persian
skhai: *to cut, strike*	caedere: *to cut*		sîmân: *cement*
بریدن، ضربه زدن	caementum: *stone chips used to make lime*	AD:217	سیمان (سمنت)
PK:917	PK:917, BL1:84		MO:1983

1400

246

سیمرغ: پرنده تیره رنگ   همریشه: سیاه

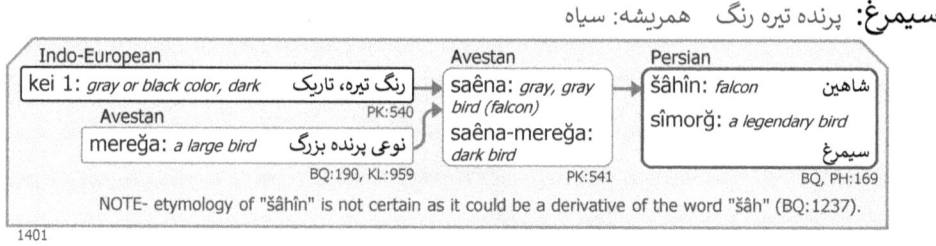

Indo-European		Avestan	Persian
kei 1: *gray or black color, dark* رنگ تیره، تاریک		**saêna:** *gray, gray bird (falcon)*	**šâhîn:** *falcon* شاهین
	PK:540	**saêna-mereğa:** *dark bird*	**sîmorğ:** *a legendary bird*
Avestan			سیمرغ
mereğa: *a large bird* نوعی پرنده بزرگ			
	BQ:190, KL:959	PK:541	BQ, PH:169

NOTE- etymology of "šâhîn" is not certain as it could be a derivative of the word "šâh" (BQ:1237).

1401

این حرف گاهی به چ یا س بدل شود.

شاخ، شاخه

Indo-European	Pahlavi	Persian
kâk: *twig, branch* شاخه، ترکه	šâk	šâx: *horn, branch* (شاخه) شاخ
COGNATE- Sanskrit "šâxa: branch"	PK:523	BQ:1219
1402		PK:523, BQ:1219, BK:525

شاد

همریشه: quiet

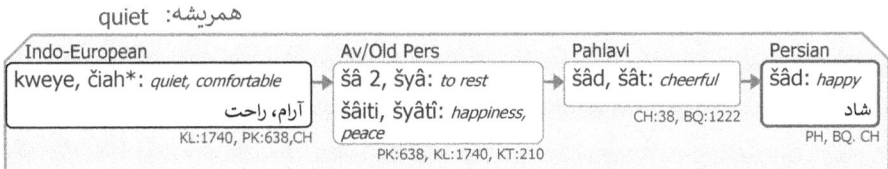

Indo-European	Av/Old Pers	Pahlavi	Persian
kweye, čiah*: *quiet, comfortable* آرام، راحت	šâ 2, šyâ: *to rest* šâiti, šyâtî: *happiness, peace*	šâd, šât: *cheerful*	šâd: *happy* شاد
KL:1740, PK:638,CH	PK:638, KL:1740, KT:210	CH:38, BQ:1222	PH, BQ. CH
1403			

شادُروان: پرده پیش در، سایبان، چادر، فرش

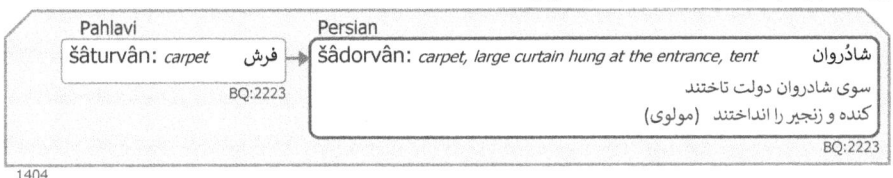

Pahlavi	Persian
šâturvân: *carpet* فرش	šâdorvân: *carpet, large curtain hung at the entrance, tent* شادُروان
BQ:2223	سوی شادروان دولت تاختند
	کنده و زنجیر را انداختند (مولوی)
1404	BQ:2223

شار

ـ رجوع شود به   شاریدن

شاریدن

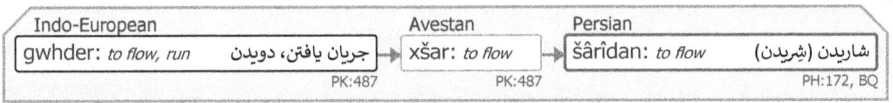

Indo-European	Avestan	Persian
gwhder: *to flow, run* جریان یافتن، دویدن	xšar: *to flow*	šârîdan: *to flow* (شریدن) شاریدن
PK:487	PK:487	PH:172, BQ
1405		

شاش

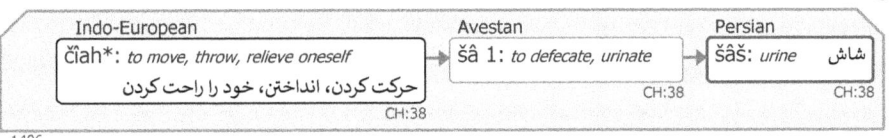

Indo-European	Avestan	Persian
čiah*: *to move, throw, relieve oneself* حرکت کردن، انداختن، خود را راحت کردن	šâ 1: *to defecate, urinate*	šâš: *urine* شاش
CH:38	CH:38	CH:38
1406		

شاگرد: "دنبال رو"

همریشه: pursue

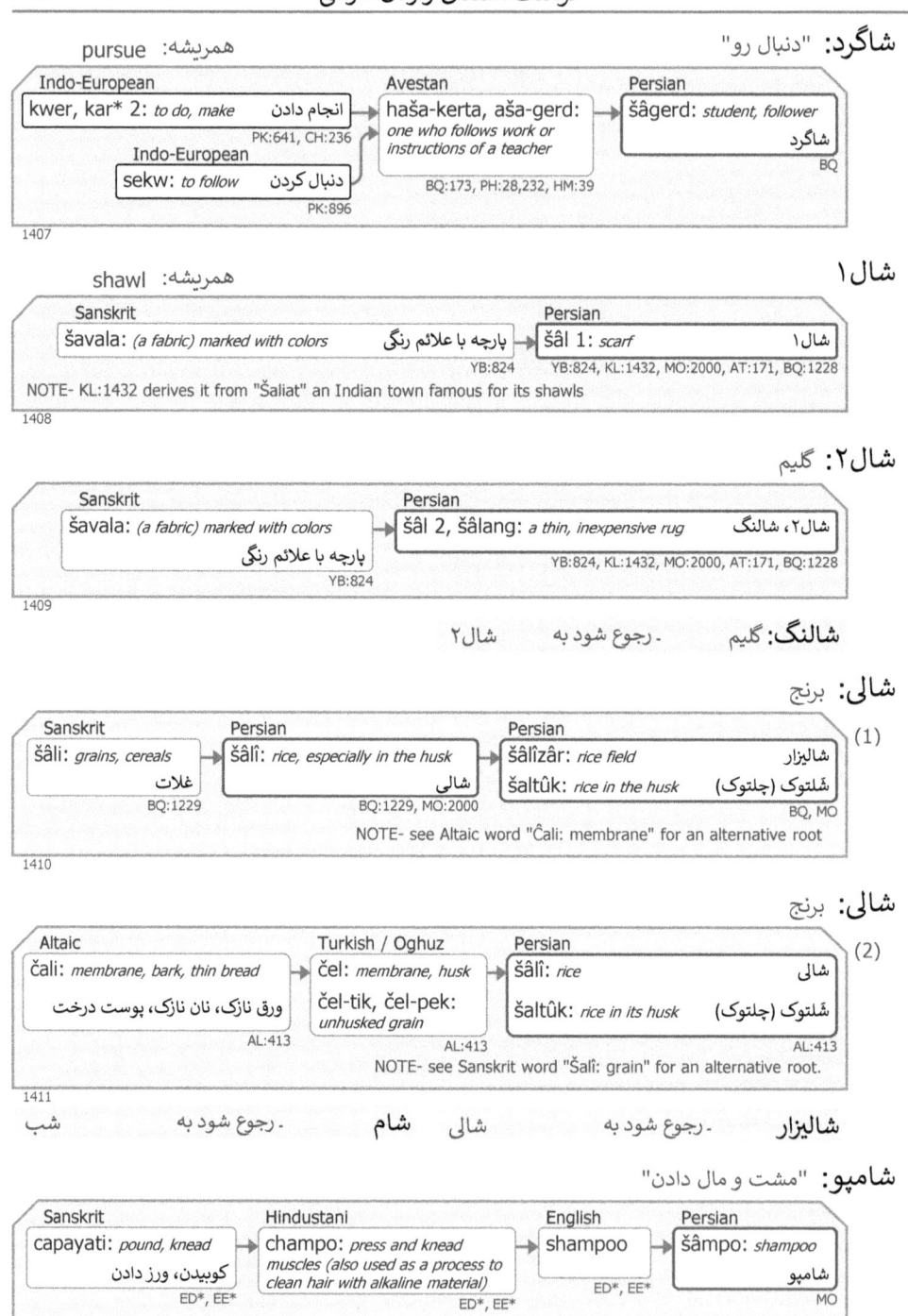

Indo-European	Avestan	Persian
kwer, kar* 2: *to do, make* انجام دادن PK:641, CH:236	haša-kerta, aša-gerd: *one who follows work or instructions of a teacher* BQ:173, PH:28,232, HM:39	šâgerd: *student, follower* شاگرد BQ
Indo-European		
sekw: *to follow* دنبال کردن PK:896		

1407

شال ۱

همریشه: shawl

Sanskrit	Persian
šavala: *(a fabric) marked with colors* پارچه با علائم رنگ YB:824	šâl 1: *scarf* شال۱ YB:824, KL:1432, MO:2000, AT:171, BQ:1228
NOTE- KL:1432 derives it from "Šaliat" an Indian town famous for its shawls	

1408

شال ۲: گلیم

Sanskrit	Persian
šavala: *(a fabric) marked with colors* پارچه با علائم رنگ YB:824	šâl 2, šâlang: *a thin, inexpensive rug* شال۲، شالنگ YB:824, KL:1432, MO:2000, AT:171, BQ:1228

1409

شالنگ: گلیم ۔ رجوع شود به   شال۲

شالی: برنج

Sanskrit	Persian	Persian	
šâli: *grains, cereals* غلات BQ:1229	šâlî: *rice, especially in the husk* شالی BQ:1229, MO:2000	šâlîzâr: *rice field* شالیزار šaltûk: *rice in the husk* شلتوک (چلتوک) BQ, MO	(1)
		NOTE- see Altaic word "Ĉali: membrane" for an alternative root	

1410

شالی: برنج

Altaic	Turkish / Oghuz	Persian	
čali: *membrane, bark, thin bread* ورق نازک، نان نازک، پوست درخت AL:413	čel: *membrane, husk* čel-tik, čel-pek: *unhusked grain* AL:413	šâlî: *rice* شالی šaltûk: *rice in its husk* شلتوک (چلتوک) AL:413	(2)
		NOTE- see Sanskrit word "Šalî: grain" for an alternative root.	

1411

شالیزار: شالی ۔ رجوع شود به   **شام** شالی ۔ رجوع شود به   شب

شامپو: "مشت و مال دادن"

Sanskrit	Hindustani	English	Persian
capayati: *pound, knead* کوبیدن، ورز دادن ED*, EE*	champo: *press and knead muscles (also used as a process to clean hair with alkaline material)* ED*, EE*	shampoo ED*, EE*	šâmpo: *shampoo* شامپو MO

1412

شانزده

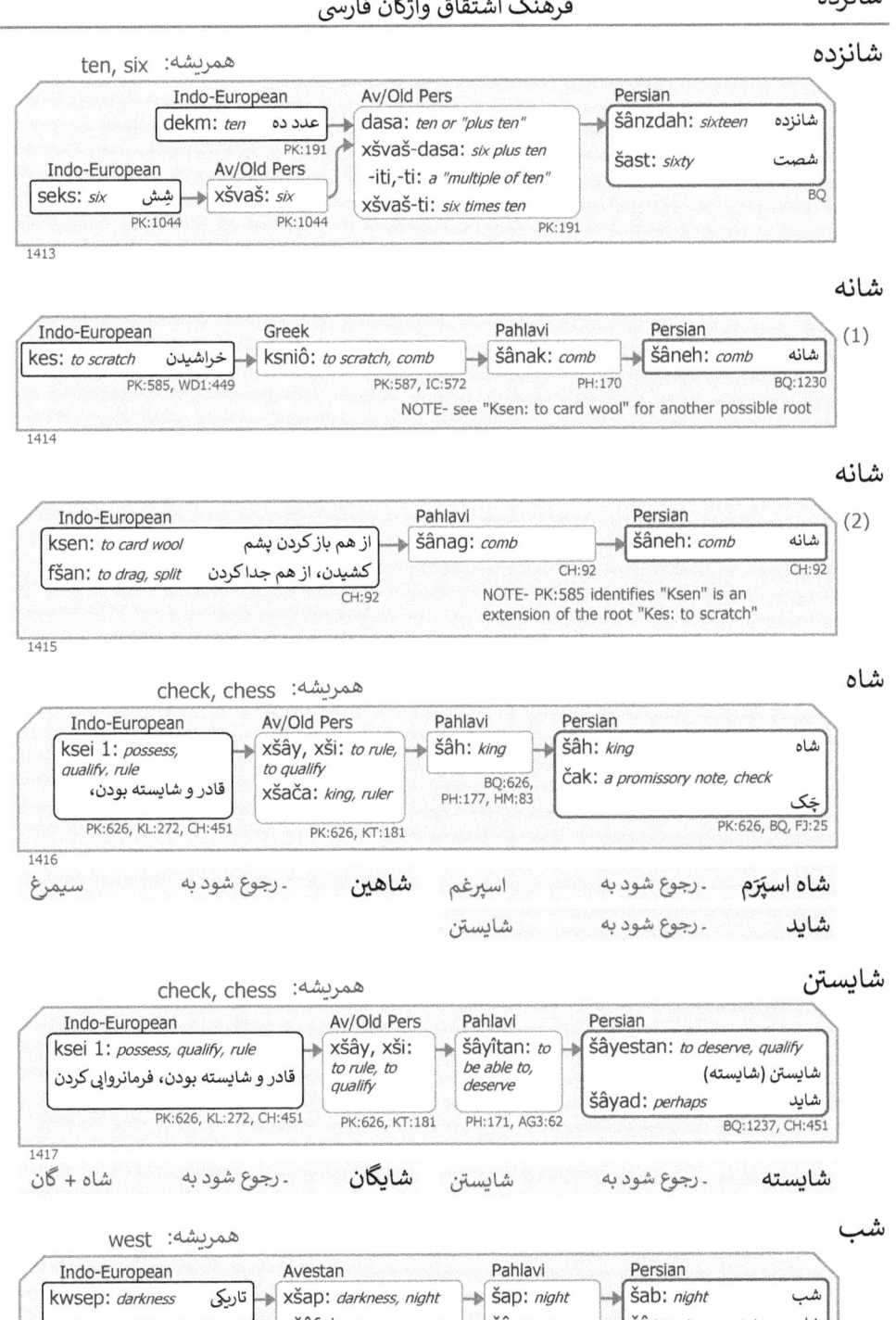

همریشه: ten, six

Indo-European	Av/Old Pers	Persian
dekm: *ten* عدد ده	dasa: *ten or "plus ten"*	šânzdah: *sixteen* شانزده
PK:191	xšvaš-dasa: *six plus ten*	šast: *sixty* شصت
Indo-European	Av/Old Pers	-iti,-ti: *a "multiple of ten"*	BQ
seks: *six* شش	xšvaš: *six*	xšvaš-ti: *six times ten*	
PK:1044	PK:1044	PK:191

1413

شانه

خراشیدن

Indo-European	Greek	Pahlavi	Persian
kes: *to scratch*	ksniô: *to scratch, comb*	šânak: *comb*	šâneh: *comb* شانه
PK:585, WD1:449	PK:587, IC:572	PH:170	BQ:1230

NOTE- see "Ksen: to card wool" for another possible root

(1)

1414

شانه

Indo-European	Pahlavi	Persian
ksen: *to card wool* از هم باز کردن پشم	šânag: *comb*	šâneh: *comb* شانه
fšan: *to drag, split* کشیدن، از هم جدا کردن	CH:92	CH:92
CH:92		

NOTE- PK:585 identifies "Ksen" is an extension of the root "Kes: to scratch"

(2)

1415

شاه

همریشه: check, chess

Indo-European	Av/Old Pers	Pahlavi	Persian
ksei 1: *possess, qualify, rule*	xšây, xši: *to rule, to qualify*	šâh: *king*	šâh: *king* شاه
قادر و شایسته بودن،	xšača: *king, ruler*	BQ:626, PH:177, HM:83	čak: *a promissory note, check* چک
PK:626, KL:272, CH:451	PK:626, KT:181		PK:626, BQ, FJ:25

1416

شاه اسپَرم ـ رجوع شود به اسپرغم   **شاهین** ـ رجوع شود به سیمرغ

شاید ـ رجوع شود به شایستن

شایستن

همریشه: check, chess

Indo-European	Av/Old Pers	Pahlavi	Persian
ksei 1: *possess, qualify, rule*	xšây, xši: *to rule, to qualify*	šâyîtan: *to be able to, deserve*	šâyestan: *to deserve, qualify* شایستن (شایسته)
قادر و شایسته بودن، فرمانروایی کردن	PK:626, KT:181	PH:171, AG3:62	šâyad: *perhaps* شاید
PK:626, KL:272, CH:451			BQ:1237, CH:451

1417

شایسته ـ رجوع شود به شایستن   **شایگان** شایستن ـ رجوع شود به شاه + گان

شب

همریشه: west

Indo-European	Avestan	Pahlavi	Persian
kwsep: *darkness* تاریکی	xšap: *darkness, night*	šap: *night*	šab: *night* شب
PK:649	xšâfniya: *night meal*	šâm: *dinner*	šâm: *dinner, night* شام
	PK:649	BQ:1229,1239	MO, BQ, PH:169, BK:992

1418

شب + دیس	شبدیز - رجوع شود به	چوپان	شبان - رجوع شود به

شبستان

همریشه: stand

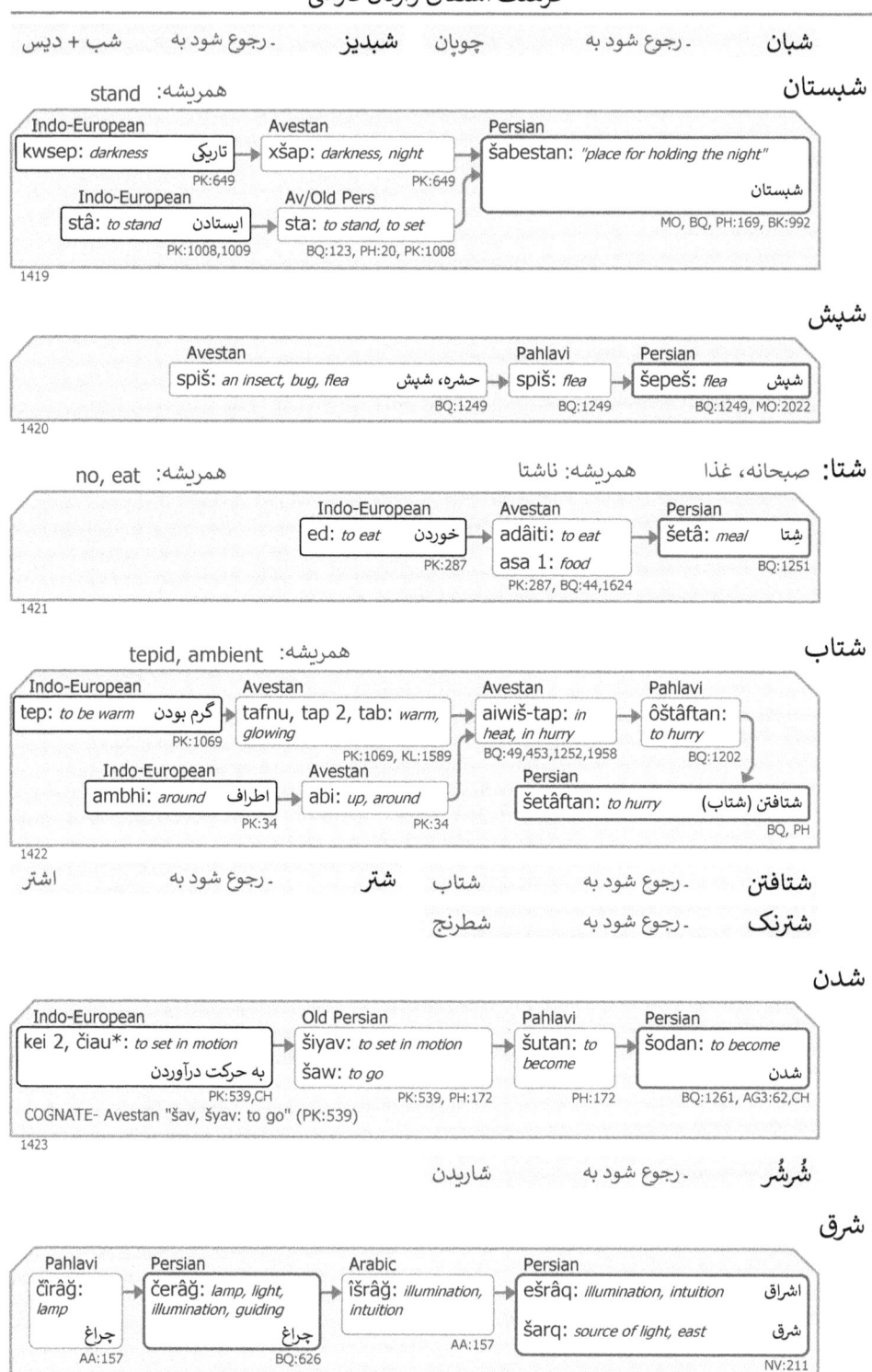

Indo-European
kwsep: *darkness* تاریکی → **Avestan** xšap: *darkness, night*
PK:649 / PK:649

Indo-European
stâ: *to stand* ایستادن → **Av/Old Pers** sta: *to stand, to set*
PK:1008,1009 / BQ:123, PH:20, PK:1008

Persian
šabestan: *"place for holding the night"*
شبستان
MO, BQ, PH:169, BK:992

1419

شپش

Avestan spiš: *an insect, bug, flea* حشره، شپش → **Pahlavi** spiš: *flea* → **Persian** šepeš: *flea* شپش
BQ:1249 / BQ:1249 / BQ:1249, MO:2022

1420

شتا: صبحانه، غذا

همریشه: ناشتا   همریشه: no, eat

Indo-European ed: *to eat* خوردن → **Avestan** adâiti: *to eat* asa 1: *food* → **Persian** šetâ: *meal* شِتا
PK:287 / PK:287, BQ:44,1624 / BQ:1251

1421

شتاب

همریشه: tepid, ambient

Indo-European
tep: *to be warm* گرم بودن → **Avestan** tafnu, tap 2, tab: *warm, glowing*
PK:1069 / PK:1069, KL:1589

Avestan aiwiš-tap: *in heat, in hurry* → **Pahlavi** ôštâftan: *to hurry*
BQ:49,453,1252,1958 / BQ:1202

Indo-European ambhi: *around* اطراف → **Avestan** abi: *up, around*
PK:34 / PK:34

Persian šetâftan: *to hurry* شتافتن (شتاب)
BQ, PH

1422

اشتر	شتاب	شتر - رجوع شود به	شتافتن - رجوع شود به
شطرنج		شترنک - رجوع شود به	

شدن

Indo-European
kei 2, čiau*: *to set in motion* به حرکت درآوردن šaw: *to go* → **Old Persian** šiyav: *to set in motion* → **Pahlavi** šutan: *to become* → **Persian** šodan: *to become* شدن
PK:539,CH / PK:539, PH:172 / PH:172 / BQ:1261, AG3:62,CH

COGNATE- Avestan "šav, šyav: to go" (PK:539)

1423

شاریدن	شُرِشُر - رجوع شود به

شرق

Pahlavi čîrâğ: *lamp* چراغ → **Persian** čerâğ: *lamp, light, illumination, guiding* چراغ → **Arabic** išrâq: *illumination, intuition* → **Persian** ešrâq: *illumination, intuition* اشراق / šarq: *source of light, east* شرق
AA:157 / BQ:626 / AA:157 / NV:211

1424

شرم: خجلت و حیا

همریشه: harm

Indo-European	Avestan	Pahlavi	Persian
kormo, fšar* 1: *suffering, shame* رنج بردن، شرمنده شدن PK:615, CH:92	fšarema: *pain, shame* PK:615, CH:92	šarm BQ:1264	šarm: *shame* شرم PH:172, BQ:1264

1425

شِریدن ـ رجوع شود به شاریدن

شستن

Indo-European	Avestan	Pahlavi	Persian
kseud: *water, to clean in water* آب، پاک کردن در آب PK:625, WD1:502	xšaod, xšaud: *flow* PK:625, WD1:502, CH:455	šustan: *clean* BQ:2267	šostan: *to clean, wash* شستن (شوی۲، شور۲) PH, BQ, AG3

1426

شُش همریشه: هوا

Indo-European	Avestan	Pahlavi	Persian
kwes: *to pant, to breathe fast* نفس نفس زدن PK:631, GT6:284, CH:369	suši, suš: *the lungs* PK:631, BK:260	suš: *lung* TV:192	šoš: *lung* شُش PH:173, BQ:1266, CH:369

1427

شِش

Indo-European	Av/Old Pers	Pahlavi	Persian
seks: *six* شِش PK:1044	xšvaš: *six* PK:1044	šaš: *six* BQ:1266	šeš: *six* شِش BQ:1266

1428

شَصت ـ رجوع شود به شانزده

شطرنج: "چهار مهره"   همریشه: چهار، انگشت   همریشه: four, anchor

Indo-European	Sanskrit	Pahlavi	Persian
ang: *to bend* خم کردن PK:46	angam: *part* catur-anga: *four parts (castle, Knight, Bishop and Pawn)* PK:46, BQ:1254	catrang	Satranj: *chess* (شطرنج (شترنگ، کترنگ تا جزء از بیست و چهارش نبود خانه نرد همچو در سی و دو خانه است اساس شترنگ (نجار) BQ:1254, ES:404
Indo-European kwetwer: *four* چهار PK:642			

1429

شغال همریشه: jackal (from šoğâl)

Sanskrit	Pahlavi	Persian
srgâla: *howler* زوزه کش KL:823, MO:2050	šağâl: *coyote* MO:2050	šağâl, šoğâl: *coyote* (شغال (شکال، شگال KL:823

NOTE- BQ:1270 indicates that "Srgâla" may be from Babylonia

1430

شَفش: شاخه، سیم   همریشه: سیف

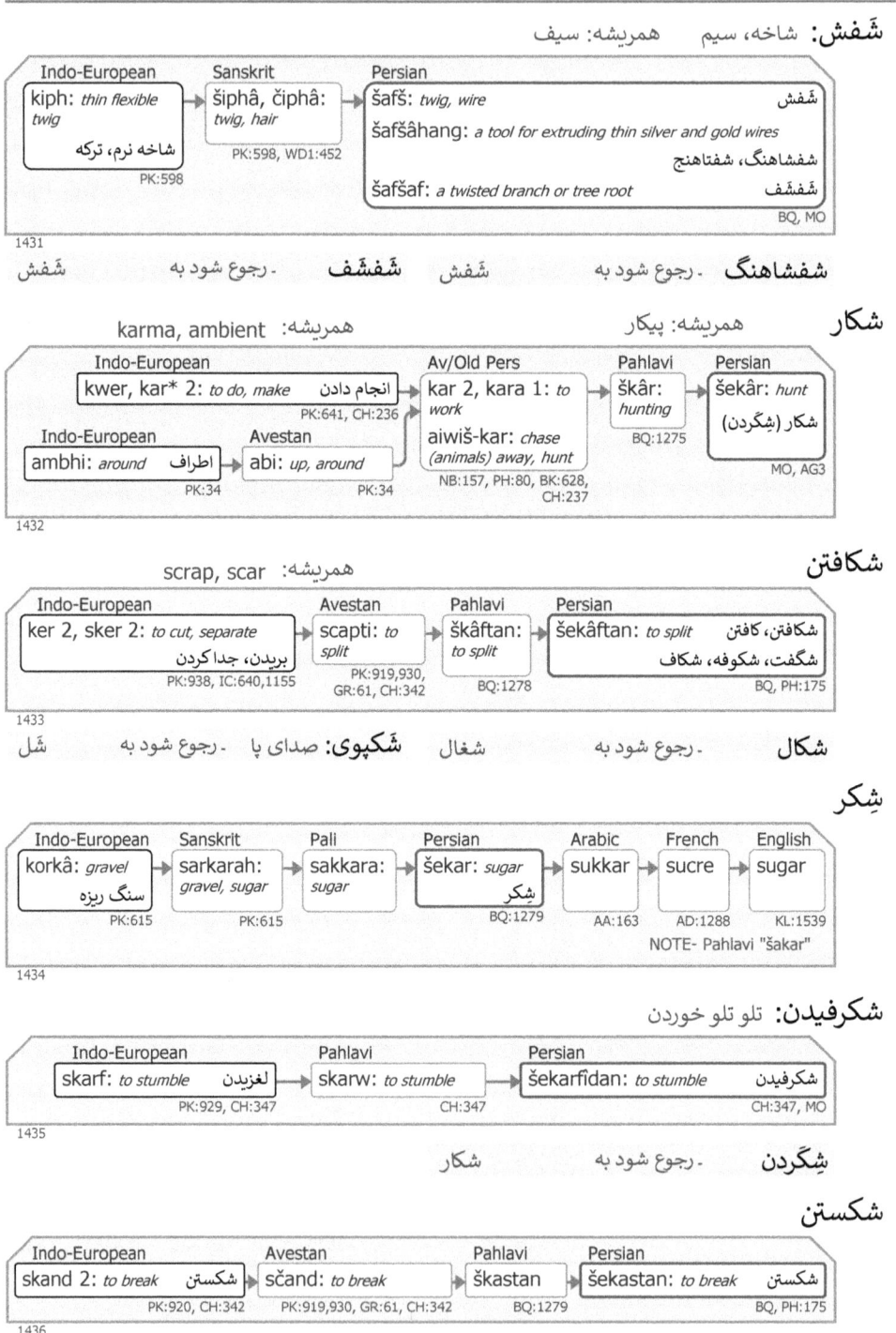

Indo-European	Sanskrit	Persian
kiph: *thin flexible twig* شاخه نرم، ترکه PK:598	šiphâ, čiphâ: *twig, hair* PK:598, WD1:452	šafš: *twig, wire* شَفش šafšâhang: *a tool for extruding thin silver and gold wires* شفشاهنگ، شفتاهنج šafšaf: *a twisted branch or tree root* شَفشَف BQ, MO

1431

شفشاهنگ ـ رجوع شود به   شَفش   شَفشَف   ـ رجوع شود به   شَفش

شکار
همریشه: پیکار   همریشه: karma, ambient

Indo-European		Av/Old Pers	Pahlavi	Persian
kwer, kar* 2: *to do, make* انجام دادن PK:641, CH:236		kar 2, kara 1: *to work* aiwiš-kar: *chase (animals) away, hunt* NB:157, PH:80, BK:628, CH:237	škâr: *hunting* BQ:1275	šekâr: *hunt* شکار (شگردن) MO, AG3
Indo-European	Avestan			
ambhi: *around* اطراف PK:34	abi: *up, around* PK:34			

1432

شکافتن
همریشه: scrap, scar

Indo-European	Avestan	Pahlavi	Persian
ker 2, sker 2: *to cut, separate* بریدن، جدا کردن PK:938, IC:640,1155	scapti: *to split* PK:919,930, GR:61, CH:342	škâftan: *to split* BQ:1278	šekâftan: *to split* شکافتن، کافتن شگفت، شکوفه، شکاف BQ, PH:175

1433

شکال ـ رجوع شود به   شغال   شَکپوی: صدای پا   ـ رجوع شود به   شَل

شِکر

Indo-European	Sanskrit	Pali	Persian	Arabic	French	English
korkâ: *gravel* سنگ ریزه PK:615	sarkarah: *gravel, sugar* PK:615	sakkara: *sugar*	šekar: *sugar* شکر BQ:1279	sukkar AA:163	sucre AD:1288	sugar KL:1539

NOTE- Pahlavi "šakar"

1434

شکرفیدن: تلو تلو خوردن

Indo-European	Pahlavi	Persian
skarf: *to stumble* لغزیدن PK:929, CH:347	skarw: *to stumble* CH:347	šekarfidan: *to stumble* شکرفیدن CH:347, MO

1435

شِگردن ـ رجوع شود به   شکار

شکستن

Indo-European	Avestan	Pahlavi	Persian
skand 2: *to break* شکستن PK:920, CH:342	scand: *to break* PK:919,930, GR:61, CH:342	škastan BQ:1279	šekastan: *to break* شکستن BQ, PH:175

1436

شکله

Indo-European	Sanskrit	Persian
kâk: *twig, branch* شاخه، ترکه	šakala: *part, piece*	šeklah: *slice, piece, a torn piece of garment* شکله
PK:523	PK:523	BQ:1280

1437

شکم

رجوع شود به ـ   اشکم

شکنجه

	Pahlavi	Persian
	šikênjak: *torture* زجر و آزار	šekanjeh: *torture* شکنجه
	BQ:1283	BQ:1283

1438

شکوفه

رجوع شود به ـ   شکافتن

شُکوه

همریشه: show

Indo-European	Pahlavi	Persian
keu 3, skeu: *to watch, see, hear* دیدن، شنیدن	škôh: *grace*	šokûh: *glory* شُکوه
	PK:587 AP:382	PK:588
COGNATE- Old Persian "au-šaudîhtwi: to trust";/ Avestan "čevîšî: hope" (PK:587,588)		

1439

شکیبا

Old Iranian	Pahlavi	Persian
skaip: *to wait* منتظر بودن	škêb: *patient*	šakîbîdan: *to be patient* (شکیبا) شکیبیدن
	AG3:63 AG3:63	AG3:64, MO

1440

| شگال | رجوع شود به ـ | شکیبا | شکیبیدن |
| رجوع شود به ـ شغال | | | |

| | رجوع شود به ـ شکافتن | | شگفت |

شَل: پا

همریشه: colon, cylinder

Indo-European	Persian	Persian
skel: *bent, curved* خمیده	šal 1: *leg, thigh* شل	šelang: *step* شلنگ
PK:928	šalvâr: *"like legs", pants* شلوار	šalpûy: *sound from foot steps* (شلپوی) شلبوی
NOTE- CH:207 derives šalvâr from a different root meaning "Leg covers"	PH:175, BQ	توانگر بنزدیک زن خفته بود زن از خواب شلبوی مردی شنود (شهید بوشکور بلخی)
		PH:175, BQ

1441

| شَلتوک | رجوع شود به ـ | شَل | شَلبوی: صدای پا ـ رجوع شود به پا |
| رجوع شود به ـ شالی | | | |

| شلوار | رجوع شود به ـ | شَل | شلنگ ـ رجوع شود به شَل |

شما

همریشه: you

Indo-European	Avestan	Pahlavi	Persian
yu: *you* شما	yûš, yûšmat: *you*	šmah	šomâ: *you* شما
PK:513	PK:513	BQ	PH:176, BQ:1291

1442

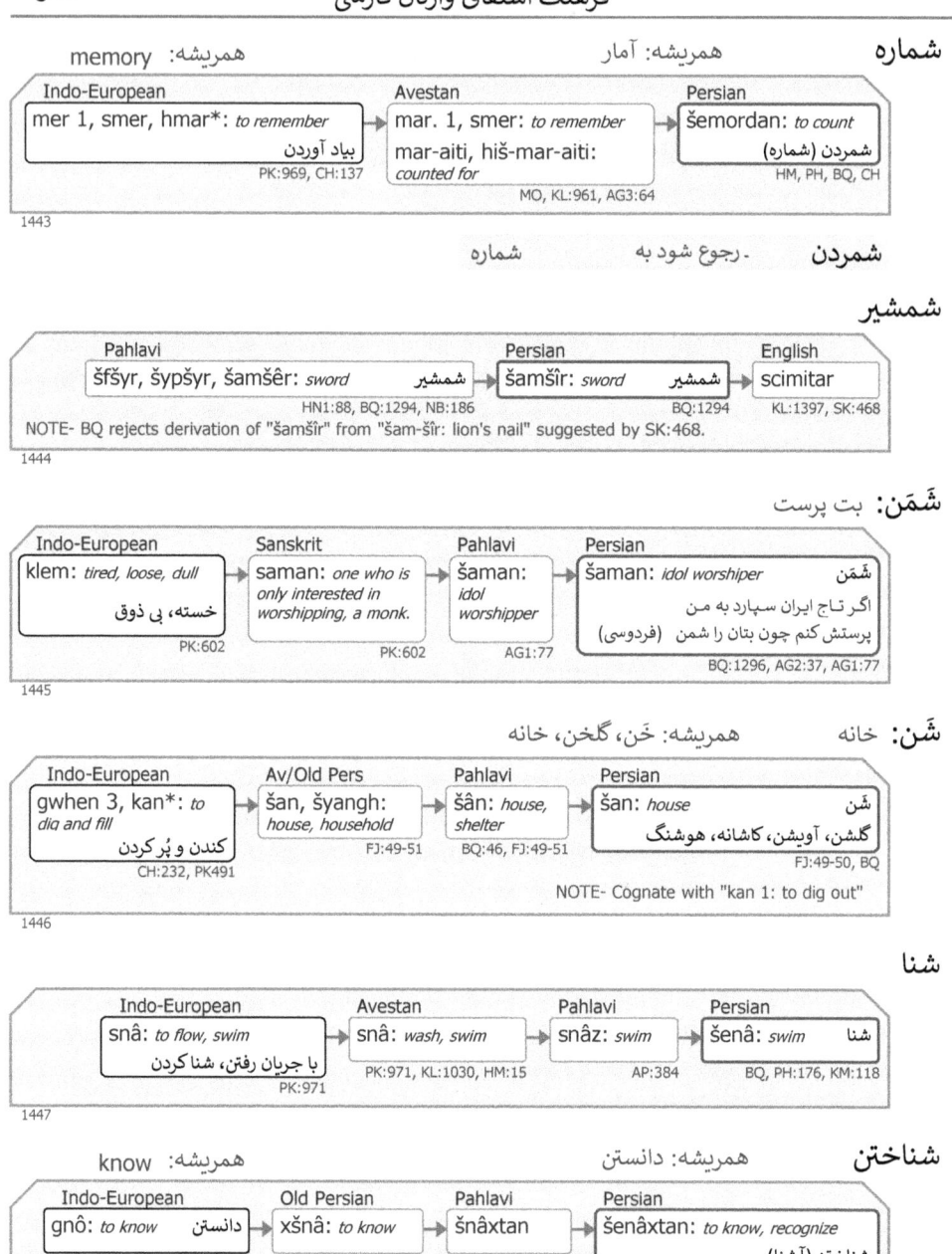

شماره

همریشه: memory   همریشه: آمار

Indo-European	Avestan	Persian
mer 1, smer, hmar*: *to remember* بیاد آوردن PK:969, CH:137	mar. 1, smer: *to remember* mar-aiti, hiš-mar-aiti: *counted for* MO, KL:961, AG3:64	šemordan: *to count* شمردن (شماره) HM, PH, BQ, CH

1443

شمردن   ـ رجوع شود به   شماره

شمشیر

Pahlavi	Persian	English
šfšyr, šypšyr, šamšêr: *sword* شمشیر HN1:88, BQ:1294, NB:186	šamšîr: *sword* شمشیر BQ:1294	scimitar KL:1397, SK:468

NOTE- BQ rejects derivation of "šamšîr" from "šam-šîr: lion's nail" suggested by SK:468.

1444

شَمَن: بت پرست

Indo-European	Sanskrit	Pahlavi	Persian
klem: *tired, loose, dull* خسته، بی ذوق PK:602	saman: *one who is only interested in worshipping, a monk.* PK:602	šaman: *idol worshipper* AG1:77	šaman: *idol worshiper* شَمَن اگر تـاج ایران سپارد به من پرستش کنم چون بتان را شمن (فردوسی) BQ:1296, AG2:37, AG1:77

1445

شَن: خانه   همریشه: خَن، گلخن، خانه

Indo-European	Av/Old Pers	Pahlavi	Persian
gwhen 3, kan*: *to dig and fill* کندن و پُر کردن CH:232, PK491	šan, šyangh: *house, household* FJ:49-51	šân: *house, shelter* BQ:46, FJ:49-51	šan: *house* شَن گشن، آویشن، کاشانه، هوشنگ FJ:49-50, BQ

NOTE- Cognate with "kan 1: to dig out"

1446

شنا

Indo-European	Avestan	Pahlavi	Persian
snâ: *to flow, swim* با جریان رفتن، شنا کردن PK:971	snâ: *wash, swim* PK:971, KL:1030, HM:15	snâz: *swim* AP:384	šenâ: *swim* شنا BQ, PH:176, KM:118

1447

شناختن   همریشه: دانستن   همریشه: know

Indo-European	Old Persian	Pahlavi	Persian
gnô: *to know* دانستن PK:376	xšnâ: *to know* PK:376, BQ:1298	šnâxtan BQ:1298	šenâxtan: *to know, recognize* شناختن (آشنا) BQ

1448

شنبه

همریشه: Sabbath

Akkadian	Hebrew	Persian
šabatu: *to cut, stop working*	šâbat: *to stop work*	šanbeh: *Saturday, day of rest*
قطع کردن، دست برداشتن از کار		شنبه
ZM:67, BQ:1300	BQ:1300	MO:2081, BQ:1300

1449

شَندف: دف خانگی (شن + دف)

Indo-European	Av/Old Pers	Pahlavi	Persian
gwhen 3, kan*: *to dig and fill*	šan, šyangh: *house, household*	šân: *house, shelter*	šandaf: *house tambourine*
کندن و پُر کردن			شندف
CH:232, PK491	FJ:49-51	BQ:46, FJ:49-51	FJ:49-50, BQ

Sumerian	Akkadian	Aramaic	Arabic
dub: *tablet, scripture*	duppu: *tablet*	dappa: *skin for writing tablet*	daf: *a tambourine made of animal skin on a frame*
لوحه، نوشته			
ZM:19, BQ:823	ZM:19, BQ:823		MO:1540

1450

شنگبیل

مقایسه: زنجبیل   همریشه: ginger

Indo-European	Sanskrit	Pahlavi	Persian
ker 1: *head, horn*	srnga: *horn*	šanga-vîr, singiber	šangabîl: *ginger*
سر، شاخ	sringa-vera: *horn-shaped root of ginger*		شنگبیل
PK:574, KL:261,657	AD:1522, KL:657	BR:42	MO:1751, BR:42

1451

شنگرف: رنگ سرخ، سنگ معدن جیوه   همریشه: cinnabar

Old Persian	Persian
sinkadruš: *the red ore of mercury (mercuric sulfide) used as a pigment*	šangarf: *red lead, cinnabar, red pigment*
سنگ معدن سرخ رنگ جیوه که در رنگرزی بکار میرفته	شنگرف (زنجرف)
MO:2083	MO:2083, BQ:1302

1452

شنوشه: عطسه   همریشه: sneeze

Indo-European	Pahlavi	Persian
skêu: *to sneeze*	šanôšag: *to sneeze*	šonûšeh: *sneeze*
عطسه کردن		شنوشه (اشنوسه، سنوسه)
PK:838,953	AP:91	مرا امروز توبه سـود دارد
		چنان چون دردمندان را شنوشه (رودکی)
		PK:953, BQ:1102,1304

1453

شنیدن

همریشه: listen

Indo-European	Avestan	Pahlavi	Persian
kleu 1, srau*: *to hear*	sru, srav, xšnu: *to hear*	ašnûdan: *to hear*	šenîdan: *to hear*
شنیدن	dâuš-sravah: *ill-famed*	du-srav: *ill-famed*	شنیدن (اشنودن)
PK:605, CH:356	PH:177	AG3:64	BQ:1304

1454

شوخ

Indo-European	Persian
skaivos: *sinister, odd, strange*	šûx: *vulgar, rude, a joker*
شوم، عجیب و غریب	شوخ
WD2:537, IC:1146	IC:1146, MO:2085

1455

شور۱

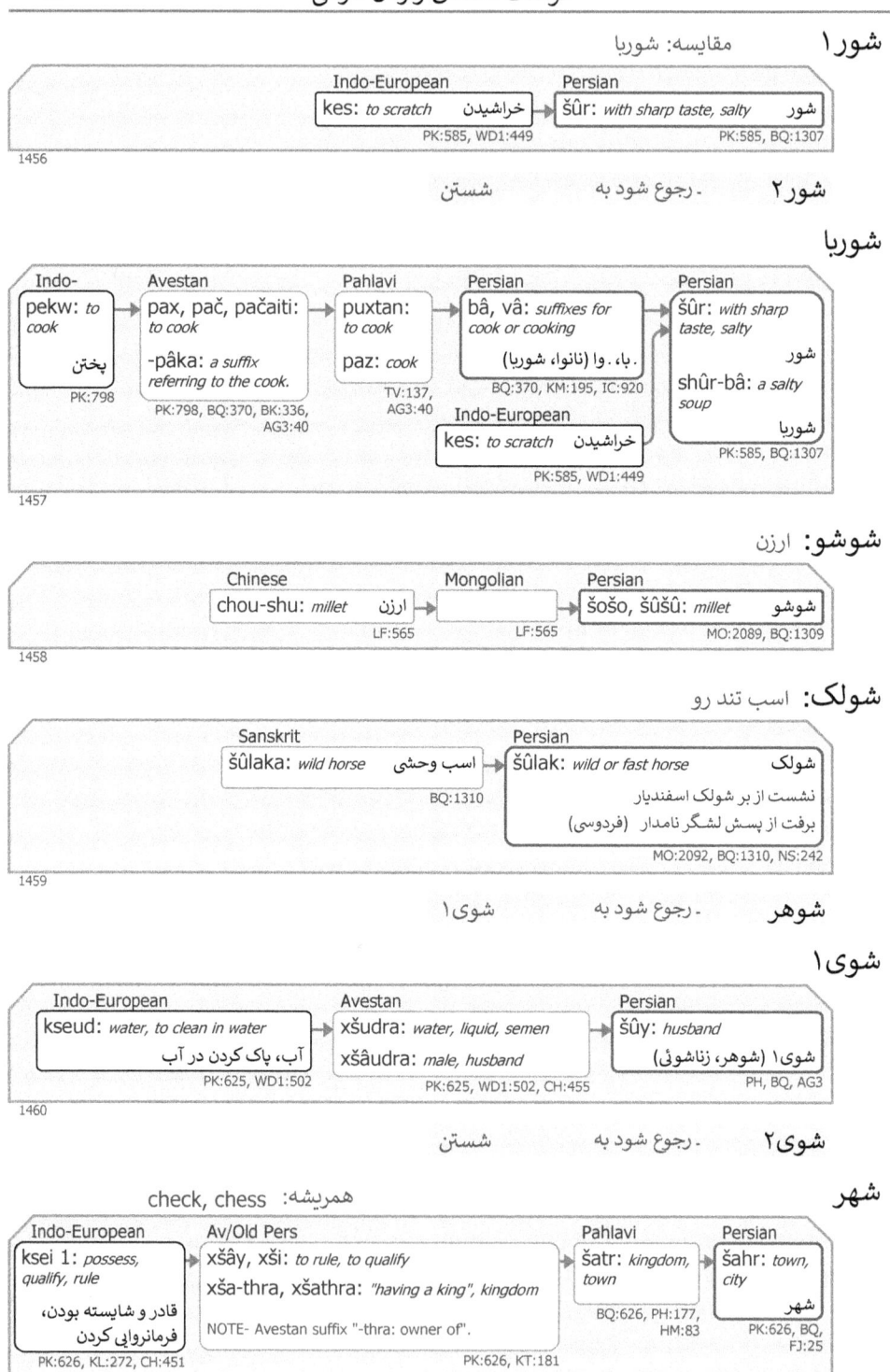

مقایسه: شوریا

Indo-European — kes: to scratch   خراشیدن   → **Persian** — šûr: with sharp taste, salty   شور
PK:585, WD1:449   PK:585, BQ:1307
1456

شور۲   ـ رجوع شود به   شستن

شوریا

Indo- pekw: to cook   پختن   PK:798

Avestan pax, pač, pačaiti: to cook
-pâka: a suffix referring to the cook.
PK:798, BQ:370, BK:336, AG3:40

Pahlavi puxtan: to cook
paz: cook
TV:137, AG3:40

Persian bâ, vâ: suffixes for cook or cooking
با، .وا (نانوا، شوریا)
BQ:370, KM:195, IC:920
Indo-European kes: to scratch   خراشیدن
PK:585, WD1:449

Persian šûr: with sharp taste, salty   شور
shûr-bâ: a salty soup   شوریا
PK:585, BQ:1307
1457

شوشو: ارزن

Chinese chou-shu: millet   ارزن   LF:565 → **Mongolian**   LF:565 → **Persian** šošo, šûšû: millet   شوشو
MO:2089, BQ:1309
1458

شولک: اسب تند رو

Sanskrit šûlaka: wild horse   اسب وحشی   BQ:1310 → **Persian** šûlak: wild or fast horse   شولک
نشست از بر شولک اسفندیار
برفت از پسش لشگر نامدار (فردوسی)
MO:2092, BQ:1310, NS:242
1459

شوهر   ـ رجوع شود به   شوی۱

شوی۱

Indo-European kseud: water, to clean in water
آب، پاک کردن در آب
PK:625, WD1:502

Avestan xšudra: water, liquid, semen
xšâudra: male, husband
PK:625, WD1:502, CH:455

Persian šûy: husband
شوی۱ (شوهر، زناشوئی)
PH, BQ, AG3
1460

شوی۲   ـ رجوع شود به   شستن

شهر

همریشه: check, chess

Indo-European ksei 1: possess, qualify, rule
قادر و شایسته بودن، فرمانروایی کردن
PK:626, KL:272, CH:451

Av/Old Pers xšây, xši: to rule, to qualify
xša-thra, xšathra: "having a king", kingdom
NOTE- Avestan suffix "-thra: owner of".
PK:626, KT:181

Pahlavi šatr: kingdom, town
BQ:626, PH:177, HM:83

Persian šahr: town, city
شهر
PK:626, BQ, FJ:25
1461

شهرام: ـ رجوع شود به   شاه + رام

شهریور: "شهر یا کشور مطلوب"   همریشه: check, chess

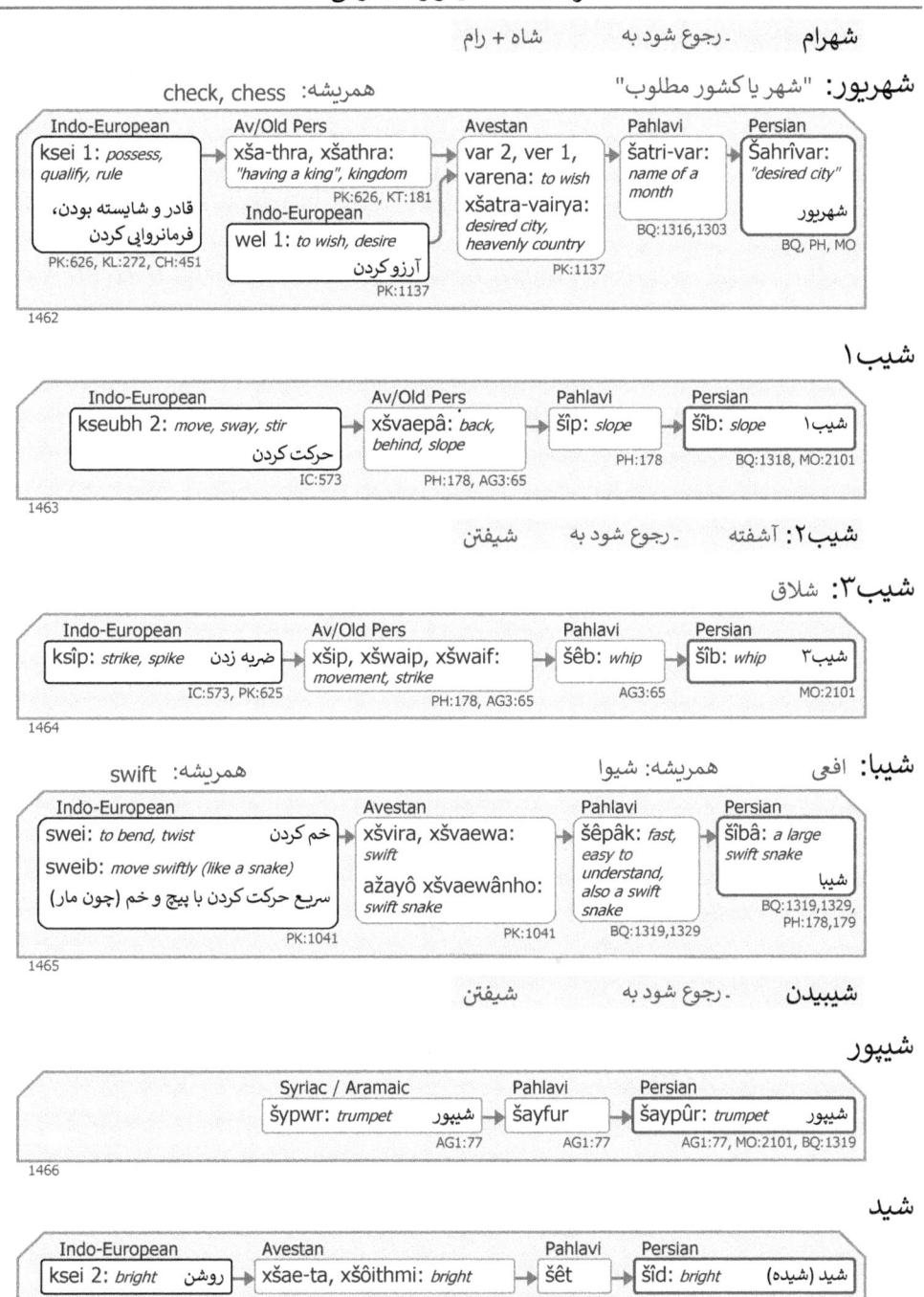

1462

شیب۱

1463

شیب۲: آشفته   ـ رجوع شود به   شیفتن

شیب۳: شلاق

1464

شیبا: افعی   همریشه: شیوا   همریشه: swift

1465

شیبیدن   ـ رجوع شود به   شیفتن

شیپور

1466

شید

1467

258

شیدا

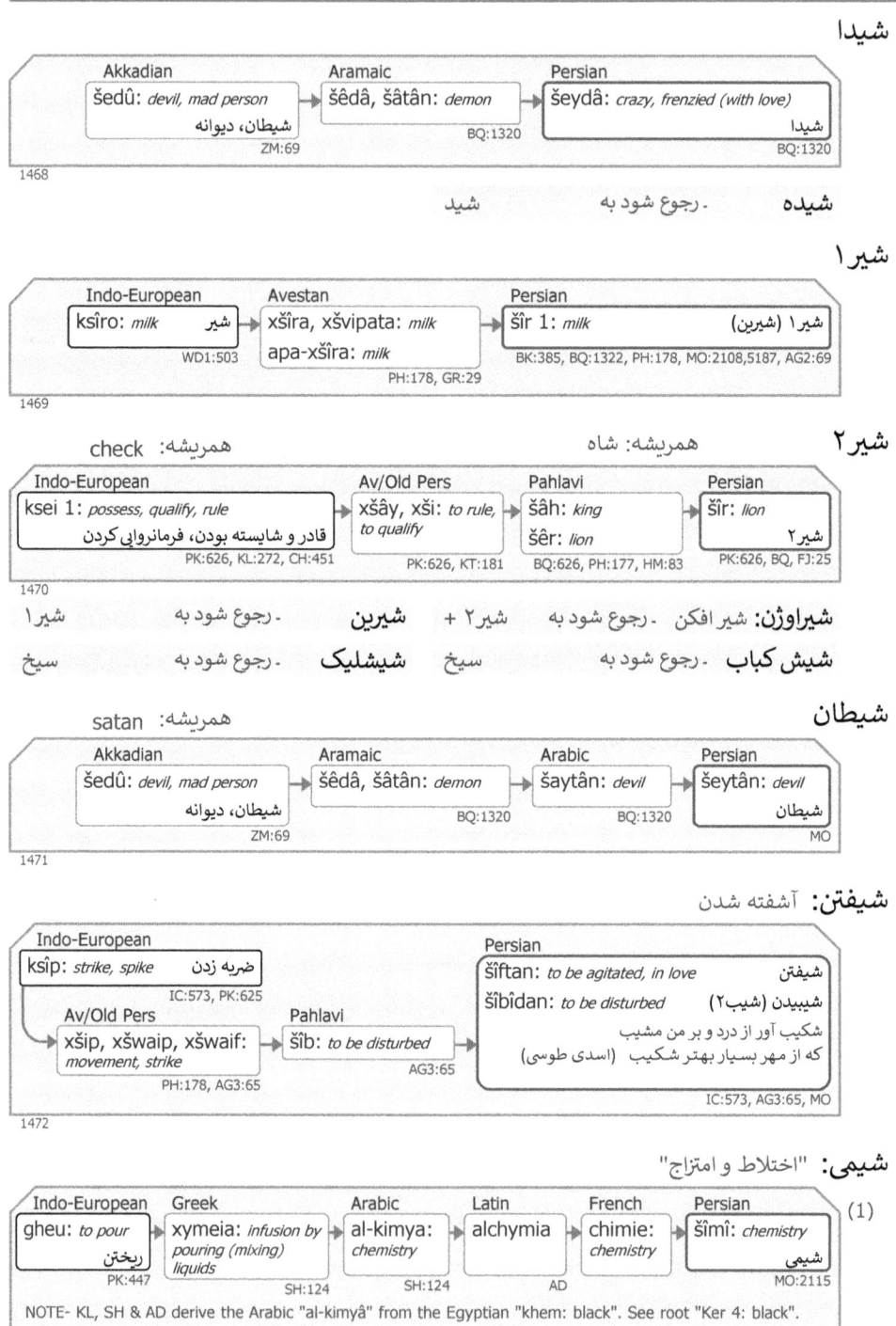

Akkadian
šedû: *devil, mad person*
شیطان، دیوانه
ZM:69

Aramaic
šêdâ, šâtân: *demon*
BQ:1320

Persian
šeydâ: *crazy, frenzied (with love)*
شیدا
BQ:1320

1468

شیده ۔ رجوع شود به شید

شیر۱

Indo-European
ksîro: *milk* شیر
WD1:503

Avestan
xšîra, xšvipata: *milk*
apa-xšîra: *milk*
PH:178, GR:29

Persian
šîr 1: *milk* (شیرین) شیر ۱
BK:385, BQ:1322, PH:178, MO:2108,5187, AG2:69

1469

شیر۲

همریشه: check   همریشه: شاه

Indo-European
ksei 1: *possess, qualify, rule*
قادر و شایسته بودن، فرمانروایی کردن
PK:626, KL:272, CH:451

Av/Old Pers
xšây, xši: *to rule, to qualify*
PK:626, KT:181

Pahlavi
šâh: *king*
šêr: *lion*
BQ:626, PH:177, HM:83

Persian
šîr: *lion*
شیر۲
PK:626, BQ, FJ:25

1470

شیراوژن: شیر افکن ۔ رجوع شود به شیر۲   **شیرین** شیر۲ + شیرین ۔ رجوع شود به شیر۱

شیش کباب ۔ رجوع شود به سیخ   **شیشلیک** سیخ ۔ رجوع شود به سیخ

شیطان

همریشه: satan

Akkadian
šedû: *devil, mad person*
شیطان، دیوانه
ZM:69

Aramaic
šêdâ, šâtân: *demon*
BQ:1320

Arabic
šaytân: *devil*
BQ:1320

Persian
šeytân: *devil*
شیطان
MO

1471

شیفتن: آشفته شدن

Indo-European
ksîp: *strike, spike* ضربه زدن
IC:573, PK:625

Av/Old Pers
xšip, xšwaip, xšwaif: *movement, strike*
PH:178, AG3:65

Pahlavi
šîb: *to be disturbed*
AG3:65

Persian
šîftan: *to be agitated, in love* شیفتن
šîbîdan: *to be disturbed* (شیب) شیبیدن
شکیب آور از درد و بر من مشیب
که از مهر بسیار بهتر شکیب (اسدی طوسی)
IC:573, AG3:65, MO

1472

شیمی: "اختلاط و امتزاج"

Indo-European
gheu: *to pour*
ریختن
PK:447

Greek
xymeia: *infusion by pouring (mixing) liquids*
SH:124

Arabic
al-kimya: *chemistry*
SH:124

Latin
alchymia

French
chimie: *chemistry*
AD

Persian
šîmî: *chemistry*
شیمی
MO:2115

(1)

NOTE- KL, SH & AD derive the Arabic "al-kimyâ" from the Egyptian "khem: black". See root "Ker 4: black".

1473

شیمی: "صنعت مصری برای استحاله مواد"

(2)

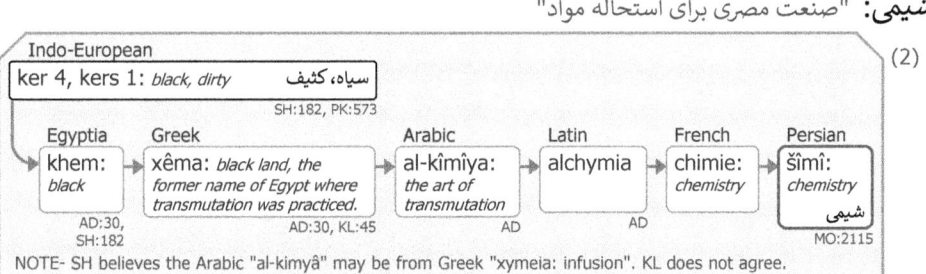

Indo-European

ker 4, kers 1: *black, dirty*   سیاه، کثیف
SH:182, PK:573

Egyptia	Greek	Arabic	Latin	French	Persian
khem: *black*	**xêma:** *black land, the former name of Egypt where transmutation was practiced.*	**al-kîmîya:** *the art of transmutation*	**alchymia**	**chimie:** *chemistry*	**šîmî:** *chemistry* شیمی
AD:30, SH:182	AD:30, KL:45	AD	AD		MO:2115

NOTE- SH believes the Arabic "al-kimyâ" may be from Greek "xymeia: infusion". KL does not agree.

1474

شیوا: فصیح   همریشه: شیبا   همریشه: swift

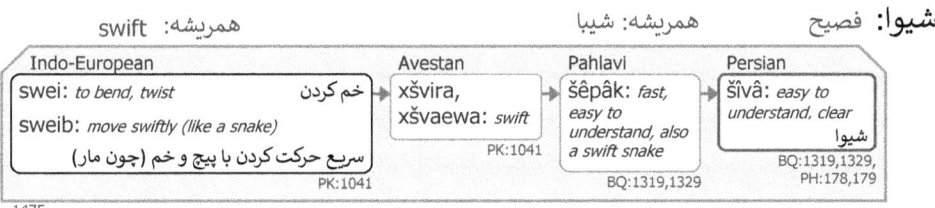

Indo-European	Avestan	Pahlavi	Persian
swei: *to bend, twist* خم کردن **sweib:** *move swiftly (like a snake)* سریع حرکت کردن با پیچ و خم (چون مار) PK:1041	**xšvira, xšvaewa:** *swift* PK:1041	**šêpâk:** *fast, easy to understand, also a swift snake* BQ:1319,1329	**šîvâ:** *easy to understand, clear* شیوا BQ:1319,1329, PH:178,179

1475

شیون

Indo-European	Av/Old Pers	Pahlavi	Persian
xšai*: *weep, lament* گریستن، نالیدن CH:452	**Xšî:** *grief, poverty* غم، فقر **Xšaivan:** *grief, crying* غم، گریه BQ:1329	**šêvan:** *crying*	**šîvan:** *crying* شیون BQ:1329, CH:5045

1476

صابون

همریشه: soap

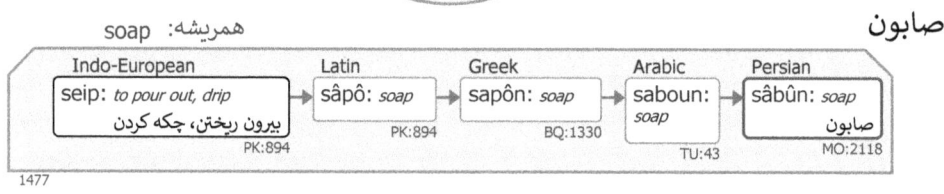

Indo-European	Latin	Greek	Arabic	Persian
seip: to pour out, drip	sâpô: soap	sapôn: soap	saboun: soap	sâbûn: soap
بیرون ریختن، چکه کردن				صابون
PK:894	PK:894	BQ:1330	TU:43	MO:2118

1477

صد

همریشه: hundred

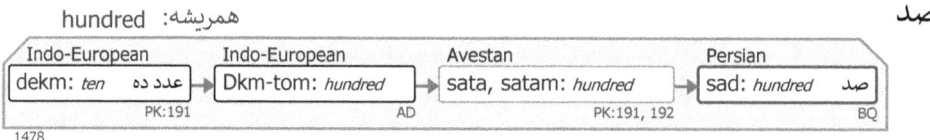

Indo-European	Indo-European	Avestan	Persian
dekm: ten عدد ده	Dkm-tom: hundred	sata, satam: hundred	sad: hundred صد
PK:191	AD	PK:191, 192	BQ

1478

صداع

همریشه: سدیم   همریشه: سر درد   soda

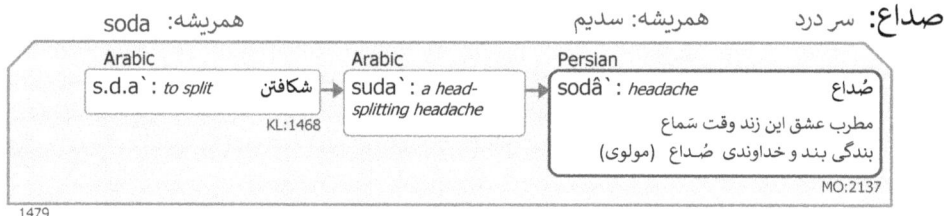

Arabic	Arabic	Persian
s.d.a`: to split شکافتن	suda`: a head-splitting headache	sodâ`: headache صُداع
KL:1468		مطرب عشق این زند وقت سَماع
		بندگی بند و خداوندی صُداع (مولوی)
		MO:2137

1479

صراط

همریشه: راه   همریشه: گستردن، بستر   street, strategy

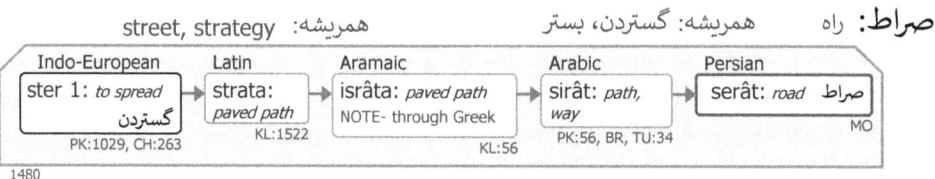

Indo-European	Latin	Aramaic	Arabic	Persian
ster 1: to spread گستردن	strata: paved path	isrâta: paved path NOTE- through Greek	sirât: path, way	serât: road صراط
PK:1029, CH:263	KL:1522	KL:56	PK:56, BR, TU:34	MO

1480

صرّاف

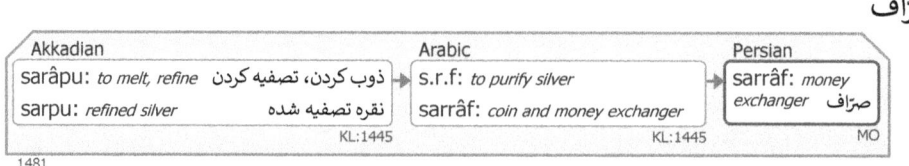

Akkadian	Arabic	Persian
sarâpu: to melt, refine ذوب کردن، تصفیه کردن	s.r.f: to purify silver	sarrâf: money exchanger صرّاف
sarpu: refined silver نقره تصفیه شده	sarrâf: coin and money exchanger	
KL:1445	KL:1445	MO

1481

صفر

همریشه: zero

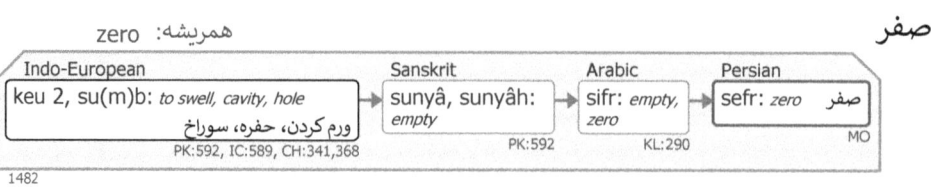

Indo-European	Sanskrit	Arabic	Persian
keu 2, su(m)b: to swell, cavity, hole	sunyâ, sunyâh: empty	sifr: empty, zero	sefr: zero صفر
ورم کردن، حفره، سوراخ			
PK:592, IC:589, CH:341,368	PK:592	KL:290	MO

1482

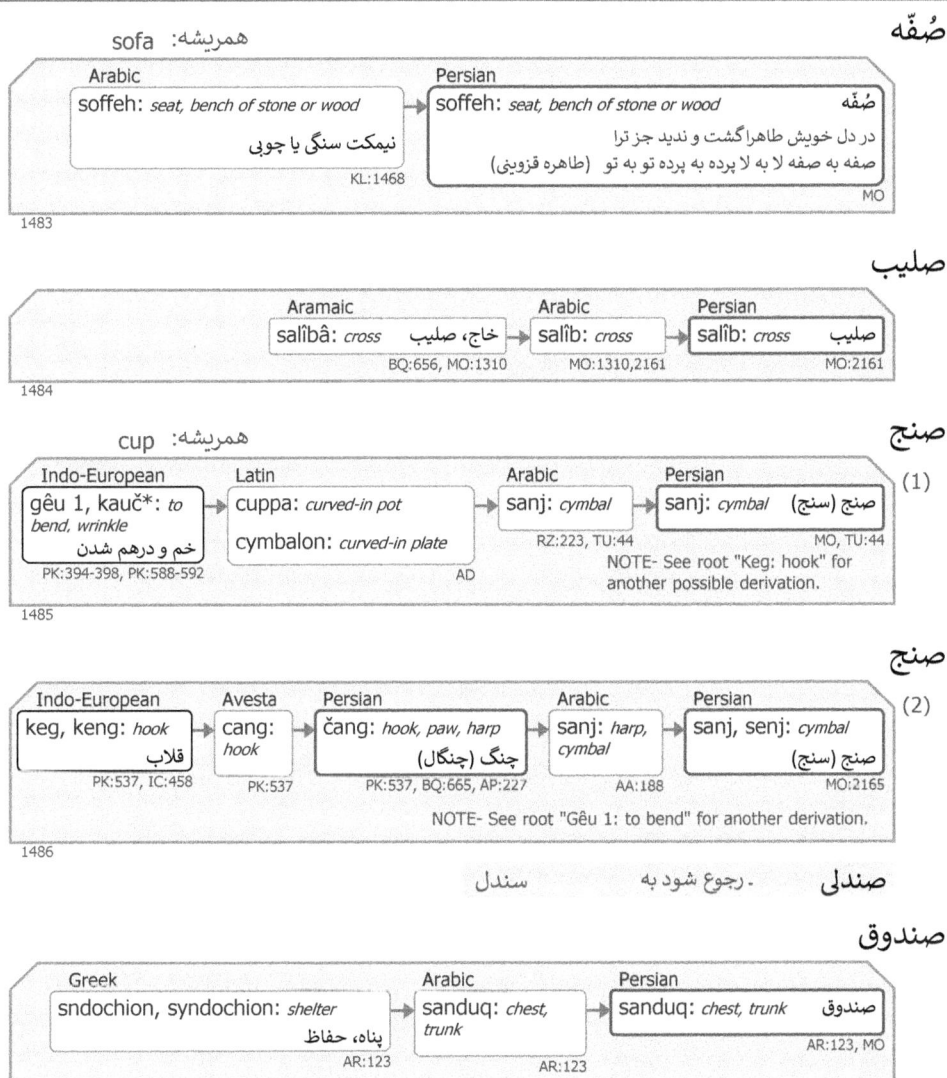

صُفّه

صلیب

صنج
(1)

صنج
(2)

صندلی

صندوق

صُفّه

همریشه: sofa

Arabic	Persian
soffeh: *seat, bench of stone or wood*	صُفّه soffeh: *seat, bench of stone or wood*
نیمکت سنگی یا چوبی	در دل خویش طاهراگشت و ندید جز ترا
KL:1468	صفه به صفه لا به لا پرده به پرده تو به تو (طاهره قزوینی) MO

1483

صلیب

Aramaic	Arabic	Persian
salîbâ: *cross* خاج، صلیب	salîb: *cross*	salîb: *cross* صلیب
BQ:656, MO:1310	MO:1310,2161	MO:2161

1484

صنج (1)

همریشه: cup

Indo-European	Latin	Arabic	Persian
gêu 1, kauč*: *to bend, wrinkle*	cuppa: *curved-in pot*	sanj: *cymbal*	صنج (سنج) sanj: *cymbal*
خم و درهم شدن	cymbalon: *curved-in plate*	RZ:223, TU:44	MO, TU:44
PK:394-398, PK:588-592	AD		NOTE- See root "Keg: hook" for another possible derivation.

1485

صنج (2)

Indo-European	Avesta	Persian	Arabic	Persian
keg, keng: *hook*	cang: *hook*	čang: *hook, paw, harp*	sanj: *harp, cymbal*	sanj, senj: *cymbal*
قلاب		چنگ (چنگال)		صنج (سنج)
PK:537, IC:458	PK:537	PK:537, BQ:665, AP:227	AA:188	MO:2165

NOTE- See root "Gêu 1: to bend" for another derivation.

1486

صندلی . رجوع شود به سندل

صندوق

Greek	Arabic	Persian
sndochion, syndochion: *shelter*	sanduq: *chest, trunk*	sanduq: *chest, trunk* صندوق
پناه، حفاظ		
AR:123	AR:123	AR:123, MO

1487

ضحّاک   مقایسه: اژدها

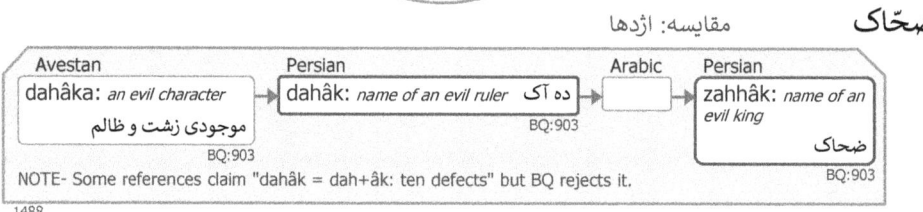

Avestan	Persian	Arabic	Persian
dahâka: *an evil character*	dahâk: *name of an evil ruler* ده آک		zahhâk: *name of an evil king*
موجودی زشت و ظالم	BQ:903		ضحاک
BQ:903			BQ:903

NOTE- Some references claim "dahâk = dah+âk: ten defects" but BQ rejects it.

1488

طاس ‎ ‎ - رجوع شود به ‎ ‎ ‎ تیشه

طاووس

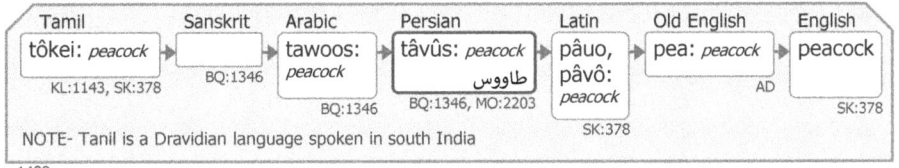

Tamil	Sanskrit	Arabic	Persian	Latin	Old English	English
tôkei: *peacock*		tawoos: *peacock*	tâvûs: *peacock* طاووس	pâuo, pâvô: *peacock*	pea: *peacock*	peacock
KL:1143, SK:378	BQ:1346	BQ:1346	BQ:1346, MO:2203	SK:378	AD	SK:378

NOTE- Tanil is a Dravidian language spoken in south India

1489

طبل

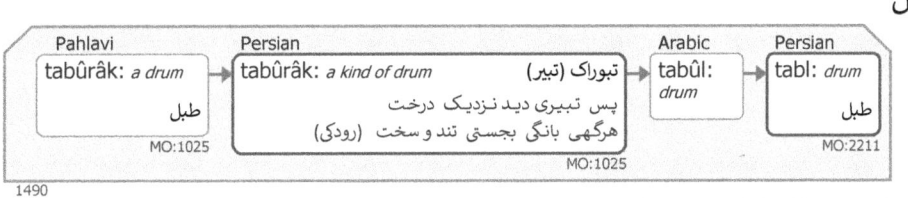

Pahlavi	Persian	Arabic	Persian
tabûrâk: *a drum* طبل	tabûrâk: *a kind of drum* تبوراک (تبیر) پس تبیری دید نزدیک درخت هرگهی بانگ بجستی تند و سخت (رودکی)	tabûl: *drum*	tabl: *drum* طبل
MO:1025	MO:1025		MO:2211

1490

طراز ‎ ‎ - رجوع شود به ‎ ‎ ‎ تراز

طلسم ‎ ‎ همریشه: چرخ ‎ ‎ ‎ ‎ همریشه: talisman, wheel

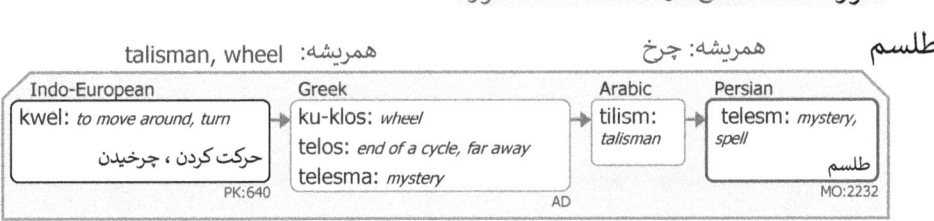

Indo-European	Greek	Arabic	Persian
kwel: *to move around, turn* حرکت کردن ، چرخیدن	ku-klos: *wheel* telos: *end of a cycle, far away* telesma: *mystery*	tilism: *talisman*	telesm: *mystery, spell* طلسم
PK:640	AD		MO:2232

1491

طلق ‎ ‎ مقایسه: تالک ‎ ‎ ‎ ‎ همریشه: talc, talcum

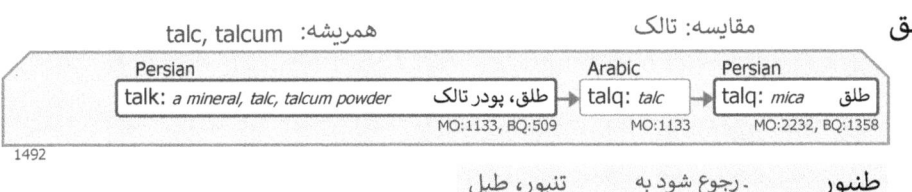

Persian	Arabic	Persian
talk: *a mineral, talc, talcum powder* طلق، پودر تالک	talq: *talc*	talq: *mica* طلق
MO:1133, BQ:509	MO:1133	MO:2232, BQ:1358

1492

طنبور ‎ ‎ - رجوع شود به ‎ ‎ ‎ تنبور، طبل

طوفان

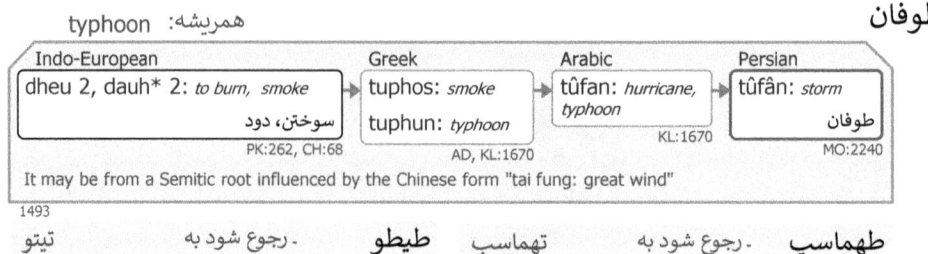

همریشه: typhoon

Indo-European	Greek	Arabic	Persian
dheu 2, dauh* 2: *to burn, smoke* سوختن، دود PK:262, CH:68	tuphos: *smoke* tuphun: *typhoon* AD, KL:1670	tûfan: *hurricane, typhoon* KL:1670	tûfân: *storm* طوفان MO:2240

It may be from a Semitic root influenced by the Chinese form "tai fung: great wind"

1493

تینتو   ـ رجوع شود به   طیطو   تهماسب   ـ رجوع شود به   طهماسپ

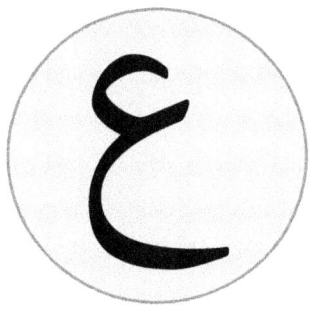

عار   همریشه: average

Arabic	Arabic	Persian
`awar: he damaged` `خراب کرد`	`awar: damaged goods` KL:133	`âr 2: damage, shame` عار `avâr: defect, damaged goods` عوار گنگ باد آن آن کس که اندر طعن تو گوید سخن کور باد آن آن کس که اندر عرض تو جوید عوار (فرخی) MO

1494

عروس: سفید   (مستقل از واژه عربی "عروس")

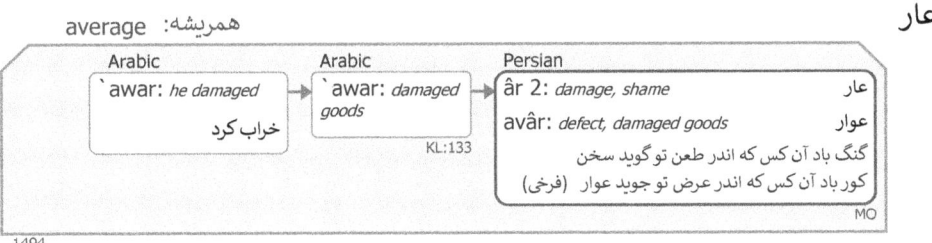

Indo-European	Avestan	Pahlavi	Persian
el 2: red or brown used in animal and tree names رنگ سرخ یا قهوه ای PK:302, KL:509	auruša: pale red, white PK:302, JS1:42	arûs: white BQ:55, JS1:42	arus: white عروس JS1:42

COGNATE- Sanskrit "arusah: color of fire" (JS1:42)

1495

عسگر   مقایسه: لشگر

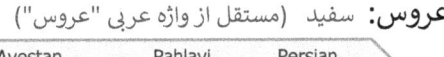

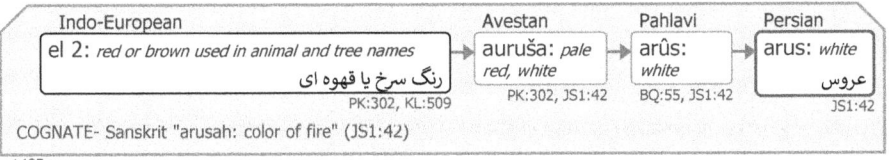

Indo-European	Latin	Arabic
ark, areg, herk: to hold, guard حفاظت کردن PO:65, DV:51, ED*	arceo: defend ex-ercitus: ward off, defend AR:13, DV:51	askar: defending troops, army AR:13

Indo-European	Latin	Persian
eghs: out بیرون، دور DV:195	ex-: out, away DV:195	asgar: troops, army عسگر AR:13

NOTE- ZV1:113 claims Arabic askar is from Persian laškar.

1496

عفریته   همریشه: friend, positive

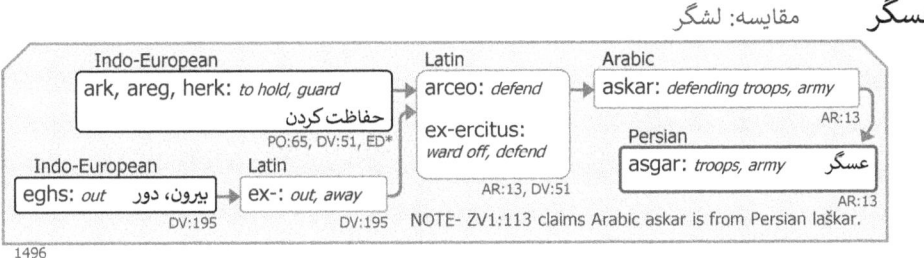

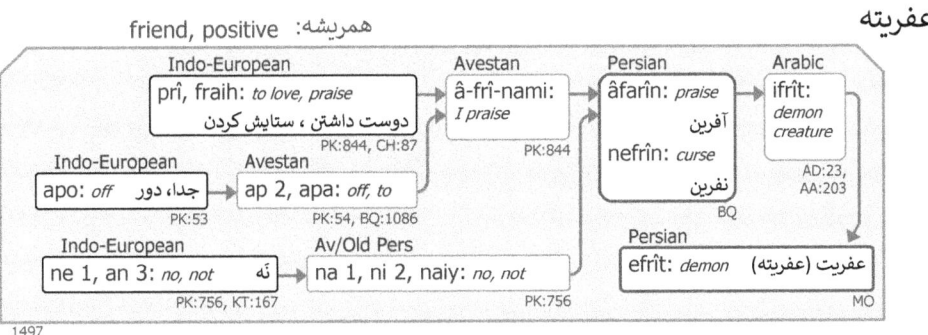

Indo-European	Avestan	Persian	Arabic
prî, fraih: to love, praise دوست داشتن ، ستایش کردن PK:844, CH:87	â-frî-nami: I praise PK:844	âfarîn: praise آفرین nefrîn: curse نفرین BQ	ifrît: demon creature AD:23, AA:203

Indo-European	Avestan		
apo: off جدا، دور PK:53	ap 2, apa: off, to PK:54, BQ:1086		

Indo-European	Av/Old Pers	Persian	
ne 1, an 3: no, not نَه PK:756, KT:167	na 1, ni 2, naiy: no, not PK:756	efrît: demon عفریت (عفریته) MO	

1497

عقرب

همریشه: scorpion

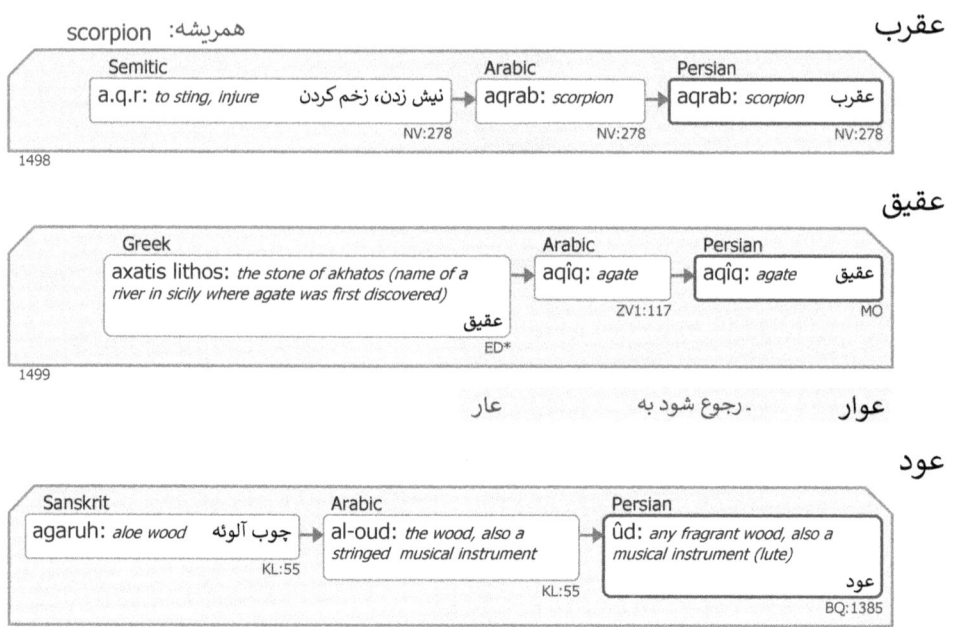

Semitic	Arabic	Persian
a.q.r: *to sting, injure* نیش زدن، زخم کردن	aqrab: *scorpion*	aqrab: *scorpion* عقرب
NV:278	NV:278	NV:278

1498

عقیق

Greek	Arabic	Persian
axatis lithos: *the stone of akhatos (name of a river in sicily where agate was first discovered)* عقیق	aqîq: *agate*	aqîq: *agate* عقیق
ED*	ZV1:117	MO

1499

عوار

عوار   رجوع شود به   عار.

عود

Sanskrit	Arabic	Persian
agaruh: *aloe wood* چوب آلوئه	al-oud: *the wood, also a stringed musical instrument*	ûd: *any fragrant wood, also a musical instrument (lute)* عود
KL:55	KL:55	BQ:1385

1500

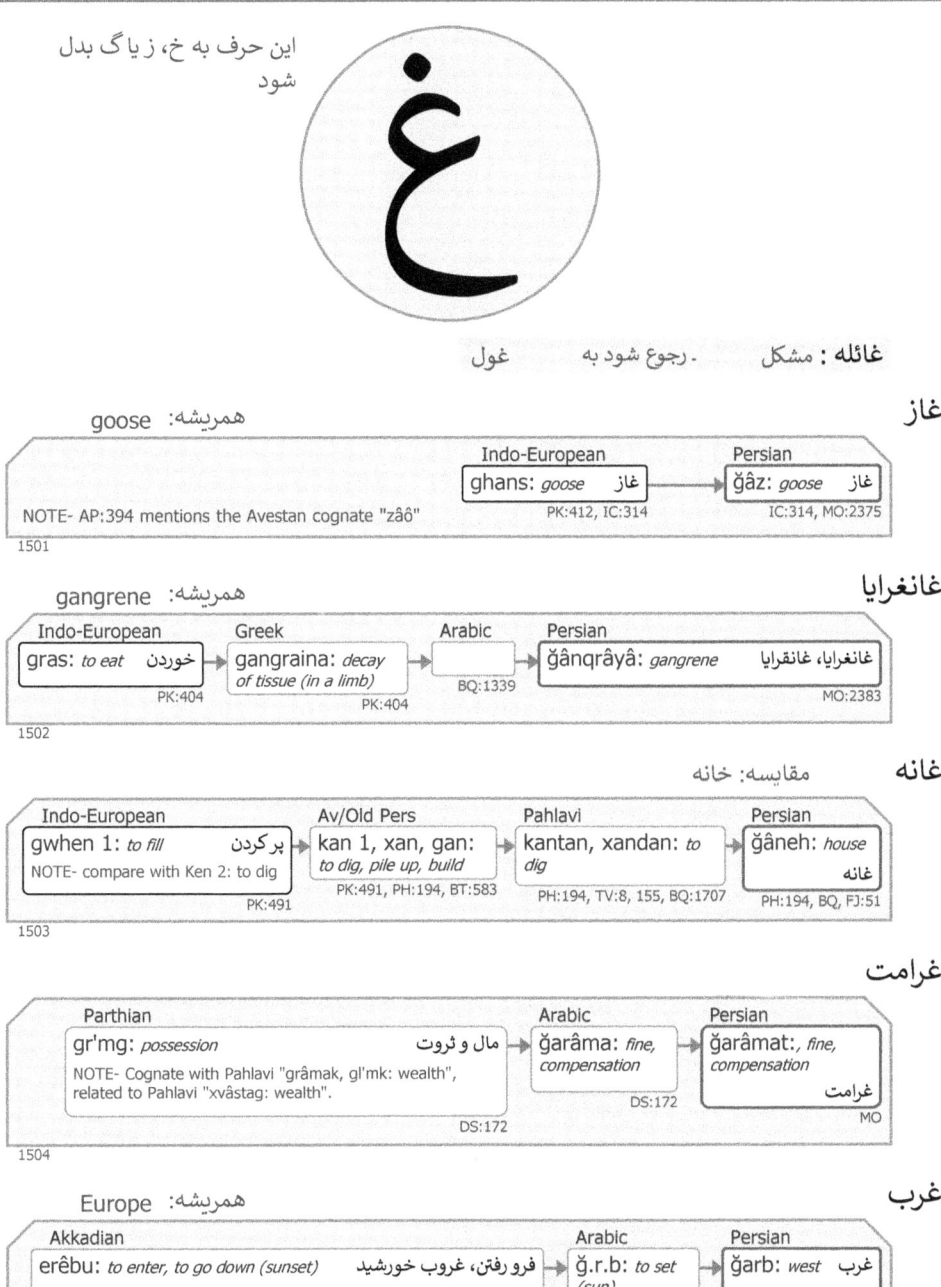

این حرف به خ، ز یا گ بدل شود

غائله : مشکل ـ رجوع شود به   غول

غاز

همریشه: goose

Indo-European	Persian
ghans: *goose* غاز PK:412, IC:314	ǧâz: *goose* غاز IC:314, MO:2375

NOTE- AP:394 mentions the Avestan cognate "zâô"

1501

غانغرایا

همریشه: gangrene

Indo-European	Greek	Arabic	Persian
gras: *to eat* خوردن PK:404	gangraina: *decay of tissue (in a limb)* PK:404	BQ:1339	ǧânqrâyâ: *gangrene* غانغرایا، غانقرایا MO:2383

1502

غانه

مقایسه: خانه

Indo-European	Av/Old Pers	Pahlavi	Persian
gwhen 1: *to fill* پرکردن NOTE- compare with Ken 2: to dig PK:491	kan 1, xan, gan: *to dig, pile up, build* PK:491, PH:194, BT:583	kantan, xandan: *to dig* PH:194, TV:8, 155, BQ:1707	ǧâneh: *house* غانه PH:194, BQ, FJ:51

1503

غرامت

Parthian	Arabic	Persian
gr'mg: *possession* مال و ثروت NOTE- Cognate with Pahlavi "grâmak, gl'mk: wealth", related to Pahlavi "xvâstag: wealth". DS:172	ǧarâma: *fine, compensation* DS:172	ǧarâmat:, *fine, compensation* غرامت MO

1504

غرب

همریشه: Europe

Akkadian	Arabic	Persian
erêbu: *to enter, to go down (sunset)* فرو رفتن، غروب خورشید ZM:64, KL:550	ǧ.r.b: *to set (sun)* ZM:640,854	ǧarb: *west* غرب MO

1505

غربال

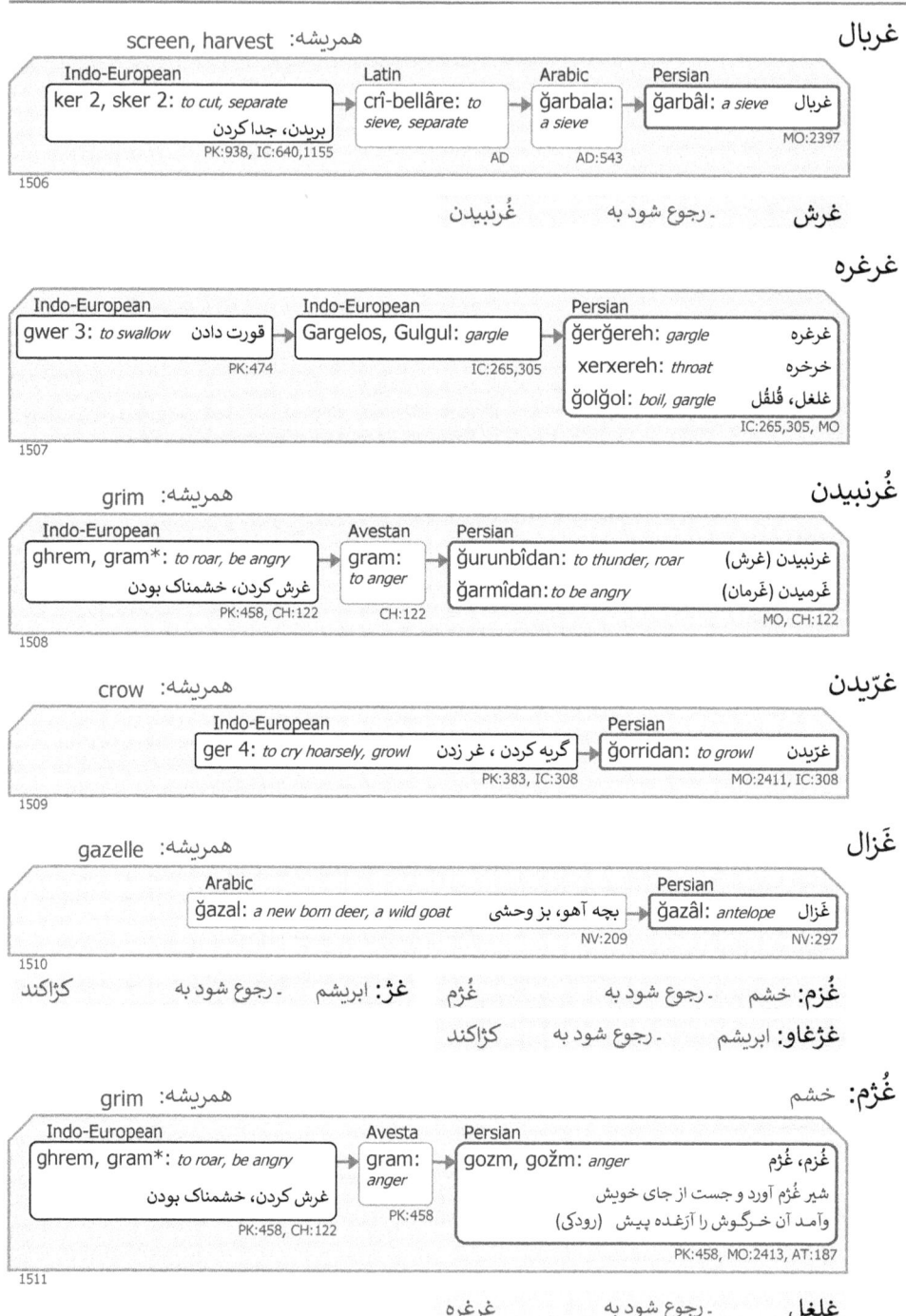

همریشه: screen, harvest

Indo-European	Latin	Arabic	Persian
ker 2, sker 2: *to cut, separate* بریدن، جدا کردن PK:938, IC:640,1155	crî-bellâre: *to sieve, separate* AD	ğarbala: *a sieve* AD:543	ğarbâl: *a sieve* غربال MO:2397

1506

غرش ـ رجوع شود به   غُرنبیدن

غرغره

Indo-European	Indo-European	Persian
gwer 3: *to swallow* قورت دادن PK:474	Gargelos, Gulgul: *gargle* IC:265,305	ğerğereh: *gargle* غرغره xerxereh: *throat* خرخره ğolğol: *boil, gargle* غلغل، قُلقُل IC:265,305, MO

1507

غُرنبیدن

همریشه: grim

Indo-European	Avestan	Persian
ghrem, gram*: *to roar, be angry* غرش کردن، خشمناک بودن PK:458, CH:122	gram: *to anger* CH:122	ğurunbîdan: *to thunder, roar* غرنبیدن (غرش) ğarmîdan: *to be angry* غرمیدن (غرمان) MO, CH:122

1508

غرّیدن

همریشه: crow

Indo-European	Persian
ger 4: *to cry hoarsely, growl* گریه کردن ، غر زدن PK:383, IC:308	ğorridan: *to growl* غرّیدن MO:2411, IC:308

1509

غَزال

همریشه: gazelle

Arabic	Persian
ğazal: *a new born deer, a wild goat* بچه آهو، بز وحشی NV:209	ğazâl: *antelope* غزال NV:297

1510

غُزم: خشم ـ رجوع شود به   **غژ:** ابریشم **غژ:** ابریشم ـ رجوع شود به   کژاکند

غژغاو: ابریشم ـ رجوع شود به   کژاکند

غُزم: خشم

همریشه: grim

Indo-European	Avesta	Persian
ghrem, gram*: *to roar, be angry* غرش کردن، خشمناک بودن PK:458, CH:122	gram: *anger* PK:458	gozm, gožm: *anger* غزم، غُزم شیر غُزم آورد و جست از جای خویش وآمد آن خرگوش را آزغده پیش (رودکی) PK:458, MO:2413, AT:187

1511

غلغل ـ رجوع شود به   غرغره

269

غنودن

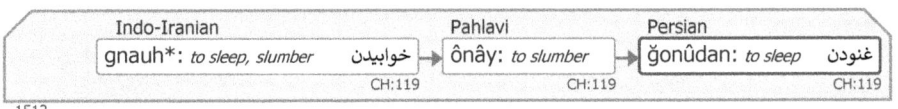

Indo-Iranian	Pahlavi	Persian
gnauh*: *to sleep, slumber* خوابیدن	ônây: *to slumber*	ğonûdan: *to sleep* غنودن
CH:119	CH:119	CH:119

1512

غوز

همریشه: cove, cup

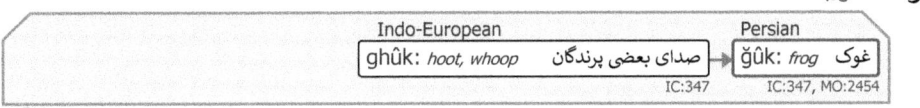

Indo-European	Pahlavi	Persian
gêu 1, kauč*: *to bend, wrinkle* خم و درهم شدن	kws, gust: *curve*	ğûz: *a lump on the back bone*
PK:394-398, PK:588-592	CH:248	غوز (قوز، کوژ، غوزک، قوزک)
NOTE- Compare with root "Kam 2: to bend"		PK:395, PK:589

1513

غوک: قورباقه

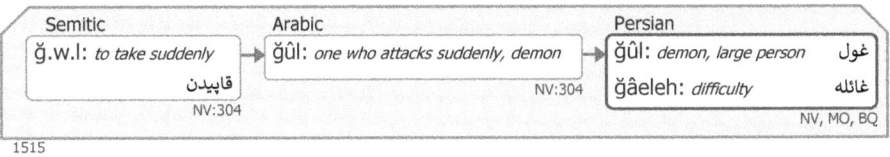

Indo-European	Persian
ghûk: *hoot, whoop* صدای بعضی پرندگان	ğûk: *frog* غوک
IC:347	IC:347, MO:2454

1514

غول۱

Semitic	Arabic	Persian
ğ.w.l: *to take suddenly* قاپیدن	ğûl: *one who attacks suddenly, demon*	ğûl: *demon, large person* غول
NV:304	NV:304	ğâeleh: *difficulty* غائله
		NV, MO, BQ

1515

غول۲   . رجوع شود به   آغل

این حرف به ب، و یا ر بدل شود.

ف

فارس ـ رجوع شود به **پارس۱**   **فاز** ـ رجوع شود به   **فتو**

فاژ: خمیازه

همریشه: yawn

Indo-European		Persian
ghêi 3: *to yawn* خمیازه کشیدن	→	فاژ (فاژیدن) :fâž: *yawn*
PK:419, IC:418		IC:418, MO:2470, AT:120

1516

فاژیدن: خمیازه کردن ـ رجوع شود به   **فاژ**

فاشیسم

همریشه: band

Indo-European	Latin	Italian	French	Persian
bhendh: *to bind, fasten* بستن	fascis: *bundle*	fascismo: *bundle, (a political) group*	fascism	fâšizm: *dictatorship of political "groups"* فاشیسم
PK:127	KL:152,576	KL:576		MO:2471

1517

فالوده ـ رجوع شود به   **پالوده**

ـ فام۱: پسوند رنگ

همریشه: photo

Indo-European	Avestan	Sogdian	Persian
bhâ 1: *to shine* درخشیدن	bama, bâ,	b`m: *color, brilliance*	fâm: *a suffix meaning color* فام۱
PK:104	PK:104, GR:97	BQ:1437, GR:97	GR:97, HN2:100

1518

فام۲ ـ رجوع شود به   **وام**   **فانتوم:** شبه ـ رجوع شود به   **فتو**

فانوس

همریشه: phosphor, photo

Indo-European	Greek	Persian
bhâ 1: *to shine* درخشیدن	phôs: *light* phânôs: *torch*	fânûs: *lantern* فانوس
PK:104	KL:1170	BQ:1437

1519

فئودال: ملاک بزرگ   همریشه: پشم

Indo-European	Latin	French	Persian
pek: *wool, to pluck wool* پشم، پشم کندن peku: *woolly animals, cattle, property* حیوانات پر پشم، احشام، دارایی	feudum: *property* AD		feodâl: *large land owner* فئودال MO
PK:797			

1520

فتال: پراکنده   ـ رجوع شود به   افتالیدن

فتو: نور   همریشه: فانوس، بامداد   همریشه: beacon

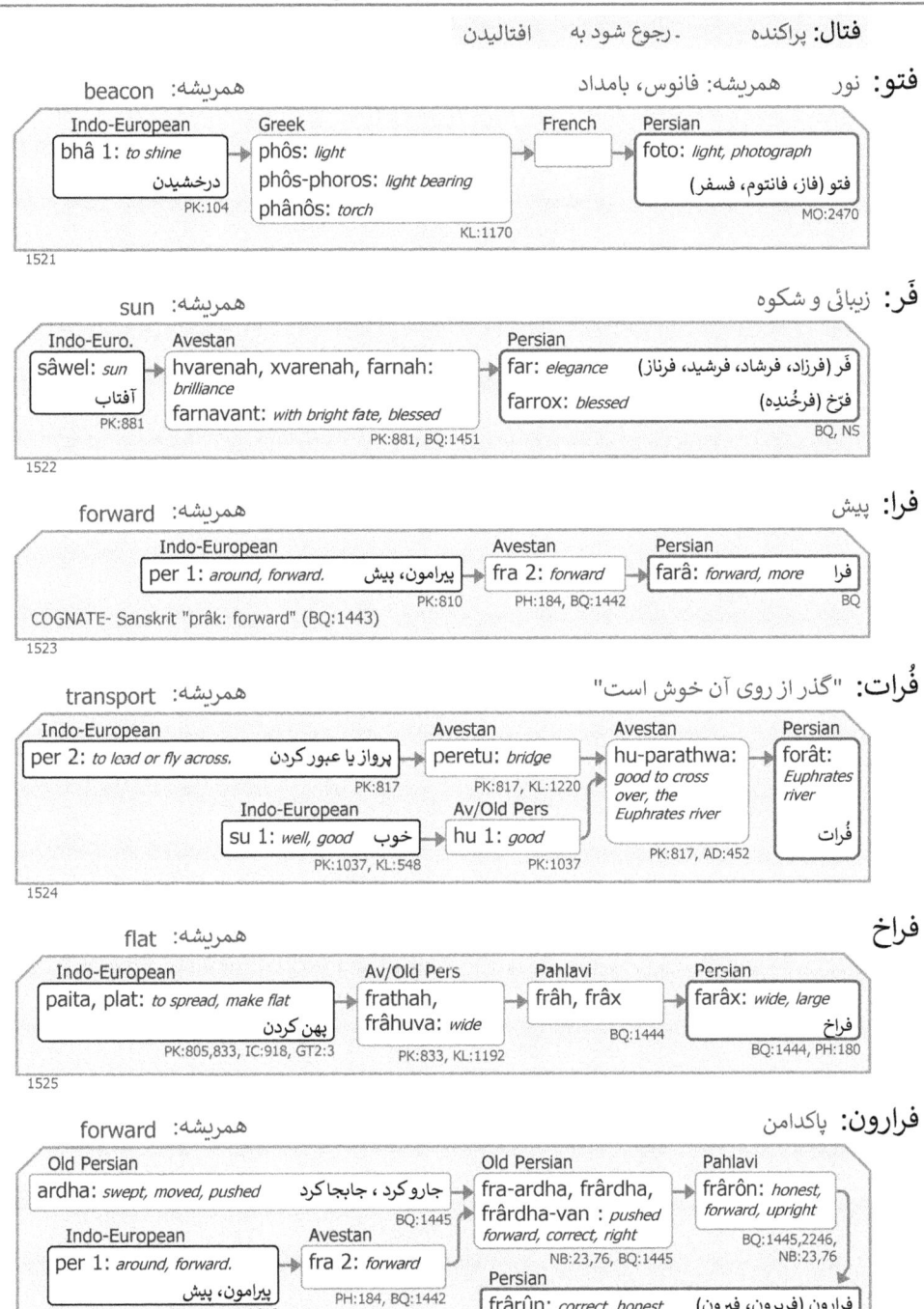

فَر: زیبائی و شکوه   همریشه: sun

فرا: پیش   همریشه: forward

فُرات: "گذر از روی آن خوش است"   همریشه: transport

فراخ   همریشه: flat

فرارون: پاکدامن   همریشه: forward

فتو: نور — beacon

Indo-European	Greek	French	Persian
bhâ 1: *to shine* درخشیدن PK:104	phôs: *light* phôs-phoros: *light bearing* phânôs: *torch* KL:1170		foto: *light, photograph* فتو (فاز، فانتوم، فسفر) MO:2470

1521

فَر: زیبائی و شکوه — sun

Indo-Euro.	Avestan	Persian
sâwel: *sun* آفتاب PK:881	hvarenah, xvarenah, farnah: *brilliance* farnavant: *with bright fate, blessed* PK:881, BQ:1451	far: *elegance* فَر (فرزاد، فرشاد، فرشید، فرناز) farrox: *blessed* فَرخ (فرخُنده) BQ, NS

1522

فرا: پیش — forward

Indo-European	Avestan	Persian
per 1: *around, forward.* پیرامون، پیش PK:810	fra 2: *forward* PH:184, BQ:1442	farâ: *forward, more* فرا BQ

COGNATE- Sanskrit "prâk: forward" (BQ:1443)

1523

فُرات: "گذر از روی آن خوش است" — transport

Indo-European	Avestan	Avestan	Persian
per 2: *to load or fly across.* پرواز یا عبور کردن PK:817	peretu: *bridge* PK:817, KL:1220	hu-parathwa: *good to cross over, the Euphrates river* PK:817, AD:452	forât: *Euphrates river* فُرات
su 1: *well, good* خوب (Indo-European) PK:1037, KL:548	hu 1: *good* (Av/Old Pers) PK:1037		

1524

فراخ — flat

Indo-European	Av/Old Pers	Pahlavi	Persian
paita, plat: *to spread, make flat* پهن کردن PK:805,833, IC:918, GT2:3	frathah, frâhuva: *wide* PK:833, KL:1192	frâh, frâx BQ:1444	farâx: *wide, large* فراخ BQ:1444, PH:180

1525

فرارون: پاکدامن — forward

Old Persian	Old Persian	Pahlavi
ardha: *swept, moved, pushed* جاروکرد، جابجاکرد BQ:1445	fra-ardha, frârdha, frârdha-van : *pushed forward, correct, right* NB:23,76 BQ:1445	frârôn: *honest, forward, upright* BQ:1445,2246, NB:23,76
per 1: *around, forward.* پیرامون، پیش (Indo-European) PK:810	fra 2: *forward* (Avestan) PH:184, BQ:1442	frârûn: *correct, honest* فرارون (فریرون، فیرون) (Persian) MO:2499

1526

فراز: پیش، بالا

Avestan	Pahlavi	Persian
frank: *forward* پیش	frač, fraz: *forward*	farâz: *forward, above* فراز
BQ:1446	BQ:1446, JS1:297	BQ:1446, JS1:297

COGNATE- Sanskrit "prâč: forward" (BQ:1446)

1527

فرازیدن ۔ رجوع شود به   افراشتن

فرامرز: "بخشنده همه گناهان"

Indo-European	Avestan	Persian
mêlg, marz?: *to wipe off, rub, milk* لمس کردن، پاک کردن، دوشیدن	â-marz: *wipe out sins*	farâmarz: *"forgiver of all sins"*
PK:722, CH:180, 269	fra-â-marz: *one who forgives all sins*	فرامرز
Indo-European		
per 1: *around, forward.* پیرامون، پیش	PK:722, BQ:1448, PH:12	MO
PK:810		

1528

فراموش

مقایسه: خاموش از همین ریشه

Indo-European	Indo-European	Sanskrit	Persian
mer 2: *to rub away, die* فرسودن، مردن	Mers, Marš: *to forget* فراموش کردن	pra-marš: *to forget*	farâmûš: *(to) forget* فراموش
PK:735,970	PK:737, CH:268	BQ:708, 1448	BQ:706,1448

1529

فراموشیدن

mortal :همریشه   همریشه: پژمردن، مردن

Indo-European	Indo-Euro.	Av/Old Pers	Pahlavi	Persian
mer 2: *to rub away, die* فرسودن، مردن	Mers, Marš: *to forget* فراموش کردن	muš, fra-â-muš: *to forget*	frâmûštan: *to forget*	farâmûšîdan: *to forget* فراموشیدن
PK:735,970	PK:737, CH:268	AG3:65	AG3:65	AG3:65, MO:2506

NOTE- BQ:1448 derives this word from Sanskrit "pra-marš: to forget"

1530

فراوان

full :همریشه

Indo-Euro.	Indo-European	Avestan	Persian
pel 1: *to fill* پر کردن	Pelu: *a quantity of, a group of* تعداد یا گروه	pouru, paourus: *much, many*	farâvân: *plenty* فراوان
PK:799	PK:799, CH:299	KT:196, PK:800, IC:974	IC:956,974, MO:2508

COGNATE- Old Persian "Paru, parav: much, many" (KT:196, PK:800)

1531

فَربُد، فربود: راست و درست   همریشه: فرخ، فرزاد   sun :همریشه

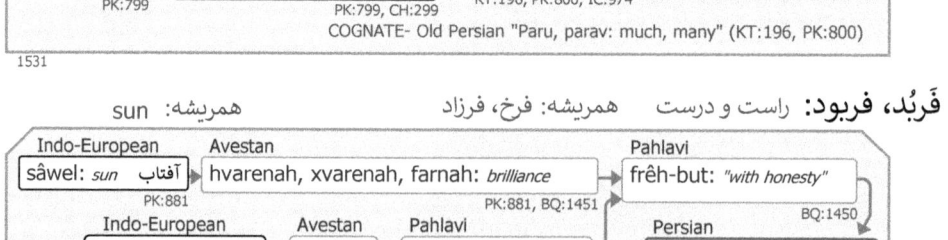

Indo-European	Avestan	Pahlavi
sâwel: *sun* آفتاب	hvarenah, xvarenah, farnah: *brilliance*	frêh-but: *"with honesty"*
PK:881	PK:881, BQ:1451	BQ:1450
Indo-European	Avestan	Pahlavi	Persian
per 3: *oppose, hit* مقابل	paiti 2: *oppose*	paitiš, pat, pêš: *in front, leader, owner*	farbod: *true and honest* فَربُد (فربود)
PK:815-818	PK:815	BQ:440	BQ:1450

1532

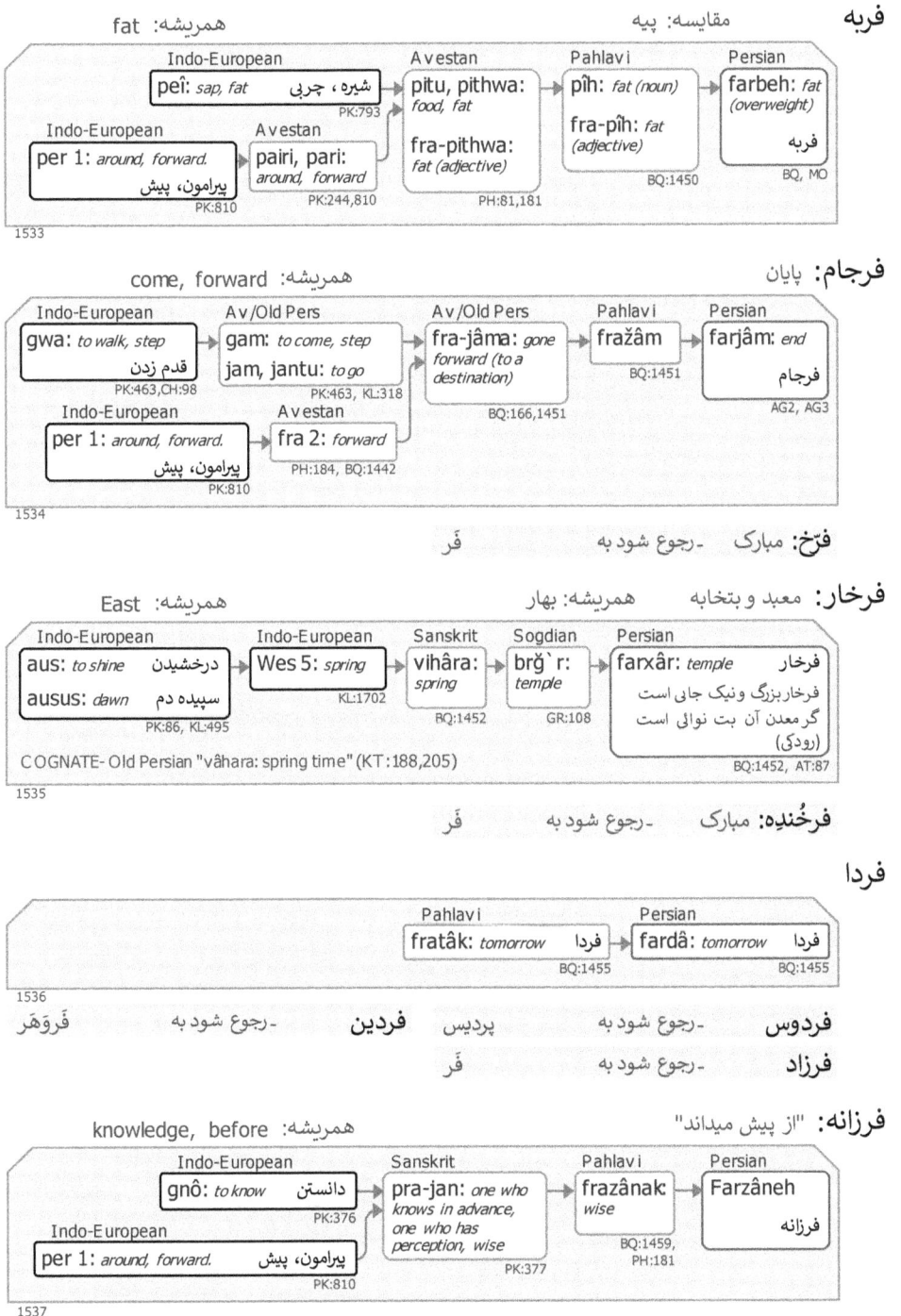

فربه: مقایسه: پیه   همریشه: fat

1533

فرجام: پایان   همریشه: come, forward

1534

فتخ: مبارک ‐رجوع شود به فَر

فرخار: معبد و بتخابه   همریشه: بهار   همریشه: East

1535

فرخُنده: مبارک ‐رجوع شود به فَر

فردا

1536

فردوس ‐رجوع شود به پردیس   فردین ‐رجوع شود به فَرَوَهَر

فرزاد ‐رجوع شود به فَر

فرزانه: "از پیش میداند"   همریشه: knowledge, before

1537

فرزند

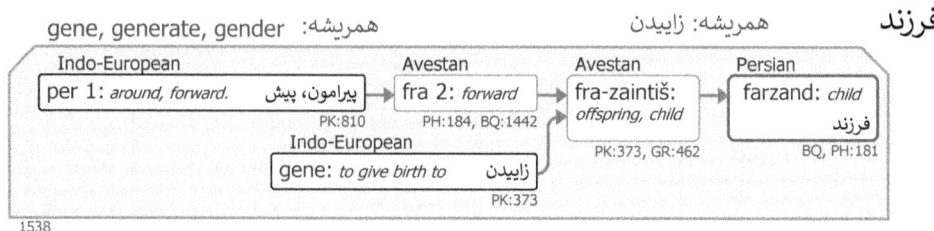

1538

فرزین: "شخص یا عامل مهم" چون وزیر در شطرنج

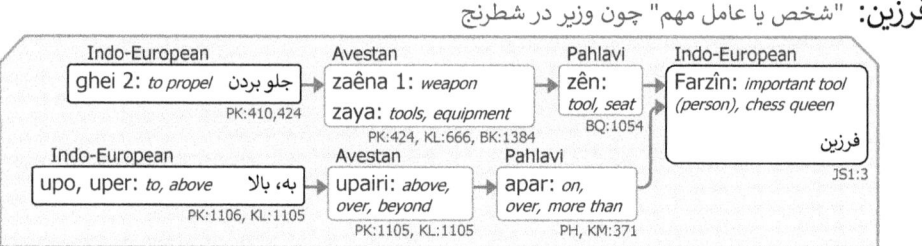

1539

فَرَسب: شاه تیر چوبی که بدان بام خانه را پوشانند

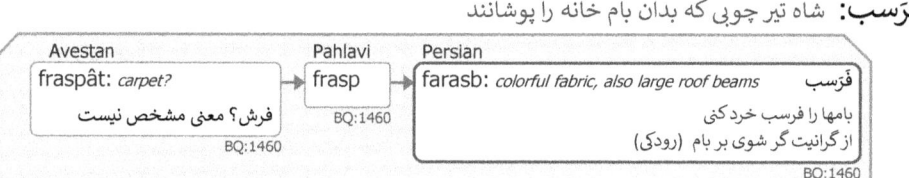

1540

فرستادن (1)

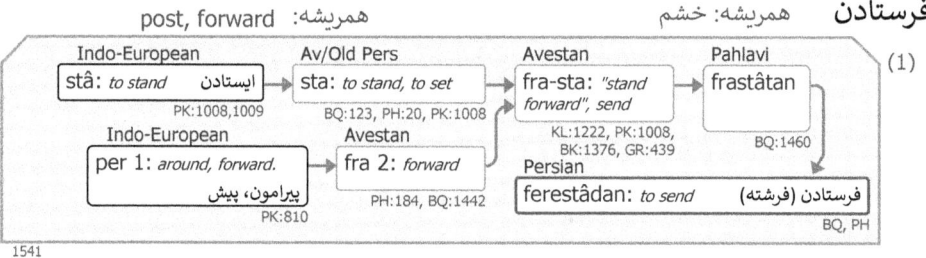

1541

فرستادن (2)

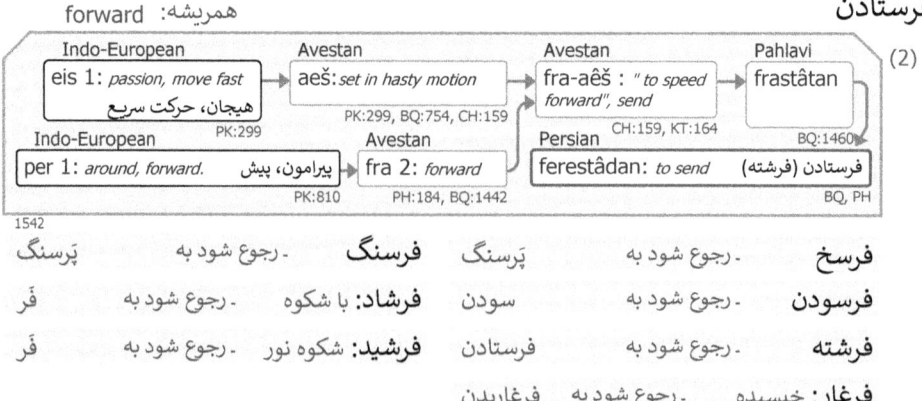

1542

پَرسنگ	فرسنگ. رجوع شود به	پَرسنگ. رجوع شود به	فرسخ
فَر	فرشاد: با شکوه. رجوع شود به	سودن. رجوع شود به	فرسودن
فَر	فرشید: شکوه نور. رجوع شود به	فرستادن. رجوع شود به	فرشته
		فرغاریدن. رجوع شود به	فرغار: خیسیده

فرغاریدن: خیساندن   همریشه: آغار

(1)

Indo-European	Sanskrit	Persian	
gherto: *milk, butter* شیر، کره PK:446	ğar: *milk, also anything wet* â-gar: *to soak, also to swallow* PK:446, KM:40	farğârîdan: *to soak* farğâr: *soaked* farğandeh: *rotten* BQ, AT, MO	فرغاریدن، فرغردن فرغار فرغنده

1543

فرغاریدن: خیساندن   همریشه: آغار

(2)

Indo-European	Sogdian	Persian	
gwel, gar*: *to drip, soak, throw* خیساندن PK:471, CH:108	ğ'yr, ğ'r: *to soak* CH:108	farğârîdan: *to soak* farğâr: *soaked* farğandeh: *rotten* BQ, AT, MO	فرغاریدن، فرغردن فرغار فرغنده
Indo-European per 1: *around, forward.* پیرامون، پیش PK:810	Avestan fra 2: *forward* PH:184, BQ:1442		

1544

فرغر: حوضچه

(1)

Indo-European	Sanskrit	Persian	
gherto: *milk, butter* شیر، کره PK:446	ğar: *milk, also anything wet* â-gar: *to soak, also to swallow* PK:446, KM:40	farğar: *water puddles in a dried river bed* farğan: *new river* BQ, AT, MO	فرغر فرغن

1545

فرغر: حوضچه

(2)

Indo-European	Sogdian	Persian	
gwel, gar*: *to drip, soak, throw* خیساندن PK:471, CH:108	ğ'yr, ğ'r: *to* CH:108	farğar: *water puddles in a dried river bed* farğan: *new river*	فرغر فرغن
Indo-European per 1: *around, forward.* پیرامون، پیش PK:810	Avestan fra 2: *forward* PH:184, BQ:1442	ازآب دریا گفتی همی بگوش آمد که شهریارا دریا تولی و من فرغر (فرخی) BQ, AT, MO	

1546

فرغردن: خیساندن   -رجوع شود به   فرغاریدن   **فرغن:** جوب   -رجوع شود به   فرغر

فرغنده: پوسیده   -رجوع شود به   فرغاریدن

فَرفَر: با عجله

Indo-European	Indo-European	Persian	
per 1: *around, forward.* پیرامون، پیش PK:810	Per-per-os: *flighty, giddy* PK:810,811, IC:927	farfar: *in hurry* برداشت کلک و کاغذ و فَرفَر نوشت فی الفوراین قصیدهٔ مطبوع آبدار (انوری) IC:927, MO:2521	فَرفَر

1547

فرق   همریشه: traffic

Arabic	Persian	
f.r.q: *to split, divide* فرق گذاشتن، تقسیم کردن tafrîq: *distribution* پخش KL:1637	farq: *difference, dividing line* NV:313	فرق

1548

فرمان

فرمان

(1) همریشه: آزمودن   همریشه: measure, before

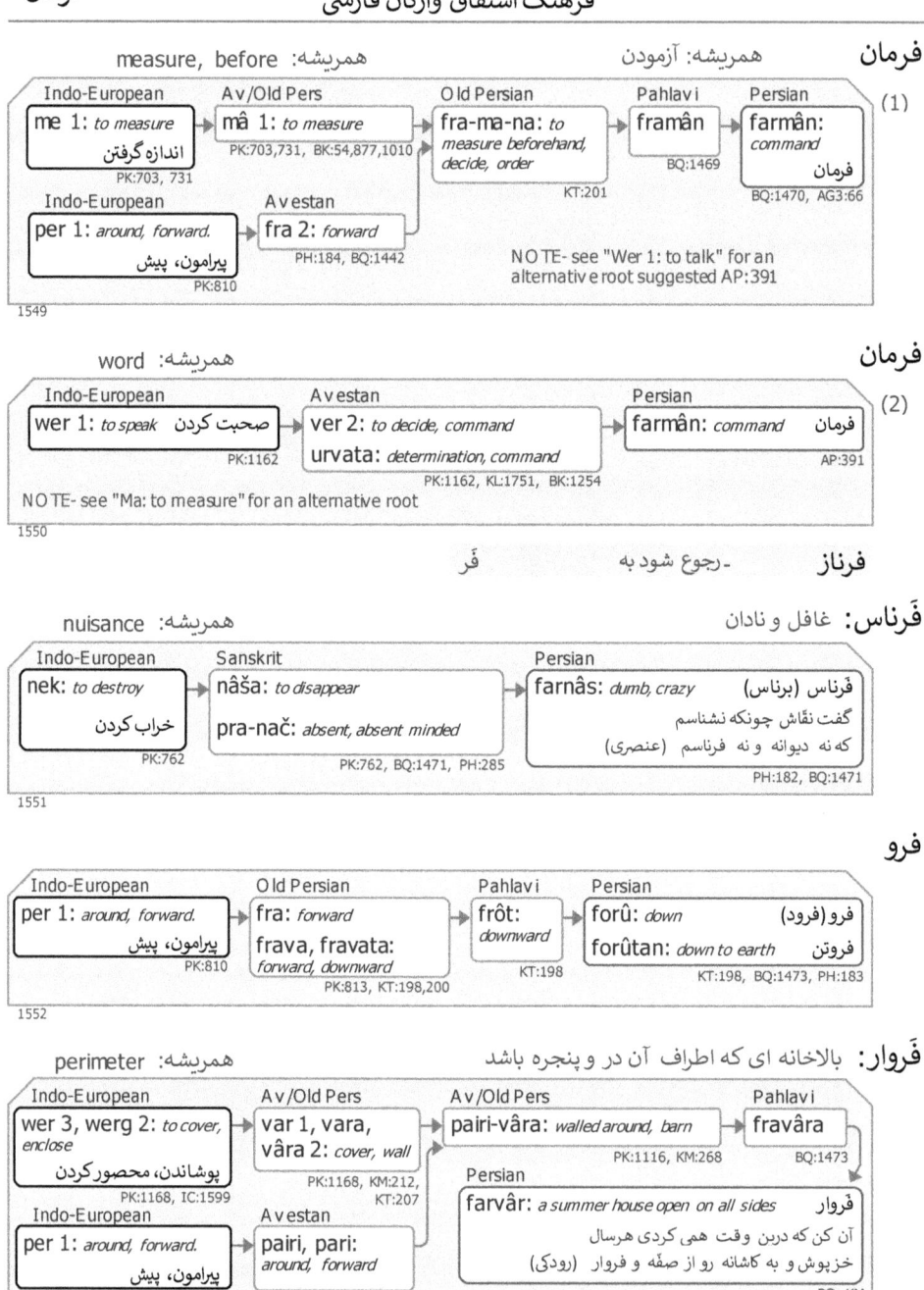

فرمان

(2) همریشه: word

فرناز   ـرجوع شود به   فَر

فَرناس: غافل و نادان   همریشه: nuisance

فرو

فَروار: بالاخانه ای که اطراف آن در و پنجره باشد   همریشه: perimeter

فروتن   ـرجوع شود به   فرو + تن

277

فروختن: "فراخواندن مشتری"

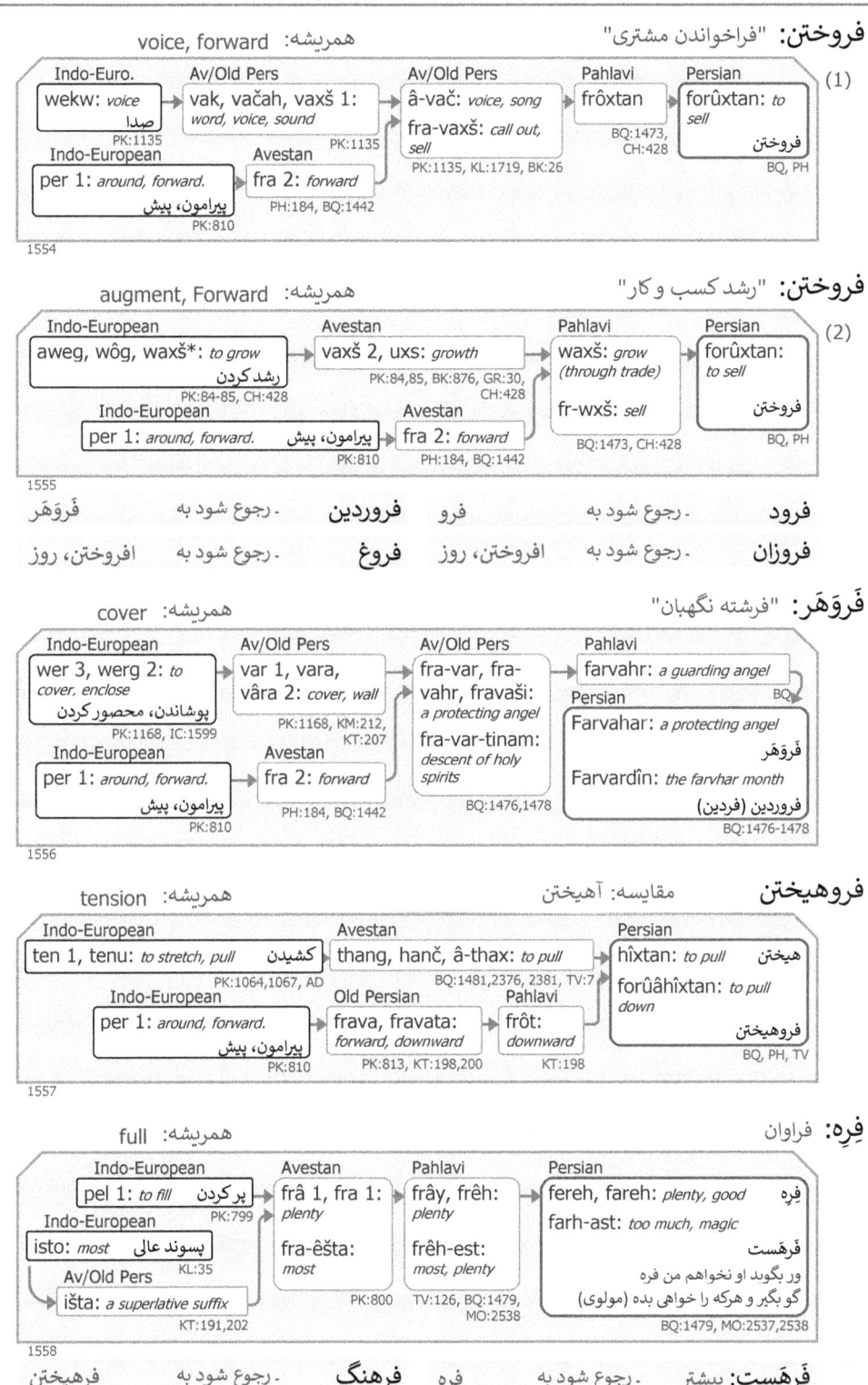

همریشه: voice, forward

Indo-Euro.
wekw: *voice*
صدا
PK:1135

Av/Old Pers
vak, vačah, vaxš 1:
word, voice, sound
PK:1135

Av/Old Pers
â-vač: *voice, song*
fra-vaxš: *call out, sell*
PK:1135, KL:1719, BK:26

Pahlavi
frôxtan
BQ:1473,
CH:428

Persian
forûxtan: *to sell*
فروختن
BQ, PH

(1)

Indo-European
per 1: *around, forward.*
پیرامون، پیش
PK:810

Avestan
fra 2: *forward*
PH:184, BQ:1442

1554

فروختن: "رشد کسب و کار"

همریشه: augment, Forward

Indo-European
aweg, wôg, waxš*: *to grow*
رشد کردن
PK:84-85, CH:428

Avestan
vaxš 2, uxs: *growth*
PK:84,85, BK:876, GR:30,
CH:428

Pahlavi
waxš: *grow (through trade)*
fr-wxš: *sell*
BQ:1473, CH:428

Persian
forûxtan:
to sell
فروختن
BQ, PH

(2)

Indo-European
per 1: *around, forward.*
پیرامون، پیش
PK:810

Avestan
fra 2: *forward*
PH:184, BQ:1442

1555

فَروَهَر   · رجوع شود به   **فروردین**   فرو   · رجوع شود به   **فرود**

افروختن، روز   · رجوع شود به   **فروغ**   افروختن، روز   · رجوع شود به   **فروزان**

فَروَهَر: "فرشته نگهبان"

همریشه: cover

Indo-European
wer 3, werg 2: *to cover, enclose*
پوشاندن، محصور کردن
PK:1168, IC:1599

Av/Old Pers
var 1, vara, vâra 2: *cover, wall*
PK:1168, KM:212, KT:207

Av/Old Pers
fra-var, fra-vahr, fravaši:
a protecting angel
fra-var-tinam:
descent of holy spirits
BQ:1476,1478

Pahlavi
farvahr: *a guarding angel*
BQ

Persian
Farvahar: *a protecting angel*
فَروَهَر
Farvardîn: *the farvhar month*
فروردین (فردین)
BQ:1476-1478

Indo-European
per 1: *around, forward.*
پیرامون، پیش
PK:810

Avestan
fra 2: *forward*
PH:184, BQ:1442

1556

فروهیختن   مقایسه: آهیختن

همریشه: tension

Indo-European
ten 1, tenu: *to stretch, pull*   کشیدن
PK:1064,1067, AD

Avestan
thang, hanč, â-thax: *to pull*
BQ:1481,2376, 2381, TV:7

Persian
hîxtan: *to pull*
هیختن
forûâhîxtan: *to pull down*
فروهیختن
BQ, PH, TV

Indo-European
per 1: *around, forward.*
پیرامون، پیش
PK:810

Old Persian
frava, fravata:
forward, downward
PK:813, KT:198,200

Pahlavi
frôt:
downward
KT:198

1557

فِره: فراوان

همریشه: full

Indo-European
pel 1: *to fill*   پرکردن
PK:799

Indo-European
isto: *most*
پسوند عالی
KL:35

Av/Old Pers
išta: *a superlative suffix*
KT:191,202

Avestan
frâ 1, fra 1:
plenty
fra-êšta:
most
PK:800

Pahlavi
frây, frêh:
plenty
frêh-est:
most, plenty
TV:126, BQ:1479,
MO:2538

Persian
fereh, fareh: *plenty, good*
فِره
farh-ast: *too much, magic*
فَرهَست
ور بگوید او ونخواهم من فره
گو بگیر و هرکه را خواهی بده (مولوی)
BQ:1479, MO:2537,2538

1558

فَرهَست: بیشتر   · رجوع شود به   **فرهنگ**   فِره   · رجوع شود به   فروهیختن

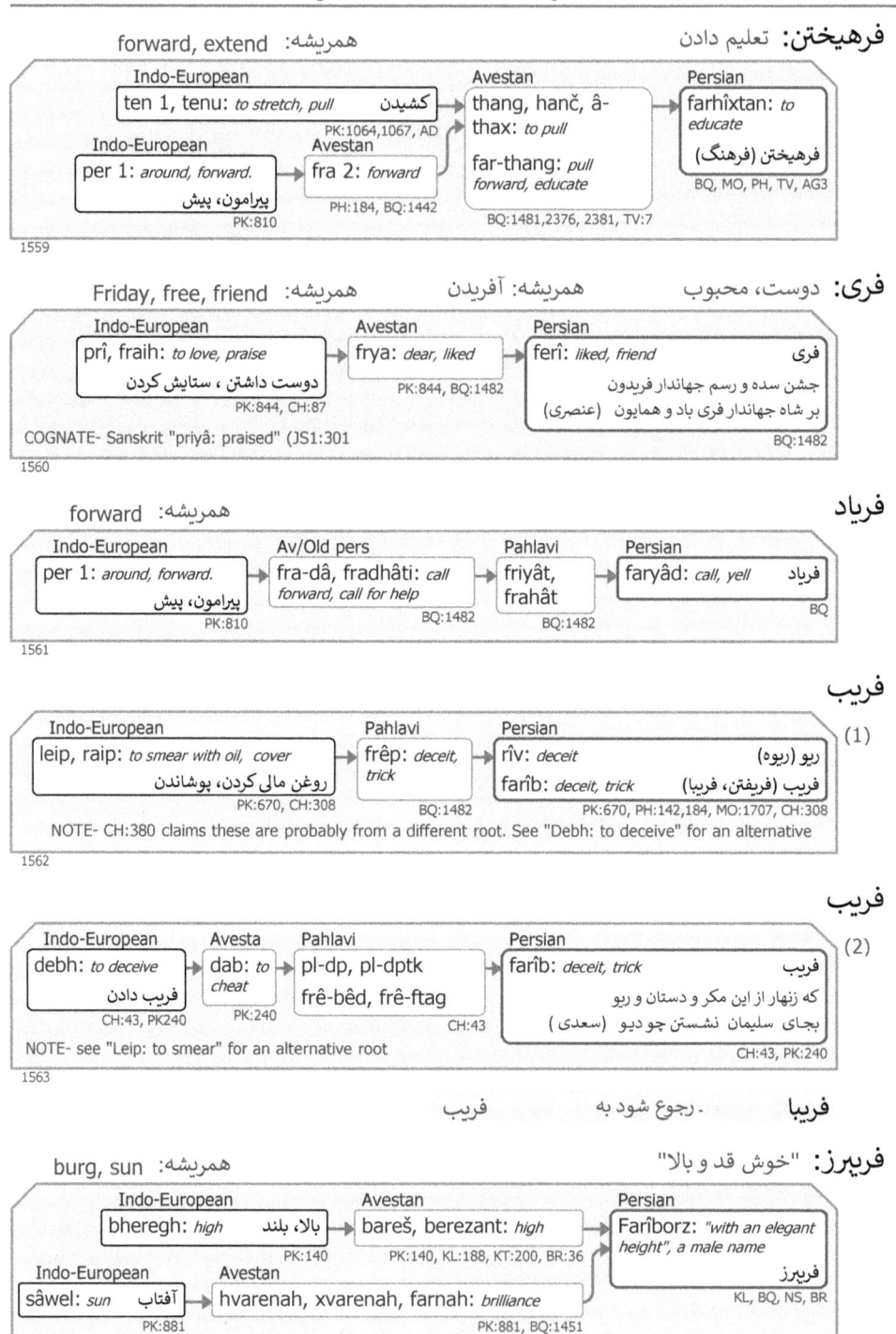

فرهیختن: تعلیم دادن

همریشه: forward, extend

Indo-European
ten 1, tenu: *to stretch, pull*   کشیدن
PK:1064,1067, AD

Indo-European
per 1: *around, forward.*
پیرامون، پیش
PK:810

Avestan
fra 2: *forward*
PH:184, BQ:1442

Avestan
thang, hanč, â-thax: *to pull*

far-thang: *pull forward, educate*
BQ:1481,2376, 2381, TV:7

Persian
farhîxtan: *to educate*
فرهیختن (فرهنگ)
BQ, MO, PH, TV, AG3

1559

فری: دوست، محبوب   همریشه: آفریدن   همریشه: Friday, free, friend

Indo-European
prî, fraih: *to love, praise*
دوست داشتن ، ستایش کردن
PK:844, CH:87

Avestan
frya: *dear, liked*
PK:844, BQ:1482

Persian
ferî: *liked, friend*   فری
جشن سده و رسم جهاندار فریدون
بر شاه جهاندار فری باد و همایون (عنصری)
BQ:1482

COGNATE- Sanskrit "priyâ: praised" (JS1:301)

1560

فریاد

همریشه: forward

Indo-European
per 1: *around, forward.*
پیرامون، پیش
PK:810

Av/Old pers
fra-dâ, fradhâti: *call forward, call for help*
BQ:1482

Pahlavi
friyât, frahât
BQ:1482

Persian
faryâd: *call, yell*   فریاد
BQ

1561

فریب (1)

Indo-European
leip, raip: *to smear with oil, cover*
روغن مالی کردن، پوشاندن
PK:670, CH:308

Pahlavi
frêp: *deceit, trick*
BQ:1482

Persian
rîv: *deceit*   ریو (ریوه)
farîb: *deceit, trick*   فریب (فریفتن، فریبا)
PK:670, PH:142,184, MO:1707, CH:308

NOTE- CH:380 claims these are probably from a different root. See "Debh: to deceive" for an alternative

1562

فریب (2)

Indo-European
debh: *to deceive*
فریب دادن
CH:43, PK240

Avesta
dab: *to cheat*
PK:240

Pahlavi
pl-dp, pl-dptk
frê-bêd, frê-ftag
CH:43

Persian
farîb: *deceit, trick*   فریب
که زنهار از این مکر و دستان و ریو
بجای سلیمان نشستن چو دیو (سعدی)
CH:43, PK:240

NOTE- see "Leip: to smear" for an alternative root

1563

فریبا   . رجوع شود به   فریب

فریبرز: "خوش قد و بالا"

همریشه: burg, sun

Indo-European
bheregh: *high*   بالا، بلند
PK:140

Avestan
bareš, berezant: *high*
PK:140, KL:188, KT:200, BR:36

Indo-European
sâwel: *sun*   آفتاب
PK:881

Avestan
hvarenah, xvarenah, farnah: *brilliance*
PK:881, BQ:1451

Persian
Farîborz: *"with an elegant height", a male name*
فریبرز
KL, BQ, NS, BR

1564

فریدون: "شریف زاده"   همریشه: آبتین

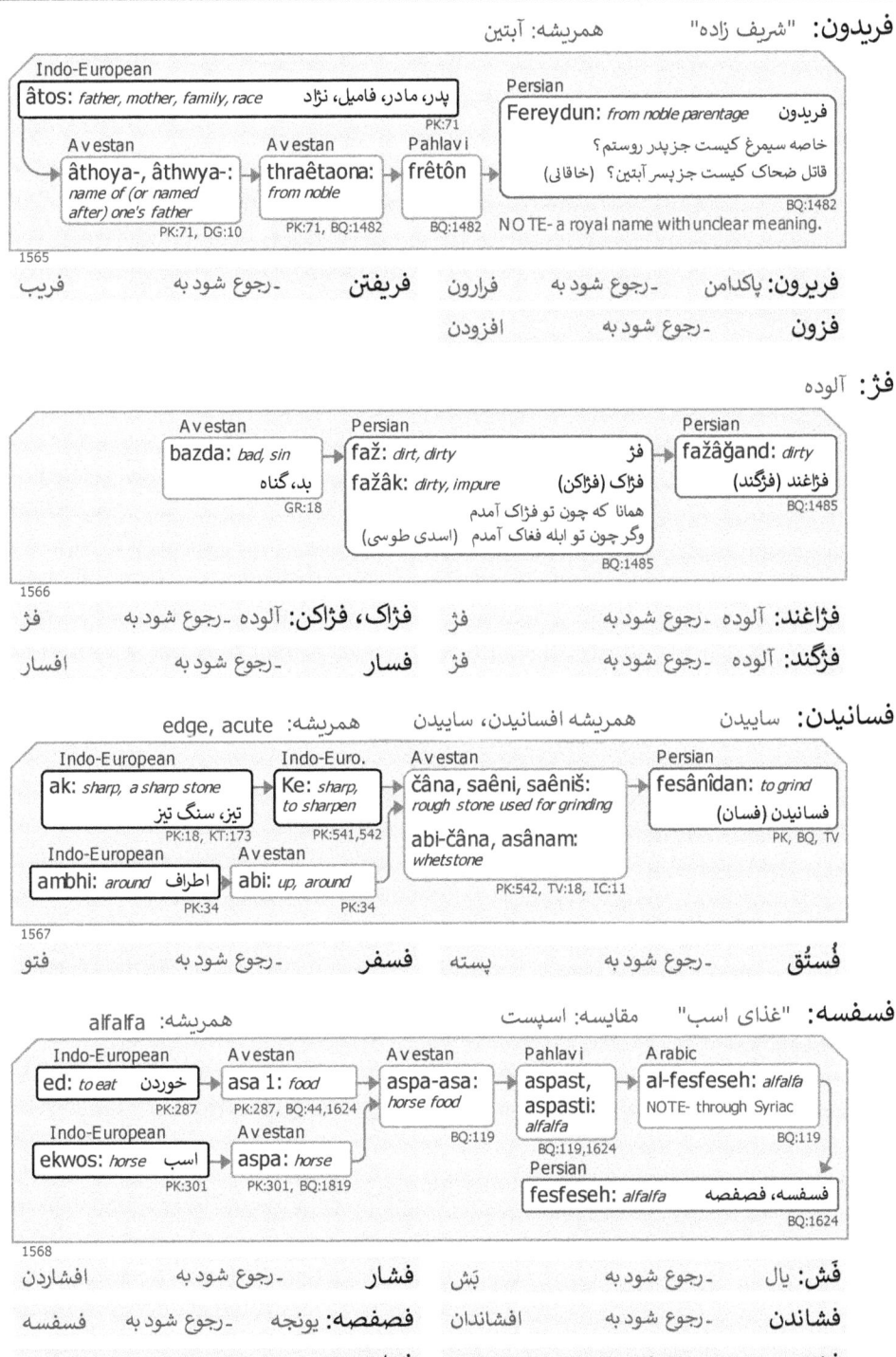

1565

فریرون: پاکدامن   ـرجوع شود به   فرارون   **فریفتن**   ـرجوع شود به   فریب

فزون   ـرجوع شود به   افزودن

فژ: آلوده

1566

فژاغند: آلوده ـرجوع شود به   فژ   **فژاک، فژاکن:** آلوده ـرجوع شود به   فژ

فژگند: آلوده ـرجوع شود به   فژ   **فسار**   ـرجوع شود به   افسار

فسانیدن: ساییدن   همریشه افسانیدن، ساییدن

1567

فُستُق   ـرجوع شود به   پسته   **فسفر**   ـرجوع شود به   فتو

فسفسه: "غذای اسب"   مقایسه: اسپست   همریشه: alfalfa

1568

فَش: یال   ـرجوع شود به   بَش   **فشار**   ـرجوع شود به   افشاردن

فشاندن   ـرجوع شود به   افشاندان   **فصفصه:** یونجه   ـرجوع شود به   فسفسه

فغ   ـرجوع شود به   بغ   **فغان:** زاری   ـرجوع شود به   افغان

فغستان   ـ رجوع شود به   بغستان

فغفور: "پسر خدا"   مقایسه: بیدخت

فگار: آزرده   ـ رجوع شود به   افگار

فلاخن

همریشه: forward

فلز

فَلَس   مقایسه: پول

فلسفه   مقایسه: سفسطه

فلفل

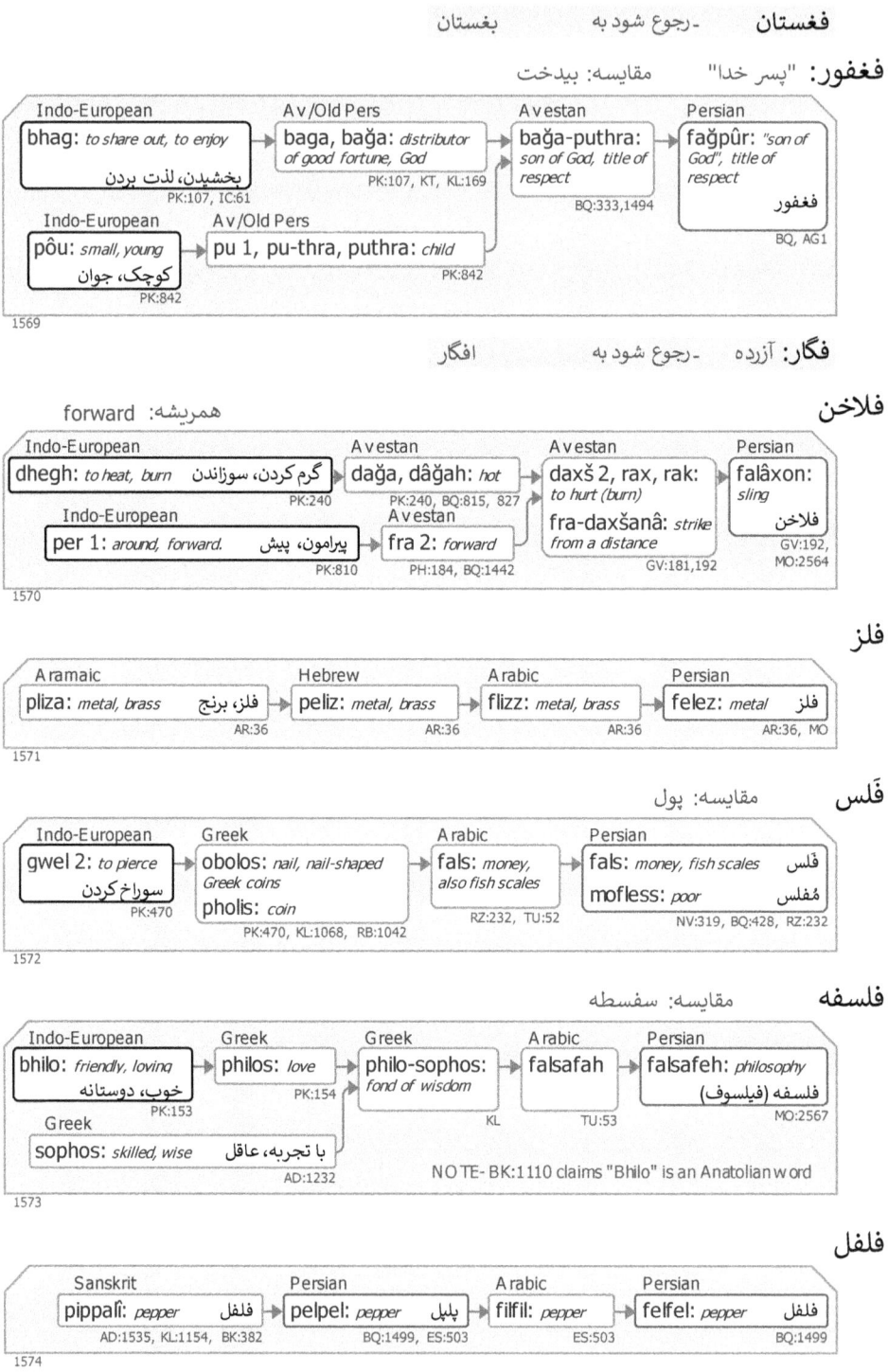

فلوت   مقایسه: عود

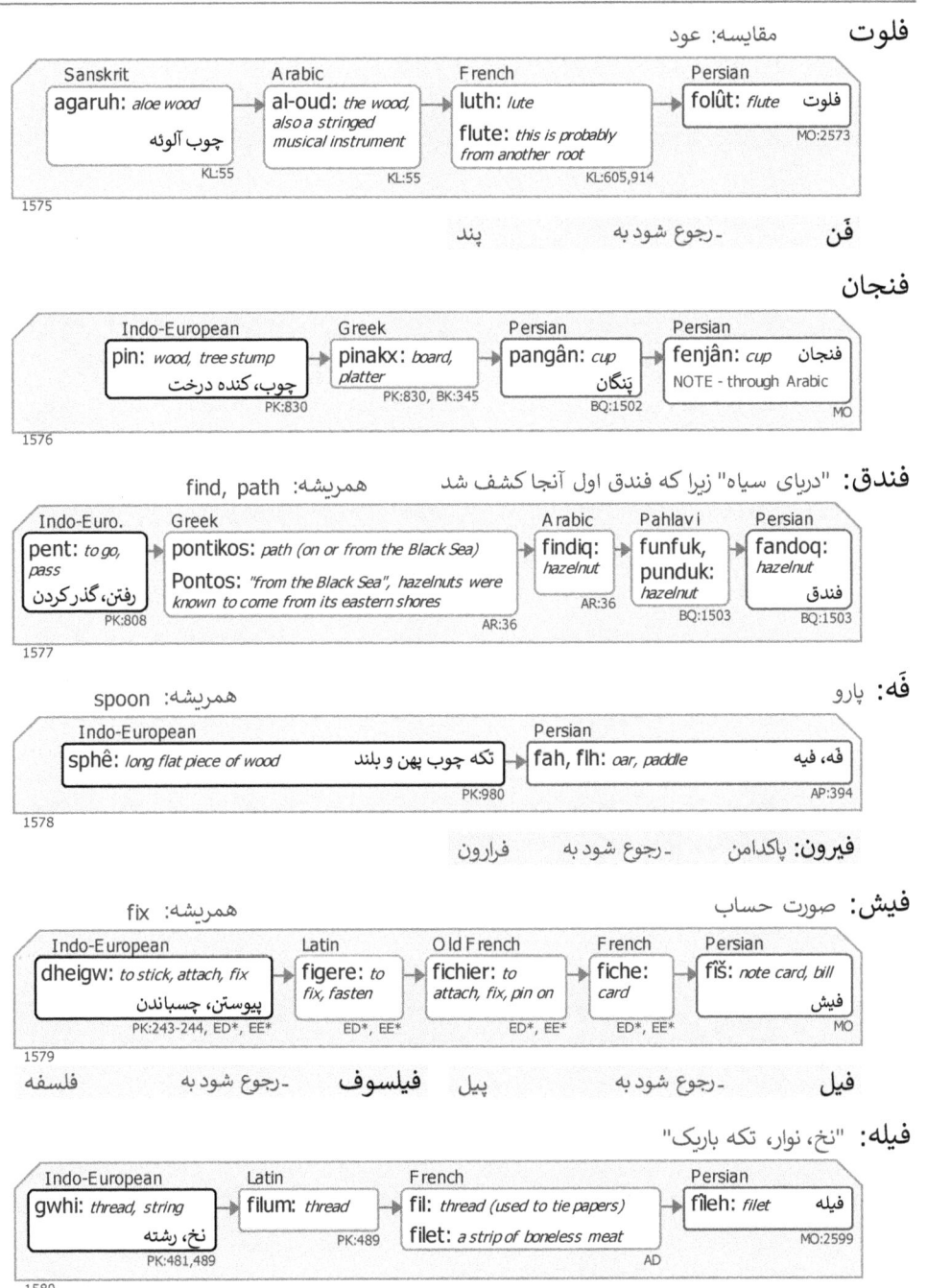

فلوت

Sanskrit	Arabic	French	Persian
agaruh: *aloe wood* چوب آلوئه KL:55	al-oud: *the wood, also a stringed musical instrument* KL:55	luth: *lute* flute: *this is probably from another root* KL:605,914	folût: *flute* فلوت MO:2573

1575

فَن   -رجوع شود به   پند

فنجان

Indo-European	Greek	Persian	Persian
pin: *wood, tree stump* چوب، کنده درخت PK:830	pinakx: *board, platter* PK:830, BK:345	pangân: *cup* پنگان BQ:1502	fenjân: *cup* فنجان NOTE - through Arabic MO

1576

فندق: "دریای سیاه" زیرا که فندق اول آنجا کشف شد   همریشه: find, path

Indo-Euro.	Greek	Arabic	Pahlavi	Persian
pent: *to go, pass* رفتن، گذر کردن PK:808	pontikos: *path (on or from the Black Sea)* Pontos: *"from the Black Sea", hazelnuts were known to come from its eastern shores* AR:36	findiq: *hazelnut* AR:36	funfuk, punduk: *hazelnut* BQ:1503	fandoq: *hazelnut* فندق BQ:1503

1577

فَه: پارو   همریشه: spoon

Indo-European		Persian
sphê: *long flat piece of wood* تکه چوب پهن و بلند PK:980		fah, flh: *oar, paddle* فه، فیه AP:394

1578

فیرون: پاکدامن   -رجوع شود به   فرارون

فیش: صورت حساب   همریشه: fix

Indo-European	Latin	Old French	French	Persian
dheigw: *to stick, attach, fix* پیوستن، چسباندن PK:243-244, ED*, EE*	figere: *to fix, fasten* ED*, EE*	fichier: *to attach, fix, pin on* ED*, EE*	fiche: *card* ED*, EE*	fîš: *note card, bill* فیش MO

1579

فیل   -رجوع شود به   پیل   **فیلسوف**   **فیلسوف**   -رجوع شود به   فلسفه

فیله: "نخ، نوار، تکه باریک"

Indo-European	Latin	French	Persian
gwhi: *thread, string* نخ، رشته PK:481,489	filum: *thread* PK:489	fil: *thread (used to tie papers)* filet: *a strip of boneless meat* AD	fîleh: *filet* فیله MO:2599

1580

فیه: پارو   -رجوع شود به   فَه

قابوس ـ رجوع شود به   کی۳

قاطر: "از نسل خر"   همریشه: hard

Indo-European	Avestan	Sogdian	Persian
kar 1: *hard* سخت	xara: *a harsh-voiced animal, donkey*	xr: *donkey* xara-tara: *related to a donkey, mule*	qâter: *mule* قاطر
PK:531, IC:1056,1632	GR:166	GR:166	MO:2615

1581

قالب ـ رجوع شود به   کالب

قانون: "نی یا چوب اندازه گیری"، معیار   همریشه: cane, canal, canon

Indo-European	Av/Old Pers	Arabic	Greek	Arabic
gwhen 3, kan*: *to dig and fill* کندن و پُر کردن	kan 1, xan, gan: *to dig, pile up, build*	qanah: *reed, cane* qanat: *underground water*	kanon: *yard stick, rule* KL:232	qânun: *law* BQ:1516
CH:232, PK491	PK:491, PH:194, BT:583	KL:232, ES:539,545	Persian qânun: *rule, law* (قانون۲) قانون	BQ:1516, MO:2875

NOTE- These words also reached the Greek and Latin languages through Semitic languages

1582

قایق

Turkish	Persian
kay-guk, kayik: *boat* قایق، کشتی	qâyeq: *boat* قایق
KL:220, EE*	MO, RZ:214

1583

قباد: محبوب   همریشه: شُکوه، کیان   همریشه: see, hear

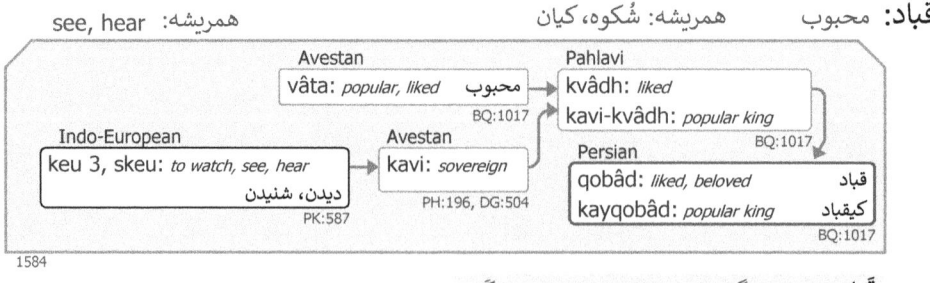

Avestan	Pahlavi
vâta: *popular, liked* محبوب BQ:1017	kvâdh: *liked* kavi-kvâdh: *popular king* BQ:1017

Indo-European	Avestan	Persian
keu 3, skeu: *to watch, see, hear* دیدن، شنیدن PK:587	kavi: *sovereign* PH:196, DG:504	qobâd: *liked, beloved* قباد kayqobâd: *popular king* کیقباد BQ:1017

1584

قباریس: نوعی گیاه   ـ رجوع شود به   گَبَر

قُبّه

مقایسه: کُبّه

Iranian	Arabic	Persian
gabbah: *dome, vault, blister* گنبد ، طاق ، تاول AS:123	qabbah: *arched, bent* NOTE- KL:46 claims this is from the Semitic root "Q.b.b: to be bent" ES:520, AS:120	qobbeh: *dome, vault* قُبّه MO:2637, NV:323

1585

همریشه: camp

Indo-European	Latin	Persian
kam 2, kamp: *to bend, a vault* خم کردن، حفره PK:524,525, CH:229	campus: *bent land, valley* Campania: *an area in Italy famous for its scales* PK:525	capân: *a weighing scale* کپان (قپان) MO:2896, RZ:222, AA:216

1586

قُراب: شیشهٔ شراب ـ رجوع شود به   قُرّابه

قُرّابه: شیشهٔ شراب

Arabic	Persian	English
qirbah, qirrâbah: *a leathern bottle* بطری چرمی، مَشک AD:202	Qarrâbeh: *a glass bottle (for wine)* قرابه (قُراب) NV:328, MO	carboy: *large glass bottle* KL:238

1587

مقایسه: کارت   همریشه: carton, chart, card   قرطاس

Greek	Arabic	Persian
čartês: *leaf of papyrus* برگ پاپیروس NOTE- Probably from an Egyptian origin AD:203, KL:239	qertâs: *paper* TU:55, BR:342	qertâs: *paper* قرطاس MO:2659

1588

قرمز: "ساخته شده از کرم"   همریشه: worm

Indo-European	Sanskrit	Persian
wer 2, kwermi: *to turn, bend* چرخیدن، خم شدن PK:1142-1157, PK:649	krmi: *worm*	qermez: *red* قرمز MO:2663
Indo-European gene: *to give birth to* زاییدن PK:373	krmi-ja: *made from worms (a red* PK:649	

1589

همریشه: garden, court   قَرن

Indo-European	Greek	Arabic	Persian
gher 1: *to grab, enclose* گرفتن ، محصور کردن PK:442, 444	ğr-on-os, chronos, xronos: *that which encloses all things, time* KL:284	qarn: *a century* TU:56	qarn: *century* قَرن MO:2665

1590

قرنطینه

همریشه: چهار ، چهل

همریشه: four

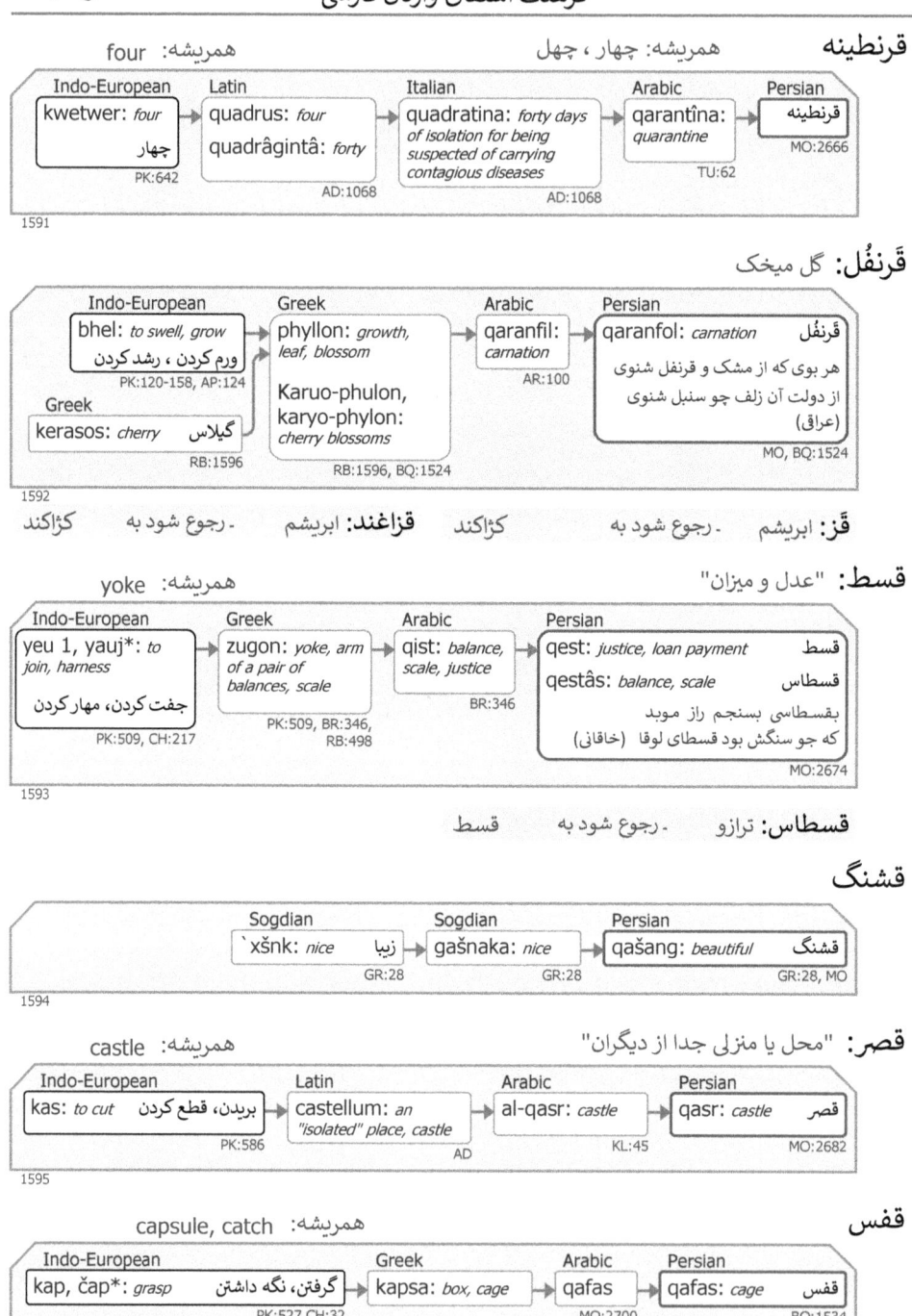

قَرنُفُل: گل میخک

قَز: ابریشم   - رجوع شود به   کژاکند   **قزاغند:** ابریشم   کژاکند   - رجوع شود به   کژاکند

قسط: "عدل و میزان"

همریشه: yoke

قسطاس: ترازو   - رجوع شود به   قسط

قشنگ

قصر: "محل یا منزلی جدا از دیگران"

همریشه: castle

قفس

همریشه: capsule, catch

قفقاز: "با یخهای درخشان"   همریشه: کریستال   همریشه: raw, crust, crystal

Indo-European	Greek	Latin	Arabic	Persian
kû 1: *to burn (also firewood)* سوزاندن (هیزم) PK:595	kau: *burning, shining* kau-casos: *(mountains) shining with ice* KL:252	caucasus: *mountains between Caspian and Black sea.*		qafqâz: *Caucasia* قفقاز MO5:1474
Indo-European kreu: *blood, crust, ice* خون، پوسته سخت، یخ PK:621, KL:252				

COGNATE- Avestan "xru: bloody flesh;/ xruždra: hard" (PK:621, KL:377)

1597

قفیز: پیمانه غلات   ـ رجوع شود به   کویز

ققنوس: مرغ آتش   همریشه: سوختن   همریشه: cygnet

Indo-European	Greek	Arabic	Persian
keuk: *to shine, be white* درخشیدن، سفید بودن PK:597, RB:799	kuknos: *(white) swan* BQ:1535, AR:99, RB:799	qaqus: *phoenix* AR:99	ğoğnûs: *phoenix* قوقنوس (ققنُس) ترا دنیا خوش آمد ای برادر چو ققنوس این زمان در سوی آذر (عطار) BQ, MO

1598

قُلزُم

Indo-European	Greek	Arabic	Persian
kleu 2: *to wash, rinse* شستن، آب کشیدن PK:607, DV:122, ED*	klysma: *water used for washing* AR:103, PK:607	qulzum: *large body of water, sea* AR:103	qolzom: *sea* دریا به دریای قلزم به جوش آرد آب نخارد سر از کین افراسیاب (فردوسی) MO, AR:103

1599

قُلقُل   ـ رجوع شود به   غرغره

قلم   همریشه: caramel

Indo-European	Greek	Arabic	Persian
kolemos: *reed, cane* تره، نی PK:612	kalamos: *a reed (used as a pen)* PK:612	qalam: *pen* TU:57	qalam: *pen* قلم MO:2715

1600

قلیا   ـ رجوع شود به   قلیه

قلیه: "گوشتی که بر تابه بریان شده باشد"   همریشه: alkali, alkaline

Arabic	Arabic	Persian
q.l.y: *to roast in a pan, to barbeque meat* بریان کردن، پختن گوشت ED*	alqaliy: *burnt ashes, alkaline material* ED*, EE*	qalyeh: *meat cooked or roasted in a pan* قلیه qalyâ: *burnt ashes, alkaline material* قلیا MO

1601

قمیص   همریشه: شُمیز   همریشه: chemise

Indo-European	Greek	Latin	Arabic	Persian
kem 2: *to cover* پوشاندن PK:556, GT6:122	kamision: *shirt* BR:352	camisia: *shirt* PK:556	qamîs: *cotton shirt* BR:352	qamîs: *cotton shirt* قمیص MO:2729

1602

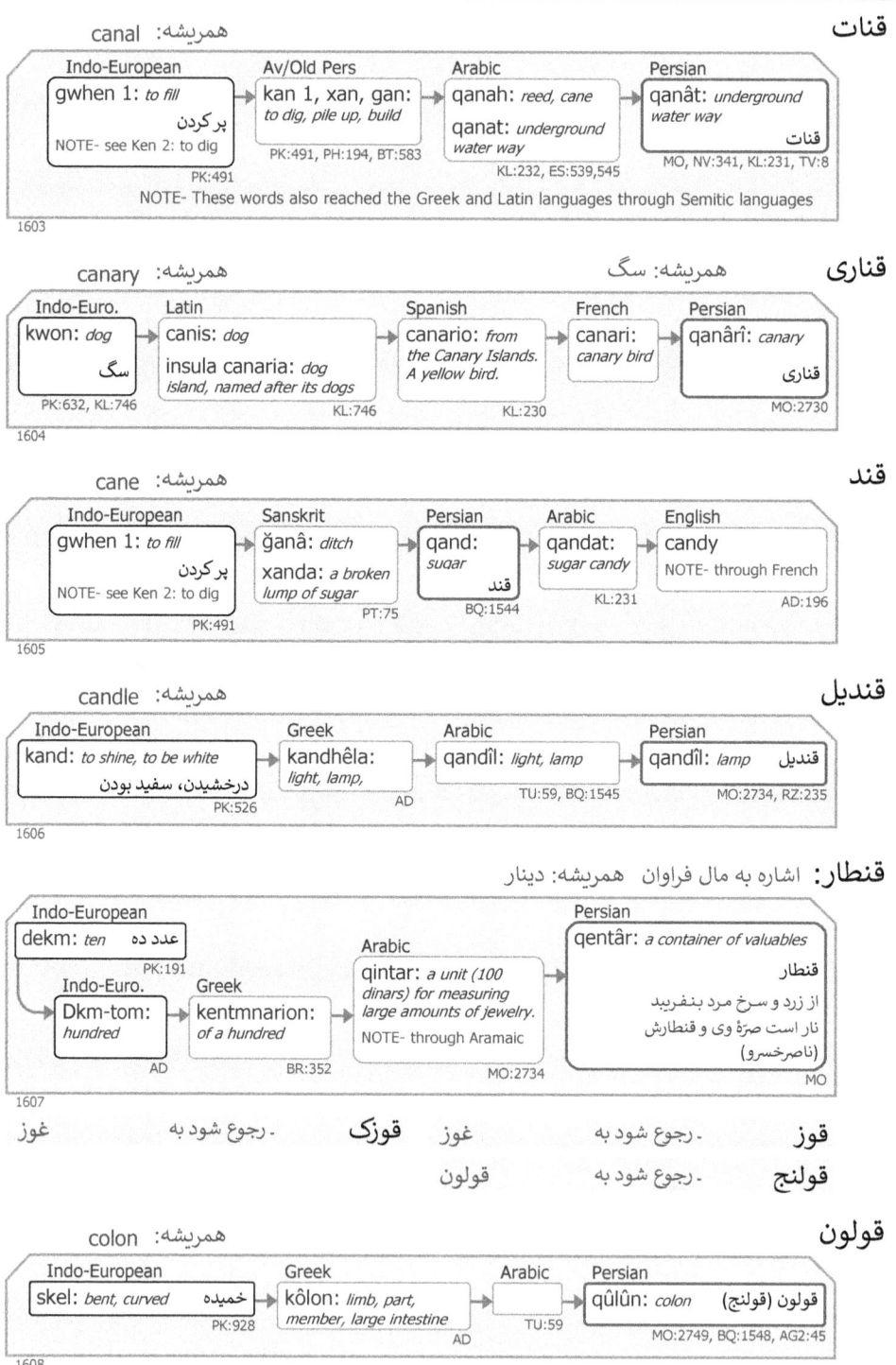

قنات

همریشه: canal

Indo-European	Av/Old Pers	Arabic	Persian
gwhen 1: *to fill* پر کردن NOTE- see Ken 2: to dig PK:491	kan 1, xan, gan: *to dig, pile up, build* PK:491, PH:194, BT:583	qanah: *reed, cane* qanat: *underground water way* KL:232, ES:539,545	qanât: *underground water way* قنات MO, NV:341, KL:231, TV:8

NOTE- These words also reached the Greek and Latin languages through Semitic languages

1603

قناری

همریشه: سگ   همریشه: canary

Indo-Euro.	Latin	Spanish	French	Persian
kwon: *dog* سگ PK:632, KL:746	canis: *dog* insula canaria: *dog island, named after its dogs* KL:746	canario: *from the Canary Islands. A yellow bird.* KL:230	canari: *canary bird*	qanârî: *canary* قناری MO:2730

1604

قند

همریشه: cane

Indo-European	Sanskrit	Persian	Arabic	English
gwhen 1: *to fill* پر کردن NOTE- see Ken 2: to dig PK:491	ğanâ: *ditch* xanda: *a broken lump of sugar* PT:75	qand: *sugar* قند BQ:1544	qandat: *sugar candy* KL:231	candy NOTE- through French AD:196

1605

قندیل

همریشه: candle

Indo-European	Greek	Arabic	Persian
kand: *to shine, to be white* درخشیدن، سفید بودن PK:526	kandhêla: *light, lamp,* AD	qandîl: *light, lamp* TU:59, BQ:1545	qandîl: *lamp* قندیل MO:2734, RZ:235

1606

قنطار: اشاره به مال فراوان   همریشه: دینار

Indo-European		Persian
dekm: *ten* عدد ده PK:191		qentâr: *a container of valuables* قنطار
Indo-Euro. Dkm-tom: *hundred* AD	Greek kentmnarion: *of a hundred* BR:352	
	Arabic qintar: *a unit (100 dinars) for measuring large amounts of jewelry.* NOTE- through Aramaic MO:2734	از زرد و سرخ مرد بنفرید نار است صرّهٔ وی و قنطارش (ناصرخسرو) MO

1607

قوز	ـ رجوع شود به	غوز	قوزک	ـ رجوع شود به	غوز
قولنج	ـ رجوع شود به	قولون			

قولون

همریشه: colon

Indo-European	Greek	Arabic	Persian
skel: *bent, curved* خمیده PK:928	kôlon: *limb, part, member, large intestine* AD	TU:59	qûlûn: *colon* قولون (قولنج) MO:2749, BQ:1548, AG2:45

1608

قهرمان: "ماهر در کار، کار بلد"

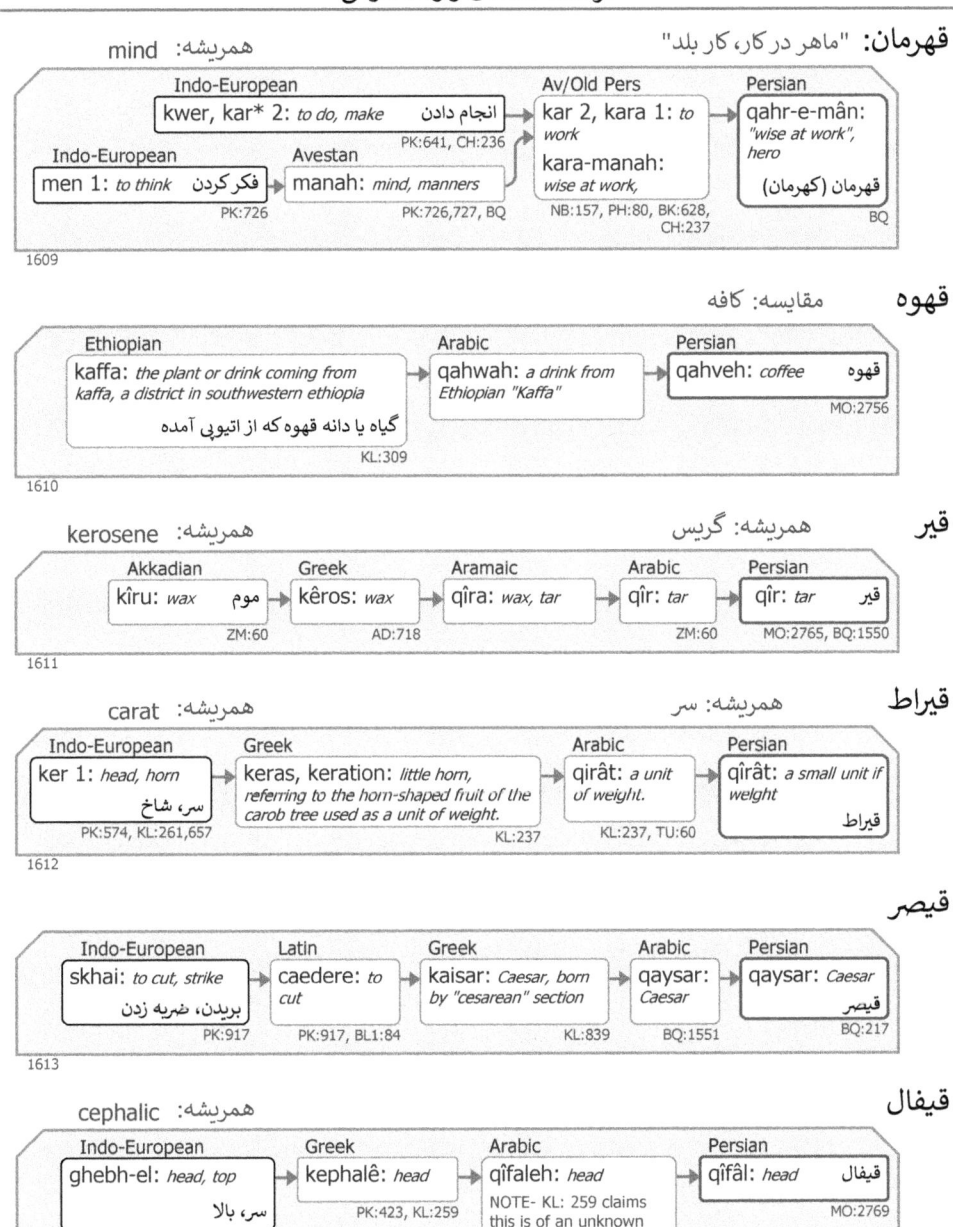

همریشه: mind

Indo-European
kwer, kar* 2: to do, make   انجام دادن
PK:641, CH:236

Indo-European
men 1: to think   فکر کردن
PK:726

Avestan
manah: mind, manners
PK:726,727, BQ

Av/Old Pers
kar 2, kara 1: to work
kara-manah: wise at work,
NB:157, PH:80, BK:628, CH:237

Persian
qahr-e-mân: "wise at work", hero
قهرمان (کهرمان)
BQ

1609

قهوه   مقایسه: کافه

Ethiopian
kaffa: the plant or drink coming from kaffa, a district in southwestern ethiopia
گیاه یا دانه قهوه که از اتیوپی آمده
KL:309

Arabic
qahwah: a drink from Ethiopian "Kaffa"

Persian
qahveh: coffee   قهوه
MO:2756

1610

قیر   همریشه: گریس   همریشه: kerosene

Akkadian
kîru: wax   موم
ZM:60

Greek
kêros: wax
AD:718

Aramaic
qîra: wax, tar

Arabic
qîr: tar
ZM:60

Persian
qîr: tar   قیر
MO:2765, BQ:1550

1611

قیراط   همریشه: سر   همریشه: carat

Indo-European
ker 1: head, horn
سر، شاخ
PK:574, KL:261,657

Greek
keras, keration: little horn, referring to the horn-shaped fruit of the carob tree used as a unit of weight.
KL:237

Arabic
qirât: a unit of weight.
KL:237, TU:60

Persian
qîrât: a small unit if weight
قیراط

1612

قیصر

Indo-European
skhai: to cut, strike
بریدن، ضربه زدن
PK:917

Latin
caedere: to cut
PK:917, BL1:84

Greek
kaisar: Caesar, born by "cesarean" section
KL:839

Arabic
qaysar: Caesar
BQ:1551

Persian
qaysar: Caesar
قیصر
BQ:217

1613

قیفال   همریشه: cephalic

Indo-European
ghebh-el: head, top
سر، بالا
PK:423

Greek
kephalê: head
PK:423, KL:259

Arabic
qîfaleh: head
NOTE- KL: 259 claims this is of an unknown
MO:2769, KL:259

Persian
qîfâl: head   قیفال
MO:2769

1614

این حرف به خ یا غ بدل شود.

ک.

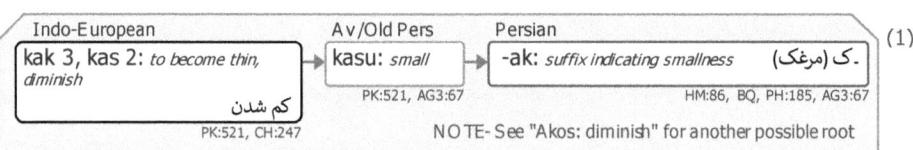

(1)

Indo-European	Av/Old Pers	Persian
kak 3, kas 2: *to become thin, diminish*	kasu: *small*	-ak: *suffix indicating smallness* (مرغک) ک.
کم شدن	PK:521, AG3:67	HM:86, BQ, PH:185, AG3:67
PK:521, CH:247		NOTE- See "Akos: diminish" for another possible root

1615

ک.

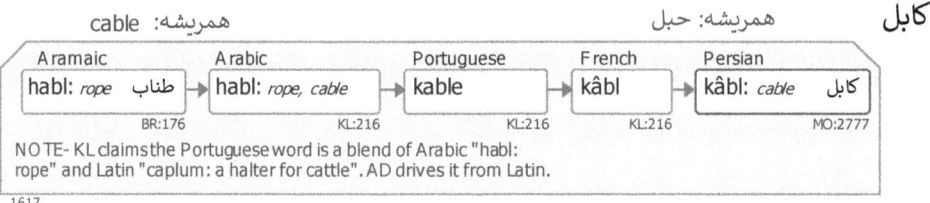

(2)

Indo-European	Pahlavi	Persian
akos: *suffix indicating small size*	-ak	-ak: *a suffix indicating small size* (مرغک، دخترک) ک
پسوند تحقیر	MO:2775	IC:9, MO:2775
IC:9		NOTE- See "Kak: small size" for another possible root

1616

کابل   همریشه: حبل

cable :همریشه

Aramaic	Arabic	Portuguese	French	Persian
habl: *rope* طناب	habl: *rope, cable*	kable	kâbl	kâbl: *cable* کابل
BR:176	KL:216	KL:216	KL:216	MO:2777

NOTE- KL claims the Portuguese word is a blend of Arabic "habl: rope" and Latin "caplum: a halter for cattle". AD drives it from Latin.

1617

کاتوره: سرگیجه

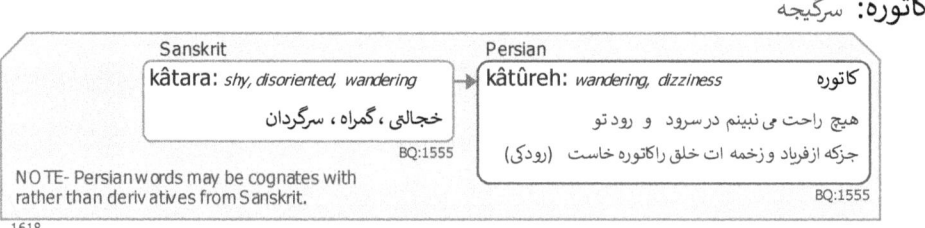

Sanskrit	Persian
kâtara: *shy, disoriented, wandering*	kâtûreh: *wandering, dizziness* کاتوره
خجالتی ، گمراه ، سرگردان	هیچ راحت می نبینم در سرود و رود تو
BQ:1555	جزکه ازفریاد و زخمه ات خلق راکاتوره خاست (رودکی)
	BQ:1555

NOTE- Persian words may be cognates with rather than derivatives from Sanskrit.

1618

کاچ

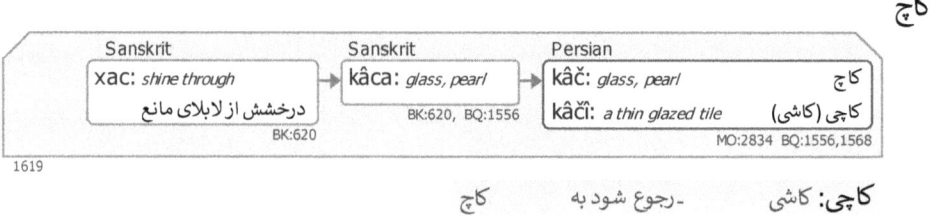

Sanskrit	Sanskrit	Persian
xac: *shine through*	kâca: *glass, pearl*	kâč: *glass, pearl* کاچ
درخشش از لابلای مانع	BK:620, BQ:1556	kâči: *a thin glazed tile* (کاشی) کاچی
BK:620		MO:2834 BQ:1556,1568

1619

کاچی: کاشی   ـرجوع شود به   کاچ

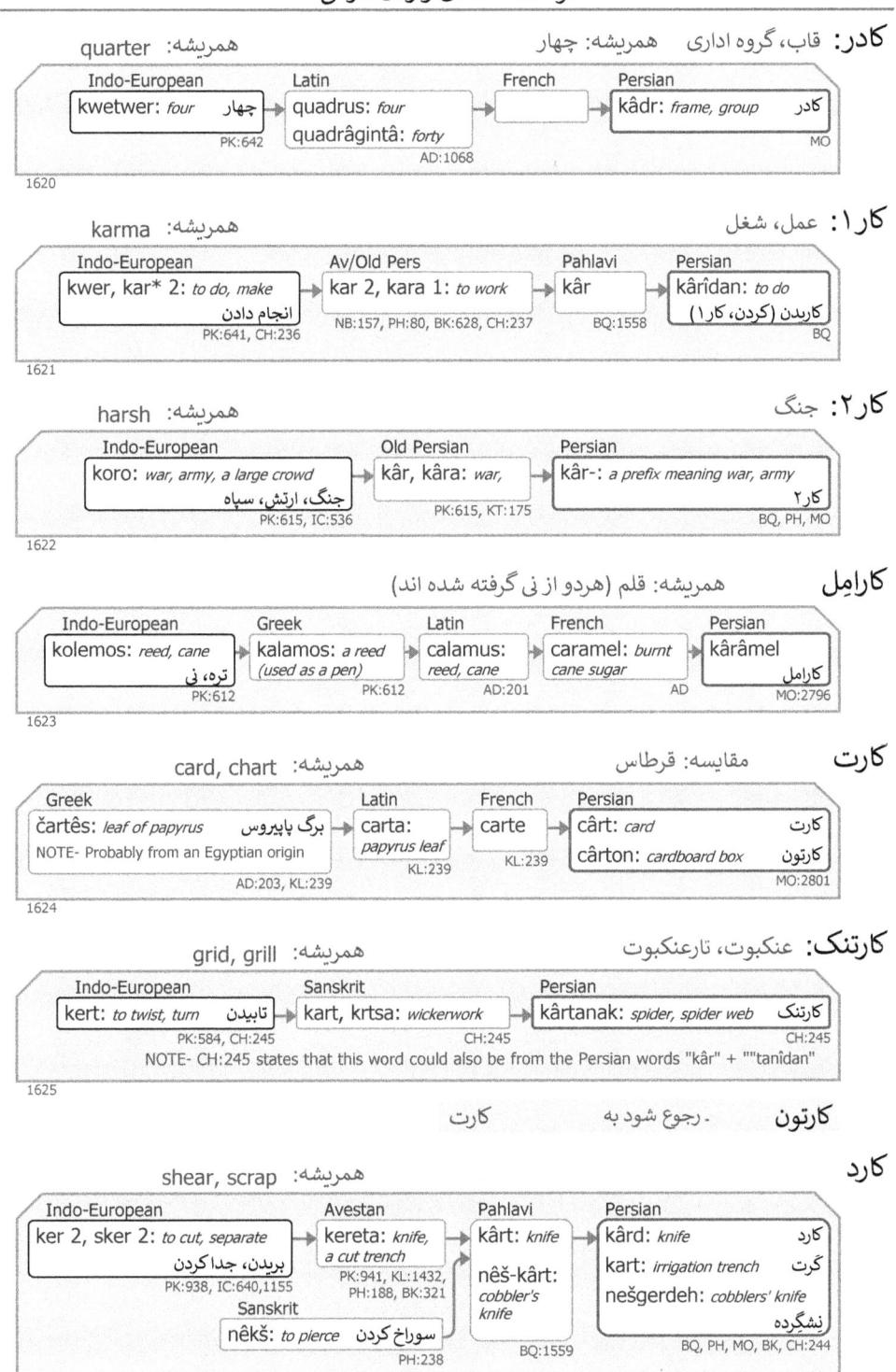

کادر: قاب، گروه اداری   همریشه: چهار   همریشه: quarter

Indo-European	Latin	French	Persian
kwetwer: four چهار	quadrus: four quadrâgintâ: forty		kâdr: frame, group کادر
PK:642	AD:1068		MO

1620

کار۱: عمل، شغل   همریشه: karma

Indo-European	Av/Old Pers	Pahlavi	Persian
kwer, kar* 2: to do, make انجام دادن	kar 2, kara 1: to work	kâr	kârîdan: to do کاریدن (کردن، کار۱)
PK:641, CH:236	NB:157, PH:80, BK:628, CH:237	BQ:1558	BQ

1621

کار۲: جنگ   همریشه: harsh

Indo-European	Old Persian	Persian
koro: war, army, a large crowd جنگ، ارتش، سپاه	kâr, kâra: war,	kâr-: a prefix meaning war, army کار۲
PK:615, IC:536	PK:615, KT:175	BQ, PH, MO

1622

کارامِل   همریشه: قلم (هردو از نی گرفته شده اند)

Indo-European	Greek	Latin	French	Persian
kolemos: reed, cane تره، نی	kalamos: a reed (used as a pen)	calamus: reed, cane	caramel: burnt cane sugar	kârâmel کارامل
PK:612	PK:612	AD:201	AD	MO:2796

1623

کارت   مقایسه: قرطاس   همریشه: card, chart

Greek	Latin	French	Persian
čartês: leaf of papyrus برگ پاپیروس NOTE- Probably from an Egyptian origin	carta: papyrus leaf	carte	cârt: card کارت cârton: cardboard box کارتون
AD:203, KL:239	KL:239	KL:239	MO:2801

1624

کارتنک: عنکبوت، تارعنکبوت   همریشه: grid, grill

Indo-European	Sanskrit	Persian
kert: to twist, turn تابیدن	kart, krtsa: wickerwork	kârtanak: spider, spider web کارتنک
PK:584, CH:245	CH:245	CH:245

NOTE- CH:245 states that this word could also be from the Persian words "kâr" + ""tanîdan"

1625

کارتون   . رجوع شود به   کارت

کارد   همریشه: shear, scrap

Indo-European	Avestan	Pahlavi	Persian
ker 2, sker 2: to cut, separate بریدن، جدا کردن PK:938, IC:640,1155	kereta: knife, a cut trench PK:941, KL:1432, PH:188, BK:321	kârt: knife nêš-kârt: cobbler's knife	kârd: knife کارد kart: irrigation trench گرت nešgerdeh: cobblers' knife نِشگِرده
	Sanskrit		
	nêkš: to pierce سوراخ کردن PH:238	BQ:1559	BQ, PH, MO, BK, CH:244

1626

کارزار: "میدان جنگ"   همریشه: cycle, hurry, harbor

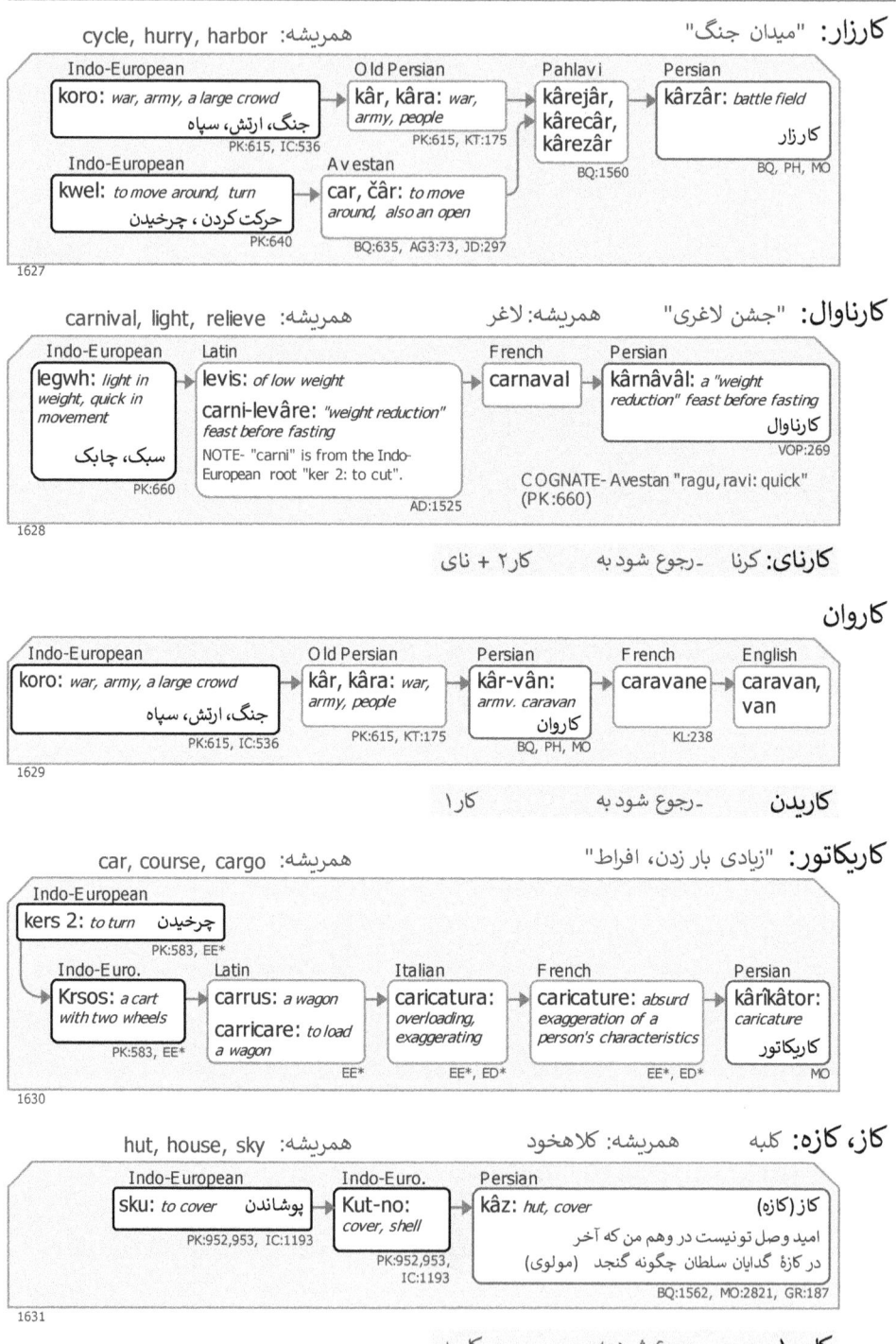

کارناوال: "جشن لاغری"   همریشه: لاغر   همریشه: carnival, light, relieve

COGNATE- Avestan "ragu, ravi: quick"
(PK:660)

کارنای: کرنا   -رجوع شود به   کار۲ + نای

کاروان

کاریدن   -رجوع شود به   کار۱

کاریکاتور: "زیادی بار زدن، افراط"   همریشه: car, course, cargo

کاز، کازه: کلبه   همریشه: کلاهخود   همریشه: hut, house, sky

کاس۱   -رجوع شود به   کاسه

کاس۲ : خوک، گراز

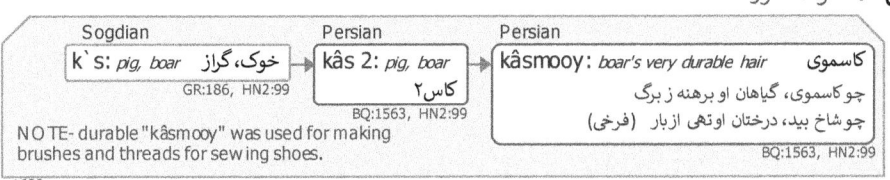

NOTE- durable "kâsmooy" was used for making brushes and threads for sewing shoes.

1632

کاست

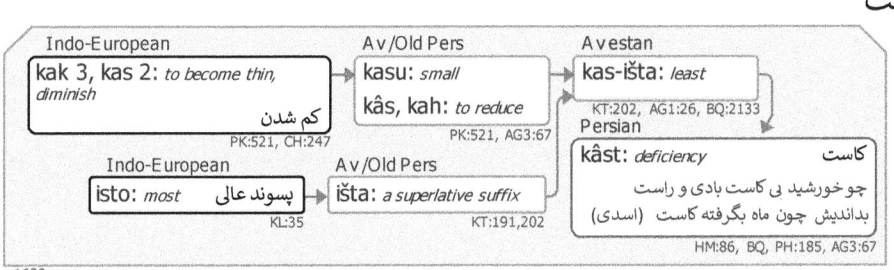

1633

کاستن

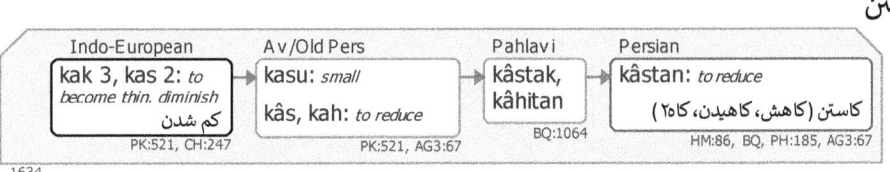

1634

کاسموی: موی گراز ـرجوع شود به   کاس۲

کاسه

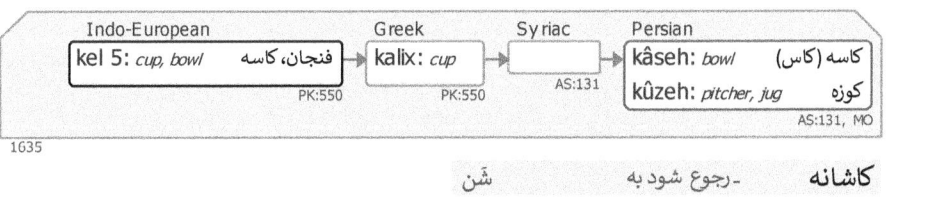

1635

کاشانه   ـرجوع شود به   شَن

کاشتن   همریشه: wheel, culture

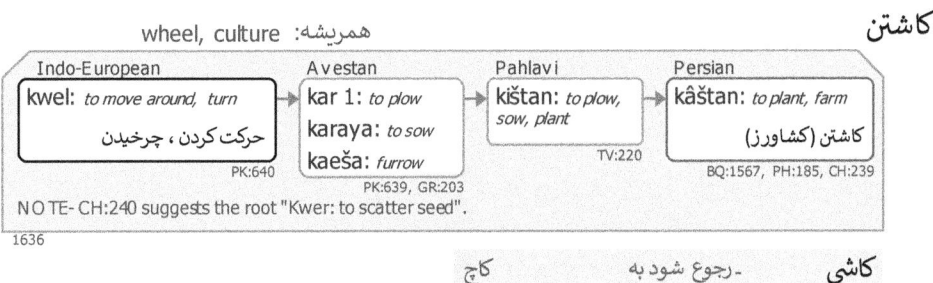

NOTE- CH:240 suggests the root "Kwer: to scatter seed".

1636

کاشی   ـرجوع شود به   کاچ

کاغذ

Turkish	Pahlavi	Persian
kagaz: *tree bark* پوست درخت	kâgad: *paper*	kâǧaz: *paper* کاغذ
LF:559	LF:559, AA:225	BQ:1569

NOTE- Chinese paper was imported into Iran (Samarghand) as early as 650 AD but the word "kâǧaz" was not borrowed from the Chinese word "Ku-Ĉih".

1637

کافتن - رجوع شود به شکافتن

کافه مقایسه: قهوه

Ethiopian	Arabic	Turkish	Italian	French	Persian
kaffa: *the plant or drink coming from kaffa, a district in southwestern ethiopia* گیاه یا دانه قهوه که از اتیوپی آمده	qahwah: *a drink from Ethiopian "Kaffa"*	qhve': *coffee*		cafe'	kâfeh: *coffee house* کافه
	KL:309	AD:258			MO:2851

1638

کافور

Sanskrit	Pahlavi	Persian
karpurah: *camphor tree* درخت کافور	kâpûr: *camphor*	kâfûr: *camphor* کافور
KL:229	BR:356, BQ:1571	BQ:1571

1639

کاک همریشه: cake

Indo-European	Persian	Arabic	Persian
kak 2: *a round object (loaf), cake* گرد، قرص (نان)	kâk: *dry hard bread, a dry cookie* کاک	ka`k: *a dry bread*	ka`k: *dry bread* کعک
PK:349, BQ:1572	BQ:1572	AA:233	BQ:1572

Note- This word could be of an Egyptian origin

1640

کال: زمین شکافته، کانال

Indo-European	Persian
kard*: *keep down, subside* پایین نگه داشتن، فروکش کردن	kal: *ditch, ravine, canal* کال
CH:239	CH:239

این لغت یا متروک شده و یا استفاده از آن بسیار محدود میباشد.

1641

کالا

Indo-European	Greek	Pahlavi	Persian
ped, pod: *foot* پا PK:790, AP:148	kalo-podion: *wooden foot used as a shoe mold, shape* kalo-podein: *wooden foot, mold*	kal-pâd: *fabrication mold, shape, body* NOTE- IC: derives it from Avestan "kehrp: flesh", from Indo-European "Kwrp, Kwerp: shape, body"	kâlâ: *manufactured (molded) goods* کالا
Indo-European kû 1: *to burn (also firewood)* سوزاندن (هیزم) PK:595	AD:1365, KL, PK:595,790	BQ:1075, 1095	MO:2858, IC:1047

1642

کالب

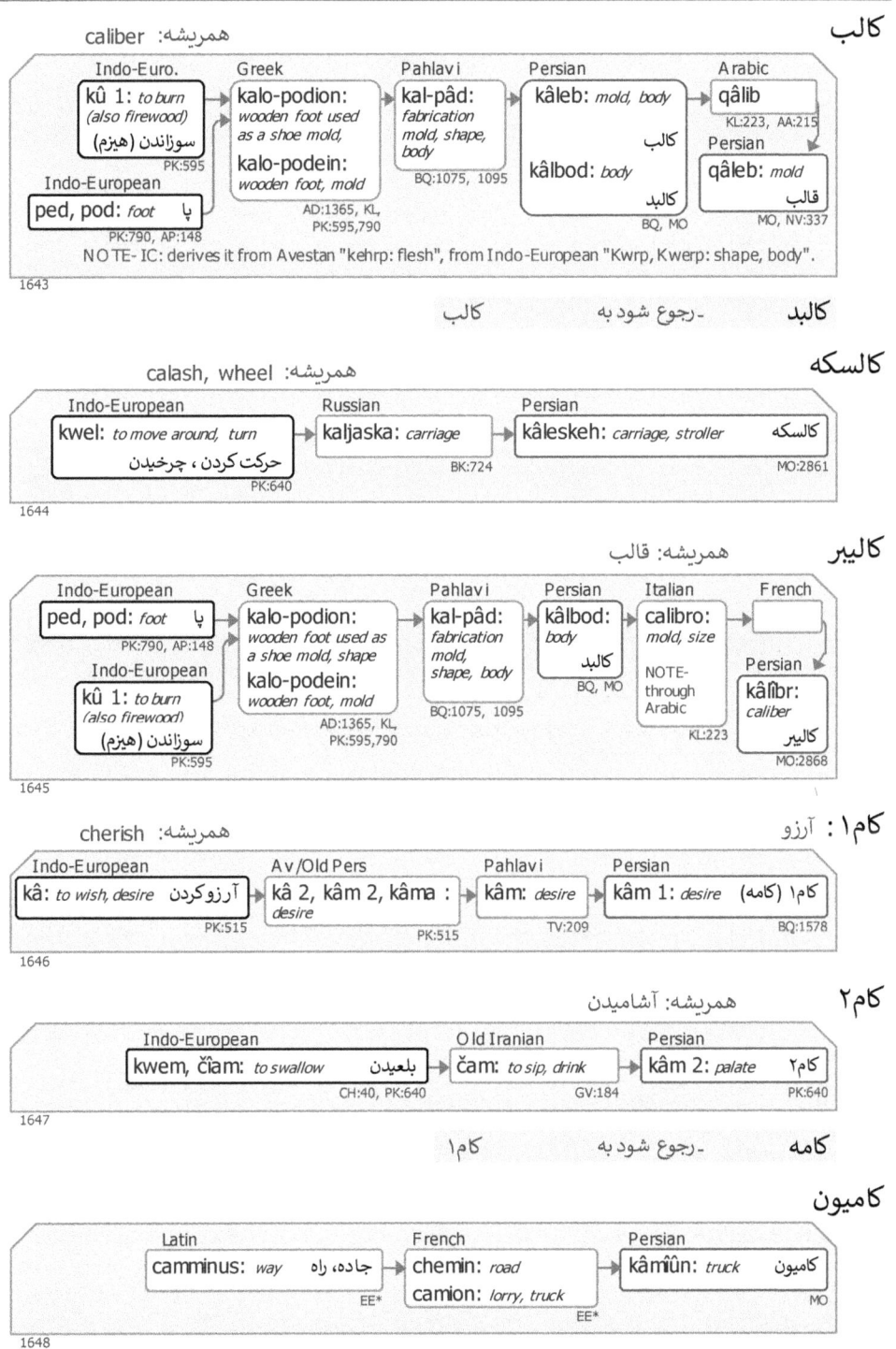

همریشه: caliber

Indo-Euro.	Greek	Pahlavi	Persian	Arabic
kû 1: to burn (also firewood) سوزاندن (هیزم) PK:595	kalo-podion: wooden foot used as a shoe mold, kalo-podein: wooden foot, mold	kal-pâd: fabrication mold, shape, body BQ:1075, 1095	kâleb: mold, body کالب kâlbod: body کالبد	qâlib KL:223, AA:215
Indo-European ped, pod: foot پا PK:790, AP:148	AD:1365, KL, PK:595,790		BQ, MO	Persian qâleb: mold قالب MO, NV:337

NOTE- IC: derives it from Avestan "kehrp: flesh", from Indo-European "Kwrp, Kwerp: shape, body".

1643

کالبد ‏-رجوع شود به ‏کالب

کالسکه

همریشه: calash, wheel

Indo-European	Russian	Persian
kwel: to move around, turn حرکت کردن ، چرخیدن PK:640	kaljaska: carriage BK:724	kâleskeh: carriage, stroller کالسکه MO:2861

1644

کالیبر

همریشه: قالب

Indo-European	Greek	Pahlavi	Persian	Italian	French
ped, pod: foot پا PK:790, AP:148	kalo-podion: wooden foot used as a shoe mold, shape	kal-pâd: fabrication mold, shape, body	kâlbod: body کالبد	calibro: mold, size NOTE- through Arabic	
Indo-European kû 1: to burn (also firewood) سوزاندن (هیزم) PK:595	kalo-podein: wooden foot, mold AD:1365, KL, PK:595,790	BQ:1075, 1095	BQ, MO	KL:223	Persian kâlîbr: caliber کالیبر MO:2868

1645

کام۱: آرزو

همریشه: cherish

Indo-European	Av/Old Pers	Pahlavi	Persian
kâ: to wish, desire آرزوکردن PK:515	kâ 2, kâm 2, kâma : desire PK:515	kâm: desire TV:209	kâm 1: desire (کامه) کام۱ BQ:1578

1646

کام۲

همریشه: آشامیدن

Indo-European	Old Iranian	Persian
kwem, čiam: to swallow بلعیدن CH:40, PK:640	čam: to sip, drink GV:184	kâm 2: palate کام۲ PK:640

1647

کامه ‏-رجوع شود به ‏کام۱

کامیون

Latin	French	Persian
camminus: way جاده، راه EE*	chemin: road camion: lorry, truck EE*	kâmîûn: truck کامیون MO

1648

کان ‏-رجوع شود به ‏کندن

294

کاناپه: "تخت مجهز به پشه بند"

همریشه: canopy

Greek	Greek	Latin	French	Persian
kônôs: mosquito پشه	kôkôpein: Egyptian couch with mosquito nets	canopeum: mosquito net	canape': "bed-curtain", couch	kânâpeh: couch, originally a "couch with mosquito nets" کاناپه
ED*, EE*	ED*, EE*	ED*, EE*	ED*, EE*	MO

1649

کانال

همریشه: قنات

Indo-European	Av /Old Pers	Arabic	Latin	French	Persian
gwhen 3, kan*: to dig and fill کندن و پُرکردن	kan 1, xan, gan: to dig, pile up, build	qanah: reed, cane qanat: underground water	canalis: water pipe		kânâl: canal, channel کانال
CH:232, PK491	PK:491, PH:194, BT:583	KL:232, ES:539,545	KL		MO

NOTE- These words also reached the Greek and Latin languages through Semitic languages

1650

کاندید

همریشه: قندیل

Indo-European	Latin	French	Persian
kand: to shine, to be white درخشیدن، سفید بودن	candidus: glowing white candidâtus: candidate (due to their white toga)	candidat	kândîd: candidate کاندید (کاندیدا)
PK:526	KL:231		MO:2874

1651

کانون۱ : بخاری، آتشدان

Akkadian	Syriac	Arabic	Persian
kânûnu: fireplace آتشدان			kânûn: fireplace کانون۱ چو گیرد آتش خشم تو بالا نیابد از دو عالم نیم کانون (انوری)
MO:2875, BQ:1580	MO:2875	MO:2875	BQ:1580, MO:2875

1652

کاوُش	قانون	ـرجوع شود به	کانون۲
کَی۳		ـرجوع شود به	کاووس

کاویدن

مقایسه: کافتن   همریشه: scar, scrap, shear

Indo-European	Avestan	Persian
ker 2, sker 2: to cut, separate بریدن، جدا کردن	kaf, kâf: to break	kâvîdan: to break open, split کاویدن (کفتن، کاوُش)
PK:938, IC:640,1155	PK:919,930, GR:61, CH:342	BQ, PH:175

1653

کاه۱

Indo-European	Sanskrit	Pahlavi	Persian
kuâtos: straw کاه	Kâča: straw	kah: straw	kâh: straw کاه۱
IC:1021	PH:186	PH:186	BQ:1583, IC:1021

1654

کاهش	کاستن	ـرجوع شود به	کاه۲
کاستن		ـرجوع شود به	کاهیدن

گَبَر: نوعی گیاه

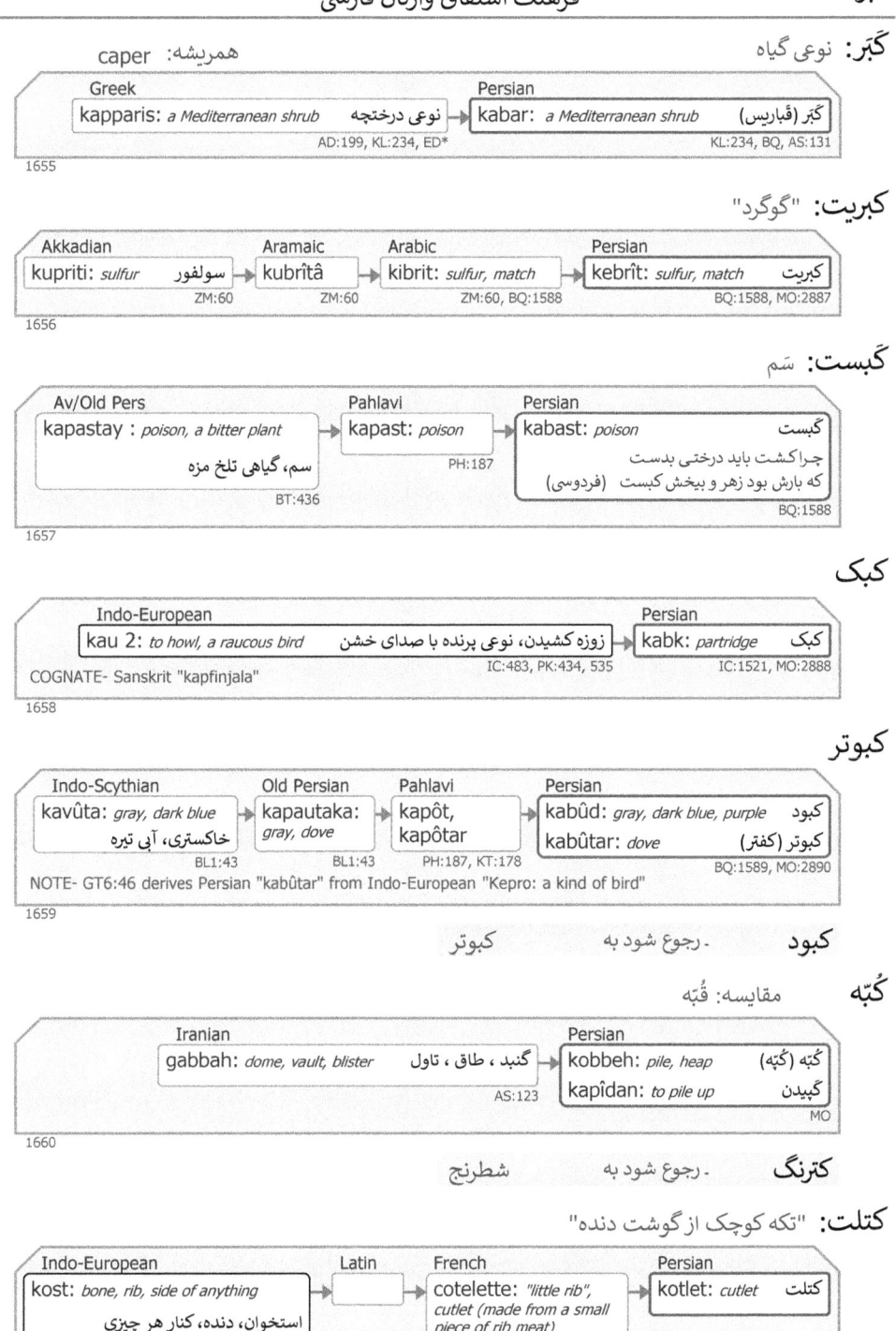

همریشه: caper

Greek	Persian
kapparis: *a Mediterranean shrub* نوعی درختچه	kabar: *a Mediterranean shrub* گَبَر (قَباریس)
AD:199, KL:234, ED*	KL:234, BQ, AS:131

1655

کبریت: "گوگرد"

Akkadian	Aramaic	Arabic	Persian
kupriti: *sulfur* سولفور	kubrîtâ	kibrit: *sulfur, match*	kebrît: *sulfur, match* کبریت
ZM:60	ZM:60	ZM:60, BQ:1588	BQ:1588, MO:2887

1656

گَبست: سَم

Av/Old Pers	Pahlavi	Persian
kapastay : *poison, a bitter plant*	kapast: *poison*	kabast: *poison* گبست
سم، گیاهی تلخ مزه	PH:187	چراکشت باید درختی بدست
BT:436		که بارش بود زهر و بیخش گبست (فردوسی)
		BQ:1588

1657

کبک

Indo-European	Persian
kau 2: *to howl, a raucous bird* زوزه کشیدن، نوعی پرنده با صدای خشن	kabk: *partridge* کبک
IC:483, PK:434, 535	IC:1521, MO:2888

COGNATE- Sanskrit "kapfinjala"

1658

کبوتر

Indo-Scythian	Old Persian	Pahlavi	Persian
kavûta: *gray, dark blue* خاکستری، آبی تیره	kapautaka: *gray, dove*	kapôt, kapôtar	kabûd: *gray, dark blue, purple* کبود / kabûtar: *dove* کبوتر (کفتر)
BL1:43	BL1:43	PH:187, KT:178	BQ:1589, MO:2890

NOTE- GT6:46 derives Persian "kabûtar" from Indo-European "Kepro: a kind of bird"

1659

کبود ۰رجوع شود به کبوتر

کُبّه مقایسه: قُبّه

Iranian	Persian
gabbah: *dome, vault, blister* گنبد ، طاق ، تاول	kobbeh: *pile, heap* کُبّه (گُبّه) / kapîdan: *to pile up* گبیدن
AS:123	MO

1660

کترنگ ۰رجوع شود به شطرنج

کتلت: "تکه کوچک از گوشت دنده"

Indo-European	Latin	French	Persian
kost: *bone, rib, side of anything* استخوان، دنده، کنار هر چیزی		cotelette: *"little rib"*, cutlet (made from a small piece of rib meat)	kotlet: *cutlet* کتلت
PK:616		AD:327, ED*	

1661

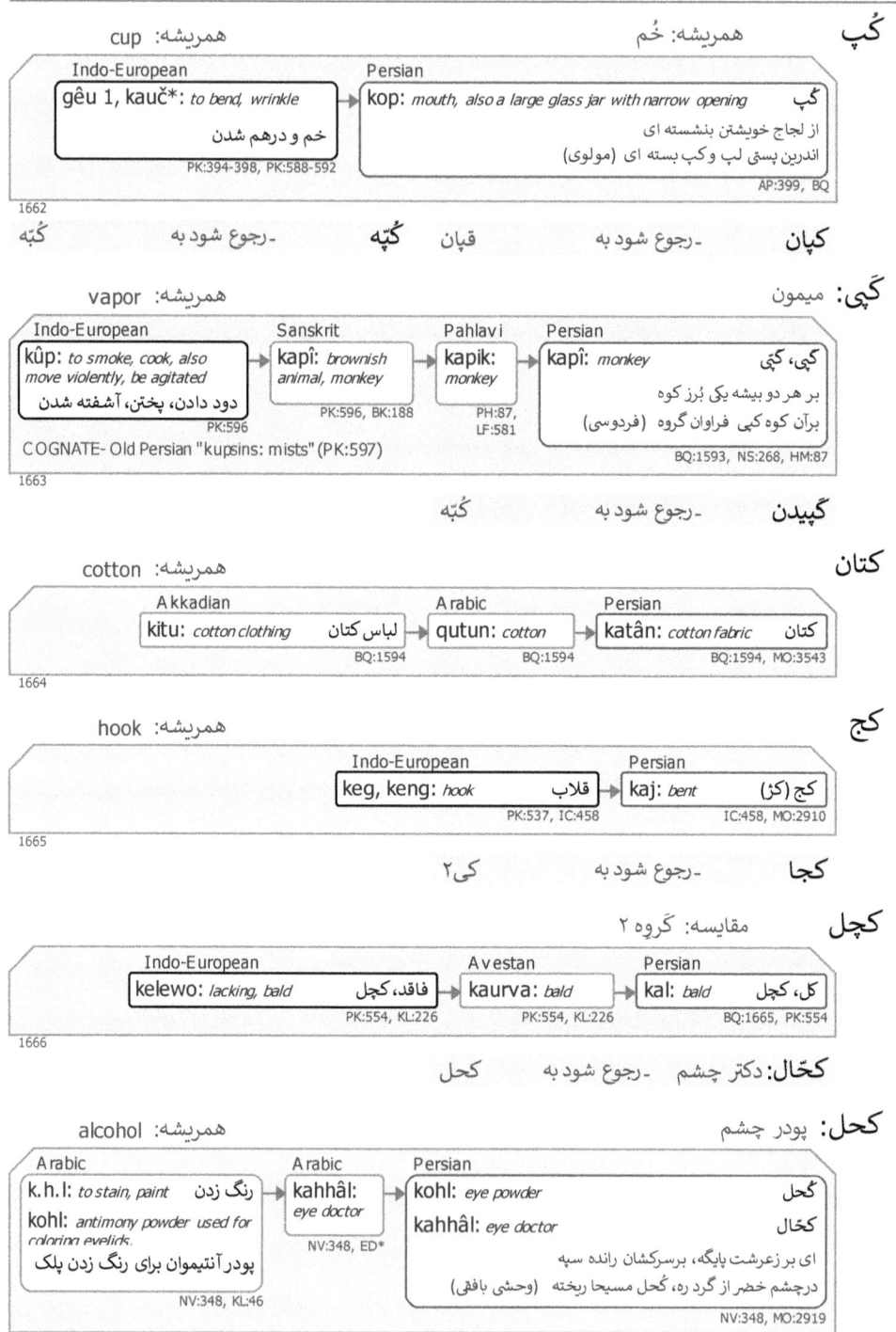

همریشه: خُم   کُپ

کُپ

همریشه: cup

Indo-European
gêu 1, kauč*: *to bend, wrinkle*

خم و درهم شدن

PK:394-398, PK:588-592

Persian
kop: *mouth, also a large glass jar with narrow opening*   کُپ

از لجاج خویشتن‌بنشسته ای
اندرین پستی لب و کپ بسته ای (مولوی)

AP:399, BQ

1662

کپان   -رجوع شود به   قپان   **کُپّه**   -رجوع شود به   کُبّه

گَپی: میمون

همریشه: vapor

Indo-European
kûp: *to smoke, cook, also move violently, be agitated*

دود دادن، پختن، آشفته شدن

PK:596

Sanskrit
kapî: *brownish animal, monkey*

PK:596, BK:188

Pahlavi
kapik: *monkey*

PH:87, LF:581

Persian
kapî: *monkey*   گَپی، کَپی

بر هر دو بیشه یکی بُرز کوه
برآن کوه کپی فراوان گروه (فردوسی)

BQ:1593, NS:268, HM:87

COGNATE- Old Persian "kupsins: mists" (PK:597)

1663

گَپیدن   -رجوع شود به   کُبّه

کتان

همریشه: cotton

Akkadian
kitu: *cotton clothing*   لباس کتان

BQ:1594

Arabic
qutun: *cotton*

BQ:1594

Persian
katân: *cotton fabric*   کتان

BQ:1594, MO:3543

1664

کج

همریشه: hook

Indo-European
keg, keng: *hook*   قلاب

PK:537, IC:458

Persian
kaj: *bent*   (کژ) کج

IC:458, MO:2910

1665

کجا   -رجوع شود به   کی۲

کچل   مقایسه: گروه ۲

Indo-European
kelewo: *lacking, bald*   فاقد، کچل

PK:554, KL:226

Avestan
kaurva: *bald*

PK:554, KL:226

Persian
kal: *bald*   کل، کچل

BQ:1665, PK:554

1666

کحّال: دکتر چشم   -رجوع شود به   کحل

کحل: پودر چشم

همریشه: alcohol

Arabic
k.h.l: *to stain, paint*   رنگ زدن
kohl: *antimony powder used for coloring eyelids.*

پودر آنتیموان برای رنگ زدن پلک

NV:348, KL:46

Arabic
kahhâl: *eye doctor*

NV:348, ED*

Persian
kohl: *eye powder*   کُحل
kahhâl: *eye doctor*   کحّال

ای بر زعرشت پایگه، برسرکشان رانده سپه
درچشم خضر از گرد ره، کُحل مسیحا ریخته (وحشی بافقی)

NV:348, MO:2919

1667

کد . . : پیشوند به معنی خانه، محل

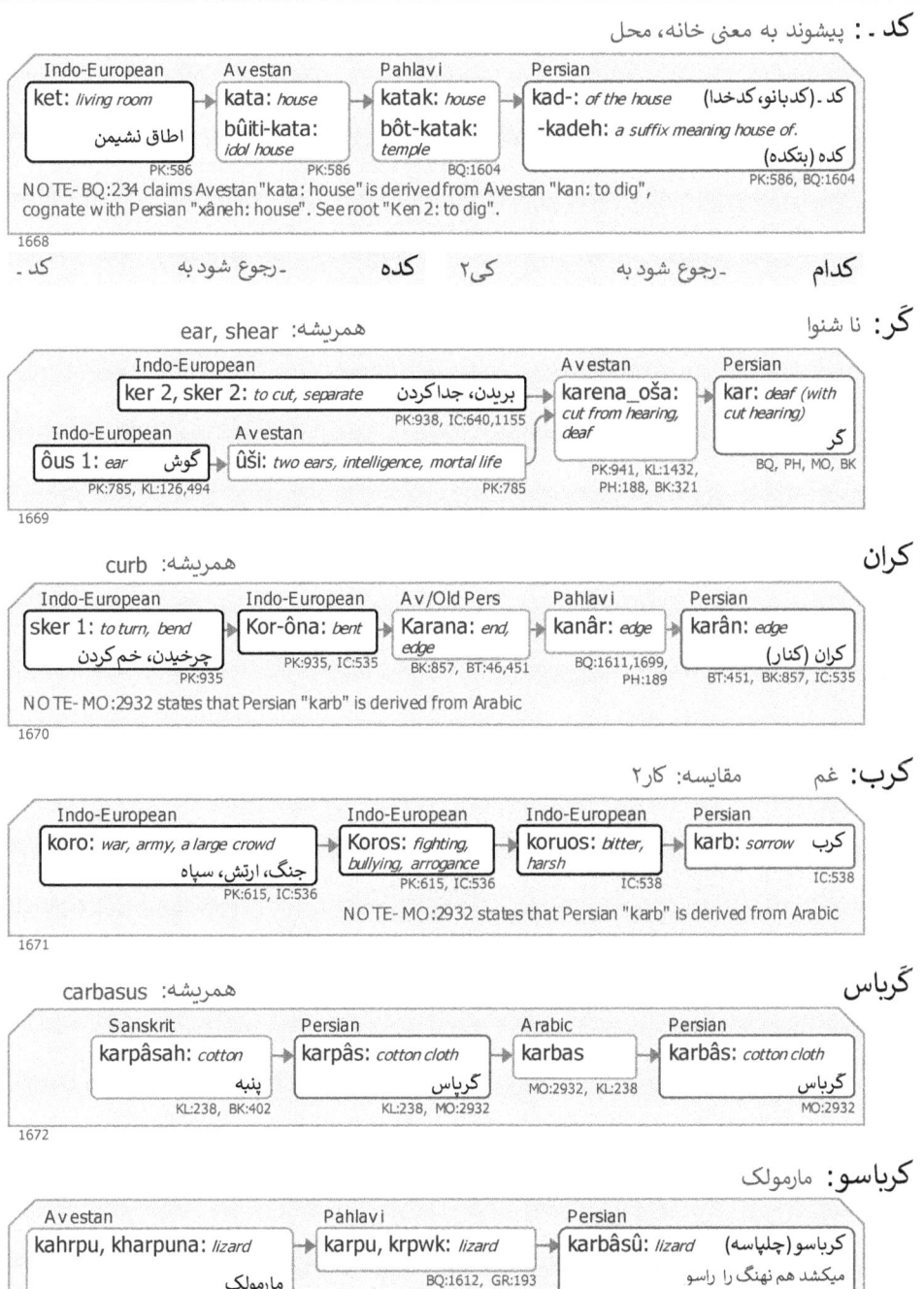

کد . .

Indo-European	Avestan	Pahlavi	Persian
ket: *living room* اطاق نشیمن	kata: *house* bûiti-kata: *idol house*	katak: *house* bôt-katak: *temple*	kad-: *of the house* کد ـ (کدبانو، کدخدا) -kadeh: *a suffix meaning house of.* کده (بتکده)
PK:586	PK:586	BQ:1604	PK:586, BQ:1604

NOTE- BQ:234 claims Avestan "kata: house" is derived from Avestan "kan: to dig", cognate with Persian "xâneh: house". See root "Ken 2: to dig".

1668

کدام ـرجوع شود به کی۲ **کده** ـرجوع شود به کد ـ

گَر: نا شنوا همریشه: ear, shear

	Indo-European		Avestan	Persian
	ker 2, sker 2: *to cut, separate* بریدن، جدا کردن PK:938, IC:640,1155		karena_oša: *cut from hearing, deaf*	kar: *deaf (with cut hearing)* گر
Indo-European		Avestan		BQ, PH, MO, BK
ôus 1: *ear* گوش PK:785, KL:126,494		ûši: *two ears, intelligence, mortal life* PK:785	PK:941, KL:1432, PH:188, BK:321	

1669

کران همریشه: curb

Indo-European	Indo-European	Av/Old Pers	Pahlavi	Persian
sker 1: *to turn, bend* چرخیدن، خم کردن PK:935	Kor-ôna: *bent* PK:935, IC:535	Karana: *end, edge* BK:857, BT:46,451	kanâr: *edge* BQ:1611,1699, PH:189	karân: *edge* کران (کنار) BT:451, BK:857, IC:535

NOTE- MO:2932 states that Persian "karb" is derived from Arabic

1670

کرب: غم مقایسه: کار۲

Indo-European	Indo-European	Indo-European	Persian
koro: *war, army, a large crowd* جنگ، ارتش، سپاه PK:615, IC:536	Koros: *fighting, bullying, arrogance* PK:615, IC:536	koruos: *bitter, harsh* IC:538	karb: *sorrow* کرب IC:538

NOTE- MO:2932 states that Persian "karb" is derived from Arabic

1671

گرباس همریشه: carbasus

Sanskrit	Persian	Arabic	Persian
karpâsah: *cotton* پنبه KL:238, BK:402	karpâs: *cotton cloth* کرپاس KL:238, MO:2932	karbas MO:2932, KL:238	karbâs: *cotton cloth* گرباس MO:2932

1672

کرباسو: مارمولک

Avestan	Pahlavi	Persian
kahrpu, kharpuna: *lizard* مارمولک BQ:1612, GR:193	karpu, krpwk: *lizard* BQ:1612, GR:193	karbâsû: *lizard* کرباسو (چلپاسه) میکشد هم نهنگ را راسو مرگ عقرب بود ز کرباسو (آذری طوسی) MO:2933

1673

گرت ـرجوع شود به کارد **کردن** ـرجوع شود به کار۱

گَرس: چرک روی جراحت که بسته و سخت شده باشد

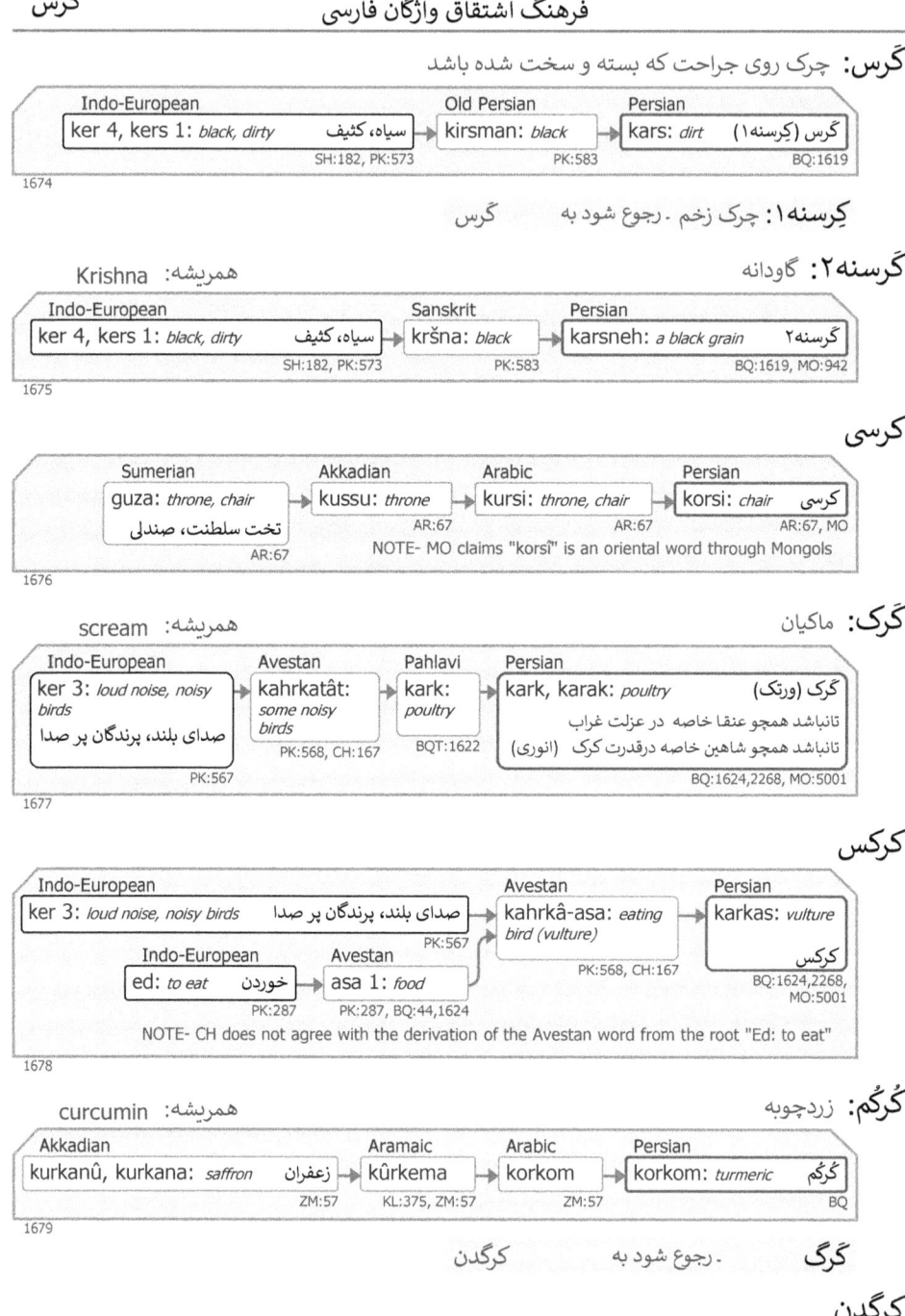

1674

Indo-European	Old Persian	Persian
ker 4, kers 1: *black, dirty* سیاه، کثیف	kirsman: *black*	kars: *dirt* گرس (کِرسنه۱)
SH:182, PK:573	PK:583	BQ:1619

کِرسنه۱: چرک زخم ۔ رجوع شود به   گرس

گَرسنه۲: گاودانه

همریشه: Krishna

Indo-European	Sanskrit	Persian
ker 4, kers 1: *black, dirty* سیاه، کثیف	kršna: *black*	karsneh: *a black grain* گرسنه۲
SH:182, PK:573	PK:583	BQ:1619, MO:942

1675

کرسی

Sumerian	Akkadian	Arabic	Persian
guza: *throne, chair* تخت سلطنت، صندلی	kussu: *throne*	kursi: *throne, chair*	korsi: *chair* کرسی
AR:67	AR:67	AR:67	AR:67, MO

NOTE- MO claims "korsî" is an oriental word through Mongols

1676

گَرک: ماکیان

همریشه: scream

Indo-European	Avestan	Pahlavi	Persian
ker 3: *loud noise, noisy birds* صدای بلند، پرندگان پر صدا	kahrkatât: *some noisy birds*	kark: *poultry*	kark, karak: *poultry* گرک (ورتک) تانباشد همچو عنقا خاصه در عزلت غراب تانباشد همچو شاهین خاصه درقدرت کرک (انوری)
PK:567	PK:568, CH:167	BQT:1622	BQ:1624,2268, MO:5001

1677

کرکس

Indo-European	Avestan	Persian
ker 3: *loud noise, noisy birds* صدای بلند، پرندگان پر صدا PK:567	kahrkâ-asa: *eating bird (vulture)* PK:568, CH:167	karkas: *vulture* کرکس BQ:1624,2268, MO:5001

Indo-European	Avestan
ed: *to eat* خوردن PK:287	asa 1: *food* PK:287, BQ:44,1624

NOTE- CH does not agree with the derivation of the Avestan word from the root "Ed: to eat"

1678

کُرکُم: زردچوبه

همریشه: curcumin

Akkadian	Aramaic	Arabic	Persian
kurkanû, kurkana: *saffron* زعفران	kûrkema	korkom	korkom: *turmeric* کُرکُم
ZM:57	KL:375, ZM:57	ZM:57	BQ

1679

گَرگ   ۔ رجوع شود به   کرگدن

کرگدن

Akkadian	Syriac	Arabic	Persian
kurkizannu: *rhinoceros* کرگدن	karkedânâ	karkadan	karg, kargadan: *rhinoceros* گرگ، کرگدن
ZM:51	ZM:51	ZM:51	BQ:1622, NS:270

1680

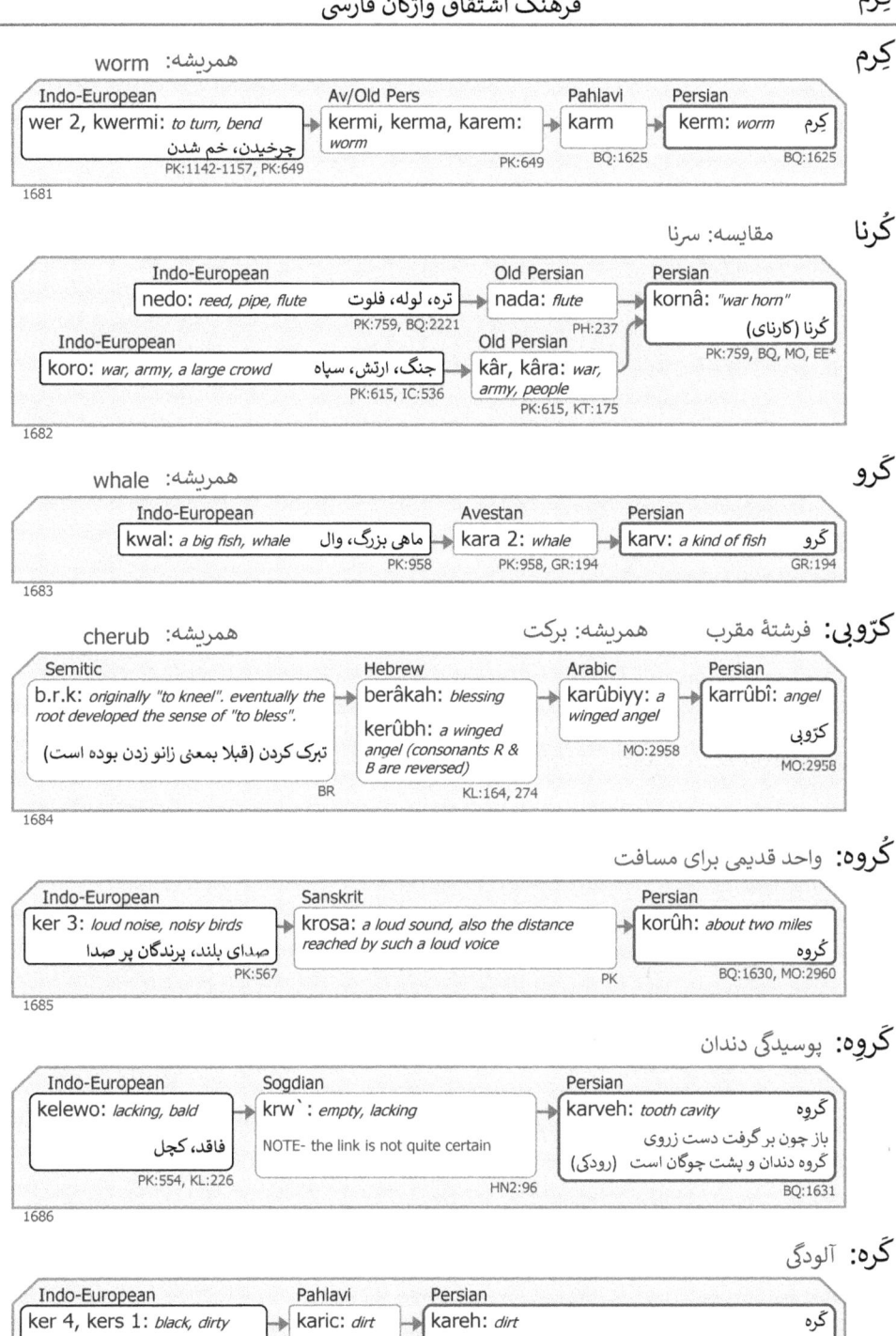

کِرم

همریشه: worm

Indo-European	Av/Old Pers	Pahlavi	Persian
wer 2, kwermi: *to turn, bend* چرخیدن، خم شدن PK:1142-1157, PK:649	kermi, kerma, karem: *worm* PK:649	karm BQ:1625	kerm: *worm* کِرم BQ:1625

1681

کُرنا

مقایسه: سرنا

Indo-European	Old Persian	Persian
nedo: *reed, pipe, flute* تره، لوله، فلوت PK:759, BQ:2221	nada: *flute* PH:237	kornâ: *"war horn"* کُرنا (کارنای) PK:759, BQ, MO, EE*
koro: *war, army, a large crowd* جنگ، ارتش، سپاه PK:615, IC:536	kâr, kâra: *war, army, people* PK:615, KT:175	

1682

گَرو

همریشه: whale

Indo-European	Avestan	Persian
kwal: *a big fish, whale* ماهی بزرگ، وال PK:958	kara 2: *whale* PK:958, GR:194	karv: *a kind of fish* گَرو GR:194

1683

کَرّوبی: فرشتهٔ مقرب   همریشه: برکت   همریشه: cherub

Semitic	Hebrew	Arabic	Persian
b.r.k: *originally "to kneel". eventually the root developed the sense of "to bless".* تبرک کردن (قبلا بمعنی زانو زدن بوده است) BR	berâkah: *blessing* kerûbh: *a winged angel (consonants R & B are reversed)* KL:164, 274	karûbiyy: *a winged angel* MO:2958	karrûbî: *angel* کَروبی MO:2958

1684

گُروه: واحد قدیمی برای مسافت

Indo-European	Sanskrit	Persian
ker 3: *loud noise, noisy birds* صدای بلند، پرندگان پر صدا PK:567	krosa: *a loud sound, also the distance reached by such a loud voice* PK	korûh: *about two miles* گُروه BQ:1630, MO:2960

1685

گَرْوِه: پوسیدگی دندان

Indo-European	Sogdian	Persian
kelewo: *lacking, bald* فاقد، کچل PK:554, KL:226	krw`: *empty, lacking* NOTE- the link is not quite certain HN2:96	karveh: *tooth cavity* گَروه باز چون بر گرفت دست زروی گروه دندان و پشت چوگان است (رودکی) BQ:1631

1686

گَره: آلودگی

Indo-European	Pahlavi	Persian
ker 4, kers 1: *black, dirty* سیاه، کثیف SH:182, PK:573	karic: *dirt* PK:573	kareh: *dirt* گَره چون دست و پای پاک نبینمت جان و دل این هردو پاک بینم و آن هردو با گره (ناصرخسرو) PK:573, BQ, MO

1687

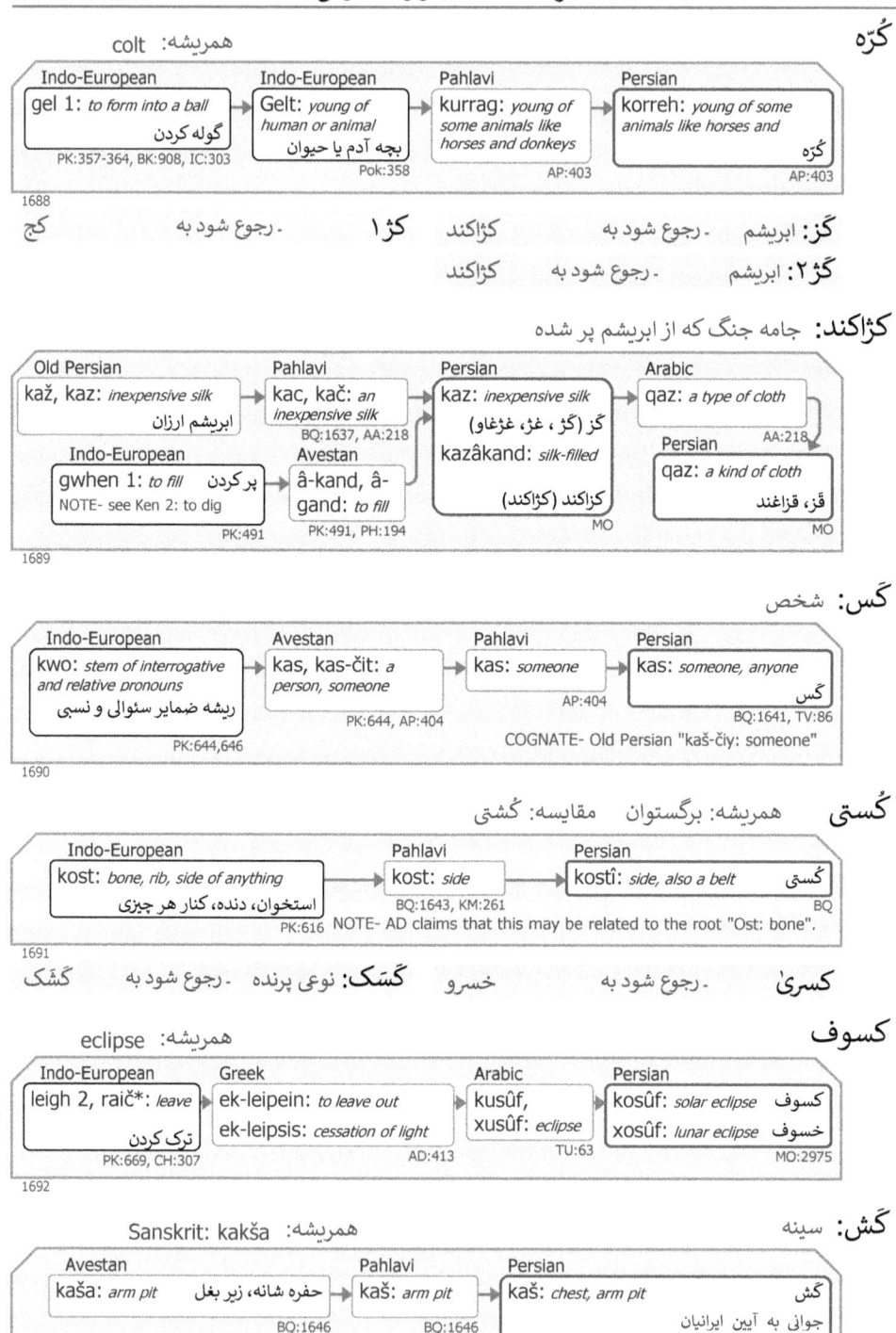

گُرّه

همریشه: colt

Indo-European	Indo-European	Pahlavi	Persian
gel 1: *to form into a ball* گوله کردن PK:357-364, BK:908, IC:303	Gelt: *young of human or animal* بچه آدم یا حیوان Pok:358	kurrag: *young of some animals like horses and donkeys* AP:403	korreh: *young of some animals like horses and* گُرّه AP:403

1688

گَژ ۱   رجوع شود به   گِژاکند   **گَز:** ابریشم   رجوع شود به   کج

گَژ ۲: ابریشم   رجوع شود به   گِژاکند

گِژاکند: جامه جنگ که از ابریشم پر شده

Old Persian	Pahlavi	Persian	Arabic
kaž, kaz: *inexpensive silk* ابریشم ارزان	kac, kač: *an inexpensive silk* BQ:1637, AA:218	kaz: *inexpensive silk* گز (گژ ، غژ، غژغاو) kazâkand: *silk-filled* کزاکند (کژاکند) MO	qaz: *a type of cloth* AA:218
Indo-European gwhen 1: *to fill* پر کردن NOTE- see Ken 2: to dig PK:491	**Avestan** â-kand, â-gand: *to fill* PK:491, PH:194		**Persian** qaz: *a kind of cloth* قَز، قزاغند MO

1689

گَس: شخص

Indo-European	Avestan	Pahlavi	Persian
kwo: *stem of interrogative and relative pronouns* ریشه ضمایر سئوالی و نسبی PK:644,646	kas, kas-čit: *a person, someone* PK:644, AP:404	kas: *someone* AP:404	kas: *someone, anyone* گَس BQ:1641, TV:86

COGNATE- Old Persian "kaš-čiy: someone"

1690

گُستی   همریشه: برگستوان   مقایسه: گُشتی

Indo-European	Pahlavi	Persian
kost: *bone, rib, side of anything* استخوان، دنده، کنار هر چیزی PK:616	kost: *side* BQ:1643, KM:261	kostî: *side, also a belt* گُستی BQ

NOTE- AD claims that this may be related to the root "Ost: bone".

1691

کَسریٰ   رجوع شود به   خسرو   **گَسَک:** نوعی پرنده   رجوع شود به   گَشک

کسوف

همریشه: eclipse

Indo-European	Greek	Arabic	Persian
leigh 2, raič*: *leave* ترک کردن PK:669, CH:307	ek-leipein: *to leave out* ek-leipsis: *cessation of light* AD:413	kusûf, xusûf: *eclipse* TU:63	kosûf: *solar eclipse* کسوف xosûf: *lunar eclipse* خسوف MO:2975

1692

گَش: سینه   همریشه: Sanskrit: kakša

Avestan	Pahlavi	Persian
kaša: *arm pit* حفره شانه، زیر بغل BQ:1646	kaš: *arm pit* BQ:1646	kaš: *chest, arm pit* گَش جوانی به آیین ایرانیان گشاده گش و تنگ بسته میان (اسدی طوسی) BQ:1646

1693

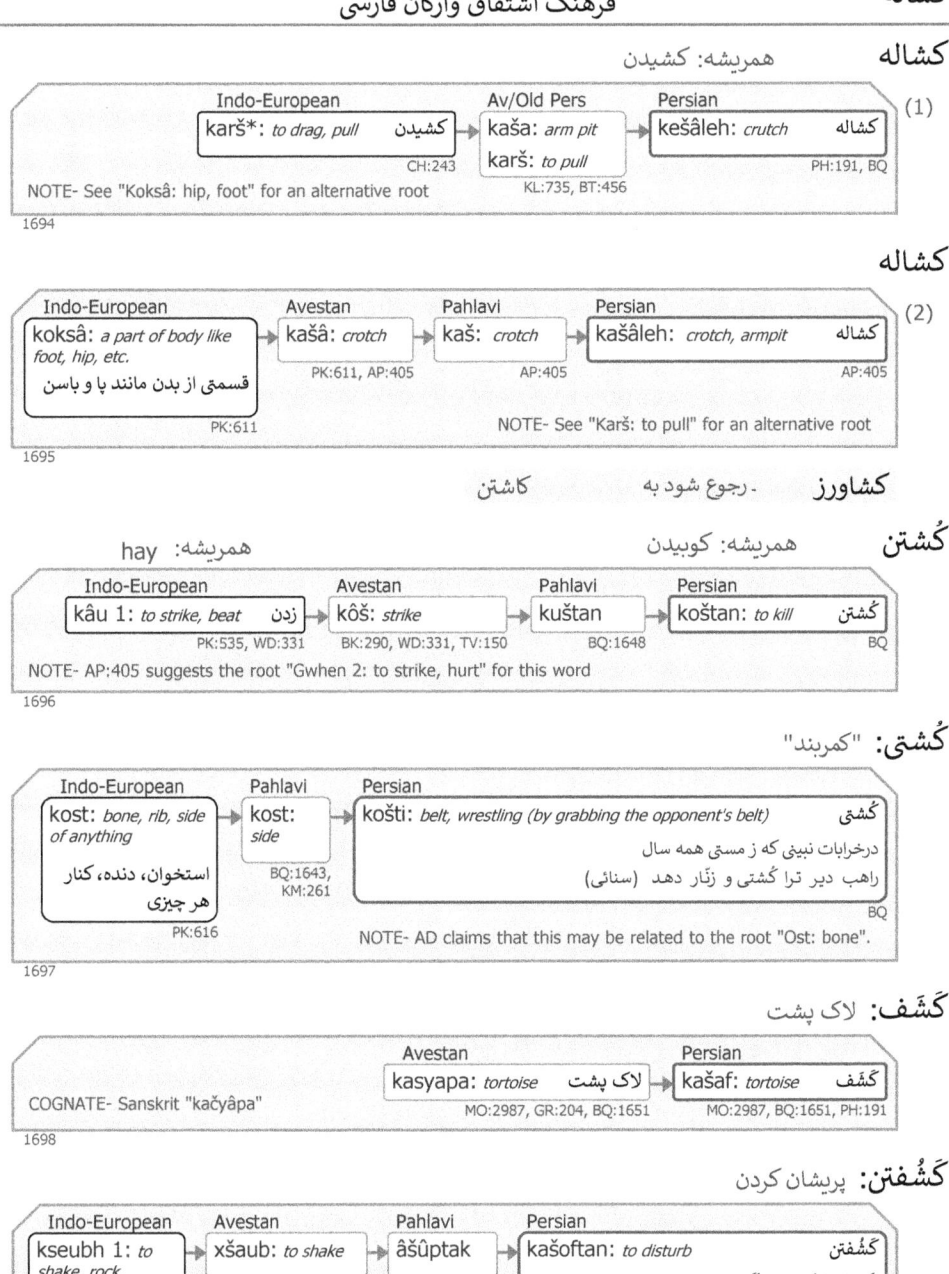

کشاله   همریشه: کشیدن

(1)

Indo-European	Av/Old Pers	Persian
karš*: *to drag, pull* کشیدن	kaša: *arm pit* karš: *to pull*	kešâleh: *crutch* کشاله
CH:243	KL:735, BT:456	PH:191, BQ

NOTE- See "Koksâ: hip, foot" for an alternative root

1694

کشاله

(2)

Indo-European	Avestan	Pahlavi	Persian
koksâ: *a part of body like foot, hip, etc.* قسمتی از بدن مانند پا و باسن	kašâ: *crotch*	kaš: *crotch*	kašâleh: *crotch, armpit* کشاله
PK:611	PK:611, AP:405	AP:405	AP:405

NOTE- See "Karš: to pull" for an alternative root

1695

کشاورز   ـ رجوع شود به   کاشتن

کُشتن   همریشه: کوبیدن   همریشه: hay

Indo-European	Avestan	Pahlavi	Persian
kâu 1: *to strike, beat* زدن	kôš: *strike*	kuštan	koštan: *to kill* کشتن
PK:535, WD:331	BK:290, WD:331, TV:150	BQ:1648	BQ

NOTE- AP:405 suggests the root "Gwhen 2: to strike, hurt" for this word

1696

کُشتی: "کمربند"

Indo-European	Pahlavi	Persian
kost: *bone, rib, side of anything* استخوان، دنده، کنار هر چیزی	kost: *side*	košti: *belt, wrestling (by grabbing the opponent's belt)* کشتی
PK:616	BQ:1643, KM:261	درخرابات نبینی که ز مستی همه سال راهب دیر ترا کُشتی و زنّار دهد (سنائی) BQ

NOTE- AD claims that this may be related to the root "Ost: bone".

1697

گَشَف: لاک پشت

	Avestan	Persian
COGNATE- Sanskrit "kačyâpa"	kasyapa: *tortoise* لاک پشت	kašaf: *tortoise* گشف
	MO:2987, GR:204, BQ:1651	MO:2987, BQ:1651, PH:191

1698

گُشُفتن: پریشان کردن

Indo-European	Avestan	Pahlavi	Persian
kseubh 1: *to shake, rock,* تکان دادن	xšaub: *to shake*	âšûptak	kašoftan: *to disturb* گشفتن
PK:625	PK:625, AG3:26	BL1:11	یکی را خانه شادی گشفته یکی را باغ پیروزی شکفته (ویس و رامین) PK:625, BQ, MO, AG3:26

1699

گَشَک: "پرنده سریع"

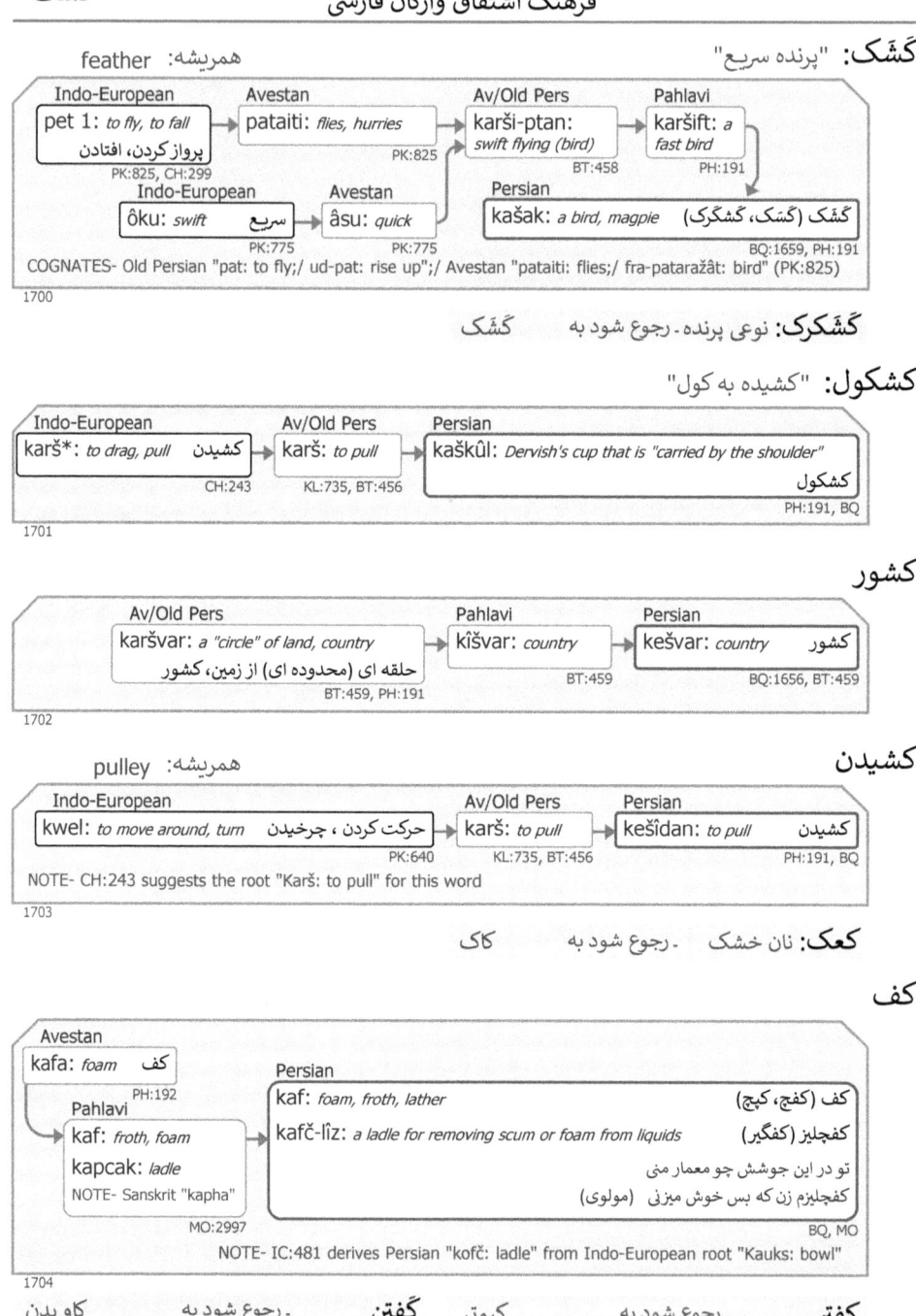

همریشه: feather

Indo-European
pet 1: *to fly, to fall*
پرواز کردن، افتادن
PK:825, CH:299

Avestan
pataiti: *flies, hurries*
PK:825

Av/Old Pers
karši-ptan: *swift flying (bird)*
BT:458

Pahlavi
karšift: *a fast bird*
PH:191

Indo-European
ôku: *swift*   سریع
PK:775

Avestan
âsu: *quick*
PK:775

Persian
kašak: *a bird, magpie*   گشک (گشک، گشگرک)
BQ:1659, PH:191

COGNATES- Old Persian "pat: to fly;/ ud-pat: rise up";/ Avestan "pataiti: flies;/ fra-pataražât: bird" (PK:825)

1700

گَشَگرک: نوعی پرنده ـ رجوع شود به   گَشک

کشکول: "کشیده به کول"

Indo-European
karš*: *to drag, pull*   کشیدن
CH:243

Av/Old Pers
karš: *to pull*
KL:735, BT:456

Persian
kaškûl: *Dervish's cup that is "carried by the shoulder"*
کشکول
PH:191, BQ

1701

کشور

Av/Old Pers
karšvar: *a "circle" of land, country*
حلقه ای (محدوده ای) از زمین، کشور
BT:459, PH:191

Pahlavi
kîšvar: *country*
BT:459

Persian
kešvar: *country*   کشور
BQ:1656, BT:459

1702

کشیدن

همریشه: pulley

Indo-European
kwel: *to move around, turn*   حرکت کردن ، چرخیدن
PK:640

Av/Old Pers
karš: *to pull*
KL:735, BT:456

Persian
kešîdan: *to pull*   کشیدن
PH:191, BQ

NOTE- CH:243 suggests the root "Karš: to pull" for this word

1703

کعک: نان خشک ـ رجوع شود به   کاک

کف

Avestan
kafa: *foam*   کف
PH:192

Pahlavi
kaf: *froth, foam*
kapcak: *ladle*
NOTE- Sanskrit "kapha"
MO:2997

Persian
kaf: *foam, froth, lather*   کف (کفج، کپج)
kafč-lîz: *a ladle for removing scum or foam from liquids*   کفچلیز (کفگیر)

تو در این جوشش چو معمار منی
کفچلیزم زن که بس خوش میزنی (مولوی)
BQ, MO

NOTE- IC:481 derives Persian "kofč: ladle" from Indo-European root "Kauks: bowl"

1704

کاویدن   رجوع شود به ـ   **گفتن**   کبوتر   رجوع شود به ـ   **کفتر**

کف   رجوع شود به ـ   **کفچلیز**: کفگیر   کف   رجوع شود به ـ   **کفج**

کفش

Pahlavi	Persian
kafš: *shoe, boot* کفش، پوتین	kafš: *shoe* (کفش (کفاش
MO:3005	MO

1705

ککه: مدفوع

Indo-European	Persian
kakka: *to defecate* ریدن	kekeh, kaka: *excrement* ککه
COGNATE- Sanskrit "cack" and "kaknas" PK:521	AP:409, BQ

1706

گُل: خَمیده، کج

همریشه: شل   همریشه: colon, cylinder

Indo-European	Greek	Persian
skel: *bent, curved* خمیده	skhelos, kellos: *crooked*	kol: *crooked* گُل
		بدانگه که گیرد جهان گرد و میغ
		گُل پشت چوگانت گردد ستیغ (بوشکور)
PK:928	WD:597	WD:597, PH:192, MO:3012
COGNATE- Avestan "skarena: round"		

1707

گل   . رجوع شود به   کچل

کلاس

همریشه: council

Indo-European	Latin	French	Persian
kel 6: *to shout, call*	classis: *summons, a group of people*		kelâs: *class* کلاس
فریاد زدن، صدا زدن برای گردهمایی			
PK:548	PK:548	AD:248	MO:3015

1708

کلاغ   . رجوع شود به   ورغنه

کلاه

همریشه: helmet

Indo-European	Pahlavi	Persian
kel 2: *to cover* پوشاندن	kulâf: *cover, hat*	kolâh: *hat* کلاه
PK:553	PH:192,193, HM:88	BQ, AA:233

1709

کلاهخود   . رجوع شود به   خود۲

کلبه

همریشه: hole

Indo-European	Pahlavi	Persian
kel 2: *to cover* پوشاندن	kurpak: *shelter, hut*	kolbeh: *hut* کلبه
PK:553	PH:192,193, HM:88	BQ, AA:233

1710

کلنجار

همریشه: harsh

Indo-European	Old Persian	Persian
koro: *war, army, a large crowd*	kâr, kâra: *war, army, people*	kalanjâr: *fight, quarrel*
جنگ، ارتش، سپاه		کلنجار
PK:615, IC:536	PK:615, KT:175	BQ, PH, MO

1711

گلند   . رجوع شود به   کلنگ

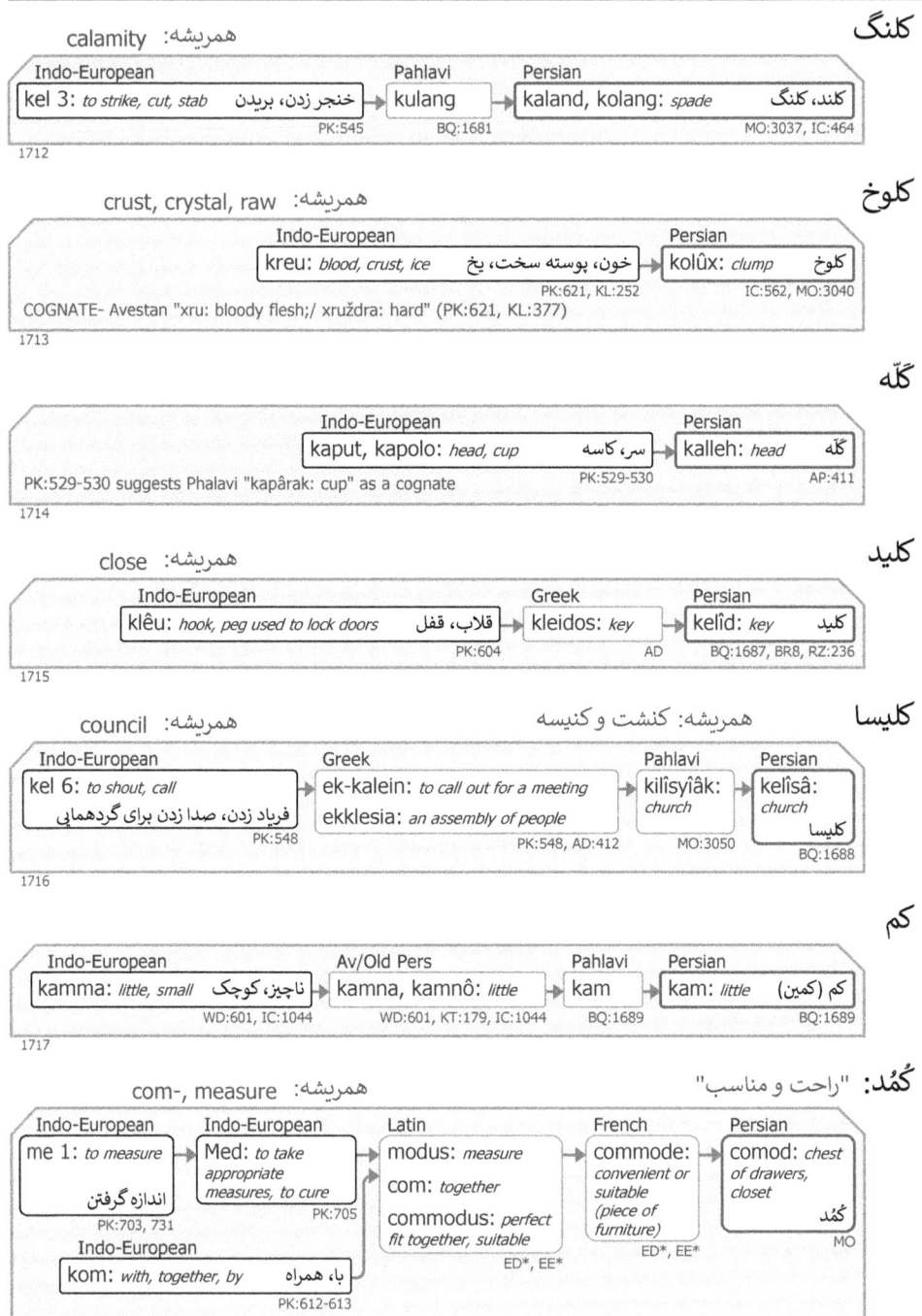

کلنگ

همریشه: calamity

Indo-European	Pahlavi	Persian
kel 3: *to strike, cut, stab* خنجر زدن، بریدن	kulang	kaland, kolang: *spade* کلند، کلنگ
PK:545	BQ:1681	MO:3037, IC:464

1712

کلوخ

همریشه: crust, crystal, raw

Indo-European	Persian
kreu: *blood, crust, ice* خون، پوسته سخت، یخ	kolûx: *clump* کلوخ
PK:621, KL:252	IC:562, MO:3040

COGNATE- Avestan "xru: bloody flesh;/ xruždra: hard" (PK:621, KL:377)

1713

گلّه

Indo-European	Persian
kaput, kapolo: *head, cup* سر، کاسه	kalleh: *head* گلّه
PK:529-530	AP:411

PK:529-530 suggests Phalavi "kapârak: cup" as a cognate

1714

کلید

همریشه: close

Indo-European	Greek	Persian
klêu: *hook, peg used to lock doors* قلاب، قفل	kleidos: *key*	kelîd: *key* کلید
PK:604	AD	BQ:1687, BR8, RZ:236

1715

کلیسا

همریشه: کنشت و کنیسه   همریشه: council

Indo-European	Greek	Pahlavi	Persian
kel 6: *to shout, call* فریاد زدن، صدا زدن برای گردهمایی	ek-kalein: *to call out for a meeting* / ekklesia: *an assembly of people*	kilîsyîâk: *church*	kelîsâ: *church* کلیسا
PK:548	PK:548, AD:412	MO:3050	BQ:1688

1716

کم

Indo-European	Av/Old Pers	Pahlavi	Persian
kamma: *little, small* ناچیز، کوچک	kamna, kamnô: *little*	kam	kam: *little* کم (کمین)
WD:601, IC:1044	WD:601, KT:179, IC:1044	BQ:1689	BQ:1689

1717

کُمُد: "راحت و مناسب"

همریشه: com-, measure

Indo-European	Indo-European	Latin	French	Persian
me 1: *to measure* اندازه گرفتن	Med: *to take appropriate measures, to cure*	modus: *measure* / com: *together* / commodus: *perfect fit together, suitable*	commode: *convenient or suitable (piece of furniture)*	comod: *chest of drawers, closet* کُمُد
PK:703, 731	PK:705	ED*, EE*	ED*, EE*	MO
Indo-European				
kom: *with, together, by* با، همراه				
PK:612-613				

1718

کمر: میان

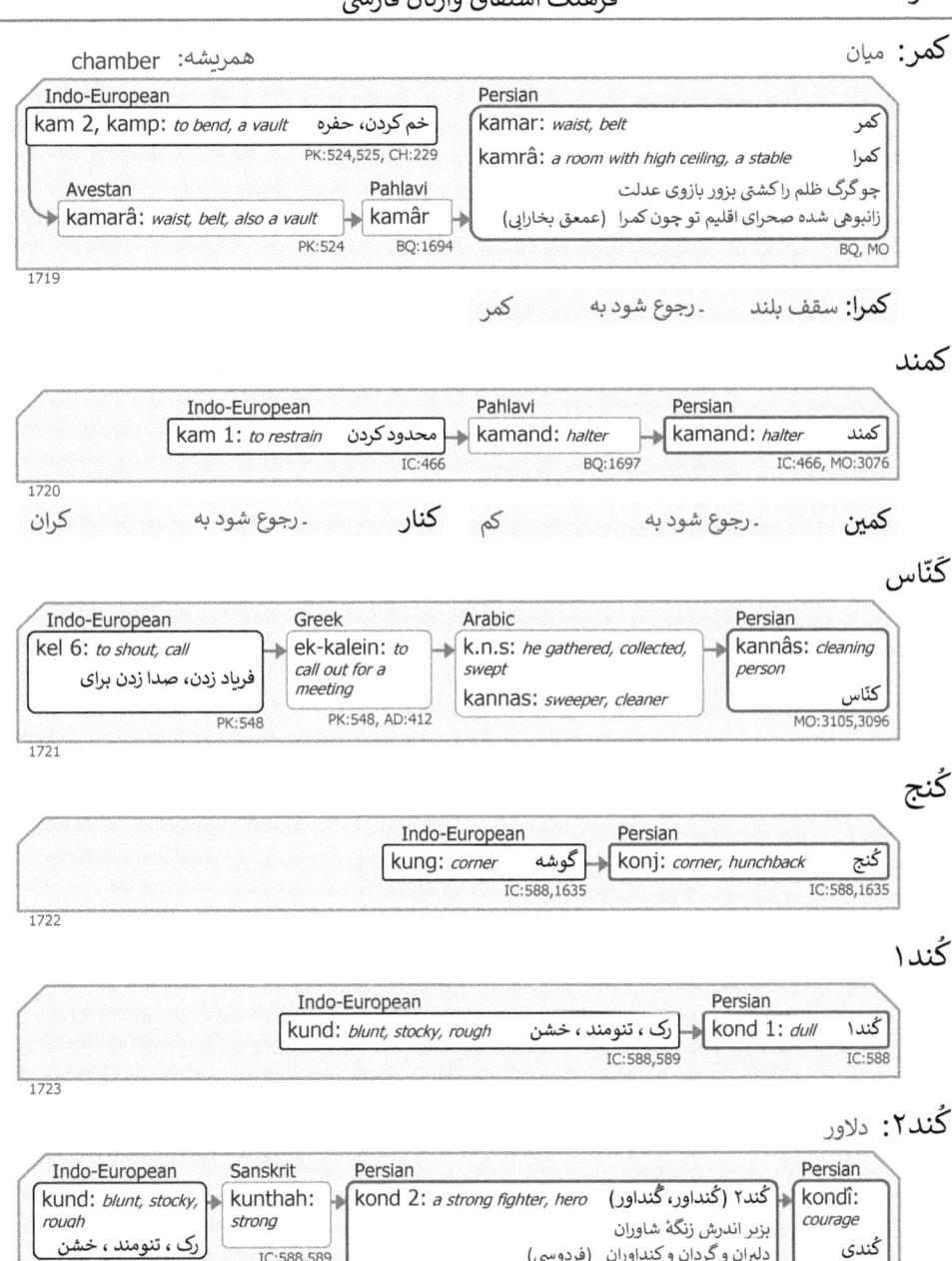

کمرا: سقف بلند ۔ رجوع شود به   کمر

کمند

کمین ۔ رجوع شود به   کم   **کنار** ۔ رجوع شود به   کران

کنّاس

کُنج

کُند۱

کُند۲: دلاور

کُنداور: دلاور ۔ رجوع شود به   کُند۲

306

کُندر

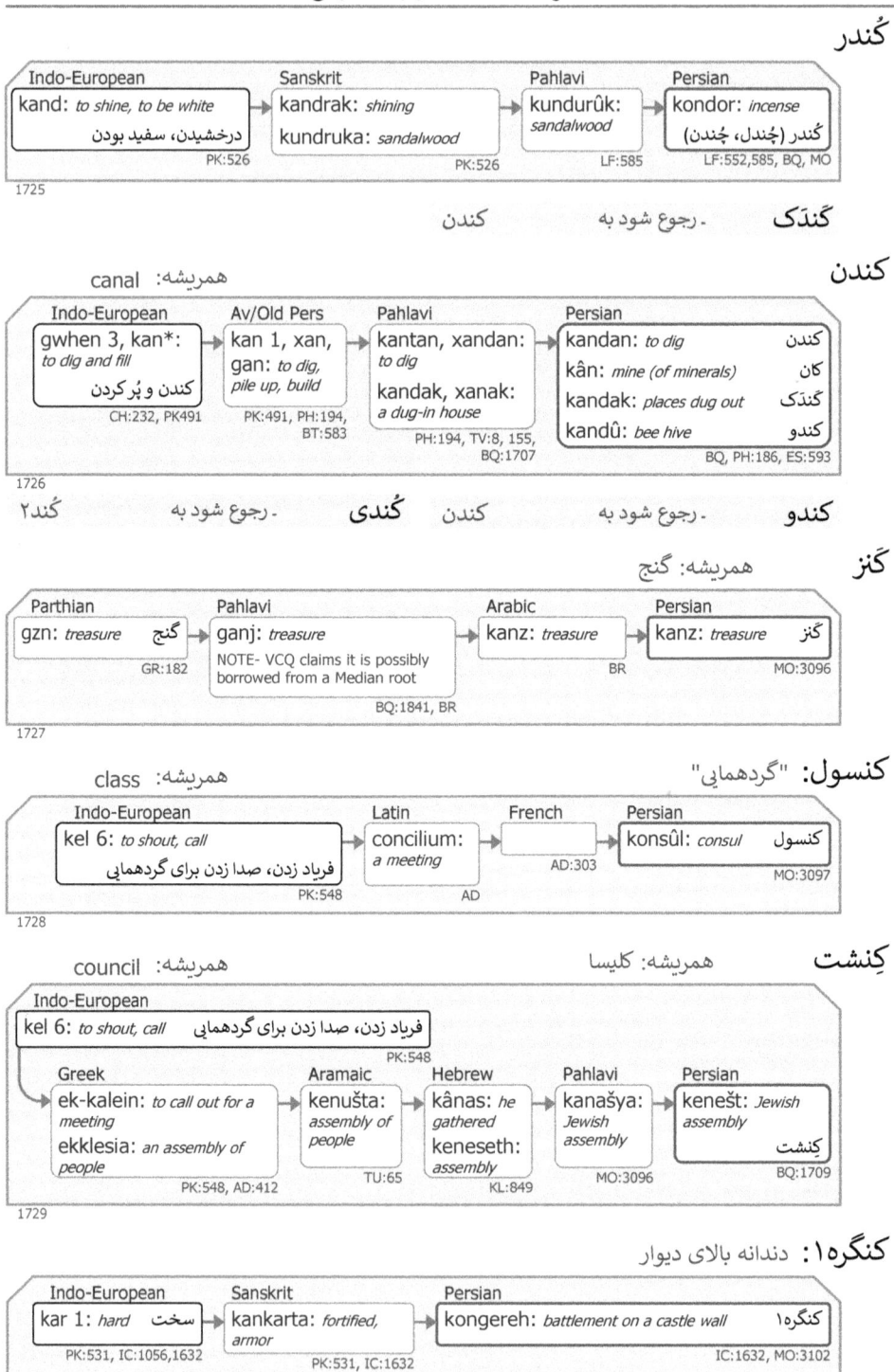

Indo-European	Sanskrit	Pahlavi	Persian
kand: *to shine, to be white* درخشیدن، سفید بودن	kandrak: *shining* kundruka: *sandalwood*	kundurûk: *sandalwood*	kondor: *incense* کندر (چندل، چندن)
PK:526	PK:526	LF:585	LF:552,585, BQ, MO

1725

گَندَک ‑ رجوع شود به   کندن

کندن

همریشه: canal

Indo-European	Av/Old Pers	Pahlavi	Persian
gwhen 3, kan*: *to dig and fill* کندن و پُر کردن	kan 1, xan, gan: *to dig, pile up, build*	kantan, xandan: *to dig* kandak, xanak: *a dug-in house*	kandan: *to dig* کندن kân: *mine (of minerals)* کان kandak: *places dug out* گندک kandû: *bee hive* کندو
CH:232, PK491	PK:491, PH:194, BT:583	PH:194, TV:8, 155, BQ:1707	BQ, PH:186, ES:593

1726

کندو   کندی ‑ رجوع شود به کندن   گُندی   ‑ رجوع شود به کند۲

گَنز

همریشه: گنج

Parthian	Pahlavi	Arabic	Persian
gzn: *treasure* گنج	ganj: *treasure* NOTE‑ VCQ claims it is possibly borrowed from a Median root	kanz: *treasure*	kanz: *treasure* گنز
GR:182	BQ:1841, BR	BR	MO:3096

1727

کنسول: "گردهمایی"

همریشه: class

Indo-European	Latin	French	Persian
kel 6: *to shout, call* فریاد زدن، صدا زدن برای گردهمایی	concilium: *a meeting*		konsûl: *consul* کنسول
PK:548	AD	AD:303	MO:3097

1728

کِنشت   همریشه: کلیسا   همریشه: council

Indo-European				
kel 6: *to shout, call* فریاد زدن، صدا زدن برای گردهمایی				
PK:548				
Greek	Aramaic	Hebrew	Pahlavi	Persian
ek-kalein: *to call out for a meeting* ekklesia: *an assembly of people*	kenušta: *assembly of people*	kânas: *he gathered* keneseth: *assembly*	kanašya: *Jewish assembly*	kenešt: *Jewish assembly* کِنشت
PK:548, AD:412	TU:65	KL:849	MO:3096	BQ:1709

1729

کنگره۱: دندانه بالای دیوار

Indo-European	Sanskrit	Persian
kar 1: *hard* سخت	kankarta: *fortified, armor*	kongereh: *battlement on a castle wall* کنگره۱
PK:531, IC:1056,1632	PK:531, IC:1632	IC:1632, MO:3102

1730

کنگره۲: همایش   همریشه: گراییدن   همریشه: congress

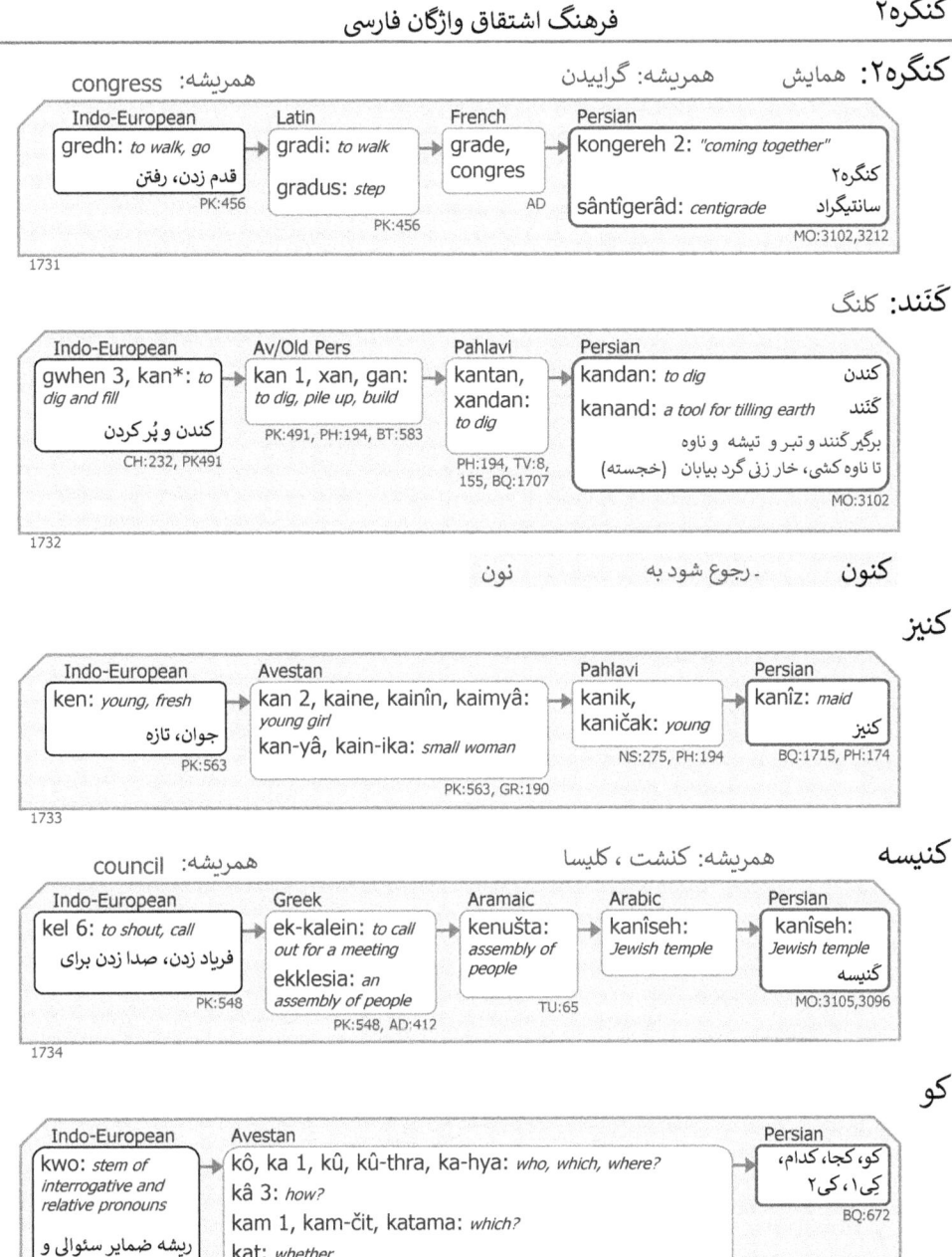

کنگره۲: همایش

Indo-European	Latin	French	Persian
gredh: *to walk, go* قدم زدن، رفتن PK:456	gradi: *to walk* gradus: *step* PK:456	grade, congres AD	kongereh 2: *"coming together"* کنگره۲ sântîgerâd: *centigrade* سانتیگراد MO:3102,3212

1731

گَنَند: کلنگ

Indo-European	Av/Old Pers	Pahlavi	Persian
gwhen 3, kan*: *to dig and fill* کندن و پُرکردن CH:232, PK491	kan 1, xan, gan: *to dig, pile up, build* PK:491, PH:194, BT:583	kantan, xandan: *to dig* PH:194, TV:8, 155, BQ:1707	kandan: *to dig* کندن kanand: *a tool for tilling earth* گَنَند برگیر گنند و تبر و تیشه و ناوه تا ناوه کشی، خار زنی گرد بیابان (خجسته) MO:3102

1732

کنون   .رجوع شود به   نون

کنیز

Indo-European	Avestan	Pahlavi	Persian
ken: *young, fresh* جوان، تازه PK:563	kan 2, kaine, kainîn, kaimyâ: *young girl* kan-yâ, kain-ika: *small woman* PK:563, GR:190	kanik, kaničak: *young* NS:275, PH:194	kanîz: *maid* کنیز BQ:1715, PH:174

1733

کنیسه   همریشه: کنشت ، کلیسا   همریشه: council

Indo-European	Greek	Aramaic	Arabic	Persian
kel 6: *to shout, call* فریاد زدن، صدا زدن برای PK:548	ek-kalein: *to call out for a meeting* ekklesia: *an assembly of people* PK:548, AD:412	kenušta: *assembly of people* TU:65	kanîseh: *Jewish temple*	kanîseh: *Jewish temple* کنیسه MO:3105,3096

1734

کو

Indo-European	Avestan	Persian
kwo: *stem of interrogative and relative pronouns* ریشه ضمایر سئوالی و نسبی PK:644,646	kô, ka 1, kû, kû-thra, ka-hya: *who, which, where?* kâ 3: *how?* kam 1, kam-čit, katama: *which?* kat: *whether* ka-da, ka-tha: *when?* katâra: *which of the two? either* PK:644,648, BQ:1748, PH:196	کو، کجا، کدام، کی۱، کی۲ BQ:672

1735

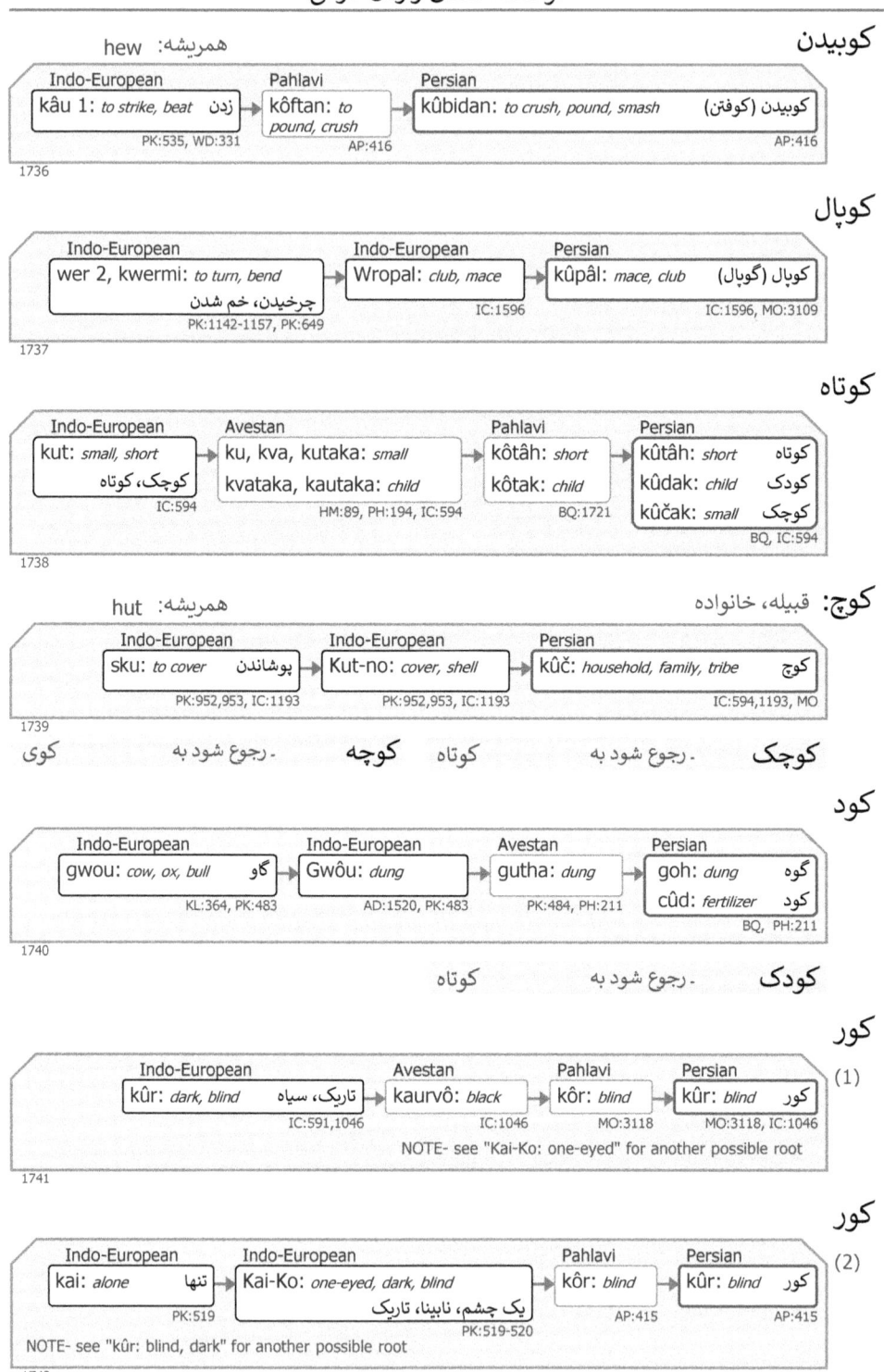

کوبیدن

همریشه: hew

Indo-European — **kâu 1**: *to strike, beat* زدن — PK:535, WD:331

Pahlavi — **kôftan**: *to pound, crush* — AP:416

Persian — **kûbidan**: *to crush, pound, smash* کوبیدن (کوفتن) — AP:416

1736

کوپال

Indo-European — **wer 2, kwermi**: *to turn, bend* چرخیدن، خم شدن — PK:1142-1157, PK:649

Indo-European — **Wropal**: *club, mace* — IC:1596

Persian — **kûpâl**: *mace, club* کوپال (گوپال) — IC:1596, MO:3109

1737

کوتاه

Indo-European — **kut**: *small, short* کوچک، کوتاه — IC:594

Avestan — **ku, kva, kutaka**: *small* / **kvataka, kautaka**: *child* — HM:89, PH:194, IC:594

Pahlavi — **kôtâh**: *short* / **kôtak**: *child* — BQ:1721

Persian — **kûtâh**: *short* کوتاه / **kûdak**: *child* کودک / **kûčak**: *small* کوچک — BQ, IC:594

1738

کوچ: قبیله، خانواده

همریشه: hut

Indo-European — **sku**: *to cover* پوشاندن — PK:952,953, IC:1193

Indo-European — **Kut-no**: *cover, shell* — PK:952,953, IC:1193

Persian — **kûč**: *household, family, tribe* کوچ — IC:594,1193, MO

1739

کوچک . رجوع شود به **کوچه**   کوتاه   . رجوع شود به   کوی

کود

Indo-European — **gwou**: *cow, ox, bull* گاو — KL:364, PK:483

Indo-European — **Gwôu**: *dung* — AD:1520, PK:483

Avestan — **gutha**: *dung* — PK:484, PH:211

Persian — **goh**: *dung* گوه / **cûd**: *fertilizer* کود — BQ, PH:211

1740

کودک . رجوع شود به   کوتاه

کور (1)

Indo-European — **kûr**: *dark, blind* تاریک، سیاه — IC:591,1046

Avestan — **kaurvô**: *black* — IC:1046

Pahlavi — **kôr**: *blind* — MO:3118

Persian — **kûr**: *blind* کور — MO:3118, IC:1046

NOTE- see "Kai-Ko: one-eyed" for another possible root

1741

کور (2)

Indo-European — **kai**: *alone* تنها — PK:519

Indo-European — **Kai-Ko**: *one-eyed, dark, blind* یک چشم، نابینا، تاریک — PK:519-520

Pahlavi — **kôr**: *blind* — AP:415

Persian — **kûr**: *blind* کور — AP:415

NOTE- see "kûr: blind, dark" for another possible root

1742

کوره

کوره

همریشه: carbon

Indo-European	Persian
ker 5, kur: *heat, fire* حرارت، آتش PK:571, IC:590	kûreh: *fireplace, oven, kiln* کوره IC:590, MO:3121

1743

کوزه . رجوع شود به **کوژ** کاسه . رجوع شود به غوز

کوس: طبل

Indo-European	Pahlavi	Persian
kaus: *to pound, beat* کوبیدن، کوفتن CH:228, PK:535	kôs- to beat, pound CH:228	kôs: *drum* کوس (کوسیدن) CH:228

1744

کوشش . رجوع شود به کوشیدن **کوشک** . رجوع شود به گوشه

کوشیدن

Indo-European	Avestan	Pahlavi	Persian
kâu 1: *to strike, beat* زدن PK:535, WD:331	kau-kušati: *tries, fights* BK:290, WD:331, TV:150	hôxšîtan BQ:1731	kûšîdan: *to try, to fight* کوشیدن (کوشش) BQ

1745

کوفتن . رجوع شود به کوبیدن

کوفیّه: "سرپوش"

همریشه: cephalic

Indo-European	Greek	Italian	Arabic	Persian
ghebh-el: *head, top* سر، بالا PK:423	kephalê: *head* PK:423, KL:259	cuffia: *headband, scarf* TU:65	kûfiyyah: *scarf* TU:65	kûfiyyeh: *scarf* کوفیّه MO:3127

1746

کوکو: فاخته

Indo-European	Persian
kau 2: *to howl, a raucous bird* زوزه کشیدن، نوعی پرنده با صدای خشن IC:483, PK:434, 535	kûkû: *cuckoo, owl* کوکو AP:417

1747

کوه

همریشه: cove

Indo-European	Av/Old Pers	Pahlavi	Persian
gêu 1, kauč*: *to bend, wrinkle* خم و درهم شدن PK:394-398, PK:588-592	kaofa: *mountain* kava: *humped* PK:591,592, KL:391	kôf: *mountain* PH:195	kûh: *mountain* کوه kowhân: *camel's hump* کوهان (کوهه) abar-Kûh: *tall mountain, name of a city* ابرکوه (ابرقوه) BQ, WD1, JS1:3
NOTE- Compare with root "Kam 2: to bend"			

1748

کوهان . رجوع شود به کوه **کوهسار** کوه . رجوع شود به کوه + سرای

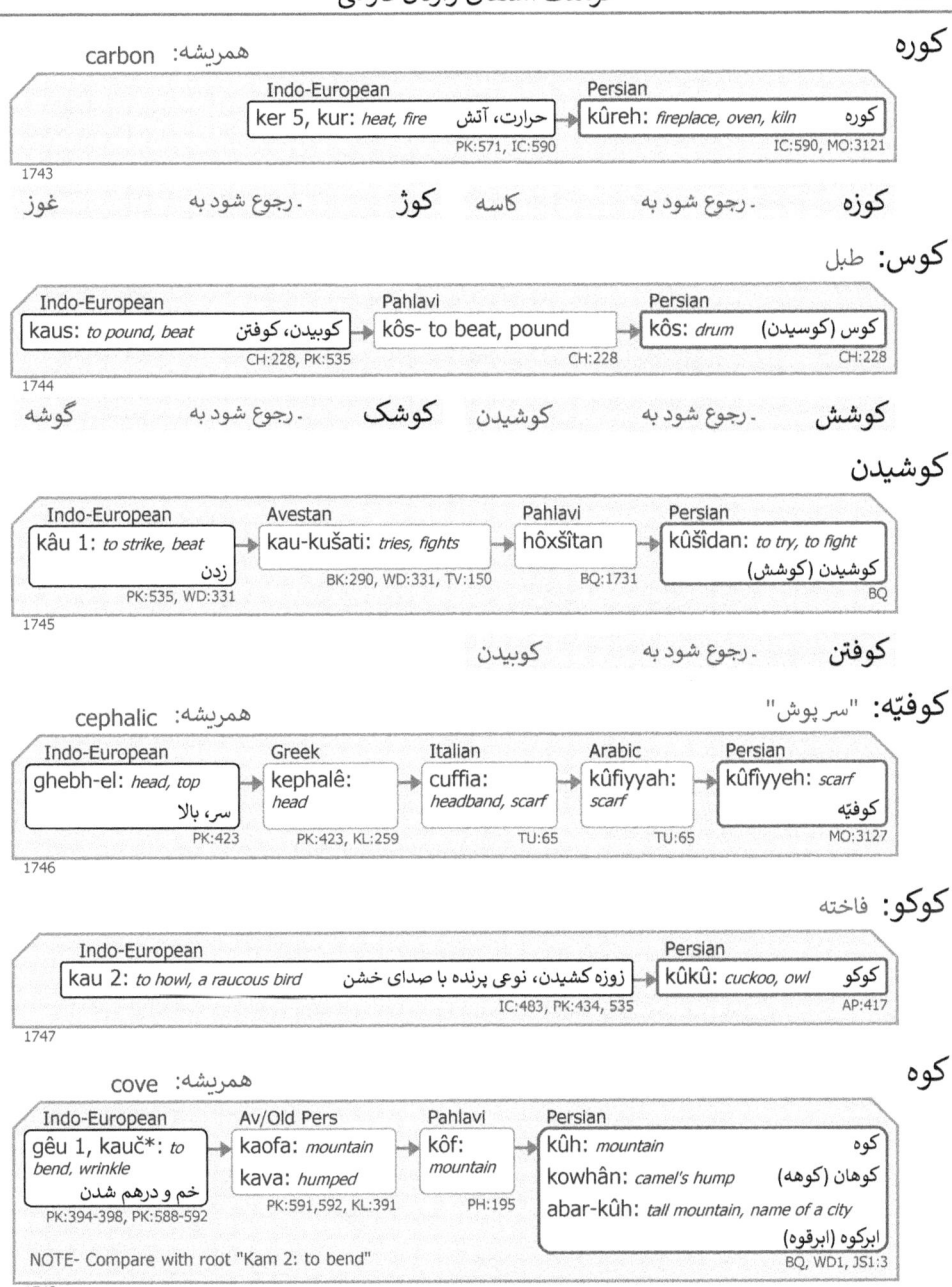

کوی

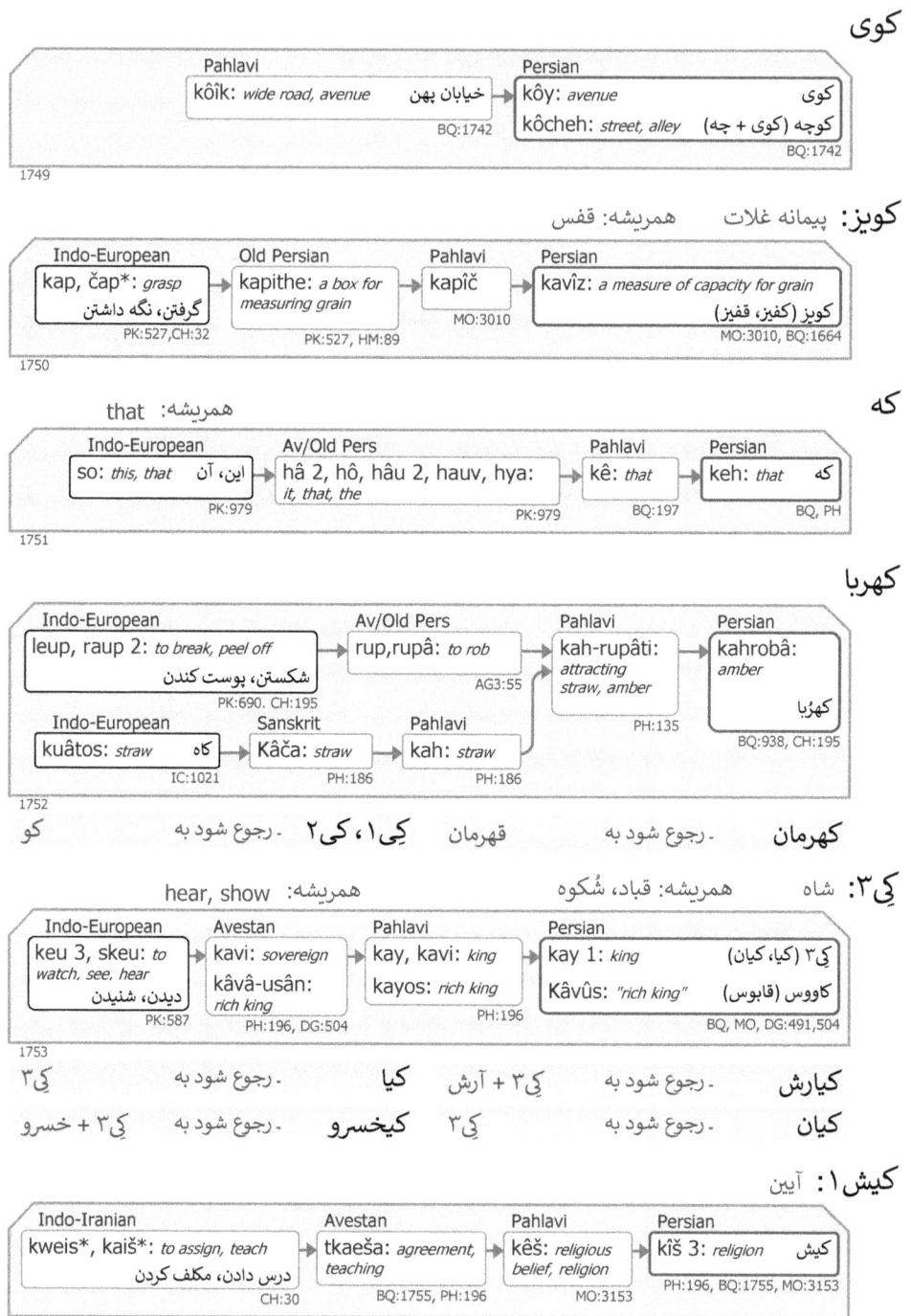

کویز: پیمانه غلات   همریشه: قفس

1750

که

همریشه: that

1751

کهربا

1752

کهرمان ـ رجوع شود به   قهرمان   کِی۱، کِی۲ ـ رجوع شود به   کو

کِی۳: شاه   همریشه: قباد، شُکوه   همریشه: hear, show

1753

کیارش ـ رجوع شود به   کِی۳ + آرش   **کیا** ـ رجوع شود به   کِی۳

کیان ـ رجوع شود به   کِی۳   **کیخسرو** ـ رجوع شود به   کِی۳ + خسرو

کیش۱: آیین

1754

کیش۲: ترکش

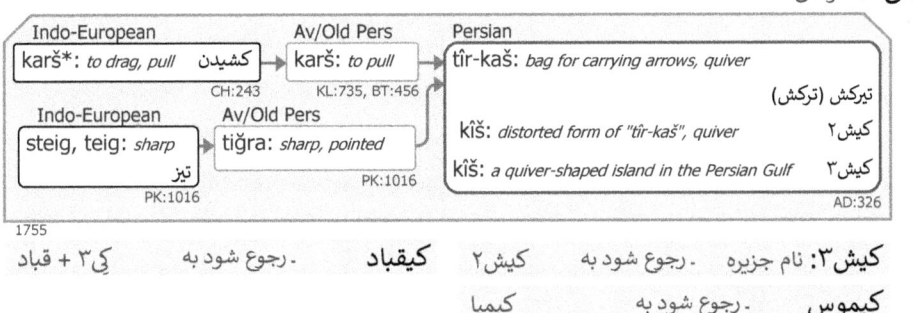

1755

کیش۳: نام جزیره   .رجوع شود به   کیش۲   **کیقباد**   .رجوع شود به   کی ۳ + قباد   قباد

کیموس   .رجوع شود به   کیمیا

کیمیا: "اختلاط و امتزاج"

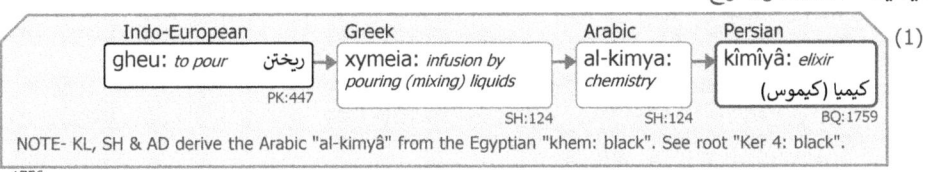

1756

کیمیا: "صنعت استحاله مصری"

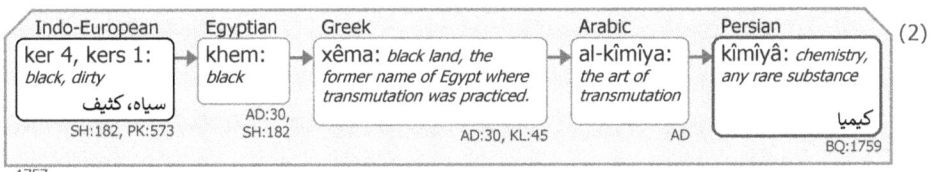

1757

کین

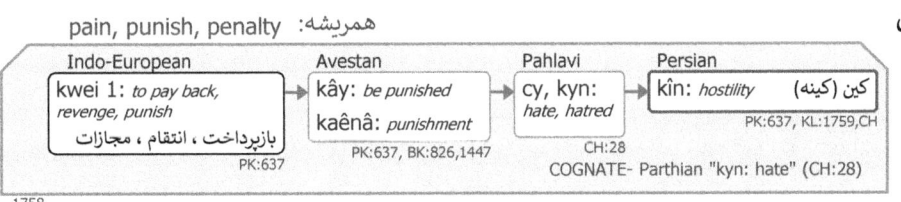

1758

کیوسک: کوشک   .رجوع شود به   گوشه

کیومرث: "انسان فانی"

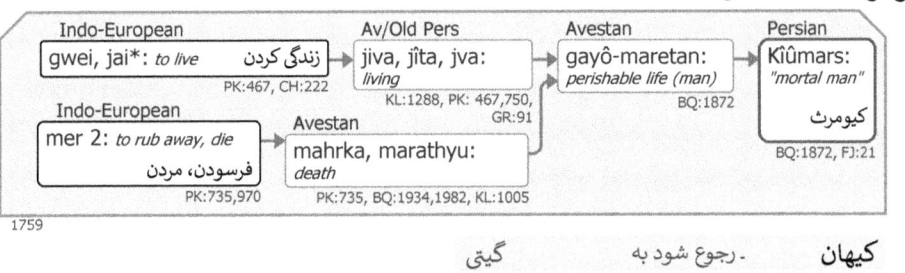

1759

کیهان   .رجوع شود به   گیتی

312

این حرف گاه به غ یا و بدل
شود.

گ ـ

Indo-European		Av/Old Pers		Persian	
wi: *part, apart* جدا		wi, vî, vi: *apart, against*		g-: *a prefix meaning apart, against, analyze, etc.*	گ ـ
PK:1175,1176		PK:1175, KT:204		مثال: گداختن, گریختن, گسستن, گسیختن, گشادن	
				BQ	

1760

گات ـ رجوع شود به گاه۱۵   **گادن** ـ رجوع شود به   گاییدن

گاز۱: پارچه زخم بندی   همریشه: gauze:

Old Persian	Pahlavi	Persian	Arabic	French	Persian
kaž, kaz: *inexpensive silk*	kac, kač: *an inexpensive silk*	kaz: *inexpensive silk*	qaz: *a type of cloth*	gaze: *a loosely woven cotton fabric*	gâz: *a surgical dressing*
ابریشم ارزان		گز (گژ ، غژ، غژغاو)			گاز
	BQ:1637, AA:218	MO	AA:218		MO:3166

1761

گاز۲

Indo-Iranian		Pahlavi	Persian
gaz*: *to bite, string* گاز زدن، نیش زدن		gaz-: *to string*	gâz: *bite* گاز
CH:117		CH:117	CH:118

1762

گام   همریشه: هنگام، پیغام

همریشه: come:

Indo-European	Av/Old Pers	Avestan	Pahlavi	Persian
gwa: *to walk, step* قدم زدن	gam: *to come, step*	gâman: *step*	gâm	gâm: *step* گام
PK:463,CH:98	PK:463, KL:318	PK:463	BQ:1765	PH:11, BQ

1763

- گان، - گانه

Pahlavi	Persian
kân, kânak: *belonging to a group (of numbers), similar, deserving*	gân: *similar, deserving* (گانه) گان.
مانند، پسوند گروه مثل یگان وصدگان	یگانه، رایگان، شایگان
JD:151	JD:151, BQ:1765

1764

313

گاو

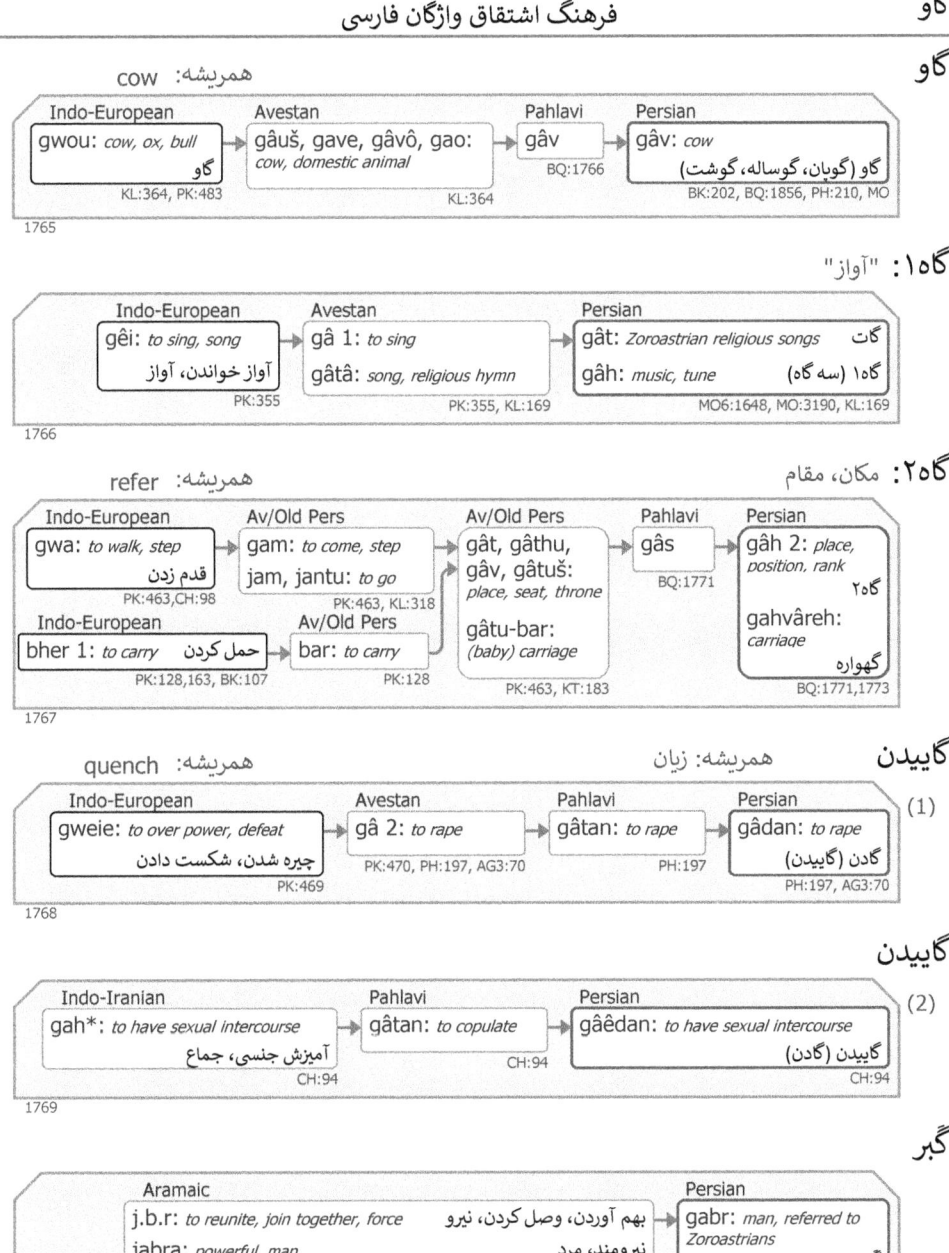

همریشه: cow

Indo-European
gwou: cow, ox, bull
گاو
KL:364, PK:483

Avestan
gâuš, gave, gâvô, gao:
cow, domestic animal
KL:364

Pahlavi
gâv
BQ:1766

Persian
gâv: cow
گاو (گوپان، گوساله، گوشت)
BK:202, BQ:1856, PH:210, MO

1765

گا۱۵: "آواز"

Indo-European
gêi: to sing, song
آواز خواندن، آواز
PK:355

Avestan
gâ 1: to sing
gâtâ: song, religious hymn
PK:355, KL:169

Persian
gât: Zoroastrian religious songs   گات
gâh: music, tune   (سه گاه) ۱۵گاه
MO6:1648, MO:3190, KL:169

1766

گا۲۵: مکان، مقام

Indo-European
gwa: to walk, step
قدم زدن
PK:463,CH:98

Indo-European
bher 1: to carry   حمل کردن
PK:128,163, BK:107

Av/Old Pers
gam: to come, step
jam, jantu: to go
PK:463, KL:318

Av/Old Pers
bar: to carry
PK:128

Av/Old Pers
gât, gâthu,
gâv, gâtuš:
place, seat, throne

gâtu-bar:
(baby) carriage
PK:463, KT:183

Pahlavi
gâs
BQ:1771

Persian
gâh 2: place,
position, rank
۲۵گاه

gahvâreh:
carriage
گهواره
BQ:1771,1773

1767

گاییدن   همریشه: زیان   همریشه: quench

(1)

Indo-European
gweie: to over power, defeat
چیره شدن، شکست دادن
PK:469

Avestan
gâ 2: to rape
PK:470, PH:197, AG3:70

Pahlavi
gâtan: to rape
PH:197

Persian
gâdan: to rape
گادن (گاییدن)
PH:197, AG3:70

1768

گاییدن

(2)

Indo-Iranian
gah*: to have sexual intercourse
آمیزش جنسی، جماع
CH:94

Pahlavi
gâtan: to copulate
CH:94

Persian
gâêdan: to have sexual intercourse
گاییدن (گادن)
CH:94

1769

گَبر

Aramaic
j.b.r: to reunite, join together, force   بهم آوردن، وصل کردن، نیرو
jabra: powerful, man   نیرومند، مرد
KL:633

Persian
gabr: man, referred to
Zoroastrians
گبر
MO:3193

NOTE- BQ: 1774 does not agree with this derivation.

1770

گَپ   ـ رجوع شود به   گفتن

گت: بزرگ (گت و گنده)

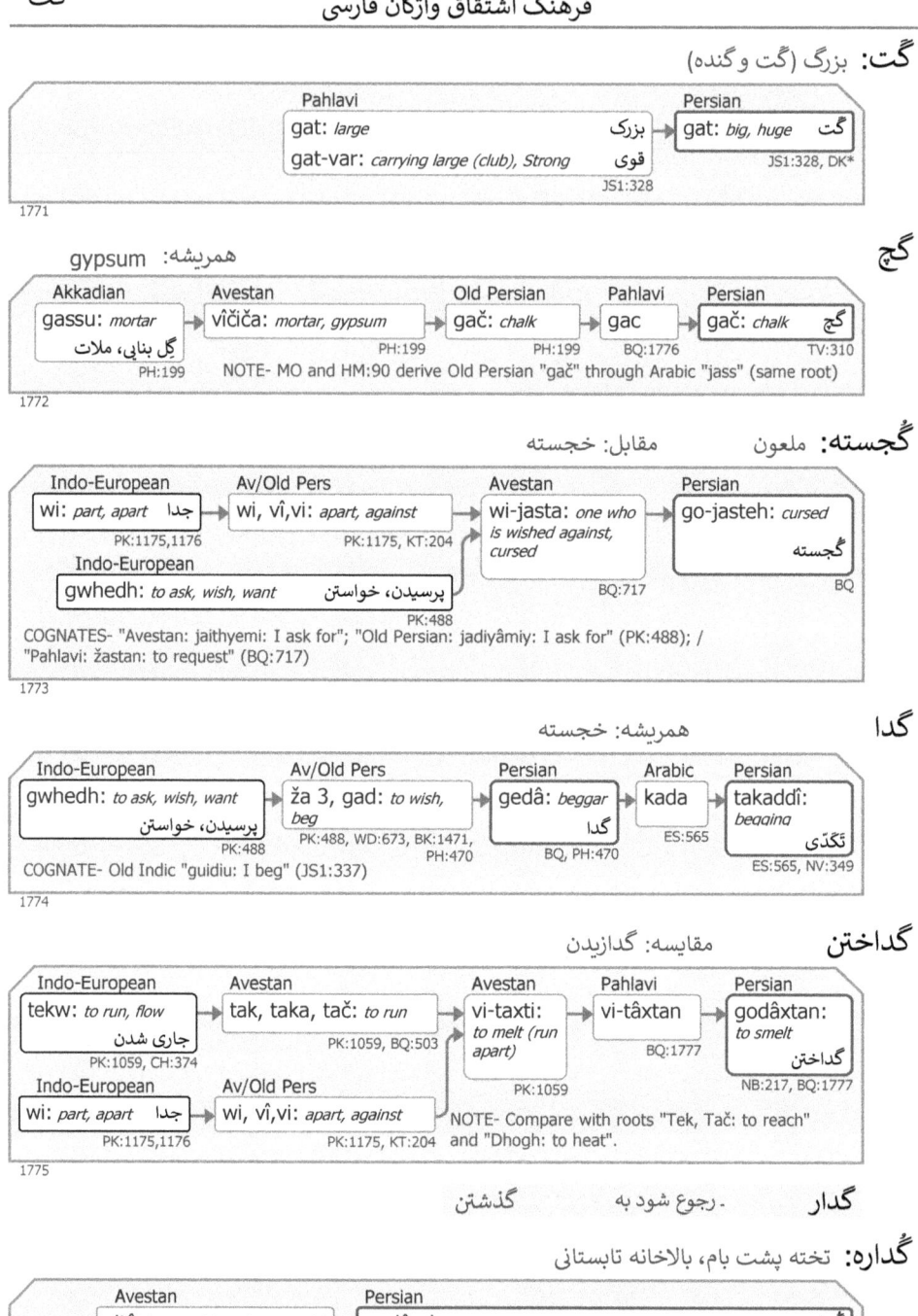

Pahlavi
- gat: *large* — بزرگ
- gat-var: *carrying large (club), Strong* — قوی
JS1:328

Persian
- gat: *big, huge* — گت
JS1:328, DK*

1771

گچ

همریشه: gypsum

Akkadian
gassu: *mortar*
گل بنایی، ملات
PH:199

Avestan
vîčiča: *mortar, gypsum*
PH:199

Old Persian
gač: *chalk*
PH:199

Pahlavi
gac
BQ:1776

Persian
gač: *chalk* — گچ
TV:310

NOTE- MO and HM:90 derive Old Persian "gač" through Arabic "jass" (same root)

1772

گجسته: ملعون مقابل: خجسته

Indo-European
wi: *part, apart* — جدا
PK:1175,1176

Av/Old Pers
wi, vî,vi: *apart, against*
PK:1175, KT:204

Avestan
wi-jasta: *one who is wished against, cursed*
BQ:717

Persian
go-jasteh: *cursed*
گجسته
BQ

Indo-European
gwhedh: *to ask, wish, want* — پرسیدن، خواستن
PK:488

COGNATES- "Avestan: jaithyemi: I ask for"; "Old Persian: jadiyâmiy: I ask for" (PK:488); / "Pahlavi: žastan: to request" (BQ:717)

1773

گدا   همریشه: خجسته

Indo-European
gwhedh: *to ask, wish, want*
پرسیدن، خواستن
PK:488

Av/Old Pers
ža 3, gad: *to wish, beg*
PK:488, WD:673, BK:1471, PH:470

Persian
gedâ: *beggar*
گدا
BQ, PH:470

Arabic
kada
ES:565

Persian
takaddî: *beqqinq*
تگّدی
ES:565, NV:349

COGNATE- Old Indic "guidiu: I beg" (JS1:337)

1774

گداختن   مقایسه: گدازیدن

Indo-European
tekw: *to run, flow*
جاری شدن
PK:1059, CH:374

Avestan
tak, taka, tač: *to run*
PK:1059, BQ:503

Avestan
vi-taxti: *to melt (run apart)*
PK:1059

Pahlavi
vi-tâxtan
BQ:1777

Persian
godâxtan: *to smelt*
گداختن
NB:217, BQ:1777

Indo-European
wi: *part, apart* — جدا
PK:1175,1176

Av/Old Pers
wi, vî,vi: *apart, against*
PK:1175, KT:204

NOTE- Compare with roots "Tek, Tač: to reach" and "Dhogh: to heat".

1775

گدار . رجوع شود به گذشتن

گداره: تخته پشت بام، بالاخانه تابستانی

Avestan
vitâra: *wood boards* — تخته
BQ:1777

Persian
godâreh: *summer house, boards used to cover roofs* — گداره
BQ:1777, DK*

1776

گدازیدن

همریشه: داغ

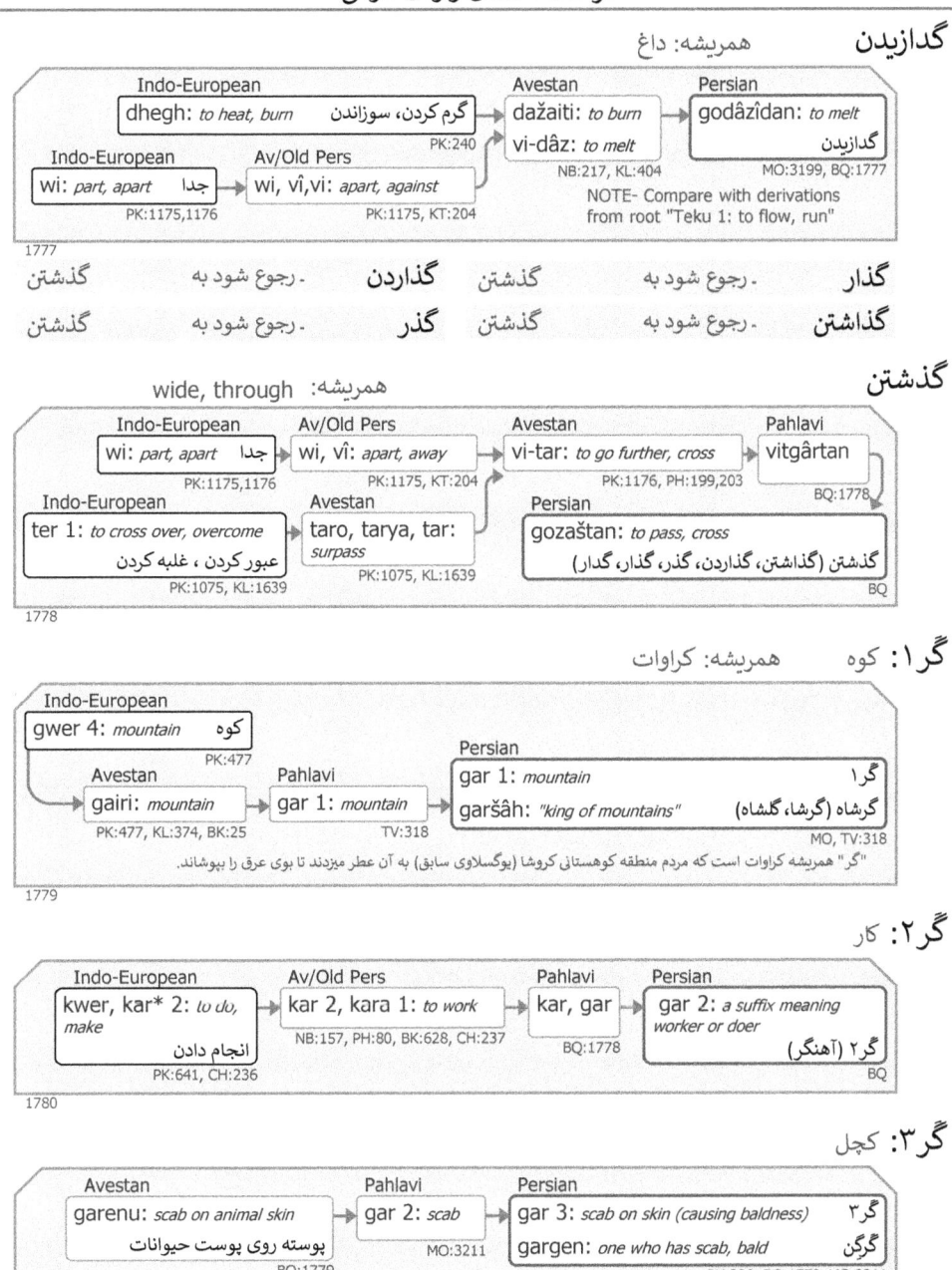

Indo-European
dhegh: *to heat, burn* گرم کردن، سوزاندن
PK:240

Indo-European
wi: *part, apart* جدا
PK:1175,1176

Av/Old Pers
wi, vî,vi: *apart, against*
PK:1175, KT:204

Avestan
dažaiti: *to burn*
vi-dâz: *to melt*
NB:217, KL:404

Persian
godâzîdan: *to melt*
گدازیدن
MO:3199, BQ:1777

NOTE- Compare with derivations from root "Teku 1: to flow, run"

1777

| گذشتن | . رجوع شود به | گذشتن | گذاردن | گذشتن | . رجوع شود به | گذشتن | گذار |
| گذشتن | . رجوع شود به | گذشتن | گذر | گذشتن | . رجوع شود به | گذشتن | گذاشتن |

گذشتن

همریشه: wide, through

Indo-European
wi: *part, apart* جدا
PK:1175,1176

Av/Old Pers
wi, vî: *apart, away*
PK:1175, KT:204

Avestan
vi-tar: *to go further, cross*
PK:1176, PH:199,203

Pahlavi
vitgârtan
BQ:1778

Indo-European
ter 1: *to cross over, overcome*
عبور کردن ، غلبه کردن
PK:1075, KL:1639

Avestan
taro, tarya, tar: *surpass*
PK:1075, KL:1639

Persian
gozaštan: *to pass, cross*
گذشتن (گذاشتن، گذاردن، گذر، گذار، گدار)
BQ

1778

گر ۱: کوه

همریشه: کراوات

Indo-European
gwer 4: *mountain* کوه
PK:477

Avestan
gairi: *mountain*
PK:477, KL:374, BK:25

Pahlavi
gar 1: *mountain*
TV:318

Persian
gar 1: *mountain* گر۱
garšâh: *"king of mountains"* گرشاه (گرشا، گلشاه)
MO, TV:318

"گر" همریشه کراوات است که مردم منطقه کوهستانی کروشا (یوگسلاوی سابق) به آن عطر میزدند تا بوی عرق را بپوشاند.

1779

گر ۲: کار

Indo-European
kwer, kar* 2: *to do, make*
انجام دادن
PK:641, CH:236

Av/Old Pers
kar 2, kara 1: *to work*
NB:157, PH:80, BK:628, CH:237

Pahlavi
kar, gar
BQ:1778

Persian
gar 2: *a suffix meaning worker or doer*
گر۲ (آهنگر)
BQ

1780

گر ۳: کچل

Avestan
garenu: *scab on animal skin*
پوسته روی پوست حیوانات
BQ:1779

Pahlavi
gar 2: *scab*
MO:3211

Persian
gar 3: *scab on skin (causing baldness)* گر۳
gargen: *one who has scab, bald* گرگن
PH:200, BQ:1779, MO:3211

1781

گراز

. رجوع شود به   وُراز

گرازیدن: خرامیدن

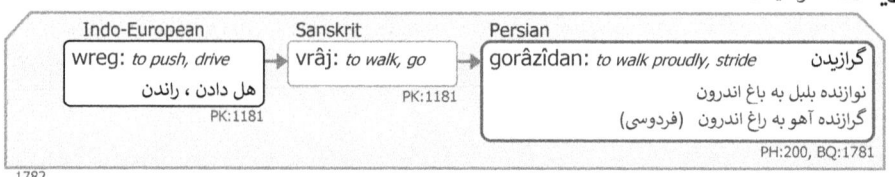

گراس: لقمه

گرامی

همریشه: grace, agree

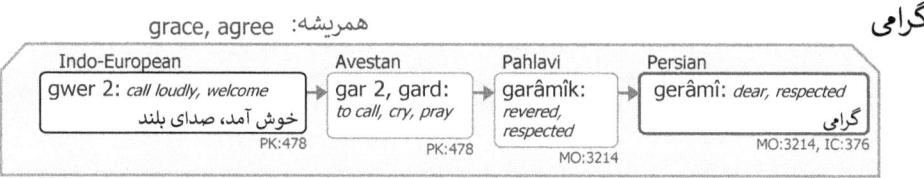

گران

همریشه: gravity

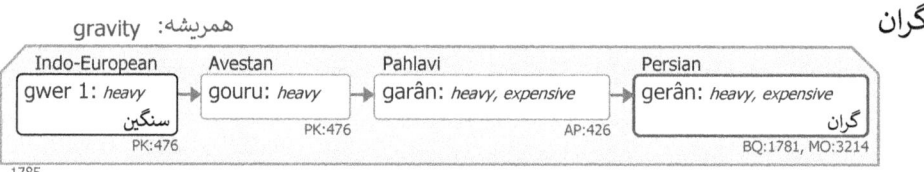

گراییدن

همریشه: grade

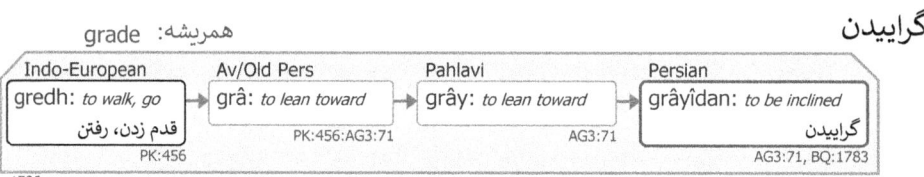

گربه

همریشه: روباه

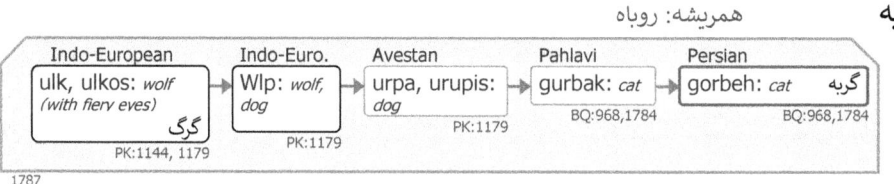

گُرد۱: پهلوان

گِرد۲: مدور   همریشه: گردیدن

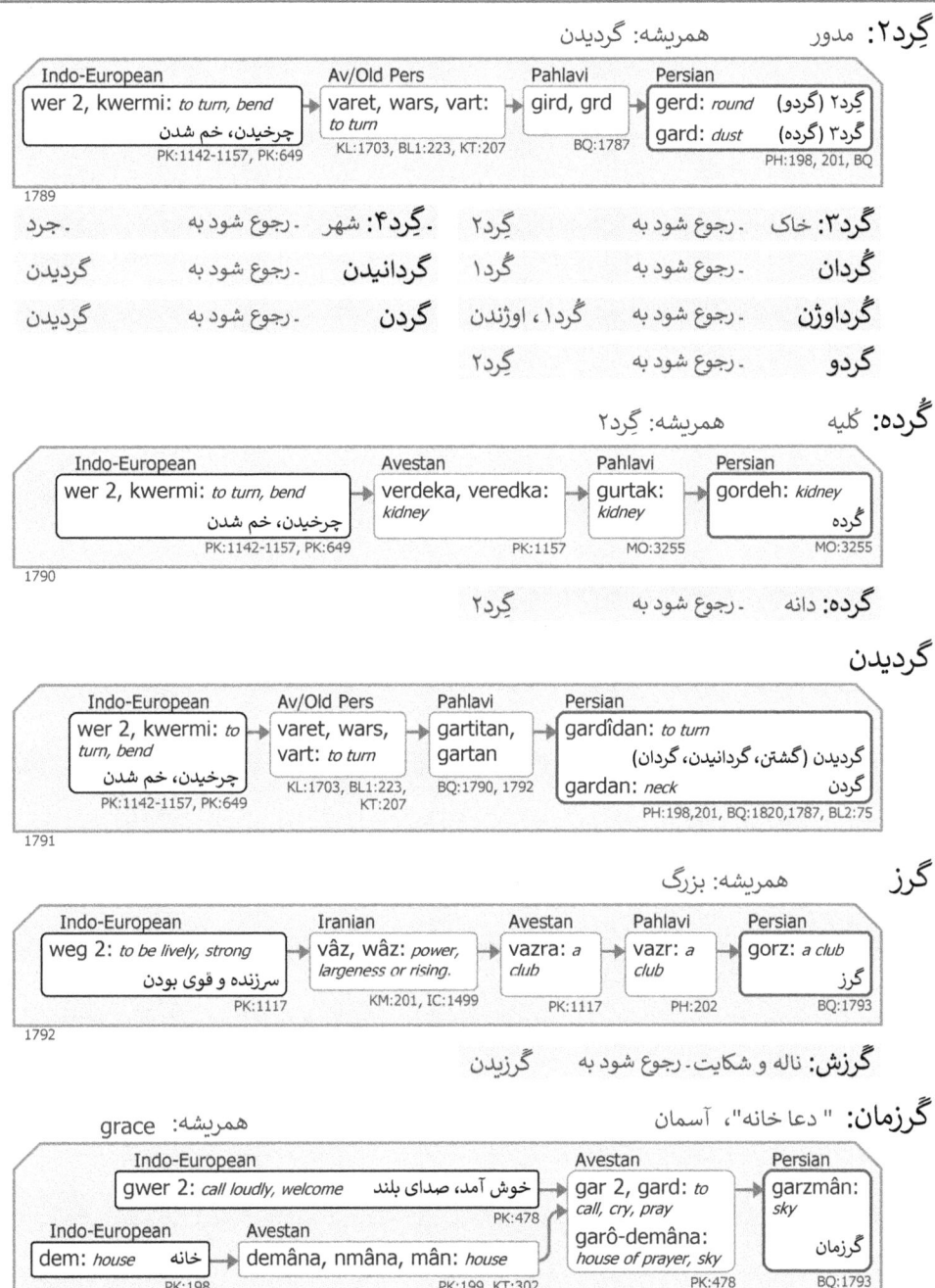

Indo-European	Av/Old Pers	Pahlavi	Persian
wer 2, kwermi: *to turn, bend* چرخیدن، خم شدن PK:1142-1157, PK:649	varet, wars, vart: *to turn* KL:1703, BL1:223, KT:207	gird, grd BQ:1787	gerd: *round* گِرد۲ (گردو) gard: *dust* گِرد۳ (گرده) PH:198, 201, BQ

1789

گرد۳: خاک ـ رجوع شود به   گِرد۲   **.گِرد۴:** شهر ـ رجوع شود به   .جرد

گُردان ـ رجوع شود به   گُرد۱   **گردانیدن** ـ رجوع شود به   گردیدن

گرداوژن ـ رجوع شود به   گُرد۱، اوژندن   **گردن** ـ رجوع شود به   گردیدن

گردو ـ رجوع شود به   گِرد۲

گُرده: کلیه   همریشه: گِرد۲

Indo-European	Avestan	Pahlavi	Persian
wer 2, kwermi: *to turn, bend* چرخیدن، خم شدن PK:1142-1157, PK:649	verdeka, veredka: *kidney* PK:1157	gurtak: *kidney* MO:3255	gordeh: *kidney* گُرده MO:3255

1790

گرده: دانه   ـ رجوع شود به   گِرد۲

گردیدن

Indo-European	Av/Old Pers	Pahlavi	Persian
wer 2, kwermi: *to turn, bend* چرخیدن، خم شدن PK:1142-1157, PK:649	varet, wars, vart: *to turn* KL:1703, BL1:223, KT:207	gartitan, gartan BQ:1790, 1792	gardîdan: *to turn* گردیدن (گشتن، گردانیدن، گردان) gardan: *neck* گردن PH:198,201, BQ:1820,1787, BL2:75

1791

گرز

همریشه: بزرگ

Indo-European	Iranian	Avestan	Pahlavi	Persian
weg 2: *to be lively, strong* سرزنده و قوی بودن PK:1117	vâz, wâz: *power, largeness or rising.* KM:201, IC:1499	vazra: *a club* PK:1117	vazr: *a club* PH:202	gorz: *a club* گرز BQ:1793

1792

گِرزش: ناله و شکایت ـ رجوع شود به   گِرزیدن

گَرزمان: " دعا خانه"، آسمان

همریشه: grace

Indo-European	Avestan	Persian
gwer 2: *call loudly, welcome* خوش آمد، صدای بلند PK:478	gar 2, gard: *to call, cry, pray* garô-demâna: *house of prayer, sky* PK:478	garzmân: *sky* گرزمان BQ:1793
Indo-European **Avestan**		
dem: *house* خانه demâna, nmâna, mân: *house* PK:198 PK:199, KT:302		

COGNATE- Old Persian "mâna: house;/ mânya: domestic" (KT:191-202)

1793

گرزه: مار، موش

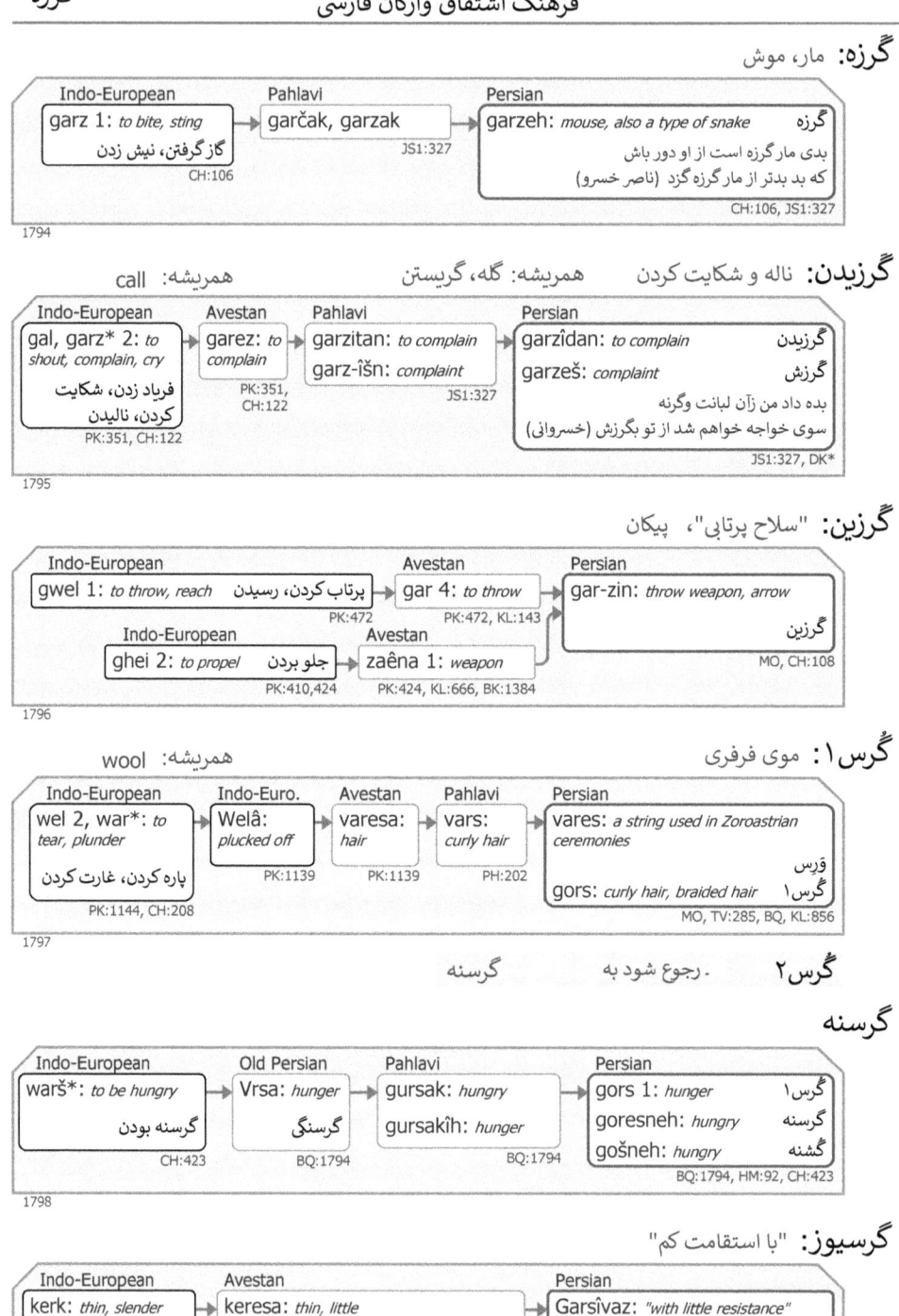

Indo-European	Pahlavi	Persian
garz 1: *to bite, sting* گاز گرفتن، نیش زدن CH:106	garčak, garzak JS1:327	garzeh: *mouse, also a type of snake* گرزه بدی مار گرزه است از او دور باش که بد بدتر از مار گرزه گزد (ناصر خسرو) CH:106, JS1:327

1794

گرزیدن: ناله و شکایت کردن   همریشه: گله، گریستن   همریشه: call

Indo-European	Avestan	Pahlavi	Persian
gal, garz* 2: *to shout, complain, cry* فریاد زدن، شکایت کردن، نالیدن PK:351, CH:122	garez: *to complain* PK:351, CH:122	garzitan: *to complain* garz-îšn: *complaint* JS1:327	garzîdan: *to complain* گرزیدن garzeš: *complaint* گرزش بده داد من زآن لبانت وگرنه سوی خواجه خواهم شد از تو بگرزش (خسروانی) JS1:327, DK*

1795

گرزین: "سلاح پرتابی"، پیکان

Indo-European	Avestan	Persian
gwel 1: *to throw, reach* پرتاب کردن، رسیدن PK:472	gar 4: *to throw* PK:472, KL:143	gar-zin: *throw weapon, arrow* گرزین MO, CH:108
ghei 2: *to propel* جلو بردن PK:410,424	zaêna 1: *weapon* PK:424, KL:666, BK:1384	

1796

گرس۱: موی فرفری   همریشه: wool

Indo-European	Indo-Euro.	Avestan	Pahlavi	Persian
wel 2, war*: *to tear, plunder* پاره کردن، غارت کردن PK:1144, CH:208	Welâ: *plucked off* PK:1139	varesa: *hair* PK:1139	vars: *curly hair* PH:202	vares: *a string used in Zoroastrian ceremonies* وَرس گرس۱ gors: *curly hair, braided hair* MO, TV:285, BQ, KL:856

1797

گرس۲ ـ رجوع شود به   گرسنه

گرسنه

Indo-European	Old Persian	Pahlavi	Persian
warš*: *to be hungry* گرسنه بودن CH:423	Vrsa: *hunger* گرسنگی BQ:1794	gursak: *hungry* gursakîh: *hunger* BQ:1794	gors 1: *hunger* گرس۱ goresneh: *hungry* گرسنه gošneh: *hungry* گشنه BQ:1794, HM:92, CH:423

1798

گرسیوز: "با استقامت کم"

Indo-European	Avestan	Persian
kerk: *thin, slender* نازک، لاغر PK:581	keresa: *thin, little* keresa-vazda: *with "little power"* PK:581, BQ:1795, KL:672	Garsîvaz: *"with little resistance"* گرسیوز BQ:1795

1799

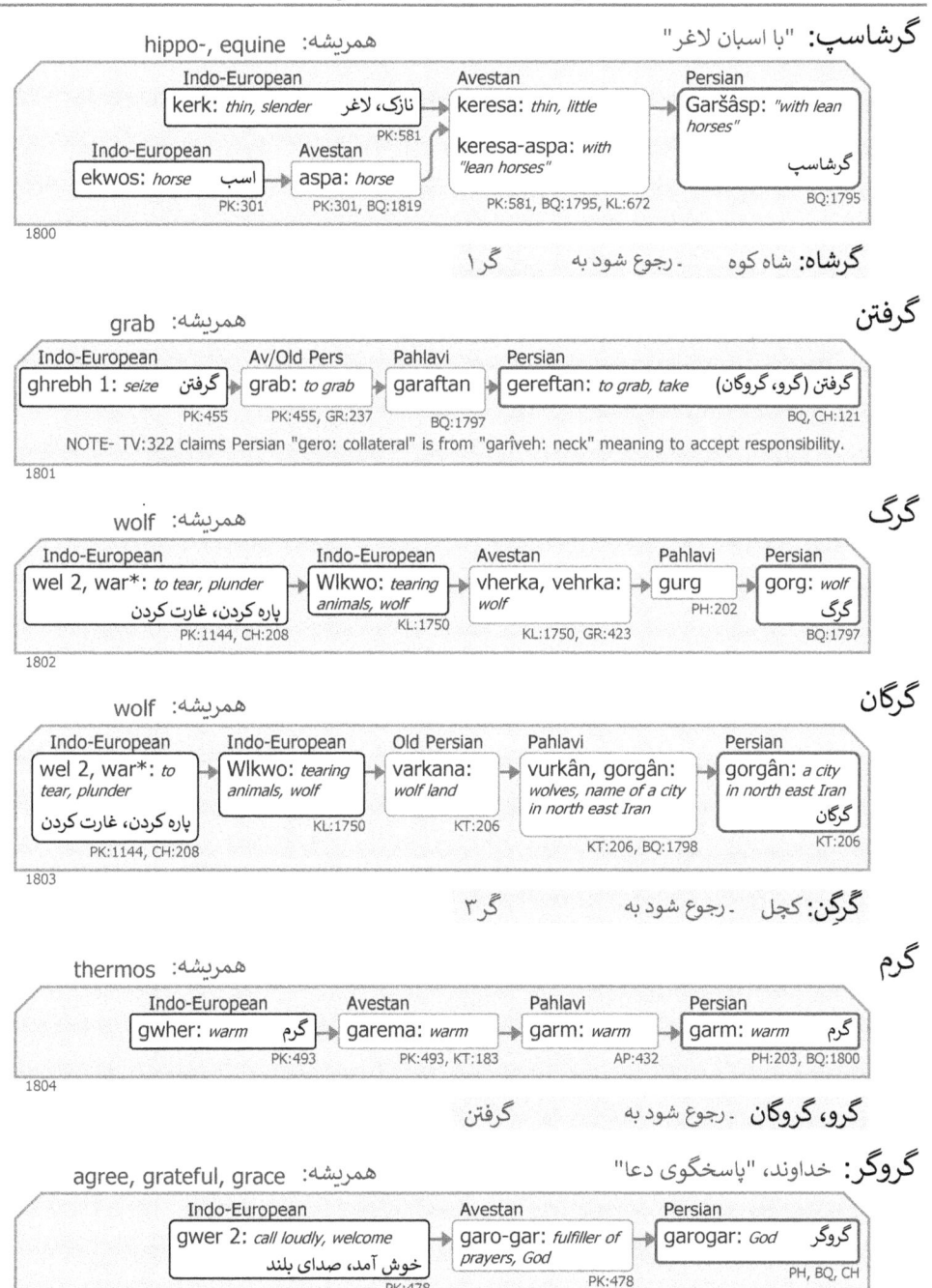

گرشاسپ: "با اسپان لاغر"

همریشه: hippo-, equine

Indo-European — kerk: *thin, slender* — نازک، لاغر — PK:581

Indo-European — ekwos: *horse* — اسب — PK:301

Avestan — aspa: *horse* — PK:301, BQ:1819

Avestan — keresa: *thin, little* / keresa-aspa: with "lean horses" — PK:581, BQ:1795, KL:672

Persian — Garšâsp: *"with lean horses"* — گرشاسپ — BQ:1795

1800

گرشاه: شاه کوه ـ رجوع شود به   گر ۱

گرفتن

همریشه: grab

Indo-European — ghrebh 1: *seize* — گرفتن — PK:455

Av/Old Pers — grab: *to grab* — PK:455, GR:237

Pahlavi — garaftan — BQ:1797

Persian — gereftan: *to grab, take* — گرفتن (گرو، گروگان) — BQ, CH:121

NOTE- TV:322 claims Persian "gero: collateral" is from "garîveh: neck" meaning to accept responsibility.

1801

گرگ

همریشه: wolf

Indo-European — wel 2, war*: *to tear, plunder* — پاره کردن، غارت کردن — PK:1144, CH:208

Indo-European — Wlkwo: *tearing animals, wolf* — KL:1750

Avestan — vherka, vehrka: *wolf* — KL:1750, GR:423

Pahlavi — gurg — PH:202

Persian — gorg: *wolf* — گرگ — BQ:1797

1802

گرگان

همریشه: wolf

Indo-European — wel 2, war*: *to tear, plunder* — پاره کردن، غارت کردن — PK:1144, CH:208

Indo-European — Wlkwo: *tearing animals, wolf* — KL:1750

Old Persian — varkana: *wolf land* — KT:206

Pahlavi — vurkân, gorgân: *wolves, name of a city in north east Iran* — KT:206, BQ:1798

Persian — gorgân: *a city in north east Iran* — گرگان — KT:206

1803

گرگِن: کچل ـ رجوع شود به   گر ۳

گرم

همریشه: thermos

Indo-European — gwher: *warm* — گرم — PK:493

Avestan — garema: *warm* — PK:493, KT:183

Pahlavi — garm: *warm* — AP:432

Persian — garm: *warm* — گرم — PH:203, BQ:1800

1804

گرو، گروگان ـ رجوع شود به   گرفتن

گروگر: خداوند، "پاسخگوی دعا"

همریشه: agree, grateful, grace

Indo-European — gwer 2: *call loudly, welcome* — خوش آمد، صدای بلند — PK:478

Avestan — garo-gar: *fulfiller of prayers, God* — PK:478

Persian — garogar: *God* — گروگر — PH, BQ, CH

1805

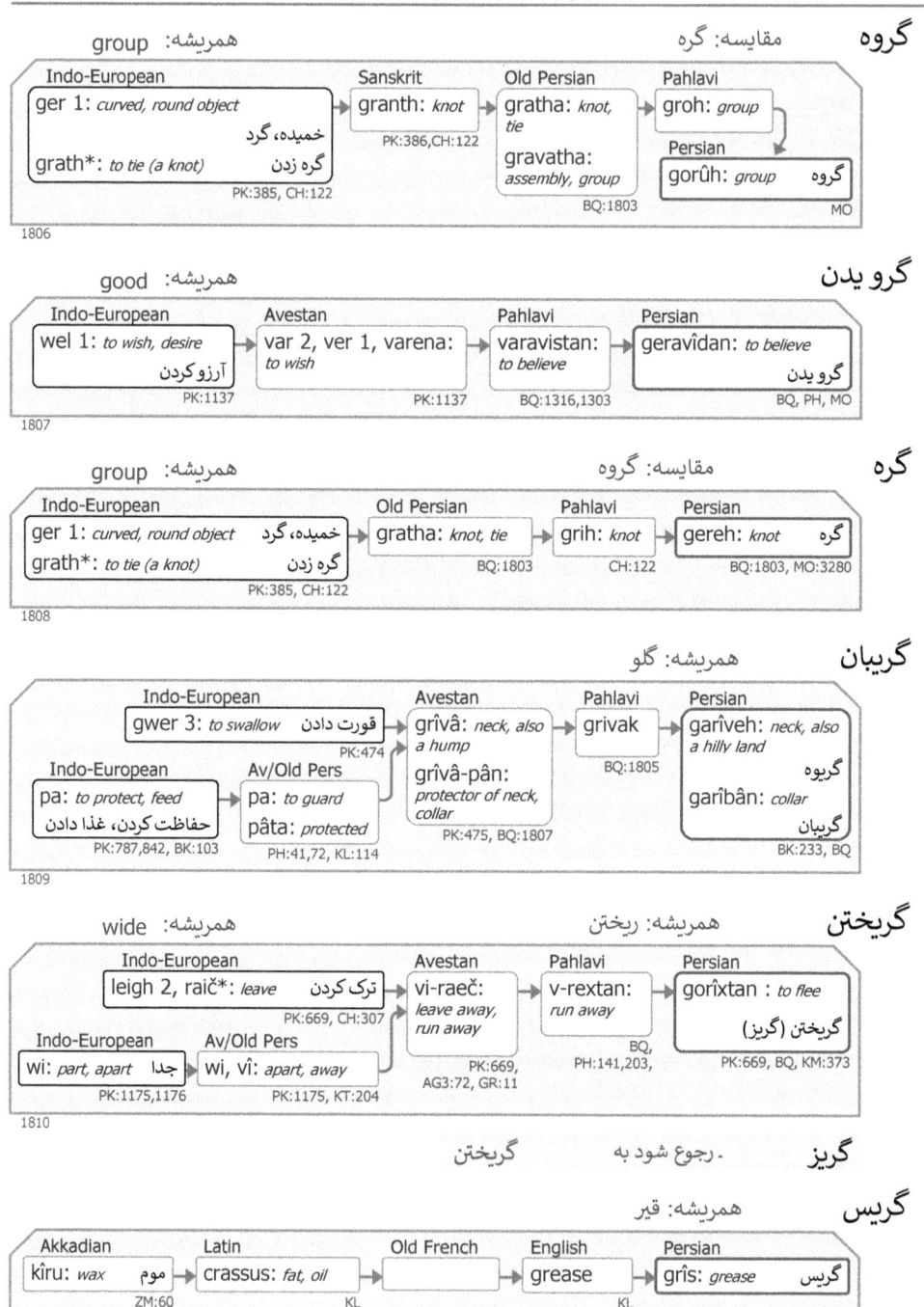

گروه مقایسه: گره

همریشه: group

Indo-European
ger 1: *curved, round object*
خمیده، گرد
grath*: *to tie (a knot)*
گره زدن
PK:385, CH:122

Sanskrit
granth: *knot*
PK:386,CH:122

Old Persian
gratha: *knot, tie*
gravatha: *assembly, group*
BQ:1803

Pahlavi
groh: *group*

Persian
gorûh: *group*
گروه
MO

1806

گرو یدن

همریشه: good

Indo-European
wel 1: *to wish, desire*
آرزو کردن
PK:1137

Avestan
var 2, ver 1, varena: *to wish*
PK:1137

Pahlavi
varavistan: *to believe*
BQ:1316,1303

Persian
geravîdan: *to believe*
گرو یدن
BQ, PH, MO

1807

گره مقایسه: گروه

همریشه: group

Indo-European
ger 1: *curved, round object*
خمیده، گرد
grath*: *to tie (a knot)*
گره زدن
PK:385, CH:122

Old Persian
gratha: *knot, tie*
BQ:1803

Pahlavi
grih: *knot*
CH:122

Persian
gereh: *knot*
گره
BQ:1803, MO:3280

1808

گریبان همریشه: گلو

Indo-European
gwer 3: *to swallow*
قورت دادن
PK:474

Indo-European
pa: *to protect, feed*
حفاظت کردن، غذا دادن
PK:787,842, BK:103

Av/Old Pers
pa: *to guard*
pâta: *protected*
PH:41,72, KL:114

Avestan
grîvâ: *neck, also a hump*
grîvâ-pân: *protector of neck, collar*
PK:475, BQ:1807

Pahlavi
grivak
BQ:1805

Persian
garîveh: *neck, also a hilly land*
گریوه
garîbân: *collar*
گریبان
BK:233, BQ

1809

گریختن همریشه: ریختن

همریشه: wide

Indo-European
leigh 2, raič*: *leave*
ترک کردن
PK:669, CH:307

Indo-European
wi: *part, apart*
جدا
PK:1175,1176

Av/Old Pers
wi, vî: *apart, away*
PK:1175, KT:204

Avestan
vi-raeč: *leave away, run away*
PK:669, AG3:72, GR:11

Pahlavi
v-rextan: *run away*
BQ,
PH:141,203,

Persian
gorîxtan : *to flee*
گریختن (گریز)
PK:669, BQ, KM:373

1810

گریز . رجوع شود به گریختن

گریس همریشه: قیر

Akkadian
kîru: *wax*
موم
ZM:60

Latin
crassus: *fat, oil*
KL

Old French
KL

English
grease

Persian
grîs: *grease*
گریس

1811

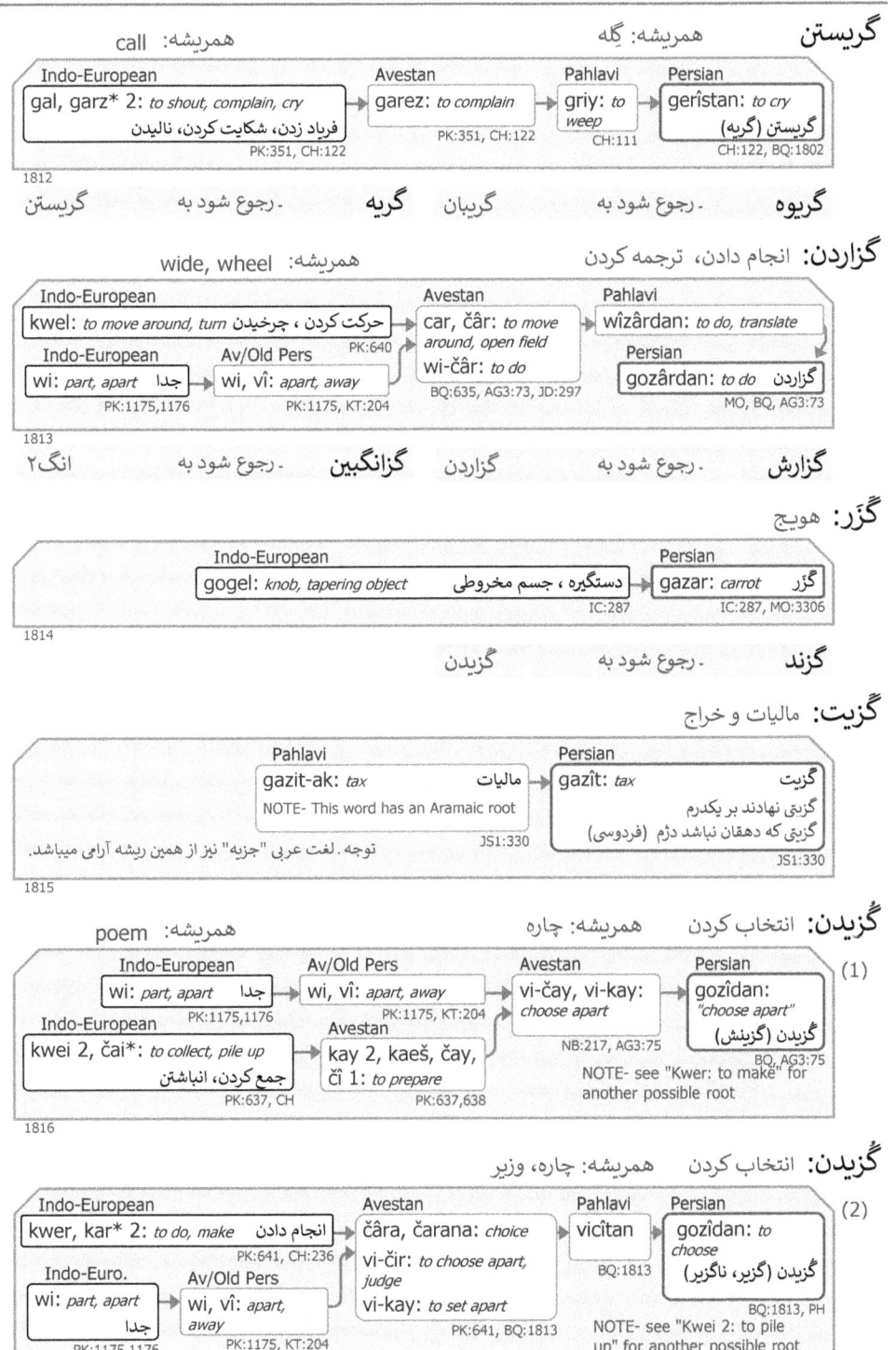

گریستن
همریشه: گِله   همریشه: call

Indo-European
gal, garz* 2: *to shout, complain, cry*
فریاد زدن، شکایت کردن، نالیدن
PK:351, CH:122

→ **Avestan**
garez: *to complain*
PK:351, CH:122

→ **Pahlavi**
griy: *to weep*
CH:111

→ **Persian**
gerîstan: *to cry*
گریستن (گریه)
CH:122, BQ:1802

1812

گریوه - رجوع شود به **گریه**   **گریبان** - رجوع شود به   گریستن

گزاردن: انجام دادن، ترجمه کردن
همریشه: wide, wheel

Indo-European
kwel: *to move around, turn* حرکت کردن، چرخیدن
PK:640

Indo-European
wi: *part, apart* جدا
PK:1175,1176

Av/Old Pers
wi, vî: *apart, away*
PK:1175, KT:204

→ **Avestan**
car, čâr: *to move around, open field*
wi-čâr: *to do*
BQ:635, AG3:73, JD:297

→ **Pahlavi**
wîzârdan: *to do, translate*

→ **Persian**
gozârdan: *to do*
گزاردن
MO, BQ, AG3:73

1813

گزارش - رجوع شود به گزاردن   **گزانگبین** - رجوع شود به   انگ۲

گَزَر: هویج

Indo-European
gogel: *knob, tapering object* دستگیره، جسم مخروطی
IC:287

→ **Persian**
gazar: *carrot* گَزَر
IC:287, MO:3306

1814

گزند - رجوع شود به   گزیدن

گزیت: مالیات و خراج

Pahlavi
gazit-ak: *tax* مالیات
NOTE- This word has an Aramaic root
JS1:330

Persian
gazît: *tax* گزیت
گزیتی نهادند بر یکدرم
گزیتی که دهقان نباشد دژم (فردوسی)
JS1:330

توجه. لغت عربی "جزیه" نیز از همین ریشه آرامی میباشد.

1815

گزیدن: انتخاب کردن
همریشه: چاره   همریشه: poem

(1)

Indo-European
wi: *part, apart* جدا
PK:1175,1176

Av/Old Pers
wi, vî: *apart, away*
PK:1175, KT:204

Indo-European
kwei 2, čai*: *to collect, pile up*
جمع کردن، انباشتن
PK:637, CH

Avestan
kay 2, kaeš, čay, čî 1: *to prepare*
PK:637,638

→ **Avestan**
vi-čay, vi-kay: *choose apart*
NB:217, AG3:75

→ **Persian**
gozîdan: *"choose apart"*
گزیدن (گزینش)
BQ, AG3:75
NOTE- see "Kwer: to make" for another possible root

1816

گزیدن: انتخاب کردن
همریشه: چاره، وزیر

(2)

Indo-European
kwer, kar* 2: *to do, make* انجام دادن
PK:641, CH:236

Indo-Euro.
wi: *part, apart* جدا
PK:1175,1176

Av/Old Pers
wi, vî: *apart, away*
PK:1175, KT:204

→ **Avestan**
čâra, čarana: *choice*
vi-čir: *to choose apart, judge*
vi-kay: *to set apart*
PK:641, BQ:1813

→ **Pahlavi**
vicîtan:
BQ:1813

→ **Persian**
gozîdan: *to choose*
گزیدن (گزیر، ناگزیر)
BQ:1813, PH
NOTE- see "Kwei 2: to pile up" for another possible root

1817

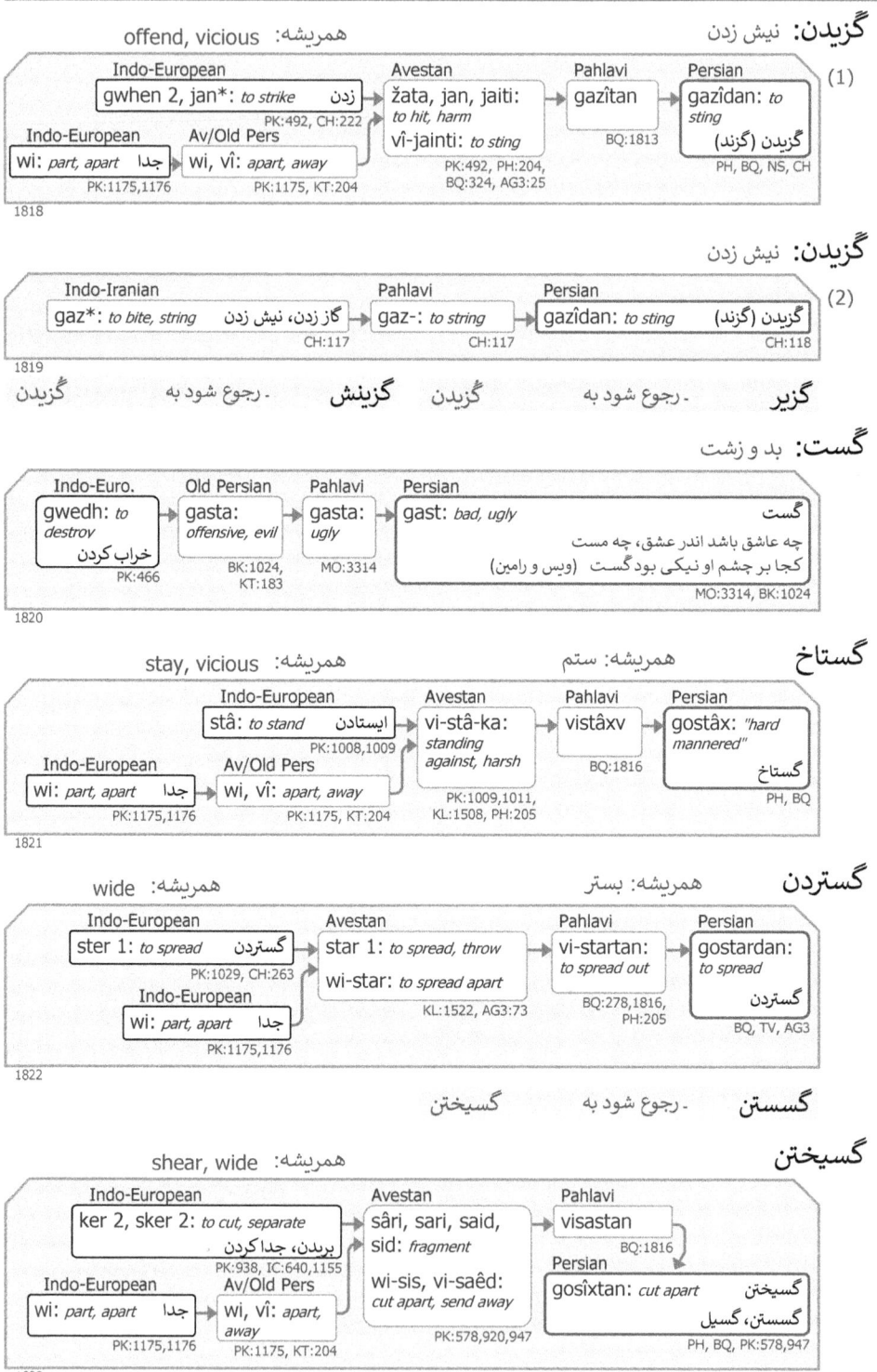

گزیدن: نیش زدن   همریشه: offend, vicious   (1)

Indo-European
gwhen 2, jan*: *to strike* زدن
PK:492, CH:222

Indo-European   Av/Old Pers
wi: *part, apart* جدا   wi, vî: *apart, away*
PK:1175,1176   PK:1175, KT:204

Avestan
žata, jan, jaiti: *to hit, harm*
vî-jainti: *to sting*
PK:492, PH:204, BQ:324, AG3:25

Pahlavi
gazîtan
BQ:1813

Persian
gazîdan: *to sting*
گزیدن (گزند)
PH, BQ, NS, CH

1818

گزیدن: نیش زدن   (2)

Indo-Iranian
gaz*: *to bite, string* گاز زدن، نیش زدن
CH:117

Pahlavi
gaz-: *to string*
CH:117

Persian
gazîdan: *to sting*
گزیدن (گزند)
CH:118

1819

گزیر - رجوع شود به   گزیدن   **گزینش**   **گزیدن** - رجوع شود به   گزیدن

گست: بد و زشت

Indo-Euro.
gwedh: *to destroy* خراب کردن
PK:466

Old Persian
gasta: *offensive, evil*
BK:1024, KT:183

Pahlavi
gasta: *ugly*
MO:3314

Persian
gast: *bad, ugly* گست
چه عاشق باشد اندر عشق، چه مست
کجا بر چشم او نیکی بود گست (ویس و رامین)
MO:3314, BK:1024

1820

گستاخ   همریشه: ستم   همریشه: stay, vicious

Indo-European
stâ: *to stand* ایستادن
PK:1008,1009

Indo-European   Av/Old Pers
wi: *part, apart* جدا   wi, vî: *apart, away*
PK:1175,1176   PK:1175, KT:204

Avestan
vi-stâ-ka: *standing against, harsh*
PK:1009,1011, KL:1508, PH:205

Pahlavi
vistâxv
BQ:1816

Persian
gostâx: *"hard mannered"*
گستاخ
PH, BQ

1821

گستردن   همریشه: بستر   همریشه: wide

Indo-European
ster 1: *to spread* گستردن
PK:1029, CH:263

Indo-European
wi: *part, apart* جدا
PK:1175,1176

Avestan
star 1: *to spread, throw*
wi-star: *to spread apart*
KL:1522, AG3:73

Pahlavi
vi-startan: *to spread out*
BQ:278,1816, PH:205

Persian
gostardan: *to spread*
گستردن
BQ, TV, AG3

1822

گستن - رجوع شود به   گسیختن

گسیختن   همریشه: shear, wide

Indo-European
ker 2, sker 2: *to cut, separate* بریدن، جداکردن
PK:938, IC:640,1155

Indo-European   Av/Old Pers
wi: *part, apart* جدا   wi, vî: *apart, away*
PK:1175,1176   PK:1175, KT:204

Avestan
sâri, sari, said, sid: *fragment*
wi-sis, vi-saêd: *cut apart, send away*
PK:578,920,947

Pahlavi
visastan
BQ:1816

Persian
gosîxtan: *cut apart*
گسیختن
گستن، گسیل
PH, BQ, PK:578,947

1823

گسیل ـ رجوع شود به   گسیختن

گَش: خوشحال

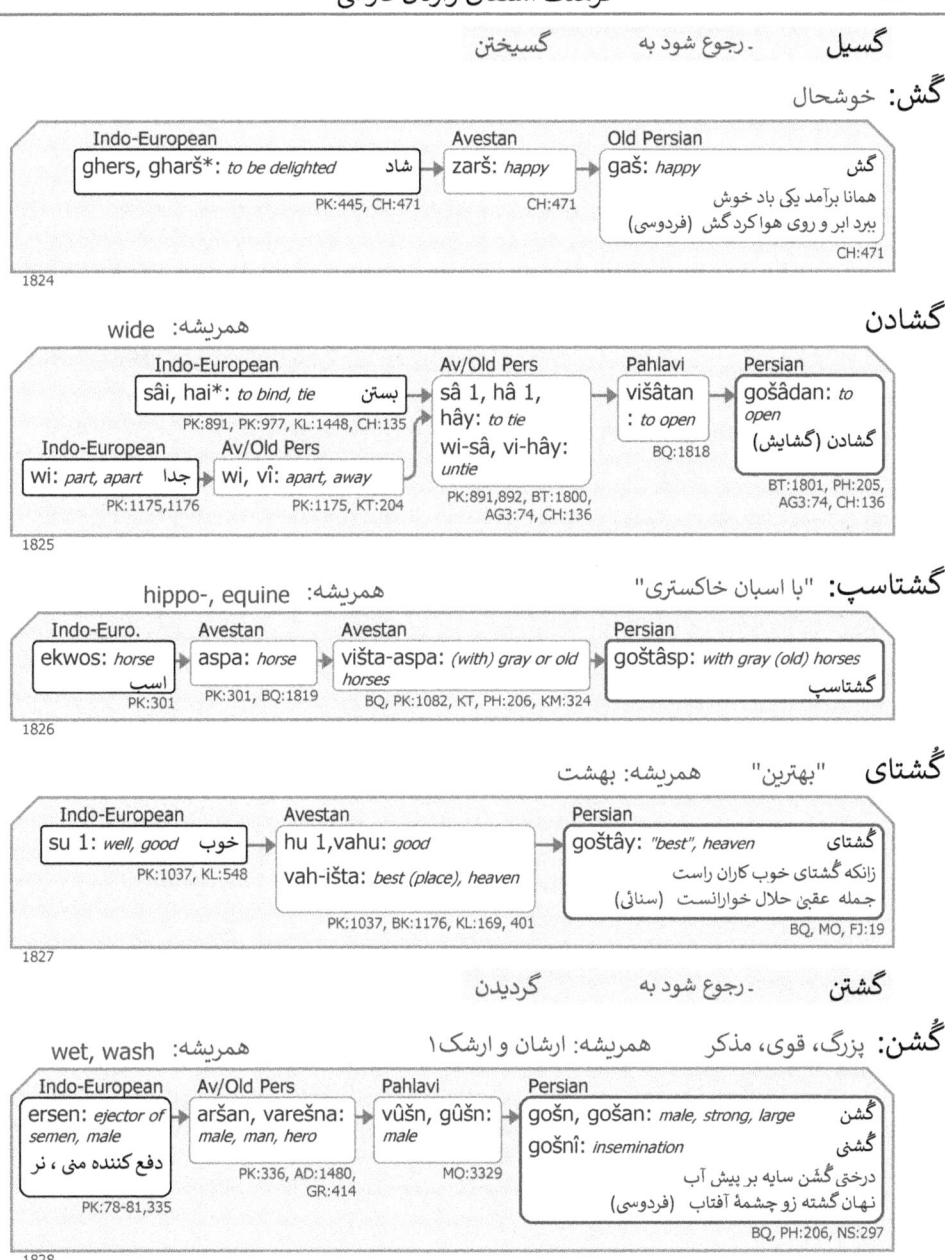

Indo-European	Avestan	Old Persian
ghers, gharš*: *to be delighted* شاد	zarš: *happy*	gaš: *happy*
PK:445, CH:471	CH:471	**گش**

همانا برآمد یکی باد خوش
ببرد ابر و روی هوا کرد گش (فردوسی)
CH:471

1824

گشادن

همریشه: wide

Indo-European	Av/Old Pers	Pahlavi	Persian
sâi, hai*: *to bind, tie* بستن	sâ 1, hâ 1, hây: *to tie*	višâtan : *to open*	gošâdan: *to open*
PK:891, PK:977, KL:1448, CH:135	wi-sâ, vi-hây: *untie*	BQ:1818	گشادن (گشایش)
Indo-European	Av/Old Pers	PK:891,892, BT:1800, AG3:74, CH:136	BT:1801, PH:205, AG3:74, CH:136
wi: *part, apart* جدا	wi, vî: *apart, away*		
PK:1175,1176	PK:1175, KT:204		

1825

گشتاسپ: "با اسبان خاکستری"

همریشه: hippo-, equine

Indo-Euro.	Avestan	Avestan	Persian
ekwos: *horse* اسب	aspa: *horse*	višta-aspa: *(with) gray or old horses*	goštâsp: *with gray (old) horses*
PK:301	PK:301, BQ:1819	BQ, PK:1082, KT, PH:206, KM:324	گشتاسپ

1826

گُشتای "بهترین"   همریشه: بهشت

Indo-European	Avestan	Persian
su 1: *well, good* خوب	hu 1,vahu: *good*	goštây: "best", *heaven* گشتای
PK:1037, KL:548	vah-išta: *best (place), heaven*	زانکه گشتای خوب کاران راست
	PK:1037, BK:1176, KL:169, 401	جمله عقبیٰ حلال خوارانست (سنائی)
		BQ, MO, FJ:19

1827

گشتن ـ رجوع شود به   گردیدن

گُشن: بزرگ، قوی، مذکر   همریشه: ارشان و ارشک۱   همریشه: wet, wash

Indo-European	Av/Old Pers	Pahlavi	Persian
ersen: *ejector of semen, male* دفع کننده منی ، نر	aršan, varešna: *male, man, hero*	vûšn, gûšn: *male*	gošn, gošan: *male, strong, large* گشن
PK:78-81,335	PK:336, AD:1480, GR:414	MO:3329	gošnî: *insemination* گشنی

درختی گُشن سایه بر پیش آب
نهان گشته زو چشمهٔ آفتاب (فردوسی)
BQ, PH:206, NS:297

1828

گشناسب ـ رجوع شود به   گشنسپ

گشنسپ: "با اسبان قوی"

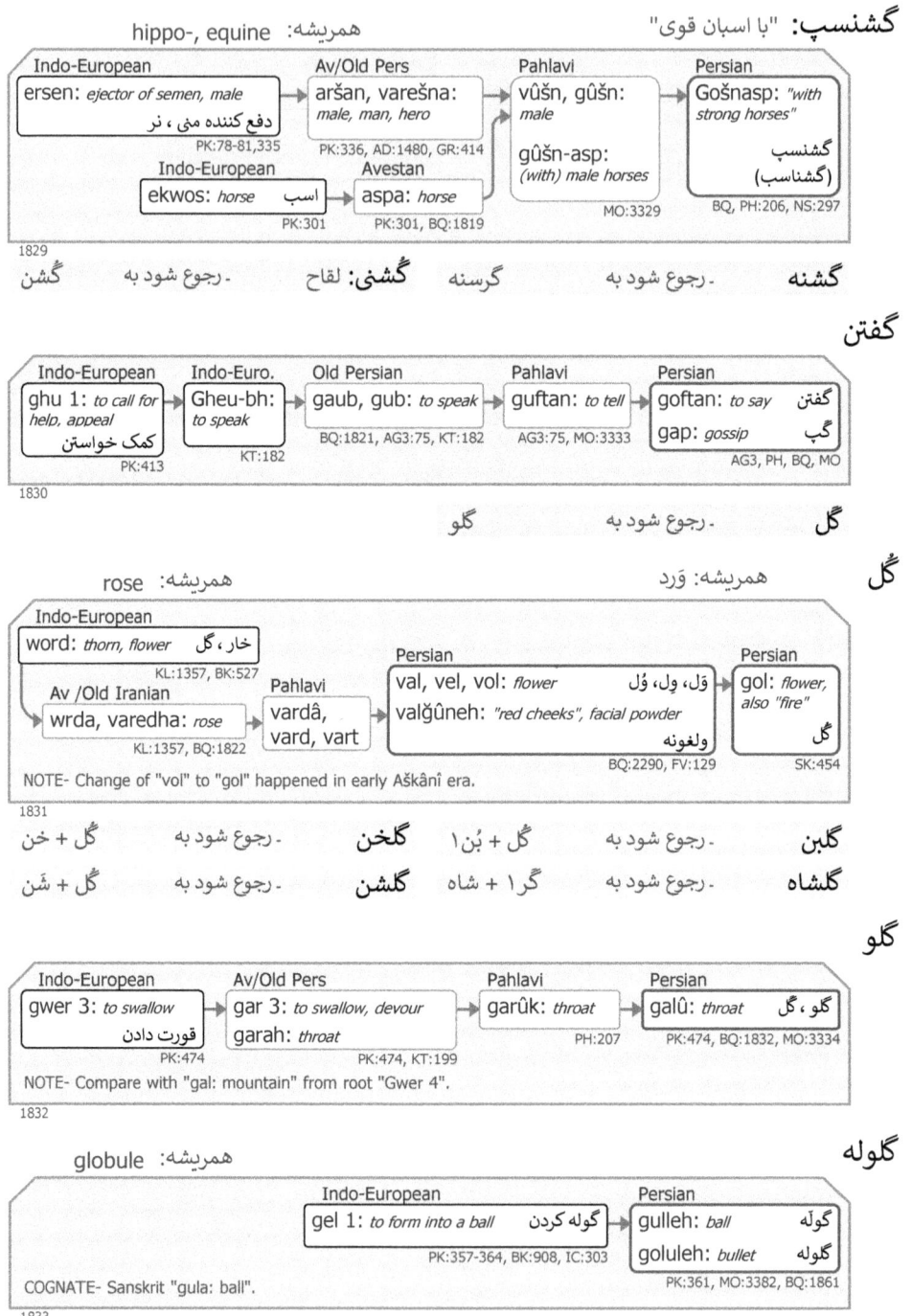

همریشه: hippo-, equine

Indo-European
ersen: *ejector of semen, male*
دفع کننده منی ، نر
PK:78-81,335

Av/Old Pers
aršan, varešna: *male, man, hero*
PK:336, AD:1480, GR:414

Pahlavi
vûšn, gûšn: *male*
gûšn-asp: *(with) male horses*
MO:3329

Persian
Gošnasp: *"with strong horses"*
گشنسپ
(گشناسپ)
BQ, PH:206, NS:297

Indo-European
ekwos: *horse* اسب
PK:301

Avestan
aspa: *horse*
PK:301, BQ:1819

1829

گشنه   .رجوع شود به   گرسنه   **گشنی:** لقاح   .رجوع شود به   گشن

گفتن

Indo-European
ghu 1: *to call for help, appeal*
کمک خواستن
PK:413

Indo-Euro.
Gheu-bh: *to speak*
KT:182

Old Persian
gaub, gub: *to speak*
BQ:1821, AG3:75, KT:182

Pahlavi
guftan: *to tell*
AG3:75, MO:3333

Persian
goftan: *to say* گفتن
gap: *gossip* گپ
AG3, PH, BQ, MO

1830

گل   .رجوع شود به   گلو

گُل

همریشه: وَرد

همریشه: rose

Indo-European
word: *thorn, flower* خار ، گل
KL:1357, BK:527

Av /Old Iranian
wrda, varedha: *rose*
KL:1357, BQ:1822

Pahlavi
vardâ, vard, vart

Persian
val, vel, vol: *flower* وَل، ول، وُل
valğûneh: *"red cheeks", facial powder*
ولغونه
BQ:2290, FV:129

Persian
gol: *flower, also "fire"*
گل
SK:454

NOTE- Change of "vol" to "gol" happened in early Aškânî era.

1831

گلبن   .رجوع شود به   گُل + بُن۱   **گلخن**   .رجوع شود به   گل + خن

گلشاه   .رجوع شود به   گر۱ + شاه   **گلشن**   .رجوع شود به   گل + شَن

گلو

Indo-European
gwer 3: *to swallow*
قورت دادن
PK:474

Av/Old Pers
gar 3: *to swallow, devour*
garah: *throat*
PK:474, KT:199

Pahlavi
garûk: *throat*
PH:207

Persian
galû: *throat* گو ، گل
PK:474, BQ:1832, MO:3334

NOTE- Compare with "gal: mountain" from root "Gwer 4".

1832

گلوله

همریشه: globule

Indo-European
gel 1: *to form into a ball* گوله کردن
PK:357-364, BK:908, IC:303

Persian
gulleh: *ball* گوله
goluleh: *bullet* گلوله
PK:361, MO:3382, BQ:1861

COGNATE- Sanskrit "gula: ball".

1833

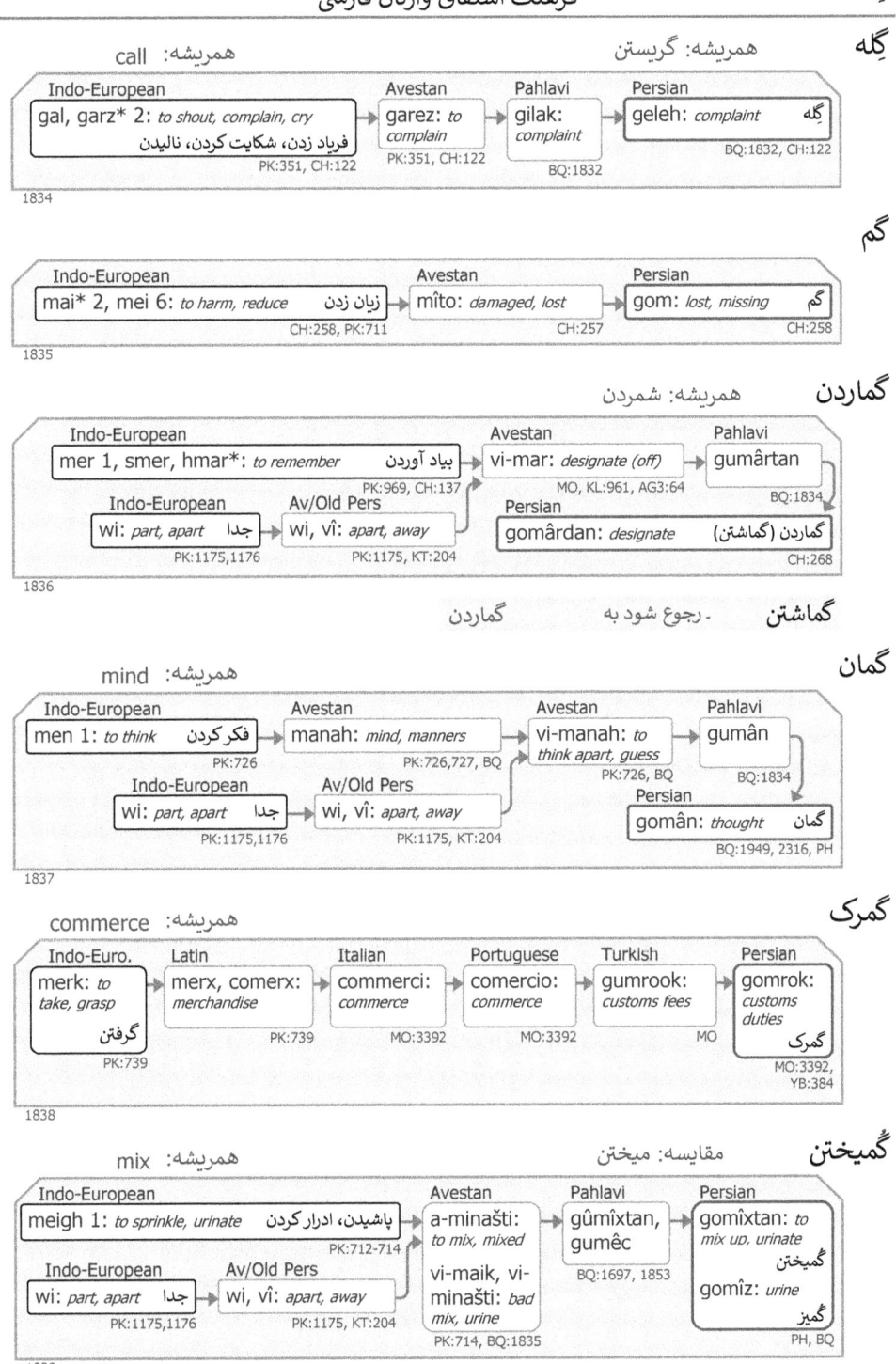

گِله

همریشه: گریستن

همریشه: call

Indo-European
gal, garz* 2: *to shout, complain, cry*
فریاد زدن، شکایت کردن، نالیدن
PK:351, CH:122

Avestan
garez: *to complain*
PK:351, CH:122

Pahlavi
gilak: *complaint*
BQ:1832

Persian
geleh: *complaint* گِله
BQ:1832, CH:122

1834

گم

Indo-European
mai* 2, mei 6: *to harm, reduce* زیان زدن
CH:258, PK:711

Avestan
mîto: *damaged, lost*
CH:257

Persian
gom: *lost, missing* گم
CH:258

1835

گماردن

همریشه: شمردن

Indo-European
mer 1, smer, hmar*: *to remember* بیاد آوردن
PK:969, CH:137

Avestan
vi-mar: *designate (off)*
MO, KL:961, AG3:64

Pahlavi
gumârtan
BQ:1834

Indo-European
wi: *part, apart* جدا
PK:1175,1176

Av/Old Pers
wi, vî: *apart, away*
PK:1175, KT:204

Persian
gomârdan: *designate* گماردن (گماشتن)
CH:268

1836

گماشتن . رجوع شود به **گماردن**

گمان

همریشه: mind

Indo-European
men 1: *to think* فکر کردن
PK:726

Avestan
manah: *mind, manners*
PK:726,727, BQ

Avestan
vi-manah: *to think apart, guess*
PK:726, BQ

Pahlavi
gumân
BQ:1834

Indo-European
wi: *part, apart* جدا
PK:1175,1176

Av/Old Pers
wi, vî: *apart, away*
PK:1175, KT:204

Persian
gomân: *thought* گمان
BQ:1949, 2316, PH

1837

گمرک

همریشه: commerce

Indo-Euro.
merk: *to take, grasp* گرفتن
PK:739

Latin
merx, comerx: *merchandise*
PK:739

Italian
commerci: *commerce*
MO:3392

Portuguese
comercio: *commerce*
MO:3392

Turkish
gumrook: *customs fees*
MO

Persian
gomrok: *customs duties* گمرک
MO:3392, YB:384

1838

گمیختن

مقایسه: میختن

همریشه: mix

Indo-European
meigh 1: *to sprinkle, urinate* پاشیدن، ادرار کردن
PK:712-714

Avestan
a-minašti: *to mix, mixed*

vi-maik, vi-minašti: *bad mix, urine*
PK:714, BQ:1835

Pahlavi
gûmîxtan, gumêc
BQ:1697, 1853

Persian
gomîxtan: *to mix up, urinate* گمیختن
gomîz: *urine* گمیز
PH, BQ

Indo-European
wi: *part, apart* جدا
PK:1175,1176

Av/Old Pers
wi, vî: *apart, away*
PK:1175, KT:204

1839

گمیز: ادرار . رجوع شود به **گمیختن**

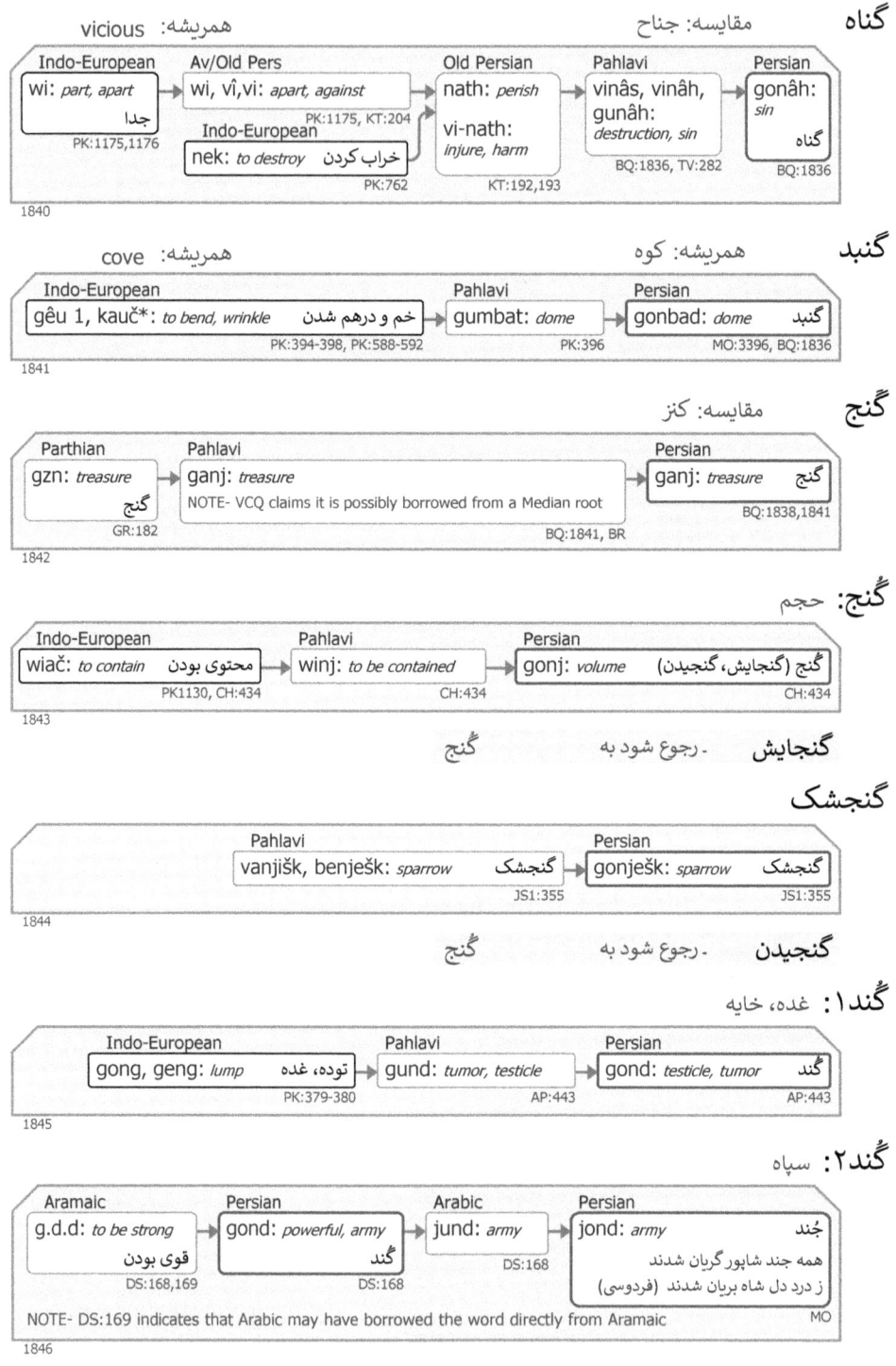

گناه

مقایسه: جناح

همریشه: vicious

| Indo-European | Av/Old Pers | Old Persian | Pahlavi | Persian |

Indo-European — wi: *part, apart* جدا — PK:1175,1176

Av/Old Pers — wi, vî,vi: *apart, against* — PK:1175, KT:204

Indo-European — nek: *to destroy* خراب کردن — PK:762

Old Persian — nath: *perish* / vi-nath: *injure, harm* — KT:192,193

Pahlavi — vinâs, vinâh, gunâh: *destruction, sin* — BQ:1836, TV:282

Persian — gonâh: *sin* گناه — BQ:1836

1840

گنبد

همریشه: کوه — همریشه: cove

Indo-European — gêu 1, kauč*: *to bend, wrinkle* خم و درهم شدن — PK:394-398, PK:588-592

Pahlavi — gumbat: *dome* — PK:396

Persian — gonbad: *dome* گنبد — MO:3396, BQ:1836

1841

گنج

مقایسه: کنز

Parthian — gzn: *treasure* گنج — GR:182

Pahlavi — ganj: *treasure* / NOTE- VCQ claims it is possibly borrowed from a Median root — BQ:1841, BR

Persian — ganj: *treasure* گنج — BQ:1838,1841

1842

گنج: حجم

Indo-European — wiač: *to contain* محتوی بودن — PK1130, CH:434

Pahlavi — winj: *to be contained* — CH:434

Persian — gonj: *volume* گنج (گنجایش، گنجیدن) — CH:434

1843

گنجایش ۔ رجوع شود به گنج

گنجشک

Pahlavi — vanjišk, benješk: *sparrow* گنجشک — JS1:355

Persian — gonješk: *sparrow* گنجشک — JS1:355

1844

گنجیدن ۔ رجوع شود به گنج

گُند۱: غده، خایه

Indo-European — gong, geng: *lump* توده، غده — PK:379-380

Pahlavi — gund: *tumor, testicle* — AP:443

Persian — gond: *testicle, tumor* گند — AP:443

1845

گُند۲: سپاه

Aramaic — g.d.d: *to be strong* قوی بودن — DS:168,169

Persian — gond: *powerful, army* گند — DS:168

Arabic — jund: *army* — DS:168

Persian — jond: *army* جُند
همه جند شاپور گریان شدند
ز درد دل شاه بریان شدند (فردوسی) — MO

NOTE- DS:169 indicates that Arabic may have borrowed the word directly from Aramaic

1846

گَند: فساد، بوی بد   مقایسه: گست

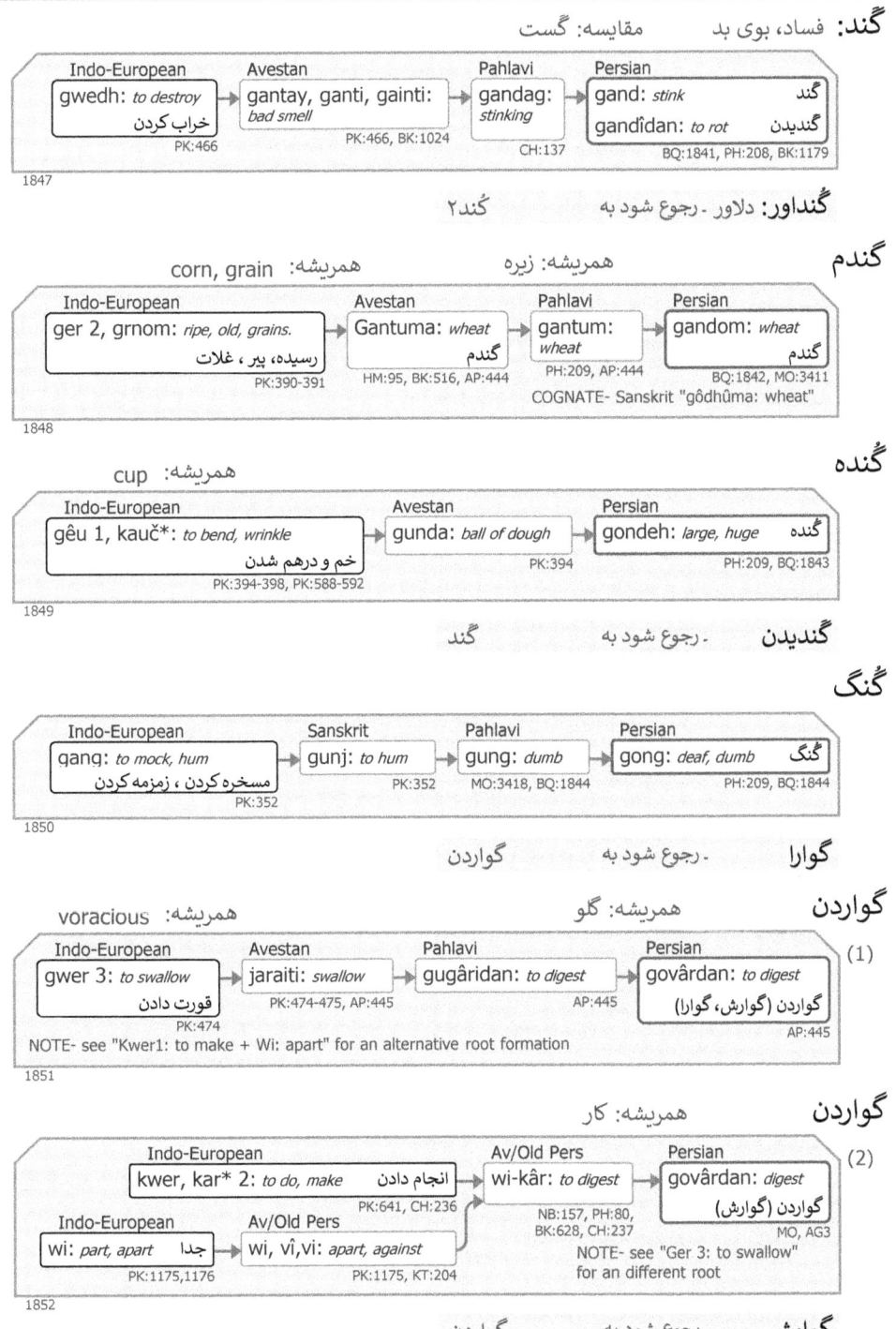

Indo-European	Avestan	Pahlavi	Persian
gwedh: to destroy خراب کردن PK:466	gantay, ganti, gainti: bad smell PK:466, BK:1024	gandag: stinking CH:137	gand: stink گند / gandîdan: to rot گندیدن BQ:1841, PH:208, BK:1179

1847

گُنداور: دلاور ۔ رجوع شود به   گند۲

گندم   همریشه: زیره   همریشه: corn, grain

Indo-European	Avestan	Pahlavi	Persian
ger 2, grnom: ripe, old, grains. رسیده، پیر، غلات PK:390-391	Gantuma: wheat گندم HM:95, BK:516, AP:444	gantum: wheat PH:209, AP:444	gandom: wheat گندم BQ:1842, MO:3411

COGNATE- Sanskrit "gôdhûma: wheat"

1848

گُنده   همریشه: cup

Indo-European	Avestan	Persian
gêu 1, kauč*: to bend, wrinkle خم و درهم شدن PK:394-398, PK:588-592	gunda: ball of dough PK:394	gondeh: large, huge گنده PH:209, BQ:1843

1849

گَندیدن   ۔ رجوع شود به   گند

گُنگ

Indo-European	Sanskrit	Pahlavi	Persian
ganq: to mock, hum مسخره کردن ، زمزمه کردن PK:352	gunj: to hum PK:352	gung: dumb MO:3418, BQ:1844	gong: deaf, dumb گنگ PH:209, BQ:1844

1850

گوارا   ۔ رجوع شود به   گواردن

گواردن   همریشه: گلو   همریشه: voracious   (1)

Indo-European	Avestan	Pahlavi	Persian
gwer 3: to swallow قورت دادن PK:474	jaraiti: swallow PK:474-475, AP:445	gugâridan: to digest AP:445	govârdan: to digest گواردن (گوارش، گوارا) AP:445

NOTE- see "Kwer1: to make + Wi: apart" for an alternative root formation

1851

گواردن   همریشه: کار   (2)

Indo-European	Av/Old Pers	Persian
kwer, kar* 2: to do, make انجام دادن PK:641, CH:236	wi-kâr: to digest NB:157, PH:80, BK:628, CH:237	govârdan: digest گواردن (گوارش) MO, AG3

Indo-European	Av/Old Pers
wi: part, apart جدا PK:1175,1176	wi, vî,vi: apart, against PK:1175, KT:204

NOTE- see "Ger 3: to swallow" for an different root

1852

گوارش   ۔ رجوع شود به   گواردن

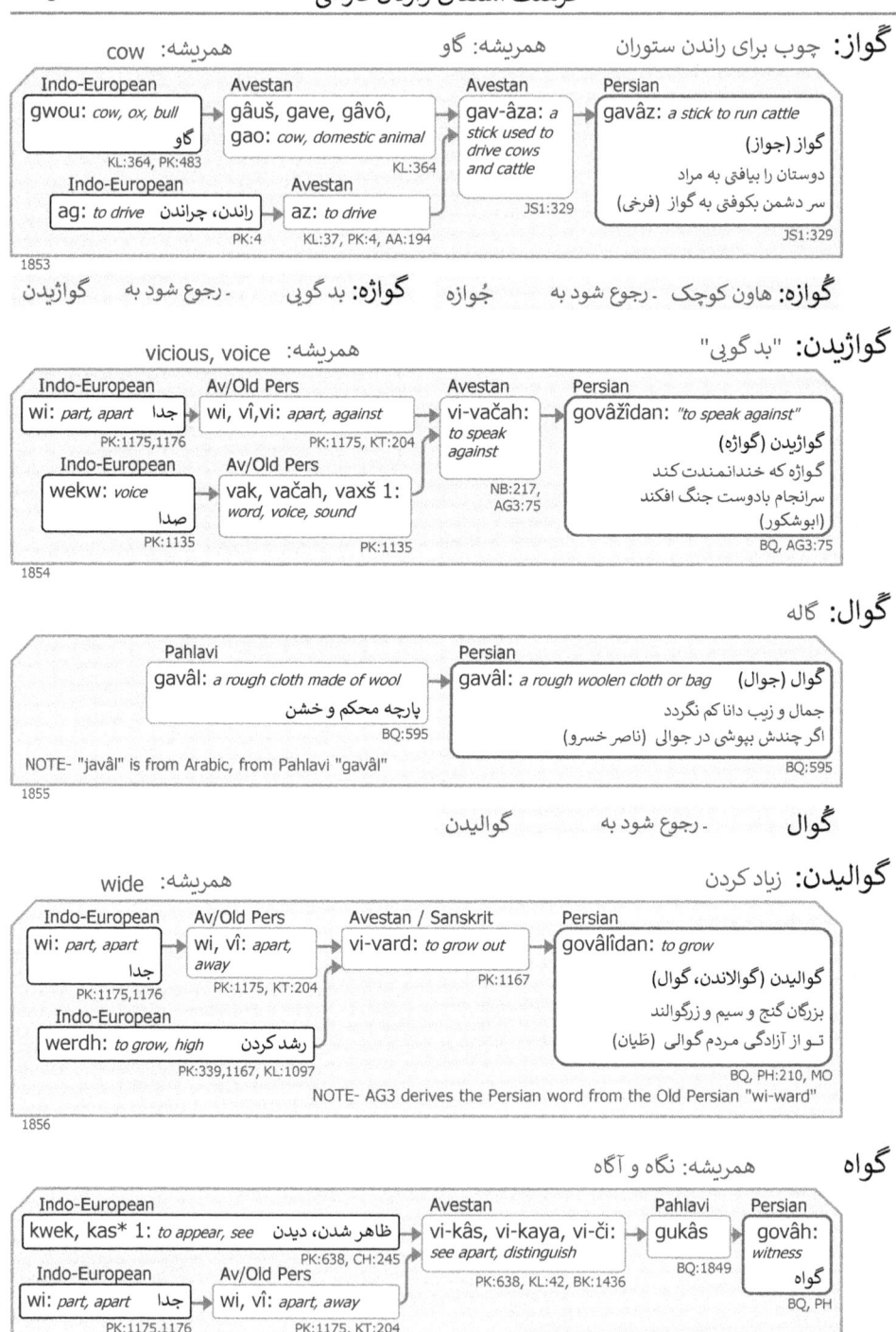

گواز: چوب برای راندن ستوران   همریشه: گاو   همریشه: cow

Indo-European	Avestan	Avestan	Persian
gwou: cow, ox, bull گاو KL:364, PK:483	gâuš, gave, gâvô, gao: cow, domestic animal KL:364	gav-âza: a stick used to drive cows and cattle JS1:329	gavâz: a stick to run cattle گواز (جواز) دوستان را بیافتی به مراد سر دشمن بکوفتی به گواز (فرخی) JS1:329
Indo-European	Avestan		
ag: to drive راندن، چراندن PK:4	az: to drive KL:37, PK:4, AA:194		

1853

گواز: هاون کوچک   .رجوع شود به   جُوازه   **گواژه:** بد گویی   .رجوع شود به   گواژیدن

گواژیدن: "بد گویی"   همریشه: vicious, voice

Indo-European	Av/Old Pers	Avestan	Persian
wi: part, apart جدا PK:1175,1176	wi, vî,vi: apart, against PK:1175, KT:204	vi-vačah: to speak against NB:217, AG3:75	govâžîdan: "to speak against" گواژیدن (گواژه) گواژه که خندانمندت کند سرانجام بادوست جنگ افکند (ابوشکور) BQ, AG3:75
Indo-European	Av/Old Pers		
wekw: voice صدا PK:1135	vak, vačah, vaxš 1: word, voice, sound PK:1135		

1854

گوال: گاله

Pahlavi	Persian
gavâl: a rough cloth made of wool پارچه محکم و خشن BQ:595	gavâl: a rough woolen cloth or bag (گوال (جوال جمال و زیب دانا کم نگردد اگر چندش ببوشی در جوالی (ناصر خسرو) BQ:595

NOTE- "javâl" is from Arabic, from Pahlavi "gavâl"

1855

گوال   .رجوع شود به   گوالیدن

گوالیدن: زیاد کردن   همریشه: wide

Indo-European	Av/Old Pers	Avestan / Sanskrit	Persian
wi: part, apart جدا PK:1175,1176	wi, vî: apart, away PK:1175, KT:204	vi-vard: to grow out PK:1167	govâlîdan: to grow گوالیدن (گوالاندن، گوال) بزرگان گنج و سیم و زرگوالند تـو از آزادگی مردم گوالی (ظیان) BQ, PH:210, MO
Indo-European			
werdh: to grow, high رشد کردن PK:339,1167, KL:1097			

NOTE- AG3 derives the Persian word from the Old Persian "wi-ward"

1856

گواه   همریشه: نگاه و آگاه

Indo-European	Avestan	Pahlavi	Persian
kwek, kas* 1: to appear, see ظاهر شدن، دیدن PK:638, CH:245	vi-kâs, vi-kaya, vi-či: see apart, distinguish PK:638, KL:42, BK:1436	gukâs BQ:1849	govâh: witness گواه BQ, PH
Indo-European	Av/Old Pers		
wi: part, apart جدا PK:1175,1176	wi, vî: apart, away PK:1175, KT:204		

1857

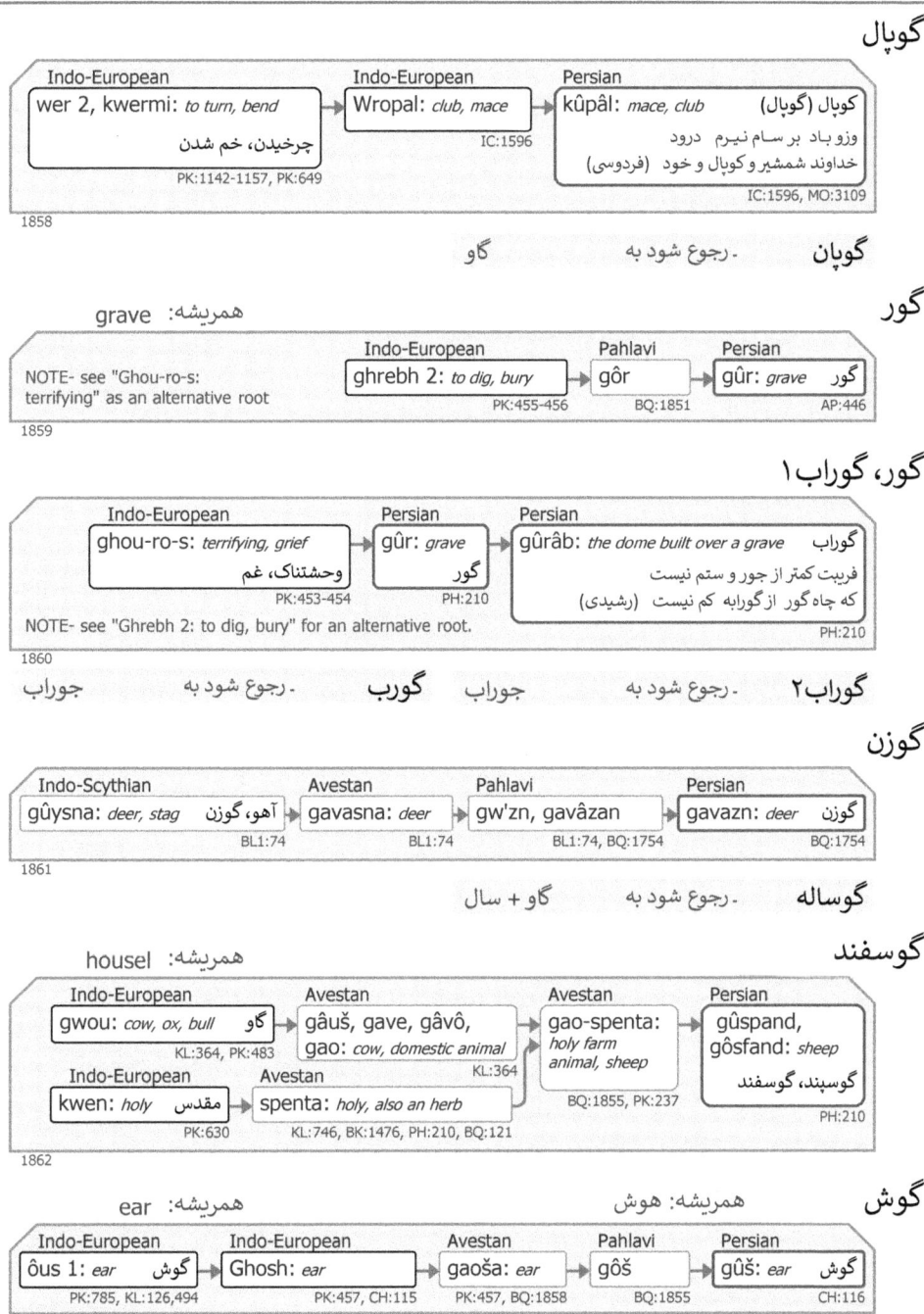

گوپال

Indo-European
wer 2, kwermi: *to turn, bend*

چرخیدن، خم شدن

PK:1142-1157, PK:649

Indo-European
Wropal: *club, mace*

IC:1596

Persian
kûpâl: *mace, club*

کوپال (گوپال)
وزو باد بر سام نیرم درود
خداوند شمشیر و کوپال و خود (فردوسی)

IC:1596, MO:3109

1858

گوپان ۔ رجوع شود به گاو

گور

همریشه: grave

NOTE- see "Ghou-ro-s: terrifying" as an alternative root

Indo-European
ghrebh 2: *to dig, bury*

PK:455-456

Pahlavi
gôr

BQ:1851

Persian
gûr: *grave* گور

AP:446

1859

گور، گوراب۱

Indo-European
ghou-ro-s: *terrifying, grief*

وحشتناک، غم

PK:453-454

Persian
gûr: *grave*

گور

PH:210

Persian
gûrâb: *the dome built over a grave* گوراب
فریبت کمتر از جور و ستم نیست
که چاه گور از گوراب کم نیست (رشیدی)

PH:210

NOTE- see "Ghrebh 2: to dig, bury" for an alternative root.

1860

گوراب۲ ۔ رجوع شود به جوراب **گورب** جوراب ۔ رجوع شود به جوراب

گوزن

Indo-Scythian
gûysna: *deer, stag* آهو، گوزن

BL1:74

Avestan
gavasna: *deer*

BL1:74

Pahlavi
gw'zn, gavâzan

BL1:74, BQ:1754

Persian
gavazn: *deer* گوزن

BQ:1754

1861

گوساله ۔ رجوع شود به گاو + سال

گوسفند

همریشه: housel

Indo-European
gwou: *cow, ox, bull* گاو

KL:364, PK:483

Indo-European
kwen: *holy* مقدس

PK:630

Avestan
gâuš, gave, gâvô, gao: *cow, domestic animal*

KL:364

Avestan
spenta: *holy, also an herb*

KL:746, BK:1476, PH:210, BQ:121

Avestan
gao-spenta: *holy farm animal, sheep*

BQ:1855, PK:237

Persian
gûspand, gôsfand: *sheep*

گوسپند، گوسفند

PH:210

1862

گوش

همریشه: ear   همریشه: هوش

Indo-European
ôus 1: *ear* گوش

PK:785, KL:126,494

Indo-European
Ghosh: *ear*

PK:457, CH:115

Avestan
gaoša: *ear*

PK:457, BQ:1858

Pahlavi
gôš

BQ:1855

Persian
gûš: *ear* گوش

CH:116

1863

گوشاسب ۔ رجوع شود به بوشاسپ **گوشت** گاو

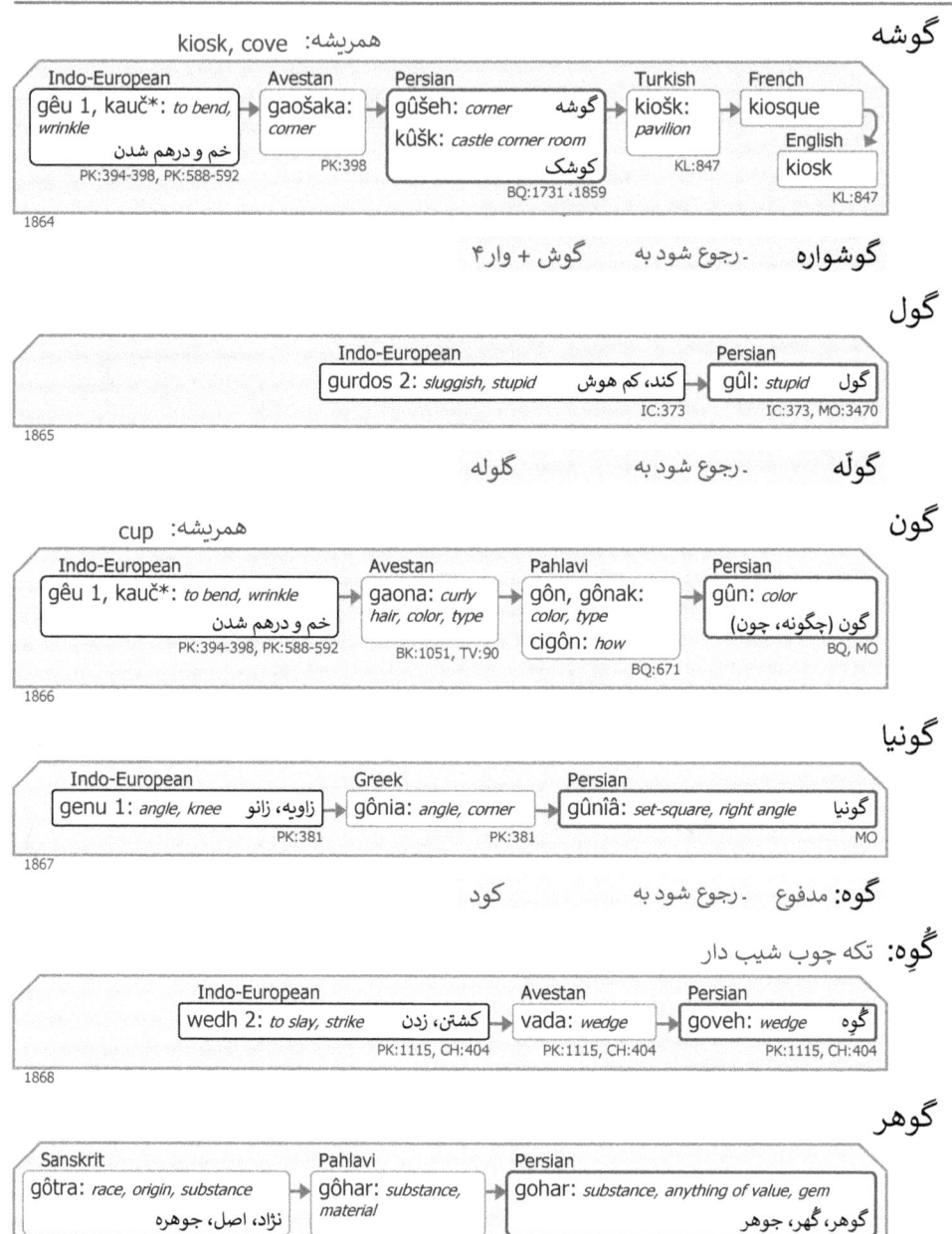

گوشه

همریشه: kiosk, cove

Indo-European	Avestan	Persian	Turkish	French
gêu 1, kauč*: *to bend, wrinkle* خم و درهم شدن PK:394-398, PK:588-592	gaošaka: *corner* PK:398	gûšeh: *corner* گوشه kûšk: *castle corner room* کوشک BQ:1731، 1859	kiošk: *pavilion* KL:847	kiosque English kiosk KL:847

1864

گوشواره .رجوع شود به   گوش + وار۴

گول

Indo-European	Persian
gurdos 2: *sluggish, stupid* کند، کم هوش IC:373	gûl: *stupid* گول IC:373, MO:3470

1865

گوڵه .رجوع شود به   گلوله

گون

همریشه: cup

Indo-European	Avestan	Pahlavi	Persian
gêu 1, kauč*: *to bend, wrinkle* خم و درهم شدن PK:394-398, PK:588-592	gaona: *curly hair, color, type* BK:1051, TV:90	gôn, gônak: *color, type* cigôn: *how* BQ:671	gûn: *color* گون (چگونه، چون) BQ, MO

1866

گونیا

Indo-European	Greek	Persian
genu 1: *angle, knee* زاویه، زانو PK:381	gônia: *angle, corner* PK:381	gûnîâ: *set-square, right angle* گونیا MO

1867

گوه: مدفوع   .رجوع شود به   کود

گُوِه: تکه چوب شیب دار

Indo-European	Avestan	Persian
wedh 2: *to slay, strike* کشتن، زدن PK:1115, CH:404	vada: *wedge* PK:1115, CH:404	goveh: *wedge* گُوه PK:1115, CH:404

1868

گوهر

Sanskrit	Pahlavi	Persian
gôtra: *race, origin, substance* نژاد، اصل، جوهره PH:211	gôhar: *substance, material* PH:211	gohar: *substance, anything of value, gem* گوهر، گُهر، جوهر BQ:1862, AA:101, RZ:249, NS:302

1869

گوهَریدن: معامله پایاپای کردن

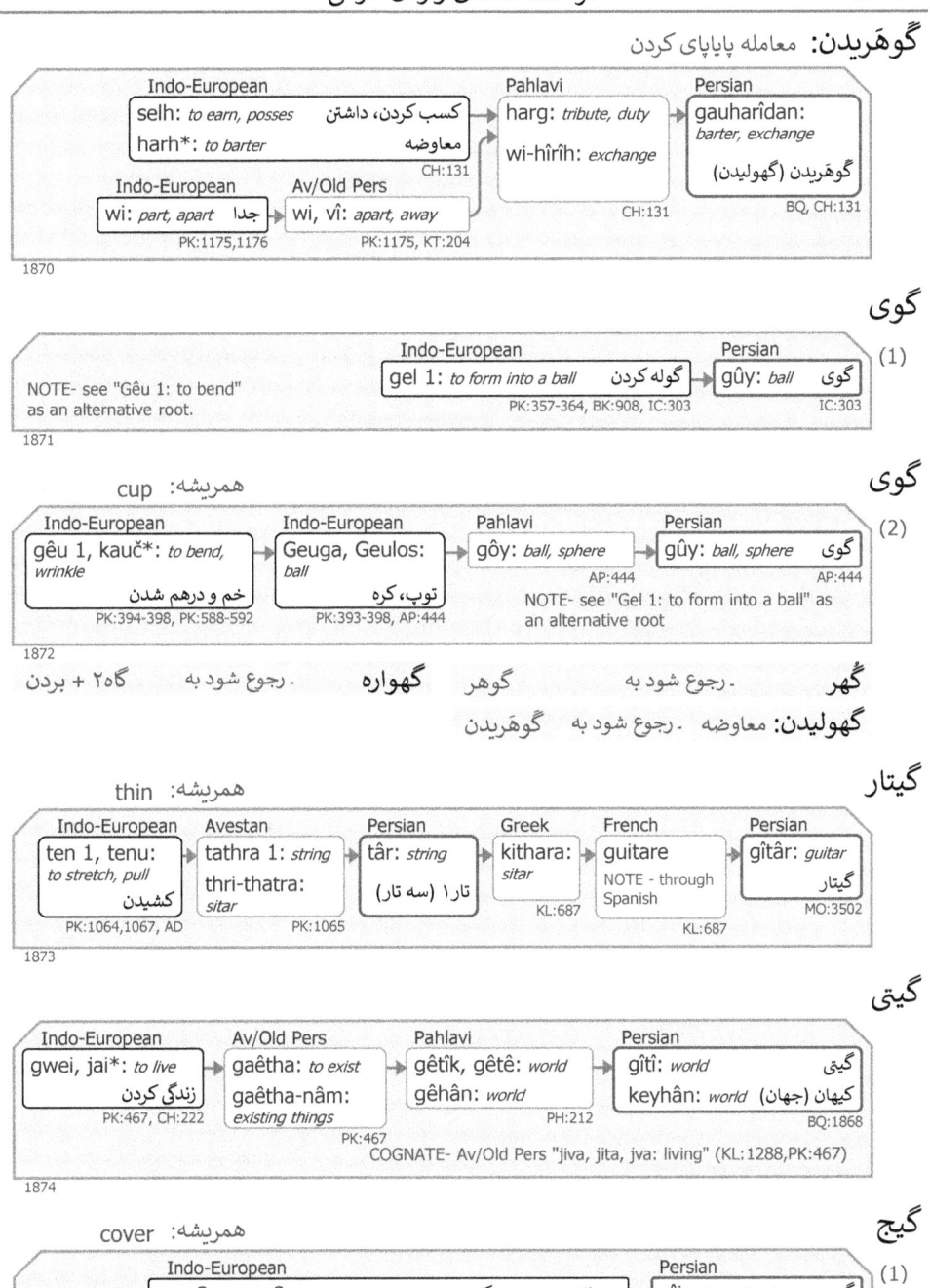

گوی (1)

گوی (2)

گُهر . رجوع شود به گوهر   گهواره . رجوع شود به گ ۲۵۰ + بردن

گهولیدن: معاوضه . رجوع شود به گوهَریدن

گیتار

گیتی

گیج (1)

گیج

(2)

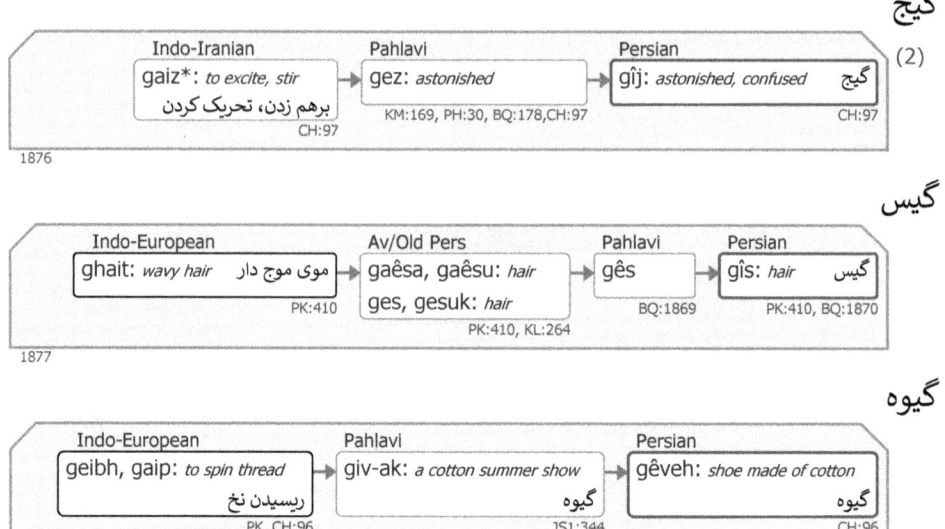

Indo-Iranian	Pahlavi	Persian
gaiz*: *to excite, stir* برهم زدن، تحریک کردن CH:97	gez: *astonished* KM:169, PH:30, BQ:178,CH:97	gîj: *astonished, confused* گیج CH:97

1876

گیس

Indo-European	Av/Old Pers	Pahlavi	Persian
ghait: *wavy hair* موی موج دار PK:410	gaêsa, gaêsu: *hair* ges, gesuk: *hair* PK:410, KL:264	gês BQ:1869	gîs: *hair* گیس PK:410, BQ:1870

1877

گیوه

Indo-European	Pahlavi	Persian
geibh, gaip: *to spin thread* ریسیدن نخ PK, CH:96	giv-ak: *a cotton summer show* گیوه JS1:344	gêveh: *shoe made of cotton* گیوه CH:96

1878

این حرف گاه به ر بدل شود.

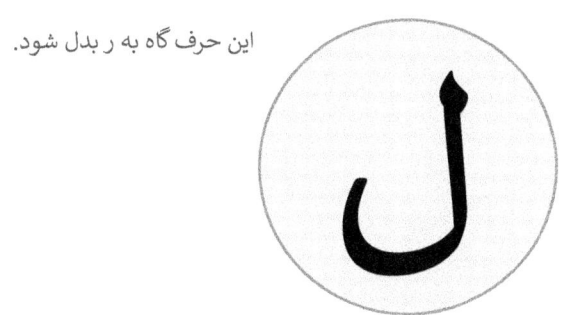

لابه: چاپلوسی، فریب

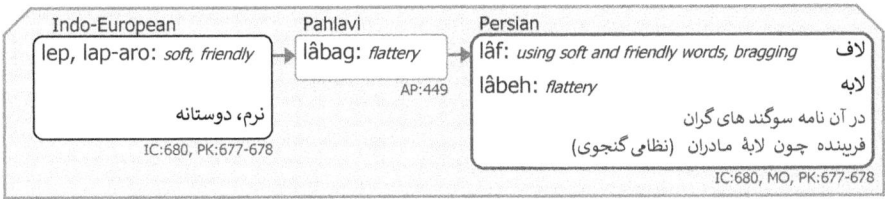

Indo-European	Pahlavi	Persian
lep, lap-aro: *soft, friendly*	lâbag: *flattery*	lâf: *using soft and friendly words, bragging* لاف
نرم، دوستانه	AP:449	lâbeh: *flattery* لابه
IC:680, PK:677-678		در آن نامه سوگند های گران
		فریبنده چون لابهٔ مادران (نظامی گنجوی)
		IC:680, MO, PK:677-678

1879

لاجورد: "شهر قبیله لاج"

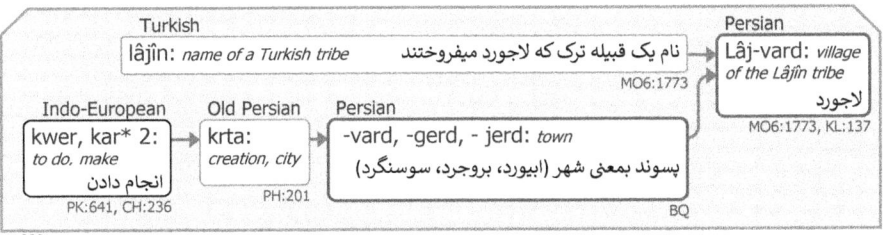

Turkish		Persian
lâjîn: *name of a Turkish tribe* نام یک قبیله ترک که لاجورد میفروختند		Lâj-vard: *village of the Lâjîn tribe*
	MO6:1773	لاجورد
Indo-European	Old Persian	Persian	MO6:1773, KL:137
kwer, kar* 2: *to do, make*	krta: *creation, city*	-vard, -gerd, - jerd: *town*	
انجام دادن		پسوند بمعنی شهر (ابیورد، بروجرد، سوسنگرد)	
PK:641, CH:236	PH:201	BQ	

1880

لاخ

Indo-European	Persian
lêsos: *place, space, area* محل، منطقه	lâx: *a suffix meaning place of* لاخ (سنگلاخ)
IC:680	IC:680, MO:3522

1881

لادن

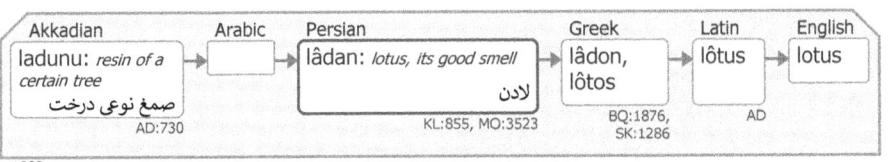

Akkadian	Arabic	Persian	Greek	Latin	English
ladunu: *resin of a certain tree*		lâdan: *lotus, its good smell*	lâdon, lôtos	lôtus	lotus
صمغ نوعی درخت		لادن		AD	
AD:730		KL:855, MO:3523	BQ:1876, SK:1286		

1882

لاغر

همریشه: carnival, light

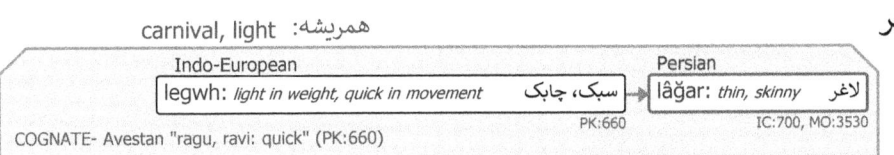

Indo-European	Persian
legwh: *light in weight, quick in movement* سبک، چابک	lâğar: *thin, skinny* لاغر
PK:660	IC:700, MO:3530
COGNATE- Avestan "ragu, ravi: quick" (PK:660)	

1883

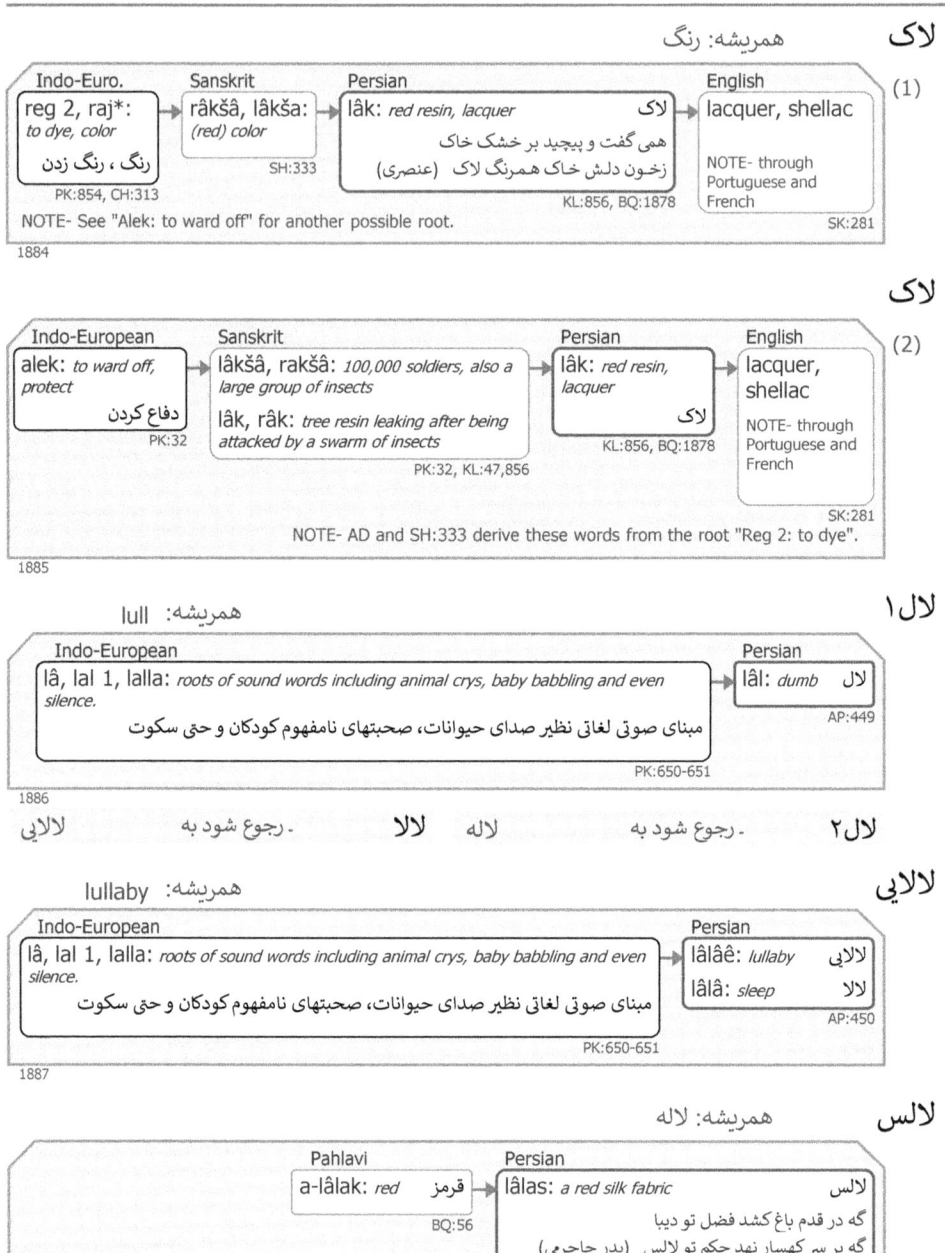

لاک همریشه: رنگ   لاک (1)

Indo-Euro.	Sanskrit	Persian	English
reg 2, raj*: to dye, color رنگ ، رنگ زدن PK:854, CH:313	râkšâ, lâkša: (red) color SH:333	lâk: red resin, lacquer لاک همی گفت و پیچید بر خشک خاک زخون دلش خاک همرنگ لاک (عنصری) KL:856, BQ:1878	lacquer, shellac NOTE- through Portuguese and French SK:281

NOTE- See "Alek: to ward off" for another possible root.

1884

لاک   لاک (2)

Indo-European	Sanskrit	Persian	English
alek: to ward off, protect دفاع کردن PK:32	lâkšâ, rakšâ: 100,000 soldiers, also a large group of insects lâk, râk: tree resin leaking after being attacked by a swarm of insects PK:32, KL:47,856	lâk: red resin, lacquer لاک KL:856, BQ:1878	lacquer, shellac NOTE- through Portuguese and French SK:281

NOTE- AD and SH:333 derive these words from the root "Reg 2: to dye".

1885

لال۱ همریشه: lull   لال

Indo-European	Persian
lâ, lal 1, lalla: roots of sound words including animal crys, baby babbling and even silence. مبنای صوتی لغاتی نظیر صدای حیوانات، صحبتهای نامفهوم کودکان و حتی سکوت PK:650-651	lâl: dumb لال AP:449

1886

لال۲ لالا . رجوع شود به لاله   لالایی

لالایی همریشه: lullaby   لالایی

Indo-European	Persian
lâ, lal 1, lalla: roots of sound words including animal crys, baby babbling and even silence. مبنای صوتی لغاتی نظیر صدای حیوانات، صحبتهای نامفهوم کودکان و حتی سکوت PK:650-651	lâlâê: lullaby لالایی lâlâ: sleep لالا AP:450

1887

لالس همریشه: لاله   لالس

Pahlavi	Persian
a-lâlak: red قرمز BQ:56	lâlas: a red silk fabric لالس گه در قدم باغ کشد فضل تو دیبا گه بر سر کهسار نهد حکم تو لالس (بدر جاجرمی) BQ

1888

لالک

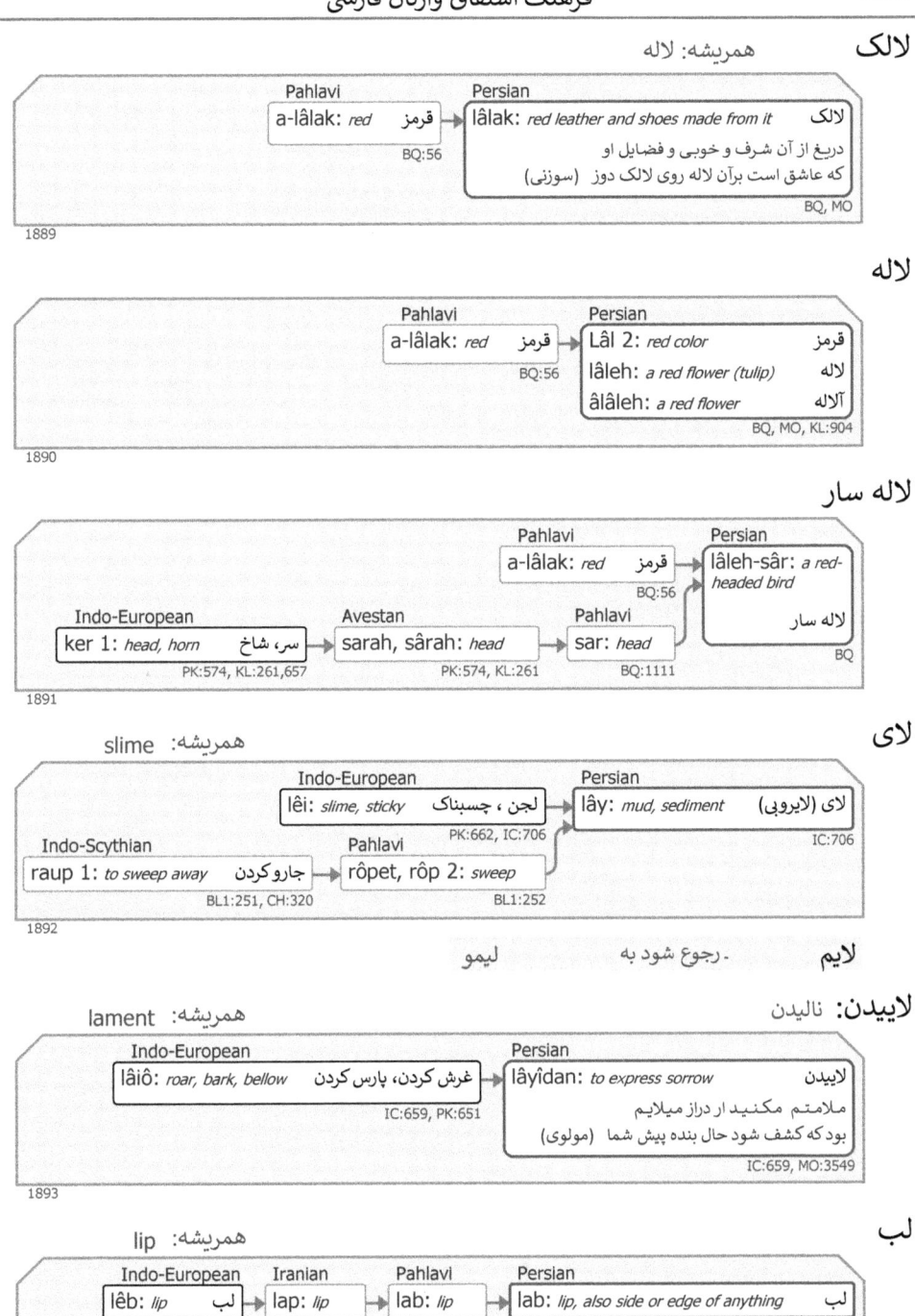

لالک
همریشه: لاله

Pahlavi
a-lâlak: *red* قرمز

Persian
lâlak: *red leather and shoes made from it* لالک
دریغ از آن شرف و خوبی و فضایل او
که عاشق است برآن لاله روی لالک دوز (سوزنی)
BQ, MO

BQ:56

1889

لاله

Pahlavi
a-lâlak: *red* قرمز

Persian
Lâl 2: *red color* قرمز
lâleh: *a red flower (tulip)* لاله
âlâleh: *a red flower* آلاله
BQ, MO, KL:904

BQ:56

1890

لاله سار

Pahlavi
a-lâlak: *red* قرمز

Persian
lâleh-sâr: *a red-headed bird* لاله سار
BQ

BQ:56

Indo-European
ker 1: *head, horn* سر، شاخ
PK:574, KL:261,657

Avestan
sarah, sârah: *head*
PK:574, KL:261

Pahlavi
sar: *head*
BQ:1111

1891

لای
همریشه: slime

Indo-European
lêi: *slime, sticky* لجن ، چسبناک
PK:662, IC:706

Persian
lây: *mud, sediment* لای (لایروبی)
IC:706

Indo-Scythian
raup 1: *to sweep away* جارو کردن
BL1:251, CH:320

Pahlavi
rôpet, rôp 2: *sweep*
BL1:252

1892

لایم
رجوع شود به ـ لیمو

لاییدن: نالیدن
همریشه: lament

Indo-European
lâiô: *roar, bark, bellow* غرش کردن، پارس کردن
IC:659, PK:651

Persian
lâyîdan: *to express sorrow* لاییدن
ملامتم مکنید ار دراز میلایم
بود که کشف شود حال بنده پیش شما (مولوی)
IC:659, MO:3549

1893

لب
همریشه: lip

Indo-European
lêb: *lip* لب
PK:655

Iranian
lap: *lip*
BQ:1885

Pahlavi
lab: *lip*
MO:3551

Persian
lab: *lip, also side or edge of anything* لب
PH:212, MO:3551

1894

لَت: تکه پارچه

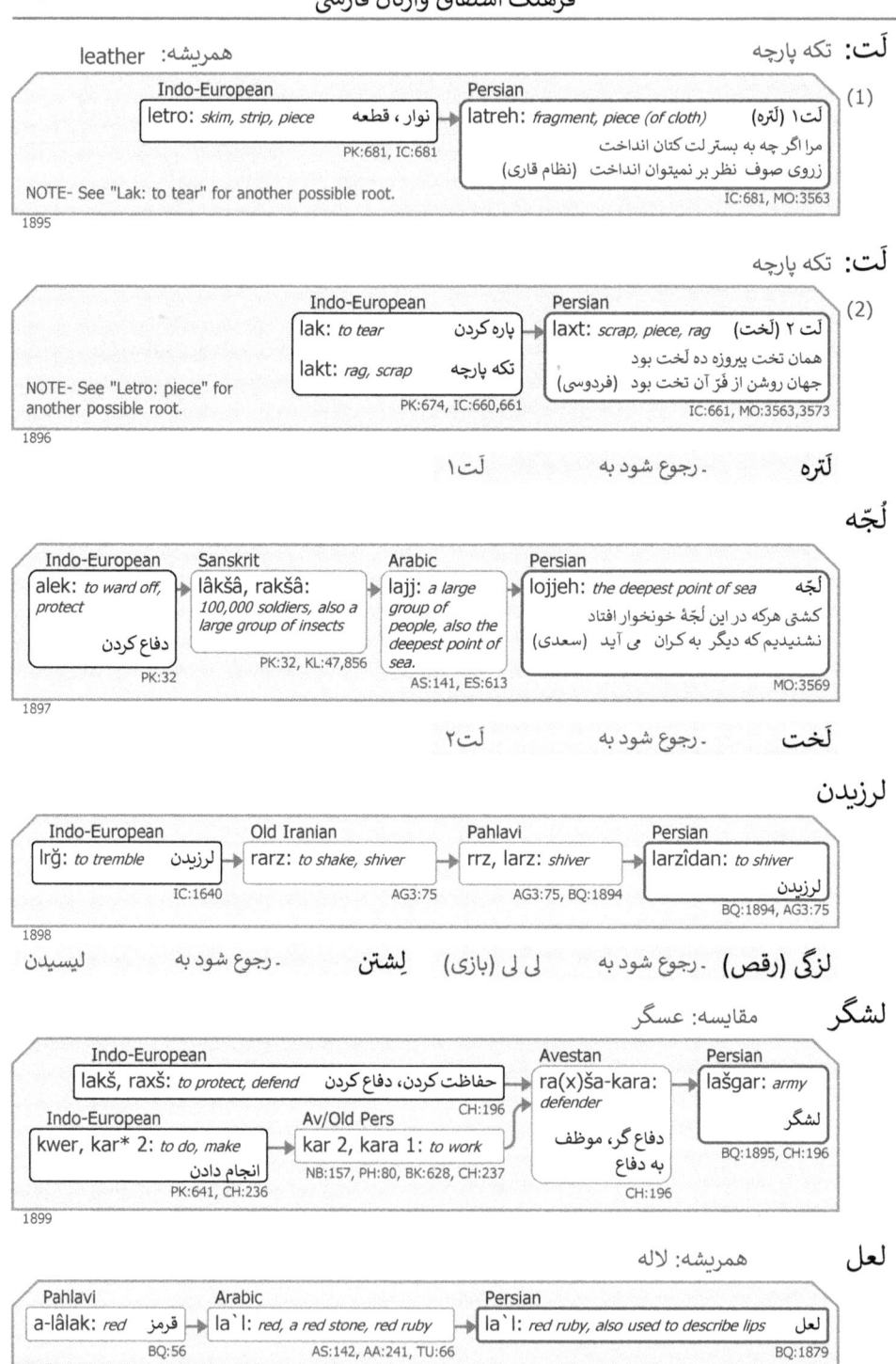

همریشه: leather

Indo-European

letro: *skim, strip, piece*   قطعه ، نوار

PK:681, IC:681

Persian (1)

latreh: *fragment, piece (of cloth)*   (لَتره) ۱ لَت

مرا اگر چه به بستر لت کتان انداخت
زروی صوف نظر بر نمیتوان انداخت   (نظام قاری)

IC:681, MO:3563

NOTE- See "Lak: to tear" for another possible root.

1895

لَت: تکه پارچه

Indo-European

lak: *to tear*   پاره کردن

lakt: *rag, scrap*   تکه پارچه

PK:674, IC:660,661

Persian (2)

laxt: *scrap, piece, rag*   (لَخت) ۲ لَت

همان تخت پیروزه ده لَخت بود
جهان روشن از فّر آن تخت بود   (فردوسی)

IC:661, MO:3563,3573

NOTE- See "Letro: piece" for another possible root.

1896

لَتره   . رجوع شود به   لَت۱

لُجّه

Indo-European

alek: *to ward off, protect*

دفاع کردن

PK:32

Sanskrit

lâkšâ, rakšâ: *100,000 soldiers, also a large group of insects*

PK:32, KL:47,856

Arabic

lajj: *a large group of people, also the deepest point of sea.*

AS:141, ES:613

Persian

lojjeh: *the deepest point of sea*   لُجّه

کشتی هرکه در این لُجّهٔ خونخوار افتاد
نشنیدیم که دیگر به کران می آید   (سعدی)

MO:3569

1897

لَخت   . رجوع شود به   لَت۲

لرزیدن

Indo-European

lrğ: *to tremble*   لرزیدن

IC:1640

Old Iranian

rarz: *to shake, shiver*

AG3:75

Pahlavi

rrz, larz: *shiver*

AG3:75, BQ:1894

Persian

larzîdan: *to shiver*

لرزیدن

BQ:1894, AG3:75

1898

لزگی (رقص)   . رجوع شود به   لی لی (بازی)   لِشتَن   . رجوع شود به   لیسیدن

لشگر   مقایسه: عسگر

Indo-European

lakš, raxš: *to protect, defend*   حفاظت کردن، دفاع کردن

CH:196

Indo-European

kwer, kar* 2: *to do, make*

انجام دادن

PK:641, CH:236

Av/Old Pers

kar 2, kara 1: *to work*

NB:157, PH:80, BK:628, CH:237

Avestan

ra(x)ša-kara: *defender*

دفاع گر، موظف
به دفاع

CH:196

Persian

lašgar: *army*

لشگر

BQ:1895, CH:196

1899

لعل   همریشه: لاله

Pahlavi

a-lâlak: *red*   قرمز

BQ:56

Arabic

la`l: *red, a red stone, red ruby*

AS:142, AA:241, TU:66

Persian

la`l: *red ruby, also used to describe lips*   لعل

BQ:1879

1900

لقلق، لقلقه   . رجوع شود به   لکلک

لَک: صد هزار

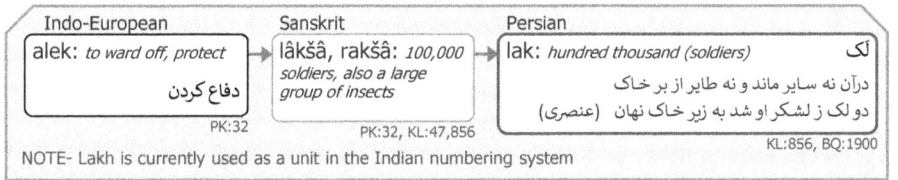

Indo-European	Sanskrit	Persian
alek: *to ward off, protect* دفاع کردن PK:32	lâkšâ, rakšâ: *100,000 soldiers, also a large group of insects* PK:32, KL:47,856	لک lak: *hundred thousand (soldiers)* درآن نه سایر ماند و نه طایر از بر خاک دو لک ز لشکر او شد به زیر خاک نهان (عنصری) KL:856, BQ:1900

NOTE- Lakh is currently used as a unit in the Indian numbering system

1901

لکلک

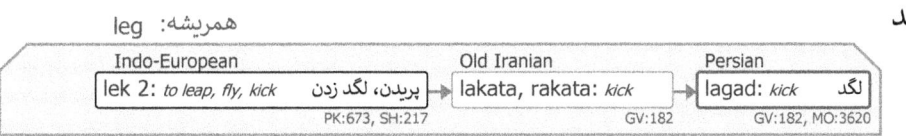

Akkadian	Arabic	Persian
laqalaqa: *flamingo, stork* فلامینگو ، لک لک ZM:52	laqlaq: *stork* laqlaqeh: *stork's cry* MO:3616, ZM:52	لکلک (لقلق، لغلغ) laklak, laqlaq: *stork* لقلقه (لغلغه) laqlaqeh: *slang speech* BQ:1902

1902

لگد

همریشه: leg

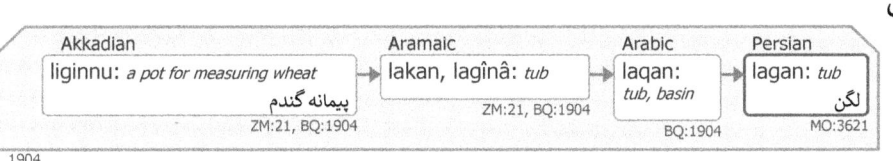

Indo-European	Old Iranian	Persian
lek 2: *to leap, fly, kick* پریدن، لگد زدن PK:673, SH:217	lakata, rakata: *kick* GV:182	لگد lagad: *kick* GV:182, MO:3620

1903

لگن

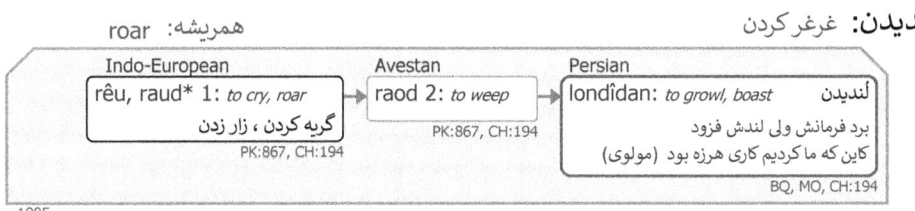

Akkadian	Aramaic	Arabic	Persian
liginnu: *a pot for measuring wheat* پیمانه گندم ZM:21, BQ:1904	lakan, lagînâ: *tub* ZM:21, BQ:1904	laqan: *tub, basin* BQ:1904	lagan: *tub* لگن MO:3621

1904

لُندیدن: غرغر کردن

همریشه: roar

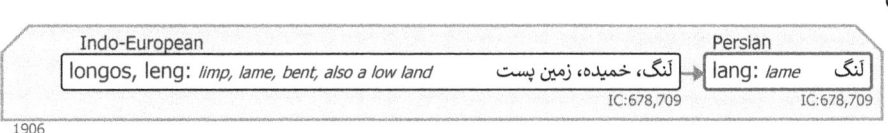

Indo-European	Avestan	Persian
rêu, raud* 1: *to cry, roar* گریه کردن ، زار زدن PK:867, CH:194	raod 2: *to weep* PK:867, CH:194	لندیدن londîdan: *to growl, boast* برد فرمانش ولی لندش فزود کاین که ما کردیم کاری هرزه بود (مولوی) BQ, MO, CH:194

1905

لَنگ

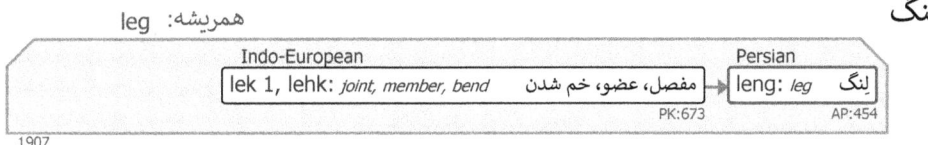

Indo-European	Persian
longos, leng: *limp, lame, bent, also a low land* لنگ، خمیده، زمین پست IC:678,709	لنگ lang: *lame* IC:678,709

1906

لِنگ

همریشه: leg

Indo-European	Persian
lek 1, lehk: *joint, member, bend* مفصل، عضو، خم شدن PK:673	لنگ leng: *leg* AP:454

1907

لنگر

همریشه: anchor

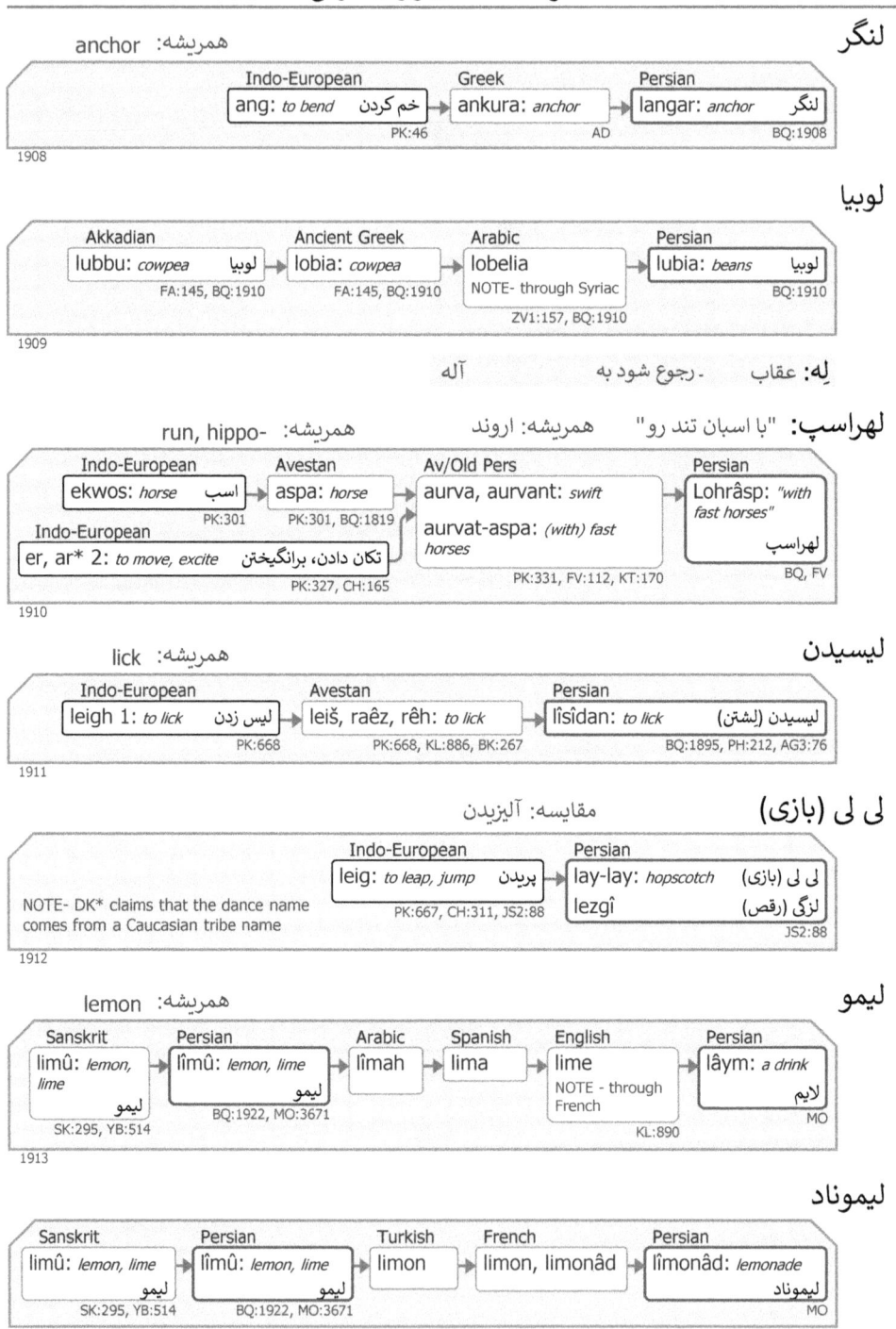

Indo-European	Greek	Persian
ang: to bend خم کردن	ankura: anchor	langar: anchor لنگر
PK:46	AD	BQ:1908

1908

لوبیا

Akkadian	Ancient Greek	Arabic	Persian
lubbu: cowpea لوبیا	lobia: cowpea	lobelia NOTE- through Syriac	lubia: beans لوبیا
FA:145, BQ:1910	FA:145, BQ:1910	ZV1:157, BQ:1910	BQ:1910

1909

لِه: عقاب   .رجوع شود به   آله

لهراسپ: "با اسبان تند رو"

همریشه: اروند   همریشه: run, hippo-

Indo-European	Avestan	Av/Old Pers	Persian
ekwos: horse اسب	aspa: horse	aurva, aurvant: swift	Lohrâsp: "with fast horses" لهراسپ
PK:301	PK:301, BQ:1819		
Indo-European er, ar* 2: to move, excite تکان دادن، برانگیختن		aurvat-aspa: (with) fast horses	
PK:327, CH:165		PK:331, FV:112, KT:170	BQ, FV

1910

لیسیدن

همریشه: lick

Indo-European	Avestan	Persian
leigh 1: to lick لیس زدن	leiš, raêz, rêh: to lick	lîsîdan: to lick لیسیدن (لشتن)
PK:668	PK:668, KL:886, BK:267	BQ:1895, PH:212, AG3:76

1911

لی لی (بازی)

مقایسه: آلیزیدن

	Indo-European	Persian
NOTE- DK* claims that the dance name comes from a Caucasian tribe name	leig: to leap, jump پریدن	lay-lay: hopscotch لی لی (بازی)
	PK:667, CH:311, JS2:88	lezgî لزگی (رقص)
		JS2:88

1912

لیمو

همریشه: lemon

Sanskrit	Persian	Arabic	Spanish	English	Persian
limû: lemon, lime لیمو	lîmû: lemon, lime لیمو	lîmah	lima	lime NOTE - through French	lâym: a drink لایم
SK:295, YB:514	BQ:1922, MO:3671			KL:890	MO

1913

لیموناد

Sanskrit	Persian	Turkish	French	Persian
limû: lemon, lime لیمو	lîmû: lemon, lime لیمو	limon	limon, limonâd	lîmonâd: lemonade لیموناد
SK:295, YB:514	BQ:1922, MO:3671			MO

1914

این حرف گاهی به ن بدل شود.

م

مَ .

Indo-European: **mê 3:** *no, not* — خیر، علامت نفی (PK:703, KT:210)
→ Av/Old Pers: **mâ 2:** *no, not*; **mâ-tya:** *that not, lest* (PK:703, KT:201)
→ Pahlavi: **mâ** (BQ:2058)
→ Persian: **ma-:** *a prefix for negating verbs* — مَ . (مرو، مگو، مباد) (MO:3677)

1915

ـُ م

همریشه: maximum

Indo-European: **êmos:** *a suffix meaning most or last* — پسوند صفت عالی (IC:257)
→ Avestan: **-emô:** *most or extreme* (IC:257)
→ Persian: **-om:** *a suffix indicating the order of a number* — ـُ م (دوّم، چهارُم) (IC:257)

1916

ما

همریشه: us, our

Indo-European: **ne 2:** *our, us* — ما، متعلق به ما (PK:758)
→ Avestan: **na 2:** *us*; **ahma, ahmâka :** *we* (PK:758, KL:1683)
→ Pahlavi: **amâg, amâh:** *we, us* (BQ:1931, TV:232)
→ Persian: **mâ:** *we, us* — ما (BQ:1931)

1917

ماچ: بوسه

همریشه: مکیدن، مزیدن

Indo-European: **maič*, mač*:** *to suck* — مکیدن (CH:357-360)
→ Avestan: **maêkant:** *oozing* (CH:357-360)
→ Pahlavi: **mêz, myc, micîtan:** *to suck, taste* (CH:357-360, BQ:2002)
→ Persian: **mâč:** *kiss* — ماچ (CH:357-360)

1918

مادر

همریشه: ممه

همریشه: mammal

Indo-European: **mâ:** *breast* — پستان (PK:694, BK:103)
Indo-European: **ter 2, tar:** *a kinship term* — پسوند گروه یا فامیل (PT:863)
→ Indo-European: **Mâ-ter:** *feeder (of the family), mother* — مسئول غذا، مادر (PK:694, BK:103)
→ Avestan: **mâtar:** *mother* (PK:694, SK:336)
→ Pahlavi: **mâtar:** *mother*; **matak:** *female*; **mâdiyânag, mâyag:** *essence* (BQ:1933, TV:237)
→ Persian: **mâdar:** *mother* — مادر; **mâdeh:** *female* — ماده (مادیان، ماکیان); **mâyeh:** *essence, value* — مایه (BQ:1933,1946,1964, PH:213, MO:3716, TV:237)

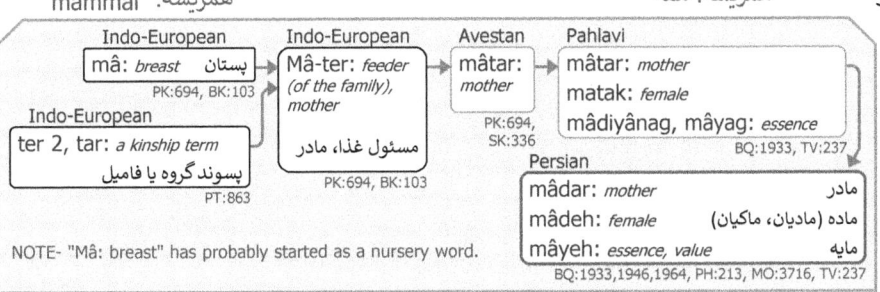

NOTE- "Mâ: breast" has probably started as a nursery word.

1919

مادراندر	۔رجوع شود به	مادر + اندر۲	**ماده**	۔رجوع شود به	مادر
مادیان	۔رجوع شود به	مادر			

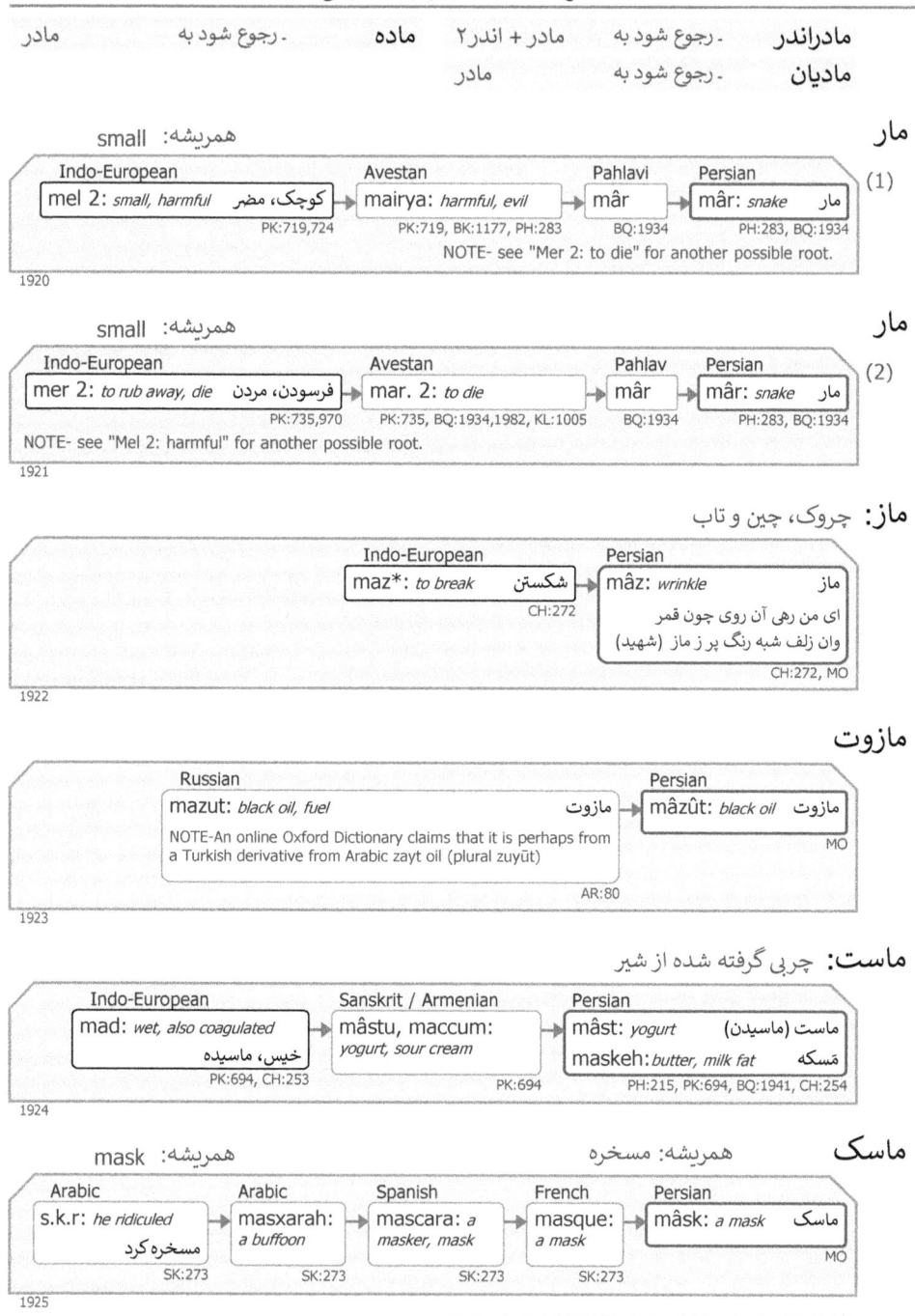

همریشه: small

** مار** (1)

Indo-European	Avestan	Pahlavi	Persian
mel 2: *small, harmful* کوچک، مضر	mairya: *harmful, evil*	mâr	mâr: *snake* مار
PK:719,724	PK:719, BK:1177, PH:283	BQ:1934	PH:283, BQ:1934

NOTE- see "Mer 2: to die" for another possible root.

1920

همریشه: small

مار (2)

Indo-European	Avestan	Pahlav	Persian
mer 2: *to rub away, die* فرسودن، مردن	mar. 2: *to die*	mâr	mâr: *snake* مار
PK:735,970	PK:735, BQ:1934,1982, KL:1005	BQ:1934	PH:283, BQ:1934

NOTE- see "Mel 2: harmful" for another possible root.

1921

ماز: چروک، چین و تاب

Indo-European	Persian
maz*: *to break* شکستن	mâz: *wrinkle* ماز
CH:272	ای من رهی آن روی چون قمر
	وان زلف شبه رنگ پر ز ماز (شهید)
	CH:272, MO

1922

مازوت

Russian	Persian
mazut: *black oil, fuel* مازوت	mâzût: *black oil* مازوت
NOTE-An online Oxford Dictionary claims that it is perhaps from a Turkish derivative from Arabic zayt oil (plural zuyūt)	MO
AR:80	

1923

ماست: چربی گرفته شده از شیر

Indo-European	Sanskrit / Armenian	Persian
mad: *wet, also coagulated* خیس، ماسیده	mâstu, maccum: *yogurt, sour cream*	mâst: *yogurt* ماست (ماسیدن)
PK:694, CH:253	PK:694	maskeh: *butter, milk fat* مَسکه
		PH:215, PK:694, BQ:1941, CH:254

1924

همریشه: mask   همریشه: مسخره

ماسک

Arabic	Arabic	Spanish	French	Persian
s.k.r: *he ridiculed* مسخره کرد	masxarah: *a buffoon*	mascara: *a masker, mask*	masque: *a mask*	mâsk: *a mask* ماسک
SK:273	SK:273	SK:273	SK:273	MO

1925

ماسیدن	۔رجوع شود به	ماست

ماش

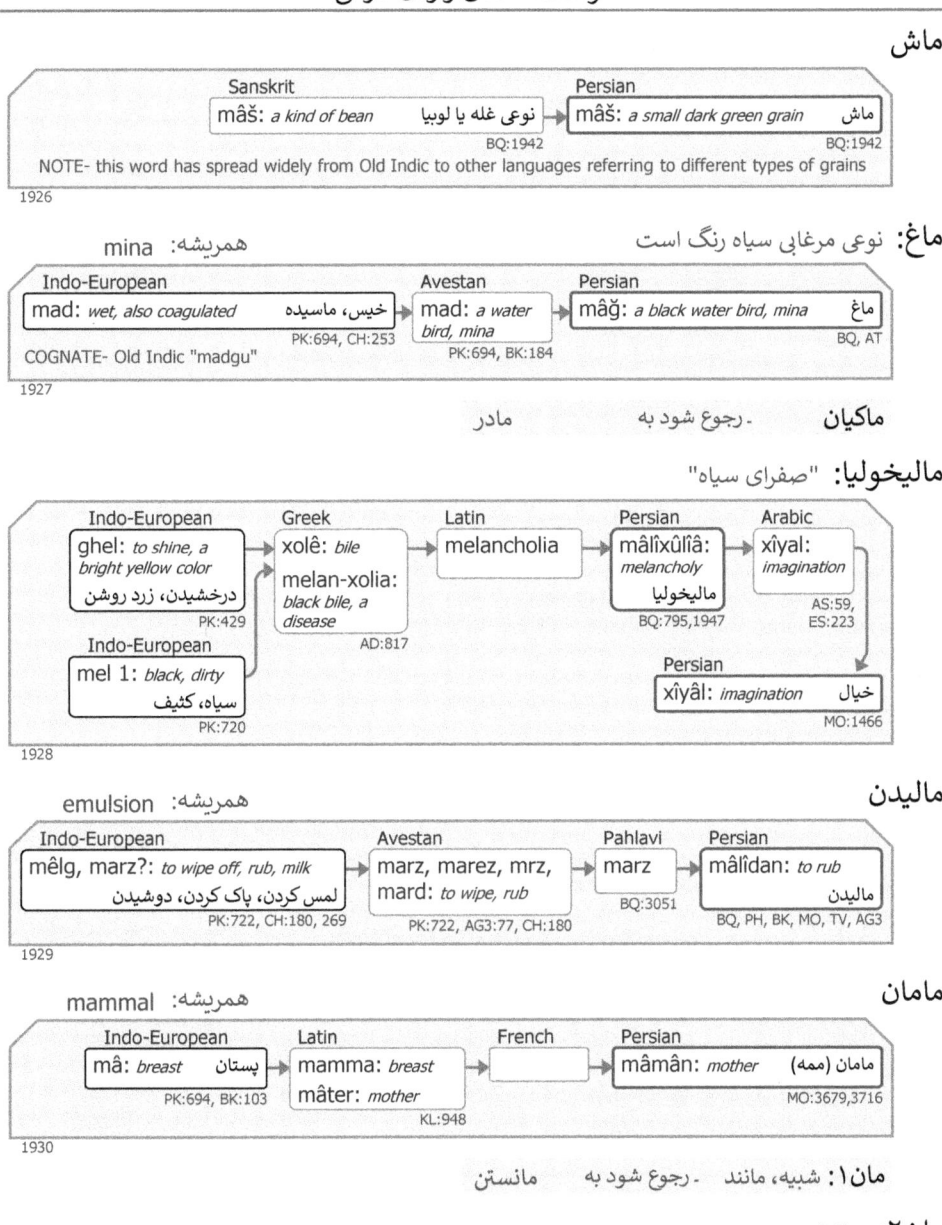

Sanskrit		Persian	
mâš: *a kind of bean*	نوعی غله یا لوبیا	mâš: *a small dark green grain*	ماش
	BQ:1942		BQ:1942

NOTE- this word has spread widely from Old Indic to other languages referring to different types of grains

1926

ماغ: نوعی مرغابی سیاه رنگ است

همریشه: mina

Indo-European		Avestan		Persian	
mad: *wet, also coagulated*	خیس، ماسیده	mad: *a water bird, mina*	mâğ: *a black water bird, mina*	ماغ
PK:694, CH:253		PK:694, BK:184		BQ, AT	

COGNATE- Old Indic "madgu"

1927

ماکیان - رجوع شود به مادر

مالیخولیا: "صفرای سیاه"

Indo-European	Greek	Latin	Persian	Arabic
ghel: *to shine, a bright yellow color* درخشیدن، زرد روشن PK:429	xolê: *bile* melan-xolia: *black bile, a disease* AD:817	melancholia	mâlîxûlîâ: *melancholy* مالیخولیا BQ:795,1947	xîyal: *imagination* AS:59, ES:223
Indo-European mel 1: *black, dirty* سیاه، کثیف PK:720			Persian xîyâl: *imagination* خیال MO:1466	

1928

مالیدن

همریشه: emulsion

Indo-European	Avestan	Pahlavi	Persian
mêlg, marz?: *to wipe off, rub, milk* لمس کردن، پاک کردن، دوشیدن PK:722, CH:180, 269	marz, marez, mrz, mard: *to wipe, rub* PK:722, AG3:77, CH:180	marz BQ:3051	mâlîdan: *to rub* مالیدن BQ, PH, BK, MO, TV, AG3

1929

مامان

همریشه: mammal

Indo-European	Latin	French	Persian
mâ: *breast* پستان PK:694, BK:103	mamma: *breast* mâter: *mother* KL:948		mâmân: *mother* مامان (ممه) MO:3679,3716

1930

مان۱: شبیه، مانند - رجوع شود به مانستن

مان۲: خانواده

همریشه: domestic

Indo-European	Avestan	Pahlavi	Persian
dem: *house* خانه PK:198	demâna, nmâna, mân: *house* garô-demâna: *prayer house, sky* PK:199, KT:302	mân: *house* BQ:894,1949	mân: *house* مان۲ (دودمان) TV:239

COGNATE- Old Persian "mâna: house;/ mânya: domestic" (KT:191-202)

1931

. **مان۳**: پسوند بمعنی پندار و رفتار

همریشه: mind

Indo-European	Avestan	Persian
men 1: *to think* فکر کردن PK:726	manah: *mind, manners* PK:726,727, BQ	- mân, -man: *suffixes for thoughts and manners.* مان۳، .من۳ مثال: اهریمن، بهمن، دشمن، قهرمان، منش، هومن BQ, PH, FJ

1932

ماندن

همریشه: remain

Indo-European	Av/Old Pers	Pahlavi	Persian
men 2: *to remain* ماندن PK:729	man 2: *await* KL:934, PH:215, KT:202	mân-stan: *to stay* PH:215	mândan: *to stay* ماندن BQ:1950, CH:74

1933

مانستن: شباهت داشتن

همریشه: measure, symmetry

Indo-European	Indo-European	Avestan	Persian
me 1: *to measure* اندازه گرفتن PK:703, 731	mân: *to resemble* شبیه بودن CH:272	man 1: *to resemble* PK:726,727, BQ	mânastan: *to resemble* مانستن (مانند، مان۱) شادمان، درزمان، آسمان، همان BQ

1934

مانند   . رجوع شود به   مانستن

ماه

همریشه: measure, month, moon

Indo-European	Indo-European	Av/Old Pers	Persian
me 1: *to measure* اندازه گرفتن PK:703, 731	Mênôt: *moon used to measure time* ماه برای اندازه گیری زمان PK:703, 731	mâ 1: *to measure* mâh, mâhya: *moon, month* PK:703,731, BK:54,877,1010	mâh: *moon, month* ماه PK:731, BQ:1956, 1958, TV:37,113

1935

ماهی

همریشه: ماغ

Indo-European	Avestan	Pahlavi	Persian
mad: *wet, also coagulated* خیس، ماسیده PK:694, CH:253	masya: *fish* PK:694, BK:184	mâhik, mâhîg: *fish* AP:465	mâhî: *fish* ماهی BQ, AT

1936

ماهیچه   . رجوع شود به   موش

مایده

همریشه: میزبان   همریشه: mitigate

Indo-European	Avestan	Pahlavi	Arabic	Persian
mei 1: *soft, mild* نرم، ملایم PK:711	mayazda: *a special meal of Zoroastrians, guests* PK:712, MO:4494	mayazd, mâz: *feast* BQ:2076, BR:370	mâ`da: *meal* AS:148, BR:370	mâedeh: *food* مایده MO:3674

1937

مایه   . رجوع شود به   مادر

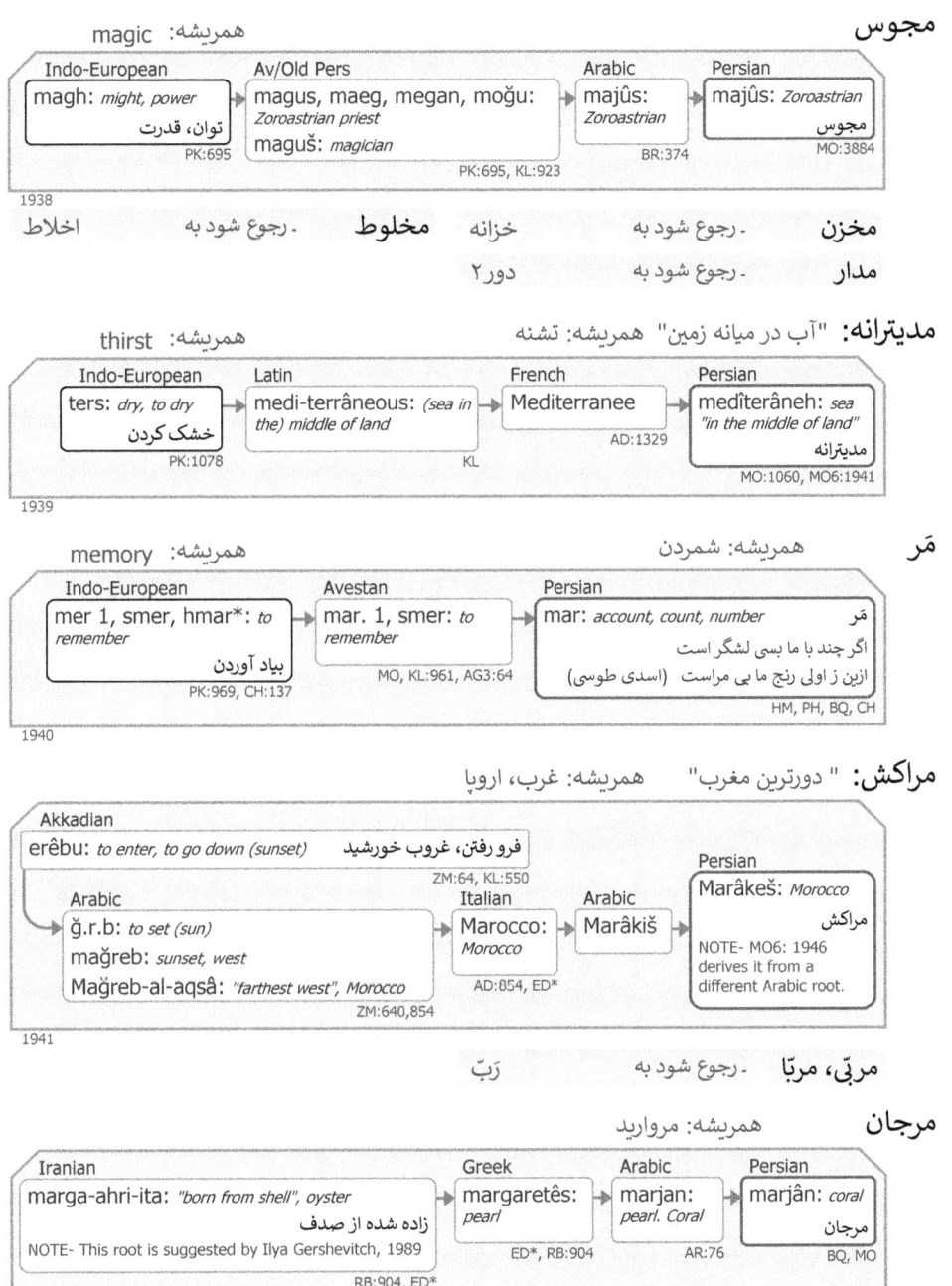

مجوس   همریشه: magic

Indo-European	Av/Old Pers	Arabic	Persian
magh: *might, power* توان، قدرت PK:695	magus, maeg, megan, moǧu: *Zoroastrian priest* maguš: *magician* PK:695, KL:923	majûs: *Zoroastrian* BR:374	majûs: *Zoroastrian* مجوس MO:3884

1938

مخزن   ـ رجوع شود به   خزانه   **مخلوط**   ـ رجوع شود به   اخلاط

مدار   ـ رجوع شود به   دور۲

مدیترانه: "آب در میانه زمین" همریشه: تشنه   همریشه: thirst

Indo-European	Latin	French	Persian
ters: *dry, to dry* خشک کردن PK:1078	medi-terrâneous: *(sea in the) middle of land* KL	Mediterranee AD:1329	medîterâneh: *sea "in the middle of land"* مدیترانه MO:1060, MO6:1941

1939

مَر   همریشه: شمردن   همریشه: memory

Indo-European	Avestan	Persian
mer 1, smer, hmar*: *to remember* بیاد آوردن PK:969, CH:137	mar. 1, smer: *to remember* MO, KL:961, AG3:64	mar: *account, count, number* مَر اگر چند با ما بسی لشگر است ازین ز اولی رنج ما بی مراست (اسدی طوسی) HM, PH, BQ, CH

1940

مراکش: " دورترین مغرب"   همریشه: غرب، اروپا

Akkadian				
erêbu: *to enter, to go down (sunset)* فرو رفتن، غروب خورشید ZM:64, KL:550				Persian Marâkeš: *Morocco* مراکش NOTE- MO6: 1946 derives it from a different Arabic root.
Arabic ǧ.r.b: *to set (sun)* maǧreb: *sunset, west* Maǧreb-al-aqsâ: *"farthest west", Morocco* ZM:640,854	Italian Marocco: *Morocco* AD:854, ED*	Arabic Marâkiš		

1941

مربّی، مربّا   ـ رجوع شود به   رَبّ

مرجان   همریشه: مروارید

Iranian	Greek	Arabic	Persian
marga-ahri-ita: *"born from shell", oyster* زاده شده از صدف NOTE- This root is suggested by Ilya Gershevitch, 1989 RB:904, ED*	margaretês: *pearl* ED*, RB:904	marjan: *pearl. Coral* AR:76	marjân: *coral* مرجان BQ, MO

1942

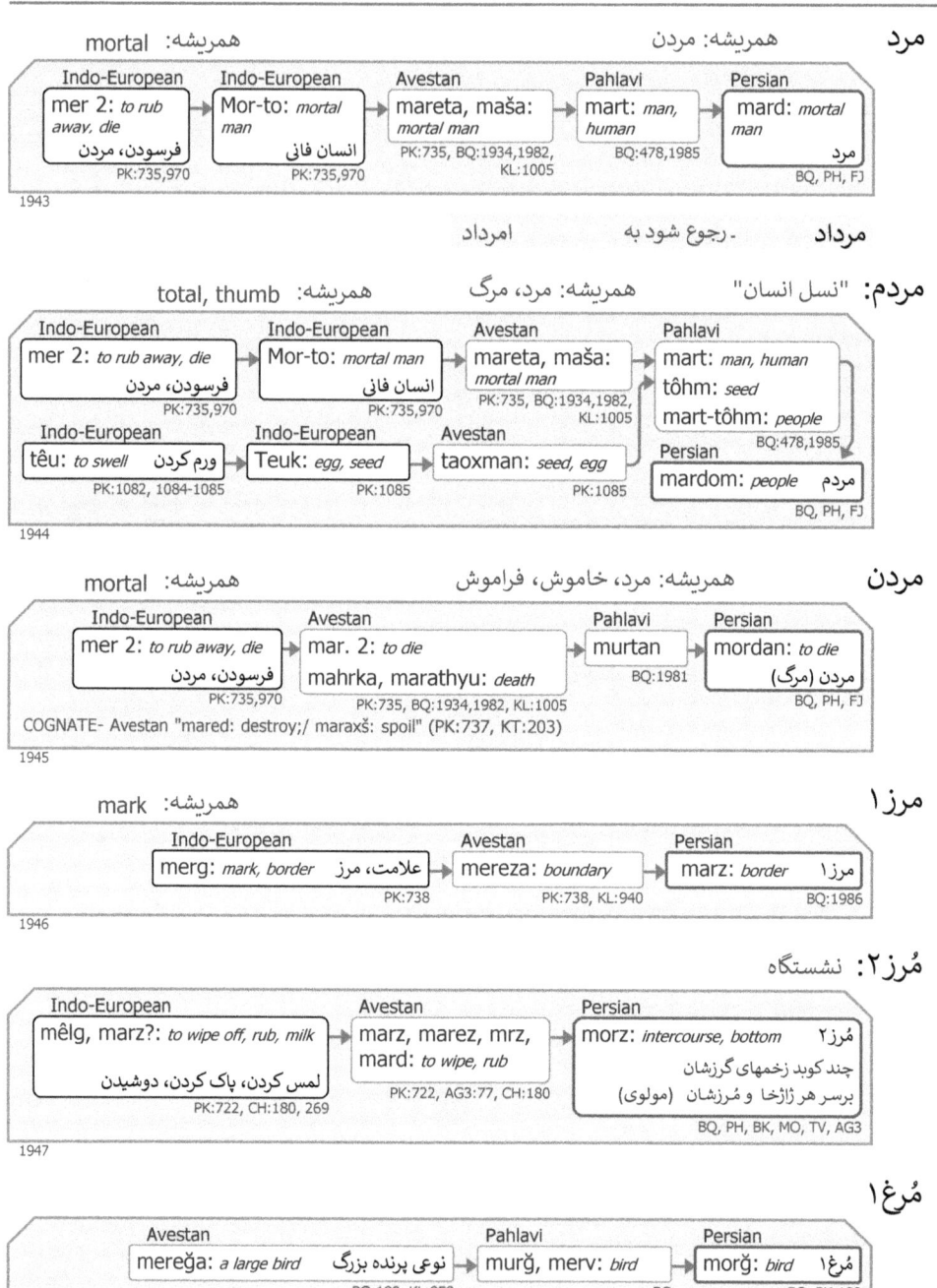

مرد

همریشه: مردن

همریشه: mortal

Indo-European	Indo-European	Avestan	Pahlavi	Persian
mer 2: *to rub away, die*	Mor-to: *mortal man*	mareta, maša: *mortal man*	mart: *man, human*	mard: *mortal man*
فرسودن، مردن	انسان فانی			مرد
PK:735,970	PK:735,970	PK:735, BQ:1934,1982, KL:1005	BQ:478,1985	BQ, PH, FJ

1943

مرداد ـ رجوع شود به امرداد

مردم: "نسل انسان"

همریشه: مرد، مرگ

همریشه: total, thumb

Indo-European	Indo-European	Avestan	Pahlavi
mer 2: *to rub away, die*	Mor-to: *mortal man*	mareta, maša: *mortal man*	mart: *man, human*
فرسودن، مردن	انسان فانی		tôhm: *seed*
PK:735,970	PK:735,970	PK:735, BQ:1934,1982, KL:1005	mart-tôhm: *people*
			BQ:478,1985
Indo-European	Indo-European	Avestan	Persian
têu: *to swell*	Teuk: *egg, seed*	taoxman: *seed, egg*	mardom: *people* مردم
ورم کردن			BQ, PH, FJ
PK:1082, 1084-1085	PK:1085	PK:1085	

1944

مردن

همریشه: مرد، خاموش، فراموش

همریشه: mortal

Indo-European	Avestan	Pahlavi	Persian
mer 2: *to rub away, die*	mar. 2: *to die*	murtan	mordan: *to die*
فرسودن، مردن	mahrka, marathyu: *death*	BQ:1981	مردن (مرگ)
PK:735,970	PK:735, BQ:1934,1982, KL:1005		BQ, PH, FJ

COGNATE- Avestan "mared: destroy;/ maraxš: spoil" (PK:737, KT:203)

1945

مرز۱

همریشه: mark

Indo-European	Avestan	Persian
merg: *mark, border*	mereza: *boundary*	marz: *border* ۱مرز
علامت، مرز		
PK:738	PK:738, KL:940	BQ:1986

1946

مُرز۲: نشستگاه

Indo-European	Avestan	Persian
mêlg, marz?: *to wipe off, rub, milk*	marz, marez, mrz, mard: *to wipe, rub*	morz: *intercourse, bottom* ۲مُرز
لمس کردن، پاک کردن، دوشیدن		چند کوبد زخمهای گرزشان
PK:722, CH:180, 269	PK:722, AG3:77, CH:180	برسر هر ژاژخا و مُرزشان (مولوی)
		BQ, PH, BK, MO, TV, AG3

1947

مُرغ۱

Avestan	Pahlavi	Persian
mereğa: *a large bird*	murğ, merv: *bird*	morğ: *bird* ۱مُرغ
نوعی پرنده بزرگ		
BQ:190, KL:959	BQ	BQ, BK:183

1948

مَرغ۲

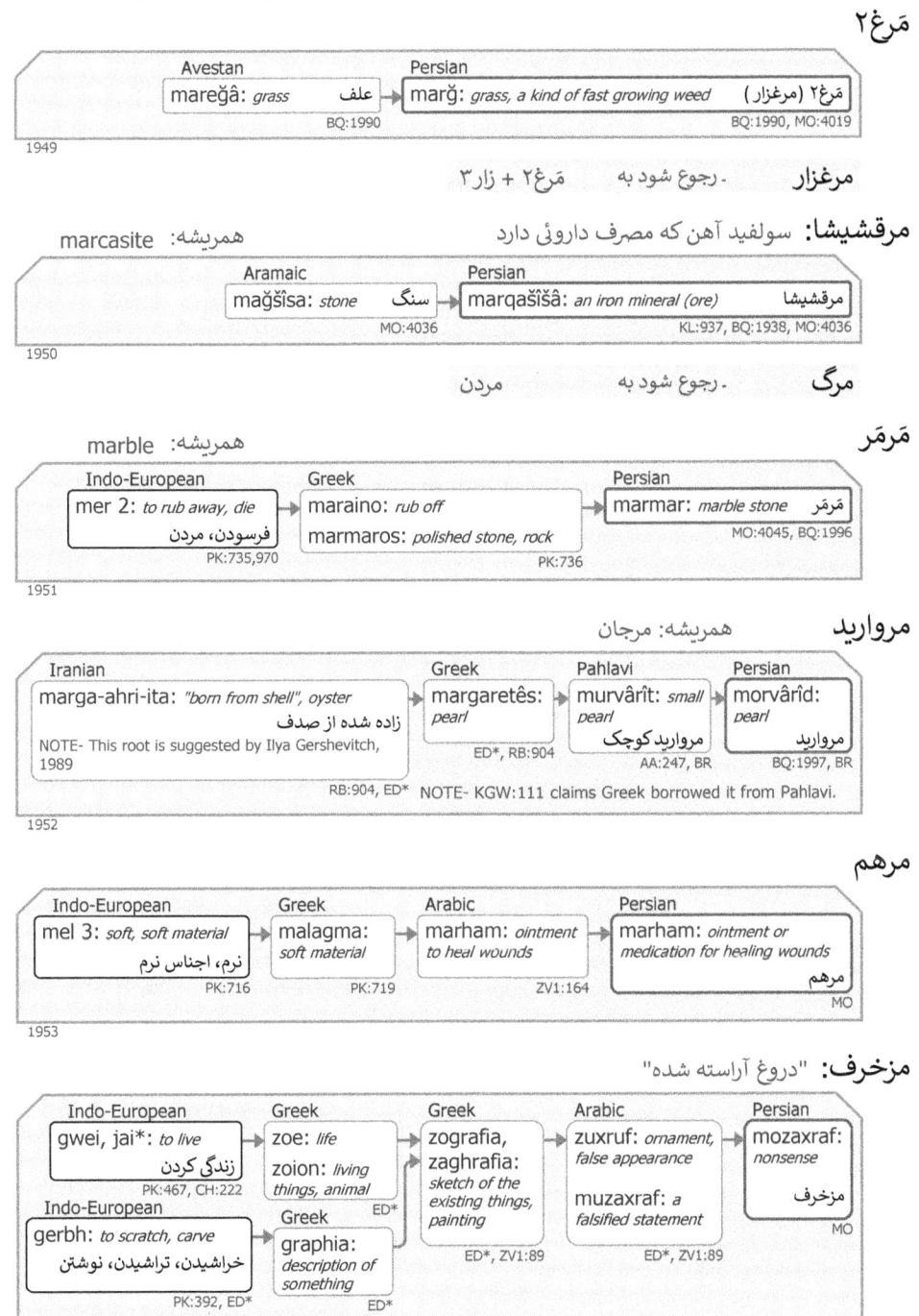

مرغزار   . رجوع شود به   مَرغ۲ + زار۳

مرقشیشا: سولفید آهن که مصرف داروئی دارد

مرگ   . رجوع شود به   مردن

مَرمَر

مروارید   همریشه: مرجان

مرهم

مزخرف: "دروغ آراسته شده"

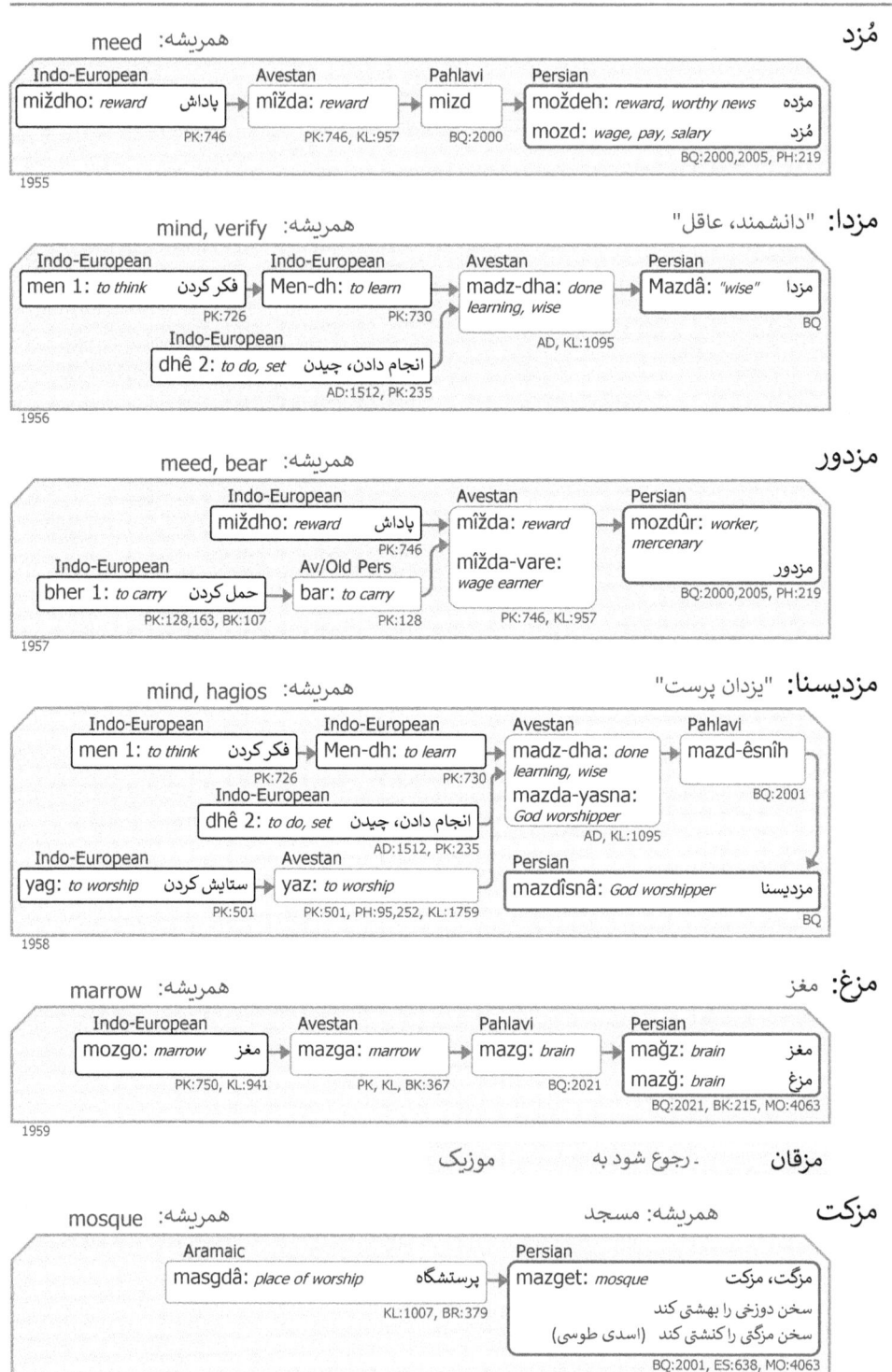

مُزد

همریشه: meed

Indo-European	Avestan	Pahlavi	Persian
miždho: *reward* پاداش	mîžda: *reward*	mizd	moždeh: *reward, worthy news* مژده
PK:746	PK:746, KL:957	BQ:2000	mozd: *wage, pay, salary* مُزد
			BQ:2000,2005, PH:219

1955

مزدا: "دانشمند، عاقل"

همریشه: mind, verify

Indo-European	Indo-European	Avestan	Persian
men 1: *to think* فکر کردن	Men-dh: *to learn*	madz-dha: *done learning, wise*	Mazdâ: *"wise"* مزدا
PK:726	PK:730	AD, KL:1095	BQ
	dhê 2: *to do, set* انجام دادن، چیدن		
	AD:1512, PK:235		

1956

مزدور

همریشه: meed, bear

Indo-European	Avestan	Persian
miždho: *reward* پاداش	mîžda: *reward*	mozdûr: *worker, mercenary*
PK:746	mîžda-vare: *wage earner*	مزدور
bher 1: *to carry* حمل کردن	bar: *to carry*	
PK:128,163, BK:107	PK:128	PK:746, KL:957	BQ:2000,2005, PH:219

1957

مزدیسنا: "یزدان پرست"

همریشه: mind, hagios

Indo-European	Indo-European	Avestan	Pahlavi
men 1: *to think* فکر کردن	Men-dh: *to learn*	madz-dha: *done learning, wise*	mazd-êsnîh
PK:726	PK:730	mazda-yasna: *God worshipper*	BQ:2001
	dhê 2: *to do, set* انجام دادن، چیدن	AD, KL:1095	
	AD:1512, PK:235		
yag: *to worship* ستایش کردن	yaz: *to worship*	Persian	
PK:501	PK:501, PH:95,252, KL:1759	mazdîsnâ: *God worshipper* مزدیسنا	BQ

1958

مزغ: مغز

همریشه: marrow

Indo-European	Avestan	Pahlavi	Persian
mozgo: *marrow* مغز	mazga: *marrow*	mazg: *brain*	maǧz: *brain* مغز
PK:750, KL:941	PK, KL, BK:367	BQ:2021	mazǧ: *brain* مزغ
			BQ:2021, BK:215, MO:4063

1959

مزقان   موزیک   ـ رجوع شود به

مزکت   همریشه: مسجد   همریشه: mosque

Aramaic	Persian
masgdâ: *place of worship* پرستشگاه	mazget: *mosque* مزگت، مزکت
KL:1007, BR:379	سخن دوزخی را بهشتی کند
	سخن مزگتی را کنشتی کند (اسدی طوسی)
	BQ:2001, ES:638, MO:4063

1960

347

مِزنا: ترازو

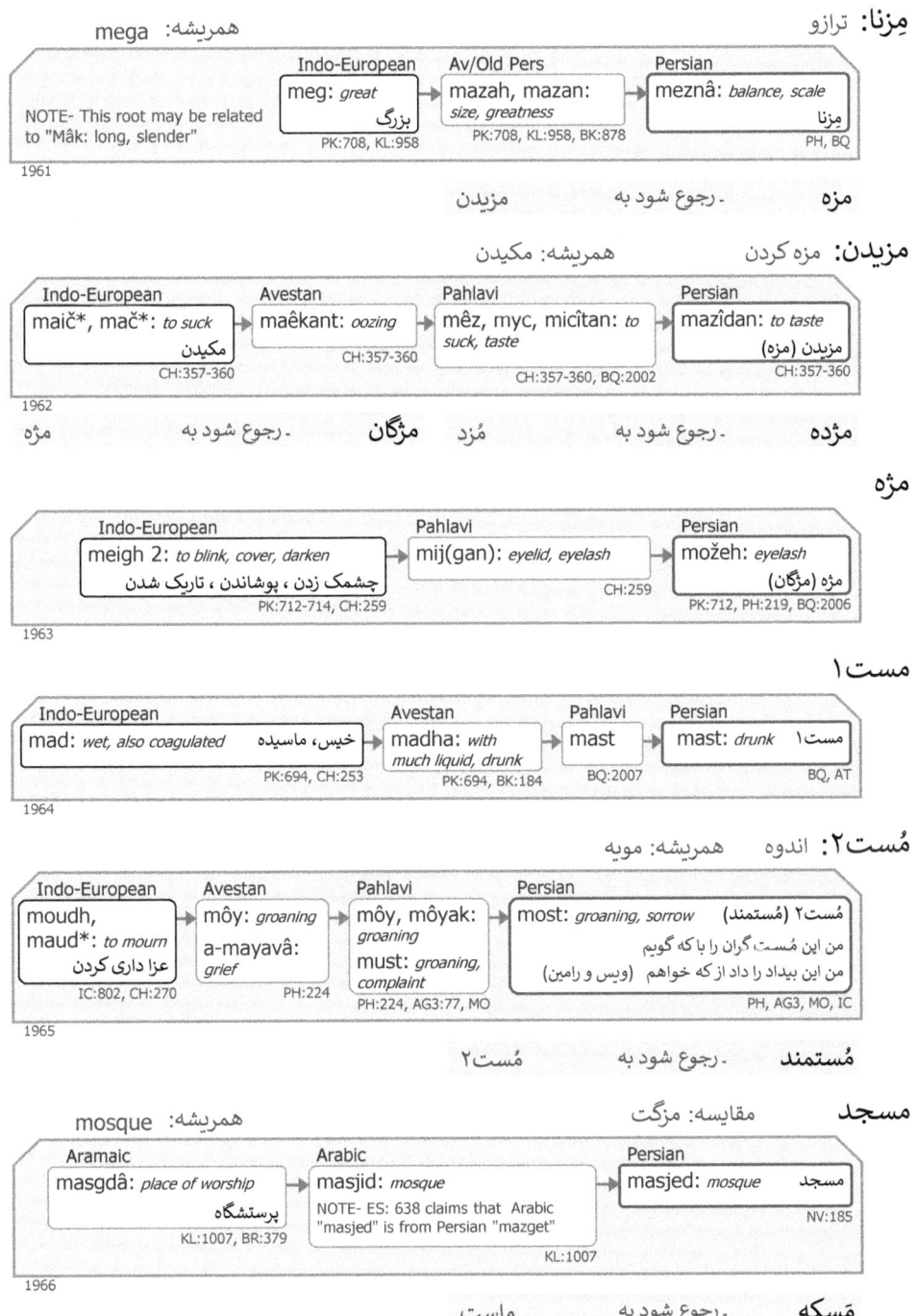

همریشه: mega

| NOTE- This root may be related to "Mâk: long, slender"
1961 | Indo-European
meg: *great*
بزرگ
PK:708, KL:958 | Av/Old Pers
mazah, mazan: *size, greatness*
PK:708, KL:958, BK:878 | Persian
meznâ: *balance, scale*
مزنا
PH, BQ |

مزه ـ رجوع شود به مزیدن

مزیدن: مزه کردن

همریشه: مکیدن

| Indo-European
maič*, mač*: *to suck*
مکیدن
CH:357-360 | Avestan
maêkant: *oozing*
CH:357-360 | Pahlavi
mêz, myc, micîtan: *to suck, taste*
CH:357-360, BQ:2002 | Persian
mazîdan: *to taste*
مزیدن (مزه)
CH:357-360 |

1962

مژده ـ رجوع شود به **مُزد** **مژگان** ـ رجوع شود به **مژه**

مژه

| Indo-European
meigh 2: *to blink, cover, darken*
چشمک زدن ، پوشاندن ، تاریک شدن
PK:712-714, CH:259 | Pahlavi
mij(gan): *eyelid, eyelash*
CH:259 | Persian
možeh: *eyelash*
مژه (مژگان)
PK:712, PH:219, BQ:2006 |

1963

مست۱

| Indo-European
mad: *wet, also coagulated* خیس، ماسیده
PK:694, CH:253 | Avestan
madha: *with much liquid, drunk*
PK:694, BK:184 | Pahlavi
mast
BQ:2007 | Persian
mast: *drunk* مست۱
BQ, AT |

1964

مُست۲: اندوه   همریشه: مویه

| Indo-European
moudh, maud*: *to mourn*
عزا داری کردن
IC:802, CH:270 | Avestan
môy: *groaning*
a-mayavâ: *grief*
PH:224 | Pahlavi
môy, môyak: *groaning*
must: *groaning, complaint*
PH:224, AG3:77, MO | Persian
most: *groaning, sorrow* مُست۲ (مُستمند)
من این مُست، گران را با که گویم
من این بیداد را داد از که خواهم   (ویس و رامین)
PH, AG3, MO, IC |

1965

مُستمند ـ رجوع شود به **مُست۲**

مسجد مقایسه: مزگت

همریشه: mosque

| Aramaic
masgdâ: *place of worship*
پرستشگاه
KL:1007, BR:379 | Arabic
masjid: *mosque*
NOTE- ES: 638 claims that Arabic "masjed" is from Persian "mazget"
KL:1007 | Persian
masjed: *mosque* مسجد
NV:185 |

1966

مَسکه ـ رجوع شود به ماست

مشت۱

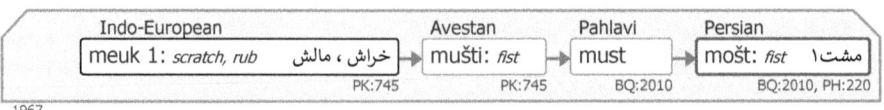

Indo-European	Avestan	Pahlavi	Persian
meuk 1: *scratch, rub* خراش ، مالش	mušti: *fist*	must	mošt: *fist* مشت۱
PK:745	PK:745	BQ:2010	BQ:2010, PH:220

1967

مُشت۲: مشتمال . رجوع شود به مُشتن

مُشتن

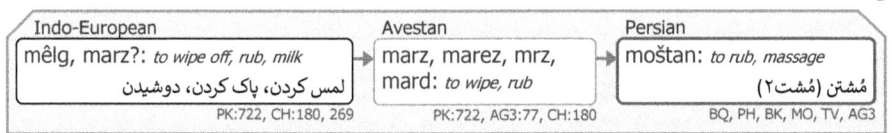

Indo-European	Avestan	Persian
mêlg, marz?: *to wipe off, rub, milk* لمس کردن، پاک کردن، دوشیدن	marz, marez, mrz, mard: *to wipe, rub*	moštan: *to rub, massage* مُشتن (مُشت۲)
PK:722, CH:180, 269	PK:722, AG3:77, CH:180	BQ, PH, BK, MO, TV, AG3

1968

مُشک

همریشه: موش   همریشه: muscle

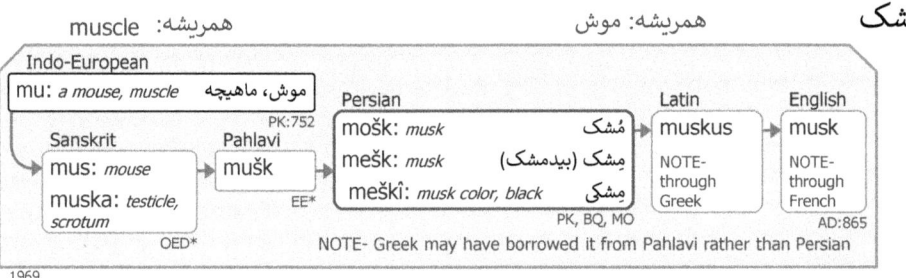

Indo-European			Persian	Latin	English
mu: *a mouse, muscle* موش، ماهیچه			mošk: *musk* مُشک	muskus	musk
		PK:752	mešk: *musk* مِشک (بیدمشک)	NOTE-through Greek	NOTE-through French
Sanskrit	**Pahlavi**		meškî: *musk color, black* مِشکی		
mus: *mouse*	mušk				
muska: *testicle, scrotum*	EE*				AD:865
OED*			PK, BQ, MO		
			NOTE- Greek may have borrowed it from Pahlavi rather than Persian		

1969

مِشک

. رجوع شود به مُشک

مَشک

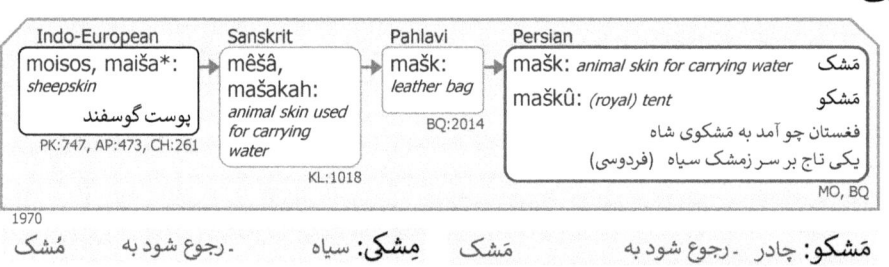

Indo-European	Sanskrit	Pahlavi	Persian
moisos, maiša*: *sheepskin* پوست گوسفند	mêšâ, mašakah: *animal skin used for carrying water*	mašk: *leather bag*	mašk: *animal skin for carrying water* مَشک maškû: *(royal) tent* مَشکو
PK:747, AP:473, CH:261	KL:1018	BQ:2014	فغستان چو آمد بر مَشکوی شاه یکی تاج بر سر زمشک سیاه (فردوسی)
			MO, BQ

1970

مَشکو: چادر . رجوع شود به   مَشک   مِشکی: سیاه   . رجوع شود به   مُشک

مشیا: آدم

همریشه: مرد، مرگ   همریشه: mortal

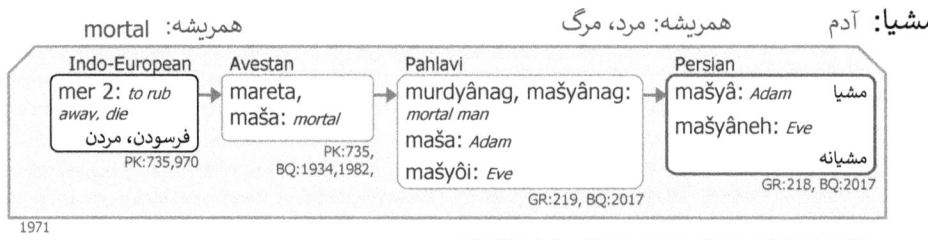

Indo-European	Avestan	Pahlavi	Persian
mer 2: *to rub away, die* فرسودن، مردن	mareta, maša: *mortal*	murdyânag, mašyânag: *mortal man* maša: *Adam* mašyôi: *Eve*	mašyâ: *Adam* مشیا mašyâneh: *Eve* مشیانه
PK:735,970	PK:735, BQ:1934,1982,	GR:219, BQ:2017	GR:218, BQ:2017

1971

مشیانه: حوا   . رجوع شود به   مشیا

مصطکی

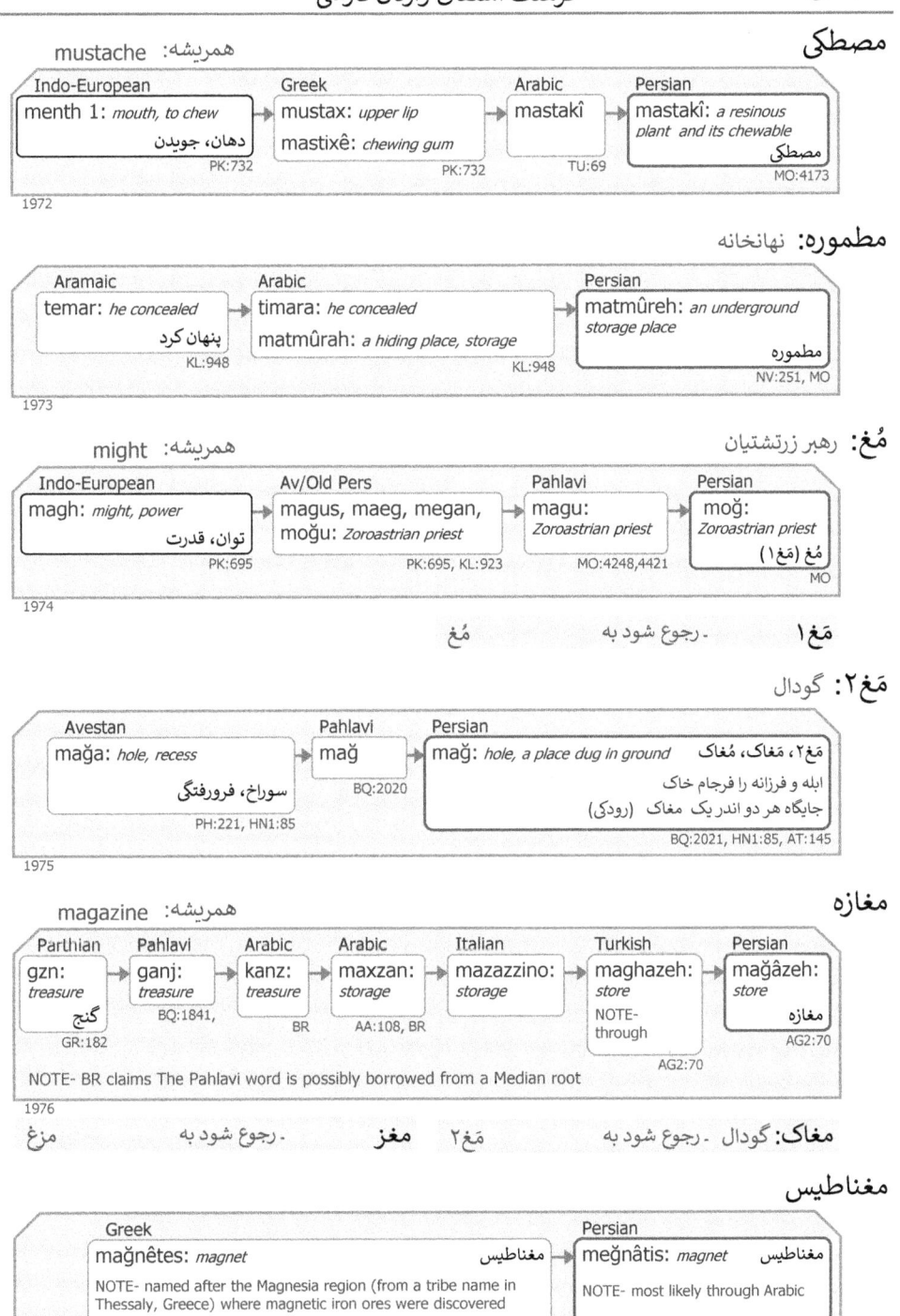

همریشه: mustache

Indo-European	Greek	Arabic	Persian
menth 1: *mouth, to chew* دهان، جویدن PK:732	mustax: *upper lip* mastixê: *chewing gum* PK:732	mastakî TU:69	mastakî: *a resinous plant and its chewable* مصطکی MO:4173

1972

مطموره: نهانخانه

Aramaic	Arabic	Persian
temar: *he concealed* پنهان کرد KL:948	timara: *he concealed* matmûrah: *a hiding place, storage* KL:948	matmûreh: *an underground storage place* مطموره NV:251, MO

1973

مُغ: رهبر زرتشتیان   همریشه: might

Indo-European	Av/Old Pers	Pahlavi	Persian
magh: *might, power* توان، قدرت PK:695	magus, maeg, megan, moğu: *Zoroastrian priest* PK:695, KL:923	magu: *Zoroastrian priest* MO:4248,4421	moğ: *Zoroastrian priest* مُغ (مَغ۱) MO

1974

مَغ۱ ـ رجوع شود به   مُغ

مَغ۲: گودال

Avestan	Pahlavi	Persian
mağa: *hole, recess* سوراخ، فرورفتگی PH:221, HN1:85	mağ BQ:2020	mağ: *hole, a place dug in ground* مَغ۲، مغاک، مُغاک ابله و فرزانه را فرجام خاک جایگاه هر دو اندر یک مغاک (رودکی) BQ:2021, HN1:85, AT:145

1975

مغازه

همریشه: magazine

Parthian	Pahlavi	Arabic	Arabic	Italian	Turkish	Persian
gzn: *treasure* گنج GR:182	ganj: *treasure* BQ:1841,	kanz: *treasure* BR	maxzan: *storage* AA:108, BR	mazazzino: *storage*	maghazeh: *store* NOTE- through AG2:70	mağâzeh: *store* مغازه AG2:70

NOTE- BR claims The Pahlavi word is possibly borrowed from a Median root

1976

مغاک: گودال ـ رجوع شود به   مَغ۲   **مغز**   ـ رجوع شود به   مزغ

مغناطیس

Greek	Persian
mağnêtes: *magnet* مغناطیس NOTE- named after the Magnesia region (from a tribe name in Thessaly, Greece) where magnetic iron ores were discovered AR:80, ODE*	meğnâtis: *magnet* مغناطیس NOTE- most likely through Arabic BQ, MO

1977

مُغیلان: بته یا درخت خاردار   همریشه: غول

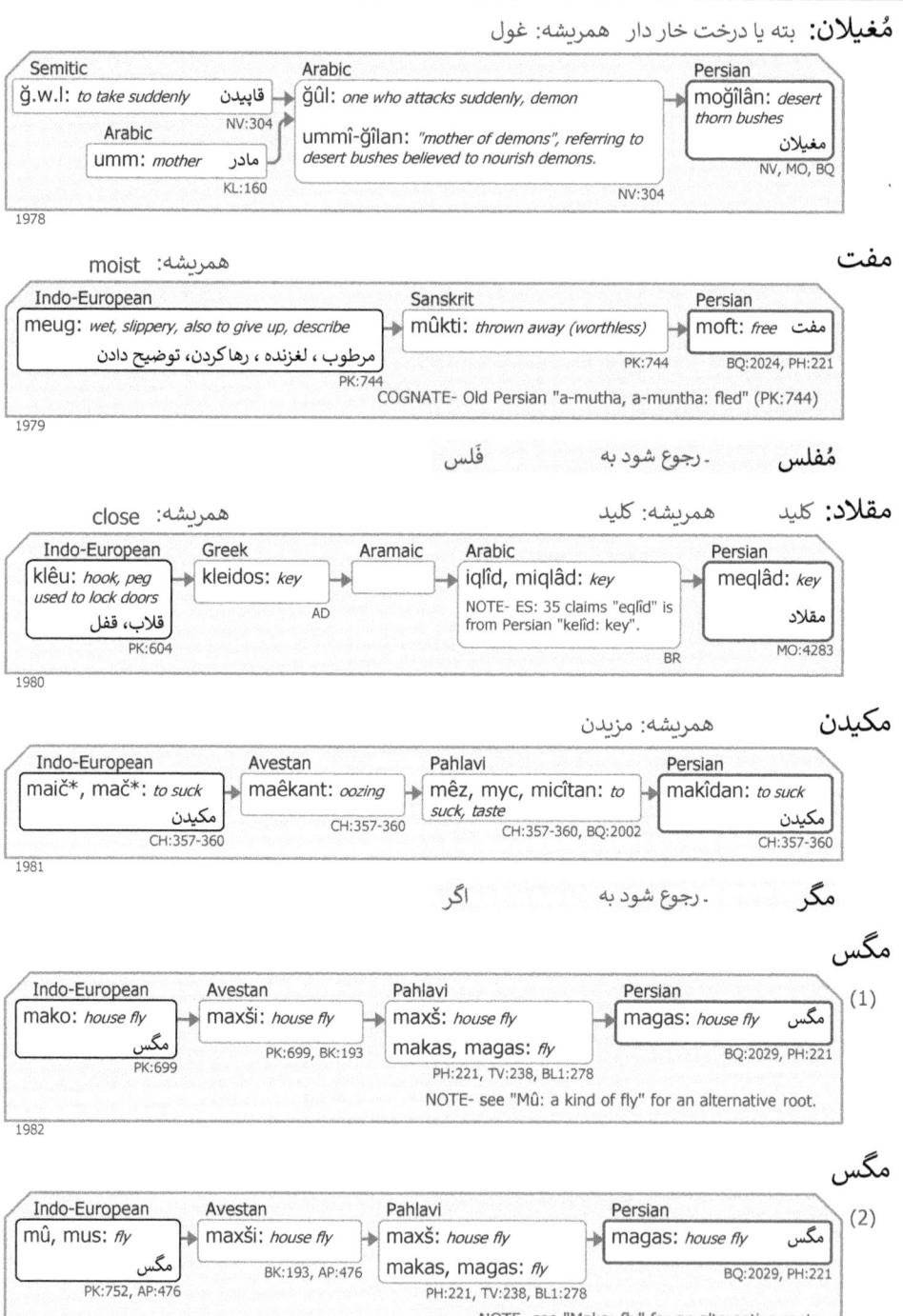

مفت

همریشه: moist

1979

مُفلس   رجوع شود به .   فَلَس

مقلاد: کلید   همریشه: کلید

1980

مکیدن   همریشه: مزیدن

1981

مگر   رجوع شود به .   اگر

مگس (1)

1982

مگس (2)

1983

مُل

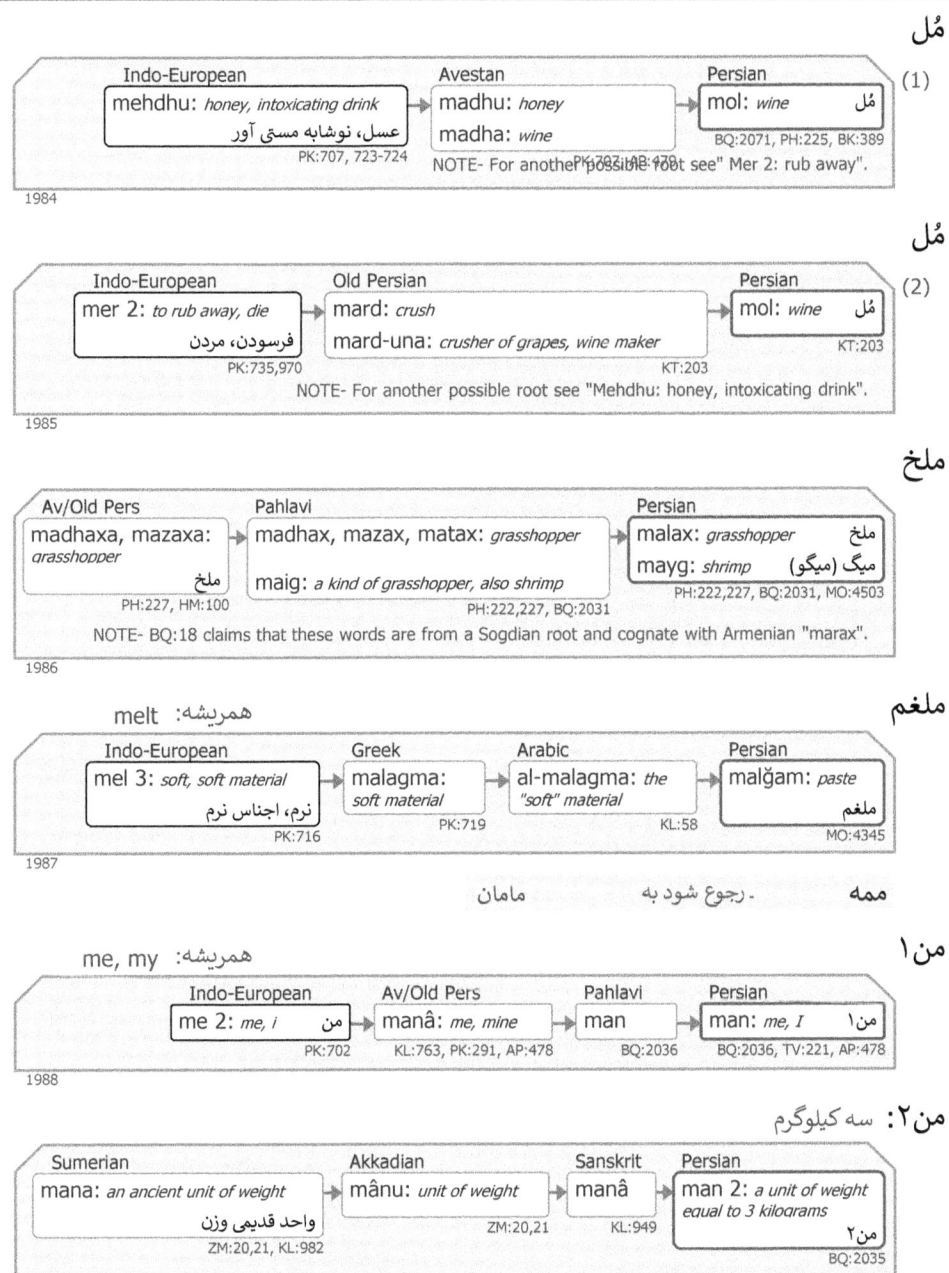

مُل (1)

Indo-European
mehdhu: *honey, intoxicating drink*
عسل، نوشابه مستی آور
PK:707, 723-724

Avestan
madhu: *honey*
madha: *wine*

Persian
mol: *wine*   مُل
BQ:2071, PH:225, BK:389

NOTE- For another possible root see "Mer 2: rub away".

1984

مُل (2)

Indo-European
mer 2: *to rub away, die*
فرسودن، مردن
PK:735,970

Old Persian
mard: *crush*
mard-una: *crusher of grapes, wine maker*
KT:203

Persian
mol: *wine*   مُل
KT:203

NOTE- For another possible root see "Mehdhu: honey, intoxicating drink".

1985

ملخ

Av/Old Pers
madhaxa, mazaxa: *grasshopper*
ملخ
PH:227, HM:100

Pahlavi
madhax, mazax, matax: *grasshopper*
maig: *a kind of grasshopper, also shrimp*
PH:222,227, BQ:2031

Persian
malax: *grasshopper*   ملخ
mayg: *shrimp*   میگ (میگو)
PH:222,227, BQ:2031, MO:4503

NOTE- BQ:18 claims that these words are from a Sogdian root and cognate with Armenian "marax".

1986

ملغم

همریشه: melt

Indo-European
mel 3: *soft, soft material*
نرم، اجناس نرم
PK:716

Greek
malagma: *soft material*
PK:719

Arabic
al-malagma: *the "soft" material*
KL:58

Persian
malğam: *paste*
ملغم
MO:4345

1987

ممه   .رجوع شود به   مامان

من۱   همریشه: me, my

Indo-European
me 2: *me, i*   من
PK:702

Av/Old Pers
manâ: *me, mine*
KL:763, PK:291, AP:478

Pahlavi
man
BQ:2036

Persian
man: *me, I*   من۱
BQ:2036, TV:221, AP:478

1988

من۲: سه کیلوگرم

Sumerian
mana: *an ancient unit of weight*
واحد قدیمی وزن
ZM:20,21, KL:982

Akkadian
mânu: *unit of weight*
ZM:20,21

Sanskrit
manâ
KL:949

Persian
man 2: *a unit of weight equal to 3 kilograms*
من۲
BQ:2035

1989

من۳: رفتار   .رجوع شود به   مان۳ .   **منار**   .رجوع شود به   نور

مَنج: زنبور عسل

همریشه: mildew

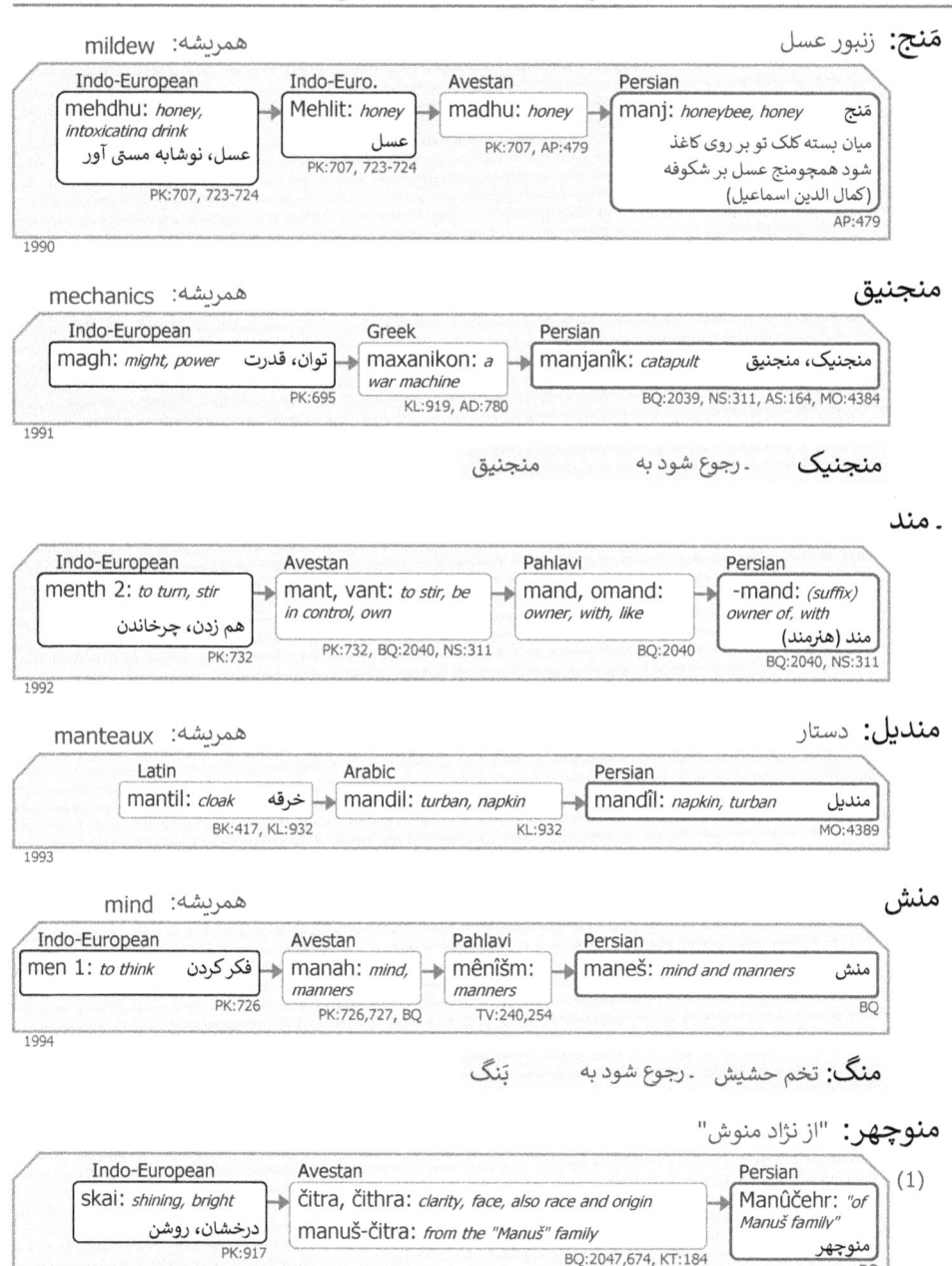

Indo-European	Indo-Euro.	Avestan	Persian
mehdhu: *honey, intoxicating drink* عسل، نوشابه مستی آور PK:707, 723-724	Mehlit: *honey* عسل PK:707, 723-724	madhu: *honey* PK:707, AP:479	manj: *honeybee, honey* مَنج میان بسته کلک تو بر روی کاغذ شود همچومنج عسل بر شکوفه (کمال الدین اسماعیل) AP:479

1990

منجنیق

همریشه: mechanics

Indo-European	Greek	Persian
magh: *might, power* توان، قدرت PK:695	maxanikon: *a war machine* KL:919, AD:780	manjanîk: *catapult* منجنیک، منجنیق BQ:2039, NS:311, AS:164, MO:4384

1991

منجنیک ـ رجوع شود به   منجنیق

ـ مند

Indo-European	Avestan	Pahlavi	Persian
menth 2: *to turn, stir* هم زدن، چرخاندن PK:732	mant, vant: *to stir, be in control, own* PK:732, BQ:2040, NS:311	mand, omand: *owner, with, like* BQ:2040	-mand: *(suffix) owner of, with* مند (هنرمند) BQ:2040, NS:311

1992

مندیل: دستار

همریشه: manteaux

Latin	Arabic	Persian
mantil: *cloak* خرقه BK:417, KL:932	mandil: *turban, napkin* KL:932	mandîl: *napkin, turban* مندیل MO:4389

1993

منش

همریشه: mind

Indo-European	Avestan	Pahlavi	Persian
men 1: *to think* فکر کردن PK:726	manah: *mind, manners* PK:726,727, BQ	mênîšm: *manners* TV:240,254	maneš: *mind and manners* منش BQ

1994

منگ: تخم حشیش   ـ رجوع شود به   بَنگ

منوچهر: "از نژاد منوش"

Indo-European	Avestan	Persian
skai: *shining, bright* درخشان، روشن PK:917	čitra, čithra: *clarity, face, also race and origin* manuš-čitra: *from the "Manuš" family* BQ:2047,674, KT:184	Manûčehr: *"of Manuš family"* منوچهر BQ

(1)

1995

منوچهر: "با چهره مردانه"

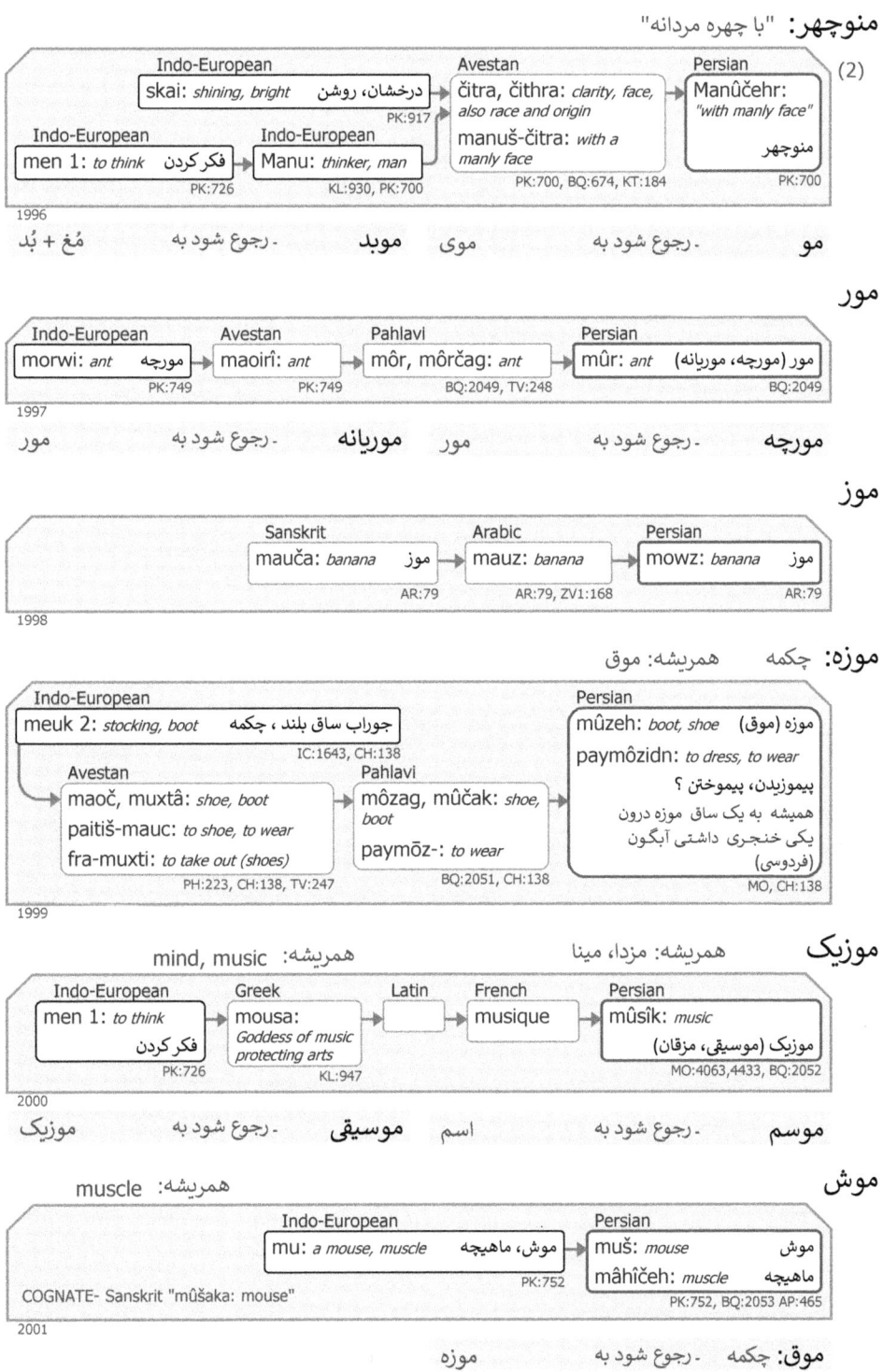

(2)

Indo-European	Avestan	Persian
skai: shining, bright درخشان، روشن PK:917	čitra, čithra: clarity, face, also race and origin	Manûčehr: "with manly face" منوچهر PK:700
	manuš-čitra: with a manly face PK:700, BQ:674, KT:184	

Indo-European	Indo-European
men 1: to think فکر کردن PK:726	Manu: thinker, man KL:930, PK:700

1996

مو   . رجوع شود به   موی   **موبد**   رجوع شود به .   مُغ + بُد   مو

مور

Indo-European	Avestan	Pahlavi	Persian
morwi: ant مورچه PK:749	maoirî: ant PK:749	môr, môrčag: ant BQ:2049, TV:248	mûr: ant (مور (مورچه، موریانه BQ:2049

1997

مورچه   . رجوع شود به   مور   **موریانه**   رجوع شود به .   مور

موز

Sanskrit	Arabic	Persian
mauča: banana موز AR:79	mauz: banana AR:79, ZV1:168	mowz: banana موز AR:79

1998

موزه: چکمه   همریشه: موق

Indo-European	Persian
meuk 2: stocking, boot جوراب ساق بلند، چکمه IC:1643, CH:138	mûzeh: boot, shoe (موزه (موق paymôzidn: to dress, to wear پیموزیدن، پیموختن ؟ همیشه به یک ساق موزه درون یکی خنجری داشتی آبگون (فردوسی) MO, CH:138

Avestan	Pahlavi
maoč, muxtâ: shoe, boot paitiš-mauc: to shoe, to wear fra-muxti: to take out (shoes) PH:223, CH:138, TV:247	môzag, mûčak: shoe, boot paymôz-: to wear BQ:2051, CH:138

1999

موزیک

همریشه: مزدا، مینا   همریشه: mind, music

Indo-European	Greek	Latin	French	Persian
men 1: to think فکر کردن PK:726	mousa: Goddess of music protecting arts KL:947		musique	mûsîk: music (موزیک (موسیقی، مزقان MO:4063,4433, BQ:2052

2000

موسم   . رجوع شود به   اسم   **موسیقی**   رجوع شود به .   موزیک

موش

همریشه: muscle

Indo-European	Persian
mu: a mouse, muscle موش، ماهیچه PK:752	muš: mouse موش mâhîčeh: muscle ماهیچه PK:752, BQ:2053 AP:465

COGNATE- Sanskrit "mûšaka: mouse"

2001

موق: چکمه   . رجوع شود به   موزه

موک: نیش

موم، مومیا: "قیری که در مومیایی کردن بکار میرفته"

موی

مویه: زاری   همریشه: مُست۲

موبیدن   -رجوع شود به   مویه   مَه   -رجوع شود به   مهتاب

مِه ۱

مِه ۲   همریشه: mega

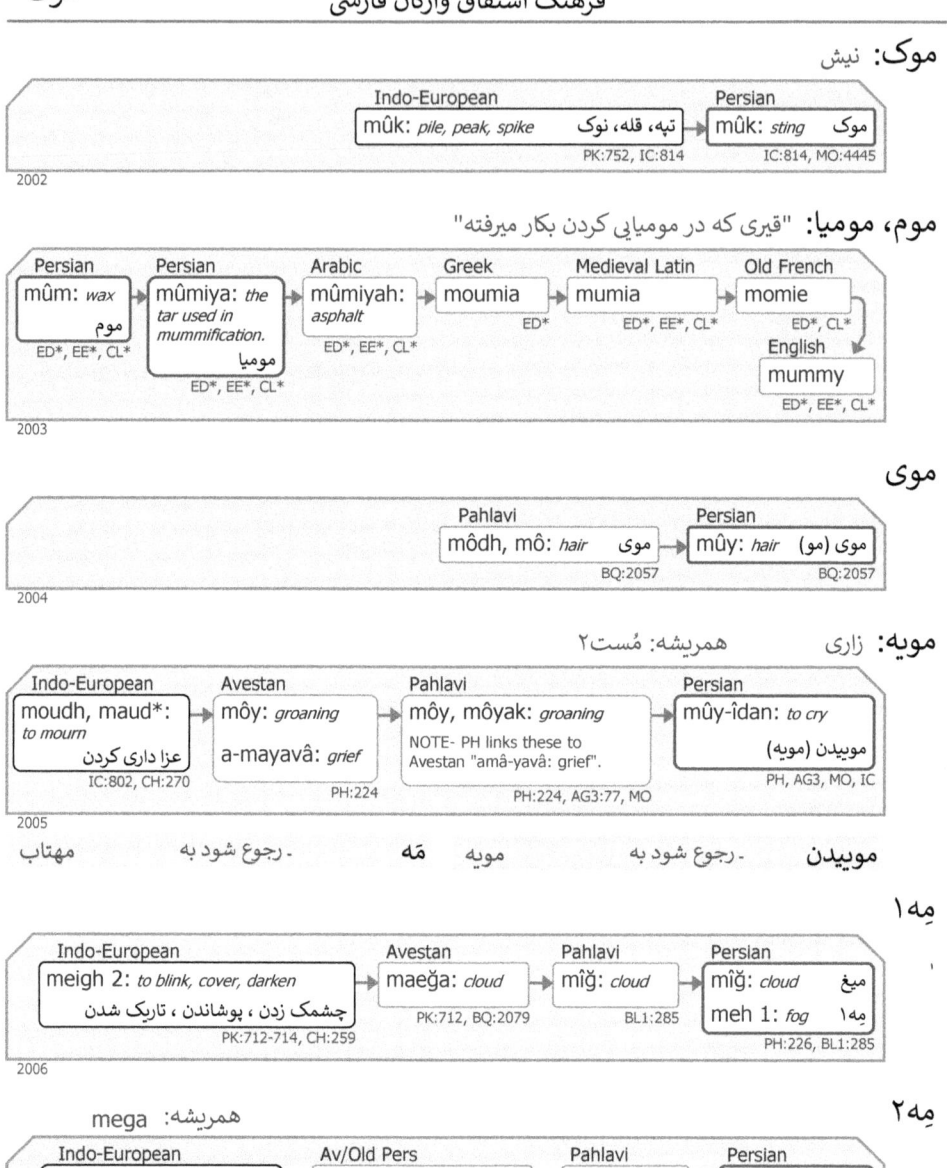

مهتاب

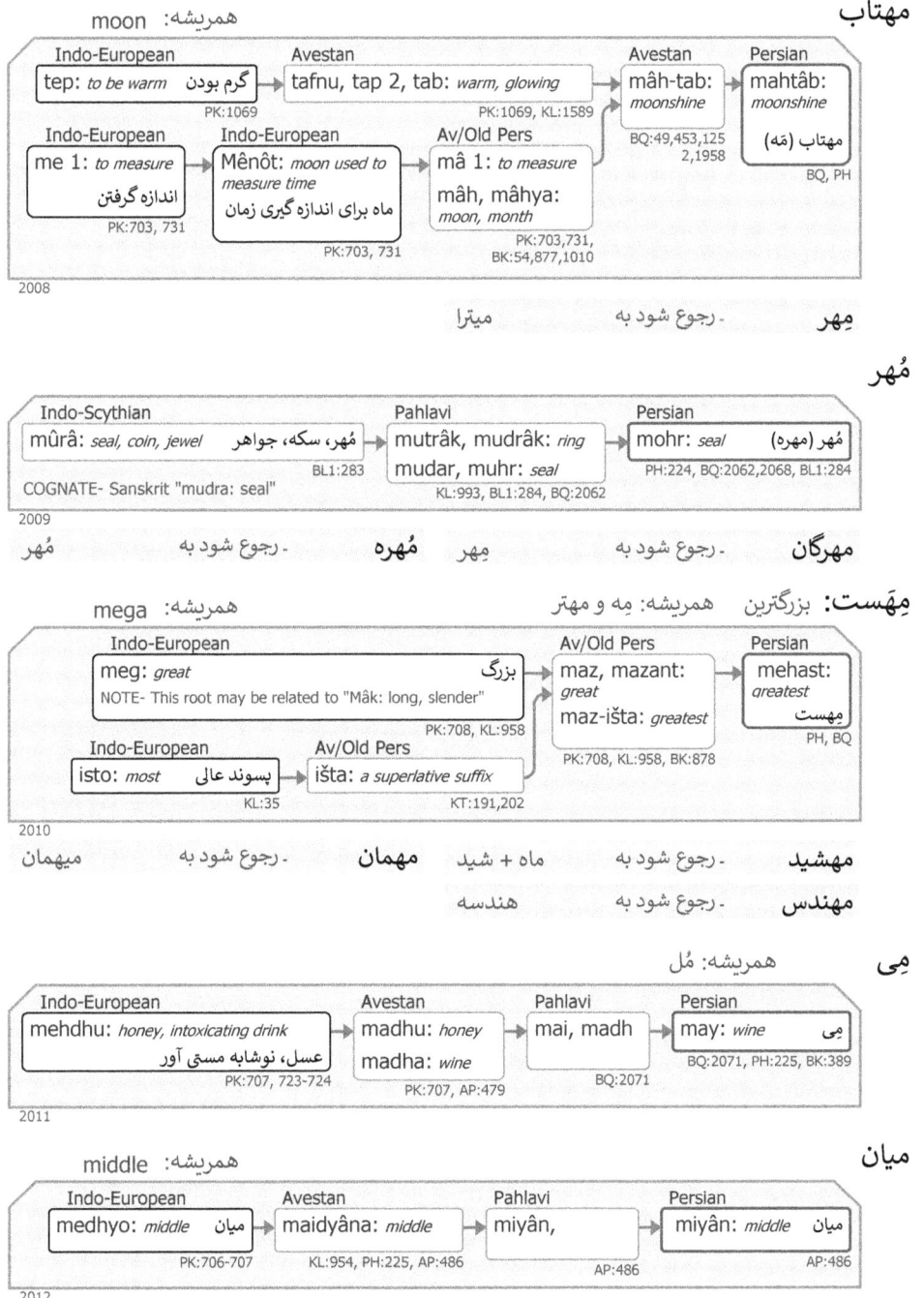

مهتاب   همریشه: moon

Indo-European	Avestan	Avestan	Persian
tep: *to be warm* گرم بودن	tafnu, tap 2, tab: *warm, glowing*	mâh-tab: *moonshine*	mahtâb: *moonshine*
PK:1069	PK:1069, KL:1589	BQ:49,453,125 2,1958	مهتاب (مه)

Indo-European	Indo-European	Av/Old Pers		BQ, PH
me 1: *to measure* اندازه گرفتن	Mênôt: *moon used to measure time* ماه برای اندازه گیری زمان	mâ 1: *to measure* mâh, mâhya: *moon, month*		
PK:703, 731	PK:703, 731	PK:703,731, BK:54,877,1010		

2008

میترا   . رجوع شود به   مِهر

مُهر

Indo-Scythian	Pahlavi	Persian
mûrâ: *seal, coin, jewel* مُهر، سکه، جواهر	mutrâk, mudrâk: *ring* mudar, muhr: *seal*	mohr: *seal* مُهر (مهره)
BL1:283	KL:993, BL1:284, BQ:2062	PH:224, BQ:2062,2068, BL1:284

COGNATE- Sanskrit "mudra: seal"

2009

مُهر   . رجوع شود به   مِهر   **مُهره**   **مهرگان**   . رجوع شود به   مِهر

مِهَست: بزرگترین   همریشه: مِه و مهتر   همریشه: mega

Indo-European	Av/Old Pers	Persian
meg: *great* بزرگ NOTE- This root may be related to "Mâk: long, slender" PK:708, KL:958	maz, mazant: *great* maz-išta: *greatest*	mehast: *greatest* مهست PH, BQ
Indo-European	Av/Old Pers	
isto: *most* پسوند عالی	išta: *a superlative suffix*	PK:708, KL:958, BK:878
KL:35	KT:191,202	

2010

میهمان   **مهمان**   . رجوع شود به   ماه + شید   **مهشید**

هندسه   . رجوع شود به   **مهندس**

مِی

همریشه: مُل

Indo-European	Avestan	Pahlavi	Persian
mehdhu: *honey, intoxicating drink* عسل، نوشابه مستی آور	madhu: *honey* madha: *wine*	mai, madh	may: *wine* مِی
PK:707, 723-724	PK:707, AP:479	BQ:2071	BQ:2071, PH:225, BK:389

2011

میان

همریشه: middle

Indo-European	Avestan	Pahlavi	Persian
medhyo: *middle* میان	maidyâna: *middle*	miyân,	miyân: *middle* میان
PK:706-707	KL:954, PH:225, AP:486	AP:486	AP:486

2012

میترا: فرشته محبت، آفتاب

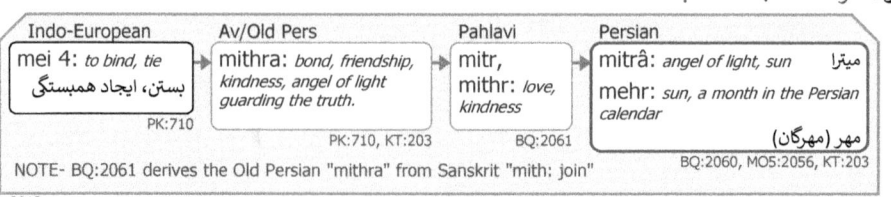

Indo-European	Av/Old Pers	Pahlavi	Persian
mei 4: *to bind, tie* بستن، ایجاد همبستگی PK:710	mithra: *bond, friendship, kindness, angel of light guarding the truth.* PK:710, KT:203	mitr, mithr: *love, kindness* BQ:2061	mitrâ: *angel of light, sun* میترا mehr: *sun, a month in the Persian calendar* مهر (مهرگان) BQ:2060, MO5:2056, KT:203

NOTE- BQ:2061 derives the Old Persian "mithra" from Sanskrit "mith: join"

2013

میخ   همریشه: ammunition

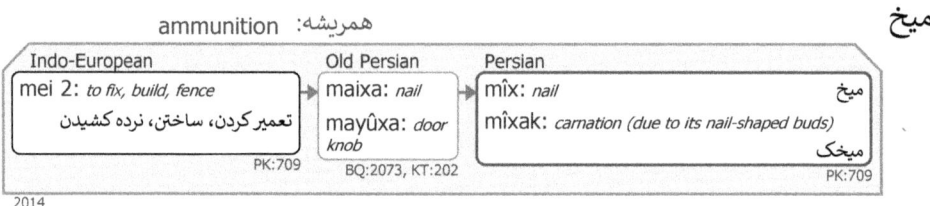

Indo-European	Old Persian	Persian
mei 2: *to fix, build, fence* تعمیر کردن، ساختن، نرده کشیدن PK:709	maixa: *nail* mayûxa: *door knob* BQ:2073, KT:202	mîx: *nail* میخ mîxak: *carnation (due to its nail-shaped buds)* میخک PK:709

2014

میختن: ادرار کردن   همریشه: mist

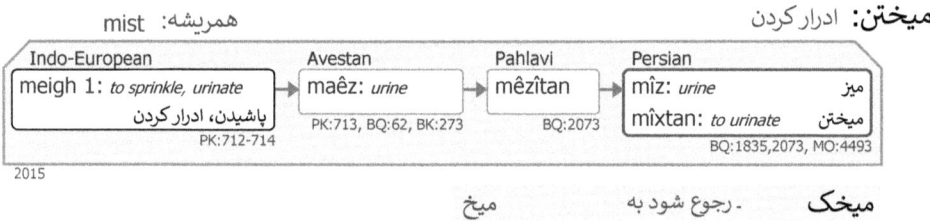

Indo-European	Avestan	Pahlavi	Persian
meigh 1: *to sprinkle, urinate* پاشیدن، ادرار کردن PK:712-714	maêz: *urine* PK:713, BQ:62, BK:273	mêzîtan BQ:2073	mîz: *urine* میز mîxtan: *to urinate* میختن BQ:1835,2073, MO:4493

2015

میخک   ـ رجوع شود به   میخ

میرزا   همریشه: gentleman, generate

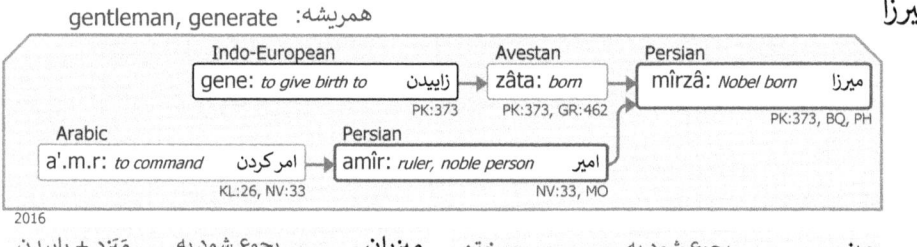

Indo-European	Avestan	Persian
gene: *to give birth to* زاییدن PK:373	zâta: *born* PK:373, GR:462	mîrzâ: *Nobel born* میرزا PK:373, BQ, PH
Arabic a'.m.r: *to command* امر کردن KL:26, NV:33	Persian amîr: *ruler, noble person* امیر NV:33, MO	

2016

میز ـ رجوع شود به میختن   **میزبان** ـ رجوع شود به مَیَزد + پاییدن

مَیَزد: میهمان

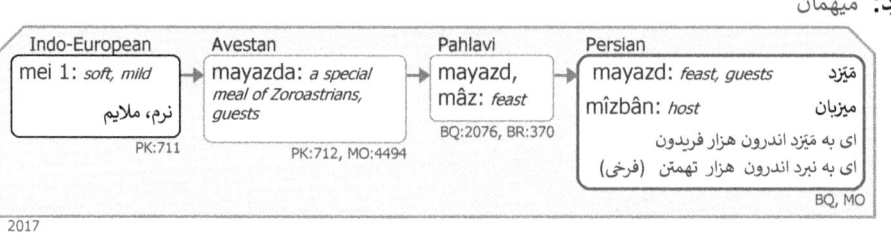

Indo-European	Avestan	Pahlavi	Persian
mei 1: *soft, mild* نرم، ملایم PK:711	mayazda: *a special meal of Zoroastrians, guests* PK:712, MO:4494	mayazd, mâz: *feast* BQ:2076, BR:370	mayazd: *feast, guests* مَیَزد mîzbân: *host* میزبان

ای به مَیَزد اندرون هزار فریدون

ای به نبرد اندرون هزار تهمتن   (فرخی)

BQ, MO

2017

میزراه   ـ رجوع شود به   میختن + راه

میش

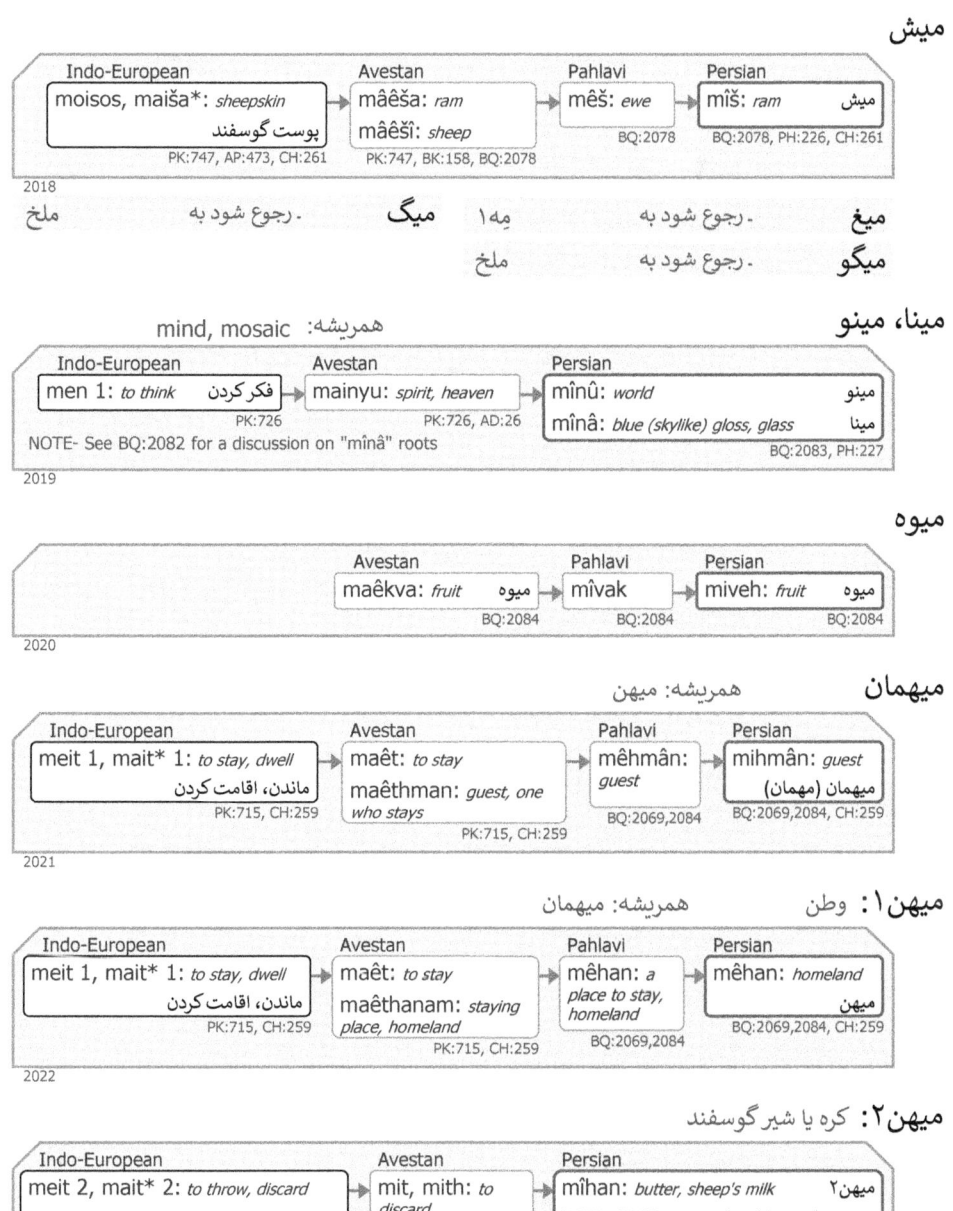

Indo-European	Avestan	Pahlavi	Persian
moisos, maiša*: *sheepskin* پوست گوسفند PK:747, AP:473, CH:261	mâêša: *ram* mâêši: *sheep* PK:747, BK:158, BQ:2078	mêš: *ewe* BQ:2078	mîš: *ram* میش BQ:2078, PH:226, CH:261

2018

میغ . رجوع شود به **مِه ۱ه** . رجوع شود به ملخ

میگو . رجوع شود به **میگ** . رجوع شود به ملخ

مینا، مینو

همریشه: mind, mosaic

Indo-European	Avestan	Persian
men 1: *to think* فکر کردن PK:726	mainyu: *spirit, heaven* PK:726, AD:26	mînû: *world* مینو mînâ: *blue (skylike) gloss, glass* مینا BQ:2083, PH:227

NOTE- See BQ:2082 for a discussion on "mînâ" roots

2019

میوه

Avestan	Pahlavi	Persian
maêkva: *fruit* میوه BQ:2084	mîvak BQ:2084	miveh: *fruit* میوه BQ:2084

2020

میهمان

همریشه: میهن

Indo-European	Avestan	Pahlavi	Persian
meit 1, mait* 1: *to stay, dwell* ماندن، اقامت کردن PK:715, CH:259	maêt: *to stay* maêthman: *guest, one who stays* PK:715, CH:259	mêhmân: *guest* BQ:2069,2084	mihmân: *guest* میهمان (مهمان) BQ:2069,2084, CH:259

2021

میهن۱: وطن

همریشه: میهمان

Indo-European	Avestan	Pahlavi	Persian
meit 1, mait* 1: *to stay, dwell* ماندن، اقامت کردن PK:715, CH:259	maêt: *to stay* maêthanam: *staying place, homeland* PK:715, CH:259	mêhan: *a place to stay, homeland* BQ:2069,2084	mêhan: *homeland* میهن BQ:2069,2084, CH:259

2022

میهن۲: کره یا شیر گوسفند

Indo-European	Avestan	Persian
meit 2, mait* 2: *to throw, discard* دور ریختن، پرت کردن PK:968, CH:260	mit, mith: *to discard* CH:260	mîhan: *butter, sheep's milk* میهن۲ NOTE- CH:261 states that this word may be influenced with the root Maiša: sheep. CH:260, BQ

2023

این حرف گاهی به م یا ل بدل شود.

نا ، نا .

همریشه: no

Indo-European	Av/Old Pers	Pahlavi	Persian
ne 1, an 3: *no, not* نَه	na 1, ni 2, naiy: *no, not*	nê: *no*	na: *no* (نا .) نَه
PK:756, KT:167	PK:756	BQ:2211	BQ:2210

2024

ناب

Indo-European	Avestan	Pahlavi	Persian
ab 1: *water* آب	âp: *water, water glitter*	na-âp: *with no added water, pure*	nâb: *pure* ناب
PK:1	KL:2		BL1:3
Indo-European	Av/Old Pers		
ne 1, an 3: *no, not* نَه	na 1, ni 2, naiy: *no, not*	BR, BL1:3	
PK:756, KT:167	PK:756		

2025

نابیوسان: ناگاه . رجوع شود به بیوسیدن   **ناخدا** ناو + خدا . رجوع شود به

ناخن

همریشه: nail

Indo-European	Sanskrit	Pahlavi	Persian
nogh: *nail* ناخن	nakhâ, naxâ: *nail*	nâxun: *nail*	nâxon: *nail* ناخن
PK:780	PK:780, TV:258	TV:258, PH:228	PK:780, BQ:2089, BK:245, KL:1028

2026

نار   . رجوع شود به نور

نارد، ناردین: سُنبل هندی

Indo-European	Sanskrit	Persian	Greek	English
nedo: *reed, pipe, flute* تره، لوله، فلوت	nadah: *reed*	nard 2: *spikenard* نرد۲، نارد، ناردین	nardos NOTE- through Arabic	nard, spikenard NOTE- through Latin
PK:759, BQ:2221	PK:759, PH:237	PH:237, BQ:2093	AD	KL:1028, AA:257

2027

نارگیل

همریشه: narghile

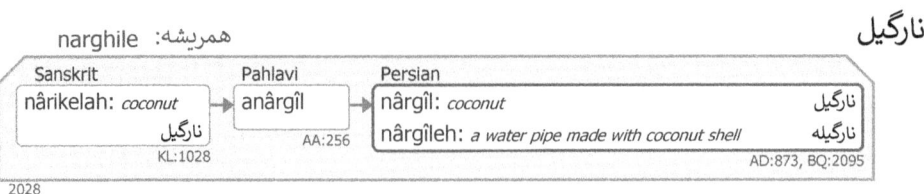

Sanskrit	Pahlavi	Persian
nârikelah: *coconut* نارگیل	anârgîl	nârgîl: *coconut* نارگیل
KL:1028	AA:256	nârgîleh: *a water pipe made with coconut shell* نارگیله
		AD:873, BQ:2095

2028

نارنج، نارنگ

همریشه: orange

Sanskrit	Persian	Arabic	Persian
naranga: *orange tree*	nâreng: *a citrus fruit*		nârenj: *a citrus fruit*
درخت پرتقال	نارنگ (نارنگی)		نارنج
YB:642	YB:642, BQ		MO

NOTE- European words like "orange" are derived from Persian through Arabic

2029

نارون: نارین - رجوع شود به بُن۱

ناز، نازک

Indo-European	Old Iranian	Pahlavi	Persian
nôğ: *whim, triviality, fancy*	nâz: *happiness, pride*	nâz: *to be happy, mince*	nâz: *affected manners, pride* ناز
هوس، ناچیز		nâčuk: *delicate*	nâzok: *thin, delicate* نازک
IC:848, 1236	AG3:77	AG3:77	AG3:77, PH:228

2030

ناشتا - رجوع شود به نا + شتا

ناف، نافه

همریشه: nave

Indo-European	Avestan	Pahlavi	Persian
nobh: *nave, hub* ناف، مرکز	nâf, nâfah, nafa, nâfô: *nave*	nâf nâfak	nâf: *nave* ناف
PK:314			nâfeh: *musk bag* نافه
	PK:314	BQ:2100	KL:1032, PH:228, BQ:2100

NOTE- BQ:2100 claims "naveh" is cognate with "nâf"

2031

ناگاه - رجوع شود به نا + آگاه

ناگزیر - رجوع شود به گزیدن

نال - رجوع شود به نای

نالیدن

Indo-European	Av/Old Pers	Persian
neu: *to cry, wail*	nard: *to cry*	nâlîdan: *to moan* نالیدن
گریه کردن، نالیدن		NOTE- HM:103 derives "nâlîdan" from Sanskrit "nard: to cry".
PK:767, CH:274	AG3:77	AG3:77

2032

نام

همریشه: name

Indo-European	Av/Old Pers	Pahlavi	Persian
nomn: *name* نام	nâma, nâman: *name*	nâm	nâm: *name* نام (نامه)
PK:321	PK:321, KT:193	BQ:2106	BQ, PH:229

2033

ناموس: "قانون و قواعد"

همریشه: number, economy

Indo-European	Greek	Arabic	Persian
nem 1: *to assign, take*	nomos: *law*	namûs: *law, rules*	nâmûs: *rules, dignity, family*
اختصاص دادن، گرفتن			ناموس
PK:763	AD	BQ:2106, MO:4629	

2034

نامه - رجوع شود به نام

نان

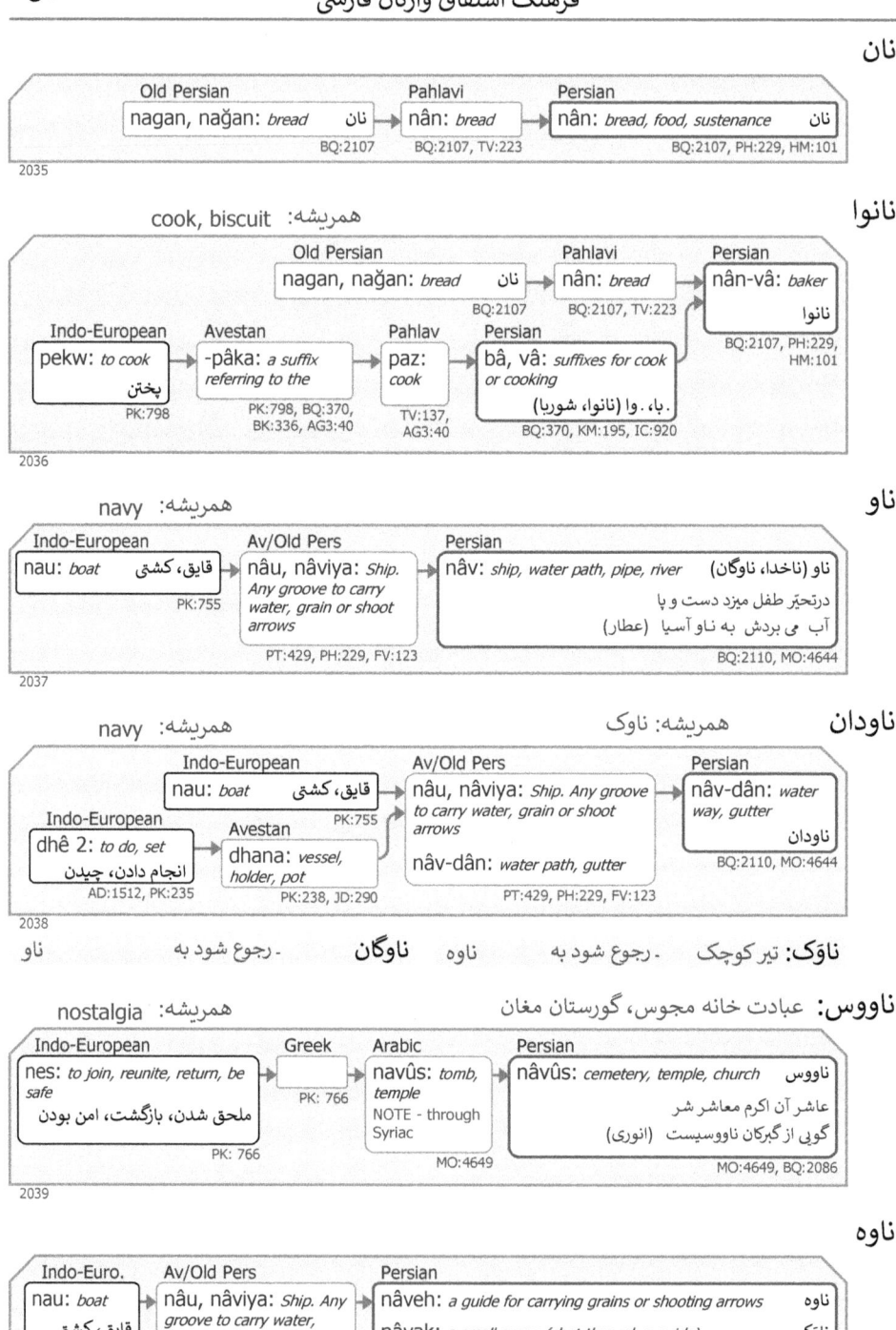

Old Persian
nagan, naǧan: *bread* نان
BQ:2107

Pahlavi
nân: *bread*
BQ:2107, TV:223

Persian
nân: *bread, food, sustenance* نان
BQ:2107, PH:229, HM:101

2035

نانوا

همریشه: cook, biscuit

Old Persian
nagan, naǧan: *bread* نان
BQ:2107

Pahlavi
nân: *bread*
BQ:2107, TV:223

Persian
nân-vâ: *baker*
نانوا
BQ:2107, PH:229, HM:101

Indo-European
pekw: *to cook*
پختن
PK:798

Avestan
-pâka: *a suffix referring to the*
PK:798, BQ:370, BK:336, AG3:40

Pahlav
paz: *cook*
TV:137, AG3:40

Persian
bâ, vâ: *suffixes for cook or cooking*
با، .وا (نانوا، شوریا).
BQ:370, KM:195, IC:920

2036

ناو

همریشه: navy

Indo-European
nau: *boat* قایق، کشتی
PK:755

Av/Old Pers
nâu, nâviya: *Ship. Any groove to carry water, grain or shoot arrows*
PT:429, PH:229, FV:123

Persian
nâv: *ship, water path, pipe, river* ناو (ناخدا، ناوگان)
درتحیّر طفل میزد دست و پا
آب می بردش به ناو آسیا (عطار)
BQ:2110, MO:4644

2037

ناودان

همریشه: navy همریشه: ناوک

Indo-European
nau: *boat* قایق، کشتی
PK:755

Av/Old Pers
nâu, nâviya: *Ship. Any groove to carry water, grain or shoot arrows*
nâv-dân: *water path, gutter*
PT:429, PH:229, FV:123

Persian
nâv-dân: *water way, gutter*
ناودان
BQ:2110, MO:4644

Indo-European
dhê 2: *to do, set*
انجام دادن، چیدن
AD:1512, PK:235

Avestan
dhana: *vessel, holder, pot*
PK:238, JD:290

2038

ناوَک: تیر کوچک ‎- رجوع شود به **ناوگان** ناوه ‎- رجوع شود به ناو

ناووس: عبادت خانه مجوس، گورستان مغان

همریشه: nostalgia

Indo-European
nes: *to join, reunite, return, be safe*
ملحق شدن، بازگشت، امن بودن
PK:766

Greek
PK: 766

Arabic
navûs: *tomb, temple*
NOTE - through Syriac
MO:4649

Persian
nâvûs: *cemetery, temple, church* ناووس
عاشر آن اکرم معاشر شر
گویی از گبرکان ناووسیست (انوری)
MO:4649, BQ:2086

2039

ناوه

Indo-Euro.
nau: *boat*
قایق، کشتی
PK:755

Av/Old Pers
nâu, nâviya: *Ship. Any groove to carry water, grain or shoot arrows*
PT:429, PH:229, FV:123

Persian
nâveh: *a guide for carrying grains or shooting arrows* ناوه
nâvak: *a small arrow (shot through a guide)* ناوَک
MO, BQ, NS:321

2040

361

ناو یدن: تلو تلو خوردن (شبیه حرکت کشتی)

همریشه: navy

Indo-Euro.	Av/Old Pers	Persian
nau: *boat* قایق، کشتی PK:755	nâu, nâviya: *Ship.* *Any groove to carry water, grain or shoot arrows* PT:429, PH:229, FV:123	nâvânîdan: *to bend something (shape like a boat)* ناوانیدن nâvîdan: *to walk while moving to the sides (like a ship)* ناو یدن چو مست هر طرفی می رُفتی و می ناوی که شب گذشت کنون نوبت دعاست، مَحُسب (مولوی)

MO

2041

ناهنجار ۔رجوع شود به هنجار **ناهید** ۔ رجوع شود به آناهیتا

نای مقایسه: کرنا، سرنا

Indo-European	Old Persian	Pahlavi	Persian
nedo: *reed, pipe, flute* تره، لوله، فلوت PK:759, BQ:2221	nada: *flute* PH:237	nâdh BQ:2113	nâi, nay, nâl: *flute, windpipe* نای، نی، نال خشم تو آذر است و حسود تو نال خشک مر نال خشک را رسد از آذر آذرنگ (سوزنی) PK:759, BQ, MO, EE*

2042

نبرد: مبارزه مقایسه: آورد همریشه: suppress

Indo-European	Indo-European	Avestan	Pahlavi
per 3: *oppose, hit* مقابل PK:815-818	Perg, Part: *to fight* جنگیدن PK:818, CH:298	peret: *fight against* ni-part: *fight down* PK:818, CH:298	ni-part BQ:2115
nî: *down* پایین KL:1042	ni 1: *down* KL:1042		nabard: *battle* نبرد BQ:2115, PH:230

2043

نَبَس: نوه از دختر ۔رجوع شود به نوه **نُبی** ۔ رجوع شود به نوشتن

نَبید: شراب

Indo-European	Av/Old Pers	Persian
pô, pe: *to drink* نوشیدن PK:839, CH:289	pitu, pîta, ni-pîta: *juice* CH:289, BQ:2117	Nabîd: *wine* نَبید (نَبید) CH:289, BQ:2117, MO

2044

نَبیذ: شراب ۔رجوع شود به نَبید

نبیره همریشه: نوه همریشه: nephew

Indo-European	Av/Old Pers	Pahlavi	Persian
nepôt: *grandson* نوه پسر neptis: *grand daughter* نوه دختر PK:764, IC:836	napât, napâ: *grandson* naptis: *grand daughter* KL:1039, PK:764, KT:193, IC:836	napîrak, navîrak: *great-grandchild* BQ:2117	namîreh: *great-grandchild* نبیره BQ:2117

2045

نخ

Indo-European	Avestan	Pahlavi	Persian
nask: *twist, twine* پیچ دادن، تاباندن IC:825	naska: *thread* IC:825	nax: *thread* MO:4683	nax: *thread, string* نخ IC:825, MO:4683

2046

نخست

همریشه: نزد

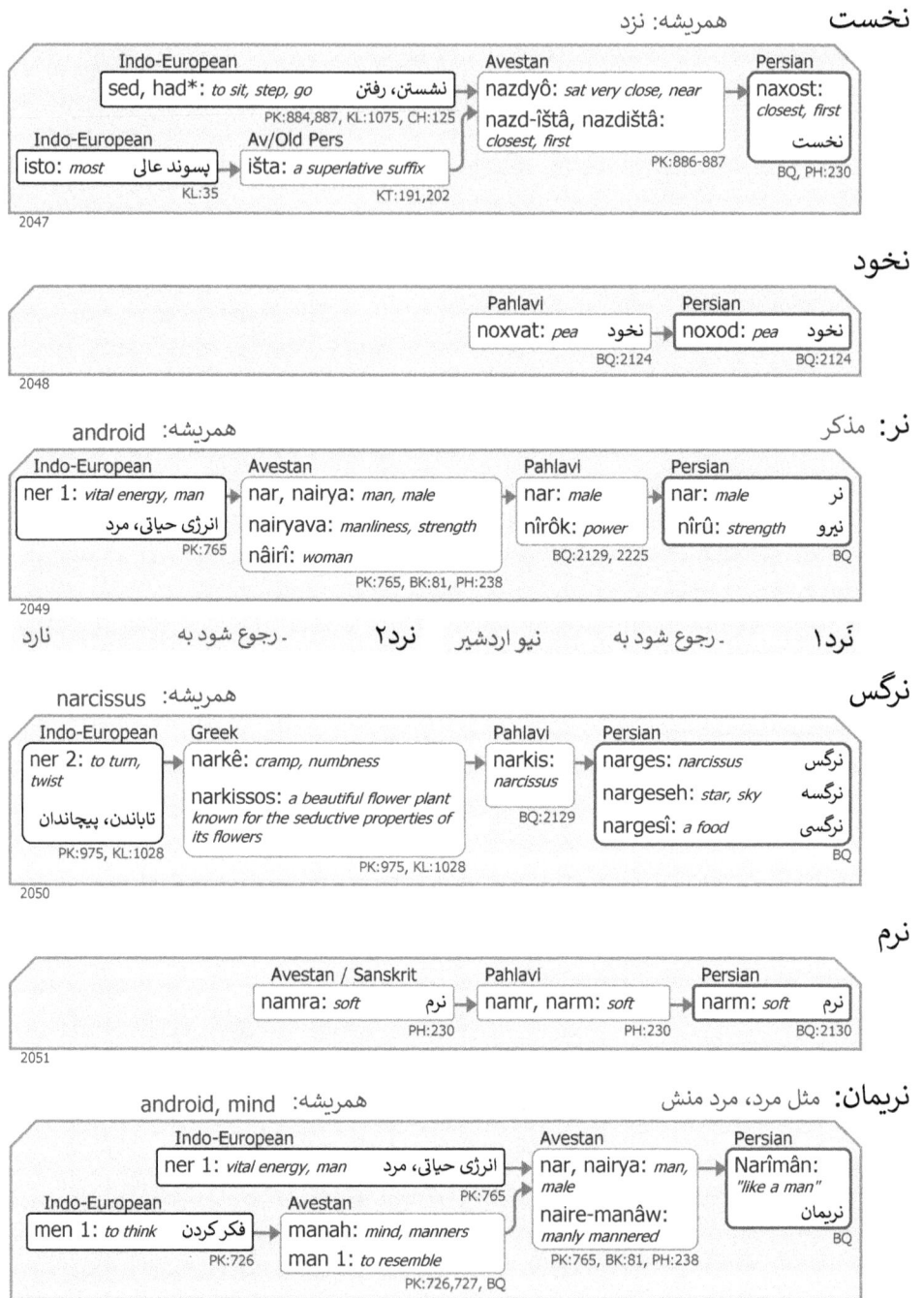

Indo-European	Avestan	Persian
sed, had*: to sit, step, go نشستن، رفتن	nazdyô: sat very close, near	naxost:
PK:884,887, KL:1075, CH:125	nazd-îštâ, nazdištâ:	closest, first

Indo-European	Av/Old Pers
isto: most پسوند عالی	išta: a superlative suffix

KL:35 KT:191,202 PK:886-887 BQ, PH:230

2047

نخود

Pahlavi	Persian
noxvat: pea نخود	noxod: pea نخود
BQ:2124	BQ:2124

2048

نر: مذکر

همریشه: android

Indo-European	Avestan	Pahlavi	Persian
ner 1: vital energy, man	nar, nairya: man, male	nar: male	nar: male نر
انرژی حیاتی، مرد	nairyava: manliness, strength	nîrôk: power	nîrû: strength نیرو
PK:765	nâirî: woman	BQ:2129, 2225	BQ
	PK:765, BK:81, PH:238		

2049

نَرد۱ ۔رجوع شود به نیو اردشیر **نرد۲** ۔رجوع شود به نارد

نرگس

همریشه: narcissus

Indo-European	Greek	Pahlavi	Persian
ner 2: to turn, twist	narkê: cramp, numbness	narkis: narcissus	narges: narcissus نرگس
تاباندن، پیچاندن	narkissos: a beautiful flower plant known for the seductive properties of its flowers		nargeseh: star, sky نرگسه
PK:975, KL:1028	PK:975, KL:1028	BQ:2129	nargesî: a food نرگسی
			BQ

2050

نرم

Avestan / Sanskrit	Pahlavi	Persian
namra: soft نرم	namr, narm: soft	narm: soft نرم
PH:230	PH:230	BQ:2130

2051

نریمان: مثل مرد، مرد منش

همریشه: android, mind

Indo-European	Avestan	Persian
ner 1: vital energy, man انرژی حیاتی، مرد	nar, nairya: man, male	Narîmân: "like a man"
PK:765	naire-manâw: manly mannered	نریمان

Indo-European	Avestan
men 1: to think فکر کردن	manah: mind, manners
PK:726	man 1: to resemble

PK:726,727, BQ PK:765, BK:81, PH:238 BQ

2052

نزار: ضعیف و لاغر

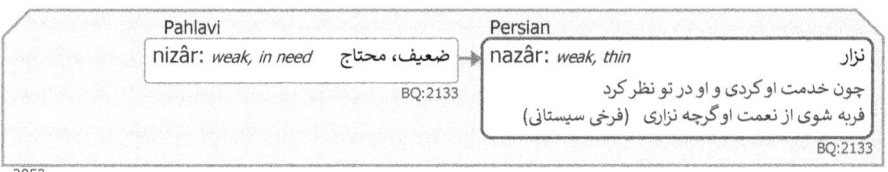

نزد، نزدیک   همریشه: sit

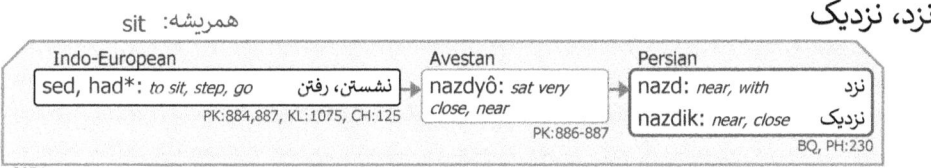

نژاد   همریشه: nation, genus

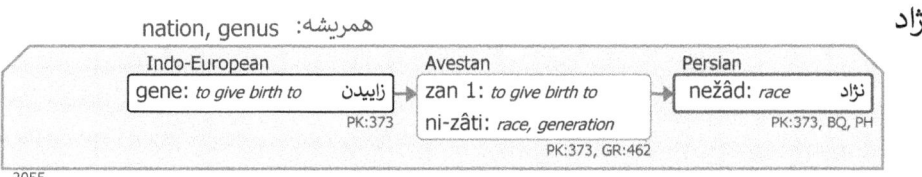

نژند: اندوهگین   همریشه: offend

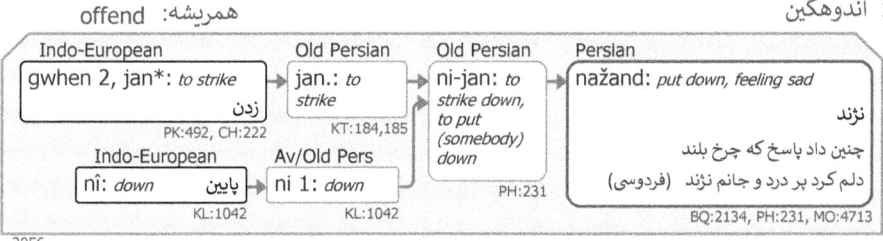

نُس: پوزه   همریشه: بینی   همریشه: nose

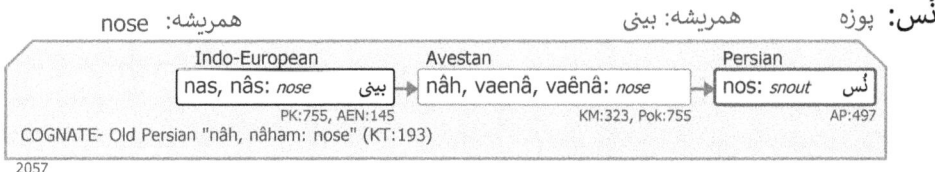

نَسا: جسد، فساد

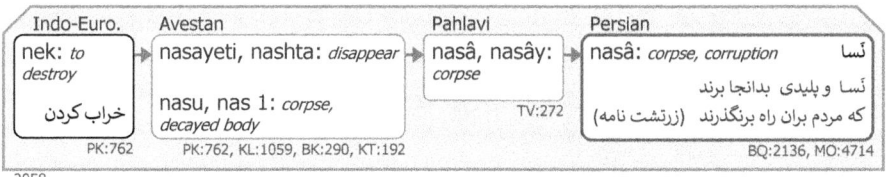

نَستوه: خسته نشدنی ـ رجوع شود به   ستوه

نُسخه

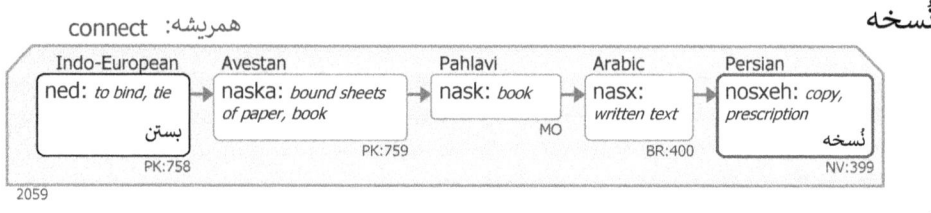

نُسک: نام هر دفتر از دفاتر پازند.

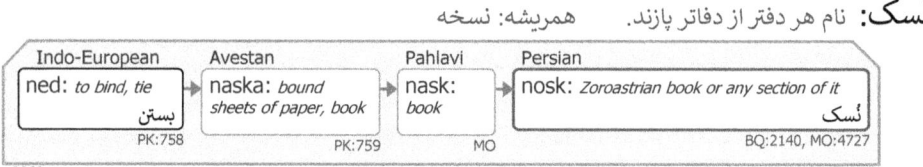

نشان

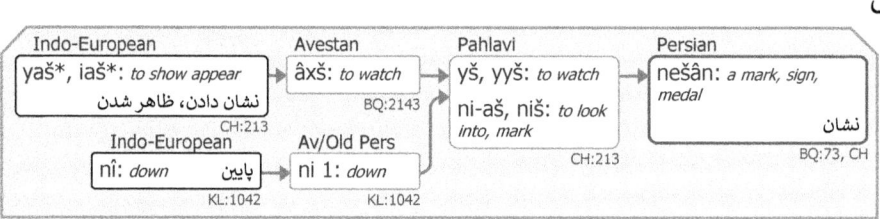

نشستن

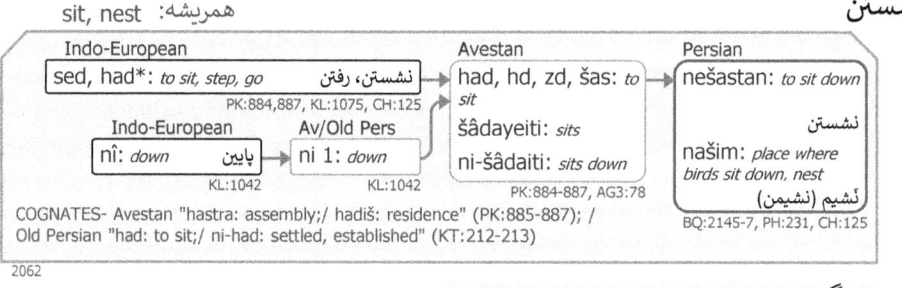

نِشگِرده: چرم بُر ـ رجوع شود به   کارد

نشیب

مقایسه: شیب۱

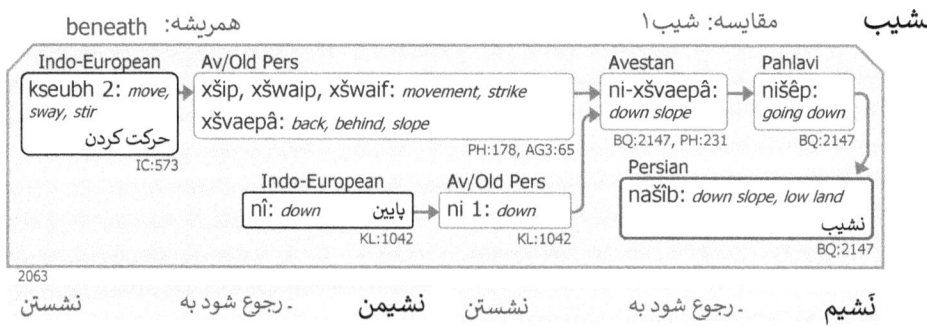

نُشیم   ـ رجوع شود به   نشستن   **نشیمن**   نشستن   ـ رجوع شود به   نشستن

نطرون: سدیم

همریشه: nitrogen

Akkadian	Hebrew	Greek	Arabic	Persian
nitiru: *natron* نطرون	nither	natron	natrûn	natrûn: *sodium* نطرون
ZM:61	ZM:61, KL:1031	KL:1049	KL:1031	MO:4745

2064

نَغام: زشت

همریشه: no, nude

Indo-European	Indo-European	Persian
nogw: *naked* عریان	Gumnos: *naked*	na-ğâm: *not beautiful, ugly* نغام
PK:769	PK:769, IC:364	چون صورت و کار دیو را دیدی

Indo-European	Av/Old Pers	بگذار طریقت نغامش را
ne 1, an 3: *no, not* نَه	na 1, ni 2, naiy: *no, not*	(ناصرخسرو)
PK:756, KT:167	PK:756	IC:364, MO:4760

2065

نغوشا: طرفداران مانی　　مقایسه: نیوشیدن

همریشه: beneath, ear

Indo-European	Indo-Euro.	Avestan	Avestan	Pahlavi
ôus 1: *ear* گوش	Ghosh: *ear*	gaoša: *ear*	ni-gaoša: *to listen*	ni-ğôšâg: *follower of the Mânî religion, also a "non-Moslem"*
PK:785, KL:126,494	PK:457, CH:115	PK:457, BQ:1858	PK:454	AG2:71

Indo-European	Av/Old Pers	Persian
nî: *down* پایین	ni 1: *down*	nağûšâ: *the followers of Mânî religion* نغوشا
KL:1042	KL:1042	AG2:71, MO:4746

2066

نغوشیدن: شنیدن　.رجوع شود به　نیوشیدن

همریشه: نفتالین

Akkadian	Aramaic	Arabic	Persian	(1)
nabatu: *to shine* درخشیدن	naftâ	naft	naft: *oil, kerosene* نفت	
nabtu, naptu: *light, lamp oil* نور، روغن چراغ	KL:1027	KL:1027	KL:1027, BQ:2155, ZM:60, MO:4777	
ZM:60				
NOTE- See "Nebh: moisture" for another possible root.				

2067

همریشه: نم

Indo-European	Avestan	Persian	(2)
nebh, nembh: *cloud, moisture* ابر، رطوبت	nab, napta: *humidity, moisture*	naft: *oil, kerosene* نفت	
PK:315	PK:316	TV:282, PH:232, BQ:2155, PK:316	
	NOTE- See Akkadian "Nabatu: to shine" for another possible root.		

2068

همریشه: نفت

Akkadian	Aramaic	Greek	Persian
nabatu: *to shine* درخشیدن	naftâ	naphta: *oil*	naftâlîn: *naphthalene* نفتالین
nabtu, naptu: *light, lamp oil* نور، روغن چراغ	KL:1027	NOTE- SK: 344 derives this from Persian "naft".	NOTE- through French
ZM:60		KL:1027	MO

2069

نفرت　.رجوع شود به　تنفر　**نفرین**　.رجوع شود به　نَه + آفرین

نقره

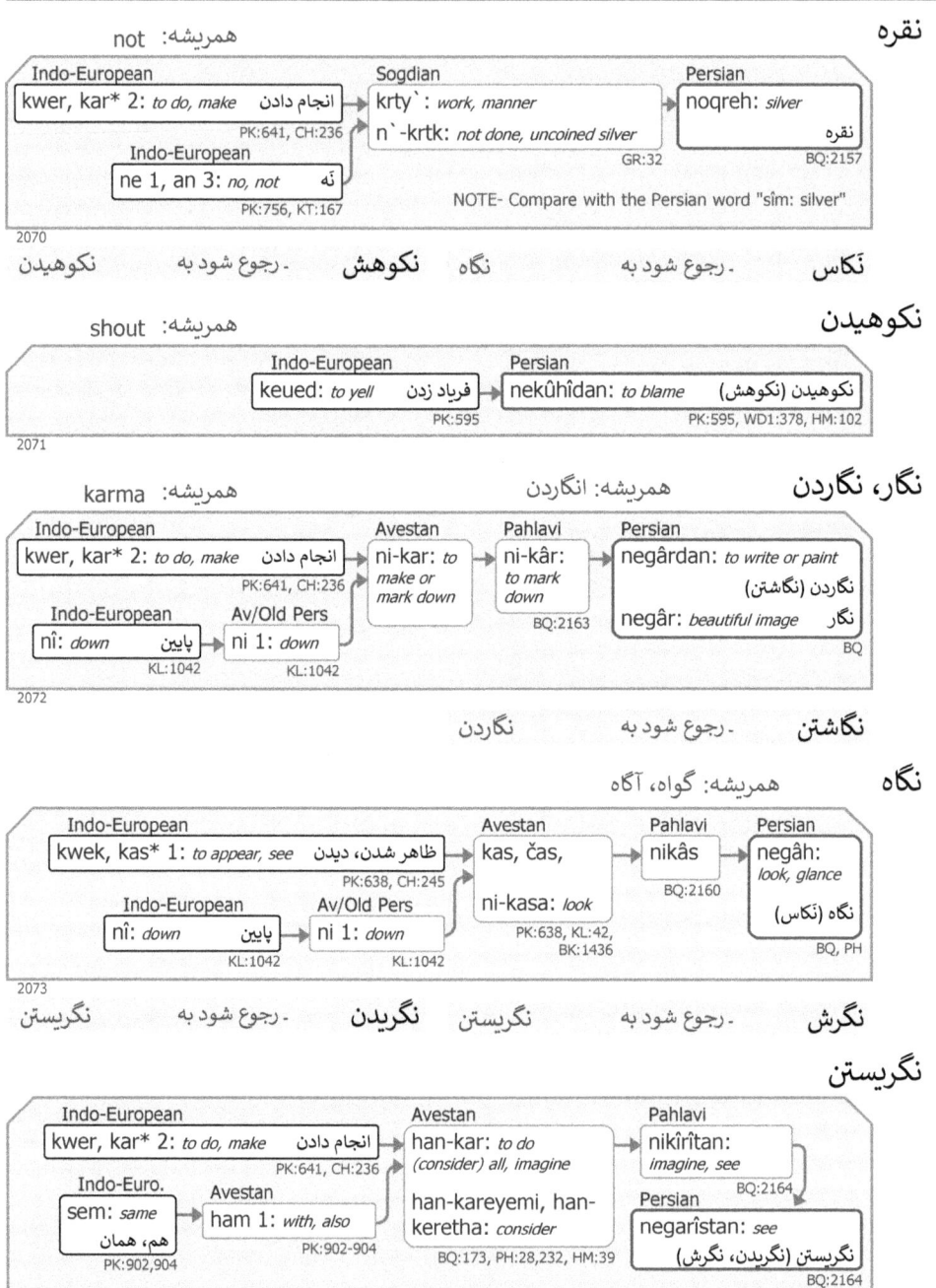

همریشه: not

Indo-European	Sogdian	Persian
kwer, kar* 2: _to do, make_ انجام دادن PK:641, CH:236	krty`: _work, manner_ n`-krtk: _not done, uncoined silver_	noqreh: _silver_ نقره

Indo-European
ne 1, an 3: _no, not_ نه
PK:756, KT:167

GR:32

BQ:2157

NOTE- Compare with the Persian word "sîm: silver"

2070

نکاس · رجوع شود به نگاه نکوهش · رجوع شود به نکوهیدن

نکوهیدن

همریشه: shout

Indo-European	Persian
keued: _to yell_ فریاد زدن PK:595	nekûhîdan: _to blame_ نکوهیدن (نکوهش) PK:595, WD1:378, HM:102

2071

نگار، نگاردن

همریشه: انگاردن همریشه: karma

Indo-European	Avestan	Pahlavi	Persian
kwer, kar* 2: _to do, make_ انجام دادن PK:641, CH:236	ni-kar: _to make or mark down_	ni-kâr: _to mark down_ BQ:2163	negârdan: _to write or paint_ نگاردن (نگاشتن) negâr: _beautiful image_ نگار BQ

Indo-European
nî: _down_ پایین
KL:1042

Av/Old Pers
ni 1: _down_
KL:1042

2072

نگاشتن · رجوع شود به نگاردن

نگاه

همریشه: گواه، آگاه

Indo-European	Avestan	Pahlavi	Persian
kwek, kas* 1: _to appear, see_ ظاهر شدن، دیدن PK:638, CH:245	kas, čas, ni-kasa: _look_ PK:638, KL:42, BK:1436	nikâs BQ:2160	negâh: _look, glance_ نگاه (نکاس) BQ, PH

Indo-European
nî: _down_ پایین
KL:1042

Av/Old Pers
ni 1: _down_
KL:1042

2073

نگرش · رجوع شود به نگریستن نگریدن · رجوع شود به نگریستن

نگریستن

Indo-European	Avestan	Pahlavi
kwer, kar* 2: _to do, make_ انجام دادن PK:641, CH:236	han-kar: _to do (consider) all, imagine_ han-kareyemi, han-keretha: _consider_ BQ:173, PH:28,232, HM:39	nikîrîtan: _imagine, see_ BQ:2164

Indo-Euro.
sem: _same_ هم، همان
PK:902,904

Avestan
ham 1: _with, also_
PK:902-904

Persian
negarîstan: _see_ نگریستن (نگریدن، نگرش)
BQ:2164

2074

نگون

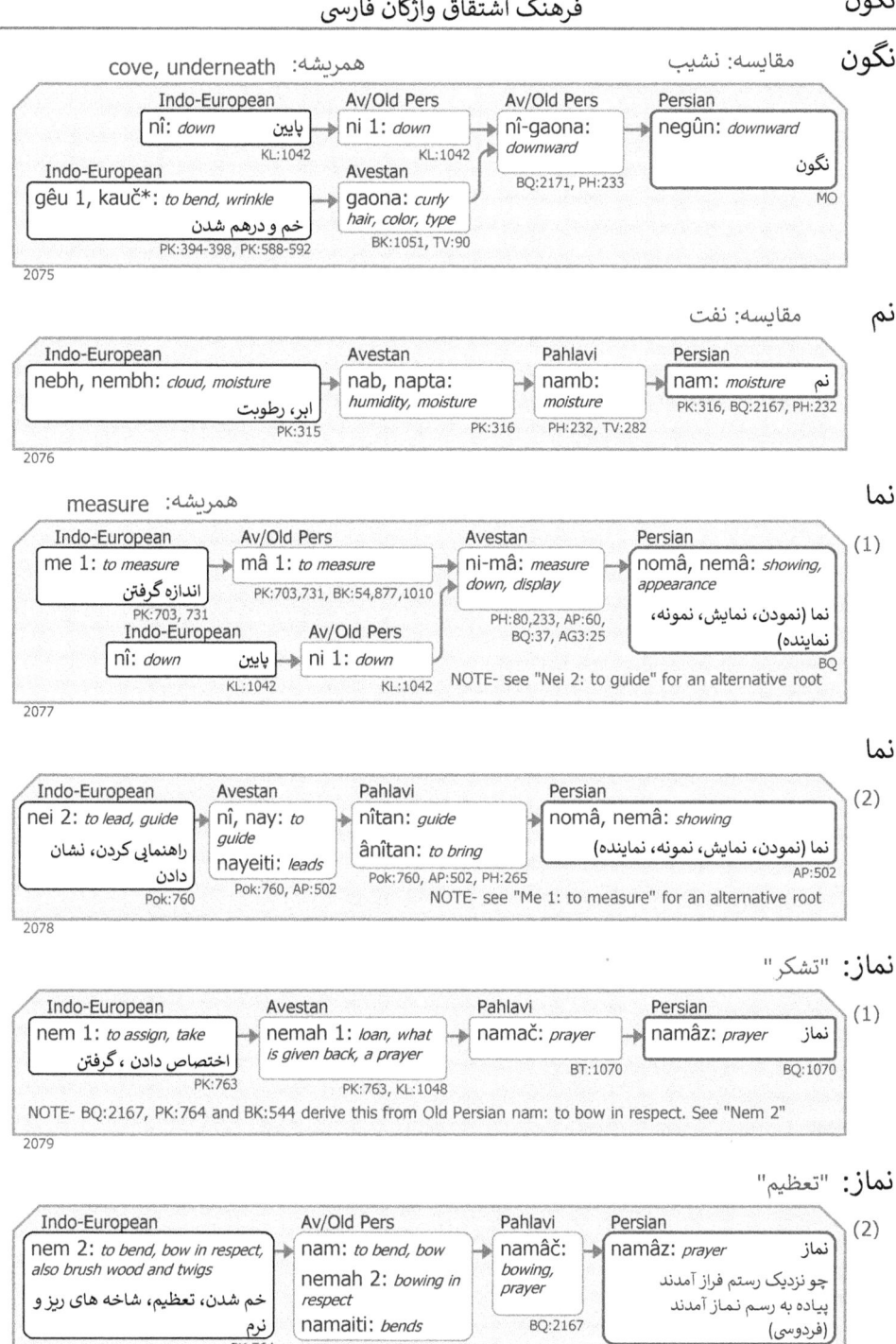

مقایسه: نشیب

نگون

همریشه: cove, underneath

2075

مقایسه: نفت

نم

2076

همریشه: measure

نما (1)

2077

نما (2)

2078

نماز: "تشکر" (1)

2079

نماز: "تعظیم" (2)

2080

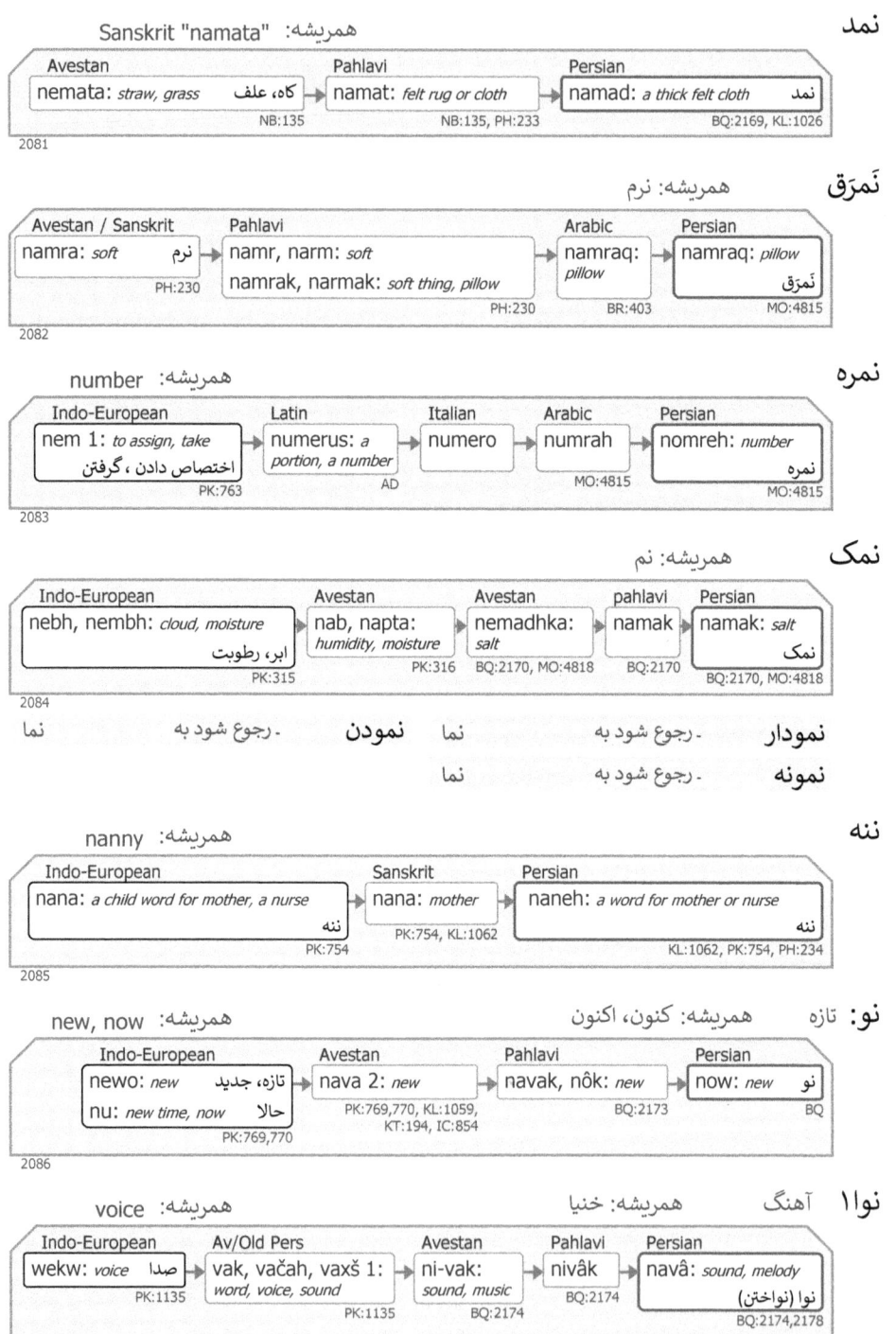

نمد

همریشه: Sanskrit "namata"

Avestan	Pahlavi	Persian
nemata: *straw, grass* كاه، علف	namat: *felt rug or cloth*	namad: *a thick felt cloth* نمد
NB:135	NB:135, PH:233	BQ:2169, KL:1026

2081

نَمرَق

همریشه: نرم

Avestan / Sanskrit	Pahlavi	Arabic	Persian
namra: *soft* نرم	namr, narm: *soft* namrak, narmak: *soft thing, pillow*	namraq: *pillow*	namraq: *pillow* نَمرَق
PH:230	PH:230	BR:403	MO:4815

2082

نمره

همریشه: number

Indo-European	Latin	Italian	Arabic	Persian
nem 1: *to assign, take* اختصاص دادن ، گرفتن	numerus: *a portion, a number*	numero	numrah	nomreh: *number* نمره
PK:763	AD		MO:4815	MO:4815

2083

نمک

همریشه: نم

Indo-European	Avestan	Avestan	pahlavi	Persian
nebh, nembh: *cloud, moisture* ابر، رطوبت	nab, napta: *humidity, moisture*	nemadhka: *salt*	namak	namak: *salt* نمک
PK:315	PK:316	BQ:2170, MO:4818	BQ:2170	BQ:2170, MO:4818

2084

نمودار - رجوع شود به   نما   نمودن   نما   - رجوع شود به   نما

نمونه - رجوع شود به   نما   نما

ننه

همریشه: nanny

Indo-European	Sanskrit	Persian
nana: *a child word for mother, a nurse* ننه	nana: *mother*	naneh: *a word for mother or nurse* ننه
PK:754	PK:754, KL:1062	KL:1062, PK:754, PH:234

2085

نو: تازه   همریشه: کنون، اکنون   همریشه: new, now

Indo-European	Avestan	Pahlavi	Persian
newo: *new* تازه، جدید nu: *new time, now* حالا	nava 2: *new*	navak, nôk: *new*	now: *new* نو
PK:769,770	PK:769,770, KL:1059, KT:194, IC:854	BQ:2173	BQ

2086

نوا١   آهنگ   همریشه: خنیا   همریشه: voice

Indo-European	Av/Old Pers	Avestan	Pahlavi	Persian
wekw: *voice* صدا	vak, vačah, vaxš 1: *word, voice, sound*	ni-vak: *sound, music*	nivâk	navâ: *sound, melody* نوا (نواختن)
PK:1135	PK:1135	BQ:2174	BQ:2174	BQ:2174,2178

2087

نوا۲: ضمانت، وسایل زندگی   همریشه: پاییدن

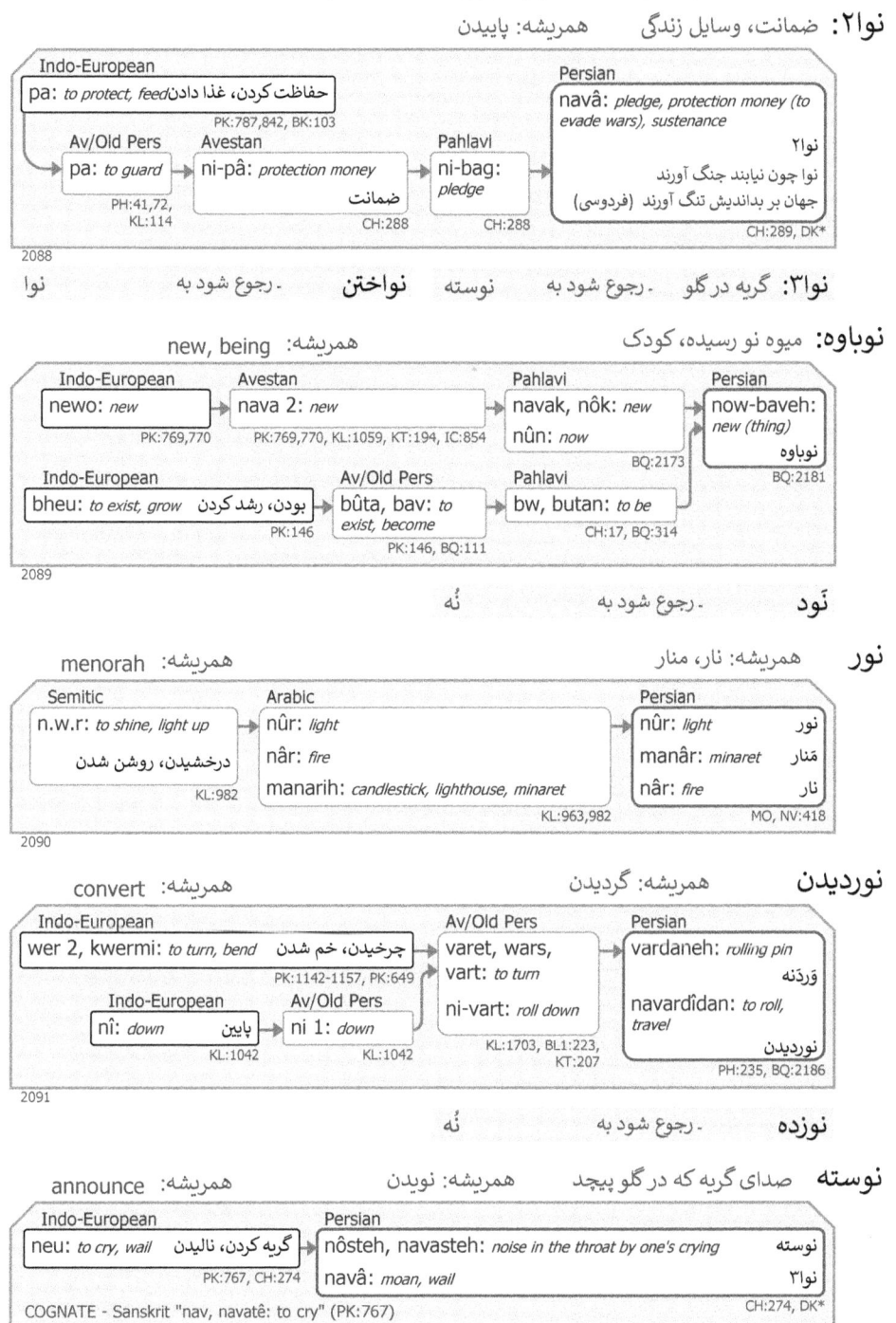

2088

نوا۳: گریه در گو   . رجوع شود به   **نواختن**   نوسته   . رجوع شود به   نوا

نوباوه: میوه نو رسیده، کودک   همریشه: new, being

2089

نَود   . رجوع شود به   نُه

نور   همریشه: نار، منار   همریشه: menorah

2090

نوردیدن   همریشه: گردیدن   همریشه: convert

2091

نوزده   . رجوع شود به   نُه

نوسته   صدای گریه که در گو پیچد   همریشه: نوید   همریشه: announce

2092

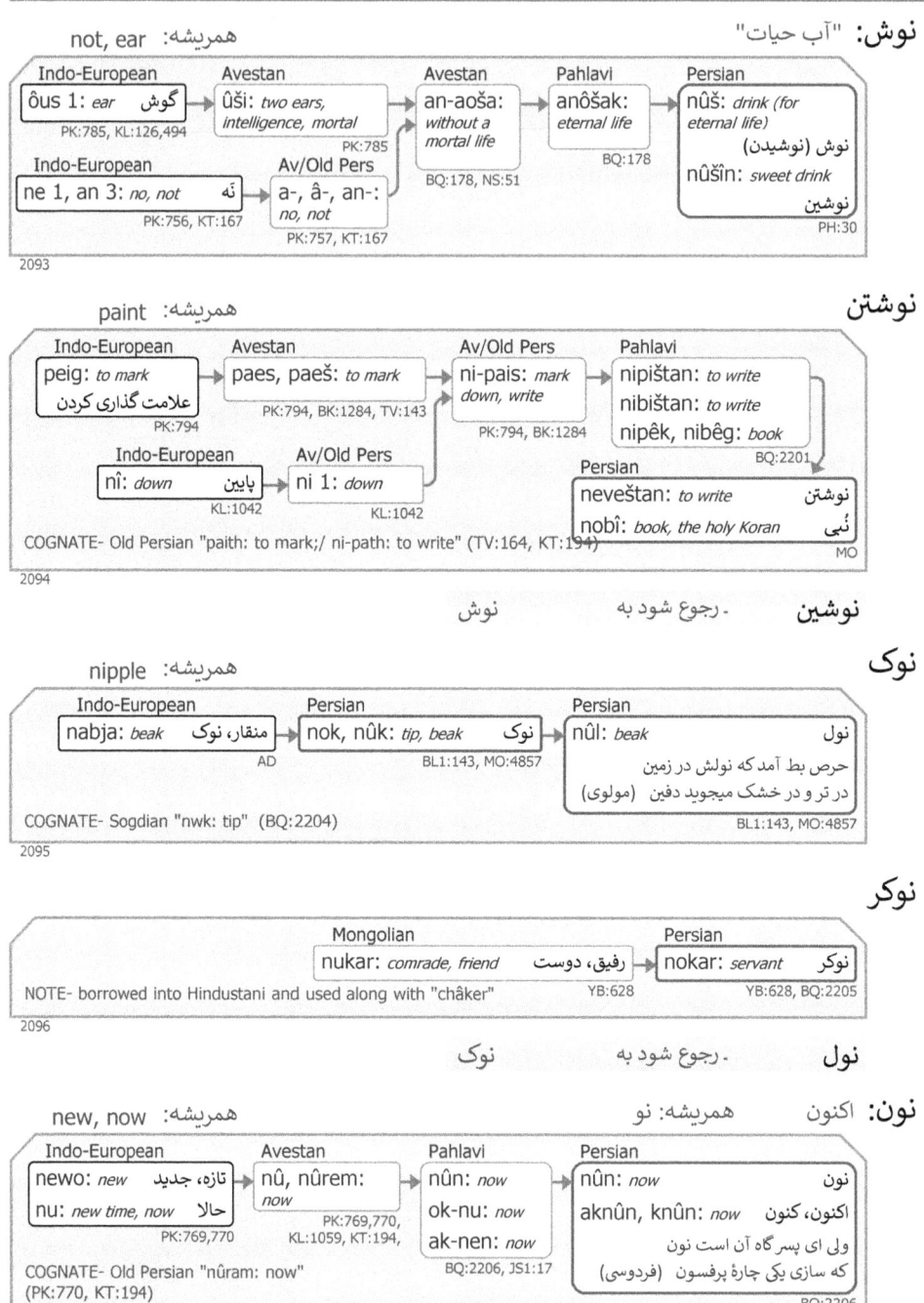

نوش: "آب حیات"

همریشه: not, ear

Indo-European	Avestan	Avestan	Pahlavi	Persian
گوش ôus 1: *ear* PK:785, KL:126,494	ûši: *two ears, intelligence, mortal* PK:785	an-aoša: *without a mortal life* BQ:178, NS:51	anôšak: *eternal life* BQ:178	nûš: *drink (for eternal life)* نوش (نوشیدن) nûšîn: *sweet drink* نوشین PH:30
Indo-European		Av/Old Pers		
نه ne 1, an 3: *no, not* PK:756, KT:167		a-, â-, an-: *no, not* PK:757, KT:167		

2093

نوشتن

همریشه: paint

Indo-European	Avestan	Av/Old Pers	Pahlavi
peig: *to mark* علامت گذاری کردن PK:794	paes, paeš: *to mark* PK:794, BK:1284, TV:143	ni-pais: *mark down, write* PK:794, BK:1284	nipištan: *to write* nibištan: *to write* nipêk, nibêg: *book* BQ:2201
Indo-European	Av/Old Pers		Persian
nî: *down* پایین KL:1042	ni 1: *down* KL:1042		neveštan: *to write* نوشتن nobî: *book, the holy Koran* نُبی MO

COGNATE- Old Persian "paith: to mark;/ ni-path: to write" (TV:164, KT:194)

2094

نوشین . رجوع شود به   نوش

نوک

همریشه: nipple

Indo-European	Persian	Persian
nabja: *beak* منقار، نوک AD	nok, nûk: *tip, beak* نوک BL1:143, MO:4857	nûl: *beak* نول حرص بط آمد که نولش در زمین در تر و در خشک میجوید دفین (مولوی) BL1:143, MO:4857

COGNATE- Sogdian "nwk: tip" (BQ:2204)

2095

نوکر

Mongolian	Persian
nukar: *comrade, friend* رفیق، دوست YB:628	nokar: *servant* نوکر YB:628, BQ:2205

NOTE- borrowed into Hindustani and used along with "châker"

2096

نول . رجوع شود به   نوک

نون: اکنون   همریشه: نو   همریشه: new, now

Indo-European	Avestan	Pahlavi	Persian
newo: *new* تازه، جدید nu: *new time, now* حالا PK:769,770	nû, nûrem: *now* PK:769,770, KL:1059, KT:194,	nûn: *now* ok-nu: *now* ak-nen: *now* BQ:2206, JS1:17	nûn: *now* نون aknûn, knûn: *now* اکنون، کنون ولی ای پسر گاه آن است نون که سازی یکی چارهٔ پرفسون (فردوسی) BQ:2206

COGNATE- Old Persian "nûram: now" (PK:770, KT:194)

2097

نوه

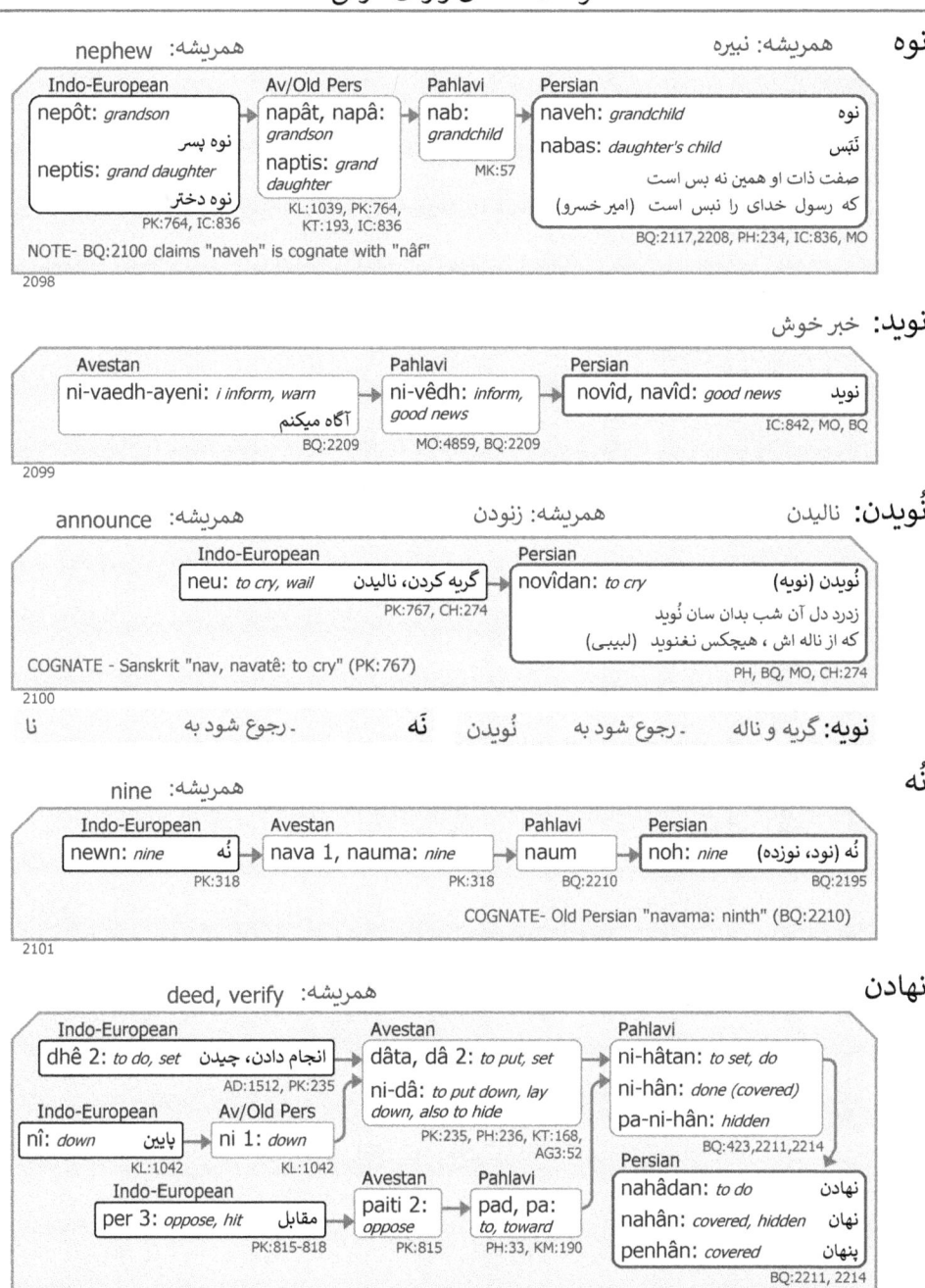

همریشه: نبیره

نوه همریشه: nephew

Indo-European
nepôt: grandson
نوه پسر
neptis: grand daughter
نوه دختر
PK:764, IC:836

Av/Old Pers
napât, napâ: grandson
naptis: grand daughter
KL:1039, PK:764, KT:193, IC:836

Pahlavi
nab: grandchild
MK:57

Persian
naveh: grandchild نوه
nabas: daughter's child تَبَس
صفت ذات او همین نه بس است
که رسول خدای را نبس است (امیر خسرو)
BQ:2117,2208, PH:234, IC:836, MO

NOTE- BQ:2100 claims "naveh" is cognate with "nâf"

2098

نوید: خبر خوش

Avestan
ni-vaedh-ayeni: i inform, warn
آگاه میکنم
BQ:2209

Pahlavi
ni-vêdh: inform, good news
MO:4859, BQ:2209

Persian
novîd, navîd: good news نوید
IC:842, MO, BQ

2099

نُویدن: نالیدن همریشه: زنودن همریشه: announce

Indo-European
neu: to cry, wail گریه کردن، نالیدن
PK:767, CH:274

Persian
novîdan: to cry (نُویدن (نویه
زدرد دل آن شب بدان سان نُوید
که از ناله اش، هیچکس نغنوید (لبیبی)
PH, BQ, MO, CH:274

COGNATE - Sanskrit "nav, navatê: to cry" (PK:767)

2100

نویه: گریه و ناله ـ رجوع شود به **نُویدن** ـ رجوع شود به **نَه** نا

نُه همریشه: nine

Indo-European
newn: nine نُه
PK:318

Avestan
nava 1, nauma: nine
PK:318

Pahlavi
naum
BQ:2210

Persian
noh: nine (نُه (نود، نوزده
BQ:2195

COGNATE- Old Persian "navama: ninth" (BQ:2210)

2101

نهادن همریشه: deed, verify

Indo-European
dhê 2: to do, set انجام دادن، چیدن
AD:1512, PK:235

Indo-European
nî: down پایین
KL:1042

Av/Old Pers
ni 1: down
KL:1042

Indo-European
per 3: oppose, hit مقابل
PK:815-818

Avestan
dâta, dâ 2: to put, set
ni-dâ: to put down, lay down, also to hide
PK:235, PH:236, KT:168, AG3:52

Avestan
paiti 2: oppose
PK:815

Pahlavi
pad, pa: to, toward
PH:33, KM:190

Pahlavi
ni-hâtan: to set, do
ni-hân: done (covered)
pa-ni-hân: hidden
BQ:423,2211,2214

Persian
nahâdan: to do نهادن
nahân: covered, hidden نهان
penhân: covered پنهان
BQ:2211, 2214

2102

نهان ـ رجوع شود به نهادن

نهفتن

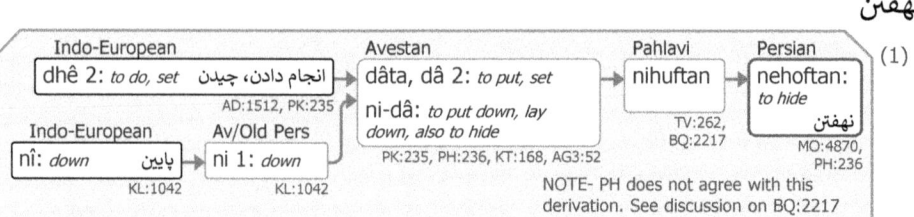

(1)

نهفتن

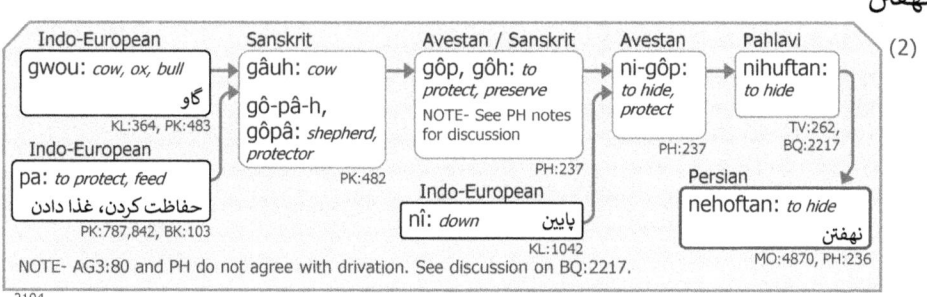

(2)

نهنگ

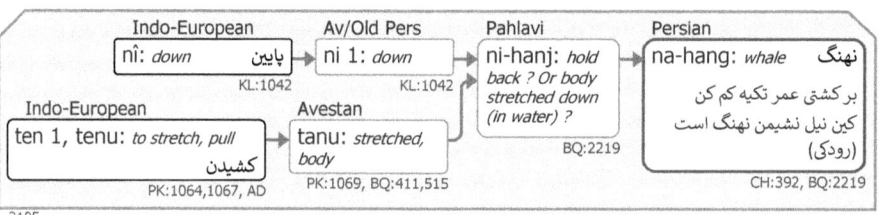

نُهور: چشم، رویت

همریشه: sun

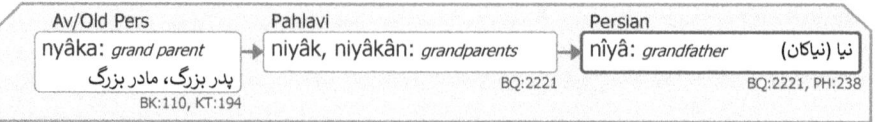

نی ‌   .رجوع شود به   نای

نیا: پدربزرگ

Av/Old Pers	Pahlavi	Persian
nyâka: *grand parent* پدر بزرگ، مادر بزرگ BK:110, KT:194	niyâk, niyâkân: *grandparents* BQ:2221	nîyâ: *grandfather* (نیاکان) نیا BQ:2221, PH:238

2107

نیاز، نیازی

همریشه: آز   همریشه: anxious, anger

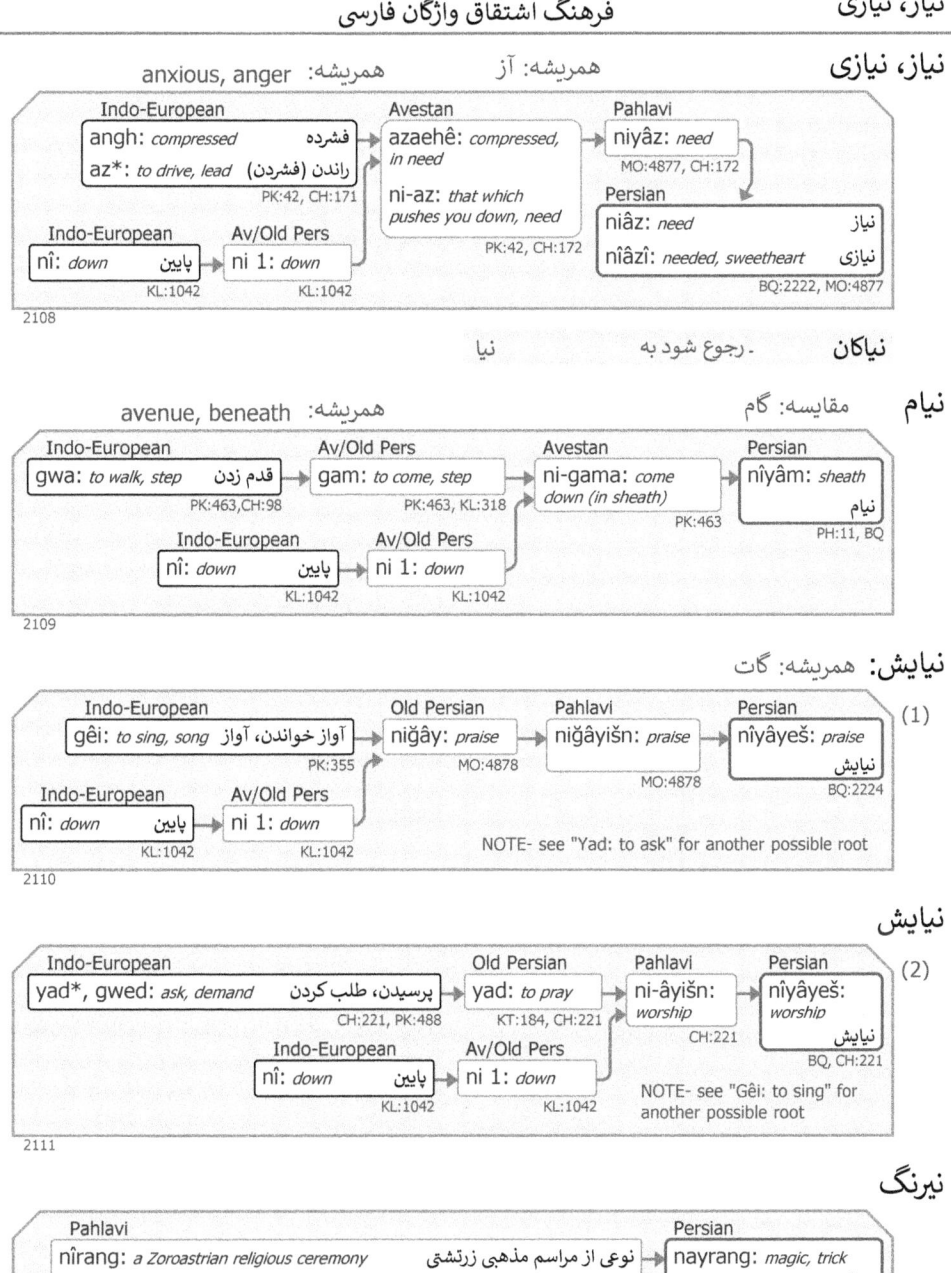

2108

نیاکان   ـ رجوع شود به   نیا

نیام   مقایسه: گام   همریشه: avenue, beneath

2109

نیایش: همریشه: گات

(1)

NOTE- see "Yad: to ask" for another possible root

2110

نیایش

(2)

NOTE- see "Gêi: to sing" for another possible root

2111

نیرنگ

NOTE- The meaning and usage of this word changed after people accepted Islam

2112

نیرو   ـ رجوع شود به   نر

نیروانا: "فنا در خالق هستی"

همریشه: wind

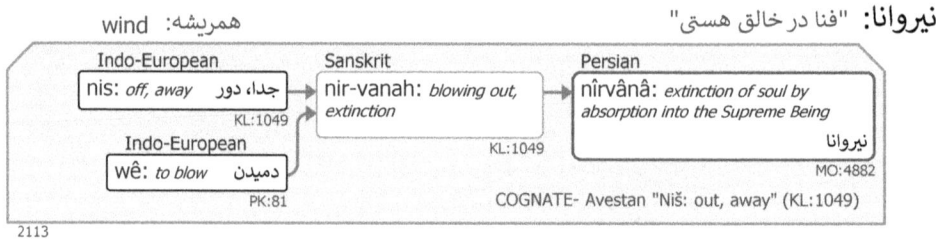

2113

نیز

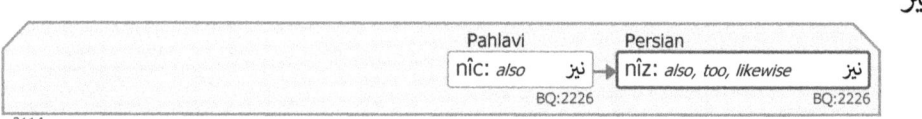

2114

نیزه

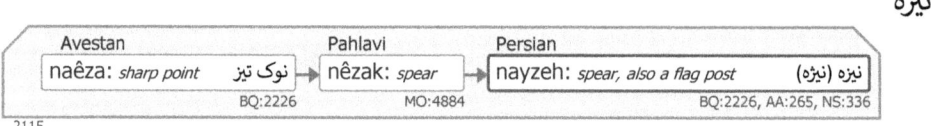

2115

نیست

همریشه: is, not

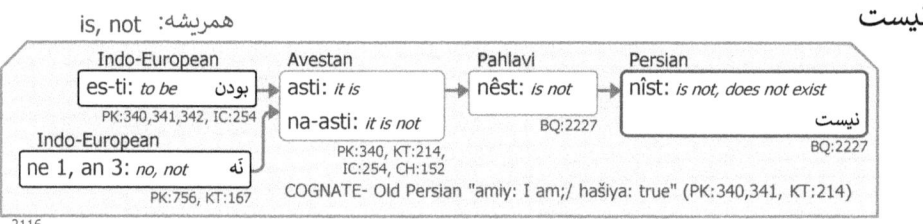

2116

نیش

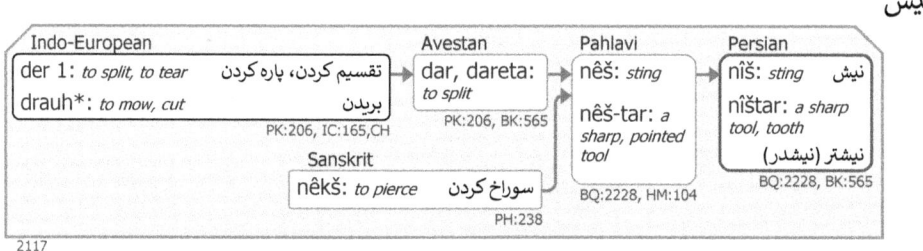

2117

نیشابور: "شاهزادهٔ نیکو"

همریشه: check, chess

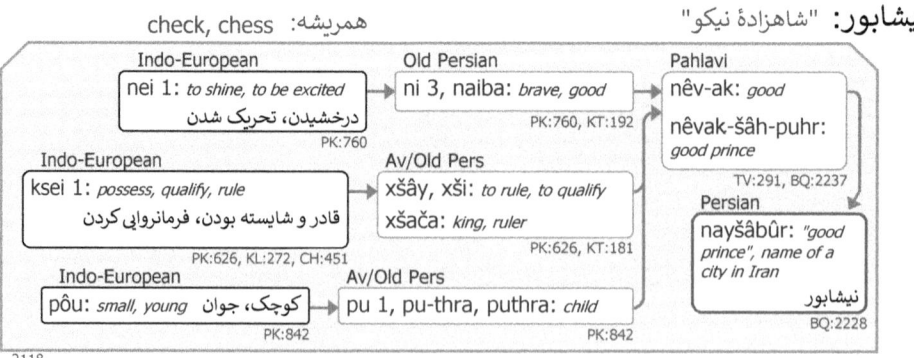

2118

375

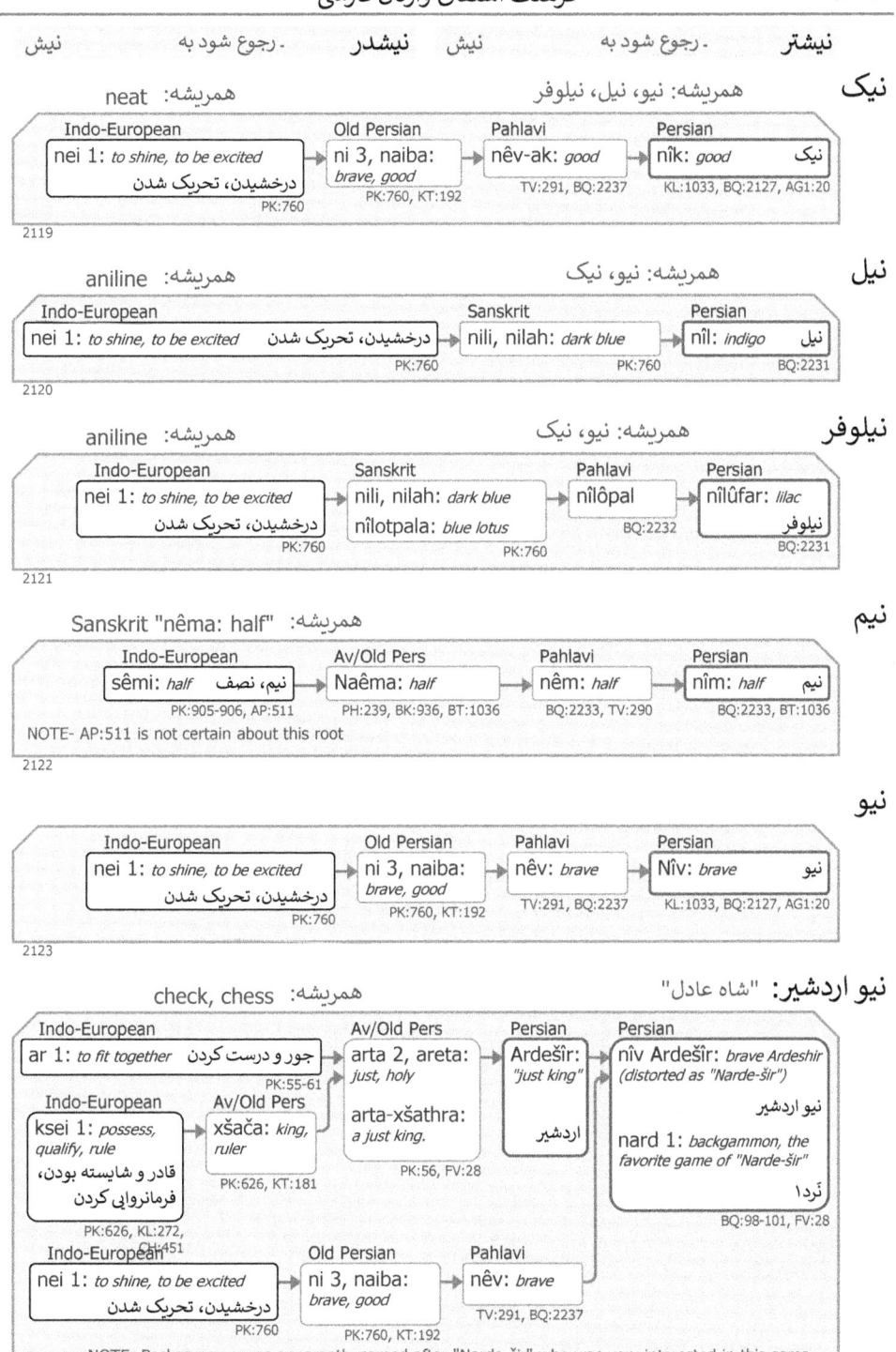

نیوشیدن   مقایسه: گوش   همریشه: beneath, ear

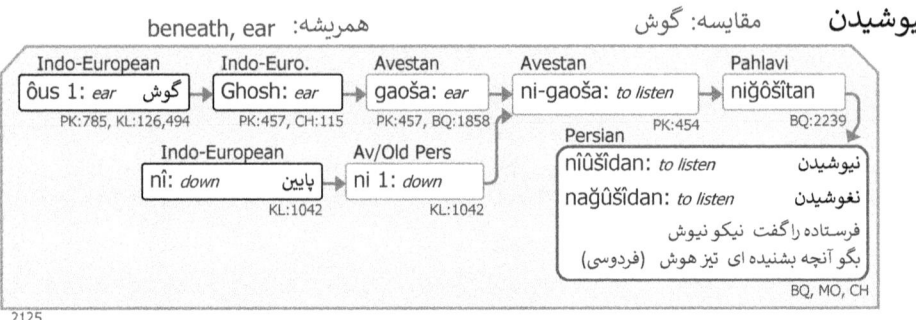

2125

377

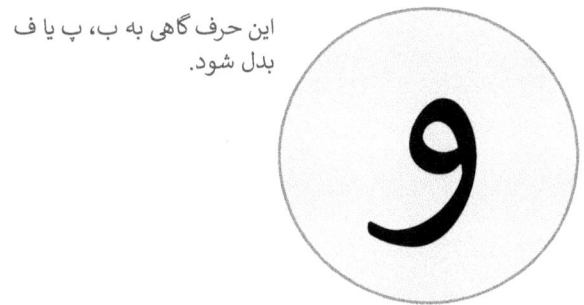

این حرف گاهی به ب، پ یا ف بدل شود.

وُ: حرف ربط و عطف است

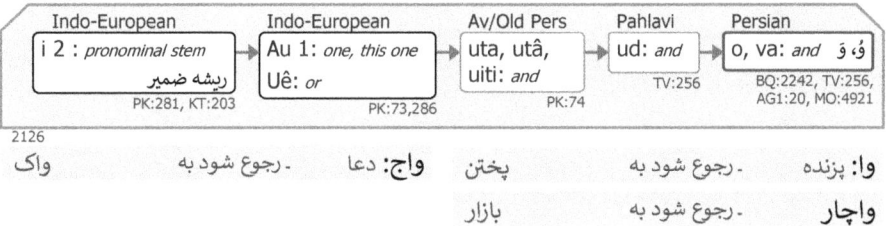

Indo-European	Indo-European	Av/Old Pers	Pahlavi	Persian
i 2 : *pronominal stem* ریشه ضمیر PK:281, KT:203	Au 1: *one, this one* Uê: *or* PK:73,286	uta, utâ, uiti: *and* PK:74	ud: *and* TV:256	o, va: *and* وُ، وَ BQ:2242, TV:256, AG1:20, MO:4921

2126

وا: پزنده .رجوع شود به پختن **واج:** دعا .رجوع شود به **واک**

واچار .رجوع شود به بازار

واخیدن: پنبه زدن و پاک کردن آن

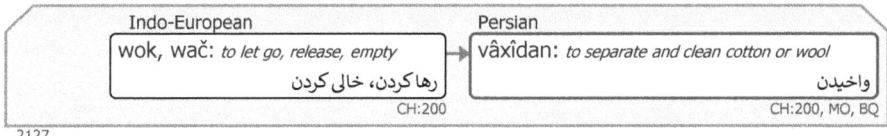

Indo-European	Persian
wok, wač: *to let go, release, empty* رها کردن، خالی کردن CH:200	vâxîdan: *to separate and clean cotton or wool* واخیدن CH:200, MO, BQ

2127

وار۱: دیوار

Indo-European	Av/Old Pers	Persian
wer 3, werg 2: *to cover, enclose* پوشاندن، محصور کردن PK:1168, IC:1599	var 1, vara, vâra 2: *cover, wall* PK:1168, KM:212, KT:207	vâr 1: *wall* وار۱ BQ

2128

وار۲: مانند، شبیه

همریشه: *resemble, same*

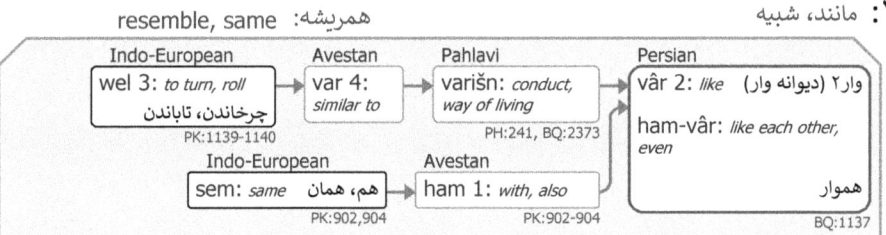

Indo-European	Avestan	Pahlavi	Persian
wel 3: *to turn, roll* چرخاندن، تاباندن PK:1139-1140	var 4: *similar to*	varišn: *conduct, way of living* PH:241, BQ:2373	vâr 2: *like* وار۲ (دیوانه وار) ham-vâr: *like each other, even*
sem: *same* هم، همان PK:902,904	ham 1: *with, also* PK:902-904		هموار BQ:1137

2129

وار۳: جشن

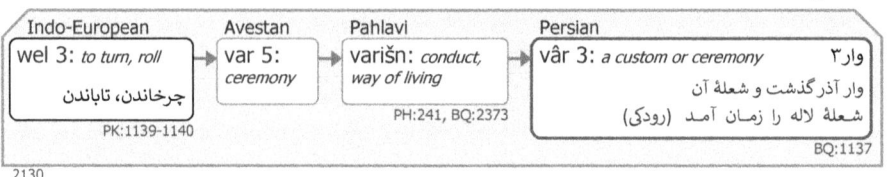

2130

ـ وار۴: پسوند به معنی بار

همریشه: burden

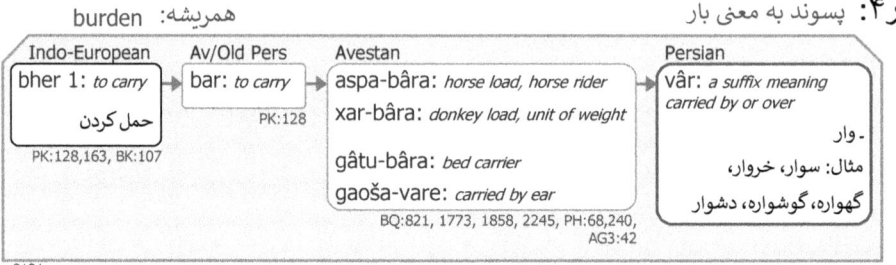

2131

وارستن   ـ رجوع شود به   رَستن

وارون   مقایسه: فرارون

همریشه: off

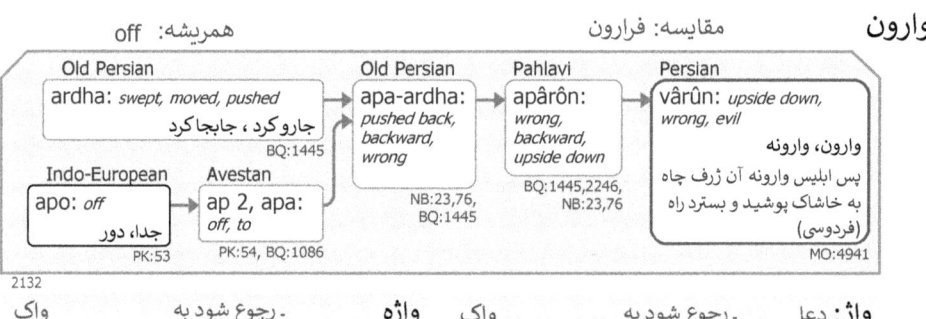

2132

واژ: دعا   ـ رجوع شود به   واک   **واژه**   واک   ـ رجوع شود به   واژه

واس: علوفه ستور

2133

واستر: مزرعه

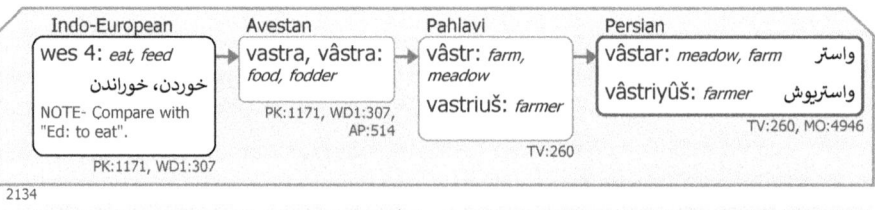

2134

واستریوش: کشاورز ـ رجوع شود به   واستر   **واش:** علوفه ستور ـ رجوع شود به   واس

واشه: شاهین   ـ رجوع شود به   باز۲

واک: صدا

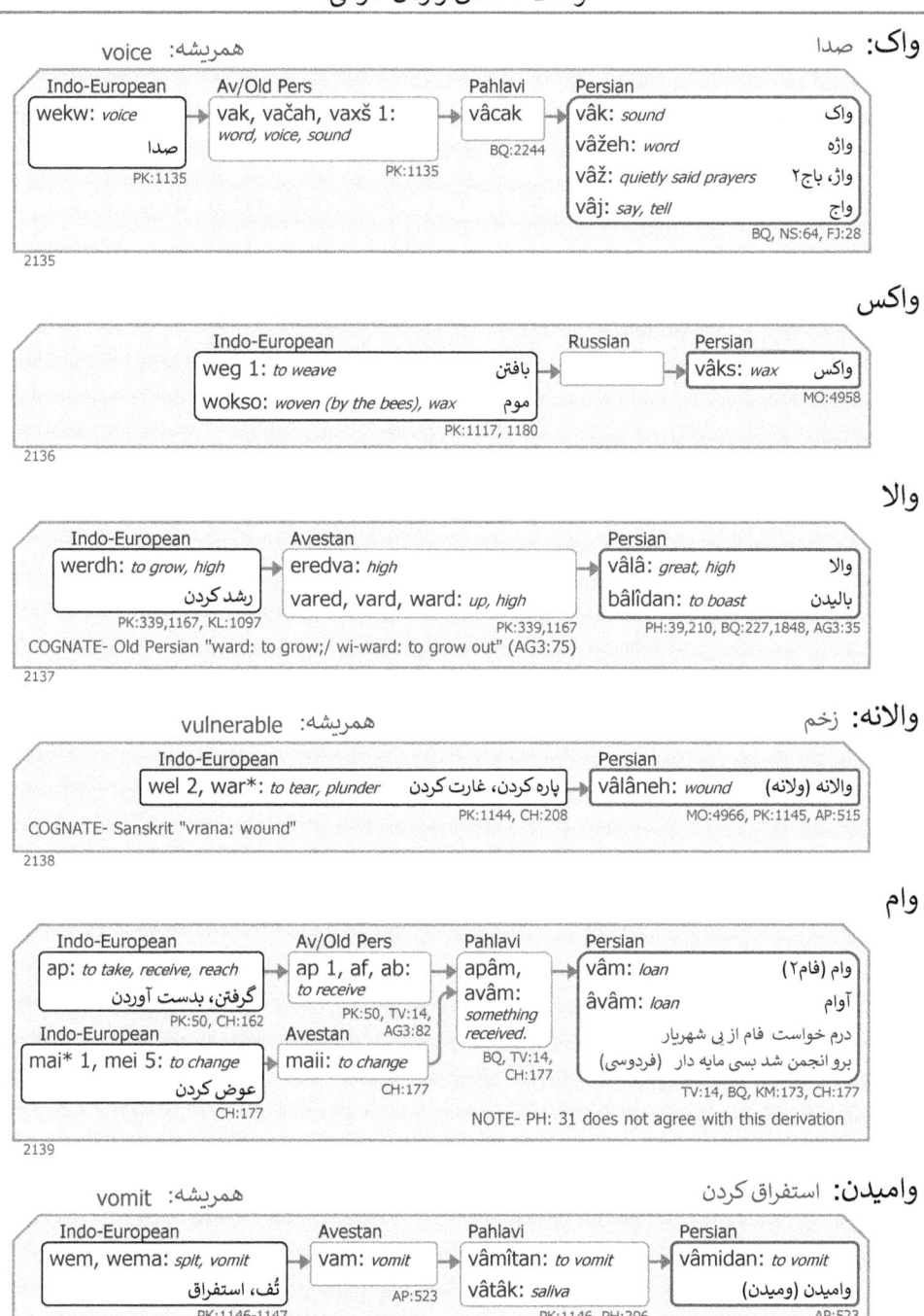

همریشه: voice

Indo-European
wekw: voice
صدا
PK:1135

Av/Old Pers
vak, vačah, vaxš 1:
word, voice, sound
PK:1135

Pahlavi
vâcak
BQ:2244

Persian
vâk: sound — واک
vâžeh: word — واژه
vâž: quietly said prayers — واژ، باج۲
vâj: say, tell — واج
BQ, NS:64, FJ:28

2135

واکس

Indo-European
weg 1: to weave — بافتن
wokso: woven (by the bees), wax — موم
PK:1117, 1180

Russian

Persian
vâks: wax — واکس
MO:4958

2136

والا

Indo-European
werdh: to grow, high
رشد کردن
PK:339,1167, KL:1097

Avestan
eredva: high
vared, vard, ward: up, high
PK:339,1167

Persian
vâlâ: great, high — والا
bâlîdan: to boast — بالیدن
PH:39,210, BQ:227,1848, AG3:35

COGNATE- Old Persian "ward: to grow;/ wi-ward: to grow out" (AG3:75)

2137

والانه: زخم

همریشه: vulnerable

Indo-European
wel 2, war*: to tear, plunder — پاره کردن، غارت کردن
PK:1144, CH:208

Persian
vâlâneh: wound — (والانه (ولانه
MO:4966, PK:1145, AP:515

COGNATE- Sanskrit "vrana: wound"

2138

وام

Indo-European
ap: to take, receive, reach
گرفتن، بدست آوردن
PK:50, CH:162

Indo-European
mai* 1, mei 5: to change
عوض کردن
CH:177

Av/Old Pers
ap 1, af, ab:
to receive
PK:50, TV:14, AG3:82

Avestan
maii: to change
CH:177

Pahlavi
apâm,
avâm:
something
received
BQ, TV:14, CH:177

Persian
vâm: loan — (وام (فام۲
âvâm: loan — آوام
درم خواست فام ازی بی شهریار
برو انجمن شد بسی مایه دار   (فردوسی)
TV:14, BQ, KM:173, CH:177

NOTE- PH: 31 does not agree with this derivation

2139

وامیدن: استفراق کردن

همریشه: vomit

Indo-European
wem, wema: spit, vomit
تُف، استفراق
PK:1146-1147

Avestan
vam: vomit
AP:523

Pahlavi
vâmîtan: to vomit
vâtâk: saliva
PK:1146, PH:296

Persian
vâmidan: to vomit
(وامیدن (ومیدن
AP:523

COGNATE - Persian "vâtâk: saliva" is mentioned by Pokorny but not found in Dehkhoda (PK:1146)

2140

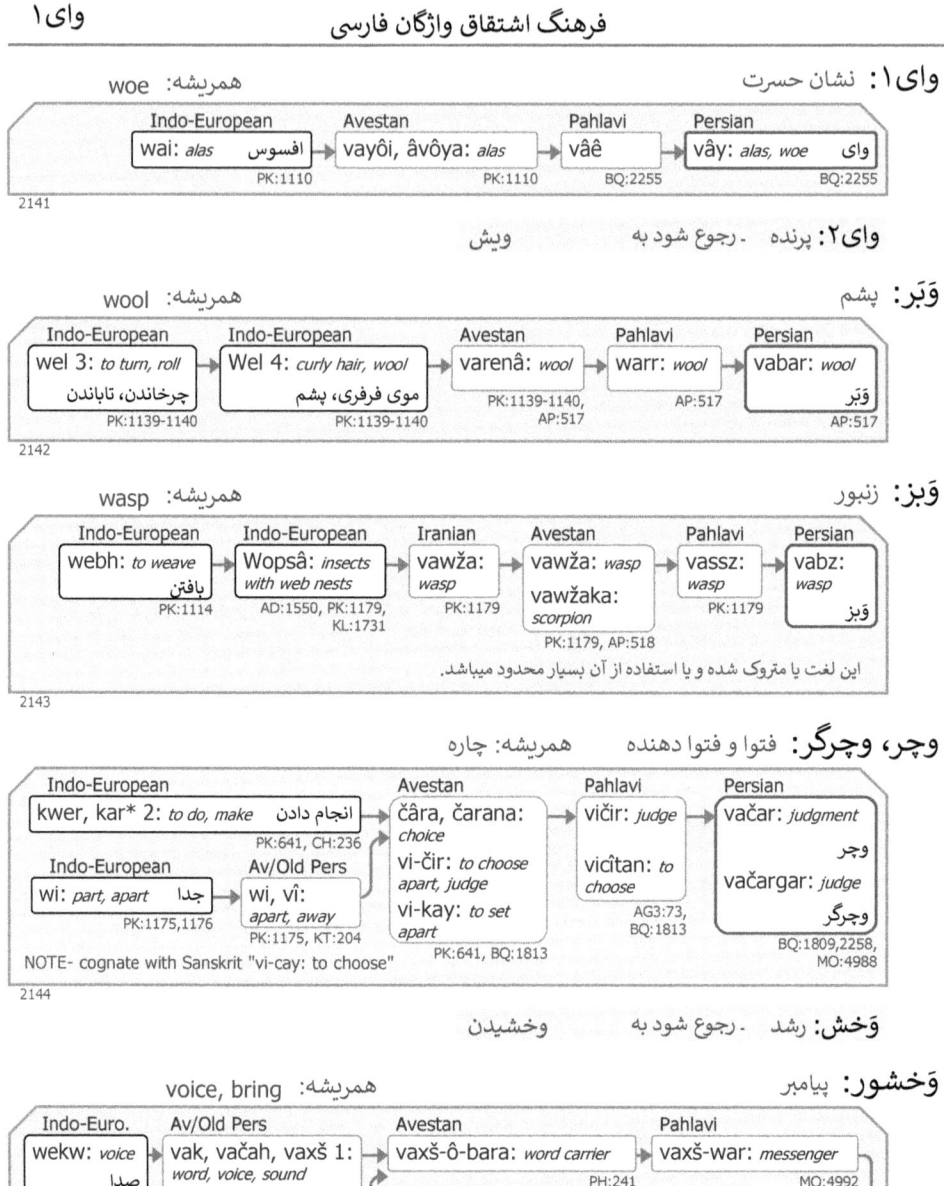

وای۱: نشان حسرت　　همریشه: woe

وای۲: پرنده　- رجوع شود به　ویش

وَبَر: پشم　　همریشه: wool

وَبز: زنبور　　همریشه: wasp

این لغت یا متروک شده و یا استفاده از آن بسیار محدود میباشد.

وچر، وچرگر: فتوا و فتوا دهنده　　همریشه: چاره

NOTE- cognate with Sanskrit "vi-cay: to choose"

وَخش: رشد　- رجوع شود به　وخشیدن

وَخشور: پیامبر　　همریشه: voice, bring

به گفتار وَخشور خود راه جوی
دل از تیرگیها بدین آب شوی　(فردوسی)

وخشیدن: رشد کردن   همریشه: هوخشتَّر

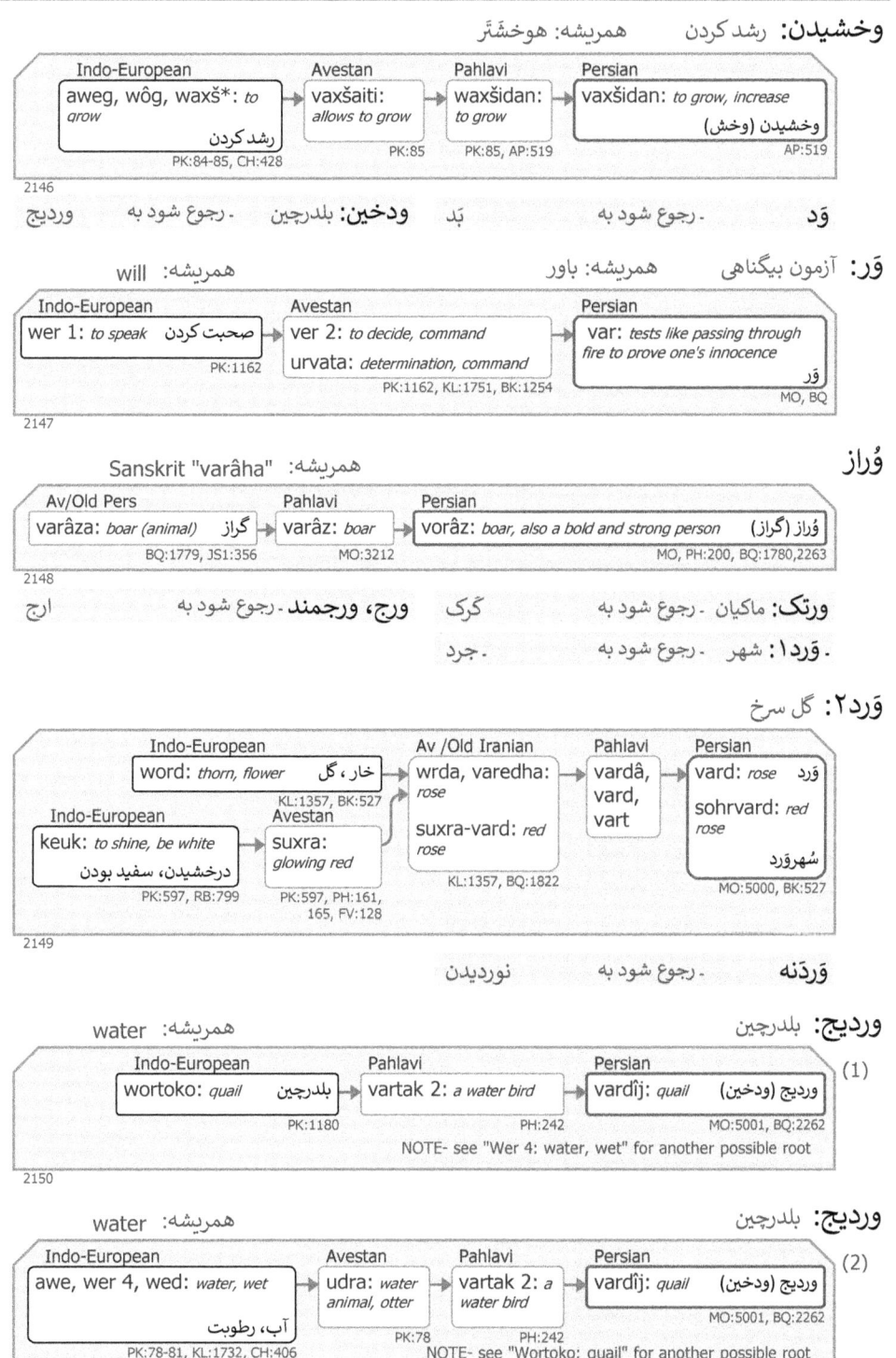

Indo-European	Avestan	Pahlavi	Persian
aweg, wôg, waxš*: to grow رشد کردن	vaxšaiti: allows to grow	waxšidan: to grow	vaxšidan: to grow, increase وخشیدن (وخش)
PK:84-85, CH:428	PK:85	PK:85, AP:519	AP:519

2146

وَد. ـ رجوع شود به   بَد   **ودخین:** بلدرچین ـ رجوع شود به   وردیج

وَر: آزمون بیگناهی   همریشه: باور   همریشه: will

Indo-European	Avestan	Persian
wer 1: to speak صحبت کردن	ver 2: to decide, command urvata: determination, command	var: tests like passing through fire to prove one's innocence وَر
PK:1162	PK:1162, KL:1751, BK:1254	MO, BQ

2147

وُراز   همریشه: Sanskrit "varâha"

Av/Old Pers	Pahlavi	Persian
varâza: boar (animal) گراز	varâz: boar	vorâz: boar, also a bold and strong person وُراز (گراز)
BQ:1779, JS1:356	MO:3212	MO, PH:200, BQ:1780,2263

2148

ورتک: ماکیان ـ رجوع شود به   گرک   **ورج، ورجمند** ـ رجوع شود به   ارج

وَرد۱: شهر ـ رجوع شود به   جرد

وَرد۲: گل سرخ

Indo-European	Av /Old Iranian	Pahlavi	Persian
word: thorn, flower خار، گل KL:1357, BK:527	wrda, varedha: rose	vardâ, vard, vart	vard: rose وَرد
Indo-European Avestan	suxra-vard: red rose		sohrvard: red rose
keuk: to shine, be white درخشیدن، سفید بودن	suxra: glowing red		سُهرورد
PK:597, RB:799	PK:597, PH:161, 165, FV:128	KL:1357, BQ:1822	MO:5000, BK:527

2149

وَردَنه ـ رجوع شود به   نوردیدن

وردیج: بلدرچین   همریشه: water

Indo-European	Pahlavi	Persian	(1)
wortoko: quail بلدرچین	vartak 2: a water bird	vardîj: quail وردیج (ودخین)	
PK:1180	PH:242	MO:5001, BQ:2262	

NOTE- see "Wer 4: water, wet" for another possible root

2150

وردیج: بلدرچین   همریشه: water

Indo-European	Avestan	Pahlavi	Persian	(2)
awe, wer 4, wed: water, wet آب، رطوبت	udra: water animal, otter	vartak 2: a water bird	vardîj: quail وردیج (ودخین)	
PK:78-81, KL:1732, CH:406	PK:78	PH:242	MO:5001, BQ:2262	

NOTE- see "Wortoko: quail" for another possible root

2151

ورز - رجوع شود به ورزیدن

ورزاو: گاو نر

```
Indo-European                    Pahlavi                    Persian                      (1)
wâka, wakâ: cow    گاو    →    varzâ, warzâg: cow    →    varzâ: bull    ورزاو
                   PK:1111, AP:521                      AP:521                      AP:521
NOTE- See "gwou: cow" for a different root
2152
```

ورزاو: "گاو ورزیده" که برای شخم زدن بکار میرود

```
Indo-European            Avestan              Pahlavi              Persian                      (2)
werg 1: to work    →    vareza: work    →    varezâ: strong    →  varzâv: strong bull
کار کردن                                                           used for farming
PK:1168          PK:1168, KL:1751, BK:537    BQ:2270              ورزاو (برزه گاو)
Indo-European            Avestan              Pahlavi                            BQ:252,2270
gwou: cow, ox, bull  گاو → gâuš, gave, gâvô, gao:  →  gâv
                          cow, domestic animal        گاو
KL:364, PK:483                                     BQ:1766
                      cow, domestic animal
                          KL:364
NOTE- See "wâka: cow" for a different root
2153
```

ورزش - رجوع شود به ورزیدن

ورزیدن

```
Indo-European            Avestan              Pahlavi              Persian
werg 1: to work    →    vareza: work    →    varzîtan    →       varzîdan: to work    ورزیدن (ورزش)
کار کردن                                                          barz, varz: work    برز، ورز
PK:1168          PK:1168, KL:1751, BK:537    BQ:2270              barz-gar: farmer    برزگر
COGNATE- Old Persian "vatd: work" (KT:207)                                            BQ, MO
2154
```

وَرِس: ریسمان - رجوع شود به گُرس۲

ورغ: بند آب   همریشه: divert

```
Indo-European            Sanskrit             Persian
wer 2, kwermi: to   →   varj: to turn    →   varğ: a dam made to turn water around    ورغ (برغ، برغاب)
turn, bend              around
چرخیدن، خم شدن                                دل برد و مرا نیز بمردم نشمرد
PK:1142-1157, PK:649    PK:1154              گفتارچه سوداست که ورغ آب ببرد  (فرخی)
                                                                          BQ:258,2273, PH:242
2155
```

ورغنه: شاهین:"قاتل برّه"   همریشه: offend

```
Indo-European            Av/Old Pers          Pahlavi              Persian
weren: lamb    بره  →   varnak: lamb    →    varrak: lamb    →    varğeneh: falcon
PK:1170                 PK:1170              vâra-ğna, vâren-žar,  ورغنه
Indo-European            Old Persian         varâğ: lamb killer   kalâğ: crow    کلاغ
gwhen 2, jan*: to strike  زدن → jan.: to strike  (referred to falcon or crow)  BQ, PK:1170, PH:192,
PK:492, CH:222          KT:184,185           PK:1170, BQ:268      GR:398
2156
```

وَروَره: سنجاب

```
Indo-European            Persian
wer 6: squirrel    سنجاب  →  varvareh: squirrel    وَروَره
PK:1166                      PK:1166521:آی
2157
```

وریزه -رجوع شود به برنج۲

وَزَغ: قورباغه

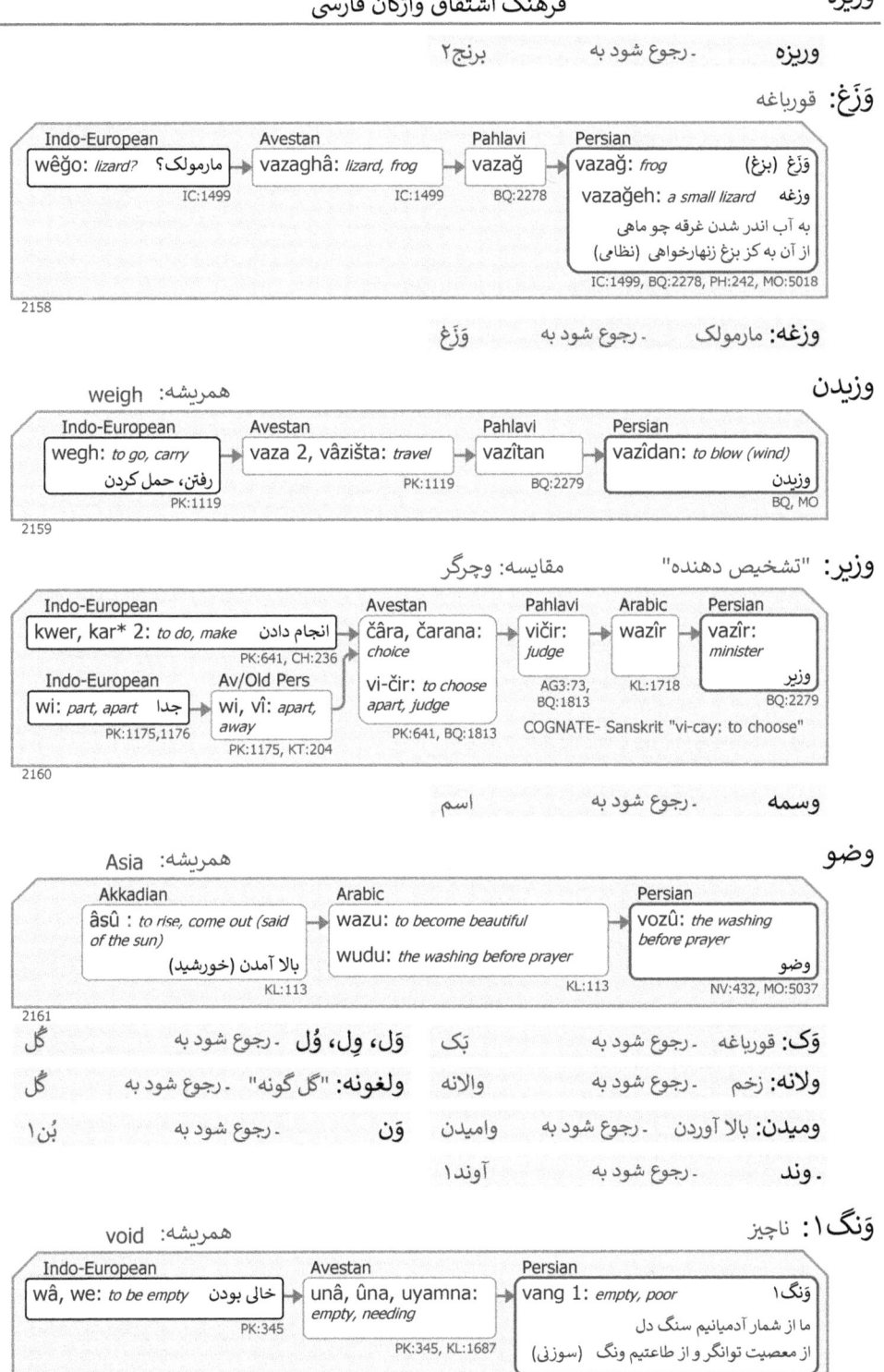

Indo-European	Avestan	Pahlavi	Persian
wêğo: lizard? مارمولک؟	vazaghâ: lizard, frog	vazağ	vazağ: frog وَزغ (بزغ)
IC:1499	IC:1499	BQ:2278	vazağeh: a small lizard وزغه

به آب اندر شدن غرقه چو ماهی
از آن که ز بزغ زنهارخواهی (نظامی)

IC:1499, BQ:2278, PH:242, MO:5018

2158

وزغه: مارمولک -رجوع شود به وَزَغ

وزیدن همریشه: weigh

Indo-European	Avestan	Pahlavi	Persian
wegh: to go, carry رفتن، حمل کردن	vaza 2, vâzišta: travel	vazîtan	vazîdan: to blow (wind) وزیدن
PK:1119	PK:1119	BQ:2279	BQ, MO

2159

وزیر: "تشخیص دهنده" مقایسه: وچرگر

Indo-European		Avestan	Pahlavi	Arabic	Persian
kwer, kar* 2: to do, make انجام دادن		čâra, čarana: choice	vičir: judge	wazîr	vazîr: minister وزیر
PK:641, CH:236			AG3:73, BQ:1813	KL:1718	BQ:2279
Indo-European	Av/Old Pers	vi-čir: to choose apart, judge			
wi: part, apart جدا	wi, vî: apart, away				
PK:1175,1176	PK:1175, KT:204	PK:641, BQ:1813	COGNATE- Sanskrit "vi-cay: to choose"		

2160

وسمه -رجوع شود به اسم

وضو همریشه: Asia

Akkadian	Arabic	Persian
âsû : to rise, come out (said of the sun) بالا آمدن (خورشید)	wazu: to become beautiful	vozû: the washing before prayer وضو
	wudu: the washing before prayer	
KL:113	KL:113	NV:432, MO:5037

2161

وَک: قورباغه -رجوع شود به بَک **وَل، وِل، وُل** -رجوع شود به گل

ولانه: زخم -رجوع شود به والانه **ولغونه:** "گل گونه" -رجوع شود به گل

ومیدن: بالا آوردن -رجوع شود به وامیدن **وَن** -رجوع شود به بُن۱

وند -رجوع شود به آوند۱

وَنگ۱: ناچیز همریشه: void

Indo-European	Avestan	Persian
wâ, we: to be empty خالی بودن	unâ, ûna, uyamna: empty, needing	vang 1: empty, poor وَنگ۱
PK:345	PK:345, KL:1687	ما از شمار آدمیانیم سنگ دل

از معصیت توانگر و از طاعتیم وَنگ (سوزنی)

NOTE- HM:105 has doubts about this etymology.

PK:345, PH:243, BQ:2293

2162

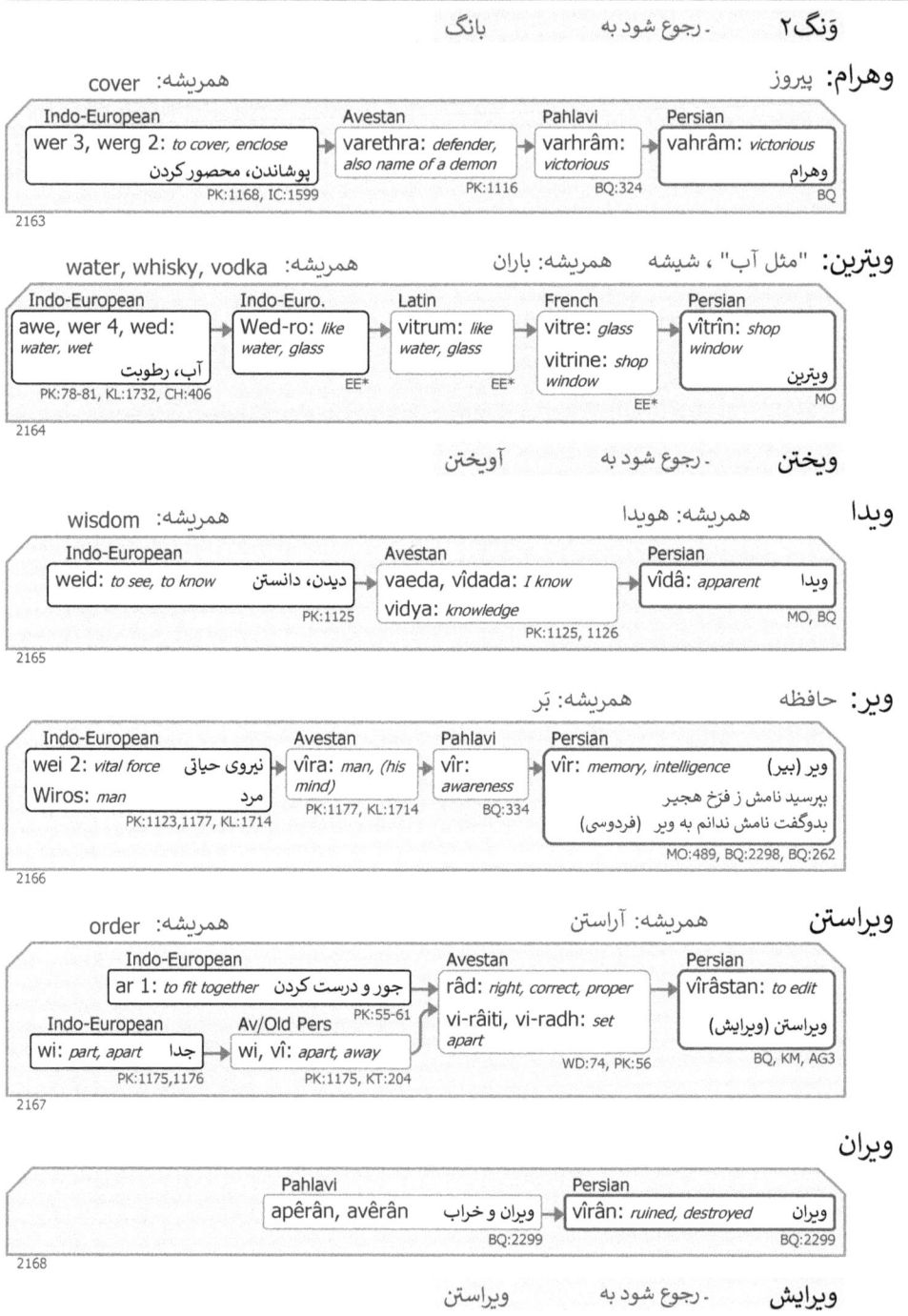

وَنگ ۲ - رجوع شود به   بانگ

وهرام: پیروز

همریشه: cover

Indo-European	Avestan	Pahlavi	Persian
wer 3, werg 2: *to cover, enclose* پوشاندن، محصور کردن	varethra: *defender, also name of a demon*	varhrâm: *victorious*	vahrâm: *victorious* وهرام
PK:1168, IC:1599	PK:1116	BQ:324	BQ

2163

ویترین: "مثل آب" ، شیشه   همریشه: باران   همریشه: water, whisky, vodka

Indo-European	Indo-Euro.	Latin	French	Persian
awe, wer 4, wed: *water, wet* آب، رطوبت	Wed-ro: *like water, glass*	vitrum: *like water, glass*	vitre: *glass* vitrine: *shop window*	vîtrîn: *shop window* ویترین
PK:78-81, KL:1732, CH:406	EE*	EE*	EE*	MO

2164

ویختن - رجوع شود به   آویختن

ویدا   همریشه: هویدا   همریشه: wisdom

Indo-European	Avestan	Persian
weid: *to see, to know* دیدن، دانستن	vaeda, vîdada: *I know* vidya: *knowledge*	vîdâ: *apparent* ویدا
PK:1125	PK:1125, 1126	MO, BQ

2165

ویر: حافظه   همریشه: بَر

Indo-European	Avestan	Pahlavi	Persian
wei 2: *vital force* نیروی حیاتی Wiros: *man* مرد	vîra: *man, (his mind)*	vîr: *awareness*	vîr: *memory, intelligence* ویر (بیر) بپرسید نامش ز فرّخ هجیر بدوگفت نامش ندانم به ویر (فردوسی)
PK:1123,1177, KL:1714	PK:1177, KL:1714	BQ:334	MO:489, BQ:2298, BQ:262

2166

ویراستن   همریشه: آراستن   همریشه: order

Indo-European	Avestan	Persian
ar 1: *to fit together* جور و درست کردن	râd: *right, correct, proper* vi-râiti, vi-radh: *set apart*	vîrâstan: *to edit* ویراستن (ویرایش)
PK:55-61		

Indo-European	Av/Old Pers		
wi: *part, apart* جدا	wi, vî: *apart, away*	WD:74, PK:56	BQ, KM, AG3
PK:1175,1176	PK:1175, KT:204		

2167

ویران

Pahlavi	Persian
apêrân, avêrân ویران و خراب	vîrân: *ruined, destroyed* ویران
BQ:2299	BQ:2299

2168

ویرایش - رجوع شود به   ویراستن

385

ویژه: "پاک"   همریشه: پرویز

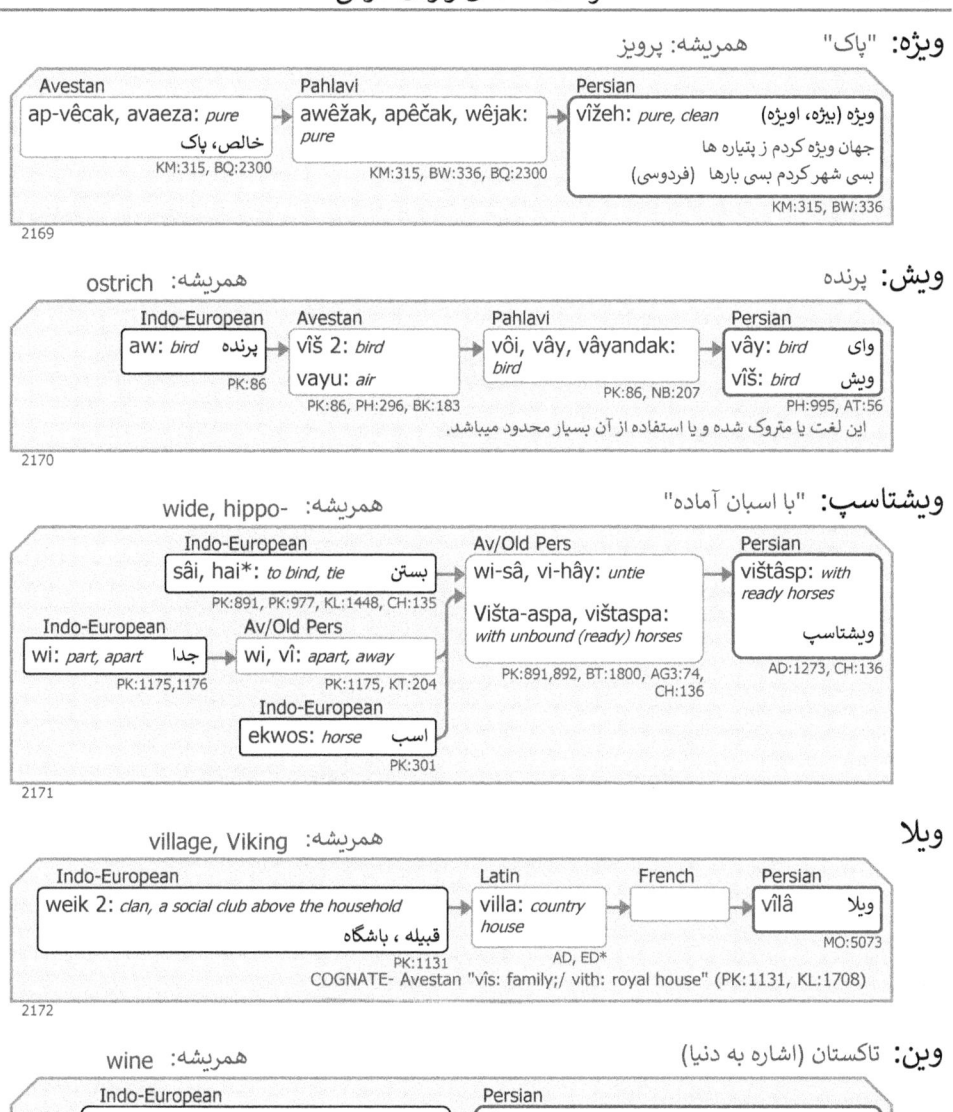

ویژه: "پاک" همریشه: پرویز

Avestan	Pahlavi	Persian
ap-vêcak, avaeza: *pure* خالص، پاک	awêžak, apêčak, wêjak: *pure*	vîžeh: *pure, clean* ویژه (بیژه، اویژه)

KM:315, BQ:2300   KM:315, BW:336, BQ:2300

جهان ویژه کردم ز بتیاره ها
بسی شهر کردم بسی بارها (فردوسی)
KM:315, BW:336

2169

ویش: پرنده   همریشه: ostrich

Indo-European	Avestan	Pahlavi	Persian
aw: *bird* پرنده	vîš 2: *bird* vayu: *air*	vôi, vây, vâyandak: *bird*	vây: *bird* وای vîš: *bird* ویش

PK:86   PK:86, PH:296, BK:183   PK:86, NB:207   PH:995, AT:56

این لغت یا متروک شده و یا استفاده از آن بسیار محدود میباشد.

2170

ویشتاسپ: "با اسبان آماده"   همریشه: -wide, hippo

Indo-European	Av/Old Pers	Persian
sâi, hai*: *to bind, tie* بستن	wi-sâ, vi-hây: *untie*	vištâsp: *with ready horses* ویشتاسپ

PK:891, PK:977, KL:1448, CH:135

Indo-European	Av/Old Pers
wi: *part, apart* جدا	wi, vî: *apart, away*

PK:1175,1176   PK:1175, KT:204

Višta-aspa, vištaspa: *with unbound (ready) horses*

Indo-European
ekwos: *horse* اسب

PK:301

PK:891,892, BT:1800, AG3:74, CH:136   AD:1273, CH:136

2171

ویلا   همریشه: village, Viking

Indo-European	Latin	French	Persian
weik 2: *clan, a social club above the household* قبیله ، باشگاه	villa: *country house*		vîlâ ویلا

PK:1131   AD, ED*   MO:5073

COGNATE- Avestan "vîs: family;/ vith: royal house" (PK:1131, KL:1708)

2172

وین: تاکستان (اشاره به دنیا)   همریشه: wine

Indo-European	Persian
win: *wine* شراب	vîn: *black grape, color, vineyard (world ?)* وین
NOTE- This is probably a Mediterranean word.	اگر زندگانی بود دیر باز

AD:1547

براین وین خرّم بمانم دراز (فردوسی)
ES:695, AS:159, BQ:2302, NS:341

2173

این حرف گاهی به ح، ج یا خ بدل شود.

ها: نشانه جمع (پسوند)

همریشه: Sanskrit "sâti"

Avestan	Avestan	Pahlavi	Persian
hâ: *to join, attach* وصل کردن	hâiti: *part, section*	hât: *attachment*	hâ: *sign of plural* ها
BQ:2303	BQ:2303	BQ:2303	BQ:2303

2174

هار: گردن، گردنبند

همریشه: series, sort

Indo-European	Sanskrit	Persian
ser 3: *to line up, arrange, sort* ردیف کردن	sarat: *thread* hâra: *string of beads*	hâr: *string of beads, necklace, neck* هار گزیده سواران برون از شمار بران باد پایان آهخته هار (فردوسی)
PK:911, IC:1131	IC:1131, MO:5081	IC:1131, MO:5081

COGNATE- Avestan "hara: mountain range" (IC:1131)

2175

هاسر: واحد قدیمی زمان یا فاصله

Indo-European	Avestan	Pahlavi	Persian
sâen: *to be late, a period of time* تاخیر داشتن، مدتی از زمان	hâthra: *a time period*	hâsr, hâsar: *a unit of time*	hâsr: *a unit of time* هاسر
PK:889	PK:890	TV:3	PH:280

NOTE- On page 67 of "Pajhoheshi dar Asatir Iran", "hâser" is defined as a unit of length about 700 meters

2176

هاله

همریشه: helium

Indo-European	Greek	Persian
sâwel: *sun* آفتاب	helios: *sun*	hâleh: *halo, hue* هاله
PK:881	AD	MO:5091, TU:75

2177

هامون

همریشه: same

Indo-European	Avestan	Persian
sem: *same* هم، همان	hama 1: *same, equal, flat level*	hâmûn: *land with same (flat) elevation* هامون
PK:902,904	PK:902-904	BQ, PH

2178

هامین: تابستان

همریشه: summer

Indo-European	Avestan	Persian
sam: *summer* تابستان	ham 2, hama 2: *summer*	hâmin, hamin: *summer* هامین، همین
PK:905	PK:905, KL:1541	PH:280

این لغت یا متروک شده و یا استفاده از آن بسیار محدود میباشد.

2179

هان: پیر   . رجوع شود به   آنا

هاون

همریشه: هوم   همریشه: soak, suck

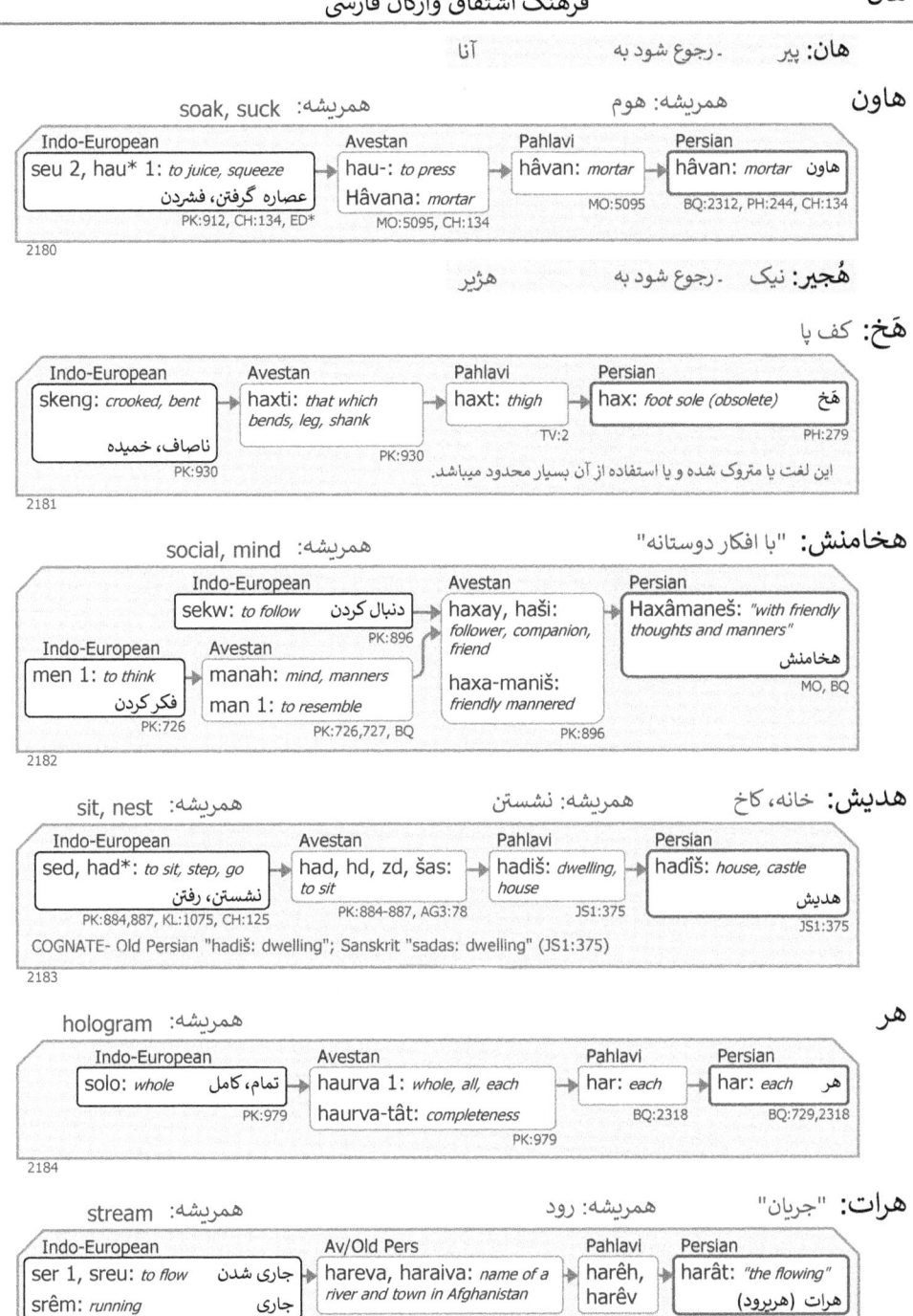

Indo-European	Avestan	Pahlavi	Persian
seu 2, hau* 1: *to juice, squeeze* عصاره گرفتن، فشردن PK:912, CH:134, ED*	hau-: *to press* Hâvana: *mortar* MO:5095, CH:134	hâvan: *mortar* MO:5095	hâvan: *mortar* هاون BQ:2312, PH:244, CH:134

2180

هُجیر: نیک   . رجوع شود به   هژیر

هَخ: کف پا

Indo-European	Avestan	Pahlavi	Persian
skeng: *crooked, bent* ناصاف، خمیده PK:930	haxti: *that which bends, leg, shank* PK:930	haxt: *thigh* TV:2	hax: *foot sole (obsolete)* هَخ PH:279

این لغت یا متروک شده و یا استفاده از آن بسیار محدود میباشد.

2181

هخامنش: "با افکار دوستانه"

همریشه: social, mind

Indo-European	Avestan	Persian
sekw: *to follow* دنبال کردن PK:896	haxay, haši: *follower, companion, friend*	Haxâmaneš: *"with friendly thoughts and manners"* هخامنش MO, BQ

Indo-European	Avestan	
men 1: *to think* فکر کردن PK:726	manah: *mind, manners* man 1: *to resemble* PK:726,727, BQ	haxa-maniš: *friendly mannered* PK:896

2182

هدیش: خانه، کاخ

همریشه: نشستن   همریشه: sit, nest

Indo-European	Avestan	Pahlavi	Persian
sed, had*: *to sit, step, go* نشستن، رفتن PK:884,887, KL:1075, CH:125	had, hd, zd, šas: *to sit* PK:884-887, AG3:78	hadiš: *dwelling, house* JS1:375	hadîš: *house, castle* هدیش JS1:375

COGNATE- Old Persian "hadiš: dwelling"; Sanskrit "sadas: dwelling" (JS1:375)

2183

هر

همریشه: hologram

Indo-European	Avestan	Pahlavi	Persian
solo: *whole* تمام، کامل PK:979	haurva 1: *whole, all, each* haurva-tât: *completeness* PK:979	har: *each* BQ:2318	har: *each* هر BQ:729,2318

2184

هرات: "جریان"

همریشه: رود   همریشه: stream

Indo-European	Av/Old Pers	Pahlavi	Persian
ser 1, sreu: *to flow* جاری شدن srêm: *running* جاری PK:909,1003, KT:205, IC:1276	hareva, haraiva: *name of a river and town in Afghanistan* PK:909	harêh, harêv BQ:2319	harât: *"the flowing"* هرات (هریرود) BQ

2185

هراز: "رود بزرگ"

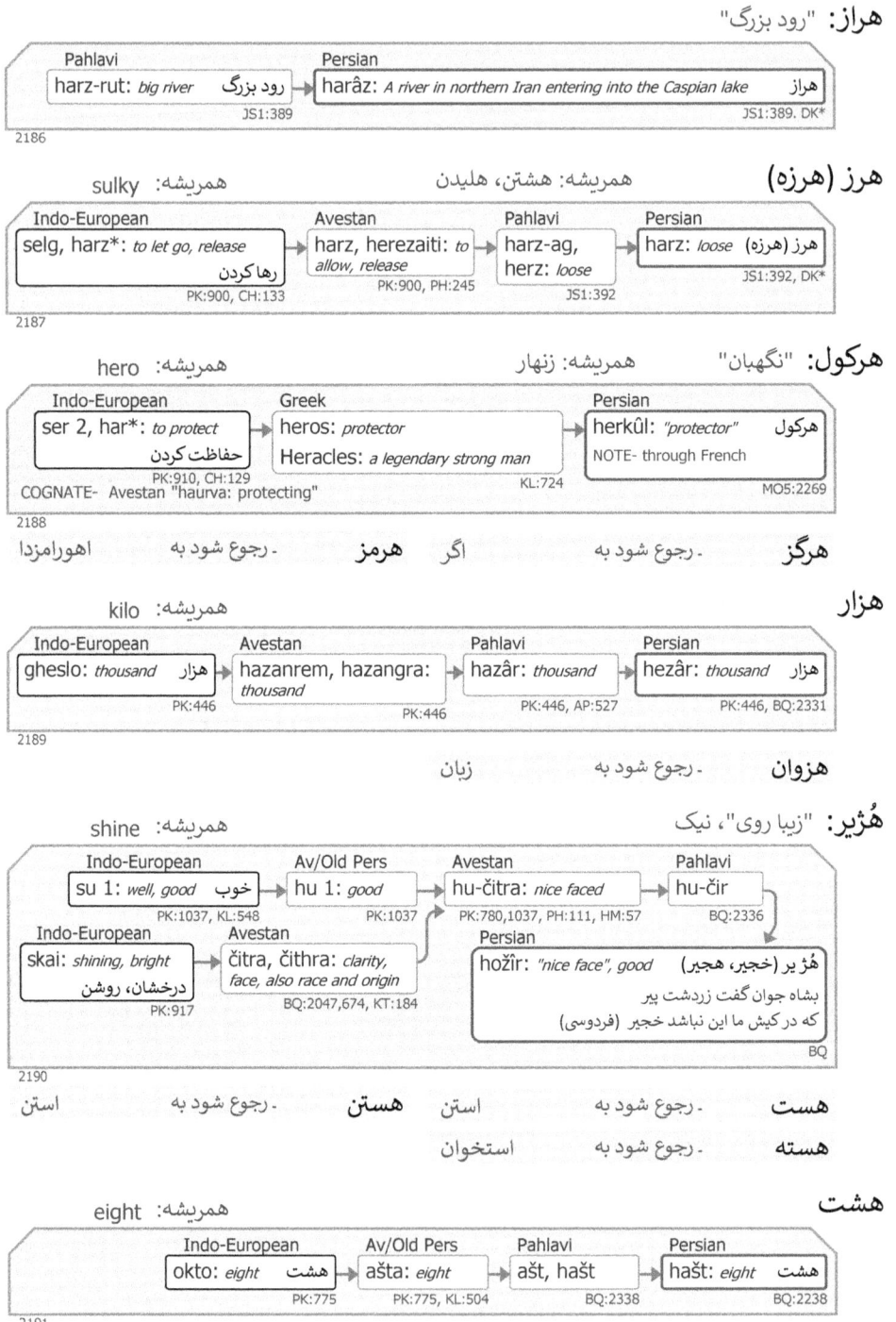

Pahlavi
harz-rut: big river   رود بزرگ
JS1:389

Persian
harâz: A river in northern Iran entering into the Caspian lake   هراز
JS1:389. DK*

2186

هرز (هرزه)

همریشه: هشتن، هلیدن   همریشه: sulky

Indo-European
selg, harz*: to let go, release   رها کردن
PK:900, CH:133

Avestan
harz, herezaiti: to allow, release
PK:900, PH:245

Pahlavi
harz-ag, herz: loose
JS1:392

Persian
harz: loose   (هرزه) هرز
JS1:392, DK*

2187

هرکول: "نگهبان"

همریشه: زنهار   همریشه: hero

Indo-European
ser 2, har*: to protect   حفاظت کردن
PK:910, CH:129
COGNATE- Avestan "haurva: protecting"

Greek
heros: protector
Heracles: a legendary strong man
KL:724

Persian
herkûl: "protector"   هرکول
NOTE- through French
MO5:2269

2188

هرگز   . رجوع شود به   اگر   **هرمز**   . رجوع شود به   اهورامزدا

هزار

همریشه: kilo

Indo-European
gheslo: thousand   هزار
PK:446

Avestan
hazanrem, hazangra: thousand
PK:446

Pahlavi
hazâr: thousand
PK:446, AP:527

Persian
hezâr: thousand   هزار
PK:446, BQ:2331

2189

هزوان   . رجوع شود به   زبان

هُژیر: "زیبا روی"، نیک

همریشه: shine

Indo-European
su 1: well, good   خوب
PK:1037, KL:548

Av/Old Pers
hu 1: good
PK:1037

Avestan
hu-čitra: nice faced
PK:780,1037, PH:111, HM:57

Pahlavi
hu-čir
BQ:2336

Indo-European
skai: shining, bright   درخشان، روشن
PK:917

Avestan
čitra, čithra: clarity, face, also race and origin
BQ:2047,674, KT:184

Persian
hožir: "nice face", good   هُژیر (خجیر، هجیر)
بشاه جوان گفت زردشت پیر
که در کیش ما این نباشد خجیر (فردوسی)
BQ

2190

هست   استن   . رجوع شود به   استن   **هستن**   استن

هسته   . رجوع شود به   استخوان

هشت

همریشه: eight

Indo-European
okto: eight   هشت
PK:775

Av/Old Pers
ašta: eight
PK:775, KL:504

Pahlavi
ašt, hašt
BQ:2338

Persian
hašt: eight   هشت
BQ:2238

2191

هشتن: رها کردن

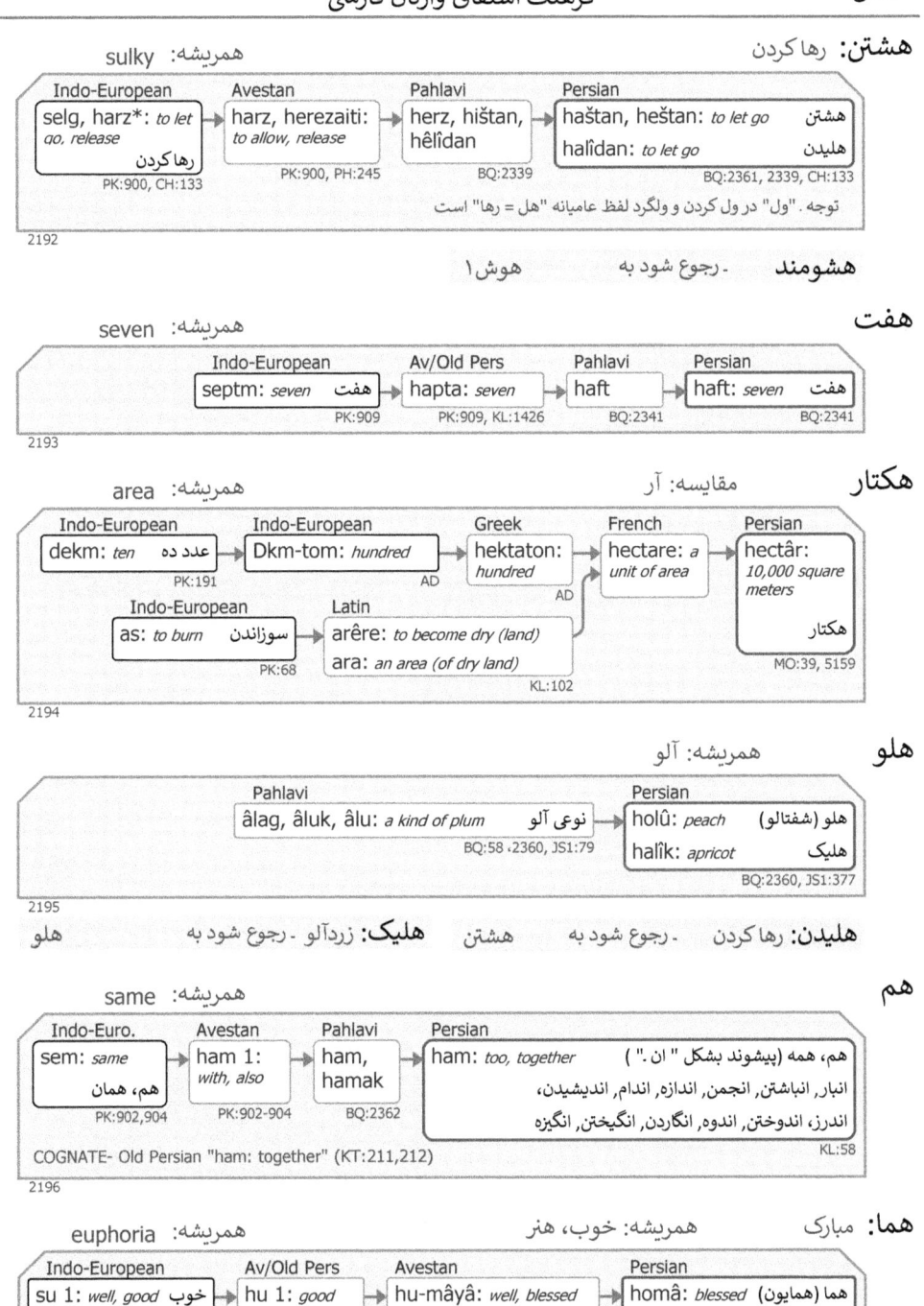

همریشه: sulky

Indo-European	Avestan	Pahlavi	Persian
selg, harz*: *to let go, release* رها کردن	harz, herezaiti: *to allow, release*	herz, hištan, hêlîdan	haštan, heštan: *to let go* هشتن halîdan: *to let go* هلیدن
PK:900, CH:133	PK:900, PH:245	BQ:2339	BQ:2361, 2339, CH:133

توجه . "ول" در ول کردن و ولگرد لفظ عامیانه "هل = رها" است

2192

هشومند ـ رجوع شود به   هوش۱

هفت   همریشه: seven

Indo-European	Av/Old Pers	Pahlavi	Persian
septm: *seven* هفت	hapta: *seven*	haft	haft: *seven* هفت
PK:909	PK:909, KL:1426	BQ:2341	BQ:2341

2193

هکتار   مقایسه: آر   همریشه: area

Indo-European	Indo-European	Greek	French	Persian
dekm: *ten* عدد ده	Dkm-tom: *hundred*	hektaton: *hundred*	hectare: *a unit of area*	hectâr: *10,000 square meters* هکتار
PK:191	AD	AD		MO:39, 5159

Indo-European	Latin
as: *to burn* سوزاندن	arêre: *to become dry (land)* ara: *an area (of dry land)*
PK:68	KL:102

2194

هلو   همریشه: آلو

Pahlavi	Persian
âlag, âluk, âlu: *a kind of plum* نوعی آلو	holû: *peach* هلو (شفتالو) halîk: *apricot* هلیک
BQ:58، 2360, JS1:79	BQ:2360, JS1:377

2195

هلیدن: رها کردن ـ رجوع شود به   هشتن   **هلیک: زردآلو**   هلو

هم   همریشه: same

Indo-Euro.	Avestan	Pahlavi	Persian
sem: *same* هم، همان	ham 1: *with, also*	ham, hamak	ham: *too, together* هم، همه (پیشوند بشکل " ان .") انبار، انباشتن، انجمن، اندازه، اندام، اندیشیدن، اندرز، اندوختن، اندوه، انگاردن، انگیختن، انگیزه
PK:902,904	PK:902-904	BQ:2362	KL:58

COGNATE- Old Persian "ham: together" (KT:211,212)

2196

هما: مبارک   همریشه: خوب، هنر   همریشه: euphoria

Indo-European	Av/Old Pers	Avestan	Persian
su 1: *well, good* خوب	hu 1: *good*	hu-mâyâ: *well, blessed*	homâ: *blessed* هما (همایون)
PK:1037, KL:548	PK:1037	BQ, PH:108	BQ

2197

هَمار: تعداد ـ رجوع شود به   آمار

همال: مانند، همتا، رفیق

همریشه: similar

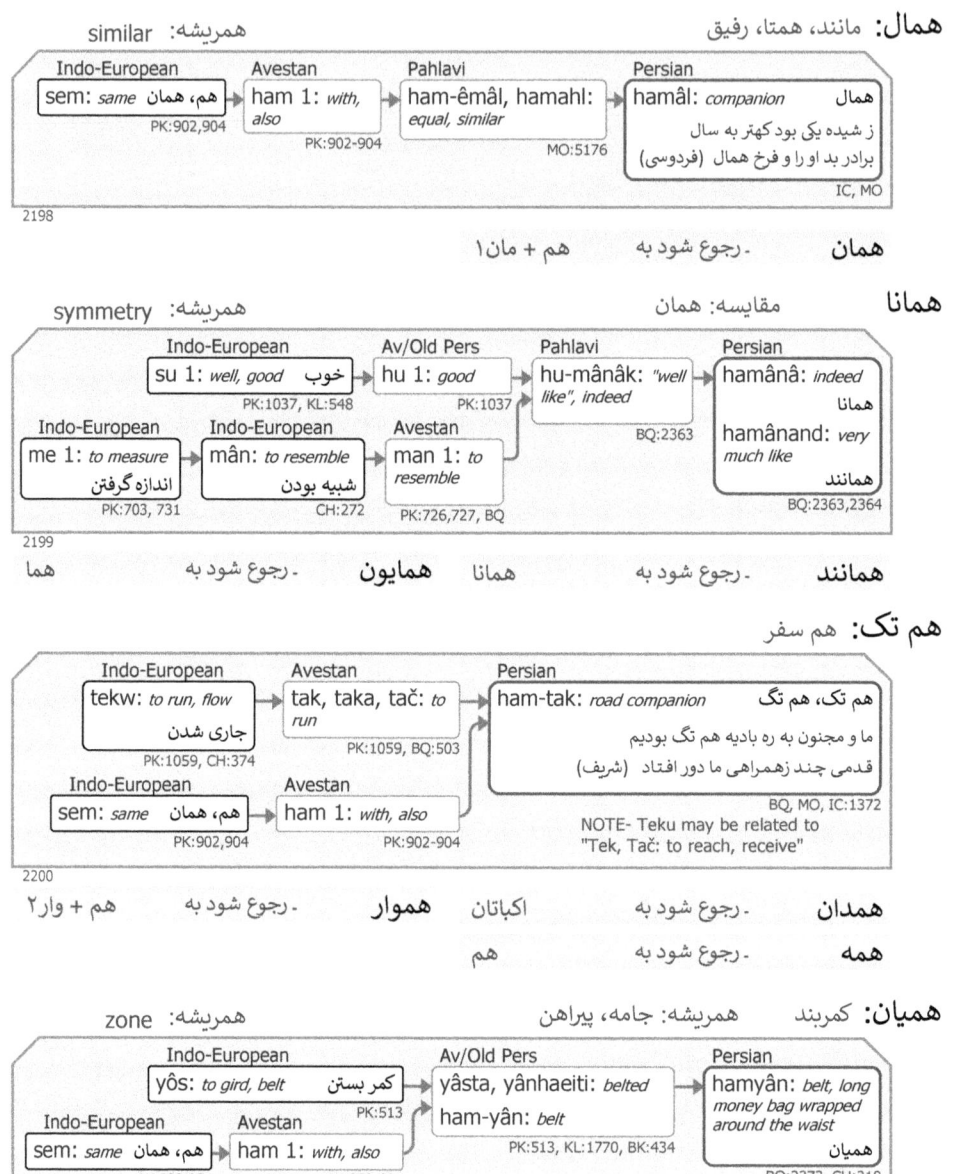

Indo-European	Avestan	Pahlavi	Persian
sem: same هم، همان	ham 1: with, also	ham-êmâl, hamahl: equal, similar	hamâl: companion همال
PK:902,904	PK:902-904	MO:5176	ز شیده یکی بود کهتر به سال

برادر بد او را و فرخ همال (فردوسی)

IC, MO

2198

همان ۔رجوع شود به   هم + مان۱

همانا   مقایسه: همان   همریشه: symmetry

Indo-European	Av/Old Pers	Pahlavi	Persian
su 1: well, good خوب	hu 1: good	hu-mânâk: "well like", indeed	hamânâ: indeed همانا
PK:1037, KL:548	PK:1037	BQ:2363	hamânand: very much like همانند

Indo-European	Indo-European	Avestan	
me 1: to measure اندازه گرفتن	mân: to resemble شبیه بودن	man 1: to resemble	
PK:703, 731	CH:272	PK:726,727, BQ	BQ:2363,2364

2199

همانند ۔رجوع شود به   همانا   **همایون** ۔رجوع شود به   هما

هم تک: هم سفر

Indo-European	Avestan	Persian
tekw: to run, flow جاری شدن	tak, taka, tač: to run	ham-tak: road companion هم تک، هم تگ
PK:1059, CH:374	PK:1059, BQ:503	ما و مجنون به ره بادیه هم تگ بودیم
Indo-European	Avestan	قدمی چند زهمراهی ما دور افتاد (شریف)
sem: same هم، همان	ham 1: with, also	BQ, MO, IC:1372
PK:902,904	PK:902-904	NOTE- Teku may be related to "Tek, Tač: to reach, receive"

2200

همدان ۔رجوع شود به   اکباتان   **هموار** ۔رجوع شود به   هم + وار۲

همه ۔رجوع شود به   هم

همیان: کمربند   همریشه: جامه، پیراهن   همریشه: zone

Indo-European	Av/Old Pers	Persian
yôs: to gird, belt کمر بستن	yâsta, yânhaeiti: belted	hamyân: belt, long money bag wrapped around the waist
PK:513	ham-yân: belt	
Indo-European	Avestan	همیان
sem: same هم، همان	ham 1: with, also	
PK:902,904	PK:902-904	PK:513, KL:1770, BK:434 BQ:2373, CH:210

2201

391

هَمیستَر: دشمن، رقیب

همریشه: dismiss, omit

Indo-European	Avestan	Pahlavi	Persian
smeit: *to throw, send forward* پرتاب کردن، به جلو فرستادن PK:968	maêth: *to send, throw* hamista: *thrown down, oppress* hamaêstar: *oppressor* PK:968, KL:988	hamêstâr: *enemy* hamêstagân: *awkward situation* TV:53	hamîstar: *enemy* همیستَر hamîstakân: *a place between hell and heaven* همیستکان PH:279, MO:5185

این لغت یا متروک شده و یا استفاده از آن بسیار محدود میباشد.

2202

هَمیستَکان: برزخ ـ رجوع شود به هَمیستَر

همیشه

	Pahlavi	Persian
	hamêšak: *always* دائما BQ:2374	hamîšeh: *always* همیشه BQ:2374

2203

همین ـ رجوع شود به هامین **هُنام** ـ رجوع شود به اندام

هَنبان ـ رجوع شود به انبان **هنج**: کشیدن ـ رجوع شود به هنجیدن

هنجار: راه

همریشه: tone

Indo-European	Avestan	Persian
ten 1, tenu: *to stretch, pull* کشیدن PK:1064,1067, AD	thang, hanč, â-thax: *to pull* BQ:1481,2376, 2381, TV:7	hanjâr: *path* هنجار (ناهنجار) ز هنجار دیگر درآمد به روم فروماند گنج اندرون مرز و بوم (نظامی گنجوی) BQ, MO, PH, TV, AG3

2204

هنجیدن: کشیدن

همریشه: هیختن همریشه: tone

Indo-European	Avestan	Persian
ten 1, tenu: *to stretch, pull* کشیدن PK:1064,1067, AD	thang, hanč, â-thax: *to pull* BQ:1481,2376, 2381, TV:7	hanjîdan: *to pull or dig out* هنجیدن (هنج، آهنجیدن) BQ, MO, PH, TV, AG3

2205

هند

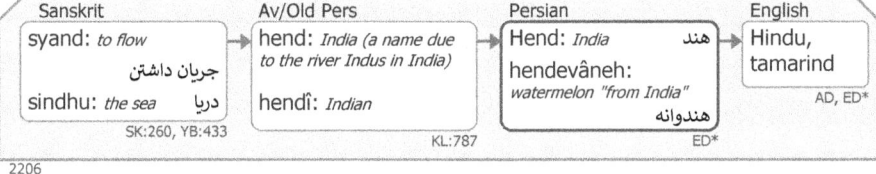

Sanskrit	Av/Old Pers	Persian	English
syand: *to flow* جریان داشتن sindhu: *the sea* دریا SK:260, YB:433	hend: *India (a name due to the river Indus in India)* hendî: *Indian* KL:787	Hend: *India* هند hendevâneh: *watermelon "from India"* هندوانه ED*	Hindu, tamarind AD, ED*

2206

هندسه: "اندازه گیری"   همریشه: اندازه

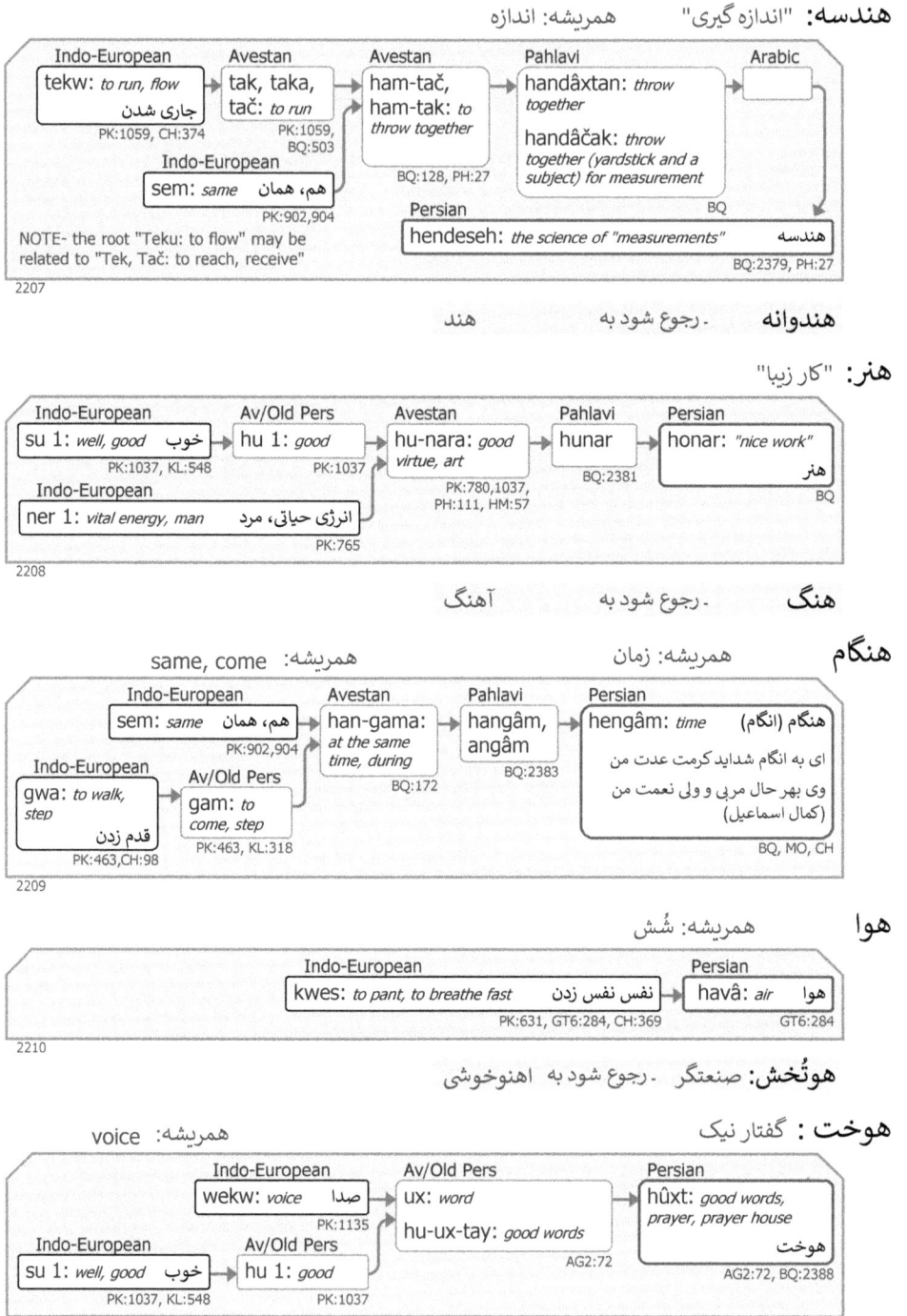

هندوانه   . رجوع شود به   هند

هنر: "کار زیبا"

هنگ   . رجوع شود به   آهنگ

هنگام   همریشه: زمان   همریشه: same, come

هوا   همریشه: شُش

هوتُخش: صنعتگر   . رجوع شود به   اهنوخوشی

هوخت : گفتار نیک   همریشه: voice

هُوَخشَتَر: "خوب رشد کرده"، نام سومین شاه ماد

همریشه: augment, authority

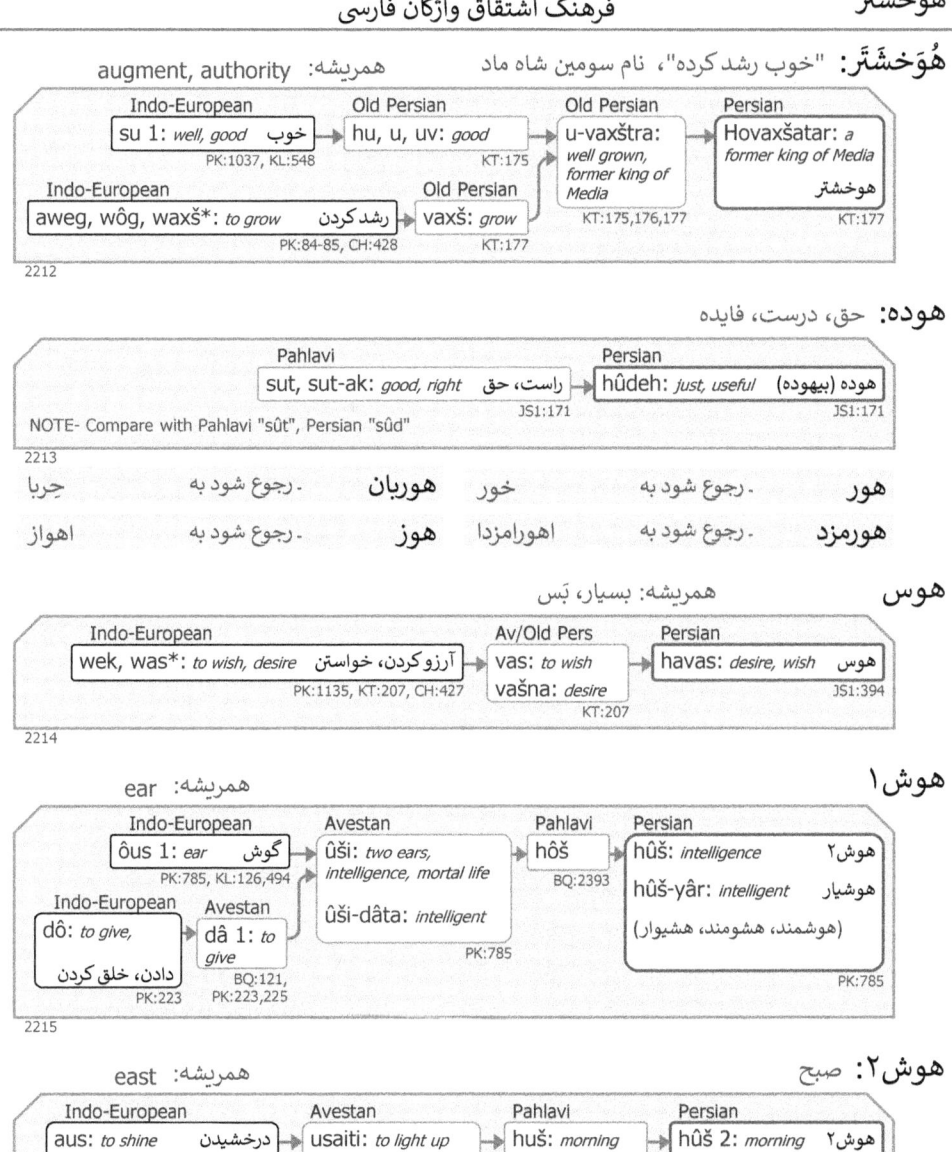

Indo-European	Old Persian	Old Persian	Persian
su 1: *well, good* خوب PK:1037, KL:548	hu, u, uv: *good* KT:175	u-vaxštra: *well grown, former king of Media* KT:175,176,177	Hovaxšatar: *a former king of Media* هوخشتر KT:177
Indo-European		Old Persian	
aweg, wôg, waxš*: *to grow* رشد کردن PK:84-85, CH:428		vaxš: *grow* KT:177	

2212

هوده: حق، درست، فایده

Pahlavi	Persian
sut, sut-ak: *good, right* راست، حق JS1:171	hûdeh: *just, useful* هوده (بیهوده) JS1:171

NOTE- Compare with Pahlavi "sût", Persian "sûd"

2213

هور	.رجوع شود به	خور	هوربان	.رجوع شود به	حِربا
هورمزد	.رجوع شود به	اهورامزدا	هوز	.رجوع شود به	اهواز

هوس   همریشه: بسیار، بَس

Indo-European	Av/Old Pers	Persian
wek, was*: *to wish, desire* آرزو کردن، خواستن PK:1135, KT:207, CH:427	vas: *to wish* vašna: *desire* KT:207	havas: *desire, wish* هوس JS1:394

2214

هوش۱   همریشه: ear

Indo-European	Avestan	Pahlavi	Persian
ôus 1: *ear* گوش PK:785, KL:126,494	ûši: *two ears, intelligence, mortal life* ûši-dâta: *intelligent*	hôš BQ:2393	hûš: *intelligence* هوش۲ hûš-yâr: *intelligent* هوشیار (هوشمند، هشومند، هشیوار)
Indo-European	Avestan		
dô: *to give,* دادن، خلق کردن PK:223	dâ 1: *to give* BQ:121, PK:223,225		PK:785
			PK:785

2215

هوش۲: صبح   همریشه: east

Indo-European	Avestan	Pahlavi	Persian
aus: *to shine* درخشیدن ausus: *dawn* سپیده دم PK:86, KL:495	usaiti: *to light up* ušâ: *east, dawn* ušas-tara: *east* PK:86, BK:871	huš: *morning* TV:67	hûš 2: *morning* هوش۲ PH:281, TV:67

2216

هوشمند	.رجوع شود به	هوش۱

هوشنگ: "خوش خانه یا معمار خوب"   مقایسه: شَن

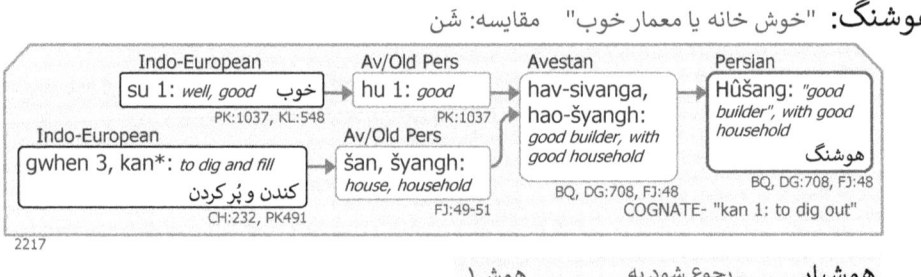

هوشیار   ـ رجوع شود به   هوش۱

هوم: نام گیاهی پر شیره و مقدس نزد اقوام آریایی   همریشه: soak, suck

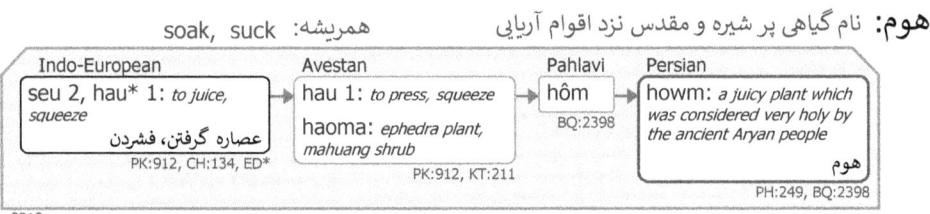

هومن: "نیک رفتار"   همریشه: mind

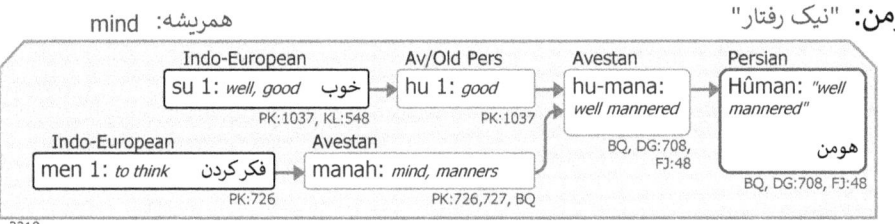

هویدا

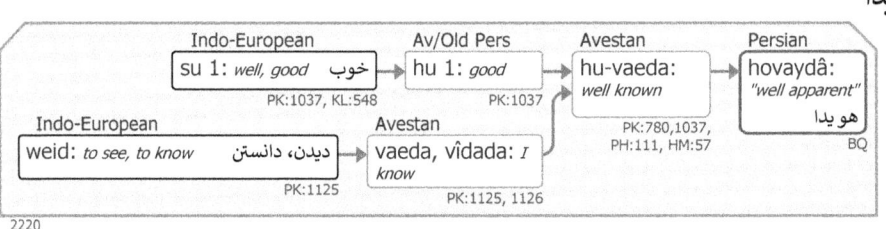

هیچ

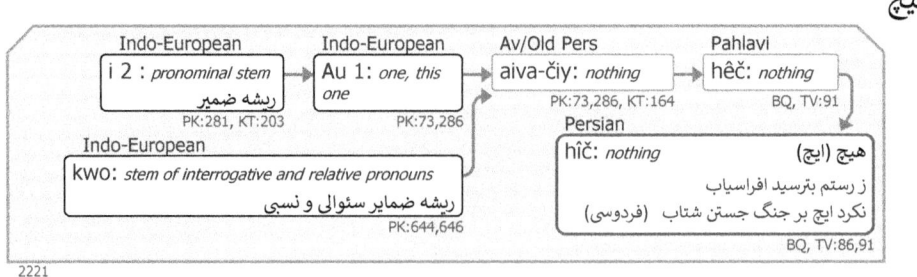

هیختن کشیدن   همریشه: هنجیدن، آهیختن   همریشه: tension

Indo-European	Avestan	Persian
ten 1, tenu: *to stretch, pull* کشیدن	thang, hanč, â-thax: *to pull*	hîxtan: *to pull* هیختن
PK:1064,1067, AD	BQ:1481,2376, 2381, TV:7	BQ, PH, TV

2222

هیرید   ـ رجوع شود به   بُد

هیرک: بچه حیواناتی نظیر بز و گوسفند   همریشه: year

Indo-European	Indo-Euro.	Avestan	Pahlavi	Persian
i 1, ei, ai*: *to go* رفتن	Yero: *year*	yâr, yâra: *year*	yâirka: *one year old.*	hîrak: *a baby animal* هیرک
PK:293,501, KL:825, CH:154	PK:296, KL:1761	PK:296, KL:1796	PH:249	BQ:2406

2223

هیزم   همریشه: anneal

Indo-European	Av/Old Pers	Pahlavi	Persian
aidh: *to burn* سوزاندن	aesmo: *heat* hêzum: *fire wood*	hêzam, êsim	hîzom: *firewood* هیزم hîmeh: *firewood* هیمه
PK:11, CH:157, KL	PK:11	BQ:2407	BQ:2407, PH:249

2224

هیکل: معبد، بتخانه

Sumerian	Akkadian	Arabic	Persian
egal, ekal: *temple* معبد	ekalu: *temple*	haikal: *temple, statue* NOTE- through Hebrew	haykal: *temple, idol house* هیکل چنان دان که این هیکل از پهلوی بود نام بتخانه ار بشنوی (لغت فرس)
BQ:2408, AR:40	AR:40	BQ:2408, AR:40	BQ:2408, AR:40

2225

هیمالیا: "خانه برف"   همریشه: زمستان

Indo-European	Sanskrit	Persian
ghei 1: *winter* زمستان	hima: *snow* hima-alaya: *home of snow*	hîmâlâyâ: *"home of snow"* هیمالیا
PK:425	PK:425	MO6:2320

2226

هیمه   ـ رجوع شود به   هیزم

هیولا: عنصر، مایه، ماده   همریشه: sill

Indo-European	Greek	Arabic	Persian
swel, sel: *wood, beam, board* چوب، تخته	hulê, hylê: *wood, matter, raw material*	hayula: *matter*	hayulâ: *matter* هیولا، هیولی
PK:898	AR:41, ED*	AR:41	MO, AR:41

2227

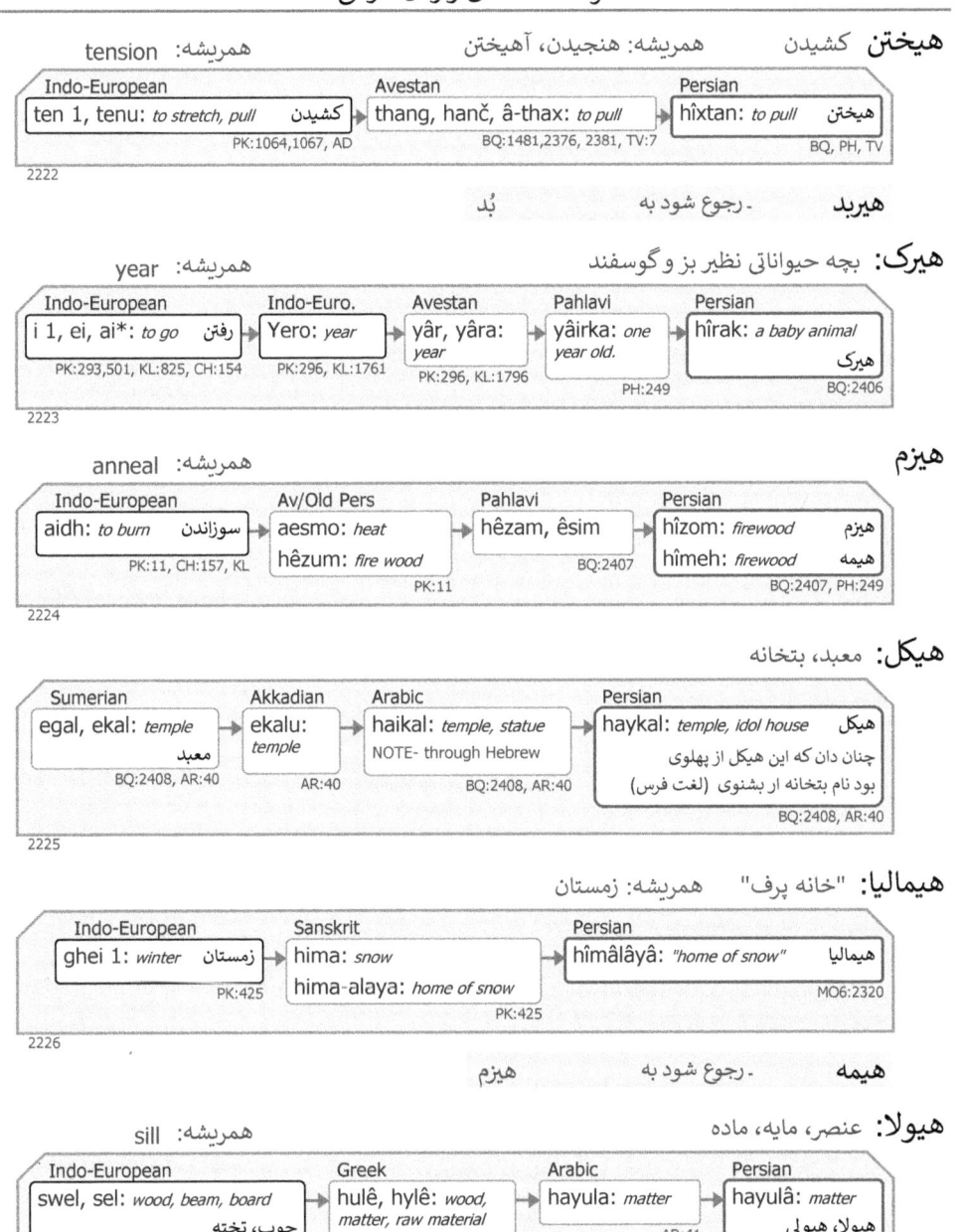

این حرف گاهی به ل، ه یا ز بدل شود.

ـ ی: یای نسبت مانند چوبی، آهنی، آبی

Pahlavi	Persian
- ik, - ikâ: *like* شبیه، مانند JS1:418	- î: *a suffix for making adjectives like Fars-î* پسوند " ی " برای نشان دادن نسبت مانند چوبی، خاکی، اراکی JS1:418

2228

یا

همریشه: one, none, any

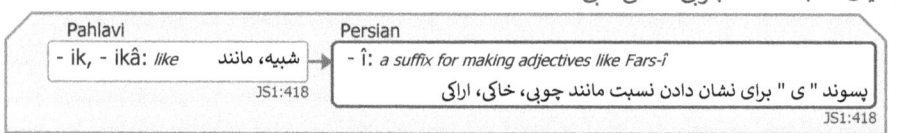

Indo-European	Indo-Euro.	Av/Old Pers	Pahlavi	Persian
i 2 : *pronominal stem* ریشه ضمیر PK:281, KT:203	Uê: *or* PK:73,286	va, vâ: *or* PK:73,286, KT:164	ayâb, ayâ, ayâo: *or* BQ, TV:91	یا yâ: *or* BQ, TV:86,91

2229

یابیدن   رجوع شود به   **یافتن**

یاد

همریشه: even

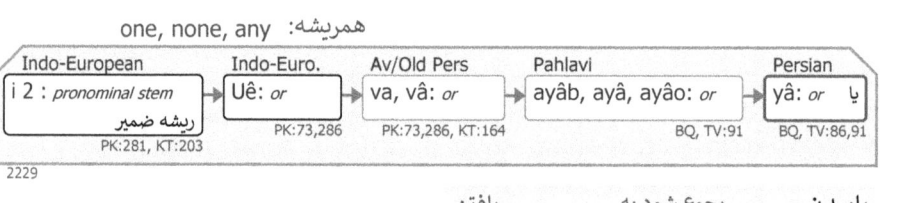

Indo-European	Avestan	Pahlavi	Persian
yem: *hold together (pair)* جفت، جفت کردن PK:505	yata, yâta, ya: *remember* PK:505	yât, âyât PH:250	یاد yâd: *memory* BQ:2412, TV:85, AG1:22

2230

یار

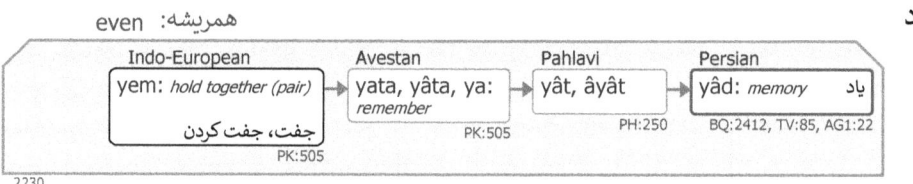

Pahlavi	Persian
âyâr, âyârih: *friend, help* دوست، کمک BQ:2413	یار yâr: *friend, helper* BQ:2413

2231

یازده

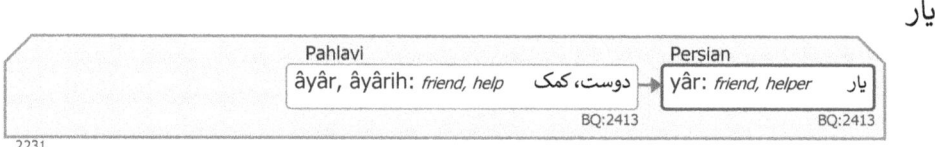

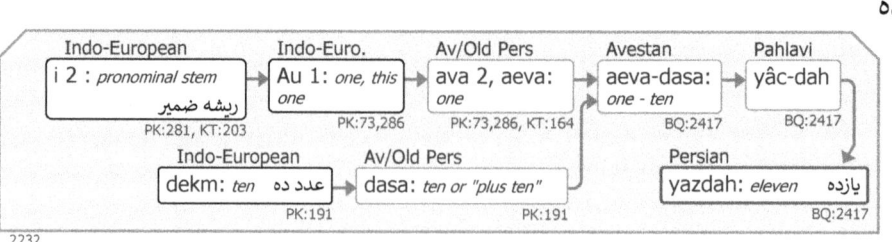

Indo-European	Indo-Euro.	Av/Old Pers	Avestan	Pahlavi
i 2 : *pronominal stem* ریشه ضمیر PK:281, KT:203	Au 1: *one, this* *one* PK:73,286	ava 2, aeva: *one* PK:73,286, KT:164	aeva-dasa: *one - ten* BQ:2417	yâc-dah BQ:2417
Indo-European	Av/Old Pers		Persian	
dekm: *ten* عدد ده PK:191	dasa: *ten or "plus ten"* PK:191		یازده yazdah: *eleven* BQ:2417	

2232

یازیدن: بالیدن، قصد کردن

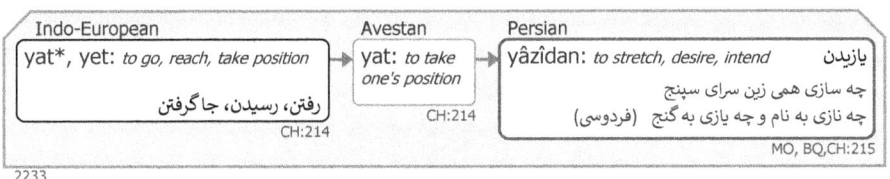

Indo-European	Avestan	Persian
yat*, yet: *to go, reach, take position* رفتن، رسیدن، جا گرفتن	yat: *to take one's position* CH:214	yâzîdan: *to stretch, desire, intend* یازیدن چه سازی همی زین سرای سپنج چه نازی به نام و چه یازی به گنج (فردوسی) MO, BQ,CH:215
CH:214		

2233

یاسه: آرزو

همریشه: جادو   همریشه: jealous, zeal

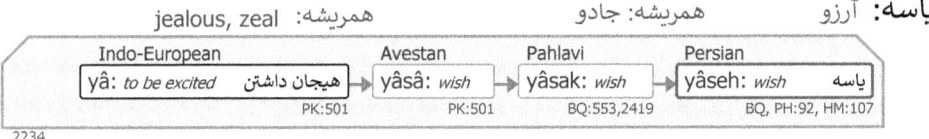

Indo-European	Avestan	Pahlavi	Persian
yâ: *to be excited* هیجان داشتن PK:501	yâsâ: *wish* PK:501	yâsak: *wish* BQ:553,2419	yâseh: *wish* یاسه BQ, PH:92, HM:107

2234

یافتن

همریشه: وام   همریشه: couple

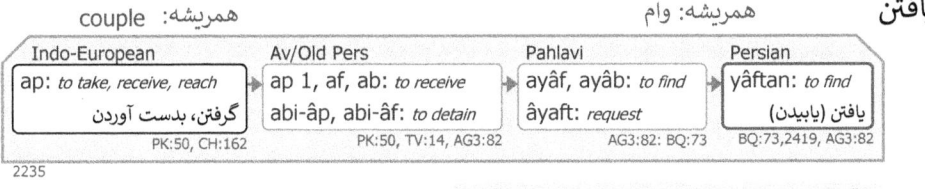

Indo-European	Av/Old Pers	Pahlavi	Persian
ap: *to take, receive, reach* گرفتن، بدست آوردن PK:50, CH:162	ap 1, af, ab: *to receive* abi-âp, abi-âf: *to detain* PK:50, TV:14, AG3:82	ayâf, ayâb: *to find* âyaft: *request* AG3:82: BQ:73	yâftan: *to find* یافتن (یابیدن) BQ:73,2419, AG3:82

2235

یاقوت

رجوع شود به   یاکند

یاکند

همریشه: hyacinth

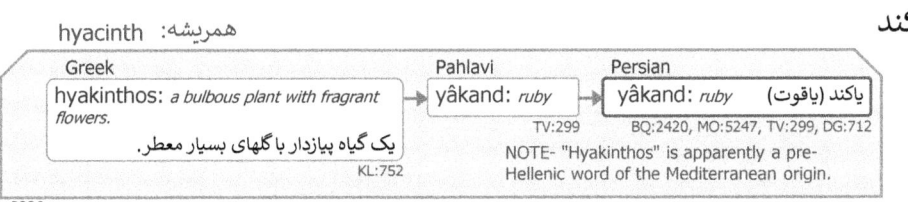

Greek	Pahlavi	Persian
hyakinthos: *a bulbous plant with fragrant flowers.* یک گیاه پیازدار با گلهای بسیار معطر. KL:752	yâkand: *ruby* TV:299	yâkand: *ruby* یاکند (یاقوت) BQ:2420, MO:5247, TV:299, DG:712 NOTE- "Hyakinthos" is apparently a pre-Hellenic word of the Mediterranean origin.

2236

یاور: ابزار خُرد کردن غلات

Avestan	Persian
yâvarenâ: *a stone or tool for beating and crushing grains* سنگ برای خرد کردن گندم PH:252	yâvar: *stone or other objects used for crushing grains* یاور BQ:2422

2237

یخ

همریشه: ice

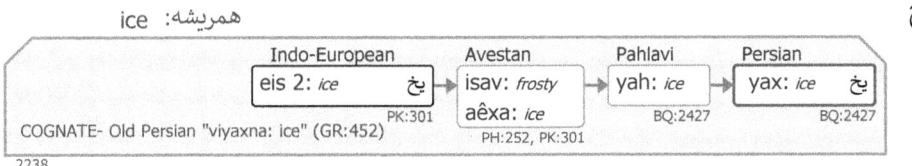

Indo-European	Avestan	Pahlavi	Persian
eis 2: *ice* یخ PK:301	isav: *frosty* aêxa: *ice* PH:252, PK:301	yah: *ice* BQ:2427	yax: *ice* یخ BQ:2427

COGNATE- Old Persian "viyaxna: ice" (GR:452)

2238

یرقان: "مرغ زردی که باور میشد دیدنش یرقان را علاج کند"

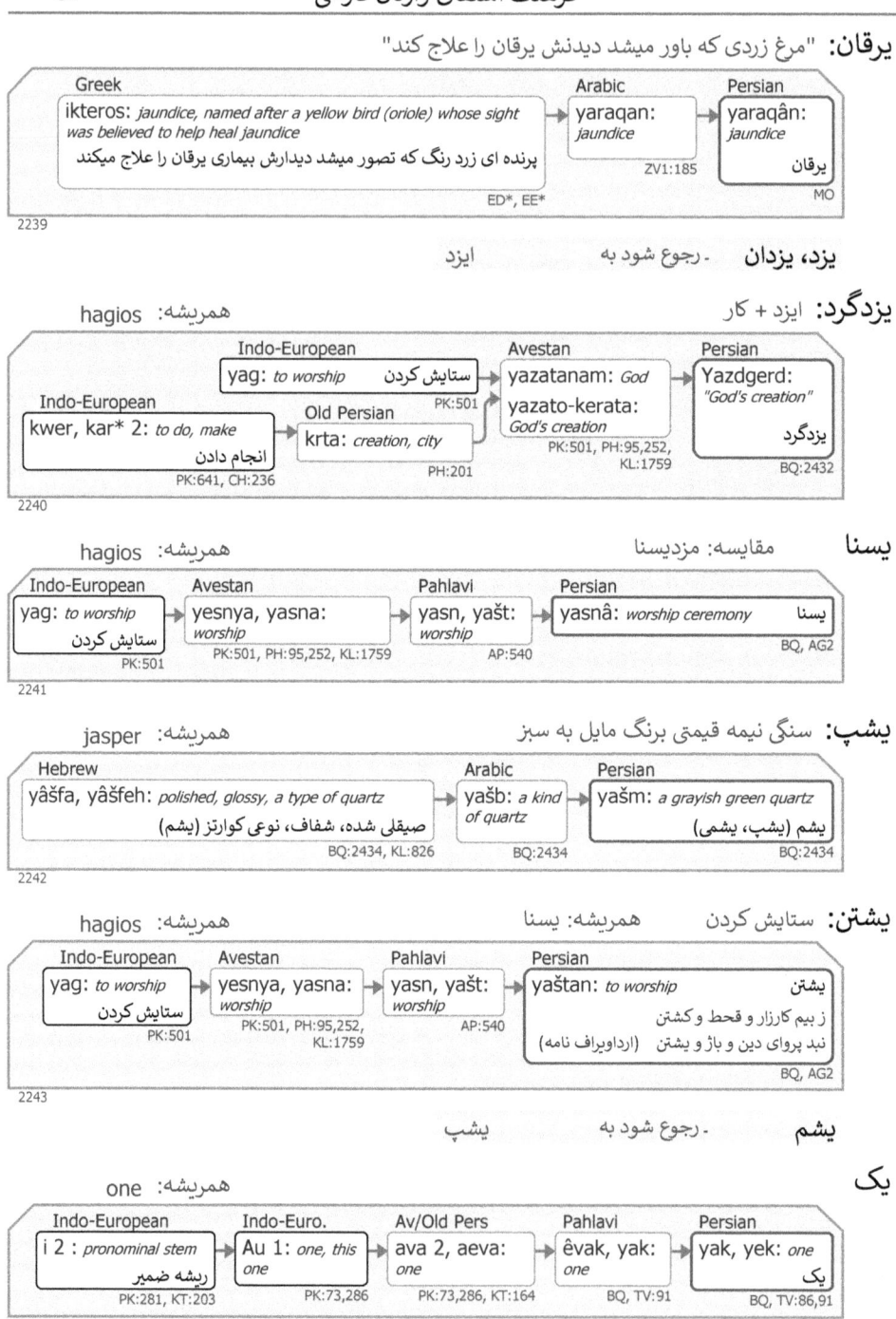

یزد، یزدان - رجوع شود به .   **ایزد**

یزدگرد: ایزد + کار

یسنا   مقایسه: مزدیسنا

یشپ: سنگ نیمه قیمتی برنگ مایل به سبز

یشتن: ستایش کردن   همریشه: یسنا

یشم - رجوع شود به .   یشپ

یک

یکتا - رجوع شود به .   **یگانه**   تای   یک + گان

. یل: پسوند بمعنی خدا

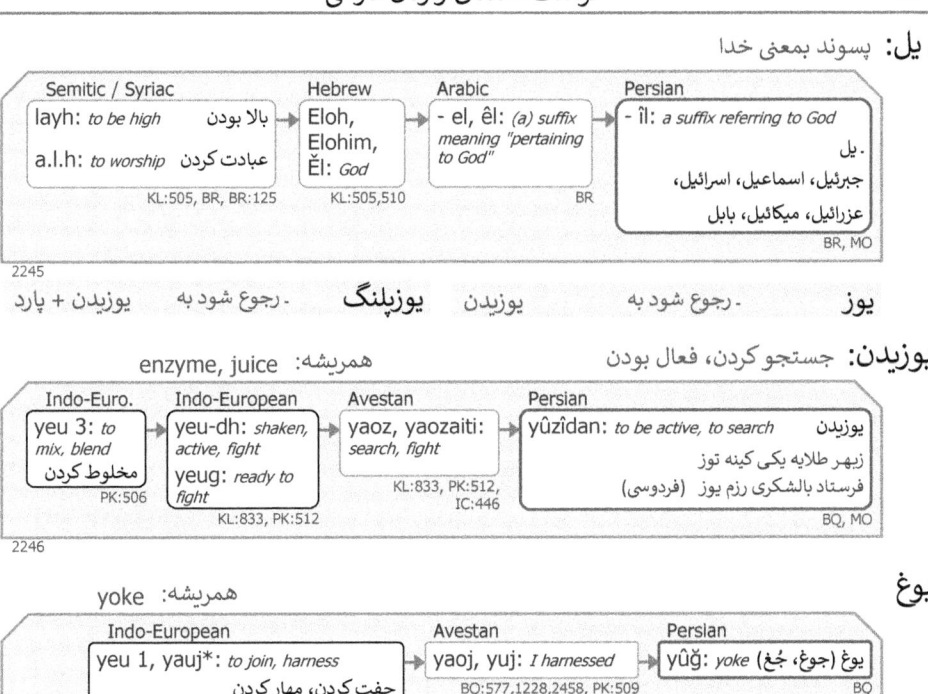

Semitic / Syriac	Hebrew	Arabic	Persian
layh: *to be high* بالا بودن a.l.h: *to worship* عبادت کردن KL:505, BR, BR:125	Eloh, Elohim, Ěl: *God* KL:505,510	- el, êl: *(a) suffix meaning "pertaining to God"* BR	- îl: *a suffix referring to God* یل . جبرئیل، اسماعیل، اسرائیل، عزرائیل، میکائیل، بابل BR, MO

2245

یوز ۰ رجوع شود به   یوزیدن   **یوزپلنگ**   یوزیدن ۰ رجوع شود به   یوزیدن + پارد

یوزیدن: جستجو کردن، فعال بودن

همریشه: enzyme, juice

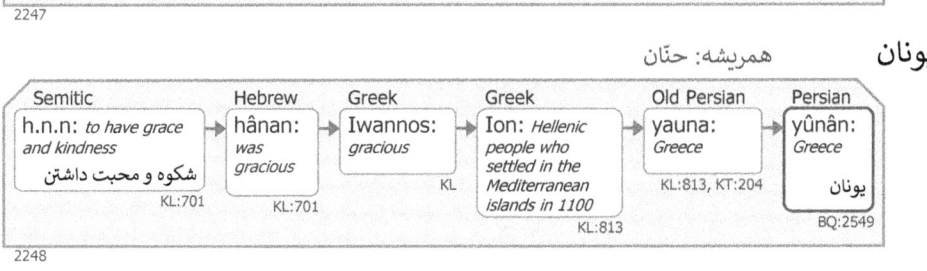

Indo-Euro.	Indo-European	Avestan	Persian
yeu 3: *to mix, blend* مخلوط کردن PK:506	yeu-dh: *shaken, active, fight* yeug: *ready to fight* KL:833, PK:512	yaoz, yaozaiti: *search, fight* KL:833, PK:512, IC:446	yûzîdan: *to be active, to search* یوزیدن زیهر طلایه یکی کینه توز فرستاد بالشکری رزم یوز (فردوسی) BQ, MO

2246

یوغ

همریشه: yoke

Indo-European	Avestan	Persian
yeu 1, yauj*: *to join, harness* جفت کردن، مهار کردن PK:509, CH:217	yaoj, yuj: *I harnessed* BQ:577,1228,2458, PK:509	yûğ: *yoke* یوغ (جوغ، جُغ) BQ

2247

یونان

همریشه: حتّان

Semitic	Hebrew	Greek	Greek	Old Persian	Persian
h.n.n: *to have grace and kindness* شکوه و محبت داشتن KL:701	hânan: *was gracious* KL:701	Iwannos: *gracious* KL	Ion: *Hellenic people who settled in the Mediterranean islands in 1100* KL:813	yauna: *Greece* KL:813, KT:204	yûnân: *Greece* یونان BQ:2549

2248

نمودارهای ناتمام

1

همریشه: own

Indo-European	Avestan	Persian
aik: *to possess, own* مالک بودن PK:298, KL:1106	îs, îše, îšti, âêšâ 1: *wealth, power* îsvan, išvan: *wealthy* PK:298, KL:1106, BK:771,772	?

2249

2

همریشه: on, upon

Indo-European	Av/Old Pers	Persian
an 3: *on, upon, above, to* روی، بالای PK:39	ana: *on, upon* anu, anuv: *to, after, along* anu-i: *going along* PK:39, KL:67, KT:164	?

2250

3

همریشه: umbrella

Indo-European	Avestan	Persian
andho: *blind, dark* کور، تاریک PK:41	anda, ando: *blind* PK:41, BK:323	?

2251

4

همریشه: best

Indo-European	Avestan	Persian
bhad: *good* خوب PK:106	badra: *good fortune, luck* hu-badra: *(with) good luck, lucky* PK:106, KL:167	?

2252

5

Indo-European	Avestan	Persian
bhen: *to strike* ضربه زدن PK:126	ban: *to be sick* banta: *sick* banay: *to make sick* KL:145, BK:304	?

2253

6

همریشه: to

Indo-European	Avestan	Persian
de: *demonstrative stem* ضمیر یا ریشه اشاره PK:181	dim: *him, her, he, she* dit: *it* -da 5: *toward, to* PK:183, KL:1622	?

2254

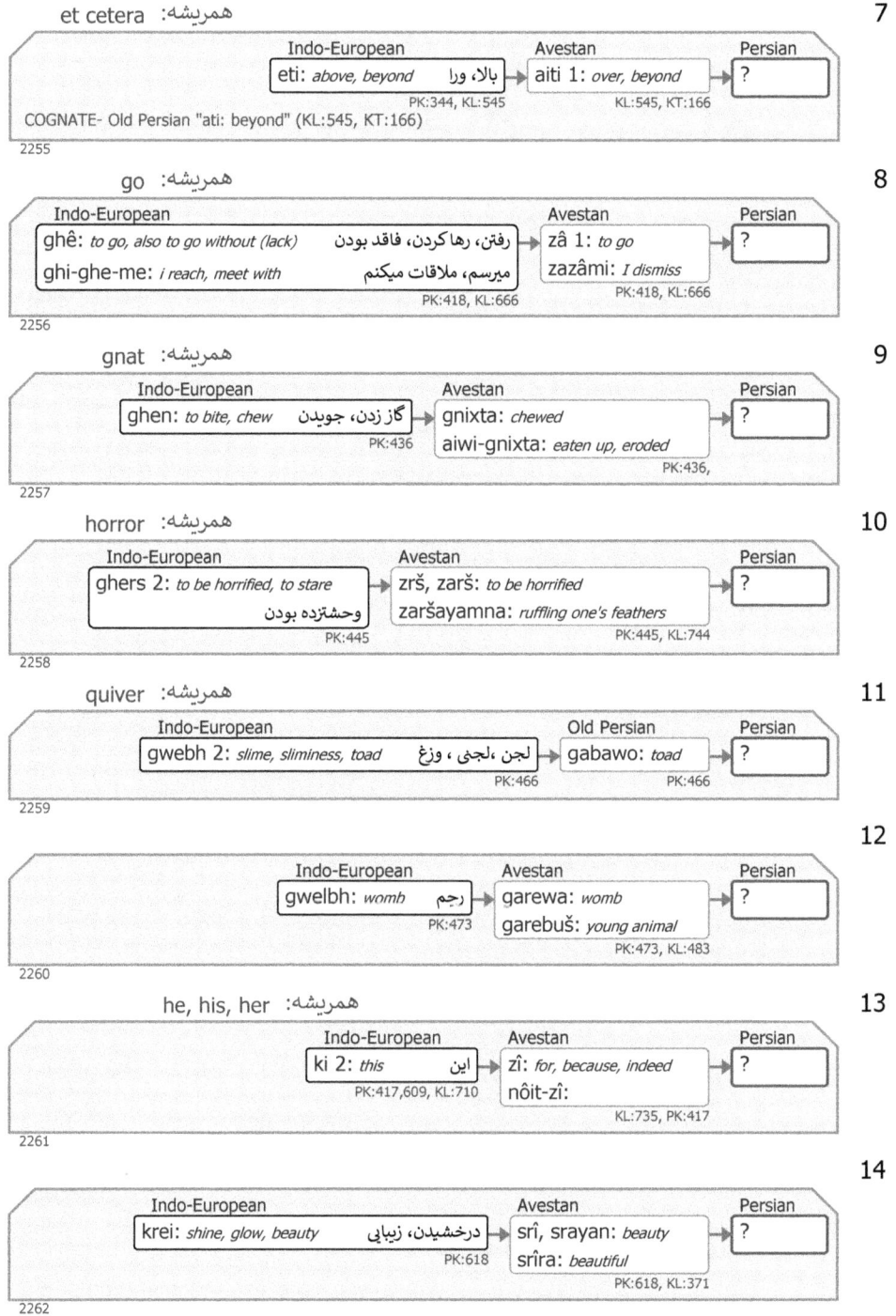

7

همریشه: et cetera

Indo-European
eti: *above, beyond* — بالا، ورا
PK:344, KL:545

Avestan
aiti 1: *over, beyond*
KL:545, KT:166

Persian
?

COGNATE- Old Persian "ati: beyond" (KL:545, KT:166)

2255

8

همریشه: go

Indo-European
ghê: *to go, also to go without (lack)* — رفتن، رها کردن، فاقد بودن
ghi-ghe-me: *i reach, meet with* — میرسم، ملاقات میکنم
PK:418, KL:666

Avestan
zâ 1: *to go*
zazâmi: *I dismiss*
PK:418, KL:666

Persian
?

2256

9

همریشه: gnat

Indo-European
ghen: *to bite, chew* — گاز زدن، جویدن
PK:436

Avestan
gnixta: *chewed*
aiwi-gnixta: *eaten up, eroded*
PK:436,

Persian
?

2257

10

همریشه: horror

Indo-European
ghers 2: *to be horrified, to stare* — وحشتزده بودن
PK:445

Avestan
zrš, zarš: *to be horrified*
zaršayamna: *ruffling one's feathers*
PK:445, KL:744

Persian
?

2258

11

همریشه: quiver

Indo-European
gwebh 2: *slime, sliminess, toad* — لجن ،لجنی ، وزغ
PK:466

Old Persian
gabawo: *toad*
PK:466

Persian
?

2259

12

Indo-European
gwelbh: *womb* — رحم
PK:473

Avestan
garewa: *womb*
garebuš: *young animal*
PK:473, KL:483

Persian
?

2260

13

همریشه: he, his, her

Indo-European
ki 2: *this* — این
PK:417,609, KL:710

Avestan
zî: *for, because, indeed*
nôit-zî:
KL:735, PK:417

Persian
?

2261

14

Indo-European
krei: *shine, glow, beauty* — درخشیدن، زیبایی
PK:618

Avestan
srî, srayan: *beauty*
srîra: *beautiful*
PK:618, KL:371

Persian
?

2262

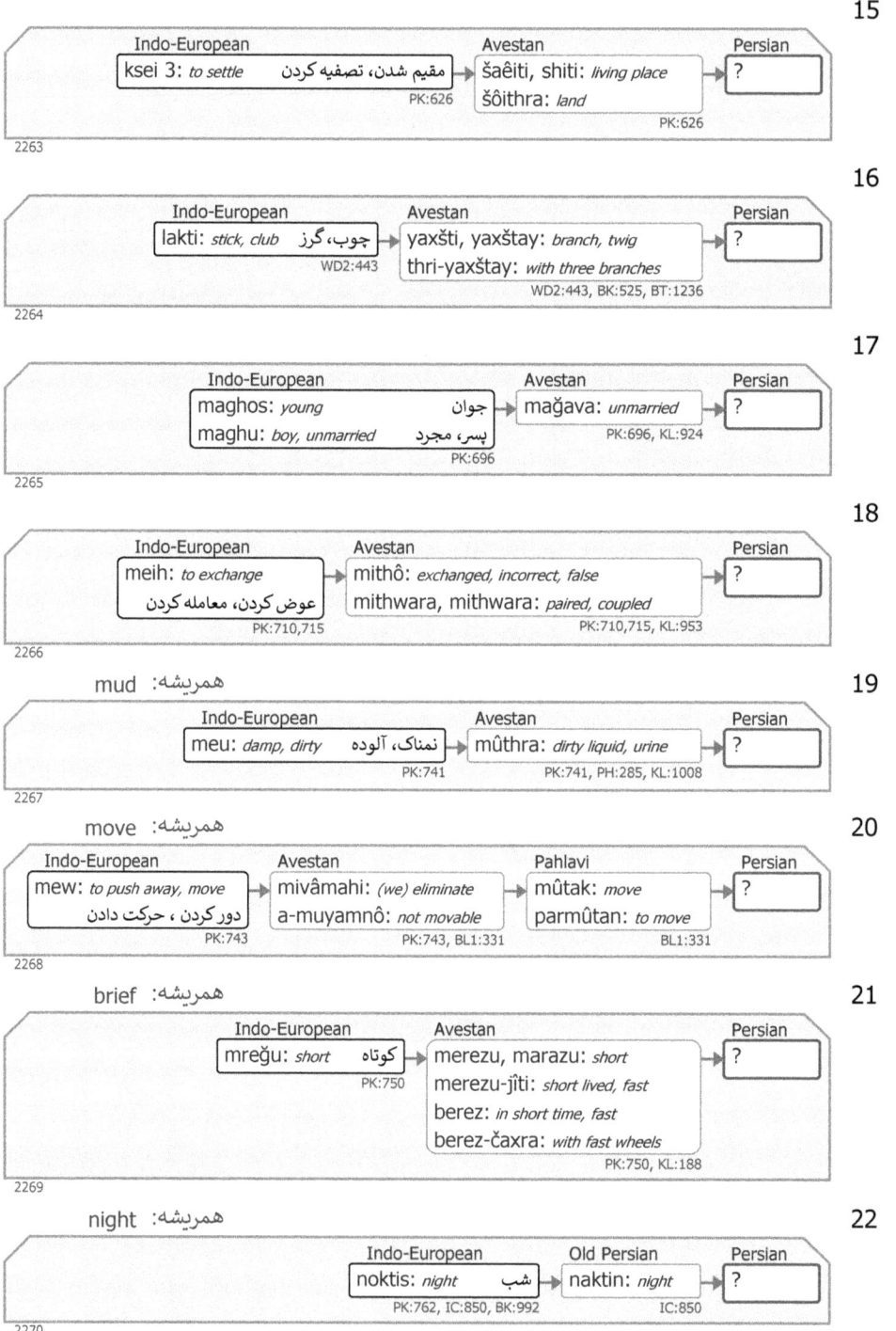

15

Indo-European
ksei 3: *to settle* — مقیم شدن، تصفیه کردن
PK:626

Avestan
šaêiti, shiti: *living place*
šôithra: *land*
PK:626

Persian
?

2263

16

Indo-European
lakti: *stick, club* — چوب، گرز
WD2:443

Avestan
yaxšti, yaxštay: *branch, twig*
thri-yaxštay: *with three branches*
WD2:443, BK:525, BT:1236

Persian
?

2264

17

Indo-European
maghos: *young* — جوان
maghu: *boy, unmarried* — پسر، مجرد
PK:696

Avestan
mağava: *unmarried*
PK:696, KL:924

Persian
?

2265

18

Indo-European
meih: *to exchange*
عوض کردن، معامله کردن
PK:710,715

Avestan
mithô: *exchanged, incorrect, false*
mithwara, mithwara: *paired, coupled*
PK:710,715, KL:953

Persian
?

2266

همریشه: mud

19

Indo-European
meu: *damp, dirty* — نمناک، آلوده
PK:741

Avestan
mûthra: *dirty liquid, urine*
PK:741, PH:285, KL:1008

Persian
?

2267

همریشه: move

20

Indo-European
mew: *to push away, move*
دور کردن ، حرکت دادن
PK:743

Avestan
mivâmahi: *(we) eliminate*
a-muyamnô: *not movable*
PK:743, BL1:331

Pahlavi
mûtak: *move*
parmûtan: *to move*
BL1:331

Persian
?

2268

همریشه: brief

21

Indo-European
mreğu: *short* — کوتاه
PK:750

Avestan
merezu, marazu: *short*
merezu-jîti: *short lived, fast*
berez: *in short time, fast*
berez-čaxra: *with fast wheels*
PK:750, KL:188

Persian
?

2269

همریشه: night

22

Indo-European
noktis: *night* — شب
PK:762, IC:850, BK:992

Old Persian
naktin: *night*
IC:850

Persian
?

2270

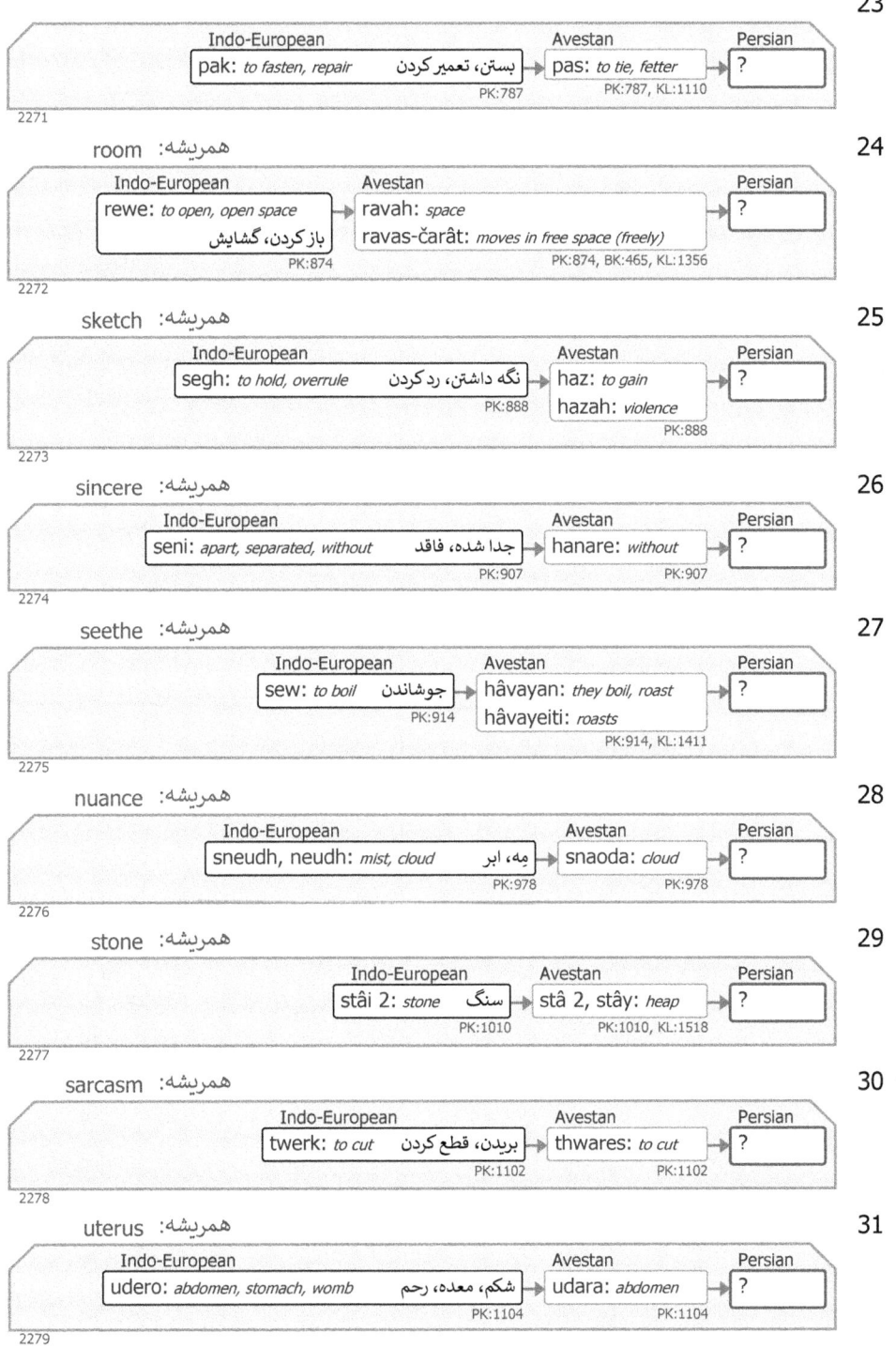

23

Indo-European
pak: *to fasten, repair* بستن، تعمیر کردن
PK:787

Avestan
pas: *to tie, fetter*
PK:787, KL:1110

Persian
?

2271

همریشه: room

24

Indo-European
rewe: *to open, open space* باز کردن، گشایش
PK:874

Avestan
ravah: *space*
ravas-čarât: *moves in free space (freely)*
PK:874, BK:465, KL:1356

Persian
?

2272

همریشه: sketch

25

Indo-European
segh: *to hold, overrule* نگه داشتن، رد کردن
PK:888

Avestan
haz: *to gain*
hazah: *violence*
PK:888

Persian
?

2273

همریشه: sincere

26

Indo-European
seni: *apart, separated, without* جدا شده، فاقد
PK:907

Avestan
hanare: *without*
PK:907

Persian
?

2274

همریشه: seethe

27

Indo-European
sew: *to boil* جوشاندن
PK:914

Avestan
hâvayan: *they boil, roast*
hâvayeiti: *roasts*
PK:914, KL:1411

Persian
?

2275

همریشه: nuance

28

Indo-European
sneudh, neudh: *mist, cloud* مه، ابر
PK:978

Avestan
snaoda: *cloud*
PK:978

Persian
?

2276

همریشه: stone

29

Indo-European
stâi 2: *stone* سنگ
PK:1010

Avestan
stâ 2, stây: *heap*
PK:1010, KL:1518

Persian
?

2277

همریشه: sarcasm

30

Indo-European
twerk: *to cut* بریدن، قطع کردن
PK:1102

Avestan
thwares: *to cut*
PK:1102

Persian
?

2278

همریشه: uterus

31

Indo-European
udero: *abdomen, stomach, womb* شکم، معده، رحم
PK:1104

Avestan
udara: *abdomen*
PK:1104

Persian
?

2279

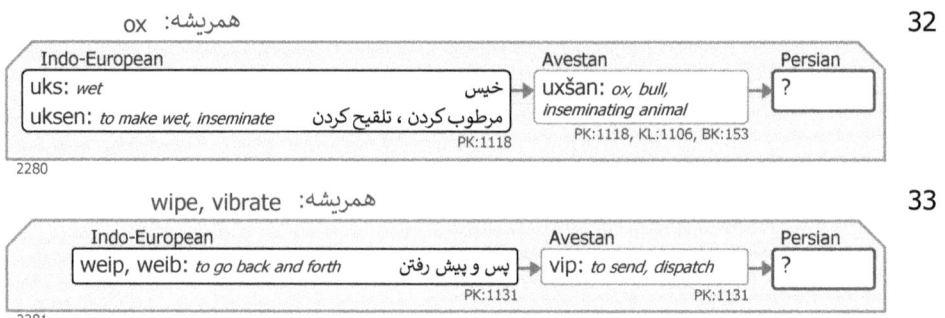

همریشه: ox

Indo-European

uks: *wet*
خیس

uksen: *to make wet, inseminate*
مرطوب کردن ، تلقیح کردن

PK:1118

Avestan

uxšan: *ox, bull, inseminating animal*

PK:1118, KL:1106, BK:153

Persian

?

2280

همریشه: wipe, vibrate

Indo-European

weip, weib: *to go back and forth*
پس و پیش رفتن

PK:1131

Avestan

vip: *to send, dispatch*

PK:1131

Persian

?

2281

فهرست ها

فهرست لغات در زبانهای مختلف

فهرست ریشه ها همراه بالغات
فارسی مشتق از آنها

Index of Words

Index of Words

Index of Words

Index of Words

Index of Words

Index of Words

Index of Words

A62

Index of Words

Index of Words

Index of Words

Index of Words

Index of Words

Index of Words

Index of Words

Index of Words

Index of Words

Index of Words

Index of Words

A50

Index of Words

Index of Words

Index of Words

Index of Words

Index of Words

Index of Words

Index of Words

Index of Words

Index of Words

Index of Words

Index of Words

Index of Words

Index of Words

Index of Words

Index of Words

Index of Words

Index of Words

Index of Words

Index of Words

Index of Words
in different Languages

xâč: *cross*

خاج

xad: *to beat*

آبخست, خَستن, خسته

xaf*: *cough*

خفیدن

xâk: *dust*

خاک, خاکستر

xalen: *birch tree*

خدنگ

xan: *ruler*

خان, خانم

xand: *laughter*

خنده

xand-ak > see xand

xapak: *suffocate*

خَتَک, خپه, خفه

xarmâ(v) > see armâv

xâz*: *fight*

پرخاش, خاش

xitai: *name of a tatar dynasty that ruled beijing 936-1122. they were from xitan*

ختن

xšad*: *to forgive*

بخشودن, بخشیدن۲

xšai*: *weep*

شیون

`xšnk: *nice*

قشنگ

xvaini: *cover*

خوان, خوانچه

xyâr: *cucumber*

خیار

---

yâ: *to be excited*

جادو, یاسه

yad*: *ask*

نیایش

yag: *to worship*

ایزد, جشن, مزدیسنا, یزد, یزدان, یزدگرد, یسنا, یشتن

yâma: *cup*

جام

yamb*: *to move*

جنبیدن

yantra: *tool*

جَندَره

yaš*: *to show appear*

آیشه, ایش, ایشه, نشان

yaska: *sickness*

جَسک

yau 1: *move*

جو۱, جوب, جوی, جوبار

yau* 2: *to separate*

جدا

yauj* > see yeu 1

yekwer: *liver*

جگر

yelek > see ijlak

yem: *hold together (pair)*

جم, جمشید, دشیاد, یاد

yes: *to boil*

جَستن, جهیدن, جوشیدن

yeu 1: *to join*

جُغ, جفت, جوغ, چفت, زوج, قسط, قسطاس, یوغ

yeu 2: *young*

جوان

---

yeu 3: *to mix*

جُستن, جوییدن, یوز, یوزپلنگ, یوزیدن

yeu 4 > see yau* 2

yôs: *to gird*

بارجامه, پاجامه, پیراهن, پیژامه, جامه, چمدان, زنّار, همیان

yu: *you*

شما

zauša: *raising a noise*

زوش

z.b.d: *to extract butter from milk*

زُبده

zgwes: *to extinguish*

زخم

zi: *to adorn*

دیبا, دیباج, دیبه, زَوار۲, زیب, زیبا, زیبنده, زیبیدن, زیور

zîk: *calendar*

زیگ

weik 1: *to shake*

آونگ, آویختن, آویز, انگیختن, انگیزه, بریزن, بیختن, بیز, بیزش, پرویزن, ویختن

weik 2: *clan*

ویلا

weis: *to rot*

بیش۱

wek: *to wish*

بَس, بسنده, بسیار, بیوسیدن, پیوسیدن, نابیوسان, هوس

wekw: *voice*

آوا, آواز, باج۲, بانگ, پَتواز, پژواک, خُنیا, فروختن, گواژه, گواژیدن, نوا۱۱, هوخت, واج, واژه, واک, وَخشور, وَنگ۲

wel 1: *to wish*

آری, آور, آوری, باور, شهریور, گرویدن

wel 2: *to tear*

آوار۱, بَرده, گُرس۱, گرگ, گرگان, والانه, ولانه

wel 3: *to turn*

بار۲, دربار, هموار, وار۲, وار۳, وَبَر

wem: *spit*

وامیدن, ومیدن

wema > see wem

wen: *to wish*

بُن۲, بنفش, بنفشه

wep: *to throw*

برف

wer 1: *to speak*

باور, فرمان, وَر

---

wer 2: *to turn*

برغ، برغاب, قرمز, کرم, کوپال, گِرد۲, گَرد۳, گردانیدن, گردن, گرده, گُرده, گردو, گردیدن, گشتن, گویال, نوردیدن, وَردنه, ورغ

wer 3: *to cover*

باره۲, بارو, برزن, برواره, بهرام, پروار, دیوار, فردین, فروار, فروردین, فَروَهَر, گیج, وار ۱, وهرام

wer 4 > see awe

wer 5: *to burn*

سماور

wer 6: *squirrel*

وَروَره

werd: *raised point*

werdh: *to grow*

بالیدن, گوال, گوالیدن, والا

weren: *lamb*

بَرّه, کلاغ, ورغنه

werg 1: *to work*

آلرژی, ارغنون, انرژی, بَرز, برزه گاو, ورز, ورزاو, ورزش, ورزیدن

werg 1: *nourished*

پروردن

werg 2 > see wer 3

wes 1: *wet*

اشتر, باه, خون, زرتشت, شتر

wes 2: *to buy*

بها

wes 3: *to wear*

آستر, ایوان, بام۲, بان۲, بانو, بهانه, پوست

wes 4: *eat*

واس, واستر, واستریوش, واش

---

wet: *year*

بچّه, بیطار

wetos > see wet

wi: *part*

بستر, بیدار, بیست, بیمار, جُناح, گ هِ, گُجسته, گداختن, گدار, گدازیدن, گذار, گذاردن, گذاشتن, گذر, گذشتن, گریختن, گریز, گزاردن, گزارش, گزند, گزیدن, گزیر, گزینش, گستاخ, گستردن, گستن, گسیختن, گسیل, گشادن, گماردن, گماشتن, گمان, گمیختن, گناه, گهولیدن, گوارا, گواردن, گوارش, گواژه, گواژیدن, گوال, گوالیدن, گواه, گوهریدن, ناگزیر, وجر, وچرگر, وزیر, ویراستن, ویرایش, ویشتاسپ

wiač: *to contain*

گنج, گنجایش, گنجیدن, ویرایش, ویشتاسپ

win: *wine*

وین

wôg > see aweg

wok: *to let go*

واخیدن

word: *thorn*

رُز۲, گل, گلبن, گلخن, گلشن, وَرد۲, وَل، ول, وُل, ولغونه

wortoko: *quail*

ودخین, وردیج

wrais* > see wreik

wreg: *to push*

گرازیدن

wreik: *to turn*

ابریشم, رشتن, رشته, ریسمان, ریسیدن, ریشتن

xac: *shine through*

کاچ, کاچی, کاشی

Roots of Persian Words

tulupos: *lump*

تُرُب

tund* > see Teud

tur > see tuer

turd: *hard*

تُرد

tuxš: *to be busy*

اهنوخوشی، تخشا، تخشیدن، هوتُخش

ul: *to go*

الغ

ulk: *wolf (with fiery eyes)*

تهمورث، روباه، گربه

ulkos > see ulk

umm: *mother*

اُمّ، اَمَل، اُمّی، خان، خانم، مُغیلان

uper > see upo

upo: *to*

آبسال، اَبر، ابرزین، امید، باور، باید، بَر۲، بردیه، برگستوان، برمنش، برهیختن، بَرواره، به، بیو، بیوگ، پچگم، پدید، پرویز، پسندیدن، پشگم، پگاه، زَبَر، فرزین

urigh: *rice*

اُرز، برنج۲، وریزه

urine > see čamiš

urmak: *to strike*

اردو

urmut > see amrôt

uroiks: *twist*

ریش۲، ریشه

urvan: *spirit*

انوشیروان، روان۲

vac: *frog*

تَک، وَک

vanjišk: *sparrow*

گنجشک

vant*: *an ownership suffix*

آوند۱، آوند۲، دماوند، وند

var: *to cover*

بَرم

varâza: *boar (animal)*

گراز، وُراز

vata: *small*

بَد، وَد

vâta: *popular*

قباد، کیقباد

vâtâm: *almond*

بادام

vatin-ganah: *eggplant*

بادنجان

vât-rang: *a kind of citrus plant*

بادرنگ، بالنگ

vitâra: *wood boards*

گداره

vîvâp: *without water*

بیابان

wâ: *to be empty*

وَنگ۱

wač > see wok

wai: *alas*

وای۱

wakâ > see wâka

wâka: *cow*

برزه گاو، ورزاو

war* > see wel 2

warš*: *to be hungry*

گُرس۲، گرسنه، گشنه

warz* > see werg 1

was* > see wek

wasama: *he marked*

اسم، سِمَت، موسم، وسمه

waxš* > see aweg

wd: *up*

آزمایش، آزمودن، اُزدودن، استردن، اِسکنه، اُشنان، اوج، زاب، زاهیدن، زدودن، زنودن، زنویه، زنویدن، زه، زهاب، زهدان، زهیدن، سپری، ستردن، ستوه، سگال، نَستوه

we > see wâ

wê: *to blow*

اندروا، باد، بادآس، نیروانا

webh: *to weave*

آبافت، آبفت، اَبفت، بافتن، وَبز

wed > see awe

wedh 1: *to marry*

بیو، بیوگ

wedh 2: *to slay*

گُوه

weg 1: *to weave*

واکس

weg 2: *to be lively*

باختن، بازنده، بازیدن، بزرگ، گرز

wegh: *to go*

باز۲، باشه، پرواز، واشه، وزیدن

wêğo: *lizard?*

بَزَغ، وَزَغ، وزغه

wegwh > see eueguh

wei 1: *to bend*

بید، بیشه

wei 2: *vital force*

بَر۱، بیر، ویر

weid: *to see*

اساطیر، اسطوره، اوستا، پژوهیدن، هویدا، ویدا

weidh: *to select*

بریزن، بیختن، بیز، بیزش، بیوه، پرویزن

A25

Roots of Persian Words

tât: *a suffix for making abstract nouns*

خرداد

tau*: *to throw*

پرت، پرتاب

tauj: *to gather*

اندوختن, اندوزیدن, توختن۲, دوختن۳

tâvant > see tâvat

tâvat: *so much*

تا, تک

taxra: *bitter*

تلخ

tebus: *side*

تو۲, سو, سوق, سوی

teig > see steig

tek: *to stretch*

پرداختن۲

teks: *to build from wood*

آرشیتکت, تاس, تخته, تراشیدن, تَش, تشت, تیشه, طاس

tekw: *to run*

انداختن, اندازه, پرداختن۱, تاختن, تازیانه, تازیدن, تخش, تکیدن, گداختن, مهندس, هم تک, هندسه

tel: *to lift*

اطلس, تراز, ترازو, طراز

tem: *dark*

تار۲, تاریک, تَم, تیره

temar: *he concealed*

مطموره

temh: *to be tired*

تاسیدن

---

ten 1: *to stretch*

آبستن, آختن, آنتن, آهختن, آهنجیدن, آهنگ, آهیختن, اخته, برهیختن, پشوتن, تابیدن۱, تار۱, تافتن۱, تَر۲, ترانه, تَن, تنافُر, تنافور, تنبل, تنش, تنفر, تُنُک, تَنیدن, توره, توله, فرهنگ, فرهیختن, فروهیختن, گیتار, ناهنجار, نفرت, نهنگ, هنج, هنجار, هنجیدن, هنگ, هیختن

ten 2: *to thunder*

تُندر

tenk: *to become firm and thick*

ترخینه, تلخینه, تنجیدن, تَنگ, تَهم, تهمتن, تهمورث, رُستم

tenu > see ten 1

tep: *to be warm*

آفتاب, پرتو, تاب, تابان, تابستان, تابش, تابه, تابیدن۲, تافتن۲, تب, تپیدن, تفت, تفسیدن, شتاب, شتافتن, مَه, مهتاب

ter 1: *to cross over*

اندر۲, پدراندر, پسراندر, تر۱, ترابری, ـ ترین, دختراندر, ـ سار۱, سرا, سُرادِق, سرای, کوهسار, گدار, گذار, گذاردن, گذاشتن, گذر, گذشتن, مادراندر

ter 2: *a kinship term*

آزرمیدخت, برادر, بیدخت, پدر, خواهر, داماد, دختر, ـ دُر, مادر, مادراندر, ماده, مادیان, ماکیان, مایه

ter 3: *to rub*

استردن, ستردن

terd: *to pierce*

افتالیدن, فتال

terp 2 > see ster 3

ters: *dry*

تراس, تشنه, مدیترانه

teter: *chatter*

تذرو

---

têu: *to swell*

تخم, تُند۲, تهماسب, توان, توبره, توده, توش, ثور, ستوه, طهماسب, مردم, نَستوه

Teud: *push*

تُند۱

teus: *empty*

تَه, تهی

thrah* > see tres

thranč* > see trenk

thwanj*: *to get*

الفاختن, الفنجیدن

tiegu: *to approach shyly*

سیج

tien: *store*

تیم, تیمچه

titi: *imitation of a bird song*

تیتو, طیطو

tôkei: *peacock*

طاووس

trei: *three*

سه, سوم, سی

trenk: *to compress*

تَرنجیدن

trep: *to tremble*

چابک, سبُک

tres: *to tremble*

ترسا, ترسیدن, سهستن, سهم, سهمناک

trp: *to satisfy*

تولف

tu: *you*

تو۱

tuer: *to hurry*

توریدن, تولیدن

tu-kûe: *strong people*

ترک, ترکمن

A24

steg: *to cover*

تاج, تاجور, تایر, تَجَر, تَزر

steig: *sharp*

ترکش, تیر, تیز, تیغ, دجله, دیاله, ستیز, ستیزه, کیش۲, کیش۳

ster 1: *to spread*

بستر, خاکستر, صراط, گستردن

ster 2: *star*

ستاره

ster 3: *stiff*

تُرش, تره, تریکو

ster 4: *barren*

استرلیزه, سَتروَن

sterp > see ster 3

steu 1: *to praise*

افدستا, خَستو۲, ستایش, ستاییدن, ستوان۱, ستودن

steu 2: *to push*

تباه

stewe: *to cluster*

توپ

stoigh: *to stride*

أُسطُقس

stomen: *mouth*

آستَم

storos: *a type of bird (sparrow?)*

سار۳

su 1: *well*

آلگوریتم, آناهیتا, آهو۲, اردیبهشت, انجیل, اهنوخوشی, اوستا, بَه, بهشت, بهمن, حور, خجسته, خُرّم, خُسُر, خسرو, خُسُرو, خُسوره, خشنود, خشو, خُنیا, خوارزم, خوب, خوش, داریوش, فُرات, کسرٰی, کیخسرو, گُشتای, ناهید, هُژیر, هما, همانا, همانند, همایون, هنر, هوتُخش, هوخت, هُوَخشتَر, هوشنگ, هومن, هویدا

su 2: *wild boar*

خوک, سفلیس

su(m)b > see keu 2

su(m)p*: *to beautify*

سفره

sub* > see su(m)p*

suîg: *jump*

خاستن, خزیدن, خیزیدن, رستاخیز

sukurna: *porcupine*

سُغُر, سُگُر

šûlaka: *wild horse*

شولک

summaq: *red*

سماق

sup > see rup

sure: *acid*

سرکه, سکنجبین

šurmênu: *cypress tree*

سَرو

sust: *soft*

سُست

svas: *thresh*

خُست, خُوست

swâd: *sweet*

خواستن, خواهش, خوای

swei: *to bend*

شیبا, شیوا

sweid: *to sweat*

خوی, خیساندن, خیو, خیوه

swekwo: *resin*

اپیون, افیون

swel: *to eat*

آبخور, آخُر, آخور, خوردن, خَوَرنَق, خورنگاه

swen: *to sound*

آخوند, افغان, خنیدن, خواندن, فغان

swep: *to sleep*

بَختَک, خسبیدن, خُفتَک, خُفتَن, خَفج, خفسیدن, خواب

swer: *to press*

خاراندن, خَستن, خسته, خلبان, خَله, خَلیدن, خوره۱

swerd: *dirty*

خوال

syndochion > see sndochion

šypšyr > see šfšyr

šypwr: *trumpet*

شیپور

tabaco: *a pipe for smoking*

تنباکو

tabrak: *ax*

تبر

tabûrâk: *a drum*

تنبور, طبل

tač* > see tek

tâl: *to grow*

تالار

tâl: *to grow*

تالار

talk: *a mineral*

تالک, طلق

tamh* > see temh

tanûr: *fire*

تنور

tar > see ter 2

tarê: *to humiliate*

تَر۳, تردامن, تردست, ترمنش

targumânu: *interpreter*

ترجمه

tarp: *to lie*

تَرفند, تروند

A23

Roots of Persian Words

skaivos: *sinister*	**snaithiš**: *weapon*	**spinakion**: *spinach*
شوخ	سَتی	اسیناخ, اسفناج
skand 1: *to climb*	**sndochion**: *shelter*	**spiš**: *an insect*
اسکله	صندوق	شپش
skand 2: *to break*	**sneigwh**: *snow*	**spongo**: *fluffy*
شکستن	سنهر	اسفنج, سپنج
skarf: *to stumble*	**so**: *this*	**spyeu**: *to spit*
شکرفیدن	او, ایشان, که	تُف, تفنگ
skarna > see sukurna	**soffeh**: *seat*	**srau*** > see kleu 1
sked: *to cover*	صُفّه	**srêno**: *thigh*
چادر, چتر	**solo**: *whole*	ران
skel: *bent*	جائلیق, خرداد, هر	**sresk**: *to drip*
شَکپوی, شَل, شَلپوی, شلنگ, شلوار, قولنج, قولون, گل	**sophos**: *skilled*	سرشک
	سفسطه, فلسفه, فیلسوف	**sreu** > see ser 1
sker 1: *to turn*	**šôšen**: *lotus*	**srgâla**: *howler*
کران, کنار	سوسن	شغال, شکال, شگال
sker 2 > see ker 2	**spek**: *to look*	**srîra**: *satisfied*
skeu > see keu 3	اسقف, پاس, پاسبان, سپاس, سکوبا	سیر۱
skêu: *to sneeze*		**srisâ**: *file*
اشنوسه, سنوسه, شنوشه	**spelgh**: *spleen*	اژه
skeud: *to throw*	سپُرز	**sru**: *lead (metal)*
پژوهیدن, چُست	**spen** > see pend	سرب
skhai: *to cut*	**sper**: *sparrow*	**srva** > see sru
چیلان, چیلنگر, سمنت, سیمان, قیصر	پرستو, سار۳	**stâ**: *to stand*
	spereg: *to swell*	آستان, آشتی, ارتش, اِستاخ, استاد, استاک, استان, استاندارد, استخر, استوانه, اسطبل, اوستام, اوستان, ایستادن, بغستان, بیستون, پرستار, پرستیدن, پشت, تابستان, رستوران, ساس۱, سِتاک, ستان, سُتُرگ, ستم, ستور, ستون, سکا, سیستان, شبستان, فرستادن, فرشته, فغستان, گستاخ
skordh: *small*	اسپرغم, اسپرود, اسفراج, اسفرود, شاه اسپَرَم	
خُرد		
s.k.r: *he ridiculed*	**sphallein**: *cause to fall*	
ماسک	آسفالت, اسفالت, زفت	
sku: *to cover*	**sphê**: *long flat piece of wood*	
خود۲, سکوره, کاز, کازه, کلاهخود, کوچ	فَه, فیه	
skweht*: *tremble*	**sphel**: *to split*	**stâi**: *to steal*
چندش	سپار, سپر	ستادن
smer > see mer 1	**spher**: *move*	**stebh**: *support*
snâ: *to flow*	آتمسفر, اسپهر, سپاردن, سپردن, سپری, سپهر	استبرق, استبرک, استوار, استوان۲, ستبر, ستنبه, سُتوان۲
أشنان, شنا	**spheud** > see peud	

Roots of Persian Words

ریشهٔ لغات فارسی

salîbâ: *cross*

چلیپا، صلیب

sam: *summer*

هامین، همین

sam*: *to agree*

سامه

šamšêr > see šfšyr

sapz: *green*

سبز

saq: *sack*

ساک

sarâpu: *to melt*

صرّاف

sâsân: *dervish*

ساسان

šâturvân: *carpet*

شادُروان

saus: *dry*

خشک، خوشیدن

šavala: *(a fabric) marked with colors*

شال۱، شال۲، شالنگ

sâwel: *sun*

جربا، خاور، خراسان، خور، خورشید، خَوَرَه۲، فَر، قَرْبُد، فریبود، فَرّخ، فرخُنده، فرزاد، فرشاد، فرشید، فرناز، فریبرز، نُهور، هاله، هور، هوربان

scetka: *counter*

چرتکه

s.d.a`: *to split*

سدیم، صداع

sê: *to sift*

سطل

sed: *to sit*

آهسته، پسندیدن، خرسند، نخست، نزد، نزدیک، نشستن، نَشیم، نشیمن، هدیش

šedû: *devil*

شیدا، شیطان

seiku: *to flow*

بشنجیدن، پشنجیدن، خیساندن

seip: *to pour out*

صابون

seks: *six*

شانزده، شیش، شَصت

sekw: *to follow*

از، اسکناس، سجلّ، سقرلات، شاگرد، هخامنش

selh: *to earn*

گهولیدن، گوهریدن

selp: *fat*

چرب

sem: *same*

اکباتان، اگر، ان ـ ۱، انبار، انباز، انباشتن، انباغ، انبوه، انجام، انجمن، انجوخ، انجوختن، انجوغ، انجیدن، انداختن، اندازه، اندام، اندرز، اندوختن، اندودن، اندوزیدن، اندوه، اندیشیدن، انگردن، انگاشتن، انگم، انگیختن، انگیزه، پُر، توختن۲، دوختن۳، سماور، مگر، مهندس، نگرش، نگریدن، نگریستن، هامون، هرگز، هم، هم تک، همال، همان، همدان، همه، هموار، همیان، هُنام، هندسه، هنگام، وار۲

sêma: *marked*

سیم۲، هنگام، وار۲

sêmi: *half*

نیم

sen 1: *to prepare*

افندی

sen 2: *old*

آنا، سنا، هان

senh > see sen 1

---

ser 1: *to flow*

رَم، رمه، رمیدن، رود۱، روضه، رون، سیرُم، هرات

ser 2: *to protect*

زنهار، زنیهار، هرکول

ser 3: *to line up*

سیری، هار

sernh > see srisâ

sês: *moth*

سوس

seu 1: *self*

خدا، خدیو، خو، خواجه، خواهر، خود۱، خوش، ناخدا

seu 3: *to give birth*

رود۲

s.f.r: *(to be) yellow*

زعفران

šfšyr: *sword*

شمشیر

sighr: *garlic*

سیر۲

šikênjak: *torture*

شکنجه

sik-ke: *detail of the house entrance*

سگّو

sinkadruš: *the red ore of mercury (mercuric sulfide) used as a pigment*

زنجرف، شنگرف

sîp: *apple*

سیب

skabh: *to support*

پچگم، پشگم

skai: *shining*

چهره، سایه، منوچهر، هُژیر

skaip: *to wait*

شکیبا، شکیبیدن

pûlâfat: *steel* پولاد	rauh*: *to pluck* رودن	reudh: *red* روناس, روی۲, رویگر, رویین
pûlâft > see pûlâfat	raup 1: *to sweep away* جاروب, رُفتن, روبیدن, لای	reug: *to vomit* آروغ, رُغ
pulâka: *ball of rice* پلو	raup 2 > see leup	reuğmen: *oil* روغن
purgos: *tower* برج	rauxšn* > see leuk	reuto: *intestines* اشکم, روده, شکم
pwt: *Buddha* بُت	rauž*: *to please* آرزو, ریز۱, ریژ	rezg: *to plait* رَغزه
pyrgos > see purgos	raxš > see lakš	r.f.a': *to repair* رفو
qâter: *smoke* سِدر	raz* > see redh	rk-tho: *bear (animal)* آرشام, ارشام, خرس
qirbah: *a leathern bottle* قَراب, قَرابه	redh: *to escape* راز, رستگار, رَستن, رهیدن, وارستن	rôspîk: *prostitute* روسپی
qirrâbah > see qirbah	reg 1: *straight* آدرس, آرازش, افراختن, افراز, افراشتن, راست, رج, رده, رزم, رژه, رژیم, ریال, فرازیدن	rup: *shoulder* سُفت
q.l.y: *to roast in a pan* قلیا, قلیه	reg 2: *to dye* آبزنجن, افرنگ, اورنجن, اورنگ, رَجیدن, رزیدن, رنگ, لاک	r.z.m: *to bundle up* رزمه
rabba: *to be great* تربیت, رَبّ, رُب, مربّا, مربّی, مربّا	rei 1: *possession* راد, رای	šabatu: *to cut* سَبْت, شنبه
ragâ: *city of "ray" in the south of tehran.* رازق, رازگی, رازی, ری	rei 2: *to hurt* ریز۲, ریزه, ریش۱	sač > see kak 1
rağâ > see ragâ	rek: *to tie* رَسَن	sâd > see sked
raič* > see leigh 2		sâen: *to be late* هاسر
raika: *sand* ریگ	rekph > see raš*	sâi: *to bind* سِتَور, گشادن, ویشتاسپ
raip > see leip	rem: *to rest* آرام , آرامش, آرمیدن, پدرام, خُرَم, رام, رامش, رامین, شهرام	saka: *an Aryan tribe in Iran* ساس۱, سکا, سیستان
raiš* > see rei 2	rêp: *to crawl* ترویج, رایج, رَفتن, روا, رواج, روان۱, روش, روند	sakah: *teak wood* ساج
raj* > see reg 2	resg > see rezg	salamandra: *salamander* سمندر
rand*: *to scrape* رندیدن, رنده	ret: *to roll* اَرابه, اَرابه, ارتش, اسپریس, ترهّات, راه, راهب, رایگان, رده, رژه, میزراه	šâli: *grains* چلتوک, شالی, شالیزار, شَلتوک
raš*: *to harm* رَشیدن	rêu: *to cry* لُئندیدن	
raub > see leubh		
rauč* > see rauž*		
raud 2 > see leudh		
raud* 1 > see rêu		

pel 1: *to fill*

اُباردن, اُباشتن, انبار, انباشتن, اوباردن, اوباش, برنا, پُر, پروین, تنافر, تنافور, تنبل, تنفر, فراوان, فِره, فَهَرست, نفرت

pel 2: *pale*

پارسا, پیر

pel 3: *dust*

باروت, پودر

pelpel: *butterfly*

پروانه

pend: *twist*

پینه

penkwe: *five*

پنج

pent: *to go*

پند, فَن, فندق

per 1: *around*

تَدَرزه, برقوق, بشنجیدن, پار, پارسال, پالیز, تَدَرزه, پراکندن, پرت، پرتاب, پرتو, پرچین, پرداختن۱, پرداختن۲, پردیس, پرستار, پرستیدن, پرگار, پَرگنه, پَرماسیدن۱, پَرماسیدن۲, تَرزندوش, پرواز, پرواز, پروردن, تَریر, پریروز, پژمردن, پشت, پشنجیدن, پیار, پیراستن, پیرامون, پیراهن, پیرایه, پیروز, جالیز, فرا, فرارون, فرامرز, فربه, فرجام, فردوس, فردین, فرزانه, فرزند, فرستادن, فرشته, فرغار, فرغاریدن, فرغر, فرغردن, فرغن, فرغنده, قَرفَر, فرمان, فرهنگ, فرهیختن, فرو, قَروار, فروتن, فروختن, فرود, فروردین, فَروَهَر, فروهیختن, فریاد, فریرون, فلاخن, فیرون

per 2: *to lead or fly across.*

بار۳, بَر, تَرند, پرنیان, پریدن, پُل, فُرات, فرغر, فرغردن, فرغن, فرغنده, قَرفَر, فرمان, فرهنگ, فرهیختن, فرو, قَروار, فروتن, فروختن, فرود, فروردین, فَروَهَر, فروهیختن, فریاد, فریرون, فلاخن, فیرون

per 3: *oppose*

آورد, بادافره, بُد, بد, بدرود, بند, به, بیغاره, بیوسیدن, پ - , پاداش, پادافره, پادزهر, پاسخ, پَتَّت, پَتواز, پتیاره, پدرام, پدرود, پذیرفتن, پذیره, پرهیختن, پرهیز, پژمان, پژوهیدن, پشیمان, پنهان, پیاله, پیام, پیچ, پیچیدن, پیدا, پیش, پیشانی, پیشوا, پیکان, پیکر, پیغاله, پیغام, پیکار, پیکان, پیکر, پیمان, پیمانه, پیمودن, پیوستن, پیوسیدن, دُرود۲, فَرُبُد, فربود, نابیوسان, نبرد, نهادن, نهان

per 4: *to give*

پاره, نهادن, نهان

perd: *speck*

پارد, پارس۲, پاشیدن, پلنگ, یوزپلنگ

perk 1 : *to ask*

بادافره, پادافره, پرسیدن

perk 2: *rib*

پهلو۱

pers > see perd

persna: *heel*

پاشنه

pestêno: *breast*

پستان

pet 1: *to fly*

افتادن, پَتَّر, پَست, گَسَک, گَشَک, گَشَکرک

pet 2: *to spread*

پهن

peu: *to purify*

پاک

peud: *to press*

پو, پود, پویا, پوییدن, پوییدن, تکاپو

peuk: *to prick*

سپوختن۱, سپوختن۲, سپوزگار, سپوزیدن

pikho > see piko

piko: *lump*

پیختن

pilo: *hair*

پیله

pin: *wood*

پَنگان, فنجان

pippalî: *pepper*

پلپل, فلفل

plat > see paita

pliza: *metal*

فلز

plou: *flea*

پشه

pô: *to drink*

پاتیل, نَبید, نَبیذ

pod > see ped

pôl : *to touch*

پالیدن۲, سنتور

pôu: *small*

آبستن, پسر, پور, پوران, فغفور, نیشابور

prî: *to love*

آفریدن, آفرین, عفریته, فری

pu 1: *to blow*

پوک

pu 2: *to decay*

پوده, پوسیدن

puk 1: *bundled together*

بَساک, پَساک

puk 2: *puff*

پُف

Roots of Persian Words

ریشه لغات فارسی

nizâr: *weak*	**ost**: *bone*	**parth**: *the name of a tribe in khorâsân who rose to power and pushed the greeks out of iran in 250 bc.*
نزار	است۲, استخوان, خستو۱, هسته	
nobh: *nave*	**ôus 1**: *ear*	
ناف, نافه	آشکار, انوشه, انوشیروان, گر, گوش, گوشواره, نغوشا, نغوشیدن, نوش, نوشین, نیوشیدن, هشومند, هوش۱, هوشمند, هوشیار	پارت, پهلبُد, پَهلُو۲, پهلوی
nôğ: *whim*		**parti > see parth**
ناز, نازک		**parvan**: *knot*
nogh: *nail*		پاپژ, پَژ, پژواک
ناخن	**ôus 2**: *mouth*	**pâšin > see pâcin**
nogw: *naked*	زاب, زاهیدن, زه۲, زهاب, زهدان, زهیدن	**pati-daiza**: *to gather*
برهنه, ژیمناستیک, نَغام	**ozgho**: *branch*	پاییز
nomn: *name*	ازغ, ازگ۱, ازم	**pauk > see puk 2**
دشنام, نام نامه	**pa**: *to protect*	**paus***: *to dress*
noxvat: *pea*	آباد, آبادان, آذربایجان, اردوان, استوان۲, باب۲, بابا, بابک, بان۱, برگستوان, بطریق, پادشاه, پاده, پالایش, پالودن, پالوده, پالونه, پالیدن۱, پایستن, پاینده, پاییدن, پدر, پناه, پناه, پهره, چوپان, جربا, دریان, سُتوان۲, سروان, شبان, فالوده, گریبان, گریوه, میزبان, نهفتن, نوا۲, هوریان	**payda**: *to spread*
نخود		بیرق
nukar: *comrade*		**pe > see pô**
نوکر		**ped**: *foot*
n.w.r: *to shine*		پا, پاپژ, پاجامه, پای, پایین, پَل, پی, پیاده, پیژامه, پیک, دارابزین, زرافه, قالب, کالا, کالب, کالبد, کالیر
منار, نار, نور		
nyâka: *grand parent*	**pâcin**: *male goat*	**peg**: *breast*
نیا, نیاکان	پازن	پنکه
oies: *pole*	**pad-**: *duck*	**peî**: *sap*
خیش, خیشکار	بَط	انگ۲, انگبین, پنیر, په, پینو, پیه, دُژپیه, دُشپیل, دُشپیه, دُمَل, دنبل, سکنجبین, فربه, گزانگبین
ôku: *swift*	**pais**: *crush*	
آهو۱, گَستک, گَشک, گَشکرک	پست	
om: *raw*	**paita**: *to spread*	**peig**: *to mark*
خام	پرده, فراخ	پیسه, پیشه, نُبی, نوشتن
ome: *to move with energy*	**parîkâ**: *sweet heart*	**peis > see pais**
آرشام, ارشام	بلقیس, پری	**pek**: *wool*
ong > see ang	**parrak**: *step*	پشم, چوپان, شبان, فئودال
op: *work*	پله	
خوب	**pârsa**: *name of an Aryan (indo-european) tribe who migrated to Persia (iran) about 4000 years ago.*	**pekw**: *to cook*
opop: *a bird sound*		ابا, با, برقوق, بیسکویت, پختن, پز, پَزیدن, شوریا, نانوا, وا
پوپک, پوپو		
orghi: *testicle*		
ارکیده	پارس۱, پاسارگاد, پشملبا, فارس	
oruza > see ariza		

A18

mûk: *pile*	ndheros > see ndhos	nemata: *straw*
موک	ndhos: *under*	نمد
mûm: *wax*	زیر	nembh > see nebh
موم، مومیا	ne 1: *no*	nepôt: *grandson*
mûrâ: *seal*	آ ـ ۲، آزرمیدخت، آسفالت، آن ـ	ح، ص، ض، نَبَس، نبیره، نوه
مُهر، مُهره	۱، آناهیتا، آهو۲، ۱، اتُم،	ner 1: *vital energy*
mus > see mû	اسفالت، الماس، امرداد،	اسکندر، نر، نریمان، نیرو، هنر
nâ: *to help*	امشاسپند، ان ـ ۲، انکار، انوشه،	ner 2: *to turn*
پناه	انوشیروان، انیر، انیران۱، انیران۲،	نرگس
nabatu: *to shine*	برنا، خَشن، خشیسار، خشین،	nes: *to join*
نفت، نفتالین	سایه، ستوه، عفریته، مرداد، نا،	ناووس
nabja: *beak*	ناب، ناهید، نَستوه، نغام، نقره،	neu: *to cry*
نوک، نول	نوش، نوشین، نیست	زنودن، زنویه، زنوبیدن، نالیدن،
naêza: *sharp point*	ne 2: *our*	نوا۳، نوسته، نُوبیدن، نوبه
نیزه	ما	newn: *nine*
nagan: *bread*	nebh: *cloud*	نُه، نَود، نوزده
نان، نانوا	ابر، ابرآمون، نفت، نم، نمک	newo: *new*
nağan > see nagan	ned: *to bind*	اکنون، کنون، نو، نوباوه، نون
namra: *soft*	نُسخه، نُسک	nî: *down*
نرم، نَمرَق	nedo: *reed*	پنهان، نبرد، نُبی، نژند، نشان،
nana: *a child word for*	زرّافه، سرنا، سرنای، کارنای، کُرنا،	نشستن، نشیب، نَشیم، نشیمن،
mother	نارد، ناردین، نال، نای، نی	نغوشا، نغوشیدن، نَکاس، نگار،
ننه	nei 1: *to shine*	نگاردن، نگه، نگون، نما، نمایش،
naranga: *orange tree*	آبنیک، انبیق، رونق، رونیک،	نماینده، نمودار، نمودن، نمونه،
نارنج، نارنگ	ثَرد۱، نیشابور، نیک، نیل، نیلوفر،	نهادن، نهان، نهفتن، نهنگ،
nârikelah: *coconut*	نیو اردشیر	نوردیدن، نوشتن، نیاز، نیازی، نیام،
نارگیل	nei 2: *to lead*	نیایش، نیوشیدن، وَردَنه
nas: *nose*	نما، نمایش، نماینده، نمودار،	nîc: *also*
بینی، نُس	نمودن، نمونه	نیز
nâs > see nas	nek: *to destroy*	nîrang: *a Zoroastrian*
nask: *twist*	برناس، جُناح، فَرناس، گناه، نَسا	*religious ceremony*
نخ	nêkš: *to pierce*	نیرنگ
nau: *boat*	کارد، گرت، نَشگِرده، نیش، نیشتر،	nis: *off*
ناخدا، ناو، ناو یدن، ناودان، ناوَک،	نیشدر	نبروانا
ناوگان، ناوه	neku: *to reach*	nitiru: *natron; carbonate*
n.b.b: *to make hollow*	آسیدن	*of soda*
انبوب، باب۱، بابِل	nem 1: *to assign*	نطرون
	ناموس، نماز، نمره	ni-vaedh-ayeni: *i inform*
	nem 2: *to bend*	نوید
	نماز	

Roots of Persian Words

mauča: *banana*

موز

maud* > see moudh

maug*: *to err*

آسموغ, آشموغ

maz*: *to break*

ماز

mazaxa > see madhaxa

mazut: *black oil*

مازوت

me 1: *to measure*

آرمئیتی, آزمایش, آزمودن, آسمان, آمادن، آماده, آرمَتی, پَرماسیدن۲, پیمان, پیمانه, پیمودن, فرمان, کُمُد, مان۱, مانستن, ماندن, ماه, مَه, مهتاب, مهشید, نما, نمایش, نماینده, نمودار, نمودن, نمونه, همانا, همانند

me 2: *me*

من۱

mê 3: *no*

مَ ـِ

medhyo: *middle*

میان

meg: *great*

مزنا, مِه۲, مِهست

mehdhu: *honey*

مُل, مَنج, می

mei 1: *soft*

مایده, میزبان, مَیَزد

mei 2: *to fix*

میخ, میخک

mei 3: *to go*

سَمت

mei 4: *to bind*

مِهر, میترا

mei 5 > see mai* 1

mei 6 > see mai* 2

meig: *to mix*

آمیختن, آمیزش

meigh 1: *to sprinkle*

گمیختن, میختن, میز, میزراه

meigh 2: *to blink*

مژگان, مژه, مه۱, میغ

meit 1: *to stay*

مهمان, میهمان, میهن۱

meit 2: *to throw*

میهن۲

mel 1: *black*

خیال, مالیخولیا

mel 2: *small*

مار

mel 3: *soft*

مرهم, ملغم

mêlg: *to wipe off*

آمرزیدن, پَرماسیدن۱, فرامرز, مالیدن, مُرز۲, مُشت۲, مُشتن

men 1: *to think*

اسپندارمذ, اسفندارمذ, اهریمن, اهورا, اهورامزدا, اورمزد, ایرمان, برمنش, بهمن, پژمان, پشیمان, دُژم, دُژمان, دُژوان, دشمن, سپندارمذ, سفندارمذ, قهرمان, کهرمان, گمان, . مان۳, مان۳, منش, مزدیسنا, مزقان, موزیک, موسیقی, مینا, مینو, نریمان, هخامنش, هرمز, هورمزد, هومن

men 2: *to remain*

امید, ماندن

menth 1: *mouth*

مصطکی

menth 2: *to turn*

.مند

mer 1: *to remember*

آمار, شماره, شمردن, گماردن, گماشتن, مَر, هَمار

mer 2: *to rub away*

امرداد, امشاسپند, بیمار, پژمردن, خاموش, فراموش, فراموشیدن, کیومرث, مار, مرد, مرداد, مردم, مردن, مرگ, مَرمَر, مشیا, مشیانه, مُل

mereğa: *a large bird*

سیمرغ, شاهین, مُرغ۱

merg: *mark*

مرز۱

merg: *mark*

مرز۱

merk: *to take*

گمرک

meug: *wet*

مفت

meuk 1: *scratch*

مشت۱

meuk 2: *stocking*

پیموزیدن, موزه, موق

miždho: *reward*

مُزد, مزدور, مژده

mô > see môdh

môdh: *hair*

مو, موی

moisos: *sheepskin*

مَشک, مَشکو, میش

morwi: *ant*

مور, مورچه, موریانه

moudh: *to mourn*

مُست۲, مُستمند, مویه, موییدن

mozgo: *marrow*

مزغ, مغز

mu: *a mouse*

ماهیچه, مُشک, مِشک, مِشکی, موش

mû: *fly*

مگس

Roots of Persian Words

lehk > see lek 1

lêi: *slime*

لای

leig: *to leap*

آلیختن, آلیز, آلیزیدن, لزگی
(رقص), لی لی (بازی)

leigh 1: *to lick*

اُشنه, لِشتن, لیسیدن

leigh 2: *leave*

آبریز, اِبریق, پرهیختن, پرهیز,
خسوف, ریختن, کسوف, گریختن,
گریز

leip: *to smear with oil*

ریو, ریوه, فریب, فریا, فریفتن

leith: *to go forth*

رستاخیز

lek 1: *joint*

لِنگ

lek 2: *to leap*

لگد

leng > see longos

lep: *soft*

لابه, لاف

lêsos: *place*

لاخ

letro: *skim*

لَت

leu: *to smear*

آلاییدن, آلودن, اندودن, پالایش,
پالودن, پالوده, پالونه, پالیدن۱,
فالوده

leubh: *to grow mad and be afflicted with love*

آلوفتن

leudh: *to grow*

حور, رز۱, رُستم, رُستن, روستا,
روضه, رونق, رونیک, روی۱,
روییدن

leuh > see rauh*

---

leuk: *light*

آذرخش, آرش, افروختن, انیران۲,
درخش, درخشیدن, درفش۱,
دیروز, رازق, رخش, رخشان,
رخشیدن, رزق, روز, روزن, روزنه,
روشن, کیارش

leup: *to break*

ریودن, کهربا

liginnu: *a pot for measuring wheat*

لگن

limû: *lemon*

لایم, لیمو, لیموناد

lithra: *a scale*

رطل

lohrk: *weasel*

راسو

lonče > see lonche

lonche: *lance*

رُمح

longos: *limp*

لَنگ

lrǧ: *to tremble*

لرزیدن

lubbu: *cowpea*

لوبیا

mâ: *breast*

مادر, مادراندر, ماده, مادیان,
ماکیان, مامان, مایه, ممه

mač* > see maič*

mad: *wet*

ماست, ماسیدن, ماغ, ماهی,
مست۱, مَسکه

madhaxa: *grasshopper*

ملخ, میگ, میگو

maêkva: *fruit*

میوه

maǧa: *hole*

مَغ۲, مغاک

---

magh: *might*

مجوس, مُغ, مَغ۱, منجنیق,
منجنیک, موبد

maǧnêtes: *magnet*

مغناطیس

maǧšîsa: *stone*

مرقشیشا

mai* 1: *to change*

آوام, فام۲, وام

mai* 2: *to harm*

گم

maič*: *to suck*

ماچ, مزه, مزیدن, مکیدن

maiša* > see moisos

mait* 1 > see meit 1

mait* 2 > see meit 2

mako: *house fly*

مگس

mana: *an ancient unit of weight*

من۲

mantil: *cloak*

مندیل

mareǧâ: *grass*

مَرغ۲, مرغزار

marga-ahri-ita: *"born from shell"*

مرجان, مروارید

marz? > see mêlg

mâš: *a kind of bean*

ماش

masgdâ: *place of worship*

مزکت, مسجد

mat: *ick*

آماج

mauč*: *to learn*

آموختن

Roots of Persian Words

ریشه لغات فارسی

kû 1: to burn (also firewood)

قالب، قفقاز، کالا، کالب، کالبد، کالیر

kû 2: spike

سوزن، سوک۲، سوگ۲

kuâtos: straw

کاه۱، کهربا

kuei: white

اسپهر، سپهر، سپید، سفید

kulanjâ: a plant (alpina galanga)

خلنج، خلنگ

kund: blunt

گند۱، گند۲، گنداور، گندی، گنداور

kung: corner

گنج

kûp: to smoke

گی

kupriti: sulfur

کبریت

kur > see ker 5

kûr: dark

کور

kûrb > see gûrb

kurkana > see kurkanû

kurkanû: saffron

گرگم

kurkizannu: rhinoceros

گرگ، کرگدن

kut: small

کوتاه، کوچک، کودک

kwal: a big fish

گرو

kwei 1: to pay back

کین

kwei 2: to collect

انجیدن، پرچین، پیچ، پیچیدن، توختن۱، چیدن، چینه۱، گزیدن، گزیر، گزینش، ناگزیر

kweis*: to assign

کیش۱

kwek: to appear

آگاه، چاشت، چاشنی، چشم، چشیدن، گواه، ناگاه، نَکاس، نگاه

kwel: to move around

بازار، بازرگان، جال، چالاک، چالش، چالیدن، جَرا، چرخ، چریدن، چلیدن، .زار۳، طلسم، کارزار، کاشتن، کالسکه، کشاورز، کشیدن، گزاردن، گزارش، واچار

kwem: to swallow

آشامیدن، چمان۲، چمانه، چمیدن۲، کام۲

kwen: holy

اسپنتا، اسپند، اسپندارمذ، اسفند، اسفندارمذ، اسفندیار، افسنتین، امشاسپند، سپنتا، سپندارمذ، سفندارمذ، گوسفند

kwer: to do

آهنگر، افگار، انگاردن، انگاشتن، پرگار، پیکر، - جرد، چار، چاره، دارابگرد، سگال، شاگرد، شکار، شگردن، فگار، قهرمان، کار۱، کاریدن، کردن، کهرمان، گر۲، گزیدن، گزیر، گزینش، گوارا، گواردن، گوارش، لاجورد، لشگر، ناگزیر، نقره، نگار، نگاردن، نگرش، نگریدن، نگریستن، وچر، وجرگر، وزیر، یزدگرد

kwermi > see wer 2

kwes: to pant

شُش، هوا

kwetwer: four

چَتوَر، چهار، چهارم، چهل، دارابزین، شترنک، شطرنج، قرنطینه، کادر، کترنگ

kweye: quiet

آشیانه، شاد

kwo: stem of interrogative and relative pronouns

ایچ، چگونه، چند، چه، چون، چی، چیز، کَس، کو، کی۱، کی۲، هیچ

kwon: dog

سگ، قناری

kwri: to buy

خریدن

kwsep: darkness

شام، شب، شبدیز، شبستان

lâ: roots of sound words including animal crys

لال۱، لالا، لالایی

ladunu: resin of a certain tree

لادن

lâiô: roar

لاییدن

lâjîn: name of a Turkish tribe

لاجورد

lak: to tear

لَت

lakš: to protect

لشگر

lal 1 > see lâ

lalla > see lâ

lanğ: to droop

رنج

lap-aro > see lep

laqalaqa: flamingo

لقلق، لقلقه، لكلك

layh: to be high

الله، جبرئیل، .یل

lêb: lip

لب

legwh: light in weight

کارناوال، لاغر

Roots of Persian Words

kes: *to scratch*

خَسیدن, خِشنود, خوش, شانه, شورا۱, شوربا

ket: *living room*

کد .

keu 1: *to shine*

زرَفِه, سرنا، سرنای, سور

keu 2: *to swell*

سُفتن, سُمبه, سُنبه, سود, سوراخ, صفر

keu 3: *to watch*

شُکوه, قابوس, قباد, کاووس, کی۳, کیا, کیارش, کیان, کیخسرو, کیقباد

keued: *to yell*

نکوهش, نکوهیدن

keuk: *to shine*

افسوس, زُهره, سرخ, سهراب, شهرورد, سوختن, سوز, سوزاک, سوزان, سوزِش, سوک۱, سوگ۱, سوگند, ققنوس, وَرد۲

khâd: *to bite*

خاییدن

khalkos: *copper or copper alloy with tin*

اخلاط, خِلط, مخلوط

kharpuna > see kahrpu

k.h.l: *to stain*

الکل, کخّال, کحل

ki* 1: *to freeze*

چاییدن

kiês: *bug*

ساس۲

kiph: *thin flexible twig*

سیف, شِفش, شفشاهنگ , شَفشَف

kîru: *wax*

قیر, گریس

kitu: *cotton clothing*

تُنکه, کتان

---

klei: *to lean*

اقلیم

klem: *tired*

شَمَن

klêu: *hook*

کلید, مقلاد

kleu 1: *to hear*

اشنودن, خُسُر, خسرو, خُسور, خُسوره, خُشو, سراییدن, سروا، سرواد, سرودن, سُروش, شنیدن, کسریٰ, کیخسرو

kleu 2: *o wash*

قُلزُم

klis: *adhere*

سرشت, سریش

klou-ni: *buttock*

سُرون۲, سَرین

kôîk: *wide road*

کوچه, کوی

koksâ: *a part of body like foot*

کشاله

kolemos: *reed*

قلم, کارامِل

kom: *with*

کُمُد

kônôs: *mosquito*

کاناپه

korâčak: *a roll of bread*

گِراس

korkâ: *gravel*

ساخارین, ساکارُز, سوخاری, شکر

kormo: *suffering*

شَرم

koro: *war*

پیکار, کار۲, کارزار, کارنای, کاروان, کرب, گُرنا, کلنجار

---

kost: *bone*

برگستوان, کتلت, کُستی, کُشتی

kram: *to walk*

خرامیدن

krep: *body*

خراستر, خِزَفستَر, خَستَر

kreu: *blood*

قفقاز, کلوخ

k`s: *pig*

کاس۲, کاسموی

ksei 1: *possess*

اردشیر, افشین, پادشاه, چک, خشایار, شاه, شاید, شایستن, شایسته, شایگان, شهر۲, شهرام, شهریور, شیر۲, شیراوژن, گلشاه, نَرد۱, نیشابور, نیو اردشیر

ksei 2: *bright*

آذرخش, جمشید, خَشَن, خشیسار, خشین, خورشید, درخش, درخشیدن, درفش۱, رخش, رخشان, رخشیدن, روشن, شید, شیده, مهشید

ksen: *to card wool*

شانه

ksero: *dry*

اکسیر

kseubh 1: *to shake*

آشفتن, آشوب, گُشُفتن

kseubh 2: *move*

شیب۱, نشیب

kseud: *water*

اَیُخشُت, شستن, شور۲, شوهر, شوی۱, شوی۲

ksîp: *strike*

شیب۲, شیب۳, شیبیدن, شیفتن

ksîro: *milk*

شیر۱, شیرین

ksudros: *coarse*

خُرد

A13

Roots of Persian Words

ریشهٔ لغات فارسی

kar* 2 > see kwer	kaz > see kaž	ken: *young*
		کنیز
kard*: *keep down*	kaž: *inexpensive silk*	keng > see keg
کال	غژ، غژغاو، قژ، قزاغند، گز، گژ۲، کژاکند، گاز۱	kens: *to announce*
karpâsah: *cotton*		افسانه، افسون
گرباس	keanos: *to lie down*	ker 1: *head*
karpurah: *camphor tree*	اقیانوس	افسار، افسر، زنجبیل، سار۴، سالار، سر، سُرو، سروان، سَرون۱، شنگبیل، فسار، قیراط، لاله سار
کافور	keg: *hook*	
karš*: *to drag*	چنگ، سنج، صنج، کج، کژ۱	ker 2: *to cut*
ترکش، کشاله، کشکول، کیش۲، کیش۳	kei 1: *gray or black color*	اگر، چرم، خوک، ریسک، سرگین، سگال، سودن، سیلی، شکافتن، شکوفه، شگفت، غربال، فرسودن، کارد، کافتن، کاو یدن، کاوُش، گر، گرت، گفتن، گسستن، گسیختن، گسیل، مگر، نشگرده، هرگز
karšvar: *a "circle" of land*	سام، سیامک، سیاه، سیاوش، سیمرغ، شاهین	
کشور	kei 2: *to set in motion*	
kas: *to cut*	شدن	
قصر	kei 3: *to lie down*	ker 3: *loud noise*
kas 2 > see kak 3	اریکه	خروج، خروس، خروشیدن، سرفه، گرک، کرکس، گروه، ورتک
kâs 3: *to command*	keku: *club*	
پاسخ، ساستا، سُخن	چاقو، چکاد، چکش	ker 4: *black*
kas* 1 > see kwek	kel 1: *cold or warm*	پیخال، چرده، سمور، شیمی، گرس، کرسنه۱، گرسنه۲، گره، کیموس، کیمیا
kaša: *arm pit*	آبسال، افسردن، سال، سرد، سرما، گوساله	
گش	kel 2: *to cover*	ker 5: *heat*
kasyapa: *tortoise*	کلاه، کلبه	کوره
گَشَف	kel 3: *to strike*	kerasos: *cherry*
kâtara: *shy*	گند، کلنگ	قَرنفُل
کاتوره	kel 4: *light and dark spots*	kerd 1: *heart*
kâu 1: *to strike*	چرمه	دل
گُشتن، کوبیدن، کوشش، کوشیدن، کوفتن	kel 5: *cup*	kerd 2: *row*
	کاس۱، کاسه، کوزه	سرده
kau 2: *to howl*	kel 6: *to shout*	kerdh > see skordh
کبک، کوکو	کلاس، کلیسا، گنّاس، کنسول، کنشت، کنیسه	kerk: *thin*
kauč* > see gêu 1		گرسیوز، گرشاسپ
kaus: *to pound*	kelewo: *lacking*	kers 1 > see ker 4
کوس	کچل، گروه، کل	kers 2: *to turn*
kavûta: *gray*	kem 1: *stick*	کاریکاتور
کبوتر، کبود، کفتر	سیم۱	kert: *to twist*
kay-guk: *boat*	kem 2: *to cover*	کارتنک
قایق	قمیص	
kayik > see kay-guk		

haya > see haem

hebni: *ebony tree*

آبنوس

herk > see ark

herk > see hixra

hixra: *filth*

چرک

hmar* > see mer 1

h.š.š: *to dry vegetable*

حشیش

huaid* > see sweid

huan* > see swen

huar* > see swer

hûzâyê: *name of a native tribe in southwest iran (remnant of the elamite)*

اهواز, حوز, خوز, خوزستان, هوز

h.y.y: *to live*

حوّا, حیات

i 1: *to go*

باید, پتّت, جا, جاروب, جَن, جیناک, هیرک

i 2: *pronominal stem*

استاد, اِم, امروز, ایچ, ایدر, ایدون, ایمه, این, پندار, پنداشتن, هیچ, ؤ, یا, یازده, یک, بیگانه

iaš* > see yaš*

iâtom: *going*

جادّه

ies > see yes

ieuo: *grain*

جو۲, جُوازه, گُوازه

ijlak: *sleeveless coat*

جلیقه

isto: *most*

اردیبهشت, بهشت, فِره, فَرهَست, کاست, مِهست, نخست

jai* > see gwei

jan* > see gwhen 2

---

jangalah: *wasteland covered with wild growths*

جنگل

j.b.r: *to reunite*

جبر, جبرئیل, گبر

jiau* > see geu 3

kâ: *to wish*

کام۱, کامه

kâd: *sorrow*

سار۲

kafa: *foam*

کف, کفچ, کفچلیز

kaffa: *the plant or drink coming from kaffa*

قهوه, کافه

kafš: *shoe*

کفش

kaftân: *a silk-filled war garment*

خفتان, خفدان

kagaz: *tree bark*

کاغذ

kahrpu: *lizard*

چلپاسه, کرباسو

kai: *alone*

کور

kaiš* > see kweis*

kâk: *twig*

شاخ, شاخه, شکله

kak 1: *to enable*

آسغده, بسغده, بسیج, ساختن, سازش, سخت, سزا, سزیدن

kak 2: *a round object (loaf)*

کاک, کعک

kak 3: *to become thin*

.ک, کاست, کاستن, کاه۲, کاهش, کاهیدن

---

kakis: *spike*

سگک

kakka: *to defecate*

ککه

kam 1: *to restrain*

کمند

kam 2: *to bend*

چپ, چپه, چفته, چم۱, چمان۱, چماندن, چمیدن۱, چنبر, خَم, قپان, کپان, کمر, کمرا

kamma: *little*

کم, کمین

kamp > see kam 2

kân: *belonging to a group (of numbers)*

-گان, -گانه

kan* > see gwhen 3

kânak > see kân

kand: *to shine*

چندل, چندن, سَندَروس, سندل, صندلی, قندیل, کاندید, گُندر

kânûnu: *fireplace*

کانون۱

kap: *grasp*

چاپیدن, چسبیدن, چفسیدن, قفس, قفیز, کویز

kapastay: *poison*

گَبست

kapho: *hoof*

سَفَل, سُم, سُنب

kapolo > see kaput

kapparis: *a Mediterranean shrub*

قَباریس, گَبر

kaput: *head*

گَلّه

kar 1: *hard*

خار, خارا, خاریدن, خر, خربزه, خرچنگ, خِرد, خروار, قاطر, کنگره۱

gras: *to eat*

غانغرایا

gredh: *to walk*

سانتیگراد, کنگره۲, گراییدن

ğreîos > *see glei*

gr'mg: *possession*

غرامت

grnom > *see ger 2*

gûrb: *stocking*

جوراب, گوراب۲, گورب

gurdos 1: *brave*

گرد۱, گردان

gurdos 2: *sluggish*

گول

gûysna: *deer*

گوزن

guza: *throne*

کرسی

gwa: *to walk*

آغاز, آمدن, آینده, اکباتان, انجام, انجمن, انگام, پیام, پیغام, جاه, خانقاه, خورنگاه, دیابت, زمان, فرجام, گام, گه۲ه, گهواره, نیام, همدان, هنگام

gwag: *cry*

زاغ, زکیدن, ژاژ, ژکیدن

gwebh 1: *to dip*

ژرف

gwed > *see yad**

gwedh: *to destroy*

گست, گند, گندیدن

gwei: *to live*

آژیر, جهان, جیوه, زندگ, زنده, زیبق, زیرک, زیستن, ژیوه, کیهان, کیومرث, گیتی, مزخرف

gweie: *to over power*

زیان, گادن, گاییدن

---

gwel: *to drip*

آغار, آغاردن, آغاریدن, آغر, آغردن, آغشتن, فرغار, فرغاریدن, فرغر, فرغردن, فغن, فغنده

gwel 1: *to throw*

ابلیس, گرزین

gwel 2: *to pierce*

پول, فلس, مفلس

gwen: *woman*

زن

gwer 1: *heavy*

گران

gwer 2: *call loudly*

آژیر, بیغاره, پیغاره, گرامی, گرزمان, گروگر

gwer 3: *to swallow*

پیاله, پیغاله, خرخره, ژرد, غرغره, غلغل, قلقل, گریبان, گریوه, گل, گلو, گوارا, گواردن, گوارش

gwer 4: *mountain*

گر۱, گرشاه, گلشاه

gwet: *resin*

بتون

gwhder: *to flow*

آبشار, سرشار, شار, شاریدن, شرشر, شریدن

gwhedh: *to ask*

تگدّی, خجسته, گجسته, گدا

gwhen 1: *to fill*

غانه, غژ, غژغاو, قز, قزاغند, قنات, قند, گز, گز۲, کژاکند

gwhen 2: *to strike*

آجدن, آزدن, آژدن, انگژه, اوژدن, اوژندن, بهرام, پادزهر, زدن, زه۳, زد, زهر, زه, شیراوژن, کلاغ, گزند, گزیدن, نژند, ورغنه

---

gwhen 3: *to dig and fill*

آبشن, آکندن, آویشن, اِسکنه, افکندن, بالاخانه, بالکن, پراکندن, پرگنه, پیکان, خانقاه, خانه, خانی, خن, خندق, سمرقند, شَن, شندف, قانون, کاشانه, کان, کانال, کانون۲, گندَک, کندن, کندو, گنند, گلشن, هوشنگ

gwher: *warm*

گرم

gwhi: *thread*

زه۱, فیله

ğ.w.l: *to take suddenly*

غول۱, مغیلان

gwou: *cow*

برزه گاو, توده, جواز, کود, گاو, گواز, گوپان, گوساله, گوسفند, گوشت, گوه, نهفتن, ورزاو

gzn: *treasure*

جنازه, خزانه, کنز, گنج, مخزن, مغازه

hâ: *to join*

ها

habl: *rope*

حبل, کابل

had* > *see sed*

haem: *character*

خیم, دژخیم

hai* > *see sâi*

haič* > *see seiku*

halak: *mad*

آلَک, آلَکی

ham-bak: *jam*

انبه

hanbân > *see anbân*

har* > *see ser 2*

harn* > *see srisâ*

hau* **2** > *see seu 3*

hauš* > *see saus*

genu 2: *chin*	**gharš*** > see ghers	**gheugh**: *to hide*
چانه, زنخ, زنخدان	**ghdies**: *yester*	آغال۲, آغل, غول۲
geph: *mouth*	دی۲	**ghlâd**: *to sound*
دهان, زفر	**ghebh-el**: *head*	زرّاد, زره
ger 1: *curved*	قیفال, کوفیّه	**ghou-ro-s**: *terrifying*
گره, گروه	**ghei 1**: *winter*	گور, گوراب۱
ger 2: *ripe*	دی۱, زم, زمستان, زمهریر, هیمالیا	**ghrebh 1**: *seize*
آزرمیدخت, زار۱, زال, زر۲, زرتشت, زرمان, زیره, گندم	**ghei 2**: *to propel*	پذیرفتن, گرفتن, گرو, گروگان
ger 3: *to awaken*	آبزین, ابزرین, ابزار, افزار, زنجیر, زندان, زنهار, زوار۱, زین, زینهار, سفینه, فرزین, گرزین	**ghrebh 2**: *to dig*
بیدار	**ghêi 3**: *to yawn*	گور
ger 4: *to cry hoarsely*	فاژ, فاژیدن	**ghrem**: *to roar*
زار۲، زاری, غرّیدن	**gheidh**: *wish for*	غرش, غُرنبیدن, غُرم, غُرُم
gerbh: *to scratch*	آغالیدن	**ghu 1**: *to call for help*
مزخرف	**gheis**: *to frighten*	خدا, خدیو, خواجه, گپ, گفتن, ناخدا
gêu 1: *to bend*	زشت	**ghu 2**: *tongue*
آغوش, ابرقوه, ابرکوه, اکواب, انجوخ, انجوختن, انجوغ, چگونه, چون, خُم, خمره, زرگون, زیرکونیم, سرگین, سنج, صنج, غوز, قوز, قوزک, کُپ, کوژ, کوشک, کوه, کوهان, کوهسار, کیوسک, گنبد, گنده, گوشه, گون, گوی, نگون	**ghel**: *to shine*	زبان, هزوان
	آرسنیک, خیال, زر۱, زرد, زردک, زرگون, زرنیخ, زریر, زهره, زیرکونیم, مالیخولیا	**ghuel**: *crooked*
	gheled: *ice*	تزویر, زور۳
	ژاله	**ghûk**: *hoot*
		غوک
geu 2: *to hasten*	**ghengh**: *to proceed*	**gieu** > see geu 3
ابزار, افزار, افزودن, زاو, زاوَر, زوار۱, زود, زور۱, فزون	جنگ, خنگ, زنگ	**glei**: *to start*
geu 3: *to chew*	**gher 1**: *to grab*	دریا, زراه
جویدن	آزار, آزردن, - جرد, رزده, قرن	**gnauh***: *to sleep*
geus: *to love*	**gher 2**: *to wish*	غنودن
دوست	زار۴	**gnô**: *to know*
ghâgwh: *young animal*	**ghers**: *to be delighted*	آشنا, دانستن, دانش, زند, زندیق, شناختن, فرزانه
زاغ	گش	**gogel**: *knob*
ghaido: *goat*	**gherto**: *milk*	گِزر
زاق	آغشتن, فرغار, فرغاریدن, فرغر, فرغردن, فرغن, فرغنده	**gong**: *lump*
ghait: *wavy hair*	**ghesto**: *hand*	گَند۱
گیس	آستین, دست, دستار, دستگاه	**gôtra**: *race*
ghans: *goose*	**gheu**: *to pour*	جوهر, گُهر, گوهر
غاز	رفوزه, زوت, زوتر, زور۲, شیمی, کیموس, کیمیا	**gram*** > see ghrem

Roots of Persian Words

ens: meet with hostile intent

اهریمن

epi: at

اسقف

er: to move

آرغنده, آریغ, ارغنده, اروند, الوند, پتیاره, پذیره, راندن, رسیدن, ریدن, ریغ, ریم, ریمه, لهراسپ

ere: to have bad will

ارشک۲, رَشک

erêbu: to enter

اروپا, غرب, مراکش

erek: flea

رشک

ereš > see arš

eres 1: to flow

ارشان, ارشک۱, رگ, ریواس, ریوند

eres 2: to pierce

خِشت۲

erezu > see arš

ersen: ejector of semen

ارشاسپ, خشایار, سیاوش, گشن, گشناسپ, گشنسپ, گُشنی

eskopo: door threshold

آشکوب

es-ti: to be

اسانس, است۱, اِستن, نیست, هست, هستن

êter: internal (insignificant) organs

خوار

eueguh: to speak solemnly

پاسخ

fraih > see prî

fran(g)rasyan: scary

افراسیاب

---

frank: forward

فراز

fra-sanga: a distance of about five kilometers

پَرسنگ, فرسخ, فرسنگ

fraspât: carpet?

فَرسپ

fratâk: tomorrow

فردا

f.r.q: to split

ترافیک, فرق

fšân: spread

افشاندن, افشون

fšar* 1 > see kormo

fšar* 2: o press (for making an intoxicating drink)

افشاردن, افشره, فشار

gabbah: dome

قُبّه, کُبّه, کُپّه, گِپیدن

gah*: to have sexual intercourse

گادن, گاییدن

gaip > see geibh

gaiz*: to excite

انگیختن, انگیزه, گیج

gal: to shout

گرزش, گرزیدن, گریستن, گریه, گِله

gan: to seize

زغن

gang: to mock

گُنگ

gar* > see gwel

garenu: scab on animal skin

گر۳, گرگن

garz 1: to bite

گرزه

---

garz* 2 > see gal

gassu: mortar

گچ

gat: large

گت

ğaulos: vessel

زورق

gavâl: a rough cloth made of wool

جَوال, گوال

gaz*: to bite

گاز ۲, گزند, گزیدن

ğazal: a new born deer

غَزال

gazit-ak: tax

گَزیت

g.d.d: to be strong

جُند, گُند۲

ğdhem: earth

آلگوریتم, خوارزم, زَمی, زمین

gêi: to sing

افغان, فغان, گات, گاه، نیایش

geibh: to spin thread

گیوه

gel 1: to form into a ball

گِرِه, گلوله, گولَه, گوی

gel 2: to swallow

زالو, زلو

ğem > see ğdhem

geme: to marry

داماد

gene: to give birth to

آزاد, جِن, زادن, زاییدن, فرزند, قرمز, میرزا, نژاد

geng > see gong

genu 1: angle

زانو, گونیا

Roots of Persian Words

dhen: *to flow*
دانیدن, دَن, دَنان, دَنیدن

dher 1: *to hold*
اندرز, بَدَرزه, بسیار, بهادر, پَدَرزه, پندار, پنداشتن, داراب, دارابگرد, دارو۲, داریوش, داشتن, درز, درزمان, درزن, درزی, درزی, درمان

dher 2: *to confuse*
تراخم

dheu 1: *to flow*
دوک, دویدن

dheu 2: *to burn*
اندوه, دود, دودمان, طوفان

dheu 3: *to shine*
اَزدودن, اندودن, زدودن

dheugh: *to milk*
آزرمیدخت, بیدخت, دختر, دوختن۲, دوشیدن, دوشیزه, دوغ

dheye: *to see*
آدینه, آذین, آینه, آیین, اندیشیدن, بینا, پدید, پیدا, جان, دیدن, دیم, دیمه, دین۱, سیما

dhîs: *village*
دخو, دِه, دهخدا, دهقان, دهگان

dhragh 1: *to pull*
درشکه

dhragh 2 > see dher 2

dhreu: *to call on*
درای, دراییدن

dhreugh: *to deceive*
دروغ, دُروَند

dhûs: *whir*
دوک

dhwer: *door*
بندر, در, درب, دربان, دربند

dînu: *law*
تمدّن, دین۱, دِین۳

---

dô: *to give*
اسفندیار, بغداد, پاداش, دادار, دادن, داشن, دَشت۲, دهش, دی۱, هشومند, هوش۱, هوشمند, هوشیار

dolmak: *to wind*
دلمه

dous: *arm*
دوش۲

drassoman: *as much as one can hold in the hand*
دِرَم, دِرهم

drau* > see dhreu

drauš* **1**: *to make a mark*
دروش

drauš* **2**: *to grind*
درشت

dregh: *unwilling*
درو یش, دریغ, درپوزگی

dub: *tablet*
دبستان, دبیر, دَف, دیوان, شَندف

dumb: *tail*
تنبک, دُم, دُمَل, دُنب, دُنبک, دنبل, دنبلان, دنبه

dumuzi: *shepherd god*
تموز

dus: *bad*
جوجه, دزد, دُزِ ـ, دُزُپیه, دژخیم, دُژُم, دُژمان, دُژوار, دُژوان, دُش ـ, دُشبیل, دُشبیه, دشخوار, دشمن, دشنام, دشوار, دشیاد, دُمَل, دنبل, دوزخ, ژوژه

duvariya-ûn: *outside*
بیرون

dvarya-ûn > see duvariya-ûn

d.v.r: *to turn*
دارا۱, دایره, دَهر, دور۲, دیار, دیّار, مدار

---

dwo: *two*
ابلیس, بیش۲, بیسکویت, دگر, دو, دوازده, دوجین, دوم, دویست, دیگر, دیهیم

ed: *to eat*
آش, آلفاآلفا, اسپست, خراستر, خِرَفستّر, خَستّر, دندان, دنده, سپست, شتا, فسفسه, فصفصه, کرکس, ناشتا

eg(n)is: *fire*
اخگر

eghs: *out*
عسگر

ei > see i 1

eis 1: *passion*
خشم, خشمن, فرستادن, فرشته

ekwos: *horse*
آلفاآلفا, ارجاسپ, ارشاسپ, اسب, اسپاه, اسپریس, اسپست, اسپهان, استر, اسوار, اصفهان, تهماسپ, جاماسپ, سپاه, سپست, سوار, طهماسپ, فسفسه, فصفصه, گرشاسپ, گشتاسپ, گشناسپ, گشنسپ, لهراسپ, ویشتاسپ

el 1: *to bend*
آرنج, آرش۱

el 2: *red or brown used in animal and tree names*
آل, آلبالو, آلک, آلگونه, آله۱, عروس

elu-ephas: *elephant*
پیل, پیلاس, فیل

embhi: *honey*
انغوزه, انگ۲, انگبین, انگژه, سکنجبین, گزانگبین

êmos: *a suffix meaning most or last*
دوم, سوم, ـُم

en: *in*
آری, آور, آوری, اندر۱, اندروا, اندرون, ایستادن

Roots of Persian Words

čînar: *poplar* چنار، چنال	**darz*** > see dher 1	**der 2**: *to run* درون
čine: *grain* چینه۲	**dau** > see dheu 1	**derk**: *to see* ترخون
čîrâğ: *lamp* اشراق، چراغ، سراج، شرق	**dauh 1** > see leu	**deru**: *wood* بدرود، پدرود، دار۲، دارکوب، دارو۱، داربه، درخت، درست، درواخ، دُرود۱، دُرود۲، درودگر، درونه
čirya: *brave* چیره	**dauh* 2** > see dheu 2	
čîxâ : *point* سیخ، شیش کباب، شیشلیک	**daxš*** > see dek	**deu 1**: *to penetrate* دوش۱
člyk: *hit by a blow* چالیک، چلیک	**d.b.r**: *to buzz* زنبور	**deu 2**: *going away* دور۱
čop: *stick* چوب، چوگان	**dê**: *to bind* دام۲، دیهیم	**deuk**: *to lead* دوختن۱، دوزندگی، دوزیدن، دوش۳
čoti > see scetka	**debh**: *to deceive* ریو، ربوه، فریب، فریبا، فریفتن	**dhars**: *to dare* درشت، دلیر
čubûq: *smoking pipe with wooden stem* چپق	**dei**: *to shine* دیبا، دیباج، دیبه، دیو، دیوانه، زاوش	**dhê 1**: *to suckle milk* دانگ، دانه، دایه، دایی
dâ 1: *to divide* بیدستر، داس، داو، داوطلب، دهره	**deik**: *to show* ۔ دیز، ۔ دیس	**dhê 2**: *to do* آپادانا، اسپهان، اصفهان، اندام، اهورا، اهورامزدا، اورمزد، پنام، پنهان، داد، داستان، ۔ دان، داور، دستان، دستور، زندان، زهدان، مزدا، مزدیسنا، ناودان، نهادن، نهان، نهفتن، هرمز، هُنام هورمزد
dâ 2: *to flow* دانوب	**dek**: *teach* دخش۱، دشت۱، دَشن	
dah 1 > see dhê 1	**dekm**: *ten* بیست، چهل، دَه، دوازده، دوجین، دویست، دینار، سی، شانزده، شصت، صد، قنطار، هکتار، یازده	
dah 2 > see dê		**dhedh**: *nurse* دادا، دَدَه۲
dahâka: *an evil character* ضحّاک	**del**: *long* دراز، درنگ، دیر، دیرند	**dhegh**: *to heat* داش، داغ، دخش۲، دخمه، ذغال، زغال، سکار، فلاخن، گدازیدن
dâlman: *eagle* دال، دالمن	**dem**: *house* الماس، دودمان، گزمان، مان۲	
danh* > see dens	**dema**: *to tame and domesticate animals* الماس، دام۱	**dheigh**: *to form out of clay* پالیز، پردیس، جالیز، دِز، دزفول، دِژ، دژبان، دژپل، دژدار، دیزی، دیگ، دیوار، فردوس
daqal: *fruit of palm tree* دقّل	**denk**: *to bite* دَد، دندان، دنده	
darb*: *to join* درفش۲	**dens**: *to teach* دستور	
	deph: *to stamp* دفتر	**dheigw**: *to stick* فیش
darf > see darb*	**der 1**: *to split* دَرد، درفش۱، درّه، درو، دُرودن، دریدن، نیش، نیشتر، نیشدر	**dhem**: *to make vapor* آماس، دَم، دما، دماوند، دمیدن
darh*: *to have pain* درد		

Roots of Persian Words

bheregh: *high*

آرزو, ابر, بالا, بالاخانه, بالار, بالاگر, بالکن, بَر۲, بردیه, بُرز, برزخ, برزوی, برمنش, برهمن, بروزیه, بُش, بلند, زَبَر, فریبرز

bheru: *to boil*

بلوا

bheu: *to exist*

أروَر, اورور, بُت, بودن, بوم۲, بومَهن, نوباوه

bheudh: *to be aware*

بو, بودا, بوی۱, بیوسیدن, پیوسیدن, نابیوسان

bheug: *to purify*

بُخت, پوزش, پوزیدن

bhilo: *friendly*

سفلیس, فلسفه, فیلسوف

bhôi: *to fear*

پاک, بیم, بیمه

bhôu: *joy*

بوی۲, بوبه

bhreus: *swollen*

بَر۴

bhru 1: *eyebrow*

ابرو, بُرو

bhru 2: *beam*

باهو۲

bhugo: *male animal of various kinds*

بُز

bhun: *base*

بُن۱, بُنه, بنیاد, گبن, نارون, وَن

bigâr > see bekâr

bistak: *pistachio*

پسته, فُستُق

blou > see plou

bôb: *carpet*

بوب

---

boqčâ: *linen for wrapping clothes in it*

بغچه

b.r.k: *originally "to kneel". eventually the root developed the sense of "to bless".*

برکت, کَروبی

bu: *lip*

بوس

bûcak > see bûjîna

bûjîna: *cucumber*

خربزه

bûnai: *naked*

برهنه

busmâ: *perfume*

بَشام, بلسام

bûšyastâ: *the sleep demon*

بوشاسپ, گوشاسپ

byûrru: *ten thousand*

بیوَر

č'a: *tea*

چای

čaêčasta: *bright*

چیچست, خنجست

cağ: *seek*

چغیدن

čag* > see čak*

čai* > see kwei 2

čaih*: *to sew*

آجیدن, آزیدن, آژیدن

čak*: *to strike*

چاک

ča-kar: *obedient*

چاکر

čali: *membrane*

چَلتَپک, چلتوک, شالی, شالیزار, شَلتوک

čamiš

چامیدن, چامین

čamišn > see čamiš

camminus: *way*

کامیون

čao: *to print*

چاپ, چاو

čap* > see kap

čapar: *wall*

چَپَر

capayati: *pound*

شامپو

čark: *a hunting bird*

چَرغ

čartês: *leaf of papyrus*

خربطه, قرطاس, کارت, کارتون

čât: *well*

چاه

čat* > see skweht*

čaud* > see skeud

čellem: *a small box*

چَلَم, چلیم

chiang-yu: *soybean oil*

سویا

chou-shu: *millet*

شوشو

čiah* > see kweye

čîah*: *to move*

شاش

čiam > see kwem

čiau* > see kei 2

čih* > see ki* 1

cîm: *reason*

چَم۲

A5

Roots of Persian Words

awe: *water*

باران, بارگین, ودخین, وردیج,
ونترین

aweg: *to grow*

آغال۱, أغور, بنفش, بنفشه,
پیروز, فروختن, هُوَخشَثرَ, وَخش,
وخشیدن

axatis lithos: *the stone of akhatos (name of a river in sicily where agate was first discovered)*

عقیق

ayer: *day*

پار, پارسال, پَرندوش, پریر,
پریروز, پیرار

âzarm: *honor*

آزرم

baba: *baby words*

بَبَه, بریط

bačak: *bad deed*

بزه

bâd* > see bhedh

bâl: *corn*

بلال

bâl-ak: *wing*

بال

balût: *oak*

بلوط

bamb: *bang*

بَم

bamia: *okra*

بامیه

bangha > see banha

banha: *hemp*

بَنج, بَنگ, منگ

banz* > see bhengh

baoj: *to rescue*

بوختن

---

bârig: *narrow*

باریک

barq: *shine*

برق, زبرجد, زمرد

baru: *to chew*

أباردن, أباشتن, اوباردن, اوباش

bašn: *height*

بَشن

batiaxê: *a bowl (of wine)*

باده, بادیه, باطیه

baud*: *to feel*

بوس

bazda: *bad*

فَژ, فژاغند, فژاک, فژاکن, فژگند

bêgânak: *stranger*

بیگانه

bekâr: *forced labor? (not work?)*

بیگر, بیگاری

bêlûr: *an indian city famous for its crystal*

برلیان, بُلور

benješk > see vanjišk

berenža: *brass*

برنج۱, برنز

beu 1: *root of muffled sounds*

بوتیمار, بوف, بوم۱

beu 2: *to swell*

بوق, پاکت

bhâ 1: *to shine*

بام۱, بامداد, فاز, ـفام۱, فانتوم,
فانوس, فتو, فسفر

bhâ 2: *to speak*

پزشک

bhabhâ: *bean*

باقلا

---

bhag: *to share out*

اتابک, انباز, انباغ, باج۱, باژ, باغ,
بَخت, بخشیدن۱, بذله, بَرخ, بزم,
بغ, بغداد, بغستان, بهادر, بهره,
بیدخت, بیستون, بیگ, بیگم, فغ,
فغستان, فغفور

bhâghu: *elbow*

بازو, باهو۱

bhê: *indeed*

ب . بله, بیا

bhedh: *to press*

بستن۲

bheğh: *outside*

ابی, باز۳, بجز, بی, بیدستر, جُز

bhel: *to swell*

آنفلوآنزا, بالش, بالین, بَرسَم, برگ,
بلغم, بلغه, بلیط, بلیت, بودجه,
قَرنفُل

bhendh: *to bind*

بستن۱, بند, بندر, بنده, پیوستن,
دربند, فاشیسم

bhengh: *to be thick*

باز۱, دَبز

bher 1: *to carry*

آوردن, استوار, اسوار, انبر, بار۱,
بارجامه, باره۱, بَر۳, برادر, بردن,
بَرید, ترابری, خانقاه, خاور,
خاویار, خروار, خورنگاه, داور,
دژوار, دستور, دشخوار, دشوار,
سوار, گاه۲, گهواره, مزدور, ـوار۴,
وَخشور

bher 2: *to cook*

برشته, بریان, بریجَن

bher 3: *to cut*

بریدن, بیل

bher 4: *bright*

بر, بَبَر, بور, بوره

bhereg: *to shine*

ابلق, ابلک, برازنده, برازیدن

A4

Roots of Persian Words

ang: *to bend*

انگ۱, انگشت, انگور, انگولک, جوجه, ژوژه, شترنک, شطرنج, کترنگ, لنگر

angh: *compressed*

آز, جُوازه, گُوازه, نیاز, نیازی

angwhi: *snake*

اژدر, اژدها

anjihr: *fig*

انجیر

anôr: *watery*

انار

anta: *little*

آند, اندک

ap: *to take*

آوام, آیفت, فام۲, وام, یابیدن, یافتن

apak > see apânk

apâk > see apânk

apa-kienak > see ap-genak

apânk: *again*

باز۴

apâxtara: *north*

اباختر, اختر, باختر, بدخشان, بلخ

apêrân

ویران

ap-genak: *glass*

آبگینه

âpilak > see âbilag

apo: *off*

آ. ۱, آپادانا, آختن, آراستن, آرایش, آغار, آغاردن, آغاریدن, آغاز, آغر, آغردن, آغشتن, آغُدم, آکندن, آمادن, آماده, آمدن, آهختن, آهیختن, آورد, آینده, اخته, افگار, بافدُم, بخشودن, بخشیدن۲, پس, پوست, سپاردن, سپردن, عفریته, فگار, وارون

ap-vêcak: *pure*

اویژه, بیژه, پرویز, ویژه

a.q.r: *to sting*

عقرب

ar 1: *to fit together*

آراستن, آرایش, آرمئیتی, آرتا, ارد, اردشیر, اردلان, اردوان, اردیبهشت, آرم, آرمَتی, اسپندارمذ, اسفندارمذ, اشو, پیراستن, پیرایه, چرا, راد۱, رَد, سپندارمذ, سفندارمذ, نَرد۱, نیو اردشیر, ویراستن, ویرایش

ar* 2 > see er

ardeba: *a unit of volume in ancient egypt*

اَردَب

ardha: *swept*

فرارون, فریرون, فیرون, وارون

areg > see ark

arg: *to shine*

ارزیز

ariza: *pine*

ارز۲

ark: *to hold*

ارک, ارگ, ارگبُد, عسگر

arkh > see arx

arkhein: *to rule*

بطریق

armâv: *date*

خُرما

arš > see ere

arš: *truth*

آرشیا

aršya > see arš

arx: *master*

آرشیتکت, آرشیو

arzan: *millet*

ارزن, ارژن

as: *to burn*

آر, هکتار

âs: *to arrive*

خراسان

âsa > see âs

ašgab: *leather worker*

اسکاف

asksâ: *axis*

آسه

âsû: *to rise*

آسیا۲, وضو

ater: *fire*

آتش, آذر, آذربایجان

âtos: *father*

آبتین, آتبین, دده۱, فریدون

au: *away*

أباردن, أباشتن, افتادن, اوباردن, اوباش, اوژدن, اوژندن, خرسند, شیراووژن

aulos: *jaw*

آرواره

aus: *to shine*

بهار, فرخار, هوش۲

autos: *self*

افندی

avaeza > see ap-vêcak

avêrân; ruined > see apêrân

av-sud: *charm*

افسانه, افسون

aw: *bird*

خاویار, خایه, وای۲, ویش

`awar: *he damaged*

عار, عوار

awd: *strange*

افدستا

A3

Roots of Persian Words

ریشهٔ لغات فارسی

ab 1: *water*

آب۱, آب۲, آبان, آبخست, آبخور, آبرو, آبریز, آبزین, آبشن, آبنیک, آخُر ، آخور, آس, آسیاب, آفتاب, آوند۲, آویشن, ابریق, اَبّهت, انبیق, دریا, زاب, زهاب, ناب

ab 2: *father*

ابراهیم, بوزینه

abâ: *to assemble together*

بازار, بازرگان, واچار

abâr: *lead*

آبار

âbilag: *blisters*

آبله

âdhâmah: *earth*

آدم

ag: *to drive*

آژانس, تراز, ترازو, جواز, طراز, گواز

agaru: *to hire*

اجاره, اجرت, انجیل

agaruh: *aloe wood*

عود, فلوت

âgerepta: *premeditated crime*

آگرفت

agh(lo): *fear*

آخر, آک, آکل, آکله, اخ, اَفِد, افدیدن, آک

ağra: *limit*

انیران۲

agurru: *baked clay*

آجر, آگور

âi: *hay*

آی, ای

ai* > see i 1

aidh: *to burn*

اِتِر, اثیر, خِشت۱, هیزم, هیمه

aig-: *goat*

ازگ۲

aios: *metal*

آهن, آیَخشُت

aiw: *vitality*

برنا, جاوید, خدا, خدیو, خواجه, ناخدا

ak: *sharp*

آس, آسمان, آسیاب, اپسان, افسان, افسانیدن, اقاقیا, بادآس, ساییدن, سَختن, سنجیدن, سنگ, سوهان, فسانیدن

akos: *suffix indicating small size*

ـک

akostan > see akustan

akru: *tear*

آرس, اشک

aksas > see asksâ

akustan: *hang*

آکستن

akwa: *water*

آله۲

al 1: *beyond*

آریا, آلرژی, اراک, آران, اردلان, انیر, انیران۱, ایران, ایرانویج, ایرج, ایرمان

al 2: *to grind*

آرد

âlag: *a kind of plum*

آلو, هلو, هلیک

a-lâlak: *red*

آلاله, لال۲, لالس, لالک, لاله, لاله سار, لعل

âlêiô: *to wander*

آوار۲, آواره

alek: *to ward off*

اسکندر, لاک, لُجّه, لَک

algwh: *worth*

ارج, ارجاسپ, ارز۱, ارزش, ارزیدن, ارژنگ, ورج, ورجمند

âlu > see âlag

âluk > see âlag

amalaka: *emblic tree*

آمُلَج, آمُلَه

am-bak > see ham-bak

ambarôt > see amrôt

ambhi: *around*

آستین, آبزنجَن, ابریشم, اپسان, افتالیدن, افراختن, افراز, افراشتن, افرنگ, افروختن, افزودن, افسار, افسان, افسانیدن, افسر, افسوس, افشاندن, افشون, افغان, افکندن, انبر, اورنجن, اورنگ, رشتن, رشته, ریسمان, ریسیدن, ریشتن, شتاب, شتافتن, شکار, شِگردن, فتال, فرازیدن, فزون, فسار, فسانیدن, فغان

amča: *plough*

آماج

âmon: *full*

آمودن, ابرآمون

a'.m.r: *to command*

میرزا

amrôt: *pear*

امرود

an 1: *breath*

اهورا, اهورامزدا, اورمزد, برزخ, دوزخ, هرمز, هورمزد

an 2: *other*

آن۲, اندر۲, پدراندر, پسراندر, دختراندر, مادراندر

an 3 > see ne 1

anbân: *a bag made of sheep hide*

انبان، انبانه

ang: *coal*

انگِشت

Index of Roots

With derived Persian Words

Table of Contents

* <u>Reverse Pagination</u>

Pagination of the Persian Dictionary is from right to left.

A Brief Description

This Persian Etymology book is arranged as a dictionary of Persian words where the derivation of each word and the evolution of its meaning from its Indo-European root(s) are displayed in a simple chart as shown in the samples below. Persian words from Semitic and other roots are also included.

This dictionary explains the etymology of over 3400 Persian words. Their derivation paths pass through some 40 different languages. An index of words is provided for each language. The original meanings of words, if different from their current usage, are shown in quotations.

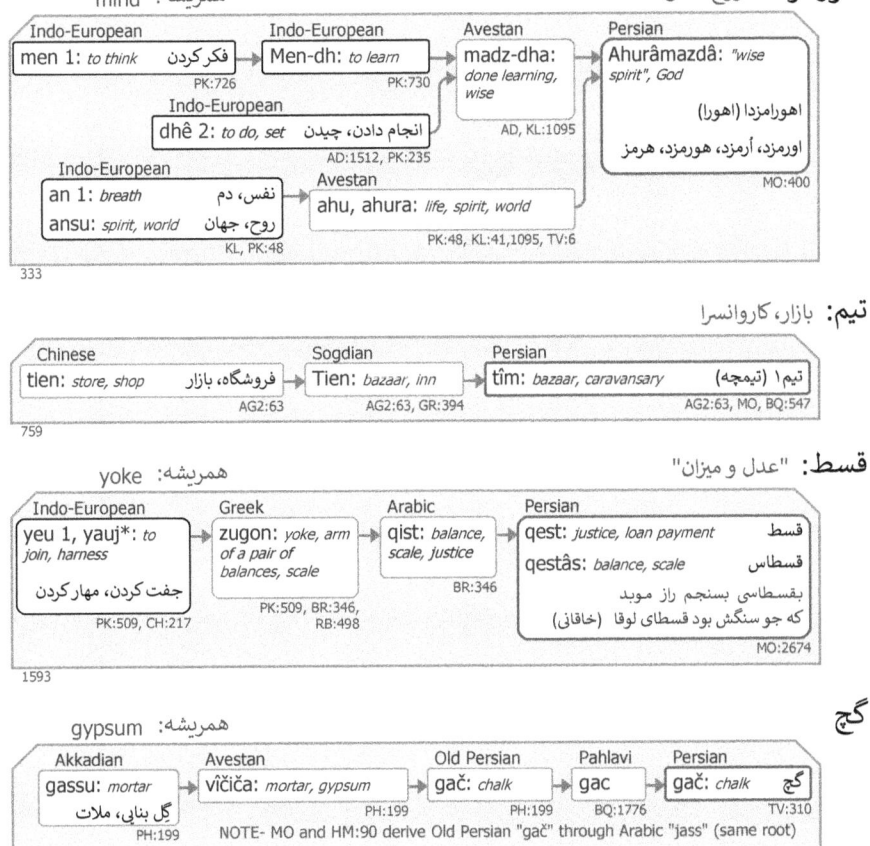

Persian Etymology
from Indo-European and other Roots

Copyright © 2024, Dr. Ali Nourai
ISBN   Paperback   979-8-218-34167-1
Library of Congress Control Number: 2023924494

Rev. date: 2/4/2024

Publisher's Cataloging-in-Publication Data

Names: Nourai, Ali, 1953- .
Title: Persian etymology : from Indo-European and other roots / Dr. Ali Nourai.
Description: 2024 edition. | Dublin, OH : Lexis Books Publishing, 2024. |
    Includes b&w language charts. | Includes indexes and bibliographic
    references. | Summary: Displays the etymology of over 3400 Persian
    words from Indo-European and other roots in simple charts. Their
    derivation paths pass through 40 different languages. A word index is
    provided for each language. The original meanings of words, if different
    from their current usage, are shown in quotations.
Identifiers: LCCN 2023924494 | ISBN 9798218341671 (pbk.)
Subjects: LCSH: Persian language – Etymology – Dictionaries. | Iranian
    languages – Etymology – Dictionaries. | Indo-European languages –
    Etymology – Dictionaries. | BISAC: FOREIGN LANGUAGE STUDY / Persian.
Classification: LCC PK6363 N68 2024 | DDC 491 N--dc23
LC record available at https://lccn.loc.gov/2023924494

Lexis Books Publishing
Printed in the United States of America

Persian
Etymology

From
Indo-European and other
Roots

Dr. Ali Nourai